P9-DYP-271

ENCYCLOPEDIA OF WORLD BIOGRAPHY

SUPPLEMENT

23

ENCYCLOPEDIA OF WORLD BIOGRAPHY

SUPPLEMENT

$$\frac{A}{Z}$$ **23**

GALE®

THOMSON

™

GALE

Detroit • New York • San Diego • San Francisco • Cleveland • New Haven, Conn. • Waterville, Maine • London • Munich

THOMSON
—★—
™
GALE

Encyclopedia of World Biography Supplement, Volume 23

Project Editor
Andrea Kovacs Henderson

Editorial
Laura Avery, Luann Brennan, Leigh Ann
DeRemer, Jennifer Mossman, Tracie Ratiner

Editorial Support Services
Andrea Lopeman

Permissions
Margaret A. Chamberlain

Imaging and Multimedia
Dean Dauphinais, Leitha Etheridge-Sims,
Lezlie Light, Dan Newell, David G. Oblender,
Robyn V. Young

Manufacturing
Stacy Melson

LIBRARY OF CONGRESS CATALOGING-IN-PUBLICATION DATA

ISBN 0-7876-5285-7
ISSN 1099-7326

Printed in the United States of America

10 9 8 7 6 5 4 3 2

CONTENTS

INTRODUCTION vii

ADVISORY BOARD ix

ACKNOWLEDGMENTS xi

OBITUARIES xiii

TEXT 1

HOW TO USE THE INDEX 455

INDEX 457

The study of biography has always held an important, if not explicitly stated, place in school curricula. The absence in schools of a class specifically devoted to studying the lives of the giants of human history belies the focus most courses have always had on people. From ancient times to the present, the world has been shaped by the decisions, philosophies, inventions, discoveries, artistic creations, medical breakthroughs, and written works of its myriad personalities. Librarians, teachers, and students alike recognize that our lives are immensely enriched when we learn about those individuals who have made their mark on the world we live in today.

Encyclopedia of World Biography Supplement, Volume 23, provides biographical information on 200 individuals not covered in the 17-volume second edition of *Encyclopedia of World Biography* (*EWB*) and its supplements, Volumes 18, 19, 20, 21, and 22. Like other volumes in the *EWB* series, this supplement represents a unique, comprehensive source for biographical information on those people who, for their contributions to human culture and society, have reputations that stand the test of time. Each original article ends with a bibliographic section. There is also an index to names and subjects, which cumulates all persons appearing as main entries in the *EWB* second edition, the Volume 18, 19, 20, 21, and 22 supplements, and this supplement— more than 8,000 people!

Articles. Arranged alphabetically following the letter-by-letter convention (spaces and hyphens have been ignored), articles begin with the full name of the person profiled in large, bold type. Next is a boldfaced, descriptive paragraph that includes birth and death years in parentheses. It provides a capsule identification and a statement of the person's significance. The essay that follows is approximately 2,000 words in length and offers a substantial treatment of the person's life. Some of the essays proceed chronologically while others con-fine biographical data to a paragraph or two and move on to a consideration and evaluation of the subject's work. Where very few biographical facts are known, the article is necessarily devoted to an analysis of the subject's contribution.

Following the essay is a bibliographic section arranged by source type. Citations include books, periodicals, and online Internet addresses for World Wide Web pages, where current information can be found.

Portraits accompany many of the articles and provide either an authentic likeness, contemporaneous with the subject, or a later representation of artistic merit. For artists, occasionally self-portraits have been included. Of the ancient figures, there are depictions from coins, engravings, and sculptures; of the moderns, there are many portrait photographs.

Index. The *EWB Supplement* index is a useful key to the encyclopedia. Persons, places, battles, treaties, institutions, buildings, inventions, books, works of art, ideas, philosophies, styles, movements—all are indexed for quick reference just as in a general encyclopedia. The index entry for a person includes a brief identification with birth and death dates *and* is cumulative so that any person for whom an article was written who appears in the second edition of *EWB* (volumes 1–16) and its supplements (volumes 18–23) can be located. The subject terms within the index, however, apply only to volume 23. Every index reference includes the title of the article to which the reader is being directed as well as the volume and page numbers.

Because *EWB Supplement,* Volume 23, is an encyclopedia of biography, its index differs in important ways from the indexes to other encyclopedias. Basically, this is an index of people, and that fact has several interesting consequences. First, the information to which the index refers the reader on a particular topic is always about people associated with that topic. Thus the entry "Quantum theory (physics)" lists articles on people associated with quantum theory. Each article may discuss a person's contribution to quantum theory, but no single article or group of articles is intended to provide a comprehensive treatment of quantum theory as such. Second, the index is rich in classified entries. All persons who are subjects of articles in the encyclopedia, for example, are listed in one or more classifications in the index—abolitionists, astronomers, engineers, philosophers, zoologists, etc.

The index, together with the biographical articles, make *EWB Supplement* an enduring and valuable source for biographical information. As school course work changes to reflect advances in technology and fur-

ther revelations about the universe, the life stories of the people who have risen above the ordinary and earned a place in the annals of human history will continue to fascinate students of all ages.

We Welcome Your Suggestions. Mail your comments and suggestions for enhancing and improving the *Encyclopedia of World Biography Supplement* to:

The Editors
Encyclopedia of World Biography Supplement
Gale Group
27500 Drake Road
Farmington Hills, MI 48331-3535
Phone: (800) 347-4253

ADVISORY BOARD

ACKNOWLEDGMENTS

Photographs and illustrations appearing in the *Encyclopedia of World Biography Supplement*, Volume 23, have been used with the permission of the following sources:

AFP/CORBIS: Alain Resnais, Donald Rumsfeld

AP/WIDE WORLD PHOTOS: Pedro Almodovar, Lance Armstrong, John Ashcroft, Mildred Bailey, Albert Beveridge, Bonnie Blair, Mel Brooks, Carol Burnett, Dick Button, Thomas Cech, Chung Ju Yung, Johann Deisenhofer, Michael Dell, John Elway, Geraldine Farrar, Kenichi Fukui, Walter Gilbert, Tom Hanks, Malvina Hoffman, Helen Elna Hokinson, Anna Hyatt Huntington, Ilya Kabakov, Urho Kekkonen, Yuan Tseh Lee, Jose Arcadia Limon, Bruce McCandless, Joni Mitchell, Pauli Murray, Camille Paglia, Sigmar Polke, Charley Pride, Stanley B. Prusiner, Bernard Rands, Sumner Murray Redstone, Ishmael Reed, Condoleezza Rice, Randall Robinson, Edith Sampson, Alexander Schindler, Ntozake Shange, Christina Stead, Juanita Kidd Stout, Andrei Tarkovsky, Samuel Chao Chung Ting, Al Unser, Ellen Gould White, Jeana Yeager, Steve Yzerman

ARCHIVE PHOTOS, INC.: Al Pacino

ARCHIVES OF THE HISTORY OF AMERICAN PSYCHOLOGY, THE UNIVERSITY OF AKRON: Christine Ladd-Franklin

ARTE PUBLICO PRESS: Lola Rodriguez de Tio

JERRY BAUER: Louise Erdrich, Jamaica Kincaid

BEINECKE LIBRARY, YALE UNIVERSITY: Jean Toomer

BETTMAN/CORBIS: Tenley Albright, Margaret Lucas Cavendish, Leadbelly, William Murray, Oscar Peterson, Mark Spitz

CORBIS: Amy Beach, Jakob Bernoulli, Lucrezia Bori, Georg Brandes, Clare of Assisi, Frances Benjamin Johnston, Alice Neel, Paul V, Arno Penzias, Mary Edwards Walker

CORBIS SYGMA: Alfonso Garcia Robles, Meryl Streep, Mitsuko Uchida

CRISTIE'S IMAGES/CORBIS: Benedict XIV

CHRIS FELVER: Gerhard Richter

FISK UNIVERSITY LIBRARY: Charlemae Hill Rollins

FRANK DRIGGS COLLECTION/GETTY IMAGES: Ernesto Lecuona

GETTY IMAGES: Xavier Cugat, David Geffen, Ellen Gleditsch, Dorothy Height, Guy Lombardo, Roman Polanski

THE GRANGER COLLECTION, NEW YORK: Claudio Arrau, Isabella Bird, Innocent IV, Pauline Johnson, Matilda Sissieretta Joyner, Henrietta Swan Leavitt, Marianne North, Samuel Romilly, Mary Church Terrell, Theodore Newton Vail

CAROLINA HERRERA: Carolina Herrera

DAVID HO: David Ho

HULTON/ARCHIVE, GETTY IMAGES: Jane Campion, Clement I, Kyung Wha Chung, Marie-Olympe de Gouges, Ludwig Holberg, Gjergj Kastrioti-Skanderbeg, Khalid bin Abdul Aziz Al-Saud, Horace Liveright, William Oughtred, Sandor Petofi, Bertel Thorvaldsen, Vigilius

HULTON DEUTSCH COLLECTION/CORBIS-BETTMAN: Yousuf Karsh, Mike Leigh, Alan Charles MacLaurin Mackerras, Gilbert Murray, Paul Signac

THE KOBAL COLLECTION: Elinor Glyn

LIBRARY OF CONGRESS: Gertrude Atherton, Mary Austin

PHOTO RESEARCHERS, INC.: Sophia Jex-Blake

REUTERS NEW/MESIA INC./CORBIS Patrick Roy

UNIVERSITY OF OKLAHOMA, WORLD LITERATURE TODAY AND GIL JAIN: Luisa Valenzuela

UPI/BETTMAN: Kateri Tekakwitha, Mary Lou Williams

JACK VARTOOGIAN: John Lee Hooker

YALE UNIVERSITY OFFICE OF PUBLIC AFFAIRS: Sidney Altman

OBITUARIES

The following people, appearing in volumes 1-22 of the *Encyclopedia of World Biography,* have died since the publication of the second edition and its supplements. Each entry lists the volume where the full biography can be found.

AGNELLI, GIOVANNI (born 1920), Italian industrialist, died in Turin, Italy, on January 24, 2003 (Vol. 1).

BALAGUER Y RICARDO, JOAQUIN (born 1907), Dominican president, died of heart failure in Santo Domingo, Dominican Republic, on July 14, 2002 (Vol. 1).

BANZER SUAREZ, HUGO (born 1926), Bolivian president, died of a heart attack in Santa Cruz, Bolivia, on May 5, 2002 (Vol. 1).

BELAUNDE TERRY, FERNANDO (born 1912), Peruvian president, died of complications following a stroke in Lima, Peru, on June 4, 2002 (Vol. 2).

BERIO, LUCIANO (born 1925), Italian composer, died in Rome, Italy, on May 27, 2003 (Vol. 2).

BRINKLEY, DAVID (born 1920), American journalist, died due to complications following a fall in Houston, Texas, on June 11, 2003 (Vol. 8; group entry entitled "Huntley and Brinkley").

CELA Y TRULOCK, CAMILO JOSE (born 1916), Spanish author, died of heart disease in Madrid, Spain, on January 17, 2002 (Vol. 3).

CHADWICK, LYNN RUSSELL (born 1914), English sculptor, died in Stroud, England, on April 25, 2003 (Vol. 18).

CHARGAFF, ERWIN (born 1905), Austrian biochemist, died of natural causes in New York, New York, on June 20, 2002 (Vol. 3).

EBAN, ABBA (born 1915), Israeli statesman, diplomat, and scholar, died near Tel Aviv, Israel, on November 17, 2002 (Vol. 5).

FRANKENHEIMER, JOHN (born 1930), American filmmaker, died of complications following a stroke in Los Angeles, California, on July 6, 2002 (Vol. 22).

GADAMER, HANS-GEORG (born 1900), German philosopher, classicist, and interpretation theorist, died in Heidelberg, Germany, on March 14, 2002 (Vol. 6).

GALTIERI, LEOPOLDO FORTUNATO (born 1926), Argentine president, died of heart and respiratory ailments in Buenos Aires, Argentina, on January 12, 2003 (Vol. 6).

GARDNER, JOHN W. (born 1912), American educator, public official, and political reformer, died in Palo Alto, California, on February 16, 2002 (Vol. 6).

GOULD, STEPHEN JAY (born 1941), American paleontologist, died of cancer in New York, New York, on May 20, 2002 (Vol. 6).

HAMPTON, LIONEL (born 1908), American jazz musician, died of natural causes in New York, New York, on August 31, 2002 (Vol. 22).

HEYERDAHL, THOR (born 1914), Norwegian explorer, anthropologist, and author, died of cancer in Colla Micheri, Italy, on April 18, 2002 (Vol. 18).

ILLICH, IVAN (born 1926), American theologian, educator, and social critic, died in Bremen, Germany, on December 2, 2002 (Vol. 8).

JENKINS, ROY HARRIS (born 1920), British politician and author, died in Oxfordshire, England, on January 5, 2003 (Vol. 8).

JORDAN, JUNE (born 1936), Jamaican-American poet and activist, died if breast cancer in Berkeley, California, on June 14, 2002 (Vol. 8).

LEBED, ALEXANDER IVANOVICH (born 1950), Russian general and politician, died in a helicopter accident in Siberia, Russia, on April 28, 2002 (Vol. 18).

LIPPOLD, RICHARD (born 1915), American sculptor, died in Roslyn, New York, on August 22, 2002 (Vol. 9).

LUNS, JOSEPH (born 1911), Dutch political leader, died after a long illness in Brussels, Belgium, on July 17, 2002 (Vol. 10).

MARCUS, STANLEY (born 1905), American businessman, died in Dallas, Texas, on January 22, 2002 (Vol. 19).

MAULDIN, BILL (born 1921), American cartoonist, died of pneumonia in Newport Beach, California, on January 22, 2003 (Vol. 10).

MERTON, ROBERT K. (born 1910), American sociologist, died in New York, New York, on February 23, 2003 (Vol. 10).

MINK, PATSY TAKEMOTO (born 1927), American politician, died of pneumonia in Honolulu, Hawaii, on September 28, 2002 (Vol. 18).

MOYNIHAN, DANIEL PATRICK (born 1927), American politician, died of complications following abdominal surgery in Washington, D.C., on March 26, 2003 (Vol. 11).

NE WIN (born 1911), Burmese political leader, died in Yangon, Myanmar, on December 5, 2002 (Vol. 11).

NOZICK, ROBERT (born 1938), American philosopher, died of stomach cancer in Cambridge, Massachusetts, on January 23, 2002 (Vol. 11).

PERUTZ, MAX (born 1914), English crystallographer and biochemist, died of cancer in Cambridge, England, on February 6, 2002 (Vol. 12).

RAWLS, JOHN (born 1921), American political philosopher, died of heart failure in Lexington, Massachusetts, on November 24, 2002 (Vol. 13).

REBER, GROTE (born 1911), American radio astronomer, died in Tasmania, Australia, on December 20, 2002 (Vol. 21).

RIESMAN, DAVID (born 1909), American sociologist, writer, and social critic, died in Binghamton, New York, on May 10, 2002 (Vol. 13).

RIVERS, LARRY (born 1923), American artist, died of liver cancer in Southampton, New York, on August 14, 2002 (Vol. 13).

ROGERS, FRED (born 1928), American television host, died of stomach cancer in Pittsburgh, Pennsylvania, on February 13, 2003 (Vol. 18).

ROSTOW, WALT WHITMAN (born 1916), American educator, economist, and government official, died in Austin, Texas, on February 13, 2003 (Vol. 13).

SHAPEY, RALPH (born 1921), American composer, conductor, and teacher, died of heart and kidney failure in Chicago, Illinois, on June 13, 2002 (Vol. 14).

SISULU, WALTER MAX ULYATE (born 1912), South African activist, died in South Africa on May 5, 2003 (Vol. 14).

SNEAD, SAM (born 1912), American golfer, died from complications following a stroke in Hot Springs, Virginia, on May 23, 2002 (Vol. 21).

SOELLE, DOROTHEE (born 1929), German theologian, political activist, and feminist, died in Goeppingen, Germany, on April 27, 2003 (Vol. 14).

TODD, REGINALD STEPHEN GARFIELD (born 1908), Zimbabwean politician, died from complications following a stroke in Bulawayo, Zimbabwe, on October 13, 2002 (Vol. 18).

UNITAS, JOHNNY (born 1933), American football player, died of a heart attack in Baltimore, Maryland, on September 11, 2002 (Vol. 20).

VANCE, CYRUS R. (born 1917), American secretary of the Army and secretary of state, died of pneumonia in New York, New York, on January 12, 2002 (Vol. 15).

WEAVER, PAT (born 1908), American television executive, died of pneumonia in Santa Barbara, California, on March 15, 2002 (Vol. 19).

WHITE, BYRON R. (born 1917), American U.S. deputy attorney general and U.S. Supreme Court justice, died of pneumonia in Denver, Colorado, on April 15, 2002 (Vol. 16).

WILDER, BILLY (born 1906), American film director, screenwriter, and producer, died of pneumonia in Beverly Hills, California, on March 27, 2002 (Vol. 21).

WILLIAMS, TED (born 1918), American baseball player, died of cardiac arrest in Inverness, Florida, on July 5, 2002 (Vol. 19).

ZINDEL, PAUL (born 1936), American author and playwright, died of cancer in New York, New York, on March 27, 2003 (Vol. 18).

Abraham

The patriarch Abraham (c. 1996 BC–1821 BC) started with humble beginnings as a son of Ur. Abraham is now regarded as one of the most influential people in all of history. The world's three largest monotheistic religions—in fact possibly monotheism itself—found their beginnings with him. Over 3 billion people in the modern world cite Abraham as the "father" of their religion. Abraham was promised by his God descendants as numerous as the stars of the sky, but today two branches of his family, the Jews and the Muslims, continue to battle for his birthright.

Birth of a Patriarch

In the Torah, Abraham's story is found in Lekh Lekha. In the Bible, it is the same, in Genesis, but is also commented on in the New Testament. In the Koran, Abraham can be found mentioned throughout, revered as one of the great prophets of the Muslim faith. In all three holy books, and in all three faiths, Abraham is revered as a father and a founder. The Bible calls him "our spiritual faith." Archaeology knows him as literally impossible to trace. History calls him the father of monotheism and originator of a great battle—spanning centuries—for pride and a little place: the land of Israel.

Abraham was born Abram, son of Terah, at the beginning of the second millennium BC in Ur, the capital of Mesopotamia at the height of its splendor as a highly developed ancient world. According to Jewish tradition, he was the son of an idol maker and smashed all of his fathers idols—except one—in a story that foreshadows his devotion to one God. The Koran tells of a time when Abram confronts his father about his idol worship and is condemned to burn in a furnace by King Nimrod of Babylon, but God protected him. His family left Ur—in modern day Iraq—to travel northwest along the trade route and the Euphrates River to the city of Haran. Abram settled down in Haran—in modern day Israel—with his family. He married Sarai and entered into a lifelong partnership with her. At the time, Haran—as well as all the neighboring cities and countries—was a land devoted to polytheism.

Abraham's Calling

Abram was in Haran at age 75 when he got the call from God to leave his home and family behind and follow God into a strange land that He would give him. *Time* quoted Thomas Cahill, author of *The Gifts of the Jews,* calling the move "a complete departure from everything that has gone before in the evolution of culture and sensibility." Abram took his wife, his nephew, Lot, and his possessions and departed. Abram moved south into the land of Canaan, a land inhabited by a warrior people called the Canaanites. He settled temporarily in Shechem and Beth-el. God told Abraham his descendants would inherit the Canaanite land.

Egyptian Layover

A famine in the land forced Abram and his people to move on to Egypt. Fearful that Pharoah would kill Abram for his beautiful wife, Abram asked Sarai to pretend she was his sister instead. Pharoah noted Sarai and took her as a concubine. For this, God struck the Pharoah with a plague and revealed Sarai's true identity. Angry with Abram, Pharoah

returned Sarai and asked them to leave Egypt. Abram left with carts of wealth.

Renewal of Abraham's Calling

Abram returned to Canaan with Lot and Sarai, but Lot and Abram had a dispute over grazing land for their herds. Breaking with tradition, Abram allowed Lot—the younger of the two—to chose the land he would take. Lot chose the fertile plain to the east, and Abram took the hills to the west. Lot's land included the cities of Sodom and Gomorrah. After Abram was again settled, God came to Abram and renewed his promise; that Abram would inherit for his descendants all the land he could see in every direction.

Lot moved to Sodom and was captured when local tribes attacked the city. Abram—who had grown wealthy and distinguished—armed his men and pursued Lot's kidnappers, regaining Lot and his possessions. Again God affirmed his promises to Abram, Abram now being well advanced in years and without offspring. God reaffirmed that He would give the land from the Nile to the Euphrates to Abram's descendants, but only after they had spent 400 years as slaves.

The First Son

With God having more than once affirmed his promise of numerous progeny to Abram, Sarai made a suggestion. In the ancient world, it was a custom to offer a substitute to bear a child to ensure the continuation of the family. Sarai offered her Egyptian handmaid, Hagar, to Abram to bear

them a child. Abram consented, and at the age of 86 Hagar bore him a son, Ishmael.

The Second Son

Thirteen years after the birth of Ishmael, God once again appeared to Abram and renewed His covenant with Abram through the sign of circumcision and even expanded the promises: if Abram would "walk before [the LORD] and be upright" then God would make Abram the "father of a multitude of nations." God changed Abram's name to Abraham, which means "the father of many nations," and He changed Sarai's name to Sarah, meaning "princess." God also revealed that the promises would not come to Abraham through Ishmael, but through another son that would be born to Sarah in a years' time. Abraham laughed at this seemingly absurd promise, because Abraham was 99 at the time and Sarah was 89. When Abraham laughed, God said the boy's name would be Isaac, which means "he laughs."

God came again to speak to Abraham, in the guise of a traveler with companions (who were two angels). They were on their way to Sodom to destroy the city for its wickedness. Abraham boldly bargained with God on behalf of Lot, and because of Abraham's favor, God relented: if there were just ten righteous people in Sodom, God would not destroy it. During God's and the angels' visit, Abraham served them Bedouin hospitality: a goat, water, and other food. Later, God could not find even ten righteous in Sodom, but spared Lot's family by warning them to leave before he destroyed the city. Lot's wife was turned to a pillar of salt when she turned to view Sodom as she fled.

A year later, Sarah gave birth to Isaac. Sarah grew increasingly jealous of Hagar and Ishmael, and Abraham relented to allow Sarah to send them out into the wilderness. God saved Hagar and Ishmael and promised Ishmael would also father a great nation through 12 sons, assumed by tradition to be the 12 Arab tribes. According to Christian and Jewish scripture, God stipulated, though, that the covenant would flow through Isaac's line. In Talmudic tradition, Ishmael was later down-played, cast as a bully to younger brother Isaac. According to the Koran, Hagar and Ishmael made a journey to Mecca where they build a home and Abraham often visited them.

The Offering

According to Judaism and Christianity, Isaac is the son whom the offering story is about. According to Islamic interpretation, Ishmael is the son in the story. Either way, Abraham was asked in a test of faith by God to take one of his sons onto Mount Moriah and sacrifice him as a burnt offering. At the time, children were often sacrificed as burnt offerings to a variety of deities. Abraham submitted, despite the fact that he "loved" his son. He took the son up on the mountain and prepared to sacrifice him. At the last moment, God told him to stay his hand and a ram appeared in the bushes. Abraham and his son slayed the ram as an offering, instead. God reiterated His promises to Abraham again, at this point, and made the covenant binding. Because Abraham had faith in the One God, God showed Himself different from other gods who desired human sacrifice and started His history with a people: the Jews or the Muslims. Christianity also lays claim to this story as the foreshadowing of the sacrifice of Jesus Christ.

Death of a Patriarch

After Sarah died, two things happened. The Koran tells the story of Abraham and Ishmael making a journey to retrieve the Kaaba—Islam's great shrine—from the sands. Also, Abraham sent a servant to find a suitable wife for Isaac among Abraham's relatives. The servant returned with Rebekah and Rebekah married Isaac and had Esau and Jacob. The Jewish covenant would pass down through Jacob, who would have twelve sons who would become the twelve tribes of Israel. Likewise, Jacob's sons would include Joseph and Judah, and the birthright would continue through Joseph and the scepter through Judah, which is important for the establishing of Jesus Christ in the line of the covenant.

Abraham married Keturah and had six more sons. Abraham died at 175 years old and was buried in a cave in Hebron with Sarah, before he could inherit the land of Canaan. Both Isaac and Ishmael attended the funeral.

His Descendants Today

The five repetitions of daily Muslim prayer begin and end with reference to Abraham. Several rituals during the hajj—the Muslim pilgrimage to Mecca—throw back to Abraham's life. The Jews feature the story of Abraham nearly sacrificing Isaac during their New Year celebrations. Christian children around the world sing "Father Abraham had many sons. . . . And I am one of them and so are you." Pope John Paul II spent a lifetime dreaming of walking the steps of Abraham's journey and has a special place in his heart for the Biblical Abraham.

There has been a trend in the 1990s and 2000s to use Abraham as a figure and tool for reconciliation. Interfaith activists have scheduled Abraham lectures, Abraham speeches, and Abraham "salons" worldwide. Bruce Feiler's *Abraham: A Journey to the Heart of Three Faiths* was published to a welcome reception. David Van Biema in *Time* notes, "It is a staple premise of the interfaith movement, which has been picking at the problem since the late 1800s, that if Muslims, Christians, and Jews are ever to respect and understand one another, a key road leads through Abraham." But Biema also says, "He is like a father who has left a bitterly disputed will" and points out that Abraham's story has at its core a theme of exclusivity.

The Israeli settler movement is largely fueled by the concept that Abraham's covenant with God grants the Jewish people the Holy Land. Meanwhile, Christians misused passages on Abraham written by Paul in the New Testament to encourage anti-Semitism and possibly the Crusades. There are also discrepancies about which of his sons did what. The Muslims and Jews have two totally different stories on which son was exalted and inherited the birthright. The Koran also claims that Abraham was the first Muslim, not a Jewish prophet. Biema says, "His story constitutes a kind of multifaith scandal, a case study for monotheism's darker side." Tad Szulc says in *National Geographic*, "The important

thing, we are told, is to assess the meaning and legacy of the ideas Abraham came to embody. He is most famously thought of as the father of monotheism. . . . The stories do, however, describe his hospitality and peaceableness and, most important, his faith and obedience to God."

Books

Corduan, Winfried, *Neighboring Faiths,* InterVarsity Press, 1998.
Fieser, James and John Powers, *Scriptures of the West,* McGraw Hill, 1998.
Holy Bible, New Living translation, Tyndale House Publishers, 1996.
House, Paul R., *Old Testament Survey,* Broadman Press, 1992.
Murphy-O'Connor, Jerome, *Holy Land,* Oxford University Press, 1998.
Qur'an, translation, Tahrike Tarsile Qur'an, Inc., 1999.
Schechter, Solomon, *Aspects of Rabbinic Theology,* Jewish Lights Publishing, 1993.
Student Map Manual: Historical Geography of the Bible Lands, Pictorial Archive (Near Eastern History) Est., 1983.

Periodicals

Asia Africa Intelligence Wire, October 21, 2002.
Bible Review, April 2002.
Midstream, November 2001.
National Geographic, December 2001.
Time, September 30, 2002.

Online

"Biography of Abraham," http://www.logon.org/_domain/abrahams-legacy.org/al-biog.html (February 10, 2003). ☐

Tenley Emma Albright

In 1953, American figure skater Tenley Albright (born 1935) became the first "triple crown winner" ever, as she captured the World, North American, and United States ladies figure skating titles. However, she faced her ultimate challenge as she competed with a serious foot injury in the 1956 Olympic Games. Despite her pain, she skated away with the top prize, becoming the first American woman to win a gold medal in Olympic figure skating.

As *Sports Illustrated for Women* selected the top 100 female athletes of all time, writer Richard Deitsch reflected, "Few skaters have ever combined athleticism and artistic grace as successfully as Tenley Albright." Barbara Matson of the *Boston Globe* added, "Albright's athletic story is one of courage and strength of spirit. . . . She is [number one] in the celebrated history of American women in Olympic figure skating."

Early Years

Tenley Emma Albright was born on July 18, 1935, in Newton Centre, Massachusetts, the daughter of Hollis, a prominent Boston surgeon, and Elin (Peterson) Albright. She

Reflecting back on her illness, Albright noted that she really was not scared about being sick. She recalled in the Academy of Achievement interview, "The fear I had was staying in the hospital overnight. I couldn't imagine anything worse." She continued, "But no one told me how serious it was. In fact, they took the sign 'polio' off my door, hoping I wouldn't realize how sick I was. Looking back, I don't think I ever knew how sick I was, because it never occurred to me that I couldn't and wouldn't get better."

Albright recovered and was soon released from the hospital. Since she was still weak, the doctors encouraged her to return to ice skating, feeling that the exercise would improve her strength. The doctors were correct in their assessment; just four months after her polio attack, Albright won her first important competition: the Eastern Juvenile Skating Championship.

Won Olympic Silver

As noted in her profile on Hickoksports.com, "In her early teens, Tenley Albright had two ambitions: To become a surgeon, like her father, and to win a gold medal in figure skating." Albright worked hard and was soon winning more competitions. At age 13, Albright won the U.S. Ladies Novice championship, and at age 14, she won the U.S. Ladies Junior title.

In the Academy of Achievement interview, Albright reflected on her determination and noted, "If you don't fall down, you aren't trying hard enough, you aren't trying to do things that are hard enough for you. So, falling down is part of learning for whatever you do, and it certainly is for skating."

To the surprise of many, Albright made the 1952 Olympic figure skating team. In the *United States 1952 Olympic Book—Quadrennial Report,* it was noted, "From the foregoing, it will be seen that our skaters placed very well in this difficult competition." The book added that Albright "skated brilliantly to gain second place in the ladies' event."

Winning the silver medal at the Winter Olympics was considered quite an accomplishment for Albright, as she had never been the United States national champion. She won that title a month after the Olympics, winning the first of five consecutive national championships. A year later, at the age of 17, Albright became the first American woman to win the World Championship in ladies figure skating.

Prepared for Her Shot at Gold

Albright's daily routine included getting up before four a.m. each day, so she could practice before breakfast, and then going to school in Cambridge, Massachusetts. And while waiting her turn to skate at competitions, Albright did her homework.

Her dedication to her studies paid off. In 1953, she entered Radcliffe College as a pre-med student, with the intention of following in her father's footsteps and becoming a surgeon. She continued her demanding schedule, still rising by four a.m. each morning to practice before classes. Generally, she skated seven hours per day and successfully

also had a younger brother, Niles. She received her first pair of ice skates at the age of eight. The *Boston Globe*'s Matson noted, "Like many New Englanders, [Albright] skated on a flooded backyard at first, but as her love for the sport grew and her talent began to show, she headed to the Skating Club of Boston for lessons."

Although Albright was hard-working and devoted when it came to academics, she was unsure how serious she was about ice skating. As noted in *Great Women in Sports,* "Albright had to be persuaded to put the same amount of concentration into her skating. After a stern lecture by her coach, Maribel Vinson, the youngster decided to buckle down. . . . "

In a 1991 interview with the Academy of Achievement, Albright reflected, "I like to think that I was good in the compulsory figures. That wasn't the part I enjoyed. The jumps, the spins, the dance steps, the choreography, and especially that feeling [of] trying to fly, was what I really liked. . . . " Guided by her coach, Albright hoped the results would soon follow. Instead she would soon face a potentially life-changing illness.

Diagnosed with Polio

Illness almost ended Albright's career before it began. In 1946, she contracted polio, an extremely serious viral disease that often leaves its victims partially paralyzed. In the Academy of Achievement interview, Albright recalled, "When I came down with polio, at first nobody knew whether I ever would walk again or not."

balanced her training and school. Her dedication on the ice also paid off. She successfully defended her national title in 1954 and 1955 and won a second World Championship in 1955.

In her athlete profile from the *U.S. Olympic Committee Web site,* Albright talked about the demands of competition. She recalled, "When I was competing, we were outdoors. So despite all my preparation, I never knew whether I would be skating in a snowstorm or whether it would be raining or windy. I've learned to expect the unexpected."

Although Albright continued to excel and win titles, a talented rival, American skater Carol Heiss, emerged. In her interview with the Academy of Achievement, Albright noted, "And anyone who has won anything knows what it's like not to win. And I remember the day when I kept on hearing 'Well, someone has to lose.' And it occurred to me . . . someone has to win, too. So you might as well give it a good hard try." Recognizing that Heiss was a tough competitor, Albright decided to take a leave of absence from school in order to focus and train for the 1956 Olympics.

Olympic Gold Medal

The stage was set. Cortina d'Ampezzo, Italy, was the host city of the 1956 Winter Olympics. The town had been selected to host the Winter Olympics in 1944, but World War II led to the cancellation of the games.

These Winter Olympics were also special in that they were the first to be internationally televised. In *The History of the Olympics,* Martin Tyler and Phil Soar noted, "Millions of people watched on television, and 13,000 gaily expectant onlookers packed the newly built stands . . . for the opening of the seventh Winter Olympics. . . . "

"The road to an Olympic gold medal in figure skating is never easy," noted Frank and Clare Gault, in *Stories from the Olympics—From 776 B.C. to Now.* But if Albright was feeling the pressure, she did not show it. In her Academy of Achievement interview, Albright noted, "I didn't work on skating to be the best woman skater on the planet. What appeals to all of us is to do something that is a challenge."

Albright was facing two major challenges in Cortina. Heiss was a fierce competitor and also wanted Olympic gold. In addition, Albright suffered an injury two weeks before the competition. As noted in *Great Women in Sports,* Albright fell on the ice and seriously hurt her foot, cutting her right ankle to the bone. Her father came to Italy and repaired her ankle, but many believed this injury would take Albright out of the running for the top prize. However, Gault and Gault noted in *Stories from the Olympics—From 776 B.C. to Now,* "She was determined not to miss another chance at the Olympic gold medal."

Albright had worked too hard for too long to give up. As noted in *Great Women in Sports,* Albright stated, "The one thing I want to be able to do after it's over is say that was my best. It's better to lose that way than to win with something less than that." After the compulsory figures, Albright and Heiss were in first and second place respectively, and their scores were very close. That meant Albright's final program had to be free of mistakes in order to win.

It came down to the free skate. Tyler and Soar noted in *The History of the Olympics* that Albright "presented a wonderfully delicate programme, dramatically timed to *Tales of Hoffman* in a seemingly effortless, graceful style, ending splendidly with a rapid cross-foot spin." Gault and Gault added, "Despite her handicap, she skated a flawless program and won her long-sought prize." Albright had become the first American woman to win an Olympic gold medal in ladies figure skating.

In the Academy of Achievement interview, Albright remembered receiving her gold medal. She recalled, "When I was standing on the podium, outdoors in the mountains with the spotlights in the night they gave out the Olympic gold medal, I could hardly believe it. I suddenly felt as if I knew everybody in the United States."

Retired From Skating to Attend Medical School

Shortly after winning her gold medal, Albright's hometown had a parade for their Olympic champion. Yet, she had little time to celebrate her victory, as more competitions quickly followed. Heiss won the World Championship, but Albright responded by winning the U.S. Championship a month later. However, it appeared that Heiss would now be the leading woman on the ice.

After winning her gold medal, Albright enrolled in summer school in order to catch up with her classmates and graduate on time. Within the year, Albright retired from competitive skating, having turned down lucrative offers to skate professionally and earned her bachelor's degree from Radcliffe. She entered Harvard Medical School in the fall of 1957. She was one of only six women in a class of 130 students. From the late 1900s into the turn of the century, figure skating, especially professional figure skating, has become quite a lucrative spectator sport. As noted in *Great Women in Sports,* Albright "the consummate amateur . . . has never received a single paycheck from her skating."

In her Academy of Achievement interview, Albright reflected on starting medical school. She said, "Once again, I felt like a real beginner. And I'll never forget those first few months." She continued, "But I found myself very anxious to get to working with patients. And it took me a while to understand that we weren't going to just start right in there." But according to the Academy of Achievement Web site, Albright soon realized that "the discipline and dedication she learned on the road to becoming a world champion figure skater helped prepare her for her career in medicine."

Career as a Physician and Researcher

Albright graduated from medical school and followed in her father's footsteps, becoming a surgeon. She practiced medicine in Boston and was involved in blood plasma research at the Harvard Medical School. In addition, Albright also served her community and tried to help others. She served on the Board of Directors of the American Cancer Society and chaired the National Library of Medicine Board of Regents. Albright also led international efforts to eliminate polio when she was a member of the World Health Assembly.

Awards, Honors, and Family Life

Albright married and had three daughters: Lilla Rhys, Elin, and Elee. Talking about how skating relieved some of her daily stresses, Albright told *WomenSports* magazine, "It almost alarms me how free I feel on the ice. I don't think about the hospital or the groceries or the kids—I'm just in touch with myself. It's exciting when your whole body is moving in synchronous motion."

Albright divorced and later remarried in 1981. She and her second husband, Gerald W. Blakeley, Jr., settled in the Boston area. She retired from her medical practice in the 1990s.

Since stepping out of the limelight of ladies figure skating, Albright has received many honors. In 1976, Albright was inducted into the U.S. Figure Skating Hall of Fame, the World Figure Skating Hall of Fame, and the Hall of Sports—Academy of Achievement. She was named to the Olympic Hall of Fame in 1988 and was named one of the "100 Greatest Female Athletes" by *Sports Illustrated for Women* in 2000. In addition, her alma mater inducted her into the Harvard University Hall of Fame, and she has served on the U.S. Olympic Committee and the International Olympic Committee.

Books

Bruccoli, Matthew J., and Richard Layman, editors, *American Decades: 1950-1959,* Gale Research Inc., 1994.

Bushnell, Asa S., editor, *United States 1952 Olympic Book—Quadrennial Report, United States Olympic Committee,* United States Olympic Association, 1952.

Gault, Frank, and Clare Gault, *Stories from the Olympics—From 776 B.C. to Now,* Walker and Company, 1976.

Great Women in Sports, Visible Ink Press, 1996.

The Olympic Games: Athens 1896-Sydney 2000, Dorling Kindersley Publishing, Inc., 2000.

Tyler, Martin, and Phil Soar, editors, *The History of the Olympics,* Galahad Books, 1980.

Periodicals

WomenSports, January 1975.

Online

"About Tenley Albright," *Women's History,* http://womens history.about.com (January 18, 2003).

"Albright was first, foremost," *Boston Globe,* http://www.boston .com/sports/top100/players/98.htm (January 18, 2003).

"Athlete Profile—Tenley Albright," United States Olympic Committee, http://www.usolympicteam.com (January 18, 2003).

"Biography—Tenley Albright," HickokSports.com, http://www .hickoksports.com/ (January 18, 2003).

"Hall of Fame—NewFund," New England Women's Sports Hall of Fame by New Fund, http://www.newfund.org/files/ hallFame.htm (January 18, 2003).

"Institute for International Sport—Scholar Athlete Hall of Fame," Institute for International Sport, http://www.international sport.com/sa_hof/hof_inductees_99.html (January 18, 2003).

"Tenley Albright," Important Women in American History, http://www.lams.losalamos.k12.nm.us/heacock/Women/ Albright/tenley.htm (January 18, 2003).

"Tenley Albright, Figure Skating," *Sports Illustrated/CNN.com,* http://sportsillustrated.cnn.com/siforwomen/top_100/47/ (January 18, 2003).

"Tenley Albright, M.D. Profile," The Hall of Sports—Academy of Achievement, http://www.achievement.org/ (January 18, 2003).

"U.S. Hall of Fame," The Skating Source, http://www.skating source.com/ushall.shtml (January 29, 2003).

"U.S. Ladies Olympic Champions," United States of America Ladies Figure Skating Olympic Champions, http://tiger .towson.edu/users/abrown10/skate.html (January 18, 2003).

"USOC—Hall of Fame," U.S. Olympic Hall of Fame, http:// www.olympic-usa.org/about_us/programs.hof.htm (January 29, 2003).

"World Hall of Fame," The Skating Source, http://www.skating source.com/worldhall.shtml (January 29, 2003). □

Pedro Almodovar

Spanish film director Pedro Almodovar (born 1949) was a leader of New Spanish Cinema in the post-Franco era. Known for films such as *Women on the Verge of a Nervous Breakdown,* Almodovar was praised for his insightful depiction of women. After a creative downturn in the 1990s, a mature Almodovar emerged at the end of the decade and into the 2000s, with films like *All About My Mother.*

Almodovar was born on September 25, 1949 (some sources say 1951), in Calzada de Calatrava, La Mancha, Spain. This is a small village in a remote part of Spain. Almodovar moved with his family to Extremadura, Spain, when he was eight. There, his father ran a local gas station and made wine at home. The family included his mother, Francisca Caballero, two sisters, and one brother.

Almodovar showed promise as a writer from an early age. When he was about ten years old, he won a prize for an essay he wrote about the immaculate conception. Almodovar had a very intensely Roman Catholic upbringing, which he wanted to escape.

Moved to Madrid

The day after Almodovar finished high school in 1968, he moved to Madrid, Spain. Because could not afford college, he supported himself by holding a number of odd jobs. He sold books and made jewelry. Eventually, he found a real job to support himself. From 1970 to 1981, Almodovar was employed by the national phone company, first as a clerk then as an administrator. Though he really did not fit in, he needed the steady income.

While Almodovar had a number of legitimate jobs, he also had a creative side. In the late 1960s and early 1970s, he wrote comic strips and articles for underground publications such as *Star, Vibora,* and *Vibraciones.* In the 1970s, he contributed to other newspapers like *El Pais, Diario 16,* and *La Luna.* For *La Luna,* Almodovar had a cartoon character

Patti Diphusa that he did under a pseudonym. He also wrote a soft-porn novel and some X-rated comics.

Within a few years, Almodovar moved into arts and theater. He joined an avant garde theatre group, Los Golidardos, and did some acting. There he met actors and actresses who would later be stars in his films, such as Carmen Maura and Antonio Banderas.

Made Early Movies

From about 1974 through 1978, Almodovar began to experiment with films, making super-8 shorts. In 1978, he made a feature length movie in super-8, *F—, F—, F—me, Tim.* Later that year, he made his first feature in 16mm format, *Salome.*

In 1980, Almodovar made his first feature film that received commercial release. *Pepi, Luci, Bom and Other Girls on the Heap* was filmed on 16mm that was blown up to 35mm for release. It was funded by friends and made for about $60,000. The story focused on women from northern Spain who were in the big city. As with many of his most popular films, *Pepi, Luci, Bom* featured a colorful style and many characters that lived on the fringes of society.

Emerged as Leader of New Spanish Cinema

In the early 1980s, Almodovar began making low budget feature films that were supported by government funds and other producers' money. In 1981, he directed his first feature, *Labyrinth of Passion,* for which he also he also

composed and performed the score. This complex movie about love was Almodovar's first starring Banderas, who would become a film star in America in the 1990s.

Almodovar began getting some early international notice with his third feature, *Dark Habits* (1983). This was his first feature that was popular outside of Spain. The plot attacked the hypocrisy of the Roman Catholic Church in black comic fashion. The story focused on nuns who put on fake miracles to fund their cocaine and heroin habits.

In 1984, Almodovar had his first international hit, *What Have I Done to Deserve This?* This was another black comedy/satire-type movie about a dysfunctional family. Slightly based on his own past, the story had such characters and plot strands as a cleaning woman with an addition to speed and a Madrid housewife who sells her son to a homosexual dentist. The housewife also kills her husband and makes soup with his remains that she serves to the police.

As Almodovar continued to make such films, he was recognized as the leader of New Spanish Cinema and the head of La Movida (The Movement), the post-Franco Spanish pop culture scene. General Francisco Franco had been the fascist dictator of Spain for three and a half decades before his death in 1975. While much of Almodovar's work was a reaction against the repressive culture of Franco, he ignored the dictator's existence in his films. Almodovar had been influenced by American directors like Billy Wilde and Preston Sturges, who had done irreverent comedies decades earlier.

Though Almodovar was gay, he did not think of himself as a gay filmmaker. Many of his films concerned universal passions and concerns and featured women at their center. He was often praised for his insightful depiction of women. While Almodovar used a narrative structure that appealed to American audiences, his films were permissive and irreverent, international and democratic. They had mainstream appeal, despite their sometimes disturbing use of satire.

In 1985, Almodovar formed his first production company, El Deseo, with brother Agustin. The following year he directed *Matador,* which had at its center two characters for whom killing equals sex. Retired bullfighting star Diego and Maria, a lawyer, are linked because of their shared desire. This film bucks many conventions and showed how Almodovar's movies are full of interesting details.

Almodovar directed his first big budget film in 1987, *Law of Desire.* This marked the first time Almodovar produced his own movie, which he would do many times in the future, but the film still received much state money. *Law of Desire* was a love story with a triangle of homosexual and transsexual love at its center, again starring Banderas. Almodovar was criticized for depicting unprotected gay sex in the movie.

Had American Hit with *Women on the Verge*

One of biggest hits of Almodovar's career came in 1988 with *Women on the Verge of a Nervous Breakdown.* Starring Maura and Banderas, the farce was more conservative than his previous movies but attracted a wider audience. The plot focused on the lives of out-of-control, lonely, abandoned women in a 48-hour period. Maura played Pepa, a self-important soap opera star who is dumped by her lover via answering machine. Interesting consequences come into play after she tries and fails to kill herself. The film was inspired by the one-person play *The Human Voice* by Jean Cocteau.

Women on the Verge was the highest grossing film in Spain in 1988 and one of the best successes in Spanish box office history. The feminist film was also the highest grossing foreign film in the United States in 1989. In the United States, it did $7 million in ticket sales and was nominated for an Academy Award as best foreign film. American critics like Vincent Canby of the *New York Times* praised the film. He wrote, "In *Women on the Verge of a Nervous Breakdown,* Mr. Almodovar sets out to charm rather than shock. That he succeeds should not come as a surprise. The common denominator of all Almodovar films, even the one that winds up in an ecstatic murder-suicide pact, is their great good humor."

Almodovar was less conservative on his follow-up to *Women on the Verge,* 1990's *Tie Me Up! Tie Me Down!* The plot focused on the kidnapping of a woman, a porn and horror flick actress named Marina. She is taken by Ricki, a recently released mental patient who was obsessed with her and wants her to fall in love with him. Marina is also admired by the director of her films. *Tie Me Up!* becomes a love story as Marina does fall for Ricki.

Tie Me Up! was rated X in the United States. Critics were also not as kind, with many regarding it as inferior to *Women on the Verge.* Despite this potential problem, the film attracted $4 million in box office in the United States.

In the early 1990s, Almodovar made two wacky movies that did not do nearly as well at the box office. In 1991, he did *High Heels,* a comic melodrama which was not particularly successful. More filmgoers were offended by *Kika* (1993), which featured characters dying for love. The title character was a woman who never changes her loving attitude no matter what happens to her. Some audiences were offended by a rape scene that was played for laughs. Critics were not positive in their reviews. Shawn Levy wrote in *Film Comment,* "*Kika* is so filled with coincidences, contrivances, and unforeseeable interlockings that it feels like an entire season's worth of a primetime soap opera played in two hours on a bullet train. . . ."

Up to this time, Almodovar's movies had been very comic in nature. But in 1995, he created *The Flowers of My Secret,* which seriously addressed the idea of self-revelation. While the story focused on women, specifically a romance writer whose marriage is failing, it is much less comic. The writer can no longer write romances, so she starts writing under her own name. The film grossed about $1 million in the United States.

Addressed Franco Regime

With his next major film, Almodovar achieved several firsts in his career. *Live Flesh* (1998) was loosely based on the novel of the same name by Ruth Rendell. This was the first time Almodovar did a film based on another's material.

He also addressed the issue of Franco which had previously been taboo for him.

Live Flesh was a crime drama with elements of noir. It was not as stylized as his previous features but still had violent love, a common element of his movies. The story focused on five people linked by a murder and how it affected their lives over a number of years. *Live Flesh* played well in Spain, in part because it was topical about the potential of the current government.

Won Awards with *All About My Mother*

Almodovar retained his serious attitude for his next movie, *All About My Mother (Todo Sobre Mi Madre;* 1999). This was the first film in what many critics considered the mature Almodovar era. The film was a melodrama, with comedic elements, about a nurse named Manuela. Her teenage son Estaban dies when he is hit by a car, and she searches for his father, a transvestite. Her desperation and life changes form the core of the story. *All About My Mother* won more awards than any other of Almodovar's films, including the director's prize at the Cannes Film Festival and the best foreign language film at the Academy Awards.

The mature Almodovar continued to push his boundaries. In 2002, he wrote and directed *Talk to Her (Hable Con Ella),* a romantic comedy. The film was set in a hospital where two women were in a coma: Lydia, a bullfighter, and Alicia, a dancer. Both have male caretakers who become friends. For the first time in one of his films, the primary characters were men. This film received much critical praise and was nominated for a British Academy Award for best original screenplay. Almodovar was nominated for an Academy Award for best director for *Talk to Her* and his screenplay for the film was nominated for the writing (original screenplay) Academy Award. Almodovar walked away from the 2003 Academy Awards with the Oscar for writing (original screenplay) for *Talk to Her.*

As a filmmaker, Almodovar retained his own unique vision of Spanish life and the kind of characters he chose to depict, but grew past his own limits. He told *Time International* in 1999, "I've been making movies for the past 20 years—and, really, the same kind of movie. Sometimes I was accused of being scandalously modern, sometimes an opportunist. But now critics have realized that whatever it is I do, it is authentic. They see how close I feel to the characters in the margin. Characters at the margin of life are at the center of my movies."

Books

Pendergast, Tom, and Sara Pendergrast, eds., *International Dictionary of Films and Filmakers-2: Directors,* St. James Press, 2000.

Periodicals

Associated Press, November 20, 2002.
Boston Globe, December 18, 1988; February 24, 1989; December 25, 2002.
Daily Telegraph, August 17, 2002; August 23, 2002.
Economist, April 1, 2000.
Film Comment, May-June 1994.

Financial Times, August 10, 2002.
Houston Chronicle, December 29, 2002.
New York Times, September 16, 1988; September 18, 1988;
    September 23, 1988; February 11, 1990; April 22, 1990;
    January 18, 1998.
Newsweek International, May 31, 1999.
Seattle Times, December 27, 2002.
Time, January 30, 1989.
Time International, December 13, 1999.
Toronto Star, January 18, 1989.
Variety, April 20, 1998.

Online

"75th Annual Academy Awards," Oscar.com, http://www.oscar
    .com (March 24, 2003). ☐

Sidney Altman

Research by molecular biologist Sidney Altman (born 1939) has helped unravel many of the mysteries surrounding deoxyribonucleic acid (DNA), the chemical at the heart of the cells of all living things that controls their structure and purpose. For their discovery—in independently conducted studies—that ribonucleic acid (RNA) serves not only as a transmitter of genetic information but also acts as an agent of change in living cells, Altman and Thomas R. Cech in 1989 were awarded the Nobel Prize in Chemistry.

Altman's discovery of catalytic RNA has shaken the very foundations of the biosciences, altering their central principle. Even more significantly, it has had a profound impact on our understanding of how life on earth began and developed. Scientists have known that the flow of genetic information from DNA to protein requires enzymes and other proteins. Altman's discovery has gone a long way toward answering one of the most puzzling questions confronting bioscientists who have long sought to determine which was the first biomolecule-DNA or protein? In light of Altman's research, it now appears that RNA molecules were the first biomolecules to contain both the genetic information and play a role as biocatalysts. His discovery of catalytic RNA has also given gene technology researchers a new tool with the potential for creating a new defense against infection. In 1997 Altman himself experimented with a method to combat bacteria's resistance to antibiotics by inserting artificial genes in bacteria to make them more sensitive to ampicillin and chloramphenicol, two widely used antibiotics.

Showed an Early Interest in Science

Altman was born on May 8, 1939, in Montreal, Quebec, the second son of poor immigrant parents. His father, Victor, worked in a grocery store in the city's Notre Dame de Grace neighborhood, where Altman grew up. His mother, Ray Arlin, had worked in a textile mill before marrying Victor but looked after the home and her children by the time Sidney was born. Altman's parents instilled in him an appreciation for the value of hard work. As he wrote in his autobiographical profile on the Nobel Prize Web site, "It was from them that I learned that hard work in stable surroundings could yield rewards, even if only in infinitesimally small increments." As a boy, he liked sports and writing, but his greatest love was reading. An avid reader as a boy, Altman possessed a broad taste in books, including novels, sports books, and books about science. His early interest in science was sparked by two events, "the first being the appearance of the A-bomb," he recalled in his autobiographical profile. "The mystique associated with the bomb, the role that scientists played in it, and its general importance could not fail to impress even a six-year-old. About seven years later I was given a book about the periodic table of the elements. For the first time I saw the elegance of scientific theory and its predictive power. . . . [W]hile I was growing up, Einstein was presented as a worthy role model for a young boy who was good at his studies. I added various writers of fiction and stars of ice hockey and baseball to my pantheon."

After graduating from West Hill High School in Montreal, Altman headed off to the United States to study physics at the Massachusetts Institute of Technology (MIT). He'd originally planned to attend McGill University in Montreal, but when a high school friend suggested that they apply together to attend MIT, Altman agreed. As it turned out, Altman was accepted, but his friend was not. Although

Altman's father's grocery business had prospered during Sidney's high school years, there was some concern in the Altman household about their ability to meet the expenses of Sidney's schooling at MIT. On top of that, Altman himself was not really sure he wanted to go to MIT. However, after a few weeks at his new college, any doubts he may have had were dispelled. According to his profile in Science.ca, Altman found he enjoyed living away from home, on top of which he was very much impressed by the caliber of his fellow students. During his final semester at MIT, Altman took an introductory course in molecular biology, a subject that by then had begun to generate a great deal of excitement in the scientific community. The course familiarized Altman with nucleic acids and molecular genetics, laying the groundwork for his future encounters with these subjects. In 1960 he graduated from MIT and worked for the next two years as a teaching assistant in the Department of Physics at Columbia University.

In 1962 Altman moved to the University of Colorado Medical School to work as a research assistant under Leonard S. Lerman and to study molecular biology. As an assistant to Lerman, he worked mainly on research into the replication of the T4 bacteriophage, a substance that infects bacterial cells in much the same way that a virus infects human cells. In 1967 Altman earned his Ph.D. in biophysics from the University of Colorado and went to work briefly as a research assistant in molecular biology at Vanderbilt University. Later in 1967 he won a grant from the Damon Runyon Memorial Foundation for Cancer Research that allowed him work as a research fellow in molecular biology at Harvard University. For the next two years, he worked under noted biochemist Matthew Meselson, continuing his research into the genetic structure of the T4 bacteriophage. In 1969, with the help of Lerman, Altman won a fellowship to work in the Cambridge, England, laboratory of Sydney Brenner and DNA co-discoverer Francis Crick.

Made an Important Discovery

It was while working at the Brenner and Crick lab that Altman made an important discovery that helped to lay the groundwork for his later discovery of catalytic RNA. While working on mutant cells with malfunctioning tRNA (transfer RNA), Altman tried an experiment to see if he could isolate a special type of RNA called precursor-RNA. He took a glass plate (to which a thin layer of gel had been applied to one side) and put on it a few drops of material that had been prepared from the mutant cells. The glass plate was then placed into a strong electrical field. According to Altman's profile at Science.ca, "This technique, called electrophoresis, is a standard method for separating chemical compounds. The electric field causes different compounds to move across the gel at different speeds." Altman then waited for several hours and laid photographic film on top of the gel. "Tiny amounts of radioactive tracer atoms in the RNA emit X-rays that will leave characteristic bands on the film," his profile at Science.ca continued. When the film was taken to the darkroom to be developed, Altman knew within minutes that he had discovered the first radiochemically pure precursor to a tRNA molecule, the first step on the path to the discovery of catalytic RNA.

Altman stayed on for another year at Brenner and Crick's lab, before returning to the United States in 1971 to accept a post as an assistant professor in Yale University's biology department. A year later, he married Ann Korner, with whom he had two children, Daniel and Leah. In 1975 Altman was promoted to associate professor at Yale. Three years later he attracted wide attention in molecular biology circles when he published the results of an experiment conducted by one of his graduate students. The experiment demonstrated that the RNase P enzyme was at least partially made up of RNA, which meant that RNA played an integral role in the enzyme's activity. This finding contradicted the widely held belief among molecular biologists that enzymes were made up of protein, not nucleic acids.

In 1980 Altman was made a full professor at Yale. A year later, Thomas Cech of the University of Colorado independently published a study with conclusions very similar to those of Altman. Cech reported that his research had shown that the precursor RNA from the protozoan *Tetrahymena* were reduced to their final size as tRNA without the assistance of protein, suggesting that the precursor RNA catalyzed this transformation itself. Cech's findings lent considerable weight to Altman's earlier conclusions about the role of RNA in the activity of the RNase P enzyme. Further buttressing the findings of both Altman and Cech was research into the catalytic activity of RNase P conducted by Cecilia Guerrier-Takada, a colleague of Altman's at Yale. Guerrier-Takada's studies discovered catalysis even in the control experiments that used the RNA sub-unit of RNase P (the M1 RNA) but which contained no protein. Her findings laid the groundwork for a finding by Altman that the M1 RNA displayed all the classical properties of a catalyst, especially since it remained unchanged by the reaction. This finding by Altman removed any remaining doubt that RNA could function as an enzyme.

Won Nobel Prize for Discovery

In 1984 Altman, who was now chairman of Yale's biology department, became a naturalized American citizen, although he retained his Canadian citizenship. A year later he was named dean of Yale College, a post in which he served for the next four years. As dean, he helped to win an expanded role for science education in all of Yale's curricula. The crowning glory of Altman's career in scientific research came in 1989 when he and Thomas Cech were jointly awarded the Nobel Prize in Chemistry for their independent studies demonstrating the catalytic ability of RNA. It is hard to overestimate the importance of their discovery, which proved conclusively that nucleic acids were the building blocks of life, acting as both genetic codes and enzymes. According to *Notable Scientists: From 1900 to the Present,* in presenting the award to Altman and Cech, the Nobel Academy described their discovery as one of "the two most important and outstanding discoveries in the biological sciences in the past 40 years," the other being the discovery by Crick and James D. Watson of DNA's double-helix structure. The findings of Altman and Cech about the catalytic properties of RNA have provided geneticists with a strong foundation for research into possible medical applications. It seems reasonable to believe that if RNA enzymes can cut additional sequences of tRNA from a strand of precursor tRNA, medical professionals could possibly use RNA enzymes to cut infectious RNA from the genetic system of someone infected with a viral disease.

A member of the National Academy of Sciences, the American Society of Biological Chemists, and the Genetics Society of America, Altman also received the Rosenstiel Award for Basic Biomedical Research in 1989. In 1991 he was selected to present the DeVane lecture series at Yale on the topic "Understanding Life in the Laboratory." In a 1997 address to incoming freshmen, posted on Yale University's Web site, Yale President Richard C. Levin offered this quote from Altman on the joys of discovery: "When I was a post-doc, I did an experiment that resolved a problem that I had been working on for a year or more. When I saw the result, there was not only the feeling of relief you get when you stop banging your head against a wall, but, more important, I then understood some of the puzzling results that had been published by others in the years before. The feeling of great satisfaction at having solved my problem as well as having illuminated others kept me floating on air for weeks."

Books

Complete Marquis Who's Who, Marquis Who's Who, 2001.
Encyclopedia Britannica, Encyclopedia Britannica, Inc., 2003.
Newsmakers 1997, Issue 4, Gale Research, 1997.
Notable Scientists: From 1900 to the Present, Gale Group, 2001.

Periodicals

Maclean's, October 21, 1991.

Online

"Discovery," Yale Office of Public Affairs, http://www.yale.edu/opa/president/fresh_97.html (May 13, 2003).
"Profile for Sidney Altman," Canadian Institute for Advanced Research, http://www.ciar.ca/web/prmem.nsf/d099c4392bc3a987852569350064ed37/03a8947dfe5217bd852567350070f5de!OpenDocument (February 8, 2003).
"The RNA World," Nobel e-Museum, http://www.nobel.se/chemistry/articles/altman/index.html (February 7, 2003).
"Sid Altman, Molecular Biology," *Science.ca,* http://www.science.ca/scientists/scientistprofile.php?pID=3 (February 8, 2003).
"Sidney Altman-Autobiography," Nobel e-Museum, http://www.nobel.se/chemistry/laureates/1989/altman-autobio.html (February 7, 2003).
"Sidney Altman: Nobel Laureate in Chemistry, 1989," *Hypothesis,* http://www.hypothesis.it/nobel/eng/bio/altman.htm (February 8, 2003). □

Roberto Arlt

After failing out of primary school and educating himself mainly on the streets of Beunos Aires, Roberto Arlt (1900–1942) would grow to distinguish himself as an important Argentine short story writer, novelist, playwright, and journalist. Equally criticized for his rough use of language and praised for his innovative approach to Spanish, Arlt left his mark on Argentina. Despite dreams of becoming a successful inventor, and his entrance into journalism only to support his creative writing career financially, his *Aquafuertes portenas* newspaper column (later in book form) would become one of the classics of Argentine literature. In the words of the *International Dictionary of Theatre,* "Arlt incorporates ideas and techniques to create his own unique literary world of bizarre dream sequences and nightmarish characters, fueled by a strong social conscience."

Early Life

Arlt was born Roberto Godofredo Christophersen Arlt on April 2, 1900, to a German immigrant, glass-blower and postcard artist, Karl, and an Italian homemaker, Catalina (maiden name, Iobstraibitzer) in the *Flores Barrio* (the District of Flowers) in Beunos Aires, Argentina. (There is dispute over Arlt's exact birthday between April 2, 7, and 26). German was the language used in the home, and Arlt's parents, who immigrated in their thirties, never gained full usage of Spanish. Arlt had two sisters and both died from tuberculosis. One died at a very young age, and the other, Lila, died in 1936.

The Arlt family was poor, and Karl Arlt traveled to the provinces for months at a time to work, but never succeeded in improving his family's economic situation. Karl Arlt was a tyrant who abused his children. Arlt attended several schools as a child, but was expelled somewhere between the ages of eight and ten and was discarded as useless. He learned mainly on the streets and in the library, where he passed most of his time. In the library, he read Russian authors Maxim Gorky, Leo Tolstoy, and Fyodor Dostoevsky. He published his first short story between the ages of 14 and 16 in *Revista Popular* and left home in 1916.

He attended the Naval School of Mechanics from 1919 to 1920 and served in the Argentine armed forces in Córdoba during the same period. To make ends meet, Arlt was employed as a book store clerk, an apprentice to a tinsmith, a painter, a mechanic, a vulcanizer, a brick factory manager, a newspaper manager, and a port worker. He never did too well at any of these jobs. He spent much of his free time in the taverns, especially the café La Punalada, and shady spots of Buenos Aires, making acquaintances with the seedy patrons who would later populate his writing.

Journalist

Between 1914 and 1916, the same time he was starting his fiction writing career, Arlt began writing for newspapers: *Ultima Hora, Critica (Critical)* (in 1927), and *Don Goyo* (beginning in 1926). He interned with writer and journalist Ricardo Guiraldes from 1925 to 1927 and published with Guiraldes's magazine, *Prow.* Much later he wrote for *El mundo (The World).*

Arlt began his journalistic work as a way to make money and to introduce himself into Argentine literary circles. It turned out to be more than that. His daily columns for *El mundo,* "Aquafuertes portenas" ("Porteno Etchings"), appeared from 1928 to 1942 (compiled first in book form in 1936) and earned him nation-wide fame. In the column, he shared his opinions about society, economics, and politics. His journalism proved to be his most popular offering to society. On the day his column appeared each week, *El mundo* sold twice as many copies. In 1935, he was sent to Spain by *El mundo* as a correspondent, where he wrote his *Spanish Etchings.* It was one of the few times in his life that Arlt left Beunos Aires. Arlt wrote for *El mundo* until he died. His articles in *Don Goyo* have also been published in collections.

Novelist

Arlt presented his first short story, *Jehovah* in 1916. He wrote part of his first novel as a column, *"Las ciencias ocultas en la ciudad de Buenos Aires"* ("The Occult Sciences in the City of Buenos Aires"), when he was 19. He published his first novel, *El jugete rabioso (The Rabid Toy),* in 1926. *El Poder de la Palabra* online cited *El jugete rabioso* as "one of the best Argentine novels. . . . [With a] flood of autobiographical and picaresque characters, [it] expresses anguish and violence with the rough, most alive linguistic support." *El jugete rabioso* found little acceptance in critical circles, but was given much attention by the youth of Buenos Aires.

In 1929, Arlt published *Los siete locos (The Seven Madmen),* which was to be his only English language success and his most notable novel. None of his other works have been translated into English. *Los siete locos* won a municipal award, but the critics read it as a realistic book and criticized it for bad grammar and craftsmanship. The book was meant to be experimental and expressionistic. *Los lanzallamas (The Flame Throwers)* was the sequel novel to *Los siete locos.* Both *Los siete locos* and *Los lanzallamas* were influenced by Dostoevsky. Both reveal the underside of Buenos Aires life, with its delinquents, prostitutes, and ruffians. They have been credited with portraying the epitome of the alienated man in modern society. Arlt's first three novels are sometimes considered a trilogy. In 1931, Arlt published *El amor brujo (Love of the Sorcerer),* his last novel.

Arlt's writing style was innovative. He was the first novelist to use language from lower- and middle-class Spanish, including the language of thieves *(lunfardo),* the language of Beunos Aires *(portenos),* vulgarities, foreign language, Castilian Spanish, scientific language, and lyricism. He also regularly wrote using the informal form of "you:" "voseo." He broke the literary rules of tradition at every turn and populated his work with the unpleasant and grossly urban. Arlt was quoted in *Contemporary Authors* speaking to the stuffy, literary traditions of his time, "Today, amid the babble of an inevitably crumbling social edifice, it is impossible to linger over embroidery." He also cited the new and changing ideas of people as being a reason to reject the censures of "linguistic purity." Arlt assumed that language was ever changing, even living.

He published two short story collections, *El jorabadito (The Little Hunchback)* in 1933 and *El criador de gorilas (The Gorilla Breeder)* in 1941. *El jorabadito* was Arlt's favorite of all his books. *El criador de gorilas* contained 15 of his short stories. The short stories reinforced Arlt's style, continuing the use of confused chronology, fragmentation, chaos, and "warped personalities" in a downward-spiraling society. After Arlt wrote his fourth novel, he discovered theater, a medium he then dedicated his career to.

Playwright

Prueba de amor (Test of Love) and *El fabricante de fantasmas (The Ghost Manfacturer)* were Arlt's first dramatic endeavors. His story *Trescientor millones (The Three Hundred Million)* was populated with more of Arlt's grotesque characters. It incorporated a theme that would run though his plays, the tension between reality and illusion (also present in *Saverio el cruel* and *El fabricante de fantasmas*). *Trescientor millones, Saviero el cruel,* and *El fabricante de fantasmas* were the most significant of his plays. In all three, Arlt is said in *International Dictionary of Theatre* to: "[present] the fantasy world as bewitching in contrast to dull, prosaic reality. Nevertheless, to enter the realm of the imagination is to lose control and ultimately to encounter madness and death." Some of Arlt's other plays and play collections include *Escenas de un grotesco, La isla desierta (The Desert Island), Africa, La fiesta del hierro, El desierto entra en la ciudad, La juerga de los polichinelas,* and *Un hombre sensible.* His plays contain an indebtedness to Dostoevsky and continue portrayal of the grotesque and madness and also continue Arlt's social criticism.

Further Success

Arlt's work influenced later Spanish writers Gabriel Garcia Marquez and Jorge Luis Borges. His work has met with favor and respect since the 1960s. *Contemporary Authors* stated, "His books have been enthusiastically accepted by Argentine writers who see in Arlt a proponent of anti-literary and anti-establishment writing." Arlt's short stories, novels, journalism, and plays have been joined and printed in collections by influential publishing houses. In 1984, *The Seven Madmen* was translated to English.

Other Facets

Arlt's dream was to become distinguished as an inventor, but he continuously met with failure. He formed the ARNA society, an inventing business with Pascual Naccaratti and installed a small chemistry laboratory in Lanús, Argentina. Arlt secured a patent for reinforced rubber, but it failed commercially.

Arlt married Carmen Antinucci in 1923 and they had a daughter, Mirta, that same year. Antinucci secretly suffered from tuberculosis when she married Arlt, and he never quite forgave her for not telling him. The couple stayed in Córdoba because of her health and she died in 1929. Arlt married Elizabeth Shine in 1939. She gave birth to a child soon after his death. Arlt died of a heart attack on July 26, 1942, in Buenos Aires, Argentina.

Books

Contemporary Authors, The Gale Group, 2000.
Dictionary of Hispanic Biography, The Gale Group, 1996.
International Dictionary of Theatre, Volume 2: Playwrights, St. James Press, 1993.

Online

"Author," http://cervantesvirtual.com/bib_author/Arlt/ (February 10, 2003).
"*El Poder de la Palabra,*" http://www.epdlp.com/arlt.html (February 10, 2003).
"Roberto Arlt," http://www.jbeilharz.de/autores/arlt.html (February 10, 2003).
"Roberto Godofredo Christophersen Arlt," http://www.literatura .org/index.html (February 10, 2003). □

Lance Armstrong

Lance Armstrong (born 1971) will certainly be remembered for being an outstanding athlete and four-time winner of the Tour de France, but he will touch more lives through the Lance Armstrong Foundation and the Race for the Roses charity bike ride, which raise money for cancer research and assistance.

A Good Mother

Lance Armstrong was born in Plano, Texas, on September 18, 1971. His biological father moved out when he was a baby, and he and his mother were on their own. When he was three-years-old, his mother was remarried to a man named Terry Armstrong. Terry Armstrong also formally adopted Lance. There was very little money, but his mother worked hard to provide him with a good life. When he was seven-years-old, she worked out a deal with the local bike store and bought him a Schwinn Mag Scrambler.

He was a child who like to do things on his own and in his own way. "I have loved him every minute of his life, but God, there were times when it was a struggle," his mother told the *New Yorker.* "He has always wanted to test the boundaries."

Armstrong was athletic from the beginning. He enjoyed biking and swimming but did not do as well with football. In the fifth grade he won a distance running race. A few months later he joined the local swim club where he quickly advanced. He would ride his bike ten miles to early morning practices, then ride to school, and ride back again to swim in the afternoons.

Armstrong Began Competing

As a young teenager, Armstrong saw an advertisement for a junior triathlon called IronKids, that combined biking, swimming, and running. Armstrong won and loved it. He began competing regularly in swimming, biking, and running events, sometimes separately and sometimes combined. In his mid-teens, his mother and Terry Armstrong divorced and it was just the two of them again.

In 1987, when he was sixteen-years-old, he was invited to the Cooper Institute in Dallas, Texas. The Cooper Institute was a leader in fitness and aerobic conditioning research. Armstrong was given a VO2 Max test to measure the amount of oxygen his lungs consumed during exercise. His levels were the highest ever recorded at the clinic.

Opportunites Knocked

At age sixteen, Armstrong became a professional triathlete. He became the national rookie of the year in spring triathlons, and both he and his mother realized that he had a serious future. Soon it became clear that he would become a cyclist. He began training with more experienced riders and was beginning to make money in races. He began traveling farther to races that were more prestigious. During his senior year in high school, he qualified to train with the U.S. Olympic team in Colorado Springs, Colorado, and to travel to Moscow, Russia, to ride in his first international race.

After graduation in 1989, he was named to the U.S. National Cycling team and started working with Chris

Carmichael who began coaching him. Through Carmichael he learned that winning races involved strategy and tactics, as well as strength and speed. In 1991, he became the U.S. National Amateur Champion. The following year he rode in the 1992 Olympic games in Barcelona, Spain, and finished 14th. Immediately following the Olympic games, he turned professional. He placed last in his first professional race, but two weeks later he took second place in a World Cup race in Zürich, Switzerland. A man named Jim Ochowicz, who signed him with the Motorola cycling team, was watching him.

Armstrong had a good year in 1993, winning ten titles. He became the 1993 World Champion in Oslo, Norway. He was also the U.S. PRO Champion and won a stage of the Tour de France, although he later was unable to finish the race. In 1994, he won the Thrift Drug Triple Crown. He was steadily making a name for himself in the cycling world.

In 1995, during the Tour de France, his friend and teammate Fabio Casartelli was killed during a high-speed descent. The team decided to keep riding in his honor after Casartelli's wife paid them a visit and asked them to go on. Once again, Armstrong won a stage in the race. That year he came in 36th place, and it was his first time to finish the esteemed race.

The following year, 1996, started out well. Armstrong won his second Tour DuPont and had several career victories. He signed a two million dollar contract with the French cycling team, Cofidis. He had a new Porsche and a new home in Austin, Texas. However, during the Tour de France he was forced to drop out after being diagnosed with bronchitis. He rode for the 1996 U.S. Olympic team in Atlanta, Georgia, but was disappointed with a twelfth-place finish.

Cancer

Shortly after his 25th birthday he began coughing up blood. On October 2, 1996, he was diagnosed with testicular cancer that had spread to his abdomen, lungs, lymph nodes, and brain. The following day he underwent surgery to remove one of his testicles. "At that point, he had a minority chance of living another year," Craig Nichols, his principal oncologist told the *New Yorker*. "We cure at most a third of the people in situations like that."

Standard treatment for the brain tumors is radiation, but its effects can result in a slight loss of balance. "Not enough to affect the average person, but certainly enough to keep someone from riding a bicycle down the Alps," said medical oncologist Lawrence Einhorn in the August 9, 1999, issue of *Sports Illustrated*. "We chose surgery instead of radiation for Lance. It's slightly riskier, but he had only two tumors and they were in a position where a surgeon could get to them."

Armstrong also chose a non-traditional route for his chemotherapy. The usually prescribed drug, bleomycin, normally produces fewer side effects of nausea and vomiting. However, bleomycin also could slightly diminish lung capacity, so Armstrong was given ifosamide, "taking the short-term discomfort for the long-term gain," said Einhorn.

During treatment, especially between rounds of the chemotherapy, Armstrong kept riding his bike as much as he could. "Why did I ride when I had cancer?" Armstrong asks rhetorically in his autobiography, *It's Not About the Bike*. "Cycling is so hard, the suffering is so intense that it's absolutely cleansing. You can go out there with the weight of the world on your shoulders, and after a six-hour ride at a high pain threshold, you feel at peace."

While undergoing chemotherapy, Armstrong began talking with doctors about launching a charitable foundation to raise awareness about cancer. He and some cycling friends also came up with the idea of starting a charity bicycle race around Austin, Texas, and decided to call it the Ride for the Roses. The Foundation began to give him a new feeling of purpose.

Love And Marriage

A month after his chemotherapy treatment ended, while he still had no hair, or even eyebrows, he met Kristin Richard at a press conference announcing the launch of the Lance Armstrong Foundation and the Ride for the Roses. She was an account executive for an advertising and public relations firm assigned to help promote the event, and everyone called her Kik (pronounced "Keek"). After the first Ride for the Roses was over, they began finding excuses to see one another. "I got to know Lance when he was standing on the edge between life and death," Kristen said in the December 16, 2002, issue of *Sports Illustrated*. "It was awesome to be part of. I felt he showed me the view from that cliff. That bonds two people. And if you get to come back from that edge, it changes your life. You never want to miss out on anything fun or beautiful or scary again." The two were married on May 8, 1998.

During the same period, Armstrong was attempting to make a comeback into cycling. His first attempts did not go well. He would tire easily and get depressed. "In an odd way, having cancer was easier than recovery—at least in chemo I was *doing* something instead of just waiting for it to come back," he wrote in his autobiography. It did not help his morale when he could not find a team to take him on. His previous contract with Cofidis had been renegotiated while he was undergoing treatment. He was considered a bad public relations risk. He considered himself very lucky when the newly formed United States Postal Service team accepted him.

Better Than Ever

In 1998, he became determined to overcome the difficulties and get back to riding competitively. In the last half of the year, he won the Tour de Luxembourg, the Rheinland-Pfalz Rundfahrt in Germany, and the Cascade Classic in Oregon. By 1999, he decided he was ready to try the Tour de France again. He spent the spring training in Europe through the Alps and the Pyrenees. The Tour de France is a three-week ride through the villages of France, up and down the mountains, with a new stage each day. He knew he would have to train hard to endure the strenuous course. The *New Yorker* reported "Armstrong now says that cancer was the best thing that ever happened to him. Before becoming ill, he didn't care about strategy or tactics or teamwork—and nobody (no matter what his abilities) becomes a great cyclist without mastering those aspects of the sport." When the time came for the race, Armstrong was ready. He came out strong on the very first day. Soon he was wearing the yellow jersey that indicates the leader on a regular basis. He rode strong, all the way to the Champs-Elysees in Paris, winning the Tour de France on his first attempt after surviving cancer. Then, he won it again a year later. The following year, in the July 30, 2001, issue of *Sports Illustrated,* Rick Reilly wrote, "Unless the Eiffel Tower falls on him, Armstrong will become the fifth man to win the Tour de France three times in a row." Sure enough, he won. Then, he did it again in 2002.

Cycling is a big part of Armstrong's life, but it is not his whole life. The Ride for the Roses has grown larger each year and has become an entire weekend event, including a rock concert called Rock for the Roses. The Lance Armstrong Foundation has grown to provide information, services, and support for cancer patients through education, research grants, and community programs. The 2002 Ride for the Roses raised $2.7 million and drew 20,000 people.

Armstrong says that having cancer completely changed the way he looked at life. "I thought I knew what fear was, until I heard the words you have cancer," he stated in the *Buffalo News.* "My previous fears, fear of not being liked, fear of being laughed at, fear of losing my money, suddenly seemed like small cowardices. Everything now stacked up differently, the anxieties of life—a flat tire, losing my career, a traffic jam—were reprioritized into need versus want, real problem as opposed to minor scare. A bumpy plane ride was just a bumpy plane ride, it wasn't cancer."

Armstrong and Kristen now have three children, son Luke and twin daughters Isabelle and Grace. They live in Austin, Texas, but also own a home in Nice, France.

"Lance Armstrong is more than a bicyclist now, more than an athlete," wrote Rick Reilly in *Sports Illustrated* where Armstrong was named "Sportsman of the Year." "He's become a kind of hope machine."

Books

Armstrong, Lance, *It's Not About the Bike: My Journey Back to Life,* Thorndike Press, 2000.

Periodicals

Buffalo News, June 4, 2000.
New Yorker, July 15, 2002.
PR Week, October 14, 2002.
Sports Illustrated, December 16, 2002.

Online

"Lance Armstrong Foundation," *Lance Armstrong Foundation website,* http://www.laf.org (January 30, 2003).
"Sportsman of the Year," *Sports Illustrated,* http://sports illustrated.cnn.com (January 15, 2003). □

Lillian Hardin Armstrong

American musician Lillian "Lil" Hardin Armstrong (1898–1971) ranks alongside Jelly Roll Morton and James P. Johnson as one of the great early jazz pianists. "I was just born to swing, that's all," she once said. "Call it what you want, blues, swing, jazz, it caught hold of me way back in Memphis and it looks like it won't ever let go." Armstrong's statement, ironically, was portentous. After a distinguished fifty-year musical career, she died on stage, at a memorial concert for Louis Armstrong.

Armstrong was born on February 3, 1898, in Memphis, Tennessee. She received piano and organ lessons as a child in Memphis and served as a pianist and organist in church and in her school. Her mother and grandmother hated popular music and considered the blues vulgar. In fact, she was beaten for having a copy of W. C. Handy's "St. Louis Blues." Later, she recalled playing "Onward Christian Soldiers" in church one day "with a definite beat," somewhat to the consternation of her minister.

Armstrong received her formal music training at Fisk University, the Chicago College of Music (earning a teacher's certificate in 1924), and the New York College of Music (earning a diploma in 1929). She left Fisk in 1917 when her family moved to Chicago, and her professional career began there with a job as a "song-plugger" at Jones's Music Store on South State Street.

At Jones's Music Store, Armstrong learned and demonstrated all the music available at the store and was billed as "The Jazz Wonder Child." It was here that she met Jelly Roll Morton, probably the greatest jazz pianist of the era. Their encounter has become legendary among jazz historians. Armstrong and Morton traded renditions of standards of the day, and he demonstrated his heavy, foot-stomping style. She took this as an important lesson. From that day forward, she played with a heavy-handed, aggressive rhythmic style that became her trademark throughout her career.

Armstrong was well known and respected by her peers. Compliments by musicians were typically like those of George "Pops" Foster, the great bass player, who referred to her as "a great piano player and a great musician." In her day the piano was the centerpiece of the rhythm section, charged with maintaining the beat and fundamental chord structure to free the clarinet, trumpet, or cornet soloists for their flights of fancy. The piano was not necessarily a focus for solo playing, as Armstrong herself attests: "It wasn't the style during the King Oliver days for the pianist to play many solos. Sometimes I'd get the urge to run up and down the piano and make a few runs and things, and Joe ["King" Oliver] would turn around and look at me and say, 'We have a clarinet in the band.' "

Her four-beat, solid style guaranteed Armstrong's acceptance among her peers and a good following among devotees. As a pianist, her early jobs included accompanying singers, among them the blues great Alberta Hunter. Armstrong was also a good organizer and led her own band for many years. Her other talents included arranging, composing, and singing.

Armstrong's career in jazz extended more than fifty years and centered in Chicago and New York. She got her first playing jobs through contacts made at Jones's Music Store. Her first major band experience was with the Original New Orleans Creole Jazz Band, playing at the De Luxe Cafe. The band included Lawrence Duhé on clarinet, Sugar Johnson and Freddie Keppard on cornets, Roy Palmer on trombone, Sidney Bechet on clarinet and soprano saxophone, Tubby Hall on drums, Jimmy Palao on violin, Bob Frank on piccolo, and Wellman Braud on bass. It is about this band that Armstrong told one of her most famous tales: When she asked in what key they were playing their first number, they told her, " 'Key, we don't know what key. Just when you hear two knocks, start playing.' So I just hit everything on the piano, so whatever key they was in, I would be in it too. Oh, after a second I could feel what key they were playing, because at that time I don't think they used over five chords. In fact, I'm sure they didn't."

The Original New Orleans Creole Jazz Band played in a pure, swinging New Orleans style and was quite successful. The audience frequently contained some of the leading musicians and stars of the day, including Bill "Bojangles" Robinson, the vaudeville team of Walker and Williams, Eddie Cantor, Al Jolson, and Sophie Tucker. King Oliver and Johnny Dodds came over one evening to hear the band and invited Armstrong to join their band, King Oliver's Creole Jazz Band, playing at the Lincoln Gardens (later the Royal Gardens). In 1922, Louis Armstrong joined him, and the full complement of Oliver's band then included Oliver and Louis Armstrong on cornets, Honoré Dutrey on trombone, Johnny Dodds on clarinet, Baby Dodds on drums, Bill Johnson on banjo, and Armstrong on piano. This band, of course, has become one of the most famous in all of jazz history and formed the nucleus for Louis Armstrong's Hot Five and Hot Seven recording sessions.

Armstrong Called Major Figure in Jazz Field

It must have been quite a heady experience for a young woman in her first few engagements to be playing with the jazz greats of her day who brought the pioneering New Orleans style of traditional jazz to Chicago. It is certainly a testament to Armstrong's talent and ability. Moreover, she was apparently the first woman to enter the jazz field as a major figure and retain that stature and acceptance throughout her career.

Becoming friends almost from the day he joined the band, she and Louis Armstrong were married in 1924. Lil Armstrong eventually "encouraged Louis to leave Oliver and join Fletcher Henderson in New York. It was she who helped Louis Armstrong to become a better music reader and it was she, with her formal training and broad knowledge of musical form, who realized his enormous talent." In New York with Henderson, when Louis Armstrong played at

the Roseland Ballroom, Lil Armstrong was not satisfied seeing that her husband was not given featured billing. She organized a band in Chicago and brought him back to the Dreamland, where he was featured as "The World's Greatest Trumpet Player." His other ventures included the recording sessions with his Hot Five and Hot Seven from 1925 through 1928. From this point Louis Armstrong's career took off like a rocket. The Armstrong marriage followed the course of their careers: fused at first, but then divergent, and they were divorced in 1938.

Lil Armstrong's subsequent experiences were diverse. She played with many bands, including those of Oliver, Freddie Keppard, Elliot Washington, Hugh Swift, and Louis Armstrong. She led and played in an all-woman swing group called the Harlem Harlicans from about 1932 to 1936. The group included such notables as Alma Scott (Hazel Scott's mother) on reeds, Leora Mieux (Fletcher Henderson's wife) on trombone, and Dolly Hutchinson on trumpet. She also led her own group out of Buffalo, remnants of Stuff Smith's band, including Jonah Jones and George Clarke, from 1933 to 1935. She fronted this band "wearing slinky white gowns, top hat, and wielding a baton." This was, of course, during the depth of the Great Depression, and it is a testament to Armstrong's talent and skill that she was able to get jobs and keep the band together.

Armstrong worked as a session pianist for Decca Records in the late 1930s and appeared in the Broadway shows *Hot Chocolate* (1929) and *Shuffle Along* (1933). While at Decca, she recorded under the name Lil Hardin with soloists and a pick-up band that included numerous stars of the day, among them Red Allen, Chu Berry, Buster Bailey, and Jonah Jones.

She returned to Chicago in the 1940s and continued her career with several long engagements at local clubs, including The Three Deuces. She made several tours, including one to Europe in 1952. She was coaxed out of semiretirement to play at a memorial concert for Louis Armstrong in 1971 and died on stage on August 27.

Books

Berendt, Joachim E., *The Jazz Book,* Lawrence Hill, 1981.
Cerulli, Dom, Burt Korall, and Mort L. Nasatir, *The Jazz Word,* Da Capo Press, 1987.
Chilton, John, *Who's Who of Jazz: Storyville to Swing Street,* Chilton Book Co., 1972.
Collier, James L, *Louis Armstrong; An American Genius,* Oxford University Press, 1983.
Dahl, Linda, *Stormy Weather: The Music and Lives of a Century of Jazzmen,* Pantheon Books, 1984.
Foster, George M., *Pops Foster,* University of California Press, 1971.
Harrison, Max, Charles Fox, and Eric Thacker, *The Essential Jazz Records: Ragtime to Swing,* Greenwood Press, 1984.
Hazeldine, Mike, *Grove's Dictionary of Jazz,* Macmillan, 1988.
Hodier, Andre, *Jazz: Its' Evolution and Essence,* Grove Press, 1956.
Jones, Max, and John Chilton, *Louis: The Louis Armstrong Story,* Da Capo Press, 1988.
Mezzrow, Milton, *Really the Blues,* Random House, 1946.
Nanry, Charles, *The Jazz Text,* Van Nostrand, 1979.

Placksin, Sally, *American Women in Jazz, 1900 to the Present*, Seaview Books, 1982. □

Claudio Arrau

Musical genius, prodigy, and boy wonder are some of the words most often used to describe Claudio Arrau (1903–1991). Regarded by many music critics as a master interpreter and impassioned artist, Arrau enjoyed a stellar, if sometimes unorthodox, career that spanned over 80 years. Arrau was born on February 6, 1903, in Chillan, Chile. His father died less than 12 months after he was born, but his mother, an amateur pianist, recognized and nurtured his musical genius and became his first teacher.

Chilean legend says that Arrau could read music before he could read words. He made his formal performing debut in Chile at the age of five, playing selections composed by Wolfgang Amadeus Mozart, Ludwig van Beethoven, and Frederic Chopin. It became clear long before he reached ten years of age that his talents surpassed those of the available teachers and that his musical education would require the molding of a master mentor. In 1912 Arrau was sent to study with Martin Krause at the Stern Konservatorie in Berlin at the expense of the Chilean government.

It was through Krause that Arrau was first linked to the music of Beethoven in what would prove to be a profound lifelong musical and spiritual connection. Arrau's life was threaded to the composer's through a direct line of four teachers: Beethoven taught Karl Czerney, who taught Franz Liszt, who taught Krause. Once Arrau left Chile, Krause was his only teacher.

Young Arrau's introduction to the European concert scene came early. He performed before royalty and in salons and in 1914, at the age of 11, made his formal recital debut in Berlin, marking the official start of his career as a solo pianist. In 1922 he made his London debut in a recital with Dame Nellie Melba and the violinist Branislaw Hubermann.

Life in Berlin provided Arrau with the opportunity to bathe in the richness of European culture. Arrau considered it the duty of every great artist to become not only proficient in his or her field of expertise, but also to know as much as possible about all art—painting, sculpture, literature, and theater. He collected Etruscan and pre-Columbian art and was knowledgeable about European classic literature. Arrau felt that his appreciation of the wide range of arts and culture helped inform his interpretations of the music he played. Arrau's concert schedule, which over the course of his life took him all around the globe, enabled him to indulge in his interest in the world around him. Whether in Europe, America, Australia, South Africa, Israel, India, or Japan, the young pianist studied the local art and culture and collected artifacts.

Martin Krause died in 1918, when Arrau was in his late teens, an event that deeply shook the young musician. Arrau was further rocked in 1923 and 1924 by a disastrous U.S. reception on his first tour there. Performing with the Boston Philharmonic and the Chicago Symphony, Arrau found that U.S. acceptance of his style and work came slowly. Mournful about the loss of his mentor and concerned about maintaining his career, Arrau experienced a period of emotional, artistic, and financial insecurity. He eventually found a psychological and spiritual mentor in Jungian analyst Dr. Hubert Abrahamsohn, with whom he remained close throughout his life.

Arrau adhered to Carl Jung's notion of the "collective unconscious" in which the psychologist posits that the same universal aspects of human experience lie dormant in all people, clothed in symbolism, waiting to be exposed, felt, and lived. Arrau willingly underwent analysis throughout his life because he believed that if he could tap into his unconscious he could set in motion powerful creativity. He remained humble within this context, acknowledging his creativity as something available to all humans, his talent a gift.

Arrau's accomplishments and the honors he received throughout his career were myriad. In 1927 he won the International Prize for Pianists in Geneva, which helped build his early reputation as a Bach pianist. This link to the composer became firmly established in 1935 when Arrau completed the entire cycle of Johann Sebastian Bach's keyboard works. After completing the cycle, though, he decided that the harpsichord was the most appropriate instrument on which to play Bach's works and chose not to play them again. He did, however, find this cyclical approach to composers' works satisfying. For example, he played a cycle of Beethoven's works in Mexico City in 1938 and later did the same with compositions by Mozart and Franz Schubert.

Arrau married soprano Ruth Schneider in 1940 and shortly thereafter left Germany to live in New York City. He and his wife had children after moving to the United States. Although he lived there for years, he did not become a naturalized U.S. citizen until 1979.

Arrau's Mastery Acknowledged

In 1991, *New York Times* music critic Donal Henahan called Arrau's musical contributions "exemplary," noting in particular his detailed interpretations of Beethoven. "Arrau played a great deal of 19th-century music with great virtuosity and insight, but also with a well-tailored refinement that prompted critics early in his career to characterize his style as 'aristocratic,' a somewhat misleading label that stuck with him."

But Arrau was not merely a traditionalist. In fact, his musical taste and affinities varied greatly. Although primarily considered a Beethoven specialist, he also played the modern music of Arnold Schoenberg, Igor Stravinsky, and Ferruccio Busoni before they achieved fame in their own right. Whatever the composition, music critics found that Arrau's playing was marked by a thoughtfulness and consideration of detail not often evident in others' work.

Arrau was also regarded by many as a man of particularly sensitive and passionate temperament. He found it difficult, and often emotionally painful, to live up to the expectations thrust upon him by the public, the artistic and financial communities, and himself. Because he was so focused on his emotional life, he was considered by some to be temperamental. He would on occasion cancel performances if he felt that his spiritual affinity to a piece was out of balance.

In addition to his musical talents, Arrau was a man of great political passion and conscience. On one occasion he performed a benefit concert that raised $190,000 in contributions for Amnesty International's campaign for the release of political prisoners around the world. In addition, he refused to play in his native Chile for years in protest against the Marxist government of Salvadore Allende and later that of the right-wing military dictatorship of Augusto Pinochet. He did return to his homeland in 1981, though, arriving to a hero's welcome. The Chilean government declared a day of national mourning when he died. A nephew reported at the time that Arrau had claimed that, while his mind and intellect belonged to Germany, his heart was still with Chile.

Although Arrau was a dedicated teacher for many years, in his later life he became disillusioned with teaching because he saw a trend in the musical world towards placing an emphasis on technique rather than the personal development of the artist. He was committed to the notion that a pianist not only had to know myriad aspects of culture to be a well-rounded artist, but also must know him or herself emotionally. Arrau felt that many of his students were unwilling to take such steps. Still, he found comfort in having chosen and adhered to his own personal path of growth and exploration.

Arrau gave up performing after his wife died in 1989. He had been scheduled to perform a recital, his first in three years, when he died on June 9, 1991, in Murzzuschlag, Austria, at the age of 88 after undergoing intestinal surgery. He is best remembered for his personalized interpretations of the work of some of the greatest piano masters of all time, as well as his willful artistic spirit.

Books

The Annual Obituary, 1991, edited by Deborah Andrews, St. James Press, 1992.
The New Grove Dictionary of Music and Musicians, Vol. 1, edited by Stanley Sadie, Macmillan Publishers Limited, 1980.
Newsmakers, Gale Research, 1992.

Periodicals

New York Times, June 16, 1991. □

John David Ashcroft

U.S. Attorney General John Ashcroft (born 1942) was one of the most powerful members of President George W. Bush's cabinet. Ashcroft served as a state attorney general, Missouri governor, and U.S. senator prior to becoming U.S. attorney general. His conservative social views made him a controversial figure in the Bush administration.

Religious Upbringing

Ashcroft's paternal grandfather emigrated to the United States from Northern Ireland at the beginning of the twentieth century. Shortly after arriving, he was severely burned in a gasoline explosion and almost died. He thereafter dedicated his life to full-time Christian evangelism. Eventually he joined the Assembly of God Church.

Robert Ashcroft followed his father into the ministry. On May 9, 1942, while Robert and his wife, Grace, were living in Chicago, their son John was born. The Ashcrofts later moved to Springfield, Missouri, to be closer to the headquarters of the Assembly of God.

Robert Ashcroft served as president of three colleges affiliated with the Assembly of God. According to an article that appeared in the *New Yorker* in 2002, he began each day with a prayer that included the words, "Keep us from accident, injury, and illness. But most of all keep us from

evil." As attorney general, Ashcroft would continue his father's practice of morning group prayer.

Scholastic Achievements

As a student at Hillcrest High School in Springfield, Ashcroft was president of his class. He also played basketball and was captain and quarterback of the football team, and he earned a football scholarship to Yale University. At Yale, a knee injury kept him out of intercollegiate football, though he did well in intramural sports. Following his graduation with honors from Yale in 1964, Ashcroft attended the University of Chicago Law School on a scholarship.

While at the University of Chicago, Ashcroft met his future wife, Janet Roede, another law student. They were married in 1967. After graduating from law school, Ashcroft took his wife back to Springfield, where he opened a law practice. He also began teaching at Southwest Missouri State University.

Political Head Start

While still an undergraduate, Ashcroft had worked as a summer intern for his congressman. When the congressman declined to seek re-election in 1972, Ashcroft ran as a replacement candidate in the Republican Party primary, but lost the bid for the nomination with nearly 45 percent of the vote. Soon after, the 30-year-old Ashcroft was asked to fill an unexpired term as state auditor. However, Ashcroft failed to win election to the office two years later.

Missouri's attorney general John Danforth then hired Ashcroft as a legal assistant. (One of the other junior lawyers in Danforth's office was future Supreme Court Justice Clarence Thomas.) In 1976, when Danforth ran for the United States Senate, Ashcroft was elected to replace him as attorney general.

As Missouri's attorney general, Ashcroft made a single appearance before the United States Supreme Court, arguing a set of state statutes, including one that required all second-trimester abortions to be performed in a hospital. Ashcroft won re-election as attorney general in 1980, and he was selected chairman of the non-partisan National Association of Attorneys General.

Governor of Missouri

In 1984, Ashcroft ran successfully for governor of Missouri. As governor, he balanced eight consecutive state budgets. He also served as chairman of the Education Commission of the States. *Fortune* magazine named him one of the top ten education governors, and he made Missouri one of the best managed states financially. In 1991, he was elected chairman of the non-partisan National Governors Association.

But as Missouri's governor, Ashcroft also drew attention for opposing abortion rights and school desegregation. He attempted to appoint a task force to tighten Missouri's restrictive abortion law after the Supreme Court upheld the state's law in 1989. And a year later, he proposed limiting the number of abortions a woman could have to one.

Term limits prevented Ashcroft from seeking re-election in 1992, so in 1993 he ran for chairman of the Republican National Committee. But after meeting opposition from pro-choice Missouri Republicans, he abandoned the race. When Senator Danforth announced that he would not seek re-election in 1994, Ashcroft successfully ran for the open seat.

U.S. Senator

During his single six-year term in the Senate, Ashcroft served on the Senate Judiciary Committee and as chairman of the Constitution Committee. He sponsored seven proposed constitutional amendments, none of which won Congressional approval. The amendments would have banned abortions, prohibited burning the American flag, allowed line-item vetoes, required a balanced federal budget, required a super-majority vote in Congress for tax increases, established term limits for federal office holders, and made it easier to pass a constitutional amendment.

Ashcroft also attempted to abolish the National Endowment for the Arts for funding projects he considered indecent. He also blasted "activist" judges and opposed the appointment of David Satcher as Surgeon General because Satcher had a record of supporting abortion rights. A member of the National Rifle Association, Ashcroft also opposed nearly all gun control legislation. During the Monica Lewinsky scandal, Ashcroft was the first senator to call on President Clinton to resign if the allegations of misconduct proved true. Ashcroft's voting record in the Senate won him 100 percent approval ratings from the American Conservative Union and the Christian Coalition, and zero ratings from the Americans for Democratic Action, the League of Conservation Voters, and the National Organization for Women.

Ashcroft toyed with the idea of seeking the 2000 Republican presidential nomination, but instead focused on re-election to the Senate. Ashcroft's opponent Mel Carnahan died in a plane crash three weeks before the 2000 election. State officials decided it was too late to reprint the ballots, so Ashcroft officially ran against a dead man. After Carnahan posthumously won the election, his widow agreed to accept the Senate appointment. Ashcroft did not challenge that arrangement, even though his defeat seemed to place him on the threshold of political oblivion.

Attorney General

President-elect George W. Bush resurrected Ashcroft's career on December 22, 2000, when he nominated Ashcroft to be U.S. attorney general. Ashcroft's nomination ran into major opposition in the Senate over his conservative religious and political beliefs, including his opposition to abortion. Ashcroft was confirmed, but the 42 votes against him in the Senate was the largest number ever cast against an attorney general's confirmation. Following the contentious confirmation, Ashcroft vowed to renew the war on drugs, reduce violence due to firearms, and combat discrimination.

In the war on terrorism that followed the September 11, 2001, attacks on the United States, Ashcroft was accused of creating an atmosphere in which any opposition to his policies was seen as unpatriotic, if not subversive. Under policies put in place by the Bush administration, suspected terrorists were to be held on the slightest of charges to keep them off the streets. In the past, even organized crime figures or suspected spies had been granted their liberties until they actually committed crimes.

Ashcroft, along with Colin Powell and Donald Rumsfeld, emerged as one of the most powerful members of Bush's cabinet. Ashcroft became the administration's persona for the war on terrorism and took a number of controversial steps in its pursuit—including detaining over 1,000 people on charges not made public, deciding to monitor selected attorney-client conversations, and setting in place plans to try alleged war criminals in military tribunals.

Ashcroft continued to pursue his faith-based agenda as attorney general, even though he stated that he did not believe religious doctrine can or should be imposed. When he took over as attorney general in 2001, Ashcroft introduced prayer sessions in which up to 30 participants studied Bible passages and prayed. Ashcroft's sessions drew criticism for posing a conflict between church and state, until meetings with President Bush in the wake of the terrorist attacks pre-empted the prayer meetings.

In 2002, Ashcroft told Jeffrey Toobin of the *New Yorker,* "[T]here are standards that are moral and spiritual and eternal that I want to live up to. And people who win the battle write the history, and they may or may not get it right. I want to do what's right in God's sight."

Not surprisingly, Ashcroft's presumption that he would be able to interpret God's wishes for others drew criticism. He caused a stir when he had curtains erected around two twelve-foot art deco statues in the Justice building, one of which portrayed a partially unclad figure, prompting charges of prudishness and intolerance from his critics. And he gave no sign that he was prepared to compromise on his views about abortion—his Justice Department asked a federal appeals court to uphold a law banning "partial birth" abortions.

Political Phoenix

Ashcroft established a well-deserved reputation for turning defeat into victory. He told Toobin: "When I lost the race for Congress, I became state auditor. When I lost the race for state auditor, I became attorney general. When I lost the race for national committee chairman, I became a United States senator. When I lost the race for senator, I became the Attorney General."

By April 2002, Ashcroft enjoyed a 76 percent approval rating, according to a Gallup poll. Although Ashcroft stated that he had retired from electoral politics, some analysts saw him as a successor to Vice-President Dick Cheney should Cheney's health become a problem before the 2004 election.

Personal

Ashcroft was the author of *Lessons from a Father to His Son.* He was the co-author with his wife Janet (who taught law at Howard University) of two college law textbooks. The Ashcrofts have three children, a daughter and two sons, and one grandchild. Ashcroft enjoyed spending holidays on his 150-acre farm on the outskirts of his hometown of Springfield.

Ashcroft also enjoyed playing the piano. In 2003, he told *The American Enterprise,* "I play the piano almost every day, because it's a way to express ideas and to experiment. I also play the guitar a little bit, and the mandolin a little bit. Music, as I see it, is the study of relationships—tonal relationships—and in all of life, nothing is more important than relationships." Ashcroft is also an accomplished baritone; in the Senate, he was known as one of the Singing Senators, along with Trent Lott, Jim Jeffords, and Larry Craig.

Not without a sense of humor, Ashcroft told Toobin in the *New Yorker,* "There are only two things necessary in life—WD-40 and duct tape. . . . WD-40 for things that don't move that should, and duct tape for things that do move but shouldn't."

Periodicals

American Enterprise, January–February 2003.
New Yorker, April 15, 2002.
Time, May 28, 2001.

Online

"Attorney General John Ashcroft," *United States Department of Justice,* http://www.usdoj.gov/ag/ashcroftbio.html (January 2003).

"Profile: John Ashcroft," *BBC News,* http://news.bbc.co.uk/1/hi/
    world/americas/1120440.stm (January 2003). ☐

Gertrude Atherton

**American author Gertrude Atherton (1857–1948)
wrote many novels and other works set in California,
primarily in San Francisco. Many of her works consider themes related to the West, social ideas, and
women.**

Atherton was born Gertrude Horn on October 30,
1857, in San Francisco, California, the only child of
Thomas L. Horn and Gertrude Franklin Horn. Her
father was a businessman with a tobacco and cigar business
from Connecticut, while her mother was a Southern belle
who had been born in New Orleans. Atherton's mother
married Thomas Horn mostly for his money.

The Horns had a tough marriage that ended in divorce
when Atherton was two. Until the divorce, Atherton lived in
relative wealth. After the divorce, her parents both remarried and she had one half-brother and two half-sisters.
Immediately following her parents' divorce, Atherton lived
on a ranch owned by her maternal grandfather, Stephen
Franklin, in San Jose, California. He was a relative of Benjamin Franklin and worked as a newspaper editor and secretary of the Bank of California. Atherton credits her
grandfather with introducing her to serious literature, and
she read books in his library while growing up. She lived
there from 1859 to 1865, until her mother married to a man
she did not like, John Frederick Uhlhorn. They returned
when Uhlhorn left the family in 1870.

Though Atherton was well read because of her readings
in her grandfather's library, she did not receive much in the
way of a formal, organized education. She began writing on
her own when she was 14 years old. Atherton did attend St.
Mary's Hall School in Benicia, California. When she was 17
years old, she was a student at the Sayre Institute in Lexington, Kentucky. Atherton was sent there because it was
thought she might have tuberculosis and need treatment.
She did not finish her education there, but returned home.
Atherton was a very difficult child, and she later admitted
that she tried to be.

Married Atherton

When Atherton returned to California from Kentucky,
she found that her mother was dating a man 14 years
younger than her. George H. Bowen Atherton was a
wealthy heir. George Atherton decided he was more
attracted to daughter than mother and asked the 17-year-
old-girl to marry him. Atherton agreed, and they eloped in
early 1876. Because of the marriage, Atherton's relationship
with her mother ended.

The marriage was not particularly successful. The couple lived at Fair Oaks, the Atherton estate. Atherton's life
was run by her mother-in-law, who was a Chilean aristo-

crat, and her husband, who did not support her ambitions to
write. George Atherton was very jealous. He did not even
like Atherton to read on her own. Though the marriage
produced two children, George Goñi (who died at age six)
and Muriel Florence, Atherton was bored there. She allowed her children to be raised by her mother-in-law.

Wrote First Novel

On the sly while living at Fair Oaks, Atherton wrote her
first novel, *The Randolphs of Redwood.* This work was
based on a local scandal in society. It was first published in
serial fashion in the San Francisco-based publication
Argonaut in 1882. Its publication created a family scandal
in part because of the sexually suggestive scenes, though it
was published in the periodical anonymously. *The Randolphs* was later published as a novel in 1899 under the title
A Daughter of the Vine. Despite the objections of her husband and his family, Atherton continued to write by herself,
primarily at night. Her output included another novel as
well as stories.

Atherton was freed from her life at Fair Oaks when her
husband died in 1887 while sailing on a Chilean warship.
He died of a kidney hemorrhage. After his death, Atherton
left California and traveled to New York City. She then went
to Europe on several occasions, traveling to England,
France, and Germany. Atherton moved back to California in
1890.

Became Prolific Author

Atherton's widowhood allowed her time to write and do research. When she returned to California, she began doing many interviews and research on California. Many of her works from this time period feature strong heroines and are often set in her native state. They include: *What Dreams May Come* (1888), a story about reincarnation that was ignored by critics; *Hermia Suydam* (1889), which focuses on the love life of a single woman and was harshly criticized for being immoral; *Los Cerritos* (1890), her first novel set in California, specifically a French Convent; *The Dooms-woman* (1892), set in California in the Spanish period, this novel explores the conflict between Mexican and American cultures in a tragic love story; and *Before Gringo Came* (1894), about Old California and the missions.

Writing novels was not Atherton's only profession. She also wrote a weekly column for the *San Francisco Examiner* called "A Woman in Her Variety." There, she found a mentor in American author Ambrose Bierce, who praised *The Doomswoman*. When Atherton went east again to New York City in 1892, she also did some journalism work to make money.

Journalism was never Atherton's primary focus. She continued to write novels. It was in this time period that she wrote *Patience Sparhawk and Her Times*. But because Atherton could not secure a publisher, she moved to England in 1895. During her four years in that country, she published six novels.

Published *Patience Sparhawk*

Patience Sparhawk was published in London in 1897 and proved to be Atherton's first novel of significance. She was appreciated first as an author in Europe, where this book was popular. This was the first novel that introduced what became known as the new Western-American woman—a character featured in three other novels by Atherton. The story focuses on a woman who lived in the West in the 1890s who tried to succeed and overcome her low birth to be self-reliant and passionate. The novel offers Atherton's take on the argument about how much heredity versus environment affects a person.

Atherton also received critical acclaim for *The Californians* (1898), another novel that explores the themes of man versus woman and of nature. It also reflects conflicts with which Atherton was very familiar. In it, a woman tries to fight an oppressive Spanish society. *American Wives and English Husbands* (1898)—which was later republished as *Transplanted* in 1919—also features an independent woman, an American from California who marries an English gentleman. The novel explores the tensions in their marriage and different civilizations. This novel also attracted attention and received critical praise.

Returned to the United States

In 1899, Atherton returned to the United States and immediately began working on a novel about politics in the United States. She did research in Washington, D.C., observing the political process and meeting President William McKinley. The novel was published in 1900 as *Senator North,* and the main character was based on Eugene Hall of Maine. The novel reflects the political tensions of the time.

Atherton became as famous in the United States as she was in Europe with the 1902 publication of her fictionalized biography of Alexander Hamilton, *The Conqueror.* This was one of the first biographical novels. To write it, Atherton did much research, reading hundreds of books and traveling to the British West Indies where Hamilton was born. Though the book received mixed reviews, it sold a million copies.

Between 1903 and 1910, Atherton lived in San Francisco and Munich, Germany. She lost much in terms of papers in the San Francisco earthquake and fire in 1906. Strong women still figured prominently in her books. In *Ancestors* (1907), she wrote about a woman who is financially independent and who has a friendship with a rich British aristocrat, bringing them together with values and friendship instead of expected love. Atherton believed that *Tower of Ivory* (1910), a study of genius set in Munich, was her best novel, though most critics disagreed.

Atherton wrote a number of works about women's rights and the early feminist movement. They include *Julia France and Her Times* (1912), which was originally a play. In the novel, the title character, France, is a suffrage campaigner in England. Atherton took on other social issues. In 1914, she published *Perch of the Devil,* which is set in Butte, Montana, during the War of the Copper Kings.

Covered World War I

During World War I, Atherton returned to Europe to cover the conflict for the *New York Times.* While there, she also did charity work related to the war. Two novels came out of the experience: *The Living Present* (1917) and *The White Morning* (1918). In *The White Morning,* she explores the idea of German women revolting against Kaiser Wilhelm.

By the early 1920s, Atherton was in her sixties and underwent a treatment to rejuvenate older women by using radioactive x-rays to stimulate their ovaries and other sex glands. She used the experience as the basis for her best-selling novel *Black Oxen* (1923), which relates the story of the doctor who did these treatments, Dr. Eugen Steinach. *Black Oxen* also concerns romantic elements and was later adapted for film.

By this point in her life, Atherton primarily lived in San Francisco. Though she lived in California, she wrote a number of works about ancient Greece. In 1927, she published the fictionalized biography of Pericles and Aspasia entitled *The Immortal Marriage.* Like her other historical works, it contains many authentic details. Atherton also wrote *The Jealous Gods* (1928) about the Athenian general Alcibiades and *Dido, Queen of Hearts* (1929), about Dido, the woman reputed to have founded Carthage.

Two of Atherton's later novels return to her early themes. In *The House of Lee* (1940), she wrote about California and three generations of aristocratic women who face changes in money and social standing. *The Horn of Life* (1942) focuses on self-reliant women who marry for common interests and the character of the man, instead of money.

Atherton also reflected on herself later in her career. In 1932, she published an autobiography, *Adventures of a Novelist.* While she omitted some facts about her life, she also recounted her way of being different. While *My San Francisco: A Wayward Biography* (1946) was mostly about the city in which she was born, it also had many autobiographical elements.

Over the course of her writing career, Atherton published more than 56 books, mostly novels. Her best years were in the 1890s and early 1900s when she was regarded as one of the best women authors in the United States. Generally though, critics had a mixed view of Atherton. Many believed that she wrote too much without care, while others praised her use of realism, women characters as heroines, and what was going on in California in her time period.

One observer, Grant Overton, wrote in *The Women Who Make Our Novels* in 1928, "Almost without exception her fiction has been made the vehicle for ideas—not single, dominating ideas but casual, highly incisive judgments on everything under the sun. She lards her narratives with opinions, but it is not thereby rendered more tender. . . . Aristocratic in all her attitudes, she prefers frankness and is not afraid of coarseness."

Atherton was still writing near her death. She had a stroke about a month before she died on June 14, 1948, in San Francisco. As Brian St. Pierre wrote in the *San Francisco Chronicle,* "Though poorly educated and ill-prepared for much of a life, Atherton made herself, by sheer force of will and hard work, into a force to be reckoned with. Luck had nothing to do with her success . . . ."

Books

Benbow-Pfalzgraf, Taryn, ed., *American Women Writers: A Critical Reference Guide,* Volume 1, St. James Press, 2000.

Garraty, John A. and Mark C. Carnes, eds., *American National Biography,* Oxford University Press, 1999.

James, Edward T., ed., *Notable American Women 1607-1950: A Biographical Dictionary,* Volume 1, The Belknap Press, 1971.

Magill, Frank N., ed., *Great Lives from History: American Women Series,* Volume 1, Salem Press, 1995.

McHenry, Robert, ed., *Her Heritage: A Biographical Encyclopedia of Famous American Women,* Merriam-Webster, 1994.

Overton, Grant, *The Women Who Make Our Novels,* Dodd, Mead and Company, 1928.

Sadler, Geoff, ed., *Twentieth-Century Western Writers,* St. James Press, 1991.

Periodicals

San Francisco Chronicle, January 20, 1991. □

Mary Hunter Austin

American author Mary Hunter Austin (1868–1934) primarily wrote fiction and essays, with many of her works focusing on Native American culture. The novel *The Land of Little Rain* (1903) was her best known work.

Early Traumas and Inspiration

Austin was born on September 9, 1868, in Carlinville, Illinois, the fourth of six children born to George and Susannah (Graham) Hunter. George Hunter was a lawyer who emigrated from Yorkshire, England, in 1851. Austin's mother was of Scotch-Irish and French descent.

A veteran of the Civil War who had reached the rank of captain, George Hunter was ill for much of his daughter's young life with malaria that he had contracted in the conflict. He died when she was ten years old. A short time after, Austin's most supportive and understanding sister, Jennie, died of diphtheria. These deaths greatly affected Austin's life. Her mother ignored her, did not understand her, and was far more concerned with her older brother. Thus, from an early age, Austin looked to herself for support.

At the age of five, she had a spiritual experience that led to her formulating her own private religion. She also communicated with an inner, deeper personality that she called the "Inknower," "Genius," or "I-Mary." Austin later said that she drew from this part of herself when she wrote. She was often in a trance when she wrote.

From an early age, Austin had wanted to be a writer, but writing became her life after her father and sister died. She began writing poems at ten, immersed herself in academics and was a good student.

In 1884, Austin entered Blackburn College in Carlinville to study art and later changed her major to science. She also spent some time at the State Normal School in Bloomington, Illinois, in 1885. In 1888, she graduated from Blackburn College with a degree in science.

After Austin graduated, she moved to California with her mother and brother Jim. The family settled on a desert homestead near the San Joaquin Valley. Austin grew to love the desert. She taught school in Mountain View, California, but would spend much time alone in the desert at night. She was also friendly with those who were not part of white society, such as Native Americans and Chinese laborers in the area.

Difficult Family Life

In May 1891, Austin married Stafford Wallace Austin, who was a teacher and grape grower. He later became the manager of an irrigation project that failed, causing the couple many hardships. Adding to their challenges was that their daughter, Ruth, was born with mental disabilities.

Because of her husband's failures, including his inability to keep another job as a superintendent of schools, Austin had to return to teaching, and soon she also began to look to writing for income. The family moved between desert towns in California. Austin taught at the Methodist Academy in Bishop from 1895 to 1897, the Lone Pine School in 1897, and the Normal School in Los Angeles in 1899. Eventually, Austin put her daughter in an institution because she could not care for her.

Austin often wrote stories and poems for the amusement of her students. In 1892, she sold her first short story and soon began contributing to the magazine *Overland Monthly*. Many of her early works were about Native Americans and the desert. She had been taking notes and writing sketches since moving to the desert.

The Land of Little Rain

In 1903, Austin published her first book, *The Land of Little Rain*, which became a classic and her best known work. It consisted of 14 sketches that focused on the Mojave Desert and the Native Americans who lived there. Many essays concerned the battle between life and death. The book gave her instant fame.

While Austin was becoming a successful writer, her marriage failed. Her husband was not compassionate and could not support her intellectually, physically, or financially. She left her husband in 1903 or 1905 and divorced him in 1914.

During this period she was described by a visitor quoted by Grant Overton in *The Women Who Make Our Novels:* "Mrs. Austin has an Indian-like solemnity, a pervading shyness. All that she says has a certain value. She speaks seldom. Her utterance is rather slow and her remarks are usually grave. The desert has cloistered her."

Beginning in 1904, Austin lived in Carmel, California, where she built a home. At different times, Austin also lived in an artist colony there, as well as in Los Angeles and Greenwich Village in New York City. She associated with bohemian authors such as Jack London.

Austin began writing about one book a year. She published *The Basket Woman* (1904) about Paiute Indian legends. In 1905, *Isidro,* a romantic novel about missions in California, went to press. One of her more successful books was *The Flock* (1906). This follow-up to *The Land of Little Rain* focused on sheep herding and sheep raising in the desert Southwest. An underlying theme of the book was how people abused the land.

Austin's failed marriage also served as source material. In 1908, she published the novel *Santa Lucia,* a book about women and marriage. In this novel, she argued against the conventions of the day, in particular the taboo against wives working outside the home and the mandate that husbands should take charge of family finances even if they were not equipped to do so.

Traveled to Italy for Cure

In 1910, Austin traveled to Italy because she was told by a doctor that she was dying of breast cancer. There, she studied prayer techniques under the tutelage of the Roman Catholic church. Austin believed that her prayers cured her cancer.

Austin resumed writing, and two works were directly influenced by her experience in Italy. They were *Christ in Italy: Being the Adventures of a Maverick among Masterpieces* (1912) and *The Man Jesus: Being a Brief Account of the Life and Teachings of the Prophet of Nazareth* (1915).

On her way back to the United States, Austin stopped in London. There she learned that she had a wide audience that included such authors as W.B. Yeats, George Bernard Shaw, and H.G. Wells.

When Austin returned to the United States, she first went to New York, where her drama *The Arrow Maker* was being prepared for staging. This play was produced in the spring of 1911. It was about an ambitious Paiute medicine woman. Austin wrote another play, *Fire,* also about Native Americans, which was produced in Carmel in 1912.

Published *Woman of Genius*

From 1912 to 1924, Austin split her time between New York and California, though she lived primarily in New York City. In 1912, she published what many believed was her best novel, *A Woman of Genius.* This work, which featured some autobiographical elements, was about women having to chose between marriage and career. As in many of her books about women, Austin also explored how and why women were subjugated by men. This early feminist novel led to Austin later being embraced by the women's movement of the 1970s.

Austin continued to address social issues, though in a heavy-handed manner, with *The Ford* (1917) and *No. 26 Jayne Street* (1920). The latter explored the idea of an equal marriage. Many critics preferred her books about Native Americans.

Active in New Mexico

After recovering from a nervous breakdown, Austin in 1924 moved to New Mexico, where she built an adobe which she named La Casa Querida. That same year, she published *The Land of Journeys' Ending,* a collection of sketches about New Mexico and Arizona. Austin became an activist while living in Santa Fe and Taos, New Mexico. She was involved in conserving the arts and handicrafts of Native Americans. In 1927, she was a representative for New Mexico at the Seven States Conference concerning the proposed Boulder Dam and related water diversion problems.

Late in her career, Austin published a number of different kinds of works. In 1928, she published her only collection of poetry, targeted at children, entitled *The Children Sing in the Far West.* Four years later, she published her autobiography, *Earth Horizon.* Writing in the third person, Austin covered the whole of her life and philosophies, including her experiences with God, her love of the Southwest, her difficult family life, and feminism. In 1934, she published *One-Smoke Stories,* a collection of short stories and sketches about Native American legends and folk tales, many with Southwestern themes.

Lasting Impact

In all, Austin published 32 books and over 250 articles. Most were about Native Americans and their heritage and nature but others dealt with such topics as socialism, feminism, and issues of the day. Austin was also a lecturer and public speaker. She spoke in a number of places about Native Americans, including her ideas about the sources of their poetic rhythms. She was also a social activist who was part of the suffrage and birth control movements and a socialist sympathizer.

While beginning a new novel, Austin suffered a heart attack and died in her sleep on August 13, 1934, in Santa Fe. She was cremated and her ashes set in a cave in the mountains.

Austin did not live the typical life of a woman of her era and that was reflected in her writing. Stacy Alaimo wrote in *Studies in American Fiction:* "Austin sought in nature a place that was not domesticated and that did not domesticate women. . . . No utilitarian ground, Austin's land pulsates spiritually, aesthetically, and erotically. Sometimes Austin celebrates the borderland as a place to think beyond the confines of gender; sometimes she couples women and nature through mutual strength and resistance to male domination. Often, by picturing the land as a mistress, Austin creates a feminine land that counters domestic ideology and conjoins women and nature not as a victims but as powerful allies."

Book

Adamson, Lynda G., *Notable Women in American History: A Guide to Recommended Biographies and Autobiographies,* Greenwood Press, 1999.

Benbow-Pfalzgraf, Taryn, ed., *American Women Writers: A Critical Reference Guide,* Volume 1, St. James Press, 2000.

Garraty, John A., and Mark C. Carnes, eds., *American National Biography,* Oxford University Press, 1999.

James, Edward T, ed., *Notable American Women, 1607-1950: A Biographical Dictionary,* Volume 1, Belknap Press, 1971.

Kester-Shelton, Pamela, ed., *Feminist Writers,* St. James Press, 1996.

Overton, Grant, *The Women Who Make Our Novels,* Dodd, Mead, and Company, 1928.

Sadler, Geoff, *Twentieth-Century Western Writers,* St. James Press, 1991.

Snodgrass, Mary Ellen, *Encyclopedia of Frontier Literature,* ABC-CLIO, 1997.

Periodicals

Boston Globe, September 27, 1998.

Studies in American Fiction, Spring 1998.

Studies in the Novel, Spring 1998. ☐

B

Henk Badings

A prolific composer of more than 600 works, Henk Badings (1907–1987) is one of the best known figures in twentieth-century Dutch music. A favorite of critics and avant garde theorists, Badings wrote many works in the traditional diatonic scale but is most famous for his electronic and microtonal music. The Russian composer, conductor, and pianist Nicolas Slominsky described Badings's musical style in David Ewen's book *Composers Since 1900: A Biographical and Critical Guide* as "romantic modernism . . . in his melodic material he often uses a scale of alternating whole tones and semitones."

Hendrik Herman Badings was born on January 17, 1907, in Bandung, Java, Indonesia, to Dutch parents. His mother and father died when he was eight years old, and he was sent back to the Netherlands to live with a guardian. Although he studied violin and exhibited obvious talent, he was forbidden to pursue a career in music. Instead, Badings studied geology and mining technology at the Technical University of Delft. He graduated with honors in 1931 and began to work as a lecturer, assistant, and researcher in the school's paleontology and historic geology department.

Composed First Symphony

Badings's interest in music had never abated, however, and he had continued to study independently. Shifting his focus from performance to composition, he wrote his first piece, a violin concerto, in 1928. During his later years at Delft, he studied briefly with the famous Dutch performer, critic, and composer Willem Pijper. Although their musical styles were completely different, Pijper influenced his young pupil sufficiently to write his First Symphony in 1930. The composition was premiered by the Concertgebouw Orchestra in Amsterdam while Badings was still a university student.

The work generated a great deal of public interest, especially since the composer was a virtual unknown. His Second Symphony, which followed two years later, was equally well received. His Third Symphony, composed in 1934, is one of his best known orchestral works and one that helped establish his international reputation as a composer. In that same year Badings took teaching posts at both the Rotterdam Music Conservatory and the Amsterdam Music Lyceum. He became a co-director of the Amsterdam school in 1937, when he was given the job of overhauling the school's teaching methods.

In the 1930s, while Badings was composing his first symphonies, he also produced smaller works, such as the *Largo en Allegro* in 1935 and the Symphonic Variations a year later. During this period his music was "predominantly elegiac, with generally dark orchestral colours and thick harmonies," according to Stanley Sadie in *The New Grove Dictionary of Music and Musicians*. David Ewen remarked on Badings's "serious, tragic overtones" during this period of composition. Even his famous Third Symphony is characterized by music Ewen calls "tragic and sparse . . . [that] seems to herald the coming war in a similar fashion to Vaughan Williams's Symphony no. 4 of the same year."

Beginning in 1941 the mood of his music began to lift, and he produced lighter, more playful pieces that are exemplified by his 1941 ballet *Orpheus en Euridike* and the comic opera *Liefde's listen (Love's intrigues)* in 1944. He composed smaller works during this period as well, including the well-known String Quartet no. 3.

Accused of Nazi Collaboration

During the German occupation of the Netherlands, Badings was installed as head of the State Music Conservatory in the Hague. Being given such a prominent position earned him much enmity, however, and many viewed his acceptance of the job as proof of his Nazi sympathies. According to Mark Morris in the *Guide to 20th-Century Composers,* the Nazis themselves lauded him as "the very model of a Nationalist Socialist artist." In 1946 Badings was convicted of collaboration and banned from all professional associations and activities for two years. David Ewen in *Composers Since 1900* says he was "completely exonerated" of these charges in 1947. Less enthusiastic, *Baker's Biographical Dictionary of Musicians* states cryptically instead that he "was permitted to resume his career." Whether or not he was wrongly accused, the stigma of whispered Nazi collaboration continued to hang over him and protests accompanied the premieres of his works for many years afterward.

Experimented with Alternative Tonalities

From the earliest days of his career Badings was fascinated with alternative tonalities, exploring music based on hexatonic (six-note) and octatonic (eight-note) scales. (Western music is based on the diatonic scale, with seven notes per scale in a familiar series of whole and half steps.) Despite these avant-garde leanings, much of his work is surprisingly melodic and traditional, marked by counterpoint and conventional thematic structure.

Despite the social and political turmoil of the 1940s, Badings produced some of his most important works during this decade. His third and fourth violin concerti debuted in 1944 and 1946, respectively; his Fourth Symphony premiered in Rotterdam in 1947. His Fifth Symphony, written in 1948 to commemorate the 60th anniversary of the Concertgebouw Orchestra, demonstrates his increasing interest in different tonalities—nondiatonic scales of six, seven, and eight notes.

Composed Electronic Music

Bading's interest in polytonal (nontraditional) composition led him to explore electronic music beginning in the early 1950s, although he continued to write more conventional orchestral pieces as well. His radio opera *Orestes,* first broadcast in 1954, combines *musique concrète* (the earliest type of electronic music, which uses recorded sounds that are altered and distorted) and acoustic instruments. The opera won the Prix Italia in 1954 and was later broadcast in an English translation by the BBC. His opera *Salto mortale (Death leap),* which won the Salzburg Award in the International Competition of Television Societies in 1959, was the first to use an entirely electronic score. Ewen calls *Martin Korda, D.P.* Badings's 1960 opera, his "most successful use of electronic sounds . . . [Set in a] displaced persons' camp . . . Badings uses electronics to

suggest the nightmarish quality of a hallucination. Loudspeakers throughout the auditorium helped make the audience acutely conscious of the experience of terrifying unreality."

In 1951 Badings developed and expanded his theories in *Tonaliteitsproblemen in de nieuwe muziek (Tonality problems in new music),* a paper published by the Flemish Academy of Sciences. He began to compose his most ambitious pieces yet, using a 31-tone octave first proposed by the seventeenth-century Dutch scientist Christiaan Huygens. In this musical system the whole tones are divided into fifths, each of which is called a *diése.* Several of these microtonal pieces were composed for a unique 31-tone organ that had been designed by the Dutch physicist Adriaan Fokker; *Reeks van kleine klankstukken in selectieve toonsystemen foor 31-toonsorgel (Series of small sound pieces in selected tone systems for 31-tone organ)* and *Suite van kleine klankstukken (Suite of small sound pieces)* were both composed in 1954.

Working with the Philips Company in Eindhoven, Badings helped establish an electronic music studio in 1956. The studio became part of the University of Utrecht in 1961, with Badings retained as its director. This was his first academic foothold since 1946, and he taught acoustics and information theory at the university for 16 years. In that same year he began a 10-year stint as a professor of composition at the Staatliche Hochschule für Musik in Stuttgart, Germany. His international work as a visiting professor took him to the University of Adelaide, Australia; Point Park College, Pittsburgh, Pennsylvania; and South Africa.

In 1959 Badings began to use computers to both compose and analyze music. His Toccata 1 and Toccata 2, for example, were based on a series of electronically generated tones. By using computers to study the mathematical relationships between notes and applying it to Haydn's works, he also developed a method of dating musical compositions based on the probabilities inherent in their tonalities and harmonies.

Won Prizes and Critical Acclaim

Badings's music was almost always commissioned and was usually a critical success as well. In addition to the Prix Italia and Salzburg Awards, he won a string of honors that began with the Sienese Accademia Chigiana Prize for his Piano Quintet in 1952; the Paganini Prize, awarded for two violin sonatas in 1953; and his Double Piano Concerto, which won the Marzotto Prize in 1954. He earned a second Prix Italia in 1971 for the oratorio *Ballade van die bloeddorstige Jagter (Ballad of the bloodthirsty hunter);* the Sweelinck Prize, awarded by the Dutch government, for lifetime achievement in 1972; a medal of arts, sciences, and letters from the Académie Française in 1981; and a posthumous award for the best European choral composition in 1988.

Badings lived in Maarheeze, the Netherlands, for the last 15 years of his life. He died there on June 26, 1987.

Books

Ewen, David, *Composers Since 1900: A Biographical and Critical Guide,* H. W. Wilson & Co., 1969.

Greene, David Mason, *Greene's Biographical Encyclopedia of Composers,* Doubleday & Co., 1985.

Klemme, Paul, *Henk Badings, 1907–1987: Catalog of Works,* Detroit Studies in Music Bibliography, no. 71, Harmonie Park Press, 1993.

Morris, Mark, *A Guide to 20th-Century Composers,* Methuen, 1996.

Sadie, Stanley, editor, *New Grove Dictionary of Music and Musicians,* Volume 2, Macmillan, 1980.

Slominsky, Nicolas, editor, *Baker's Biographical Dictionary of Musicians,* Volume 1, Schirmer, 1990.

Online

"Badings, Henk" *Encyclopedia Britannica,* http://www.britannica.com/eb/article?eu=11848&=0&=badings= (February 12, 2003).

"The Development of 31-Tone Music," Huygens-Fokker Foundation, Centre for Microtonal Music, http://www.xs4all.nl/~huygensf/doc/beerart.html (February 12, 2003).

"Henk Badings," Huygens-Fokker Foundation, Centre for Microtonal Music, http://www.xs4all.nl/~huygensf/english/badings.html (February 12, 2003).

"Microtonal Musical Instruments, Huygens-Fokker Foundation, Centre for Microtonal Music, http://www.xs4all.nl/~huygensf/english/instrum.html#fokker (February 12, 2003).
□

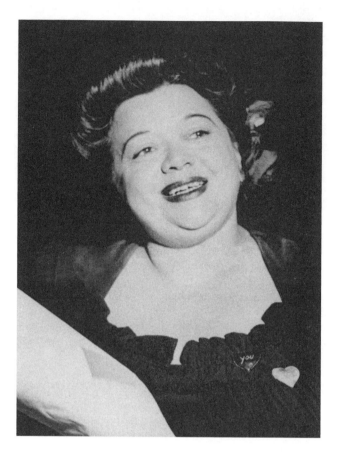

Mildred Bailey

One of the first female singers to make a name for herself in the American pantheon of jazz, Mildred Bailey (1907–1951) managed to capture the subtleties of the era's African American blues and ragtime music. Bailey early on developed her own unique way to underline the meaning of the words she sang. She performed with some of the finest musicians of the swing era—including Benny Goodman, Paul Whiteman, Coleman Hawkins, and Red Norvo, her husband for most of the 1930s. Plagued by health problems for much of her life, she died when she was only 44 years old in 1951.

Many jazz lovers had a hard time reconciling Bailey's high, dulcet tones with her rather corpulent body. During the hey-days of the Swing Era, she and Norvo, her husband at the time, were dubbed "Mr. and Mrs. Swing." Influenced by the stylings of Ethel Waters, Connie Boswell, and Bessie Smith, she developed a uniquely soft yet swinging delivery that delighted nightclub audiences wherever she appeared throughout the United States. Although she is perhaps best remembered for her work in jazz, Bailey enjoyed a good deal of success in popular music as well. Although she appeared with some of the most successful bands of the Swing Era, she ended her career as a solo performer, drawing thousands of appreciative fans to her appearances at some of New York City's most popular jazz clubs.

Began Performing at an Early Age

Bailey was born Mildred Rinker on February 27, 1907, in Tekoa, a small town in eastern Washington state, close to the border with Idaho. While she was still quite young, Bailey moved with her mother and three brothers to nearby Spokane. Her mother, who was part Native American, schooled Bailey and her brothers in Native American traditions, and the family often visited relatives on the Coeur d'Alene Indian Reservation in nearby Idaho. Bailey learned music from her mother and began performing at an early age, playing the piano and singing in movie theaters in the early 1920s. Her interest in jazz was shared by older brother Al and a neighborhood friend, Harry Lillis (Bing) Crosby. In writing the liner notes for one of her early albums, Crosby recalled, as quoted in *Dictionary of American Biography:* "Mildred Bailey gave me my start. She took off Hollywood for newer and broader fields, and a year or so later, Al and I followed her there. She introduced us to Marco [Wolff], at that time a very big theatrical producer, and we were on our way—with a lot of her material, I might add. She was *mucha mujer,* with a heart as big as Yankee Stadium."

By the mid-1920s, Bailey, who had married and divorced at an early age, retaining nothing of her first husband but his last name, was headlining at a club in Hollywood, performing a mixture of pop, vaudeville standards, and early jazz tunes. In quick succession she worked as a "song demonstrator," toured with the dance revue of Fanchon and Marco Wolff, and was a solo vocalist on Los Angeles radio station KMTR. Bailey's first big break came when she sent a demo record to popular bandleader Paul Whiteman. The bandleader had already hired Crosby and Bailey's older brother, Al Rinker, to appear with his band as the "Rhythm Boys." Impressed with Bailey's vocal stylings, Whiteman hired her to sing with his band, making her one of the first female singers to be featured with a major dance orchestra. In 1932 Bailey gained added fame when she recorded Hoagy Carmichael's "Rockin' Chair," written especially for her. It became Bailey's signature song and earned her the moniker "The Rockin' Chair Lady."

Bailey developed a relationship with jazz xylophonist Red Norvo (Kenneth Norville) not long after he joined the Whiteman band in 1931. Shortly thereafter the couple was married. Not long after they were wed, Norvo left Whiteman to start his own band and Bailey went off on her own to build a career for herself as a radio vocalist. Norvo's band soon ran into trouble and appeared likely to break up. Bailey offered to join the group as vocalist in an effort to prevent disbandment. Some of the finest work of Bailey's career came from her collaboration with Norvo. Working together, the couple came to be known as "Mr. and Mrs. Rhythm." One of the most memorable of their collaborations was on the album *Smoke Dreams*.

In a review of *Smoke Dreams* (reissued by Definitive Records in 1999) that appears on the *Songbirds* web site, Jeff Austin wrote: "The Red Norvo Orchestra with Mildred Bailey had an unmistakable sound, with Bailey's feather-light vocals paralleled by the delicacy and grace of Norvo's xylophone, all couched in light, ever-swinging arrangements by the likes of Eddie Sauter. The title track, 'Smoke Dreams,' epitomizes what made Bailey/Norvo different than anyone else. Legend very credibly has it that, subsequent to Sauter's being the object of a Bailey rage, he fashioned for her an arrangement that would be any other singer's worst nightmare, riddled with ear-bending dissonance that might have permanently traumatized most other lady band singers. Undaunted, Bailey sails serenely through the din—and one is left wondering what other band (save, perhaps, for Stan Kenton ten years later) might have attempted a chart so avant-garde."

Bailey and Norvo Divorced

Other songs closely identified with Bailey during her years with Norvo's band include "I've Got My Love to Keep Me Warm" and "Weekend of a Private Secretary." Although they remained close friends, Bailey and Norvo realized by the end of the 1930s that their marriage was no longer working and divorced. They continued to work together from time to time, however. About 1940, economic pressures forced Norvo to reduce the size of his group, freeing Bailey to once again pursue her solo career. Through the first half of the 1940s she was backed on her recordings by some of the era's finest musicians, including Johnny Hodges, Mary Lou Williams, Teddy Wilson, Roy Eldridge, Coleman Hawkins, Bunny Berigan, Artie Shaw, Benny

Goodman, and Tommy and Jimmy Dorsey. Having performed with scores of African American musicians throughout her career, Bailey took an extremely enlightened view of race relations and at one point in her career had sung at a benefit in Harlem's Savoy Ballroom to aid the Scottsboro Boys.

Famed record producer John Hammond worked with Bailey on a number of her recordings in the late 1930s and early 1940s. In his liner notes for the three-LP retrospective album, *Mildred Bailey: Her Greatest Performances* (1962), which are discussed on the *Songbirds* Web site, Hammond asserted: "Mildred was resentful that she was not a commercial success, and there was always a battle between us over the kind of accompaniment she should have on records." Taking sharp issue with Hammond's observations is reviewer Austin. In his review of Bailey's *All of Me* (reissued by Definitive in 1999), Austin wrote: "This idea has been recycled time and again in biographical material about Bailey. Not only is it probably untrue, it casts her in a slightly pathetic light. Hammond's remark is particularly strange when one considers that commercial success in terms of hit records had infinitely less to do with accompaniment than with material. Any singer wanting to hit it big on jukeboxes would not have recorded such a wealth of unusual songs by Willard Robison. . . . More importantly, documentary evidence exists in interviews about Bailey with Bing Crosby, Johnny Mercer (both of whom knew a great deal about commercialism), and her brother Al, that Bailey resolutely wouldn't compromise on material, and simply wasn't interested in doing what it took to make herself a commercial entity. According to Crosby, she frankly didn't want to work all that hard."

Superstardom Eluded

Whatever the reasons may have been, superstardom eluded Bailey. The singer blamed her plumpness for her lack of commercial success, while others suggested that it was really Bailey's temper and sharp tongue that were her undoing. There's plenty of evidence that Bailey felt especially bitter towards better-looking female vocalists, many of whom she felt lacked her talent. Throughout her life, Bailey blamed her obesity on a glandular condition, although many of her friends attributed it instead to her great love of food.

Bailey continued to perform and record until the mid-1940s. She appeared on Benny Goodman's Camel Caravan radio program and was given her own radio program for a brief period in the mid-1940s. However, mounting health problems forced her to step away from her career by mid-decade. A longtime diabetic, Bailey also suffered from a heart condition and hardening of the arteries. With her two pet dachshunds, she retired to a farm in upstate New York, returning to the New York City club circuit now and again for a solo engagement. She was a particular favorite at the Café Society. Bailey got some financial help from composer Jimmy Van Heusen, who arranged to split her medical bills with Frank Sinatra and longtime friend Bing Crosby. Finally, by the early 1950s, Bailey's health had deteriorated to such an extent that she was forced to give up performing altogether. On December 12, 1951, Bailey died penniless at Poughkeepsie Hospital in Poughkeepsie, New York.

Enjoyed Resurgence in Popularity

A unique talent in almost every respect, Bailey will long be remembered as one of the great jazz stylists of her time. Although her singing—swinging, straightforward, and delivered with superb diction—was very much of her time, it remains fresh and sparkling. Perhaps Bailey's career was best summed up by jazz musician Loren Schoenberg in his review of *The Complete Columbia Recordings of Mildred Bailey* (released by Mosaic on CD in 2002) for National Public Radio's (NPR's) *Jazz Reviews.* Schoenberg wrote: "Mildred Bailey was one of the greatest jazz singers in the Swing Era. Yet today her name is unknown, largely because the great majority of recordings have been out of print for decades. Like Louis Armstrong, Mildred Bailey could transform the most hackneyed Tin Pan Alley trite into something beautiful and, at times, profound." Of Bailey's rendition of the 1938 tune, "I Can't Face the Music," Schoenberg wrote that "the phrasing is worthy of Maria Callas or of Armstrong. However, Bailey had something that Armstrong never had—a genius for an arranger. Eddie Sauter was one of the most original arranger/composers to emerge . . . in the 1930s."

Late in the 20th century and in the early years of the new millennium, Bailey's work enjoyed a resurgence in popularity as a number of her recordings of the 1930s and 1940s were reissued on compact disc. She received another posthumous honor in September 1994 when the U.S. Postal Service issued a 29-cent stamp bearing her image as part of its Pop, Jazz, and Blues Legends series. Bailey's vocal style has often been likened to that of jazz great Billie Holiday, whom Bailey, husband Red Norvo, and record producer John Hammond discovered singing in a small club in New York City. Bailey's influence is also seen in the work of Bing Crosby and Tony Bennett. Sadly, Bailey's low self-esteem, body image problems, and failing health prematurely crippled her career and kept her from developing into the superstar she so richly deserved to be.

Books

Almanac of Famous People, 6th ed., Gale Research, 1998.
Dictionary of American Biography, Supplement 5: 1951–1955, American Council of Learned Societies, 1977.

Online

"100 Jazz Profiles: Mildred Bailey (1907–1951)," *BBC-Radio 3,* http://www.bbc.co.uk/radio3/jazz/jazzprofiles/bailey.shtml (February 8, 2003).
The Complete Columbia Recordings of Mildred Bailey, NPR Jazz Reviews, http://www.nprjazz.org/reviews/jrcd.mbailey.html (February 9, 2003).
"Mildred Bailey," *All Music Guide,* http://www.allmusic.com/cg/amg.dll?p = amg& = 1Mildred + Bailey (February 8, 2003).
"Mildred Bailey," *Slipcue.com E-Zine,* http://www.slipcue.com/music/jazz/artists/mildredbailey.html (February 9, 2003).
"Mildred Bailey," *Solid!,* http://www.parabrisas.com/d_baileym .html (February 8, 2003).
"Mildred Bailey," *Songbirds,* http://www.mrlucky.com/song birds/html/oct99/9910_bailey.html (February 8, 2003). □

Amy Beach

The best known woman composer of her time period and the first in the United States, Amy Beach (1867–1944) did not just create small pieces, but large orchestral works, and other complex compositions were part of her repertoire. She was the first American woman to write a symphony, and this was especially important because she received all her training in the United States.

Born Amy Marcy Cheney on September 5, 1867, in Henniker, New Hampshire, Beach was the only child of Charles Abbor Cheney and Clara Imogene (Marcy) Cheney. Her father was a mathematician and businessman who worked in paper manufacturing business that his father owned, who later had his own paper importing business. Her mother was a musician, a singer, and pianist.

Beach exhibited talent from an early age. She began singing tunes on pitch and with accuracy when she was a year old and she had also taught herself to read by the time she was three. The Cheney family moved to the Boston, Massachusetts, area in 1871, and it was at this time that Beach began composing her own melodies, mainly waltzes.

Began Piano Lessons

When Beach was six years old, she started taking formal piano lessons with her mother as her first teacher. Within a year, Beach was playing Ludwig van Beethoven and Frederic Chopin; she gave her first recital by the time she was seven. Beach went on to have a number of good teachers as a young piano student. They included Carl Baermann (who was a student of Franz Liszt) and Ernst Perabo. Beach's innate sense of harmony and form helped her to achieve in her studies. Although her parents were advised that she would benefit from studying at a European conservatory—rather than in the United States—they chose to keep her home.

As with her musical training, Beach's academic education was also home-centered. Her mother taught her at home for six years. She then attended a private school run by W. L. Whittemore. Beach particularly enjoyed natural science and languages like French and German. While she was encouraged academically, it was within the limits of what was expected of young women in this time period.

Though Beach became known as a composer, she only took one class in music theory. When she was 15 years old, she took a harmony course taught by Junius Welch Hill. Also in this time period, she wrote her first published piece, a song to the poem of Henry Wadsworth Longfellow "The Rainy Day."

Gave First Recitals

In October 1883, Beach gave her first significant public recital at the Boston Music Hall. For the event, she played Ignaz Moscheles's *G Minor Concerto* with the orchestra

and as a soloist. She also performed Chopin's *Rondo in E-flat*. Between 1883 and 1885, Beach gave several more recitals in Boston.

One of Beach's last public recitals was with the Boston Symphony Orchestra; she played Chopin's *F Minor Concerto*. In addition to her recitals, she appeared as a soloist with the Theodore Thomas Orchestra and the Boston Symphony Orchestra. For all her public appearances, Beach generally received many positive reviews.

Married Dr. Beach

On December 2, 1885, Beach was married to Dr. Henry Beach, who was 24 years her elder and a widower. Dr. Beach was a surgeon and professor at Harvard. He had followed her career from the time she was a child in part because he was also a musician, albeit on an amateur level.

After the marriage, Beach did not perform in public except for charity functions. Any time she performed, her fees were donated to charity. She did this at the request of her husband, who wanted her to be a wife and not a concert pianist. Upon her marriage, Beach was known publicly as Mrs. H. H. A. Beach.

Focused on Composing

Dr. Beach did not want his wife to perform, but he did encourage her musical career. It was at his suggestion that she began composing. He did not encourage her to formally study the subject of composition believing that it might inhibit her originality. It was because of these restrictions that Beach became a virtually self-taught composer.

To begin her training, Beach studied music theory, counterpoint, musical form, and instrumentation on her own. She studied Bach's fugues by writing out her version of one of his works then comparing it to the original. Beach taught herself orchestration by writing notations of themes she heard at concerts, looking at the original score, and then putting the versions side by side.

Beach's first works were poems that she liked, set to her original music. While she would continue to do these kinds of pieces throughout her career, Beach would do much larger and more complex pieces including major orchestral works, as well as choral works, chamber works, church music, and cantatas.

First Major Work Performed

In 1892, after three years of labor, Beach's first major work was performed, *Mass in E-flat major,* numbered Opus 5. It was for chorus, vocal quartet, soloists, orchestra, and organ. The mass was performed by the Handel and Haydn Society with the Boston Symphony Orchestra. This marked the first time a composition written by a woman was performed by these groups. It was received positively.

That same year, Beach had her second work performed, an aria entitled *Eilende Wolken,* for contralto and orchestra, based on Friedrich von Schiller's *Mary Stuart.* Beach was asked to write this for Mrs. Carl Alves, who had been the alto soloist for the premiere of *Mass in E-flat major.* The first performance of *Eilende Wolken* was given by the Symphony Society of New York. Again, this was the first work arranged by a woman to be performed by this group.

Women remained the focus of Beach's next major work. She was commissioned to write a piece for the dedication for the Women's Building at the World's Columbia Exposition in Chicago. *Festival Jubilate* (Opus 17) was written for chorus and orchestra and premiered in 1893.

Wrote First Symphony

In 1896, Beach wrote the *Gaelic Symphony* (also known as the *Symphony in E-minor),* which was the first symphony ever written by an American woman and the first symphony written by a woman and performed by an American orchestra. It was based on Gaelic themes. After its premiere at the Boston Symphony, it was performed throughout the United States. An article by David Wright in the *New York Times* quoted Boston composer George Whitefield Chadwick as writing that the symphony was: "full of fine things, melodically, harmonically, orchestrally, and mighty well built besides."

Beach wrote a number of other significant works in the late 1890s and first decade of the 1900s. In 1897, the *Sonata in A-minor* for violin and piano premiered. Beach herself played in the first performance with Franz Kneisel. At the 1900 premier of the *Piano Concerto in C-sharp minor* (opus 454), Beach also performed, this time with the Boston Symphony. Beach received worldwide fame with her 1899 composition to the Robert Browning poem "The Year's at the Spring'' (opus 44, number 1). Another frequently performed work was her *Quintet for Pianoforte and Strings* (opus 67), an instrumental piece.

While Beach was becoming an established and respected composer, she was also concerned with struggling musicians. Before her husband's death, she had events in her home every Wednesday in which she encouraged and introduced young musicians to the elite of Boston's society: social, musical, and artistic.

Death of Husband Changed Career

After Dr. Beach's death in 1910, Beach spent a few years in Europe, from 1911 to 1914. There, she did much performing and composing, both to acclaim. Beach's goal in travelling to Europe was to become an established solo performer as well as composer. She found much praise, especially in Germany. In Leipzig and Berlin, her *Gaelic Symphony* was performed to much commendation.

When World War I broke out, Beach was forced to return to the United States in 1914. The year after she returned, she moved to New York City, which remained her home base for the rest of her life. After her return, she toured as a pianist and continued composing.

Beach's years played out with her touring in the winter and practicing and composing in the summer. She spent her summers at her cottage in Cape Cod, Massachusetts, until 1921, when she began spending her summers as a fellow in the MacDowell Colony in Peterborough, New Hampshire. Many of her compositions in this time period were played at New York's St. Bartholomew's Episcopal Church, where she was essentially the composer in residence.

Beach still composed other types of works, however. In 1916, she wrote a work commissioned by the Chamber Music Society of San Francisco. This was called *Theme and Variations for Flute and String Quartet* (opus 80). In 1932, she wrote her first opera, *Cabildo,* a chamber opera in one act; Nan Bagby Stephens wrote the opera's libretto, and it premiered in February 1945 in Athens, Georgia. In 1938, she wrote *Piano Trio* (Opus 150), which was a arrangement for piano, violin, and piano.

All but three of Beach's numbered works were published—an amazing accomplishment for a composer of American origin. She composed approximately 300 total works, including 128 songs for poems. Many of her songs for poems were popular, especially the three by Browning which were set to music, ''Ecstasy,'' ''Ah, Love, but a Day,'' and ''The Year's at the Spring.'' Stylistically, she was influenced by romanticism, especially early in her career, and such French composers as Brahms and Debussy. Beach was also among the first to be influenced by the idea of creating an American-style of music and using folk music as source material, including ideas from Native Americans, African Americans, and Alaskan Inuits.

During her lifetime, Beach received much acclaim in the United States as the country's foremost woman composer. However, some critics thought that she was too sentimental. She was also criticized for her reliance on chromatics. Others believed she had great technical skills

and was very lyrical, she was also praised for her use of altered chords and enharmonic modulations.

Beach died of a heart ailment in New York City on December 27, 1944. She was a very generous person, even in death. In her will, she donated the royalties from her work to the MacDowell Colony. Although interest in the composer faded after her death, there was a revival of interest in her work in the late 1990s as feminists realized how innovative she was. As Michael Anthony in the *Star Tribune* wrote, ''Late in her long, productive life as a pianist and composer, Amy Beach, who died in 1944, said that being a woman hadn't held her back as a musician.''

Books

Adamson, Lynda G., *Notable Women in American History: A Guide to Recommended Biographies and Autobiographies,* Greenwood Press, 1999.
American Cultural Leaders, ABC-CLIO Interactive, 2001.
Garraty, John A., and Mark C. Carnes, eds., *American National Biography,* Volume 2, Oxford University Press, 1999.
Hitchcock, H. Wiley, and Stanley Sadie, eds., *The New Grove Dictionary of American Music,* Volume 1, Macmillan, 1986.
James, Edward T., *Notable American Women, 1607-1950: A Biographical Dictionary,* Volume 1, The Belknap Press, 1971.
McHenry, Robert, ed., *Her Heritage: A Biographical Encyclopedia of Famous American Women,* Merriam-Webster, 1994.
Uglow, Jennifer, *The Macmillan Dictionary of Women's Biography,* Macmillan, 1982.

Periodicals

Commercial Appeal, July 27, 2002.
New York Times, September 6, 1998; September 22, 1998; January 31, 1999.
Star Tribune, August 27, 2000. □

Benedict XIV

Pope Benedict XIV (1675–1758) was one of the most eminent popes of his century and considered by his contemporaries one of Europe's leading learned minds of the day. His 17-year pontificate was remarkable for several advancements in canon law, in which he was an expert, and reforms that revealed his scholarly, progressive mind. When he was still a cardinal, he wrote a treatise on parapsychological phenomena that helped establish firm guidelines for the canonization of saints.

Bolognese Heritage

B orn Prospero Lorenzo Lambertini in the city of Bologna on March 31, 1675, the future Pope Benedict XIV was the son of a senator, Marcello Lambertini, in that city. The Lambertinis were an esteemed family in Bologna but, by the time of this second son's birth, had suffered financial hardships because of flooding on their

estates. A promising student at an early age, Benedict went to Rome at the age of 13 in 1688 to study at the Clementine College, which had been established by Pope Clement VIII to educate young Italian men of a devout nature. At the age of 16 he was invited by the rector of the college to deliver a discourse, in Latin, on the Trinity. Word of his remarkable intellect reached the new pope, Innocent XII, who invited him for a private meeting and granted him a stipend that allowed him to enter the University of Rome. Beginning in 1692 Benedict studied theology, canon law, and civil law there. He earned his doctorate two years later, at the age of 19, in the faculties of theology and law.

Benedict initially held a post as an advocate in Rome's ecclesiastical courts and became a priest at the age of 23, in 1698. The following year he became an assistant to an Auditor of the Rota, one of the secret tribunals within the church that handled serious ecclesiastical matters. In this capacity Benedict first became familiar with the intricacies of the canonization process, which at the time was a type of hearing in which a prosecutor, called the *advocatus diaboli,* or devil's advocate, challenged evidence presented that the deceased holy person in question had led an exemplary life and that miracles could be attributed to his or her piety.

Advanced through Church Ranks

In 1702, Benedict was named to the devil's advocate post himself and held it for more than twenty years. He became one of the ablest holders of the office, famous in Rome for the zeal, clarity, and wit that he deployed in

hearings. He held other posts concurrently, including serving in the Congregation of Rites and as a consultant on canon law. In 1724, Pope Benedict XIII made him archbishop of Theodosia "in partibus," a term denoting that the city had been conquered by Muslims and its Christian hierarchy ousted, but a titular head remained. He was made a cardinal in 1728, and his characteristically wry sense of humor was evident in a letter he wrote to a friend, musing, "One must have a very firm belief in the Pope's infallibility to think he has made no mistake over my promotion," according to his biographer, Renée Haynes, in *Philosopher King: The Humanist Pope Benedict XIV.*

In 1731 Pope Clement XII named Benedict archbishop of Bologna, a cause for great celebration in his native city. He spent the next nine years there, during which time he wrote extensively when not busy with administrative matters. He finished his *De beatificatione servorum Dei et canonizatione beatorum (Of the Beatification of the Servants of God, and of the Canonization of the Blessed),* which set forth important ground rules for judging miracles. Benedict admitted that miracles attributed to the grace of God were possible, but should be distinguished from those that were the result of otherwise explainable natural phenomena. He wrote that there were three kinds of paranormal phenomena: from God, from the Devil, and neutral. He wrote extensively on the miracles and incidents of sudden healing attributed to past saints throughout the ages. In a superstitious age, he assured readers that such phenomena as comets and shooting stars are entirely natural and not evidence of the supernatural.

Witty Remark Taken Seriously

In February of 1740 Clement XII died, and Benedict was summoned to Rome to take part in the top-secret conclave of cardinals to elect a successor from among themselves. The conclave remained deadlocked for many months, and so one day he rose and told his colleagues, according to the *Catholic Encyclopedia,* "If you wish to elect a saint, choose Gotti; a statesman, Aldobrandini; an honest man, elect me." An old friend of his, Cardinal Aquaviva, formally proposed Benedict's name, and he was elected unanimously—save for his own vote. Surprised, he accepted, as he told the conclave, "for three reasons; so as not to resist God's will; so as not to be ungrateful for your kindness; and so as to finish our assembly, which has lasted so long that I think it is giving scandal to the world at large," according to Haynes in the *Philosopher King* biography.

Taking the name Benedict in honor of the pope who had made him archbishop, he was crowned in St. Peter's Basilica on August 22. Upon taking office, he eschewed formality in his meetings with other prelates and politicians and did not practice nepotism, which was common in his era and beyond. Popes often gave munificent offices and appointments to nephews in their family; instead the new pope wrote to his nephew and told him not to come to Rome unless invited—and the invitation never came. He reduced the papal household expenses and ordered that granaries be built in every town and village in the Papal States to alleviate hunger among the poor. In Rome, he liked to explore the city on foot, as he had done in Bologna, and was known to wander into some of its more dangerous neighborhoods and genially chat with denizens.

A Progressive Pontiff

In ecclesiastical matters, Benedict issued his first important decree regarding the matter of the Eastern-rite churches, which had been split from the Roman church for some centuries. His 1742 bull *Etsi pastoralis* prohibited any attempts to Latinize them. He established four academies in a bid to make the holy men of Rome more learned: one for Roman history, another sacred history and ecclesiastical learning, another on the history of the Councils, and the fourth on the liturgy. He himself lectured at one of them every Monday. In his native city, Bologna, he endowed its university and embellished its cathedral.

In a more pressing matter of the day, Benedict weighed in with a strong opinion on the matter of anti-Semitism. At the time, Jews were gaining more social and economic rights— once they were prohibited from owning land or growing their own food—and were no longer relegated to the ghettoes of the medieval era. Anti-Semitism remained strong in some places in Europe, however, and the bishops of Poland sent a letter of complaint to Benedict that asked for new edicts against Jews there. Benedict replied in his encyclical *A quo primum* that none were necessary and reminded them that St. Bernard had cautioned against singling out the Jews for persecution, for "they are eminent reminders for us of the Lord's suffering." On the matter of usury, or charging interest on a loan, Benedict established a commission of cardinals to deal with the topic. It had been prohibited for Christians since the early Middle Ages, and by papal decree officially since Pope Clement V in 1311. Because of this prohibition, some great Jewish banking fortunes had arisen. The pope's 1745 commission issued their recommendations to maintain the ban. The Pope then wrote the encyclical *Vix pervenit* that same year. It noted that not all interest is usurious, and that scholars should decide the matter.

Decried Superstitious Habits

Regarding Islam, Benedict formally prohibited Christians from using Muslim names, which had become common in some places like Serbia as a means to avoid certain taxes. In other realms of his empire Benedict warned against the rise of fanatical cults, confirmed the decrees of his predecessors that priests—save for the Fate bene Fratelli order—were forbidden to practice pharmacy and issued the 1741 bull *Dei miseratione* on marriage practices. Divorces had become more common, and Benedict warned the judges responsible for the grants of dissolution of Christ's words, "Whom God hath joined, let no man put asunder." Benedict implemented a "defender of marriage" for each diocese, charged with the duty of adjudicating all such divorce cases. A 1748 bull *Magnæ nobis admirationis* set parameters for marriages between Catholics and Protestants, conceding that they were permissible if both parties agreed that the children of such unions were to be brought up in the Catholic faith. Elsewhere, the pope agreed to reduce the number of holidays of obligation, which some

bishops had argued were keeping the poor from working and thus brought hardship to their families. Benedict also ordered that all churches in the Papal States should be cleaned and renovated and, following his duties as bishop of Rome, undertook the same in that city; under this decree the mosaics of St. Paul's Basilica were repaired.

In administrative matters, Benedict established a formal college of consistorial advocates, as he had once been, designed to provide advice to the pontiff. One of his more lasting achievements, however, was to end a controversial practice of the Jesuit missionaries in South America. There they had established *reducciones,* or reductions, which were settlements established for the local Native Americans in order to convert them to a Christianized, European way of life. They were often sites of cruelty, which led to uprisings and martyrdoms of the Jesuit priests. Benedict's *Immensa pastorum principis* disbanded these in Paraguay and Argentina. The pope also stepped in and issued orders regarding conflicts between Jesuit and Capuchin missionaries in India and China. He reached a 1753 concordat with King Ferdinand VI of Spain that rescinded the monarch's right to name archbishoprics and bishoprics in his country. An *Apostolicum* issued that same year sent missions to England, which had emerged from a long and bitter war between Catholics and Protestants in the previous century.

Friendly with Voltaire

Benedict was well respected throughout Europe, during an era when the Catholic Church was declining in influence as Protestantism and the ideas of the Enlightenment took hold. He corresponded with famed French philosopher and author François Marie Arouet de Voltaire, who dedicated a 1744 play, *Mahomet,* to Benedict. The pope was roundly excoriated in some quarters for his links to the maverick French intellectual, whose name was symbolic with the Enlightenment, an important movement of the eighteenth century that stressed secular thought over spiritual dogmatism. Benedict also endured criticism from the superiors of religious orders for frequently granting requests from monks, priests, and nuns to be freed of their religious vows. In other matters, he regularly chastised members of the clergy who came to him with petitions that certain religious objects be granted his blessing. "This just shows," he wrote, according to Haynes's *Philosopher King,* "how religion is dishonoured by intolerable abuses, and how it is that people dare to traffic in holy things."

The pope's health worsened in 1758, after a long battle with gout, and he died on May 3, 1758, in Rome. A year before his death, the English author Horace Walpole wrote an inscription for a bas-relief portrait of Benedict honoring him as, according to *Philosopher King,* "Prospero Lambertini/Bishop of Rome/By the name of Benedict XIV/Who, though an absolute Prince/reigned as harmlessly/as a Doge of Venice./He restored the luster of the Tiara/by those arts alone/by which He attained it,/his Virtues./Beloved by Papists/esteemed by Protestants:/a priest without insolence or interest;/a Prince without favourites,/a Pope without nepotism;/an Author without vanity;/in short a Man/whom neither Wit nor Power/could spoil.

"The Son of a favourite Minister,/but One who never courted a Prince/nor worshipped a Churchman,/offers in this free Protestant Country/This deserved Incense/to the Best of the Roman Pontiffs."

Books

Catholic Encyclopedia, Volume II, Robert Appleton Company, 1907, Online Edition, 2002.
Encyclopedia of Occultism and Parapsychology, fifth edition, Gale, 2001.
Haynes, Renée, *Philosopher King: The Humanist Pope Benedict XIV,* Weidenfeld and Nicolson, 1970.

Online

"A quo primum," *Papal Library website,* http://papal-library .saint-mike.org/BenedictXIV/Encyclicals/A_Quo_Primum .html (March 3, 2002). □

Joseph Bernier

Joseph Bernier (1852–1934) led expeditions to the farthest reaches of Canada's Arctic wilderness in the early twentieth century. Bernier had once dreamed of reaching the North Pole and planting the Canadian flag there, but instead plied the Hudson Bay and Arctic Sea waters in his durable ship, the *Arctic,* and proclaimed Canadian sovereignty over the scattered islands and Inuit communities in the region. He made some dozen trips before his final 1925 voyage, establishing important political, social, and economic ties to the region for Canada and awakening interest in its northernmost territories.

Seafaring Family

Bernier, born on January 1, 1852, in L'Islet, Quebec, was French Canadian by birth. He grew up in L'Islet, a town on the St. Lawrence River, outside of Quebec City. His family's origins in the area dated back to 1656, and he came from a long line of shipbuilders and sailors. Several of them, including Bernier's father, earned the designation *capitaine au long cours,* or deep-sea captain. Bernier himself made his first ocean voyage when he was still a toddler with both parents on the *Zillah.* The vessel was captained by his father and traveled as far as Malta on a mission to bring supplies to British forces during the Crimean War.

Bernier was schooled in L'Islet, but was indifferent to his studies save for the subject of geography. He showed far more interest in his father's line of work, which came to involve sailing newly-constructed ships to England for sale there. Around 1864, when Bernier was 12, his father built a ship of his own and named it the *Saint-Joseph* in his son's honor. On this vessel Bernier learned the rigors of the seafaring life firsthand, serving as a lowly apprentice on several

ocean crossings. A terrible case of seasickness was cured by his father's rather harsh method: the 13-year-old was tied to the front of the ship as it pitched and rolled through rough waters for two hours.

Became Ship Captain

At the age of 17, Bernier was made the *Saint-Joseph*'s captain by his father, making him purportedly the youngest ocean-going captain in Canadian history. His father built a second ship, the *Saint-Michel,* and he served as captain of that after 1870. Around this time he married Rose Caron, a native of L'Islet. He spent the next two decades in the same line of work as his father, sailing ships to England and acting as a sales agent. In all, he made 269 Atlantic crossings during his lifetime. In 1895, he was offered a position as governor of the Quebec jail and accepted it. He read avidly during this time, meeting and questioning whaling captains and traders who had ventured into Canada's northernmost areas. He dreamed of sailing there and perhaps even reaching the North Pole. He began lecturing on the topic and soon won the support of the Quebec Geographical Society. Realizing he needed to provide for his family before embarking upon such a journey, which might stretch nearly two years in duration, he learned of a steamship that had run aground off the coast of Newfoundland. He hired a salvage company and managed to free her, took her to Montreal for refitting, and sold the vessel at auction for $30,000.

Still, Bernier estimated that an Arctic expedition would cost at least $150,000 and realized he needed government support. Beginning in 1900 he traveled to Ottawa and petitioned Prime Minister Wilfrid Laurier regularly, but Laurier was uneasy about committing funds for a project that seemed foolhardy at best. The islands and fjords of Canada's northernmost regions—much of it until recently in the possession of the Hudson Bay Trading Company—were littered with the carcasses of ships that had become icebound or met with other trouble. The most famous of these was the 1845 expedition led by British explorer Sir John Franklin in search of the elusive Northwest Passage—the commercial sea route from the Atlantic to the Pacific. Franklin and his 129 men became icebound, and no word was heard from them for eight years. More than 40 search parties were sent out to find them, and the highly publicized expedition and resulting tragedy served to highlight the dangers of the treacherous cold and ice of the lands in Canada north of the Arctic Circle.

Argued for North Pole Expedition

Bernier was undaunted, however. Lecturing frequently in order to drum up public support, as Laurier had suggested, he was fond of telling audiences the tale of an American ship, the *Jeannette,* which became frozen in the ice near Wrangel Island off the coast of Siberia in 1879. When the ice moved, so did the ship, in a northwesterly direction, and finally parts of it were found on the eastern coast of Greenland. Bernier told his rapt listeners that the discovery meant that the ship's parts traveled across the Arctic Sea around the North Pole. He believed that if a vessel was strategically placed, it would drift near enough the Pole so that a sled voyage could be made there to stake a claim. To date, only the Norwegian explorer Fridtjof Nansen, attempting to use this drift method, had come close to the Pole on a 1896 voyage.

With support from the Canadian government still unforthcoming, Bernier was dismayed to learn that an American, Robert E. Peary, was trying to reach North Pole on foot via Greenland. In 1903 diplomatic relations between Canada and the United States soured briefly over what became known as the Alaska Boundary Dispute, and members of a British commission sided with the American claims and a strip of land in British Columbia was handed over to the United States. The public outcry in Canada was strong, and it ignited a nationalist fervor to claim the Pole. Thus in 1904 the Canadian Parliament enacted legislation that granted Bernier's planned expedition a sum of $200,000.

Plan Thwarted

Bernier, though in his late 50s by then, eagerly prepared for the arduous voyage. He found a German vessel that had made a trip to the Antarctic, the *Gauss,* and had it refitted and rechristened the *Arctic.* Then, Bernier was sent word that the planned expedition was to be postponed, and that he and his ship—which technically belonged to the Canadian government—were to be sent to the northern end of Hudson Bay with a Canadian North West Mounted Police officer. The officer conducted a criminal investigation of a ship captain in the area suspected of selling alcohol to the Inuit, which was against the law at the time. Bernier told a newspaper reporter some years later that he believed the Canadian government called off his North Pole quest when it learned that Peary was about to make another try.

There could serve another purpose to such a trip northward, Bernier believed: Canada could stake claims on the scattered islands of the Arctic Circle. Some of them had been claimed by Franklin's party, but the British government granted Canada sovereignty over them in 1880. Bernier was a proponent of the Sector Theory, which held that Canada should possess the right to all territory from its mainland to the North Pole. Customarily a government would send settlers to such places, but the forbidding Arctic climate discouraged this prospect. Finally winning approval for his voyage, Bernier gathered a learned crew of metal workers, botanists, meteorologists, and other professionals, along with experienced sailors, and set out on his first expedition in July of 1906.

Staked Claims in Arctic

Bernier's *Arctic* sailed through Lancaster Sound and the Prince of Wales Strait. It crossed the Arctic Circle on August 11, 1906, and at Albert Harbor the captain hired two Inuit men, Monkeyshaw and Cameo, to accompany them further. Bernier landed on Bylot and Somerset Islands, making an official Canadian claim on both. At Beechey Island he found a rock left behind by the Franklin party, and built a cairn over the inscription. Bernier's explorations of the islands found other evidence of the ill-fated Franklin expedition, and some of the items were brought back for deposit in the National Archives of Canada.

In all, Bernier made another eleven trips to the Arctic over the next 19 years. His three before 1909 established Canadian sovereignty on the islands of the region. He officially claimed the last of these, Banks and Victoria, for Canada on Dominion Day of 1909. He gathered his crew for a ceremony that day, erecting a cairn and a plaque; with that act, Canada now claimed all territory from the Yukon in the west to Baffin Land, which was adjacent to Greenland, and all land north of that to the Pole.

Friendly with Inuit

During World War I, Bernier's ship made mail runs and carted supplies to the European front. After the war, he began making trips to Inuit communities like Pond Inlet, where he set up a trading post. Over the next few years he worked to establish a foothold for Canadian government administration of the region. After being deputized a special fisheries officer in Ottawa, he issued permits to whalers and fishermen in the area. He also helped establish Royal Canadian Mounted Police posts. During all of his trips, Bernier made copious notes and from these a wealth of scientific information about navigation, weather, and plant life in the region was gleaned. One member of his party studied the Inuit tongue, Inuktitut, and made a dictionary.

Bernier's missions were forgotten for many years, but the Inuit who met him during his expeditions remembered him fondly even generations later. He treated these hearty, indigenous people with respect and often plied them with questions about how to survive the cold. He even adopted their dress and always invited them aboard the ship to see its marvels. Generous supplies of pilot biscuits, or hardtack, that he left behind helped stave of hunger during the lean winter months in some places. One of his crew members was his wife's nephew, Wilfrid Caron, who decided to stay behind at Pond Inlet. Caron married an Inuit woman, with whom he had children, and Caron descendants lived in the area still at the onset of the twenty-first century.

Bernier's wife Rose died in 1917, and in 1919 he married Alma Lemieux. His last trips to the Eastern Arctic were the first annual patrols of seas by the Canadian government, between 1922 and 1925. After he retired, he settled in the Quebec community of Lévis and continued to lecture. He died of a heart attack on Christmas Eve of 1934 at the age of 82. He is still remembered by many Inuit communities in Nunavut, as this area of Canada has been called since 1999, and often referred to by his Inuit name, which means white bear. "Kapitaikallak helped in a big way," a resident, Nutaraq Cornelius, was quoted as saying by *Nunatsiaq News* writer Jane George. "He taught us about rifles. He showed us that by using the binoculars we can see things from far away." Still, confusion over official Canadian policies remained. "People did not understand that the land had been claimed by the government," Cornelius pointed out. "Inuit learned about this much later. He had warned the people of the change that is coming in the following years. . . . It's true, these events happened a long time ago. But even after these many, many years, you can still see the Kapitaikallak isn't forgotten today. We still remember him. We know about him."

Books

Fairley, T. C. and Charles E. Israel, *The True North: The Story of Captain Joseph Bernier,* Macmillan, 1957.

Periodicals

Nunatsiaq News, October 26, 2001. □

Jakob Bernoulli

Swiss mathematician Jakob Bernoulli (1654–1705) devoted his career to the study of calculating complex numerical formulas. Sometimes called Jacques or James Bernoulli to distinguish him from other prominent family members, he was the first in a long line of Bernoulli mathematicians that furthered the discipline greatly during the Age of Reason. He and his younger brother Johann engaged in a spirited, if not sometimes malicious, professional rivalry. Both, noted in an essay in *DISCovering World History,* "contributed to these sometimes-peevish arguments and mild polemics that nevertheless broadened the scope of calculus."

Earned Theology Degree

Jakob Bernoulli was born in Basel, Switzerland, on January 6, 1654. The Bernoulli family was originally of Belgian origin and had been spice merchants in the Spanish Netherlands for some time before 1583. In that year, Bernoulli's druggist grandfather moved the family to Basel, Switzerland, to escape after anti-Protestant religious persecution by a Roman Catholic ruling dynasty. In Basel, Bernoulli's father Nikolaus held civil posts on the town council and served as a magistrate after marrying a woman from a prominent banking family in the city.

As a young man, Bernoulli studied at the University of Basel, where he followed his father's wishes and earned a degree in philosophy in 1671 and then a theology degree five years later. Disinclined to enter the ministry, he studied mathematics and astronomy in his spare time. In 1676, he found work as a tutor in another Swiss city, Geneva, and then lived two years in France, during which time he studied the works of mathematician and philosopher René Descartes. Around this time, Bernoulli began his *Meditationes,* a scientific diary. He traveled to the Netherlands in 1681 and then on to England; as he had in France, he came to know prominent mathematicians of the day and began what would become a lifelong correspondence. Among them were Anglo-Irish physicist Robert Boyle, often referred to as the father of modern chemistry.

Settled in Basel

Initially, Bernoulli was fascinated by the relationship of mathematics to the cosmos, and his first scientific papers dealt with gravity and the path of comets. He formulated a theory on the origins of comets, which later proved incorrect. Back in Basel by 1682, Bernoulli published his *De gravitate aetheris,* a treatise on the theory of gravity, which caused a stir in learned European circles at the time. In the city of his birth, he taught mechanics at the university after 1683 and conducted experiments in the field as well. He began publishing his findings in two top European journals of scientific study at the time, *Journal des sçavans* and *Acta eruditorum,* the latter published out of Leipzig, Germany. He was offered a position in the church at one point, but declined it. In 1684 he married Judith Stupanus, with whom he had a son and a daughter.

Bernoulli's pamphlet on parallels of logic and algebra appeared in 1685, again furthering his reputation, and in 1687 he was offered a post at the University of Basel as a professor of mathematics. He retained the job for the rest of his life. He began to delve into the works of Gottfried Wilhelm von Leibniz, a German philosopher and mathematician who enjoyed great prominence during this era. Primarily a philosopher known for his views on consistent rationalism, Leibniz was also an eminent mathematician who devised the first calculating machine, though it did not function well due to mechanical difficulties. Around 1676 Leibniz developed his fundamental principles of calculus, the branch of mathematics that investigates continuously changing quantities. In a 1684 issue of *Acta eruditorum,* Leibniz published his theories on the differential calculus, which involves the study of the limit of a quotient as a denominator nears zero. Leibniz called this process "infinitesimal calculus," a term that denoted quantities smaller than any definable finite quantity, yet still larger than zero; the "infinitesimal" part was later abandoned.

Influenced by Leibniz

Bernoulli worked studiously from Leibniz's findings. "Misunderstood by most of his colleagues, Leibniz's discovery nevertheless attracted a small following of mathematicians who realized the tremendous analytical power of calculus," asserted an essay in *Notable Mathematicians.* "Among Leibniz's followers, Bernoulli was among the first who completely grasped the essence of calculus, and he proceeded, in numerous contributions to Acta eruditorum, to develop the foundations of calculus." Bernoulli also worked on Leibniz's quandary over the isochronous curve, and he wrote an important treatise in 1687 on geometry that determined a way to divide any triangle into four equal parts with two perpendicular lines.

Bernoulli's long and illustrious career was marred by the rivalry with his younger brother, Johann, who also became an eminent mathematician in his day. Again, their father had strongly discouraged Johann's interest in this science, and the younger Bernoulli duly studied the more practical discipline of medicine at the University of Basel in the early 1680s; at the time, however, he also studied mathematics under his brother. Johann took a post as professor of mathematics at the University of Gröningen in the Netherlands in 1694, and the antagonism between the two intensified over the years. Their arguments usually centered around mathematical riddles that were then standard methods for scientists of the day to exchange ideas throughout Europe. A scholar would devise a problem, solve it, and then send it out for others to solve under deadline.

Declared Superiority of His Work

In 1689, Bernoulli published his *Treatise on Infinite Series,* later known as the "Bernoulli inequality," but its proof had been conducted by Johann. "With uncharacteristic fraternal affection, Jakob even prefaced the argument with an acknowledgement of his brother's priority," wrote William Durham in his *Journey Through Genius: The Great Theorems of Mathematics.* The brothers also argued most vociferously over the riddle of the catenary curve, a term used to denote a line similar to a chain, fixed at two points, and hanging under its own weight. The riddle asked mathematicians to solve the equation for the curve. A generation before, the Italian astronomer, mathematician, and physicist Galileo had believed it to be a parabola, or a plane curve made up from all points equidistant from a given fixed point and a given fixed line. This proved false, and Bernoulli attempted to use calculus to solve it. He explored the possibilities in a 1690 paper, but his brother solved it before he finished. Johann delivered a wounding version of events, according to a source quoted in Durham's book. "The efforts of my brother were without success; for my part, I

was more fortunate, for I found the skill (I say it without boasting, why should I conceal the truth?) to solve it in full. . . . It is true that it cost me study that robbed me of rest for an entire night . . . but the next morning, filled with joy, I ran to my brother, who was still struggling miserably with this Gordian knot without getting anywhere, always thinking, like Galileo, that the catenary was a parabola. Stop! Stop! I say to him, don't torture yourself any more to try and prove the identity of the catenary with the parabola, since it is entirely false."

Another famous quandary for the brothers Bernoulli involved the brachistochrone problem (from the Greek term meaning "shortest time"). In 1696, Johann published a riddle in *Acta Eruditorum* which invited others to determine the curve of quickest descent between two given points A and B, assuming that B does not lie right beneath A. Johann believed it was a cycloid curve, but his proof was wrong. "Jakob solved the problem using a detailed but formally correct technique," explained the essay in *DISCovering World History.* "Johann recognized that the problem could be rephrased in such a way that existing solutions could be adapted to the solution of this problem. Johann solved the problem in a more ingenious way, but Jakob recognized that his approach could be generalized."

The brothers disputed one another's works in the pages of leading scientific publications during their respective careers. Bernoulli, however, was more critical by nature and often entered into vituperative battles with his superiors at the University of Basel as well. "Each became the other's fiercest competitor in mathematical matters, until their attempts at one-upmanship seem, in retrospect, almost comical," noted Dunham in *Journey Through Genius.*

Intrigued by Mollusk Shell

Bernoulli was fascinated by the mathematical properties of curves, especially the logarithmic spiral, a figure similar to the chambered nautilus mollusk shell in nature with its perfectly symmetrical spirals. It is also referred to as a *spira mirabilis,* or "wonderful spiral." As the essay in *Notable Mathematicians* explained, "Bernoulli noticed that the logarithmic spiral has several unique properties, including self-similarity, which means that any portion, if scaled up or down, is congruent to other parts of the curve." He was so intrigued by its shape that he requested his tombstone sport the motif, along with the Latin phrase *Eadem mutata resurgo* (Though changed, I arise again the same). Bernoulli died on August 16, 1705, in Basel, Switzerland. His brother succeeded him in his post as professor of mathematics at the University of Basel.

One of Bernoulli's best known works was published posthumously in 1713: *Ars conjectandi (The Art of Conjecture),* which involves probability theory. Described as "a highly innovative work" in an essay in *World of Scientific Discovery,* the tome "discussed what came to be known as the Bernoullian numbers and the Bernoulli theorem, and analyzed games of chance according to variations in players dexterity, expectation of profit, and other variables." It endured as an important tract on probability theory well into the modern age. A street in Paris's Eighth Arrondissement is named in his honor. His nephew, Johann's son Daniel, formulated the Bernoulli principle, which involves the speed and properties of liquid or gas.

Books

Dunham, William, *Journey Through Genius: The Great Theorems of Mathematics,* Wiley, 1990.
Notable Mathematicians, Gale Research, 1998.
Simonis, Doris, *Scientists, Mathematicians, and Inventors: Lives and Legacies,* Oryx, 1999.
World of Scientific Discovery, second edition, Gale, 1999.

Online

DISCovering World History, Gale, 1997.
U*X*L Science, U*X*L, 1998. □

Albert Jeremiah Beveridge

When he entered the U.S. Senate in 1899 at age 36, Albert Jeremiah Beveridge (1862–1927) was hailed as one of America's most influential young leaders. An advocate of U.S. imperialism overseas, he foresaw the growth of America as a world power during the early twentieth century. Over the course of his political career, Beveridge became a supporter of progressive social policies, working to enact pure food, child labor, and tariff reform laws. His later work as a historian won him wide acclaim.

A brilliant orator and charismatic political leader, U.S. Senator Albert J. Beveridge first rose to fame in 1898 as a fervent exponent of American expansion overseas. His efforts to secure a colonial presence for the United States were rooted in a deeply-held nationalism and faith in big business. Over time, though, Beveridge evolved into a critic of America's political and business elites, joining with like-minded Republican reformers to help spearhead the Progressive movement of the early 1900s. After leaving the Senate, he embarked upon a second career as a historian, authoring highly-regarded biographies of John Marshall and Abraham Lincoln.

Outstanding Young Orator

Born on a farm in Highland County, Ohio, on October 6, 1862, Beveridge was the only child of Thomas Henry Beveridge (a farmer and Union soldier) and his second wife, Francis Parkinson Beveridge. In 1865, the family moved to another farm in Moultree County, Illinois, where the son grew up under harsh conditions. By age 14, he was working as a railroad hand and, a few years later, managed a logging crew. Determined to rise above his poor beginnings, Beveridge studied the classical works of Plutarch and Caesar, winning him financial sponsorship to Indiana's Ashbury College (now DePauw University). While still an undergraduate, he won local renown as a political orator, stumping for Republican presidential candidate James G. Blaine in

1884. Even in his early speeches, Beveridge's fervent nationalism and support for a strong Federal government were evident.

Beveridge went on to earn a law degree in 1887. That same year, he moved to Indianapolis and married fellow Ashbury student Katherine Langsdale. Specializing in civil cases, he quickly became a leading member of the Indiana bar, at times facing ex-President Benjamin Harrison as opposing counsel. Beveridge continued to rise in Republican Party circles as well, speaking widely during the 1892 and 1896 presidential campaigns. His well-reasoned orations emphasized short, incisive phrases and contrasted with the more ornate speechmaking styles of the era. By age 30, he was considered one of the leading political orators in the United States.

In 1898, Beveridge gained national fame as a persuasive advocate of U.S. colonial expansion following the Spanish-American War. His appeals to his country's sense of overseas destiny had a visionary quality to them. Beveridge saw control of Cuba and the Phillipines as pivotal to American commercial expansion in the twentieth century. In his famous 1898 "March of the Flag" speech, he ridiculed the idea of that Spain's former possessions could govern themselves. "Shall we turn these people back to the reeking hands from which we have taken them?" he asked. "Shall we save them from these nations to give them the self-rule of tragedy? It would be like giving a razor to a babe and telling it to shave itself."

U.S. Senator at Age 36

Such bold declarations helped to advance Beveridge's political career. In 1899, he outmaneuvered several veteran office-holders to become the Republican choice for U.S. Senator from Indiana. His election at age 36 made him one of the youngest members in American history. From the start, Beveridge stood out from his colleagues as a brash, independent voice. A few months prior to taking his Senate seat, he traveled to the war-torn Philippines to witness conditions first-hand. He quickly became an important voice in American foreign policy, gaining far more attention than most freshman Senators. His eloquence in urging America to accept its place as a world power took on a messianic tone. "We will not renounce our part in the mission of our race, trustee, under God, of the civilization of the world," he told his fellow senators in a January 9, 1900, speech. "And we will move forward to our work, not howling out regrets like slaves whipped to their burdens, but with gratitude for a task worthy of our strength, and thanksgiving to Almighty God that He has marked us as His chosen people, henceforth to lead in the regeneration of the world."

While Beveridge's self-dramatizing manner rankled some Republican elders, he was valued as a firm supporter of conservative economic policy and overseas expansion. Many predicted great things for him, including the presidency. Recalling Beveridge's early days in the Senate, journalist William Allen White wrote in his 1946 autobiography: "He was an eager young man. . . . His ambition was obvious and sometimes a bit ridiculous, but always innocent and shameless like a child's indecencies. His was a warm personality, gentle, kindly."

In the early 1900s, Beveridge gradually began to move away from his uncritical support of American big business. A long-time believer in an activist federal government, he now sought to direct its powers towards regulation of industry and commerce. Following his re-election in 1905, he worked in the Senate to revise tariff laws and bolster the Interstate Commerce Commission's power to fix railroad rates. He was especially prominent in support of meat inspection and child labor laws, bringing him the opposition of meat packing and manufacturing interests. Beveridge began to criticize the excessive influence of big business in politics as well. "I do not object to capital," he wrote in a 1906 magazine article. "I defend it—only let it attend to its own business. And public life and special legislation for its own benefit are not its business. . . ."

Progressive Leader

In these and other battles, Beveridge had a sometimes fitful ally in President Theodore Roosevelt. By 1907, he had become a leading figure in the emerging Progressive movement, working to spur on Roosevelt to support reformist legislation. Aided by Robert M. LaFollette of Wisconsin, Jonathan P. Dolliver of Iowa, Moses Clapp of Minnesota, and other Senate insurgents, he attacked the entrenched power of the Republican Old Guard and its close association with big business. His battles with the autocratic Senator Nelson W. Aldrich of Rhode Island were especially bitter. Despite this, he remained loyal to his party and

campaigned vigorously for Republican presidential nominee William H. Taft in 1908. He became disillusioned, however, when Taft supported the Payne-Aldrich tariff bill, which progressives viewed as an attempt to block meaningful tariff reform. Beveridge's clashes with the Old Guard leadership alienated him from Indiana's more conservative Republicans, leading to his defeat for re-election in 1911.

Though out of the Senate, Beveridge remained a force in politics, supporting Roosevelt's bid for the 1912 Republican presidential nomination and subsequent candidacy as the leader of the newly-formed Progressive (or "Bull-Moose") Party. He delivered the keynote address at the party's national convention in Chicago, declaring in favor of "social brotherhood as against savage individualism . . . mutual helpfulness instead of a reckless competition." Beveridge ran as the Progressive nominee for governor of Indiana that fall. In the end, though, both he and Roosevelt were defeated.

Beveridge devoted much of the next two years to making the Progressives a viable party. He campaigned extensively for its candidates and made an unsuccessful bid for his old Indiana U.S. Senate seat as the party's nominee in 1914. Two years later, though, Roosevelt effectively ended the Progressive Party by refusing to accept its presidential nomination. Beveridge returned to the Republican fold that year, though he supported Democrat Woodrow Wilson's anti-interventionist stance in World War I, as well as many of Wilson's domestic policies. He spoke out against suppression of political dissidents after the U.S. entered the war in 1917. Most of all, he actively opposed American participation in the League of Nations, denouncing it as a surrender of national sovereignty.

Won Acclaim as Historian

In 1922, Beveridge ran for the U.S. Senate in Indiana once again, winning the Republican primary but losing to Democrat Samuel M. Ralston in the general election. Turning away from active politics, he devoted himself almost exclusively to writing history for the remainder of his life. His career as an author began back in 1903 with the publication of *The Russian Advance,* a study of international politics. *What Is Back of the War* (1915) collected a series of interviews with European leaders and drew some criticism for its supposedly pro-German tilt. *The Life of John Marshall* (four volumes, 1916–1919) is regarded as his most important work. Benefiting from careful research, this biography of the great U.S. chief justice showed its author to be a graceful, meticulous prose stylist and discerning historian. Both critically and commercially successful, *The Life of John Marshall* won the Pulitzer Prize in 1920.

For his next literary subject, Beveridge turned to Abraham Lincoln. Sifting through long-unseen documents and letters, he found many of his own long-held political beliefs altered in the process. Ultimately, Beveridge stripped away the hero-worship surrounding Lincoln and found him to be a complex, imperfect politician and human being. He was still in the process of rewriting his manuscript when he died of a heart attack at his Indianapolis home on April 27, 1927. Though left incomplete, his *Abraham Lincoln, 1809–1858* (two volumes, 1928) was a substantial contribution to Lincoln scholarship.

A truly independent political mind, Beveridge adhered to a strongly nationalistic faith that embraced both liberal social reforms and aggressive foreign policy. He was remembered by his contemporaries for his intense energy and self-confidence, especially at the start of his political career. Wrote journalist Mark Sullivan in his memoirs: "At all times, in every circumstance, Beveridge had a sense of responsibility for the United States, concern that it should be well managed, care that no ill should befall it."

Books

Bowers, Claude G., *Beveridge and the Progressive Era,* Houghton Mifflin, 1932.
Leech, Margaret, *In The Days of McKinley,* Harper & Brothers, 1959.
Morris, Edmund, *Theodore Rex,* Random House, 2001.
The Record of American Diplomacy, edited by Ruhl J. Bartlett, Alfred A. Knopf, 1948.
Sullivan, Mark, *The Education of an American,* Doubleday, Doran & Co., 1938.
White, William Allen, *The Autobiography of William Allen White,* Macmillan, 1946. □

Isabella Bird

Isabella Bird (1831–1904) was an English traveler who made a remarkable series of journeys at the end of the 19th century. Bird was born in the English county of Yorkshire on October 15, 1831. Her father was an Anglican clergyman and her mother was the daughter of a clergyman. Bird was a small woman and suffered from several ailments during her childhood. In 1850 she had an operation to remove a tumor from her spine. The operation was only partially successful, and she suffered from insomnia and depression. Her doctor recommended that she travel, and in 1854 her father gave her 100 pounds and told her she was free to go wherever she wanted. She used it to travel to North America and stayed for several months in eastern Canada and the United States. On her return she used the letters she had written to her sister, Hennie, as the basis for her first book, *The Englishwoman in America*.

Hawaii and the Rocky Mountains

Bird's father died in 1858 and she and her sister and mother moved to Edinburgh in Scotland, where she lived for the rest of her life. She took other short trips during the following years, including three to North America and one to the Mediterranean. However, the turning point in her life came in 1872 when she traveled to Hawaii.

She had taken a ship from San Francisco headed for New Zealand, but decided to get off in Hawaii and stayed there for six months. During that time she learned how to ride a horse astride, which ended the backaches she suffered from riding sidesaddle, and she climbed up to the top of Hawaii's volcanic peaks. Later, she wrote about her pleasure in "visiting remote regions which are known to few even of the residents, living among the natives, and otherwise seeing Hawaiian life in all its phases." She recorded her happy visit in *Six Months in the Sandwich Islands,* published in 1875.

Leaving Hawaii, Bird went to the west coast of the United States. From San Francisco she traveled alone by horse to Lake Tahoe and then to the Rocky Mountains and Colorado. During that trip she had many adventures, including riding alone through a blizzard with her eyes frozen shut, spending several months snowed in a cabin with two young men, and being wooed by a lonely outlaw. All these tales she told in her book *A Lady's Life in the Rocky Mountains,* published in 1879.

Japan

From San Francisco Bird went to Japan, where she hired a young Japanese man of 18 to be her translator. They traveled together to the northern part of Hokkaido, the northernmost part of the country, where she stayed among members of the Ainu tribe, the original, non-Japanese, inhabitants of the islands. Her experiences formed the basis for her book *Unbeaten Tracks in Japan,* published in 1880. From Japan she traveled to Hong Kong, Canton, Saigon, and

Singapore. From Singapore she traveled among the Malay states of the Malayan Peninsula for five weeks.

When Bird returned to England she was famous for her books about Hawaii and the Rocky Mountains. However, shortly after her return her sister died from typhoid. Bird married the doctor who had taken care of her, Dr. John Bishop, in 1881. They were happy together, but he died only five years after the marriage.

India and the Middle East

Following Bishop's death, Bird set out again on her travels. In 1888 she left for India. While there she established the Henrietta Bird Hospital in Amritsar and the John Bishop Memorial Hospital in Srinigar. She traveled to Kashmir and to Ladakh in the far north on the border with Tibet. During her travels one of her horses lost its footing while crossing a river. The horse drowned and Bird suffered two broken ribs. On her return to Simla in northern India she met up with Major Herbert Sawyer who was on his way to Persia. The two traveled together through the desert in midwinter and arrived in Tehran half-dead. After depositing the major at his new duty station, Bird set out alone and spent the next six months traveling at the head of her own caravan through northern Iran, Kurdistan, and Turkey.

On her return to England, Bird spoke out against the atrocities that were being committed against the Armenians in the Middle East and met with Prime Minister William Gladstone and addressed a Parliamentary committee on the question. By this time she was extremely well known in her native land and was made a fellow of the Royal Scottish Geographical Society and the first woman fellow of the Royal Geographical Society. However, she was not happy being still and in 1894 she set out again.

Bird traveled first to Yokohama in Japan and from there into Korea. She spent several months in that country and then was forced to leave at the outbreak of the Sino-Japanese War that was to lead to the occupation of Korea by Japan. She went to Mukden in Manchuria and photographed Chinese soldiers headed for the front. She then went back into Korea to view the devastation of the war. From Korea she went to the Yangtze River in China in January 1896. She traveled by sampan up the river as far as she could go and then went overland into the province of Sichuan. There she was attacked by a mob that called her a "foreign devil" and trapped her in the top floor of a house, which they then set on fire. She was rescued at the last minute by a detachment of soldiers. At another place she was stoned and knocked unconscious. She then traveled into the mountains bordering Tibet before returning home in 1897.

Back in Britain she wrote *The Yangtze Valley and Beyond,* which was published in 1900. She made her last trip to Morocco in 1901. On her return she became ill and died in Edinburgh on October 7, 1904.

Further Reading

A collection of Bird's writings edited by Cicely Paalser Haveley is titled *This Grand Beyond: Travels of Isabella Bird Bishop* (1984). A biography of note is Pat Barr's *A Curious Life for a Lady: The Story of Isabella Bird, a Remarkable Victorian Traveler* (1970). There are chapters on Bird in Mignon Rittenhouse, *Seven Women Explorers* (1964); Dea Birkett, *Spinsters Abroad: Victorian Lady Explorers* (1989); and Marion Tinling, *Women into the Unknown* (1989). □

Bonnie Blair

Speed skating champion Bonnie Blair (born 1964) is the most highly decorated American Winter Olympic athlete in history with six medals. She holds five gold medals, for the 500-meter and 1,000-meter events, as well as a bronze medal for the 1,000-meter event. Since her retirement from competition in 1995 at the age of 31, she has turned her stellar Olympic performances into a successful career as a motivational speaker and corporate spokesperson.

Learned to Skate at Two

B onnie Kathleen Blair was born on March 18, 1964, in the Hudson River town of Cornwall, New York, and grew up in Champaign, Illinois. She was the youngest of six children, all of whom learned to skate at an early age. Blair herself was introduced to the sport when she was just two years old. She was so small at the time that her parents could not find skates that fit her, so she had to wear shoes under her skates. By the time she was four years old, Blair was racing, and she loved it, competing against her older brothers and sisters and others in elementary and junior high school. Blair later ran on her high school track team, where, she later claimed, she did not stand out among her peers. She ran wherever her coach decided he was missing a body—on the long jump, high jump, short distances, and relays. She also tried her hand at gymnastics for a while.

Blair's introduction to competitive skating was as a pack racer on short tracks where she competed against many people in one race. She was 16 years old when she began Olympic-style racing, which pits only two racers against each other in a competition based on time. In her teens, Blair began to apply herself to the sport of speed skating as she never had before, largely at the encouragement of her friend Dave Silk, who competed on the men's U.S. team. "He's the hardest worker on the team," Blair later told Angus Phillips in the *Washington Post,* "and he got me into that, too. In Champaign, I'd miss a workout or two. But Dave gave me real direction."

Competed Internationally at 18

In 1982, when Blair was 18 years old, her trainers wanted to take her to Europe to compete outside of the United States for the first time. She agreed to go, but she lacked the backing to finance the trip. So, the police department in Champaign stepped in to raise money for her trip, holding a series of raffles and bake sales. Also, Jack Sikma, a

professional basketball player for the Milwaukee Bucks, donated $1,500 for her trip.

Blair's European trip had the desired effect, sharpening her skills for more competition. The year following her return from Europe, she won the 1983 U.S. indoor speed skating championship, a title she won again in 1984. Also in 1984, Blair competed at the Winter Olympics held in Sarajevo, Yugoslavia. She did not win any medals, but it proved a valuable experience for her. In 1985, Blair won the North American indoor speed skating championship, and in 1986, she again won the U.S. indoor title. Now a world-class speed skater, Blair went on to set a world speed skating record in 1987, racing 500 meters in 39.43 seconds.

Won First Olympic Gold Medal

Blair won her first gold medal at the 1988 Winter Olympics held in Calgary, Canada. Her win in the 500-meter event broke the world record, which had been set only minutes before by the East German skater Christa Rothenburger. With a new world record of 39.1 seconds, Blair became the first American woman since 1976 to win a gold medal in speed skating. Also at the 1988 Olympics, Blair won the bronze medal for the 1,000-meter event.

At the Olympics, Blair was cheered on by her large extended family, including her parents, her brother Chuck, her sister Mary, along with Mary's husband and children, her sister Susie, her brother Rob and his wife and child, her sister Angela, and her uncle Lennie, along with the friends of all of her family members.

Blair would in later years recall that first Olympic gold medal victory as the high point of her career. "That's not to say I didn't have other great memories," she told Paula Parrish in the *Rocky Mountain News,* "but I think that had the biggest impact." And, as she told Barbara Matson in the *Boston Globe,* "Crossing that [finish] line was the happiest moment of my life."

Continued Olympic Winning Streak

No longer a relative unknown, Blair was considered a favorite when she headed to the 1992 Winter Olympics held in Albertville, France. She surpassed her 1988 Olympic performance, taking home the gold medal not only in the 500-meter event, but in the 1,000-meter race as well. To win the 500-meter event, Blair beat Chinese skater Ye Qiaobo by 18 hundredths of a second. In winning the 1,000-meter event, Blair again beat Ye, this time by a mere two hundredths of a second. It was the first time a woman had won two Olympic gold medals for the 500-meter event in two successive Winter Olympics. Her stellar performance at the 1992 Olympics also earned Blair the Sullivan Award as the Best Amateur Athlete in the United States. Blair dedicated her successes in Albertville to the memory of her father, who had died on Christmas Day 1989.

With her gold medals and winning personality to match, Blair captured the imagination of the American public, becoming a media darling and a favorite among fans. She became almost as well known for her entourage of family and friends—a group deemed the Blair Bunch that had grown to more than 60 people by 1994—who went with her to each of her Olympic competitions to cheer her on from the stands.

Now unquestionably a star, in 1994 Blair went on to her third Winter Olympics, which were held in Lillehammer, Norway. There she won two more gold medals, for both the 500-meter and the 1,000-meter races. It was another first for a female athlete—no other woman had ever won five Olympic gold medals for individual events. Her total of six Olympic medals (five gold and a bronze) also made her the most successful American Winter Olympian in history. To celebrate, she climbed into the stands, still wearing her skates, to hug her family and friends.

This victory was bittersweet for Blair, since she knew it was to be the last Olympics in which she would compete. She was grateful for all of her successes, however, and for all the wonderful memories they gave her. Most of all, she told Karen Rosen in the *Atlanta Journal and Constitution* in 1998, "I'm really grateful for VCRs so I can go back and relive it."

Retired in 1995

Blair competed as a speed skater one more season following her last Olympic win. During this last season, she shattered her world record time for the 500-meter sprint—twice. Her final, record-breaking time for the 500-meter sprint was 38.99 seconds. After this, at the age of 31, she felt she was ready to retire from competitive skating. "I just thought it was the right time," she said of her retirement to

Heather McCabe in the *Houston Chronicle.* ''It was a nice ending.''

Following her retirement from competitive skating, Blair remained extremely active, both in her sport and outside of it. She went to work coaching the U.S. women's speed skating team, based in Milwaukee, Wisconsin. She and her husband, fellow speed skater Dave Cruikshank, made their home in Milwaukee, and Blair kept up a heavy travel schedule, flying to different cities around the country to meet various corporate endorsement obligations. Blair has also become an accomplished motivational speaker, addressing audiences on such topics as ''Achieving Your Personal Best.'' She has also made television commercials for such major corporations as McDonald's and AT&T. She counts herself lucky in being able to maintain such an active retirement, noting that not all Olympic gold medalists have been as fortunate.

After the turn of the twenty-first century, Blair still found herself involved in speed skating, even though she no longer competed. Instead, she skated vicariously through her husband, who competed in international events. Cruikshank had skated in four Olympics by 1998, and he narrowly missed qualifying for the U.S. team for the 2002 Olympics. Blair later credited her husband's continuing involvement in the sport with helping her to make the transition from competition to civilian life.

Stayed in the Public Eye

At the beginning of the 2002 Winter Olympics, Blair again took the spotlight when she became the last torchbearer on the Wisconsin segment of the Olympic torch run in January. She skated twice around the Pettit National Ice Center for a cheering crowd of ten thousand fans before lighting the Olympic caldron set up at the Center. Blair was touched by the adulations of the crowd, saying that she had never heard any group of spectators cheer so hard for her.

In addition to her ongoing endorsement commitments, Blair serves as a sports commentator on the ABC television network and sits on the board of directors of the U.S. speed skating team. Blair has also been involved in the American Brain Tumor Association's efforts to combat this little-understood disease; in 1987, Blair's brother Rob was diagnosed with brain cancer that was deemed terminal. Ten years later, however, doctors were able to remove about half of the tumor, giving Blair and her family hope for a cure.

Encased in a glass tabletop in her house, Blair's gold medals have become part of her daily landscape. ''The kids eat cereal on top of it,'' she told Parrish, ''but it's got a heavy top, so nothing gets underneath.'' Blair lives in Delafield, Wisconsin, with her husband and their son Grant and daughter Blair.

Periodicals

Atlanta Journal and Constitution, February 9, 1998.
Boston Globe, January 9, 2002.
Houston Chronicle, August 13, 1996.
Milwaukee Journal Sentinel, January 6, 2002; February 18, 2002.
Rocky Mountain News, February 15, 2002.
Sports Illustrated for Women, February 2002.
Toronto Star, January 11, 1995; March 19, 1995.
USA Today, October 17, 1995.
Washington Post, February 24, 1988.

Online

''Bonnie Blair,'' HickokSports.com, http://www.hickoksports .com/biograph/blairbon.shtml (March 10, 2003).
''Bonnie Blair,'' Infoplease.com, http://www.infoplease.com/ ipsa/A0109013.html (March 10, 2003). □

Lucrezia Bori

Opera singer Lucrezia Bori (1887–1960), known for years as the grande dame of the Metropolitan Opera, was one of its most beloved sopranos. In 19 seasons, more than 600 performances, and 29 roles with the company, her grace, style, and musicality made her a critically acclaimed and enormously popular star. Her artistic integrity, personal dignity, and lack of temperamental behavior also made her one of opera's most gracious figures. Following an illustrious stage career, her tireless dedication to fundraising efforts for the Metropolitan Opera earned her the nickname ''the opera's Joan of Arc.''

Bori was born Lucrecia Borja y González de Riancho on December 24, 1887, in Valencia, Spain, the daughter of a well-to-do army officer. She was a descendant of Renaissance Italy's powerful Borgia family; her name in Italian, in fact, was Lucrezia Borgia. Her family, however, insisted she change it for the stage. Bori made her first public appearance at a benefit concert in Valencia at age six. After a convent education, Bori at 16 decided to become a singer and went to Milan, Italy, for coaching. She made her professional debut at the Teatro Adriano in Rome on October 31, 1908, as Micaela in *Carmen.* Bori was subsequently hired by the Italian opera house La Scala the following season, where the promising young artist so enchanted German composer Richard Strauss that he insisted she sing the role of Octavian in the local premier of his *Der Rosenkavalier* in 1911.

Premiered at the Metropolitan Opera

Bori's long association with the Metropolitan Opera began in 1910 in Paris, when she was invited to replace an indisposed colleague as Manon in Puccini's *Manon Lescaut* with the touring New York company. After an enthusiastic response to her portrayal, two more performances were added and quickly sold out. Her first American appearance was in the same role at age 24, opposite the legendary Italian tenor Enrico Caruso, performed on the opening night of the Metropolitan Opera's 1912–1913 season in New York. A critic of that era quoted in the *Record Collector* praised Bori's performance as an ''exquisite exhibition of legato singing'' and ''exquisite diction, impeccable intonation and moving pathos.''

As Bori was enjoying the peak of her success, her career took a fateful and dramatic turn. Nodules on her vocal chords required delicate throat surgery in 1915, followed by five years of lonely convalescence. In a *New York Times* article she described her harrowing period of recovery, during which she once forced herself to be absolutely silent for two months. "I felt," she said, "as must those stricken with blindness just as the sun of spring flooded the world." Her discipline and courage were instrumental in her triumphant comeback to the Met in 1921, and her career flourished in the 15 years that followed.

Bori was known for her remarkably clear, true voice and dramatic prowess, capable of expressing passion as well as vulnerability and whimsical charm. Some of Bori's most famous roles included Mimi in *La Bohème;* Norina in *Don Pasquale;* Juliette in *Roméo et Juliette;* and Violetta in *La Traviata,* among others. Of her recordings, critic C. J. Luten wrote in *Opera News:* "Not everyone takes to her somewhat acidulous voice, but who can resist what she does with it? She radiates vivacity in Juliette's waltz . . . and in the Norina-Malatesta duet from *Don Pasquale.* Her legato, long line and pathetic accent . . . are masterful."

Bori's farewell performance at the Met, on March 29, 1936, was a moving tribute to a brilliant career still in its prime. After singing selections from *La Traviata* and *Manon,* the audience stood and cheered for 20 minutes in homage, with women weeping and men stamping their feet. Bori was later quoted in the *New York Times:* "I have no illusions

about the length of time a singer may sing. I want to finish while I am still at my best."

Ensured Met's Survival Through Fundraising Work

Bori's "second career" with the Metropolitan Opera began in the early 1930s, when the company's survival seemed threatened by the Depression. In addition to a demanding singing schedule, Bori took on many outside engagements as the head of fundraising committees, including writing letters, meeting with benefactors, and traveling. In 1933, she was praised by Paul D. Cravath, then president and chairman of the Met board, who told the *New York Times* that Bori "did more than anyone else to make opera at the Metropolitan . . . a financial possibility." In 1935, she became the first active artist and the first woman elected to the board of directors of the Metropolitan Opera. In 1942, she was elected president of the Metropolitan Opera Guild.

On May 2, 1960, Bori suffered a cerebral hemorrhage. She died in New York on May 14 at age 71, and funeral rites were held at St. Patrick's Cathedral. Bori, who never married, is buried in the Borja family plot in Valencia. Her will provided for the establishment of the Lucrezia Bori Foundation for charitable, educational, and literary purposes.

Periodicals

Chicago Tribune, July 14, 1991.
New York Times, May 15, 1960; May 18, 1960; May 22, 1960; May 24, 1960.
Opera News, November 1983; December 19, 1987; January 18, 1992.
Record Collector, December 1973. □

Georg Brandes

Georg Brandes (1842–1927) was an influential Danish literary critic whose interpretations of such writers as Henrik Ibsen, August Strindberg, and Bjørnsterne Bjørnson are credited with bringing Scandinavian literature into the mainstream of European culture. Similarly, his analyses of major nineteenth-century German, French, and English authors, including John Stuart Mill and Friedrich Nietzsche, also served to alleviate the cultural gap that separated Danish readers from the central currents of European thought. According to Neil Christian Pages in *Scandinavian Studies,* "Brandes was without exaggeration the most influential European literary critic and commentator at the close of the nineteenth and the beginning of twentieth century.... A prolific scholar, biographer, and essayist, Brandes's pan-European approach transgressed literary and national boundaries combining art and political activism in an astute manner."

Literature and Social Reform

Brandes was born to Jewish parents in Copenhagen, Denmark, on February 4, 1842. By all accounts an excellent student, he studied law and philosophy at the University of Copenhagen and early on developed an antireligious point of view. After completing a master's degree in 1864 he continued his studies, taking a doctorate in aesthetics and publishing his dissertation, *Den franske æsthetik i vore dage,* in 1870. During this period he produced the collection of essays *Æsthetiske studier* (1868), which presented theoretical discussions of comedy and tragedy, and he translated John Stuart Mill's *The Subjection of Women* into Danish. Brandes maintained that literature should serve to reform society through confronting controversial social issues, and his early work was strongly influenced by the German philosopher G.W.F. Hegel and the French critic Hippolyte Taine, who sought to apply the methods of scientific investigation to the interpretation of literature and culture. In describing Brandes's critical perspective, biographer Bertil Nolin wrote that to Brandes "Literature was a weapon in an ideological debate, an instrument for the continuous change of values and social situations."

During 1870 and 1871 Brandes traveled outside Denmark, meeting with Mill (whose *Utilitarianism* he would translate in 1872), and with the Norwegian playwright Henrik Ibsen, the author of *Peer Gynt* (1867), whose works embodied the realistic ideals Brandes advocated. Returning to Denmark he began lecturing at the University of Copenhagen on the relationship between literature and cultural progress and published these lectures in *Emigrant-litteraturen* (*The Emigrant Literature,* 1872); *Den romantiske skole i Tydakland* (*The Romantic School in Germany,* 1873); *Reactionen i Frankrig* (*The Reaction in France,* 1874); *Naturalismen i England* (*Naturalism in England,* 1875), the first volumes of his monumental survey of European literature; and *Hovedstrømninger i det nittende aarhundredes litteratur* (*Main Currents in Nineteenth-Century Literature,* 1872–1890). Featured in *The Emigrant Literature* are analyses of French writers who were influenced by time spent outside their homeland, including Vicomte de Chateaubriand, who fled to London during the Reign of Terror and served later governments as ambassador to Rome, and the novelist Madame de Staël (1766–1817), who was banished from Paris by Napoleon after the publication of *Delphine* (1802), a novel sympathetic to divorce, Protestantism, and the British. Brandes's consideration of French literature is continued in *The Reaction in France,* offering considerations of the political agitator and former priest Félicité de Lamennais, who predicted the rise of a revolutionary working class, and the Romantic writer Victor Hugo, among others. In *Naturalism in England* Brandes considered the works of such poets as William Wordsworth, Percy Bysshe Shelley, and Lord Byron, particularly praising Byron's liberalism.

Brandes expected to take a position within the faculty of the University of Copenhagen, but his appointment was denied owing to his Jewish background and the radical nature of his views, including his avowed atheism. During the mid-1870s Brandes undertook the publication of the journal *Det nittende aarhundrede* with his brother Edvard, but when this enterprise failed, he left Denmark. For the next five years Brandes lived in Berlin, during which time he became personally acquainted with many leading writers and wrote analyses of a number of European thinkers, including the English Conservative leader Benjamin Disraeli and the Danish existentialist philosopher Søren Kierkegaard. The volume on Kierkegaard is considered important as the earliest extended consideration of Kierkegaard's philosophy, and, when translated in 1879, the first to introduce Kierkegaard's thinking to an international audience.

The Critic Outside the Academy

With private financial support, Brandes returned to Copenhagen in 1883 and became well known as a public lecturer, unaffiliated with the university. During the ensuing decades his renown and influence grew as he published a number of significant studies and after 1887 became a leading proponent of the works of the German philosopher Friedrich Nietzsche. Largely unknown at the time, Nietzsche was in the final two years of lucidity when he and Brandes began corresponding. In Brandes's 1889 essay, "Friedrich Nietzsche: En afhandling om aristokratisk radikalisme," he presented the earliest systematic treatment of Nietzsche's philosophy and technique. As quoted by Pages in *Scandinavian Studies,* Brandes introduced readers to this obscure writer by declaring, "Nietzsche appears to me the most interesting writer in German literature at the present time. Though little known even in his own country, he is a thinker of a high order, who fully deserves to be studied, discussed, contested, and mastered. Among many good qualities he has that of imparting mood and setting thoughts in motion." Nietzsche, in a letter quoted in *Scandinavian Studies,* later approved Brandes's characterization of his work as "aristocratic radicalism," calling that phrase "the cleverest thing I have yet read about myself." Through Brandes's efforts—he lectured on Nietzsche in Copenhagen and developed a theoretical framework for Nietzsche's works—Nietzsche gained prominence, but not before the philosopher had succumbed to madness, and he died in 1900. Brandes later issued the volume *Friedrich Nietzsche* (1909), which included biography, criticism, and correspondence.

Among Brandes's works of this period are the final two volumes of *Main Currents in Nineteenth-Century Literature,* as well as a monumental three-volume consideration of Shakespeare (1895–1896) and the travel books *Intryk fra Polen* (*Impressions of Poland,* 1888) and *Intryk fra Rusland* (*Impressions of Russia,* 1888). Nolin identified *Den romantiske skole i Frankrig* (*The Romantic School in France,* 1882), the fifth volume of *Main Currents,* as "the most substantial volume" of the series. In it Brandes focused on the period 1824 to 1848, analyzing works by Hugo, George Sand, Stendhal, Honoré de Balzac, Alfred de Musset, and Charles-Augustin Sainte-Beuve, a literary critic with whom Brandes is often compared. The final volume of the survey, *Det unge Tydakland* (*Young Germany*) was published in 1890. Brandes here examined the influence of Heinrich Heine, Karl Ludwig Börne, and Karl Ferdinand Gutzkow, and other advocates of the Young Germany movement in the mid-nineteenth century.

In the literary biography *William Shakespeare* Brandes combined literary evaluation with psychological portrait, attempting to elucidate the life of the writer through his works. Brandes, as quoted by René Wellek in *A History of Modern Criticism: The Late Nineteenth Century, 1750–1950,* expressed the opinion that "given the possession of forty-five important works by any man, it is entirely our own fault if we know nothing whatever about him. The poet has incorporated his whole individuality in these writings, and there, if we can read aright, we shall find him." Brandes's travelogues were praised by Hjalmar Hjorth Boyesen in *Essays on Scandinavian Literature* as showing "a faculty to enter sympathetically into an alien civilization, to seize upon its characteristic phases, to steal into its confidence . . . and coax from it its intimate secrets." In the English journal the *Spectator,* a contemporary reviewer of *Impressions of Russia* asserted that Brandes "has drawn a portrait of the Russian State that in depth of insight, range of knowledge, and vividness of presentation, surpasses every contribution we are acquainted with."

Controversial to the End

Brandes was at last made a professor of the University of Copenhagen in 1902. His memoir, *Barndom og første ungdom* (*Reminiscences of My Childhood and Youth*) was published in 1906. Though now ensconced in the academy,

with many of his formerly controversial ideas gaining acceptance, Brandes remained an iconoclast throughout his career. He was a vocal opponent of the First World War and in 1925 elicited wide criticism when he published *Sagnet om Jesus (Jesus: A Myth),* a treatise in which he proclaimed that Jesus had never existed. Inspired in part by Nietzsche's concept of the *Übermensch,* or Superman, Brandes focused much of his later career on producing biographies of extraordinary historical personages, including Wolfgang von Goethe (1914–1915), Voltaire (1916–1917), Julius Caesar (1918), and Michelangelo (1921). Brandes died on February 19, 1927.

While Brandes's criticism has been surpassed and is little known today, his role as an early supporter of the Scandinavian writers Ibsen, Strindberg, and Kierkegaard remains significant as does his advocacy of the works of Nietzsche, whose influence continued throughout the twentieth century. In an assessment of Brandes written in the late 1890s, William Morton Payne wrote in the *Bookman,* "That the work of Brandes, taken as a whole, has been a contribution of great value to contemporary criticism can hardly be denied even by those the least in sympathy with his ideals. It more than makes up in light what it lacks in sweetness, and it has the stimulating quality that comes from freshness of thought and unconventionality of utterance." Near the end of his life, Brandes was hailed by Robert Herndon Fife in an introduction to Julius Moritzen's *Georg Brandes in Life and Letters,* as "unique in his contribution to the development of European thought. . . . He is the only critic who has ever completely identified himself with the whole of Europe's culture and the entire spirit of the age." And in *Essays in German and Comparative Literature* Oskar Seidlin, assessing Brandes's lasting significance, noted, "His critical conceptions and analyses may be completely outmoded tomorrow; but his instinct for the truly great, his fight for the recognition of the new, will testify for him. . . . He was a great discoverer, and he had the courage of his discoveries."

Books

Boyesen, Hjalmar Hjorth, *Essays on Scandinavian Literature,* Charles Scribner's Sons, 1895.

Moritzen, Julius, *Georg Brandes in Life and Letters,* D.S. Colyer, 1922.

Nolin, Bertil, *Georg Brandes,* Twayne, 1976.

Seidlin, Oskar, *Essays in German and Comparative Literature,* University of North Carolina Press, 1961.

Twentieth-Century Literary Criticism, The Gale Group, 1983.

Wellek, René, *A History of Modern Criticism: The Late Nineteenth Century, 1750–1950,* Yale University Press, 1965.

Periodicals

Bookman, April 1897.

Scandinavian Studies, Summer 2000.

Spectator, May 17, 1890. □

Mel Brooks

Mel Brooks (born 1926) transformed traditional burlesque and Jewish humor into a hit-and-miss career writing and directing film parodies of traditional Hollywood genres. His biggest success came late in his career when he adapted his first film, *The Producers,* into a smash Broadway musical.

From Catskills to Television

Mel Brooks was born Melvin Kaminsky in Brooklyn, New York, on June 28, 1926. He was a short and often sickly child, and his peers often ridiculed him. Reacting to this treatment, he learned how to strike back with stinging forms of abusive and satirical humor.

After serving in the U.S. Army in World War II in Europe as a combat engineer, Brooks took his talent for insults and pratfalls to the Catskills resorts, then famous for nurturing Jewish comics. For several years he performed the role of a "toomler," a kind of court jester who would stage impromptu monologues or pretend to insult the resort staff and the customers. The roots of Brooks's comedy were in vaudeville and burlesque, two dying forms of entertainment that emphasized physical humor, insults, sight gags, and

outrageous lampooning. Among his many gags was leaping into the swimming pool fully clothed with a suit and tie.

Brooks's style of humor was perfectly suited to early television. In 1950, desperate to get a job writing gags and skits for pioneering TV comedian Sid Caesar, Brooks auditioned by falling to his knees before Caesar and singing a comic song about himself. Caesar hired the young comic to concoct jokes for his hit series *Your Show of Shows.* Among the writers Brooks worked with in Caesar's stable were Woody Allen, playwright Neil Simon, and Carl Reiner. It was during these years that Brooks honed his gift for sharp, sometimes mean satire and rapid-fire wordplay. By the time Brooks parted ways with Caesar in the mid-1950s, he was earning $2,500 per show, a substantial amount in those days.

Brooks remained in television, though without regular income, as a gag writer and script doctor. He also worked on dialogue and scripts for radio and theater and occasionally appeared as a comic on television variety shows, such as 1962's *Timex All-Star Comedy Show.* One of his frequent skit partners was Reiner, with whom he developed a sketch called "The 2,000-Year-Old Man," in which Brooks played a smart-alecky Jewish curmudgeon who has seen it all and has comments on everything in history. With variations and elaboration, this routine developed into a staple on television shows and the two comics eventually had a hit record album on their hands. "The 2,000-Year-Old Man" was Brooks's first big success.

In 1964 Brooks married actress Anne Bancroft, with whom he would have four children. That same year he did the voice-over on a cartoon film titled *The Critic,* playing the equivalent of the 2000-Year-Old Man commenting on modern art. The film won an Academy Award for Best Animated Short Subject. In 1965 Brooks and writer Buck Henry developed the hit television show *Get Smart,* a comic spoof of the spy genre. Starring Don Adams as the bumbling secret agent Maxwell Smart, *Get Smart* became one of the most popular shows of the late 1960s. After television audiences began to turn away from comedy and variety shows in favor of drama in the next decade, and as his radio work dried up, Brooks would see his income plummet.

Springtime for Hitler

Buoyed by the success of *Get Smart,* Brooks wrote and directed the low-budget movie *The Producers,* which was released in 1968. Starring Zero Mostel and including a role for Brooks, *The Producers* is a tall tale about a down-and-out theatrical producer named Max Bialystock (Mostel) who is persuaded by corrupt accountant Leo Bloom (Gene Wilder) to deliberately stage a money-losing play and abscond with the excess cash finagled from their naive, elderly investors. The two hire a neo-Nazi director and a drug-crazed hippie star (Dick Shawn) to stage a musical comedy called *Springtime for Hitler,* a light-hearted romp featuring the German Chancellor who waged war on Europe and exterminated six million Jews. When the show turns out to be a success, Bloom and Bialystock find themselves in trouble.

The Producers was an outrageous and risky venture that depended on audiences laughing at the idea of a Hitlerian musical little more than two decades after the end of the war, during a time when many older adults with firsthand experience of World War II and the Holocaust were still living. In fact, the film is the epitome of Brooks's satirical attitude, and his belief that show business knows no bounds. Despite its low budget, *The Producers* was hailed as something of a minor comic masterpiece. Unfortunately, it flopped at the box office and was unable to buoy Brooks's sinking income.

After getting an acting role in the black comedy *Putney Swope* in 1969, Brooks wrote and directed *The Twelve Chairs,* an adaptation of a 1928 Russian novel about a former aristocrat who has hidden his fortune in a dozen chairs. Less a satire than a straight comedy and complete with chase scenes and comic suspense—and another role for Brooks—*The Twelve Chairs* was also a flop, both commercially and critically.

In 1974, after several dry years, Brooks signed on with Warner Brothers to do a film based on a satirical Western story called ''Tex X.'' ''Richard Zanuck and David Brown had it and didn't know what to do with it,'' Brooks told an interviewer for *Entertainment Weekly* years later. ''They asked me to direct. I said, I don't do things I don't write. So write it, they said. I didn't really want to. But I was broke. My wife, Anne Bancroft, was pregnant. And frankly, 'Tex X' was a really good idea.'' Tasteless, politically incorrect—in the film Brooks plays an Indian chief—and retitled *Blazing Saddles,* the film became Brooks's first big hit.

With the blockbuster success of *Blazing Saddles,* Brooks was off and running. Brooks was nominated for a 1974 Oscar award for Best Song for his penning of the title tune from *Blazing Saddles.* By the end of the same year Brooks had released a second hit, *Young Frankenstein,* starring Wilder. Following Brooks's formula, *Young Frankenstein,* shot in black and white, lampoons the granddaddy of all monster/horror movies by imagining Wilder as the great scientist's grandson who creates his own monster. Full of scatological humor, plot twists, silliness, and loving bows to monster movies of the past, *Young Frankenstein* managed to appeal both to critics and audiences, and it was nominated for Academy Awards for best adapted screenplay and for best sound.

Brooks cast himself in the lead role of his next film, *Silent Movie,* as a director who wants to return to the silent-movie era. His old boss, Sid Caesar, played the producer who approves the project. Among the stars appearing in the film was Bancroft. A very chancy project, the entire movie had no dialogue other than a single word—spoken, ironically, by famous mime Marcel Marceau. Full of sight gags yet nostalgic and sweeter than most Brooks films, *Silent Movie* was not a big box-office hit.

In 1977 Brooks took a detour from sarcasm by directing a little-known, little-seen, schmaltzy family film titled *Poco Little Dog Lost.* He also released his next big project, *High Anxiety,* a parody of Alfred Hitchcock thrillers. Vulgar and often repetitive, *High Anxiety* again starred Brooks in the lead role opposite Cloris Leachman. Brooks's efforts re-

sulted in success when he was nominated for Golden Globe awards for best musical or comedy as well as for best actor in a musical or comedy.

In 1980 Brooks tried something new. Purchasing the rights to *The Elephant Man,* a screenplay about the abuse suffered by a grotesquely deformed man in Victorian England, he hired virtual unknown David Lynch to direct the drama. Although Brooks produced the film he had his name removed from all publicity so audiences not confuse the film as a satirical comedy. With little fanfare, Brooks went on to produce several other serious films in the 1980s and the early 1990s, including *Frances* and *84 Charing Cross Road.*

Winter for Mel

Brooks's style of humor had become less popular by the 1980s, and he began using some of his favorite gags repeatedly. No joke was too tawdry and no target too sacrosanct. His 1981 film *The History of the World, Part I* was such a box-office disaster that *Part II* was never attempted. Beginning with this film, during the decade his scattershot humor ranged widely to create a series of comic vignettes ranging from the Stone Age to the French Revolution and including parodies of Hollywood Biblical epics and more recent films such as *2001: A Space Odyssey* and *Star Wars.* He extended the parody of George Lucas's blockbuster sci-fi adventure in the 1987 release *Spaceballs.* In between, he filmed a remake of Ernst Lubitsch's *To Be or Not to Be,* a story about a Polish theater troupe during the early years of the Nazi occupation. Brooks and Bancroft star as the leading duo in the troupe.

Also in the 1980s, Brooks produced and contributed his vocal talent to an animated version of *The 2000-Year-Old Man* and acted in and produced several more films. In 1990 he did the voice-over of the character Mr. Toilet Man in *Look Who's Talking, Too.* Later in the decade he released three more feature films, playing his customary roles as writer-director-producer-actor in *Life Stinks, Robin Hood: Men in Tights,* and *Dracula: Dead and Loving It,* the last film in 1995. He also produced 1992's *The Vagrant* and acted in *The Little Rascals, The Silence of the Hams* (a little-seen satire), *Screw Loose,* and two episodes of the television hit sitcom *Mad about You.*

Well into his 70s by 2000, Brooks appeared to be at the conclusion of a successful if spotty career as a leading practitioner of crude and sometimes inspired satire. He was considered almost a relic of a bygone era, one of the last American comics to take the traditions of burlesque and Catskills humor into the 1960s and beyond by blending his gift for satire and insult with a knack for parodying the tradition of Hollywood. Nobody would have predicted that he was about to achieve a new pinnacle of success.

The Producers on Broadway

In the years after it first appeared, Brooks's *The Producers* achieved increasing popularity and appreciation. Many critics began to refer to it as a comedy classic, and it became a cult favorite. At the urging of DreamWorks studio executive David Geffen and Bancroft, Brooks penned a musical version of *The Producers* designed for the stage. Opening on April 19, 2001, and starring Nathan Lane and Matthew Broderick, the show became a mega-hit on Broadway. In fact, within a year, it had broken all Broadway box-office records, and it received a record 12 Tony awards, one for every nomination, and two of them going to Brooks as author of the show's music and lyrics. In his acceptance speeches, as quoted in *Back Stage,* Brooks thanked his wife "for sticking with me through thin" and added: "I'd like to thank Hitler for being such a funny guy onstage."

In the opinion of some critics, *The Producers* reflects an earlier era when shows were not as afraid of lampooning sensitive subjects. A contributor to *Time* called it "one of the best translations of a beloved movie to the stage ever. . . . The show delivers such a wealth of vaudeville exuberance that the few quibbles (a rather lumpy second act) are likely to fade away." Explaining the appeal of the show in the same article, Brooks said: "You can't compete with a despot on a soapbox. The best thing is to make him ludicrous."

Despite its popularity, the musical also had its detractors, some of whom took issue with the way *The Producers* mocks gays, Jews, and Germans. Brooks reacted by defending his approach. "There are always holier-than-thou guys," he told Nancy Shute of *U.S. News & World Report.* "There isn't a subject that's taboo."

Late in 2002 a touring version of the play began making the rounds of U.S. theaters, with plans for a London production in 2004. Buoyed by the astonishing success of his stage remake, Brooks was laying plans for revamping *Young Frankenstein* as a musical. Meanwhile, 2002 found him busy on his memoir. "I have always been a huge admirer of my own work," Brooks told John F. Baker of *Publishers Weekly,* adding: "I'm one of the funniest and most entertaining writers I know. And I just can't wait to read my book."

Books

Sarris, Andrew, *St. James Film Directors Encyclopedia,* Visible Ink Press, 1998.
Thomson, David, *A Biographical Dictionary of Film,* Alfred A. Knopf, 1994.

Periodicals

Back Stage, June 8, 2001.
Daily Variety, June 19, 2002; August 15, 2002.
Entertainment Weekly, March 1, 2000; May 25, 2001; December 6, 2002.
People, December 31, 2001
Publishers Weekly, January 20, 2003.
Time, April 16, 2001.
U.S. News & World Report, August 20, 2001.
Variety, September 10, 2001.

Online

"Mel Brooks," *All Movie Guide,* http://www.allmovie.com (February 7, 2003). □

Natalie Curtis Burlin

Natalie Curtis Burlin (1875–1921) was an American ethnomusicologist who began the movement to transcribe the traditional songs of Native American tribes. She also published a four-volume collection of African American spirituals. Her work helped preserve the folk songs of both groups.

Born Natalie Curtis in New York City on April 26, 1875, Burlin attended the prestigious National Conservatory of Music there, intending to become a concert pianist. She also studied in France and Germany with some of the best-known musicians of her day, including Arthur Friedheim, Anton Seidl, and Ferruccio Busoni.

Fascinated by Native American Music

While visiting Arizona in 1900, Burlin abandoned her plans for a concert career. The Native American culture she discovered there, and particularly its music, so entranced her that she decided to focus exclusively on transcribing, collecting, and preserving the tribes' songs and stories. Given the state of Native American culture at the time, she was convinced that they would be lost without an active effort to preserve them.

By the beginning of the twentieth century all the tribes of the western United States had been forced onto reservations. There the Federal Bureau of Indian Affairs pursued a relentless assimilation policy: Native American children were forced to attend government schools, where they had to cut their hair, adopt western dress, and speak only English. They were also forbidden to sing any native songs; anyone who did so, even an adult, was likely to incur the authorities' wrath.

In 1903 Burlin established a base on the Hopi reservation in Arizona, where she used an Edison recorder to capture the tribal songs on wax cylinders; often, however, she found it simpler to work only with pencil and paper. To her dismay, though, she found that many Native Americans were reluctant to sing for her, fearful that to do so would bring punishment. "[W]ill not the superintendent be angry if you do this thing?" asked one chief in *The Indians' Book.* "Are you sure that you will not bring trouble upon us? White people try to stop our songs and dances, so I am fearful of your talk."

Fought to Record Native American Songs

Burlin also had to tread carefully. The Natalie Curtis Burlin website contains her reminiscence that "[A] friendly scientist on the reservation advised me that if I wished to continue my self-appointed task of recording native songs (which were at that time absolutely forbidden in all the government schools), I must keep my work secret, lest the school superintendent in charge evict me from the reservation!"

Burlin was so dismayed by the conditions under which the Native Americans were forced to live that she became determined to force a change. Capitalizing on a family friendship with President Theodore Roosevelt, she went to the White House to bring the Native Americans' plight to Roosevelt's attention and explain the need to preserve their native art and culture. Burlin's plea was successful, as detailed in the preface to *The Indians' Book:* "Thus, for example, the singing of Indian songs in the Indian schools came to be not only officially permitted, but encouraged. . . . Congress . . . found funds sufficient for a short-lived effort to record officially the music of the various tribes. At last the Indian child in the government school and the adult on the reservation were allowed a freedom of racial consciousness and a spiritual liberty theretofore almost tyrannically denied."

Called Tawi-Mana (song maid) by the tribes, Burlin was given official permission to record Native American songs, and Roosevelt himself became personally involved in the project, eventually traveling to the reservation in 1913 for the Hopi flute and snake ceremonies. The visit was detailed in "Theodore Roosevelt in Hopi Land," an article Burlin wrote for *Outlook* magazine.

Published *The Indians' Book*

The Indians' Book, published in 1907, was a collection of songs and stories gathered from 18 tribes. Lavishly illustrated with photographs and artwork contributed by Native American artists, it contained Burlin's meticulous handwritten transcriptions of songs, although she noted in the chapter on the Hopi Native Americans that "[t]o seize on paper the spirit of . . . [such] music is a task as impossible as to put on canvas the shimmer and glare of the desert." The songs were interspersed with stories of Burlin's travels among the Indians, illustrating not only the unique aspects of each tribe's culture but their humanity.

Burlin held herself to a strict standard, refusing to add or delete anything from the songs she transcribed. The book's title reflected her overwhelming belief that she was only "the white recorder," as she called herself. She described her technique in the chapter on Hopi Indians: "[I]n rhythmic monotone the old man crooned beside me. Long and diligently I worked. . . . It was no light task to fix the chant in musical notation. I saw the question in the chief's eyes: 'I have sung the song; why does it take so long to make those black marks on the paper?' And I said, 'Lolomai [Very Good One], you know that when the Hopi sets a trap for the blackbird, sometimes it is long before he can catch his fluttering prey. Your song is a wild blackbird to me, and it may be that the sun will move far along the sky before I have captured it.'"

Once transcribed and recorded, the Native American music brought to light by Burlin caught the attention of other musicians. One of them, her former teacher Ferruccio Busoni, used a collection of Native American melodies as the basis of his *Indian Fantasy*. The piece was first performed in 1915 by the Philadelphia Orchestra, conducted by the famous director Leopold Stokowski. The Natalie Curtis Burlin website quotes her reaction: "With the first bars of the orchestral introduction . . . the walls melted away, and I was

in the West, filled again with that awing sense of vastness, of solitude, of immensity."

Became Interested in African American Music

Burlin's work with Native Americans convinced her of the need to promote minority rights in American society. Although she continued to travel in the American West and remained a lifelong advocate for Native Americans, Burlin broadened her scholarly focus in the years following *The Indians' Book* publication. Around 1910 she began to record and transcribe African American music at the Hampton Institute in Hampton, Virginia, a university established in 1868 to educate former slaves. The famous philanthropist George Foster Peabody, who funded much of her work, was a trustee at Hampton. Like Burlin, he wanted to expand educational opportunities for blacks.

The following year, Burlin and the violinist David Mannes founded the Music School Settlement for Colored People in New York, intending, as the website explains, "to preserve and develop black music and provide musical education for children." Her efforts did not stop there, however. In 1912 Burlin was among a group of musicians who sponsored the first concert featuring black musicians at Carnegie Hall. The audience ranged from well-known professional musicians to everyday folks who simply loved music; music editors from the New York papers were also in attendance. Burlin was thrilled with the 125-member Clef Club orchestra directed by James Reese Europe. The website quotes her: "It was an astonishing sight, that Negro orchestra . . . Europe uplifted his baton and the orchestra began (with an accuracy of 'attack' that many a great band might envy) . . . [A]s one looked through the audience, one saw heads swaying and feet tapping in time to the incisive rhythm, and when the march neared the end, and the whole band burst out singing as well as playing, the novelty of this climax—a novelty to the whites, at least—brought a very storm of tumultuous applause."

In 1917, Burlin married Paul Burlin, an artist who was also enchanted by the beauty of the American Southwest. They were married in Taos, New Mexico, which had already become known as an artists' colony, thanks in part to Natalie Burlin's efforts. The couple created "The Deer Dance," a pageant based on Pueblo Indian ceremonies. Burlin—now Natalie Curtis Burlin—based the music on native songs, and her husband designed sets and costumes.

Published *Negro Folk-Songs*

In 1918 Burlin, in association with the Hampton Institute, published the first of four volumes entitled *Negro Folk-Songs,* each one a collection of songs for a male quartet. Books I and II were collections of spirituals; Books III and IV were, as noted on the title page, "work- and play-songs." As she had with *The Indians' Book,* Burlin strove to record, not change, the music she heard, noting in the foreword to the first volume: "These notations of Negro folk-songs are faithful efforts to place on paper an exact record of the old traditional plantation songs *as sung by Negroes*. . . . I have added nothing and I have striven to omit nothing." True to

Burlin's philanthropic ideals, all proceeds from the volumes went to the Hampton Institute.

As she had on the Native American reservations, Burlin used her Edison recorder to capture the songs' intricate harmonies and rhythms. "I lack entire faith in the study of wax records afar from the live voice of the singer," Burlin noted in the Foreword to Book II, " . . . [but] the phonograph with its wealth of recorded detail . . . [is] an invaluable adjunct to the higher spiritual task of assimilating the folk-idiom and translating it mentally into terms of notation."

Her interest in the *Negro Folk-Songs* books led Burlin to study the roots of black American music. She spent a year working with two African students at Hampton, one a Zulu from Natal (now South Africa), the other from Portugeuse East Africa (now Mozambique), recording their songs and learning about the religions and cultures of their respective societies. She intended to include these African songs in the American volumes, but decided instead to publish them separately as *Songs and Tales from the Dark Continent* in 1920.

Challenged White Hegemony

The Burlins moved to Paris in 1921. Her husband, who had begun to explore abstract and expressionist art, found the cultural climate in the United States too restrictive and chafed at the criticism he encountered even from fellow artists. He found the European arts community more supportive. The move was a welcome one for his wife, whose earlier studies in Paris had made her familiar with the city. It also enabled her to attend the International Congress of Art History, held that year in Paris, as a delegate.

For all of her care and concern for the peoples she studied and whose rights she promoted, Burlin's views, seen with the clarity of historical distance, seem condescending. She referred to the Native Americans as "simple people" and "children of the desert" and portrayed their culture in an unrealistic and idealized light. Her views of African Americans could be considered patronizing: "The Negroes possess an intuitive gift for part-singing," she noted in the foreword to Book I. "This instinct, transplanted to America and influenced by European music, has flowered into the truly extraordinary harmonic talent found in the singing of even the most ignorant Negroes of our Southern States." It "makes one wonder at the possibilities of the race," she mused in Book IV.

In her day, however, Natalie Curtis Burlin was ahead of her time in her advocacy for the rights of all peoples and all cultures. The preface to *The Indians' Book* quotes her fervent belief that "only when we admit that each race owes something to the other, only when we realize our vast mutual human indebtedness, may we hope for . . . inter-racial . . . tolerance, understanding, and co-operation. . . ." Speaking to the Congress of Art History, she railed against "the everlasting monopoly of the white race," and praised the "12 million Negroes who are 'good enough' Americans to die for American ideals in our wars." She defended America's multicultural heritage, saying, "All America is not New England, but an agglomeration of races with a rich and diverse folklore."

The speech, unfortunately, would prove to be one of her last public pronouncements. Only a few weeks later, on October 23, 1921, she was struck and killed by a speeding automobile in Paris while stepping off a streetcar.

Books

Burlin, Natalie Curtis, *The Indians' Book: An Offering by the American Indians of Indian Lore, Musical and Narrative, to Form a Record of the Songs and Legends of Their Race,* Dover, 1968.
Burlin, Natalie Curtis, *Negro Folk-Songs: The Hampton Series, Books I–IV,* Schirmer, 1918-1919.

Online

"Natalie Curtis Burlin," http://www.nataliecurtis.org (February 12, 2003).
"Natalie Curtis Burlin," *Encyclopedia Britannica,* http://www.britannica.com/eb/article?eu = 137709& = 0& = burlin = (February 12, 2003).
"Natalie Curtis Burlin," Women in American History, *Encyclopedia Britannica,* http://search.eb.com/women/articles/Burlin_Natalie_Curtis.html (Februray 12, 2003). □

Carol Burnett

For 11 years beginning in 1967, Carol Burnett (born 1933) was the undisputed leader in television entertainment. On her long-running program for the CBS television network, *The Carol Burnett Show,* the multi-talented Burnett expanded and upgraded the concept of the television variety show, mixing song and dance routines, elegant costumes, and zany humor sketches in ways that appealed to a massive populous audience. She was one of the first actors to be allowed complete control of every aspect of the show's creation, without excessive interference from network brass. Since the show's final season in 1978, Burnett has remained active as a producer, actor, and playwright who is respected by her colleagues for her strong work ethic and adored by her audiences for her decidedly unpretentious demeanor.

Burnett was born on April 26, 1933, in San Antonio, Texas; her family moved to Hollywood, California when she was three. Her father suffered from alcoholism and chronic tuberculosis; her mother was a quick-tempered alcoholic who aspired to become a writer within Hollywood social circles. Her parents divorced when she was eight and Burnett was raised by her grandmother on her mother's side, a feisty old woman who instilled the young girl with values, as well as taking her to the movies up to eight times a week (Burnett's signature ear-tug at the close of her shows was a tribute to "Nanny"). "You might say 'poor' thing when you heard my parents drank and we were

on relief," the actor told *Newsday* reporter Blake Green in 1999, "but that was the way it was with everyone in that neighborhood. I never had a picture that anything could be different, except in the movies, and I knew that was fantasy."

When Burnett started college, she got a job as an usher at a Warner Brothers-owned movie theater. She was fired after she refused to seat a couple during the last five minutes of an Alfred Hitchcock movie. When Burnett was given her star on the Hollywood Walk of Fame in 1975, she asked that it be placed in front of that theater.

Burnett attended UCLA in 1951, originally to pursue a degree in English writing. She attended an actor's workshop and was so significantly enamored with the craft that she decided it would be her calling. As part of her final exam for her theater major, her theater professor made the class perform at an elegant black-tie party he was holding. A patron attending the party who saw Burnett perform gave her a small amount of money to go to New York City, in the hopes of entering show business. She graduated in 1954, left California for New York City and married her first husband, classmate Don Saroyan, soon afterwards. After a few stints in local shows, nightclubs, and some high-profile appearances on Jack Paar and Ed Sullivan's television shows, Burnett made it to the Broadway stage in a big way; in May 1959, she had landed the lead role as Princess Winnifred Woebegone in *Once Upon A Mattress* (a stage adaptation of the fable "The Princess And The Pea"), under the direction of the acclaimed director George Abbott.

While appearing in *Once Upon A Mattress,* Burnett was discovered by representatives for television personality Garry Moore, who had a successful evening variety show on CBS. She auditioned for the show and after a few guest appearances, she was added to the full-time cast of *The Garry Moore Show* in November of that year; she stayed on until 1962. Audiences were enamored by Burnett's physical comedy, goofball facial contortions, and self-deprecating antics. While working on the Moore show, Burnett still found the time to record an album, appear in plays, host a radio show, and guest star in television shows, including an episode of *The Twilight Zone.* Her success had taken a toll on her marriage, however, and in late September of that year, she and Saroyan divorced.

After leaving the *The Garry Moore Show,* Burnett appeared on Broadway in the short-lived *Fade Out-Fade In,* some television specials, and opposite Dean Martin in her first film, *Who's Been Sleeping In My Bed?* She was offered the lead role in a musical comedy called *The Luckiest People* but suggested to the producers that they instead cast a then-unknown actress named Barbara Streisand (the show was later retitled *Funny Girl*). In May 1963, she married Joe Hamilton, a successful television producer she met on the set of the Moore show. But Burnett's biggest accomplishment was yet to come. During her frenetic schedule, representatives from CBS kept enticing the multi-talented performer with offers to perform in her own television show. Finally, on September 11, 1967, *The Carol Burnett Show* premiered on the network, with Burnett at center-stage, alongside a cast of regulars including Harvey Korman, Lyle Waggoner, and Vicki Lawrence.

The show was a vehicle for Burnett's range of talents, as well as a distillation of what she enjoyed in her various show-business experiences. She would start every show with a question-and-answer session with the audience, an idea she borrowed from her stint on Garry Moore's show (Moore never filmed his pre-show audience interactions for broadcast). Over the next 11 years, the show had amassed a dedicated following of viewers who tuned in to see an array of Burnett creations ranging from the lonely charwoman (a trademark character that Burnett never really thought that highly of); the high-strung Eunice Higgins (which fostered a spin-off show, *Mama's Place,* starring Lawrence as the elderly matron); and the highly inept office secretary Wanda Wiggins. The troupe was quite fond of doing parodies of television soap operas and classic movies. One of the show's most famous moments was during a parody of the motion picture *Gone With The Wind* (titled *Went With The Wind*). Then-fledgling designer Bob Mackie outfitted Burnett's Scarlett O'Hara character in a gown made of hanging curtains—with the rod still attached. That skit generated the longest laugh (reportedly ten minutes) from a studio audience in the history of the show. Veteran comedic actor Tim Conway joined the cast full time in 1975, adding an element of surprise with his keen improvising skills. Many viewers would tune into the show each night to see Conway routinely crack-up Burnett and the rest of the cast in mid-scene.

Sensing that the program had run its course, Burnett decided in February 1978 to end the show on a high note instead of wearing out her welcome. After 11 years, 286 shows, and being honored by her peers with 22 Emmy Awards, *The Carol Burnett Show* ended on March 17, 1978. The two-hour show included a recap of classic footage, some long-running characters with new routines (Eunice Wiggins and Mama finally saw a family counselor), some guest appearances, and Burnett reprising her charwoman character for a final emotional farewell. As author J. Randy Taraborrelli succinctly stated in his 1988 Burnett biography, *Laughing Till It Hurts,* "She tugged on her ear in recognition of Nanny. And then she turned around and walked into television history."

In the years immediately following the show, Burnett became involved in a number of projects for film, stage, and television. She appeared in two movies directed by Robert Altman, 1978's *A Wedding* and 1979's *H.E.A.L.T.H.* She teamed up with actor Charles Grodin for a TV movie based on author Erma Bombeck's book, *The Grass Is Always Greener Over The Septic Tank,* in October 1978. The following year, she starred opposite Ned Beatty in a television movie, *Friendly Fire,* about a couple's search to find the truth about a son's death in Vietnam.

Working on the politically charged film sparked Burnett to voice her political beliefs publicly for the first time in her career; she was an advocate of the Women's Rights Movement and regularly spoke out in support of the Equal Rights Amendment. When her eldest daughter, Carrie, developed a drug addiction problem, Burnett and her husband got her medical treatment and went public with the story afterwards, a move that distanced her from much of the routinely secretive Hollywood elite, yet endeared her to the hearts of regular people who had friends and loved ones going through the same torment. Burnett appealed publicly for stricter drug laws and railed against stores that routinely sold drug paraphernalia.

Unlike many show-business denizens, Burnett has continued to make her private life public in an effort to stall sensationalist stories in gossip magazines. In the mid-1970s, the *National Enquirer* printed an anecdote that she was being drunk and disorderly in a Washington, D.C. restaurant. Incensed by the fabrication—and personally wounded because of how alcohol destroyed her parents—Burnett sued the paper. After seven years in the courts, a jury sided with the actor and awarded her a hefty sum. She gave the proceeds to charity.

In July 1981, she appeared as the treacherous Miss Hannigan in the film version of the musical, *Annie* and starred alongside Elizabeth Taylor in the HBO production, *Between Friends,* in 1984. Burnett's workload had put a strain on her marriage to producer Hamilton, and the two divorced in the spring of 1984.

In 1986, Burnett turned to writing, putting together *One More Time,* a memoir of her early childhood years growing up in Texas and California that took the form of an open letter to her three daughters, Carrie, Jody, and Erin. She returned to Broadway in 1995 in the comedic farce *Moon Over Buffalo* and appeared in several television specials. She also performed in the 1999 Stephen Sondheim tribute, *Putting It Together.*

In 1998, at the suggestion of her eldest daughter Carrie (herself a writer and actor), Burnett and Carrie collaborated on the script for a play based on *One More Time.* The project, *Hollywood Arms* (named after the building that housed the one-room apartment Carol and her grandmother lived in) was both fruitful and troubling for Burnett, as Carrie was under medical supervision for cancer. Sadly, Burnett's daughter died from lung cancer in January 20, 2002, just prior to the rehearsals before the project's Halloween 2002 premiere. When *Newsweek* writer Marc Peyser asked Burnett if her daughter would be proud of *Arms* landing on Broadway, she responded, "No matter what happens to our play, my baby and I went the distance. For that, I'm grateful."

During the writing of *Hollywood Arms,* Burnett took time out to do a speaking tour of the United States. The format of the program was the same question-and-answer sessions that ran at the beginning of each episode of her network series. The fact that audiences paid to see and hear Burnett answer questions, reminisce on her career, accept complements, and do her classic Tarzan yell, was a testimony to her affable and charismatic personality.

In November 2001, at age 69, Burnett secretly wed her third husband, Brian Miller, a percussionist for the Hollywood Bowl Orchestra. And although Burnett has been given generous offers to return to network television to host her own program, she has steadfastly refused. She cites the high cost of mounting a variety show production (back in the day, many of designer Mackie's gowns alone fell within the $30,000 to $50,000 price range) as well as having to deal with meddling "suits" from network offices making "suggestions" and demanding changes. Her original show has remained in syndication for years (under the title *Carol Burnett And Friends),* edited to a half-hour format with the musical numbers excised, due to regulations from the Musicians Union.

Books

Burnett, Carol, *One More Time,* Random House, 1986.
Taraborrelli, J. Randy, *The Complete Life and Career of Carol Burnett,* William Morrow and Company, Inc., 1988.

Periodicals

AP Online, June 1998; December, 2001.
Associated Press, September 1995.
Associated Press Newswires, November 1998; January, 2002.
Canadian Press, December 2001; January 2002; November 2002.
CBS News: 60 Minutes, November 1999; January 2000.
Chicago Sun-Times, October 1994.
Chicago Tribune, June 1996.
CNN: Larry King Live, October 2002.
Dallas Morning News, February 1995.
Hartford Courant, November 1999.
Houston Chronicle, November 2001.
Interview, October 1994.
Kitchener-Waterloo Record, April 2002.
Los Angeles Times, October 2000.
Newsday, May 1999; November 1999.
Newsweek, October 2002.
People, October 1997.

Press-Enterprise, June 1996.
Providence Journal, June 2002.
San Antonio Express-News, August 1996.
Syracuse Herald American, October 1996.
Tulsa World, October 1996; April 1998.
USA Today, November 2001.
Wall Street Journal, November 2002.
WWD, September 1996.

Online

"Carol Burnett," *Famous Texans,* http://www.famoustexans .com/carolburnett.htm (February 13, 2003).
"The Carol Burnett Show," *Yesterdayland,* http://www .yesterdayland.com/popopedia/shows/primetime/pt1351 .php (February 13, 2003).
"The Facts: Carol Burnett," *E!Online,* http://www.eonline.com/ Facts/People/Bio/0,128,2402,00.html (February 13, 2003). □

Dick Button

Dick Button (born 1929), a dominant force in figure skating in the late 1940s and early 1950s, was instrumental in developing the sport in America. He is the only male figure skater to clench the "grand slam" of skating, winning the United States, North American, European, World, and Olympic championships in the same year. Button later became a somewhat controversial commentator on figure skating for television.

Richard Totten Button was born on July 18, 1929, in Englewood, New Jersey, the son of George and Evelyn B. (Totten) Button. He and his two older brothers, Jack and George, were raised in wealth and privilege. Button began skating when he was five years old, using his brothers' old skates.

When Button was 11 years old, he received his first pair of skates for Christmas. He wanted figure skates, but received hockey skates from his father. The skates were exchanged, but Button's burgeoning figure skating career was almost cut short again. The youngster was 5'2" and weighed 160 lbs. His first coach did not believe he had any ability and would never learn to skate.

Early Skating Success

Button's parents found him another coach. He was first taught by Joe Carroll in New York City in 1942 and eventually would train with a coach who would become famous for instructing Olympians, Swiss-born Gustave Lussi. Button attended public schools in Englewood, New Jersey, until high school, when he attended the private Englewood School for Boys. For the next ten years, during his summers off from school, Button would train with Lussi in Lake Placid, New York, where the 1932 Winter Olympics had been held.

Button soon proved he had great natural ability. Combined with intense training and great coaching, he soon had success in competition. Button also grew into a 6'1" frame. In 1943, he placed second at the Eastern States novice single championships. Showing his competitive spirit, Button was unhappy with his second place win. Later that year, he won first title. Button won the major novice singles championship at the Middle Atlantic States competition. He went on to win national men's novice (1944) and junior titles (1945).

In 1946, Button capped his rise to the top of American men's figure skating by winning the U.S. national senior singles championship, in Chicago, Illinois. He was only 16 years old at the time, the youngest man to win the title. Button had to come from behind to win, as he placed second after compulsory figures. This marked the first and only time a figure skater won the novice, junior, and senior titles in succession. Button would go on to win the men's singles title every year through 1952.

Changed Skating Style

Button competed at the 1947 World Championships, the first World's held since 1939 because of World War II. He placed second to Hans Gerschweiler, though some believed Button should have won. This finish prompted Button to change his skating style. In addition to becoming more precise in his school figures, more importantly, he became more bold and daring in his free skate.

The new approach in free skate allowed Button to emphasize power in his spins and jumps, becoming more artistically daring. He also focused on developing new jumps and spins, especially jumps. Button was encouraged in his pursuit by Lussi, who was a disciplinarian but also supported Button's quest for innovation. Button's work in this area paid off in 1948 when he won his first world championship. This marked the beginning of his fame as a powerful figure skater. Button would go on to win the world championship every year through 1952.

While Button was reaching the summit of the figure skating world, he still attended Englewood Boys School. He lettered in football and played baseball there, but figure skating was his main focus. Button skated for hours every day, rising early for school, to skate, and to pursue other sports. He graduated in 1947 then took a year off of school to train for the 1948 Olympics.

To practice for the Olympics, Button competed in the 1948 European championships in Prague, Czechoslovakia. Not only did this competition assist Button in preparing for the Olympic games, it allowed him to show off his newly developed style to the judges so they might be more favorable later on. It was the first time an American competed, and Button impressed the judges enough to win the title. After this victory, non-Europeans were excluded from competing for the championship.

Won First Olympic Gold

Button cemented his status as a leading figure skater at the 1948 Winter Olympics in St. Moritz, Switzerland. This was the first time the Olympics had been held since 1936. Button was leading after school figures, then won the gold medal with his free skate.

Button's free skate was innovative for several reasons. He did two moves on the ice that had not been done before in world competition. Button did the first double axel (a jump that rotated in the air for two-and-a-half rotations) and the Button camel (the first version of the flying camel, a jump into a spin). Button landed the double axel for the first time two days before the competition, then landed it perfectly in competition.

Button won the Olympic Gold Medal when eight of nine judges gave him first place. In 1948, Button won all five major championships: Olympic, European, World, North American, and United States. He was the only American to accomplish it, and the first man to ever do it. Button's win marked the beginning of American influence in skating, which had been dominated by Europeans for a number of years. Button's new style made free skate more important than the compulsory figures, which had previously been the more important part of competition. Eventually, figures would be eliminated and it was the free skate that would attract audiences.

Entered Harvard University

In the fall of 1948, Button entered Harvard University. He could have gone to Yale University, but Yale would not let him take time off to compete as a skater. While attending college, Button continued to win the World and U.S. championships, as well as a number of North American championships.

In 1949, Button won the Sullivan Award as the United States' outstanding amateur athlete. This was the first time a figure skater won the prestigious award, the finest honor an amateur athlete could receive. Button's win also showed the increased importance of figure skating.

As Button continued to win major competitions, he also was more innovative as a skater. He developed a number of jump combinations. In 1949, he came up with the double loop combo of two double loops. In 1950, Button devised a triple double loop. In 1951, he did a double axel, double loop. These combinations would go on to become something many high level skaters would learn.

Won Second Olympic Gold

In 1952, Button repeated his gold medal victory at the Olympic Games in Oslo, Norway. Again, button achieved something no skater had done before. He landed a triple loop in his free skate program, the first time he or any skater had done a triple jump in competition. Button was in the lead after school figures, but would have lost the gold medal had he not landed the triple loop.

The evolution of Button's triple loop was one of frustration. Button had spent the summer of 1951 trying to execute the jump, but some coaches thought it would be impossible. He became so focused on the triple loop that it negatively affected his ability to do his other jumps. Button finally let it go for a while, only to try again just before Christmas in 1951. This time, Button finally got the feel for jump and was able to do it at the Olympic Games.

Button liked winning gold medals, but he told Vinny DiTrani of The Record, "Being handed the gold medal is like being presented the Nobel Prize for peace. It's a thrill, but there were even greater thrills along the way when you were doing the things for world peace that earned you the honor."

Retired as an Amateur

In 1952, Button graduated from Harvard with his B.A. The university later gave him a special Harvard "H" for athletics. He also retired from amateur competition. Button became a professional figure skater touring with the Ice Capades during his vacations from Harvard Law School. Button graduated from law school in 1956 and passed the bar in Washington, D.C., but never really practiced. He continued to skate, appearing in a Goodwill Tour of Moscow, USSR, in 1959.

Became Commentator

In the early 1960s, Button started for ABC and other television networks as a color/expert commentator for figure skating competitions. He was considered as controversial for his opinions as he was hard on skaters. Some considered him fair, but others believed he played favorites.

Describing his technique as an announcer, Button told Jane Leavy of the Washington Post, "I have carte blanche to say anything I want. I've never been cut, called down, or told to shut up. When I've asked for guidance, they say, 'Tell it the way you see it.' If anyone holds back, I do. I'm reporting skating to 200 million people in the country. Probably only 25,000 to 50,000 understand the sport and only 1,000 really understand. My job is to educate them and make them aware of it." Button won an Emmy for his commentary in 1981 as Outstanding Sports Personality Analyst.

Button was also associated with television in another way. He formed a television production company with partner Paul Feigay, Candid Productions. This company produced sport and entertainment series that included national and world figure skating and gymnastics, horse shows, and national pentathlon. Button's company also created sports-oriented programs, such as *The Superstars, The Superteams,* and *The Battle of the Network Stars.* These were reality, made-for-television sports competitions that were very popular in the 1970s, but also continued to air in the 1980s and 1990s. Button also created figure skating championships through this company, including the World Professional Figure Skating Championship in 1980.

Button, involved in another aspect of the entertainment world, invested in and produced a number of stage productions in New York City, primarily on Broadway. Among these productions were *Sweet Sue* with Mary Tyler Moore and *Artist Descending a Staircase.* Button also did some appearances himself. He skated in *Hans Brinker and the Silver Skates* for television and was an actor in movies like *The Young Doctors* and stage productions such as *South Pacific.*

Married to Slava Kohout, with whom he had two children, Emily and Edward, Button was considered one of the best figure skaters ever. International Figure Skating publisher, Mark A. Lund, as quoted by *Business Wire* when

Button was selected to be man of the century for figure skating, said "No other individual in the 20th century represents the sport better than Dick Button. From his technical innovations to his creation of the world of professional figure skating competitions with the World Pro, Dick Button has by far had the most influence on the sport during the last century."

Books

Hickok, Ralph, *A Who's Who of Sports Champions,* Houghton Mifflin, 1995.
The Lincoln Library of Sports Champions, 2001.
Malone, John, *The Encyclopedia of Figure Skating,* Facts on File, Inc., 1998.
Porter, David L., ed., *Biographical Dictionary of American Sports: Basketball and Other Indoor Sports,* Greenwood Press, 1989.

Periodicals

Boston Globe, January 14, 1992; February 10, 1995.
Business Wire, December 22, 1999.
Calgary Herald, January 3, 2001.
New York Times, February 21, 1992.
Record, February 14, 1992.
Sports Illustrated, June 20, 1988.
Washington Post, February 23, 1980.

Online

"Athlete Profile-Richard T. (Dick) Button," Olympic USA, http://www.olympic-usa.org/athlete_profiles/d_button.html (February 9, 2003).
"Dick Button, Expert Commentator, Figure Skating," ABC Sports, http://espn.go.com/abcsports/columns/button_dick/bio.html (February 9, 2003). □

C

Jane Campion

Australian director and screenwriter Jane Campion (born 1954) created a number of films with strong female protagonists starting in the late 1980s. Among the best known of her works was the Academy-award-winning film *The Piano* (1993).

Campion was born on April 30, 1954, in Wellington, New Zealand, the daughter of Richard Campion and Edith Armstrong. Her father was a theater director and her mother was an actress. They had met when both were students at the Old Vic in England. Together, they co-founded the New Zealand Players. Campion was raised in Wellington, with her older sister, Anna, with whom she would later collaborate, and her younger brother, Michael.

While Campion was interested in acting, she did not immediately follow the family tradition. Instead, she attended Victoria University in Wellington and earned a bachelor's degree in structural anthropology. She then went to Europe where she studied art in Venice, among other places. Eventually, she went to London where she worked as an assistant for a filmmaker who did documentaries and commercials. She also studied at the Chelsea School of Arts in London.

Became Interested in Film

Campion finished her diploma in art at the Sydney College of Arts in Sydney, Australia. She majored in painting and sculpting, but she discovered her true calling during her last year at the college, when she began making super-8 films. Her first short film, *Tissues* (1980), got her into film school.

In 1981, Campion entered the Australian Film Television and Radio School. There, she made three significant short films. She was the director, writer, and editor of *Peel* (1982), which focused on a power struggle over discipline between a father and a son. In 1984, she made *Passionless Moments* and *Girl's Own Story,* the latter focusing on brother-sister incest.

After graduating from the school in 1984, Campion spent several years working with the government-funded Women's Film Unit. She wrote and directed *After Hours* (1984) a film about sexual harassment. Campion then moved into television. She directed an episode of the series *Dancing Daze.* In 1985, she directed her first television movie, *Two Friends,* which was released theatrically in the United States in 1996. The film focused on a female friendship and how it changed over time and was told in reverse chronological order.

Early Features

In 1986, Campion won the Palme D'Or at the Cannes Film Festival for best short film for *Peel,* garnering her much attention. She then began working on the script, with former boyfriend Gerald Lee, for what became her first feature film, *Sweetie.* The disturbing black comedy was released in 1989 and won several prizes.

Sweetie focuses on a dysfunctional family. The movie tells the story of Kay, a shy woman who is engaged to Louis but cannot enjoy life. Her already sad world is turned upside down when her sister, Dawn, also known as Sweetie, enters her life again. Dawn is obese, mentally unstable, and uncontrollable, and she was doted on by her parents her whole life. Dawn was led to believe that she was bound for show

business since childhood, and her actions and needs take over her entire family and the movie.

Audiences and critics often had extreme reactions to *Sweetie,* positive and negative. Vincent Canby of the *New York Times* wrote: "It is funny, though one doesn't often laugh at it, and sad, without ever asking for tears. Instead, it demands that it be taken on its own spare terms without regard to the sentimental conventions of other movies. At its best, it is audaciously unreasonable."

In 1990, Campion directed her second feature, originally made for New Zealand television as a miniseries. It was *Angel at My Table,* a movie about author Janet Frame adapted from her autobiography. The film had a dreamy, slow quality and focused on how men controlled, betrayed, and condemned Frame.

Angel at My Table depicts all of Frame's tragic life. After a difficult childhood, Frame worked briefly as a teacher before having a nervous breakdown. She was misdiagnosed as a schizophrenic and forced to live in a mental institution for eight years. After receiving hundreds of electroshock treatments, Frame was nearly lobotomized until a doctor discovered that she had won a literary prize for poetry. Frame left the institution and eventually found her calling as a writer.

Though *Angel at My Table* received mixed reviews in the United States, it was generally liked. The film won a number of prizes, including the Silver Lion at the Venice Film Festival. In many ways, this was Campion's break-through film, setting the stage for her biggest artistic triumph, *The Piano* (1993).

Acclaimed for *The Piano*

Though *The Piano* began with some development money from the Australian Film Commission, the film was Campion's first big-budget production, financed with French money. Campion had been working on the script since 1984, and she had long wanted to do a story about the colonial days of New Zealand.

Set in 1850, *The Piano* focuses on a mute Scottish woman named Ada, who does not speak only because she chooses not to. Her only means of communication is her piano. She has an illegitimate, young daughter, who is just as free-spirited as her mother. Ada enters into an arranged marriage with a New Zealander and moves to that country. Her new husband, Stewart, is a farmer who will not take the piano to their new home. He sells it to a man, Baines, who lives with the natives. Baines offers to give the piano back to Ada if she teaches him to play. Ada and Baines eventually become lovers, and after several plot turns, Ada leaves her husband for him.

The Piano was a huge international hit. It won numerous awards, including the Palme d'Or at Cannes. Campion was the first female director to win that award. She was also nominated for the Academy Award for best director.

Campion was developing a solid reputation as a film director. Actor Sam Neill, who played Stewart, told Mary Cantwell of the *New York Times Magazine,* "Jane works in an unusually intimate way with people. When you're an actor, you're always putting yourself in other people's hands anyway, and she repays the gesture many times over. Jane's interested in complexity, not reductiveness, and very sure of what she's doing. If you have an opinion contrary to hers, she listens with the greatest care and consideration, then does what she had in mind all along."

The same year that *The Piano* was released, Campion formed a production company, Big Shell Films, with her producer-director husband Colin Englert. Also that year, the couple had a son, Jasper, who died 12 days after birth. In 1994, their daughter Alice was born.

Later Films

Campion's films after *The Piano* could not match its success. In 1996, she directed an adaptation of Henry James' novel *The Portrait of a Lady.* The story focuses on Isabel Archer (Nicole Kidman), an American expatriate who lets her potential die and enters into an unhappy marriage with Gilbert Osmond. Reviews of the film were mixed and box office returns paltry.

In 1999, Campion directed and co-wrote, with her sister Anna, *Holy Smoke,* a contemporary story about religion, cults, and male-female relationships. The plot focuses on Ruth Barroon, a young woman from the suburbs of Sydney, Australia, who joins a religious cult in India to find enlightenment and spirituality. Ruth returns to her home after a desperate visit by her mother. When she comes home, she finds that her family has tricked her and hired a deprogammer, J.P. Waters, to force her out of the cult. Ruth ends up manipulating Waters, and the pair become lovers.

While many critics praised the themes of the movie, the script was seen as conventional and obvious. As Janet Maslin wrote in the *New York Times,* "as *Holy Smoke* moves from its early mix of rapture and humor into this more serious, confrontational stage, it runs into trouble. For one thing, the characters as written are an impressionable young woman and a tough older man. . . . And it doesn't help that the screenplay . . . threatens to become heavy-handedly ideological beneath its outward whimsy."

Campion's next movie was a Hollywood production. In 2002, she adapted the best-selling novel, *In the Cut.* Her first film set in the United States, *In the Cut* is an erotic thriller focused on a female linguist who falls in love with a cop who is investigating a serial killer. Originally, *In the Cut* was supposed to star Kidman, but she was replaced by Meg Ryan. Campion encountered problem when Miramax dropped the film, but it was scheduled for distribution in 2003.

Throughout her career, Campion was generally regarded as an important original female voice who depicted strong women characters. As Jay Carr of the *Boston Globe* wrote in 1999, "With her embrace of the bizarre and the private, Jane Campion has become film's poet of the human interior. It's not so much her way of focusing on the suppressed voices of women that marks her art. Rather, it's her stubborn belief that these voices will be heard, sooner or later, one way or another. . . . Campion's films are genuflections to the staying power of powerless woman."

Books

Pendergast, Tom, and Sara Pendergast, eds., *International Dictionary of Films and Filmmakers-2: Directors,* St. James Press, 2000.

Periodicals

Associated Press, January 24, 1990.
Boston Globe, June 14, 1991; February 3, 1999.
Film Comment, November-December 1996.
New York Times, October 6, 1989; January 14, 1990; September 19, 1993; December 3, 1999.
Toronto Star, February 25, 2000.
United Press International, 1989.
Vancouver Sun, February 15, 2000.
Variety, May 21, 2001.
Village Voice, November 30, 1999.
Washington Post, June 21, 1991.
Washington Times, February 12, 2000.

Online

"In the Cut," Yahoo! Movies, http://movies.yahoo.com/shop?d =hp&=prev&=1809404536 (February 9, 2003). □

Thomas Campion

An English poet best known during his lifetime as an author of Latin poetry, Thomas Campion (1567– **1620) is chiefly remembered for his songs for voice and lute and a number of masques celebrating occasions at court. He produced theoretical writings on music composition and in *Observations in the Art of English Poesie* (1602) called for the use of classical meter in English poetry.**

Campion was born to John and Lucy Campion in St. Andrew's parish, Holborn, on February 12, 1567. His father died in 1576, and his mother, who was the daughter of one of the queen's sergeants-at-arms, remarried but was soon widowed. After remarrying again, Campion's mother died herself, and from 1580 he was raised by his stepfather, Augustine Steward. Campion was educated at Peterhouse, Cambridge, but left in 1584 without taking a degree. During the late 1580s he studied law at Gray's Inn, where he developed an interest in musical arts and participated in dramatic performances but never completed his legal training. Based on evidence in his writings, biographers believe he left England in 1591 to accompany Robert Devereux, Second Earl of Essex, on a military campaign to Rouen, in Normandy.

Campion's first published works are believed to be unsigned lyrics included by Thomas Newman in an edition of Sir Philip Sidney's *Astrophel and Stella* in 1591. His first attributed work, the Latin volume *Thoma Campiani Poemata,* was published in 1595 and contained epigrams, elegies, and other verse works, including "Ad Thamesin," an epic recounting the defeat of the Spanish Armada.

In 1601 Campion and his friend, Philip Rosseter, a musician in the court of King James, collaborated on the volume *A Booke of Ayres.* Campion contributed the first 21 songs and a prose exposition on music theory. Campion related the composition of an ayre to that of an epigram in poetry, praising simplicity and condemning the popular madrigal style of the era as overly complex. He wrote in the preface to *Book of Ayres,* "what Epigrams are in poetrie, the same are ayres in musick, then in their chief perfection when they are short and well seasoned." His musical contributions to the volume include "Though You Are Young and I Am Old;" "Come, Let Us Sound with Melody," a rendering of Psalm 19 in Sapphic meter; and "I Care Not for These Ladies."

Observations in the Art of English Poesie, Campion's treatise on poetry, was published in 1602. In it he denounced rhyming verse as facile and inartistic and advocated instead the use of classical, quantitative meters, that is meters based on quantity—determined by duration, or the time it takes to express a syllable—rather than on accent. As an example of his theory, he exhibited "Rose-Cheekt Lawra:" "Rose-cheekt Lawra, come / Sing thou smoothly with thy beawties / Silent musick, either other / Sweetely gracing."

During this same period Campion went abroad to pursue medical studies at the University of Caen in Normandy. He returned to England a degreed physician and set up a medical practice in London in 1605. While his profession provided necessary income, he continued his artistic pursuits, and in 1607 he produced the *Lord Hay's Masque,* a presentation at the court of King James celebrating the marriage of James Hay, a Scottish courtier later created first Earl of Carlisle, to Honora Denny, the daughter of a wealthy English nobleman. Depicting the resolution of a disagreement between Diana and the knights of Apollo through the intervention of Hesperus, the masque reflects the symbolic union of Scotland and England in the nuptial occasion and the actual union of the countries under James's rule.

Campion returned to theoretical writing with *A New Way of Making Fowre Parts in Counter-point,* published circa 1610. In it he advocates using the bass line rather than the tenor as the basis of musical harmony, a shift in composition that Anthony Burgess called "innovative" in a 1970 review of Campion's works.

In November 1612, during the preparations for Campion's next court masque (a celebration of the marriage of Princess Elizabeth to Frederick, Elector Palatine), the sudden, unexpected death of Henry, the Prince of Wales, inspired Campion's *Songs of Mourning,* a collection of elegies with accompanying music by Giovanni Coprario. In February 1613 Campion's *The Lord's Masque* was at last performed at court, with scenery and decoration by the celebrated architect Inigo Jones. Within the following year Campion was commissioned to write two additional masques for the family of the influential Lord Chamberlain, Thomas Howard, Earl of Suffolk. The first of these was a production mounted for the entertainment of Queen Anne as she traveled between London and Bath in April 1613, making a stop in Reading. Known as *The Caversham Entertainment* after the location in which it was performed, the production drew on traditional pastoral themes and characters and was divided into two parts, the first occurring out of doors as the queen's entourage approached the estate, and the second presented indoors on the following evening. Later in the same year Campion composed an entertainment on the occasion of the marriage of Suffolk's daughter, the Countess of Essex, a seventeen-year-old divorcee, to Robert Carr, Earl of Somerset. The success of the masque as an entertainment, published in 1614 as *The Description of a Maske: Presented in the Banqueting Roome at Whitehall on Saint Stephen's Night Last,* has been overshadowed by the subsequent events that involved the unwitting Campion and others close to the Howard family in a murder plot. Somerset's friend, Sir Thomas Overbury, who had strongly opposed the marriage, was imprisoned on false charges and slowly poisoned by Frances Howard. Campion, though questioned and cleared during the investigation, had unknowingly collected the bribe that secured the silence of tower guards in the matter.

In addition to the masques composed during 1613, Campion also published *Two Books of Ayres.* The first part of the collection contains songs of a religious or devotional nature, including "Never Weather-Beaten Saile," which, according to Elise Bickford Jorgens in the *Dictionary of Literary Biography,* "illustrates [Campion's] intricate and careful creation of musical and verbal rhythm out of the

accentual pattern of the words and the sensitive distribution of the vowel sounds."

The second part of the volume comprises love songs, including "The Peaceful Western Wind" and "There Is None, O None but You," both of which critic Thomas MacDonagh characterized in 1913 as "masterpieces of melody." According to biographer Walter Davis, "In the texts of the songs" of 1613, Campion "developed contrast, the literal and factual, and he was developing a style that would culminate in a dry realistic tone that encouraged a vibrant complexity of attitude. In his music he was incorporating many different voices, and was moving toward heightened speech rather than suggestive dance melody as a model for what music should be." In 1617 Campion published a final song book, *Third and Fourth Books of Ayres.* MacDonagh praised the collection for presenting "an ever new variety of rhythm and rime and colour," citing such works as "Thrice Toss These Oaken Ashes in the Air" and "Now Winter Nights Enlarge," which concludes, "The Summer hath his joyes, / And Winter his delights; / Though Love and all his pleasures are but toyes, / They shorten tedious nights."

Tho. Campiani Epigrammatum Libri II. Umbra. Elegiarum liber unus, Campion's final work, was published in 1619. This work enlarges and revises his earlier Latin poetry, including *Ad Thamesin,* and presents a number of new epigrams on medical subjects and elegies on love and faithfulness. *Umbra* narrates the tragic story of Iolde and her son Melampus. According to Dana F. Sutton, "the poem deals with destructive dreams and beguiling false visions" and through its subtext suggests that "physical beauty, and the love it engenders is a destructive snare and delusion."

Campion died in London on March 1, 1620, and was buried at St. Dunstan's in the West, Fleet Street.

In the century following his death, Campion's reputation diminished as new styles of music and poetry evolved. Interest in his compositions was revived during the early twentieth century with the publication of *Campion's Works,* edited by Percival Vivian in 1909. Commentators of the era generally favored the achievement of his lyrics over his songwriting, a view held by Bruce Pattison, who in 1946 called Campion "the finest lyric poet of his age." A later estimation, advanced by Anthony Burgess in 1970, holds that "Campion is possibly unique in possessing a total mastery of both crafts ... and a precise knowledge of the relationship between them. In both he was not merely an inspired empiric but a powerful theorist." Of his dramatic works, biographer David Lindley has noted in the *Dictionary of Literary Biography* that "Campion's masques are significant examples of their kind. In them may be traced the evolution of the early Jacobean masque, its music and scene design. Each of them offers an interesting gloss on the significant political events they celebrated. If their symbolism is fully and sympathetically understood then oftenrepeated criticism of Campion's lack of structural ability is shown to be false." In 1996 Jorgens summarized, "Campion's importance for nondramatic literature of the English Renaissance lies in the exceptional intimacy of the musical-poetic connection in his work. While other poets and musicians talked about the union of the two arts, only Campion produced complete songs wholly of his own composition, and only he wrote lyric poetry of enduring literary value whose very construction is deeply etched with the poet's care for its ultimate fusion with music."

Books

Davis, Walter R., *Thomas Campion,* Twayne Publishers, 1987.
Ing, Catherine, *Elizabethan Lyrics: A Study in the Development of English Metres and Their Relation to Poetic Effect,* Chatto & Windus, 1968.
Lindley, David, *Thomas Campion,* E.J. Brill, 1986.
MacDonagh, Thomas, *Thomas Campion and the Art of English Poetry,* Hodges, Figgis, 1913. Reprint, Russell & Russell, 1973.
Wilson, Christopher, *Words and Notes Coupled Lovingly Together: Thomas Campion, A Critical Study,* Garland, 1989.

Periodicals

ANQ: A Quarterly Journal of Short Articles, Notes, and Reviews, July 1988.
English Studies: A Journal of English Language and Literature, April 1988.
The Spectator, January–June 1970.

Online

Sutton, Dana F. "The Latin Poetry of Thomas Campion (1567-1620): A Hypertext Edition," http://eee.uci.edu/~papyri/campion/ (February 7, 2003).
"Thomas Campion (1567–1620)," http://www.luminarium.org/renlit/campion.htm (February 6, 2003). □

Ion Luca Caragiale

Often considered the voice of Romanian literature and his native country's best playwright, Ion Luca Caragiale (1852–1912) reflected the language, people, and concerns of Romania in his work. Caragiale was best known for his eight plays—most of which were social comedies—though he also had an extensive body of fiction, dramatic criticism, other works of nonfiction, and one novella to his name.

Caragiale was born on January 30, 1852, in Haimanalele, in what was to become Romania. He was the son of Luca and Ecaterina (nee Karaba) Caragiale. His father was the eldest of three sons, who all had careers in the theater as actors, directors, and playwrights, and were of Greek origin. Luca Caragiale began as an actor, but later became a judge, lawyer, and administrator of an estate. Caragiale also had a sister.

As a child, Caragiale received his education in Ploesti, beginning in 1857. It was not a complete or particularly even education at a local grammar school, then the Ploesti Gymnasium for three years, from 1864 to 1867. In many ways, Caragiale was largely self-taught and cultivated his own study of literature.

Studied Acting in Bucharest

When Caragiale was 16, he went to Bucharest to enter the family business. He entered the acting school run by one of his uncles, Iorgiu "Costache" Caragiale. The uncle ran the Bucharest Drama Conservatory. While a student there, he studied acting, mime, and dramatic recitation. While Caragiale wanted a career in the theater, his studies were cut short because of the death of his father when he was 18 years old. He then became the sole supporter of his mother and sister.

To financially provide for his mother and sister, Caragiale worked a number of jobs, while also building a career in the theater and in publishing. He was employed in a tobacco factory, a beer garden, as a copyist for the Prahova County Court House, private tutor, and translator of French literature. In 1870, he worked as a prompter for the National Theatre in Bucharest. Caragiale was also the proofreader of two newspapers and a freelance journalist.

Published First Works

In the early 1870s, Caragiale began publishing sketches and poetry. In 1873 and 1875, he had sketches published in the satirical review *Ghimpele.* In 1874, Caragiale published his first poem in a review published in Bucharest. He then moved on to working as a freelance journalist, often writing theater criticism for a number of publications including *Romania libera* and *Convorbiri literare.* Caragiale also held several positions in running publications. In 1877, he was the publisher of *Clapomul,* a humor periodical. Caragiale both wrote for and was a member of the editorial board of *Timpul* from 1878 to 1881.

Thus, before Caragiale ever established himself as a playwright, he was somewhat known, at least in Bucharest, for his literary works. In his writing for *Convorbiri literare,* Caragiale was a recognized member of the literary circle, Junimea (which means youth). The journal was their publication. He eventually became a leader in the group, though he was forced out after ten years in the early 1880s because of his critical attitude.

Began Writing Plays

By the late 1870s, Caragiale began writing the plays that would cement his reputation as an important playwright in Romania. In both his plays and the prose he wrote for much of his life, he displayed an ear for the language, customs, and manner of Romanians, especially the common person, and successfully used them in comic and satirical ways. Caragiale was very observant of the human condition and our tendency towards mistakes and used what he saw and heard in his stories, which often focused on social conflicts and political corruptions. The plays, especially, were full of action and fast-paced, employing stock characters who spoke witty dialogue but often failed to succeed in their goal.

Caragiale's first foray into writing plays was two translations of French works into verse done in 1878, *Roma Invinsa* and *Lucretia Borgia.* His first original work of important was *O noapte furtunoasa sau numarul (A Stormy Night,* or *Number 9;* 1879 or 1880). The story was centered around a love triangle between a man, Dumitrache, and wife, Veta, and the assistant of the husband/wife's lover, Chririac. Dumitrache is a jealous and mean man who is employed as the head of the civil guard. Because of his worries about his wife, he has his assistant, Chririac, guard his home, though his assistant is already his wife's lover. When Rica, his wife's sister's lover, comes to the home in error, the intricacies of the relationship are nearly revealed. Though the play was later considered important, it was originally banned from performance and labeled immortal and unpatriotic.

A second significant play from the same time period was also a satire, but more of a political comedy with similar elements of social commentary. *Conul Leonida fata cu reaciunea (Mr. Leonida and the Reactionries;* 1880) also featured a couple at its center. The provincial man, Mr. Leonida, relates the story of the Romanian republic that existed for a brief three weeks, to his wife Efimita. A republican, he also tells her his idea for a utopian society. Later that night, shots ring out. At first, Leonida believes that the revolution is taking place, and later, that they reactionaries are after him because of his ideas. Both assumptions are wrong, and he learns that the shots are coming from a Shrove Tuesday celebration.

Though *Conul Leonida* did not have the same controversial opening as *A Stormy Night,* when Caragiale originally wrote it, the play featured two aristocratic characters at its center. Theater officials would not allow the play to be performed until he changed them to two provincials. This allowed the characters to be viewed as more farcical and satirical by the audience. While Caragiale was gaining much notoriety as a playwright, he was also still holding other jobs to support his family. From 1881 to 1884, he served as an inspector of schools.

Wrote *A Lost Letter*

In 1884, Caragiale wrote what many consider his masterpiece as a playwright, *O scrisoare pierduta (A Lost Letter;* 1884). This was a comic satire about political corruption, which explores the victory of a blackmailer in a provincial government election. Like Caragiale's other important plays, *A Lost Letter* features a love triangle. The letter referred to in the title is from the wife of a candidate to an election official and is romantic in nature. The letter is lost and found by others who want to win the election and/or bring down the candidate. Caragiale's depiction of the events surrounding this election is very cynical, with most of the characters not even being likable. Despite this, the play had a long life and was performed for many years.

Another significant play of this time period was *D'ale carnavalului (Carnival Adventures* or *Carnival Scenes;* 1885). This complex farcical comedy was set in Bucharest during carnival time. The story focuses on romantic intrigues among the lower class characters. Several couples deceive each other and their lovers. Originally, *Carnival Adventures* was only performed twice because it was considered violent and crude.

As Caragiale became established as a significant playwright in Romania, he briefly held a post of importance there. For a few months at the end of 1888 and the beginning of 1889, he was the director general of the National Theatre in Bucharest. As a playwright, Caragiale was also maturing. In 1889 or 1890, he wrote *Napasta* (also known as *False Accusations, Injustice,* and *False Witness),* which was a tragedy-comedy but more serious than his other works. It was often compared to Fydor Dostoyevsky's novel *Crime and Punishment* and Leo Tolstoy's *The Power of Darkness.* The central character is a woman named Anca. She is a widow who has remarried to the man, Dragomir, who killed her husband. He was not convicted of the crime, but his friend Ion was. The play focuses on Anca's revenge on Dragomir. Like his other plays, *Napasta* was controversial in its time period.

Stopped Writing Plays

After *Napasta,* Caragiale did not write plays for the most part because he did not make much money at it and he needed to take care of his own family. In 1889, he married Alexandrina Burelly, with whom he had one son, Luca Ion—who also grew up to be a writer—and daughter Ecaterina. The couple also had another daughter who died in infancy. (Caragiale also had an illegitimate son, Mateiu Caragiale, who also became a writer.) Caragiale again returned to non-theater-related jobs, but continued to write short stories, fiction, and non-fiction in periodicals.

In 1892, Caragiale published two collections of short stories. Many of these stories retained his comic bite and reflected Romanian life. They often showed the life of lower class people like peasants and clerks. One famous short story published that year was "O faclie de Paste" ("The Easter Torch"), a condemnation of anti-Semitism. He published another collection of fictional pieces in 1901.

In the 1890s, Caragiale again returned to publishing work in a multi-faceted way. In 1893, he was the founder and editor of *Mortful roman,* a humor magazine. It was revived in 1901. In 1894, he was the producer, with George Cosbuc and Ioan Slavici, of the magazine *Vatra,* a family publication. He was also a contributor to *Vointa nationala* in 1895 and *Universul* between 1899 and 1901. Though Caragiale worked in publishing, he also continued non-related occupations as well. He was a civil servant at the Romanian Department of State Monopolies between 1899 and 1901.

Lived in Voluntary Exile

In 1901, Caragiale was sued by a theater critic for plagiarism. This caused much psychological stress for him, though he eventually proved his innocence. Such incidents led to his decision to move his family to Berlin, Germany, in 1904. That year, he received a long-awaited and previously disputed inheritance from an aunt. Caragiale had never really been happy in Romania, in part because he felt unappreciated as a writer in his native country. He also continued to have problems supporting his wife and children there.

While in exile, Caragiale continued to write, often contributing sketches and stories to periodicals published in Romania. In 1907, he published *Din primavara pana in toamna (From Spring to Fall),* a sociological piece of commentary that was originally published in *Die Zeit,* a German magazine. Two years later, he published a novella, *Kir Ianulea (Lord Ianulea).* This was his version of Niccolo Machiavelli's stage play *The Marriage of Belphagor.* In this fantasy, an imp from hell is sent to investigate human women on earth by the devil. The title refers to the name and form the imp takes when he lives in Bucharest as a Greek merchant. In this form, he marries a shrew and is bankrupted by her. Negoita, a man, saves him. The imp gives his rescuer wealth. The imp goes back to hell, while his wife and Negoita to heaven.

Caragiale died in Berlin, Germany, on July 9, 1912, of arteriosclerosis. He was buried there, but later he was reburied in Romania. Though Caragiale had a following and name recognition in Romania during his lifetime, he was also criticized and unappreciated there. After his death, he became more recognized for his importance to Romanian drama. Fifty years after his death, he was given a week-long tribute in which his plays were performed. Caragiale's plays seemed especially relevant when the Communists were in control and were oppressive. In the 1980s, his plays were banned until the dictator Nicolae Ceausescu was taken out of power in 1989.

Though Caragiale only wrote eight plays, he was arguably the best playwright produced in Romania. He was the first playwright to reflect the realities, speech, and manner of Romanian people and life and influenced other playwrights including the Romanian-born Eugene Ionesco. As Eric D. Tappe wrote in his book *Ion Luca Caragiale,* "He prided himself on his knowledge of Romanian and would say: 'Not many are masters of it as I am.'"

Books

The Columbia Encyclopedia, Columbia University Press, 2002.
Frucht, Richard, ed., *Encyclopedia of Eastern Europe: From the Congress of Vienna to the Fall of Communism,* Garland Publishing, Inc., 2000.
The Hutchison Dictionary of the Arts, Helicon Publishing, Ltd., 1998.
Kunitz, Stanley J. and Vincent Colby, eds., *European Authors 1000-1900: A Biographical Dictionary of European Literature,* H.W. Wilson Company, 1967.
Magill, Frank N., *Critical Survey of Drama: Foreign Language Series: Authors: A-Chi,* Salem Press, 1986.
McGraw-Hill Encyclopedia of World Drama, McGraw-Hill, 1984.
Peacock, Scot, ed., *Contemporary Authors,* Vol. 157, Gale, 1998.
Tappe, Eric D., *Ion Luca Caragiale,* Twayne Publishers, Inc., 1974. □

Jacob Cats

Jacob Cats (1577–1660), seventeenth-century poet, moralist, and statesman, was one of the leading poets in the golden age of Dutch literature. His emblem books, which reflected a stolid Calvinist philosophy, exhorted readers to virtuous and industrial lives.

Enormously popular, the books became the source of many well-known maxims and proverbs, giving him the title of "Father Cats," a fond soubriquet still used by modern Dutch to describe him.

Jacob Cats was born on November 10, 1577, the youngest of four brothers in Brouwershaven, Zeeland, the southernmost province of what is now the Netherlands. After his mother's death and his father's remarriage, Cats and his three brothers were sent to live with an uncle in the same province. After attending school in Zierikzee, Cats began his legal studies at the University of Leiden, then traveled to France to earn a doctor of laws degree in Orléans. After a further period of study and work in Paris, he returned to the Netherlands. Settling in the Hague, he began to work as a lawyer, where, the *1911 Edition Encyclopedia* notes, "his pleading in defence of [a] wretched creature accused of witchcraft brought him many clients and some reputation."

His success in the courtroom gave him the means to consider marriage, but an engagement was broken off when he contracted a mysterious, debilitating fever that lasted for two years. Desperate for treatment, he went to England, but was unable to find any relief. He went back to Holland, resigned to death, but received a new lease on life when he was unexpectedly "cured" by a charlatan.

Restored to health, Cats went to Middelburg, Zeeland, in 1603, where he opened a law practice. Two years later he married a wealthy heiress, Elisabeth van Valkenburg, and settled down to a prosperous existence. The Twelve Years' Truce (1609–1621), an interruption of the Eighty Years' War that eventually gave the Dutch their independence from Spain, was a period of comparative tranquility. In this favorable climate Cats and his brothers became wealthy draining and reclaiming land that had been flooded during the war— a profitable undertaking in a country where most of the land lies below sea level.

A successful businessman, Cats became a prominent political figure in the cities of Middleburg, and later, Dordrecht. He was appointed an advocate, or pensionary, a public servant that conducted much official municipal business. From 1636 to 1651 he served as Grand Pensionary of Holland, the most powerful of the Netherlands provinces. This prominent position had national importance, giving him a role in foreign policy. He was sent on at least two diplomatic missions, both to England: one in 1627 to Charles I and a second, unsuccessful venture 25 years later to Oliver Cromwell.

Like Dante and Chaucer before him, however, Cats was more than a mere civil servant. He is best known as a poet and author of emblem books—illustrated collections of didactic and moralistic (although clever and often humorous) poetry. These books, which had become popular in Europe, had begun with *Liber emblemata* published in 1531 by Andrea Alciato, an Italian lawyer.

Emblem books were immensely popular, especially among the pious and hard-working Calvinists of the Netherlands. In recent years they have also become valued as treasure troves of sociological and historical detail, illustrating not only many facets of daily life in the seventeenth century, but the moral and philosophical ideals that imbued the era as well. The books were perfect fodder for the relatively new printing industry, and the savvy Dutch soon cornered the market in printing them for both foreign and domestic audiences.

Most emblem book pages consisted of an illustration that was intended to drive home and amplify the moralistic verse printed along with it. At first examination, the two did not always appear to go together. For example, Cats combined a picture of a top and the whip that drove it—a common child's toy—with a warning against sloth and indolence. The Humanities Advanced Technology and Information Institute at the University of Glasgow, Scotland, quoted Cats's explanation: "The top spins merrily on the floor, whipped by a biting cord, and the harder one hits the better it spins. But let up a bit with the whip and it falls in the dust. From then on it won't do a single turn, but lie forever like a block. One never watches it better than in times of sorrow and unhappiness. For if anyone lives without pain, he rusts at once from idleness. When man has too much leisure, you see, that's when the heart yearns for lust."

Cats's first book *Sinne-en minnebeelden (Portraits of morality and love)* was published in 1618, when he was forty years old. The book, divided into three sections, contains prose, poetry, Bible verses, quotations from the classics, and common proverbs in Dutch, French, and Latin. Each illustration was accompanied by three different texts, each of which was designed to give three different—but always instructive—interpretations: the first romantic, the second social, and last religious. This combination of texts, styles, and languages in various degrees of complexity made the book accessible to a broad public. Illustrations were expensive, however, and at least two editions were published. One version had reproduced each of the 51 illustrations in all three sections; a second, cheaper printing contained only one set of images.

The images for many of Cats's books were supplied by Adriaan van de Venne, a well-known artist of the time. He drew literally hundreds of illustrations for the books, and they were, in turn, reproduced by master engravers. Other artwork for Cats's books were imitations of van de Venne, including a famous image depicting matrimony as a fisherman's trap.

In 1620 Cats published *Self-strydt,* a retelling in verse of Joseph and Potiphar's wife that became popular enough to warrant an English translation 60 years later. Entitled *Self-Conflict: Or, The powerful Motions between the Flesh & Spirit,* it was, as the subtitled explained further, a meditation "Represented in the person and upon the occasion of Joseph, when by Potiphar's Wife he was enticed to Adultery." In the foreword, the translator, John Quarles, praised both Cats's "incomparable mind" and the "profitablest [sic] variety of delight, both Moral and Divine," that could be found in his works. Like Cats, Quarles hoped that this story of

Joseph, which he later reprinted under the title *Triumphant Chastity,* would give readers "Sovereign Antidotes to kill or enervate such (else irresistible) Charms, either in the birth or riper growth," within themselves.

Houwelyck (Marriage) was published in 1625, the first of Cats's two great works on love and marriage. The title page shows the six stages of a woman's life: maid, lover, bride, wife, mother, and widow, each illuminated with an accompanying illustration. Like most of Cats's work, it was written in verse and filled with religious and moral instruction. Its popularity can be gauged by its sales: more than 50,000 were printed in the 30 years following its debut.

Cats was widowed in 1630, a terrible blow that saddened him greatly. Searching for a way to distract himself from his grief and loneliness, he began construction of his estate Sorgvliet (Fly from care), situated near the Hague, to fill his days. He also continued to write, publishing his most famous book, *Spiegel van den ouden en nieuwen tijdt (Mirror of old and new times),* in 1632. Written in colloquial rather than classical Dutch, this oft-quoted, homespun volume has become the source of many Dutch sayings. Leiden University has an original edition that contains handwritten notes and comments from the author.

In 1639, at what was probably the height of his fame, Cats's portrait was painted by famed court artist Michiel Janszoon van Miereveld. Now housed in the Rijksmuseum in Amsterdam, the poet and statesman gazes out of a frame adorned by Homer, Virgil, Ovid, Horace, and the Cats family crest, captioned by a line of his own poetry (in archaic Dutch): *Als ick dit beelt aensie en van mijn eerste jaren, / Soo leer ick dat de tijt verloopt gelyck de haren (When I see this image of my former years / I see how time recedes, just like my hair).*

Cats continued to publish in the decades that followed. *Trou-ringh (Wedding Ring),* his second poetic exposition on conjugal bliss, appeared in 1637. He published his most heartfelt autobiographical musings in his later years: *Gedachten op slapelooze nachten (Thoughts on sleepless nights)* in 1661; *Ouderdom, buyten-leven en hof-gedachten op Sorgvliet (Old age, country life, and garden thoughts at Sorgvliet)* in 1656; and his autobiography, *Twee en tachtigh-jarigh leven (Eight-two years of my life).* This last volume, which occupied him until his death, was not published until 1734.

In his time Cats was tremendously popular and extremely influential, shaping not only contemporary thought but image as well—artists often based their paintings on his well-known poems and stories. Even after his death his works were reprinted and translated, and it was said that every Dutch home had both a Bible and a book by Cats. His pithy aphorisms remain in modern use, although his dense and difficult texts are now prized more for their historical value than their literary content. The people of his native town of Brouwershaven erected a statue honoring him in 1829; his estate, Sorgvliet, now called Catshuis (Cats house), has become the official residence of the Dutch prime minister.

Jacob Cats died on September 12, 1660, and was buried in the Kloosterkerk in the Hague.

Books

Cats, Jacob. *Self-Conflict: Or, The Powerful Motions between the Flesh & Spirit,* 1680.

Heywood, Thomas, *Pleasant Dialogues and Dramma's,* 1637.

Online

"Cats, Jacob," *1911 Encyclopedia,* http://52.1911encyclopedia .org/C/CA/CATS_JACOB.htm (February 16, 2003).

"Cats, Jacob," *Encyclopedia Britannica,* http://www.britannica .com/search?query=cats%2C%20jacob&=&=N (February 16, 2003).

"Child Playing with a Top," The Humanities Advanced Technology and Information Institute, University of Glasgow, Scotland, http://www.hatii.arts.gla.ac.uk/MultimediaStudent Projects/00-01/9704597r/mmcourse/project/html/ Mainpages/child_playing_with_a_top.htm (February 16, 2003).

"The Dutch Golden Age," Electronic Text Centre Leiden, University of Leiden, http://www.etcl.nl/goldenage (February 16, 2003).

"Emblem Book," *Encyclopedia Britannica,* http://www.britannica .com/eb/article?eu=33075&=0&=emblem%20book&= (February 16, 2003).

"Emblem Books," Bryn Mawr College Library Special Collections, http://www.brynmawr.edu/Library/SpecColl/Guides/ Emblems/emblems.html (February 16, 2003).

"Emblem Books," Netnik.com, http://www.netnik.com/ emblemata/index.html (February 16, 2003).

Huwelick title page, Koninklijke Bibliotheek, National Library of the Netherlands, http://www.kb.nl/kb/kbschool/hr/site/ subject_huwelijkrelaties.gen.html (February 16, 2003).

"Jacob Cats," Albany Institute of History & Art, http://www .albanyinstitute.org/resources/dutch/dutch.whoswho.htm (February 16, 2003).

"Jacob Cats: *Buyten Leven op Sorgvliet,*" Belmont Abbey College, http://www.bac.edu/library/rarebooks/Buyten.htm (February 16, 2003).

"Jacob Cats," Koninklijke Bibliotheek, National Library of the Netherlands, http://www.kb.nl/kb/100hoogte/hh-en/hh050- en.html (February 16, 2003).

"Jacob Cats," Kunstbus Encyclopedie, http://www.kunstbus.nl/ verklaringen/jacob+cats.html (February 16, 2003).

"Jacob Cats," Rijksmuseum, Amsterdam, http://www.rijks museum.nl/uk/index.htm (February 16, 2003).

"Masters Great and Small Represented in Netherlandish Prints from the New York Public Library," New York Public Library, http://www.nypl.org/admin/pro/press/neterlandish.html (February 16, 2003).

"Nearly Complete Literary Works of Jacob Cats," Asher Rare Books, http://www.asherbooks.com/index.phtml?page=/ main_stock.phtml/subject/27/1/Emblems.html (February 16, 2003).

"Panorama's Catshuis," Website of the Prime Minister and the Ministry of General Affairs, http://www.minaz.nl/english/ ministry/vr_tour/html/1-cat_lr.htm | (February 16, 2003).

"Word and Image," The English Emblem Book Project, Pennsylvania State University Libraries http://emblem.libraries.psu .edu/home.htm (February 16, 2003). □

Margaret Lucas Cavendish

Margaret Cavendish (1623–1673) was one of the first prolific female science writers. As the author of approximately 14 scientific or quasi-scientific books, she helped to popularize some of the most important ideas of the scientific revolution, including the competing vitalistic and mechanistic natural philosophies and atomism. A flamboyant and eccentric woman, Cavendish was the most visible of the "scientific ladies" of the seventeenth century.

Margaret Lucas was born into a life of luxury near Colchester, England, in 1623, the youngest of eight children of Sir Thomas Lucas. She was educated informally at home. At the age of eighteen, she left her sheltered life to become Maid of Honor to Queen Henrietta Maria, wife of Charles I, accompanying the queen into exile in France following the defeat of the royalists in the civil war. There she fell in love with and married William Cavendish, the Duke of Newcastle, a 52 year-old widower, who had been commander of the royalist forces in the north of England. Joining other exiled royalists in Antwerp, the couple rented the mansion of the artist Rubens. Margaret Cavendish was first exposed to science in their informal salon society, "The Newcastle Circle," which included the philosophers Thomas Hobbes, René Descartes, and Pierre Gassendi. She visited England in 1651-52 to try to collect revenues from the Newcastle estate to satisfy their foreign creditors. It was at this time that Cavendish first gained her reputation for extravagant dress and manners, as well as for her beauty and her bizarre poetry.

Published Original Natural Philosophy

Cavendish prided herself on her originality and boasted that her ideas were the products of her own imagination, not derived from the writings of others. Cavendish's first anthology, *Poems, and Fancies,* included the earliest version of her natural philosophy. Although English atomic theory in the seventeenth century attempted to explain all natural phenomena as matter in motion, in Cavendish's philosophy all atoms contained the same amount of matter but differed in size and shape; thus, earth atoms were square, water particles were round, atoms of air were long, and fire atoms were sharp. This led to her humoral theory of disease, wherein illness was due to fighting between atoms or an overabundance of one atomic shape. However in her second volume, *Philosophical Fancies,* published later in the same year, Cavendish already had disavowed her own atomic theory. By 1663, when she published *Philosophical and Physical Opinions,* she had decided that if atoms were "Animated Matter," then they would have "Free-will and Liberty" and thus would always be at war with one another and unable to cooperate in the creation of complex organisms and minerals. Nevertheless, Cavendish continued to view all matter as composed of one material, animate and

intelligent, in contrast to the Cartesian view of a mechanistic universe.

Challenged Other Scientists

Cavendish and her husband returned to England with the restoration of the monarchy in 1660 and, for the first time, she began to study the works of other scientists. Finding herself in disagreement with most of them, she wrote *Philosophical Letters: or, Modest Reflections upon some Opinions in Natural Philosophy, maintained by several Famous and Learned Authors of this Age, Expressed by way of Letters* in 1664. Cavendish sent copies of this work, along with *Philosophical and Physical Opinions*, by special messenger to the most famous scientists and celebrities of the day. In 1666 and again in 1668, she published *Observations upon Experimental Philosophy*, a response to Robert Hooke's *Micrographia*, in which she attacked the use of recently-developed microscopes and telescopes as leading to false observations and interpretations of the natural world. Included in the same volume with *Observations* was *The Blazing World* was a semi-scientific utopian romance, in which Cavendish declared herself "Margaret the First."

Invited to the Royal Society

More than anything else, Cavendish yearned for the recognition of the scientific community. She presented the universities of Oxford and Cambridge with each of her publications and she ordered a Latin index to accompany the writings she presented to the University of Leyden,

hoping thereby that her work would be utilized by European scholars.

After much debate among the membership of the Royal Society of London, Cavendish became the first woman invited to visit the prestigious institution, although the controversy had more to due with her notoriety than with her sex. On May 30, 1667, Cavendish arrived with a large retinue of attendants and watched as Robert Boyle and Robert Hooke weighed air, dissolved mutton in sulfuric acid, and conducted various other experiments. It was a major advance for the scientific lady and a personal triumph for Cavendish.

Cavendish published the final revision of her *Philosophical and Physical Opinions*, entitled *Grounds of Natural Philosophy*, in 1668. Significantly more modest than her previous works, in this volume Cavendish presented her views somewhat tentatively and retracted some of her earlier, more extravagant claims. Cavendish acted as her own physician, and her self-inflicted prescriptions, purgings, and bleedings resulted in the rapid deterioration of her health. She died in 1673 and was buried in Westminster Abbey.

Although her writings remained well outside the mainstream of seventeenth-century science, Cavendish's efforts were of major significance. She helped to popularize many of the ideas of the scientific revolution and she was one of the first natural philosophers to argue that theology was outside the parameters of scientific inquiry. Furthermore, her work and her prominence as England's first recognized woman scientist argued strongly for the education of women and for their involvement in scientific pursuits. In addition to her scientific writings, Cavendish published a book of speeches, a volume of poetry, and a large number of plays. Several of the latter, particularly *The Female Academy*, included learned women and arguments in favor of female education. Her most enduring work, a biography of her husband, included as an appendix to her 24 page memoir, was first published in 1656 as a part of *Nature's Pictures*. This memoir is regarded as the first major secular autobiography written by a woman.

Books

Alic, Margaret, *Hypatia's Heritage: A History of Women in Science from Antiquity through the Nineteenth Century,* Beacon Press, 1986.
Battigelli, Anna, *Margaret Cavendish and the Exiles of the Mind,* University Press of Kentucky, 1998.
Grant, Douglas, *Margaret the First: A Biography of Margaret Cavendish, Duchess of Newcastle, 1623–1673,* University of Toronto Press, 1957.
Kargon, Robert Hugh, *Atomism in England from Hariot to Newton,* Clarendon, 1966.
Meyer, Gerald Dennis, *The Scientific Lady in England 1650–1760: An Account of her Rise, with emphasis on the Major Roles of the Telescope and Microscope,* University of California Press, 1955.
Schiebinger, Londa, *The Mind Has No Sex? Women in the Origins of Modern Science,* Harvard University Press, 1989.

Periodicals

Journal of English and Germanic Philology, April 1952. ☐

Thomas Robert Cech

American biochemist Thomas R. Cech (born 1947) received the Nobel Prize in 1989 for his ground-breaking discovery of the role of the RNA molecule not only as a molecule of heredity, but also as a biocatalyst.

Discovered Science at an Early Age

Thomas Robert Cech was born on December 12, 1947, in Chicago, Illinois, to Robert Franklin Cech, a physician, and Annette Marie Cerveny Cech, a homemaker. The family moved to Iowa City where Cech was raised and attended school. His father, though medicine was his chosen field, was also extremely interested in physics and all sciences in general, a fascination that spread quickly to his son. It was as early as the fourth grade when Cech began collecting rocks and wondering about their formation. In later school years he could be found visiting with professors at the nearby University of Iowa about other earth sciences. This desire for knowledge and curiosity for things scientific would lead him to his life's work and future success.

Cech entered Grinnell College in 1966 and found that he enjoyed studying literature and history as well as the sciences, but it was chemistry that he pursued. As he honed in on his studies and through undergraduate research experience, he discovered that he was "attracted to biological chemistry because of the almost daily interplay of experimental design, observation, and interpretation," he later recalled in *Les Prix Nobel,* as noted in his autobiography from the website of The Nobel Foundation. His choice of study would prove to be a wise decision.

It was while an undergraduate at Grinnell, he recalled in his Nobel Prize autobiography, that he met Carol Lynn Martinson "over the melting point apparatus" in a chemistry lab. They graduated from Grinnell and married in 1970. Thomas and his new wife chose the University of California, Berkeley for their graduate studies. He was fortunate to have John Hearst as a thesis advisor, one who had a contagious interest in chromosome function and structure and greatly assisted Thomas in his studies. The Cechs received their Ph.D.'s in 1975 and accepted jobs in the Northeast; Carol went to Harvard and Thomas took a position with the Massachusetts Institute of Technology (M.I.T.) where he began his post doctorate research.

After working at M.I.T. for some years, the couple moved to Boulder and both joined the faculty at the University of Colorado in 1978. It was around this time that Cech had resolved to concentrate on more specific genetic material. From *Notable Scientists,* "He was particularly interested in what enables the DNA molecule to instruct the body to produce the various parts of itself," a process called gene expression. Though he had done some genetic research in the 1970s, he now purposed to "discover the proteins that govern the DNA transcription process onto RNA." What he and his research team would soon discover would shake the scientific community and rewrite textbooks.

Ribonucleic Acid

To understand Cech's groundbreaking discoveries, one must first appreciate the workings of chemical reactions. Most reactions are in need of a catalyst, a molecule that can aid a chemical reaction without being altered or consumed. Nearly all the reactions that take place in any living cell require the workings of a biocatalyst, which we call enzymes. Enzymes work in myriad locations in the human body: in the liver to break down alcohol, for instance. Before the research of Cech and his team was released, all enzymes were thought to be proteins. The workings of proteins and their functions are controlled by the hereditary entities called genes.

Gene expression is a fascinating scientific field. Genes of every living thing are composed of deoxyribonucleic acid, more widely known as DNA. All the genetic information for an organism is contained in the DNA and is arranged as a string of codes that work together to dictate the protein design. In order to facilitate protein synthesis, however, the code must first be transcribed into another type of nucleic acid, ribonucleic acid (RNA). Scientists commonly assumed that DNA was the template of the genetic code in the nucleus of the cell. The code was somehow imprinted on the three different types of RNA and the RNA was a passive participant that simply relayed the genetic material to the enzymes of the cell. It was the enzymes, they thought, that were the catalysts for chemical reactions that occurred in the cell. Scientists believed that RNA needed the presence of an enzyme for these reactions to take place.

Prior to Cech's research, it was widely known that there were three types of RNA: messenger RNA, the form of RNA that mediates the transfer of genetic information from the cell nucleus to ribosomes (a minute round particle composed of RNA and protein that serves as the site of assembly for polypeptides encoded by messenger RNA) in the cytoplasm, where it serves as a template for protein synthesis; ribosomal RNA, which imparts the messenger's structure within the ribosome; and transfer RNA, which helps to establish amino acids in the proper order in the protein chain as it is being assembled. In the late 1970s a researcher named Phillip A. Sharp along with others found that the DNA and the RNA product that resulted after transcription were actually different: there were portions of the DNA that had not been coded and were left off of the RNA. These non-coded sections of DNA were termed introns.

Cech and his team were not interested in introns to begin with, but these sections of DNA soon proved too important to ignore. They became fascinated with the intron function and with DNA splicing altogether. How were the introns, the portions of DNA that held no code, removed during RNA transcription? This question drove Cech and his team to delve further into the process.

At the same time, another scientist whom Cech would later share an honor with was also studying transcription. Sidney Altman was independently studying an RNA-cutting enzyme, which is made up of a combination of one protein and one RNA molecule, from the bacterium *Escherichia coli*. When the enzyme was split and the protein split from the nucleic acid, it was no longer functional. But when the pieces were rejoined, the enzyme was restored and usable. This was the first time it was shown that an RNA molecule was essential for a catalytic reaction. It would be several years, however, before Altman could take the next step with his research.

Meanwhile, at the University of Colorado, Cech began his own RNA investigation. With the use of a single-celled pond organism called *Tetrahymena thermophila*, Cech and a colleague named Arthur Zaug scrutinized the pre-ribosomal RNA of the organism just as it underwent transcription. He first isolated the unspliced RNA and added some material taken from the nucleus of the *Tetrahymena*, along with other ingredients to be used as energy for the reaction. It was in this nucleic material, according to their supposition, that the catalyst necessary for transcription was found. The results of the experiment, however, were much different than they expected. Cech discovered that isolated, unprocessed RNA without any nucleic additives would begin to splice itself even without the presence of an outside catalyst. The RNA molecule amazingly cut itself into pieces and rejoined the important genetic fragments.

Cech's work was first met with some hostility and debate as it upended and challenged many long-standing beliefs about the nature of enzymes. In fact, Cech himself was not entirely sure of his results. Skeptical scientists held that the organism used to conduct the experiments had atypical RNA or that the RNA molecule was not a true enzyme because it did not contain properties and characteristics found in other enzymes. Skepticism was proved untrue, however, when other scientists also found RNA enzymes. It was Sidney Altman who established that RNA was capable of completing the actions of an enzyme on substances other than itself, another concern of unconvinced scientists.

As with most scientific breakthroughs, the discovery of the role and function of RNA had and continues to have effects more far-reaching than even Cech could have imagined. It has astonishing potential in the area of disease, as the RNA molecule can be cut at certain points, destroying the parts that cause genetic disorders or infections. It may lead to the cure of countless health problems. Cech's research has also led scientists to hypothesize that the RNA molecule was the first bit of life on our planet. Since it can replicate without the need for an outside catalyst, it is believed to be the first self-reproducing system.

Awarded the Nobel Prize

Cech and Altman were awarded the Nobel Prize for Chemistry in 1989 for their independent work that demonstrated the catalytic properties of RNA, a groundbreaking discovery in the scientific community. Whereas the RNA molecule had been previously thought to act only in conjunction with a catalyst, now Cech had shown that it performed its function without an outside enzyme. Altman proved that the molecule carried out functions consistent with other enzymes.

Since the research of the 1980s, Cech has received numerous awards and honors and has become a sought-after lecturer at institutions around the country. He earned the Passano Foundation Young Scientific Award and the Harrison Howe Award in 1984. Besides the highest honor of receiving the Nobel Prize, he was also awarded an honorary doctorate degree from his alma mater Grinnell College in 1987. Within the next year he was elected to both the United States Academy of Sciences and the American Academy of Arts and Sciences.

Four years after Cech's discovery he had it patented. When two Australian scientists who had been working on similar technology sold their findings to a French pharmaceutical company, Cech decided to take them to court for patent violation and was awarded an inclusive patent in 1991. Although some feared that this would hinder the development of research in this area, it was unnecessary as Cech later sold his rights to the United States Biochemical Corporation.

Cech's work has been recognized by many national and international awards and prizes. He was promoted to full professor of chemistry at the University of Colorado in 1983. He was also elected president of the Howard Hughes Medical Institute in 2000. He continues to research both the RNA molecule as well as other areas of biochemistry. As for his personal life, Cech and his wife welcomed two daughters into their family, Allison, born in 1982, and Jennifer, born in 1986. Despite the busy schedule of a professor and researcher, Cech and his family enjoy backpacking, ski trips, and entertaining.

Books

Contemporary Heroes and Heroines, Book IV, Gale Group, 2000.

Notable Scientists: From 1900 to the Present, Gale Group, 2001.

Online

"37th IUPACK Congress-27th GDCh General Meeting," International Union of Pure and Applied Chemistry website, http://www.iupac.org/publications/ci/1999/november/ 37thcongress.html (January 25, 2003).

"The 1989 Nobel Prize in Chemistry," Nobel e-Museum website, http://www.nobel.se/chemistry/laureates/1989/press .html (January 30, 2003).

"Enzymatic RNA Molecules and the Replication of Chromosome Ends," Howard Hughes Medical Institue website, http://www .hhmi.org/research/investigators/cech.html (January 21, 2003).

"RNA Catalysis and the Replication of Chromosome Telomeres," The University of Colorado website, http://www.Colorado .edu/chemistry/faculty/Cech/ (January 21, 2003).

"Thomas R. Cech—Autobiography," Nobel e-Museum Website, http://www.nobel.se/chemistry/laureates/1989/cech-autobio .html (January 30, 2003). □

Chikamatsu Monzaemon

Japanese playwright Chikamatsu Monzaemon (1653–1725) is best known for his tragedies involving ordinary men and women in the kansai, or western part, of Japan, where his works were first presented in the late seventeenth and early eighteenth centuries. During his career, Chikamatsu wrote about 100 puppet and kabuki stage plays. In these works, natural human emotions keep the characters alive as their human passions come into conflict with the rational principles and ethics that serve as the foundations of society. The plays go on to treat human weakness and the need for maintaining dignity in the face of crisis.

Chikamatsu's use of lower class characters in his tragedies is rather unique in world drama, where tragic characters have most often been members of the upper classes. In Chikamatsu's most famous plays, his characters violate the rules of society—often by committing a crime such as theft, adultery, or murder—and occasionally end up meeting a tragic end, either by their own hand or by society's. But in most of the works, the tragic hero is redeemed by his or her love, confession, or penitence.

Chikamatsu's plays were printed during his lifetime to allow people to practice his singing roles or read the poetry. The chanter, who described the setting of the acts, was given the most beautiful passages to recite.

Beginnings

Chikamatsu Monzaemon was born in 1653 in the Echizen province, what later became Fukui, Japan. Of aristocratic descent, Chikamatsu was the second son in a prosperous samurai family. (The samurai were professional warriors traditionally bound to a lord or daimyo.) When Chikamatsu was around ten years old, his father became a masterless samurai (ronin) and moved the family to Kyoto. Without a formal relationship to a feudal lord, Chikamatsu's father was deprived of a fixed stipend.

At the age of eighteen, some of Chikamatsu's poems appeared in a poetry collection entitled *Takaraura (The Treasure House)* published by Yamaoka Genrin. Chikamatsu studied a traditional form of poetry known as haiku and Japanese classical literature with Genrin, while serving as a page for a nobleman in Kyoto. It has been suggested that Chikamatsu first became acquainted with the celebrated actor Uji Kaganojo while running errands for this nobleman.

Entered the Theatre

Chikamatsu's decision to enter the theatre could not have pleased his wellborn parents. But he may have been constrained in his choice of occupation by his father's ronin status, which left the son with few options for achieving samurai rank. And although Chikamatsu's association with the Japanese nobility certainly enriched his understanding of the world, it probably provided very little in the way of financial remuneration. It has been surmised that Chikamatsu's other option would have been to become a poetry teacher. Some have suggested that he may have been persuaded to pursue a career in the theatre after he saw Uji Kaganojo's success.

The Soga Heir

Although it is not known when Chikamatsu first began writing puppet plays, his earliest known work of this genre was *Yotsugi Soga (The Soga Heir)*, which was written for Uji Kaganojo in 1683. The play met instant success and brought fame to the 30-year-old playwright. The rather crudely written piece treated a well-known story involving two brothers, Onio and Dosaburo, who had formerly served as retainers to another pair of brothers, the Sogas, before the Sogas were put to death. In most versions of the story, the subject was the successful revenge of the two retainers and their subsequent deaths. But in Chikamatsu's treatment, the story became more complex.

Chikamatsu adds a scene in a brothel where the two lovers of the late Soga brothers are employed. The two women are distressed at not having heard from their sweethearts, unaware that they have both been killed. When the two alleged murderers of the brothers show up wanting to sleep with the women, the retainer Onio chases them away, not knowing who they are.

Having now learned of their lovers' deaths, the two prostitutes next travel to the Soga brothers' village, intending to tell their lovers' mother of her sons' deaths. After the old woman learns that her sons are dead, one of the prostitutes informs her that she has given birth to her son's child, a boy named Sukewaka. The boy is at the time staying with an aunt.

A short while later, the villains visit the prostitutes, looking for Sukewaka. After the two women pretend to be in love with them, the murderers try to enlist their help in killing Onio and Dosaburo. Hiding inside large chests, they wait for the two retainers to show up. But when Onio and Dosaburo arrive, they are accompanied by an enormously strong friend, who places large boulders on the chests. When one of the villains tries to get out, he is crushed to death by the weight of the stones. The second villain is taken captive, and the victors leave for the capital to celebrate.

In the final scene, the surviving villain is released so as not to mar the festivities with bloodshed. Sukewaka is given the Soga family lands. The emperor's consort declares that she has come to realize that prostitutes, far from being debased creatures, are in fact the models of fidelity in love. At the emperor's request, the prostitutes do an improvisational dance to retrace the history of courtesans. At the end of the play Sukewaka and his mother exit amid assurances that the Soga clan will flourish for years to come.

Kagekiyo Victorious

Chikamatsu's next puppet play, entitled *Shusse Kagekiyo (Kagekiyo Victorious)*, was written for a younger rival of Kaganojo in 1686. In the play, Kagekiyo's mistress learns that her lover is going to marry a woman of high birth. Out of revenge, she betrays Kagekiyo's hiding place to his enemies. After Kagekiyo is captured and bound, his mistress appears before him with their two sons to beg his apology. But he disowns his children, and she kills the children and then herself before his eyes. In the final scene, it is revealed that the goddess Kannon has substituted her own head for Kagekiyo's at his execution, so Kagekiyo is safe. He then makes peace with his old enemy.

Kabuki Interlude

Kabuki is a form of Japanese drama in which the actors use stylized movements, dances, and songs to perform comedies or tragedies. Many critics feel that Chikamatsu's early kabuki plays were inferior to his puppet plays, possibly because he had to write for conventional roles that did not allow for the complexity of some of his puppet characters.

Chikamatsu wrote most of his plays for the kabuki theatre between 1688 and 1703. Although he had written *Yugiri Shichiren Ki (The Seventh Anniversary of Yugiri's Death)* in 1684, in the ensuing four years he wrote mostly for the puppet theatre.

The best known of Chikamatsu's kabuki plays was *Keisei Mibu Dainembutsu* (roughly translated *Courtesans and the Great Recitation of the Name of Buddha at the Mibu Temple*). The play was written to coincide with the public display of a secretly kept statue of Buddha at a famous temple. The strength of the play derived from the freedom it gave to the actors to display their own particular strengths. In this play within a play, a loyal retainer is assigned the role of a woman. So disguised, the retainer overhears a plan by his master's stepmother and her brother to steal the family treasure, a religious statue. Pursuant to winning the villains' confidence, the retainer is required to kill his daughter to protect his master's reputation.

Return to the Puppet Theater

In 1703, Chikamatsu shifted his efforts back to the puppet theatre. He may have been motivated by the departure of the actor who appeared in his kabuki works from the stage, or possibly by the tendency of kabuki actors to take liberties with his text while performing his works. In any case, Chikamatsu's decision to return to the puppet theatre would have long-lasting impact. It meant, for example, that the puppet theatre would be the most popular form of drama for the next 50 years because it would be puppets who performed the works of the country's pre-eminent dramatist.

At the time that Chikamatsu was writing, audiences were accustomed to spending an entire day at the puppet theatre and were not always attentive to everything that was happening on the stage. For Chikamatsu, the challenge of the puppet theatre was to impart lifeless puppets with a variety of emotions and thereby capture the audience's attention. Chikamatsu did not hesitate to have his characters say things that a real person would not utter in order to maximize the pleasure in the play's performance.

Chikamatsu scored a major success in 1703 with a play about a lovers' double suicide entitled *Sonezaki Shinju (The Love Suicides at Sonezaki)*. In the play, which was based on an actual event, Tokubei is in love with the prostitute Ohatsu. After he refuses to marry the woman chosen for him by his uncle, he is obliged to give back her dowry money. But Tokubei is tricked out of the money by a friend, and Tokubei and Ohatsu, facing separation, decide to commit suicide together.

In 1715, Chikamatsu achieved his greatest success up to then with the puppet play *Kokusenya Kassen (The Battles of Coxinga)*, which tells the story of Coxinga, the son of a Chinese father and Japanese mother, who leaves Japan with the intention of restoring the Ming rulers to the throne of China and defeating the Tartar usurpers.

Chikamatsu's masterpiece, *Shinju Ten no Amijima (The Love Suicides at Amijima)* was written in 1721. Again dealing with a lovers' double suicide, the play tells the story of Jihei, who is in love with two women, his wife Osan and a prostitute named Koharu. To keep Jihei and Koharu from committing a double suicide, Osan suggests her husband buy Koharu's contract. But the plan is thwarted by the arrival of Osan's father, who takes his daughter away. Jihei then has no choice but to go through with the lovers' suicide. But out of concern for his wife, he arranges the suicide so that it appears that the lovers have died independently.

Final Works

Between 1720 and 1722, the 70-year-old Chikamatsu wrote ten plays in 25 months. In the earlier of these plays, the male heroes come across as depraved as they proceed to destroy the world around them. But the later plays in this group involve more noble characters of a higher social class. According to C.A. Gerstle, writing in *Hero as Mur-*

derer in the Plays of Chikamatsu, the playwright decided to look at the persons at the top of society who were ultimately responsible for the depravity among the lower classes.

Following this prodigious two-year output, Chikamatsu produced nothing for 16 months until his last play was performed in 1724. This final play, *Tethered Steed and the Eight Provinces of Kanto,* addresses the familiar theme of rivalry over love, with the hero willing to die for his honor after stealing his brother's fiancée. In the ensuing conflict between honor and love, the offended brother offers mercy in an exchange for an apology. The offending sibling finally gives up his pride and submits to his brother's demands. Chikamatsu's final statement as a playwright turned out to be a paean to idealism over self-destruction.

Chikamatsu died in the early part of 1725, less than a year after *Tethered Steed and the Eight Provinces of Kanto* was performed.

Books

Gerstle, C.A., *Hero as Murderer in the Plays of Chikamatsu,* University of London, 1994.

Keene, Donald, *Four Major Plays of Chikamatsu,* Columbia University Press, 1998.

—, *World Within Walls: Japanese Literature of the Pre-Modern Era, 1600–1867,* Charles E. Tuttle Company, 1978. □

Chung Ju Yung

Chung Ju Yung (1915–2001) founded Korea's Hyundai Group, which remained his country's most powerful *chaebol,* or family-run conglomerate, for years. Chung's assemblage of corporate entities, which he was said to run by relying heavily upon his famous iron will, included the automaker Hyundai as well as large construction, shipbuilding, and electronics concerns. In his later years, Chung entertained political ambitions and ran for president of South Korea.

Stole Family Cow

Chung Ju Yung was born on November 25, 1915, in Tongchon, located in the northern section of Korea, then annexed to Japan. At the time of Chung's birth, Korea had been under harsh Japanese colonial rule for five years; the northern regions would eventually fall under communist domination as North Korea in 1948. Chung was the oldest in a family of eight that eked out a living on the land, and he was forced to abandon his education after grade school in order to work to help support his family. He attempted to run away on two occasions, and after stints on a railway construction site and as a dock worker, he secretly sold the family cow and fled from home with the money. After walking to Seoul, one of Korea's larger cities, Chung found a job working at a rice shop as a bicycle delivery

person. He eventually bought the business, on credit, but harsh Japanese military rule made owning businesses difficult for Koreans. A small truck and repair garage he established in 1940 languished under the same harsh economic restrictions.

By the end of World War II and the ouster of the Japanese, Chung had begun a family with his wife, Byun Joong Suk, whom he had married at the age of 15 in 1930. Several of his brothers had by now also followed him from Tongchon to Seoul. At the war's close Japan had been vanquished by Allied forces, and Korea prepared for political and economic independence. With a major reconstruction effort underway, Chung moved from automobile-servicing to the construction industry and won several lucrative early contracts from the U.S.-run military government in the southern half of the country. His company's growth was again affected by the outbreak of war as northern and southern Korea battled alongside their respective controlling superpowers between 1950 and 1953. Following the war Chung's Hyundai Engineering and Construction thrived.

Company Expanded Alongside Country

Like those of other large chaebols, the fortunes of Chung's Hyundai group were boosted due to ties with South Korea's political elite. A military junta came to power in 1961 under Park Chung Hee, and the following year Chung's company won the Ssoyangang Dam project; it also built the Kyongbu (Seoul-Pusan) Expressway, South Korea's first major highway, which was completed in 1970. Park was determined to industrialize South Korea in order to free it from dependence on foreign aid, and Chung's business interests continued to expand along with this government policy. In the late 1960s he built an automobile manufacturing plant in Ulsan, on the country's southeastern coast. Initially it built two Ford Motor Company models for the South Korean domestic market, but in 1974 unveiled the first true Hyundai, the Pony. Chung's younger brother, Chung Se Yung, was put in charge of the auto group.

Chung kept expanding his Hyundai chaebol to include 86 companies at its largest. He was known to be a strong-willed business foe, constantly striving to stay ahead of other top Korean chaebols like Samsung and Daewoo. In 1971 Chung met with bankers from London's esteemed Barclays house in the hopes of gaining financing to begin a shipbuilding firm. To quell the bank's doubts, he showed them a 500-*won* bank note with an illustration of the world's first ironclad ship, built in Korea in 1592. As with all of Chung's other ventures, Hyundai Heavy Industries thrived and within 30 years had become the largest builder of merchant ships in the world. In the early 1980s, worried about the dominance of Samsung in the electronics market, Chung launched Hyundai Electronics, which soon flourished as a maker of semiconductor chips for computers. The tycoon's formidable business skills landed him a post as head of South Korea's Olympic Bidding Committee, and he was instrumental in drafting South Korea's winning proposal to host the 1988 Summer Games. The international sporting event was a turning point in the small, overcrowded nation's image.

A Demanding Boss and Parent

Daily breakfast meetings with his sons, who became top executives, took place at 5:30 a.m., but Chung was oftentimes awake hours before. The Hyundai chief "managed his sprawling industrial empire with an iron hand that befitted a Confucian patriarch," explained *Financial Times* writer John Burton. "He was said to hurl ashtrays and to slap managers who displeased him." Both Hyundai's automobile manufacturing and shipbuilding concerns were based in Ulsan, and it eventually became known informally as "Hyundai City." In time, South Korea itself would even be dubbed the "Republic of Hyundai" by critics observing the dominance of Chung's brand in all sectors of the Korean economy. The Hyundai name seemed to be everywhere in South Korea. It built trains, bridges, ships, and a plethora of consumer goods besides cars. Chung's close ties with the ruling governments, which were military in character until 1992, helped him battle labor-union movements, especially one at the Ulsan shipyard in the 1980s that dragged on for five years. At the time, South Koreans worked six-day weeks, with little vacation time, and earned some of the lowest wages in the industrialized world. Government riot police finally stepped in to quell the unrest at Ulsan in 1987, but a pro-democracy movement had taken hold countrywide, and the military juntas under Park and his successors were now considered illegitimate holders of power.

Despite his success in South Korea, Chung was interested in expanding his company beyond his country's bor-

ders. In the 1970s Hyundai Engineering and Construction bid for and won lucrative contracts for projects in the Middle East, including the construction of a vast oil terminal port facility. In 1985 Hyundai Motors produced its first cars for the American market and within a few years had made South Korea one of just a handful of export nations to hold a share of the U.S. automobile market. Yet Chung was eyeing a market closer to home: the heavily armed, isolated, and repressive socialist state of North Korea, where he still had family. Since the end of the Korean War in 1953, relations between the two Koreas were frosty at best; North Korea spent heavily on defense, and at one time boasted the fifth largest armed forces in the world; South Korea, meanwhile, was home to several thousand U.S. troops stationed at bases and alongside South Korean forces at the tense demilitarized zone (DMZ) that divided the two nations. North Korea maintained that South Koreans harbored a secret desire to be "liberated," while keeping its own citizens in a constant state of high alert by warning them that the U.S. and South Korea were planning to invade.

Returned Home with Cow

In 1989 Chung made a highly publicized visit to North Korea and announced that he would fund a tourism project in the Keumkang Mountains of his home province. He hoped to create a special coastal tourism zone in the east, near the DMZ, as a place where long-separated family members could reunite briefly. The plan fell through, however, and at times Chung, now in his 70s, began to voice criticism over his government's policies toward North Korea. In 1992 he announced he would be giving up several company posts in order to run for president. He launched his United People's Party (UUP) in February of 1992, but was bested by Kim Young Sam, President Roh Tae Woo's chosen successor. Chung won just 16 percent of the vote, but the UPP took 30 seats in the National Assembly. Kim became the first civilian president of the nation since the Korean War, and along with the new mood of democracy—and an impressive hike in the South Korean standard of living—came calls to dismantle the power of the chaebols.

Chung's political ambitions brought trouble for Hyundai. He was investigated and found guilty of diverting some $81 million in company funds to finance his campaign; his three-year sentence was suspended due to age, but several Hyundai officials were jailed and the state rescinded its policy of making favorable loans to the company. The government also began auditing Hyundai and Chung-family tax returns. Chung was still an ardent supporter of reconciliatory policies with the North and in 1998, following reports of widespread starvation in North Korea, he became the first civilian to cross the DMZ since the end of the Korean War. Prior to this moment, all travel between the two countries had to go through a third country, usually the Soviet Union or China. Chung, now 75 years old, walked the last part of the trip on foot. He brought with him 500 head of cattle from his own nearby farm as a gift to Tongchon, remarking that it was a gesture of reparation for taking his father's cow back in 1933. His visit was a major news event in South Korea; "Television networks interrupted their regular broadcasts with live footage of the trucks rumbling through the streets of Seoul on their way north," reported *Time International* correspondent Stella Kim. "Early Tuesday, the convoy stopped just short of the border, where more than 1 million heavily armed troops face off in a tense armistice. . . . A Buddhist priest in gray robes walked along the row of trucks, banging on a wooden block and praying that the animals would "survive until reunification.' "

Sons Warred with One Another

Chung met with North Korean leader Kim Jong Il, and within two years a North-South summit had taken place; this time Hyundai agreed to a $942 million investment plan in the north. Yet Chung faced more pressing concerns back in Seoul: a power struggle had erupted between his two oldest sons, with one enlisting the help of a South Korean government determined to break up the powerful chaebols. Chung had fathered nine children in all, but only five were likely born to his wife; the others were registered as part of his family anyway. There were two tragedies: the eldest, Chung Mong Pil, died in a car accident in 1982 and another, Chung Mong Woo, committed suicide in 1990. Mong Pil would have inherited control of the Hyundai empire at some point—the traditional chaebol practice—and the second eldest son, Chung Mong Koo, was thought to be next in line to succeed the father.

As the eldest living son, Chung Mong Koo was made chief of Hyundai Motors in 1998 and Chung gave his third son, Chung Mong Hun, the more lucrative construction and chip businesses. This launched an intense rivalry some say was fueled by the Chung sons' lack of allegiance to their family unit due to long-simmering resentment over legitimacy issues. Soon the infighting at the upper levels of the Hyundai Group reached an unparalleled level of acrimony, as Chung's health grew more frail and family members attempted to acquire control over parts of the business empire via stock deals. In 1999 Hyundai's combined sales stood at $80 billion, making Chung's empire the largest of the five main chaebols in South Korea during the last genuine year of their existence. Chung by then had been ordered to spin off some of the Hyundai businesses by the South Korean government, but the obstinate tycoon refused until debtors forced his hand in May of 2000.

Though he was said to be worth $6.2 billion, Chung lived in a modest home built from leftover construction materials from his company. He walked the three-mile trek to his office in Seoul daily until his health began to falter. He was an ardent fan of the Internet and liked to sing karaoke. He died of pneumonia on March 21, 2001, in Seoul, South Korea. His son Chung Mong Joon served as organizer of South Korea's hosting of the World Cup soccer tournament in 2002. After his death, the elder tycoon continued to generate respect; noted *Guardian* obituary writer Aidan Foster-Carter, Chung "personified his country's ascent from poverty to global success."

Periodicals

Automotive News, July 10, 2000.
Daily Telegraph (London, England), March 22, 2001.
Economist, November 23, 1991; January 11, 1992; June 13, 1992; December 12, 1992; June 20, 1998; February 6, 1999.
Financial Times, July 1, 2000; November 8, 2000; January 29, 2002.
Forbes, December 19, 1983.
Fortune, February 10, 1992.
Guardian (London, England), March 28, 2001.
Independent (London, England), June 17, 1998.
International Herald Tribune, June 20, 1998; March 28, 2000; June 10, 2000; March 23, 2001.
Newsweek International, September 4, 2000.
New York Times, March 22, 2001.
Time International, June 29, 1998.
Times (London, England), March 22, 2001. □

Kyung Wha Chung

Kyung Wha Chung (born 1948) led the way for Korean musicians to excel in the western world. Arriving as a child to study in New York City, Chung made the study of the violin her life's work.

On March 26, 1948, Kyung Wha Chung was born in Seoul, Korea, to Won Sook Lee and Chun Chai. She grew up in a family with eight siblings, all of whom had early training in music. They all began with piano lessons. "Both my parents were music lovers," stated Chung on the *Asia Week* website. "Music was part of our education, and there was always music-making at home." A friend of her father gave her a violin to play at the young age of six. She immediately found she could express herself with the instrument. "The violin," she noted in *Asia Week,* "is very close to the human voice." Soon she was playing in a trio with her sister Myung Wha, who was getting proficient on cello, and brother Myung Whun, who stuck with the piano.

Talented Child Musician Headed to New York City

Her older sister, Myung So, was very skilled on the flute and went to America to study at Juilliard in New York City. In 1961, Chung followed and shared an apartment with her sister. Chung also began studying at Juilliard with the well-known Ivan Galamian. Living in New York City, struggling to learn a new language and to live away from home and family in Korea, was difficult. "To put it mildly, I started a whole new life," Chung told the *Shanghai Star.* "From that time on, my commitment to music was the beacon that showed the way for me." Galamian was extremely firm with her about understanding that she would have a career as a concert violinist and would not have time to have a family. He said that it was unacceptable for a woman to have both. "Mr. Galamian loved me deeply," said Chung, according to the January/February 1999 issue of the *American Record Guide,* "but that did not change how he felt about female students. He had already been let down by a number of girl prodigies who abandoned their professional goals in their teens, or who had run off and got married." At each lesson,

he would remind her that she was not to get married and have children. She would always respond that it was her intention to become a concert violinist. Later, she would tell *Asia Week*, "I was shocked by the high standard of the music there, and my only goal was to reach that high level."

In 1967, at age 19, she gained a great deal of attention when she won the 25th international Leventritt Competition at Carnegie Hall in New York City, sharing first prize with Pinchas Zukerman. This brought her engagements throughout the United States and Europe. This further led to an opportunity that served as a springboard to her career. She got her London debut by replacing Itzhak Perlman in the Tchaikovsky Concerto with André Previn and the London Symphony. "Sometimes one person's mischance becomes another person's chance," Chung is quoted as stating on the *Amazon.com* website. "After winning the Leventritt, I began to perform in America and Europe. But it was the London debut that really launched my international career. It was very successful, though at first everything seemed to be against me: I had stepped in at the last moment, and there was so much confusion that I hardly had any rehearsal, but as a result the musicians were all the more concentrated at the performance. The communication with the audience was very strong, so the event was a wonderful experience. The concert was a benefit and not supposed to be reviewed, but the critic with the *Financial Times* wrote one of the best reviews I have ever received in my life. It was really quite embarrassing—he simply said I was better than everybody else, mentioning a lot of names. I just ignored it, but it was a gold mine for the managers, and I got engagements all over

Europe. I always feel very strange when I have to cancel a concert, but then I think, *Maybe this will give a young artist the chance of a lifetime."* She further stated, "For a young player, replacing another artist can be the first stepping stone to a career. I got my London debut by replacing Perlman in the Tchaikovsky Concerto with André Previn and the London Symphony. Shortly afterward, Renata Tebaldi canceled a recording session and London Records asked me to record the Tchaikovsky and Sibelius concertos instead. My recording career started when they offered me an exclusive contract. And I got my German debut because Lorin Maazel engaged me for his Berlin Festival when Boris Christoff pulled out."

Her success was so great that she was immediately booked for three more London concerts, a tour of Japan, and a television appearance. Engagements with the London Philharmonic, Berlin Philharmonic, and Cleveland Orchestra followed, firmly establishing her international career. Chung quickly gained recognition throughout the world as a high caliber performer. She was appearing with all of the major orchestras and conductors throughout North America, Europe, and the Far East. *Asia Week* contends that she was a leader in showing that Asians could master the western classical tradition, quoting Kyung Soo Won, the conductor of the Seoul Philharmonic Orchestra as saying, "Until she became a world-class violinist, it was only remotely possible for a Korean to achieve that kind of success. It was like a dream in the clouds. But she showed it was possible." In 1972, the South Korean government awarded her with their highest honor by presenting her with the Medal of Civil Merit. Kyung Soo Won stated in *Asia Week* that she has a skill and style all her own by saying, "Her tone and technique are unique. These days, young musicians all play the same, but she is markedly different from all the others."

Chung Changed the Rules

In 1981, her long-time instructor, Galamian, to whom she had consistently promised that she would never marry, passed away. A few years later, in 1984, when she was 35, Chung broke her promise and got married to a British businessman. When her first son, Frederick, was born, she worked hard to keep at least part of her promise to Galamian, by being determined to not let motherhood affect her work, maintaining the same schedule and taking young Frederick along with her in a basket everywhere. However, when her second son, Eugene, was born, she found that Galamian had been right and that she could no longer keep up. She cut back on her performance schedule, reducing it from 120 performances each season down to 60. "For me, because motherhood came rather late, it was the most incredible experience to have my children, so they became my first priority, and I wanted to be with them," Chung stated. "As far as music and performing are concerned, I tried to narrow it down to a certain kind of continuous project—recording—so I did concerts that were related to preparing for the recordings," she told *American Record Guide* in the January/February 1999 edition.

In 1988, she signed a contract to record exclusively with EMI Classics. "Recordings are so personal for me," she said to the *Rocky Mountain News.* "Nothing is ever permanent in an interpretation—but that's not the case with a record. You have to leave something of your soul on that compact disc. The problem is, your soul is not perfect, so a recording never will be." However, recording obviously agreed with her as she won a Gramophone Award for the recording of the "Bartók Violin Concerto No. 2" and the two rhapsodies with the City of Birmingham Symphony Orchestra and Sir Simon Rattle. She also began recording more with her brother and sister, and they called themselves the Chung Trio. Her brother, Myung Whun Chung, was a winner of the 1974 Tchaikovsky Piano competition and has been music director of the Paris Opera and head of the Orchesstra of the Academia Santa Cecilia in Rome. Her sister, Myung Wha, plays the cello and has won the Geneva International Competition. In 1994, they released Beethoven's "Piano Trios Op. 11 and 97" which received great critical acclaim. The trio is well known in Korea, but also widely recognized throughout the world. She is quoted on *Amazon.com* as saying, "We have played together all our lives." The Chung Trio made a number of recordings including a performance of the Beethoven Triple Concerto with the Philharmonic Orchestra for Deutsche Grammophon in the 1995–1996 season.

When Chung did tour, she would take her children with her when they were not in school. She also took them to Korea several times to experience the culture. Both the children learned to speak Korean. "That was important for me," Chung told *Asia Week.* Both children have also studied music extensively. Chung is considered an icon on Korea. She considers herself Korean, although she only lived there for a small percentage of her life, now living in southern England and New York City. "I'm Korean, and there's nothing that will change that," she told *Asia Week.*

In 2000, she won another Gramophone Award for her recording of the Strauss and Respighi Violin Sonatas with Krystian Zimmerman.

Chung Returned to Full Concert Schedule

As her children grew older, Chung began to expand her performing schedule once again, but she did not slow down on her recordings. In February of 2001, her recording of *Vivaldi's Four Seasons,* played with the St. Luke's Chamber Ensemble, was released. *Sensible Sound* called her a "magnificent violinist" and stated, "Chung's interpretation is best described as elegant. Her phrasing is elegant, her tempos are elegant, her command of nuance is elegant." Later that year, in November, she released the recording of "Symphony No. 5; Brahms: Violin Concerto" with Sir Simon Rattle and the Vienna Philharmonic. "Kyung Wha Chung can be a firebrand violinist, but here she's very much the aristocrat. She supplies gleaming tone and rhythmic acuity, but also delicacy and tenderness. Her hushed, high flickerings in the Joachim cadenza are breathtaking," stated the *Dallas Morning News.*

Even as an experienced concert violinist and recording artist, Chung sometimes will still get nervous. "Funnily enough, even after having been on all the major stages of the world, it took me a long time to get rid of those feelings of anxiety when I performed in New York. Every time I walked out in Carnegie Hall, I felt as though I were 19, about to play for the Leventritt Competition on that stage. I went to Carnegie Hall last December, to perform the Beethoven Concerto, and my children were sitting there with a big smile. I suddenly thought this is simply wonderful!" she told *American Record Guide.*

Chung continues to practice for several hours every day. When she has time, she enjoys gardening and teaching students. Chung remains one of the most sought-after international violin players.

Periodicals

American Record Guide, January/February 1999.
Dallas Morning News, November 13, 2001.
Rocky Mountain News, January 25, 1998.
Sensible Sound, August/September 2001.
Shanghai Star, April 11, 2000.

Online

"Kyung Wha Chung," *EMI Classics website,* http://www.emiclassics.com/artists/biogs/chung.html (February 17, 2003).
"Music of Chance," *Amazon.com website,* http://www.amazon.com (February 17, 2003).
"The Virtuoso: Chung Kyung Wha," *Asia Week website,* http://www.pathfinder.com/asiaweek/95/20greats/chung.html (February 17, 2003). □

Clare of Assisi

Clare of Assisi (1194–1253) was one of the most influential women in the early medieval period of Roman Catholic church history. A follower of Francis of Assisi, Clare founded her own order, the Poor Clares, based on his tenets of charity and humility. She is thought to be the first woman in the history of the church to write her own rule, or guidelines for the religious life of her order.

Of Noble Italian Birth

Clare was born Chiara Offreduccio di Favaronne in Assisi, a hillside town in central Italy, in July of 1194. She was the eldest daughter in an affluent, landowning Umbrian family that had links to the Roman nobility of the past. Her father was Favorino Scifi, count of Sasso-Rosso, and her mother Ortolana also hailed from an aristocratic lineage. Growing up, Clare lived at both her family's villa in Assisi and a castle on the mountainside of Mount Subasio. She was likely schooled at some point, for the writings that survive her display a good grasp of Latin.

Clare was said to be a devout, pious child from an early age, but her family planned an advantageous marriage for

her, and she resisted. When she was 18, she heard Francis of Assisi preach and was deeply moved by his words. He had come back to Assisi, his hometown, to preach Lenten sermons at the church of San Giorgio. Twelve years her senior, Francis hailed from a well-to-do cloth merchant family, but a stint in the army and a year as a prisoner of war in Perugia caused a religious awakening, and he became an ascetic. By the time Clare heard his sermons, Francis was called "Poverello" and was known throughout much of Christian Europe. His Franciscan order, founded in 1209, was the first mendicant, or beggar, order in Europe, created in what was then a radical attempt to follow Christ's teachings. It followed a verse from the Gospel of Matthew, which counseled, according to *Butler's Lives of the Saints,* "Freely have you received, freely give. . . . Do not possess gold . . . nor two coats nor shoes not a staff. . . . Behold I send you as sheep in the midst of wolves." Unlike other monastic communities, some of which were quite wealthy in land, the Franciscan communities were forbidden to own any property or worldly goods.

Founded Order

Desiring to join such a community herself, Clare sought out Francis, and according to her official church biography, went to Mass at the Assisi cathedral on Palm Sunday, the Sunday before Easter. Instead of joining the queue to receive the palm leaf—an act that recalled a biblical incident in which Christ entered Jerusalem and to welcome him, believers cut boughs from trees and tossed them in his path—Clare remained in prayer, and the bishop then reportedly

went to her and placed a palm in her hand. She was said to have fled her father's home that night, on March 20, 1212, with the help of her aunt Bianca and another woman. They met Francis, as arranged, at a small chapel called Porziuncula that served as the spiritual home of his order, and Clare made her vows before him and accepted a rough brown tunic as her habit and a thick veil.

Francis first sent Clare to live with a community of Benedictine nuns in San Paolo, near Bastia, and at one point her relatives—it is thought that her father may have died by this time—learned of her whereabouts and attempted to bring her home by force. She resisted, however, reportedly clinging to the altar and declaring she would be the bride of no other except for Christ. While staying at another Benedictine monastery in Panzo, she was joined by her younger sister Agnes. Soon Francis found them a substandard dwelling next to the chapel of San Damiano, and with this Clare established with him a women's religious community that she called "Order of Poor Ladies;" it later became known as the Poor Clares. The order was unusual in that its first members were women from well-to-do families, inspired by Clare's devotion. Daughters of the famed Ubaldini family of Florence were among some of the first postulates.

Reputation Spread Across Europe

Against her objections, Francis made Clare abbess of her order in 1215, and she is believed never to have left the San Damiano abbey for the 40 years between then and her death. Another sister, Beatrix, also followed her there, as did her widowed mother and aunt Bianca. Like Francis's Friars Minors order, her idea swiftly spread throughout Italy and beyond, and several other communities of Poor Clares were founded. As abbess, she was known for the rigors of her penance and often fasted so drastically that she became sick; during the forty days of Lent, for example, she took only bread and water. The Poor Clares did not sleep on mattresses, rather on homely beds fashioned from twig and hemp and went barefoot at all times. They begged for food, never ate meat, and refrained from all unnecessary speech. "The foundress recommended this holy silence as the means to avoid innumerable sins of the tongue," noted *Butler's Lives of the Saints,* "and to preserve the mind always recollected in God and free from the dissipation of the world which, without this guard, penetrates even the walls of cloisters."

Clare was determined that her order should live as Francis's community of friars, without assets or land, subsisting only on daily charity. This was a radical proposition for religious communities in the early Middle Ages, for many possessed large estates that they farmed to survive; others took in students or made crafts that they then sold for subsistence; the Franciscan tenet believed that such work distracted them from fulfilling their religious vocation, to serve God. Clare's order had no formal written rule, or constitution, in its early years, save for a brief one written by Francis. In 1219, the Poor Clares came under the protection of Cardinal Ugolino when Francis joined one of the Holy Crusades, and Ugolino drew up a rule based on that of St. Benedict. It did not, however, contain the injunction for absolute poverty—instead allowing for the possession of common property—and Clare objected to this; the Clares were a cloistered order, and Ugolino believed it impractical that the women should go begging. Nevertheless, it was approved by Pope Honorius III that year; after several years of her entreaties, Clare won her case. On September 17, 1228, Ugolino, now Pope Gregory IX, granted her order the *Privilegium Paupertatis,* or "Privilege of Poverty." It was the first such decree kind issued by a pope and read in part: "It is evident that the desire of consecrating yourselves to God alone has led you to abandon every wish for temporal things. . . . Since, therefore, you have asked for it, we confirm by Apostolic favour your resolution of the loftiest poverty and by the authority of these present letters grant that you may not be constrained by anyone to receive possessions. To no one, therefore, be it allowed to infringe upon this page of our concession or to oppose it with rash temerity."

In his later years, when Francis was blind and ill, Clare was said to have constructed a small hut for him at San Damiano, where he wrote his "Canticle of the Sun." She herself carried out less of the penitential punishments for which she was known in earlier years. In writing to Agnes, daughter of the Bohemian king and founder of a Poor Clares community in Prague, she cautioned the abbess to be less drastic in her own mortifications, "so that living and hoping in the Lord you may offer Him a reasonable service and a sacrifice seasoned with the salt of prudence," *Butler's Lives of the Saints* quoted her as writing to Agnes.

Famously Repelled Looting Army

Clare lived during a tumultuous period in Italian history, and in 1234 San Damiano's walls were transgressed by soldiers in the army of the Holy Roman emperor, Frederick II. Clare was ill in bed but reportedly rose and went to the window with a ciborium, a chalice-like vessel that was used at the time to house the Eucharist. She was said to have raised the ciborium at the soldiers—some of them Saracen, or Muslim—who had mounted a ladder, and they fell over backwards and fled. Because of this story, Clare is sometimes depicted holding this object in artistic representations. She also repelled another attack, it was said, a few weeks later by prayer, reminding the sisters that the city of Assisi had nourished them through charity, and they owed it to render assistance in return in the form of prayer. She was a revered figure in Assisi, and reports that she was near death caused Pope Innocent IV to visit her on her deathbed. She died on August 11, 1253, in Assisi and was said to have uttered as her final words, according to *Butler's Lives of the Saints,* "Go forth in peace, for you have followed the good road. Go forth without fear, for He that created you has sanctified you, has always protected you, and loves you as a mother. Blessed be thou, O God, for having created me."

Clare was canonized two years later by Pope Alexander IV. Clare's remains lie in the church of Santa Chiara in Assisi. Her feast day is celebrated August 12, and some 750 years after her death, there are roughly 20,000 members of her Poor Clares order in 76 countries. They still live by the rule that she wrote, which stated that they live only by

charity. Some communities are known as "urbanist," after an allowance by Pope Urban IV in 1263 that allowed some of them to possess land if they so chose. There were other reforms enacted in the fifteenth century under the direction of St. Colette in France. Clare is the patron saint of embroiderers, eye diseases, goldsmiths and gold workers, laundry workers, telephones, television, and television writers.

Books

Butler's Lives of the Patron Saints, edited and with additional material by Michael Walsh, Harper & Row, 1987.
Butler's Lives of the Saints, edited, revised, and supplemented by Herbert J. Thurston and Donald Attwater, Christian Classics, 1981.
Catholic Encyclopedia, Volume IV, Robert Appleton Company, 1908, Online Edition, 2002.

Periodicals

America, September 24, 1994.
Commonweal, April 22, 1994.
Ecumenical Review, April 1994. □

Clement I

Clement I (died 101) is believed to have been the third pope, after Saints Linus and Anacletus; some modernists who consider the apostle Paul to be the first pope refer to Clement I as the fourth pope. Although little is known about the life of Clement I, scholars believe he led the Roman Church during the turbulent years of the last decade of the first century A.D.

Clement I—sometimes called Saint Clement or Clemens Romanus—was one of the first of the Apostolic Fathers and the first pope about whom anything definite is now known. Working closely with Saints Peter and Paul, the two founding fathers of the Christian church who preached alongside Jesus prior to Christ's crucifixion in 33 A.D., he was likely a follower of the apostle Paul and was schooled by Paul in Rome. Accepting the Christian faith as a young man and working as a missionary preaching the word of the crucified Jesus, Clement I was eventually ordained a bishop by the apostle Peter and served a leadership role in the Roman church before being exiled to the Crimea, where he died in 101 A.D.

Although several letters have been attributed to Clement I throughout the ages, only one exists with definite authenticity: a letter dated circa 96 addressed to the Church of Corinth, which had become established during the reign of St. Paul and which was at the time experiencing internal dissension. Clement's epistle is noteworthy because it bridges the chasm between inspired and uninspired Christian writings. Clement's feast is celebrated on November 23.

The Life of Clement I

Because little is known of the life and death of Clement I, much scholarly speculation has resulted. Although his name is of Latin origin, his epistle to the Corinthians is written in Greek. While it is possible that, as an educated Roman, he wrote in Greek for the sake of his audience, several distinctly non-Roman elements in his letter have let some to speculate that Clement I was born outside the Roman empire. He may also have been a non-Latin dependent of a Roman household.

References to the Old Testament made in Clement's letter to the Church of Corinth have suggested to some scholars that the letter-writer was of Jewish extraction. However, because he does not appear to have been familiar with Hebrew, and because references within the epistle—including mention of the mythological phoenix that rises from the ashes of its parent—suggest a Gentile upbringing, Clement's Jewish origin remains in doubt. Some have proposed that he was a Hellenistic Jew, while still others have speculated that he was a Jewish freedman or son of a freedman of the emperor's household. Another theory holds that Clement I was a convert to Judaism who later became a Christian. In any case, the Old Testament was, during Clement's adult years, the principle sacred canon of the Christian Church; thus, it is not surprising that he would be well versed in it regardless of whether or not he had ties to Judaism.

An ancient church fresco dating to the fifth century corresponds to a legend in which Clement I was the son of a Roman nobleman named Faustinus and raised by Tiberius (42 B.C.–37 A.D.), second emperor of Rome. According to one account, when Clement I was five years old his mother left for Athens in response to a dream. After hearing nothing from his wife for a lengthy period, Faustinus went in search of his wife, leaving his young son to the care of the Roman emperor. Many years later, according to this legend, Clement I was taken to Palestine, where he met Saint Peter and rediscovered his lost family.

Second-century historian Saint Hegesippus (died 180), in his *Five Memorials of Ecclesiastical Affairs,* is reported by later historian Eusebius of Caesarea (c. 264–340)—a Palestinian scholar known as the father of Roman Catholic history—to write that Clement I was a contemporary of the apostles Peter and Paul. This view is echoed in the writings of Alexandrian scholar Origen (c. 185–c. 254). Greek theologian Saint Irenaeus (c. 130–200) writes that Clement I "saw the blessed Apostles and conversed with them, and had yet ringing in his ears the preaching of the Apostles and had their tradition before his eyes, and not he only for many were then surviving who had been taught by the Apostles." Tertullian, in his *De Praescript* of 199, writes that Clement I was ordained a bishop by Saint Peter, echoing the most widely accepted view.

Although it is traditional to refer to Clement I as "pope," early works refer to him simply as the bishop of Rome, a position he was likely granted as a reward for his missionary zeal. Although Clement I was most likely ordained a bishop by Saint Peter and appointed by Peter to be, as his successor, the first pope, he may in fact have declined the position for several decades due to his relative youth and served instead under others for many years.

Historian Saint Epiphanius (c. 315–403) was unable to verify whether or not Clement I was actually ordained by Saint Peter or whether he was perhaps appointed bishop by another church elder. In his letter Clement I refers to the deaths of the apostles Peter and Paul in a manner that suggests that these deaths were not distant events. But he also notes that many of the presbyters or elders ordained by the apostles at Corinth were already dead. It therefore appears that Clement I may have lived among those who had known the apostles Paul and Peter in Rome, if he did not know the apostles himself.

Dating Clement's Episcopate

In his letter to Corinth, Clement I himself never refers to his personal authority as a bishop of the Church, although this may have been a tactical decision in light of the fact that the churches of Rome and Corinth had not yet come to recognize a single Church leader of overarching authority. In later years the leaders of the Roman Church would become dominant within the Christian faith.

According to Eusebius of Caesarea, the first references to the dates of Clement I's episcopate are found in the writings of Hegesippus and Dionysius of Corinth (c. 180). Eusebius writes that Clement I was made bishop of Rome in the 12th year of the reign of the Roman Emperor Domitianus (reigned 81–96), whose alienation of the upper classes resulted in a period of terror and ended in his assassination.

Hegesippus, who circa 160 compiled the first record of the popes and their episcopates, lists the dates of Clement's episcopate as 90 to 99, in the midst of the schism within the Church of Corinth. More recent scholars have placed the beginning of Clement's reign anywhere from 88 to 96 A.D. Eusebius also links Clement's reign with the rise in troubles at Corinth, a situation that existed through the end of the first Christian century.

Noted Church historian Saint Jerome (c. 342–420) writes that among his own contemporaries most "Latins" believed that Clement I was the immediate successor to Saint Peter, but that he was in fact the fourth pope. Hegesippus and Irenaeus also identify Clement I as the fourth pope (after Peter), but two other early sources identify him as the third pope, and one other source as the fifth pope. Hegesippus's list appears to have been used in chronologies compiled as late as the fourth century. Among twentieth-century scholars, he is most often cited as the third pope after saints Linus and Anacletus.

Epistle to the Church of Corinth

In the last decade of the first Christian century some elders in the Church of Corinth spearheaded a move against other of the church leaders, resulting in a split or schism among the region's Christians. Clement's now-famous letter was sent to urge peace and unity. It begins with a reference to the persecution of the Roman Church, presumably by Emperor Domitianus, by way of explanation of his delay in writing. In addition to being unpopular among the Roman wealthy class, Domitianus also made frequent attacks on Christians, killing or exiling some and confiscating the goods of others.

In his letter Clement I notes the high esteem in which the Corinthian Church had previously been held, and traces its current problems to jealousy. The just have always been persecuted, he notes, adding that the actions of only a few have caused the current disgraceful situation within the Church of Corinth. Clement I urges these few Corinthians to repent and asks his fellow believers to forsake evil and approach God with purity. He adds that discipline and subordination in the Church, as within an army, are necessary. The letter ends in a beautiful prayer bearing traces of Jewish devotional language: "May the grace of our Lord Jesus Christ be with you and with all men in all places, who have been called by God and through Him, through whom is glory and honor, power and greatness, and eternal dominion unto Him from the ages past and for ever and ever. Amen."

Although this letter to the Church of Corinth was written in the name of the Church of Rome, most authorities have credited it to Clement I. The style of the letter is simple and understated and, although writing in Greek, its author does not employ a classical style. The epistle makes no mention of Clement I by name, but rather identifies itself as the work of "the church of God which resides as a stranger in Rome." The fact of Clement's authorship is based on the attribution of subsequent historians, such as Irenaeus, who writes: "Under this Clement I no small sedition took place among the brethren at Corinth and the Church of Rome sent

a most sufficient letter to the Corinthians, establishing them in peace, and renewing their faith, and announcing the tradition it had recently received from the Apostles."

Dating the Epistle

Many scholars place the date of Clement's epistle to the Church of Corinth at between 93 and 97, based on the document's reference to persecutions that are believed to have occurred during Domitianus's reign, as well as to the writer's reference to the church at Corinth as being "ancient" and to Christians who were persecuted under the earlier emperor Nero as being of advanced age.

Some scholars have argued for a date of around 70 for the epistle due to its author's references to events involving Peter and Paul that sound as though these event had recently occurred. Still others have argued that the document was written between 125 and 135, based on certain references to the document external to itself.

Evidence that the epistle was written at an early date in Church history comes from the fact that letter addresses a quarrel at Corinth over the authority of the presbyters, with some members of that church arguing against order or hierarchy in the church. The very nature of the dispute would only have arisen during the first Christian century when the Church was governed by a group of presbyters or elders. In fact, the word "bishop," which comes from a Greek phrase meaning "supervisor," was during Clement's day synonymous with the term "elder."

A Martyr to the Faith

The Epistle to the Church of Corinth is the only document believed to have been written by Clement I. A second letter, known as the Second Epistle of Clement to the Corinthians, is considered by scholars to be spurious. Other apparently apocryphal documents once attributed to Clement I are two Epistles to Virgins, the Apostolical Constitutions, the Apostolic Canons, the Testament of Our Lord, and five other letters.

Although it is not known what effect Clement's letter had on the quarrel at Corinth, the Corinthian Church came to revere the letter and held it second in value only to the epistles Saint Paul had written. Clement's letter was for many years reopened on Sundays and read aloud to the Christian congregation. It became one of the best-known of the early Christian writings and served as a model upon which many subsequent church documents were based. It also had the effect of placing Clement I in a position second only to that of the apostles.

Clement I is believed to have died in 101, a year after the end of his pontificate, and was succeeded by Pope Evaristus. The Roman theologian Rufuinus (c. 345–410) was the first to refer to Saint Clement as a martyr, and in 417 Pope Zosimus wrote in a letter that Clement I had given his life for the Christian faith. There are at least two other references to Clement's martyrdom dating to the fifth century. Some modern scholars are of the opinion that Pope Clement I may have been confused with a martyred consul also named Clement. On the other hand, since there is no tradition that he was buried in Rome, Clement I may have died while in exile.

An apparently apocryphal account of Clement's martyrdom dating to no earlier than the fourth century relates that he converted over 400 individuals to the Christian faith before being banished from Rome to the Crimea—modern-day Russia—by an angry Emperor Trajan (c. 53–117). Trajan was a militant leader who conquered both Mesopotamia and Armenia. In the Crimea, it is said, Clement I quenched the thirst of 2,000 Christians by means of a miracle. In retribution for this act, Trajan had Clement I bound to an anchor and thrown into the Black Sea. A shrine of white marble miraculously encased his corpse; each year when the tide receded some two miles this shrine containing the martyr's bones was said to become visible to those on shore.

Around 868 Slavic apostle Saint Cyril dug up some bones in the Crimea along with an anchor, and he believed these to be the relics of Saint Clement. These relics were deposited by Pope Hadrian II in the altar of the basilica of Saint Clement in Rome, along with the relics of Saint Ignatius of Antioch. The modern church of Saint Clement at Rome was constructed as late at the early 12th century by Paschal II, following the destruction of parts of the city by the Normans. However, an older church dating to the fourth century lies under the present building.

Books

Duffy, Eamon, *Saints and Sinners: A History of the Popes,* Yale University Press, 1997.

Holland, H. S., *The Apostolic Fathers,* Society for Promoting Christian Knowledge, 1913.

Kelly, J. N. D., *The Oxford Dictionary of Popes,* Oxford University Press, 1986.

Online

Brusher, Joseph, S.J., "St. Clement I," *Popes through the Ages,* http://www.ewtp.com/library (March 20, 2003).

Catholic Encyclopedia, http://www.newadvent.org/ (January 2003).

"First Epistle of Clement to the Corinthians by by Pope Saint Clement I of Rome," Patron Saints Index, http://www.catholic-forum.com (March 20, 2003). □

Xavier Cugat

Xavier Cugat (1900–1990), a classically trained violinist who conducted with his bow, was known in his lifetime as the Rumba King. He is credited with pushing Latino music and dance into popularity in America during the first half of the 20th century.

Best-known for having popularized the rumba in the United States during the 1930s, Xavier Cugat's Latin-influenced band lead the way in a new music craze among the dancing and radio-listening public. A dramatic showman who often wore huge South American hats on stage and who led his band with the wave of a violin

bow, Cugat performed in the ritziest of clubs, on the radio, and in the movies. Having made his professional start as a child prodigy playing classical violin, Cugat was never apologetic about his switch to popular music. He was quoted in the *Los Angeles Times* as saying, "I play music . . . make an atmosphere that people enjoy. It makes them happy. They smile. They dance. Feel good—who be sorry for that?" Cugat's several marriages, extramarital affairs, and divorces made headlines, but these events did not cause him to repine. He credited his irrepressible interest in women to a Latin temperament and once said he'd marry each of his four wives over again.

Born on January 1, 1900, near Barcelona, Spain, and christened Francisco de Asis Javier Cugat Mingall de Brue y Deulofeo, Cugat was two years old when his father moved the family to Havana, Cuba. Two years later, a neighbor and violinmaker gave the boy a quarter-sized violin as a Christmas present. Cugat's exceptional talents were soon evident, as he developed into a musical prodigy. He played professionally when he was just nine years old, and at age twelve he became first violinist for the Teatro Nacional Symphonic Orchestra.

Tenor Enrico Caruso met Cugat in Havana when he was performing there with the Metropolitan Opera Company, and he enlisted the boy as his accompanist for an American tour. The subsequent events of Cugat's teen years are somewhat obscure. He is known to have played the violin on a WDY broadcast in 1917, which made him one of the first violinists to perform on radio, and some sources list

Cugat as having moved to the United States with his parents in 1915. But the bandleader once told the *Los Angeles Times* a far different story, one where he began by working 14 hours a day for a room, meals, and no pay. "[Caruso died] shortly after I got to New York . . . and there I was, no friends and not a word of English. And not much money," he said. In any case, Cugat was disappointed in his musical career. Although he played Carnegie Hall twice, toured the United States and Europe with a symphony orchestra, and became a soloist for the Los Angeles Philharmonic, the money—and critical response—was not satisfactory to Cugat.

He then gave up playing the violin for a job with the *Los Angeles Times* as a cartoonist. Caruso had taught Cugat how to draw caricatures and the young man hoped to use this skill to improve his prospects. Cugat had considerable talents as an artist but soon grew tired of the situation. Quoted in a *Los Angeles Times* obituary, Cugat explained, "When they tell you to be funny by 10:30 tomorrow morning . . . I can't do it—I finally quit, and get these six guys to play commercial music with me." Also joining Cugat on the bandstand was his wife-to-be Carmen Castillo as lead singer. The year was 1928 and Latin music was not yet popular. However, the band would land a gig playing during intermissions at the famed Coconut Grove in Los Angeles. At the time, a Gus Arnheim band with singer Bing Crosby was the main act. While in Los Angeles, Cugat also played the violin with two performers on a daily broadcast on KFWB radio.

Fame at the Waldorf-Astoria Hotel

The job that served as Cugat's springboard to fame was at the new Starlight Roof at the Waldorf-Astoria hotel in New York City. The bandleader made a modest start there in 1933 but was soon ensconced in the hotel's "Cugat Room." His dance band played at the posh hotel for 16 years and Cugat became the Waldorf-Astoria's highest-paid bandleader, making $7,000 a week plus a cut of the cover charge take. In 1934 Cugat's band played a three-hour network radio program on Saturday nights.

During a time when dance band leaders Benny Goodman and Glenn Miller were immensely popular, Cugat benefited from a conflict between the American Society of Composers, Authors and Publishers (ASCAP) and the radio networks. ASCAP withheld its music from broadcasts, forcing dance bands to play mostly tired public-domain songs. Cugat, however, had some 500 non-ASCAP Latin tunes at his disposal and had soon attracted a national audience. He became known as the "Rumba King." Some of the performers that Cugat in turn helped to popularize were Desi Arnaz, Dinah Shore, Lina Romay, and Miguelito Valdes. He wrote and recorded hundreds of songs, including "Chiquita Banana," "Rumba Rhapsody," "Kasmiri Love Song," "Rain in Spain," "Babalu," "My Shawl," "Rendezvous in Rio,"

"Walter Winchell Rumba," "Is It Taboo," and "I'll Never Love Again."

Cugat made the leap to the silver screen in 1942, appearing in *You Were Never Lovelier,* which starred Rita Hayworth. Cugat had met the actress in California many years before, when she was a dancer known as Margarita Cansino. With his band, Cugat appeared in many more films—often as himself. He was repeatedly seen on screen with the swimming actress Esther Williams; among their motion pictures together were *Neptune's Daughter, Bathing Beauty, This Time for Keeps,* and *On an Island With You.* Cugat's caricatures were also featured in some of his films and on a "curtain of stars" in Grauman's Chinese Theater in Hollywood. These events followed an earlier interest in movie making on the part of Cugat, who had previously made films including an ill-fated production during the early sound era. In 1928 he had spent $35,000 to produce a Spanish-language film, only to discover that there were as yet no sound projectors in Latin America.

Cugat's personal life made news many times, as he wed and divorced four times. His marriage to Castillo ended unhappily in 1944. The bandleader was married to Lorraine Allen from 1947 to 1952, when—with the help of private detectives—she caught him in a compromising position in a hotel room with the band's lead singer, Abbe Lane. Cugat wed Lane that same year and stayed married some 14 years, until he found her with another man. In 1966 he married the much younger singer-guitarist Charro Baeza, who is better known by her first name alone. This marriage ended in 1978 and was said to be the only amicable divorce. Cugat's reflections on his love life were recalled in the *Los Angeles Times:* "I like women—all women. . . . Also, there is my temperament. I am Latin. I excite. For me, this is life."

Although the Latin music craze that had swelled in the 1930s and 1940s died down, Cugat remained extremely popular. His band was often booked in Las Vegas and he performed until 1969, when Cugat suffered a stroke and became partially paralyzed. The bandleader recovered from the stroke but his health was never the same. After his divorce from Charro, Cugat moved to Barcelona, where he lived for 18 years—until his death in 1990. He had been suffering from heart and lung problems and was in intensive care at the Quiron Clinic when he died.

Books

Contemporary Authors, Gale, 1991.
Newsmakers, Gale, 1991.

Periodicals

Los Angeles Times, October 28, 1990.
New York Times, October 28, 1990.

Online

All-Music Guide, www.allmusic.com (February 2003). □

D

Saint David

Saint David (c. 520–c. 601) is the patron saint of doves, poets, and Wales. One source calls him "perhaps the most celebrated of British saints." Another gives him credit for evangelizing much of Wales. The body of information available about him today is thin in substantiated fact but rich with tradition, including even King Arthur and a sea monster. Saint David's mere existence may provide evidence that Christianity in Wales persisted in tact and uninterrupted since Roman times.

Rhygyfarch Embellished Story

Most information about Saint David comes from the writings of an eleventh-century monk named Rhygyfarch (also Rhygyvarch, Rhigyfarch, and Ricemarch), son of Bishop Sulien, of Saint David's Cathedral, Saint David's favorite of the churches he established. Rhygyfarch claimed to have gathered his information from old written sources, but those have not survived. Rhygyfarch's life of Saint David is regarded by many scholars as suspect because it contains many implausible events and because he had a stake in enhancing Saint David's history so as to support the prestige of the Welsh church and its independence from Canterbury, the center of the English church (still Catholic at the time). According to David Hugh Farmer in *The Oxford Dictionary of Saints,* Rhygyfarch's history of Saint David "should be treated as propaganda, which may, however, contain some elements of true tradi-

tion." Another source considers Rhygyfarch's biography "traditional, symbolic tales of a great religious leader." Saint David's existence at least does not seem to be in doubt; it is attested to in written records from earlier dates. The earliest is an Irish Catalogue of the Saints of 730. Another is an Irish Martyrology of 800.

Saint David Born

One legend says Saint David's birth was foretold to Saint Patrick (about 373–464) by an angel 30 years in advance. In the traditions surrounding Saint David, his mother is said to be a woman named Non, now Saint Non, who may have been a nun at the cloister called Ty Gwyn, near Whitesand Bay. She may also have been the daughter of a chieftain in Pembrokeshire. She is said to have been very beautiful, and it was her great beauty that is said to have driven Saint David's father, Sant, or Xantus, a local chieftain or king, perhaps related to King Arthur, to rape her. (Other traditions say Sant and Non were married, and she became a nun later in her life.) She became pregnant with Saint David. Yet another legend says that during her pregnancy she entered the church of Saint Gildas in Wales, and he was struck dumb. He realized the Welsh church must be intended for the future Saint David and left for Ireland. In any case, Non is said to have given birth during a storm (so violent as to have deterred a local ruler who planned to kill Saint David in order to eliminate a rival for power in the realm) at a spot overlooking Saint Bride's Bay, south of today's Saint David's Cathedral. The year is given variously as 454, 487, 520, 542, and 544. A medieval chapel named for Saint Non was built at the spot; it is today in ruins. Non's son was baptized at Porth Clais by Saint Ailbhe, who may have been Non's nephew. Miracles marked the event: a new spring erupted and sight was restored to a blind monk, Movi, holding the baby.

Excelled in School

Saint David went to school at a monastery called Hen Vynyw, or Henfynyw, in Cardigan. Rhygyfarch wrote, "He grew up full of grace and lovely to behold. And there it was that holy David learnt the alphabet, the psalms, the lessons for the whole year and the divine office; and there his fellow disciples saw a dove with a golden beak playing at his lips and teaching him to sing the praise of God." One source points out he would have learned Latin there and studied mathematics, astronomy, and music. After Hen Vynyw, he went to an unidentified island (one source says it was the Isle of Wight) to study for the priesthood under a Welsh scribe, Saint Paulinus. A legend says that Paulinus had gone blind from crying so much as he prayed, and that Saint David restored his sight with a gentle touch. Another legend says that an angel told Paulinus to send Saint David out to evangelize the British.

Founded Monasteries

As a traveling priest, Saint David is said to have founded 10 or 12 monasteries. The number is disputed, but several have been authenticated. He also allegedly cleansed deadly water at Bath and turned it into a warm and healing pool. Another legend says some monks tried to poison Saint David's bread, but Saint Schuthyn rode to Saint David one night from Ireland on the back of a sea monster to warn him, and Saint David blessed the bread, counteracting the poison. There is consensus that he ended his evangelizing travels in Mynyw, or Menevia, in extreme southwest Wales (where Saint David's Cathedral is today) and founded his major abbey there, training "many great pastors and eminent servants of God," according to Father Alban Butler on the Catholic Forum website. Butler described Mynyw as "formed by nature for solitude, being . . . almost cut off from the rest of the island." Another source calls the site "lovely and lonely."

Wrote Strict Rule

Saint David's monks followed a very strict rule "in the spirit of penance," according to Father Butler. Others say Saint David adapted his rule from that of monks in Egypt. "Every moment of the day had its duties," wrote Amy Steedman, one interpreter of Saint David's life. Wearing animal skins, they labored in the fields, plowing without farm animals; "every man his own ox," Saint David is reported to have said. Speaking was severely restricted, and they were to pray, silently if not aloud, at all times. When not in the fields, they prayed, studied, and wrote. They ate bread, vegetables, and salt and drank only water and a little milk. Following the evening meal, the only one of the day, they prayed for three hours before going to bed, then awoke at dawn. Because he didn't allow the consumption of wine or other spirits, Saint David is nicknamed "The Waterman." The monks were to pray continuously from evening on Friday until daybreak on Sunday, with only an hour after Saturday Matins for rest. Farmer noted, "David devoted himself to works of mercy and practised frequent genuflexions and total immersion in cold water as his favourite austerities."

Father Butler wrote that if someone wished to join Saint David's monastery, he had to wait outside for 10 days, "during which time he was tried by harsh words, repeated refusals, and painful labours, that he might learn to die to himself. When he was admitted, he left all his worldly substance behind him."

Combatted Pelagian Heresy

A man who lived over a hundred years before Saint David played a role in the next major event in the traditional telling of Saint David's life. The monk Pelagius, born in Britain in about 354, visited Rome in approximately 380. Although Pelagius was not a priest, he was a popular religious leader who placed a high value on asceticism, or self-denial, as a way of drawing closer to God. The self-indulgent excess he saw in Rome shocked him, and he blamed it on the doctrine of salvation by grace, the idea that people cannot earn salvation by good works but that only God can bestow it. To counteract this doctrine, which Pelagius thought led to moral degradation, he insisted humans were responsible for their own salvation. For this he was declared a heretic and excommunicated in 417 by Pope Innocent I.

By the fifth century, Pelagius's heresy, called Pelagianism, was widespread in Britain. It was suppressed, but legend says it sprang up again in Saint David's lifetime, and a meeting of church officials, called a synod, took place at Brefi, in Cardigan, in about 519, to suppress it again. Saint David was invited to attend. Although he spoke to the assembly only reluctantly, his words were compelling, and legend says a hill rose up under his feet so that everyone could see and hear him and a white dove came and sat on his shoulder as he spoke. (He is represented in church art standing on his hill with the dove on his shoulder.) He not only put down the heresy, but was elected primate of the Cambrian, or Welsh, church unanimously. The incumbent primate, Dubricius, even resigned in Saint David's favor. Saint David accepted on the condition that the headquarters of the see be transferred to his home monastery in Mynyw (now Saint David's Cathedral). Some traditions say the legendary King Arthur approved the relocation of the see.

Made Pilgrimage to Jerusalem

Other stories of Saint David say that after a vision, he traveled to Jerusalem with two companions to aid the patriarch, and that the patriarch of Jerusalem, John III, consecrated him archbishop. Back in Wales, he allegedly assembled a Synod of Victory to officially celebrate the end of the Pelagian heresy in Britain. This synod also presumably ratified a set of rules written by Saint David for the "regulation of the British church," but Rhygyfarch maintained the writings were lost to "age and negligence, and also . . . the frequent attacks of pirates."

Died in Mynyw

Saint David died in his monastery at Mynyw, some say at the age of 142 or 147 (he is credited with predicting the day), and an observer watched angels carry Saint David's soul up to heaven. Saint David's last words to his monks are said to be, "Be joyful, and keep your faith and your creed.

Do those little things that you have seen me do and heard about.'' The year of his death varies; it may have been in 560, 589, or 601.

Sanctified

In 1120 Pope Callistus II declared David a saint. *Butler's Lives of the Saints* casts doubt on a legend that the pope also declared that visiting Mynyw twice would be ''equal to one visit to Rome'' in indulgence value. Saint David's feast day is March 1 (his mother Saint Non's is March 3), and according to *Butler's Lives,* ''There can . . . be no question that he was a highly popular saint in his own country. More than fifty pre-Reformation churches in South Wales are known to have been dedicated in his honour. Moreover, even in England, Archbishop Arundel in 1398 ordered his feast to be kept in every church throughout the province of Canterbury.'' Although the monastery Saint David built is gone, today's Saint David's Cathedral, much of it dating from the twelfth century, is Wales's largest cathedral.

Saint David Symbolized

Several symbols are associated with Saint David. William Shakespeare referred to the Welsh custom of wearing leeks or daffodils in Saint David's honor on March 1 as ''an ancient tradition begun upon an honourable request,'' as quoted in Farmer's *Oxford Dictionary.* Some say the custom comes from a battle between the Welsh and the Saxons; Saint David reportedly wanted the Welsh to wear leeks in their hats so they could recognize other Welsh. Saint David's day now is marked by festivals that feature singing, dancing, and reciting, and the leek and the daffodil are national symbols of Wales.

Other symbols associated with Saint David come from yet another legend about his birth: An angel told Saint David's father, Sant, in a dream that when he went hunting the next day, he would kill a stag and find a fish and a beehive. The stag, said to eat snakes, represents Christianity's conquering Satan (the serpent); the fish represents Saint David's abstinence from liquor; and the bees represent his wisdom and spirituality.

Books

Farmer, David Hugh, *The Oxford Dictionary of Saints,* Oxford University Press, 1987.

Gill, Elaine, *The Celtic Saints,* Cassell, 1995.

Guiley, Rosemary Ellen, *The Encyclopedia of Saints,* Facts On File, 2001.

McBrien, Richard P., *Lives of the Saints,* HarperSanFrancisco, 2001.

Thurston, Herbert J., and Donald Attwater, eds., *Butler's Lives of the Saints,* Christian Classics, 1956.

Online

Butler, Alban, www.catholic-forum.com/saints/std08002.htm (March 1, 2003).

''David of Wales B (AC),'' http://users.erols.com/saintpat/ss/0301 .htm (March 1, 2003).

''Dewi of Wales,'' http://elvis.rowan.edu/~kilroy/JEK/03/01.html (March 1, 2003).

Halpert, Jane H., ''On Being Welsh–Saint of Small Things,'' *World and I,* March 2001, http://web3.infotrac.galegroup .com (March 15, 2003).

''Pelagius,'' Encyclopaedia Britannica Library, 2003, CD-ROM.

''Rhigyfarch,'' http://www.saintdavid.org.uk/stories.htm/page11 .htm (March 1, 2003).

''Saint David's,'' Encyclopaedia Britannica Library, 2003, CD-ROM.

''St. Dewi, Bishop of Mynyw,'' http://www.earlybritishkingdoms .com/bios/dewi.html (March 15, 2003).

''St. Gildas Badonicus,'' http://www.earlybritishkingdoms.com/ bios/gildas/html (March 15, 2003).

Steedman, Amy, ''Saint David of Wales,'' http://www.catholic-forum.com/saints/std08001.htm (March 1, 2003).

''A Stormy Night,'' http://www.saintdavid.org.uk/stories.htm/ page2.htm (March 1, 2003).

''Wales,'' Encyclopaedia Britannica Library, 2003, CD-ROM. □

Marie-Olympe de Gouges

French author and activist Marie Olympe de Gouges (1748–1793) achieved modest success as a playwright in the 18th century, but she became best known for her political writing and support of the French Revolution. Considered a feminist pioneer, de Gouges was an advocate of women's rights. Her most famous work was *The Declaration of the Rights of Woman,* (1791). Even in revolutionary France, feminist ideas were considered radical. In 1793, she was executed for crimes against the government.

Early Life

Marie-Olympe de Gouges was born Marie Gouzes in Montauban, in southern France, on December 31, 1748. The facts about her true parentage are somewhat vague, and de Gouges herself contributed to the confusion by encouraging rumors about her illegitimacy.

It is commonly believed that she was born and raised in a modest family, the daughter of Pierre Gouze, a butcher, and Anne Olympe Moisset, a maidservant. However, it was rumored that de Gouges's mother, who reportedly was a beautiful women and unhappy in her marriage, had an affair with a person of high social rank, Marquis Lefranc de Pompignan. The marquis, many claimed, was de Gouge's real father. Another circulated rumor suggested that de Gouges was the illegitimate daughter of King Louis XV. When asked about her true parentage, de Gouges would only answer somewhat ambiguously. Fueling the speculation about de Gouge's illegitimate birth was the fact the Pierre Gouze's name did not appear on any significant documents relating to his daughter's paternity. However, it is now generally believed today that Gouze was indeed her real father. Whatever the true facts about her parentage, she actually lived with Gouze, who died when she was two years old. During her youth, de Gouges already

demonstrated the kind of rebelliousness that would come into play in her adult life.

In 1765, when she was 17, de Gouges married a French officer, Louis Aubrey. Two years later, they had a son. Aubrey was much older than de Gouges and he died three years into the marriage. Following his death, and displaying her characteristic rebelliousness, de Gouges refused to accept her position as a widowed mother or the designation of "Widowed Aubrey," a personal stance that was counter to the social convention. Even more, she vowed never to remarry.

Moved to Paris

Abandoning her son, de Gouges went to Paris in 1770 to seek fame as a writer. For her pen name she chose simply Olympe de Gouges, a variation of both her mother and father's names. She actively sought to achieve her ambition, propagating the rumors of her illegitimate birth. It has been suggested that she started, or at least encouraged, the rumors because she believed that, by tying her lineage to a marquis, she'd gain her entrance into the higher social circles that she aspired. Also, she most likely believed that a blood tie with Marquis Lefranc of Pompignan, who was a well-known author, would help her establish her own reputation as a writer. The rumor gained currency in her lifetime even though no proof existed of its truth.

During this period, she furthered her career by meeting and establishing connections with the most famous writers and philosophers of the time, and she worked her way into the highest social circles. Remaining resolute in her desire never to marry again, she reportedly became the mistress of several men of high social rank and she divided herself between her many lovers and her writing. A self-educated woman, de Gouges wrote plays, novels, and sociopolitical pamphlets. Her dramatic works included *Le Mariage inattendu de Chérubin* and *Zamore et Mirza ou l'Heureux naufrage.*

Her career as a playwright turned out to be somewhat disappointing, as it resulted in only modest success. She was poorly educated, could barely read for a good portion of her life, and her grammar and punctuation were terrible. As a result, her writing tended to be plodding, verbose, and awkward. However, greatly affected by current events, she would soon enter the phase of her career that proved the most productive and thematically significant. She began turning out political works that helped influence the course of human rights, specifically for women. Paris, in the late 1780's, was a political focal point. France was a country in turmoil and on the verge of an influential and inspiring, though bloody, revolution that would attract the attention of the world. De Gouges was swept up in the fervor of the times.

Although most of her fellow citizens were exuberantly political, and even fanatically revolutionary, de Gouges initially took a moderate stance. Reforms she suggested in her political materials were intended to bring about change without sacrificing the social stability. Indeed, de Gouges had friends in the French royalty that was about to be overthrown, but her works often attempted to negatively depict the extremists on both sides of the political spectrum: the royalists, or monarchists, and the revolutionaries. As the storms of revolution swirled, de Gouges still considered herself a royalist. Her 1788 piece *Droits de la femme* articulated advanced revolutionary ideals while expressing her sympathies for the French monarchy. Also in 1788, she published her *Patriotic Remarks,* wherein she presented a large program of social reforms and advocated for the dismantling of the monarchial government. The document also outlined the abuses of the elite social class. One of her works was a political satire, *Project of a Patriotic Case By Citoyenne,* involving a "voluntary tax."

But de Gouges would become disillusioned by the French monarchy's inaction, and she would encourage the French king Louis XVI to abdicate his throne and put in its place a regent government. She felt that this would be a workable solution to an ever-growing crisis. The citizens had armed themselves, the Bastille had been stormed, and blood was literally flowing in the streets. De Gouges would remain a royalist until Louis XVI escaped from the country, a move that further increased the growing chaos. From that point on, her political material become more pointed and she sided more strongly with the revolutionaries.

In 1789, after Louis XVI's escape, she produced two more satires, *Cry of Wise by a Woman* and *To Save the Fatherland.*

Feminist Thought

The sociopolitical works that de Gouge produced during this period focused strongly on the issues of civil rights, particularly the rights of women, which she deemed were "natural" and "inalienable." Her dedication to and advocacy for these issues stemmed from her much broader belief in the complete equality of all human beings.

The revolution created the type of environment that fostered innovative ideas such as feminism. One of the feminist organizations created during this period was the Society of Republican and Revolutionary Women. Its members encouraged de Gouges to develop a document that would essentially serve as a declaration of rights for women. She set out to produce the work, which would eventually be published as the *Declaration of the Rights of Woman and of the Citizen* in 1791.

In the meantime, her name was becoming widely known in radical circles, just as it had a few years earlier when she established her standing in the bourgeois. In October 1789, the year the French Revolution came to a boil, she proposed a radical reform platform to the French National Assembly, a governing body comprised of the nation's new leaders. Appearing before this board, she advocated for the complete legal equality of the sexes, more job opportunities for women, a legal alternative to the private dowry system, better education for young girls, and the establishment of a national theater that would show only plays written by women.

Declaration of Women's Rights

Finally published in September of 1791, the *Declaration of the Rights of Woman (Déclaration of the Droits de la Femme et de la Citoyenne)* was, in a way, a response to the *Declaration of the Rights of Man and the Citizen* that was published in 1789 and was to the French Revolution what the Declaration of Independence was to the American Revolution. De Gouge's declaration called for an extension of the rights demanded in the latter including complete freedom of speech, the right to vote, and the opportunity to seek public office. Lest anyone miss her point, de Gouge employed the same kind of language and rhetoric that characterized the male "Declaration."

De Gouge dedicated the work to Queen Marie Antoinette, hoping that the royal would support women's rights. The work consists of a preamble, 17 articles, and an epilogue. Her words were provocative and incited women to action. In the epilogue, de Gouge proclaimed, "Woman, wake up; the tocsin of reason is being heard throughout the whole universe; discover your rights. The powerful empire of nature is no longer surrounded by prejudice, fanaticism, superstition, and lies. The flame of truth has dispersed all the clouds of folly and usurpation. Enslaved man has multiplied his strength and needs recourse to yours to break his chains. Having become free, he has become unjust to his companion. Oh, women, women! When will you cease to be blind? What advantage have you received from the Revolution?"

Essentially, the *Declaration of the Rights of Woman and of the Citizen* stated that women were equal to men in every respect and thus were entitled to the same rights. The work would create enemies for de Gouge; she believed that because many women participated in the French Revolution, they would or should automatically receive the newfound rights extended to the male citizenry.

Accused of Sedition

De Gouge's outspokenness would eventually lead to her arrest, conviction, and execution. The government that came to power after the overthrow of the monarchy demonstrated no tolerance for perceived subversion or even criticism. In a way, one tyranny replaced another, and de Gouge had placed herself in a rather tenuous situation. She felt she had the right to speak out on the behalf of the citizenry and to assert the rights of women. But in doing so, she violated traditional social boundaries that even the revolutionaries held inviolable, thus invoking the ire of the ruling body. Also, she harshly criticized Maximilien Robespierre, the recognized leader of the new government. Her advocacy of women's rights combined with this criticism, which she published as *Pronostic de Monsieur Robespierre pour an animal amphibie,* as well as her previous support of King Louis XVI, led to accusations of sedition. In retrospect, and given the tenor of the times, de Gouge's publications of the criticism and "Declaration" were highly impetuous and imprudent actions.

Sent to Trial

At the time of her arrest, she was known publicly as Marie Olympe de Gouges, femme of letters. She was 38 years old and lived in the Pont-Neuf section of Paris, on rue du Harlay. A review of her trial proves enlightening, as it provides a typical example of the persecution that befell the revolutionaries who criticized the new government that arose in the wake of the monarchy's downfall. As this new government, the so-called National Convention, grew stronger, it took on the force of a "Reign of Terror."

De Gouges was charged on July 25, 1793, with having written works contrary to the wants and needs of the entire nation and directed against those in power. She was imprisoned and her writings were reviewed by a public prosecutor the next day. Her interrogation began on August 6, 1793. Following the review and her interrogation, it was determined that she had produced writings that were considered an attack on the sovereignty of the people and that she had questioned and openly provoked civil war and sought to arm citizens against one another.

The public prosecutor assigned to her case expressed great indignation for de Gouges and her writings, claiming that she stated "perfidious intentions," as it is written in the *Life, Liberty, Fraternity: Exploring the French Revolution* website. Describing de Gouges as "criminal," the prosecutor ascribed to her "hidden motives" against the sovereignty of the citizens of France and accused her of seeking to reestablish the monarchial government. He also criticized her for alleged inappropriate behavior during her public hearing, accusing her of smirking during her hearing, shrugging her shoulders at the accusations, raising her eyebrows at various statements, and smiling at spectators.

The prosecutor drew up formal accusations and de Gouge was held for trial. She was found guilty and condemned to death according to article one of the new constitution, quoted by the *Life, Liberty, Fraternity: Exploring the French Revolution* website, "Whoever is convicted of having composed or printed works or writings which provoke the dissolution of the national representation, the reestablishment of royalty, or of any other power attacking the sovereignty of the people, will be brought before the Revolutionary Tribunal and punished by death."

In an attempt to escape the guillotine blade, de Gouges claimed she was pregnant. She was examined by doctors and midwives, who determined that her claim was false.

Executed by Guillotine

De Gouge was executed in Paris on November 3, 1793, put to death by guillotine, the instrument that had taken the lives of so many royals and members of the bourgeoisie during the revolution, as well as the lives of many staunch and true revolutionaries who dared defy or criticize the implacable government that rose to power. According to reports in the *Life, Liberty, Fraternity: Exploring the French Revolution* website, de Gouge ascended the scaffold at 4 p.m., looked into the assembled crowd, and said, "Children of the Fatherland, you will avenge my death."

Following the execution, a published report, quoted in an article by Jone Johnson Lewis, stated that "Olympe de Gouges, born with an exalted imagination, mistook her delirium for an inspiration of nature. She wanted to be a man of state. She took up the projects of the perfidious people who want to divide France. It seems the law has punished this conspirator for having forgotten the virtues that belong to her sex."

Before her death, she wrote to her son, as seen on the Bibliotheca Augustana website, "Good-bye, my son, I will not live any more when you receive this letter. You will repair the injustice which one makes to your mother." In a public statement, she wrote, "Think of me and remember the action that I carried out in favour of the women! I am certain that we will triumph one day!"

Books

Darline Gav Levy, H. Applewhite, and M. Johnson, eds., *Women in Revolutionary Paris,* University of Illinois Press, 1979.

Online

Johnson Lewis, Jone, "Olympe de Gouges and the Rights of Women," *About.com: Women's History,* http://womenshistory.about.com/library/weekly/aa071099.htm (March 15, 2003).

"Marie Gouze, known as Olympe de Gouges," *History on Line,* www.histoire-en-ligne.com/article.php3?id_article=195 (March 15, 2003).

"Marie Olympe Aubry de Gouges, Declaration of the Rights of Women (1791)," *The University of Adelaide Department of History,* http://www.arts.adelaide.edu.au/personal/DHart/ETexts/Enlightenment/Rights/GougesWomen.html (March 15, 2003).

"Olympe de Gouges," *Women of the French Revolution,* www.furman.edu/~pecoy/projects/gouges/ (March 15, 2003).

"Olympe de Gouges 1748-1793," *Bibliotheca Augustana,* http://translate.google.com/translate?hl=en&=fr&=http://www.fh-augsburg.de/~harsch/gallica/Chronologie/18siecle/DeGouges/gou_fils.html&=/search%3Fq%3Ddegouges%2Bidol%25C3%25A2trie%26hl%3Den%26l%3D%26ie%3DUTF-8%26sa%3DG (May 21, 2003).

"The Trial of Olympe de Gouges," *Life, Liberty, Fraternity: Exploring the French Revolution,* http://chnm.gmu.edu/revolution/d/488/ (March 15, 2003). □

Marie le Jars de Gournay

Marie le Jars de Gournay (1565–1645) was one of Renaissance France's most active literary figures. She served as the posthumous editor for the works of famed essayist Michel de Montaigne, and in her own writings espoused a strongly feminist point of view that made her a woman far ahead of her time. A generation after her death, de Gournay was honored as one of the seventy most famous women of all time by Jean de la Forge in the 1663 volume *Circle of Learned Women*.

Barred from School

De Gournay was born on October 6, 1565, in Paris, where her father Guillaume enjoyed royal patronage as an officeholder during the reigns of Charles IX and Henry III. She was the first of six children in her family, and when she was three years old, her father acquired an estate in Picardy, a region in northern France. The property, Gournay-sur-Aronde, also gave him a minor nobility title, but the family did not live there until after his death in 1577. De Gournay's mother decided to relocate the family there in order to live more cheaply than in Paris; the death of Guillaume de Gournay had caused some financial difficulties, which were exacerbated by general economic troubles in France at the time during its contentious Wars of Religion.

De Gournay's brothers were sent away to school, but she was not. Had they received an education at home with tutors, she might have enjoyed some access to learning; thus she took it upon herself to learn by reading avidly and teaching herself Latin. She became proficient enough to translate works from Virgil, the classical Roman poet, and then moved on to the study of Greek. At the time, French Humanist thought stressed that a familiarity with the classics would breed a virtuous intellect. De Gournay still retained a respect for the teachings and tenets of the Roman Catholic church, however, and also read the works of church fathers such as St. Jerome.

Met Montaigne

Around 1584, de Gournay came across the new second edition of Montaigne's *Essais,* published just a few years earlier to widespread public debate. A renowned scholar, Montaigne hailed from a landowning family and had served as the mayor of Bordeaux. His essays discussed a range of topics, from friendship to intellectual curiosity to human fallibility and were written in a lively style that greatly influenced other writers of the era and beyond. As editors Richard Hillman and Colette Quesnel wrote in a preface to one of de Gournay's works in translation, *Apology for the Woman Writing and Other Works,* "the *Essays* were a radically innovative work in their time, not least for their author's complex self-portrayal, which makes him a fascinating presence within his own work; they also apply abundant classical learning to a wide variety of moral, political, and philosophical questions of contemporary concern, which are often treated in a manner at once iconoclastic and profound."

Deeply intrigued by Montaigne's ideas and literary style, de Gournay traveled to Paris in 1588 to meet him. At the time, she was 23 years old, and Montaigne 32 years her senior; afterward, he journeyed to Picardy, where she was still living with her family and spent three months there. He termed her his *fille d'alliance* or "adoptive daughter," which was a common mentor-student relationship at the time among intellectuals. In Picardy, she later asserted, Montaigne recounted to her a tragic love story that she drew upon to craft the plot of her first and only novel, *Le Proumenoir de M. de Montaigne, par sa fille d'alliance* ("The Promenade of Monsieur de Montaigne, by his adoptive daughter"). She sent the manuscript on to him after he returned to his home in Gascony.

Settled Family Finances

De Gournay's literary ambitions were both stalled and set free by family matters. Orphaned with the death of her mother in 1591, she was forced to undertake the education of two more brothers—while her own formal schooling never materialized—and find a husband for her sister, each of which were costly enterprises that depleted the family's already diminished assets. Yet her mother, scholars believe, likely viewed de Gournay's goal to live independently—both free of marriage and free to write—with more than some disdain, and the death of her parent allowed de Gournay to pursue her ambitions once she had provided for her younger siblings' futures. During this period, Montaigne died, and the news did not reach de Gournay until the following year. She was crushed but did visit his widow, who treated her kindly and gave her the notes for a new edition of the *Essais* slated for publication. By this time de Gournay's novel *Le Proumenoir* had been published, and though it was not a commercial or critical success at the time, it is considered one of the first modern psychological novels by a male or female author. Its plot centers on a princess in ancient Persia, Alinda, who balks at the prospect of an arranged marriage and instead elopes. The vessel carrying the newlyweds is shipwrecked in Thrace, and the

ruler there involves her in an intrigue; eventually her husband Leontin betrays her, and Alinda commits suicide.

Returning to Picardy, de Gournay diligently went to work on revising the new edition according to Montaigne's notes and wrote "Preface. . . , sa fille d'alliance" for the 1595 edition of *Essais.* In this preface, she answered critical remarks made by Montaigne's detractors and drew criticism herself in part for her strident tone, wrote Hillman and Quesnel. "She was widely viewed as having impertinently mingled her own interests with those of Montaigne—a veritable usurpation of the 'father' by the 'daughter.'"

Led Literary Life

Eventually de Gournay's family business matters were settled, and she was left with a small income that enabled her to travel on occasion and live independently. She went to Brussels and Antwerp in 1597, where she met well-known authors and was surprised to find herself somewhat feted. After 1599 she lived in Paris with one servant, who remained with her until her death and devoted her energies to writing essays, verse, and literary criticism. She revised *Proumenoir* and frequented the famed salon of the former French queen, Margot, who wrote as Marguerite de Valois. Margot's husband, Henry IV, had demanded an annulment so that he could be free to marry his mistress, and de Gournay was also active in Henry's court. When this Protestant king was assassinated in 1610, the death was blamed on a faction loyal to the Jesuits, the Roman Catholic religious order, and de Gournay involved herself in the controversy by defending the Jesuit cause in her published writings. Characteristically, her arguments on such topical matters were "tightly focused, highly articulate, and dauntingly indignant," wrote Hillman and Quesnel in *Apology for the Woman Writing.*

After obtaining a small pension from Henry IV's son, Louis XIII, de Gournay enjoyed a prolific period during the 1620s. She published a series of important tracts, later cited as prime examples of feminist reasoning, during this time. They began with *Egalite des hommes et des femmes* ("The Equality of Men and Women") in 1622, which traced the history of misogyny in Western European civilization back to the apostle Paul and his first epistle to the Corinthians, which set forth the reasons that women were to be barred from ministry in the early Christian church. De Gournay also espoused equal access to education for men and women alike. She mused about the backhanded praise often leveled at women like herself who had achieved some merit in the arts, noting that the highest compliment of the day was in itself damning praise—"the supreme excellence women may achieve is to resemble ordinary men," she asserted. In the same essay, she noted that "If, therefore, women attain less often than men to the heights of excellence, it is a marvel that the lack of good education—indeed, the abundance of outright and blatantly bad education—does not do worse and prevent them from doing so entirely."

Espoused Provocative Ideas

Her two major next work, *Grief des dames* ("Complaint of Women" or, alternately, "The Ladies' Grievance") appeared in 1626 in a volume of her collected works, *L'Ombre de la Demoiselle de Gournay* ("The Shadow of Miss Gournay"). *L'Ombre* also contained two other essays, *Apologie pour celle qui escrit* ("Apology for the Woman Writing") and *Peincture de moeurs* ("Character Portrait"). De Gournay also wrote poetry, and much of her verse had a strong feminist strain, focusing on themes of marital love or the French heroine Joan of Arc and the legendary Amazon women. "The writer's ultimate figurations of female triumph . . . are women who excelled in the ultimate masculine sphere, epitomizing the fulfillment of her aspiration to beat men at their own game," noted Hillman and Quesnel.

In her literary criticism, De Gournay often resisted prevailing trends. In a 1624 essay, she defended the works of Pierre de Ronsard, the leader of the so-called Pléiade poets who took their name from an Alexandrian group of the classical era. Ronsard, who died in 1585, had fallen out of favor by de Gournay's time, but she attempted to revive his reputation, wrote Hillman and Quesnel, "by pretending to have discovered a more 'modern' authorial revision of one of his pieces, which she proceeded to publish with a dedication to the king. In fact, the 'revision' was her own work (and not particularly distinguished at that)." For such acts de Gournay was often mocked and derided in print for her views and was victimized by the occasional practical joke; in one notorious example, she was told that King James I of England desired a profile of her work for a planned compilation of the lives of famous men and women of the time, and she duly wrote an autobiographical sketch and sent it in. "Copie de la vie de la Demoiselle de Gournay" (Representation of the life of Miss de Gournay) appeared in print later in one of the last works published during her lifetime, the 1641 collection *Les Advis ou les Presens de la Demoiselle de Gournay*. The tome contained revisions of her feminist tracts as well.

Mocked, Then Forgotten

In her later years, De Gournay continued to be the occasional target of ridicule. "Her taste and talent for controversy seems to have been particularly provocative," wrote Hillman and Quesnel, particularly in the twilight of her career, they noted, when "it became easier not only to stamp her as a holdover from a remote era but to make fun of her eccentricities. These were real enough, running the gamut from rashness—of tongue, temper, and judgment—to a shameless thirst for praise and a fascination with alchemy. Humorous stories were recounted at her expense; she was the object of practical jokes, the target of satire in print, even of caricature on the stage." Despite such scorn, de Gournay had attained enough of a reputation to earn another pension, this one from King Louis XIII's influential chief minister, Cardinal Richelieu, in 1634; she was also involved in the founding of the prestigious Académie Française that same year, created to further and protect the French language.

De Gournay was read by some in the generation of women scholars who immediately followed her, such as Anna Maria van Schurman and Marguerite Buffet. She continued to work on several subsequent new editions of Montaigne's *Essais* before her death in Paris on July 13, 1645. Her reputation languished until the early nineteenth century, which coincided with revival of interest in Montaigne's works. Much of her work did not appear in English translation until the late 1980s.

Books

De Gournay, Marie le Jars, *Apology for the Woman Writing and Other Works,* edited and translated by Richard Hillman and Colette Quesnel, University of Chicago Press, 2002.

Periodicals

Renaissance Quarterly, Summer 1997.

Online

"Marie le Jars de Gournay (1565–1645)," Other Women's Voices, http://home.infionline.net/~ddisse/gournay.html (May 16, 2003). □

Johann Deisenhofer

Biochemist and biophysicist Johann Deisenhofer (born 1943) devised a way to use X-ray technology to map the chemical reactions central to plant photosynthesis, earning him the Nobel Prize in Chemistry in 1988.

D eisenhofer has spent his career investigating the design and composition of molecular structures. Through his work at the Max-Planck Institute for Biochemistry in his native Germany, Deisenhofer gained experience in the application of X-ray technology as a tool to analyze the structure of crystallized substances. During the 1980s his work aiding a group of German biologists in studying plant photosynthesis—the process whereby light energy from the sun is converted into the chemical energy that maintains life—resulted in the first-ever mapping of the structure of those molecules involved in the chemical reaction integral to the conversion process.

From Farm to Laboratory

Deisenhofer was born on September 30, 1943, in Zusamaltheim, Bavaria (now Germany), a small village located near the city of Munich. His parents, Johann and Thekla (Magg) Deisenhofer, were farmers and they raised Johann with the expectation that, as the only son in their small family, he would take over the responsibility of running the family farm when his father retired. However, the young boy showed more aptitude for academics than he did for farming, and his parents reluctantly came to the conclusion that their son was an intellectual rather than a farmer. In 1956, 13-year-old Johann was sent away to a series of

Munich, where he studied under the direction of Institute director Robert Huber and where he also became well versed in the technique of X-ray crystallography. X-ray crystallography—first used in 1912 by German scientist Max Theodore Felix von Laue to create X-ray diffraction images and employed as well during the mid-twentieth century by University of Cambridge biologists James Watson and Francis Crick as a means of confirming their model of the DNA molecule—is a technique whereby the atomic structure of a purified and crystallized water-soluble substance is studied by exposing the crystal to bursts of radiation of a predetermined and controlled wavelength. Because the internal atomic structure of water-soluble crystals is ordered into a system of lattices, the wavelength of the X-rays used to scatter the subject crystal's electrons and the measurement of the intensity of the scattered electrons can be combined to allow scientists to map out the crystal's electron and atomic structure. During his research into X-ray crystallography, Deisenhofer focused specifically on a project with fellow student Wolfgang Steigemann wherein the two Ph.D. candidates attempted to determine the atomic structure of Bovine Pancreatic Trypsin Inhibitor. Deisenhofer obtained his Ph.D. from the Max-Planck Institute in 1974, his thesis based on his successful work with Steigemann.

After graduation Deisenhofer stayed at the Max-Planck Institute, content to work alongside Huber as a research scientist. He continued to make advances in the applications for X-ray crystallography and was appointed a staff scientist at the lab in 1976. To supplement his lab work, Deisenhofer also developed a facility with computers and was able to design computer programs that could process the data obtained from the X-ray techniques and produce a map of the atomic structure of the substance in question. As the computers available to the lab became more sophisticated, so did Deisenhofer's programs. Meanwhile, the findings of his work with Steigemann on the Bovine Pancreatic Trypsin Inhibitor while a Ph.D. candidate were published to favorable peer reviews in a 1975 edition of the journal *Acta Crystallographica*.

Technical Advances Hastened Project

In 1979 Huber and his laboratory associates were joined by German biophysicist Hartmut Michel, who was engaged in the ongoing study of photosynthesis in the hopes of finding a way to obtain a thorough analysis of the molecules involved in the complex chemical-reaction process. Even in the late twentieth century, the detailed process of photosynthesis remained a mystery to scientists, although it was known that an understanding of the structure of the proteins present in cell membranes would be the key to understanding the photosynthetic light-chemical energy transfer. The reason: the light energy sent to the electron in the cell membrane fuels the reaction during which the protein transmits that energy through the cell wall in a chemical form. In September of 1981 Michel successfully hit upon a way to crystallize the photosynthetic reaction center of a purple bacterium called *Rhodopseudomonas viridis*. He came to Huber for advice, and Huber sent Michel to Deisenhofer, reasoning that with his experience in

boarding schools, and he graduated from Augsburg's Holbein Gymnasium—a gymnasium is the German equivalent of a North American high school—seven years later in 1963. After passing Germany's mandatory qualifying exam, he earned a state scholarship that allowed him to attend the Technical University in Munich. Prior to enrolling at school, however, Deisenhofer was required to perform a year and a half of compulsory military service, after which he left with the rank of private.

In Munich at last, Deisenhofer decided to focus his studies on physics, the logical outgrowth of the fascination with astronomy he had developed while observing the night sky as a boy and reading popular books by such authors as Fred Hoyle during his years at the gymnasium. The more he explored his academic major, however, the more he found himself drawn specifically to the study of solid-state physics: the study of the composition and structure of condensed matter and solids. During his hours in the laboratory he was inspired by a professor to explore the new and growing area of physics called biophysics: the study of biology using the principles of physical science. In 1971, the same year he graduated with a diploma in physics from Munich's Technical University, Deisenhofer successfully published his first scientific paper in *Physical Review Letters*. His university thesis meanwhile focused on the detection of terahertz-phonons in a ruby.

Deciding to continue his education in biophysics, in June of 1971 Deisenhofer enrolled as a doctoral candidate at the prestigious Max-Planck Institute for Biochemistry near

X-ray crystallography, Deisenhofer would find a way to analyze and map the photosynthetic reaction center.

In less than three years Deisenhofer, with the aid of several assistants, was able to use X-ray crystallography techniques to map the more than 10,000 atoms within the membrane protein complex of *Rhodopseudomonas viridis* and produce the first three-dimensional structural analysis of a photosynthetic reaction center. Measuring the X-ray diffraction was accomplished quickly with the aid of electronic devices that had replaced the standard X-ray film or more primitive devices used only a few years before. However, the actual computer modeling process went much slower. In fact, two years were needed by Deisenhofer as he repeatedly refined his model of the membrane protein. Using custom-designed software and a high-speed computer to quickly perform the myriad of calculations required to establish the location within the cell of each of the many thousands of atoms contained in that single crystallized protein, the German biophysicist painstakingly supervised the slow formation of the model, a process akin to watching a photograph develop in a darkroom. A computer graphics program he devised took the data relating to X-ray diffraction, combined it with the predetermined wavelength of the relevant radiation, and translated the resulting data into a three-dimensional computer model that has been for scientists a welcome replacement for the classic ball-and-stick models of decades past. Of the future of X-ray crystallography, Deisenhofer predicted to *Southwestern Medicine* contributor David Doremus: "Progress in this field will closely parallel progress in the development of computers. That's what makes me optimistic—computers have fantastic capabilities now compared to 10 years ago."

Amid the excitement that broke out within the scientific community at the news of Deisenhofer and Michel's accomplishment, a writer in *New Scientist* heralded the efforts of the scientists at the Max-Planck Institute as "the most important advance in the understanding of photosynthesis" since the mid-1960s, as quoted in *Notable Scientists: From 1900 to the Present*. Deisenhofer later recalled of his experience in the award-winning project in his autobiography for the Nobel e-Museum: "It was a special privilege to belong to the very small group of people who saw the structural model of this molecule grow on the screen of a computer workstation, and it is hard to describe the excitement I felt during this period of the work."

Received Nobel Prize in Chemistry

In 1988 the Royal Swedish Academy of Sciences announced that the recipients of that year's Nobel Prize in Chemistry were Deisenhofer, Huber, and Michel. In addition to paving the way for the creation of artificial photosynthetic reaction centers, their findings were acknowledged for their potential as tools to gain knowledge about other biologic functions, such as the function of cell hormones, respiration, nutrition, and nerve impulses.

The Nobel Prize changed Deisenhofer's world. Instead of working quietly in his laboratory in Germany, he was now a celebrity of sorts, and he and his award-winning colleagues were asked to present papers and appear at a host of science-related functions. In addition to the Nobel Prize, Deisenhofer was a co-recipient, with Michel, of the American Physical Society's Biological Physics Prize in 1986 and Germany's Otto-Bayer Prize two years later. His other honors include the Knight Commander's Cross of the German Order of Merit and the Bavarian Order of Merit, while honorary degrees have been conferred on him from Drury College of Springfield, Missouri, and Burdwan University of West Bengal, India. A fellow of the American Association for the Advancement of Science since 1992 and named an Argonne fellow in 2001, Deisenhofer also belongs to the American Crystallographic Association, the German and U.S. affiliates of the Biophysical Society, the German Society for Biological Chemistry, the Protein Society, Academia Europaea, Sigma Xi, and has been an honored foreign associate of the U.S. National Academy of Sciences since 1997. He also serves on the University of Chicago board of governors for the Argonne National Laboratory and was inducted into the Texas Science Hall of Fame in 2002. After moving to the United States and establishing a permanent residence in this country, Deisenhofer applied for and was granted dual U.S./German citizenship.

Leaving the Max-Planck Institute and moving to the United States in February of 1988, Deisenhofer accepted the Virginia and Edward Linthicum Distinguished Chair in Biomolecular Science at the University of Texas Southwestern Medical Center (UTSMC) at Dallas. In addition to his role as Regental Professor and professor of biology at UTSMC he also accepted a position as an investigator at the Dallas unit of the Howard Hughes Medical Institute, where he is able to promote the use of X-ray crystallography in the study of water-soluble proteins, membrane proteins, and other macromolecules and develop additional crystallographic software. Early in his tenure at the Texas research center he also met the woman who would become his wife, microbiology professor and fellow Howard Hughes Medical Institute investigator Kirsten Fischer Lindahl. Deisenhofer and Lindahl were married in 1989 and continue to make their home near Dallas, Texas.

Although Deisenhofer has a reputation for being shy and totally involved in his work, he also finds time to enjoy music and chess, swimming and skiing, and is an amateur history buff. As an outgrowth of his lab work, in 1993 he joined fellow scientist James R. Norris of the Argonne National Laboratory in writing the two-volume book *The Photosynthetic Reaction Center,* based on research emanating from his Nobel Prize-winning investigation into photosynthesis. Other research by Deisenhofer has been published in *Science, Journal of Molecular Biology, Journal of Biological Chemistry, EMBO Journal, Nature,* and other scientific journals. Among his continuing goals as a scientist is the ability to discover the rules defining the three-dimensional structure of proteins. By learning this, the biophysicist reasons, scientists will be a good deal closer to understanding the basic structural component of all life on Earth.

Books

Notable Scientists: From 1900 to the Present, Gale Group, 2001.

Periodicals

Physics Today, February 1989.

Science, November 4, 1988.

Scientific American, December 1988.

Southwestern Medicine (University of Texas Southwestern Medical Center), 1991.

Time, October 31, 1988.

Online

"Dr. Johann Deisenhofer," Texas Hall of Fame for Science, Mathematics and Technology, http://www.texasscience summit.org/halloffame/scannedinfo/newdeisenhoferbio1 .htm (December 28, 2002).

"Johann Deisenhofer–Autobiography," Nobel e-Museum, http://www.nobel.se/chemistry/laureates/1988/deisenhofer-autobio.html (February 11, 2002).

"Johann Deisenhofer, Ph.D.," University of Texas Southwestern, http://www.swnt240.swmed.edu/gradschool/webrib/ deisenhofer.htm (September 11, 2002). □

Michael Saul Dell

One of the most successful executives in the highly competitive personal computer industry, American businessman Michael Dell (born 1965) has shepherded his company—Dell Computer Corporation—from an idea hatched in his college dorm room in 1984 into one of the world's largest PC manufacturers. The company, launched by Dell with an initial investment of only $1,000, has generated revenue of tens of billions of dollars since its creation. The company has prospered while adhering to Dell's original concept of selling computers directly to its customers and avoiding middleman markups in order to keep costs down. Along the way, Dell has expanded its product line to include not only personal computers but network servers, storage systems, handheld computers, and a wide array of computer services as well.

ell, who dropped out of college at the age of 19 to pursue his dream of a direct-sales PC empire, had a net wealth hovering around $20 billion at the beginning of 2003. As chief executive officer of Dell Computer, he successfully steered his company through the treacherous economic waters of the early new millennium. To keep his company at the top of its game—a neck-and-neck competitor with Hewlett Packard for the title of world's largest PC company—Dell has launched a number of marketing innovations, not the least of which has been his skillful use of the Internet as a sales tool. As of late 2002, Dell Computer was recognized as the largest online commercial seller of PC systems with average online sales of

more than $50 million per day. Dell has also used the World Wide Web to deliver faster and more efficient service to its customers.

Bitten by the Computer Bug at an Early Age

Michael Saul Dell was born in Houston, Texas, on February 23, 1965. The son of Alexander (an orthodontist) and Lorraine Dell (a stockbroker), he first got interested in computers when he was in the seventh grade. In an interview with Esther Wang of the *Daily Texan,* Dell recalled: "Computers were just starting to come into being in terms of the personal computer in the late '70s, early '80s. I got some exposure to the first personal computers, became really interested in the product and what I could envision about how that could change society and business and culture and education and everything else, and that caught my interest pretty early." He got his first computer—an Apple II—in 1979 when he was 14. Dell also was a born entrepreneur, earning a quick $2,000 from a stamp and baseball card trading enterprise he operated through the mail when he was only 12 years old. He also found innovative ways to drum up business for the newspaper delivery route he operated while in high school. Dell would obtain the names and addresses of newlyweds in his delivery area and mail them an introductory offer of two weeks' free service. His clever sales strategy earned him more than $18,000, enough to buy his own fully-equipped BMW even before he was old enough to drive.

Although he was a fairly good student, Dell grew impatient with the slow pace of school and at the age of 8 sent by mail for information about obtaining a high school equivalency diploma, hoping that he might be able to bypass the rest of his public school obligation. His parents, however, balked at this notion and insisted that Michael complete his schooling conventionally. After he graduated from high school, Michael was sent to the University of Texas at Austin, where his parents hoped he might eventually study to be a doctor. It was during his freshman year in college that Dell launched his direct sales computer business. He had already gained some experience in taking apart and then reassembling computers and soon realized that he could make money by adding components to basic units and selling them for a profit. With an initial investment of $1,000 he began operating his business out of his dorm room, much to the chagrin of his roommates, who at one point barricaded his door with piles of computer equipment. His roommates' enmity notwithstanding, Dell's business skyrocketed. By the end of his freshman year, he was taking in roughly $80,000 a month.

Incorporated as PCs Unlimited

In the summer of 1984 Dell incorporated his business as PCs Unlimited and moved its headquarters from his dormitory room to a storefront in Austin. In its first year of business, the company sold computer equipment manufactured by other computer companies, such as IBM and Compaq, to which were added various optional features. In July 1985, PCs Unlimited introduced its first proprietary model, the Turbo PC, which featured the Intel 8088 processor and operated at 8 Mhz. To help expand his business, Dell borrowed money from his family but was soon able to repay it as his company's annual sales climbed to the $30 million mark. In 1987 Dell renamed his company Dell Computer Corporation and a year later took it public with an initial offering of 3.5 million shares at $8.50 each. By the end of 1988, Dell's annual sales had reached $159 million.

The late 1980s brought some major changes in Dell's personal life, even as his fledgling computer company continued to expand at an exponential rate. In February 1988 he was introduced to Susan Lieberman, a real estate agent who had recently relocated to Austin from Dallas. The daughter of noted Baylor University Medical Center cancer surgeon Zelig "Zeke" Lieberman, Susan had grown up in the affluent North Dallas neighborhood of Russwood Acres. After graduating from W.T. White High School, she enrolled at Arizona State University to study fashion design and merchandising. Returning to Texas, Lieberman decided against a career in fashion and following the lead of her older brother Steve got into real estate, moving to Austin to work for Trammell Crow, a major real estate company. She and Dell met at a North Austin bistro for lunch and in the spring of 1989 they were engaged. They married on October 28, 1989.

Direct-Sales Strategy Key to Success

At the heart of his computer company's success has been its adherence to Dell's original concept of a direct-

sales model. Customers can place their orders by calling Dell's toll-free number or by logging on to the company's Web site. Their orders produce a made-to-order computer that is shipped within 36 hours. Because the company builds only to order, it has managed to keep its inventory to less than 6 percent of sales. Further slashing its inventories, Dell maintains a close relationship with most of its suppliers, many of whom have built new facilities close to Dell's headquarters outside of Austin.

By 1993 Dell's annual sales had climbed to $2 billion, although the company reported a loss of $36 million for the fiscal year, which ended January 31, 1994. That same year, Dell joined the ranks of the top five computer system manufacturers worldwide. The following year the company powered back with a profit of $149 million.

Dell was quick to recognize the potential of the Internet as a marketing tool. By 1996 the company's Web site (http://www.dell.com) was booking orders from customers. In the late 1990s Dell appeared on the company's television commercials to plug the company's newly created online technical support called "E-Support-Direct from Dell." Of the company's new advertising strategy and its growing use of the World Wide Web as a selling tool, one Dell executive said "it will leverage our position on the Internet and show how it's easier for customers to do business with us." Dell's Internet strategy paid off well, favorably impressing major customers like the Ford Motor Company. In September 1999, Ford's CEO observed: "We can interact much, much more efficiently with them [Dell] than with their rivals."

Kept Close Ties to Suppliers

Dell has continued to refine his company's Internet strategy, moving aggressively to maintain close communications with Dell's key suppliers. By the dawn of the new millennium the company had connected 90 percent of its suppliers onto Dell's factory floors via the World Wide Web, allowing suppliers to see current information on orders and thus replenish supplies only as needed. Using this and other techniques, Dell was able to cut its inventories to a mere five days' worth in 2000, a sharp reduction from 13 days' worth in 1997. By contrast rival Compaq Computer (since merged into Hewlett Packard) had more than three weeks of inventories on hand in the first quarter of 2001.

Another important element in Dell's growth strategy has been its expansion into overseas markets. As early as 1987, the company opened a subsidiary to serve the United Kingdom. In 1990 Dell opened a manufacturing facility in Limerick, Ireland, to build computers for sale in its European, Middle Eastern, and African markets. In 1993 the company expanded into the Asia-Pacific region with the opening of subsidiaries in Australia and Japan. This was followed in 1996 with the opening of an Asia-Pacific manufacturing center in Penang, Malaysia. To serve its growing market in China, Dell in 1998 opened a production center in Xiamen, China. The following year saw the opening of a factory in El Dorado do Sul, Brazil, to serve Dell's growing Latin American market.

Interviewed in October 2002 by Esther Wang of the *Daily Texan,* Dell was asked what it was that set his company apart from its competitors. In response, he pointed out that "we took a very different approach to customers. Our business, I think, understood and anticipated customer needs much better than our competitors," most of which sold their products through intermediaries and dealers, "which certainly was the industry started, but it's not the way it's evolved. Our business system has proven to be more responsive and more efficient in providing what customers want."

Expanded Product Line

Although Dell's initial success was in marketing customized personal computers, Michael Dell recognized that to continue to grow, his company would have to look beyond PCs. Underlining the need for a broader product line to reinvigorate company results was Dell's fiscal 2001 decline in sales, the first in company history. The decline was relatively small, falling from $31.9 billion in fiscal 2000 to about $31.2 billion in fiscal 2001. To diversify its product line, Dell in May 2002 introduced two new non-PC products—a big screen projector and a new line of the company's most popular server, a computer that runs PC networks. Late in 2001, to broaden its line of business devices, Dell began reselling data-storage machines manufactured by EMC Corp. It also began selling computer-network switches to compete with 3Com Corporation and Cisco.

Interviewed in November 2002 by Maria Bartiromo of the CNBC cable television network, Dell was asked how his company had managed to do so well during the economic slump of the early new millennium while the rest of the industry continued to struggle. "I think it's pretty simple," Dell replied. "We deliver better value to customers with a business model that's really focused on direct relationships. We've got a very efficient supply chain. We turn our inventory 99 times during the quarter. And so when you've got great service, great products, great value, customers beat a path to your door."

Books

Business Leader Profiles for Students, Vol. 1, Gale Research, 1999.
Complete Marquis Who's Who, Marquis Who's Who, 2001.
Gale Encyclopedia of E-Commerce, Gale Group, 2002.
Gale Encyclopedia of U.S. Economic History, Gale Group, 1999.
Newsmakers, Issue 2, Gale Research, 1996.

Periodicals

Business Week, May 14, 2001.
CNBC/Dow Jones Business Video, November 14, 2002.
Daily Texan, October 21, 2002.
Fortune, September 8, 1997.
Money, November 1, 2002.
Texas Monthly, August 2000.
Toronto Star, May 17, 2002.

Online

"Dell Computer Corporation," *Hoover's Online,* http://www.hoovers.com/annuals/3/0,2168,13193,00.html (February 10, 2003).

"Dell Computer Corporation," *Hoover's Online,* http://www.hoovers.com/quarterlies/3/0,2167,13193,00.html (February 10, 2003).
"Dell History," *Dell Computer Corporation,* http://www.dell.com/us/en/gen/corporate/access_history_fact_pak.htm (February 9, 2003).
"Welcome," *Dell Computer Corporation,* http://www.dell.com/us/en/gen/corporate/michael.htm (February 9, 2003). □

Maya Deren

Maya Deren (1917–1961) wore many hats in her brief lifetime: avant-garde filmmaker, documentarian, author, and Voudoun priestess, to name a few. Her influence, especially in independent film, has not only endured but also increased in the decades following her death. Deren was a seminal figure among independent filmmakers about whom legends sprung. Her reputation as a filmmaker rests on only seven short completed films in her lifetime and five unfinished films, though one was edited and released after her death. In the early 21st century Deren, who by then had been dead for more than 40 years, was still discussed as a fresh voice and a "past master who still matters," as the magazine *Utne Reader* declared her.

Early Years

Deren was born Eleanora Solomonovna Derenkovsky on April 29, 1917, in Kiev, Ukraine, less than two months after the Russian Revolution that forced the Tsar's abdication (but prior to the Bolshevik takeover). Her parents were members of Kiev's intelligentsia: her mother, Marie, had studied music and her father, Solomon, was a psychiatrist. The period between 1917 and 1922, Deren's early years, was a time of political and economic upheaval in Russia and Ukraine. The five-year span saw the Tsar's abdication; the two revolutions of 1917, the second of which brought the Bolsheviks to power; Russia's capitulation in the First World War; the civil war; and the formation of the Soviet Union. Furthermore, Ukraine, which had been part of the tsarist empire, declared itself an independent nation on January 22, 1918, but in 1922 it became a constituent republic of the Union of Soviet Socialist Republics (USSR). Despite all of this, the Derenkovsky family led a relatively secure life.

All of that changed by 1922. The economy was in such a shambles that even Lenin had retreated from hardline communism toward a "New Economic Policy." A more important factor in the Derenkovskys' decision to emigrate was a recurrence of pogroms (organized massacres of Jews) in Ukraine. The family eventually settled in Syracuse, New York, where Solomon Derenkovsky's brother lived. After a period of adjustment Solomon Derenkovsky set up his psychiatric practice and the family name was shortened to Deren.

Young Eleanora Deren attended primary school in Syracuse until 1930 when she was sent to Switzerland to attend Ecole Internationale de Geneve, which was founded under the auspices of the League of Nations (the immediate predecessor of the United Nations). Deren remained in Switzerland for three years studying French, German, and Russian. When she returned to the United States in 1933 she enrolled at Syracuse University, where she studied journalism until 1935. At this time Deren joined the Young People's Socialist League, a Trotskyite organization. Among the political activists she became involved with was Gregory Bardacke, whom she married in 1935. Deren and Bardacke moved to New York City, and Deren transferred to New York University (NYU) from which she graduated in 1936. At NYU Deren first became interested in photography and film. Deren then went on to study literature at Smith College in Northampton, Massachusetts; she was awarded an M.A. in 1939. By then Deren and Bardacke had divorced. Deren's initial career path was the publishing industry. She worked briefly as a writers' and publishers' factotum, all the while writing poetry herself.

Independent Filmmaker

Soon she met and began working as a secretary for Katherine Dunham, who was to have a profound influence on the directions Deren's career would take. Dunham was a choreographer and an anthropologist who had founded an African American dance company. It was while working for Dunham in Los Angeles in 1941, where Deren lived with her mother (Deren's parents ultimately divorced), that she met Alexander Hammid; ten years Deren's senior, he became another influence on her career. Hammid (original name Hackenschmied) was a Czechoslovakian refugee who came to the United States to work as a motion picture photographer for "The March of Time" newsreels. Deren and Hammid were married in 1942 and it was he who provided the stimulus for Deren's filmic imagination. During this time, possibly at Hammid's suggestion, Deren changed her first name to Maya, the Sanskrit word for illusion.

At the time of her marriage Deren was primarily a writer, with poetry, newspaper articles, short stories, and essays to her credit. One of her essays, written no doubt under the eye of Dunham, discussed religious possession in dancing—a theme that would later command her attention. In 1943 Solomon Deren died and left Deren a small inheritance with which she purchased a second-hand Bolex 16mm camera, which she and Hamid used to make the film *Meshes in the Afternoon*. While *Meshes in the Afternoon* is considered her first film by most film historians, filmmaker Stan Brakhage in his essay on Deren (published in *Film at Wit's End*) discussed the idea that a study of the photography reveals it is primarily Hammid's film: "For all the unusual things that happen within the film, its whole style of photography betrays the slick, polished, penultimate craftsmanship of the old European sensibility for which Sasha [Hammid] was known." Nevertheless Brakhage does ac-

knowledge "the real force of the film came from Maya herself."

Deren and Hammid moved to New York City where her electric personality really took off. Soon she was regularly screening *Meshes in the Afternoon* and lecturing the audience on independent filmmaking. This caused a natural friction with Hammid who felt he was being slighted. In 1943 Deren began another film, *Witch's Cradle,* but it remained unfinished. The most notable aspects of the film were that it was shot at an art gallery where a surrealist exhibition was taking place and that it included Marcel Duchamp. Deren followed up this attempt with the 15-minute film, *At Land,* which featured Deren herself on different landscapes: merticulously crawling on rocks, walking along what appears to be a cart path with a man who changes appearances. The film included brief appearances by poet and critic Parker Tyler, composer John Cage, and Hammid.

In 1945 Deren and Hammid decided to make a second film together in which Hammid would take the lead in directing and filming. The result was the 30-minute *The Private Life of a Cat.* Here again Stan Brakhage, who was a friend and something of a protégé of Deren, disputes the claim of film historians who say that Deren's imput was minimal. However *The Private Life of a Cat* did not boost Hammid's reputation the way *Meshes* had lifted Deren's. Also in 1945 Deren made *A Study in Choreography for Camera,* a 2 1/2-minute film that featured choreographer Talley Beatty who was also credited as co-director.

1946 was a busy year for Deren. She rented the Provincetown Playhouse n New York City and screened *Meshes in the Afternoon, At Land,* and *A Study in Choreography for Camera.* The program, which ran several evenings, was titled "Three Abandoned Films." She published *An Anagram of Art, Form, and Film* and received a Guggenheim Fellowship for "Creative Work in the Field of Motion Pictures." Deren was the first filmmaker to be awarded a Guggenheim fellowship. That year Deren also completed *Ritual in Transfigured Time.*

Voudoun Priestess

In 1947 she presented *Meshes in the Afternoon* at the Cannes Film Festival where it won the Grand Prix International in the category of 16mm Film, Experimental Class. It was the first time the award went to a film produced in the United States and the first time a female director was honored. Deren and Hammid were divorced that year, and Deren began making trips to Haiti to observe and film Voudoun rituals and dance. The result was that over the next eight years her focus began to shift away from film and onto Voudoun culture. Deren's involvement with Voudoun became the source of most of the legends that surrounded her life.

In between trips to Haiti, Deren completed *Meditation on Violence* (1948). This was to be her only completed film for the next seven years as she spent a total of nearly two years in Haiti working on her Voudoun ritual project. In 1949 she began but left unfinished *Medusa,* and in 1951 she abandoned *Ensemble for Somnambulists.* By time that she had met and fallen in love with a young Japanese musician, Teiji Ito. Ito was 15 years old at the time of their meeting (Deren was 43), and Deren became both his mentor and lover; they lived together in New York and traveled to Haiti. In 1953 Deren published *Divine Horsemen: The Living Gods of Haiti,* a study of Haitian deities, rituals, and practices. The work had the assistance of anthropologist Gregory Bateson and was edited by Joseph Campbell. In the book Deren defined myth as "facts of the mind made manifest in a fiction of matter." When the book was republished in 1970 Campbell wrote a second foreword (he had also written a foreword to the first edition) in which he summed up the work by saying: "It has always been my finding that the poet and the artist are better qualified both by temperament and by training to intuit and interpret the sense of the mythological figure than the university-trained empiricist. And rereading today, after twenty years, Maya Deren's celebration of the gods by whom her own life and personality were transformed, I am reconfirmed in that finding; reconfirmed, also, in my long-held belief that this little volume is the most illuminating introduction that has yet been rendered to the whole marvel of the Haitian *mystères* as 'facts of the mind.' "

By the time Deren had finished filming in Haiti she had shot more than 18,000 feet of film, but as Brakhage attests the amount of footage overwhelmed Deren and she could not complete the job of editing. Her own Voudoun practice continued, however, which may have been the reason for her inability to edit the footage. The deeper Deren became involved in the religion the harder it was for her to believe in the efficacy of the film document of the rituals. Deren's practice included regular dance rituals in her apartment as well as performing a Voudoun ritual at the marriage of dancer Geoffrey Holder, whereupon she went into a trance, witnessed by Brakhage, in which she displayed amazing physical strength and fits of violence. But Deren's Voudoun legend did not end there.

Final Film

Her final film, *The Very Eye of Night,* was completed in 1955, but because of financial problems it did not premiere until 1959. The film had its premiere in Port-au-Prince, Haiti, with a soundtrack by Teiji Ito. The delay caused a rift between Deren and her backer, lyricist John Latouche, with the supposed result being that Deren put a Voudoun curse on Latouche, who died soon afterward.

In the late 1950s Deren established the Creative Film Foundation and in 1960 she married Teiji Ito. She had also begun the "Haiku Film Project," but it never went beyond the planning stage. In 1961 Deren and Ito traveled to New England to claim his inheritance following the death of his father. Ito's family sought to block the claim and Deren became apoplectic (showing signs of a stroke). The fit, whether Voudoun inspired or not, caused her to have a cerebral hemmorage, and she lapsed into a two-week coma from which she never awoke. Deren died on October 13, 1961, in New York City. The fact that it was Friday the 13th also contributed to her legend. Some believe she was the victim of a counter-curse placed on her by friends of Latouche. Another possible (and more rational) cause of her stroke was the so-called vitamin shots Deren had been receiving. These contained amphetamines.

After her death, the Haitian footage was offered to many filmmakers to edit, but all refused. In the 1980s Teiji Ito and his new wife Cherel completed the editing process and, with a soundtrack by Ito, the completed film became *Divine Horsemen.* In 1985 the American Film Institute established the Maya Deren Award for independent filmmaking.

Books

Brakhage, Stan, *Film at Wit's End: Eight Avant-Garde Filmmakers,* McPherson & Company, 1989.
Deren, Maya, *Divine Horsemen: The Living Gods of Haiti,* McPherson & Company, 1953, 1970.

Periodicals

Utne Reader, November–December 1991.

Online

"The Life of Maya Deren," Zeitgeist Films, http://www.zeitgeistfilms.com/current/mayaderen/mayaderenbio.html (January 20, 2003).
"Maya Deren," Internet Movie Database, http://us.imdb.com/Name?Deren, + Maya (January 27, 2003). □

E

John Elway

Considered by some to be the greatest modern American football player, John Elway (born 1960) played in the position of quarterback for the Denver Broncos for 16 years, leading his team to two consecutive Super Bowl wins before retiring in 1999.

Born to Play Ball

John Elway was born in Port Angeles, Washington, on June 28, 1960. His twin sister, Jana, was born 11 minutes after him, and they joined their older sister, Lee Ann, who had been born 18 months beforehand. Elway's father, Jack, made a living as a college football coach, and he encouraged his children to be athletic from an early age. Elway's family fostered healthy competition among the siblings and they got along well; in later years, Elway recalled that playing with his sisters as a boy formed some of his happiest memories. Jack Elway remembered that the twins shared a special bond, even before they could walk or talk, "jabbering at each other in that special language twins have," quoted Michael BeDan in the *Rocky Mountain News.*

Even as a baby, Elway seemed naturally inclined to play, and when he was old enough to get on his feet, he wore out an average of a pair of sneakers every month. His sister Lee Ann remembered that his competitive spirit sometimes got in the way of having a good time while playing with him. "I love John a lot," she told Adam Schefter in the *Denver Post,* "But it wasn't always fun playing with him

because he took everything so seriously. He was just so competitive, even back then."

Meanwhile, Elway's father taught him how to play baseball in the back yard. He recognized that his son had a talent, and he aimed to nurture it. While Elway's sisters went on skiing trips, his father made him stay home for fear that he would injure himself seriously before he had a chance to play competitive sports. Until he was in the fourth grade, Elway played baseball and basketball. Then, before he entered fifth grade, his parents allowed him to play football, and there his true talent shined. In his very first game, he ran circles around the opposing team's members, scoring four touchdowns by himself. A basketball coach who was present at the game remarked to Jack Elway, as reported Adam Schefter in the *Denver Post,* "Either every kid on that field is the worst football player I've ever seen or your boy is the greatest player I've ever seen."

The family moved a great deal while Elway was growing up, as his father traveled from one college coaching position to another. Leaving Port Angeles, the family next settled in Missoula, Montana, then headed back to Washington state to live in the town of Pullman, Washington, before finally settling for good in Southern California.

Recruited by 65 Different Colleges

The young Elway learned plenty about the game of football by watching the games that his father coached at Montana State, Washington State, and California State University at Northridge. Elway often acted as ball boy for these games, and he got a chance to see a great many games up close. A star player on his high school football team, Elway attracted the attention of college athletics recruiters, eventually being courted by no less than 65 different schools. He also played high school baseball, leading the team to the

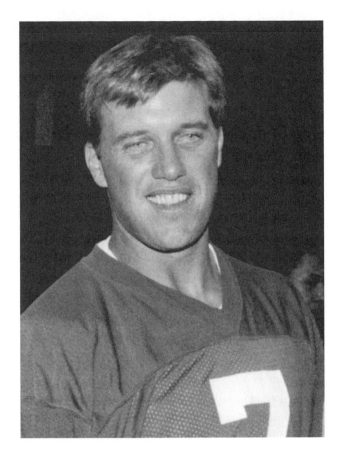

Los Angeles City championship. His outstanding perform-ance on the baseball team attracted the attention of scouts for the Kansas City Royals baseball team, which selected him for the summer draft in 1979. Elway decidedly settled on college at Stanford University, in Stanford, California. At Stanford, he immediately established a reputation as being one of the best football players in the history of the school.

Highlights of Elway's college football career included setting five major NCAA Division 1-A records, as well as nine major Pac-10 records. Of his 1,243 college career passes, Elway completed a record 774, or 62.1 percent, traveling 9,349 yards to make 77 touchdown passes. Elway also found the time to play baseball with the New York Yankees' Oneonta single-A farm team. He played his last baseball season in his second year at Stanford. Elway's twin sister, Jana, also attended college at Stanford University, where she played tennis for the school team. She went on to become a professional tennis instructor.

Became a Top Player for the
Denver Broncos

Elway became an All-American college football star at Stanford before graduating in 1983 with a degree in eco-nomics. He was the number one draft pick among profes-sional football teams in the National Football League (NFL) and proceeded to become a quarterback for the Denver Broncos. He would hold this position for his entire profes-sional football career.

Elway quickly distinguished himself as one of the best players on the Broncos' team. In 1985, he shattered the Broncos single-season record for attempts (605), comple-tions (327), passing yards (3,891), and more. In 1986, Elway led the Broncos to their first American Football Conference (AFC) Championship in almost ten years. In 1987, Elway was named the NFL's Most Valuable Player (MVP) and was named to the *Sporting News* All-NFL team. He was also named the Colorado Pro Athlete of the Year by the Colorado Sports Hall of Fame and was voted the Broncos' offensive MVP. Playing in Super Bowl XXII, he made history by becoming the first quarterback in a Super Bowl to catch a pass.

The beginning of 1989 saw Elway at his second Super Bowl in which he scored the only touchdown made by his team. In spite of a persistent shoulder injury, Elway led his team in touchdowns in 1991, with a then career high of six. In the 1992 off-season, he had his shoulder injury corrected by arthroscopic surgery. In the 1992 regular season, Elway was back in action and better than ever throwing the longest touchdown pass of his career, 80 yards.

In 1993, Elway was named AFC MVP by the NFL Play-ers Association, as well as AFC Offensive Player of the Year by United Press International (UPI) and AFC Player of the Year by *Football News.* Also this year he was named to the all-AFC team by UPI and *Football News,* as well as second team all-NFL by the Associated Press, *College and Pro Foot-ball Weekly,* and *Football Digest.* In 1995, Elway scored 26 touchdowns, made 14 interceptions, and threw for more than 300 yards five separate times—all career bests for him. His 26 touchdowns also set a record for the Broncos. He repeated this performance in 1996 with 26 touchdowns and 14 interceptions. Also in 1996, he set Broncos records for most games played (192) and most consecutive games scor-ing touchdown passes (15).

Recognition for Elway's achievements came yet again in 1997, when he received the NFL Players Association Mackey Award as the best quarterback in the AFC. Also in 1997, Elway helped the Broncos' offense become the best in the NFL for the second season in a row.

Playing with the Broncos, Elway became famous for dramatic, last-minute game-winning scores. He also topped the NFL by making first place in the history of the league in victories by a starting quarterback, first in rushing attempts by a quarterback.

During his 16 years with the Broncos, Elway played in four Super Bowls, the final two of which, Super Bowl XXXII and Super Bowl XXXIII, his team won. Also during his career with the Broncos, Elway became only the second player in NFL history to throw for over 50,000 yards, and he topped the NFL in victories for a starting quarterback and in rushing attempts by a quarterback.

During the height of his popularity, Elway was an inter-nationally recognized star: he regularly stopped to sign au-tographs wherever he went, including Europe and Asia. He took to wearing sunglasses while out in public and walking with his head down in an effort not to be recognized. He also had to change his telephone number every month or so to avoid getting thousands of telephone calls.

Retired as a Top Player in the NFL

Looking ahead to his retirement from football, Elway opened an automobile dealership in the Denver area in the 1990s. This business grew to include seven auto franchises by the turn of the century. He also became an active philanthropist, donating time and money to victims of child abuse and the Make-A-Wish Foundation. Elway decided to retire in 1999, after two Super Bowl wins in a row and 16 years as a Broncos quarterback.

Immediately following Elway's retirement announcement, the Denver Broncos Ring of Fame Committee waved its usual five-year waiting time after a player retires from the team to induct Elway into the Ring of Fame. The purpose of the Ring of Fame is to honor Broncos players and administrators who have made outstanding contributions to the team. The committee also retired Elway's jersey number, seven, making him the third player in Broncos history to have his number retired. Elway was inducted and his number retired in a halftime ceremony at Mile High Stadium in Colorado on September 13, 1999.

In March 2001, Elway sold most of his stake in his chain of auto dealerships, earning $82.5 million for the sale. Uneasy in retirement, Elway, at 42 years old, wasn't ready to turn to a life of leisure. "I didn't really know what to do," he told *Sports Illustrated*'s Josh Elliott. "I was searching for something, and that was pretty tough." He found his answer in the form of a part ownership stake in an Arena Football League (AFL) team called the Colorado Crush. The team, which intendeed to begin regularly scheduled games in 2003, gave Elway the spirit of competition and the role in a business for which he had been searching. Best of all, it allowed Elway to stay in the game of football.

Bowed by Tragedy

Elway's happiness was soon dampened by tragedy. Elway's father, Jack, died of a heart attack in April 2001. The two were very close; Elway considered his father his best friend, and Jack was the earliest supporter of Elway's football career. Elway blamed part of his father's illness on stress brought on by news that Elway's twin sister, Jana, had been diagnosed with lung cancer.

Tragedy again struck the Elway family in 2002. In July, his twin sister, Jana Elway-Sever, who had become a school teacher in San Jose, California, died after a two-year battle with lung cancer. She was 42 years old. She had been seriously ill at the time of Jack Elway's death the previous year, although she had managed to attend the funeral service.

Learned that Winning Is Not Everything

As if the deaths of Elway's father and sister had not brought enough heartache, his wife Janet moved out soon after Jana's death, taking the couple's four children with her. Elway and Janet had been married 18 years. It was a wakeup call for the football star, who realized that the pressures of his football career, and his later career as a businessperson, had stressed his family life to the breaking point.

Elway learned to shift his priorities, making more time for his family. He began to go to Janet's rented house when she was not home to pull weeds from her garden. He sent her roses every week and took the kids out for shopping trips and other excursions—things he had not done in earlier years. Responding to Elway's attentions, Janet and the kids moved back in with him within a month. Elway told *Sports Illustrated*'s Rick Reilly soon afterwards that his shift in attitude was permanent. "I'm trying to do things . . . that aren't necessarily about achieving. I want to put my family first from now on."

Periodicals

Denver Post, November 28, 1996; May 12, 1999; July 25, 2002.
Rocky Mountain News, July 25, 2002.
Sports Illustrated, June 24, 2002; August 19, 2002. .

Online

"John Elway," *NFL.com,* http://www.nfl.com (March 11, 2003).
☐

Enchi Fumiko Ueda

Enchi Fumiko Ueda (1905–1986) achieved literary fame in post-World War II Japan as a feminist before her time. Enchi typically portrayed the subordination of women by paternalistic Japanese society through supernatural themes in dreamlike settings. Her writings frequently included references to traditional Japanese texts, with which she had become familiar through her work as a translator of such premodern writings as *The Tale of Genji* into modern Japanese. Her literary allusions to traditional texts covered a wide range of genres, including tales of fiction, history, and war.

Early Life

Enchi Fumiko Ueda was born on October 2, 1905, in Tokyo, Japan. Her father was Ueda Kazutoshi (1867–1937), a professor of linguistics and philology at Tokyo University. Enchi's paternal grandmother, who was reportedly a good storyteller, introduced her granddaughter to the kabuki theatre.

As a young girl, Enchi enjoyed kabuki and tales from the novels of the late Edo period (1600–1867). Her early reading included *The Tale of Genji (Genji monogatari),* Edo novels, and modern fiction. By the time she was 13, she was reading Oscar Wilde, Edgar Allen Poe, Izumi Kyoka, Nagai Kafu, Akutagawa Ryunosuke, and Tanizaki Junichiro.

From 1918 to 1922, Enchi attended the girl's middle school at Japan Women's University. But she abandoned her studies at the middle school to study drama. Her interest in the theatre was encouraged by her father, and as a young woman, she attended the lectures of Osanai Kaoru, a noted modern Japanese dramatist. She also received private instruction, lasting until she married, in English, French, and Chinese literature.

In 1926, the twenty-one year-old Enchi published a one-act play entitled "A Birthplace" that was received well by critics. "A Birthplace" was followed two years later (1928) by "A Noisy Night in Late Spring," which was subsequently staged at the Tsukiji Little Theatre in Tokyo.

In 1930, the twenty-five-year-old Enchi married Enchi Yoshimatsu, a journalist. Following their daughter's birth, Enchi began writing novels. But early attempts in this genre, including *The Words Like the Wind* (1939), *The Treasures of Heaven and Sea* (1940), and *Spring and Autumn* (1943), failed to meet with any financial success.

In World War II, Enchi lost her property during the bombing of Tokyo. She also had a cancer operation about this time, from which she was slow to recover. Her writing lapsed until around 1951.

Post War Success

Following the war, with the loss of all her property, Enchi began writing about the oppressiveness of domestic life. Although Japan's postwar constitution guaranteed gender equality, discrimination based on gender continued unabated at all levels of society in the years immediately following the war. Most women could neither support a family nor rise to the top of their chosen professions. Women were instead largely relegated to roles as mothers and wives. In 1953, Enchi's story "Starving Days," about family misfortune and deprivation, won the Women's Literature Prize.

The Waiting Years

Enchi's *The Waiting Years,* written between 1949 and 1957, looked at the sufferings of women at the hands of the patriarchal family system. The novel is set between the 1880s and 1920s—a time when the patriarchal social and political order was evolving.

In the novel, the protagonist, Tomo, is married at the age of 15 to a government official. Later, after her husband has become a high level prefectural officer, he persuades her to allow him to keep a mistress in their home. The following passage from the novel describes Tomo's humiliation as her husband instructs her how to find a mistress for him.

"To call the girl a concubine would be making too much of it," he had said to Tomo. "She'll be a maid for you, too. . . . It's a good idea, surely, to have a young woman with a pleasant disposition about the house so that you can train her to look after things for you when you're out calling. That's why I don't want to lower the tone of the household by bringing in a geisha or some other woman of that type. I trust you, and I leave everything to you, so use your good sense to find a young—as far as possible inexperienced—girl. Here, use this for your expenses."

But Tomo's husband is not satisfied with one mistress and eventually takes a second. Later he seduces his son's

wife. Through the repeated humiliations, however, Tomo remains mistress of the household. On her death bed, she tells her husband she does not wish to be buried and instead asks to be dumped into the sea. Only at that point, after forty years of marriage, does Tomo's husband realize how much he has made her suffer.

Voices from the Past

In *Masks* (1958), Enchi creates a protagonist based on a witch-like character in the *The Tale of Genji*. The heroine of *Masks* has hopes that her son will atone for the torments her husband has caused her. But her hopes are shattered with his premature death. The woman then prevails upon her daughter-in-law to have a son to replace the one she has lost. The daughter-in-law later dies after giving birth to the son. For the mother-in-law, a daughter-in-law flawed by male domination is replaced by an untainted male heir.

In Enchi's novels, her female characters often discover suppressed shamanesses or mediums within themselves. Many of Enchi's writings attempt to supplement the voices of the women of the medieval period with modern ones of defiance. Unlike the ancient Japanese shamanesses who set out to wreak revenge on their female rivals, however, Enchi's women seek their retribution against men.

Enchi saw in Shintoism, a Japanese belief system that employed female shamanesses, a path to empowerment for women. Enchi contrasted the traditions of female subjugation in Buddhism with the indigenous Japanese Shinto religion, which left women with more power. Although modern Japanese tend to find the beliefs of Buddhism and Shintoism complementary rather than in opposition to each other, Enchi preferred to see the two belief systems in conflict. Shamanesses had appeared in the earliest Japanese folk tales, through the writings of the medieval period and beyond; however, the female shaman was traditionally a marginalized character, who existed on the outskirts of mainstream society.

Enchi seemed to have a particular fondness for writings by women of the Heian era (794–1185), especially *The Tale of Genji*, which was written by a well educated lady-in-waiting in the imperial court of the late tenth and early eleventh centuries. (Enchi would work for six years on the *Enchi Genji*, her 10-volume modern translation of *The Tale of Genji*.) The Heian era marked the emergence of Japanese women as writers of verse, fiction, and poetic diaries. These works frequently served as vehicles for the writers to criticize the subordination of women in their society.

The patriarchal Japanese society of the Heian era and the traditional practice of polygamy in the royal court left many women writers of the time resentful. Enchi was able to find a modern voice that perpetuated the tradition of women writers into the twentieth century by making her characters mediums for the mythic woman of the past. In Enchi's *The Tale of an Enchantress* (1965), she tells the story of a consort to a Heian emperor. The book won the 1966 Women's Literature Prize.

Enchi's novel *A Tale of False Oracles* (1959–1965; *Namamiko monogatari)* was one of the first to deal exclusively with female mediums and possession by spirits. Narrated in the first person, the story at first seems to be told with authority, but eventually two other narrators—one from the Heian period and another who paraphrases events in the Heian-era text being referenced—join in telling the story, with the result that the original narrator becomes discredited as a false-medium.

The influence on Enchi of the kabuki theater, where all roles were assumed by male actors, comes through in her fascination with the sort of androgynous environments that appealed to many of the women writers of the Heian era—women who were dissatisfied with the male-dominated society. Although Enchi frequently employed androgynous characters in her writing, she did not develop the concept. But the frequent appearance of androgynes in her books has suggested to some critics that she may have felt they represented a wholeness lacking in the lives of women subjugated by men.

Aging Women and Sexual Desire

In *Growing Fog* (1976), Enchi writes of an aging woman who attempts to revive her waning sexuality through liaisons with younger men. In Enchi's novel, sexual desire brings vitality and helps to overcome the fear of death.

Enchi's older women are caught between their passion and anger. On the one hand they are overwhelmed by physical desire, but at the same time they are burdened by self-loathing. As they age, they watch themselves lose their physical attractiveness while they continue to have sexual yearnings. There is a basic inequality for Enchi between men and women when they face advanced age in that men can still achieve paternity, while maternity is not an option for women.

Criticism

Literary critic S. Yumiko Hulvey has divided the themes in Enchi's work into three developmental stages. In the first, Enchi's women endure male subjugation, with only a faint hint of the presence of a female shamaness. Writings in this category included *The Waiting Years,* "Skeletons of Men," "Enchantress," and "A Bond for Two Lifetimes—Gleanings." In the second stage, middle-aged women find inner strength by tapping into the shamanistic powers of the female medium. Hulvey places Enchi's *Masks* and *A Tale of False Oracles* at this developmental stage. In Hulvey's third stage, elderly women vacillate between illusion and reality in their attempts to understand sexual desire. Hulvey assigns Enchi's trilogy *Wandering Spirit,* "The Voice of a Snake," "The Old Woman Who Eats Flowers," and *Colored Mist* to this stage.

In *Dangerous Women, Deadly Words,* literary critic Nina Cornyetz argues that the psychological depths of Enchi's characters were complicated by historical depths. For Cornyetz, it is the collective female past coupled with the individual pasts of Enchi's characters that gives rise to the actions in the narrative. The historical subordination of women thus becomes a past that produces the present. But, as Cornyetz notes, Enchi's characters do not abandon them-

selves to their fates; instead they confront the constraints of their subordination.

Enchi received numerous Japanese literary prizes, including the Bunka Kunsho, the highest award made to an individual, in 1985 from Emperor Hirohito. Before her death on November 14, 1986, of heart failure, she was elected to the Japan Art Academy. Few of Enchi's works have been translated out of Japanese.

Books

Cornyetz, Nina, *Dangerous Women, Deadly Words: Phallic Fantasy and Modernity in Three Japanese Writers,* Stanford University Press, 1999.

Online

"Enchi Fumiko," http://www.willamette.edu/~rloftus/enchi.htm (February 2003).

Excerpts from *The Waiting Years,* translated by John Bester, http://www.thejapanpage.com/html/book_directory/Detailed/203.shtml (February 2003).

Hulvey, S. Yumiko, "The Intertextual Fabric of Narratives by Enchi Fumiko," http://www.inform.umd.edu/EdRes/Colleges/ARHU/Depts/CompLit/cmltgrad/JSchaub/CMLT270SU98/readings/fumia.html (February 2003). □

Louise Erdrich

Once named one of *People* magazine's most beautiful people, Louise Erdrich (born 1954) is a Native American writer with a wide popular appeal. She is no literary lightweight, however, having drawn comparisons to such noted American authors as William Faulkner.

Louise Erdrich was the first of seven children born to Ralph Louis Erdrich and Rita Joanne (Gourneau) Erdrich. Born on June 16, 1954, in Little Falls, Minnesota, she was raised in Wahpeton, North Dakota. Her mother, of Ojibwe descent, was born on the Turtle Mountain Ojibwe Reservation while her father was of German ancestry. Both parents taught at a Bureau of Indian Affairs boarding school.

A Tradition of Storytelling

From childhood, the rich oral tradition of Ojibwa storytelling was a part of Erdrich's life. Her mother and grandparents told her many stories about life on the reservation during the Great Depression of the 1930s, as well as other tales. Erdrich's father also told stories about his relatives and the towns where he grew up. Erdrich maintains that listening to her family's stories has in some ways been her most significant literary influence. Her father introduced her to the works of William Shakespeare and encouraged all of his children to write, paying a nickel apiece for her stories—Erdrich later joked that these nickels were her first royalties. Her mother supported her efforts as well, creating book

covers for her daughter's manuscripts out of woven strips of construction paper and staples.

Living in a small town where she and her family were regarded as eccentric, Erdrich became an avid reader. Among her literary influences were Flannery O'Connor, Gabriel García Marquéz, Katherine Anne Porter, Toni Morrison, Willa Cather, Jane Austen, George Eliot, and Faulkner.

Erdrich attended a Catholic school in Wahpeton. Her grandfather, Petrice Gourneau, taught her about culture and religion; tribal chair of the Turtle Mountain Reservation, he worshiped the traditional Ojibwa religion while at the same time was a devout Catholic. Her grandfather's example inspired Erdrich's creation of the character Father Damien who appears in many of her novels.

Indeed, Erdrich has drawn on her roots, both the land and the experiences of her family, for inspiration. As Mark Anthony Rolo wrote in the *Progressive,* "Erdrich once mused that Native American literature is often about coming home, returning to the land, the language and love of ancient traditions—a theme opposite of Western literature, which is about embarking on a journey, finding adventures beyond one's beginnings."

Native American Studies

In 1972 Erdrich enrolled in Dartmouth College as part of that school's first coeducational graduating class. There she met anthropologist Michael Dorris, chair of the Native American Studies department created at Dartmouth that

same year. At Dartmouth Erdrich started writing poems and stories integrating her Ojibwa heritage and in 1975 she was awarded the Academy of Poets Prize. She received her bachelor of arts degree the following year.

Erdrich served as a visiting poet and teacher for the Dakota Arts Council for two years after college graduation. She went on to earn a master of arts in writing from Johns Hopkins University in 1979. While she began sending her work to publishers around this time, most of them sent back rejections.

Erdrich served as communications director and editor for one year for *The Circle,* a Boston Indian Council-sponsored newspaper. Following that, she worked as a text-book writer for Charles Merrill Company.

Beginning of a Partnership

In 1979 Erdrich returned to Dartmouth to do a poetry reading, where she once again met up with Dorris. Dorris became interested in Erdrich's poetry, but even more interested in the poet herself. Although the two went their separate ways for a year—Dorris to New Zealand, Erdrich returning to Dartmouth as a visiting fellow in the Native American Studies department—they continued to exchange manuscripts through the mail. They met back at Dartmouth the next year and were married on October 10, 1981.

Viewed by outsiders as having an idyllic relationship, Erdrich and Dorris collaborated on every project and wrote tender dedications to each other in their books. They had a system worked out: when both wrote comparable amounts of a draft, the work was published under both names, but when one of them wrote the entire first initial draft, that person was the author. Even in the latter case, the final product was always a result of collaboration. They did the research together, developed plot lines and characters—sometimes even drawing them to see what they looked like—and discussed all aspects of the draft before submitting it for publication.

When they were first married and needed money, Erdrich and Dorris published romantic fiction using the pen name Milou North: "*Mi*chael plus *Lou*ise plus where we live," Erdrich once explained to Shelby Grantham in the *Dartmouth Alumni Magazine.* One of their stories was published in *Redbook,* while others ran in European publications.

Erdrich received the 1982 Nelson Algren Fiction Award for "The World's Greatest Fishermen," a story that became the first chapter of her first novel, *Love Medicine.* Erdrich learned of the contest and started writing just two weeks before the submission deadline. The first draft was completed in just one day, and Dorris collaborated with her on the subsequent drafts. The final product was one of 2,000 entries judged by Donald Barthelme, Studs Terkel, and Kay Boyle.

In 1983 Erdrich was awarded the Pushcart Prize for her poem "Indian Boarding School" and the National Magazine Award for fiction for her short story "Scales." This story and another she had previously published, "The Red Convertible," also found their way into *Love Medicine.*

Prizewinning First Novel

The next year, at the age of 30, Erdrich published *Jacklight,* a book of blank verse poems collected from her graduate thesis work, and *Love Medicine,* her first novel. *Love Medicine* was a runaway success, winning the 1984 National Book Critics Circle Award for fiction, the Sue Kaufman Prize for Best First Fiction, and the Virginia McCormick Scully Award. The novel continued to win awards the following year, including the *Los Angeles Times* Award for fiction, the American Book Award from the Before Columbus Foundation, and a fiction award from the Great Lakes Colleges Association.

Love Medicine became the first of Erdrich's "Argus" novels covering several generations of three Ojibwe families living in Argus, North Dakota, between from 1912 and the 1980s. Comparisons have been drawn to the work of Southern writer William Faulkner because of Erdrich's use of multi-voice narration and nonchronological storytelling as well as the ties of her characters to the land. Erdrich's fictional town of Argus has also been compared by critics to Faulkner's Yoknapatawpha County.

The "Argus" Novels

Erdrich's second novel in the series, *The Beet Queen,* published in 1986, covers a 40-year span beginning in 1932. Through characters like orphans Karl and Mary Adare and Celestine James and her daughter, Erdrich explores the negotiated interactions between the worlds of whites, halfbreeds, and Native Americans. She followed this with a prequel, *Tracks.* Gleaned from the manuscript of the first novel she had ever started, *Tracks* explores the tensions between Native American spirituality and Catholicism. Erdrich continued the "Argus" series with *The Bingo Palace, Tales of Burning Love, The Antelope Wife,* and *The Last Report on Miracles at Little No Horse.*

Many of the characters in Erdrich's books grow and develop over time in successive novels. Katy Read in the *Globe & Mail* wrote, "Erdrich's characters do seem to have lives of their own—lives and histories and intricate relationships that meander in and out of nearly all her books."

For example, *In the Last Report on Miracles at Little No Horse,* a finalist for the National Book Award, Father Damian Modeste, first introduced in *Love Medicine,* returns. The Father's secret, it unfolds, is that he is really a former nun, Agnes DeWitt, who, through a series of events, ended up posing as a Catholic priest. Agnes spends half a century ministering to the people of an Objibwe reservation and hiding the fact that she is actually a woman.

Interest in the Unusual

Although strange things often happen in her books, Erdrich rejects the "magical realist" label, claiming that even the most unusual events are based on things that really occurred, things she has found documented in newspaper clippings and books. She collects books on strange tales and supernatural happenings and keeps notebooks which she fills with stories of odd events she has heard about. Erdrich has also done a great deal of historical research, especially family

history and local history around North Dakota. On the other hand, she admitted to Rolo, "A lot of it is plain made up."

Erdrich's second book of poems, *Baptism of Desire,* was published in 1989. That same year, her husband, Dorris, received the National Book Critics Circle Award for his nonfiction work *The Broken Chord.* The book, with a preface by Erdrich, is a memoir of Dorris's experiences as one of the first single men to adopt children; by the time he married Erdrich he had adopted three Native American children with fetal alcohol syndrome.

In 1991 the couple published their co-authored novel *The Crown of Columbus.* The book is a complicated 400-page story about a love affair between two writers and intellectuals who, at the same time they are trying to define their relationship, are also grappling with the historical figure of Columbus in their research and writing. The couple also co-authored a book of travel essays titled *Route Two.*

Tragic Turn of Events

Erdrich and Dorris had three children together in addition to the three children Dorris adopted prior to their marriage. The couple separated in 1995 in the wake of allegations of sexual abuse brought against Dorris by some of his children. After an investigation left the accusations unresolved, Dorris committed suicide in 1997. As Erdrich told a National Public Radio *Weekend Edition* commentator that during that time, "All my being was really concentrated on getting our children through it, and that's something you do minute by minute. Then, you know, there's that one day at a time."

Despite the turbulence within her personal life during the 1990s, Erdrich kept writing. In 1995 she published her first nonfiction book, *The Blue Jay's Dance,* in which she records her experience with pregnancy and the birth year of her child. The title, which refers to the way a blue jay will defiantly dance toward an attacking hawk, is a metaphor for "the sort of controlled recklessness that having children always is," Erdrich told Jane Aspinall in an article in *Quill & Quire.*

The following year Erdrich wrote the children's book *Grandmother's Pigeon.* Using the same sense of magic found in her novels, she tells the story of an adventurous grandmother who rides to Greenland on a dolphin. The eggs she leaves for her grandchildren hatch into pigeons that can send messages to her.

New Start in Minneapolis

In 1999 Erdrich and her three youngest children relocated to Minneapolis to be closer to her parents in North Dakota. In July 2000, she and her sister Heidi opened Birchbark Books, Herbs, and Native Arts in the Kenwood neighborhood of Minneapolis. The store, located in a building that was once a meat market, is decorated with a stairway made of birch trees that fell on land owned by friends in Wisconsin; the shop's focal point is an intricately carved Roman Catholic confessional Erdrich found at an architectural salvage store. Dream-catchers hang in the corners of the confessional, along with books with "sin" in the title and a framed copy of the U.S. Government's 1837 treaty with the Chippewa.

Since the late 1990s Erdrich has focused on learning the Ojibwe language and studying her tribe's culture and traditions, including its mysticism. She has also taught her youngest daughter to speak the Ojibwe language. In 2001 she finished writing *The Last Report on Miracles at Little No Horse* and also had a baby girl. The following year Erdrich wrote her first novel for young adults, the National Book Award for Young People finalist *The Birchbark House.* The story of a young Ojibwa girl named Omakayas, *The Birchbark House* also features illustrations by Erdrich. Her 2003 novel for adults, *The Master Butchers Singing Club,* returns readers to Argus, North Dakota; its main character is a German butcher named Fidelis Waldvogel, an immigrant to the United States in the 1920s.

Books

Conversations with Louise Erdrich and Michael Dorris, edited by Allan Chavkin and Nancy Feyl Chavkin, University Press of Mississippi, 1994.

Periodicals

Associated Press Newswires, March 23, 1998; March 25, 1998.
Globe & Mail (Toronto, Ontario, Canada), April 21, 2001.
News & Observer (Raleigh, North Carolina), April 22, 2001.
Progressive, April 1, 2002.
Quill & Quire, August 1995.
Star Tribune (San Diego, California), December 30, 2001.
Toronto Star, April 22, 2001.

Online

"Meet the Writers: Louise Erdrich," http://www.barnesand noble.com/writers/writer.asp?cid929573 (February 4, 2003).
"Modern American Poetry: About Louise Erdrich," http://www .english.uiuc.edu/maps/poets/a_f/erdrich/about.htm (February 4, 2003).
NPR Weekend Edition, http://www.npr.org/ (July 8, 2001).
"Voices from the Gaps: Louise Erdrich," http://voices.cla.umn .edu/authors/louiseerdrich.html (February 4, 2003). □

F

Geraldine Farrar

American opera singer Geraldine Farrar (1882–1967) was a lyric soprano with great vocal skills and dramatic flair. Often paired with tenor Enrico Caruso at New York City's Metropolitan Opera, her career was relatively short-lived because her voice had given out by 1920.

Farrar was born on February 28, 1882, in Melrose, Massachusetts, the only child of Sidney "Syd" Farrar and his wife Henrietta. A professional baseball player with the Philadelphia Phillies, Farrar's father later worked as a storekeeper. Both he and his wife were amateur musicians, and when their young daughter exhibited musical talent at an early age, they encouraged her.

Wanted to Sing

To supplement her natural talent, Farrar began taking instruction in various instruments from age five. However, when the young girl balked at practicing the piano, lessons stopped and her parents resorted to other means of encouraging their daughter in expressing herself musically. Farrar ultimately found her musical expression in singing, and at the age of 12 she played the part of a popular singer of her day, Jenny Lind, in her town's annual May Festival, singing two numbers before an appreciative home-town audience.

Although Farrar was not rigorous in practicing, she continued her lessons as a vocalist, studying with noted vocal instructor Mrs. J. H. Long in Boston in 1894. The 12-year-old Farrar also studied operatic acting and deportment

with Victor Capoul, a singing actor. Capoul is credited with changing her development as a performer and inspiring the dramatic flair Farrar later brought to her work on stage. In 1896 Farrar made her professional debut when she was paid $10 to sing a song from *Mignon* at the Melrose town hall. Later she appeared on a Boston stage to perform a selection from the *Barber of Seville.*

Trained in New York City, Europe

By the time she was 13 Farrar was living in New York City and studying with Emma Thursby. Under Thursby's tutelage, Farrar began giving recitals when she was 14 years old, and her talent caught the attention of established opera singer Nellie Melba. Melba arranged an introduction between Farrar and Maurice Grau, director of the Metropolitan Opera of New York. Although Farrar had the opportunity to be cast in a small role in one of the Met's upcoming opera productions, she turned it down.

On the advice of professionals, Farrar pursued her training in Europe, her parents borrowing money so the family could remain together while Farrar was in Paris pursuing her dream. There from 1899 to 1900, she studied with Trabadelo, a Spanish vocal coach, and also attended plays that starred Sarah Bernhardt. Her studies of Bernhardt influenced the way in which Ferraro approached the staging of her performances when she became an established opera star.

Sang Opera in Berlin

When Farrar had learned all she could from Trabadelo, she went to Berlin, Germany, to study with Francesco Graziani, who was also known for being an important vocal teacher. In 1900 Farrar auditioned and won a three-year contract with the Berlin Hofoper, the city's Royal opera house. Making her debut as Marguerite in *Faust* in 1901, Farrar was

an immediate success and was named "court singer." She was even lauded by the German royal family, the country's crown prince going so far as to become smitten with the beautiful, young vocalist. Farrar would go on to sing the role of Marguerite 60 times over the course of her career.

Soon after her first stage debut, Farrar engaged another vocal coach in Lilli Lehmann. Lehmann was important to Farrar's training because she helped the singer modulate her voice, improving Farrar's diction and forward projection, and giving her greater technical control over her voice. Farrar's roles required that she learn German, although she sung her first three roles with the company in Italian because she had not yet mastered the language.

After her contract in Berlin was up, Farrar moved to the Monte Carlo Opera, where she sang from about 1904 to 1906, making her Monte Carlo debut in Puccini's *La Bohéme* alongside costar Enrico Caruso, who would later play a significant role as her co-star in the United States. In 1905, on the strength of only five days of rehearsal, Farrar sang in *Amica* by Mascagni. She also appeared in Paris, Munich, Warsaw, and Salzburg, establishing an international reputation that preceded her when she returned to the United States. While she lived in Europe, Farrar continued to study with Lehmann.

Made Debut at the Met

On opening night of the 1906–1907 season at the Metropolitan Opera House in New York City, Farrar made her debut with the company with which she would be associated for the rest of her career. She would become its leading singing actress. In her debut, Farrar sang in *Roméo et Juliette* by Gounod.

Over the course of her career at the Met, Farrar became known for her thorough preparation, her staging, and her costumes. Her interpretations and characterizations were often very different from those previously done by operas. In addition to her strong personality, Farrar had different look than other opera singers. Rather than being overweight, she was pretty, slim, and full of grace.

Soon after Farrar arrived at the Met, a new managing director took over the well-known opera house. Arriving from Italy, Guilin Gatti-Casazza brought with him conductor Arturo Toscanini, with whom Farrar immediately became at odds due to both their unrelenting personalities. Fortunately, Farrar and Toscanini eventually resolved their problems, and she became the composer's mistress for the duration of his tenure in the United States, seven years.

In 1907 Farrar made a well-received appearance in the Met's first production of Puccini's *Madama Butterfly,* which the composer even attended. She was acclaimed in the role of Cho Cho San, and the role became the most linked to her name. Farrar had prepared for this role by studying with a Japanese actress named Fu-ji-Ko. New York audiences loved Farrar's interpretation of Cho Cho San, and although Puccini was initially reluctant, he was also eventually won over. Farrar went on to play the lead role in *Madama Butterfly* 95 more times at the Met. Caruso was also part of the initial production, and their on-stage chemistry made their performances together very popular.

Throughout her career, Farrar was known for her desire to take on new risks and challenges. One of these risks was presented to her in 1910 at the world premiere of German composer Engelbert Humperdinck's *Köngiskinder,* creating the role of the Goose Girl. She went on to sing this role 30 more times. A year later, in 1911, Farrar sang in the American premiere of *Ariane et Barbe-bleue.*

Suffered Vocal Problems

Among Farrar's strengths as an opera singer was her very wide vocal range, especially the upper register. Unfortunately, in 1913 her voice broke during a performance, prompting much discussion of why this had happened. While some blamed her vocal stress on the fact that Farrar had studied under many vocal coaches with different teaching methods, others blamed it on her wide-ranging and sometimes odd-beat repertory. In fact, Farrar had never taken care of her voice in proportion to the work she demanded of it, and although she rested, after 1913 her voice never regained the strength and vitality it had once possessed.

Despite the diminished quality of her voice, Farrar's popularity was such that she continued to be offered starring roles. In 1914 she made her debut in the title role of Bizet's *Carmen,* although that role had already been linked to another star singer. Farrar played the role 65 times on stage before appearing in the silent film version in 1915. After shooting the film, her stage versions of *Carmen* became more animated, as Farrar added more acting touches than were normally found in opera. One time, for example, she physically slapped Caruso, who played Don Juan opposite her Carmen.

Made Film Debut

Farrar's film debut in *Carmen* was directed by Cecil B. DeMille, one of the leading silent film directors of the day. Even without the sound of Farrar's voice, *Carmen* was a hit at the box office, earning her fans that were not necessarily opera fans. Discussing her performance in this film from a historical perspective, critic Richard Dyer wrote in the *Boston Globe* that "Farrar had a real screen face that the camera loves—alluring, vital, and in every moment expressive. Her face tells the story, and you can't take your eyes off her." In short, she possessed "star quality."

Farrar's agreement to appear in *Carmen* gave a varnish of respectability to a young film industry that many viewed as somewhat suspect as a credible art form. She went on to have a second career as film actress, appearing in 13 films that included *Maria Rosa* (1916), *Joan the Woman* (1917), *The Woman God Forgot* (1917), *The Turn of the Wheel* (1918), *The Hell Cat* (1918), *The World and Its Woman* (1919), *Flame of the Desert* (1920), and *The Woman and the Puppet* (1920). None of these films were opera roles; all confirmed Farrar's aptitude for acting.

While Farrar gave the silent film dignity, she also brought opera to many outside that music's traditional audience. During the Met's off-season she traveled throughout the United States in her own Pullman railroad car, singing operatic arias to crowds in small towns which had never heard such performances. By the time Farrar was 30 years old she was a celebrity.

Because of the U.S. public's interest in Farrar's life, she penned an autobiography titled *Geraldine Farrar: The Story of an American Singer, by Herself.* The book was published in 1916, the same year she was married to Lou Tellegen, a Dutch actor. The marriage was short-lived, and the couple endured a bitter divorce in 1923.

Retired from the Met

By the early 1920s Farrar's upper range had been compromised, forcing her relatively early retirement as an opera singer. Her final performance at the Met was in April 1922. She sang in *Zazá* by Leoncavallo, a role she first sang in 1920 after working with stage director and producer David Belasco. Her farewell performance was a big event; it was sold out almost immediately, and scalpers made huge profits as the singer's many fans paid huge amounts to witness her performance. After the final curtain, Farrar was followed in her open-topped car by a mob of admirers that extended up Broadway.

During her time at the Met, Farrar sang in 23 roles for 493 performances. She even had a following of teenaged groupies, dubbed the "Gerryflappers." Her best roles were considered to be in Mascagni's *Amica,* Saint-Saëns's *L'Ancêtre,* and Puccini's *Suor Angelica.*

After retiring from the Met, Farrar continued to perform in concert tours throughout the United States. While her voice had lost many vocal qualities, she retained her technical abilities, and she continued to perform in concert until November of 1931, when she took the stage at Carnegie Hall for her last concert. She remained connected to opera by serving as intermission commentator for the Met's Saturday afternoon radio broadcasts during the 1934–35 season and was active in civic activities, charity work, the Republican party, and some public speaking. During World War II Farrar volunteered for the Red Cross and corresponded with serviceman. In addition to music, Farrar explored several forms of writing, including poetry and songs. In 1938 she expanded her 1916 autobiography into a second book, *Such Sweet Compulsion,* in which she credited the spirit of her now-deceased mother with inspiring her writing.

Though Farrar no longer sang, fans could still hear her voice due to the number of recordings she made as early as 1904 and primarily during her prime. These popular recordings let fans showed how great her voice really was. Her records, like her tours, brought a larger audience that numbered in the millions to listen to opera. Referring to listening to her voice on recordings, Tim Page wrote in the *New York Times,* "Farrar's voice was one of great warmth; her high notes had a brilliant gem-like quality. There is a serene confidence to her singing, a subliminal awareness of her splendid technique and the seamless skein of her register. Hers was startlingly original singing, full of verve and passion, yet very modern, with none of the swooping into notes so prevalent at the time. Her singing always had a sense of center, a sense of control, which is one of the reasons her disks are more enjoyable to listen to today than those of many of her contemporaries."

Farrar died on March 11, 1967, in Ridgefield, Connecticut, where she lived in her retirement. To sum her life, a representative for *Opera News* quoted the singer as saying, "If I can live so that those who come in contact with me find encouragement and enrichment, that is all I ask of life. For more important to me than being a great artists will be, when the final curtain is drawn, to have succeeded in being a great human being."

Books

Adamson, Lynda G., *Notable Women in American History: A Guide to Recommended Biographies and Autobiographies,* Greenwood Press, 1999.

Farrar, Geraldine, *Geraldine Farrar: The Story of an American Singer, by Herself,* 1916, revised as *Such Sweet Compulsion,* 1938, reprinted, Books for Libraries Press, 1970.

Garraty, John, and Mark C. Carnes, editors, *American National Biography,* Oxford University Press, 1999.

Guinn, John, and Les Stone, editors, *The St. James Opera Encyclopedia: A Guide to People and Works,* St. James Press, 1997.

Hitchcock, H. Wiley, and Stanley Sadie, editors, *The New Grove Dictionary of American Music,* Macmillan, 1986.

Nash, Elizabeth, *Always First Class: The Career of Geraldine Farrar,* University Press of America, 1981.

Periodicals

Boston Globe, September 19, 1997.
New York Times, February 28, 1982.
Opera News, February 2003. □

Abraham Adolf Fraenkel

One of the fathers of modern logic, German-born mathematician Abraham Fraenkel (1891–1965) first became widely known for his work on set theory. Long fascinated by the pioneering work in set theory of fellow German Ernst Zermelo (1871–1953), Fraenkel launched research to put set theory into an axiomatic setting that improved the definitions of Zermelo's theory and proposed its own system of axioms. Within that system, Fraenkel proved the independence of the axiom of choice. The Zermelo-Fraenkel axioms of set theory, known collectively as ZF, are the standard axioms of axiomatic set theory on which, together with the axiom of choice, all of ordinary mathematics is based. When the axiom of choice is included, the resulting system is known as ZFC.

Studied at Several Universities

Abraham Adolf Fraenkel was born on February 17, 1891, in Munich, Germany. The son of Sigmund and Charlotte (Neuberger) Fraenkel, he was strongly influenced by his orthodox Jewish heritage. B.H. Auerbach-Halberstadt, Fraenkel's great-grandfather, had been widely known for his rabbinical teachings. As a child, Fraenkel was enrolled in Hebrew school and was reading Hebrew by the time he was five. Raised in a family that set a high priority on education, Fraenkel advanced rapidly in his general studies and, like most German students of that era, studied at a number of universities. He began his higher studies at the University of Munich in his hometown and studied subsequently at the German universities of Marburg, Berlin, and Breslau. In 1914, at the age of 23, Fraenkel received his doctoral degree in mathematics from the University of Breslau.

World War I broke out in August 1914, shortly after Fraenkel had completed his studies at Breslau. For the next two years, he served in the German military as a sergeant in the medical corps. He also worked briefly for the German army's meteorological service. In 1916 Fraenkel accepted a position at the University of Marburg as an unsalaried lecturer, or privatdocent. It was at Marburg that Fraenkel began his most important research in mathematical theory. On March 28, 1920, he married Malkah Wilhemina Prins. The couple eventually had four children.

Focused on Set Theory

Fraenkel's earliest research was on the p-adic numbers first described by Kurt Hensel in the late nineteenth century and on the theory of rings. Before long, however, he became deeply involved in the study of set theory, specifically the work of Ernst Zermelo, who in the early years of the twentieth century had published his controversial and innovative views on the subject. Zermelo had postulated that from any set of numbers, a single element could be selected and that definite properties of that element could be determined. This was known as the axiom of choice, but Zermelo offered no real proof for his theory, suggesting that the study of mathematics could only progress if certain axioms were simply accepted without question. For many mathematicians, Zermelo's lack of proof was unacceptable. Some, including French mathematician Jacques Hadamard, reluctantly agreed to accept Zermelo's theory until a better way could be found, while others, including Jules-Henri Poincaré, adamantly opposed acceptance of Zermelo's theory.

Without either accepting or rejecting Zermelo's theory outright, Fraenkel set about to find ways to put Zermelo's work on a firmer foundation. In the case of finite sets of numbers, Fraenkel found, Zermelo's theory already worked quite well. However, for infinite sets, Zermelo's assumptions were more questionable. Fraenkel eventually substituted a notion of function for Zermelo's idea of determining a definite property of a number in a set. In so doing, he significantly clarified Zermelo's set theory and also rid it of its dependence on the axiom of choice, which had clearly been one of the most controversial elements of Zermelo's work.

Just as Fraenkel's research built on theories advanced earlier by Zermelo, others' refinements to the work of Zermelo and Fraenkel have buttressed their theories and advanced the mathematical community's understanding of set theory. Fraenkel's system of axioms was modified by Norwegian mathematician Thoralf Skolem in 1922 to create what is known today as the ZFS system, named for Zermelo, Fraenkel, and Skolem. Within the ZFS system, it is harder to prove the independence of the axiom of choice, a goal that was not achieved until the work of American Paul Joseph Cohen in the 1960s. Cohen used a technique called "forcing" to prove the independence in set theory of the axiom of choice and the generalized continuum hypothesis.

Published Set Theory Findings

Fraenkel published his conclusions on set theory in two separate works—a popular introductory textbook published in 1919 and a 1922 research article determining the independence of the axiom of choice. The conclusions in the latter work were later included as part of the proof for a newly coined term, Ur-elements—infinite and distinct pairs of objects that do not in themselves define a set. A number of prominent mathematicians of the period questioned the validity of Ur-elements, but only three years later German physicist Wolfgang Pauli used them in his proof of the exclusion principle.

In 1922 Fraenkel was promoted to assistant professor of mathematics at the University of Marburg. His earlier work on set theory had propelled him to the forefront of set theory research, and over the next few years he published a number of articles on the subject while he continued to teach. In 1928 Fraenkel was offered a full professorship at the University of Kiel. He accepted but only a year later took a leave of absence to become a visiting professor at Jerusalem's Hebrew University. For the next two years he taught at Hebrew

University, leaving in 1931 after a disagreement with the school's administration.

Germany in Turmoil

Fraenkel's return to Germany proved to be a bittersweet occasion. His native country was in economic disarray, suffering through the effects of the worldwide economic depression and the brutal conditions imposed by the Treaty of Versailles that had ended World War I. The economic pressures on the German people had given rise to increasing intolerance, most notably a disturbing wave of anti-Semitism. For the next two years, Fraenkel resumed his teaching duties at Kiel, keeping a wary eye on the increasingly unsettled political situation in Germany. In January 1933 Adolf Hitler, leader of the National Socialist German Workers' Party, better known as Nazis, became Germany's chancellor. Fraenkel and his family left the country a month later, moving first to Amsterdam in the neighboring Netherlands.

Fraenkel and his family spent only two months in Amsterdam, closely monitoring the situation in their native Germany while there. Convinced that there would not be a quick turnaround under the Nazi regime, Fraenkel drafted a letter of resignation to the University of Kiel in April 1933 and returned to Jerusalem to teach once again at Hebrew University. Despite his earlier disagreement with the university's administration, he was warmly welcomed back to the school's faculty.

Focus of Research Changed

Following his exile from Germany, Fraenkel changed the focus of his research. Although he continued to publish texts on set theory for the remainder of his career, Fraenkel began to concentrate his studies on the evolution of modern logic and the contributions made by Jewish mathematicians and scientists in their respective fields. Fraenkel had written a number of books about the history of mathematics. In 1920 he had published an overview of the work of Carl Friedrich Gauss, who in his doctoral dissertation had proved the fundamental theorem of algebra. As early as 1930 he had begun the work of chronicling the accomplishments of Jewish mathematicians with his biography of Georg Cantor, who was half-Jewish. Cantor at that time was of greater interest to Fraenkel for the nature of his research into set theory than for his ethnic background. However, once he had resumed teaching at Hebrew University in 1933, he began a much wider study into the work of Jewish scientists and mathematicians. In 1960 Fraenkel published *Jewish Mathematics and Astronomy.*

In his research into the origins of modern logic, Fraenkel looked closely at natural numbers, describing them in terms of modern concepts of logic and reasoning. Although his research underscored the need for continuity in consideration of the number line, Fraenkel also expressed interest in opposing points of view. During this period, Fraenkel had a conversation with physicist Albert Einstein, who suggested that the prevailing theory of continuity in mathematics might some day be overtaken by the atomistic concept of the number line. Although Fraenkel himself remained unconvinced, largely because he considered math-

ematical continuity necessary to the foundation of modern calculus, he did publish an article explaining the views of the intuitionists, as Einstein and others who believed similarly were known.

Taught at Einstein Institute of Mathematics

Fraenkel was among the first professors at Hebrew University's Einstein Institute of Mathematics. Along with fellow professor Edmond Landau, Fraenkel taught mathematical logic and mathematical analysis. In 1958, while still teaching at Hebrew University, Fraenkel published an overview of his work on set theory, a textbook entitled *Foundations of Set Theory.* A year later, he retired as a professor at Hebrew University. To mark Fraenkel's 70th birthday in 1961, several members of the mathematical community put together a collection of essays and research articles related to Fraenkel's life work. The collection, *Essays on the Foundations of Mathematics,* contained contributions from mathematicians around the world. Sadly, Fraenkel never saw the book in its final form. He died in Jerusalem on October 15, 1965, only months before the book was published.

Fraenkel will be remembered for his research in set theory and modern logic. His refinements to the set theory conclusions of Ernst Zermelo, codified as the Zermelo-Fraenkel axioms, or ZF, are almost always what scientists and mathematicians mean today when they speak of "set theory." Further enhancing the value of Fraenkel's contributions to the body of mathematical theory are the clarity and precision of his writings, several of which continue to be taught in colleges and universities worldwide. In its review of Fraenkel's summation of his set theory research— *Foundations of Set Theory*—the *British Journal for the Philosophy of Science* was lavish in its praise. Its reviewer wrote that the book "is a masterly survey of its field. It is lucid and concise on a technical level, it covers the historical ground admirably, and it gives a sensible account of the various philosophical positions associated with the development of the subject . . . essential reading for any mathematician or philosopher."

Books

Contemporary Authors Online, Gale Group, 2000.
Mathematical Expeditions: Chronicles by the Explorers, Springer-Verlag, 2001.
Notable Scientists: From 1900 to the Present, Gale Group, 2001.

Online

"Adolf Abraham Halevi Fraenkel," *Groups, Algorithms, and Programming,* http://www-gap.dcs.st-and.ac.uk/~history/Mathematicians/Fraenkel.html (March 5, 2003).
"Adolf Fraenkel," *201E: Mathematical Foundations,* http://ergo.ucsd.edu/~movellan/courses/245/people/Fraenkel.html (March 9, 2003).
"P-adic Number," *Wikipedia,* http://www.wikipedia.org/wiki/p-adic+numbers (March 9, 2003).
"Paul Joseph Cohen," *Groups, Algorithms, and Programming,* http://www-gap.dcs.st-and.ac.uk/~history/Mathematicians/Cohen.html (March 9, 2003).

"Zermelo-Fraenkel Axioms," *Wikipedia,* http://www.wikipedia
.org/wiki/Zermelo-Fraenkel_axiom (March 9, 2003). □

Kenichi Fukui

Kenichi Fukui (1918–1998) was a theoretical chemist whose career was devoted to explaining the nature of chemical reactions. His work was distinguished from that of other chemists by its mathematical structure. He especially contributed to bridging the gap between quantum theory, a mathematical theory of the behavior of molecules and atoms, and practical chemistry. He made it easier both to understand and predict the course of chemical reactions, and he shared the 1981 Nobel Prize in chemistry with Roald Hoffmann.

Fukui was born October 4, 1918, in Nara on the island of Honshu, Japan. He was the eldest of three sons born to Chie and Ryokichi Fukui. His father was a merchant and factory manager who played a major role in shaping his son's career; he persuaded Fukui to study chemistry. Fukui had no interest in chemistry during high school and he described in his autobiography, from the Nobel Foundation website, that his father's persuasiveness was the "most decisive occurrence in my educational career." He enrolled at the Department of Industrial Chemistry at Kyoto Imperial University, and he remained associated with that university throughout his life. Fukui graduated from the university in 1941, and he spent most of World War II at a fuel laboratory, performing research on the chemistry of synthetic fuel.

Fukui returned to Kyoto University in 1945, when he was named assistant professor. He received his Ph.D. in engineering in 1948 and was elevated to a full professorship in physical chemistry in 1951. At the beginning of his career, his research interests ranged broadly through the areas of chemical reaction theory, quantum chemistry, and physical chemistry. But during the 1950s, Fukui began theorizing about the role of electron orbitals in molecular reactions. Molecules are groups of atoms held together by electron bonds. Electrons circle the nuclei in what are called orbitals, similar to the orbit of planets around the sun in our solar system. Whenever molecules react with one another, at least one of these electron bonds is broken and altered, forming a new bond and thus changing the molecular structure. At the time Fukui began his work, scientists understood this process only when one bond was changed; the more complex reactions, however, were not understood at all.

Theories Increased Understanding of Chemical Reactions

During the 1950s, Fukui theorized that the significant elements of this interaction occurred in the highest occupied molecular orbital of one molecule (HOMO) and the lowest unoccupied molecular orbital of another (LUMO). Fukui named these "frontier orbitals." The HOMO has high energy and is willing to lose an electron, and the LUMO has low energy and is thus willing to accept an electron. The resulting bond, according to Fukui, is at an energy level between the two starting points. Over the next decade, Fukui developed and tested his theory using complex mathematical formulas, and he attempted to use it to predict the process of molecular interaction and bonding.

Fukui continued to break new ground in theoretical chemistry through the 1960s. Other chemists began research on these same problems during this period, but Fukui's work was largely neglected. His use of advanced mathematics made his theories difficult for most chemists to understand, and his articles were published in journals that were not widely read in the United States and Europe. In an interview quoted in the *New York Times,* Fukui also attributed some of his obscurity to resistance from Japanese colleagues: "The Japanese are very conservative when it comes to new theory. But once you get appreciated in the United States or Europe, then after that the appreciation spreads back to Japan."

Two of the chemists who had been working independently of Fukui were Roald Hoffmann of Cornell University and Robert B. Woodward of Harvard, and in 1965 they came to conclusions that were similar to his, though they had arrived there along a different path. Staying away from complex math, these two developed a formula almost as simple as a pictorial representation. Taken together, the work of Fukui and the American team enabled research scientists to predict how reactions would occur and to understand many complexities never before explained. These formulae answered questions about why some reactions between molecules occurred quickly and others slowly, as well as why certain molecules reacted better with some molecules than with others. They removed much of guesswork from this area of chemistry research.

For the advancements in knowledge their work had brought, Fukui and Hoffmann were jointly awarded the 1981 Nobel Prize in chemistry. Woodward, who would probably also have shared in the prize, had died two years before. Fukui was one of the first Japanese to receive the Nobel Prize in any field, and the very first in the area of chemistry. After winning the Nobel Prize, Fukui remained at Kyoto University, and he continued to be active in his field. He continued his research on chemical reactions and expanded his formula to predict the interaction of three or more molecules.

Fukui was elected senior foreign scientist of the American National Science Foundation in 1970. In 1973, he participated in the United States-Japan Eminent Scientist Exchange Program. In 1978 and 1979, he was vice-president of the Chemical Society in Japan, and he served as their president from 1983 to 1984. In 1980, he was made a foreign member of the National Academy of Sciences, and in 1982 he was named President of the Kyoto University of Industrial Arts and Textile Fibers. He was a member of the International Academy of Quantum Molecular Science; the European Academy of Arts, Sciences, and Humanities; and the American Academy of Arts and Sciences. He served as director of the Institute for Fundamental Chemistry from 1988 until his death on January 9, 1998, in Kyoto, Japan.

Fukui was married in 1947 to Tomoe Horie. The couple had one son, Tetsuya, and one daughter, Miyako.

Books

Nobel Prize Winners, H. W. Wilson, 1987.

Periodicals

New York Times, October 20, 1981.
Physics Today, December 1981.
Science, November 6, 1981.

Online

"Kenichi Fukui-Autobiography," *Nobel e-Museum,* http://www .nobel.se/chemistry/laureates/1981/fukui-autobio.html (April 11, 2003). □

Meta Warrick Fuller

Meta Vaux Warrick Fuller (1877–1968) is celebrated for being the first American black artist to reflect African themes and folk tales in her work and for being ahead of her time in her understanding of the black experience. Fuller's career spanned over seventy years. Her sculptural works in bronze, clay, and plaster represented her comments on wartime America, racism and violence, and the African American perspective. As a young woman studying in Paris, she was encouraged by French artist Auguste Rodin and W.E.B. DuBois.

Encouraged as a Young Artist

William H. Warrick, Jr., was a master barber, and his wife, Emma (Jones) Warrick, was a hairdresser and wigmaker. Their fourth child, Meta Vaux Warrick, was born June 9, 1877, in a middle-class neighborhood in Philadelphia, Pennsylvania. She was ten years younger than her brother William and sister Blanche. Another sister, Virginia, died before Fuller was born.

As early as elementary school, Fuller's parents encouraged her interest in art and her artistic talents began to shine. In high school, she was selected to attend J. Liberty Tadd's art school for special classes once a week. In fact, a small woodcarving of Fuller's was part of the school's display at the 1893 World's Colombian Exposition in Chicago.

After graduating high school, Fuller was one of the first blacks to earn a scholarship to the Pennsylvania Museum and School for Industrial Art, which she attended for three years, until 1897. Part of her scholarship was that she produce a work for the school, which resulted in a bas-relief, which featured thirty-seven medieval figures, called *Procession of the Arts and Crafts.* Fuller won a prize for the sculpture, one of the year's best works.

Studies in Paris Challenged by Money, Race

After college, in 1899, Fuller sailed to Europe. She first stopped in England and spent a month with a friend of her mother, then continued on to Paris. A friend of Fuller's uncle, painter Henry Ossawa Tanner, had agreed to look after her there. When her train arrived in Paris, Tanner was not there to meet her. Fuller found her way to a women's youth hostel for students, called the American Girls Club, but was unwelcome. Fuller was shocked to find the club's rules excluded her because of her race.

Though the American Girls Club did not welcome Fuller, the club's director was helpful to her. The director helped her find a room to stay in and introduced her to American sculptor Augustus Saint-Gaudens. Fuller's studies in Paris had been limited by financial problems, and Saint-Gaudens helped her meet competent teachers. He suggested she take time to study drawing for a while rather than rush into sculpting. For the first year of her Paris stay, Fuller studied drawing, visited museums, and attended lectures at Académie des Beaux-Arts. With Saint-Gaudens's guidance, she had advanced to sculpting from live models by the summer of 1900.

Fuller was in the company of many notable black Americans who had come to Paris to participate in the Paris Universal Exposition in 1900. Fuller spent time with Thomas J. Calloway, the exposition commissioner; Andrew F. Hilyer, an agent of the United States Department of the Interior, and his wife, Mamie, an accomplished pianist; Alonzo Herndon; Adrian McNeal Herndon, an actress who taught at Atlanta University; and Professor W. E. B. DuBois of Atlanta University. Fuller resisted DuBois when he suggested she focus on African American subjects. She felt it would limit her work. After the exposition, Fuller registered at the Académie Colarossi to study under French sculptors.

Mentored by Master Auguste Rodin

In the summer of 1901, Fuller had a fortunate meeting. One of her fellow students at Colarossi arranged to introduce her to renowned French sculptor Auguste Rodin at the sculptor's home in Meudon. Fuller went with hopes of being accepted as one of Rodin's students and so brought with her an example of her work. He was impressed with the piece, called *The Man Eating His Heart,* and complemented her sense of form. Though he already had too many students, he did promise to visit her in Paris often to critique her work.

Fuller and Rodin shared a belief that the purpose of art was to explore human emotion. Under her French mentor, Fuller became more bold in her execution of these ideas, often embracing an ugly portrayal rather than limiting herself to aesthetically pleasing ones. During this time Fuller's work became stronger and more daring in subject as well as form. She began more consciously using her work to make a philosophical point. She illustrated the importance of duty in *Man Carrying a Dead Comrade.* She explored the struggle of the wise man who cannot alleviate human suffering in *The Wretched.*

Although Fuller shied away from focusing solely on African American themes, her work—and her world perspective—certainly was influenced by her color. Many were shocked and laughed at the grotesque face of Fuller's contribution to the 1902 Victor Hugo Centennial, a portrayal of Hugo's *Laughing Man.* In an era when African Americans were depicted humorously as slow and lazy, bug-eyed "Sambos," Fuller was commenting on the accepted images of the time with *Laughing Man.* She objected to such stereotypes and by altering her subject's face—his mouth opened grotesquely to his ears, his ears folded over his eyes—was indirectly protesting them with the piece.

Her studies in Paris began to pay off during her last year there. Rodin was drawing attention to Fuller's work and she held private showings. The press called her the "delicate sculptor of horrors," and she was the only American artist invited to show with several French artists in Paris. During that year, her work caught the attention of S. Bing, a patron of such artists as Mary Cassatt, Aubrey Beardsley, and Henri de Toulouse-Lautrec. He held a one-woman show for her at his famous modern art and design gallery, L'Art Nouveau.

Started to Follow African American Inspiration

Back in her native Philadelphia in 1902, Fuller at once set up a studio and continued to work. She found chilly receptions from local art dealers who claimed not to buy domestic work, but were not interested in her Paris sculptures either. Fuller felt that her race was the reason and found a more appreciative group in Philadelphia's black social and intellectual circles. The more she became immersed in black life in Philadelphia, the more her work began to reflect African American themes as well as European influences. She held exhibitions at her studio and was invited by local art schools and community organizations to contribute to their art shows. She showed pieces like *Two-Step* and *The Comedian,* a portrayal of dancer and singer George Walker. Both sculptures were examples of this transitional time in Fuller's work.

Fuller began to draw her inspiration more heavily from the songs of black America and from African folk tales. Before the emergence of the artists of the Harlem Renaissance, Fuller presented America with work that showed the impact of African and African American themes. Her sculptures illustrated truth, joy, and other universal facets of the human condition. Her work naturally began to take the tone of W.E.B. DuBois's suggestion to her in Paris—that she specialize in African American themes.

In 1907, on the recommendation of Thomas Calloway, whom she had met at the Paris Universal Exposition, Fuller was commissioned to sculpt a number of scenes for the Negro pavilion at the Jamestown Tercentennial Exposition. She won a gold medal for 150 figures, which represented the progress of black Americans since their 1619 arrival in Jamestown, Virginia. She was the first black woman artist to receive a federal commission.

Fire Destroyed, but Family Strengthened

Although it was not the popular view of the time, Fuller decided to combine career and marriage and wed Dr. Solomon C. Fuller in 1909. Dr. Fuller, born in Liberia, was a neurologist at Massachusetts State Hospital and a director of the pathology lab at Westborough State Hospital. The couple moved into the house they had built in Framingham, Massachusetts. The Fullers would become significant residents of the town. In 1994, Fuller Middle School in Framingham was named in their honor.

Before she was married, Fuller stored all her tools and sculptures in a Philadelphia warehouse. In 1910, before she could have the load shipped to her home in Framingham, a fire in the warehouse destroyed sixteen years' worth of her work from Paris and Philadelphia. The tragedy killed her desire to sculpt, and Fuller found solace as a wife and mother—over the next six years, she gave birth to three children, sons Solomon, Jr., William Thomas, and Perry.

However, Fuller did not stop sculpting for too long. In 1913, W.E.B. DuBois requested that she recreate one of her pieces lost in the fire, *Man Eating His Heart.* for the fiftieth-anniversary celebration of the Emancipation Proclamation in New York. The prospect seemed too painful to Fuller, who instead produced an eight-foot-tall sculpture of three figures, called *Spirit of Emancipation*. Unlike her other work at the time, the sculpture was not comprised of obvious slavery and African American symbolism, such as the discarded chains and thankful slaves bowing to the image of Abraham Lincoln that appeared in her other sculptures. *Spirit of Emancipation* was the start of the most prolific period of Fuller's life, which lasted fifty years.

Social Observations Produced Strong, Subtle Work

Where before Fuller's sculptural statements on the African American experience had utilized bold and obvious imagery, her style became more subdued. She was no less a social observer and advocate, but she made her statements more subtlety. Between 1914 and 1921, Fuller's work reflected American anxieties over the world at war. She explored the search for peace and the atrocities of war. Fuller created two anti-lynching pieces in response to the increasing violence against blacks in America, one based on the notorious Mary Turner case. She also produced a relief of a boy rising from his knees in the morning sun, hoping to inspire black youth at Atlanta, Georgia's black Young Men's Christian Association during these racially tense times.

During this period, Fuller created *Ethiopia Awakening*, a sculpture which symbolized the emergence of a new way of black thinking that anticipated the voices of the Harlem Renaissance. Using an African motif, she sought to awaken blacks to the awareness of anti-colonialism and nationhood. The sculpture was of a woman whose lower half was wrapped like a mummy, with the head of a beautiful African woman wearing an ancient Egyptian queen's headdress. In *Ethiopia Awakening*, Fuller looked to share a message of hope in Africa—a world plagued by hunger and war, compared to the prosperity of the Western world.

In 1929, Fuller responded to her increasingly crowded attic studio and her husband's concerns for her health. Dr. Fuller was worried that so much dust produced in so small a space would damage his wife's health. So she designed and had built a shoreline studio on Larned's Pond, not far from the Fuller home. The new space increased her productivity and allowed her to begin taking on students.

Grew No Less Inspired With Age

Fuller's popularity grew in the 1930s. She showed her work at local libraries and churches and with the Boston Art Club. She exhibited her work with and later became a juror for The Harmon Foundation in New York City, which was founded to support the work of young black artists. Through these types of relationships, Fuller shared work still rooted in African American culture throughout the thirties and forties.

Fuller closed up her studio in 1950 to care for her husband, who died three years later. Sick with tuberculosis, she entered a sanitarium, where she stayed until 1956. When she was again well, she started taking commissions, including one for the Palmer Institute in Sedalia, North Carolina, to sculpt its founder. She also sculpted the head and hands of ten notable black women for a set of dolls for the National Council of Negro Women in Washington, D.C.

Through her eighties, Fuller continued to produce significant and inspired commissions. *Storytime,* for the Framingham Center Library, depicts a mother reading to her children. Framingham Union Hospital, where Dr. Fuller practiced, commissioned her to sculpt a representation of working doctors and nurses. She also supported the civil rights movement by donating proceeds from the sales of her work and by letting symbols of that era inspire her. She dedicated *The Good Shepherd* to the clergymen who walked with Martin Luther King, Jr. across the Edmund Pettus bridge on March 9, 1965. When four young girls died in the bombing of the Sixteenth Street Baptist Church in Birmingham, Alabama, Fuller reacted with a piece called *The Crucifixion.*

Although Fuller initially resisted W.E.B. DuBois's idea that she specialize in African American themes in her work, she ultimately did just that. Her perspective of the black American experience led to her strongest, most recognized, and inspired works. Fuller died March 18, 1968, at age 90.

Books

Dictionary of American Women, edited by Chris Petteys, 1985.
Facts on File Encyclopedia of Black Women in America, edited by Darlene Clark Hine, 1997.

Online

Hall of Black Achievement, http://www.bridgew.edu/HOBA/fuller.htm (April 21, 2003). □

G

Griselda Gambaro

Griselda Gambaro (born 1928) is a powerful, world-renowned, prize-winning playwright, novelist, and short story writer. For decades she has been creating allegorical dramas that deal with issues relating to the oppressive political and social environment of Argentina in the 1960s, 1970s, and 1980s. Although her characters and their situations offer a commentary on Argentine society and government, Gambaro's work reached beyond the country's borders to make universal statements about power dynamics, human nature, and the role women play in the larger social order.

From Humble Beginnings to Recognition

Gambaro is a second-generation Argentine with Italian roots. She was born in Buenos Aires on July 28, 1928. Growing up as the only girl amongst four older brothers in a poor family was not easy. Her father was a postal worker of limited economic means, tending to the most basic needs of his children. As a result, the young girl had little access to books and plays, and her public schooling did not provide her with good formal education. Gambaro was highly motivated, though, and refused to be stopped by her circumstances. She taught herself about drama and literature by going to the public library and immersing herself in the works of dramatists such as Eugene O'Neill, Anton Chekhov, and Luigi Pirandello. After finishing high school in 1943, she began working in a publishing company. She later moved into business and accounting

and remained there until she married sculptor Juan Carlos Distefano by whom, she said in *Women's Voices from Latin America,* she was "emancipated." Together, they had two children, Andrea in 1961 and Lucas in 1965.

Gambaro began writing at a young age, but her work was not immediately successful. "When I was twenty-four, I published a book of stories that I don't want to remember. It was so immature, so full of the sort of imperfections that mar many first books," she confessed in *Interviews with Contemporary Women Playwrights.* In her mid-thirties, however, Gambaro suddenly started to enjoy great recognition and success as a writer. *Madrigal en ciudad,* her second volume of short stories, won an esteemed prize from Argentina's National Endowment for the Arts, which resulted in publication in 1963. At the same time, she became involved with the Instituto Torcuato Di Tella, an avant-garde foundation formed in Buenos Aires in 1958 that combined sociological studies with the fine arts until it was forced to close in 1971 due to the repressive political climate. The Instituto achieved a name for itself in the 1960s as a hot bed of groundbreaking experimental art, music, and theater. It was at the Instituto's theater that Gambaro put on a series of four plays responsible for her international success. Each of these plays—*Las paredes* ("The Walls," 1964), *El desatino* ("The Blunder," 1965), *Los siameses* ("The Siamese Twins," 1967), and *El campo* ("The Camp," 1971)—was developed alongside a corresponding prose piece. *El desatino,* for example, was also a collection of short stories, which gained attention from literary critics and won the Emecé Publishers Prize for 1964.

Major Themes

Gambaro's plays share the common theme of everyday people wrapped up in oppressive power relationships.

Gambaro's characters are victims and oppressors locked into situations in which the victim remains helpless and unable to rebel against the cruelty of his oppressor who often takes the form of friend or family member. These early plays, as Gambaro herself acknowledged in *Women's Voices from Latin America,* are largely concerned with the subject of passivity. "One often has a single theme, and I probably have mine, the problem of passivity. It must be due to personal reasons; I am a very cowardly woman. Very cowardly in every way. I'm not brave; I find it difficult to be brave. I am very preoccupied with passivity and the non-assumption of individual responsibility. In society it is that way and, also, in my plays." In *The Female Dramatist,* Gambaro was quoted as having said that she was also majorly preoccupied with "violence—its roots, manifestations, and spheres of influence, as well as the ways in which it may be perceived, masked, and denied."

Gambaro's style involved black humor, focusing on the absurdities of the Argentine political situation, and it broke with realistic drama insofar as her plays were not set in a specific time or place. The dramatist did not locate her plays literally within Argentina by use of identifiable nationalist themes or specific references to her native country. Instead the physical and mental abuse played out by her characters mirrors the reality perpetrated by the Argentine military in the 1960s through the Dirty War ending in 1983. Adding to the surreal nature of her work was the fact that the action of the plays was rarely linear or logical, and it was almost always terrifying. *Las paredes,* for example, is about a nameless Youth who is abducted and questioned by an Official and a Custodian in a well-decorated room. Nobody seems to know why he is being held captive, but the tormentors are dead set on breaking his will and torturing him, regardless. As the walls close in and the room begins to literally shrink in front of the audience's eyes, the Youth can no longer deny that he has "disappeared" from the world. Still, at the end of the play, he is unable to bring himself to walk out the open door because he is so deeply traumatized.

Years in Exile

Gambaro managed to remain in good enough favor with the Argentine regime until 1977 when her novel *Ganarse la muerte* was banned. Copies were confiscated and President Rafael Videla did not allow the book's sale. "There were raids, the army paid us 'visits' during which they looked at all the material in the house. As any material was considered subversive—Marx, Freud—a big burning of books resulted. Everyone who owned books burned them," Gambaro explained in *Interviews.* She even burned the manuscript to her visionary masterpiece, *Información para extranjeros* ("Information for Foreigners," 1971) and had to reconstruct it years later. She refused to publish it for many years because of its obvious political message and the certain negative repercussions that would ensue once it was released. The piece predicted the rise of the government's intellect police who eventually came to murder, torture, and kidnap thousands of Argentines because of their thoughts.

Gambaro and her family went into self-imposed exile for three years in Barcelona, Spain, from 1977 to 1980.

When the Argentine dictatorship's control over society began to diminish in the early 1980s, Gambaro returned home and participated—along with the foremost directors, actors, and writers in the theater community—in staging the Teatro Abierto ("Open Theater"). It was a creative protest against the government's on-going repression, and in 1981 the Teatro released 20 plays, most of which, including Gambaro's *Decir sí ("To Say Yes,"* 1981), were political attacks on the military government and the commercial nature of Argentine theater. Soon after, when the Argentine government lost the Falklands War, failing to expel the British from the Falkland Islands off Argentina's coast in 1982, Argentina began a period of extended democracy, the likes of which had not been in place in many years. The attempt to drive Great Britain from the Falklands was one of the Argentine dictatorship's last efforts to gain popularity and maintain power. When it failed, a new era of freedom began, exemplified by the fact that a formerly banned playwright, Carlos Gorostiza, was named minister of culture.

Homecoming: More Freedom and a New Voice

Since Gambaro herself had been a "prohibited" writer under the former administration, the democratic shift in Argentina's political climate affected her very personally and allowed her the freedom to influence Argentina with her bold art. Although the political climate in Argentina had calmed, the writer was no less passionate in her work. In 1987, she finally published *Información para extranjeros,* an arresting work that challenged spectators to comment on and engage the brutal actions they witnessed on a "stage" that did not have clearly defined boundaries. The stage directions called for an entire house to be used as the backdrop for some actors who perpetrated violent acts, such as murders and kidnappings, while others played children's games. The audience members encounter harmlessness or torture, depending upon which room they enter, and they were to be led by an actor/guide who interacted with spectators along the way. The surreal writing style and contrast between the actions taking place in the different rooms reflected Gambaro's belief that, "[Argentina] is a schizophrenic country, a country that lives two lives. The courteous and generous have their counterpart in the violent and the armed who move among the shadows. . . . One never really knows what country one is living in, because the two co-exist." Gambaro created a drama in which viewers were not permitted to be passive bystanders to terrible acts of violence, for the guide forced them to question and respond to their surroundings and the events that take place within them. The play, which powerfully addresses the reality of Argentina's past military regime and the way average citizens were implicated—through their silence—in the brutalization of their neighbors, was a commentary on passivity in the face of horror. It indirectly, but clearly, was a reminder of the phenomenon of *desaparecidos* ("the disappeared"). These vanished Argentine citizens, many of whom were intellectuals or politically conscious members of society, were commonly dragged off to a horrible fate, often in the dead of night, by the former dictatorship while their neighbors pretended they did not see what was happening.

During Gambaro's time in exile, the playwright had the opportunity to engage the feminist movement in Europe and develop consciousness about women and their issues. At the time, *Ganarse la muerte* had been published in France and Gambaro was invited there. "I had the opportunity to meet the feminists of France, and I began reading about the specific problems related to women. I started to realize things which, before that time, I had only felt in an instinctive way," she told Kathleen Betsko and Rachel Koenig in *Interviews*. In the 1980s, Gambaro's writing reflected, embraced, and contributed to the growing women's movement in Argentina. She created a number of plays with strong female characters. These women, like the geisha Suki in *Del sol naciente ("From the Rising Sun")* and Antígona in *Antígona Furiosa,* represented powerful models who rejected the confines of stereotypical female roles. "The title character of her 1986 play *Antígona Furiosa* hauntingly mirrors Gambaro herself. She, like Antígona and her Greek namesake, is intent on burying her dead, her disappeared ones. She renounces the traditional sphere, home and hearth, and refuses to remain silent," Elaine Parnow commented in *The Female Dramatist.*

Starting in the mid 1980s, many of Gambaro's characters—not just women—shifted in such a way that those in the victims' roles managed to confront and fight back against their oppressors. For example, marginalized characters in *Del sol naciente* joined forces at the end of the play, their solidarity and humanity undermining the oppressive system in which they found themselves. This transformation from passive characters to consciously united, active ones reflects the way in which Argentine society was unable to fight government oppression until the Falklands War brought about a group effort to overcome it.

It was only in the 1990s, after decades of recognition in Latin America and Europe, that Gambaro's work began to be performed with some frequency in the United States. In this era, her plays began changing in texture and theme—personal emotions, rather than state control became the main subject. *Penas sin importancia,* written in the early 1990s, has been described by reviewers as having a gentler tone than her previous work, reflecting the transitions—socially, economically, and politically—that have occurred in Argentina since Gambaro began writing. Since the early 1960s, Gambaro has let loose her words through plays, fiction, and essays. In the face of terror, exile, repression, and financial challenges, the dramatist has never failed to offer creative, poignant, relevant, and painfully true perspectives on politics and human nature.

Books

Betsko, Kathleen and Rachel Koenig, *Interviews with Contemporary Women Playwrights,* Beech Tree Books, 1987.
Garfield, Evelyn Picón, *Women's Voices from Latin America: Interviews with Six Contemporary Authors,* Wayne State University Press, 1985.
Marting, Diane E., editor, *Spanish American Women Writers: A Bio-Bibliographical Source Book,* Greenwood Press, 1990.
Partnow, Elaine T., editor, with Lesley Ann Hyatt, *The Female Dramatist,* Facts on File, Inc., 1998.

Online

Kozilowski, Thomas, "Griselda Gambaro," *Gale Contemporary Authors Online,* http://www.gale.com, (February 8, 2003). □

Alfonso García Robles

During his distinguished career, Mexican diplomat Alfonso García Robles (1911–1991) was a strong advocate of banning nuclear weapons. Educated in international universities as a lawyer, García Robles rose through the ranks of Mexico's diplomatic service to become a well-known and highly respected international spokesperson on nuclear disarmament. He was instrumental in bringing about the Treaty of Tlateloco, an agreement among 22 Latin-American countries that banned nuclear weapons in that part of the world. It was because of this outstanding achievement—and García Robles's tireless efforts toward global nuclear disarmament—that he received the Nobel Peace Prize in 1982.

Alfonso García Robles was born in Zamora, Mexico, on March 20, 1911. Showing intellectual promise, he studied law at the Independent National University of Mexico. Later he travelled to Europe and earned a postgraduate degree at the Institute of Superior Studies at the University of Paris. García Robles went on to earn a second postgraduate degree at the Academy of International Law in the Netherlands.

Entered Diplomatic Service

In 1939 García Robles became a member of his country's foreign service, first working as a secretary of the Mexican delegation in Sweden. In 1945 he was Mexico's delegate at the San Francisco Conference, a global summit that involved the founding of the United Nations. As a result of his efforts at this pivotal conference, he obtained a position at the United Nations Secretariat for several years.

In the late 1950s García Robles served as director general in the Mexican Ministry of Foreign Affairs. In this capacity he played a major role in his country's Law of the Sea conferences. In 1962 he was appointed Mexican Ambassador to Brazil and first became aware of a proposal that aimed to prohibit the use of nuclear weaponry in Latin America. The proposal originated in the anxiety created during the Cuban Missile Crisis of 1962, when the United States, Cuba, and the Union of Soviet Socialist Republics (USSR) were involved in a standoff many feared would lead to a nuclear war. The crisis had been sparked when the USSR attempted to secretly establish a base for nuclear missiles in Cuba, one of its communist allies. In October the missile site was discovered by CIA operatives who reported its existence to U.S. President John F. Kennedy. Because of Cuba's proximity to the southern shores of the United States,

Kennedy imposed a naval blockade around the island and demanded that Soviet Premier Nikita Khrushchev remove the missiles. The crisis came to an end on October 28, 1962, when Khrushchev accepted Kennedy's promise to decrease the number of U.S. missiles in Turkey. Although a major conflict had been averted, for two tension-filled weeks the whole world had held its breath.

In the wake of the crisis García Robles persuaded the Mexican government to support the proposed plan of nuclear non-proliferation in Latin America. He tirelessly advocated this position for several years, after which his efforts resulted in the 1967 Treaty of Tlatelolco.

Negotiated Treaty of Tlateloco

Since 1964 García Robles had served as under-secretary of foreign affairs to Mexican president Gustavo Diaz Ordaz. In this position, he was able to effectively champion the cause of international nuclear disarmament—particularly disarmament for Latin America—and this directly led to his key role in the formation of the Treaty of Tlateloco. His role in creating a nuclear-free Latin America was an extremely important and high-profile one, his efforts so integral to the cause that he became known as the "father" of the Tlatelolco treaty. This agreement, which was concluded on March 12, 1967, had been first proposed by Adolfo López Mateos, who was president of Mexico at the time. The basic idea of the agreement was that a ban on nuclear weapons in Latin America would prevent that part of the world from becoming involved in any conflicts—and

potential full-scale warfare—that could arise between the world's superpowers. García Robles conducted the negotiations, which went on for several years and called on his diplomatic skills to bring about a conclusion. Although the agreement was finalized, its ultimate goal of the agreement remained unrealized into the next century; several Latin American countries, among them Brazil and Argentina, signed the agreement but never implemented it. Still, 22 countries in that part of the world banned nuclear weapons from their territories as a result of García Robles' efforts.

Became International Figure

The Tlatelolco Treaty was the crowning achievement of García Robles's distinguished career. In all, the negotiations lasted four years and were concluded in the Tlatelolco Plaza in Mexico City. While García Robles's role eventually led to his receiving the Nobel Prize in 1982, this honor was not bestowed for the Tlatelolco Agreement alone. The Nobel Prize committee recognized the Mexican diplomat's numerous efforts toward achieving nuclear disarmament worldwide. He advocated for global disarmament in session at the United Nations, thereby gaining a reputation as one of the most reasonable and knowledgeable advocates for a nuclear weaponry ban. In 1968 he helped draft the Treaty on the Non-proliferation of Nuclear Weapons.

In the late 20th century García Robles became a major diplomatic player in world affairs. From 1971 to 1975 he served as Mexico's permanent representative to the United Nations and from 1974 to 1975 was chairman of Mexico's delegation to the General Assembly. During this time he also held the post of director in the Political Affairs Division of the U.N. Secretariat, serving as principal secretary of the special committee on Palestine and as secretary of an ad hoc committee on the Palestine question.

In 1975 García Robles became Mexico's secretary of Outer Relations, a position he held for two years. That position evolved into something larger when, in 1977, he became his country's permanent representative to the U.N. committee on disarmament, which was based in Geneva, Switzerland.

During the U.N. session on general nuclear disarmament held in Geneva in 1978—the first-ever session of its kind—García Robles became known and respected for his patient and skillful diplomacy in helping to stem a global arms race that, by that point in time, had approached alarming levels. It was largely because of his tireless efforts that the U.N. General Assembly adopted the "Final Document" that resulted the session. As one of the international representatives seeking to initiate a world-wide campaign to ban nuclear weapons, García Robles assumed the prodigious task of coordinating all of the various views from different countries and incorporating those views, along with the accompanying proposals, into this document.

In 1977 García Robles published *338 Days of Tlatelolco,* a book documenting the creation and adoption of the Latin American non-nuclear agreement. It was one of several books on international affairs he would publish during his career.

Received the Nobel Peace Prize

García Robles continued his untiring efforts toward global nuclear disarmament during the U.N. disarmament sessions held in 1982 as the second of three scheduled sessions (a third was held in 1999). This second session turned out to be less positive than the first. While supporting his idea of a world disarmament campaign, the assembly failed to adopt it.

In presenting him with the 1982 Nobel Peace Prize, the Nobel committee stated that García Robles's main contribution was in helping to create the agreement that made Latin America a nuclear-free zone. It went on to acknowledge his other efforts as well, citing the diplomat for "not only . . . almost 20 years of work on disarmament, but also vindication of the virtues of patient and methodical negotiation." García Robles shared the prize with Sweden's Alva Myrdal, a former cabinet minister, diplomat, and writer whose efforts toward world nuclear disarmament matched those of García Robles. Like García Robles, Myrdal played an active role in nuclear non-proliferation negotiations and emerged as one of the world leaders on that issue. Also like García Robles, she attempted to pressure the United States and the USSR to demonstrate greater concern for the dangers of nuclear weaponry and to come up with workable solutions to disarmament.

Cofounder of Contadora Group

Following their award, García Robles and Myrdal worked together in another important effort toward world peace: the creation of the Contadora Group, which was established in 1983 to deal with the highly volatile situation in Central America. The group's main goals are to bring to an end the terrible suffering endured by the people of Central America due to the ongoing military conflicts; to recognize the basic human rights of all citizens; and to help solve a the local crisis before it could negatively impact global peace. The idea for the group was developed by another Nobel Prize winner: Gabriel García Marquez, the Colombian writer who received the award for literature. Also contributing to the creation of the group Swedish Prime Minister Olof Palme. Together, the Contadora Group founders called for the presidents of Colombia, Mexico, Venezuela, and Panama to mediate in the Central American conflict.

In 1983 the foreign ministers of these countries met on the island of Contadora and agreed to combine their efforts in the Contadora Act on Peace and Co-operation in Central America. Reviewing the political and economic situation in this region, they then drew up a detailed plan for the formation of the Group. The plan met with the support of the U.N. Security Council and its General Assembly, as well as with that of many regional and international governing bodies. In 1985 Argentina, Brazil, Peru, and Uruguay organized groups to support the Contadora Group's advisers. That same year, the Group was awarded the Simon Bolívar Prize.

Honored in Life and Death

In 1990 the Fulbright-García Robles scholarship honoring García Robles and U.S. Senator J. William Fulbright was established to help both Mexican and U.S. citizens. García Robles passed away the following year on September 2, 1991, in Mexico City, Mexico. After his death his widow, Juanita García Robles, gifted her husband's personal 1,100-volume library to the University of Virginia. In appreciation of the donation, the university erected an exhibit to honor García Robles. The exhibit included documents, articles, and photos and emphasized the Nobel Peace Prize.

Books

Latin American Lives, Macmillan, 1998.

Online

"Alfonso García Robles Biography," *Nobel e-Museum,* http://www.nobel.se/peace/laureates/1982/robles-bio.html (March 15, 2003).

"Contadora Group and the Central American Crisis," *Global Security.com,* http://www.globalsecurity.org/military/library/report/1985/SA.htm (March 15, 2003). □

David Lawrence Geffen

David Geffen (born 1943) has emerged as one of the wealthiest individuals in rock music through his combined talents as a manager, label owner, and film producer.

Beginnings

David Geffen's father, Abraham Geffen, was only three years old in 1906 when his Jewish family packed their few belongings and left their home in Vilna, Russia, for America. Many years later, in 1930, a marriageable "Abe" Geffen would again cross the Atlantic, having decided to use his hard-earned savings to see the world. Taking leave of his job as a Western Union telegrapher, he made his way first to Europe and later to Palestine, where he met a pretty seamstress by the name of Batya Volovskaya.

Volovskaya had been born in a small village in the Ukraine in 1907. Her father was a wealthy Jewish landowner. Her mother ran a small pharmacy and cosmetology business. When she was thirteen, Volovskaya's parents sent her to live with an aunt in Romania so that she could continue her studies. After the aunt died, Volovskaya was unable to return to Russia because the Bolsheviks had cut off all communication between Russia and Romania. She chose instead to go to Palestine, where her father had relatives.

During Abe Geffen's stay in Tel Aviv, Volovskaya introduced him to the intellectual and artistic circles of that city. Although Volovskaya could not speak English, she was able to converse with Abe in Yiddish. Abe, however, returned to America alone. Back home, Abe Geffen kept up a correspondence with the young seamstress, while saving everything he could towards making a return trip to Palestine. In

1931, he succeeded in making his second trip, during which he married Volovskaya. That November, the pair arrived at Ellis Island, New York. The newlyweds took an apartment on Manhattan's Lower East Side, and their first child, a boy named Misha, was born in 1933. On February 21, 1943, their second son, David Lawrence Geffen, joined the family.

Childhood

When David Geffen was six years old, his mother had what was then called a "nervous breakdown" and had to be hospitalized. During the six months that she was in the hospital, his grandmother cared for David. The young boy exhibited emotional problems during his mother's absence, and after she was released, Batya Geffen arranged to have them both treated by a psychiatrist.

Later David's parents opened a successful corset shop. Batya, a good businesswoman, taught her youngest son the value of hard work. But his parents' long hours away from home left David unsupervised for lengthy periods. Geffen later said he used his unstructured time to attend Broadway musicals and to listen to recordings of show tune musicals.

Show Business

Geffen once claimed to have had 17 jobs between high school and the time that he was hired as an usher at the CBS-TV studios in New York, but he could not fall in love with any of them. Not at least until he got the job at CBS, where

he was allowed to watch TV rehearsals with the likes of Judy Garland and Red Skelton.

Eventually he was hired as a receptionist for a new CBS TV series called *The Reporters,* but after he made the mistake of offering some suggestions to the show's producer, he lost the job. He then approached the show's casting director, asking her whether there was anything he could do. When she asked him what it was he could do, he reportedly replied, "Nothing." The casting director jokingly suggested he might want to consider becoming an agent.

William Morris Agency

Geffen apparently took her advice seriously and applied for a job in the mailroom of the William Morris Agency. The mailroom brought Geffen into contact with everybody at William Morris, and he has said that the job was the first one he held where he knew he was in the right place.

Geffen worked his way up to agent at William Morris and became a specialist in signing and managing rock 'n' roll artists. He worked with Laura Nyro, who had recently received disappointing reviews at the Monterey Pop Festival. Geffen promoted her by keeping her out of major concerts until she had achieved a following and then booked her into Carnegie Hall, where she sold out twice. Nyro's first album on Verve had not sold well, and Geffen landed her a contract on Columbia, where her albums scored well on the record charts. With Nyro's songs selling, Geffen renegotiated her contract with Columbia and in the process made himself a millionaire—at the tender age of 27.

Formed Asylum Records

Geffen went on to sign Crosby, Stills and Nash to Atlantic Records. After Atlantic refused to sign Jackson Browne, however, Geffen formed his own label, Asylum Records, with Elliot Roberts. Asylum would eventually sign many other top West Coast artists. According to Geffen's biographer, Tom King, "Geffen . . . wanted [Asylum] to be known as a sanctuary for artists, a place where they could make their music and be free from any kind of corporate interference."

But there may have been a darker side to Geffen's decision to form Asylum. According to King, Geffen was all too willing to sabotage personal relationships to get what he wanted. "For example," King told *ABCNews.com* in 2000, "he signed the Eagles, Joni Mitchell and others to his Asylum Records label with false promises and suspect business contracts."

In any case, the label began selling in 1972-73 after Asylum had signed Browne, Joni Mitchell and Linda Ronstadt. Geffen, meanwhile, refused to let members of the band that would later become known as the Eagles record until he felt they were ready. Geffen's call proved to be on target, and the Eagles would go on to become one of rock 'n' roll's biggest acts.

Warner Brothers

Geffen's next move was to sell Asylum to the Warner/Elektra/Atlantic (WEA) distribution company for $7 million. The sale brought more money to the Eagles; at the same time WEA more than recouped the purchase price of Asylum through sales of albums by Linda Ronstadt and the Eagles. This sale would prove to be one of the few times that Geffen would undervalue his artists.

The deal also left Geffen on contract with Warner Brothers. He managed to regain control of the Asylum label after it was taken from Warner Brothers Atlantic division and combined with its Elektra operation. In 1974, Geffen scored a major coup when he cajoled Bob Dylan into signing a contract. Dylan ended up making two albums for Geffen on Elektra/Asylum, but he left after he was offered a better royalty rate elsewhere. Geffen also signed Andrew Gold, Tom Waits, and a revamped Byrds.

But Geffen was restless. He tried his hand at Los Angeles club management, and, without success, as vice-chairman of Warner Brothers Pictures. After his Warner Brothers contract expired, he chose to move on.

Cancer Diagnosis

About this time Geffen was diagnosed with bladder cancer, though a second opinion failed to confirm the earlier diagnosis. Nevertheless, in 1976 Geffen decided to retire from the music industry to attend to his perceived health problems. Four years later, he would be back.

Geffen Records

In 1980, Geffen became a consultant and formed his own record label, Geffen Records, with Warner Brothers money. He signed John Lennon, after bringing the former Beatle out of a five-year retirement, to make an album entitled "Double Fantasy" that was released in November 1980. Although Geffen Records also had contracts with Elton John and Peter Gabriel in the United States, Donna Summer, Joni Mitchell, Asia, Don Henley, Neil Young, Was (Not Was), Greg Copeland, and Lone Justice, Geffen's leading stars were not at that time at the peaks of their careers, and his label struggled. Meanwhile, Geffen invested in several Broadway musicals, including *Dreamgirls* and *Cats,* and achieved some success as a film producer (Geffen Films produced *Risky Business, Beetlejuice,* and *Little Shop of Horrors).*

In exchange for distribution rights for five years, Steve Ross of Warner Brothers agreed to sign over Geffen Records to David Geffen. The record company had not achieved any real success up until then, and Geffen had sometimes been forced to ask Ross for advances. After Geffen sold 13 million copies of one Guns N' Roses album, he tried to sell the company back to Ross. But Ross declined the offer. In 1990, Thorn-EMI attempted to buy Geffen Records for a reported $750 million, but Geffen instead sold it to MCA for approximately $530 million in stock, which made him the largest shareholder. In 1989, Geffen and MCA had more top selling albums than any other company. When Matsushita bought MCA in 1991, Geffen became a billionaire.

Gay Spokesperson

In 1992, Geffen publicly acknowledged his homosexuality at an AIDS benefit in Los Angeles. Even though Geffen's sexual preference was widely known among his associates as early as the 1960s, it was not something that he talked about very much. But Geffen's speech in Los Angeles had the effect of making him a spokesman for gay issues.

When President Clinton proposed ending the ban on homosexuals in the military, he turned to Geffen for feedback. With military officials opposing the idea on the grounds that it would be bad for morale, Geffen became a torch carrier for the president's proposal. But after a month spent trying to turn public opinion in favor of the plan, Clinton was forced to adopt a "don't ask, don't tell" compromise. Geffen, for his part, backed away from the issue, saying that overturning the ban would not be worth committing political suicide.

DreamWorks

In 1995, Geffen formed the DreamWorks movie studio with Steven Spielberg, Mo Ostin, and Jeffrey Katzenberg. Each partner contributed $33 million in start-up capital, making them title to 67 percent of the company. By 1995, they had attracted more than $2 billion that they would use to release films, television shows, interactive games, animated films, and music. DreamWorks even negotiated a partnership with Microsoft for their computer releases. One of the first achievements of the company's record division, DreamWorks SKG Music, was to extract George Michael from his Sony contract.

In October 1999, DreamWorks announced its plans to create an internet entertainment company under the name of Pop.com in a joint venture with Imagine Entertainment. The start-up was to offer short films, streaming video, live events, games, performance art, and continuing series. Pop.com's creators hoped to encourage film and video artists to create new material for the site. But after merger talks broke down in September 2000, the founders of Pop.com decided to terminate the venture. Geffen and his partners reportedly could not figure out how the start-up would be able to make any money given that only a handful of Internet users then had the high-speed connections needed to make live video interesting. The audience to sustain such a venture was still in the dream stage.

The Operator

Even though Geffen long ago made enough money to tempt him from ever doing another day's honest work, he reportedly plans to continue working for many more years. DreamWorks partner Jeffrey Katzenberg once praised Geffen's integrity as a key to his success in the entertainment business. But in an unauthorized biography, published in 2000 and entitled *The Operator: David Geffen Builds, Buys and Sells the New Hollywood,* Wall Street Journal columnist Tom King portrayed Geffen as a man with few scruples who was all too willing to betray friends and sacrifice personal relationships to get what he wanted. Not surprisingly, Geffen took affront at the portrayal.

King told *ABCNews.com* in 2000: "[Geffen] apparently doesn't like the way the book portrays him. He has told people that he thinks the book is a 'total character assassination.' It is not. In my mind, the book is a very balanced portrait of a man who has made indisputable contributions to pop culture history. At the same time, he's no boy scout. He knocked a lot of people off the ladder on his way to the top, and those people's stories are reflected in the book too."

Books

King, Tom, *The Operator: David Geffen Builds, Buys, and Sells the New Hollywood,* Random House, 2000.

Periodicals

Calonius, Erik, "Their Wildest Dreams," *Fortune,* August 16, 1999.

Online

"David Geffen," *Musicweb,* http://www.musicweb.uk.net/encyclopaedia/g/G19.HTM (January 2003).
"Hollywood's High and Mighty: Chat with the Author of a Biography of David Geffen," *ABCNews.com,* http://abcnews.go.com/sections/business/DailyNews/king_chat000417.html (January 2003). □

Walter Gilbert

American scientist Walter Gilbert (born 1932), who shared the Nobel Prize for Chemistry in 1980, became world famous for his groundbreaking research in the field of molecular biology. Admired by both fellow scientists and laymen, his efforts substantially advanced the field of genetic engineering. Because of his work, scientists have been able to manufacture genetic material in laboratories. When receiving his Nobel award, he was cited for developing a method for determining the sequence of nucleotide links in the chainlike molecules of nucleic acids. Later, he formed several commercial biotechnology firms, and he became involved in helping map the human genetic blueprint.

Early Life

Walter Gilbert was born on March 21, 1932, in Boston, Massachusetts, to Richard V. Gilbert, an economist, and Emma Cohen, a child psychologist. His father worked for the Office of Price Administration during World War II as part of President Franklin D. Roosevelt's administration. His mother proved to be an intellectually stimulating influence in the two-child household. When Gilbert was a boy, she would administer intelligence tests to his sister and him, and she educated him at home during his earliest years, teaching him how to read. In 1939, the family moved to Washington, D.C., where Gilbert attended public schools.

As a boy, Gilbert took an active interest in science, joining mineralogical and astronomical clubs. Naturally curious, he began performing his own experiments, once with nearly catastrophic results: when he was 12 years old, while his family lived in Virginia, he attempted a chemistry experiment that ended in an explosion of shattered glass. He suffered a slashed wrist and his mother had to take him to the hospital. According to her account, Gilbert was only concerned with determining what went wrong with the experiment.

In high school, he became fascinated with inorganic chemistry and nuclear physics. A youth of advanced intelligence, he would often skip school to go to the Library of Congress so he could read about Van de Graaf generators and atom smashers. "I decided to try and find out about these subjects, but there was nothing available in school," he recalled. "My grades were still good enough that the school didn't object too much." He also maintained his interest in astronomy and, as a teenager, he won a regional science fair in Washington, D.C. by making a telescope that photographed sun spots.

After high school, he attended Harvard University, where he majored in chemistry and physics. While in college, his interests became focused on theoretical physics. As a graduate student, he studied the theory of elementary particles and the quantum theory of fields. After one year of graduate school at Harvard, he transferred to the University of Cambridge in England for two years and received a doctorate degree in physics in 1957. His thesis involved dispersion relations for elementary particle scattering. While at Cambridge, he met James Watson, a young American scientist who had established a name for himself in scientific circles—and imprinted his name in genetic textbooks forever—with his groundbreaking work with DNA. That same year he returned to Harvard for a year of postdoctorate study. He also married Celia Stone, a poet he first met in high school. They would have two children, John Richard and Kate. After that, he became an assistant professor of physics at Harvard University. In the late 1950s and early 1960s, he taught several courses in theoretical physics.

Entered Molecular Biology Field

In 1960, Gilbert reached a turning point in his life when he worked with Watson and Francois Gros on an experiment that involved the identification of messenger RNA. (The experiment uncovered new information about messenger RNA—essentially, the "messenger that relayed information from DNA to the areas in the cell where proteins are manufactured.") Gilbert found experimental research exciting, and from that point on, he continued working in molecular biology, which was a new and exciting field at the time. In 1961, Gilbert gained a great deal of notoriety when he published his first paper on messenger RNA in *Nature Magazine*. He soon became a tenured biophysicist at Harvard.

Following his work with RNA, he did research into protein synthesis, again uncovering new information that would advance the field. In the mid-sixties, he worked with Benno Müller-Hill. Their collaboration resulted in the isolation of the lactose repressor, the first example of a genetic control element. Again, his research findings advanced the field as well extended his notoriety to the international level. Later in that decade, working with David Dressler, he helped invent the rolling circle model, which describes one of the two ways DNA molecules duplicate themselves.

The 1970s were also an active and fruitful period for Gilbert. In that decade, he developed a technique of using gel electrophoresis that read nucleotide sequences of DNA segments. Also, he isolated the DNA fragment to which the lactose repressor is bound, studied the interaction of the bacterial RNA polymerase and the lactose repressor with DNA, developed recombinant DNA techniques, and helped develop rapid chemical DNA sequencing. In 1974, he became an American Cancer Society Professor of Molecular Biology. Late in the decade, he worked with Lydia Villa Komaroff and Argiris Efstratiadis on the bacterial strains that expressed insulin. The work he started with DNA would eventually lead to the Nobel Prize in Chemistry in the next decade.

Entered the Business Arena

In 1979, Gilbert formed an alliance with businessmen and other scientists to help found Biogen, a commercial genetic-engineering research corporation. Reportedly, he approached this enterprise with the same enthusiasm he brought to his academic and research pursuits, learning as much as he could about patent laws and exploring management issues. For several years, Gilbert served as chief executive officer. However, he was often at odds with the company's board of directors and he resigned in 1984. Later, he would lend a hand in starting several other biological companies, including Myriad Genetics. A few years after he left Biogen, he founded the Genome Corporation, a company involved in human genome research. But the company went out of business after the stock market crash of 1987. Despite the failed venture, Gilbert's interest in genome research never flagged. When he left Biogen, he went back to Harvard, where he became a major and very high profile supporter of the Human Genome Project, a government-funded enterprise looking to build a complete map of the gene sequences in human DNA.

Won the Nobel Prize

The next decade started with Gilbert receiving the most prestigious honor a scientist can attain. His innovative work and long list of achievements up to that point culminated in 1980 when he received a share of that year's Nobel Prize in Chemistry. Still a Harvard professor at the time, he shared the award with Professor Frederick Sanger, of Cambridge University in Great Britain, and Paul Berg, of Stanford University in California. They were honored for independently developing a method for determining the sequence of nucleotide links in the chainlike molecules of the nucleic acids DNA and RNA. Their work added a great deal to the worlds knowledge about how DNA, as a carrier of the genetic traits, directs the chemical machinery of the cell. Working separately in their own labs, Gilbert and Sanger developed different methods to determine the exact sequence of the nucleotide building blocks in DNA. Together, their work resulted in the creation of effective tools that enabled continued investigations into the structure and function of the genetic material.

Sought the Origin of Genes

After Gilbert resigned from Biotech in 1984, he returned to Harvard University. Beginning in 1985, he worked as a professor in the university's departments of physics, biophysics, biochemistry, and biology. Former students fondly recalled studying under him. Gilbert's labs and classrooms provided an exciting atmosphere where all were considered equals, including the world famous educator himself. Students enjoyed working with Gilbert, as they found that he encouraged camaraderie, demonstrated humor, and possessed an infectious personality.

Gilbert also worked in Harvard's Department of Molecular and Cellular Biology where, with fellow staff members, he became involved in research, discovery, and training in biological areas including cellular biology, biochemistry, neurobiology, genetics, and bioinformatics. This led him to research involving molecular evolution and the development of the theory of the intron/exon gene structure. Essentially, Gilbert set out to discover the origins of genes and how they evolved. It is believed that such a theory, if eventually proven correct, could impact drug design, as it may allow scientists to recognize and manipulate the working parts within proteins.

Essentially, the purpose of the research was to discover where genes may have come from and what the first genes were like. In the course of the work, Gilbert came up with terms for the interrupted pattern in which genes are stored. In the intron/exon theory, exons refer to the working parts, while introns refer to the regions in between where the cell has to splice out. If the theory is proven correct, some believe the history of life on earth could be deduced from the DNA of modern genes. The intron/exon theory is somewhat controversial and has not gained total acceptance. In response, Gilbert employed extensive computer and statistical analysis to try and support it. Fellow scientist Philip Sharp, a molecular biologist at the Massachusetts Institute of Technology, who first discovered the primordial introns, an accomplishment that won him a Nobel Prize in Physiology or Medicine in 1993, remarked that solving the mystery may be impossible, but he gave Gilbert a vote of confidence: "That won't stop Wally Gilbert, of course. . . . [He] captured the imagination of the field, and still has it, I think."

What Gilbert has tried to do is to find out how the first genes were assembled in the "organic soup oceans that once covered the entire world and gave rise to life." Obviously, this is a daunting task. Modern genes contain a great deal of information, and to determine precisely how they evolved by examining their structure would be a lengthy and complex process. However, Gilbert feels the first genetic elements were simple components that predate the modern exons. The early exons became mixed and matched and constructed into long chains that would make increasingly larger genes. He believes that by studying the structure of modern genes, we could see find the early components and then determine how the mixing and matching process occurred. In his theory, the introns would be the elements that could make the mixing and matching possible.

Outside Activities

Outside of his interests in science, Gilbert enjoys Chinese cooking, playing the piano (a skill he learned later in life), and studying and collecting ancient art, particularly Greek sculpture.

Periodicals

Hilts, Philip J., "Reading the History of Life in the Text of Modern Genes, *The New York Times,* November 12, 1996.

Online

"A Conversation with Walter Gilbert," *Discover,* November 1998, http://www.findarticles.com/cf_0/m1511/11_19/57564251/p1/article.jhtml (February 10, 2003).

Cromie, William J., "Scientists Ponder Sequence of Genes," *Harvard University Gazette,* http://www.news.harvard.edu/gazette/2001/04.05/07-genes.html (February 10, 2003).

Gilbert, Walter, "Walter Gilbert-Autobiography," *Nobel e-Museum,* http://www.nobel.se/chemistry/laureates/1980/gilbert-autobio.html (February 10, 2003).

"Nobel Prize in Chemistry to Nucleic Acid Investigators," *Nobel e-Museum,* http://www.nobel.se/chemistry/laureates/1980/press.html (February 10, 2003).

"Walter Gilbert (1932–)," *Access Excellence @ the National Health Museum,* http://www.accessexcellence.org/AB/BC/Walter_Gilbert.html (February 10, 2003)

"Walter Gilbert," *International Center for Scientific Research,* http://www.cirs.net/researchers/Chemistry/GILBERT.htm (February 10, 2003). □

Ellen Gleditsch

Ellen Gleditsch (1879–1968) began her long career in chemistry as Marie Curie's assistant but quickly grew to prominence in her own right. She pioneered the field of chemical radioactivity, becoming one of the first specialists. Gleditsch established the half-life of radium and aided in proving the existence of isotopes. In addition, Gleditsch was in contact with many prominent scientists of the time, and her friendship and work connected them all.

Ellen Gleditsch was born on December 29, 1879, in Mandal, Norway, the first of ten children born to Karl Kristian Gleditsch, a teacher, and Petra Birgitte (Hansen) Gleditsch. Although poor, the Gleditsch family was an exceptionally happy and close one. Both Karl and Petra were intellectual and politically liberal. The children were exposed to cultural, musical, and natural activities in addition to their regular studies. Gleditsch's mother was an advocate of women's rights.

Gleditsch graduated from high school in 1895 as valedictorian, with her highest grades in science and mathematics. She could not enter the university because it was not open to women at the time, so she began training as a pharmacologist in Tromso, and completed her nonacademic degree in pharmacology in 1902.

Because her studies involved chemistry and her degree qualified her to take courses at Oslo University, chemist Eyvind Bodtker invited her to study at the university laboratory. In 1903, she was an assistant in the chemistry lab, and in 1906 she was permitted to take the university entrance exam, which she passed. Bodtker, who became a lifelong friend—as did most who came into contact with sociable Gleditsch—suggested she continue her training at Marie Curie's laboratory in Paris and personally saw to her appointment there in 1907.

Became Curie's Assistant

Gleditsch received a grant from philanthropic funds made available by Josephine, the dowager queen of Norway and Sweden, for her Paris studies. Although students normally paid to work in Curie's laboratory, Curie needed a chemist and gave Gleditsch responsibility for purifying radium salts in exchange for exemption from fees. Curie also asked Gleditsch to help her reproduce a recent study in

the half-life of radium: 1,686 years. Her number remained the standard for many years until it was adjusted to 1,620 years. Half-life refers to the amount of time it takes for half the atoms of a radioactive substance to decay, or decrease in amount. Measuring the half-life of radium was important in the study of radioactivity because it could be used as a constant to study other elements. This work brought her acclaim and respect in the scientific community. Smith College awarded her an honorary Doctor of Science degree, and Lyman changed his mind about having women in his lab. Boltwood even helped her to publish her results in the *American Journal of Science.*

Helped to Confirm Existence of Isotopes

Gleditsch's other significant contribution to chemistry was her part in confirming the existence of isotopes. Isotopes are two or more atoms of an element that have the same atomic number and chemical behavior, but different atomic mass and physical properties. British chemist Frederick Soddy had suggested that an element's atoms could have different atomic weights, but most scientists maintained that atomic weight was fixed within an atom and evidence otherwise was hard to find. American chemist Theodore Richards was considered the expert in the field at the time, so like many other scientists trying to prove the existence of isotopes, Gleditsch sent a lead sample to him to analyze. Gleditsch's sample was so free of errors that it was the only one that proved the existence of isotopes.

Her work finally gained her respect and she was appointed a reader in chemistry at the University of Oslo in 1916. Although it was not a tenure track position, it was an improvement over the low-paying fellowship she had before. In 1917, Gleditsch coauthored two chemistry textbooks, one of which was the first of its kind written by Scandinavians. That same year, she became a member of Oslo's Academy of Science, only the second woman to be elected.

Gleditsch was always active in promoting the reputation of women in academics. In 1919, Gleditsch cofounded the Norwegian Women Academics Association, for which she acted as president from 1924 to 1928. She also served as president of the International Federation of University Women from 1926 to 1929, a position that allowed her to travel and lecture extensively. She began a radio lecture series and wrote biographies and research papers in several languages, in order to keep the public and other scientists informed in scientific research and breakthroughs. During the 1920s Gleditsch also traveled to Curie's laboratory many times to supervise experiments and once the entire lab while Curie was in South America.

Gleditsch continued her isotope research during this time, sometimes working with her chemist sister. She published a book on isotopes which was translated into English and sold so well it had to be reprinted in a year after its publication. In 1929, the University of Oslo finally appointed her professor of chemistry, making her only the second woman at Oslo to be appointed to that level.

which British scientists claimed that copper changed to lithium when exposed to radium, a study Curie doubted. Their findings did, indeed, prove the first study wrong. Gleditsch worked closely with Curie and became a family friend to Curie and her children. Most of her work in Curie's lab involved analyzing uranium and radium in radioactive minerals.

Established Half-Life of Radium

Gleditsch returned to Norway periodically to visit her family and, in 1912, returned to stay after receiving her *Licencée ès Sciences* from La Sorbonne in Paris. She was offered a fellowship at the University of Oslo, where she supervised the laboratory and lectured on radioactivity. The university's most experienced radiochemist, she continued her study of radium's half-life, but became discouraged by isolation and the lack of equipment. Hope for better opportunities came in 1913 in the form of a scholarship from the American-Scandinavian Foundation to study the United States. That same year, both her parents and a brother died within weeks of each other and Gleditsch then took in two of her brothers to care for them.

In 1914 Gleditsch wrote to Theodore Lymann at Harvard and Bertram Boltwood at Yale, asking to work in their laboratories. Lymann informed her that no woman had ever worked in his lab and he did not intend to change that. Boltwood was more polite, trying to discourage her with claims of minimal space. Undeterred, Gleditsch went to Yale anyway and spent a year there where she established

Provided Safe Haven for Scientists

During the 1930s, Gleditsch began work at a new laboratory she had helped to plan. Soon after, the Nazis came into power. Gleditsch, always the ''mother,'' took in her brother's child during the war and offered her laboratory space in Oslo as a kind of ''safe house'' for scientists, including Marietta Blau, who were fleeing Nazi persecution in other countries. By 1940, Norway was under German occupation as well. Even though part of the university had been taken control of by Nazis, Gleditsch continued her work. She and a few of her colleagues secretly became ''guerrilla scientists,'' working with an underground organization to defy Nazi power. Gleditsch aided the university community, sometimes hiding people in her own home. They planted gardens because food was scarce, and took turns guarding them from thieves. She went undercover, pretending to be a needleworker making national costumes, so she could relay messages to people about the underground resistance movement.

In 1943, the laboratory was raided by the Germans, and all of the men were arrested. Gleditsch and the other women worked quickly to clear the lab of anything valuable, and Gleditsch hid valuable minerals in a suitcase under her bed. When she was finally arrested, her scientific knowledge and fluent German helped her to negotiate her release.

After the war and her retirement, Gleditsch worked for the newly established United Nations organization UNESCO, only to resign several years later in protest to fascist Spain becoming a member. She was granted an honorary doctorate by the University of Strasbourg in 1948 and by La Sorbonne in 1962. She was the first woman to receive the award at La Sorbonne, and it was her proudest achievement.

After her retirement, Gleditsch continued her research and wrote papers on scientific history. She still kept an office at the laboratory and continued to advise and inspire students. She gave a dinner party at her country house for her students less than a week before her death of a stroke on June 5, 1968. That same year, the Ellen Gleditsch Scholarship Foundation was established in Norway to support aspiring scientists in their educations.

Books

Rayner-Canham, Marelene F., and Geoffrey W., eds., *A Devotion to Their Science: Pioneer Women of Radioactivity,* 1997.
Shearer, Benjamin F., and Barbara S. Shearer, eds., *Notable Women in the Physical Sciences,* 1997. □

Elinor Glyn

British author Elinor Glyn (1864–1943) wrote a number of novels, many featuring strong female characters in sexually charged situations. The most scandalous was *Three Weeks,* which nearly ended Glyn's career. Later in her career she was lured to

Hollywood to write screenplays, one of which originated the idea of the "It Girl." She also directed two unsuccessful films.

Glyn was born Elinor Sutherland on October 17, 1864, in Jersey, England, the daughter of Douglas and Elinor (Saunders) Sutherland. Douglas Sutherland was a Canadian-Scottish civil engineer who died of typhoid fever when Glyn was three months old. After her father's death, Glyn, her mother, older sister Lucy—who as Lady Lucy Duff Gordon would become a successful fashion designer—and her French grandmother moved to Canada. Glyn's grandmother was a particularly strong influence on Glyn; from an aristocratic background and with strong beliefs, the elderly woman helped shape her granddaughter's outlook on life.

In 1871 Glyn's mother was remarried, and the family returned to Jersey, England. Glyn and her sister did not like their stepfather, an oppressive man, nor did Glyn want to live in Jersey. Glyn became very rebellious in all facets of her life and stuck to her own ideas. Although she did not receive much of an education because she did not like the governesses assigned to teach her through the age of 14, Glyn read a great deal of the books in her stepfather's library.

As was expected of a woman of her class, Glyn wanted to marry, but was selective in her choice of suitors. As Jane Abdy wrote in the *Financial Times,* ''Elinor was beautiful, a flame-haired temptress, too exotic and too well-dressed to be easily accepted in the society of which she sometimes adorned the fringe. Her ambition was a happy and worldly marriage.'' Finally, Glyn married when she was in her late twenties. From outward appearances, the 1892 match was favorable: Clayton Glyn was a landowner and a member of the gentry. While the couple eventually had two daughters, Margot and Juliet, Clayton Glyn spent his fortune and had a drinking problem. The marriage was essentially over in the early 1900s, by which time his wife had sought solace in the arms of other men such as Lord Milner and Lord Curzon.

Published First Novel

Before her marriage ended, Glyn saw her first novel, *The Visits of Elizabeth,* serialized in *The World* in 1900. The story, which focuses life on country-house society, reflects Glyn's ability to observe the world around her. The book was popular and successful, and Glyn used the money she made from the book's publication to travel to Italy, France, and Egypt.

In 1902 Glyn followed *The Visits of Elizabeth* with a similar work, *Reflections of Ambrosine.* Basing the work on historical facts, she employed a diary format so the novel reads like the autobiography of its subject, Ambrosine Eustasie Marquise de Galincourt, who was guillotined in 1793. Her next novel was much different. *The Damsel and the Sage: A Woman's Whimsics* presents a dialogue between the Damsel, a free and loving woman, and the Sage, who lives alone in a cave and hates women. The pair debates love, life, and the universe. The Damsel ultimately prevails and the Sage falls in love with her.

Penned Scandalous *Three Weeks*

As Glyn's career as a novelist progressed, her plots became more unrealistic and featured socially prominent, beautiful, sexually charged heroines and heroes that were dominating. In 1907 she published the work that made her almost notorious. In *Three Weeks,* she depicts an affair between Lady Henrietta, an older woman who turns out to be a queen in the Balkans, and a younger man, a handsome but rather dim Englishman. The fact that the pair makes love on a tiger-skin rug was more than enough to shock reading audiences and provoke somewhat of a scandal. The liaison produces a son, though because Henrietta is married, she is able to pass the child off as her husband's. On a more conservative note, she devotes the remainder of her life to her son's success. Still, due to the provocative sex scenes, London critics almost universally condemned *Three Weeks,* with the result that by 1916 the novel had sold more than two million copies and been translated into a number of languages. Despite the scandal Glyn made money on the book, but ultimately lost it because she trusted her husband's investment advice.

Clayton Glyn's debts bankrupted the family by 1908, forcing Glyn to write for money to support herself and her family. Despite continuing money problems, she was determined to live in a comfortable fashion and pursued other avenues of attaining such comfort. She had an affair with

Curzon, a former viceroy of India, probably with her husband's consent.

Traveled Abroad

In 1907–1908, Glyn went to the United States and lived in New York City, as well as Colorado, Nevada, and California. Despite the continuing turmoil over *Three Weeks,* she published *Elizabeth Visits America* (1909), which was written in a similar vein as her first novel and featured Glyn's own illustrations. Although it was not completely successful, her next work restored her reputation as an author.

At the end of the first decade of the 1900s, Glyn spent a winter at the Russian court at St. Petersburg and Moscow, and this experience provided the background for her 1910 novel, *His Hour.* A best seller that restored her reputation, *His Hour* focuses on an English widow who falls in love with with a Russian prince, whom she ultimately marries. Glyn also had another best seller with *The Reason Why* (1911), a book she wrote in 18 days as a means to make money.

In 1915 Clayton Glyn died, and Glyn moved to Paris, where her literary output increased. She had another big seller with *The Man and the Master* (1915), which was written in the popular romance style of the time in which the couple destined to be together does not get together until the very end. Glyn also expanded beyond novel-writing to publish stories and articles in popular magazines. She also was a war correspondent in France during World War I, visiting the trenches but writing from the Ritz hotel.

Glyn's finances improved in 1917 after she signed a contract with William Randolph Hearst for the U.S. rights to her novels. One of the first books to published under the agreement was *The Career of Katherine Bush* (1916). While the book sparked a disagreement with Hearst, who wanted the heroine to be more agreeable, Glyn refused to change her text.

Worked as Screenwriter

Because of her popularity as a novelist, like many high profile authors of the time, in 1920 Glyn was asked to come to Hollywood and write screenplays by Jesse Lasky of Famous Players-Lasky. She proved to be very successful at screenwriting, because her scripts, much like her novels, were daring and sexy. Her first script was written in 1920 for leading star Gloria Swanson. *The Great Moment* concerns an Englishwoman with social standing who falls in love with a macho American man. When she returns to her native country, she almost marries the British millionaire chosen by her father, but ends up with the American, who has created his own wealth. Glyn's second screenplay, *Beyond the Rocks,* paired Swanson with costar Rudolph Valentino to provide another hit film.

Glyn produced a number of screenplays in the 1920s. She wrote *Six Hours* and *Three Weeks (The Romance of a Queen)* in 1923; the King Vidor-directed *His Hour* in 1924; *Man and Maid* and *Love's Blindness* in 1925; and *The Only Thing* in 1926. Both *Man and Maid* and *The Only Thing* were of the same genre as *The Great Moment,* but failed at the box office. These failures forced Glyn to attempt a different kind of story. Based on her own short story, *Ritzy* (1927)—a farce about a woman hunting a duke who pretends he is poor though he loves her—did not do well at the box office either.

Defined "It Girl"

While working on screenplays for Hollywood Glyn continued to write novels, one of which was *It* (1926). The screenplay version of this story of liberated female sexuality restored Glyn's reputation as a screenwriter, although she was credited only as author, adapter, and co-producer; Hope Loring and Louis D. Lighton actually adapted the screenplay from her novel. The 1928 film starred Clara Bow, whose sultry performance as a store clerk who has a crush on her boss and ultimately wins his affections earned her the name the "It Girl." Bow's new label inspired a catch phrase of the time describing the liberated, jazz-aged, new woman and *It* became a definitive jazz age film.

Glyn followed *It* with another film starring Bow, *Red Hair* (1928). A redhead herself, she used the hair color as a symbol for passionate women, though the movie did not have much of a plot. Up to this point, all of Glyn's scripts had been for silent films. She wrote her first non-silent script, *Such Men Are Dangerous,* in 1929. That same year the 65-year-old novelist and screenwriter decided to return to England, in part because of tax demands.

Describing Glyn's role in Hollywood, Victoria Glendinning wrote in the *Washington Post:* "Elinor had a triumphant last chapter as the social arbitrator of Hollywood. Aging now, her hair dyed, her make-up over-bright, she worked on scenarios and instructed ignorant American actors on how real ladies and gentleman walked and dressed and decorated their houses. She was immensely grand."

Worked as Film Director

When Glyn returned to England in 1929, she formed her own film production company and began a film-directing career that proved less than successful. Using her own money, she directed *Knowing Men* (1929), a comic-feminist take on men as sexual harassers. The woman at the center of the film is an heiress who assumes a false identity to learn what her suitor is really like. The final product came off as very amateur, and the screenwriter, Edward Knoblock, sued to prevent it from being released. *Knowing Men* created such a scandal that it ruined Glyn's fledgling film company.

Glyn managed to direct a second film, *The Price of Things* (1929), which also proved to be a commercial disaster. After two such failures Glyn retired from film work and continued to write novels until her death. In 1936 she published her autobiography, *Romantic Adventures.*

Glyn died on September 23, 1943, in London. Moira Petty described the late novelist in *Stage* magazine as "the chick-lit author of the early 1900s, with a dash of Dorothy Parker and a dollop of Barbara Cortland."

Books

Etherington-Smith, Meredith, and Jeremy Pilcher, *The It Girls: Eleanor Glyn and Lucy, Duff Gordon,* Hamish Hamilton, 1986.
Foster, Gwendolyn Audrey, *Women Film Directors: An International Bio-Critical Dictionary,* Greenwood Press, 1995.
Schlueter, Paul, and June Schlueter, editors, *An Encyclopedia of British Women Writers,* Rutgers University Press, 1998.
Uglow, Jennifer, compiler and editor, *Dictionary of Women's Biography,* 3rd edition, Macmillan, 1982.
Unterburger, Amy L., editor, *Women Filmmakers and Their Films,* St. James Press, 1998.

Periodicals

Financial Times, October 18, 1896.
New York Times, May 5, 1987.
Stage, July 11, 2002.
Washington Post Book World, May 17, 1987. □

R.C. Gorman

R.C. Gorman (born 1931) was perhaps the leading Native American artist in the United States. Gorman's themes were universal and transcended the boundaries of the Navajo culture in which he was raised. Gorman's portraits of Navajo women were executed in a free-flowing style with vivid colors. He was sometimes called the "Picasso of American Indian artists."

Talented Ancestors

Rudolph Carl Gorman was born on July 26, 1931, in Chinle, Arizona, though some sources give his birth year as 1932. He grew up on the Navajo reservation in Chinle, Arizona, not far from Canyon de Chelly in the northeastern part of the state. The ancient home of the Anasazi and a place steeped in legend, power, and magic, the Chinle area served for centuries as a refuge for the Navajo from their Indian, Spanish, and Anglo enemies. The Navajo traditionally lived in earth-covered dwellings called hogans, while ekeing out a subsistence living from the land.

Gorman's family, like its ancestors, grazed sheep on the plains. Gorman's father, Carl Gorman, attended mission schools as a boy and eventually became a wealthy cowboy. During World War II, Carl Gorman was a member of the Navajo Code Talkers, an elite group of U.S. Marines who developed a Navajo-based communications code that the Japanese were unable to break. When Gorman was about twelve, his parents separated. Carl Gorman left to attend art school and later became a recognized painter and teacher at the University of California at Davis.

Gorman described himself in his autobiography *R.C. Gorman: The Radiance of My People* as a descendant of sand painters, silversmiths, chanters, and weavers on both sides of his family. In 1864, Gorman's paternal great-grandfather was forced to march four hundred miles during the Navajo Long March from Canyon de Chelly to Fort Sumner. At the army fort he learned the art of silversmithing, which he taught to the rest of his tribe. Later, while attending the first government school at Fort Defiance, he was given the name Nelson Carl Gorman.

Gorman's mother, though a devout Catholic, was raised in a family that still held to traditional Navajo religious practices. According to her son, she was in labor for twenty hours before he was born prematurely. The infant grew strong on a diet of coffee and goat milk prescribed by his great-grandmother.

Gorman was raised with two brothers, a sister, and several half-sisters and half-brothers. His family lived in an old stone house without running water. The local Catholic church allowed the family to use its outdoor faucet, and Gorman later recalled hauling water to the family home.

Early Interest in Art

As a boy, Gorman modeled animals and toys out of clay from the local swimming hole. Later he drew with charcoal on rocks. When he started school and discovered pencils, papers, and books, he began drawing with abandon. His first school, Chinle Public School, was a one-room structure heated with a wood stove. He recalled that his first work of art in school was a drawing of a naked woman; it brought spankings from his teacher and his mother.

In *R.C. Gorman: A Portrait,* Carl Gorman recalled the origins of his son's career: "R.C. always carried a tablet and drew, wherever we were. We were dipping sheep once, and he got a little girl to model for him. A white man working with us saw the drawing, got me, and said, 'Look. Someday he's going to be a great artist.' And it's true. He was less than ten years old at that time. I never held his hand, or led him like a teacher. His eyes were his teachers."

In 1943, Gorman enrolled in a Catholic boarding school on the Navajo reservation. In the fall of 1944, he switched to the Ganado Presbyterian Mission School. In the seventh grade, Gorman began selling his artwork to nurses and doctors at the mission school. He graduated from Ganado Mission High School in 1950.

As a child, Gorman never received instruction in the Navajo religion. "The Catholics and Protestants got to me first," he wrote in his autobiography. Although he rejected Catholicism after his experience at the Catholic boarding school, he later considered himself a good Catholic.

In the Navy

After briefly enrolling at Arizona State College (now Northern Arizona University), Gorman joined the Navy in 1951. It was at that time that he began calling himself R.C., because, he said, Rudolph Carl didn't seem to fit him. Following boot camp, Gorman was assigned to duty in Guam. He attended Guam Territorial College, intending to become a writer. During this time, he picked up pocket money by sketching girlfriends of officers and enlisted men from photographs they provided.

In 1955, after leaving the Navy, Gorman enrolled again at Arizona State College, with a major in literature and a minor in art. In the summer of 1956, he worked at Disneyland, where he dressed as a Native American and paddled a canoe.

San Francisco and Mexico

After his art began to sell, he moved to San Francisco. On a trip to Mexico, Gorman first saw the murals of Guadalajara depicting the history of the Mexican people. He later wrote in his autobiography, "Instead of trying to paint like a European, I started painting like a Mexican, I guess, except that I was using the Navajos for my subject matter." In Mexico City, Gorman saw the works of Diego Rivera and other artists. According to Gorman, "Rivera went to Europe to discover himself. I went to Mexico and discovered Rivera and myself."

Upon returning from Mexico, Gorman applied for a grant from the Navajo Tribal Council. He was awarded a scholarship to attend Mexico City College in 1958. After three months, Gorman returned to San Francisco, where he held a job in the post office at night and painted by day. Later he worked as a nude model for colleges and private art studios in the San Francisco Bay area.

Taos

In the early 1960s, Gorman relocated briefly to Houston, Texas. In 1964, he discovered Taos, New Mexico, which he loved at first sight. After he showed some slides to gallery owner Dorothy Brett of the Manchester Gallery in Taos, she agreed to handle his work. Following an extremely successful show in Taos, Gorman returned to San Francisco, where he began experimenting with landscapes, pottery, and sand paintings. In 1966, on another trip to Mexico City, Gorman did his first work in lithography. During this trip, Gorman was introduced to the noted printmaker Jose Sanchez.

When the Manchester Gallery in Taos came up for sale in the late 1960s, Gorman borrowed money from his parents and bought it. He reopened the gallery as the Navajo Gallery in 1968, starting with 55 artists. But after the others' works failed to sell, Gorman began selling only his own material. His drawings sold for $100 apiece.

Gorman's Women

Gorman said he liked to capture the beauty of his people, especially the women. As he explained in his autobiography, "Navajos always had respect for strong, powerful women who would go out and chop wood, herd sheep, have babies in the field. My Indian woman isn't glamorous but she is beautiful. She is earthy, nurturing, and it is a constant challenge to capture her infinite variety.

"I deal with the common woman who smells of the fields and maize. She lives and breathes. . . . My women work and walk on the land. They need to be strong to survive. They have big hands, strong feet. They are soft and strong like my grandmother who gave me life.

"My women are remote, withdrawn in their silence. They don't look out, but glance inward in the Indian way. You know their faces, but not a thing about their thoughts. They do not reveal whether they are looking at us or not.

"I like to think that my women represent a universal woman. They don't have to be from the reservation. They could be from Scottsdale or Africa. They're composites of many women I've known."

Gorman used live models when he drew Navajo women, but not all of his models were Navajo. He said that by throwing a blanket over a Japanese woman, he could end up with a Navajo model. In fact, one of his favorite models was a young Japanese woman.

Magic Mountain

Gorman wrote in his autobiography, "It's strange I should come to Taos. The Navajos are encircled by the four sacred mountains, and within those four mountains the Navajo feels, I think, protected, but on the other hand inhibited. I'm outside of the sacred Navajo mountains and feel like a very independent creature who is protected by another mountain that is quite magic, the Taos mountain."

Gorman was visited in Taos by many celebrities, including Elizabeth Taylor, Jacqueline Onassis, Arnold Schwartzeneggar, Tab Hunter, Alan Ginsberg, Caesar Romero, Danny DeVito, and baseball pitcher Jim Palmer.

Indian Artist

Gorman was not offended at being called an "Indian artist." He wrote in his autobiography, "I am what I am, and its obvious I'm not white, black, or Oriental. I am an Indian. I am an artist. I'm an Indian painting Indians, and if it worked out for me, then it's all well and good."

But Gorman added: "I've always felt successful. Even when I wasn't making any money, I just knew it was all there. I always believed in myself. I knew I had talent and there was just no doubt about it. I just didn't give up."

Gorman gave thought to his legacy in his autobiography: "If I'm remembered at all, I'd be very surprised and amused. I don't really think about it or worry about it. But I suppose I would like to be remembered that I was an earnest worker. That I cared. That I know anyone can get what they want if they work hard enough. After all, I'm just a little boy from the reservation who used to herd sheep at Black Mountain."

Books

Gorman, R.C., *R.C. Gorman: The Radiance of My People,* Santa Fe Fine Arts, 1992.
Parks, Stephen, *R.C. Gorman: A Portrait,* Little, Brown, 1983.

Online

"R.C. Gorman," *New Mexico Internet Access, Inc.,* http://www .highfiber.com/~lhb/bio.htm (February 2003).
"R.C. Gorman (1932–)," *Ro Gallery.com,* http://www.rogallery .w1.com/R/gorman_rc/gorman-biography.htm (February 2003). □

Earl Gilbert Graves, Jr.

American publishing magnate Earl Graves (born 1935) launched his empire in 1972 with *Black Enterprise* magazine. Coming less than a decade after new U.S. federal civil rights legislation had been enacted, the magazine soon became the standard-bearer for upwardly mobile African Americans.

Working-Class Family Upbringing

Graves was born in Brooklyn, New York, on January 9, 1935, and grew up in the Bedford-Stuyvesant neighborhood. His father worked as a shipping clerk in New York's garment district. Bedford-Stuyvesant, far from the nightclubs and jazz of Harlem, was home to many similar working-class black families. Many owned their own homes, as Graves later pointed out in an interview with *Los Angeles Times* writer Lee Romney. "I swept the sidewalk once a day and God forbid if I didn't bring the garbage cans in after the garbage had been collected," he recalled. "From that environment came the idea of wanting to do something of my own. . . ." Still, entrepreneurship seemed an unlikely avenue to success for a black man in that era; as Graves wrote in his book, *How to Succeed in Business Without Being White: Straight Talk on Making It in America,* "the concept of being black and in business was still considered to be almost seditious even when I was a student at Morgan State University in Baltimore from 1953 to 1957."

During his time at the historically black college in Baltimore, Maryland, Graves earned money by delivering flowers on campus, at a time when the local florists would not venture there. He earned a degree in economics in 1958 and served two years in the U.S. Army, leaving with the rank of captain in the elite Green Beret unit. Back home in New York City, he dabbled in real estate and worked for the Boy Scouts of America before joining the staff of New York's newly elected U.S. senator, Robert F. Kennedy, in 1964. Graves spent four years as Kennedy's administrative assistant and was in the Kennedy entourage the night the senator, campaigning to win the Democratic Party's presidential nomination, was assassinated at the Ambassador Hotel in Los Angeles in June 1968. As he told Romney in the *Los Angeles Times* interview 30 years later, "The enormity of his death stayed with me. When I went back a year later to Los Angeles, I sat up all night staring out the window thinking, 'What would it all have been had Kennedy lived?' I believe this would be a different country than we have today."

Empowerment Through Economic Success

Devastated, Graves sought a new direction in his life. While serving on an advisory board to the Small Business Administration, he launched his own management consulting firm. By the late 1960s, the civil rights movement had paved the way for black empowerment and the concept of "black capitalism." Proponents believed that a liberated

American society would come only when minority communities thrived with their own businesses.

With this in mind, Graves founded *Black Enterprise* magazine in New York City in 1970. At the time, only the Johnson Company in Chicago issued magazines targeted at black readers in the United States: *Ebony* and *Jet*. Many believed Graves was too optimistic in starting a magazine aimed at African American businesspeople. At the time, there were only about 100,000 black-owned businesses in the United States, and most of them were small, family-run, neighborhood operations. Only three of the 3,000 business leaders who were serving on the boards of Fortune 500 companies were African Americans. "Lacking capital, managerial and technical knowledge and crippled by prejudice, the minority businessman has been effectively kept out of the marketplace. We want to help change this," Graves declared in *Black Enterprise*'s first issue in August 1970.

"The BE 100"

Graves's publication was a success within its first year, becoming profitable after just ten issues. In June 1973, the magazine started listing its Black Enterprise 100, ranking the top black-owned companies in America by revenues. At the time, Berry Gordy's music and entertainment company, Motown, was number one on the list, and it remained there for a record eleven years. In time, as black-owned businesses grew in both number and revenues, the magazine expanded its rankings to list banks and insurance companies, auto dealerships, and other enterprises; it also began to publish statistics on Fortune 500 and other companies that were positive places for African Americans to work or to join as franchisees.

Graves expanded his empire over the years. He acquired several radio stations, and in 1990, in a much-heralded deal, joined with Los Angeles Lakers basketball star Earvin "Magic" Johnson to acquire the distribution rights for Pepsi-Cola products in the Washington, D.C. area. It was a $60 million deal, and their venture became the largest minority-owned franchise in the United States at that time. It was all the more remarkable because Pepsi rarely allowed outsiders to acquire its lucrative local distribution franchises. "Pepsi-Cola made the conscious decision, to their credit, to identify a minority person who could be a successful bottler," Graves told *Beverage World*'s Tim Davis. "And I wanted Washington, DC. I looked at other areas that were not necessarily minority. The population here is 80 percent minority, but the fact of the matter is that this is the seat of government for western civilization. And the beverage of choice right now is Pepsi-Cola."

Wrote Autobiography

Graves later bought out Johnson's shares and sold the Pepsi franchise back to the company in 1998, taking a post as chairman of Pepsi's customer advisory and ethnic marketing committee. By this time he also sat on the boards of several Fortune 500 corporations, among them Chrysler Corporation, Aetna Inc., American Airlines, and Federated Department Stores. "Let's be frank: African Americans are not invited to join the boards of white-owned companies because the world has run out of smart white people," he wrote in *How to Succeed in Business Without Being White*. "We are expected to add a unique business perspective and a fresh dimension, just as women are. That is a strength to be leveraged, not a deficit to be hidden away."

Graves's book appeared in 1997. Much of it was a summation of his magazine's editorial focus, with tips on dressing conservatively and how to define and assert personal career goals. A *Publishers Weekly* review found that "Graves's own reflections on the challenges faced by blacks in business" proved "more interesting" than the standard how-to fare in rest of it. True to form, Graves promoted the book tirelessly, and it enjoyed strong sales in many urban markets. When asked by Romney in the *Los Angeles Times* about what minorities needed to succeed in corporate America, Graves asserted that "a junkyard-dog mentality" was crucial, "that competitive spirit that comes from the culture in terms of having to be better, having to try harder, and having to be prepared to get up after you get knocked down."

Ardent Civil Rights Champion

Graves has often used the pages of *Black Enterprise* to call attention to unfinished civil rights business. He urged readers to support historically black colleges and to contribute to the United Negro College Fund. In one "Letter to My Grandchildren," Graves noted that many critical changes had taken place since his own childhood, opening the doors for unparalleled achievement for blacks in the United States. "It is important to remind ourselves from time to time that the entrepreneurial, professional, and economic strides and accomplishments that fill the pages of BE each month were unimaginable just a few short decades ago," he wrote. However, Graves noted, there was still work to be done, particularly with setbacks in affirmative action in the 1990s. " . . . [E]ven as we pause to congratulate ourselves, our celebration is tempered by deep concerns," he reflected. "I worry that the same legislation and policies that enabled the advances of my generation, and that of your parents' generation, will no longer exist for your generation."

For his longtime commitment to civil rights, Graves was awarded the 1999 Spingarn Medal from the NAACP, its highest honor. At the same time, he announced a new $1.23 million Earl G. Graves/NAACP Scholarship Fund. In 1995, he had given his alma mater, Morgan State University, $1 million, the largest alumni gift in the school's history. Morgan State named its business school in Graves's honor. Graves remained active in Democratic Party politics and supported the mayoral bid of Fernando Ferrer in the 2001 New York City race.

Magazine Entered Fourth Decade

Black Enterprise magazine continued to thrive. In 2001, the company, headquartered on Fifth Avenue in Manhattan, enjoyed $5.7 million in sales, with four million readers. The company also included a book publishing arm, sponsored seminars for entrepreneurs, and ran a private equity investment fund. *Washington Post* writer Linton Weeks called its founder "one of the most influential black businesspeople in the country" and said Graves "has used *Black Enterprise* to tell the community how to: work together, dress smart, pull strings, borrow money, live revengefully well."

Graves, married in 1960, lived in the posh New York suburb of Scarsdale. Two of his three sons served as executives with his company, while the third held a post with Pepsi-Cola. In addition to the Spingarn Medal, Graves was also the recipient of numerous other awards, including the Entrepreneurial Excellence Award from Dow Jones & Co. in 1992, and the Ernst & Young New York City Entrepreneur of the Year Award three years later. In all, he held 53 honorary degrees, but as he wrote in the 30th anniversary issue of his magazine in 2000, "I have always said that these awards recognize the magazine's role in uplifting African Americans. By showcasing their achievements as well as gaining a forum to address the issues of the day, we helped fuel the aspirations of generations of black entrepreneurs and business people."

In the same issue, he wrote: "We wanted to show our readers a better way and, at the same time, communicate to the business world, from Madison Avenue to Wall Street, that there was a viable black consumer market. It was my vision to show a more positive side of African American participation in the business mainstream. Along the way, we would carve a path for future generations."

Books

Business Leader Profiles for Students, Volume 1, Gale, 1999.
Contemporary Black Biography, Volume 35, edited by Ashyia Henderson, Gale, 2002.

Periodicals

Beverage World, October 1992.
Black Enterprise, August 1995; February 1998; August 2000.
Booklist, April 1, 1997.
Changing Times, November 1990.
Directors & Boards, Spring 1997.
Jet, December 21, 1998.
Library Journal, April 15, 1997.
Los Angeles Times, October 14, 1998.
Publishers Weekly, April 7, 1997.
Washington Post, June 17, 1997. □

Rafael Guastavino

Each year, thousands of tourists visit New York City and its historic structures such as Grand Central Terminal, Carnegie Hall, and the Great Hall on Ellis Island. Most tourists are not aware that the man responsible for these famous buildings was Rafael Guastavino (1842–1908), a Spanish immigrant who integrated centuries-old construction techniques into modern architecture. Guastavino left his personal stamp on the city. His work—with its great spans of curving, expressive spaces—combines grace with sturdy, enduring construction.

Adapted Ancient Building Technique

Rafael Guastavino was born in Valencia, Spain, in 1842. He was trained as an architect in Barcelona, graduating in 1872 from the Escuela de Arquitectura. Before emigrating to the United States, Guastavino established himself as a successful architect in Barcelona.

In Spain, Guastavino designed and built homes and factories for wealthy industrialists in the region of Catalin. He revived an ancient form of tile and mortar building that had been used for centuries. This technique, called the boveda catalana, or Catalan vault, featured long flat tiles placed in layers held together by a mixture of Portland cement and cow bay sand. The technique was also known as "timbrel" vaulting, a term that suggested the membrane of a timbrel, an old percussion instrument similar to a tambourine.

Guastavino would adapt the ancient technique into a method called "cohesive construction," which involved placing layers of thin, interlocking terra cotta tiles in layers of mortar to create curved horizontal surfaces including floors, stairs, roofs, and ceilings which were usually shaped like vaults or domes. Though the tiles were light, their placement enabled them to withstand a great deal of weight, resulting in self-supporting arches. The strength of the vaults and arches came from a curved geometry held in a state of monolithic cohesion. The sturdiness of Guastavino's structures has often been compared to the natural strength of eggshells. The style was both visually striking and practical: Not only were the structures strong, they were fireproof. These curved surfaces became his personal trademark, and Guastavino would employ this method when he emigrated to the United States in 1881.

Started Business in America

Guastavino wanted to emigrate to America after architectural plans he submitted to the Philadelphia Centennial Exposition earned him a medal of merit in 1876. He believed he could acquire better building materials and more job opportunities there. Five years after his award, he brought his son, Rafael Guastavino, Jr., with him to the United States. His son was nine at the time and would later go into business with his father.

In America, Guastavino worked as a builder and contractor. At first, he had trouble finding work. His techniques were not well understood in America. However, given time, he was able to establish his reputation. In 1885, he secured the first of his many patents on his vaulting system of construction.

In 1889, he founded the Guastavino Fireproof Construction Company. Promoting the vaulting technique called the "Guastavino Tile Arch System," a refinement of the fireproof construction system he first used in Spain, Guastavino advanced his reputation, and his services were soon much in demand in New York. His fire-resistant construction method was a major selling point, given the great fire that had ravaged Chicago in 1871.

Became Accomplished Architect

Today, his structuring method is a visual characteristic in many of New York City's landmark buildings. However, much of Guastavino's work during this early period involved residential architecture, including row houses on the city's Upper West Side that remained standing into the 21st century. With his techniques, Guastavino could design homes with a distinctive feature: large openings could be spanned without using timber or iron beams. Guastavino also incorporated Moorish details into these homes, including brownstone, terra cotta, and articulated brickwork. The fact that the buildings still exist are a testament to Guastavino's workmanship. He was so conscientious about quality that his company manufactured its own tiles.

Guastavino developed a reputation as an accomplished architect, and he worked with some of the best architects in the United States, including Stanford White, Richard Morris Hunt, Ralph Adams Cram, and Cass Gilbert. Guastavino greatly influenced these colleagues. They borrowed elements of his style and technique to create their own world-famous works. The same year that he formed his company, Guastavino collaborated with architects White, Charles Follen McKim, and William Rutherford Mead on the Boston Public Library, one of his best-known projects.

Guastavino's business was essentially a construction and contracting firm. He, and later his son, installed the trademark masonry floors, ceilings, vaults, domes, stairs and acoustic products in churches, museums, railroad stations, state capitols, libraries, concert halls, government and university buildings, private homes, and highway structures. In all, his firm created nearly 400 structures in New York City. By 1891 the company had offices in New York, Boston, Milwaukee, Chicago, and Providence, Rhode Island.

The company also developed successful building products, including acoustic tile. With Wallace C. Sabine, Guastavino created Rumford tiles designed to reduce echoes inside large ecclesiastical edifices. The tiles can be found in several famous churches, including St. Bartholomew and St. Thomas in New York City and the Duke University Chapel in Durham, North Carolina. In 1900, the firm opened a tile manufacturing factory in Woburn, Massachusetts.

Moved to North Carolina

In the mid-1890s, Guastavino went to Asheville, North Carolina, to work on the Biltmore House, which would become a National Historic Landmark. He decided to stay in the area, buying land and building a house near Black Mountain. In 1905, working with another renowned architect, Richard Sharp Smith, he helped design and build the St. Lawrence Catholic Church, which would later be placed on the National Register Of Historic Places.

Guastavino decided to work on the church after he tried attending services one morning and was turned away because it was too crowded. He offered his services to help build a much larger and more splendid church. Construc-

tion began in 1905 but was unfinished when Guastavino died in 1908. His son finished the project. However, the church still presents a stunning example of his style and technique. Every horizontal surface is made of his trademark combination of tile and mortar, and it features an impressive, elliptical dome. Guastavino's crypt is located in the church. Reportedly, fellow architect Smith also contributed to the design. However, it is Guastavino's unique style that dominates. His signature vaults run throughout the interior, which also features three Catalan staircases. "It's really kind of his church," said William Flynn Wescott, a North Carolina preservationist who has organized several Guastavino exhibits. "[Guastavino] contributed not only tile and construction but major funds. And of course, he's buried there."

Guastavino's business continued for many years following his death. His son, who died in 1950, took over the business, and it continued operating under a number of successors. Eventually, steel and concrete building methods were deemed more practical than Catalan vaulting, and the firm went out of business in 1962. In an interview with the *Mountain Xpress* of Asheville, North Carolina, Westcott pointed out that while Guastavino's techniques produced great beauty, they could not compete with newer, cheaper building techniques. "It's a prettier system, but people weren't willing to pay additional dollars for his system," he said.

Left a Strong Legacy

Much of Guastavino's output can be found in the northeastern United States, including 360 works in New York, 100 in Boston, 30 in Pittsburgh, and 20 in Philadelphia. Examples of his work also can be found in ten other countries. His most famous accomplishments include vaults in Grand Central Station, Saint Patrick Cathedral, Saint John the Divine Cathedral, Mount Sinai Hospital, and City Hall Station. Buildings include Grant's Tomb, the Great Hall at Ellis Island, Carnegie Hall, and the chapel at West Point. Other famous projects in other parts of the country include the Nebraska State Capitol and the U.S. Army War College in Washington, D.C.

Guastavino's distinctive architectural stamp is also a strong presence in North Carolina. Along with the St. Lawrence church, the Biltmore House, and the Duke Chapel, famous sites include the Jefferson Standard Building in Greensboro, the Motley Memorial in Chapel Hill, and St. Mary's Catholic Church in Wilmington. But it is the St. Lawrence church that remains perhaps the best-known structure in that state.

Built Many New York Landmarks

A walking tour of New York's Upper West Side reveals many of Guastavino's fingerprints, including the tiles in the Holy Trinity Church, the vehicular entrance to the American Museum of Natural History on Central Park West, and the porte-cochere at the Ansonia. Outside the Upper West Side, other Guastavino works include St. Paul's Chapel on the Columbia University campus, the Cathedral of St. John the Divine, the Western Union Building on Hudson Street, the

City Hall subway station, the Grand Central's Oyster Bar, the Church of Notre Dame, the Federal Reserve Bank, the U.S. Custom House, the Plaza and St. Regis hotels, Temple Emanu-El, Lenox Hill Hospital, the Cloisters, St. Bartholomew's and St. Vincent Ferrer churches, and the Municipal Building. Many of these structures are among the most famous and distinctive in the country. "The Guastavino system represents a unique architectural treatment that has given America some of its most monumental spaces," wrote Thomas Prudon in *Progressive Architecture.* "It deserves to be preserved and treated with care."

Guastavino Rediscovered

The visual elegance of Guastavino's work provided indelible impressions of New York City. However, until recent years, few knew who was responsible for these structures. Indeed, even when he was alive, Guastavino was not well known outside of the architectural field. Since he worked mainly as a contractor, his name did not appear on the buildings, and the public was largely unaware of the impact and significance of his work. "They are the best examples we have . . . of something that is at the same time structural, decorative and fireproof—an amazing combination of architectural and decorative elements in American architecture," said Wescott.

In the late 20th and early 21st centuries, renewed interest was generated by exhibitions that highlighted his achievements. "It's been a passion of mine to get him known," said Wescott. "He's just this incredible architect, engineer, contractor and ceramist. He is probably one of the best examples of a Renaissance man who never got any PR, and now it's time for his PR."

Periodicals

Columbia University Record, April 26, 1996.
Mountain Xpress, January 9, 2002.
Smithsonian Preservation Quarterly, Spring 1995.

Online

"Basilica of St. Lawrence, Asheville, N.C., Diocese of Charlotte," *MassTransit.com,* http://www.massintransit.com/nc/stlawrence1-nc/stl2.html (February 10, 2003).
"Rafael Guastavino Moreno," *Structurae,* http://www.structurae.de/en/people/data/des1794.php (February 10, 2003).
Stachelberg, Cas, "Structural Signatures: Raphael Guastavino on the Upper West Side, *LandmarkWest,* http://www.preserve.org/lmwest/id129.htm (February 10, 2003). □

Tom Hanks

Oscar-winning actor Tom Hanks (born 1956) embraced his budding theater career as a high school student in the San Francisco Bay area. In 1984 he established a foothold in films, starring as the romantic interest of a mermaid in the movie *Splash.* Four years and seven films later he won a Golden Globe Award and by 2000 had won back-to-back Academy Awards as best actor.

Hanks was born Thomas Jeffrey Hanks on July 9, 1956, in Concord, California. His father, Amos, was a restaurant chef; his mother, Janet, was a waitress. Hanks, the third of the couple's four children and the second of three sons, was five years old in February 1962 when his parents separated. Leaving their younger brother behind with their mother, Hanks and his two older siblings went with their father to Reno, Nevada, where they lived in a basement flat at 529 Mills Street. By April their father had married Winfred Finley, the owner of the Mills Street residence. Finley was herself divorced and living with five of her eight children, and the large Finley brood merged to become step-siblings with the Hanks children.

In 1964 the 10-member household moved to Pleasant Hills, California. Soon afterward, Amos Hanks and Finley divorced. The Hanks children were shuffled continuously between the homes of various relatives while their father established a residence near his family in the San Francisco Bay area. For a time the three children stayed in Red Bluff with their mother, who was three-times remarried by then.

After leaving Red Bluff they spent time with assorted relatives of their father in San Mateo and Oakland.

The living arrangement stabilized after Amos Hanks met and married Frances Wong who brought three daughters of her own into the marriage. Thus a large family was created anew, with six siblings in all. Hanks coped admirably with the unpredictability of his home life. He took judo lessons and participated in Little League, and the family enjoyed camping when circumstances allowed. He maintained above average grades at Oakland's Bret Harte junior high school and had by adolescence learned to be flexible above all else. Hanks, in fact, demonstrated a remarkable sense of resilience in the face of continuous upheaval. At home he and his siblings learned to fend for themselves by doing their own laundry and preparing meals as much as possible.

Found His Focus

When Hanks entered Oakland's Skyline High School in the early 1970s, he found an emotional anchor in a social group based at the First Covenant Church. Having been raised alternately as a Catholic and as a Mormon and later as a member of the Nazarene Church, he gravitated easily toward the group. In his senior year he left home and took up residence with a family from the church, supporting himself by working as a bellhop at the Oakland Hilton Hotel.

In high school, Hanks, with encouragement from a friend, joined the school's drama program. Beginning with a role in Shakespeare's *Twelfth Night,* Hanks appeared in a number of plays under the direction of the school's drama teacher, Rawley Farnsworth. Many years later, Hanks—in accepting his first Academy Award in 1994—publicly thanked Farnsworth for his help and encouragement.

After high school graduation in 1974, Hanks enrolled at Chabot Community College in nearby Hayward. For the next two years, he began a metaphorical love affair with the theater, appearing on stage and working as a stagehand. He took acting classes and developed a sincere appreciation of live theater. By the time he enrolled at California State University at Sacramento (CSUS) in 1976, his fascination with the theater could no longer be contained.

Through an extracurricular involvement with the Sacramento Civic Theater, Hanks developed a fortuitous acquaintance with director Vincent Dowling. A visitor to the Sacramento area, Dowling was affiliated with the Great Lakes Shakespearean Festival (now Great Lakes Theater Festival) in Cleveland, Ohio. Hanks appeared as Yasha in the Sacramento community theater production of Anton Chekhov's *Cherry Orchard* and at Dowling's invitation spent the summer of 1977 at the Shakespeare Festival in Cleveland as a volunteer intern.

When Hanks returned to Sacramento in the fall of 1977 he became an assistant stage manager for the Civic Theater and quickly lost interest in academics. He returned to Cleveland in the summer of 1978, where he appeared in *Two Gentlemen of Verona* at the festival and received the Cleveland Drama Critics Award for his effort. Attracted by the smell of the greasepaint, he abandoned school altogether and opted to try his luck as a professional actor. At the end of the festival season, he moved to New York City to embark on a serious acting career.

After a disappointing first season in New York, spent largely in the unemployment office, Hanks summered at the Shakespeare Festival in Cleveland for a third time in 1979. After appearing in *Do Me a Favor,* he returned to New York where a small movie role materialized in a grade B horror film—*He Knows You're Alone*—about a deranged stalker of brides. He came to mainstream notoriety soon afterward in the unlikely television role of Kip Wilson—also known as Buffy—in *Bosom Buddies,* co-starring Peter Scolari. A weekly comedy series, *Bosom Buddies* was based on an outlandish situation wherein Hanks and Scolari portrayed two advertising men who dressed up regularly as women in order to rent rooms in a women's hotel. The series ran from 1980 to 1982, and Hanks emerged from the experience secure in his name and face recognition before the viewing public.

Movie Stardom

In 1984 Hanks teamed with actor-turned-director Ron Howard in *Splash.* A whimsical romantic comedy about a man who meets a mermaid, *Splash* was a perfect vehicle to movie stardom for Hanks whose boy-next-door image had survived the quirky sitcom role of Buffy. Secure in his appeal as a comedic actor, he was cast in the spoof film *Bachelor Party* that same year. His 1985 film offerings—*Man with One Red Shoe* and *Volunteers*—were less than successful, although he did attract some attention that year in portraying an attorney named Walter Fielding, opposite Shelley Long, in *The Money Pit.* He appeared in three films in 1986; and in 1987 provided the comedy relief as detective Pep Streebek in *Dragnet.* The film, a reprise of an old detective series from the early days of television, was a mild success.

Hanks, who subscribes to a classic style of method acting, immerses himself in the experiences and feelings of each character that he portrays. In 1988 he captivated the movie-going public with in a charming movie, called *Big,* in which he depicts a 12-year-old boy in a 30-something body. To prepare for the role Hanks spent much of his time in observing and learning to mimic the mannerisms of his 13-year-old co-star in that movie. Hanks prepared for a subsequent role as a stand-up comic in *Punchline* by performing several times on-stage at a comedy club in order to comprehend the daily life of a comic.

After two lighter-side films, *The 'Burbs* and *Turner & Hooch* in 1989, and two box office duds in 1990 (*Joe Versus the Volcano* and *Bonfire of the Vanities*), Hanks took an overdue sabbatical to spend time with his family. He made a comeback in 1992 with a cameo role in *Radio Flyer.*

With his professional battery re-charged, he ramped up his output and gained 30 pounds for his next film. In the movie he played a middle-aged alcoholic baseball coach, opposite Geena Davis, Madonna, and Rosie O'Donnell, cast as lady baseball players. The film, called *A League of Their Own,* was a box office hit. He followed in 1993 with a highly controversial role, as an attorney who becomes stricken with AIDs. For his role as the homosexual Andrew Beckett, Hanks did a great deal of research, talking openly with AIDs patients and with gay men. Under careful medical supervision he lost a large amount of weight so as to appear gaunt and dying. The movie, called *Philadelphia,* earned widespread critical acclaim.

Early in 1994 Hanks won an academy award as best actor for his role as Beckett, and that same year he delivered a second successive Oscar-winning performance, as the mentally challenged hero of *Forrest Gump.* The movie depicts the serendipitous adventures of a simple-minded man named Forrest Gump, who in spite of the mental handicap lives a life that proved to be more eventful and more fulfilling than the lives of many folks with twice his IQ. Hanks successfully brought the fictional character of Gump to life on the silver screen and turned the controversial character into a beloved folk hero.

Behind the Scenes

Hanks by 1995 was earning eight-figure salaries for his films, augmented by a percentage of the box office receipts. That year he starred as the Apollo 13 commander James Lovell, a true-life astronaut who steered an aborted moon mission safely back to earth. The film, called *Apollo 13,* was directed by Howard.

Among the most powerful films of his career was the critical favorite, *Saving Private Ryan,* directed by Steven Spielberg and released in 1998. Hanks and seven other actors underwent rigorous boot camp conditions for many days in preparation for their roles as a company of soldiers in World War II. The movie grossed $190 million at the box office, and Hanks was recognized with an Oscar nomination for the effort. Equally compelling that year was Hanks's portrayal of a uniquely compassionate prison guard in *The Green Mile,* based on a Stephen King series about a supernaturally endowed inmate on Louisiana's death row in the 1930s.

Behind the scenes, Hanks contributed his voice to the character of the cowboy Sheriff Woody in a computer animated film called *Toy Story* in 1995, and to the 1999 sequel, *Toy Story 2.* He also experimented with production work. He wrote and directed *That Thing You Do!* and served as executive producer of a 12-part Emmy-winning miniseries for Home Box Office (HBO), called *From the Earth to the Moon,* in 1998.

Hanks directed the war drama *Road to Perdition* in 2001 with David Frankel and was involved in several projects in 2002 and 2003. Among them, *Lady Killers* and *Polar Express* were scheduled for release in 2004.

Family Ties

In 1977 while a student at CSUS Hanks became close friends with a classmate, Susan Dillingham. An aspiring actress herself, Dillingham went by the stage name of Samantha Lewes. The two were married in 1978. Their son Colin was born in 1978 and a daughter Elizabeth was born in 1981. Sadly the marriage was fragile and the couple divorced in the mid 1980s.

Hanks, fearful of entering into a succession of unstable relationships, went into therapy before encouraging a close relationship with a colleague, Rita Wilson, who had appeared with him in several films. They were married on April 30, 1988. Their first child, Chester, was a born in 1990; a second son, Truman Theodore, was born in 1995. Hanks, who spends virtually all of his free time with his family, maintains homes in Los Angeles, Malibu, and New York City.

The family name of Hanks might stimulate interest among history buffs because Hanks, through his father's family tree, shares a common ancestor with Nancy Hanks, the mother of Abraham Lincoln.

Books

Gardner, David, *Tom Hanks,* Blake Publishing Ltd., 1999.
Kramer, Barbara, *Tom Hanks Superstar,* Enslow Publishers Inc., 2001.
McAvoy, Jim, *Tom Hanks,* Chelsea House Publishers, 2000. □

Thomas Harriot

A contemporary of Shakespeare, Elizabeth I, Johannes Kepler, and Galilei Galileo, Thomas Harriot (1560–1621) was an English scientist and mathematician. His principal biographer, J. W. Shirley, was quoted in the website "Thomas Harriot's manuscripts," saying that in his time he was "England's most profound mathematician, most imaginative and methodical experimental scientist, and first of all Englishmen to make a telescope and turn it on the heavens." He was also an early English explorer of North America. He published very little in his lifetime, and the extensive scientific papers he left at his death suffered loss and then neglect until the twentieth century.

Educated at Oxford

Harriot was born in Oxfordshire, England, in 1560. Nothing is known about his parents except that his father was recorded as a plebeian when Harriot entered the University of Oxford on December 20, 1577. Of Harriot's early school years a boyhood friend, Tom Buckner, one day wrote, as quoted in *Thomas Harriot: Science Pioneer,* "Tom Harriot had a far greater gift for language than I had. He enjoyed reading the writings of the ancient Romans, sharpening his language abilities through disputation and debate, and writing poetry in Latin." Harriot was a good student. At Oxford he attended St. Mary's Hall with other students from the plebeian class. He became friends with two of his teachers, Richard Hakluyt, a geographer, and Thomas Allen, who had an interest in astronomy and was a suspicious figure to some because of the unusual instruments in his rooms. Harriot continued to do well in his studies and was one of only three in his class to receive a bachelor's degree in July 1580.

Sponsored by Raleigh

While Harriot was enrolled in St. Mary's Hall, Walter Raleigh had attended Oxford's Oriel College, the preserve of the gentry and nobility. Raleigh was already involved in exploration in North America when Harriot graduated. Raleigh and his half brother Sir Humphrey Gilbert had sailed with 11 ships to the Cape Verde Islands in 1578, and the ships had become badly scattered en route. Raleigh wanted someone to teach reliable navigation techniques to his ship captains. The principal at St. Mary's recommended Harriot, and Raleigh became Harriot's first patron. Harriot moved to Raleigh's London residence, Durham House.

Harriot made several investigations to prepare a course for English navigators. He interviewed ships' captains at the docks along the Thames River. His friends Allen and Hakluyt from Oxford helped him. He also read John Dee's translation of Martin Cortes' *Arte de navigation*. The result was a textbook he named *Arcticon*. Only the names of its chapters have survived; some of them were "Some Remembrances of taking the altitude of the Sonne by Astrolabe and Sea Ring," "How to find the declination of the Sonne for any time of the yeare & any place; by a speciall table called the Sonnes Regiment newly made according to late observations," and "Effect of longitude on declination."

Traveled to Virginia

When Raleigh received permission to sail to North America in 1584, Harriot may have accompanied him, but there are no records to confirm it. He is known to have sailed for the Western Hemisphere with Sir Richard Grenville in 1585. En route Harriot made many observations of the sun and stars to track his course, and he also observed a partial solar eclipse. The ship sighted Dominica in the Caribbean, then moved northward. On June 30, 1585, it anchored at Roanoke Island, off Virginia. On shore, Harriot observed the topography, flora, and fauna, making many drawings and maps, and the native people, who spoke a language the English called Algonquian. Harriot worked out a phonetic transcription of the native people's speech sounds and began to learn the language, which enabled him to converse to some extent with other natives the English encountered. Apparently Harriot favored friendly relations with the native people, but others in the party felt otherwise, and at least one of the native people was killed. At the same time, Sir Francis Drake, patrolling the Florida coast for Spanish treasure galleons to capture, heard the Spanish planned to attack the colony at Roanoke. He sailed north to warn the English and took most of them back to England in 1586. Harriot wrote his report for Raleigh and published it as *A Briefe and True Report of the New Found Land of Virginia* in 1588. Raleigh gave Harriot his own estate, in Ireland, and Harriot began a survey of Raleigh's Irish holdings. He also undertook a study of ballistics and ship design for Raleigh in advance of the Spanish Armada's arrival.

Security Shaken

Two events made Raleigh's and Harriot's lives stressful about this time. First, Raleigh's political situation became murky when he married Elizabeth Throckmorton, one of Queen Elizabeth's ladies in waiting, in 1587. He had been a favorite of Elizabeth, and the marriage may have displeased the queen. Second, the queen issued a proclamation on October 18, 1591, attacking Jesuits in England for trying to return the country to Catholicism. Perhaps in retaliation, Jesuit father Robert Parsons attacked Elizabeth's sometime friend Raleigh, as well as Harriot, accusing them of atheism.

Then in 1592, soon after Raleigh's son was born, Elizabeth imprisoned Raleigh and his family in the Tower of London. Coincidentally, one of Raleigh's ships captured a Spanish treasure ship, the *Madre de Deus*, not long after the imprisonment. With Raleigh in prison, the ship was being gradually looted. Elizabeth wanted the greater part of its fortune for England's treasury, so Raleigh and his family were released so that Raleigh could stop the looting. Harriot remained under Raleigh's patronage in Ireland, avoiding the plague that struck London in 1593.

Harriot Studied Optics, Algebra

In 1595, the Duke of Northumberland, Henry Percy, a great friend of Raleigh's, became Harriot's patron and deeded him property in Durham as well as allowing him use of a house in London. Harriot undertook a study of optics, using part of the house as a laboratory. The studies eventually led to several important discoveries concerning the refraction of light, but Harriot never published his results. He also began to analyze the forces affecting projectiles and commenced various studies in algebra. He and earlier mathematicians may have made several discoveries often credited to Rene Descartes (1596-1650). He wrote *Artis Analyticae Praxis ad Aequationes Algebraicas Resolvendas,* an algebra text, and left specific instructions for its publication in his will, but knowledgeable mathematicians reportedly think that the work which was eventually published represents Harriot's efforts poorly. His body of work in algebra is considerable. He advanced the notation system for algebra (although the "greater than" and "less than" symbols that have been credited to him are now thought to have been introduced by the editor of *Artis Analyticae Praxis*) and did novel work on the theory of equations, including cubic equations and negative and imaginary numbers.

Queen Elizabeth died in March 1603, and James I became king. Raleigh was implicated in a plot against the new king and was arrested and charged with high treason. After a failed suicide attempt, Raleigh was sentenced to death, and Harriot, who had tried to help his former friend and patron, was mentioned in the judgment as "an atheist and an evil influence." Harriot, apparently shaken, ceased scientific work for about a year. Raleigh's death sentence was withdrawn, but he remained in the Tower of London. Then Guy Fawkes was arrested on November 4, 1604, for a plot to blow up Parliament. Henry Percy's grandson was arrested with Fawkes, and Harriot was imprisoned in a place called the Gatehouse on suspicion. Later in November, Percy was imprisoned in the Tower to remain for 16 years.

Moons, Sunspots Observed

Harriot was released by the end of 1604 and quickly resumed his study of optics, still under Percy's generous patronage. He also visited Percy and Raleigh in the Tower from time to time. Harriot was working out a theory of color, and a correspondence began between him and the German astronomer Johannes Kepler, although nothing memorable seems to have resulted. Harriot went on to observe a comet, later identified as Halley's, on September 17, 1607. With his painstaking observations, later workers were able to compute the comet's orbit. Harriot also was the first in England to use a telescope to observe the heavens. He made sketches of the moon in 1609, then developed lenses of increasing magnification. By April 1611, he had developed a lens with a magnification of 32. Between October 17, 1610, and February 26, 1612, he observed the moons of Jupiter, already discovered by Galileo. While observing Jupiter's moons, he made a discovery of his own: sunspots, which he viewed 199 times between December 8, 1610, and January 18, 1613. These observations allowed him to figure out the sun's period of rotation. After this time, his scientific work dwindled.

Cancer Diagnosed

The cause of Harriot's diminished productivity may have been a cancer discovered on his nose. A doctor he consulted in 1615 made notes in which he called Harriot "a man somewhat melancloly. . . . A cancerous ulcer in the left nostril eats up the septum of his nose and in proportion to its size holds the lips hard and turned upwards. . . . This evil the patient has suffered the last two years," quoted the "Thomas Harriot" website. Harriot lost several friends during this time, and on October 29, 1618, he witnessed the public execution of his friend Raleigh.

Three days before Harriot died, he made his will. His mind was clear. He willed Percy charts and maps and his choice of books and papers. He remembered friends, servants, and Tom Buckner, a childhood friend with whom he maintained contact all his life and who had accompanied him on Grenville's trip to America. In the will, Harriot mentioned a sister, whose son he left fifty pounds, and a cousin. Most evidence suggests they were his only family when he died; it seems he never married. He remembered his servants generously, as well as Tom Buckner's wife (in whose house he died) and the Buckners' son.

Harriot died July 1 or 2 (accounts vary), 1621, in London and was buried in Saint Christopher's Parish Church, which burned in the fire of London in 1666. According to *Thomas Harriot: Science Pioneer,* after the fire an inscription was incorporated in a plaque in the Bank of England of London which reads, Harriot "cultivated all the sciences And excelled in all." The plaque calls him "A most studious searcher after truth." Harriot was several times accused of atheism during his lifetime, but the plaque adds that he was "a most devout worshiper of the Triune God."

Papers Rediscovered

Harriot's story did not end with his death. What some writers describe as his "thousands upon thousands of sheets of mathematics and of scientific observations" appeared to be lost until 1784, when they were found in Henry Percy's country estate by one of Percy's descendants. She gave them to Franz Xaver Zach, her husband's son's tutor. Zach eventually put some of the papers in the hands of the Oxford University Press, but much work was required to prepare them for publication, and it has never been done. Scholars have begun to study them, and an appreciation of Harriot's contribution began to grow in the second half of the twentieth century. Today scholars, sometimes referred to as "Harrioteers," study the details of his life and work to understand both the man and the science of his time.

Books

Staiger, Ralph C., *Thomas Harriot: Science Pioneer,* Clarion Books, 1998.

Online

Apt, Adam Jared, "Harriot, Thomas," Encyclopaedia Britannica Library, www.britannica.com, 2003.
O'Connor, J. J., and E. F. Robertson, "Thomas Harriot," www .groups.dcs.st-and.ac.uk/~history/Mathematicians/Harriot .html (March 1, 2003).
—, "Thomas Harriot's Manuscripts," www.groups.dcs.st-and.ac .uk/~history/HistTopics.Harriot.html (March 16, 2003). ☐

Dorothy Irene Height

American social activist Dorothy Height (born 1912) was an advocate of women's rights and civil rights. She shared the platform with the Martin Luther King Jr. when he delivered his "I Have a Dream" speech in 1963. The recipient of more than 50 awards from local, state, and national organizations, Height received the Presidential Medal of Freedom, the nation's highest civilian honor, in 1994.

Early Years

D orothy Irene Height was born in Richmond, Virginia, on March 24, 1912. She was the daughter of James Edward Height, a building contractor, and Fannie Burroughs Height, a nurse. When Dorothy Height was very young, the family moved to Rankin, Pennsylvania, not far from Pittsburgh, where she attended integrated schools. Although she taught Bible stories to white children at her church, she was hurt at the age of nine when her best friend, a white girl, told her that she could not play with her any longer because Height was black.

As a high school student, Height made a speech about slavery amendments to the U.S. Constitution that won her a scholarship to the college of her choice. Although she was accepted at Barnard College in New York City, when she showed up to enroll there, she was told the college's quota for blacks had been filled. Instead, she enrolled in New York University, where she earned a bachelor's degree in social sciences and a master's degree in educational psychology.

As a young woman, Height made time to join church-sponsored and civic groups. She continued her voluntary service in these organizations even after she graduated from New York University in 1932.

Welfare Caseworker

Following Height's graduation, she became a welfare caseworker. As an employee of the New York Welfare Department, Height helped the city deal with the 1935 Harlem riots. She emerged as one of the leaders in the National Youth Movement during President Franklin Roosevelt's New Deal years.

Height also volunteered in Christian activist groups. In 1937, she became an assistant director of the Harlem YWCA. She developed leadership training programs for volunteers and staff and programs promoting interracial and ecumenical education. Height worked with the national YWCA from 1944 until 1977. She founded the YWCA's Center for Racial Justice in 1965 and directed it for 12 years.

Height caught the attention of U.S. government leaders and human rights activists as a representative to international YWCA meetings. In 1966, she served on the council to the White House conference "To Fulfill These Rights." Height also worked with Delta Sigma Theta sorority, serving as its national president from 1946 to 1957. She never married.

Headed NCNW

In 1937, while escorting First Lady Eleanor Roosevelt to a National Council of Negro Women (NCNW) meeting,

Height met Mary McLeod Bethune, the NCNW's founder. Bethune asked Height to help in promoting the NCNW's agenda, which included pursuit of full and equal employment and educational opportunities for women. Height later said she learned "the value of collaboration and of building political coalitions" in NCNW.

Height assumed leadership of the NCNW in 1957 and led the organization for 41 years until she became president emerita in 1998. By then, the National Council of Negro Women had become a federation of 250 community organizations. During Height's tenure, she fought for the rights of black women and sought ways to strengthen black families. Under Height, the organization developed national and community programs aimed at combating problems such as teenage pregnancy and poor nutrition in rural communities. In 1975, Height started the only African American private voluntary organization working in Africa, building on the earlier achievements of NCNW's programs in other parts of the world.

In 2002, in honor of Height's ninetieth birthday, a gathering of friends that included TV star Oprah Winfrey, boxing promoter Don King, author Maya Angelou, the Reverend Al Sharpton, and former Washington D.C. mayor Marion Barry pledged $5 million to pay off the mortgage of the NCNW building on Washington's Pennsylvania Avenue. Height had been struggling for years to retire the debt.

Height, who was never an employee of NCNW, remained a strong advocate of volunteer work throughout her career. She said that people should realize that they can do more by working together than they can on their own.

Civil Rights Activist

While working with the NCNW, Height also worked for civil rights. In 1936 in New York, she participated in a protest against lynchings. She advocated an end to segregation in the military, a fairer legal system, and an end to racial restrictions on access to public transportation. During the 1950s, she worked on voter registration drives in the South.

By the 1960s, Height was at the forefront of the civil rights movement. She worked closely with the movement's major leaders, including King, Roy Wilkins, Whitney Young, and A. Philip Randolph, and she participated in nearly all of the major civil and human rights events of the era.

In 1964, Height initiated the NCNW's "Wednesdays in Mississippi" program, in which women activists from the North flew south to spend Wednesdays in small towns, meeting with black women. One such meeting, held in a church in Hattiesburg, Mississippi, was nearly the scene of tragedy after someone threw a Molotov cocktail through the church window. Fortunately, the bomb did not ignite.

During Height's years as a civil rights activist, she never acquired a reputation as a radical or militant. Height received little attention for her work, perhaps because the movement was dominated by men. But Height told *People* in 1998, "If you worry about who is going to get credit, you don't get much work done." James Farmer, a former leader of the Congress for Racial Equality, credited Height with bringing the women's movement into the civil rights struggle.

New Directions

Following major civil rights victories in the 1960s, Height supported initiatives aimed at eliminating poverty among southern blacks, such as home ownership programs and child care centers. There was even a program aimed at giving poor families a pig. As Height explained to *People* in 1998, "I thought if they had a pig in their backyard, no one could push them around."

In the 1980s and 1990s, the NCNW under Height's direction took on AIDS education and put in place a program to celebrate traditional African American values. In 1986, Height inaugurated the Black Family Reunion Celebration to reinforce the traditional strengths and values of the African American family. In the late 1990s, Height championed the confirmation of Alexis Herman, the first black woman to head the U.S. Department of Labor.

In 2001, Height told *Black Issues in Higher Education* that sit-ins and protest marches had been replaced by lobbying for legislation. Instead of desegregation and voting rights, the issues had become economic opportunity, educational equality, and an end to racial profiling. If Height had any regrets, one was that the righteous indignation that had spurred the civil rights movement was lacking in the new century. She asked where the country would be if the "vigor placed in fighting slavery and in the women's movement had kept pace."

Height was inducted into the National Women's Hall of Fame in 1993. She received more than 20 honorary degrees, including degrees from Harvard and Princeton Universities. In 1998, she told *People,* "I want to be remembered as someone who used herself and anything she could touch to work for justice and freedom. . . . I want to be remembered as one who tried."

Periodicals

Black Issues in Higher Education, August 16, 2001.
Jet, December 29, 1997.
People, October 19, 1998.
Richmond Times-Dispatch, February 1, 2002.

Online

"Dorothy Height, a model of social consistency," *The African American Registry,* http://www.aaregistry.com/african_american_history/772/Dorothy_Height_a_model_of_social_consistency (January 2003).
"Dorothy Height Honoring the Diversity of America," *National Women's History Project,* http://www.nwhp.org/tlp/biographies/height/height_bio.html (January 2003).
"Dorothy Irene Height," *Endarkenment.com,* http://www.endarkenment.com/eap/mission/donations/_holdings/height/ (January 2003). □

Carolina Herrera

Venezuelan fashion designer Carolina Herrera (born 1939) ran a thriving fashion empire centered around her designer clothing line that consistently won praise for its elegant, feminine lines after its launch in 1980. The longtime New Yorker was regularly hailed in the media as one of the city's most elegant women and was well-respected inside its fashion industry for her gracious manner. "In a world in which wearing borrowed haute couture on the red carpet signifies great style and erecting an East Hampton faux chateau verifies taste," observed Hal Rubenstein in a 2003 *In Style* profile, "Herrera is unassailable proof that class and poise depend less on what you have on—or what you move into—than on how you behave."

Led a Charmed Life

Herrera is the scion of an old South American family. She "was hardly bred for this sort of business success," noted *WWD* writer Lorna Koski in 1991. "She was born, in fact, on another, much more languid planet, the lost world of the traditional Latin American aristocracy.'' Born Maria Carolina Josefina Pacanins y Nino in Venezuela's capital city of Caracas on January 8, 1939, she was one of four daughters in a family whose roots on the continent stretched back to the 1500s. Her father, an aviation pioneer, served as governor of Caracas and was twice the country's foreign affairs minister. Herrera's mother and grandmother were chic women who regularly traveled to Paris to have their clothes made at the great design houses of Balenciaga and Lanvin.

Herrera's early life was a charmed one, with a governess on hand and luxurious surroundings. Still, her parents were strict with their children, as she recalled in the interview with Koski: ''I had three sisters and I grew up in a very organized house, a very disciplined house. There was a right time for having breakfast, a right way of doing everything.'' Herrera sewed clothes for her dolls, but as she grew older became less interested in needlework; instead she became a skilled equestrienne and read avidly. ''My mother believed you had to be cultivated,'' Herrera told *Town & Country* writer Annette Tapert in 1997. ''Having an inner life was very important to her. She told her four daughters, 'Beauty is the first thing to go. If you don't have anything inside you, you are going to be so lonely.' ''

Endured Failed Marriage

Herrera was married at the age of 18 to a young man from an affluent Venezuelan family. With him she had two daughters, but the marriage ended after less than a decade, as Herrera became the first person in her family ever to divorce. She moved back into her parents' home with her little girls and for a time worked in Caracas as a publicist for Emilio Pucci, the mod Italian designer. Soon she renewed an acquaintance with Reinaldo Herrera, whom she had known since she was a child. He also hailed from a well-to-do Venezuelan family, and after their 1968 marriage the pair embarked upon a romantic, jet-set lifestyle. They traveled in social circles that included Princess Margaret of Great Britain and New York artist Andy Warhol. When in Caracas, they lived with their two daughters and her two daughters from her first marriage at the 65-room Herrera family estate, La Vega, built in 1590 and thought to be the oldest continually inhabited house in the Western Hemisphere.

In her thirties, Herrera began to appear regularly on the International Best Dressed lists, and in 1980 she and her husband moved to New York with the children. Nearing 40, she considered trying some sort of fashion-related business venture and thought about fabric design. A longtime friend, fashion publicist Count Rudi Crespi, suggested that she do an entire line of clothing instead. Former magazine editor and style icon Diana Vreeland enthusiastically agreed. Others, including Herrera's husband and mother-in-law, were more skeptical. Herrera had little business sense and had collected paychecks only during her stint at Pucci.

Launched Company in Borrowed Digs

In the fall of 1980, Herrera brought to New York about 20 dresses her dressmaker had made for her in Caracas. She borrowed the Park Avenue apartment of an acquaintance and invited her friends and acquaintances to see them. Soon, buyers for some of New York's upscale fashion retailers arrived and wanted to take the entire line, but Herrera had no company and no way of putting a production deal together. Back in Caracas, she met publishing tycoon Armando de Armas, who offered to back her, and within a few months a design atelier and showroom, Carolina Herrera Ltd., opened on New York's Seventh Avenue in the fashion industry's heart. Her first full collection was shown at New York's Metropolitan Club in April 1981.

Herrera's business started small, with just a dozen employees, but soon grew rapidly. The socialites who knew her became some of her first devoted customers, and women like cosmetics tycoon Estee Lauder and former First Lady Jacqueline Kennedy Onassis became clients. The fashion trade journals were not always complimentary, however. ''I had bad reviews at the beginning,'' Herrera recalled in the interview with Tapert for *Town & Country.* ''And when you haven't been involved in this world, they really affect you. But that was good—you read the reviews and see what they found wrong and you think, 'They were right.' ''

Kennedy Wedding Dress a Hit

Some of the hallmarks of Herrera's clothing found their way into the more mainstream fashions of the 1980s. She was one of the first to use padded shoulders, believing that broader shoulders made a woman's waist appear smaller, and she loved elaborate sleeves as well. When she began designing in the early 1980s, Herrera told *National Review* interviewers John O. Sullivan and John Simon, ''the whole fashion world was going mad on layer after layer of very loose skirts and free blouses—and no shapes. I came out with a collection that was all fitted.'' Her big sleeves were novel for the day, and Herrera recalled that ''Everyone asked me: 'Why big sleeves?' I replied: 'Well, they are not that new. They have been a fashion feature from Elizabethan times, or even the Middle Ages, up to the Gibson Girls.' All I did was to adapt them to modern times. They were successful because women liked these big sleeves framing their faces.''

Herrera's company enjoyed even stronger sales after she designed the wedding dress for Caroline Kennedy in 1986. It made her a household name overnight across North America, and the ultra-feminine gown was quickly copied. Soon Herrera's business expanded to include not just her ''pret-a-porte'' or designer line and the made-to-order items for women like Onassis, but bridal wear and a lower-priced line named CH. In 1988 she launched a fragrance line with an eponymous, jasmine-heavy scent based on the memory of a jasmine bush that bloomed outside her bedroom in Caracas when she was a teenager. Lucrative licensing agreements for accessories, costume jewelry, and eyewear boosted the fortunes of her company even further. By 1990, after a decade in business, its wholesale figures reached $20 million. She celebrated by opening a new, luxurious showroom on Seventh Avenue.

Maintained Focus on Elegance

As the elaborately overdressed mood of the 1980s gave way to new styles in the next decade, Herrera's designs continued to maintain a devout clientele and attract new wearers. She admitted that the fashion industry was difficult, noting that the modern woman often had more pressing concerns than hemlines. "Fashion in the past meant that you had to have the guts to wear something different from others—to express your individual personality—but within the constraints set by formal standards of elegance and style," she mused in the *National Review* interview. "Today, people want to be free to wear what they like, in any combination they like, to be confined by no rules, and to set their own standards—yet they all end up looking exactly the same."

Herrera often began a collection by assembling luxurious fabrics and draping them over mannequins. She was frank about her abilities as a seamstress. "I have an eye for proportion, which is always the key to looking great, for mixing fabrics, and for shape," she said in an *In Style* interview with Rubenstein from 2000. "Don't ask me to cut or sew. I can't do that. But I know exactly how a shoulder should lie." A team of assistants then executed her ideas into sketches that served as the basis for a more formal process of production. "I could tell you that I'm inspired by painters or some wonderful garden or music but that all isn't true. . . . I get my inspiration from everyday life, from looking at women around me," she told *WWD* writer Irene Daria in 1989. She said that her own lifestyle and her regular visits to upscale retailers in major American cities to present her new lines helped her creations as well. "By traveling around you get to know your customer and what they need but you have to have your own point of view," she said in the same *WWD* interview. "The more you listen the more confused you get. You can't design to please the press and to be in fashion."

Expanded Empire into Europe

Herrera contracted with Puig, a Spanish cosmetics company, to produce her fragrance line, which became a tremendous success; she even created a top-selling men's scent, Herrera for Men, in 1991, and regularly added new women's products to the line. Her empire continued to expand, and in 1994 the partnership with Armas ended when he sold his share to Puig. In 2000, Herrera opened her first store, located at Madison Avenue and 75th Street in Manhattan, and looked forward to expanding her business further into Europe. Within two years, she had opened her first collection boutique outside of New York, a boite located in Madrid's upscale Salamanca district.

Herrera's daughters, now grown, began families of her own and made her a grandmother several times over. One of them, Carolina Adriana, worked at her mother's company. Husband Reinaldo served as the special projects editor for *Vanity Fair* magazine. An apartment on New York's Upper East Side was their home base, but they returned often to La Vega. Herrera was adamant that running a highly successful company such as her own could be done during a normal work week, and she claimed never to work past

5 p.m. "The moment I leave my office I draw a curtain on my work," she told *In Style*'s Rubenstein. "Because you know what is really boring? When you work and work and then work some more, and you don't realize it, but work is all you talk about all the time. Many designers have that problem. Work should be an important part of your life. But for it to be your life? That is very sad."

Books

Contemporary Fashion, St. James Press, 1995.
Newsmakers 1997, Issue 4, Gale, 1997.

Periodicals

In Style, June 1, 2000; February 1, 2003.
National Review, October 28, 1996.
New York Times, January 4, 1994.
New York Times Magazine, July 10, 1983.
Town & Country, September 1997.
W, October 2002.
WWD, March 2, 1987; March 7, 1989; May 29, 1990; June 18, 1991; October 20, 1992; August 19, 1997; July 19, 2000; May 7, 2002. □

Hiawatha

The Native American honored as a leader of the Iroquois nation in Henry Wadsworth Longfellow's "The Song of Hiawatha" is not an actual person, although Hiawatha (c. 1400) has entered American legend as such. Although the legendary Hiawatha is usually cited as a member of the Mohawk tribe, some Iroquois traditions hold that he belonged to the Onondaga tribe. Given the uncertainty about his tribal affiliation, it has been suggested that the legendary Hiawatha is in fact a composite of several historical personages. The founding of the confederacy and the time of Hiawatha have been assigned to sometime between the late 14th to the early 17th century.

Legend of the Iroquois Confederacy

The Mohawk people once inhabited what is now New York state. They were a fierce, warlike tribe whose members frequently sought to subdue neighboring tribes by attacking them. According to a traditional Iroquois legend recounted in Arthur C. Parker's *Seneca Myths and Folk Tales,* sometime after 1390 a Mohawk chief named Dekanawida recognized the hopelessness of his tribe's constant aggressions toward their neighbors. When his tribal council gathered Dekanawida spoke out against these incessant battles, pointing out that all the Mohawk warriors would eventually lose their lives if such warfare continued. Eventually frustrated by the council's lack of response to his request, Dekanawida left his tribe and journeyed to the west to escape the fighting. Reaching the shore of a lake, he paused to rest.

As he reflected, Dekanawida heard the paddling of a canoe in the lake. Looking up, he saw a man fishing for periwinkle shells by dipping his basket into the shallow water of the lake. Paddling to shore with a canoe full of quahog or round clam shells, the canoeist built a fire and proceeded to shape the shells into wampum beads. Varying in color from white to purple, these half-inch-long wampum bead were strung in patterns on elm fiber or sinew thongs and worn as belts. As he finished each belt, the canoeist touched the shells and spoke.

After the man had made the last of his wampum belts, Dekanawida announced his own presence, and the canoeist introduced himself as Hiawatha. Dekanawida asked Hiawatha about the wampum belts, and the canoeist explained that they represented the rules of life and good government. The white shells signify truth, peace, and good will, he explained, while the black shells stand for hatred, war, and an evil heart. Hiawatha went on to explain that the string in which black shells alternate with white indicates that peace should exist between tribes, while the string with white on the end and black in the middle means that wars must end and peace should be declared.

Dekanawida recognized the wisdom in Hiawatha's philosophy and thought his Mohawk kinsmen could benefit from it. Tribes speaking the same language should stop fighting each other, he realized, and instead unite against their common enemies. Hiawatha explained to Dekanawida that he had tried to share his philosophy with Chief Tadadaho of the Onondaga tribe, but that Tadadaho had forced him to leave. That was why he now professed his laws in seclusion, at the lake where Dekanawida now found him. The bands of wampum he created would one day serve to remind future generations of Hiawatha's laws and their meaning.

Dekanawida asked Hiawatha to return with him to his Mohawk village, and the two traveled east. After reaching his village, Dekanawida called a tribal council to listen to Hiawatha. The Mohawks were impressed with Hiawatha's philosophy and readily agreed to live by them. Dekanawida and Hiawatha next traveled to the neighboring Oneida and Cayuga tribes, and they too agreed to be bound by Hiawatha's guiding rules. Finally the two men journeyed to the Onadaga and confronted Chief Tadadaho. Upon learning that three of the Iroquois nations had already agreed to abide by Hiawatha's philosophy Tadadaho fled into the woods. Although the evil spirits possessing Tadadaho hung from his head as serpents, Dekanawida and Hiawatha bravely followed. Hiawatha assured Tadadaho he would be allowed to be the head chief of the Iroquois Confederacy if he promised to govern in accord with their philosophy of peace, at which Tadadaho relented and joined the confederacy. Dekanawida and Hiawatha also visited the Seneca and other tribes to the west, but only the Seneca agreed to join the Iroquois Confederacy.

Iroquois Longhouse

Dekanawida built the Iroquois Confederacy's Longhouse at Albany, New York, at the mouth of a stream emptying into the Hudson River. The longhouse is symbolic of the political structure of the confederacy. A long, narrow dwelling of over 10 feet wide and up to 250 feet long, it housed many families. At both ends were doors, while shelves for sleeping or storage ran along each side. Families in the longhouse lived in segmented units, and adjoining families shared a fire in the center aisle. Each nation in the confederacy was represented symbolically: the Mohawks, who lived furthest to the east, were portrayed as keepers of the eastern door; the Seneca, who lived to the west, kept the western door; the Onondaga, who lived in the middle, became the keepers of the central meeting fire. As keepers of the longhouse doors, the Seneca and Mohawk were expected to watch for potential danger on their fronts.

Dekanawida was given the honorary title "Pine Tree" because, according to tradition, he had a dream in which an evergreen tree grew so tall that it reached the heavens. The five supporting roots of the tree represented the five members of the confederacy. Another tradition holds that when the confederacy was founded a pine tree was uprooted and tomahawks, bows and arrows, armor, shields, and clubs were thrown into the hole where it had stood. In honor of Pine Tree, an Iroquois warrior who demonstrated particular courage became a member of the Pine Tree Society.

The Historical Confederacy

Also known as the League of the Ho-de-no-sau-nee, the Iroquois Confederacy was composed of the Mohawk, Onondaga, Seneca, Oneida, and the Cayuga tribes. Scholars trace its origins to sometime between 1400 and 1600, when the tribes came together primarily as a means of preserving peace. The Confederacy consisted of a grand council of chiefs or *sachems* made up 9 Mohawk chiefs, 8 Oneida chiefs, 14 Onondaga chiefs, 10 Cayuga chiefs, and 8 Seneca chiefs; the Tuscarora nation, which would not join the confederacy until 1717, would be represented by the Oneida. All decisions were required to be unanimous, and if a unanimous decision could not be reached nations were allowed to act on their own. The confederacy existed only to mediate disputes among tribes, not within them. It had no police powers, so could not enforce its decisions, and had no power to tax its members. The position of chief was hereditary, with appointments made for life by the women in the matriarchal Iroquois society. If the chief performed less than satisfactorily, the individual was given three chances to reform before being removed from office.

The Confederacy's Great Law set out rules for settling blood feuds. Setting the value of a human life at ten strings of wampum, the confederacy compensated a bereaved family in the case of murder with the price of its lost member as well as the price for the murderer, who was required to forfeit his of her life to the bereaved family. The Great Law had the desirable effect of bringing to a close many long-standing feuds between families.

By 1500, at which time the Iroquois Confederacy was functioning, French traders had made their way into the St.

Lawrence River valley. The confederacy doubtless had concerns about the French presence among the five nations. Now joined together, the united tribes were able to present a united defense against this new threat, as well as against hostile and longstanding threats such as the Algonquians. Their unity also guarded them against the risk of famine and other natural disasters.

Hiawatha's Legacy

Unfortunately, the Confederacy did not bring peace to the Iroquois and their neighbors. The Algonquian and other hostile tribes to the south, after being repeatedly repulsed and then attacked by the five united Iroquois nations, were eventually forced to ally themselves with European colonists. The Confederacy meanwhile sought to bring other tribes within its structure.

Following a French attack on Confederate villages during the French and Indian War, the Iroquois joined with the British to help drive the French from North America. However, they failed to unite against the Americans following the Revolutionary War that followed, and by 1851 the Iroquois confederacy was all but obsolete. Even so, the tradition of the tribal confederacy greatly impressed subsequent historians, some viewing it as a forerunner of the U.S. Constitution. Some scholars even speculated that the tribal Confederacy would have eventually dominated the Atlantic coast tribes had it not met resistance from European-born whites.

The Role of Wampum

As one of the founding chiefs, Hiawatha was assigned the position of Keeper of the Wampum. In this capacity he looked after the wampum belts with patterns representing the Great Law and the confederacy as well as those patterned in ways assigned by the council to remind the Iroquois of treaties, important personages, and other noteworthy things. Wampum belts were also carried to various villages to announce a decision reached by the Grand Council of Chiefs. When a particular wampum belt lost its significance, it could be assigned a new meaning. Among the Iroquois, wampum did not serve as a currency of exchange.

The traditions established by Hiawatha continue to be honored by the Iroquois into the 21st century. When a new leader is selected to head the chiefs of the Grand Council he takes the name Tadadaho, and the chief who takes the position of Keeper of the Wampum assumes the name Hiawatha. Observance of this tradition reminds members of the Confederacy of its origins. The original wampum belt representing Hiawatha was removed from the tribe but was eventually returned to the Onodaga by the New York State Museum in Albany.

Longfellow's "Hiawatha"

Several centuries later, in 1855, poet Henry Wordsworth Longfellow muddied the waters of history when he published "The Song of Hiawatha." In fact, the hero of Longfellow's poem is not the founder of the Iroquois nation at all, but rather an Algonquian cultural hero named Nanabozho. Apparently deciding that the name Hiawatha had a more musical ring to it than Nanabozho, Longfellow decided to assign the Algonquian hero Hiawatha's name. The unplanned result created a century and a half of historical confusion before the traditions of Native Americans came under renewed scrutiny by revisionist historians late in the 20th century.

Books

Edmonds, Margot, and Ella E. Clark, *Voices of the Winds,* Facts on File, 1989.
Page, Thomas, *The Civilization of the American Indians,* Minerva, 1986.
Parker, Arthur C., *Seneca Myths and Folk Tales,* University of Nebraska Press, 1989.
Richter, Daniel K., *The Ordeal of the Longhouse: The Peoples of the Iroquois League in the Era of European Colonization,* University of North Carolina Press, 1992.

Online

"Hiawatha," http://www.nativepubs.com/nativepubs/Apps/bios/0176Hiawatha.asp (January 20, 2003). □

David Da-I Ho

Molecular biologist David Da-I Ho (born 1952) has dedicated his career to identifying a cure for acquired immune deficiency syndrome (AIDS). His greatest contribution to the worldwide battle against AIDS came in 1996 when he combined state-of-the art AIDS medications in a way that stopped the progression of the human immunodeficiency virus (HIV), which leads to the deadly AIDS condition.

AIDS researcher David Ho was the fourth scientist to identify the cause of AIDS as a virus that attacks the body's immune system. Now chief executive officer and scientific director of the Aaron Diamond AIDS Research Center (ADARC), Ho has been at the forefront of the worldwide battle against the AIDS epidemic and remains hopeful that HIV can be eradicated.

A Strong Work Ethic

Ho was born on November 3, 1952, in Taichung, a small town in Taiwan where transportation was by means of bicycle and the only form of communications technology was a small radio. His parents, Paul and Sonia Ho, were poor but proud; they lived in a small four-room house bordering a ditch that served as an outdoor toilet. Ho's father, an engineer, had high hopes for his family. Reflecting Paul Ho's optimism, he named his first child Da-I, meaning "Great One," then boarded a freighter for the United States in 1956. Fluent in English, he enrolled in an advanced engineering degree program at the University of Southern California, Los Angeles (UCLA), determined to make a better life for his growing family. It would be nine years before

Paul Ho felt secure enough in a new job to send for his wife and two young sons.

Raised by his mother, Ho showed an early aptitude for math and science, staying after school for advanced class work and transforming the family garage into a scientific laboratory. He also exhibited the same penchant for comic books and sports as many boys his age. It was clear to all that the young boy was following the family tradition; many of his relatives were involved in science-related jobs.

In 1965 Ho arrived in the United States, where his father had established a home. David and younger brother Philip were joined by another brother, Sidney, as they settled into their new residence in an African American neighborhood in central Los Angeles. Wanting to assimilate into his new country and inspired by his Christian beliefs, Paul Ho renamed his children, and Da-I became David. While his father had spent nine years adapting to American language and culture, 12-year-old David spoke only Chinese and without even a basic knowledge of the English alphabet, the language of math became his refuge. Putting all his energy into his schoolwork, he showed the same determination as had his father. "People get to this new world, and they want to carve out their place in it," he told a *Time* contributor. "The result is dedication and a higher level of work ethic. You always retain a bit of an underdog mentality."

During his first year at school in Los Angeles, Ho was looked upon as an outcast because he never talked with his classmates and never participated in class discussions.

Within six months he had mastered the English language enough to break down his social barriers, and his grades shot up. A daily dose of television also aided in his eventual fluency in spoken English, and the game of basketball provided him with friends. By the end of high school, Ho's transcript reflected his hard work, and the decision to go to college became clear.

Deciding to go into physics, Ho applied to the best schools and ultimately enrolled at the Massachusetts Institute of Technology (MIT). Unhappy on the east coast being so far from home, he returned to California to finish his bachelor of science degree and graduated summa cum laude from the California Institute of Technology in 1974. Ho was fascinated by the ongoing advances in the area of molecular biology and the cutting-edge technology involved in gene splicing. This fascination prompted him to make a second trip east and earn a medical degree from the Harvard-MIT Division of Health Science and Technology in 1978.

A Series of Mysterious Deaths

In 1981 Ho became a resident in internal medicine at UCLA's Cedars-Sinai Medical Center and advanced to chief resident the following year. He was concerned by the large number of homosexual men who exhibited the same unusual symptoms. Their immune systems were seemingly inoperable; infections that would otherwise be easily overcome such as pneumonia and brain infection (toxoplasmosis) were suddenly proving fatal. Diagnoses ranged all over the map, from allergies to substance abuse to sexually transmitted diseases. Some researchers suspected that it was more likely a parasitic, bacterial, or viral infection that destroyed the body's immune system, and Ho was among them. He decided to make the cause of these deaths his focus. When that cause was eventually determined, it was found to be AIDS.

When the AIDS epidemic became understood in the late 1970s, it drew the best minds from the country's finest research hospitals, both bacteriologists and virologists. Ho worked first from UCLA, moving his research into the existence of a possible virus to Massachusetts General Hospital's infectious diseases unit in 1982, where he worked alongside fellow virologist Martin Hirsch. Ho was the fourth researcher to identify HIV; Paris-based researcher Luc Montagnier of the Pasteur Institute was the first to isolate the retrovirus, followed by American scientist Robert C. Gallo of the National Cancer Institute and Jay Levy of the University of California's San Francisco Medical Center.

Ho relocated to Cambridge, Massachusetts, from 1982 to 1985 to serve as a Harvard University research fellow in medicine before returning to UCLA in 1986. With the HIV virus now isolated, he was able to provide others colleagues in the battle against AIDS with much-needed information about the disease, including its neurological complications. "He was the first to show that it grows in long-lived immune cells called macrophages," a *Time* reporter explained, "and was among the first to isolate it in the nervous system and semen." Ho was also able to subdue a public scare by verifying the fact that there not sufficient HIV virus in human saliva to transmit AIDS on drinking glasses or eating utensils or while kissing. Other scientists also added pieces to the AIDS puzzle, and within a few years researchers had discovered that the virus destroys the immune system by entering T-cells, cells that help keep disease from taking hold by attaching and unlocking the CD4 receptor proteins on the cells' surface.

Research Setbacks Reoriented Search for a Cure

AIDS researchers believed that injecting AIDS patients with massive doses of CD4 protein could intercept the virus and prevent it from attaching to those CD4 receptor proteins located on the surface of T-cells. Ho and Robert Schooley of the University of Colorado Medical Center in Denver tested soluble CD4 in over 20 AIDS patients, but the results were disappointing: some HIV strains, termed "wild viruses," are able to distinguish the real CD4 proteins from the CD4 decoy particles.

Frustrated at this failed effort to stop HIV's rampage, Ho decided to start at the beginning and study the onset of the virus. Using as subjects four homosexual men who displayed the flu-like symptoms of an early HIV infection, he discovered through research that millions of infected particles are present in a patient's blood stream, even at the early stage of the disease. In fact, the level of virus particles remains a high constant during the course of the disease, resulting in its rapid spread. Ho's results mirrored those of fellow researcher Dr. Robert W. Coombs, affiliated with the Unversity of Washington School of Medicine, in proving that the virus directly damages the immune system and actively reproduces even in early stages and does not at first lie dormant as was previously believed.

In addition to his research, Ho established a teaching career, beginning as assistant professor in 1986 and rising to the post of associate professor of medicine at the UCLA Medical School three years later. In 1990 he was named chief executive officer and scientific director of the new Aaron Diamond AIDS Research Center (ADARC), the largest privately funded AIDS research center in the world, established by philanthropist Irene Diamond and based in east Manhattan, New York. He left UCLA and relocated his career as an educator at New York University, becoming professor of medicine and microbiology at the university's medical school and co-director of its Center for AIDS Research. In 1996 he moved to the Rockefeller University and a new professorship. Despite the fact that his work had increasingly taken him away from the "front line" of AIDS, the clinics, the emergency rooms, the hospitals, Ho remained dedicated to fighting the disease on a personal level. As he told Judy Woodruff in an interview with *CNN:* "I think everybody who's involved in patient care in the AIDS field has been personally affected in many different ways. We've seen too many tragedies, too many deaths, due to this virus. There's no question that myself and all of my colleagues who have cared for AIDs patients have been touched in a very deeply emotional way."

Attracting many top-notch AIDS researchers from around the world, ADARC quickly became a heavy hitter in the battle against AIDS. In addition to testing a wide variety of AIDS treatments, including herbal remedies used by AIDS patients, Ho and his team continued to focus on ways the virus might be contained and worked closely with the Centers for Disease Control in tracking the spread of AIDS. Through work at ADARC, Ho revealed that the presence of white blood cells, a byproduct of a functioning immune system in HIV patients shows that the immune system responds in combating the virus early on. Then why does the virus level in AIDS patients become so high so quickly? One possibility, Ho reasoned, was that in the earliest stages of the virus the immune system sets to work killing off viral particles; because the HIV virus replicates immediately upon infection, the disease progresses rapidly, causing the overtaxed immune system to quickly give out and the production of virus particles is then allowed to continue unabated.

"Cocktail" Therapy Proves Effective

In 1994 those battling AIDS were handed a new weapon in the form of non-nucleoside protease inhibitors, protease being an enzyme component of HIV that breaks down the proteins in the virus so that an infectious particle is formed. Developed by drug researchers, protease inhibitors stop the breakdown, bringing to a halt the replication of HIV unlike AZT, the first drug to show effectiveness, which only slows the spread of the virus. Within the year Ho and his team at ADARC had devised an experiment utilizing protease inhibitors and two other drugs, reverse transcriptase inhibitors, administering these to patients in the early stages of the disease in a "cocktail." The results were dramatic and were quickly disseminated around the world: through combination therapy Ho had halted the AIDS virus in its tracks. Even better, he showed that once the HIV is halted, the body's immune system is able to reduce viral particles to undetectable levels. And Ho's use of a combination of drugs reduces the chances that virus particles will mutate and become resistant to the drug therapy.

While many scientists have been quick to point out that Ho's drug treatment is not a cure for AIDS as it does not restore the health of organs already damaged, there is no sense of how long its positive effects will last. There is the chance that the virus may remain dormant in certain body organs, but the treatments ability to stop the advancement of HIV was the first positive news for those infected with the disease. It has also provided other researchers using techniques such as X-ray crystallography with information useful for continued work. Meanwhile, researchers have become split in their goals: some, like Ho, believe that HIV can be eradicated through the use of antiviral drug therapies, while others hope only to control the epidemic. As Ho noted to Woodruff, "We, basically, have, for the first time, staggered the virus, and the new optimism comes from the fact that we now realize maybe, just maybe, this virus is not as invincible as we have previously thought. . . . This is just a beginning of this battle, and I think we have taken the first step successfully." Overall, Ho maintains, although he continues to refine and improve the effectiveness of his protease inhibitor "cocktail," combination drug therapy is effective only in individual cases in individuals with access to physicians and expensive medicines. In order to protect the world population, the true work is in the area of AIDS prevention: vaccines and education.

Ho continues his work at ADARC, where in 2002 he and his staff of over 100 were investigating a group of antiviral proteins called alpha-defensins that seem to help some individuals remain resistant to HIV infection. He also continues in his role as an educator. In addition to serving in an advisory capacity to such organizations as the scientific advisory board of the National Cancer Institute and the American Foundation for AIDS Research, he continues to author or coauthor scientific articles in journals such as *Nature* and the *New England Journal of Medicine.* For his accomplishments in the area of AIDS research, Ho was named 1996 Man of the Year by *Time* magazine and has been honored for his work in other ways. Among his scientific prizes are the Scientific Award of the Chinese-American Medical Society, the Ernst Jung Prize in Medicine, New York City Mayor's Award for Excellence in Science and Technology, the Squibb Award, and a Presidential Citizen's Medal. Making his residence in Chappaqua, New York, Ho is married to artist Susan Kuo, with whom he has three children: Kathryn, Jaclyn, and Jonathan. He is a member of the Committee of One Hundred, a Chinese American leadership organization, in addition to several scientific groups. Interestingly, despite his high professional profile, his command of the English language, his role as director of a U.S. corporation, and his successful assimilation into U.S. culture, Ho still performs his mathematical calculations in Chinese.

Books

Notable Scientists: From 1900 to the Present, Gale, 2001.

Periodicals

Advocate, July 21, 1998.
Asian American Times, August 2001.
Chemical and Engineering News, September 30, 2002.
Gay Men's Health Crisis: Treatment Issues, May 15, 1991.
New York Times, December 14, 1989; January 31, 1990; September 27, 2002.
Rolling Stone, March 6, 1997; April 29, 1999.
Time, December 30, 1996; August 20, 2001.
Wall Street Journal, December 17, 1996.

Online

"Interview with Dr. David Ho," *CNN Interviews: Medical Detectives,* http://www.time.com/time/moy/ho.html (February 15, 2003). ☐

Malvina Cornell Hoffman

One of America's foremost sculptors, Malvina Cornell Hoffman (1885–1966) studied with the great French sculptor Auguste Rodin from 1910 until his death in 1917 and is recognized by some as "America's Rodin." Hoffman is perhaps best known for her monumental bronze series, "The Races of

Mankind," commissioned in 1930 by Chicago's Field Museum of Natural History. Hoffman first won acclaim for her bronze sculpture of Russian dancers Anna Pavlova and Mikhail Mordkin and also studied under two other sculptors—Gutzon Borgium of Mount Rushmore fame and Herbert Adams.

Hoffman's commission from the Field Museum sent the sculptor on a round-the-world odyssey that lasted for more than eight months. During her global journey, Hoffman photographed and sketched hundreds of people of different racial and ethnic groups and collected massive amounts of anthropological data. In the end she produced a total of 104 monumental bronze figures, which were first exhibited in 1932 in Paris. The sculptures were formally unveiled to the American public at the opening of the Field Museum's Hall of Man on June 6, 1933.

Showed Early Interest in Art

Hoffman was born in New York City on June 15, 1885, the youngest child of British-born pianist Richard Hoffman and Fidelia Lamson Hoffman. Her father, born in Manchester, England, came to the United States in 1847 at the age of 16. Shortly after his arrival he played for the New York Philharmonic Society. Three years later he was hired by P.T. Barnum as an accompanist for Jenny Lind, the so-called Swedish Nightingale, on her first American tour. When he was 22, he became soloist for the New York Philharmonic, a post he held for the next 30 years. During the Civil War, Hoffman organized a series of concerts for the benefit of wounded Union soldiers. Fidelia Hoffman was a native of Ipswich, Massachusetts, and the Hoffman family often spent summers on the New Hampshire seacoast nearby.

The Hoffmans' Manhattan home on West 43rd Street was a popular gathering place for the many artist and musician friends of her parents. Hoffman attended the prestigious Brearley School in Manhattan and at the age of 14 enrolled at the Art Students League. She later studied painting under John White Alexander. By the time she was 15, she had made up her mind that art would be her vocation. When she was 21, her father's health was failing, and Hoffman wanted desperately to memorialize his image. She first tried to paint his portrait in oils but was dissatisfied with the result and turned instead to clay, creating a three-dimensional likeness. The sculpture was eventually reproduced in marble. Shown the clay likeness, her father said, "My child, I'm afraid you are going to be an artist." He died two weeks later.

In 1910, a year after the death of Hoffman's father, she and her mother left New York to move to Paris, where the budding sculptor hoped to study with Auguste Rodin, the foremost sculptor of the 20th century. Desperate to gain an audience with Rodin, Hoffman was turned away from his studio five times. Unwilling to take no for an answer, she resolved that on her sixth attempt she would refuse to leave until he agreed to see her. In her 1936 memoir, *Heads and Tales,* Hoffman recalled her ultimatum to Rodin's concierge: "I shall not leave, he must admit me today." Her persistence paid off. Rodin agreed to grant her an audience and quickly recognized her talent, agreeing to take her under his wing.

Became Close Friends with Rodin

Off and on over the next seven years, until Rodin's death in 1917, the French master helped Hoffman improve her technical knowledge and understanding of carving, modeling, and foundry techniques, as well as her artistic discipline and expressive abilities. Student and teacher developed a close friendship, and when World War I broke out in 1914, Hoffman helped Rodin store his sculptures before she returned to the United States. To help finance her studies while in Paris, she worked as a studio assistant to American-born sculptor Janet Scudder. After her return to New York, Hoffman improved her understanding of the human form by studying anatomy at the city's College of Physicians and Surgeons.

While in Paris, Hoffman produced her first dance sculpture, "Russian Dancers." Long an aficionado of the ballet, Hoffman was inspired to create the sculpture after attending a Ballet Russe production of *Bacchanale* in London, featuring prima ballerina Anna Pavlova. The sculpture later was awarded first prize in an international art exposition. It was the first in a series of ballet-inspired sculptures Hoffman created. She met Pavlova in New York in 1914, and the two remained close friends until the dancer's death in 1931. To perfect her knowledge of ballet and the basic movements of its performers, Hoffman took about 30 les-

sons from Pavlova's partner. Pavlova then convinced the sculptor to make her debut in a ballet recital. Pavlova loaned Hoffman the same costume which the Russian ballerina had worn in *Bacchanale* in London and tied bunches of grapes about Hoffman's brow. Suffering stage fright, Hoffman danced to center stage at New York's Century Theater as a full orchestra provided a musical backdrop. Hoffman, overcome with nervousness, collapsed in a dead faint. It was the end of her ballet career.

While in New York in the fall of 1914, Hoffman set up a residence and studio at Sniffen Court in Manhattan's Murray Hill neighborhood. During World War I, the sculptor was active in Red Cross relief efforts and also served as the American representative for Appui aux Artistes, a Paris-based organization she had helped to found. The organization was dedicated to providing assistance to artists and models who had lost their jobs because of the war. At the close of the war, Hoffman embarked on a seven-week inspection tour of hospitals and children's centers in the Balkans at the request of Herbert Hoover, who was then serving as director of the American Relief Administration.

Unveiled "The Sacrifice"

Hoffman's first major sculpture after the war was "The Sacrifice," a massive memorial to Harvard University's war dead. The sculpture, carved in Caen stone, was commissioned by Mrs. Robert Bacon in memory of her late husband, the former U.S. ambassador to France and a hero of World War I, for display in Harvard's proposed War Memorial Chapel. While construction on the chapel continued, Hoffman's completed sculpture was exhibited at upper Manhattan's Cathedral of St. John the Divine from 1923 until 1932.

In 1925, Hoffman unveiled her most significant architectural sculpture, "To the Friendship of the English Speaking People," at Bush House in London. Consisting of two heroic stone figures and an altar for the entrance to the house, it was commissioned by American-born businessman Irving Bush. Staid Londoners were startled by the sight of Hoffman clambering over her massive statuary putting finishing touches on her work. That same year, the sculptor traveled to Zagreb, Yugoslavia, to study equestrian sculpture with Ivan Mestrovic. She also filmed Mestrovic at work on his "American Indian Groups" sculpture for Chicago's Grant Park.

In June 1924 Hoffman married violinist Samuel Grimson. Hoffman first met Grimson in 1908 when he came to the Hoffmans' Manhattan home to play chamber music with her father. A couple of years after they married, the couple moved to the Villa Asti in Paris.

By far the biggest commission of Hoffman's career came when she was approached by Stanley Field, who asked if she would be interested in participating in a massive undertaking planned by Chicago's Field Museum of Natural History. The museum hoped to put together a series of more than a hundred bronze and marble busts, heads, and life-sized figures representing all the peoples of the world. The museum wanted the sculptures completed before the 1933 opening of the Chicago World's Fair and planned to divide the work among three prominent sculptors. Hoffman wanted the whole job for herself, and she eventually persuaded Field to award the commission exclusively to her.

Toured World

Once she had struck an agreement with Field and the museum's board of directors, Hoffman, with her husband in tow, embarked on an eight-month tour to find models for her statues of the world's many ethnic groups and races. On her travels, the sculptor photographed or sketched scores of models. In Singapore a Dyak headhunter modeled for Hoffman. Deep in the jungles of the Malay Peninsula, she drew a sketch of a Saka warrior, who would not allow her interpreter or white escorts to observe them while she modeled. On Hokkaido, the northernmost of Japan's islands, Hoffman spent several days among the Ainu, sketching, photographing, and observing members of that indigenous group.

With her research complete, Hoffman went to work on the sculptures in her Paris stuido. By early 1932 she had completed 97 bronze figures, casting many of them herself. The remaining statues were carved in marble. All were completed in time for a debut exhibition at the Musee d'Ethnographie in Paris's Palais du Trocadero. In all, Hoffman's ''Races of Mankind'' series included 105 sculptures—35 full figures, 1 half-size figure, 30 busts, and 39 heads. Almost from the start, the series provoked controversy. While prominent abstract artists of the early 1930s criticized Hoffman's sculptures as either too realistic or too romantic, social scientists argued that her work relied too heavily on physical rather than cultural characteristics. Despite the criticism, almost everyone agreed that it was a monumental work of art.

In 1936 Hoffman divorced Grimson and returned from Paris to her Sniffen Court residence and studio in New York. For the next three decades she continued to work out of her New York studio, producing a number of notable sculptures, including a World War II memorial for the Epinal Memorial Cemetery in France. In 1939 Hoffman published an instructional guide to sculpture entitled *Sculpture Inside and Out.* This was followed in 1943 by *Heads and Tales,* an account of her world travels on the ''Races of Mankind'' project, and in 1965 by her autobiography, *Yesterday Is Tomorrow.* On July 19, 1966, Hoffman died at her home in Manhattan.

Periodicals

Metro Santa Cruz, March 10-17, 1999.
New York Times, July 11, 1966.

Online

''Biographical Note,'' *The Getty,* http://www.getty.edu/research/tools/special_collections/hoffman.html (February 16, 2003).
''Hoffman, Malvina,'' *Women in American History by Encyclopaedia Britannica,* http://search.eb.com/women/articles/Hoffman_Malvina.html (February 16, 2003).
''Hoffman, Malvina Cornell,'' *AskArt,* http://www.askart.com/Biography.asp (February 16, 2003).
''Malvina Hoffman,'' *The Bronze Gallery,* http://www.bronze-gallery.com/sculptors/artist.cfm?sculptorID=73 (February 16, 2003).
''Malvina Hoffman (1887-1966),'' *Cedar Rapids Museum of Art,* http://www.crma.org/collection/hoffman/hoffman.htm (February 16, 2003).
''Malvina Hoffman: A Tribute,'' *Sandy Cline Soapstone Sculpture,* http://www.sandycline.com/sculpture/malvhoff.html (February 16, 2003).
''Malvina Hoffman Remembered,'' *Lane Memorial Library,* http://www.hampton.lib.nh.us/hampton/history/vignettes/malvinahoffman.htm (February 16, 2003). □

Helen Elna Hokinson

One of the 20th century's most influential cartoonists, Helen Hokinson (1893–1949) chronicled the social comings and goings of the middle-aged American matron in the pages of the *New Yorker* for nearly a quarter century. She traded her early aspirations to become either a painter or a fashion illustrator for life as a cartoonist after one of her early cartooning efforts was accepted for publication by the newly founded magazine in 1925. Hokinson's cartoons were peopled with what came to be known as ''those Hokinson ladies.'' The ladies of Hokinson's cartoons, all of them ''slightly overweight, behatted, and ranging in mental state from outright addled to merely puzzled, populated garden clubs, library societies, civic meetings, and luncheons, and they entertained numberless notions and aspirations that were at once ridiculous and engagingly innocent,'' according to a profile of Hokinson in *Her Heritage: A Biographical Encyclopedia of Famous American Women.*

Over the next 24 years Hokinson created more than 1,700 cartoons, the majority of which were published in the *New Yorker,* gently lampooning the society matron. So gentle was Hokinson's touch, in fact, that she counted among her numerous admirers many of the plump, well-to-do middle-aged women her cartoons chided. Her earliest cartoons appeared in the *New Yorker* without caption. Before long, however, the magazine's editors began adding captions to further punch up the impact of her work. Beginning in 1931, she collaborated with James Reid Parker, a contributor of short stories to the *New Yorker,* who originated many of the scenarios for Hokinson's cartoons and also wrote the captions. In an assessment of their longtime association in the *Saturday Review of Literature,* John Mason Brown wrote: ''Theirs was the happiest of collaborations. Without any of the friction of the lords of the Savoy, they found themselves as perfectly matched as Gilbert and Sullivan. If Miss Hokinson's was the seeing eye, Mr. Parker's was the hearing ear.''

Drew Sketches of Classmates, Teachers

Hokinson was born Helen Elna Hokinson in Mendota, Illinois, on June 29, 1893. The only child of Adolph and

Mary (Wilcox) Hokinson, she spent her early years in Moline, Illinois, and Des Moines, Iowa, before returning in 1905 to Mendota. Her father, a farm machinery salesman, was the son of Swedish immigrants who had changed the family name from Haakonson to Hokinson. Her mother, an Arkansas native of English descent, was the daughter of Phineas Wilcox, a well-known lecturer known as the "Carpenter Orator." During her years at Mendota High School, Hokinson carried a sketchbook with her wherever she went, discreetly recording the events and personalities around her. She drew humorous sketches of her classmates and teachers at Mendota High, as well as some of the more interesting characters among the townspeople of Mendota.

After her graduation from high school in 1913, Hokinson persuaded her parents to let her enroll in a two-year program of study at the prestigious Chicago Academy of Fine Arts. The school promised that its program would produce commercial artists who were fully equipped to make a living. During the course of her studies in fashion illustration and design, Hokinson lived modestly at the Three Arts Club in Chicago. After completing the two-year program, she was able to secure assignments from art service agencies and department stores in the city.

Moved to New York City

Buoyed by her modest success in Chicago, Hokinson in 1920 moved to New York City, hopeful that she might do even better in the larger market the city offered. She was joined in New York the following year by fellow artist Alice

Harvey, with whom she had earlier shared a small studio in Chicago. The two moved into rooms at the Smith College Club, a newly opened residence for Smith graduates that just happened to have some accommodations available for young women who had not attended Smith. While Harvey managed to sell some of her humorous drawings to *Life* magazine, Hokinson worked mostly as a fashion illustrator for such fashionable New York stores as B. Altman, John Wanamaker, and Lord & Taylor. Both women also tried their hand at cartooning, hoping to sell one of their strips to the *Daily Mirror*. Hokinson's "Sylvia in the Big City" did appear briefly in the newspaper but was dropped after a couple of months.

In 1924 Hokinson and Harvey enrolled in courses at New York's School of Fine and Applied Art. That learning experience was to radically alter the course of Hokinson's career. She studied under Howard Giles, who taught the Jay Hambridge theory of dynamic symmetry. Looking over some of Hokinson's high school sketches, Giles was struck by the young artist's talent for "drawing true." Although some of her high school work might loosely be described as caricatures because of the humor they conveyed, Giles believed that this was due mostly to Hokinson's ability to accurately represent characteristics in her subjects that were innately funny. Giles urged Hokinson to concentrate on this form of artistic expression, capturing accurately the funny and ironic situations that unfolded around her. Hokinson took his advice and soon had abandoned fashion illustration altogether. Before long, she was turning out her slice-of-life observations in watercolor, combining the elements of dynamic symmetry she'd learned from Giles with the color theory of Denman Ross.

Cartoon Accepted by *New Yorker*

When the *New Yorker* began publishing in 1925, its editors launched a search for writers and artists whose work accurately reflected life in the city. Shortly after they'd opened their editorial offices, Hokinson submitted one of her drawings for consideration. When she checked back two weeks later, she learned that her drawing had been accepted for publication. What's more, the editors asked that she continue to send drawings each week for possible publication. It was the beginning of a long association between Hokinson and the magazine.

Typical of Hokinson's cartoons for the *New Yorker* are these: An ample matron, seated in the beauty parlor, submits stoically to the ministrations of her hairdresser, who opines, "These little curls will add to the gaiety of nations, Mrs. Balcom." In another, an equally well-padded woman of late middle age, clad in an overcoat with fur collar and sporting an imposing chapeau, has just purchased a fish in a pet store. She asks the store owner, "And when they spawn, do I do anything?" In neither of these so-called cartoons are the characters' features overly exaggerated. They are fairly accurate drawings of humorous situations that Hokinson had either observed or imagined.

Assigned to Do Magazine Covers

As Hokinson continued to turn out cartoons for the *New Yorker,* its editors began to assign her to create cover illustrations for the weekly magazine. For the cover of the magazine's October 3, 1931, issue, Hokinson drew a decidedly obese matron posing for her photograph at the feet of a giant statue of Buddha. In another charming slice-of-life cover (November 27, 1937), a middle-aged housewife puzzles over a cookbook before a table covered with the ingredients for a pumpkin pie—including a pumpkin—as members of her family look on covertly from a nearby room. For the *New Yorker* cover of February 26, 1938, Hokinson drew two obviously wealthy youngsters—brother and sister—selecting food items for themselves at a Horn & Hardart Automat as the family chauffeur patiently looks on.

Hokinson's earliest work for the *New Yorker* carried no captions. After the first year, however, the magazine's editors began supplying appropriate captions. They also began to suggest ideas for her to work on and sent her on assignments to cover various New York area events and phenomena they thought might spark a cartoon or cover idea. In 1931 Hokinson met writer James Reid Parker, who was also a regular contributor to the magazine. For the next 18 years, until her death in 1949, the two worked together on cartoons for the *New Yorker.* Parker supplied the ideas or situations, as well as the captions, while Hokinson did the artwork. The two also collaborated on a monthly cartoon—"The Dear Man"—for the *Ladies Home Journal* and handled some advertising assignments as well.

Felt Fondness for Her Subjects

In an article in the *Saturday Review of Literature,* literary critic John Mason Brown wrote of Hokinson's feelings for the subjects of her cartoons. "Miss Hokinson's fondness for them was transparent and contagious. Hers was the rarest of satiric gifts. She had no contempt for human failings. She approached foibles with affection. She could ridicule without wounding. She could give fun by making fun and in the process make no enemies." At one point in her career, Hokinson became concerned that those who saw her cartoons were laughing at, rather than with, the plump, strong-minded but occasionally befuddled women who were their principal characters. So strongly did the artist feel about her subjects that she launched a crusade to defend and explain them.

In addition to her work for the *New Yorker* and *Ladies Home Journal,* Hokinson published three books of her own cartoons: *So You're Going to Buy a Book* in 1931; *My Best Girls* in 1943; and *When Were You Built?* in 1948. After her death in 1949, the Hokinson estate brought out these additional collections of the cartoonist's work: *The Ladies, God Bless Them* in 1950; *There Are Ladies Present* in 1952; and *The Hokinson Festival* in 1956. Two of the books published posthumously—*The Ladies, God Bless Them* and *The Hokinson Festival*—included not only Hokinson's cartoons but John Mason Brown's essay about her and a memoir entitled "Helen" by longtime collaborator Parker.

Regarded Subjects as Individuals

In his memoir of Hokinson, Parker wrote of the artist's choice of subjects for her cartoons. "Her best-known sketches were of pleasantly plump, middle-aged suburban clubwomen. Most, but certainly not all, of these women were unself-consciously charming, kind, self-indulgent, ingenuous to a degree, and generally addicted to short-lived enthusiasms. But Miss Hokinson confounds us because she drew so very many women (and men), each a true individual. It is true, however, that many of Miss Hokinson's admirers were inclined to think of her women as a type, an amalgam of women exemplified by the women's club treasurer who declines to submit her monthly report 'because there is a deficit.' Miss Hokinson herself thought of her characters only as individuals, which in fact they are."

Hokinson, who never married, divided her time between an apartment in New York and cottages in Connecticut—first in Silvermine and later in Wilton. Invited to speak at the opening of the annual Community Chest drive in Washington, D.C., on November 1, 1949, Hokinson was aboard a flight from New York that collided with a Bolivian fighter plane and plunged into the Potomac River, killing all aboard. She was buried in her hometown of Mendota, Illinois.

Books

Dictionary of American Biography, Supplement 4: 1946–1950, American Council of Learned Societies, 1974.
Her Heritage: A Biography Encyclopedia of Famous American Women, Pilgrim New Media, 1994.

Online

"Helen Hokinson: Gag Cartoon: Matron at Pet Store Purchasing Fish," *Illustration House Inc.,* http://www.illustration-house.com/current/abp13/abp13_080.html (March 10, 2003).
"Helen Hokinson: Gag Cartoon: Woman at the Hairdresser's," *Illustration House Inc.,* http://www.illustration-house.com/current/abp13/abp13_081.html (March 10, 2003).
"Helen Hokinson: Well Known Cartoonist," *Mendota Museum & Historical Society,* http://www.mendotamuseums.org/helen.htm (March 8, 2003).
"Hokinson, Helen Elna," *AskART,* http://askart.com/Biography.asp (March 8, 2003).
"Polite Society: *New Yorker* Cartoons by Helen Hokinson," *Lakeview Museum,* http://www.lakeview-museum.org/pastexhibits/ps.html (March 8, 2003). □

Ludvig Holberg

Scandinavian playwright, writer, historian, and philosopher Ludvig Holberg (1684–1754) is considered the father of Danish and Norwegian literature, as well as the founder of drama for all of Scandinavia.

B orn on December 3, 1684, in Bergen, Norway, Ludvig Holberg was the youngest of twelve children born to Lieutenant Colonel Christian Nielsen

Again living in Bergen, Holberg saved money by working as a French tutor and supplemented this income by teaching other languages in Kristianland, a city located in the south of Norway. Holberg amassed enough funds to resume his travels and further his education. From 1706 to 1708, he lived in England, primarily in London.

Attended Oxford University

While in England, Holberg spent two years at the Bodeleian Library at Oxford University. He studied history, languages, and literature and was exposed to the ideas of the Enlightenment. Holberg was especially captivated by the works of Jonathan Swift, among other English authors, and Swift influenced his development as a writer. To fund his stay in England, Holberg worked as a teacher of flute and violin. Before returning to Denmark, he also studied in Leipzig in late 1708 and early 1709, then moved to Copenhagen. There he became a fellow of Borch's Kollegium, which supported scholars who had no money so they could continue to study. Holberg had already begun a book while he was living in England, *Introduction til de Fornemste Europeiske Rigers Historier (Introduction to the History of Leading European Nations),* which he published in 1711. The success of this volume led to Holberg being given a royal grant that allowed him to continue his education and travel. He also continued to tutor as well as lecture at the University of Copenhagen on the current European thought of the day.

In 1714 Holberg traveled to major cities in France, Italy, and the Netherlands using his preferred method of travel: by foot. The two years he spent walking to these cities affected his development as a writer very deeply, for he witnessed intellectual developments first hand and was exposed to the works of such writers as Moliére and theatrical genres like the commedia dell'arte.

Became Professor

When Holberg returned to Denmark in 1716 he published *Introduction til naturensog Copenhagen,* a book about natural law and natural rights. The following year he was awarded a professorship at the University of Copenhagen that gave him financial security. However, he was now required to teach metaphysics, a subject he disliked, and he avoided lecturing as much as possible. Nonetheless, in 1720 he was promoted to the University's chair of public eloquence and began teaching Latin literature and rhetoric.

While a professor, Holberg came into his own as a writer and had what he called a poetic rapture. His first work of significance was *Peder Paars,* published under the pen name Hans Mikkelsen in 1719–1720. It was the beginning of his own brand of humorous literature and the first classic in the Danish language. *Pedar Paars,* a 6,000-line epic poem, is a parody of Virgil's *Aeneid* that mocks Danish society and the social conditions of its author's day.

Wrote for First Theater in Copenhagen

In 1722 the first Danish-language theater opened in Copenhagen on Lille Grønnedgrade. Holberg wrote 25 plays for the theater, mostly comedies and satire, and many

Holberg and his wife, Karen Lem. From a family of farmers and himself a member of the Norwegian army, Lieutenant Colonel Holberg was 25 years older than his wife, who was from a merchant family. The family had been wealthy, but were considered poor by the time the playwright was two years old. Tragically, of the couple's 12 children, 6 had died as infants. Their bad luck continued with the death of Holberg's father in 1688; the family was further impoverished by one of Bergen's fires that same year. Holberg suffered another loss eight years later when his mother died, and he and his siblings were sent to live with relatives.

For the first three years after the death of his parents, Holberg lived with a pastor in Norway's Gudbrand Valley, where his interest in literature and language was noticed and somewhat supported. Unfortunately, he did not do well in school because he did not get along well with his teacher, with the result that he was sent to live with his uncle Peder Lem in Bergen. There, Holberg was educated at the Bergen Grammar School.

Desired to See World

When he was 18 years old, Holberg entered the University of Copenhagen and took his degree in theology-philosophy within two years after spending a year working as a tutor in Norway. By the time he graduated Holberg was determined to see the world and traveled to Holland in 1704. His travels were short lived, however, after he became ill in the city of Aachen. Because of a lack of funds he had to return home on foot in 1705.

were successful. Many of Holberg's plays used Danish manners, pretensions, words, and class differences as a target of satire, using stock and stereotypical characters. Among his best plays were *Den politiske Kandestøber (The Political Tinker)*; *Den Vaegelsindede (The Weathervane)*; *Jean de France*; *Jeppe paa Bjerget (Jeppe of the Hill)*; *Ulysses von Itacia*; *Den Bundeslose (The Fidget)*; and *Erasmus Montanus*.

The first play by Holberg performed there was *Den politiske Kanderstøber (The Political Tinker, 1722)*. The central character in this play, Herman von Breman, wants to become the mayor of Hamburg though he had no political experience. He becomes mayor for a day and the complexities of the office distract him.

Two other plays of significance were written by Holberg in 1722, *Jeppe of the Hill* and *Jean de France*. The former play's title character is a cuckolded peasant who gets himself so drunk that he believes he is a baron, has died, and has gone to heaven, whereupon he condemns to death those who had been his bosses. *Jeppe of the Hill* is considered by many to be Holberg's best known comedy. *Jean de France* is about a Francophile Dane who goes to Paris and tries to be French. At the same time, his fiancée Elsebet is in love with someone else, and he is gotten rid of by her servants.

Wrote *Erasmus Montanus*

In 1723 Holberg wrote *Erasmus Montanus*, another social comedy. The title character in this play is the son of a farmer who gets a college education and becomes a menace to his family and neighbors with all he has learned. Though his real name is Rasmus Berg, when he returns from school the farmer's son re-names himself Montanus and Latinizes his speech.

While Holberg was establishing himself as a successful playwright he also continued to travel. In 1725–1726, he went to Paris, and many of his plays of this period were influenced by Moliére because both playwrights used the dramatic devise of the central character being confused and his confusion driving the drama of the play. Some critics maintain that Holberg is more effective at this than Moliére because his comic characters are imbued with more human qualities than those of the French playwright.

Another significant play in this genre by Holberg was *Den stundesløse (The Fussy Man or The Fidget)*, (1726). At the center of this work is an idealistic main character, Vielgeschrey, who makes much out of the minutiae of life. He tries to marry his daughter to a man she does not want to marry, a bookkeeper because the bookkeeper has agreed to help Vielgeschrey in return. The play was very modern in its approach.

Holberg wrote several plays that were influenced by the Italian commedia dell'arte in that they are centered more on the plot or pageantry than on examining educational or moral ideas. These plays included *Henrik og Pernille (Henry and Pernilla)* and *Mascarade (Masquerades)*.

In 1727 the theater on Lille Grønnedgrade closed because of funding problems. Holberg wrote a play to commemorate its closing, *Funeral of Danish Comedy*, and continued to write plays for other venues. In 1731 he published all his performed plays plus ten new plays, then took a break from playwriting until late in life. Much of Holberg's writing output now focused on history, an interest that he would follow for about a decade.

In the early 1730s Holberg began to teach history at the university, and during the years 1732 to 1735 he authored the three volume-work *Dannemarks Riges Historie (History of Denmark)*. In this work he underscored the cultural development of Denmark; he would later supplement it with a history of the navy of Denmark and Norway. Holberg also wrote about historical subjects outside of Denmark, in 1738 publishing the two-volume *Almindelig Kirkehistorie (University History of the Church)*, a history of Christianity through Martin Luther's reformation. In 1742 he published *Den Jodiske Historie (History of the Jews)* in two volumes.

By the mid-1730s Holberg was considered a leading figure at the University of Copenhagen, although he mostly worked as an administrator. From 1735 to 1736, he was a rector of the university, and from 1737 until 1751 he served as its bursar. As Holberg's work responsibilities changed, so did the subject of his writing. After 1740 much of his work focused on morals and ethics in both fiction and nonfiction.

Published Novel

In 1741 Holberg published a political and social satire titled *Nicolai Klimii iter Subterraneum (The Journey of Niels Klim to the World Underground)*. An early science fiction novel written in Latin that focuses on a man, Klim, who falls into the center of the earth and finds a utopia where women are the dominant sex. Holberg's most popular book in Europe, *Nicolai Klimii iter Subterraneum* was translated into several languages and was enjoyed by fans of Jonathan Swift's *Gulliver's Travels* (1726). However, when the book was first released in Denmark, it was considered dangerous because of some of the ideas Holberg advanced.

Less controversial was Holberg's 1744 publication *Moralske Tanker (Moral Thoughts)*. In it Holberg outlined his philosophy, both moral and religious, and, in doing so, made a statement about the Danish Enlightenment. He revealed more about himself in the five volumes of *Epistler* (1748–1754), which contains several hundred letters and essays on various subjects, including dogmas and metaphysical ideas of the day. In 1751 he wrote *Moralske Fabler (Moral Fables)*. These 200 pieces were influenced by Ovid's *Metamorphoses* and are more cynical and negative than Holberg's previous works.

Named Baron

In 1747 Holberg was given the title of baron by the king of Denmark. He had become a very wealthy man over his lifetime, having invested the money he made from teaching and publishing on land rather than in living a lavish lifestyle. He had a number of country estates that he took care of in his old age. Holberg was particularly fond of Tersløsegaard in central Zeeland.

The year Holberg was named a baron, the new Danish National Theater was founded. He wrote six more plays for the company, but they were not as good as his previous works; while they were considered very intelligent they lacked the strong characters of his previous works.

Holberg died on January 28, 1754, in Copenhagen, Denmark. After his death, his will left his estate to the Sorø Academy to fund the teaching of modern subjects. The University of Copenhagen was not happy that he did not leave his money to them.

Long after his death, Holberg's plays in Danish were still being performed. There was critical debate over his work, though he was generally considered the father of Danish and Norwegian literature. He greatly influenced another Scandinavian playwright, Henrik Ibsen. Statues of him are located in both Norway and Denmark, at the National Theatre of Øslo and Royal Theatre of Copenhagen respectively.

As S. C. Hammer wrote in his book, *Ludvig Holberg,* "wherever you go in Denmark and Norway Holberg's name is familiar. Words and sayings of his live on the lips of both nations as colloquial terms. He sits in bronze in an armchair outside the main entrance of the Royal Theatre at Copenhagen; his noble sepulchre is at Sorø, a dreaming little site of learning in Zeeland . . . [H]e is the pride of his townsmen, who cherish his memory."

Books

Hammer, S. C., *Ludvig Holberg: The Founder of Norwegian Literature and an Oxford Student,* Blackwell, 1920.

Kunitz, Stanley J., and Vineta Colby, editors, *European Authors 1000–1900: A Biographical Dictionary of European Literature,* H. W. Wilson, 1967.

Zuck, Virpi, editor, *Dictionary of Scandinavian Literature,* Greenwood Press, 1990.

Periodicals

Financial Times, April 29, 1994. □

John Lee Hooker

American musician John Lee Hooker (1917–2001) was an influential blues artist who played a role in the development of the genre from the late 1940s through the 1990s. Playing both electric and acoustic guitar, Hooker's distinctive vocal and instrumental style also shaped the development of rock and folk music during the 1960s and 1970s.

John Lee Hooker was born on August 22, 1917 (some sources say 1920), in Clarksdale, Mississippi, the fourth of 11 children born to William and Minnie Hooker. Hooker's father was a sharecropper and Baptist minister who did not like the blues, referring to it as the "devil's music." Hooker's parents separated when he was five and divorced when he was 11 years old.

While Hooker received a limited formal education, music was an important component to his life. He first became exposed to it at church and constructed his first instrument out of a piece of string and an inner tube. Soon after her divorce, Hooker's mother was remarried to William Moore, a blues musician. Hooker credited Moore with mentoring him as a musician.

Moore taught Hooker how to play guitar, showing the boy his minimalist but very rhythmic style of playing. Soon Moore and Hooker were playing together at house parties and dances near their hometown. Though Hooker enjoyed playing with his stepfather he was unhappy living in Mississippi and when he was 14 years old he ran away from home.

Traveled to Tennessee and Midwest

Hooker first tried to join the U.S. Army, in part because during World War II a young man in uniform would attract attention from women. He made it through basic training and after three months was stationed in Detroit before it was discovered that he was underage and he was kicked out. Hooker then moved to Memphis, Tennessee. Supporting himself with day jobs such as movie theater usher, Hooker also worked as a musician at house parties because he could not get into clubs. Among the musician he played with was Robert Lockwood.

In his late teens Hooker moved to Cincinnati, Ohio, where he continued to work menial day jobs like dish washer and steel mill worker while establishing his music career at night. Because he was still a minor, Hooker could only play the blues at house parties. However, he also sang in gospel quartets like the Delta Big Four, Fairfield Four, and the Big Six. By working frequently in front of a crowd, Hooker learned the ropes of performing on stage and entertaining an audience.

In 1943 Hooker moved to Detroit, where jobs were plentiful because so many men were overseas fighting in World War II. He held day jobs washing dishes and working as a janitor in a Chrysler automobile plant until 1951. Now a legal adult, Hooker was now able to perform at the many blues clubs located near Detroit's Hastings Street.

While living in Detroit Hooker's style changed: from the country/rural folk-type blues played primarily on an acoustic guitar, he shifted to a more urban style played on an electric guitar. Part of the change was due to his encounter with Elmer Barber, a local record-store owner. Barber had heard Hooker perform and he made several primitive recordings of the young musician in the makeshift studio located in the back of his store.

Barber's recordings soon found their way to Bernie Besman, owner of a small record label, Sensation Records. It was Besman who suggested that Hooker should switch to electric guitar and include faster-paced material in his gigs at local clubs. Taking this advice, Hooker soon became one of the leading musicians in the Motor City, which at this time was witnessing a booming economy due to the men and women living there who had become wealthy due to the rise in wartime manufacturing.

Recorded First Hit Single

Hooker made his first single for Besman in 1948. "Boogie Chillen," recorded in a basement in Detroit, features only Hooker's vocals, his electric guitar, and the sound of his foot tapping the beat. When "Boogie Chillen" was released on Sensation it sold so well that the small label could not handle the demand. The single was then released on Modern Records and quickly climbed to the number-one spot on 1949's prototype R & B charts, selling a million copies.

Although Hooker did not receive the royalties he was entitled to for this and future songs, his success with "Boogie Chillen" came as a surprise to him. In 1949 he followed up his first single with ten other top-ten songs. Many of these early recordings feature only Hooker and his guitar, although fellow guitarist Eddie Kirkland sometimes appeared on recordings with him.

One reason that Hooker often recorded alone was that his beat was hard for accompanying musician to follow. By recording alone, it was easier to achieve a clean take, and the recording session took less time. Describing his sound, Hooker once told John Collis of the *Independent,* "I don't like no fancy chords. Just the boogie. The drive. The feeling. A lot of people play fancy but they don't have no style. It's a deep feeling—you just can't stop listening to that sad blues sound. My sound."

Despite becoming involved in conflicts regarding royalty issues, Hooker continued to record for Modern in

the late 1940s and early 1950s, and some of his hits of the period include "Rock House Boogie," "Crawling King Snake," and "In the Mood." One of his most popular recordings of the period, "In the Mood" was released in 1951 and sold a million copies. To ensure that he would earn enough to support his family, Hooker recorded and released material under several other names for over two dozen other labels. Some of his pseudonyms included John Lee Booker, which he used for Chess recordings, Johnny Lee, used for DeLuxe, and Texas Slim and John Lee Cooker, which he used on his recordings for the King label.

Many of Hooker's early releases influenced other bluesmen such as Buddy Guy and are considered to be early precursors to rock and roll. His blues songs incorporated the traditional blues sound with jump and jazz rhythms. Although Hooker recorded his music with little backup, he also performed with a live band at clubs in Detroit and beyond. Due to his talent, hard work, and determination, Hooker was a success on the R & B circuit throughout the 1950s.

In 1955 Hooker signed on with VeeJay Records of Chicago. For this label he changed his recording style, his subsequent recordings becoming a better reflection of his live show. Because solo blues performance was waning in popularity, Hooker started recording with a band, producing such hits as "Dimples" and "Boom Boom."

Became Hit on Folk Circuit

Even though Hooker found success performing on electric guitar, he discovered a new audience for his acoustic blues during the late 1950s. Folk music was now undergoing a revival of interest, and groups like the Weavers and blues singers like Odetta were increasingly becoming popular among young white college students. Hooker began appearing in folk clubs, coffeehouses, on college campuses, and at folk festivals as a solo artist, and did several recordings accompanying himself with acoustic guitar. Many of his songs written and recorded during this period reflect his background in Mississippi.

In 1959 Hooker released his first record album, *I'm John Lee Hooker,* on Riverside Records, his new label. This new turn in the career of the 42-year-old bluesman earned him an even wider audience, not just among white folk fans but in international markets where his records were also released.

Hooker once discussed his change from electronic band to solo folk music with Peter Watrous, telling the *New York Times* interviewer: "I played solo for a long time, so I know how to tap my feet so it sounds like a drum. It wasn't any problem to start playing the coffeehouses. I can switch to any style, you have to be versatile as a musician. I knew the white audience was out there but I didn't know how to get it. As the years go by, thing change and to me they were just people. I had no thought that British singers would start singing my songs, I had no idea what would come with that. People got more civilized."

In the 1960s Hooker began touring internationally, and the popularity of his music spread throughout the world, particularly among the more sophisticated audience. His songs also influenced emerging British rock bands such as the Rolling Stones and the Animals. Hooker continued to record on VeeJay, although he did not end his practice of laying down tracks for other labels as well.

Returned to Electric

By the mid- to late 1960s Hooker once again moved away from performing acoustic solo blues when the trend toward electric blues prompted to put together a new band. In 1965 he recorded an album with British group John Mayall and the Groundhogs. Many of Hooker's recordings during the late 1960s were albums rather than singles, and many were recorded in collaboration with bands composed of younger musicians. While many of these recording sessions produced mixed results due to Hooker's unique rhythmic stylings, his sessions with the group Canned Heat is considered one of the best. The resulting album, 1971's *Hooker 'n' Heat,* was a hit.

Though Hooker continued to record a little and play a lot during the late 1970s and 1980s, the blues had declined in popularity and demand for his music had declined. He still toured as a way to pay the mortgage on the house he owned in San Francisco, often performing with his Coast-to-Coast Blues Band and sometimes coming under fire for letting other musician carry him musically. Many of his early recordings were also repackaged and released for blues collectors.

Considered one of the top blues performers in the United States, Hooker was given a small role in the blockbuster movie *The Blues Brothers* in 1980. That same year he was inducted into the Blues Foundation Hall of Fame. In the late 1980s and 1990s his songs regained popularity, even appearing as part of film soundtracks. In the 1990s, Hooker himself began appearing in ads for Lee Jeans, Pepsi, various brands of liquor, and other products.

Recorded *The Healer*

In 1989 Hooker returned to the studio after a decade's absence and recorded *The Healer.* He was joined by several contemporary blues artists, including Bonnie Raitt and Robert Cray, as well as Latin artists Los Lobos and Carlos Santana. Produced by Hooker's former guitarist Roy Rogers, *The Healer* became one of the biggest-selling blues records of all time, selling 1.5 million copies. Hooker also won a Grammy Award for the song "I'm in the Mood," which he performs on the album with Raitt.

Hooker was inducted into the Rock and Roll Hall of Fame in 1990 and was the focus of a tribute concert at Madison Square Garden that same year. With the success of *The Healer,* he started recording again, again in collaboration with other blues artists. His 1991 recording *Mr. Lucky* was a hit on the album charts in the United Kingdom. Among the musicians he worked with on this recording were Johnny Winter, Keith Richards, Van Morrison, and Santana.

Hooker continued to perform and record into his late 70s and early 80s and found himself even more popular now than he had been earlier in his career. He continued to perform live with the Coast-to-Coast Blues Band into the 1990s, but had the added security of royalty income to rely on. Unlike many other blues and R & B artists of his generation, Hooker continued to earn royalties from his early recordings because he had wisely saved his contracts and, with the proper legal advise, went to court to ensure that recording companies continued to honor them.

After a hernia operation in 1994 made it painful for Hooker to perform, he slowed down. After the release of *Chill Out* in 1995 he retired from performing on a regular basis, although he still made occasional appearances on stage. In 1997 he opened a blues club in San Francisco called John Lee Hooker's Boom Boom Room. One of his final releases was the album *Don't Look Back* (1997), which features a cover of Jimi Hendrix's "Red House."

Hooker died in his sleep of natural causes on June 21, 2001, at his home in Los Altos, California. He had performed five days earlier and was making plans to return to the recording studio. At his death he had recorded more than 500 tracks, making him one of the most recorded blues musicians of all time. Married and divorced four times, Hooker was survived by eight children. Late in his life he had contemplated his eventual passing, telling Ben Wener of *Tulsa World:* "We all got to go one day. We live out this life as long as we can and try to make the best of it. Simple as that. That's what I've done. All my life, just try to make the best of it."

Books

Hochman, Steve, editor, *Popular Musicians,* Salem Press, 1999.
Larkin, Colin, editor, *Guinness Encyclopedia of Popular Music,* Guinness Publishing, 1995.

Periodicals

Associated Press, June 22, 2001.
Billboard, September 5, 1998; July 7, 2001.
Daily Telegraph, June 23, 2001.
Down Beat, June 1997.
Independent, July 1, 1990.
New York Times, October 16, 1990; June 22, 2001.
Ottawa Citizen, November 1, 1992.
People Weekly, October 29, 1990.
San Francisco Chronicle, February 11, 1995.
Toronto Star, December 24, 1998.
Tulsa World, August 30, 1997.
Variety, June 25, 2001. ☐

Doris Humphrey

One of the first modern dance choreographers, American Doris Humphrey (1895–1958) played a large role in determining the course of modern dance in the United States. While Martha Graham was a contemporary whose career lasted longer and had a broader influence, Humphrey, an early abstractionist, like George Balanchine, had an equally important role in developing twentieth-century

modern dance through her choreography for the ensemble.

Doris Batcheller Humphrey was born October 17, 1895, in Oak Park, Illinois. She was the only child of Horace Buckingham Humphrey, a hotel manager, composer, newspaperman, and photographer, and his wife, Julia, a musician and housekeeper at the theatrical hotel her husband managed. Humphrey's ancestors included author Ralph Waldo Emerson.

From an early age Humphrey studied dance and showed she had talent in it. Her parents encouraged her interest, and she was trained in several disciplines, including ballet. Humphrey graduated from the Francis W. Parker School in Chicago, where she studied a number of dance genres. She was taught by Mary Wood Hinman, who educated her students in a version of eurhythmics and Swedish folk dancing. Humphrey also studied ballet in master classes with the European ballet dance teachers who passed through the area, among them Ottokar Bartik and Serge Oukrainsky.

Began Teaching Dance

To help support her family, Humphrey taught dance in the Chicago area for four years after she graduated from high school. She opened her own school in Oak Park in 1913, where she taught ballroom dance, among other social and fancy dances, while her mother performed the piano accompaniment. While Humphrey was unsatisfied artistically, she had to help her parents financially, something she would do for the rest of her life. During this time, Humphrey also toured with a dance group that performed at train stations along the Santa Fe Railroad to entertain employees.

Joined Denishawn

While Humphrey's ultimate goal was to train as a professional dancer, she was not able to do so until 1917 when her parents' finances became secure. That year, she joined the Denishawn dance school and company in Los Angeles. Denishawn, founded by Ruth St. Denis and Ted Shawn, was known for its Asian and exotic influence. Humphrey began as a student, but after a short time was appointed dancer in the company and rehearsal mistress. Soon rising to the company's leading soloist, her style caught the eye of St. Denis, who influenced her as a dancer and choreographer. St. Denis and Shawn moved towards the abstract in their dances, and Humphrey performed in several "music visualization" pieces choreographed by St. Denis.

Began Choreography Career

By 1920 Humphrey had begun doing choreography, composing many of her early works with St. Denis. Among her first works was 1920's *Soaring* (with St. Denis), set to the music of Robert Schumann. Denishawn did not like Humphrey's approach to choreography, which became more experimental and self-expressive than exotic over time. She also emphasized ensemble pieces over individual works,

which was also against the school's grain. In 1925 Humphrey choreographed her first major work, which was performed to Alexander MacDowell's *Sonata Tragica,* though it was later performed without musical accompaniment.

In 1925–1926, Humphrey toured Asia with Denishawn. When she returned she and Charles Weidman, another Denishawn dancer, were put in charge of the New York City-based Denishawn House, a franchise school of the Los Angeles-based company. Humphrey and Weidman lasted a year in this position before either artistic or political policies dissolved their partnership with Denishawn. Some sources say it was because of the way Humphrey viewed movement and her need to experiment with new movement forms, while others maintain she left when Shawn wanted her to do a production of the Ziegfeld Follies.

Formed Humphrey-Weidman Dance Company

No matter what the reason, Humphrey and Weidman left Denishawn to form their own school and company in 1928. With another Denishawn dancer, Pauline Lawrence, the pair formed Humphrey-Weidman and held classes in dance technique to pay for their productions of Humphrey's new choreography, which continued to be innovative. During the Depression of the 1930s the group also received funding from the Federal Theatre Project of the Works Progress Administration.

Humphrey had spent much time studying the theory of movement and had developed her own concepts. She based much of her choreography on the principle of fall and recovery, the place between standing and the prone, motionless and unbalance. This moment in time symbolized the tension between security and adventure in the unknown.

As Jennifer Dunning wrote in the *New York Times,* Humphrey "abstracted the soul . . . in the central concept of her choreography. Falling, the recovery from a fall and the body's arc between were for her an expression of the fundamental tension and precarious balance between failure and triumph that we struggle to maintain throughout our lives."

Unlike Denishawn, which focused on spectacle, Humphrey based her choreography on feelings and physical states to create art. Movements reflected these emotions and physicalities. Many of her dances were conceptual and complex and could work with and against musical scores. There was no limit to her choreographical vocabulary as in ballet.

As Jack Anderson of the *New York Times* wrote, "When both the spirit and the shape of the steps are preserved, Humphrey's dances are genuinely impressive. And however well they may be performed in any given revival, they can be fascinating to watch simply because of their thematic or formal conception."

Many of Humphrey's early works were seen as original and distinctive. A number were inspired by nature and not done to music, including *A Water Study* (1928) and *Life of the Bee* (1929). Such works were simple and considered intelligent. The abstract *Drama of Motion* (1930) had no plot, sound, or costumes in the theatrical sense. In 1931, Humphrey choreographed *The Shakers,* one of many works that had a dramatic element to it, as well as an historical element. *The Shakers* was performed to traditional Shaker music and used boxes to define the mood because Humphrey could not afford a set.

Humphrey's company toured the United States in the 1930s, during which time her life changed in a number of ways. She was married to merchant seaman Charles Francis Woodford in June of 1932 and had one son, Charles Humphrey Woodward. Her work as a choreographer expanded to Broadway. She did dances for such Broadway productions as Moliere's *School for Husbands* (1933) and *Life Begins at 8:40* (1934).

Expanded Teaching Career

In 1934 Humphrey added another teaching position to her resume when she was put on the staff of the Bennington College of Dance. She taught at the Bennington College Summer School of Dance for eight years as well as for the High School of the Performing Arts. She also taught at Connecticut College's American Dance Festival beginning in 1948. She later taught at the 92nd St. Young Men's-Young Women's Hebrew Association and eventually served as its director.

In 1936 Humphrey choreographed her masterpiece, a trilogy titled *New Dance* which featured the three dances—"Theatre Piece," "With My Red Fires," and "New Dance"—about a social utopia where individuals were satisfied while the group worked in harmony. She continued to choreograph and perform in the late 1930s and early 1940s. Her pieces included *Passacaglia* and *Fuge in C Minor* (done to the music of J. S. Bach; 1938) as well as *Song of the West* (1940). In 1940 the Humphrey-Weidman dance company was dissolved, but Humphrey continued to work. A later piece which was regularly performed was *Partita in G Major* (1943).

Forced to Retire from Dancing

In 1944 Humphrey choreographed the last piece she would publically perform, *Inquest.* While her arthritis forced her to stop dancing, she continued to choreograph. Humphrey developed increasingly severe arthritis in her hip and suffered from arthritic seizures until her death in 1958.

Named Artistic Director of José Limón

In the mid-1940s José Limón, a Mexican dancer who had been connected to Humphrey-Weidman as a student, formed his own José Limón dance company and hired Humphrey to be the artistic director. She guided Limón's choreographing career and created some major works for him and his company: *Story of Mankind* (1947), *Deep Rhythm* (1953), and *Ruins and Visions* (1953). Many of her pieces focus on gesture. *Lament for Ignacio Sánchez Mejías* (1946) was based on the poetry of Federico García Lorca and created specially for Limón. Humphrey showed her flexibility and range as choreographer, meeting the varied demands of Limón's company. She even did some mixed media work, such as *Theatre Piece No. 2* (1956).

Helped Form Juilliard School of Dance

Though Humphrey claimed she did not like to teach, she played a big role in getting the Juilliard School of Dance open in 1952. When it opened, she was named to the faculty and given funds and space to choreograph. There, she taught creative composition and in 1955 founded the Juilliard Dance Theatre.

Humphrey died of cancer on December 29, 1958, in New York City. Though she never made much money at what she did, she never compromised her values as a dancer and artist. Over the course of her career, she choreographed 97 dances, some of which are still performed. At her death, she working on a piece choreographed to Bach's *Brandenburg Concerto No. 4,* which was produced.

After Humphrey's death her book *The Art of Making Dances* (1959) appeared, explaining how she taught dance in a way that was easy to understand. Humphrey was also working on her autobiography at the time of her death, and that book was not published until 1972.

Humphrey's contribution to modern dance in the United States has been somewhat overshadowed by that of dancer and choreographer Martha Graham, who was in many ways her contemporary and often considered the main influence of modern dance development. Like Graham, Humphrey's dances are still performed. The companies she worked with, Humphrey-Weidman and José Limón, produced many influential dancers of their own, including Sybil Shearer and Jennifer Muller. Her approach to choreography also was important.

As a contributor wrote in *The Complete Guide to Modern Dance,* "Combining an intellectual sense of craft with an emotional commitment to humane values made Humphrey design dances that were heroic in the best sense. At times her interest in the sheer mechanics of making a dance consumed her attention, but the works of her mature genius show a sympathy for human suffering or sacrifice and an artistic attempt at consolation and betterment of that condition."

Books

Cohen-Stratyner, Barbara Naomi, *Biographical Dictionary of Dance,* Schirmer, 1982.
Crane, Debra, and Judith Mackrell, *The Oxford Dictionary of Dance,* Oxford University Press, 2000.
Garraty, John A., and Mark C. Carnes, *American National Biography,* Volume 11, Oxford University Press, 1999.
McDonagh, Don, *The Complete Guide to Modern Dance,* Doubleday & Company, Inc., 1976.

Periodicals

Boston Globe, July 9, 1995.
Dance Magazine, October 1995.
New York Times, February 28, 1988; April 30, 1991; October 1, 1995. □

Alberta Hunter

One of the seminal blues and cabaret singers, Alberta Hunter (1895–1984) gained international fame in the first half of the 20th century as a recording artist and nightclub and stage performer. Many of her recordings are considered classics and her accompanists were some of the greatest jazz musicians of the era. Hunter actually had two careers as a singer; during the 20-year interlude that separated them, this strong-willed and independent-minded woman worked as a nurse in New York City.

H unter was born on April 1, 1895, in Memphis, Tennessee, and named for the doctor who delivered her. Her father, a railroad porter, abandoned the family while she was a young girl, though for years Hunter repeated the story that he had died while she was a child. Her mother eventually remarried, but Hunter did not get along with her new family and ran away from home. The exact date when this occurred has been lost, but most accounts say she was either 11 or 12 years old.

Early Success in Chicago

Hunter went to Chicago where she found work in a boarding house—her pay included room, board, and $6 a week. Captivated by Chicago's nightlife, she began sneaking into clubs. Her professional debut came in 1911 when she sang in a club in Chicago's Southside called Dago Frank's, a shady place that was a hangout for underworld characters. Hunter remained there for two years and left only after the club was closed down. Her mother joined her in Chicago soon after.

Hunter's first big connection in the music business came when she started singing in another Southside nightclub, the Elite Café. There she met ragtime pianist and songwriter Tony Jackson. Among the songs Jackson wrote was "Pretty Baby," which Hunter helped popularize. Over the next few years Hunter sang in a string of Southside Chicago nightclubs including the Panama Café, which catered to whites; the De Luxe Café; and, beginning in 1917, the fabled Dreamland Café where she established herself as one of Chicago's top blues singers. At the Dreamland she became friends with the King Oliver Creole Jazz Band, which featured Joe "King" Oliver on cornet and a young Louis Armstrong on second cornet. Hunter was especially friendly with Lil Hardin, Oliver's pianist and Louis Armstrong's first wife. Three years younger than Hunter, Hardin was also from Memphis. The Dreamland Café also drew an elite white and African American clientele; it was where Hunter first met Paul Robeson, with whom years later she would star in *Showboat* in London. Other patrons included Al Jolson and Bix Beiderbecke. On her off days and after hours Hunter worked as what was then known as a "drop-in girl," making the rounds of other nightclubs.

By 1919 Hunter was a celebrity in Chicago and began paying more attention to her image, including the rumor that she was a lesbian. In that era few performers were openly homosexual (especially blues singers, who flaunted heterosexuality) and Hunter was no exception. In January she sang at a club in Cincinnati where one of the young waiters caught her eye, an army veteran named Willard Saxby Townsend. Hunter and Townsend were married in Covington, Kentucky, on January 27, 1919, but by all accounts their marriage was never consummated. Two months after they returned to Chicago Townsend filed for divorce, which was granted in March 1923. By then Hunter was living in New York with the love of her life Lottie Tyler, niece of the African American vaudeville comedian, Bert Williams.

In the early 1920s Hunter was the queen of the Dreamland Café and indeed of the Chicago blues scene. Back then Chicago was the place to be as far as jazz and blues musicians were concerned. As Hunter herself said of the era as quoted by Frank C. Taylor and Gerald Cook in *Alberta Hunter: A Celebration in Blues:* "If you had worked in Chicago and had been recognized there, you were somebody, baby. New York didn't count then."

Whether it counted or not, Hunter was soon traveling to New York to record for a label called Black Swan records. Her earliest recordings, in May 1921, were "He's a Darned Good Man to Have Around" backed by "How Long, Sweet Daddy, How Long," "Bring Back the Joys," and "Some Day Sweetheart." On all of these, Fletcher Henderson accompanied her on piano (though the identities of the other musicians have been lost). During the next two years Hunter traveled back and forth between her performing base in Chicago and her recording base in New York. In July 1922 she recorded a slew of songs for the Paramount label, including the now-classic "Down Hearted Blues," which Hunter cowrote with pianist Lovie Austin, "Daddy Blues," and accompanied by Eubie Blake on piano, "Jazzin' Baby Blues." The next year Bessie Smith recorded "Down Hearted Blues" for Columbia Records and it became that label's first hit. Hunter, however, received very little in royalty payments—and only from Paramount. In February 1923 Hunter broke ground when she became the first African American singer to be back by an all-white band—the Original Memphis Five. Among the three songs they recorded that month was "Tain't Nobody's Biz-ness If I Do." In all Hunter recorded 14 songs in the month of February 1923 alone (the other songs were backed by Fletcher Henderson's Orchestra), all for Paramount Records. With so much recording activity, not to mention Broadway, the lure of New York became stronger and stronger for Hunter and she finally moved there in April 1923.

She was not without a job for long. On April 18 she joined the cast of the musical *How Come?* and was an immediate (and literal) "showstopper." Her singing and glamour (Hunter always appeared onstage in beautiful dresses) captured the sophisticated Broadway audience. Unfortunately most critics found little else to praise in *How Come?* and the show closed after five weeks. Meanwhile Hunter continued recording for Paramount. In May and

June 1923 she cut "Stingeree Blues" and "You Can't Do What My Last Man Did," with piano accompaniment on both songs by Fats Waller.

In 1924 Hunter, feeling slighted by Paramount, recorded five songs on the Gennett label using the name Josephine Beatty. This was a technical violation of her contract with Paramount, and as a result she lost her contract at the end of the year. The five Gennett songs became minor cult classics as Hunter was backed up by the Red Onion Jazz Babies, featuring Louis Armstrong on cornet. The following year she began recording with Okeh Records and stayed with them through 1926; she also decided to hit the vaudeville circuit. Upon returning to New York from her vaudeville tour Hunter bought an apartment on West 138th Street, which placed her both professionally and personally in the midst of the famed Harlem Renaissance.

At the end of 1926 Hunter recorded three songs for a Chicago record company, Vocalion, but they were never released. In 1927 she left Okeh to record for Victor. Among the seven Victor recordings she made that year was "Beale Street Blues," with Fats Waller on pipe organ.

Paris and London

New York was home, but Hunter was a traveling woman by nature, and in August 1927 she and Tyler embarked for Paris, where Josephine Baker was already a star. It was an opportunity to escape American racism and become recognized for her talent that Hunter could not pass up. As quoted in *Alberta Hunter: A Celebration in Blues* she said, "The Negro [sic] artists went to Europe because we were recognized and given a chance. In Europe they had your name up in lights. People in the United States would not give us that chance."

In Paris Hunter's name was indeed up in lights, and she moved in the expatriate high cultural circles of the era. She also published letters in the *Amsterdam News,* New York's most prominent African American newspaper, detailing her Parisian life, serving more or less as a correspondent. However Paris was also where she broke up with Tyler, though they remained good friends afterward. In January 1928, without Tyler who had returned to the United States, Hunter left Paris for London.

Her first professional appearance in London, two days after she arrived, was at the London Pavilion located at Picadilly Circus. Her biggest triumph of her European "tour" came in May 1928 when she performed the role of Queenie in the London stage version of *Showboat,* which also featured Paul Robeson. The musical closed after three months, but Hunter remained in London until March 1929. After a brief return to Paris to open the Paris Cotton Club she returned to the United States in May 1929. Back in the U.S. she cut two more songs, this time for Columbia Records. These were her only recordings until 1934 when she recorded 12 songs in London that were released on the HMV (His Master's Voice) label.

If she had thought her unqualified success in Paris and London would be enough to open doors in the United States she was mistaken. Other than some vaudeville work, a role in a musical called *Change Your Luck,* and a revue titled *This Way Out* (in which she appeared only for a week and was never paid), Hunter found work hard to come by. There were a few bookings in Harlem's Alhambra Theatre. By 1933 things had got so bad for her—the Great Depression having exacerbated the already hard-to-come-by bookings—that she decided to return to Paris. This time her success was a bit qualified—the economic depression was keeping people away from the nightclubs. In the spring of 1934 she went to Copenhagen, Denmark, where the reception given her by the public was even warmer than that of the French.

In July 1934 Hunter was back in London, and she effortlessly picked up where she had left off five years earlier. She toured the British and Scottish music hall circuit and recorded 12 songs including "I Travel Alone," written by Noel Coward. Originally recorded for HMV, they were later released as an LP, *The Legendary Alberta Hunter: The London Sessions–1934.* She also appeared in the first British film shot in color, *Radio Parade of 1935.* In January 1935 her British work permit was not renewed and after a brief return to Paris, Hunter returned to the United States. In 1937 following another sojourn abroad, which took her not only to Europe but Egypt as well, Hunter began singing on NBC radio. Her contract expired in early 1938, whereupon she returned to Europe. With war becoming more of a likelihood, Hunter returned to New York in the fall of 1938 and resumed her radio singing. When war did break out and Paris fell to the Nazis African American entertainers returned to New York, making competition for jobs that much stiffer. Adding to this was the next generation of singers led by Ella Fitzgerald, Billie Holliday, and Lena Horne.

By then Hunter's recording career had cooled off somewhat. In 1935 she recorded four songs for the American Record Company, which the company never released. In 1939 she recorded six songs for Decca, including another version of "Down Hearted Blues." In 1940 she recorded four songs for Bluebird, accompanied by Eddie Heywood Jr. on piano. These were her last recordings until after the war.

USO Entertainer

During the World War II, Hunter entertained troops as a member of the United Service Organizations (USO). She did various tours in the Pacific (where she experienced an air raid) and European theaters, entertaining General Eisenhower, Field Marshal Montgomery, and Marshal Zhukov. She continued entertaining troops during peacetime and later toured again with the USO during the Korean War (1950–1953). During the postwar years she also continued performing in clubs and shows.

Hunter resumed her recording career in 1946 with two small companies: Juke Box, for whom she recorded two songs, and Stash, recording just one song. In 1950 she recorded on Regal and in 1952 she cut two songs for Wheeler and four songs for Prestige/Bluesville, but her career was obviously slowing down. Never the Broadway star she had hoped to become when she moved to New York, she appeared in a number of revues and plays into the mid-1950s, but work was sporadic and when one play in particular, *Debut,* closed after four days on Broadway she decided to call it a career. Or rather, she decided to change careers.

Other Careers

On August 14, 1956, Alberta Hunter graduated from the Harlem YWCA nursing school and became a licensed practical nurse. She had lied about her age to get into the school, declaring that she was twelve years younger than she was, thus coming full circle from her earliest Chicago days when she had pretended to be older to sneak into clubs. She worked as a nurse for more than twenty years and retired in 1977 at what officials thought was the mandatory retirement age of 70; she was 82 years old. The only nod Hunter gave to her performing career during her years as a nurse was in 1961 when one of her old accompanists and songwriting partner, Lovie Austin, talked her into recording an LP for the Riverside label tiled, *Alberta Hunter with Lovie Ausin's Blues Seranaders.* The songs included "Down Hearted Blues," "Moanin' Low," "Streets Paved with Gold," and "St. Louis Blues."

After retiring as a nurse Hunter effortlessly resumed her career as a New York cabaret singer and recording artist. This second career made her a bigger star than she had previously been. In 1977 she was performing at the Cookery in New York's Greenwich Village. By the end of the year she had a recording contract with Columbia Records and had recorded the LP *Remember My Name,* the soundtrack of the film of the same name. Hunter played Carnegie Hall on June 27, 1978, and also gave command performance for the Carter White House. In 1979 she recorded the album *Amtrak Blues.* She followed this up in 1981 with *The Glory of Alberta Hunter* and in 1983 completed *Look for the Silver Lining.* Alberta Hunter died on October 17, 1984, in New York City.

Books

Taylor, Frank C. and Gerald Cook, *Alberta: A Celebration in Blues,* McGraw-Hill Book Company, 1987.

Periodicals

New York Times, October 19, 1984.

Online

"Alberta Hunter," http://www.redhotjazz.com/Hunter.html (January 27, 2003). □

Anna Hyatt Huntington

A prolific and innovative American sculptor, Anna Vaughn Hyatt Huntington (1876–1973) was one of the masters of naturalistic animal sculpture. Particularly noted for her equestrian statues, Huntington, along with her husband, helped found nearly 20 museums and wildlife preserves as well as America's first sculpture garden, Brookgreen Gardens in South Carolina.

The youngest of three children, Huntington was born Anna Vaughn Hyatt on March 10, 1876, in Cambridge, Massachusetts, to noted paleontologist Alpheus Hyatt and amateur landscape artist Aduella Beebe Hyatt. From an early age, Huntington followed the examples of her parents by acquiring both an extensive knowledge of the anatomy and behavior of animals and an enthusiasm for drawing. As a child at her family's summer home, Seven Acres, in Cape Cod and at her brother's farm, Porto Bello, in rural Maryland, Huntington developed an affection for horses; as Charlotte Streifer Rubinstein related in *American Women Artists,* "[s]earching for her once at dinnertime, her family found her lying in a field, nose to nose with a horse, watching the action of its jaw muscles as it chewed on a cud of grass." During her childhood sojourns in the countryside, Huntington also made her first clay models of horses, dogs, and other domestic animals.

Although Huntington was fascinated by the animal world, she initially entered a private school in Cambridge to study the violin and spent several years training to become a professional concert violinist. At the age of 19, while suffering from an illness—possibly nervous exhaustion—Huntington assisted her sister, Harriet Hyatt (Mayor), repair the broken foot on a sculpture the elder had produced. Pleased with the results, the elder Hyatt sister asked her to collaborate on a sculpture which included the family dog; in *Energy and Individuality in the Art of Anna Huntington, Sculptor, and Amy Beach, Composer,* Myrna Eden reported that "the sculpture group was accepted for exhibition by one of the national art societies, and purchased." Having found both enjoyment and success in her first professional sculpture, Huntington turned away from the violin to study under Boston portrait sculptor Henry Hudson Kitson. Her first one-woman show was held at the Boston Arts Club. It consisted of 40 animal sculptures. Her original plan was to open an art school. However, the death of her father and marriage of her sister to Alfred Mayor changed these early plans. Huntington left Massachusetts for New York City.

Perfected Her Art

In New York, Huntington continued her frequently self-directed studies. She attended the Art Students League, where she studied under three sculptors: George Grey Barnard, Hermon MacNeil, and Gutzon Borglum, the designer of Mount Rushmore. Preferring to work independently, Huntington left formal instruction in favor of direct observation. Over the next few years, she spent much of her time at the Bronx Zoo. As Wayne Craven explained in *Sculpture in America,* "[Huntington] became fascinated with the beauty found in the great cats of the New York zoo, particularly a prize jaguar called Senor Lopez." The figures modeled from these personal observations, including the 1902 equestrian work *Winter Noon* and the 1906 sculpture *Reaching Jaguar,* based on Senor Lopez, became Huntington's first major works.

During this period, Huntington shared several studios with other young female artists and musicians; one of these was Abastenia St. Leger Eberle, another up-and-coming sculptor. Eden related that: "Anna and Abastenia formed an artistic partnership which led them to collaborate on at least two statues: *Men and Bull,* awarded a bronze medal at the Louisiana Purchase Exposition of 1904, and *Boy and Goat Playing,* exhibited during the spring of 1905 in the gallery of the Society of American Artists." The two sculptors worked together for about two years before following their individual paths, Huntington preferring a more traditional style and Eberle favoring the more modern Ash Can style.

First Major Commissions

In *American Women Sculptors,* Rubinstein quoted Huntington as saying, "One ought to be perfectly independent in one's work and above outside influence . . . before going abroad." By 1907, Huntington felt confident enough in her abilities to travel to Europe. Choosing to forgo academic study in order to pursue her craft independently, Huntington took a studio in Auvers-sur-Oise where she modeled two more jaguars that were exhibited at the Paris Salon of 1908. In the autumn of 1908, Huntington left France for Naples, Italy, to work on a colossal lion commissioned by a high school in Dayton, Ohio. Huntington returned to the United States for the dedication ceremonies, but went back to France about a year later to commence modeling another grand-scale piece.

For years, Huntington had wanted to produce a life-sized equestrian statue of Joan of Arc, and she now devoted herself entirely to this goal. Rubinstein described this process in *American Women Sculptors:* "The sculptor . . . immersed herself in research about the saint. She traveled to Rouen and other places [Joan] had lived . . . searched the

streets of Paris for the right kind of horse and . . . brought it to her studio. . . . Shutting herself in her studio and working ten hours a day, she massed three and half tons of clay, built the armature, and carried out the work in four months." This early model garnered an honorable mention at the Paris Salon of 1910, and led to Huntington's being offered a commission by the City of New York to produce the model in bronze to honor the saint's 500th birthday. A replica of this bronze was erected in Blois, France, and the French government made Huntington a Chevalier of the Legion of Honor. Throughout this period, Huntington received several other commissions and honors, raising her career to new heights. In 1912, she was one of only 12 women in the U.S. making at least $50,000 a year; in 1915, she received the Purple Rosette from the French government; and in 1916, she won the Rodin Gold Medal from the Plastics Club of Philadelphia as well as becoming an associate of the National Academy of Design.

Marriage to Archer Huntington

Following a brief withdrawal to Cape Cod during World War I, Huntington returned to New York City to take up new works, including a standing Joan of Arc and two sculptures depicting the Greek goddess Diana. One of these, *Diana of the Chase,* won the National Academy of Design's Saltus Award in 1922. Around this time, Huntington was working with railroad heir and philanthropist Archer Milton Huntington on an upcoming Hispanic Society sculpture exhibition. The two married quietly—and suddenly—in Huntington's studio on her 47th birthday in 1923. According to *American Women Sculptors,* "[b]oth were tall, imposing figures; they shared cultural interests and a sense of noblesse oblige toward their community. It was said of Archer Huntington that wherever he put his foot down, a museum sprang up." The couple took an extended honeymoon; following their return to New York, Huntington took on several new commissions, including her second major equestrian work, *El Cid Campeador,* in honor of the medieval Spanish warrior.

From the mid-1920s on, Huntington battled tuberculosis, reducing her output dramatically. Most of Huntington's works during this time were inspired by her husband's fascination with Spanish culture; she produced a number of pieces for the New York grounds of the Hispanic Society of America, founded by her husband. In spite of decreased production, Huntington continued to enjoy public recognition, as detailed in *Sculpture in America:* "[Huntington's] *Fighting Bulls* received the Shaw Prize at the National Academy [of Design] show in 1928, and the following year she received the Grand Cross of Alfonso XII from the Spanish government; in 1930 she won the Gold Medal of the American Academy of Arts and Letters, and two years later Syracuse University gave her an honorary Doctor of Arts degree in recognition of her work." Huntington was also made an Officer of the French Legion of Honor in 1933.

Founded Brookgreen Gardens

In 1930, the Huntingtons purchased approximately 7,000 acres of former plantation land in the coastal region of

South Carolina to provide a better winter environment for Huntington's illness. The milder climate permitted Huntington to resume work, and the estate, Brookgreen Gardens, became the first modern sculpture garden when the grounds were opened to the public in 1932. The Brookgreen collection includes many works Huntington completed while living at Atalaya, the Huntingtons' winter home on the estate, including several cast in aluminum—some of the earliest sculptures to use that medium. Brookgreen also features figures by many other sculptors of the era. *A Guide to the Sculpture Parks and Gardens of America* commented that, "[d]uring the Depression years of the 1930s, the Huntingtons' acquisitions were a boon to struggling artists; in its first six years, the Brookgreen added 197 art works."

A Return to Health and Productivity

After her recovery from tuberculosis, Huntington resumed work vigorously. In 1936, the American Academy of Arts and Letters held a retrospective exhibition of 171 of Huntington's works in New York. The following year, she received the Pennsylvania Academy's Widener Gold Medal for *Greyhounds Playing.* According to *Energy and Individuality in the Art of Anna Huntington, Sculptor, and Amy Beach, Composer,* "[t]hat same year she had her first solo exhibition on the West Coast at the Palace of the Legion of Honor at San Francisco." Huntington then arranged for 65 pieces from her 1936 New York exhibition to tour the United States through 1938 and 1939.

In the late 1930s, the Huntingtons donated their Fifth Avenue townhouse to the National Academy of Design and left for a Haverstraw, New York, estate called Rocas. Huntington here acquired her own zoo featuring monkeys, bears, wolves, and wild boars for use in continued animal modeling. After a few years, the Huntingtons donated this estate and zoo to the state of New York and moved to a large farm, named Stanerigg in honor of the Huntingtons' Scottish deerhounds, in Redding, Connecticut. Huntington spent the duration of World War II on both her art and on wartime support, including the canning of produce from Victory Gardens and the sponsorship of a chapter of the Red Cross in her home at Stanerigg. Notable pieces dating from this era include two bas-reliefs at New York's Hispanic Society Museum, *Don Quixote* and *Boabdil.*

Later Accomplishments and a Lasting Body of Work

With the advent of the 1950s, modern, abstract sculpture began to replace Huntington's more traditional, academic style, much to the artist's dismay. Huntington was quoted in *American Women Sculptors* as referring to modernism "as an overwhelming flood of degenerate trash drowning sincere and conservative workers in all the arts." Her husband became ill and Huntington spent much of her

time caring for him. However, she continued to work, producing even large pieces such as the equestrian *Lady Godiva* for an art association in Indiana and a group of large figures entitled *The Torch Bearers,* installed in Madrid in 1955.

Following Archer Huntington's death, Huntington returned to full-time art work, despite being in her 80s. Between 1959 and 1966, she completed five more equestrian statues, including one of the late 19th century writer and activist José Martí; one of a young Abraham Lincoln; and one of a young Andrew Jackson. On Huntington's 90th birthday in 1966 she was still working, reportedly on a bust of the composer Charles Ives.

Around the end of the 1960s, Huntington finally retired from creative work. She died on October 4, 1973, in Redding, Connecticut, following a series of strokes. Active over a period of 70 years, Huntington is today recognized as one of America's finest animal sculptors, whose naturalistic works helped to bridge the gap between the traditional styles of the 1800s and the abstract styles of the mid-20th century. Her prominence also enabled other female artists to succeed. Her innovations in technique and display, as exhibited through her aluminum statues in Brookgreen Gardens, guarantee her place in the annals of art history.

Books

Carr, James F., *Mantle Fielding's Dictionary of American Painters, Sculptor and Engravers,* James F. Carr, 1965.

Craven, Wayne, *Sculpture in America from the Colonial Period to the Present,* Thomas Y. Crowell Company, 1968.

Eden, Myrna G., *Energy and Individuality in the Art of Anna Huntington, Sculptor and Amy Beach, Composer,* Scarecrow Press, 1987.

Falk, Peter Hastings, ed., *Who Was Who in American Art: 1564–1975,* Sound View Press, 1999.

Gaze, Delia, ed., *Dictionary of Women Artists,* Fitzroy Dearborn Publishers, 1997.

Heller, Nancy G., *Women Artists: An Illustrated History,* Abbeville Press, 1987.

McCarthy, Jane and Laurily K. Epstein, *A Guide to the Sculpture Parks and Gardens of America,* Michael Kesend Publishing, Ltd., 1996.

National Museum of Woman in the Arts, Harry N. Abrams, 1987.

Rubinstein, Charlotte Streifer, *American Women Artists from Early Indian Times to the Present,* Avon, 1982.

—, *American Women Sculptors: A History of Women Working in Three Dimensions,* G.K. Hall & Co., 1990.

Whitney Museum of American Art, *200 Years of American Sculpture,* David R. Godine, 1976.

Online

Encyclopedia Brittanica Online, "Hyatt, Anna Vaughn," http://search.eb.com/eb/article?eu=138088 (March 9, 2003).

Macy, L., ed., "The Grove Dictionary of Art Online: Hyatt Huntington, Anna," http://www.groveart.com (March 9, 2003). □

Innocent IV

Pope Innocent IV (c. 1185–1254), whose pontificate extended from June 25, 1243, to December 7, 1254, is chiefly remembered for his disputes with Emperor Frederick II and as the author of a commentary on the decretals of Pope Gregory IX.

Early Life

Born Sinibaldo dei Fieschi in Genoa, Italy, sometime between 1180 and 1190, Pope Innocent IV was a member of a powerful Italian noble family. Innocent IV's father, Hugh, the count of Lavagna, received the Fieschi name for his service to the emperor as controller of fiscal affairs. A nephew of Innocent IV would become Pope Adrian V in 1276.

Innocent studied law in Parma, where his uncle was a bishop. Innocent continued his studies in Bologna, and later references to him by Pope Honorius III suggest that he may have earned a law degree in that city. Innocent may also have taught in Bologna, but no definite evidence of that has been uncovered. Further speculation is that Innocent began work on the *Decretals of Gregory IX* while he was at Bologna.

In 1226 the future pope left school to become an auditor of the papal Curia. After Gregory IX became pope, Innocent was appointed vice-chancellor of the Roman church in 1227, and soon thereafter he became a cardinal. In 1234, Gregory appointed Innocent governor of the March, in the Papal States. But Innocent apparently remained in Rome during his governorship, because his signature appears on many papal letters from that time. In 1235 he was named Bishop of Albenga and legate of Northern Italy.

Elevated to Papacy

While Innocent was working in the Curia, relations between the emperor and the pope began to disintegrate. By 1238, Emperor Frederick II had begun claiming sovereignty over central Italy and even Rome. In response, the pope called a general council. Frederick seized two cardinals who were on their way to Rome to attend the council and held them captive on an island off the coast of Tuscany.

Pope Gregory IX died in 1241, and the College of Cardinals immediately convened to elect a new pope. But the new pope, Celestine IV, died after a reign of only fifteen days. Meanwhile, the two cardinals were still held prisoner by the emperor, and Frederick was excommunicated. The College of Cardinals could not agree on how to deal with the emperor, and the papacy remained vacant for nearly 18 months until June 1243, when the cardinals elected Innocent pope. On his elevation, Innocent took the name Innocent IV.

Prior to being elected pope, Innocent IV had been a friend of Frederick II, and the emperor sent messengers to Rome with congratulations and peace overtures. But Innocent refused to receive the messengers.

Negotiations with Frederick

Two months after his investiture, Innocent sent two legates to try to convince Frederick to release the two cardinals. He also asked his legates to find out what compensation Frederick was prepared to make for the harm he had caused the Church. If Frederick denied any wrongdoing, the legates were instructed to propose settling the matter before a council of kings, prelates, and secular princes. On March 31, 1244, Frederick promised to accede to most of the

demands of the Curia, including restoration of the Papal States, release of the cardinals, and the granting of amnesty to allies of the pope. The apparent restoration of peace could not have been more timely—the Mongols were threatening Eastern Europe and in 1244 the Muslims captured Jerusalem.

But peace remained elusive. Frederick was slow to honor his promises, and he still refused to release the cardinals. He also secretly incited civil disorder in Rome. About the time that a formal signing of the negotiated treaty between Frederick and the Church was scheduled, Innocent, mistrusting his adversary, fled Italy.

Exile in Lyons

The pope initially traveled to Sutri, Italy, and then made his way in disguise over the mountains to Civiavecchia, where a fleet was waiting to take him to Genoa. By October 1244, he was in Burgundy, and by December he had reached Lyons, France.

Upon arriving in Lyons, Innocent called a general council, the 13th ecumenical, which was convened in 1245. Although Lyons was within Frederick's empire, the pope enjoyed the protection of the French king there, so was not threatened by Frederick. Lyons also was easily accessible to many prelates without risking capture by Frederick.

First Council of Lyons

At the opening of the general council on June 26, 1245, Innocent outlined his agenda, which far exceeded his con-

cerns about Frederick. Besides his problems with the emperor, he also hoped to address problems with the clergy and difficulties with the Muslims. When the meeting opened, three patriarchs and about 150 bishops were in attendance. Also present was the Latin emperor of Constantinople. But many church leaders had been prevented from attending either by the invasions of the Tartars in the east, the Muslim incursions in Jerusalem, or intimidation by Frederick.

Innocent was particularly concerned with the Tartars, and he sent a papal envoy to the ruler of the Mongol empire. By this time, Innocent had ruled that the pope held authority over non-Christians and could punish them if they violated the laws of nature. Innocent also decreed that non-Christians were obligated to permit Christian missionaries to visit them. If they refused, Innocent believed that the pope could call for a war against them. Innocent's policy would influence future missionary endeavors by the Church for centuries to come.

Shortly before the Council at Lyons convened, Innocent once again excommunicated Frederick. During the council, he summoned Frederick to Lyons. The emperor did not show up, but instead sent his legate Thaddeus of Suessa. Although Thaddeus argued strongly in defense of Frederick, the council nevertheless ordered the emperor deposed, calling for the German princes to elect a new emperor. Some of the princes responded, and Henry Raspe, Landgrave of Thuringia, was elected emperor. When Frederick heard of his deposition, he reportedly placed a crown on his head and challenged the pope to knock it off.

But Henry died shortly thereafter, and the princes elected William, the Count of Holland, in his place. But most of the princes had abstained from voting and neither Henry nor William received wide recognition. They were too weak to challenge Frederick's son and ally, Conrad.

Innocent attempted to mount a crusade against Frederick, but his ally King Louis IX of France, the only monarch powerful enough to confront Frederick, was unwilling to sign up for such an undertaking. Instead, the French king attempted to mediate a settlement.

Last Acts

In 1248 Innocent renewed Frederick's excommunication. With Frederick's death at the end of 1250, Innocent was once again in a position to exert his authority in central Italy. Innocent set out for Rome from Lyons on April 19, 1251, arriving there in October 1253.

Following Frederick's death, Innocent campaigned for the deposition of his heirs. Innocent offered the crown of Sicily, which he controlled, to Richard of Cornwall and later to Charles of Anjou. But since Conrad's half brother Manfred still held power in Sicily, there were no takers. After Manfred submitted to the papacy, Innocent made his way into Naples in 1254. But Manfred revolted and defeated the papal army at Foggia.

Legacy

Innocent's commentary on the *Decretals of Gregory IX* was cited by almost every jurist from his contemporaries to those of the seventeenth century. Innocent is also remembered for his commentary of the First Council of Lyon.

Following precedents set by Innocent III, Innocent IV extended papal authority in the church and over secular matters. Innocent IV held that the pope could chose between two imperial candidates, depose an emperor, and exercise imperial authority when the throne was empty. As noted, although he permitted non-Christian rulers to hold power, he held that those rulers must permit Christian missionaries to proselytize in their countries.

Innocent IV believed that since Christ had the power to depose emperors, the pope held the same authority as the vicar of Christ. Innocent IV attempted to exert his influence over several potentates besides Frederick. In England, he extended his protection to Henry III against the lay and church nobility. In Austria, he confirmed the son of King Wenzel as duke and later mediated between him and the king of Hungary. In Portugal, he appointed Alfonso III as administrator of the kingdom.

His continual fighting with Frederick led to the neglect of the internal affairs of the Church, thus Italy was left desolate. Taxation by the Church increased, which prompted loud complaints from the populace. Church abuses were overlooked as the pope remained preoccupied with his struggle with the emperor.

Innocent IV, severely ill with pleurisy, died in Naples on December 7, 1254, and was buried in a tomb at the Basilica of Santa Restituta in Naples.

Books

Brecher, Joseph S., *Popes Through the Ages,* Neff-Kane, 1980.

Online

"First Council of Lyons (1245)," *Eternal Word Television Network,* http://www.ewtn.com/library/COUNCILS/LYONS1.HTM (February 2003).

Pennington, Kenneth, "Innocent IV, Pope," http://faculty.cua.edu/pennington/Medieval%20Papacy/InnocentIV.htm (February 2003).

"Pope Innocent IV," *Catholic Forum,* http://www.catholic-forum.com/saints/pope0180.htm (February 2003).

"Pope Innocent IV," *New Advent,* http://www.newadvent.org/cathen/08017a.htm (February 2003). □

J

Sophia Jex-Blake

Sophia Jex-Blake (1840–1912) led a long and difficult struggle to open the medical profession to women in Great Britain. After many years of trying to gain admittance to a Scottish medical school, she succeeded in getting Parliament to guarantee women's right to a medical education and testing. She became licensed at the age of 37 and opened a private practice in Scotland the following year, becoming the country's first female doctor. Her tenacious fight for women to have the right to become doctors opened the door for women in the medical profession.

Sophia Jex-Blake was born to a wealthy and religious family in Sussex, England, on January 21, 1840. Her father, Thomas Jex-Blake, was a retired attorney. Her mother, Maria Jex-Blake, was often sickly. Jex-Blake's parents were devoted to their children and ran a strict religious household in which dancing, theater-going, and other "worldly amusements" were forbidden. The family's older children, a son, eight years older than Sophia, and a daughter, six years older, accepted their conservative upbringing. But Sophia was an energetic and audacious child whose strong will often clashed with her parents' expectations for their Victorian daughter. Still, Sophia and her parents had a close and loving relationship throughout their lives. "No one ever had better parents than I," Sophia often said, according to a biography by Margaret Todd.

Jex-Blake was a bright, intelligent child whose thirst for knowledge was not satisfied by the schools meant to mold Victorian girls into homemakers and mothers. Jex-Blake was shuffled from school to school because her teachers and her ailing mother found it difficult to handle her excitable behavior. Jex-Blake showed little interest in marriage and was denied participation in physical activity, such as horseback riding, that she craved.

Jex-Blake took an interest in teaching, one of the few professions open to women during the mid-19th century, and in 1858 she entered Queens College, one of the first colleges for women in England. For the first time in her life, she felt intellectually challenged. She particularly liked mathematics and tutored other students in the subject. She also learned bookkeeping. While at Queens College, Jex-Blake developed a loving friendship with Octavia Hill, who later became a social reformer. The two lived together until Hill broke off the relationship, leaving Jex-Blake devastated. She remained loyal to Hill for life. Todd wrote that a friend later said, "She was never the same again. It cut her life in two."

In 1861, Jex-Blake finished her term at Queen's College and went home. The following year, she enrolled in Edinburgh Ladies' Educational Association in Scotland where she struggled to get over the loss of Hill's friendship. In addition to mathematics, Jex-Blake was very interested in religion. She had a gift for public speaking and considered becoming a missionary, but preferred teaching. She dreamed of opening a university and traveled to Germany in 1862 to study the country's education system. She took a job teaching at Grand Ducal Institute for Women in Mannheim. She was homesick and Jex-Blake had trouble in the position. Her students took advantage of the fact that she was not a strict disciplinarian. In addition, Jex-Blake was not

equipped to teach the girls dancing, singing, playing, or embroidery. Although the situation eventually improved, Jex-Blake returned home after only one year.

Traveled to America

In 1865, Jex-Blake convinced her parents to allow her to travel to the United States to study its education system. "I have such a feeling that with the new world, a new life will open," she said. In Boston, she met Dr. Lucy Sewall, a 28-year-old physician at the New England Hospital for Women and Children. Through their friendship, Jex-Blake was introduced to the field of medicine and the idea of feminism.

The trip shaped Jex-Blake's attitudes about women, education, and careers. Feminism in America was more clearly defined and advanced than in Great Britain. Jex-Blake visited schools and colleges and in 1867 published *A Visit to Some American Schools and Colleges.*

Jex-Blake's thoughts about religion changed while she was in the United States. She found that her religious ideas, which were considered mainstream in England, were extremely conservative in America. She gave up on the idea of becoming a minister, but she did later write some religious tracts.

Although she received no formal medical education, Jex-Blake worked along with Sewall and other doctors and students at the hospital. She learned practical hospital work, especially diseases of women. She worked as the hospital's bookkeeper and pharmacist. The experience convinced her that she should become a physician.

Jex-Blake wanted to attend Harvard so that she could obtain an education equal to a man's. She and another student requested admission to Harvard Medical School. When their request was denied, Jex-Blake persuaded some of the faculty to teach her and other women at Massachusetts General Hospital. Among her instructors was Dr. Oliver Wendall Holmes.

In 1868, Jex-Blake was admitted to the Women's Medical College of the New York Infirmary, a new women's college founded by Elizabeth and Emily Blackwell. (Elizabeth Blackwell was the first female physician in the United States.) However, she never attended the school because in the fall of 1869, Jex-Blake's father died and she returned to England.

The Struggle for a Medical Education

Dealing with her grief and adjusting once again to life in Great Britain, Jex-Blake contemplated her education options. She researched the history of women in medicine and wrote an essay titled, "Medicine as a Profession for Women," which was published in *Women's Work and Women's Culture.* It later appeared in her book, *Medical Women.*

Jex-Blake decided not to return to the United States. Instead, she pursued her medical education in Great Britain. In 1869, she was admitted to Edinburgh University's medical school, but the university later overturned the decision. Jex-Blake began a long and tenacious campaign for admittance, attracting international attention along the way. In 1870, Jex-Blake and four other women were admitted to the school. They had to attend separate classes for women and pay higher tuition than men. But negative pressure continued and in 1869, the university discontinued the separate classes and advised the women to seek training at a local teaching hospital, the Royal Infirmary. The hospital refused to comply. The women were harassed by opponents, although there were sympathizers among the faculty, students, and in the community.

In November, the conflict came to a head in what became known as the riot at Surgeons' Hall. When the ladies, now numbering seven, arrived for a class, 200 protesters blocked their entry to the classroom. The women were subjected to howls and jostling, according to *The Courant,* an Edinburgh newspaper. The incident earned publicity worldwide and the women gained sympathy and support. Among the seven students was Edith Pechey, a loyal friend of Jex-Blake's. They worked side-by-side throughout the struggle and remained lifelong friends.

Jex-Blake led the students to file a lawsuit against the university for failing to allow them to complete their medical education. They won the suit, but lost an appeal. The women finally took their fight to Parliament where, after a difficult battle, they succeeded in getting supporters to pass a bill that allowed all medical schools in Great Britain to admit women. However, many institutions still denied women the right to take medical exams.

Throughout the long struggle, Jex-Blake and the other women had received instruction from sympathetic faculty. Jex-Blake completed her medical education in Switzerland

and in 1877, Jex-Blake and four other women passed their medical exams at the College of Physicians in Dublin, Ireland. At the age of 37, Jex-Blake was now a licensed medical practitioner.

Established Medical Practice

Jex-Blake's strong will, which had confounded her parents and teachers when she was young, had helped her win women's right to medical education. Her determination and leadership were recognized on both sides as the driving force behind the movement. Pechey was quoted in the Jex-Blake biography, saying, "All we had done towards opening up the medical profession to women was due mainly to Miss Jex-Blake, who had got all the abuse because she had done all the work—in fact all along she had done the work of three women or . . . of ten men!"

Although she was a strong administrator, Jex-Blake was also difficult to work with. Her impulsive and autocratic manner led to a deep disappointment concerning a women's medical school she co-founded. Jex-Blake and Elizabeth Garrett Anderson founded The London School of Medicine for Women in 1874. Anderson was a London physician who had been educated in France and had introduced Jex-Blake to the cause of women's medical education in the 1860s. Jex-Blake expected to be named the London School's secretary, but because her temperament was considered inappropriate for the position, Jex-Blake was passed over in favor of Anderson.

Jex-Blake left London and established a private practice in Edinburgh, becoming Scotland's first female doctor in 1878. Eventually, she opened a cottage hospital known as the Edinburgh Hospital and Dispensary for Women and Children. She remained active in the women's medical movement as there were continuous efforts in Parliament to restrict women's ability to become doctors.

In 1881, Maria Jex-Blake died. Jex-Blake had been devoted to her mother throughout her life and the two had frequently exchanged loving and supportive letters. Jex-Blake withdrew from her practice, leaving the responsibility to a young assistant. The assistant maintained the practice and worked on laboratory experiments regarding the insolubility of fats. The experiments proved to be toxic and the assistant died. Jex-Blake was devastated by the loss of these two relationships. She gave up her practice and stayed with her friend Ursula DuPre, who nursed her back to physical and mental health. After two years, Jex-Blake moved back to Edinburgh and resumed her practice. She wrote *The Care of Infants* and a second edition of *Medical Women*.

Jex-Blake continued advocating for female medical students, who were still required to attend separate classes at the Edinburgh University. Her advocacy led to the formation of a women's college similar to the London School— the Edinburgh School of Medicine for Women, under the direction of Jex-Blake. She negotiated with a hospital to provide clinical training, making it possible for Scottish women to obtain a complete medical education for the first time.

The school functioned successfully for a year before Jex-Blake's unyielding personality clashed with students who found her to be inflexible. The bitter conflict led some students to found a new medical school for women. When many chose it over the Edinburgh School, financial difficulties arose. However, Jex-Blake was so dedicated to the cause of women's medical education that she never criticized the rival school. She supported it wholeheartedly because it advanced the cause of women's medical education.

In 1894, the Edinburgh University finally opened its medical exams to women, breaking one more barrier to women's ability to become doctors. That same year, the National Association for the Medical Education of Women honored Jex-Blake for her 25 years of dedication to women's medical education.

Retired at Age 59

The Edinburgh School of Medicine for Women remained open until 1898, when low enrollment forced its closure. Jex-Blake continued her private practice until 1899 when she retired to Sussex. Jex-Blake's business and home were acquired by Edinburgh Hospital and operated as Bruntsfield Hospital until 1989.

In retirement, Jex-Blake lived with Margaret Todd, a former student who was 20 years her junior. Todd, who was also a novelist, gave up her medical career after only five years to be with Jex-Blake. The two women spent their time reading, traveling, entertaining, and corresponding with friends. Jex-Blake remained interested in social causes, including the suffrage movement, which she supported.

Jex-Blake was very proud of her students' successes. She happily followed their careers and called them "my daughters," "my young girls," or "my doctors." She corresponded with hundreds of people during her life and kept all their letters. She also chronicled her life in voluminous diaries.

In her later years, Jex-Blake suffered a series of heart attacks and other ailments. She died on January 7, 1912, at the age of 71. She willed her possessions, including her personal papers, to Todd, who wrote a biography, *The Life of Sophia Jex-Blake,* in 1918. In accordance with Jex-Blake's wishes, Todd destroyed the personal papers after the book was published. A few months later, Todd committed suicide at the age of 58.

Books

Todd, Margaret, *The Life of Sophia Jex-Blake,* MacMillan and Co., 1918.
Women in World History: A Biographical Encyclopedia, Anne Commire, editor, Yorkin Publications, 1999. □

Pauline Johnson

Pauline Johnson (1861–1913) was the first Native American poet to have her work published in Canada and was one of the few women of her time who succeeded in supporting herself from her writings and recitals. Thousands of Canadian schoolchildren have read her poem "The Song My Paddle Sings."

J ohnson was unique in her time because she recited her own work rather than that of others. Her recitals of her own poems, anecdotes, and plays were a refreshing change for American and Canadian audiences whose usual theatrical fare was Shakespeare or Ibsen. Johnson was never able to make much money from her writing, and most of her income came from her speaking tours.

Mixed Heritage

Emily Pauline Johnson was born on March 10, 1861, near Brantford, Ontario. She was one of four children born to George Johnson, a Mohawk chief on the Six Nations Indian Reserve, and Emily Howells, a wealthy white woman originally from Bristol, England. Her paternal grandfather was Mohawk chief Smoke Johnson.

Johnson's mother was living with her family in Ohio when she decided to join her sister, who was living near Brantford. While staying there, she met George Johnson, who had been raised primarily among whites.

George and Emily Johnson were married in 1853 despite opposition from some white citizens of Brantford. Emily Johnson's brother-in-law, a minister, refused to marry the couple. George Johnson's mother was also opposed to the marriage; she was concerned their children would not be considered Mohawks. They had a private wedding but were hounded by curious onlookers after the ceremony.

George Johnson bought two hundred acres on the Indian reserve and built a mansion there that he named Chiefswood. Johnson grew up at Chiefswood. Although she had few playmates, she managed to find companionship in nature. The Grand River flowed alongside her house, and she enjoyed camping and canoeing. Chiefswood frequently played host to important visitors from England. In 1869, Prince Arthur, Duke of Connaught, who would later become governor-general of Canada, paid a visit.

Johnson's mother encouraged her daughter to read the classics in English literature, including the works of Sir Walter Scott, John Milton, and William Shakespeare. Johnson attended the Brantford Model School and also had private instruction from her governess. Her formal education ended after seven years and she did not attend college. Her father and grandfather taught her Mohawk legends.

Budding Poet

As soon as she could write, Johnson started creating poems. Her early writings were influenced by her grandfather's Indian tales and by the English poetry she heard from her mother. Canoeing would take on special significance in some of her poems, including "The Song My Paddle Sings." By the time she had reached her late teens, she was a competent poet but not yet published.

George Johnson died in 1884 at the age of 67 following a beating he received while trying to stop whites from illegally taking timber from the Six Nations Reserve. After his death, the family could not afford to remain at Chiefswood, so they rented out the house and moved to Brantford. Johnson expected to marry but found no suitors. She brought in some income by writing poems, which she published in the local newspaper and in an anthology entitled *Songs of the Great Dominion*.

Poetry Recitations

Johnson initially wanted to take up acting, but her mother objected. In the minds of many Victorian women, acting was not a reputable occupation. Instead, Johnson agreed to give poetry recitations, a highly respectable occupation for women in those days. Over the next seventeen years, Johnson recited her poems in England, New England, and Canada. During much of this period, she lived in trains and hotels. All told, she made nineteen trips across Canada and six forays into the United States. Some of her recitals were accompanied by musicians or comedians.

Although Johnson never married, she was involved with her manager and traveling partner Walter McRaye. Johnson first met McRaye in 1897, when she was 35 and near the peak of her career. McRaye, who was giving recitals of French-Canadian dialect poems throughout Canada and the United States, was 20. In 1899, the two formed a partnership; McRaye took responsibility for arranging their tours, bookings, and transportation. McRaye remained Johnson's constant companion and co-performer until she retired.

In 1892, using the Mohawk name Tekahionwake, Johnson made her reading debut at a poetry recital held at the Young Liberals Club in Toronto. At the recital, Johnson read her poem "A Cry from an Indian Wife," which argued that Canada had been taken unfairly from its first inhabitants. In "Indian Poet Princess," she asked, "If some great nation came from far away,/Wresting their country from their hapless braves,/Giving what they gave us—but wars and graves." During half the performance, she wore an evening gown, but in the other half, she dressed in buckskin embellished with silver brooches, wampum belts, a blanket, and two scalps.

Johnson toured to help defray the cost of printing her first book of poetry. She read her poetry throughout Canada. Her recitals took place in church halls, schoolhouses, and even saloons. In larger towns she might appear in an opera house.

Traveled to England

Johnson performed throughout Canada before traveling to England, where she hoped to find a publisher for her first book of poems. In England, she was warmly accepted and frequently invited to recite her poetry at private parties held by wealthy socialites.

Her first book of poetry, *The White Wampum,* appeared in 1895 while she was still in England. It included her famous poem "The Song My Paddle Sings." After her return to Canada, she again began touring while publishing in North American magazines. Besides poetry, Johnson wrote stories about Indian life, travel articles, and family stories for a variety of magazines. Because she covered a wide range of topics, she reached a diverse audience.

Johnson's second book, *Canadian Born,* appeared in 1903. Critics did not consider the poems in it as strong as those in her first collection, but the book sold well. Focusing on the shared heritage of all Canadians, Johnson emphasized the debt that her themes had to Native American culture. In the book's preface, she wrote, "White race and Red are one if they are but Canadian born." About this time, Johnson began cutting back on her public readings, having begun to feel the toll of constant traveling on her health.

Hoping to retire in England, she made a second trip there in 1906 but found no English journals or magazines willing to publish her work. The "drawing room entertainments" that had included Johnson on her visit to London twelve years earlier were no longer in vogue. She made her stage debut during this second trip in a large concert hall, billed as "E. Pauline Johnson—Tekahionwake, Indian Princess."

Vancouver

Not finding the reception she had hoped for in England, Johnson decided to make her home in Vancouver in 1909. In 1911, she published *Legends of Vancouver,* based on stories she had heard from Chief Joe Capilano of the Squamish tribe of British Columbia. Johnson's novel *The Moccasin Maker* recounted experiences of Canadian women—white, Indian and mixed-blood.

By 1911, Johnson knew that she had inoperable breast cancer. She nevertheless continued to write through the last years of her life. Many of her readers purchased her fourth book, *Flint and Feather,* which contained all of her poems in one volume, by subscription at premium rates to help defray her medical expenses. Her poem from this period, "And He Said Fight On," conveyed her determination to defeat the

illness that was taking her life: "Time and its ally, Dark Disarmament,/Have compassed me about/Have massed their armies, and on battle bent/My forces put to rout;/But though I fight alone, and fall, and die,/Talk terms of Peace? Not I."

Johnson died on March 7, 1913, in Vancouver, British Columbia, three days before her fifty-second birthday. Her ashes were placed in Vancouver's Stanley Park and later marked by a large stone. Her final book, *The Shagganappi,* was published posthumously.

Legacy

In the years immediately following Johnson's death, her work went largely ignored. But in the mid-1920s, there was renewed interest in her poetry. Canadian schoolchildren began studying "The Song My Paddle Sings." In 1961, to mark the 100th anniversary of her birth, the Canadian government issued a Pauline Johnson postage stamp, the first stamp to recognize a Canadian Indian and the first Canadian stamp to recognize a woman who was not a member of the British royal family.

Some critics believed Johnson was Canada's best Native American poet. Some others attributed her success to her theatrical talents or to her successful blending of Indian and English elements in her poetry. For her part, Johnson seemed to care little whether she was remembered as a great poet. "Forget that I was Pauline Johnson, but remember that I was Tekahionwake, the Mohawk that humbly aspired to be the saga singer of her people," she was quoted as saying in Lucie Hartley's biography, *Pauline Johnson.*

Books

Lucie Hartley, *Pauline Johnson,* Dillon Press, 1978.

Online

"E. Pauline Johnson's Legacy," *McMaster University,* http://www.humanities.mcmaster.ca/~pjohnson/legacy.html (February 2003).
"Emily Pauline Johnson (1861–1913)," *University of Minnesota Voices from the Gaps,* http://voices.cla.umn.edu/authors/EmilyPaulineJohnson.html (February 2003).
"The Pauline Johnson Archive," *McMaster University,* http://www.humanities.mcmaster.ca/~pjohnson/home.html (February 2003). □

Robert Johnson

Of all the great blues musicians, Robert Johnson (1911–1938) was probably the most obscure. All that is known of him for certain is that he recorded 29 songs; he died young; and he was one of the greatest bluesmen of the Mississippi Delta.

There are only five dates in Johnson's life that can undeniably be used to assign him to a place in history: Monday, November 23; Thursday, November 26; and Friday, November 27, 1936, he was in San

Antonio, Texas, at a recording session. Seven months later, on Saturday, June 19 and Sunday, June 20, 1937, he was in Dallas at another session. Everything else about his life is an attempt at reconstruction. As director Martin Scorsese says in his foreword to Alan Greenberg's play *Love In Vain: A Vision of Robert Johnson,* ''The thing about Robert Johnson was that he only existed on his records. He was pure legend.''

Beginnings

Robert Johnson was born in the Mississippi Delta (Hazlehurst, Mississippi) sometime around May 8, 1911, the 11th child of Julia Major Dodds, who had previously born 10 children to her husband Charles Dodds. Born illegitimate, Johnson did not take the Dodds name.

Twenty two-year-old Charles Dodds had married Julia Major in Hazlehurst, Mississippi—about 35 miles from Jackson—in 1889. Charles Dodds owned land and made wicker furniture; his family was well off until he was forced out of Hazlehurst around 1909 by a lynch mob following an argument with some of the more prosperous townsfolk. (There was a family legend that Dodds escaped from Hazlehurst dressed in women's clothing.) Over the next two years, Julia Dodds sent their children one at time to live with their father in Memphis, where Charles Dodds had adopted the name of Charles Spencer. Julia stayed behind in Hazlehurst with two daughters, until she was evicted for nonpayment of taxes.

By that time she had given birth to a son, Robert, who was fathered by a field worker named Nonah Johnson. Unwelcome in Charles Dodds' home, Julia Dodds became an itinerant field worker, picking cotton and living in camps as she moved among plantations. While she worked in the fields, her eight-year-old daughter took care of Johnson. Over the next ten years, Dodds would make repeated attempts to reunite the family, but Charles Dodds never stopped resenting her infidelity. Although Charles Dodds would eventually accept Johnson, he never would forgive his wife for giving birth to him. While in his teens, Johnson learned who his father was, and it was at that time that he began calling himself Robert Johnson.

Around 1914, Johnson moved in with Charles Dodds' family, which by that time included all of Dodds' children by Julia Dodds, as well as Dodds' mistress from Hazlehurst and their two children. Johnson would spend the next several years in Memphis, and it was reportedly about this time that he began playing the guitar under his older half-brother's tutelage.

Johnson did not rejoin his mother until she had remarried several years later. By the end of the decade, he was back in the Mississippi Delta living with his mother and her new husband, Dusty Willis. Johnson and his stepfather, who had little tolerance for music, did not get along, and Johnson had to slip out of the house to join his musician friends. Eventually he decided to run away.

It is not known whether Johnson attended school in the Delta during this time. Some later accounts say that he could neither read nor write, while others tell of his beautiful handwriting. In any case, everyone agrees that music was Johnson's first interest, and that he had gotten his start playing the jew's harp and harmonica.

Bluesman

By 1930, Johnson had married and become serious about playing the guitar. During the time that he was married, he lived with his sister and her husband. But his wife died in childbirth at the age of 16. By some accounts, Johnson briefly moved back with his mother and stepfather, where he encountered the same problems that he had found intolerable when he was growing up and soon left. In 1931, he married for a second time. By then, his fellow musicians were beginning to take note of his precocity on the guitar.

Johnson began traveling up and down the Delta, travelling by bus, hopping trains, and sometimes hitchhiking. When he arrived in a new town, he would play on street corners or in front of the local barbershop or a restaurant. He played what his audience asked for—not necessarily his own compositions. Anything he earned was based on tips, not salary. With an ability to pick up tunes at first hearing, Johnson had no trouble giving his audiences what they wanted. Also working in his favor was an ability to establish instant rapport with his audiences. In every town he stopped, Johnson would establish ties to the local community that would serve him in good stead when he passed through again a month or a year later.

Fellow musician Johnny Shines was 17 when he met Johnson in 1933. He estimated that Johnson was maybe a year older than himself. In Samuel Charters' *Robert Johnson,* the author quotes Shines as saying, ''Robert was a very friendly person, even though he was sulky at times, you know. And I hung around Robert for quite a while. One evening he disappeared. He was kind of [a] peculiar fellow. Robert'd be standing up playing some place, playing like nobody's business. At about that time it was a hustle with him as well as a pleasure. And money'd be coming from all directions. But Robert'd just pick up and walk off and leave you standing there playing. And you wouldn't see Robert no more maybe in two or three weeks. . . . So Robert and I, we began journeying off. I was just, matter of fact, tagging along.''

During this time Johnson established what would be a relatively long-term relationship with a woman who was about 15 years older than himself—the mother of future musician Robert Jr. Lockwood. But Johnson reportedly also had someone—a woman—to look after him in all of the towns he played in. Johnson would reportedly ask young women living in the country with their families whether he could go home with them, and in most cases the answer was yes. At least until their husbands came home or Johnson was ready to move on.

Recording Sessions

Around 1936, Johnson met H. C. Spier in Jackson, Mississippi, who ran a music store and doubled as a talent scout. Spier put Johnson in touch with Ernie Oertle, who offered to record the young musician in San Antonio, Texas. At the recording session, Johnson was too shy to perform in front of the musicians in the studio, so played facing the wall. In the ensuing three-day session, Johnson played 16 selections. When the recording session was over, Johnson presumably returned home with several hundred dollars in his pocket—probably more money than he had ever had at one time.

Among the songs Johnson recorded in San Antonio were "Come On In My Kitchen," "Kind Hearted Woman," and "Cross Roads Blues." "Come On In My Kitchen" included the lines: "The woman I love took from my best friend/Some joker got lucky, stole her back again,/You better come on in my kitchen, it's going to be rainin' outdoors." In "Cross Roads Blues," another of his great songs, he sang: "I went to the crossroads, fell down on my knees./I went to the crossroads, fell down on my knees./I asked the Lord above, have mercy, save poor Bob if you please./Uumb, standing at the crossroads I tried to flag a ride./Standing at the crossroads I tried to flag a ride./Ain't nobody seem to know me, everybody pass me by."

When his records began appearing, Johnson made the rounds to his relatives and the various children he had fathered to bring them the records himself. The first songs to appear were "Terraplane Blues" and "Last Fair Deal Gone Down," probably the only recordings of his that he would live to hear.

In 1937, Johnson traveled to Dallas, Texas, for another recording session. Eleven records from this session would be released within the following year. Among them were the three songs that would largely contribute to Johnson's posthumous fame: "Stones In My Heart," "Me And The Devil," and "Hell Hound On My Trail." "Stones In My Heart" and "Me And The Devil" are both about betrayal and making a pact with the devil. The terrifying "Hell Hound On My Trail" is often considered to be the crowning achievement of blues-style music.

Interestingly, six of Johnson's blues songs mention the devil or some form of the supernatural. In "Me And The Devil," he began, "Early this morning when you knocked upon my door,/Early this morning, umb, when you knocked upon my door,/And I said, 'Hello, Satan, I believe it's time to go,' " before leading into "You may bury my body down by the highway side,/ You may bury my body, uumh, down by the highway side,/So my old evil spirit can get on a Greyhound bus and ride."

Death at the Crossroads

In the last year of his life, Johnson is believed to have traveled to St. Louis and possibly Illinois. He spent some time in Memphis and traveled through the Mississippi Delta and Arkansas. By the time he died, at least six of his records had been released.

His death came on August 16, 1938, at the approximate age of 26 at a little country crossroads near Greenwood, Mississippi. He had been playing for several weeks at a country dance in a town about 15 miles from Greenwood when, by some accounts, he was given poisoned whiskey at the dance by the husband of a woman he had been seeing.

Johnson was buried in the graveyard of a small church near Morgan City, Mississippi, not far from Greenwood, in an unmarked grave. His life would be short but his music would serve as the root source for an entire generation of blues and rock and roll musicians.

Among the Mississippi Delta bluesmen believed to have exerted the strongest influences on Johnson's music are Charley Patton, Willie Brown, Howlin' Wolf, Tommy Johnson, and Son House. Peter Guralnick, in *Searching for Robert Johnson*, quotes Son House, "We'd all play for the Saturday night balls, and there'd be this little boy standing around. That was Robert Johnson. He was just a little boy then. He blew harmonica and he was pretty good with that, but he wanted to play guitar."

Books

Charters, Samuel, *Robert Johnson*, Oak Publications, 1973.
Greenberg, Alan, *Love In Vain: A Vision of Robert Johnson*, Da Capo Press, 1994.
Guralnick, Peter, *Searching for Robert Johnson*, E.P. Dutton, 1989. □

Frances Benjamin Johnston

Once called America's "court photographer" by *Life* magazine, Frances Benjamin Johnston (1864–1952) became famous doing both portraiture and documentary photography. Fortunate to know many of the rich and famous of her time, Johnston produced a body of work that serves as an important historical document. A staunch feminist and independent thinker, she campaigned to promote greater recognition of women photographers in the United States. The stark documentary style she brought to her most famous photographs would greatly influence the emerging art of photography.

Early Life and Career

An only child, Francis Benjamin Johnston was born in Grafton, West Virginia, in 1864 to affluent parents. She was raised in Washington, D.C. where her parents moved soon after she was born. In the nation's capitol, her parents were active in the high-ranking political and social circles, and their connections, particularly her mother's, would greatly benefit Johnston's education and subsequent career as a photographer. Also, Johnston drew a great deal of inspiration from the independent female role models in her family: her free-willed Aunt Nin and her mother, who worked as a journalist for the *Baltimore Sun* and the *Rochester Democrat and Chronicle*.

Johnston graduated from the Notre Dame Academy near Baltimore in 1884, where she earned the equivalent of a high school diploma. Her parents' connections to the Washington elite enabled her to study art in France, at the prestigious Academie Julien in Paris. She was one of the first

women ever to attend the school. In 1885, she returned to Washington at age 21, planning to make a living as an artist. For awhile, she drew illustrations for magazines and sometimes wrote columns. But she soon became more interested in photography because she felt it resulted in more accurate depictions than painting or drawing. Again, her mother's connections served her well, as she soon began studying photography under Thomas Smillie at the Smithsonian Institution. Smillie taught the aspiring photographer how to use a camera and work inside a dark room.

It was not long before Johnston, who received her first camera from family friend George Eastman, began establishing a name for herself as a professional photographer. As her reputation developed, she also became an advocate of women's involvement in photography, which was then a field that was dominated by men like the famous Civil War pictorial chronicler Mathew Brady. She was the first female member of the Capitol Camera Club. At the time, photography, or "pictorialism," as it was called, was a relatively new field, and its application was mainly for journalistic purposes and not as an art form. As her skills developed, Johnston would incorporate both journalistic and artistic elements into her work, which would result in a distinctive style that greatly influenced the field and made her famous.

Her mother's own journalistic activities especially benefited Johnston early in her career. Working as a newspaper reporter, her mother wrote about congressional activities as well as Washington inside information, and she knew all of the important people in the nation's capital. She was also

related to President Grover Cleveland's wife. This helped open the doors of the White House for Johnston. From the 1880s and into the 1910s, she would take pictures during the administrations of Presidents Cleveland, Harrison, McKinley, Roosevelt, and Taft. This resulted in an outstanding and historically invaluable pictorial document that depicted the members of the various first families, as well as White House staff members and visitors.

Independent Photographer and Woman

In 1889, not long after she first gained entrance into the White House, Johnston opened a studio behind her father's house. She soon developed a reputation both as a smart businesswoman and a talented photographer. Not only was she a founding member of the Business Women's Club, but her own photographs decorated the club's walls. She also developed a reputation as a free-thinking and strong-willed woman. Her independence and bohemian character was well characterized by her famous self-portrait that showed her pulling up her skirt and striking a rather manly pose while drinking a beer and smoking a cigarette. In this way, she helped symbolize the spirit of the "new woman" that was emerging during this period in the country's history. The picture was designed to shock, as it flaunted traditional values. In fact, with that single pose, Johnston managed to purposefully target many of the taboos about women's role in American society. Her aggressively feminist stance, combined with her independent nature, sometimes resulted in work that generated controversy. When she took a nude photograph of a social debutante, the young girl's father filed a lawsuit against Johnston.

With her reputation as a hard-working professional established, Johnston became a successful photojournalist and took pictures as well as wrote for many popular publications. In 1897, she published an article in *The Ladies Home Journal*, "What A Woman Can Do With A Camera," that outlined her thoughts on why she believed woman were particularly suited to photography. She also explained the training involved and how to operate a studio. Working as a freelance photographer during this period, she photographed a wide variety of people, including the famous and powerful, influential woman, and common laborers. Besides the nation's presidents she photographed President Theodore Roosevelt's high-spirited daughter Alice Roosevelt, noted feminist Susan B. Anthony, women workers in New England textile mills, iron workers, and coal miners. It is also surmised that she helped establish the tradition of school pictures for students. Once, while on assignment photographing students at a school in Washington, D.C., she was told there was no money to pay her, so she decided to offer the pictures for sale to the students' parents.

The Hampton Institute Project

In 1899, when she was 37 years old and at the height of her skills, Johnston produced a collection of photographs that would rank among her most famous and best works. By this time, her talent and ambition would direct her into taking on larger projects. That year, the Hampton Institute, in Hampton, Virginia, a vocational school founded to train ex-slaves, hired her to take pictures at the school that would be included in an exhibition about contemporary African American life.

The project demonstrated the best qualities of her work: her strong sense of pictorial composition coupled with her skillful arrangement of human subjects. Individual photographs, which depicted Hampton students in classrooms and vocational surroundings, demonstrated remarkable photographic clarity. Some were stark and intense, as Johnston played with black and white shading to a powerful effect that underscored the separation that existed between blacks and whites in American society.

Many of the pictures were presented at the Universal Exhibition in Paris in 1900 as part of the "American Negro" exhibit (organized by prominent black leaders such as W. E. B. DuBois and Booker T. Washington) and at the Pan-American Exposition in 1901.

The Hampton photographs alone would have been enough to secure Johnston's status of one of America's greatest photographers. But she had other great works ahead of her. Like the images in the Hampton collection, the other photographs that Johnston produced at this point in her career provide a rich pictorial account of the United States, as her work preserved images of settings and famous people that defined the essence of a particular period of the nation's history.

The same year she took the Hampton photographs, she took pictures aboard Admiral Dewey's battleship, the U.S.S. Olympia, when it was stationed in the Manila Bay. Like the Hampton project, this assignment provided an extensive pictorial document, as it captured life on board the ship and showed the famous admiral on the deck. It also generated a great deal of publicity and it added to her stature. This period also included her famous photographic portraits of Teddy Roosevelt and Mark Twain. At the Roosevelt White House, she took pictures of the president's children playing with their pet pony as well as the famous 1902 photo of Alice Roosevelt, which gained acclaim for perfectly capturing the essence of the president's daughter's adventurous spirit. Her famous 1906 portrait of Mark Twain has become part of America's iconography.

As her stature as a photographer grew, so did her reputation as a one of the 19th Century "liberated" women: an unmarried American female who could support herself with her own career and was strongly conscious of gender issues. Continuing to advocate on behalf of women photographers, Johnston, in 1900, organized an exhibit of women photographers for the Universal Exhibition in Paris, the same year when her Hampton photographs were exhibited. The exhibit included 148 works. The women's exhibit was presented at the Third International Photographic Congress, which was held in conjunction with the Paris exposition. Johnston received both publicity and professional recognition for her efforts.

McKinley Assassinated

Johnston's fame grew to even greater proportions in 1901 when fate brought her within intimate proximity of one of the tragedies of American history. She traveled to Buffalo to photograph a major exhibition, which was taking place in early September. Her visit coincided with that of President William McKinley, who was also attending the event, so she could take pictures of him as well. As it turned out, she would take the last picture of McKinley alive, only minutes before he was killed by an assassin's bullet.

After the assassination, Johnston made and sold postcard-sized copies of this image of McKinley speaking at the Exposition grounds the day before he was shot. It became a hugely popular seller.

Later Career

Even as she approached and then surpassed her 50s, Johnston really never slowed down in her pursuit of new projects and new subject matter. She even actively engaged in acquiring new knowledge about her profession. In 1905, Johnston, her mother, and her aunt became close friends with the Lumiere brothers in France. They taught Johnston the theory and practice of their new photographic process. By 1912, she was making "color photo-transparencies." In 1906, she took only a large project, similar in scope to the Hampton project, when she photographed the Tuskegee Institute in Alabama.

In 1910, her career direction took a significant shift when she began specializing in architectural photography. Instead of doing portraiture and journalistic pieces, Johnston now photographed striking examples of architecture as well as the homes and gardens of rich and famous people. During the period, she lived with Mattie Hewitt. The two woman shared a profession as well as a relationship for about eight years. They went their separate ways in 1917.

Johnston moved south in July of 1927 when, during a car tour of the eastern United States, she decided to settle in Virginia. Several years later, during the Great Depression, and funded by a grant from the Carnegie Institute, she again took to the road and traveled throughout the country taking photographs.

Johnston's most significant project during her architectural phase involved photographing still-standing pre-Civil War, or antebellum, mansions and early buildings throughout nine southern states. She was again funded by the Carnegie Institute. Johnston's purpose was to capture the essence and preserve a record of early architecture indigenous to the south before the buildings were lost forever.

Later Life

She moved permanently to New Orleans, Louisiana, in 1945, where she enjoyed being part of the bohemian culture. She bought a home on that city's famous Bourbon Street, where she continued her architectural photography and socialized with an eccentric, artistic crowd that included fellow photographer Joseph Whitesell.

Johnston died on March 16, 1952, in New Orleans, Louisiana. Before her death, she once stated that she was happy that she never did "marry for money." In fact, a liberated women until the day she died, Johnston never married at all. After her death, her estate donated a great deal of her photographs to the Library of Congress in Washington, D.C.

Books

Berch, Bettina, *The Woman Behind the Lens: The Life and Work of Frances Benjamin Johnston, 1864-1952,* University of Virginia Press, 2000.

Online

"Frances Benjamin Johnston," *Pan American Exposition Buffalo 1901,* http://panam1901.bfn.org/documents/panamwomen/francesjohnson.htm (March 15, 2003).

"Frances Benjamin Johnston," *Robert Leggat's History of Photography,* http://www.rleggat.com/photohistory/history/johnst_fb.htm (March 15, 2003).

"Frances Benjamin Johnston," *Women Photographers: UCR California Museum of Photography,* http://www.cmp.ucr.edu/site/exhibitions/women/johnston.html (March 15, 2003).

Rothstein, Sarah, "Making a Social Contribution: The Story of Francis Benjamin Johnston," *Women in Photography,* http://www.u.arizona.edu/ic/mcbride/ws200/grp9roth.htm (March 15, 2003).

"Stairway of Treasurer's Residence: Students at Work. Hampton Institute," *MoMA.org: The Collection: Frances Benjamin Johnston,* http://momawas.moma.org/collection/depts/photography/blowups/photo_003.html (March 15, 2003).

Tune, Howie, "Johnston Made her Mark in Photography," *Reno Gazette-Journal,* http://www.rgj.com/news/stories/html/2002/09/07/23253.php (March 15, 2003). □

Antoine Henri Jomini

Baron Antoine Henri Jomini (1779–1869) drew on his experience in the armies of French Emperor Napoleon Bonaparte to write the first systematic study of military strategy. The science of warfare as outlined in his *Précis de l'art de la guerre (The Art of War)* has been studied by military commanders in the years since Jomini's death, and it continues to influence the way modern warfare is waged, discussed, and studied.

Baron Antoine Henri Jomini rose in the ranks of the Swiss army, eventually serving under Marshall Michel Ney as chief of staff and becoming a baron in 1807. Loyal to French Emperor Napoleon Bonaparte, Jomini distinguished himself in 1806 at the battle of Jena as well as during France's takeover of Spain. His continued fame rests on his now-classic 1836 *Précis de l'art de guerre,* which advocates the use of large land forces, speed, maneuverability, and the capture of strategic points during battle. Jomini's work remained influential with military leaders throughout the 1800s, most notably during the U.S. Civil War.

Leaves Business for Battlefield

Jomini was born on March 6, 1779, in the town of Payerne, located in the Swiss canton of Vaud. His parents, of Italian descent, were of modest means and gave their son a good education. As a child he was fascinated by soldiers and the art of war and was eager to attend the Prince de Wurtemberg's military academy in Montbelliard, but his family's circumstances did not permit this. Unable to afford a commission in the Swiss Watteville regiment then under the command of the French, at age 14 he was sent to business school in Aarau with the intent that he train for a career. In April of 1795 he moved to Basle where he found a clerical position at the banking house of Monsieurs Preiswerk.

Moving to Paris in 1796, Jomini worked as a bank clerk for Monsieurs Mosselmann before leaving to become a stockbroker in partnership with another young man. Napoleon's successes in Italy at Lodi, Castiglione, and Lonato inspired Jomini to begin to write on military matters, and he began to study comparative warfare in earnest. His first published study of military operations were that of Frederick II. In 1798 he left his business career behind to reenlist in the Swiss army where he was appointed aide-de-camp to the minister of war of the Helvetic Republic.

Formulated Military Theory

In 1799 Jomini was appointed bureau chief within the Swiss war office, and in the following months, now with the rank of major, he reorganized the ministry for the Swiss War. He drew on his growing knowledge of military operations to standardize several procedures, taking advantage of his position to experiment with organizational systems and strategies. Leaving Switzerland in 1801, Jomini returned to Paris and worked for two years at a military equipment manufacturer before abandoning commerce for good and beginning the first of his books dealing with military theory and history, *Traité des grandes opérations militaires.* In this work, published in eight volumes between 1804 and 1810 and translated as *Treatise on Grand Military Operations,* Jomini presented an overview of the general principles of warfare. He included a critical history of the military actions of Frederick II, "the Great," during the Seven Years' War, contrasting them unfavorably with the battles waged by Napoleon Bonaparte. Not surprisingly, this work caught the attention of the French emperor, who eventually offered Jomini a position within his own ranks.

Jomini's *Traité des grandes opérations militaires* was the first of several works, including *Principes de la strategie* (1818), and the 15-volume, 1819-1824 work *Histoire critique et militaire des guerres de la Révolution,* which addressed the wars of the French Revolution. The grossly inept early campaigns of the French Revolution had, in fact, inspired Jomini's search for scientific principles underlying successful warfare, but he waited to publish his *Histoire critique* until most of the generals he criticized were dead. In each of his writings he described actual battles and theorized why the actions taken either were successful or failed. A child of the Enlightenment, he sought to determine the laws of military strategy, inviolate scientific principles that could be followed to wage a successful war. Such laws would, Jomini believed, provide continuity among the diverse forces at work within an army and thus make war controlled and of minimal duration.

Ironically, Jomini was at first unable to gain entrance into either the French or Russian military on the basis of his *Traité des grandes opérations militaries,* the implication being that one so young had little to teach older and far more experienced generals. Finally his work came to the attention of Marshal Ney, who took Jomini into his staff in 1805 and provided the funds necessary for the young man to publish his book. Jomini fought with the Sixth Corps against Austria at Ulm in 1805 and served as senior-aide-de-camp against the Prussian Army at Jena and Bautzen the following year. Following the 1807 peace of Tilsit, he was created Baron of the Empire on July 27, 1808, in recognition of his service. During Napoleon's campaigns to take Spain in 1808, he fought bravely and was made brigade general in 1810. When the French army retreated from Russia Jomini also handled his role commendably and was appointed brigadier general in 1813.

Throughout his career in the army of Napoleon, Jomini exhibited complete confidence in his ability to discern "correct" and "incorrect" strategies in line with his theories. Such confidence was interpreted as arrogance by many officers, including Murat and Marshal Berthier, who likely also resented the preferential treatment given to the younger man by Napoleon. In August of 1813, as the result of efforts by Berthier to discredit him and sabotage a well-earned promotion to major general following Ney's victory at the battle of Bautzen, Jomini was forced from the French ranks. Angered and humiliated at his treatment, he traded allegiances, left France, and joined the Russian Army as lieutenant general and aide-de-camp to Alexander I. Aiding in Russia in ending Napoleon's efforts to conquer Eastern Europe, Jomini was allowed to abstain from all military action that took place on French soil. Advancing to general-in-chief in the service of Russia in 1826, he became the military tutor of the Tzarevich Nicholas. As one of his final duties in the Russian military, Jomini was put in charge of organizing the Russian staff college in 1830.

Under Bonaparte, the French had revolutionized warfare by decentralizing command, using a predominately conscripted force and vesting both political and military power in a single leader. Influenced by Alexander the Great, Hannibal, and Caesar, Napoleon had little concern for individual victories or defeats, and even placed the conquest of land secondary; he focused on the overall goal of destroying his enemy through a massed concentration of force. The observation of Napoleon's battle strategy strongly influenced Jomini's theory and became the foundation of his greatest work, 1836's *Precis de l'art de la guerre,* translated in 1862 as *The Art of War,* which was written to provide military instruction for the Grand Duke of Russia, the future Nicholas I. Jomini believed that after the age of Napoleon, war would no longer be considered the private affair of individual monarchs; instead it would be waged nation against nation. In his *Precis* he defined for the first time the three main categories of military activity—strategy, tactics, and logistics—and postulated his "Fundamental Principle of War."

Jomini's "Fundamental Principle of War" involved four maxims: 1) To maneuver the mass of the army, successively upon the decisive points of a theater of war, and attack the enemy's lines of communication as frequently as possible while still protecting ones own; 2) To quickly maneuver and engage fractions of the enemy's army with the majority of one's own; 3) To focus the attack on a "decisive point," such as weak or undefended areas in the enemy lines; 4) To economize one's own force on supporting attacks so that the focus of effort could attack—preferably by surprise—the decisive point at the proper time with sufficient force. He also advocated use of the turning movement, through which an adversary was overcome by moving beyond its position and attacking from the rear, and believed that adversaries in retreat should continue to be pursued as a means of beating them psychologically. He viewed leadership as a prime requirement for military success and appraised character as "above all other requisites in a commander in chief." However, he also recognized that a commander who possessed great character but lacked intellectual training would never be a great general; the necessary characteristic of a winning general would be the combination of intellect and natural leadership. Jomini strongly advocated simplicity and praised the Napoleonic strategy of a quick victory gained by quickly massing troops, as well as the French general's objective of capturing capital cities as a signal of defeat. He also provided early definitions for modern concepts such as the "theater of operation." Jomini cared little for the political niceties of war; in his view governments choose the best commander possible, then free that person to wage war as he deems appropriate.

Influence Spanned the Centuries

Jomini's writings, which constitute over 25 translated works, continued to influence military leaders in both Europe and North America for much of the nineteenth century. His systematization of Napoleon's modus operandi became accepted military doctrine during the U.S. Civil War and was used by generals at Chancellorsville and Gettysburg. However, more recent scholars have viewed Jomini as a chronicler of pre-modern warfare. As a military strategist, he was often compared with Prussian contemporary Karl Marie von Clausewitz (1780–1831), whose 1833 treatise *Vom Kriege* was considered by many scholars to be romanticized. Unlike Clausewitz, Jomini was vague and contradicted himself on the importance of genius. Like Clausewitz, however, his focus remained on the Napoleonic "great battle" rather than the more modern war composed of multiple armed encounters. Among Jomini's other writings was a well-received 1864 *Life of Napoleon* and a political and military history of Napoleon's Waterloo campaign.

After publishing his *Precis,* Jomini retired from the Russian military. He moved to Brussels, but continued to be sought out for his expertise. In 1854 Jomini was called to advise the future Czar Nicholas I on the Crimean War and was consulted by French leader Napoleon III on the 1859 Italian campaign. Until 1888 he was considered by the

English to be preeminent among military strategists, and his books were required reading in military academies. U.S. generals such as George B. McClellan and Robert E. Lee were said to have gone into battle armed with a sword in one hand and Jomini's *Summary of the Art of War* in the other. Reported to be of sound mind as late as his nineties, Jomini continued to insist that his principles would endure despite the changing face of modern warfare as a result of the development of technological advances such as railways and telegraphs. He died on March 24, 1869, at his home in Passy, France.

Books

Charters, David A., and others, editors, *Military History and the Military Profession,* Praeger, 1992.

Earle, Edward M., editor, *Makers of Modern Strategy: Military Thought from Machiavelli to Hitler,* Princeton University Press, 1944.

Handel, Michael I., *Masters of War: Sun Tzu, Clausewitz, and Jomini,* Frank Cass, 1992.

Howard, Michael, editor, *The Theory and Practice of War,* Indiana University Press, 1975.

Jomini, Antoine Henri, *The Art of War,* translated by G. H. Mendell and W. P. Craighill, Lippincott, 1862, reprinted, Greenwood Press, 1971.

Periodicals

Galaxy, January-July 1869.

Marine Corps Gazette, December 1970; August 1988.

Military Affairs, Spring 1964; December 1974.

Military Review, February 1959.

Naval War College Review, autumn, 1990.

Online

Antoine-Henri Jomini, http://www.ostrogradsky.com (March 14, 2003). □

Matilda Sissieretta Joyner

Widely hailed as the possessor of one of the great singing voices of her day, Matilda Sissieretta Joyner (1869–1933) enjoyed a successful career as a concert and variety performer from the late 1880s to the World War I era. Joyner's career had two phases. First she was a soloist, appearing in concert halls, churches, and other venues in North America and Europe. Later, she spent two decades touring the United States as the star of an all-black variety entertainment show. It is an example of the peculiar nature of race relations in America that Joyner, whose extraordinary talent was almost universally acknowledged and whose concerts and variety shows drew mostly white audiences, never appeared in opera.

Joyner was born in Portsmouth, Virginia, as Matilda Sissieretta Joyner. The year of her birth is usually given as 1869. According to William Lichtenwanger in *Notable American Women,* no record of her birth has ever been found and the ages listed on her marriage and death records indicate that she was born around 1865. Joyner's father, Jeremiah Malachi Joyner, was a former slave and had been a body servant to his master until the end of the Civil War. After gaining his freedom, he became a minister in the Afro-Methodist Church. Joyner's mother, Henrietta, a former slave as well, was an accomplished amateur singer with a fine soprano voice. She grew up as an only child, her brother having died in infancy. In 1876, Joyner's father accepted an offer to become pastor of a church in Providence, Rhode Island, and the family moved north. A minister's salary was modest and Reverend Joyner took odd jobs to help make ends meet. Providence had a thriving black community in the 1870s and the atmosphere in the city was relatively progressive in regard to racial matters. Joyner attended the Meeting Street and Thayer Street schools, both of which had integrated student bodies and teaching personnel.

As a small child, Joyner exhibited a love for singing. "When I was a little girl, just a wee slip of a tad, I used to go about singing. I guess I must have been a bit of a nuisance then, for my mouth was always open," the adult Joyner recalled in an interview with the *Syracuse Evening Herald,* excerpts of which are included in Willia Daughtry's doctoral dissertation about Joyner. During her teenage years, Joyner made her first public appearance as a singer at the

Pond Street Baptist Church in Providence and studied voice at the Providence Academy of Music.

In 1883, Joyner married David Richard Jones, called Richard, whom Rosalyn M. Story in *And So I Sing: African-American Divas of Opera and Concert* says was described in contemporary accounts as a "handsome mulatto from Baltimore." Richard Jones had worked as a hotel bellman and as a newspaper dealer. The couple is said to have had a child who died in infancy.

Marriage does not seem to have hindered Joyner's budding professional career. She is said to have attended the New England Conservatory of Music in Boston in the mid-1880s. In 1887, Joyner made her professional debut in Boston at a concert to benefit the Irish nationalist Charles Stewart Parnell, whose political career was being jeopardized by a personal scandal. Her performance at the Parnell concert, before an audience of 5,000, drew a strongly positive reaction. The following year Joyner made her first New York appearance in a concert at Steinway Hall.

Later in 1888, Joyner sang at Wallack's Theater on Broadway, becoming the first African American to appear on stage at the prestigious theater. The attention she received at this performance led to her joining a troupe of black musicians on a tour of the West Indies. The West Indian tour lasted eight months and was a triumph. In Jamaica, Haiti, and other countries, Joyner was greeted by enthusiastic crowds and presented with jewel encrusted honors from local governments and admirers. Returning to the United States, she appeared with baritone Louis Brown in several East Coast cities and briefly returned to Providence for further study of voice. In the winter of 1890-1891, she made another tour of the West Indies.

It was during her early concert years that Joyner was dubbed the "Black Patti" by the *New York Clipper,* a theatrical newspaper. The moniker alluded to Adelina Patti, the Italian American soprano and star of the Metropolitan Opera. Joyner's managers and promoters repeated the "Black Patti" description in advertisements and it became strongly identified with her for the remainder of her career. Although Joyner adamantly disapproved of the nickname at the beginning, she then used it to her advantage in the later years. According to Daughtry, instead of finding the comparison to another artist pointless and the "black" qualification condescending, Joyner used it "as a weapon—a kind of boomerang—which drew the predominately white audience to her—an audience which expected to find a freak, a comical, awkward, unusually strange creature before it, but which found instead an artist who exhibited the same training known to the white singer of her time as well as a decorum which gave new dignity and finesse to the Negro image on the concert stage."

In February 1892, Joyner performed at the White House for President Benjamin Harrison and his luncheon guests in the Blue Room. Her vocal selections, typical of her concert repertoire at the time, were the popular songs "Home, Sweet Home," "Swanee River," and the cavatina from Meyerbeer's opera *Robert le Diable.* Enchanted by Joyner's talent, the First Lady, Caroline Harrison, presented the singer with a bouquet of White House-grown orchids. In

later years, she returned to Washington to sing for Presidents Grover Cleveland, William McKinley, and Theodore Roosevelt. African American performers at the Executive Mansion were rare but not unprecedented. According to Elise K. Kirk in *Opera News,* singer Marie Selika performed at the Rutherford B. Hayes White House in 1878, and the Fisk Jubilee Singers performed for President Chester Alan Arthur in 1882. However, it was not until 1901, when Booker T. Washington lunched with Theodore Roosevelt, that an African American was invited to the White House as a sit-down guest.

True notoriety came to Joyner in April 1892 when she was selected to be the star attraction at the Grand Negro Jubilee at New York City's Madison Square Garden. The Jubilee was a three-day extravaganza featuring hundreds of black singers and dancers and a military band. Joyner sang popular songs and opera selections, including the "Siempre libera" aria from *La Traviata.* She was said to have been the highlight of the show. Offers for bookings increased so dramatically after this appearance that it was hard for Joyner to fully absorb what had happened. "I woke up famous after singing at the Garden, and didn't know it," she said in an article quoted by *Story.*

In June 1892, Joyner signed a contract with Major J.B. Pond, a high-powered promoter and manager of entertainers and lecturers whose clients included novelist Mark Twain and clergyman Henry Ward Beecher. Pond built a program around her, featuring classical and popular music. According to *Story,* the program became "something of a forum for the best black talent of the day." Among the performers who appeared with Joyner were poet Paul Lawrence Dunbar and Joseph Douglass, a violinist and grandson of Frederick Douglass. She sometimes sang with accompaniment by black pianist Alberta Wilson, giving audiences a chance to marvel at two accomplished African American women musicians holding forth on a concert hall stage.

In 1893, under the management of Pond, Joyner earned two thousand dollars for a one-week engagement at the Pittsburgh Exposition. It was said to be the highest salary paid to a black performer up to that time. Also in 1893, she performed at the World's Columbian Exposition in Chicago where she was a top box-office draw.

Management problems began to plague Joyner's career beginning in 1893. The details are vague. It is possible that she found Pond's management style exploitative and more focused on making quick money than in fostering a long-term concert career. Other troubles are said to have stemmed when Joyner's husband, Richard, booked engagements for his wife without the permission of Pond. Her marriage was troubled due to Richard Jones's penchant for gambling and drink and his inability to hold a job. The couple divorced sometime between 1893 and 1898.

In the mid-1890s, Joyner broke with Pond and under new management participated in a charity concert at Madison Square Garden to benefit the *New York Herald*'s Free Clothing Fund. The renowned Hungarian composer Antonin Dvorak conducted the concert. Dvorak, then director of the National Conservatory of Music in New York, was an admirer of African American people and culture. Strains of black folk music can be heard in Dvorak's famous "Symphony No. 9: From the New World." At the Free Clothing Fund benefit, Joyner sang the soprano solo from Rossini's *Stabat Mater* with an all black male choir singing the chorus. "Mme. Jones was an enormous success with the audience. To those who heard her for the first time she came in the light of a revelation, singing high C's with as little apparent effort as her namesake, the white Patti," wrote a reviewer in the *New York Herald.* Joyner then performed in England, France, and Germany. In London, she participated in a Royal Command performance for the Prince of Wales (future King Edward VII) at the Royal Opera House at Covent Garden.

In 1896, Black Patti's Troubadours were formed under the auspices of New York theatrical managers Voelkel and Nolan. As the name suggests, Joyner was the main attraction of this travelling show, which also offered comedians, dancers, acrobats, jugglers, and other variety entertainers. Her appearances in the Troubadours came in what were called "Operatic Kaleidoscopes," which offered scenes from famous operas, such as *La Boehme, Rigoletto,* and *Carmen,* sung with full costumes and scenery.

Joyner's greatest dream was to sing in a full-scale opera. Many critics agreed that her voice and dramatic flair were well suited to opera. "The thought was irresistible that she would make a superb Aida, whom her appearance, as well as her voice, suggested," wrote a writer for the *Philadelphia Times,* quoted by *Story.* A few offers were made in regard to opera after her initial rise to fame in the early 1890s but nothing ever materialized. Undoubtedly, Joyner's race was the reason she never appeared with prestigious opera companies, such as the Metropolitan. It was not until the 1950s that black singers appeared with major American opera companies. However, Denis Mercier points out in *Notable Black American Women* that all-black opera performances began to be done after the turn of the century and it is unclear why Joyner never participated in any of these productions.

Black Patti's Troubadours traveled across the United States and were popular with both white and black audiences. A writer for the *Detroit Evening News,* in an article quoted by *Story,* said that "without exception the Black Patti Troubadours company is the best colored theatrical organization that has visited this city. Every member of it seems to be a star."

Despite its success, Joyner was not entirely happy as leader of the Troubadours. She felt the company was essentially a minstrel show and not the proper showcase for her serious "Operatic Kaleidoscopes." The appeal of Black Patti's Troubadours reached its peak in the first decade of the twentieth century, then began to wane along with a general decline of minstrelsy. In 1916, the company gave its final performance at the Gibson Theatre in New York City.

Joyner's career came to an end with the demise of the Troubadours. Aside from a concert at Chicago's Grand Theatre, she made no further professional appearances. Returning to Providence, she looked after her elderly mother, took in two boys who were wards of the state, and occasionally sang at local churches. To gain income, she sold off most of the possessions she had accumulated during her career, and in her last years received public assistance. She died of cancer on June 24, 1933, with only the generosity of friends preventing burial in the city's "potter's field."

Books

Dictionary of American Negro Biography, W.W. Norton, 1982.
Notable American Women, Belknap Press of Harvard University Press, 1971.
Notable Black American Women, Gale, 1992.
Rust, Brian, *The American Record Label Book,* Arlington House, 1978.
Salem, Dorothy C., ed., *African American Women: A Biographical Dictionary,* Garland Publishing, 1993.
Story, Rosalyn M., *And So I Sing: African-American Divas of Opera and Concert,* Warner Books, 1990.

Periodicals

New York Herald, January 24, 1894.
New York Times, August 27, 1893.
Opera News, November 1, 1980.
Providence Journal-Bulletin, February, 20, 1997. □

K

Ilya Kabakov

Ilya Kabakov (born 1933) is an artist of note in two distinctly polar disciplines. While living in the Soviet Union for 30 years, he was a well-known, albeit officially sanctioned, children's book illustrator. He was simultaneously amassing a substantial body of unofficial avant-garde work. Since leaving the Soviet Union in 1988, he has been prolific; he is now considered the foremost post-Stalinist Russian artist. His prime means of artistic expression has been sprawling installations largely based on Soviet-related themes.

"By any reckoning Kabakov's career has bridged an exceptional variety of situations and concerns," wrote Robert Storr in *Art in America*. "He remains better known in Europe (where he was featured in the last Venice Biennale) than in America, where he now resides. His ideas and observations raise significant questions about the development and future of installation art—which remains his principal artistic form—and about our current esthetic horizons."

Studied Art by Accident

Kabakov was born on September 30, 1933, in Dniepropetrovsk, Ukraine, to Jewish parents. His family was poor, so much so they often lived apart from each other. War also frequently uprooted Kabakov. He was first relocated in 1941 when World War II fighting extended into the Soviet Union.

By chance, Kabakov attended a professional elementary art school between the ages of 7 and 16. The school was the Leningrad Academy of Art, which had been temporarily relocated to Samarkand during World War II. A friend studying at the school decided one night to clandestinely take Kabakov into the school to look at paintings of nude women. Once inside the school, they were confronted by an adult. The boys lied to legitimize their presence there, making the excuse that they were there because Kabakov was thinking about attending the school. He was invited to apply and dashed off a few pictures—military scenes based on equipment stationed in the area—to support his application. He was accepted; he was also the only applicant.

Art was neither easy nor a passion. Kabakov claims to have been constantly frustrated by his lack of ability. "I already understood that I couldn't draw and that I had no talent for art," he told *Art in America* in 1995. "I continued to study even though I didn't like it, and my attitude toward it was like that of a trained rabbit who beats a drum: he must learn to do it, but not loving it inside and even feeling revulsion toward it. And ultimately I did learn to beat the drum fairly well, but all the while thinking to myself that it just wasn't me."

Kabakov was evacuated again when German forces began invading the Soviet Union. He was taken to Holy Trinity Monastery and Cathedral in Zagorsk. He eventually returned to Samarkand, then continued his formal education in Moscow until he was 23.

Continued Education in Moscow

Kabakov said his mother moved to Moscow to be near him while he was in boarding school, even without a special resident permit. "She became a laundry cleaner at school. But without an apartment the only place she had

Small student groups formed outside the classroom to supplant the dreary coursework. Each person would tackle a subject: philosophy, history, or poetry. Kabakov and artists Erik Bulatov, Oleg Vassilyev, and Mikhail Mezhaninov formed a clique. These students found mentors in artists such as Robert Falk, Vladimir Favorsky, and Artur Fonvizin. Under the Soviet Regime, each of these men was an unofficial artist, that is their work was not sanctioned by the state.

Sought Artistic Expression Outside the Official

Kabakov said he knew in 1955, while still in school, that he had to find an artistic form outside that which was officially dictated and sanctioned. It certainly continued his lifelong struggle with art and the creative process, but it marked an important step in his evolution and maturity. Kabakov experimented variously in genres including Abstract Expressionism and his own version of neo-Surrealism. He and his fellow artists began creating unofficial art. These pieces began to be shown in the West in 1964.

The group was known as NOMA or the Moscow Conceptual Circle of Artists. The style of art they created was called Romantic Conceptualism. This was "not so much an artistic school, but a subculture and a way of life," wrote Svetlana Boym on the ARTMARGINS website. "A group of artists, writers, and intellectuals created a kind of parallel existence in a gray zone, in a 'stolen space' carved out between Soviet institutions. Stylistically, the work of the conceptualists was seen as a Soviet parallel to pop art, only instead of the advertisement culture they used the trivial and drab rituals of Soviet everyday life—too banal and insignificant to be recorded anywhere else, and made taboo not because of their potential political explosiveness, but because of their sheer ordinariness, their all-too-human scale."

Some members' work was purchased by visiting Westerners, but Kabakov has asserted others gave away paintings in hopes of triggering some positive reaction from afar. Westerners were initially underwhelmed with the work, but this unofficial art generated buzz and attracted notice within the international art community in the 1970s and 1980s. Conceptual artists associated with this group include Vitali Komar and Alexander Melamid.

As an official artist, Kabakov worked in the Soviet Union for 30 years with the "benefit of steady work and minimal KGB scrutiny," according to Amy Ingrid Schlegel writing in the Winter 1999 issue of *Art Journal*. He has claimed in *Art in America* this art was not done for love, but because it "could be done quickly and therefore didn't take a lot of time away from your own work. . . . You should not think that we loved our illustrating. It might have been possible to love it if you had been permitted to do what you wanted, but you didn't love it because you had to do what was expected." He has also said "at the foundation of my career lies fear, ridiculous circumstances and my mother, who sacrificed everything for it." Indeed, Kabakov supported her and his in-laws throughout his sanctioned illustrating career.

Between 1969 and 1980, Kabakov created a series of 50 albums that combined art and text. "Each album told the tale of a different character, a different demented dreamer

was the room where she arranged the laundry." He related in a 1992 article on ARTMARGINS website that his mother "felt homeless and defenseless vis-a-vis the authorities, while, on the other hand, she was so tidy and meticulous that her honesty and persistence allowed her to survive in the most improbable place. My child psyche was traumatized by the fact that my mother and I never had a corner to ourselves."

He attended Moscow Secondary Art School between 1945 and 1951. He graduated from Surikov Institute of Arts in 1957. He maintained that creating art continued to be a struggle. Kabakov said in *Art in America* his education was very classical in nature, extremely similar to nineteenth-century art education but "bureaucratic and dead. . . . We all were physically present but mentally absent."

Kabakov has claimed he became an illustrator of children's books as a result of bad grades, which placed him in the school graphics program rather than in the more elite painting section. He said this discipline actually suited him well. "I read incessantly, I was crazy about books, and I would comment upon or think aloud about anything I saw. My thoughts would come to me already in the form of words. I don't know what it is, but I cannot look at a painting in silence; inside I am always talking to myself at the moment that I am viewing it," he said in *Art in America* in 1995. "Naturally, this method is very easily connected to the notion of illustration. . . . I was successful not only because I mastered what I was supposed to illustrate, but also what was expected from me."

creating an elaborate system to make life not only bearable but meaningful," wrote Amei Wallach in a feature in *Art in America*. The best known of these is "Okno" ("The Window"), which was later published. These albums became the basis of his interest in installation art.

He began working in a more conceptual style in the mid-1970s. The result were "zhek picture displays," parodies of broadsides and Soviet posters. Kabakov created the name from the acronym ZhEK, referring to the Soviet housing management. He hosted informal meetings of fellow conceptual artists at his apartment known as the Sretensky Boulevard Group, so called after the Moscow street where many of them lived.

Emigrated and Continued Prolific Creation

Kabakov attempted to emigrate from the Soviet Union three times, first in the 1970s. Each time, he changed his mind. He eventually left the Soviet Union in 1988. He is reportedly reluctant to discuss this, although immigrating to the West has obviously had a major impact on his life and art. Schlegel stated when he did leave his homeland, he chose "to exile himself from Russia physically, socially, and linguistically once the policies of perestroika and glasnost took effect in the late 1980s."

A flurry of Kabakov books was released after his emigration. A particular surge could be seen in the mid-1990s. These included his children's books as well as volumes related to his various exhibitions such as "The Palace of Projects" and "Auf dem Dach/On the Roof." Schlegel dubbed this "critical mass" of work "The Kabakov Phenomenon." His work and his prolific production plus these publications "helped make him a senior international art world star." *Artforum International* said of this generation of contemporary Soviet artists, most of the attention has been paid to Kabakov. "[H]is work comes as close as anybody's to encompassing the better part of a continent's worth of art," wrote Barry Schwabsky.

It was Kabakov's "Ten Characters" installation mounted in New York that started a series of museum installations. It was also his first solo exhibition. Wallach, writing in *Art in America* in 2000, noted since the spring of 1988, "he has for all intents and purposes been working in a series of museums. In the last 12 years he has mounted 165 installations in 148 museums in 30 countries." A 1995 book by Kabakov, *On the "Total" Installation*, explains the form and his artistic philosophies.

Moved Away from Installations

Later in his career, Kabakov began shying away from relying on the Soviet Union as a subject for his installations. One of the first of these is "Auf dem Dach/On the Roof," in which ten rooms, representing a narrative timeline of snapshots from family life, were shown from the vantage point of a rooftop. His "The Palace of Projects" and "Life and Creativity of Charles Rosenthal" marked a further turn toward other forms. Kabakov considers these works as "grand finales to his singleminded preoccupation with 'total' installation," but, added Wallach, "it is difficult to imagine that

he will forsake it altogether." As has been the case throughout his career, Kabakov continued to create prolifically. As Schlegel pointed out, Kabakov "works every day, all day. Some might say he is a workaholic. Others would interpret his work habits as a form of flood control."

He and his wife Emilia also began collaborating on public sculpture. The couple moved to Long Island, New York, around 1996. There, they built two large studios. Permanent pieces by them can be found in Italy, Japan, and Belgium. Wallach stated "according to his concept, the purpose of the sculpture is to embody a 'spirit of the place.'" Kabakov contended "The principle is that every place in our cultural life has a spirit, and . . . if you hear the spirit, if you feel it . . . what the spirit has to say is: Please do not disturb me!"

Boym submitted that "For Kabakov, art remains an inevitable, existential need and a therapy for survival. . . . The artist loves the museum not merely as an institution, but as a personal refuge. . . . Kabakov's total installations look like the artist's Noah's arks, only we are never sure if the artist escaped from hell or from paradise."

Periodicals

Artforum International, May 2000.
Art in America, January 1995; November 2000.
Art Journal, Winter 1999.

Online

"Ilya Kabakov," *Amsterdam University Library website,* http://cf .uba.uva.nl/en/news/afk/kabakov.html (February 28, 2003).
"Il'ya Kabakov," *Artnet.com,* http://www.artnet.com/library/04/ 0454/T045419.asp (February 28, 2003).
"Ilya Kabakov," *The Legacy Project: Visual Arts Library website,* http://www.legacy-project.org/artists/display.html?ID = 197 (February 28, 2003).
"Ilya Kabakov: The Soviet Toilet and the Palace of Utopias," *ARTMARGINS website,* http://www.artmargins.com/content/ feature/boym2.html (February 28, 2003). □

Yousuf Karsh

One of the greatest portrait photographers of all time, Yousuf Karsh (1908–2002) captured not only the images of hundreds of the 20th century's most memorable leaders and celebrities but also the faces of thousands of ordinary men and women whose lives formed the backbone of Canadian society. Karsh, who died at the age of 93 in July 2002, left a priceless legacy to Canada—his adopted homeland for nearly eight decades. Before his death, Karsh sold or donated all 355,000 of his negatives to Canada's National Archives in Ottawa. His photos will form the core collection of the Portrait Gallery of Canada, which was scheduled to open in 2005.

Of Karsh's accessibility to photo subjects from all walks of life, Lily Koltun, acting director of the Portrait Gallery told the *Toronto Star,* "He gave the same attention to anyone who called his studio, so the work we have from him is a wonderful cross-section of Canadian society, not just of famous people but fishermen, a sailmaker, a farmer in his field—if you look deeply in his collection, you can discover aspects to him that are quite unexpected." Equally lavish in her praise was Maia Sutnik, curator of photography at the Art Gallery of Ontario, who told the *Toronto Star,* "He brought a huge sense of the personality into his pictures. He made iconic portraits of great men and women, and he brought international acclaim to Canada." Karsh was not without his detractors, however. Some of his more vocal critics faulted the photographer for the sameness of his photo portraits, almost all of which were shot in black and white and have an extraordinarily solemn feel to them. His defenders—and they are legion—retort that this was simply Karsh's style. In its assessment of Karsh's legacy, the *Economist* likened the criticism of his work to "complaining that Rembrandt's paintings did not make you laugh."

Apprenticed to Leading Boston Photographer

Karsh was born on December 23, 1908, in the Armenian enclave of Mardin, Turkey. During the years of World War I (1914–1918), the Armenians of Turkey endured widespread persecution and privation at the hands of the Turkish government. In 1924, at the age of 16, Karsh left his native Turkey for Canada to live with his uncle, A.G. Nakash, who operated a photo studio in Sherbrooke, Quebec. Under his uncle's direction, the young Karsh learned the basics of photography. However, recognizing that Karsh needed more expert guidance to refine his skills, his uncle in 1928 sent him to Boston to apprentice under fellow Armenian John H. Garo, a well-known portrait photographer of the day. For the next couple of years, Karsh later recalled, as written in the *Independent,* that he learned about "lighting, design, and composition . . . and began to appreciate the greater dimensions of photography." Under Garo's tutelage, Karsh was exposed to some of Boston's most celebrated men and women who regularly convened at Garo's informal afternoon salons. "Even as a young man," he remembered, "I was aware that these glorious afternoons and evenings in Garo's salon were my university. There I set my heart on photographing those men and women who leave their mark on the world."

After a three-year apprenticeship under Garo, Karsh in 1931 returned to Canada. In the nation's capital of Ottawa, he opened a modest portrait studio, hoping that its location would offer him an opportunity "to photograph its leading figures and many international visitors," Karsh was quoted as saying in the *Independent.* So meager was Karsh's budget for the launch of his own studio that most of the furniture consisted of orange crates, "covered—tastefully, I thought—with monk's cloth, and if I occasionally found myself borrowing back my secretary's salary of $17 a week to pay the rent, I was still convinced, with the resilience of youth, that I had made the right choice." In his spare time, Karsh became involved with a local theater group, where he learned more about lighting and the use of artificial light in photography. It was at the theater group that the photographer first met actress Solange Gauthier, whom he married on April 27, 1939.

Studied Subjects Before Photo Shoots

Only a few years after setting up shop in Ottawa, Karsh had firmly established himself in Canadian political circles. In 1935 he was named official portrait photographer of the Canadian government, in which capacity he was frequently called upon to photograph Canadian leaders and visiting statesmen. Karsh routinely researched the lives and accomplishments of his well-known subjects. In an account of his preparations for a photo shoot, Karsh wrote, as quoted in the *Independent,* "Before I begin, I will have studied my subject to the best of my ability, and within broad limits know what I am hoping to find, and what I hope to be able to interpret successfully. The qualities that have attracted me to the subject are those that will satisfy me if I can portray them in the photograph, and that will most probably satisfy views of the picture as well. I am fascinated by the challenge of portraying greatness . . . with my camera."

Although he had already won wide acceptance in the Canadian capital, Karsh first captured international attention with his December 1941 portrait of British Prime Minister Winston Churchill. During a brief visit to Ottawa, Churchill reluctantly agreed to sit for Karsh, warning the photographer that he would give him two minutes and not a second more to take his picture. With that, Churchill lit up one of his trademark cigars. Seconds later, Karsh snatched the cigar from Churchill's lips and snapped the picture. The resulting photo, which shows a somewhat petulant Churchill scowling into the camera and was sold to *Life* magazine for only $100, eventually became the most widely reproduced portrait in the history of photography. The Churchill portrait firmly established Karsh's reputation as a world-class portrait photographer. Not long thereafter, the Canadian government asked Karsh to travel to England to shoot a series of photographs of British military leaders. *Life* magazine subsequently commissioned the photographer to do a similar series of American wartime leaders. In 1946, the year after the end of World War II, Karsh published his first book, *Faces of Destiny,* a collection of portraits of the men and women who spearheaded the Allied victories in Europe and the Pacific. That same year Karsh became a naturalized Canadian citizen.

The widely circulated Churchill portrait brought a major change in Karsh's life. No longer did he have to seek out subjects. They came looking for him, seeking immortality through his lens. To be "Karshed" was a true sign that a celebrity had arrived. Although he offered his services to those from all walks of life, there was no denying that Karsh was fascinated by those he described as "people of consequence," a group that included politicians, royalty, writers, scientists, and actors, among others. As the photographer himself observed and noted in the *Economist,* "It's the minority that make the world go around." Every Canadian prime minister from Mackenzie King to Jean Chretien sat for Karsh, as did every American president from Herbert Hoover to Bill Clinton. Although probably no one other than Karsh knows for sure, it has been estimated that he photographed 17,000 people over six decades.

Worked Briefly as Industrial Photographer

During the early 1950s Karsh worked occasionally as an industrial photographer, doing work for companies such as Ford of Canada Ltd. and Atlas Steel Ltd., but the bulk of his life's work was as a portraitist. His most famous subjects included the British royal family; a young Elizabeth Taylor; Pope Pius XII; Albert Einstein; authors Norman Mailer, George Bernard Shaw, Andre Malraux, and H.G. Wells; British Prime Minister Margaret Thatcher; and a bevy of American film stars, including Bette Davis, Humphrey Bogart, and Gregory Peck. In 1959, Karsh became the first photographer to have a one-man exhibition at the National Gallery of Canada.

Karsh gained world recognition for his portrait style, which was formal and shot almost exclusively in black and white. The most notable aspect of the photographer's unique style was his use of light to model his subject's faces in almost sculptural fashion. Karsh's portraits are shot against simple backgrounds—frequently black—and use no props or decorations that might attract attention away from the central figure of the portrait. Although some of his detractors complain that Karsh's portraits fail to capture the essence of his subjects, his supporters point out that Karsh's primary goal was the visual idealization of the legend and public image of those he photographed.

In 1961 Karsh's wife, Solange, died of cancer. A year later, on August 28, 1962, the photographer married Estrellita Maria Nachbar. He also became involved in academics, serving as visiting professor of photography at Ohio University in Athens from 1967 to 1969. In 1972 Karsh, whose "Karsh of Ontario" label was now recognized as the signature of one of the world's most famous portrait studios, moved his operation into a suite at Ottawa's fashionable Chateau Laurier Hotel. He also signed on with Boston's Emerson College as visiting professor of fine arts, a position he held until 1974.

Held in Deep Respect by Subjects

Part of Karsh's success as a portraitist may be attributable to the deep respect in which he was held by most of his subjects. According to the *Edmonton Sun,* Karsh's brother Malak, who died in 2000, said his brother's subjects freely gave of themselves "with love and respect." He said, "People knew they had a master with them and they appreciated that opportunity." For his part, Karsh preferred to refer to his photo sessions as "visits," during which he was unfailingly polite and curious, seeking to draw out his subjects' views on their own lifes' experiences as well as life in general.

Karsh maintained his studio in the Chateau Laurier Hotel until 1992, when he retired to Boston with wife Estrellita. Although he was no longer active in photography, Karsh's work continued to excite great interest worldwide. In the years following his retirement, major retrospective exhibitions of Karsh's work were held at Montreal's Museum of Fine Arts; London's National Portrait Gallery; Washington's Corcoran Gallery; the Mint Museum in Charlotte, North Carolina; the Museum of Photography, Film, and TV in Bradford, England; Boston's Museum of Fine Arts; the Detroit Institute of Art; the National Portrait Gallery of Australia; and the Tower Gallery in Yokahama, Japan. His work has also been reproduced in nearly a score of books of photography, including *Faces of Destiny* (1946), *Portraits of Greatness* (1959), *This Is Rome* (1959), *The Warren Court* (1965), *Karsh Portfolio* (1967), *This Is the Holy Land* (1970), *Faces of Our Time* (1971), *Karsh Portraits* (1976), and *Karsh Canadians* (1978).

Karsh died in Boston, Massachusetts, on July 13, 2002, from complications following surgery for diverticulitis. Perhaps Karsh himself offered the best overview of his goals as a portraitist in his 1962 autobiography, *In Search of Greatness: Reflections of Yousuf Karsh.* Echoed in *Contemporary Photographers* Karsh wrote: "I believe that it is the artist's job to accomplish at least two things—to stir the emotions of the viewer and to lay bare the soul of his subject. When my own emotions have been stirred, I hope I can succeed in stirring those of others. But it is the mind and soul of the personality before my camera that interests me most, and the greater the mind and soul, the greater my interest."

Books

Complete Marquis Who's Who, Marquis Who's Who, 2001.
Contemporary Authors, Gale Group, 2002.
Contemporary Photographers, 3rd ed., St. James Press, 1996.

Periodicals

Economist (US), July 20, 2002.
Edmonton Sun, July 14, 2002.
Independent (UK), July 15, 2002.
Toronto Star, July 15, 2002. □

Gjergj Kastrioti-Skanderbeg

Hailed as a national hero in Albania, Gjergj Kastrioti-Skanderbeg (1403–1468) successfully ousted the Ottoman Turks from his native land for over two decades, halting Turkey's efforts to spread Islam through a predominately Roman Catholic western Europe.

Kidnapped by the Ottoman Turks at a young age, Albanian freedom fighter Gjergj Kastrioti-Skanderbeg was raised under Islam and trained as a general within the ranks of the Turkish military before fleeing his captors and reconverting to Christianity in 1443. As commander of Albania's warlords, he sparked a national revolt in 1444 and held off numerous efforts by the Ottomans to take back Albania and bring that country once again under Muslim rule. Following Kastrioti-Skanderbeg's death in 1468 his Albanian forces could no longer repulse the Turks; twelve years later Albania fell once more to Turkish forces and remained part of the Ottoman Empire for many centuries, until its eventual liberation in 1912.

The Spread of the Muslim Empire

The Albanian people, descendants of the Illyrians, occupied the mountainous region of the western Balkans, a remote area extending from what is now Slovenia southward into Greece. Although known for being sociable, the Illyrians were also known for their bravery in war and aggressively maintained their lands against the many other clans throughout the Balkan region. Although influenced culturally as the result of conquest by Greece, Rome, and ultimately the Visigoths, Huns, and Ostrogoths, large numbers of Albanian peasants nonetheless managed to retain their customs, culture, and language by living in small, remote towns in the mountains where, due to the lack of roads, they were able to resist all efforts at assimilation by conquering cultures. Influenced by many years under Roman rule and subsequently made a part of the Byzantine Empire, Albania could boast a flourishing culture, established trade, and a strong economy by the middle ages; this situation would change for the worse after the region was overrun by the Ottoman Turks in 1388.

The Ottoman Empire expanded from Anatolia into the Balkans during the 1300s and by 1400 marauding Muslim armies had pierced the boundaries of the once-mighty Byzantine Empire. The city of Constantinople, built by the Roman Emperor Constantine I in 330 and the seat of the Eastern Orthodox Church, was destined to fall to Islam in little more than a half-century. Meanwhile, the Turks, known for their brutal treatment of the conquered, now extended their reach west to Bulgaria and Serbia where, due to the capitulation of a succession of competing tribal leaders, soon had the Balkans firmly under their control. Completely under Ottoman control in 1385, Albania's ruling families were allowed to retain their lands and titles, but due to their disunity they were unable to overthrow the invading armies. For the most part, the Albanian people suffered greatly under the brutal regime of their new overlord, Sultan Murad II.

A Childhood Cut Short

Into this hostile world, Kastrioti-Skanderbeg was born in the city of Krujë in northern Albania, on January 17, 1405. His father, Gjon Kastrioti, was a prince of Emathia, although the family could trace its lineage back to serf roots. To assure the loyalty of Albanian princes such as Kastrioti, Sultan Murad II established a practice of kidnapping the sons of royalty and raising them in the court of Adrianopel (now Edirne, Turkey) to become loyal Turks. As a boy of three years of age, Kastrioti-Skanderbeg and his three older brothers were taken in this manner. Tragically, his older brothers, Stanislao, Constantino, and Reposio, met their fate at the hands of their Turkish captors.

For his part, the young Kastrioti-Skanderbeg was quickly indoctrinated in the Muslim faith and was given a good education in the Turkish court. When he reached the appropriate age, he was trained for battle in the Turkish military, as was the traditional fate of Turkish teens. Given the name S'kander and eventually earning the rank of Bey—from which his second surname "Skanderbeg" was eventually derived—the intelligent and well-spoken Kastrioti-Skanderbeg proved himself on the battlefields of Asia Minor and eastern Europe. Eventually promoted to general, the former Albanian led Turkish armies against the Greeks and then north into Serbia and Hungary. It is claimed that Kastrioti-Skanderbeg was fluent in several languages, among them Arabic, Greek, Italian, Bulgarian, and Serbo-Croatian; it is also claimed that he eventually entered secret communication with highly placed persons in the powerful cities of Venice and Naples. However, believing Kastrioti-Skanderbeg to be loyal to Turkey due to his continued success on the field of battle, Murad II continued to bestow his favors on Kastrioti-Skanderbeg and granted the general the title of governor of lands in central Albania.

In 1443 Kastrioti-Skanderbeg was ordered by the sultan to attack the Hungarian forces commanded by Janos Hunyadi, a revered general known as the White Knight, for the purpose of reclaiming Nis (now Serbia) for the Ottoman Empire. While studying this new enemy, Kastrioti-Skanderbeg reportedly learned of his own Albanian origins, as well as of the tragic fate of his brothers. Now aware that his true people shared an allegiance with Hunyadi, the Turkish general arranged a secret meeting wherein the two generals conspired to thwart the Turks. Along with 300 Albanian princes, in the course of battling the Hungarians Kastrioti-Skanderbeg claimed defeat, then abandoned the Turkish army and headed toward Albania. Disguising his small regiment as acting on orders of Sultan Murad II himself, Kastrioti-Skanderbeg entered the Turkish fortifications at Krujë and that night massacred the Turkish pasha and the Muslim contingent stationed there. The following morning the Kastrioti family's standard—a red flag emblazoned with a black, double-headed eagle that has since been adopted as Albania's national flag—fluttered in the breeze over the city's castle. Here Kastrioti-Skanderbeg reportedly made his historic pronouncement: "I have not brought you liberty, I found it here, among you." In March of 1444, during a meeting of Albanian princes in the city of Lezhë, he was elected commander-in-chief of the Albanian army.

At first stunned that such a favored general would betray him, Sultan Murad II soon became infuriated and immediately amassed an army to send against the Albanians. Despite Kastrioti-Skanderbeg's inferior numbers, the battle that was waged on June 29, 1444, ended with a Turkish defeat due to the Albanian general's use of guerilla tactics. Murad amassed a second army consisting of over 15,000 men. Kastrioti-Skanderbeg once again overcame this force, his small army avoiding a conflict on open ground and instead successfully ambushing the Turkish forces as they attempted to navigate the Prizren Pass on October 10, 1445. Through his continued efforts, Kastrioti-Skanderbeg continued to defeat the Turks in battle 24 times, thereby forcing the Ottomans to remain beyond Albania's borders. His particularly spectacular victory in 1450 against the Turkish army led by Murad himself, in which the vastly outnumbered Kastrioti-Skanderbeg com-

manded only 20,000 troops, caused him to be hailed as a hero throughout Europe.

Rejoined Faith of His Father

In 1443, at the same time the 41-year-old Kastrioti-Skanderbeg broke his political allegiance to the Ottomans, he renouncing the Turkish faith of Islam and reconverted to the Roman Catholic faith of his father. With his military successes against the Turks now well known, Catholic leaders at the Vatican quickly saw an opportunity to gain a valuable ally. Hoping that the Albanian general could provide some protection for the Catholic faith in Western Europe, Pope Eugenius IV also dreamed of beginning a new crusade against Islam, this time to be led by Kastrioti-Skanderbeg. With some assistance from the Vatican, as well as from the powerful lords of Naples and Venice, Kastrioti-Skanderbeg continued to repulse successive efforts by the Turks to invade Albania over the next 25 years, including at Dibër and at Ochrida in 1462. His major supporter, King Alfonso of Naples (1416–1458), made the Albanian general his vassal in 1451. Alfonso supplied the Albanian army with needed funds, military equipment, and additional troops, and also acted as a protector by extending sanctuary to Kastrioti-Skanderbeg and his family.

After Pope Eugenius's death in February of 1447, this crusade against Islam was inherited by a series of successors, among them Popes Nicholas V, Callistus II, and, most notably Pius II. The crusades were also fueled by news of the fall of Constantinople to militant Sultan Mehmed II in 1453. At Pope Pius's death in August of 1464, Paul II was appointed pope of the Roman Catholic Church; because Pope Paul put art and antiques above any attempts to regain the city of Constantinople, no further help came to Kastrioti-Skanderbeg and his Albanian army from Rome. A battle against the Turks in 1467 left Kastrioti-Skanderbeg victorious but concerned; because of his advancing years he was finding warfare increasingly difficult. Steps to replace the 63-year-old general as commander-in-chief proved in vain; the Albanian commander contracted malaria and died in Lezhë on January 17, 1468.

At his death Kastrioti-Skanderbeg left behind him a son, Giovanni Kastrioti, born of the general's wife, Donica Arianiti. Still a young boy at the time of his father's death, Giovanni Kastrioti fled with his mother to Naples, where they were given the sanctuary once promised by King Alfonso. In 1481 Giovanni attempted to return to Albania to continue his father's work but was unsuccessful. Only a year before, little more than a decade after Kastrioti-Skanderbeg's death, Albania had succumbed once more to Turkish domination, and its new Muslim rulers now exacted a brutal revenge against the late general's military successes. The ruling families who were able to escaped; many of those of good family left behind were executed. While much of Western Europe soon came to flower as a result of the Renaissance, Albania and the east endured a withering "dark age," remaining cut off from advances in technology, science, and the arts while the Turks renewed their efforts to destroy the region's economy and culture.

Despite these dark years of Turkish rule, the memory of Kastrioti-Skanderbeg served to buoy the Albanian spirit and fuel that country's desire for independence. A statue of the Albanian hero was eventually erected in the capital city of Tirana, joining others erected elsewhere in the country. A museum dedicated to his honor was eventually installed in the family castle in Krujë. More recent generations have continued to marvel at Kastrioti-Skanderbeg's accomplishments: 16th-century French poet Pierre Ronsard honored the Albanian national hero in verse, while two centuries later Ronsard's compatriot, noted Enlightenment-era novelist and essayist François Marie Arouet de Voltaire maintained that the Byzantine Empire might have survived the Ottoman onslaught had it such a leader as Kastrioti-Skanderbeg. Italian composer Antonio Vivaldi's opera *Scanderbeg* also was written to honor the Albanian hero.

While Kastrioti-Skanderbeg's accomplishments inspired many of the artists and writers who came after him, perhaps the most ironic show of respect was that reportedly given him by his Turkish adversary. Upon retaking the city of Krujë in 1478 and locating Kastrioti-Skanderbeg's grave in Saint Nicholas Catholic Church, the Turks disinterred the general and distributed his bones, holding them as talismans that would bring them good luck.

Books

Brahaj, Jaho, and Skender Sina, *Gjergj Kastrioti Skenderbeu,* 1967.

Hutchins, Raymond, editor, *Historical Dictionary of Albania,* Scarecrow Press, 1996.

Logoreci, Anton, *The Albanians,* 1977.

Noli, Fan S., *Georges Castrioti Scanderbeg,* 1947.

Online

Albanian.com, http://www.albanian.com/main/culture/famous/skendergeg.html.

The Ottoman Conquest of Albania, http://www.workmall.com/wfb2001/albania/ (March 12, 2003). □

Urho Kekkonen

Urho Kekkonen (1900–1986) was Finland's president from 1956 to 1981. He kept the nation on a steady political course, despite continuing to keep that nation actively politically neutral to assure peaceful relations with its powerful neighbor, the Soviet Union. This policy became known as "Finlandization" by detractors.

Youth Spent in War, Journalism, Sport

Urho Kaleva Kekkonen was born on September 3, 1900, in Pielavesi, Finland, the son of a farmer. His father later became employed in some aspect of timber operations. His career has been variously de-

scribed as a sawmill operator, timber foreman, and forestry manager. His mother was a farmer's daughter. The family lived in the rural province of Kainuu. Kekkonen attended the Lyseo Lukio Kajaani. He was not an exemplary student and had to repeat the seventh grade.

Kekkonen originally planned to become a writer. He frequently wrote short stories and plays. Among his influences were Jack London, Jules Verne, and Mark Twain. His other favorite subjects were history and gymnastics.

He became a war correspondent during the Finnish Civil War, which was fought in 1916 through 1917. He fought in the White Army and reported from their positions in Eastern Finland. During his service, Kekkonen commanded an execution patrol squad. As such, he was witness to the execution of six Red Army prisoners.

After the war, Kekkonen continued his journalistic career at *Kajaanin Lehti,* a newspaper. He also worked as a magazine columnist. He was active in other organizations including the Academic Karelia Society.

He made his entry onto the world stage via international athletics where he won an Olympic gold medal in the high jump. He also was an active member of The Finnish Sports Organization and the Finnish Olympic Committee. This served as his springboard into politics.

He married Sylvi Uino, who was a writer, in 1926. They met while she was working in the secretariat of the security police. They would eventually have two children. Kekkonen graduated from the University of Helsinki with a

Bachelor of Civil Law degree in 1928. He completed his doctoral degree in 1936.

Began Ascent in Finnish Government

In 1933, Kekkonen joined the Agrarian or Maalaisliitto party, which would become known as the Center party in 1965. Among his first political jobs was a post at the ministry of agriculture. He made his ascent in Finnish politics from his post as a parliament member. He served in various national political offices between 1936 and 1956. During World War II, Kekkonen was director of the Karelian evacuees welfare center and commissioner for coordination. He was Finland's prime minister from 1950 until 1956.

Kekkonen was also known as a political columnist. He adopted numerous pseudonyms for publishing this work beginning in 1942. His noms de plumes included Pekka Peitsi ("Peter Pikestaff"), Olli Tampio, Veljenpoika, and Liimatainen. His work frequently appeared in magazines including *Suomen Kuvalehti,* even during his tenure as prime minister. He once demurred being considered as a writer, saying "I haven't even written a single poem."

In 1950, he lost his bid for the presidency to Juho Kusti Paasikivi. Kekkonen wrote a political pamphlet "Onko Maallamme Malttia Vaurastua" ("Does our country have the patience to get rich?"), published in 1954. In the document, he laid out his ideas on Finnish economic policy.

Won Election, Adopted Policy Known as "Finlandization"

Two years later when he ran again for president, he was elected by a two vote margin over Paasikivi. This was the last national election the country would hold until 1981. It was feared any open election might jeopardize Finland's relations with the neighboring Soviet Union and compromise the nation's independence. In fact, every Finnish attempt to hold a national election was said to be seen by the Soviets as a desire by the Finns to put an end to their neutrality.

Perhaps to outsiders this policy might have seemed as equal parts Finnish cowardice and Soviet bullying. It is difficult, however, to understand in a vacuum. Finland achieved political independence from Russia during the Russian Revolution. During World War II, the Soviet Union invaded Finland in 1939 and 1944, forcing its neighbor to reduce its borders. Once World War II had ended, Finland chose to adopt a policy of political neutrality for the sake of self-preservvation. This was not initiate by Kekkonen, but certainly he made sure relations with the Soviets were never in jeopardy. The nation had, under Kekkonen, become what *The New Republic* writer Joyce Lasky Shub characterized as " a silent victim of Soviet power."

Walter Laqueur, writing in *Commentary,* observed that in the 1970s Finland had to kowtow, by virtue of its proximity to Soviet Union, to display "readiness to acquiesce in Soviet wishes." This Kekkonen-extended political deference policy became known as "Finlandization." Richard Lowenthal was said to have originated the phrase in the 1960s to describe this strategic political subordination,

but Laqueur is credited with modifying the term to fit with the Finns' self-imposed submissive policies, which were adopted well before being approached by their overbearing neighbor.

Laqueur said "given Finland's geopolitical situation, it was obvious that certain concessions toward the Soviets had to be made. But I also argued that Urho Kekkonen . . . had carried this trend much too far (though he himself was not a Communist or even a socialist). It was not the policy of wisdom, maturity, and responsibility that Kekkonen and his supporters claimed, and furthermore it set a bad example for the rest of Europe."

This issue is still open to debate and has been examined closely by political commentators and historians. So too has Kekkonen's role in Finnish-Soviet relations. There is no clear consensus on these issues.

Enjoyed Reputation as an Effective Deal-Maker

Kekkonen himself, however, is said to have been a gregarious leader. Seppo Salonen, an editor of one of Finland's leading newspapers told *The New Republic* in 1983 that Kekkonen could "get anybody to do anything. When he wanted to score a point with [Soviet leaders Nikita] Khrushchev or [Leonid] Brezhnev, he'd get them into a sauna and tell them funny stories."

While in office, Kekkonen developed a reputation for following through on every deal he struck. He made good on five-year trade agreements with the Soviets throughout the 1960s. He also brought Finland to the attention of the Common Market. As a result, Finland became one of the world's leading producers of oil rigs.

Perhaps it was his earlier interest in writing or a result of his marriage to an author, but nevertheless Kekkonen made sure to keep informed about writing and the arts throughout his career. Young writers and artists were frequently guests at his residence, Tamminiemi. After Hannu Salama, the writer, was tried and convicted on blasphemy charges in connection with his writing the novel *Juhannustanssit* ("Midsummer Dance") in 1968, Kekkonen immediately pardoned him.

Kekkonen left office in 1981. There remains debate about how his retirement came about. Some suggest he was pressured into retirement. Other opinions suggest ill health led him to step down. He was succeeded by Mauno Koivisto, a Social Democrat.

Diary-Keeping Offered Insight into Kekkonen

Kekkonen continued to live in Tamminiemi until his death. He reportedly continued to write and read frequently, favoring authors such as Anatole France, Mika Waltari, and a number of other Finnish authors and works such as Machiavelli's *The Prince* and *Don Quixote.* The residence is now the Urho Kekkonen Home Museum.

About two years into his first term as president, he had started keeping a diary, a practice which he faithfully continued until 1981, shortly before his resignation. The diaries were never meant to be published, but in 2000, his son, Matti Kekkonen, and his grandson, Timo Kekkonen, consented to their publication in a four-volume set. According to the newspaper *Helsingin Sanomat*, "The only parts to be left out of the books will be Kekkonen's observations about his own family. There are to be indications in the published work whenever a cut is made."

Ironically, Kekkonen never completed his memoirs. The first volume was completed by Paavo Haavikko in 1981. Later, Juhani Suomi wrote a multi-volume biography of Kekkonen, a project that has spanned some two decades. Suomi also contributed historical perspectives to the diaries and has been credited for his ability to read Kekkonen's handwriting.

Rumors Persisted As Did Legacy Debates

Even after leaving politics and well after his death, rumor and conjecture continued to swirl about Kekkonen. One such rumor held that he had been a Soviet agent, but, says Laqueur, "they were dismissed as base calumnies by his official biographer—who denied everyone else access to the relevant archival material." When the files of the Central Committee of the Soviet Communist Party (CPSU) were eventually made public, it became clear Kekkonen and his cronies "had been paid many millions of finnmarks through the office of the KGB: some of this money was used for their election campaigns, but there were also payments for personal use." But, notes Laqueur, "perhaps he would have acted as he did even if the Soviets had never paid him a single ruble."

More controversy arose when a tell-all book by Anita Hallama was released in 2001. She claimed to have had an affair with Kekkonen that had started in the early 1960s. Her husband was the Finnish ambassador to the Soviet Union. Reuters said the publication of this correspondence between the two served to confirm the "open secret" about their relationship. Each of their spouses purportedly knew about this relationship. The book delved into how Kekkonen developed policy, purportedly even how he discussed specific issues with Hallama.

"Urho Kekkonen was a great statesman in the true meaning of the word," said Finnish Prime Minister Paavo Lipponen in a September 3, 2000, speech marking the Urho Kekkonen centenary seminar at the House of Estates. "The aim of Finland's active policy of neutrality—as Kekkonen, not the Soviet Union, understood it was to strengthen Finland's international standing. Good relations with the USSR prepared the way for consistent integration into cooperation between the Western democracies. . . . Finland was neither an outpost of the West nor a cat's-paw of the Soviet Union. When certain Western commentators saw fit to cast aspersions about us in conversation, I couldn't help asking what exactly their own countries did in 1940.

"Talk of Finlandization is justified, but in the case of foreign policy it's valid to ask which did better, the cat or the mouse. Finland came out on top in the Cold War," continued Lipponen. He says at the end of his term in office, however, Kekkonen "was interfering in the action of the Prime Minister and the Government in a way that was totally unacceptable. . . . The neo-worship and concentration of power that had grown up around the old man kept him in office too long. On the other hand, maybe Kekkonen himself knew no other way of life, and would have been unable to resist interfering in things as ex-President."

Several politicians and political commentators have noted that there has yet to be any sufficient distance from events to truly gauge what impact on Finland and the world Kekkonen might have had or to accurately determine what his legacy might be. "The jury is still out on what sort of verdict history will hand down to Kekkonen. The image of the man presented by the diaries is naturally bound to the times of which they report, in just the same way as our present image of Kekkonen is bound to what we know now. And above all we know what ultimately happened to the Soviet Union," wrote Unto Hämäläinen, in a review of the diaries published in *Helsingin Sanomat* in 2002. "Kekkonen could not even begin to guess at such an outcome, and in his weak moments he lost faith that Finland would come through intact." Kekkonen died on August 31, 1986, in Helsinki, Finland.

Books

The Columbia Encyclopedia, Seventh Edition, 2002.
Contemporary Newsmakers, Gale Research, 1986.

Periodicals

Commentary, January 1993.
The New Republic, October 31, 1983.
Reuters, September 6, 2001.

Online

"Journal entries indicate President Kekkonen considered resignation during Czech crisis of 1968: A review of Volume II of Urho Kekkonen's diaries, (ed. Juhani Suomi)," *Helsingin Sanomat* online, October 1, 2002, http://www.helsinki-hs.net/news.asp?id=20021001IE9 (February 28, 2003).

"Kekkonen diaries to appear as a book," *Helsingin Sanomat* online, August 15, 2000, http://www.helsinki-hs.net/news.asp?id=20000815xx10 (February 28, 2003).

"Prime Minister Paavo Lipponen at the Urho Kekkonen centenary seminar at the House of Estates, September 3, 2000," Ajankohtaista, http://www.valtioneuvosto.fi/vn/liston/text.lsp?r=762&=en (February 28, 2003).

"The Silenced Media: The Propaganda War between Russia and the West in Northern Europe," book review, The American Historical Review, History Cooperative online, http://www.historycooperative.org/journals/ahr/105.1/br_158.html (February 28, 2003).

"Urho Kaleva Kekkonen," Lyseo Lukio Kajaani, http://lyseolukio.kajaani.fi/english/kekkonen.htm (February 28, 2003).

"Urho Kaleva Kekkonen," Pegasos website, http://www.kirjasto.sci.fi/ukekko.htm (February 28, 2003). □

Thomas Henry Kendall

Though his education was slight and he was plagued throughout his life with a variety of personal troubles, Thomas Henry Kendall (1839–1882) perse-

vered with his verse to become Australia's best known 19th century poet. Kendall grew up on the southern coast of the continent and drew his inspiration from the surrounding natural environment as well as the local traditions.

Early Life

Kendall was born on April 18, 1839, in Kirmington, Australia, a twin son of Basil Kendall and Melinda McNally. Kendall's given names were Thomas Henry, but he was often referred to as Henry Clarence Kendall. With twin brother Basil, he was brought up among the mountains and cool rainforests of the south coast of New South Wales. Like his father before him, Basil Kendall, the poet's father, had led an adventurous life at sea before becoming a farmer. Basil and his wife settled on farmland in Kirmington, living in a primitive cottage where their sons were born.

In 1844, Basil Kendall moved his family to the coastal regions of Illawarra in the Clarence River district. Before he got married, Basil Kendall had lost almost all of one lung and, by this time, his health had begun to fail. He found it hard to support his family, which had grown to include three daughters. He died in 1851 when Henry Kendall was 12 years old.

After Basil Kendall's death, Kendall's mother moved her children back to the south coast, near Woolongong, and the family was soon scattered, the children taken in by various relatives who cared for them. Henry and his brother lived with relatives on the South Coast in Illawarra. The area was said to be especially beautiful, and the environment made an enormous impression on Kendall. The lush and beautiful surroundings influenced some of his later landscape poetry, especially in such works as "Bell Birds," "September in Australia," and "Narrara Creek."

In 1855, after a brief education, the 14-year-old Kendall followed in the footsteps of his father and grandfather and went to sea. He worked as a cabin boy on a whaling brig, the *Plumstead,* which was owned by his uncle Joseph. During the two-year voyage in the South Seas, the vessel stopped at many islands. Like the landscape of Australia, the sublime beauty of the Pacific scenery made a powerful impression on Kendall, and he referred to his experiences in two of his poems, "The Ballad of Tanna" and "Beyond Kerguelen." He found the rigors of life at sea, however, to be extremely harsh, and most of his memories of the experience were bad ones. This reaction to the experience seemed in keeping with his natural disposition. All throughout his life, even when he was a young boy, Kendall was, for the most part, unhappy. As he grew older, he was increasingly shy, inclined toward melancholy, and possessed of a keen ambition that often made him feel thwarted in his efforts. These qualities would contribute to a difficult adult life.

Started Writing Poetry

In March of 1857, he returned to Australia. Living in Sydney, and only 16 years old, he became the primary support of his mother and sisters, working at various jobs including errand boy, shop assistant, and public servant. Kendall was very devoted to his mother, who was an attractive, strong-willed woman who recognized in her son a gift for written verse. Kendall credited her with his later literary accomplishments. He always felt that he inherited his talent from her, and she helped with his education and encouraged him to write poetry.

By 1859, Kendall's poetry began to appear in newspapers and magazines published in Sydney and Melbourne. His first verse that appeared in print, published under the title "O tell me, ye breezes," appeared in *The Australian Home Companion and Band of Hope Journal.*

His poetry drew favorable notices in Australia and England and would lead to important and supportive friendships with people such as Henry Parkes, an editor; Charles Harpur, a well-known Australian poet; and Daniel Henry Deniehy, an orator and critic. In 1859, Parkes, then the editor of *The Empire,* a newspaper, published a poem, "Silent Years," signed by one "Mr. H. Kendall, N.A.P." Kendall had attached those initials to his name. They stood for Native Australian Poet. The next year, Parkes published Kendall's verses on the wreck of the *Dunbar,* titled "The Merchant Ship," which Kendall had written when he was sixteen.

Established Important Friendships

At the time, Kendall also sent some poems to *The Sydney Morning Herald,* which gained the attention of Henry Halloran, a civil servant and amateur writer, who contacted Kendall and tried to help him. Later, it was said of Kendall that he may have been unlucky in life but lucky in friendships, which proved beneficial to a young man who was shy and nervous.

During this period, Kendall's mother introduced him to Sheridan Moore, a well-known literary critic. Moore admired Kendall's work and helped to get his poetry published. Moore later would introduce Kendall to James Lionel Michael, a Grafton solicitor, who hired Kendall as his clerk. Michael was a cultured, literate man who also wrote poetry. Both a friend and an employer, Michael opened his huge, personal library to Kendall and encouraged the young man in his own poetic pursuits.

After employment in Grafton, Kendall had a somewhat nomadic work history and changed jobs and locations several times. For a while, he work in Dungog on the Williams River and then at Scone, where he only worked for a month or two before he returned to Sydney. In October of 1862, while living in Sydney, Kendall published his first volume of poetry, *Poems and Songs.* The collection gained favorable notices and proved to be popular.

More good reviews followed, including ones for his poem "The Empire" as well as for his work that appeared in the literary publication *Athenaeum* over the next four years. In 1866, his growing body of work received high praise by

G. B. Barton in his *Poets and Prose Writers of New South Wales.*

In August of 1863, Parkes used his influence to secure Kendall a clerkship in the Surveyor-General's Department in Sydney at 150 pounds a year. In 1866, he was transferred to the Colonial Secretary's Office, where he earned 200 pounds a year. He combined these positions with some journalism work and continued writing poetry. His poetry from this period would later be published in two volumes, *Leaves from an Australian Forest* (1869) and *Songs from the Mountains* (1880). The poems demonstrated his appreciation of nature and of the beautiful Australian landscape and bush.

Marriage and Financial Difficulties

In 1867, despite his natural shyness, he gave a series of lectures at the Sydney School of Arts. After one of these lectures, coincidentally titled ''Love, Courtship and Marriage,'' Kendall met Charlotte Rutter, daughter of a government medical officer and accompanied her home. They immediately fell in love and married the next year, the same year that Kendall received a prize for the best Australian poem for ''A Death in the Bush.'' The contest's judge, author Richard Hengist Horne, wrote an article in Melbourne and Sydney newspapers in which he praised Kendall as a true poet. He also stated that if the contest had awarded three prizes instead of one, Kendall would have received the other two prizes for his other submissions, ''The Glen of Arrawatta'' and ''Dungog.''

The award and the praise bolstered Kendall's confidence enough that he decided he wanted to work exclusively as a writer. He resigned his post in the Colonial Secretary's Office in March of 1869 and moved to Melbourne with his wife and their recently born daughter. Kendall opted to move to that city because, at the time, it was a center of literary activity. Still, he found it difficult to establish himself on his writing alone. He tried to work as a full-time journalist, but his efforts met with little success. His second volume of poetry, *Leaves from Australian Forests,* received good reviews but made little money.

Suffered a Nervous Breakdown

Besides the financial problems, Kendall experienced some personal tragedies. In April of 1869, Michael, his friend and former employer, was found dead in the Clarence River. Also, in June, Harpur, the fellow poet who had encouraged Kendall, passed away. Meanwhile, personal problems plagued the troubled poet. By 1870, he and his wife lived in poverty, and he was suffering a drinking problem. After they returned to New South Wales that year, Kendall suffered a nervous breakdown and was placed in an institution.

When healthy again, Kendall again sought work as a journalist, writing prose and poetry, but his earnings were small. He also established friendships with George Gordon McCrae and Lindsay Gordon, two leading figures of the Melbourne literary scene. The friendships provided Kendall with encouragement but also brought him sadness. Kendall

and Gordon had become very close, so it was devastating to Kendall when Gordon committed suicide at the age of 37.

The next two years were particularly troublesome for Kendall. The depression brought on by his friend's death further darkened his already melancholy spirit. In addition, his poor business sense and his alcoholism resulted in poverty that in turn led to a temporary breakdown of his marriage. Then, in 1871, his first-born daughter, Araluen, died. This, combined with his lack of success, led him increasingly to seek solace in alcohol. He returned to Sydney a broken man, and he would spend periods in a Sydney asylum seeking a cure for his addiction.

Attained Peace in Later Years

Fortunately for Kendall he recovered, thanks to the efforts of his devoted wife, who reconciled with him, and the help of some friends. He emerged from the darkest period of his life to find personal peace and produce his best poetic works.

Those friends—George and Michale Fagan—were timber merchants in Brisbane, and they took care of Kendall until he was well enough to take a position as storekeeper with their company. For the remaining years of his relatively short life, Kendall lived a tranquil existence with his wife and family. By this time, Kendall had two sons, and in 1876 he would have another son and a daughter.

During these final years, Kendall received some gratifying recognition for his talents. In 1879, he wrote the lyrics for the opening Cantata sung at the Sydney International Exhibition. He also won a prize for a poem he wrote about the Exhibition. In addition, his third collection of poetry, *Songs from the Mountains* (1890) earned him a huge profit. This last book published while he was still alive is generally regarded to include his best work, reflecting a greater command of the craft and demonstrating a high level of imagination.

In 1881, his old friend Parkes helped him secure the position of Inspectorship of State Forests at 500 pounds a year. The experience Kendall gained in the Fagan brothers' timber business proved especially helpful. However, by this time in his life, Kendall's health began failing, and the outdoor work drained him physically. During one of his forest inspections, he caught a chill that affected his lungs and brought about tuberculosis. He went to Sydney for treatment, but he died there on August 1, 1882, in his wife's arms. He was only 43 years old. He was buried at Waverley, which overlooked the ocean.

Kendall's wife survived him for more than 40 years. In all, they had seven children. The town Kendall in northern New South Wales was named after him. Kendall has been remembered long after his death, and a compilation of his work, *The Poetical Works of Henry Kendall,* was published in 1966.

Today, many regard his poetry to be the best produced by any Australian poet, and individual poems have been described as ''singing pictures.'' His poetry has also been described as mellifluous and highly descriptive. Modern scholars marvel that he was able to produce such a copious and effective body of work in light of his personal troubles as well as the harsh surroundings of 19th century Australia.

Books

Kendall, Henry, *Leaves from Australian Forests: Poetical Works of Henry Kendall,* Lloyd O'Neil, 1970.

Online

"Henry Kendall: Australian Poet," *ImagesAustralia.com* http://www.imagesaustralia.com/henrykendall.htm (March 15, 2003).
"Henry Clarence Kendall," *Bartleby.com,* http://www.bartleby .com/224/1202.html (March 15, 2003).
"The Poems of Henry Kendall," *Project BookRead,* http://tanaya .net/Books/phknd10/index1.html (March 15, 2003).
Stevens, Bertram, "Biographical Notes, *Henry Kendall-Preface,*" http://www.krackatinni.netfirms.com/Henry-Kendall.html (March 15, 2003). □

Khalid bin Abdul Aziz Al-Saud

Khalid bin Abdul Aziz Al-Saud (1912–1982) was Saudi Arabia's fourth king, reigning from 1975 to 1982. Like his brother, King Faisal, whom he succeeded to the throne, Khalid was most at home in the desert. His prior government service included positions as Governor of the Hijaz (from 1932 to 1934) and Minister of the Interior, starting in 1934.

The Al-Saud Royal Family

The stability of Saudi Arabia derives largely from its ruling Al-Saud family. Although outsiders have no way of knowing how large the family actually is, estimates have placed its size at between five and eight thousand adults. The size and wealth of the Al-Saud family have created a system of family politics quite unlike any previously known.

The modern history of Saudi Arabia dates to 1747 when Muhammad Bin Saud, who ruled the Arabian peninsula, allied himself with the Muslim scholar Muhammad Bin Abdul Wahhab to found the modern state. For most of the nineteenth century, control of the Arabian peninsula was in the hands of the Al-Saud family. In 1902, Abdul Rahman captured Riyadh, which marked the beginning of the unification of the region's diverse tribes into one nation that would take 30 years to achieve.

The current Kingdom of Saudi Arabia had its beginnings on September 23, 1932, when one of Abdul Rahman's sons, Abdul Aziz Bin Abdul Rahman Al-Saud (hereafter called Abdul Aziz Al-Saud), declared himself king. The kingdom's sovereignty was recognized by most of the nations of the world. In 1933, the king commissioned a survey aimed at identifying Saudi Arabia's natural resources, and four years later, oil was discovered. Commercial oil production began in 1938. Revenues from the country's oil resources drove subsequent efforts to modernize Saudi Arabia through a series of five-year development plans.

Under Abdul Aziz Al-Saud, the order of royal succession remained in question. As a result of his attempts to unify the various tribes on the Arabian peninsula, he had married many women from important tribes, and fathered 36 sons. At the time of his death, his oldest surviving sons were Saud bin Abdul Aziz and Faisal bin Abdul Aziz. The next two sons, in order of seniority, were Muhammad bin Abdul Aziz (born 1910) and Khalid bin Abdul Aziz (born 1912).

In May 1933 Saud was designated heir apparent, even though the Saudi system of succession was not based on primogeniture. Khalid, meanwhile, was acquiring authority under Faisal's supervision in the Hijaz. Starting in 1943, Saud, Faisal, Muhammad, and Khalid began assuming joint control of Saudi Arabia's destiny.

Following the death of King Abdul Aziz in 1953, his son Saud Bin Abdul Aziz inherited the throne. During his eleven-year reign, King Saud established Saudi Arabia's welfare programs and contributed to Islamic causes.

By 1960, Khalid was effectively next in line in succession to the throne, after his brother Faisal. Muhammad's health problems had kept him out of the line of succession. Khalid was by then known to have a heart problem, but he did not appear to have any interest in becoming king.

Saud was deposed by his brother Faisal in 1964, after health problems made it difficult for him to continue on the throne. Under Faisal, the country achieved sustained economic stability and growth. Faisal also instituted a major national development program based on Saudi Arabia's enormous oil revenues.

Upon becoming king, Faisal named Khalid heir designate. In 1967, Faisal appointed Interior Minister Fahd second in line to the throne after Khalid.

In March 1975, Faisal was shot to death at a reception in the royal palace. The assassination did not seem in any way related to a dispute about succession, however.

King Khalid bin Abdul Aziz Al-Saud

Following Faisal's death, a new Council of Ministers was announced in March 1975. Khalid assumed the posts of both prime minister and foreign minister. One of Faisal's sons became minister of state for foreign affairs. Fahd, meanwhile, was appointed first deputy prime minister and minister of the interior.

Khalid had the immediate advantage of being a descendant of the royal family through both parents. His mother, Jawharah bint Musa'id, was a granddaughter of Jalwi b. Turki, who was a son of the sixth Saudi emir.

In May 1975, the government announced its second five-year plan (covering 1975 to 1980), a move that required some government reorganization. Then in September, the last brother of King Abdul Aziz retired as finance minister, altering the political composition of the Council of Ministers. That October, to accommodate these developments, a major reshuffling in the Council took place. Some have speculated that Khalid and his heir apparent Fahd sought through the reshuffle to purge the council of those loyal to Faisal, and instead advance their own favorites.

Khalid had already had some training in Saudi political affairs. He had made his first appearance on the military and political stage when his father sent him on an observation mission along the Trans-Jordanian border during the Ikhwan rebellion. At the age of 19, he had stood in for his brother Faisal as acting viceroy of the Hijaz. He represented Saudi Arabia in 1934 when he signed an agreement ending war between Yemen and his country. And in 1939, he traveled with Faisal to London. He was appointed by Saud as acting prime minister in 1960, at a time when Saud was battling his half brothers for power; although the appointment meant very little in terms of a transfer of power, it established Khalid's position in the line of succession.

During Khalid's reign, he was assisted by Fahd, his first deputy prime minister. In May 1975, a royal decree assigned Fahd full responsibility for daily management of Saudi Arabia. Khalid retained the powers of king, as well as the support of the family.

Health Problems

But Khalid's absences from Saudi Arabia to deal with his health problems eventually cut into his authority. In 1972, he underwent open-heart surgery in Cleveland, Ohio. In 1977, he had hip surgery in London. Rumors eventually began to circulate that he would abdicate. Finally, in 1978, he was hospitalized in Cleveland for further heart surgery. While there seemed to be general agreement that Fahd would step in should Khalid leave the throne, there was no consensus about who would be Fahd's heir apparent. But when the king's health improved following his open-heart surgery in 1978, the issue was set aside.

Under Khalid, Saudi Arabia weathered several major political shake-ups. With the signing of the Camp David agreement in 1979, Saudi Arabia cut off its financial aid to Egypt. In November of that year, a group of Sunni Muslims barricaded themselves inside the Holy Mosque of Mecca. Although they held out for 15 days, eventually as many as 200 were killed. In 1980, Saudi Arabia assumed full control of Aramco.

Khalid's Monarchy

King Khalid and his half-brother and heir apparent Fahd shared power in a more fluid way than had Khalid and his brother, King Faisal. Like his brother, Khalid assumed the roles of both prime minister and king, but unlike King Faisal, Khalid chose to delegate many of the ministerial responsibilities to his heir apparent. But the extent of Khalid's delegation of responsibility to Fahd also fluctuated with the king's health and the political standing of Fahd.

During Khalid's reign, family rivalries were more subdued than under his predecessors. Instead, Saud family politics became characterized by the presence of multiple centers of influence. As a result, in spite of Khalid's recurring health problems, he was able to counter Fahd's political ambitions. Other centers of power, including the National Guard and the Royal Intelligence, reported directly to the king. Many government ministers refused to keep Fahd advised of their activities, frustrating Fahd's attempts to become the country's de facto prime minister.

Also contributing to the decentralization of power was the continuation in office under Khalid of princes who had built up entrenched bureaucracies during King Faisal's reign. The splitting of power between Khalid and Fahd contributed to the independence of these princes. But as older princes left their government positions, and were replaced by younger ones, the internal politics within the Saud family became complicated by the presence of shifting allegiances.

Domestic and Foreign Policy Achievements

Khalid's achievements in domestic and foreign policy were not inconsiderable, despite his suffering from a serious heart condition. As already noted, shortly after coming to the throne, Khalid initiated Saudi Arabia's second Five Year Plan, which established the infrastructure for the future prosperity of his country.

On the foreign policy front, Khalid played a role in attempting to resolve the Lebanese civil war. An Arab peace conference was held in Riyadh, Saudi Arabia, in October 1976. This conference, followed by an Arab League meeting in Cairo the same month, temporarily brought hostilities in the Lebanese Civil War to a halt. In 1981, Khalid convened a historic summit of Arab nations.

The Iran-Iraq war erupted in September 1980. Iraq had long posed a threat to the monarchies of the Arabian peninsula. After Iran recovered from the attack by Iraq, the threat of Islamic revolution seemed to replace any threat posed by Iraq. The Persian gulf principalities that had traditionally served as buffer states between Saudi Arabia and Iran and Iraq had, meanwhile, begun experiencing increased subversive activity within their borders by Iranian and Iraqi agents. After Saudi citizens were arrested in Bahrain in 1981, Saudi Arabia increased its cooperation with the mini states, and eventually formed the Gulf Cooperation Council.

The Gulf Co-operation Council (GCC) was founded in 1981 with the signing of the organization's constitution by the kings and princes of Bahrain, Kuwait, Qatar, the Kingdom of Saudi Arabia, the Sultanate of Oman, and the United Arab Emirates. Its goal included achieving unity between member states and enhancing co-operation between peoples of the region. The GCC also set out to bring into conformity laws in the member countries pertaining to economics and financial affairs; commercial, customs and transportation affairs; education and cultural affairs; social and health affairs; and communication, informational, political, legislative and administrative affairs. In addition the organization sought to encourage joint progress in science and technology.

Under Khalid, Saudi Arabia's standard of living rose considerably, and the country achieved enhanced economic and political strength in the international arena. Khalid actually oversaw the implementation of two of the country's five-year development plans, the first of these being the one that lasted from 1975 to 1979, and another that lasted from 1980 to 1984. During Khalid's reign, the country began to diversify its economy and made progress toward the completion of its infrastructure.

Khalid died on June 13, 1982, one week after civil war broke out in Lebanon. Fahd subsequently ascended to the throne.

Books

Bligh, Alexander, *From Prince to King: Royal Succession in the House of Saud in the Twentieth Century*, New York University Press, 1984.

Kechichian, Joseph A., *Succession in Saudi Arabia*, Palgrave, 2001.

Online

"King Khalid bin Abdul Aziz," http://www.saudinf.com/main/b45.htm (January 2003).

"Saudi Arabia, History," http://www.the-saudi.net/saudi-arabia/history.htm (January 2003).

"Saudi Arabia, Modern History," http://www.saudiembassy.org.uk/profile-of-saudia-arabia/history/modern-history.htm (January 2003). ☐

Jamaica Kincaid

A significant voice in contemporary literature, Jamaica Kincaid (born 1949) is widely praised for her works of short fiction, novels, and essays in which she explores the tenuous relationship between mother and daughter as well as themes of anticolonialism. A native of the island of Antigua, Kincaid is considered one of the most important women Caribbean writers. Over a career that has spanned more than three decades, Kincaid has earned a reputable place in the literary world for her highly personal, stylistic, and honest writings.

J amaica Kincaid was born Elaine Potter Richardson on May 25, 1949, in the capital city of St. John's on Antigua, a small island in the West Indies that was colonized by the British in 1632 and achieved full independence in 1981. Her mother, Annie Richardson, was an emigre from Dominica. Her stepfather, David Drew, was a carpenter and cabinetmaker. Kincaid's maternal grandmother, a Carib Indian, also played an important role in her early life. Kincaid's biological father, Roderick Potter, was never involved in her upbringing. Her family was poor: they had no electricity, running water, or plumbing in their home.

Kincaid was an only child until she was nine, at which time the first of her three brothers was born. Until their birth, Kincaid had enjoyed the sole attention of her mother, who taught her to read when she was three and had given her a copy of the *Oxford English Dictionary* when she turned seven. However, with the arrival of her brothers, Kincaid's relationship with her mother changed dramatically. She was no longer a dependent young child and her importance in her mother's eyes was severely diminished because she was female.

Although Kincaid was intellectually gifted, she was not given encouragement in the British public school she attended on the island. Her teachers frequently found her attitude rude and considered her a troublemaker. Nevertheless, she was an avid reader and spent much time at the city's library, getting to know and admire the young librarian who worked there. Kincaid's love for books was so fierce that she stole some from the library and hid them under her family's porch. The bookish and small child was not well liked by her peers, who often picked fights with her and beat her up. Discussing this period in her life, Kincaid recalled in a *Kenyon Review* interview with Moira Ferguson in 1994, "I would come home with my clothes in tatters and my face scratched up, and my mother would take me back to the person who had beaten me up and say 'fight, fight' and I couldn't fight. I would just cry and cry. . . ." Eventually, after years of abuse, when she was 11, Kincaid finally did fight back and win. After that, she was no longer tormented and she actually took on a leadership role.

As a girl there were few options available for Kincaid. She would have liked to have attended university in Antigua and remained there after becoming a teacher or a librarian, but she was not given that opportunity. Despite the shortcomings of her early education, she did acquire a strong background in English literature, studying the works of Shakespeare, Wordsworth, Keats, and the King James version of the Bible. Kincaid especially loved the works of Charlotte Bronte, reading *Jane Eyre* numerous times.

Self-Exile in the United States

In 1966, shortly after turning 17, Kincaid was sent to the United States to work as an au pair for an affluent family in Scarsdale, New York. She was expected to send money home to her family, but she would not. She received letters from home, but she did not open them. It was in this state of self-exile that Kincaid would shape her new life away from the unhappiness she had felt in Antigua. Shortly after leaving her job in Scarsdale, Kincaid found work for an Upper East Side family in New York City. After this move, she left no forwarding address and was cut off from her family until her return to Antigua 20 years later. While working in New York, Kincaid continued her education at a community college, earned a high school equivalency diploma, and began taking photography courses at the New School for Social Research. She later studied photography at Franconia College in New Hampshire on a scholarship, though she never earned a college diploma. When asked in a 1996 interview with Dwight Garner in *Salon* if she had any aspirations to become a writer when she came to the United

States, she stated flatly, "None. Absolutely none. [When] I first arrived I was incredibly depressed and lonely. I didn't know there was such a world as the literary world. I didn't know anything, except maybe how to put one foot in front of the other."

Although Kincaid was not fully aware of her literary ambitions during her childhood and early years in New York, she had gained much from her voracious reading, all of which was of an English literary tradition. She had never been exposed to West Indian literature. When speaking to Ferguson, she acknowledged that as a child she would imagine stories and conversations in her head, but she never wrote them down. It was her experiences in photography that finally made her aware of writing. After watching the French film *La Jete* and reading Alain Robbe-Grillet, Kincaid felt her burst of inspiration. She told Ferguson, "I began to write poems. I began to write of my photographs—what I would take and [how] I would set them up. I would look at what I had written down, and that is how I would take the photograph. I would write down what I thought the picture should feel like. And I would try to take a picture of what I had written down."

Entrance to Literary World

After three years as an au pair, Kincaid left to become a secretary, model, and backup singer in a New York club. In 1970, with bleached blond hair, Kincaid enjoyed a freewheeling city lifestyle, sharing with Garner that she once attended a Halloween party dressed as Josephine Baker with only some bananas wrapped around her waist. She began to contribute pieces to *Ingenue,* a teen magazine. Her first published work, "When I Was Seventeen," was an interview with Gloria Steinem about the notable feminist's own teenage years. In 1973, Elaine Potter Richardson changed her name to Jamaica Kincaid mainly to keep her anonymity since she feared her family would disapprove of her writing and mock her efforts. After her contributions to *Ingenue* and the *Village Voice,* Kincaid began to make contacts with members of New York's literary society. One friend, Michael O'Donoghue, who was a founding writer for *Saturday Night Live,* introduced Kincaid to George Trow, who wrote the "Talk of the Town" column for *New Yorker* magazine. A strong friendship developed between the two and Kincaid began to accompany Trow when he researched bits for his column, adding her observations. William Shawn, editor of the *New Yorker,* ultimately asked Kincaid to write her own "Talk of the Town" piece. She submitted notes of her observations of the West Indian Day parade, and Shawn published the notes as a finished column. Beginning in 1976, Kincaid contributed regularly to the magazine as a staff writer under Shawn's mentorship. In 1978, she published her first work of fiction, the short story "Girl," in the *New Yorker.*

Kincaid acknowledged that Shawn helped her develop her voice and encouraged her to continue writing stories. Along with the significant development as a writer Kincaid received while working at the *New Yorker,* she also met Allen Shawn, a classical composer and son of Ted Shawn. They were married in 1979.

Literary Celebrity

In "Girl" and nine other sketches, often denoted "prose poems" by critics, that appeared in the 1983 collection *At the Bottom of the River,* Kincaid plumbed her early life in Antigua, developing a series of "fictional narratives" centering on a young Caribbean girl. The stories were marked by a lyrically poetic, incantatory, rhythmic voice. Perhaps the most-discussed piece in the collection is "Girl," which is one sentence uttered by a mother to her child, listing in repetitive scrutiny a series of commands. Her breakthrough collection earned Kincaid the Morton Dauwen Zabel Award from the American Academy and Institute of Arts and Letters.

Kincaid followed the publication of *At the Bottom of the River* with the slim novel *Annie John* in 1985. In this work, Kincaid writes a coming-of-age tale that focuses on the life of a young Caribbean girl. The theme of the mother-daughter relationship in which a mother devastatingly severs her bond with her daughter is at its core. This work was well received and critics praised its rhythmic quality, evocative images, and universal themes. Many critics have noted that her most significant theme, that of the mother-daughter bond, represents the larger issue of the powerful and the powerless, particularly as this relationship operates in a colonial culture.

The personal nature of so much of Kincaid's fiction is one of its salient features, and she admits that her difficult relationship with her own mother inspired her writing, though she maintains it was an act of salvation to write her thoughts down. "Writing is really such an expression of personal growth," she admitted to Ferguson. "I don't know how else to live. For me it is a matter of saving my life. I don't know what I would do if I didn't write. It is a matter of living in the deepest way." Noting the autobiographical element to her writing, she asserted that "My writing has been very autobiographical. The events are true to me. They may not be true to other people. I think it is fair for my mother to say, 'This is not me.' It is only the mother in the books I've written. It is only the mother as the person I used to be perceived her. . . . For me it was really an act of saving my life, so it had to be autobiographical."

Angry Voice Divided Readership

With the publication of her nonfiction work *A Small Place* in 1988 and her third fictional work, *Lucy,* in 1991, Kincaid was no longer the darling of the literary world. Reviewers were divided over the angry tone expressed in both works. In *A Small Place,* described as "an anti-travel narrative," Kincaid returns to Antigua after having been gone for 20 years. She ultimately skewers the white tourist who visits Antigua with no thought to the poverty and the long-endured oppression of the colonized natives, while also pointing out the corruption of the post-independent Antiguan government. Bob Gottlieb, editor of the *New Yorker* at the time, refused to publish any of the work in the magazine due to its angry tone. In her native Antigua, the government issued an informal ban on Kincaid, restricting her visits to the island from 1985 to 1992. Seemingly unaccepting of her resentment and frustrations, V.R. Peterson of

People compared Kincaid to West Indian writer V.S. Naipaul, maintaining that "where Naipaul is humane and appreciative of the dark corners of the human condition, Kincaid seems only vituperative and intemperate."

Kincaid drew similar criticism for the novel *Lucy.* *Annie John* ends with the protagonist leaving Antigua at the age of 17, and *Lucy* begins with the eponymous protagonist leaving the Caribbean at age 19 to come to the United States to work as an au pair for a wealthy New York City family. Commentators note a more bitter tone to this novel in which Lucy will not bend to the powers that hold sway. However, most still commend Kincaid's storytelling abilities. Reviewing the novel, the *Newsweek* book critic summarized "Vinegary Lucy doesn't bother to be likable, but her shrewdness and her gumption make her good company all the same."

Familial Bonds

Kincaid returned to her familiar theme of the mother-daughter relationship and the cruel outcomes of colonization with her dark portrayal of seventy-year-old Xuela Claudette Richardson, the narrator of her novel *The Autobiography of My Mother* published in 1996. The novel, set on the island of Dominica, presents the life of the narrator and the mother whom she never knew who had died in childbirth. Xuela's life is mired in loss, and, as Andrea Stuart noted in the *New Statesman,* "[*Autobiography of My Mother*] is simultaneously one of the most beautifully written books I have read, and one of the most alienating." In 1997 this complex novel was a finalist for the National Book Critics Circle Award for fiction and the PEN Faulkner Award.

In 1997 Kincaid published *My Brother,* a memoir of her youngest brother Devon Drew, who died of AIDS in 1996 at the age of 33. This highly personal work addresses not only the relationship Kincaid had with her brother—the two were alike in personality though they had spent little time together—as well as the continued themes of her resentful relationship with her mother and the devastating outcomes of a post-colonial culture. Reviewing the work in *Time* John Skow laments that while "there is deep, honest feeling here . . . it seems long past time for this gifted writer to tell us something new." In response to such criticism, Kincaid related to Garner, "I am not troubled . . . to be seen to be of one whole cloth—that all that I write is a further development of something. Perhaps it is musical in that way. My work is a chord that develops in many different ways. I couldn't help but write these books." Central to this work is Kincaid's discovery after Drew has died that he was homosexual and the oppressive secret he had kept throughout his life. Kincaid's ability to address the personal themes within a memoir that, according to Brad Goldfarb in *Interview,* is "an almost ruthless desire to get at the truth" and still relate them to such universal themes as familial bonds and the overarching question of post-colonial issues, helped her earn a nomination for a National Book Award.

Fragrant and Thorny

As a child, Kincaid had been surrounded by plants on Antigua, and her interest in gardening developed steadily throughout her adult life. In 1985, when her husband accepted a teaching position in Bennington, Vermont, the couple moved to this idyllic community with their two young children, Annie and Harold. Leaving the confines of the city, Kincaid had ample space to garden, and she published *My Garden (Book)* in 1999. This collection of essays marks a departure from the embittered tone of her previous works and was heralded as entertaining yet intelligent due to Kincaid's artful connection between gardening and philosophical and poetic reflections. While most reviewers concede that all of Kincaid's works, despite at times her harsh tone, are complex and stylistically unique, with *My Garden (Book)*, Kincaid seemed to have expressed similarly profound observations in a more gentle, even humorous tone.

Mr. Potter, Kincaid's tenth book, is a return to a West Indian setting and characters from her family background. The narrator, Elaine Cynthia Potter Richardson, ruminates over the empty life of Roderick Potter, her father who has had no part in her life. Acknowledging the characters' obvious connections to Kincaid's own life, Susan Walker asserts in the *Toronto Star* that "it's unlikely any reader will mistake these characters for actual people. They are too encased in literary language, too distilled, almost mythic in the way they come to represent the way many people's lives are shaped by history."

While many of Kincaid's works are short in length, they have never failed to elicit respect, if at times reluctantly. Kincaid herself is a forthright person who speaks candidly. After she left the *New Yorker* in 1995, she spoke quite openly about her disgust at the "vulgarity" that the magazine produced under the editorship of Tina Brown. Her frankness, however, is always tinged with humor as she told Garner, "[Brown's] actually got some nice qualities. But she can't help but be attracted to the coarse and vulgar. I wish there was some vaccine—I would sneak it up on her."

Kincaid has been awarded honorary degrees from Williams College (1991), Long Island College (1991), Amherst College (1995), Bard College (1997), and Middlebury College (1998). She continues to write from her home in Bennington, teaching creative writing at Bennington College and Harvard University.

Books

Authors and Artists for Young Adults, Volume 13, Gale, 1994.

Concise Dictionary of American Literary Biography Supplement: Modern Writers, 1900–1998, Gale, 1998.

Contemporary Authors Online, Gale, 2001.

Contemporary Black Biography, Volume 4, Gale, 1993.

Contemporary Literary Criticism, Gale, 2002.

Contemporary Novelists, 7th ed., St. James Press, 2001.

Feminist Writers, St. James Press, 1996.

Notable Black American Women, Book 1, Gale, 1992.

St. James Guide to Young Adult Writers, 2nd ed., St. James Press, 1999.

Periodicals

Advocate, December 9, 1997.

Christian Science Monitor, January 17, 1996.

Essence, March 1996.

Interview, October 1997.

Kenyon Review, Winter 1994.

Kirkus Reviews, March 1, 2002.

Library Journal, October 1, 1999.

Literary Cavalcade, February 2001.

Maclean's, June 3, 2002.

Mother Jones, September/October 1997.

Nation, June 15, 1985; February 18, 1991; February 5, 1996; November 3, 1997.

New Statesman, October 11, 1996.

New York Times Book Review, December 5, 1999.

Newsweek, October 1, 1990.

People, September 26, 1988; December 15, 1997.

Salon, January 13, 1996; December 20, 1999.

Time, February 5, 1996; November 10, 1997.

Times, July 20, 2002.

Toronto Star, May 27, 2002.

Women's Review of Books, March 2000; September 2002.

Online

"Jamaica Kincaid," *BBC World Service,* http://www.bbc.co.uk (February 11, 2003).

"Jamaica Kincaid," *Voices from the Gaps: Women Writers of Color,* http://voices.cla.umn.edu (February 11, 2003). □

Masaki Kobayashi

Masaki Kobayashi (1916–1996) was a Japanese film director best known for injecting social criticism of Japanese traditions and norms into his chosen art form. He made each of his films carefully, meticulously. As a result, his body of work is not large in comparison with that of his contemporaries, but he remains an important figure nevertheless.

"Renowned for powerful critiques of ethical issues and a strong sense of visual detail, Kobayashi's films are surprisingly political compared to his contemporaries in Japanese cinema," wrote Mike Pinksy on the DVD Verdict website. "Although Kobayashi is not as well known abroad as some other Japanese directors, his critical reputation is based on his uncompromising scrutiny of personal responsibility and his desire to expose the uncomfortable truths about social corruptions."

Early Career Interrupted by War

There is seemingly no documentation of Kobayashi's early life or personal life other than noting he was born on January 14, 1916, in Otaru, Japan, and spent his youth on the northern island of Hokkaido, Japan, in the port city of Otaru. In 1933 Kobayashi entered Waseda University in Tokyo where he began studies in philosophy and art. He was particularly interested in Buddhist sculpture. Kobayashi had planned to continue studying art history, but the Pacific War had already begun. ''In art history I knew it would require many more years of painstaking research for me to make a contribution, and the war made the future too uncertain,'' said Kobayashi in *World Film Directors*. ''But with film, I thought there might be a chance of leaving something behind.''

Upon Kobayashi's graduation in 1941, he went to work at Shochiku Film Company in Ofuna. His job was short-lived with the advent of Japanese involvement in World War II. Kobayashi, who is often described by film historians as having been a pacifist, was drafted by the Japanese Imperial Army in 1942. He loathed the military and as a form of protest, Kobayashi refused every promotion offered to him. He was dispatched into combat first in Manchuria, then to the Ryukyu Islands. Kobayashi was captured and taken as a prisoner of war on Okinawa. He remained on Okinawa until the war ended.

Career Resumed with Lengthy Apprenticeship

Following the war, Kobayashi was able to resume his career in film and rejoin the staff at the Shochiku studios. Beginning in November 1946, he commenced what would be a six-year long apprenticeship as an assistant director. Kobayashi worked under Keisuke Kinoshita on 15 films. Kinoshita was not only Kobayashi's supervisor, he also served as his mentor. The two directors wrote one film together in 1949.

Kobayashi made his directorial debut in November 1952 with *Musoko no seishun (My Sons' Youth)*. The film followed a middle-class family with two teenage sons who were about to go on their first dates. For Kobayashi's second effort, he used a script written by his mentor titled *Magakoro (Sincere Heart)*. The script was a gift given by Kinoshita to commemorate Kobayashi's promotion within the studio.

''Kobayashi's instinct for self-preservation within the Shochiku system was correct,'' according to Audie Bock in *World Film Directors*. ''In Kinoshita he had an excellent teacher and powerful patron. While none of the early films he made under direct Kinoshita tutelage are bad films, they are more his mentor's late style than his own, and very different from what Kobayashi already knew he wanted to do as a director.''

That same year, Kobayashi decided it was time to embark on his own. The result was an independently made film called *Kabe atskui heya (Room with Thick Walls)*. For the making of this film, Kobayashi started his own production company, Shinei Productions. Shochiku Film Company agreed to distribute the film. The subject he chose to examine for this film was an unvarnished look at Japanese wartime atrocities. The script, by the novelist Kobo Abê, was based on the diaries of lower level Japanese war criminals. The film was not released until 1956. The studio feared offending Americans with its subject matter. Ultimately, the film won the nation's Peace Culture Prize for that year.

Explored Controversial Subjects in Several Films

Kobayashi went on to make four more films with Shochiku. By 1956 Kobayashi considered himself to be sufficiently well established in his career, comfortable enough to make what would be a controversial film about corruption within professional baseball, *Anata kaimasu (I'll Buy You)*. The film that followed it was no less controversial. *Kuroi kawa (Black River, 1957)* was another expose. This time Kobayashi peeked into the corruption and criminal elements surrounding the military bases in Japan.

The controversy these films stirred up dimmed in comparison to that caused by the epic film *Ningen no joken (The Human Condition)*. The epic set in World War II was based on the six-volume novel by Jumpei Gomikawa. The film follows a single male character from the period of the Japanese occupation of Manchuria through the capture of Japanese soldiers by the Russians in 1945, after the Japanese surrender. As Pinksy wrote on the DVD Verdict website, ''Kobayashi was likely drawn to the material because it parallels his own wartime experiences.''

''*The Human Condition* feels above all uncompromisingly real. Effective use of exterior locations, detailed sets, minimal use of music, and an unflinching look at the horrible effect of war on human bodies (we are shown corpses killed by steam, torture, even executions on camera) force us to confront the realities of war,'' wrote Pinksy. ''All this adds up to a strong sense that we are watching something true, like a documentary in narrative form.''

Kobayashi chose to break the film into three parts, each of which was three hours or more in length. The film was ultimately entered into the Guinness Book of Records as the longest film in existence. The first film in the trilogy is known as *No Greater Love* (1959), set in 1943. It won the San Giorgio Prize at the Venice Film Festival and is regarded as a masterpiece. The other two films in the trilogy are *Road to Eternity* (1959) and *A Soldier's Prayer* (1961). Stanley Kubrick, the noted British director of films including *2001* and *Dr. Strangelove,* was said to have been inspired by the latter film in the trilogy, portions of which he used in creating the first segment of his own war film *Full Metal Jacket*.

Decade of Frustration Followed Successes

Kobayashi made a couple of other films before choosing to make a big budget picture. This blockbuster was *Kwaidan (Kaidan, 1964)*, a film composed of four distinct ghost stories by Lafcadio Hearn, which were based on traditional Japanese tales. The project had been in the planning for years. With *Kaidan* Kobayashi also abandoned the gritty realistic style for which he had become well known in favor of exploring beauty in a more stylized manner. It was also his first color film and is regarded as his most successful. The picture won the Special Jury Prize at the Cannes Film Festival.

His work in the 1960s was among his best. An essay in *International Dictionary of Films and Filmmakers* names *Seppuku (Harakiri,* 1962) and *Joiuchi (Rebellion,* 1967) as "Kobayashi's two finest films." These films utilize "historical settings to universalize his focus on the dissident individual. The masterly blend of style and content, with the unbending ritual of samurai convention perfectly matched by cool, reticent camera movement and elegantly geometric composition, marks in these two films the peak of Kobayashi's art."

The 1970s were difficult for Kobayashi. His films were categorically rejected by the studios for their social critiques. The industry had taken a distinctively different turn, favoring exploitation films over serious art. Kobayashi, Akira Kurosawa [best known for his films *Seven Samurai* (1954) and *Rashomon* (1951)], and two other film makers formed Yonki no Kai ("The Club of the Four Knights"). The idea was for the four to collaborate on a single film project. The partnership was aborted when the filmmakers could not reach consensus. With the effort's failure, each of the participants reluctantly decided to make a film for television.

For Kobayashi, the result of this was *Kaseki*, a television film based on the book by Yasushi Inoue. The project consisted of eight, one-hour segments. Filming took Kobayashi to different locations, including Europe. The project aired on television in 1972. According to the *International Dictionary of Films and Filmmakers,* Kobayashi is said to have considered the televised version "rough footage" for the cinema version. The series was later edited to 213 minutes and released as a feature film in 1975.

Chronicled War Crimes in Documentary

Kobayashi's next project was a disappointment, but the director redeemed himself with the film *Tokyo saiban (The Tokyo Trials,* 1983), a four-and-a-half-hour documentary epic. The film chronicles the events of the Pacific counterpart to the post-World War II Nuremberg Trials. During these war crimes trials before the International Military Tribunal for the Far East, 28 high profile Japanese who had been in the military or politics during the Second World War were tried by the Allies. All were found guilty. Seven, including Hideki Tojo, the former Japanese Prime Minister, were hanged. For this documentary, Kobayashi combed thousands of reels of news footage, including 30,000 reels from the United States Pentagon.

Joan Mellen in *The Nation* explains that the film "looks at the Tokyo war-crimes trial in light of the American adventure in Vietnam; the film closes with shots of the Hiroshima bombing. So much for war guilt." It was released in the United States in 1984 and also won the FIRPRESI Award at the 1985 Berlin International Film Festival.

The last Kobayashi film was *Shokutaku no nai ie* (variously translated as either *The Empty Table, House Without a Dining Table,* or *Fate of a Family,* 1985). The work is fictional, based on real events involving a stand-off between police and radical Japanese terrorists. In the film, many of the radicals' parents are shown apologizing publicly for their children in order to save face. One of the parent's refuses, thus, Kobayashi is able to make a larger comment on contemporary society's insistence on tradition.

Remembered for Perfectionism, Social Commentary

Among his frequent collaborators was Toru Takemitsu, a composer, and actor Tatsuya Nakadai. Kobayashi and Takemitsu began working together in 1962 on *Karamiai (The Inheritance). Shokutaku no nai ie* was the last film for both masters.

Kobayashi was known as a perfectionist. He took his time on the set, possibly completing only three final takes in a day's work, which would be considered a slow pace for a director. Each of his films was carefully crafted. He even went so far as to paint sets himself.

Kobayashi's volume of production is not large compared to some of his contemporaries, such as Kurosawa, but his films are considered an important body of work. In a website dedicated to a Kobayashi retrospective at Columbia University, the corpus of his work is described as being wholly based on his experiences during the war. "Whether historical dramas or stories set in modern Japan, they reflect the director's rejection of military or social authority wielded at the expense of the individual. Few artists of any time or any culture have argued more passionately than Kobayashi against the abuse of power. None has revealed more dramatically the cost of such power for a society or an individual."

Books

International Dictionary of Films and Filmmakers, Volume 2: Directors, St. James Press, 1996.
World Film Directors, Volume 2 1945–1985, The H.W. Wilson Company, 1988.

Periodicals

Asia Africa Intelligence Wire (From The Yomiuri Shimbun/Daily Yomiuri), August 8, 2002.
The Nation, November 10, 1984.

Online

Columbia University: Japanese Film Masters, http://www .columbia.edu/cu/ealac/jfm/ (February 10, 2003).
"Deep Focus: Masaki Kobayashi (1916–1996)," DVD Verdict, October 11, 2000, http://www.dvdverdict.com/columns/ deepfocus/kobayashi.shtml (February 10, 2003). □

L

Christine Ladd-Franklin

Christine Ladd-Franklin (1847–1930) was a noted logician and psychologist who added to the literature in both fields during the late nineteenth and early twentieth centuries. She proposed the antilogism, a major contribution to the field of logic. As a psychologist, she contributed theories of color vision. Despite her contributions, she was denied acceptance in the scientific community because she was a woman.

Ladd-Franklin was born Christine Ladd in Windsor, Connecticut, on December 1, 1847. Her parents came from influential and well-to-do families. Her father, Eliphalet Ladd, was a New York merchant and the nephew of William Ladd, founder of the American Peace Society. Her mother, Augusta Niles Ladd, was the niece of John Milton Niles, former postmaster-general of the United States. Augusta Ladd was a staunch supporter of women's rights who often attended suffrage meetings. In a letter to her sister, Augusta described a lecture she had attended, saying that women belonged "every place where a man should be." Her mother's beliefs regarding women's rights had an early influence on Ladd-Franklin during a time in American history when women's sphere was expected to be the home and family.

Ladd-Franklin, known as Kitty, was the oldest of three children in the family. She spent her childhood in her native town and in New York City until the age of 12, when her mother died. She then moved to Portsmouth, New Hampshire, to live with her paternal grandmother. She did excep-

tionally well in school where she studied Greek and math alongside boys who were preparing to attend Harvard University.

Ladd-Franklin's father was very warm and supportive. Father and daughter exchanged frequent letters in which Eliphalet Ladd encouraged his daughter's educational pursuits. In an article in *American Psychologist,* Laurel Furumoto said, "Kitty's father also abundantly praised her academic achievement and communicated an unwavering belief in her potential to excel." Ladd-Franklin graduated from Wilbraham Academy as valedictorian of her class.

Ladd-Franklin aspired to a career and wanted to attend Vassar College, a new college that would offer women a curriculum comparable to men's colleges. However, she faced some obstacles. Although Ladd-Franklin's father had supported her educational endeavors, he did not believe it was necessary for her to attend college. He was also experiencing financial difficulty and could not afford to pay college tuition. Ladd-Franklin's grandmother, who had raised her after Ladd-Franklin's mother died, believed that if Ladd-Franklin attended college, she would be too old to marry after graduation. Ladd-Franklin convinced her grandmother to allow her to attend college with the argument that she was not attractive enough to find a husband and that there was a shortage of men as a result of the Civil War. Therefore, she needed education in order to support herself. Finally, her grandmother gave in. Her father also agreed.

Attended Vassar

Untold Lives states that shortly before entering Vassar, Ladd-Franklin wrote in her diary, "Vassar! Land of my longing! Mine at last. In a month I shall pace the spacious corridors and busy myself in the volumes of forgotten lore at Vassar!" Ladd-Franklin's mother's sister, Juliet Niles, an-

her diary, "Sunday evening is the most miserable time of all the week. The burdens of the morrow look impossible to be born. Teaching I hate with a perfect hatred. . . . I shall not be able to endure it another year." Ladd-Franklin did continue teaching and also published articles about mathematics in the *Educational Times,* an English periodical, and *The Analyst,* an American publication.

Earned Graduate Degree

Ladd-Franklin applied to Johns Hopkins University in Baltimore as a graduate student. Although the school did not admit women, a mathematics professor, J. J. Sylvester, noticed her application. He was familiar with her writings and persuaded the university to admit her on a special status, which allowed her to attend only lectures given by Sylvester. After a year, the university allowed her to attend other lectures and granted her a $500 annual stipend, which she held for three years. Male students who received this award were called fellows, but Ladd-Franklin was denied this title and was not even listed on the roster of students at the university. Ladd-Franklin qualified for a PhD in 1882 but was denied the degree because she was a woman. The university eventually granted her degree in 1926, when she was nearly 80 years old.

While studying mathematics at Johns Hopkins, Ladd-Franklin became interested in symbolic logic, which was taught by C. S. Peirce. She published her thesis, "The Algebra of Logic," in Peirce's *Studies in Logic by Members of the Johns Hopkins University* in 1883. Ladd-Franklin's thesis proposed a way to analyze logical statements for validity using an inconsistent triad, which she called an antilogism. *Notable Mathematicians* defines an antilogism as "three statements that are together incompatible" and lists the following example: "It is impossible that any of these measures should be idiotic, for none of them is unnecessary, and nothing that is necessary is idiotic." Ladd-Franklin's work was praised in its time and is still regarded as a major contribution to the field of logic.

While attending Johns Hopkins, Ladd-Franklin met mathematics professor Fabian Franklin, who she married in 1882. Franklin was a native of Hungary who had worked as a civil engineer and surveyor before earning his PhD in Mathematics at Johns Hopkins. As a fellow academic, Franklin was extremely supportive and proud of his wife's work. The Franklins had a son, who lived only a few days, and a daughter, Margaret.

Studied Color Theory

Ladd-Franklin began studying vision and theories of color perception. It is unclear why Ladd-Franklin became interested in vision, but one possibility, according to Furumoto, is that she had suffered from eye troubles since adolescence. Ladd-Franklin published her first paper in the field in 1887.

As a married woman, Ladd-Franklin was denied a research position at American colleges and universities. In 1891 and 1892, Ladd-Franklin, her husband, and their daughter traveled to Germany where Franklin was pursuing mathematical research. Ladd-Franklin used the opportunity

other women's rights supporter, paid Ladd-Franklin's tuition to Vassar. Ladd-Franklin was interested in physics but could not pursue that subject in college because women were denied access to laboratories. She studied mathematics instead. Ladd-Franklin attended Vassar in the 1866–1867 school year, the college's second year of operation. She then taught for a year, before returning to Vassar to complete her degree in 1869.

Eliphalet supported his daughter's career goals. *American Psychologist* reported that in 1867 he wrote, "We all miss you very much and wish you was at home but it is for your advantage and good to have some occupation and to be of some use in the world and acquire habits of independence and self-reliance and know that if you have health you can take care of yourself."

At Vassar, Ladd-Franklin met astronomy professor Maria Mitchell, who became a mentor to Ladd-Franklin. Mitchell was a renowned astronomer and the first woman admitted to the American Academy of Arts and Sciences. Ladd-Franklin excelled in Mitchell's astronomy classes and took observations for her in the college observatory, which had the third largest telescope in the country. Mitchell helped Ladd-Franklin and other women gain experience and self-confidence so they would pursue science as a career.

Ladd-Franklin earned an A.B. degree in 1869. She then taught in secondary schools in Pennsylvania, Massachusetts, and New York for nine years. Ladd-Franklin hated teaching. In 1872, according to *Untold Lives,* she wrote in to pursue research in Germany. German professors were opposed to women researchers, but Ladd-Franklin was not a threat to them. As an American, she would return home and would not compete for a teaching position in Germany.

Ladd-Franklin studied color theory in the laboratories of G.E. Müller and theories of color vision with Hermann von Helmholtz. Ladd-Franklin's study led her to propose her own color theory, which she presented to the International Congress of Psychology in London in 1892. The theory was controversial but gradually gained acceptance.

Ladd-Franklin returned to Germany alone in 1894 to do lab work with Arthur Konig, a physicist interested in color vision. During her four months there, she wrote home frequently to share her discoveries with Franklin who continued to provide encouragement and praise. The experience turned out to be a disappointment as she felt Konig was not providing good direction. According to *American Psychologist,* he also took credit for her work, causing Ladd-Franklin to lament, "what can one expect from a man!" She traveled to Germany again in 1902 to consult with Müller.

Despite the fact that Ladd-Franklin contributed to scientific literature and psychological research, she was denied a research-teaching position at a college or university. Although her work on color vision was widely accepted, without an academic affiliation, she felt illegitimate. In 1904, she was appointed lecturer in psychology and logic at Johns Hopkins. She taught one course per year, on a year-to-year basis.

In 1895, Fabian Franklin left Johns Hopkins to become editor of the *Baltimore News.* In 1909, the couple moved to New York when Franklin became associate editor of the *New York Evening Post.* Unable to obtain an official appointment, Ladd-Franklin lectured on psychology at Columbia University, although she drew no salary and was not considered faculty. She remained at Columbia until 1927.

Shunned by Male Scientists

One of her greatest disappointments was exclusion from an elite group of experimental psychologists known as the Experimentalists. Cornell University psychologist E.B. Titchener began the club in 1904 and invited the heads of psychological laboratories and up-and-coming junior faculty and graduate students to attend the informal meetings. Titchener specified that no women would be allowed to participate. Ladd-Franklin had known Titchener, who was 20 years younger than she, for many years and was incensed at her exclusion. When the group met at Columbia in 1914, Ladd-Franklin told Titchener that not inviting her to the meeting at her own university represented a medieval attitude and that his policy was "so unconscientious, so immoral,—worse than that—so unscientific." Finally, Ladd-Franklin was permitted to attend one session but was never invited back. She continued to protest the group's men-only policy, but the group continued to exclude women until long after Ladd-Franklin's and Titchener's deaths.

During the final years of her career, Ladd-Franklin studied "blue arcs," which she believed showed that active nerve fibers emit a faint light. Ladd-Franklin published *Colour and Colour Theories* in 1929. It was comprised of her major works on vision.

Ladd-Franklin died of pneumonia in New York City on March 5, 1930. She was 82 years old. Although she had made many contributions in the fields of logic and vision, she was never fully accepted in the male-dominated scientific community.

Books

Notable Mathematicians, Gale Research, 1998.
Scarborough, Elizabeth, and Laurel Furumoto, *Untold Lives: The First Generation of American Women Psychologists,* Columbia University Press, 1987.

Periodicals

American Psychologist, February 1992. □

Christopher Columbus Langdell

Christopher Columbus Langdell (1826–1906) altered the way that students of the law were educated with his development of the case law method and the treatment of law as a science. His practices were considered controversial at the time of introduction, but eventually Langdell's technique would become the basic foundation for the study of law.

Education

L angdell was born in the small farming town of New Boston, New Hampshire, on May 22, 1826. He was the son of John Langdell and Lydia Beard. He attended the local district schools and at the age of 18 he began teaching. He also worked in the textile mills in Manchester, New Hampshire. Langdell wanted to obtain further education, and in 1845, his sisters agreed to help to support him while he worked his way through Phillips Exeter Academy. After graduating, he entered Harvard University as a sophomore with the class of 1851. He did not stay at the university long before he was granted a leave of absence in order to resume teaching, presumably with the intention of obtaining more funds to continue to attend school. He then spent some time working in an Exeter Law office. When he returned to Harvard, it was not to the university, but to the Harvard Law School. He spent three years there, three times longer than most students at the time. He also worked as a student librarian from 1852 to 1854.

Langdell began practicing law in December of 1854 in New York City. He did not employ a lot of time appearing in court; instead he gained a reputation as an educated, knowledgeable lawyer. He spent a great deal of time studying at the Law Institute, and while he was there he had an opportunity to supply a reference to Charles O'Conor, the well-known lawyer and politician who was once nominated for president. O'Conor often returned to Langdell to request his help and soon thereafter others were coming to him for assistance as well.

Harvard Law School

After Langdell had been practicing law for 16 years, an old friend of his from school, Charles Eliot, was appointed as the President of Harvard Law School. Eliot invited Langdell to join him on the staff there as a Dane Professor of Law and dean of the law school. Langdell quickly accepted the positions and worked with Eliot to make changes in the way that the law students were taught. According to *A History of American Law,* "the duties of the dean were not very awesome; he was to 'keep the Records of the Faculty,' prepare 'its business,' and 'preside at its meetings in the absence of the President.'" However, Langdell, with the support of Eliot, made sweeping changes in the entire way that the law school was run. At the time, most students attended the law program for one year and achieved their degrees by attending lectures given by judges and practicing lawyers who taught at the law school as a side job. In addition, the standards for acceptance to the law school were fairly lenient, and law degrees were handed out without a great deal of testing. Langdell quickly changed all of that.

Langdell began to test students before they were accepted into the program by asking them to translate phrases in Latin from *Virgil, Cicero,* and *Caesar,* without the aid of a dictionary. In some instances, French was considered an acceptable alternative to Latin. If prospective students did not have a college degree, they were given an entrance exam. He would also quiz them on Sir Blackstone's *Commentaries on the Laws of England.* Blackstone's *Commentaries* was considered a masterwork in English law and was used to form the foundation of law in America and was the standard reference material of the 13 colonies at the time of the American Revolution. Within a year of accepting the job, Langdell had the law school changing the program from one year of study to two years. In addition, he began to require final examinations at the end of each year to assure each student was ready to move on to the next level. Five years later, the program was increased to three years, although the third year did not have to be in residence. By 1899, a three-year program in residence was a mandatory requirement.

Initially, the increase in the length of the program and the stricter entrance exams led to a decrease in the number of students. In addition, the new style of teaching was considered experimental. However, the quality of the remaining students eventually provided ample evidence of the program's success as they entered the workforce.

The curriculum of the law school classes was changed to reflect a steady stream of appropriate information. Each student was required to take a set amount of different types of courses and the courses were to be taken in an established order. The style of the teaching also changed. Lectures were no longer the standard method of learning. Instead, Langdell encouraged learning through the Socratic method so that the students were taught through questions and answers instead of through lectures. The law was not learned through memo-

rizing facts and figures. Instead, students learned through their ability to reason and recognize the science of the law. Different prior legal case decisions were brought into the classroom, and the students would discuss the principles of the law and how the laws applied to each case. Langdell felt very strongly that law was a science, and that it should be studied through its principles. In 1871, Langdell published his first casebook on contracts. He published *A Selection of Cases on the Law of Contracts* (1871), *A Selection of Cases on Sales of Personal Property* (1872), and *Cases on Equity Pleading* (1875). These texts were the first casebooks to be used as a foundation in the case method of teaching. In the preface to the *Cases on the Law of Contracts,* Langdell stated the theory of teaching on which he acted: "Law, considered as a science, consists of certain principles of doctrines. To have such a mastery of these as to be able to apply them with constant facility and certainty to the ever-tangled skein of human affairs, is what constitutes a true lawyer; and hence to acquire that mastery should be the business of every earnest student of law. . . ." In addition, brief summaries were added to each of his books regarding principles developed by the cases. Later, two of these would be published separately. *A Summary of Equity Pleading* was published in 1877 and *A Summary of the Law of Contracts* was published in 1879. Later, in 1905, *A Brief Survey of Equity Jurisdiction* was published.

Langdell began to hire young instructors who worked as teachers and scholars of the law full-time. The legal academic was a new occupation, as previously most instructors were elderly judges and lawyers who worked as instructors at the law school as a second job. The new instructors could devote all of their professional time to the study of law. Langdell hired a student, James Barr Ames, in 1873, right as he graduated from law school. He was the first full-time academic law professor. Langdell saw Ames as someone who had the ability to teach the science of law. It did not matter to Langdell that Ames had no actual experience in the practice of law. Langdell also hired the first full-time librarian at the law school. According to the Harvard Law School web site, "He believed that the Library was to law students what the laboratory was to scientists, and that its great importance demanded that vigilant improvement be made."

Case Method Faced Opposition

Initially, Langdell's methods of instruction garnered a great deal of opposition, both from outside of Harvard, as well as within. Gradually, however, the wisdom of his methods was recognized. In 1890, one of Langdell's students, William A. Keener, left his post as a Harvard professor to join the faculty of the Columbia Law School. He introduced Langdell's case method of teaching to students at Columbia.

In 1891, the American Bar Association's Committee on Legal Education, stating that the students were not taught the law, criticized the case method. There were concerns that the method created lawyers that would not fully understand the basic concepts of justice and would produce lawyers too eager to litigate and leave too many decisions to the ruling of the judges. In 1892, according to the *History Resource Center,* they further again attacked the case method, stating, "The result of this elaborate study of actual disputes, ... ignoring ... the settled doctrines that have grown out of past ones, is a class of graduates admirably calculated to argue any side of any controversy, but quite unable to advise a client when he is safe from litigation."

Gradually, the opposition died down, and the Langdell case study method won out over all of its rivals. By the 1920's, the Harvard/Langdell case method was almost universal.

The Legacy Continued

Langdell had suffered from difficulty with his eyesight since he was a young child and as he grew older, this affliction became worse. It became necessary for him to hire readers to assist him. But even the readers could not help him to maintain his position as dean; by 1895 he had to resign as the dean of the law school. His first academic law professor, James Barr Ames, replaced him as dean and continued his methods. At the time of his retirement, the case method was established not only at Harvard, but at Northwestern University, the University of Wisconsin, and the University of Cincinnati and was being taught by Harvard Law School graduates across the country. Langdell continued to teach until 1900.

Langdell passed away on July 6, 1906. He had married on September 22, 1880, to Margaret Ellen Huson, who survived him a few years. They had no children. After he died, a trust was created in his name in order to provide funding for education of poor students.

In 1905–1906 Harvard constructed what would become the principal building on the law school campus and named it Langdell Hall. It held classrooms, faculty offices, and the library. Additions were constructed in 1929. In 1997, Langdell Hall was completely renovated. The library now occupies the entire building.

Langdell's impact on the reform of legal education in the United States was immense. Despite opposition and attacks on his unorthodox methods, Langdell stood his ground and permanently altered the course of law school education and legal history.

Books

Dictionary of American Biography, American Council of Learned Societies, 1928–1936.
Friedman, Lawrence M., *American Law,* Penguin Books, 1984.
—, *A History of American Law,* Simon & Shuster, Touchstone, 1985.

Online

"Langdell Hall," *Harvard Law School web site,* http://www.law .harvard.edu/about/langdell.shtml, (March 1, 2003). □

Joseph Sheridan Le Fanu

Considered "the father of the English ghost story," Irish author Joseph Sheridan Le Fanu (1814–1873) is

recognized for combining Gothic literary conventions with realistic technique to create tales of psychological insight and supernatural terror. Among his most highly regarded works is *In a Glass Darkly* (1872), a collection of horror stories that includes the earliest example of a vampire story in English literature.

Biography

Of French Huguenot descent, Le Fanu was born in Dublin on August 28, 1814, the first son of Emma Lucretia Dobbin and Thomas Philip Le Fanu. His father, a clergyman in the Church of Ireland and nephew of the playwright Richard Brinsley Sheridan, served as the chaplain of the Royal Hibernian Military School in Phoenix Park during Le Fanu's early childhood. In 1826 the family moved to Abington in county Limerick, where Thomas Le Fanu had been appointed rector and dean of Emly. Le Fanu, who enjoyed the resources of his father's large library, was privately educated until his acceptance at Trinity College, Dublin, in 1833.

His university career was a success. He won academic honors and was active in debate and the historical society. After completing studies in classics he pursued legal studies at King's Inns in London but never took up the practice of law. His interests already lay in literary pursuits. As early as 1837 he had begun contributing to the *Dublin University Magazine*, and in 1839 he took ownership of the Irish Protestant newspaper *The Warder*. From this time on journalism constituted Le Fanu's foremost professional undertaking. He assumed a financial interest in several newspapers over the course of his career, including the *Statesman*, the *Dublin Evening Mail*, and *Dublin University Magazine*, and used these publications to promote his conservative political views.

In December 1843 Le Fanu married Susanna Bennett, the daughter of a barrister, and they had four children. Their years together were plagued by financial difficulties and ill health, and when she died in April 1858 at the age of thirty-four, it came as a life-shattering blow to Le Fanu, who blamed himself for her suffering. He wrote at the time, as quoted by Kathryn West in the *Dictionary of Literary Biography*, "The greatest misfortune of my life has overtaken me. My darling wife is gone. . . . She was the light of my life." His grief was inconsolable, and from this point on he retired from public life.

One obituary notice, quoted by Roy B. Stokes in the *Dictionary of Literary Biography*, later remarked: "He vanished so entirely that Dublin, always ready with a nickname, dubbed him 'The Invisible Prince;' and indeed he was for long almost invisible, except to his family and most familiar friends, unless at odd hours of the evening, when he might occasionally be seen, stealing, like the ghost of his former self, between his newspaper office and his home in Merrion Square; sometimes, too, he was to be encountered in an old out-of-the-way bookshop poring over some rare black letter Astrology or Demonology." However, it is during the period of his seclusion that he produced his most enduring works of fiction.

Le Fanu sold the *Dublin University Magazine*, which had become the main outlet of his short fiction, in 1869. He died in 1873. Of the effect of the seclusion of his final years on his literary work, biographer Michael H. Begnal commented, "Instead of limiting his artistic vision, it would seem that the seclusion of Sheridan LeFanu was a blessing in disguise, for it preserved him from the pitfalls of immersion in immediate social concern. Yet at the same time it induced him to concentrate upon the larger issues which were the true shapers of his time."

Early Works

Le Fanu's first published works of fiction were short stories printed in the *Dublin University Magazine* beginning in 1838. The earliest of these, "The Ghost and the Bone-Setter," draws on the Irish folk belief that the most recently deceased corpse in a cemetery must carry water to the thirsty souls already in purgatory. Though the story offers a comic explanation for the appearance of a ghost, the work is notable for introducing the character of Father Francis Purcell, a Catholic priest from Drumcoolagh in county Limerick, who serves as a connection for a number of stories later collected in *The Purcell Papers* (1880). Similarly, "The Fortunes of Robert Ardagh" employs a dual structure to tell the story of a mysterious murder, explained alternately as a

manifestation of Satanic power and a rational series of unfortunate events.

The most famous of the Purcell stories is "Strange Event in the Life of Schalken the Painter," published in May 1839. In the story, Purcell relates a tale told to him by the owner of "a remarkable picture" painted by an artist named Godfrey Schalken—a portrait of a young woman named Rose whom he had once loved. Betrothed to a wealthy stranger whose ghoulish appearance is an omen of his diabolical nature, Rose returns home in an anguished state some months after her marriage, begging not to be left alone and crying, "The dead and the living cannot be one—God has forbidden it!" She mysteriously disappears from her room, and no trace of her is ever recovered. Some time later Schalken experiences a vision of Rose beckoning him to follow her. He cannot resist, and she leads him to a richly outfitted bedchamber where she reveals—with "an arch smile, such as pretty women wear when engaged in successfully practising some roguish trick"—her demonic husband waiting for her in a black-curtained bed. The painter faints at the sight but paints a faithful representation of what he has seen.

A somewhat later tale, "The Watcher," was included in *Ghost Stories and Tales of Mystery* (1851) and revised as "The Familiar" for *In a Glass Darkly*. The story relates events leading up to the death of Captain James Barton, who is haunted by a strange figure who may or may not be a ghost, but whose relentless appearance causes Barton to lose his senses and eventually his life. In the *Dictionary of Literary Biography* Gary William Crawford called the story "remarkably sophisticated for its day," noting that "the lingering uncertainty about what happens . . . invokes a genuine frisson." A story first published in 1853, "An Account of Some Strange Disturbances in Aungier Street," again depicts the persecution of the living by the dead when two students rent a house in Dublin that had once belonged to a judge who had sentenced many convicts to hang. Only in the midst of their terror do they learn that he had ultimately hanged himself in the house in his despair and madness. The story was later revised as "Mr. Justice Harbottle" and included in *In a Glass Darkly*.

Later Career

Le Fanu published no fiction works during the period 1853 to 1861, an unsettled time in his family life, but his later period proved to be the most productive. When Le Fanu resumed his literary output he published *The House by the Churchyard* (1863), a many-faceted novel that combines comedy, mystery, history, and horror, and *Wylder's Hand* (1864), a successful tale of rivalry and murder. His next work, *Uncle Silas* (1864), is set in Derbyshire, England, and is Le Fanu's best-known Gothic mystery. In the story Maud Ruthyn is the niece of a man suspected though never proven to have committed a murder years before. A wealthy heiress, she comes under his care when her father dies and once in his household becomes herself the intended victim of a murder plot calculated by her uncle, her cousin, and an evil governess in hopes of gaining Maud's fortune. She escapes when the governess is mistakenly killed in her place, and the uncle's true character is revealed. The fourth of his sensational novels published during this period, *Guy Deverell* (1865), centers on the Marlowe estate, illegitimately acquired by Sir Jekyl Marlowe, and the efforts of Monsieur Varbarriere to reinstate the rightful heir.

Le Fanu also produced several additional novels over the next few years, including the romances *All in the Dark* (1866) and *Haunted Lives* (1868), and the mysteries *The Tenants of Malory* (1867), *A Lost Name* (1867–1868), and *The Wyvern Mystery* (1869).

In a Glass Darkly

Le Fanu's short story collection *In a Glass Darkly* contains a group of his most chilling horror tales, "Green Tea," "The Familiar," "Mr. Justice Harbottle," "The Room in the Dragon Volant," and "Carmilla," all purportedly taken from the files of Dr. Martin Hesselius, a German doctor with an interest in psychic phenomena. "Green Tea" is among the best known of Le Fanu's works of supernatural terror, and in 1947 V. S. Pritchett named it "one of the best half-dozen ghost stories in the English language." It concerns Reverend Robert Jennings, a clergyman suffering from a nervous condition. Engaged in a study of ancient religions, Jennings reports that he has been haunted by a little black monkey and suggests that perhaps it is a hallucination brought on by drinking large amounts of green tea. The presence of the monkey begins to interfere with Jennings's duties and with his research, and the creature begins to urge evil actions on the increasingly distressed clergyman. Ultimately, Jennings commits suicide.

The final tale in the collection, "Carmilla" is also the most important from a literary standpoint for it introduces the vampire legend into English literature. Set in an isolated castle occupied by an innocent young girl and her father, the story draws on conventions of the Gothic to heighten terror. Carmilla is a young woman who is brought into the castle to recuperate after a carriage accident. She gives no information about her past, but resembles a dead woman whose portrait hangs in the castle. The heroine of the tale suffers visions of a nocturnal visitor and is slowly drawn into intimate association with Carmilla, whose possessiveness and passion overpower the innocent girl. When Carmilla's true nature as a vampire is discovered, she is killed.

Le Fanu, though not as well known as Edgar Allan Poe, Bram Stoker, or Mary Shelley, remains a seminal figure in the advancement of horror writing, and his works continue to find new audiences through reprint editions. His works expanded the vocabulary of Victorian Gothic to include the deeper effects of psychological terror that characterize modern supernatural horror. In describing what set Le Fanu's stories apart, Pritchett wrote: "LeFanu's ghosts are the most disquieting of all ghosts. . . . The secret doubt, the private shame, the unholy love, scratch away with malignant patience in the guarded mind. It is we who are the ghosts. Let illness, late nights and green tea weaken the catch we normally keep clamped so firmly down, and out slink one by one all the hags and animals of moral or Freudian symbolism."

Le Fanu died on February 10, 1873, in Dublin, Ireland.

Books

Begnal, Michael H., *Joseph Sheridan Le Fanu,* Bucknell University Press, 1971.

Campbell, James L., *Supernatural Fiction Writers,* Charles Scribner's Sons, 1985.

Crawford, Gary William, *J. Sheridan Le Fanu: A Bio-Bibliography,* Greenwood Press, 1995.

Dictionary of Literary Biography, Volume 21: Victorian Novelists Before 1885, edited by Ira B. Nadel and William E. Fredeman, The Gale Group, 1983.

Dictionary of Literary Biography, Volume 178: British Fantasy and Science-Fiction Writers before World War I, edited by Darren Harris-Fain, The Gale Group, 1997.

Kollmann, Judith J., *Dictionary of Literary Biography, Volume 70: British Mystery Writers, 1860–1919,* edited by Bernard Benstock and Thomas F. Staley, The Gale Group, 1988.

Lovecraft, H. P., *Supernatural Horror in Literature,* Ben Abramson, 1945.

McCormack, W. J., *Sheridan Le Fanu,* 3rd ed., Sutton, 1997.

Melada, Ivan, *Sheridan Le Fanu,* Twayne, 1987.

Pritchett, V. S., introduction to *In a Glass Darkly* by Sheridan Le Fanu, John Lehmann, 1947.

West, Kathryn, *Dictionary of Literary Biography, Volume 159: British Short-Fiction Writers, 1800–1880,* edited by John R. Greenfield, The Gale Group, 1996.

Periodicals

Criticism, Fall 1996.

Nineteenth-Century Literature, September 1992.

Studies in Short Fiction, Winter 1987.

Studies in the Novel, Summer 1997.

Online

"Joseph Sheridan Le Fanu (1814–73)," http://lang.nagoya-u.ac.jp/~matsuoka/Fanu.html (February 11, 2003). □

Leadbelly

Leadbelly (1885–1949) was an accomplished 12-string guitar player from the Texas-Louisiana border. During his violence-torn life, Leadbelly served four prison terms for assault. At one of his performances in prison, he was discovered by John Lomax, a Harvard-trained musicologist. Lomax introduced Leadbelly to American audiences of the 1930s and 1940s through his contacts and writings. Although Leadbelly never sold many records during his lifetime, he strongly influenced several generations of folk musicians.

Louisiana Beginnings

Huddie William Ledbetter was born on Jeter Plantation in Mooringsport, Louisiana. His date of birth has been variously given as January 29, 1885, and January 21, 1888. As an only child, he enjoyed the doting affection of his parents, Wes and Sally Ledbetter. The Ledbetters were fairly well-to-do Southern blacks, having

risen from sharecroppers in Louisiana to landowners on the Texas-Louisiana border. Leadbelly's mother, born Sally Pugho, was reportedly half Indian.

Leadbelly's uncle, Terrel Ledbetter, taught his nephew to play accordion and later guitar. Leadbelly was soon playing at local parties—as well as on Shreveport's Fannin Street, a notorious red-light district, despite his mother's protests.

Leadbelly caused a scandal when he fathered a child at the age of 15 and a second child at 16. In reaction to the community's outrage, he set out on his own, supporting himself as a wandering minstrel and farm laborer. At one point, however, he became extremely sick and returned home to Mooringsport. It was during this period that he met his first wife, Lethe.

Leadbelly later claimed to have wandered around Dallas with blues singer Blind Lemon Jefferson about this time. Jefferson, who went on to sell a million records during the 1920s, had a profound influence on Leadbelly, who would later acknowledge his debt to the younger musician in a song entitled "(My Friend) Blind Lemon."

Jailed for Assault

By 1917, when Leadbelly was jailed for assault, the two musicians had gone their separate ways. Although Leadbelly's parents sold their land to pay for his legal defense, Leadbelly was sentenced to short-term hard labor. He escaped from the penitentiary by outrunning the prison dogs. After seeking refuge at his parents' farm, he was sent by his

father to New Orleans. But he disliked that city and moved on to De Kalb, Texas, in the northeastern part of the state near Arkansas. Hoping to avoid recapture, he supported himself as a farm laborer while relatives helped him.

During this period, Leadbelly played little music to avoid drawing attention to himself. He also adopted the alias Walter Boyd. He and Lethe were no longer together, and Leadbelly found other women to keep him company.

Convicted of Murder

As Walter Boyd, Leadbelly became known for the company he kept with women and for frequent fights. While traveling with friends and a relative named Will Stafford, Leadbelly got into a fight in which Stafford was fatally shot. Though Leadbelly maintained his innocence, he was convicted of murder and sentenced to 30 years of hard labor on Shaw State Farm in Texas.

Still using the name Boyd, Leadbelly served seven years of his 30-year sentence working on chain gangs. After a prison escape failed, he tried to drown himself in a lake but was apprehended. Back in prison, he used his musical talents to gain favor with the prison guards.

While Leadbelly was serving time at Shaw State Farm, his father died. Just before his death, Wes Ledbetter had tried to bribe prison officials into releasing Leadbelly. But in 1925, Leadbelly won a full pardon on his own. Oddly, the pardon came after the governor of Texas went on record as opposing pardons. The governor had visited the prison several times to hear Leadbelly sing, and Leadbelly later maintained that he won over the governor with his song "Please Pardon Me."

Following his release from prison, Leadbelly returned home to Mooringsport. While supporting himself as a truck driver, he kept himself in liquor and women by using his musical talents. By this time, Blind Lemon Jefferson's records were selling well and country blues was at the peak of its popularity. But record scouts took no notice of Leadbelly.

Another Prison Sentence

One night while performing a song titled "Mister Tom Hughes's Town," Leadbelly became involved in a brawl that left him with a horrendous scar on his neck and left the other man with permanent brain injuries. Other fights would follow, leading Leadbelly into further conflicts with the law. After a fight in which he claimed that six men tried to steal whiskey from his lunch pail, Leadbelly was convicted of assault with intent to commit murder. Court records, however, show that he was convicted of assaulting a white Salvation Army officer with a knife at a Salvation Army concert after the officer told Leadbelly to stop dancing to the music.

In 1930, Leadbelly was sentenced to ten years at the Louisiana state prison in Angola. After the authorities discovered Leadbelly's prior conviction, he was disqualified from any chance at early release. Life in Depression-era Southern prisons was not easy, and Leadbelly received beatings for minor offenses. But he adapted to the conditions at Angola and eventually was allowed to work as a laundry man and waiter. During this prison term, he acquired the habit of sleeping with the lights on.

Discovered

In 1933, a Harvard-trained expert on American folk music, John Lomax, was making his way through Southern prisons and recording musicians when he stopped at Angola and heard Leadbelly sing. Lomax made some preliminary recordings of Leadbelly's songs and returned months later with better recording equipment. Leadbelly recorded his "Please Pardon Me" song (now addressed to the governor of Louisiana) and "Goodnight Irene." Although Leadbelly later maintained that he was pardoned because the Louisiana governor had been moved by his prison song, records indicate that he was released as a cost-saving measure.

When Leadbelly was released from Angola in 1934, jobs were scarce, especially for ex-convicts. But Lomax hired him as a recording assistant and took him to New York, where Lomax was well connected with musicologists.

Sensation in New York

Leadbelly arrived in New York on December 31, 1934, and quickly created a sensation with his physical scars and prison background. His musical tradition on the 12-string guitar went back decades to roots unfamiliar in New York. He was asked to perform at elite universities, where he frightened as much as entertained his audiences.

Lomax negotiated a contract with Macmillan to write a book entitled *Negro Folk Songs as Sung by Leadbelly* that would include Leadbelly's life history, an account of his discovery by Lomax, and background details about Leadbelly's songs.

Leadbelly moved into a house in Connecticut owned by a socialite to give himself some breathing room from the publicity seekers in New York and to work with Lomax on the book. Meanwhile, the guitar player sent to Louisiana for his latest companion, Martha Promise. They were married in Wilton, Connecticut, in a highly publicized ceremony.

While in Connecticut, Leadbelly recorded songs for the Library of Congress archives. Lomax also made arrangements for Leadbelly to record under the label of the American Record Company. Although American released some of Leadbelly's recordings commercially, they sold poorly, the peak market for rural blues having passed some ten years earlier. But part of the problem was that the company insisted Leadbelly record blues rather than folk songs, even though most of his repertoire was folk music. As a result, Leadbelly never did sell many records while he was alive, even though there was a large interest among white audiences in his folk music.

Relationship with Lomax Soured

Although the relationship between Lomax and Leadbelly was at first mutually satisfactory, it gradually deteriorated. As long as Leadbelly stayed out of trouble and performed for Lomax's audiences, things went well enough. With Lomax contracted to handle Leadbelly's finances, the folk singer was totally dependent on income from Lomax,

and Lomax kept Leadbelly on a tight leash to prevent him from getting into trouble. Leadbelly increasingly resented Lomax as he discovered New York's black nightlife.

Leadbelly's violent past and emotional turbulence gave Lomax more than enough reason to be a little afraid of his discovery. Some minor disagreements and Leadbelly's failure to meet commitments led to their parting in March 1935.

Leadbelly returned to Louisiana, while Lomax moved to Texas to work on his book, which was behind schedule. Destitute, Leadbelly hired a lawyer to obtain money from Lomax. A settlement was reached in which Lomax was allowed to complete the book, and it was published in November 1936.

Darling of the Left

In March 1936, a year after he left New York, Leadbelly was back with his wife Martha. Without Lomax, Leadbelly initially floundered, but after he met lecturer Mary Barnicle of New York University, he got an introduction to left-wing political factions within New York society, which had taken a strong interest in Leadbelly's folk music.

Surviving on welfare and odd jobs, Leadbelly and his wife struggled to make ends meet. Lomax's book was not selling well. Jazz and swing now dominated popular tastes. The American folk music following and Leadbelly's audiences were largely confined to members of the political Left.

To attract a wider audience, Leadbelly added topical and protest songs about segregation to his repertoire. He also made some non-commercial recordings, a number of which ended up in the archives of East Tennessee State University.

Another Conviction

In 1939, Leadbelly was arrested for assaulting a man with a knife. He reportedly stabbed the man sixteen times. Convicted of third-degree assault, Leadbelly was sentenced to less than a year in prison. During the trial, Leadbelly made his first commercial recordings since 1935 for Musicraft, a small company with left-wing political affiliations. He received a small advance on royalties for his efforts.

The fifty-one-year-old Leadbelly began serving his fourth prison sentence in 1939. By 1940, after serving eight months, he was released and back in New York City. About this time a folk music community was springing up in New York City which would achieve tremendous growth during and after World War II.

A Living—and a Dying

Leadbelly befriended the then-unknown Woody Guthrie and invited him to move into the apartment he was sharing with his wife. Leadbelly's apartment soon became a gathering place for folk singers and the scene of all-night jam sessions. Leadbelly meanwhile made radio appearances and recorded for RCA and the Library of Congress. He also made a recording for Moe Asch's Folkway Records, which would become his principle record label.

In 1944, Leadbelly headed west to Hollywood in hopes of getting work in the studios. Although he was unable to land work in movies, he made a decent living playing club circuits. He recorded for Capitol records, which used the best recording technology that he had so far encountered. But by late 1946, he had had enough of the West Coast and returned to New York.

With the revival of Dixieland jazz and renewed interest in "origins" music, Leadbelly found his music increasingly in vogue. In 1946 a book entitled *A Tribute of Huddie Ledbetter* was published in England. Leadbelly was able to make a modest living playing in jazz clubs and giving occasional concerts. In 1949, while briefly touring in France, he was diagnosed with amyotrophic lateral sclerosis—better known as Lou Gehrig's disease. He died in New York City six months later, on December 6, 1949. He is buried in the Shiloh Baptist Church graveyard near Mooringsport, Louisiana.

Online

"Huddie William 'Leadbelly' Ledbetter," http://www.cr.nps .gov/delta/blues/people/leadbelly.htm (February 2003).
"The Leadbelly Web," *Cycad Web Works,* http://www.cycad .com/cgi-bin/Leadbelly/biog.html (January 2003).
"Ledbetter, Huddie," *The Handbook of Texas Online,* http:// www.tsha.utexas.edu/handbook/online/articles/view/LL/ fle10.html (February 2003). ☐

Henrietta Swan Leavitt

Henrietta Swan Leavitt (1868–1921) was an American astronomer of the first magnitude. Her research resulted in numerous advances within the field, the effects of which extended well beyond her lifetime. She discovered a means to rank stars's magnitudes using photographic plates, which became a standard in the field. Leavitt also discovered a means by which astronomers became better able to accurately measure extra galactic distances known as the period-luminosity relation. She also discovered more variable stars than any other astronomer in her time.

Parents Supported Her Education

Henrietta Swan Leavitt was born in Lancaster, Massachusetts, on July 4, 1868, where she was one of seven children. Her parents were Henrietta Swan Kendrick and George Roswell Leavitt, a Congregationalist minister whose parish was in Cambridge, Massachusetts. Her parents, who were said to have been strict Puritans, did encourage Leavitt to use her intellect. The majority of people in that period did not support education for women. The Leavitt family eventually relocated to Cleveland, Ohio.

Leavitt studied at Oberlin College in Ohio between 1885 and 1888. She transferred to the Society for the Collegiate Instruction of Women (which would later be known as

Radcliffe College of Harvard University) in Cambridge, Massachusetts, where she finished her A.B. degree in 1892. It was while in her senior year of college that Leavitt first became interested in astronomy.

After graduation she took another astronomy course, but then suffered a debilitating illness. It left her profoundly deaf and she stayed home for several years.

From Volunteer to Harvard Researcher

Leavitt received an appointment as a research assistant at the Harvard College Observatory in Cambridge in 1895. This was a voluntary post; her assignment was to determine stars' magnitudes by consulting photographs of the heavens. Her work impressed the staff. "She soon rose 'by her scientific ability and intense application,'" according to her biography on the Amercian Association of Variable Star Observers (AAVSO) website.

She was given a permanent position in 1902 by Edward Pickering, a noted astronomer who was head of the Harvard College Observatory. Her salary was 30 cents per hour. Leavitt was one of a group of women working at the observatory who were known as computers. It has been said that Pickering hired women in order to save money because he would have had to pay men with the same education greater salaries. Other women in this group also became well-respected astronomers, including Annie Jump Cannon and Williamina Fleming.

Leavitt was soon promoted as head of the photographic photometry department. Photometry, as its name implies, is the science of measuring stars' brightness. Employing photography in astronomy necessitated adjusting astronomers' magnitude scale to compensate for the way film registers light. This post did not give Leavitt time to indulge in theoretical work. Actually, she was given no latitude in her choice of research. Pickering would typically assign work to Leavitt on topics that interested him.

Developed Reputation as Variable Star "Fiend"

In her role in the photometry department, Leavitt was assigned to search photographic plates for variable stars in the Magellanic Clouds regions. According to *Astronomy,* "The technique for variable hunting was strikingly uncomplicated. Leavitt would simply overlay the positive plate of a region of sky on the negative plate taken on a different night. If the positive and negative star images didn't match up, she would flag a potential variable." This technique was known as superposition. By 1904 she discovered more than 200 variable stars using this method. The following year that number grew to more than 840 stars.

"What a variable-star 'fiend' Miss Leavitt is," wrote Charles Young of Princeton in a letter to Pickering. "One can't keep up with the roll of the new discoveries." It was while working at the observatory that Leavitt discovered a means to rank the magnitudes or brightness of stars on photographic plates. This ranking would become a standard used by astronomers, known as the Harvard Standard.

Worked on Several Major Research Projects

Leavitt was interested in Cepheids. These variable stars become brighter, then dim in a regular cycle. The Cepheids were named after the first star of this type to be discovered, Delta Cephei. Leavitt first made the observation in 1904 that there was a relationship between how long a Cepheid took to complete one of these cycles and its ultimate magnitude. The difficulty was that this could not be confirmed by observing these stars in this galaxy. There were too many factors that could skew the possible results. She eventually published her discovery in 1908. Leavitt continued to work on this research for four more years.

Beginning in 1907, Leavitt was asked to develop a "North Polar Sequence" by which star brightness could be described and which would serve as a standard in the field. She used 46 stars near the North Pole to represent each of the varying degrees of star magnitudes. Magnitude could not be reliably determined from photographic images nor from telescopic images. Stars typically emit light in various colors, which can confuse or trick the eye. Using this data as a basis for determining magnitude gave varied and often inaccurate results. What Leavitt did was compare and contrast the stars with each other using various images from many different telescopes. This scale she created assigned brightnesses for the stars in a range from the 4th to the 21st magnitude. Her findings were published in the *Annals of Harvard College Observatory.*

While studying photographic images of the estimated 1800 Cepheid variable stars in a system known as the Magellanic Clouds taken from Harvard's observatory in Peru in 1912, Leavitt found a direct correlation between the brightness of a Cepheid variable star and the period of its variability to confirm her theory. The Magellanic Clouds are star systems that are located just outside the Milky Way. The theoretical relationship she posited is commonly known as the period-luminosity theory. Leavitt had thought since the stars in this system are approximately the same distance from Earth, then there might be a relationship between these two factors. Her hypothesis was correct.

Expressed arithmetically, she determined the Cepheid's apparent magnitude increases linearly with the logarithm of the period. In 1912, Leavitt published her results and a table of the 25 Cepheid periods. These periods ranged in length from 1.253 days to 127 days, with an average period duration of five days. These stars' apparent brightnesses were also included in the table.

"A straight line can be readily drawn among each of the two series of points corresponding to maxima and minima, thus showing that there is a simple relation between the brightness of the variable and their periods," wrote Leavitt in 1912, as quoted on the AAVSO website. She noted that "since the variables are probably nearly the same distance from the earth, their periods are apparently associated with their actual emission of light, as determined by their mass, density, and surface brightness."

Since the stars in this system are approximately the same distance from Earth, if the range of a single Cepheid could be calculated, then that data could be used to calculate the distances to the Magellanic Clouds. The data could also then be further used to calculate the distance to even more distant Cepheids.

"The measurement and discussion of these objects present problems of unusual difficulty, on account of the large area covered by the two regions, the extremely crowded distribution of the stars contained in them, the faintness of the variables, and the shortness of their periods," according to a document published by the observatory in 1912 and quoted on the Bloomfield Science Museum website. "As many of them never become brighter than the fifteenth magnitude, while very few exceed the thirteenth magnitude at maximum, long exposures are necessary, and the number of available photographs is small."

In 1913 Leavitt's system for describing magnitudes or "North Polar Sequence" was adopted by the International Committee on Photographic Magnitudes. She established these sequences for 108 areas in the heavens. When her supervisor, Pickering, established 48 "Harvard standard regions," Leavitt calculated secondary brightness standards for each of them. These international standards were used until the methodology improved.

Using Leavitt's period-luminosity theory, a Danish astronomer was able in 1913 to calculate some star's distances only using their period. Astronomers typically used a measurement method known as the parallax method to determine distances between stars. This worked well for distances up to 100-light-years, but making these measurements was difficult. Additional work by other astronomers further refined how the relationship between absolute brightness and period could be accurately used to calculate distances greater than 10 million light-years, as well as to determine the actual distance between the Earth and a given star. This also gave astronomers a better idea as to the vastness of the heavens. It enabled Harlow Shapley to measure the size of the Milky Way galaxy.

Leavitt also discovered more variable stars during her career than had any other astronomer. Leavitt catalogued about 2400 variable stars while working at Harvard. At the time, this was about half the known variable stars. She also had discovered four novae and studied Algol-type eclipsing binary stars and asteroids as well.

Consequences of Consignment to Menial Tasks Mulled by Colleagues

As previously mentioned, Pickering dictated the work Leavitt and the other computers were to do. "If Leavitt had been free to choose her own research projects, she might have investigated the consequences of the period-luminosity relationship she had discovered," according to an excerpt from *Women of Science: Righting the Record* on a UCLA physics website. "Pickering hired people to do a specific job and didn't want them wasting their time doing anything else." That Leavitt was not given free reign to explore her passion for variable stars most likely impeded progress in the field. Cecilia Payne-Gaposchkin, one of these women who knew Leavitt, wrote that for Pickering to relegate her solely to photometry "was a harsh decision, which condemned a brilliant scientist to uncongenial work, and probably set back the study of variable stars for several decades."

Among the professional organizations of which she was a member were the American Association for the Advancement of Science and the Astronomical and Astrophysical Society of America. Leavitt was also an honorary member of the American Association of Variable Star Observers as well as a member of Phi Beta Kappa and The American Association of University Women.

"Miss Leavitt inherited, in a somewhat chastened form, the stern virtues of her puritan ancestors," Solon I. Bailey, a Harvard professor wrote of Leavitt in 1922, quoted on the AAVSO website. "She took life seriously. Her sense of duty, justice and loyalty was strong. For light amusements she appeared to care little. She was a devoted member of her intimate family circle, unselfishly considerate in her friendships, steadfastly loyal to her principles, and deeply conscientious and sincere in her attachment to her religion and church. She had the happy faculty of appreciating all that was worthy and lovable in others, and was possessed of a nature so full of sunshine that, to her, all of life became beautiful and full of meaning."

Honored by Nobel Committee

Leavitt worked at Harvard until her death. She died of cancer December 21, 1921, in Cambridge, Massachusetts. Her colleagues mourned her passing, in particular the void her death created. Some of her colleagues thought her to have been the brightest among them. She had made an irreplaceable contribution to the field.

Books

A to Z of Women in Science and Math, Facts on File, 1999.
American Science Leaders, ABC-CLIO, 2001.
American Women in Science: A Biographical Dictionary, ABC-CLIO, 1994.
Notable Scientists: From 1900 to the Present, Gale Group, 2001.
World of Scientific Discovery, 2nd ed. Gale Group, 1999.

Periodicals

Astronomy, July 2002.

Online

American Decades CD-ROM, Gale Research, 1998.
"Henrietta Swan Leavitt," CWP at UCLA, http://www.physics .ucla.edu/~cwp/Phase2/Leavitt,_Henrietta_Swan@ 871234567.html (March 3, 2003).
"Henrietta Swan Leavitt," Famous Science Innovators, Bloomfield Science Museum Jerusalem, http://www.mada.org.il/ website/html/eng/2_1_1-31.htm (March 3, 2003).
"Henrietta Swan Leavitt," Hands On Astronomy, Amercian Association of Variable Star Observers website, http://hoa.aavso .org/posterswan.htm (February 28, 2003). □

Ernesto Lecuona

Ernesto Lecuona (1896–1963) remains Cuba's best known and perhaps the nation's most prolific composer. Of his more than 1000 compositions, his most popular works remain standards in Latin music. These include popular tunes such as "Malagueña" and "Siboney." His work was not confined to popular compositions, but spanned a variety of musical forms. Lecuona was also a noted pianist and conductor.

Acknowledged as a Child Prodigy

Lecuona was born Ernesto Sixto de la Asuncion Lecuona y Casado in Guanabocoa, Cuba, on August 7, 1896. His father was a newspaper editor. His siblings, two sisters and four brothers, were all musicians. He first studied with his elder sister Ernestina, also a classically trained pianist. Several of his other siblings also studied piano. Lecuona made his performing debut at five years old. He was considered by all accounts a prodigy.

He studied music theory with Joaquin Nin, the Spanish composer and father of the writer Anais Nin. His first composition, a two-step often performed by Cuban military bands, was published when he was 11. He was frequently performing and organizing various musical groups to perform in silent movie houses as well as in ballrooms in Havana throughout his teen years. Lecuona studied at the National Conservatory in Havana, graduating in 1913 with a gold medal in performance. His educational concentra-

tion was on teaching both singing and piano. He immediately began touring throughout Europe and the Americans with a repertoire including Mozart and Bach, often playing duets with his sister Ernestina on these tours.

The year 1917 was an important one in Lecuona's career. He made his debut in New York with his first piano recital and also began his recording career. During this time his tours continued to take him outside Cuba. He was performing primarily in the Americas and in Spain. He also performed regularly on radio broadcasts.

Continued Performing, Became Prolific Composer

As a composer, Lecuona was tremendous. He created and published hundreds of songs, although the exact number varies widely. Once source credits him with composing more than 400 pieces, while another says he has produced some 1000 compositions. Lecuona studied composition under Maurice Ravel while in Paris and worked in a variety of musical forms. He remains best known for his songs, typically referred to as lighter fare by historians and critics.

Lecuona chose not to work at the piano while composing, preferring a card table. Typically, he would work in creative bursts that would produce astonishing results. He reportedly once wrote four songs that would become hits: "Blue Night," "Siboney," "Say Si Si," and "Dame tus dos rosas/Two Hearts That Pass in the Night," in a single night: January 6, 1929. The following year "Andalucia" and "Malagueña" were on the charts.

"Malagueña" is inarguably the best-known of his popular songs. It is considered his first major composition. This stirring piano instrumental has enjoyed enduring popularity as a recorded tune and in performance. Lecuona had debuted the composition at the Roxy Theatre in New York in 1927. Other notable popular tunes composed by Lecuona included "Always in My Heart," "Jungle Drums," "Dust on the Moon," "Aquella tarde," "Canto Carabili," "Como arrullo de palmas," and "Dame tus dos rosas." Some of his compositions were reworked. "Andalucia," for example, was given English lyrics and re-released in 1940 as "The Breeze and I." His "Dame tus dos Rosas" became "Two Hearts that Pass in the Night," which was a hit for big band leader, Guy Lombardo.

Becomes Noted Triple Threat

Lecuona was also in demand as a conductor throughout the 1930s and 1940s. His Cuban Boys, first known as the Palau Brothers Cuban Orchestra, was a popular dance band, which, according to *Americas* "Helped set the stage for the advent of Latin jazz and salsa." The group appeared in the film *Cuban Love Song* before being disbanded in the mid-1930s. Lecuona then became leader of the Orquesta de la Habana beginning in the late 1930s. He also conducted the Havana Casino Orchestra and continued to tour as a performer. During a particular European tour, he chose to perform his own works along with lighter compositions by various late nineteenth and early twentieth century Cuban composers.

Film scores were another popular medium for Lecuona. He was musical director of the MGM film *Under Cuban Skies* (1930). This led to work in other films including *Carnival in Costa Rica* (1947). He created a total of 11 film scores for major American studios including Warner Brothers and MGM. He also wrote scores for Mexican, Argentine, and Cuban films. Lecuona was nominated for an Academy Award in 1942 for the tune "Always in My Heart."

Lecuona appeared at New York's famed Carnegie Hall in October 1943. This was the premier for his orchestral work "Rapsodia Negra" (Black Rhapsody). This piece used Afro-Cuban instruments, atypical in so-called serious orchestral works and Cuban musicians were featured in the performance. Lecuona not only composed the piece, he also conducted and played piano for the concert that night.

"In the triple role of batonist-composer-pianist, Mr. Lecuona ranged over wide tracts of Latin-American rhythms and motifs, woven into compact lyric and symphonic form. As featured premier, Black Rhapsody proved Lecuona's grasp of native idiom and his flair for heaving rhythmic sequences," as quoted in the *Dictionary of Hispanic Biography*.

Popularity Obscures Talents

It was this continuing popularity that seemingly obscured Lecuona's merits as a serious composer of classical music, particularly later in his career. Lecuona was formally trained in composition and his body of work does in fact show remarkable breadth. He created, for example, 11 operettas and some 37 concert pieces in addition to the compositions for solo piano and the popular tunes.

As Thomas Tirino, a concert pianist who has made several recordings of Lecuona's music, observed in an interview with *Americas* this popularity "may have contributed to the lack of scholarly attention that his considerable achievements do merit," said Tirino. "His music does have a popular appeal, because of the beautiful melodies and shortness of the pieces, but the works themselves are very challenging, if you perform them in the way Lecuona intended. I believe the danger has been to stress the popular element to his music, and with his serious compositions, not to fully realize what they are and the genius behind them."

Lecuona has often been described as "the George Gershwin of Cuba," because he both composed and performed pieces bridging classical and popular music. But this "isn't quite accurate," according to *The Boston Globe*'s Richard Dyer. "although his music, like Gershwin's does cut across the divisions between concert and popular music . . . Lecuona was essentially a miniaturist, and there is an element of charm and novelty in many of the pieces." Gershwin and Lecuona, who had the same publisher, met in the 1940s and were reportedly life-long friends.

As for his abilities as a performer, Dyer observed that he was capable of creating great music, but his piano performances ultimately ranged from excellent to quite bad. "Lecuona's best music is colorful and tuneful, sultry and firey by turns; he shows considerable ingenuity in imitating idiomatic guitar effects on the piano," wrote Dyer. "There is nevertheless a wide gap between Lecuona's best and his worst—bits of Rachamaninoff keep coming into view, along with keyboard figurations that sound like Liberace or the even efforts of cocktail pianists everywhere."

Interests Extended Beyond Music

Lecuona was described as "a heavy-set, melancholic figure with famously dark eyes." He was "a popular host who invited friends to play music in his home in Jackson Heights, Queens, though he would escape on solitary walks when the company got to be too much," according to the *Dictionary of Hispanic Biography.* "Besides liking to play the piano, and collecting wood and stone sculpture of the Aztecs, Mayas, the ancient Peruvian Incas, his greatest delight is brewing strong, black Cuban coffee."

Other hobbies reportedly enjoyed by Lecuona included raising small animals and exotic birds (particularly while he was living in rural Cuba), reading mysteries (Agatha Christie was said to have been a favorite writer), and playing poker. He was a baseball fan as well as an inveterate collector who treasured antiques, cigarette lighters, and music boxes.

Lecuona lived in New York and Havana, not unexpected given his touring schedule. He also reportedly had homes in Tampa and Tallahassee, Florida. Cuban President Fulgencio Batista named him cultural attache to the Cuban Embassy in the United States in 1943. With Fidel Castro's coup in 1959, Lecuona left Cuba. He reportedly took a vow in 1960 to never play piano again until Cuba was a free nation. He chose to live abroad, splitting his time between the United States, Spain, and the Canary Islands. Lecuona was in Santa Cruz de Tenerife in the Canary Islands recuperating from a lung problem when he died of a heart attack on November 29, 1963. He is interred in Hawthorn, New York.

Left Significant Body of Work

As Carl Bauman observed in *American Record Guide* in 1997, "Lecuona, as perhaps Cuba's outstanding composer, certainly deserves to be better known." He created more than 1000 compositions, among them 176 pieces for piano and 37 orchestral pieces during his career. In a later review of another Lecuona recording in that same publication, John Boyer describes his music as "Latin music distilled for the middle-classes in the same way that Brahms and Liszt distilled Hungarian music for the consumption of 19th Century Germans."

Influenced Several Generations of Musicians Worldwide

Lecuona's music has lasted, influencing generations of musicians in various genres all over the world. "When I was a little boy growing up in Australia, one of the most popular bands on the Australian airwaves was Ernesto Lecuona and his Cuban Boys," Don Burrows, the Australian jazz musician said in a 2001 interview with *The Age*. "In those days, Cuba used to export music to all over the world and Ernesto Lecuona was as important to me in those days as Duke Ellington. So by the time I was 10, I knew every song that Ernesto Lecuona had ever written. And these boys in the band just couldn't believe that someone over the other side of the world knew as much Ernesto Lecuona as they did."

Michel Camilo, the Dominican jazz pianist, told the All About Jazz website, "The first composition I remember enjoying as a child was 'La Comparsa' by Cuban renown pianist Ernesto Lecuona, performed by my favorite uncle at the piano. He played the tune in his debut at Carnegie Hall."

"He was able to translate the Afro-Cuban rhythms and put them in tails," Camilo told *Americas*. "Technically, he was very advanced, in the tradition of Ignacio Cervantes, another Cuban pianist and composer who came before him. But Lecuona's left hand is a direct link to someone like Chopin, with the ability to translate the African syncopations."

Lecuona's music was frequently recorded by a wide range of artists during his lifetime and continues to be recorded by artists well after his passing. Among those who have recorded Lecuona songs include Desi Arnaz, Guy Lombardo, Paquito D'Rivera, Katia Labeque, Los Super Seven, and numerous others.

Books

Dictionary of Hispanic Biography, Gale Research, 1996.
The New Grove Dictionary of Music and Musicians, Macmillan Publishers Limited, 1980.

Periodicals

American Record Guide, July–August 1996; July 1997; May 2002.
Americas, November 21, 1996.
Boston Globe, February 29, 1996.

Online

"Cubans and Australians in music revival," *The Age,* February 26, 2001, http://www.theage.com.au/entertainment/2001/02/26/FFX4NDSLLJC.html (February 28, 2003).
"Ernesto Lecuona," *Space Age Pop Music website,* http://www.spaceagepop.com/lecuona.htm (February 28, 2003).
"Interview with Raul Malo," *The Mavhouse Archives,* http://www.the-mavhouse.co.uk/archives.htm (February 28, 2003).
"Michel Camilo: From Dominica to Spain and Back Again," *All About Jazz,* http://www.allaboutjazz.com/iviews/mcamilo.htm (February 28, 2003). □

Led Zeppelin

Led Zeppelin has been called the grandfathers of the "Heavy Metal" genre. At their height in the early to mid 1970s, they frequently outsold the Rolling Stones in concert tickets. And by 1973, they had sold more albums than any other band worldwide. Their anthemic song, "Stairway to Heaven," is the most-played song in the history of radio.

L ed Zeppelin was formed out of the ashes of the 1960s supergroup The Yardbirds, once featuring renowned guitarists Eric Clapton and Jeff Beck, and later, a young studio session guitarist, Jimmy Page. (Page, it is estimated, played on 50 to 90 percent of the popular rock records made in England from 1963 to 1965.) In 1965, he joined the Yardbirds, having turned down an offer to replace Eric Clapton just a year earlier. With the Yardbirds, Page and fellow guitarist Jeff Beck pioneered the two-guitar style of rock. Beck left only a year later, however, to pursue a solo career. The band continued for another year and a half, but split by 1968.

Page decided to form The New Yardbirds and sought new musicians. First, he recruited John Paul Jones, a fellow session player, to play bass and keyboards. Then, following a tip, he went to listen to a young blues singer, Robert Plant in Birmingham. Plant suggested drummer John Bonham who had played with him in the Band of Joy. The Who's drummer, Keith Moon, had said something about the new incarnation going down like a lead balloon. Thus, the name Led Zeppelin was coined.

Led Zeppelin's first British show was on October 5, 1968, at Surrey University. An unexpected American tour followed that winter, when the Jeff Beck Group cancelled their spot on a tour with Vanilla Fudge. The band's ambitious manager, Peter Grant, took the opportunity, con-

vinced all involved, and Led Zeppelin left for Los Angeles on Christmas Eve 1968.

Led Zeppelin signed with Atlantic Records and released its self-titled first album in February 1969. The band's sound had diverse influences, including the Delta blues and performers like Robert Johnson, Howlin' Wolf, Buddy Guy, The Incredible String Band, and Elvis Presley. Between Plant's incredible vocal range, and Page's utilization of the new technology of the time—including fuzzboxes, boosters, split pickups on his guitars, and super-amplifiers for the maximum distortion—the band roared into the underground rock consciousness.

Led Zeppelin's best-known song, "Stairway to Heaven," first performed at a 1971 concert in Belfast, was from their fourth album—untitled, save for four strange, runic symbols. Led Zeppelin's fourth album was recorded at Headley Grange, a converted poorhouse in Hampshire, England. Page and Jones wrote the music for "Stairway to Heaven" first, and Plant wrote most of the lyrics in one sitting. Plant later recalled to journalist Cameron Crowe in *Led Zeppelin: The Complete Studio Recordings,* "It was done very quickly. It took a little working out, but it was a fluid, unnaturally easy track. It was almost as if—uh oh—it just had to be gotten out at the time. There was something pushing it saying, 'You guys are okay, but if you want to do something timeless, here's a wedding song for you.' "

The band followed up with *Houses of the Holy* in 1973. Some of the concerts on that tour were filmed for posterity and later released in the film, *The Song Remains the Same.* Following this album, Led Zeppelin started its own label, Swan Song. Signings to the label included Dave Edmunds, Bad Company, the Pretty Things, and Maggie Bell.

In the early years, the band did not have a publicist, did not release singles, and avoided the press. While the idea had been to keep the band mysterious, the band became notorious instead when all their press had to do with riots over concert tickets and the band members and their entourage trashing hotel rooms. Nevertheless, album and concert sales climbed continuously. In the beginning, they made around $200 a night playing small clubs, but at their height were making more than $500,000 a night. After their fourth album, the band owned it's own plane, "The Starship."

Crowe, in the liner notes to *The Complete Studio Recordings,* summed it up: "The Zeppelin attitude had something to do with Peter Grant, their brilliant and imposing manager. A little bit to do with the wicked humor of Richard Cole, their road manager. Something to do with John Bonham thundering down the aisle of the Starship, performing Monty Python routines. With John Paul Jones, lost in dry ice, playing "No Quarter." It had a lot to do with Page and Plant, side-by-side, sharing a single spotlight, ripping through "Over the Hills and Far Away."

In 1974, the band returned to Headley Grange and recorded a double-album, *Physical Graffiti.* The standout song on the album was the hypnotic "Kashmir," a song the band members claim as their favorite. (Rapper Puff Daddy teamed with Page and Plant as well as Tom Morrello of Rage Against the Machine to create a reworking of "Kashmir" called "Come With Me," featuring a 70-piece orchestra, for the *Godzilla* soundtrack in 1998.) After the album's release in February 1975, the band decided to take some vacation time before touring again.

On August 4, during a trip to the Greek island of Rhodes, Plant and his wife rolled over a cliff in their car and both were seriously injured. Upcoming tours were postponed and for 18 months, it was not known whether Plant would walk again. The band released its live concert film, *The Song Remains the Same* to fill the void for their fan base during their time away. *Presence,* the band's seventh album, was recorded in Munich with Robert Plant in a wheelchair, his ankle still on the mend. The album was released in March 1976, and a tour followed the next year.

That tour was interrupted by tragedy when Plant's son Karac died at the age of five from a rare viral infection. The band abandoned their U.S. tour. "It was the toughest part of my entire life," Plant told reporter Deborah Wilker at the *Fort Lauderdale Sun-Sentinel.* "It didn't haunt me. I was just incredibly aggrieved."

Around this time, darker rumors about the band started, like stories of Page's excessive drug and alcohol use, rumors of his dabbling in black magic. There was speculation that karmic retribution was to blame for the tragedies.

James Rotondi, in *Guitar Player* magazine, recalled, "Enough preconceptions, bad raps and spurious accusations have swirled around Page over the last 30 years to fill the *National Enquirer, Blues Revue,* and an entire season of *The X-Files.*"

The band regrouped and in November and December of 1978 recorded *In Through the Out Door,* which was to be their final album. A rare single, "Fool in the Rain," was released in December 1979. A U.S. tour was planned for autumn 1980, however, their last show would be performed at the British Knebworth Festival in 1979.

On September 25, 1980, the band was assembled for rehearsals at Page's home and set to leave on tour the next day. During the night, however, Bonham was found dead in a bedroom. After drinking around 40 shots of vodka in a 12-hour period, Bonham died of asphyxiation. The remaining three members decided instantly that they could not go on without him. They later met in a London hotel room to write a statement for the press.

Page and Plant each embarked on other projects in the 1980s. Page formed The Firm, releasing a self titled first album in 1985, which had success with the single, "Radioactive." The Firm released a second album, *Mean Business,* the following year. Page released a solo album, *Outrider,* in 1988 and embarked on a brief project with David Coverdale in 1993, with one album, *Coverdale/Page.*

Plant released his first solo album, *Pictures at Eleven* in 1982, followed by *The Principle of Moments* (1983) and *Shaken 'n' Stirred* (1985). During these years, Plant distanced himself from his connections with Led Zeppelin.

Plant's stance seemed to change in 1985 when the remaining members reunited to play Live Aid concert with Bonham's son Jason on drums. Three years later, they reunited, again with Jason Bonham on drums, to play the Atlantic Records 40th Anniversary celebration. That same year, Plant released his fourth solo effort, *Now and Zen,* which contained samples of Zeppelin songs. His following solo efforts, *Manic Nirvana* (1990) and *Fate of Nations* (1993) also veered closer to his Zeppelin past.

"Led Zeppelin was so big and so successful that I wanted to distance myself from it," Plant told reporter Gary Graff in the *Houston Chronicle* in June 1988. "I was fooling myself, really. I've learned that I can lean on my past—without thinking that I'm taking the easy way out."

Hopes of a more permanent reunion sprang eternal among fans, and the remaining members of Led Zeppelin were offered $100 million to tour America. They turned it down. Two years later, Plant was still adamant about not reforming the band. He told Deborah Wilker of the *Fort Lauderdale Sun-Sentinel,* "I can't imagine anything more horrifying than three middle-aged men trying to pretend that 'Black Dog' is significant. It's inappropriate."

The mid-1990s finally saw a reunion of sorts. Plant was invited to play *MTV Unplugged* in 1994 and included Page plus a group of Egyptian, Moroccan, and Western classical musicians in addition to bassist Charlie Jones, drummer Michael Lee, and Porl Thompson of the Cure on rhythm guitar. The show was called "Unledded" and a recording of the program was released titled *No Quarter.*

In 1995, *The Sporting Life,* John Paul Jones's venture with avant-garde vocalist Diamanda Galas, was released. Jones told writer Joe Gore at *Guitar Player,* "I suppose I was disappointed that they didn't feel they had to tell me about it. (Page and Plant's project *No Quarter.*) I read it in the newspapers, which was kind of embarrassing. I'm a great Led Zeppelin fan. I thought it was a fantastic band, and I'm very proud of what we did. But Diamanda is a stunning artist, and I wouldn't want to be doing anything else right now."

In January 1995 Led Zeppelin was inducted into the Rock and Roll Hall of Fame by fellow heavy-rockers Aerosmith. "They were like Lord Byron-mad, bad and dangerous to know," Joe Perry of Aerosmith told *The Boston Globe.* "It was kind of like Howling Wolf meets the Loch Ness monster."

Led Zeppelin's record sales as strong as ever, a 1997 *Billboard* reported that Led Zeppelin were the number two-selling act of all time, according to the Record Industry Association of America (RIAA). Ten of their albums were certified at multi-platinum levels. By 1999, Led Zeppelin became the third act in music history to be awarded four or more Diamond albums, according to the RIAA.

Page and Plant continued the collaboration they'd renewed on *No Quarter* on *Walking Into Clarksdale* in 1998. The album, produced by indie-rock icon Steve Albini, represented the first new material from the duo since *In Through the Out Door* in 1979.

The two continued their solo efforts as well. Recorded over two nights in Los Angeles in October of 1999, *Jimmy Page & the Black Crowes Live at the Greek* was the first major release exclusively available online (at music-maker.com), where it could be customized by the purchaser. Page toured with The Black Crowes again the following year. Plant released his seventh solo album, *Dreamland,* in 2002, and toured behind it with his band, Strange Sensation, which again included Thompson from The Cure and Clive Deamer, drummer from Portishead. John Paul Jones released two solo CDs, 1999's *Zoomba* and *The Thunderthief,* featuring some guitar work by Robert Fripp, in 2002.

While the band had historically balked at commercializing their music, the new century saw a change of heart. First, Page and Plant licensed Zeppelin's "That's The Way" for use on the soundtrack to Cameron Crowe's 2001 film, *Almost Famous.* The film chronicled Crowe's early career as a rock journalist who, among other bands, interviewed and went on tour with Led Zeppelin. In 2002, Led Zeppelin sold a song for use in a commercial for the first time in the band's history, selling "Rock and Roll" to Cadillac. The car manufacturer has used the ad to sell its Cadillac CTS, XLR, Escalade, and Escalade EXT. In 2003, in honor of their 35th anniversary, Led Zeppelin released the *Led Zeppelin* DVD, which contains live performance footage, previously unreleased, from four of their tours during the 1970s. At the same time, the group also released *How the West Was Won,* a three-disc CD with live material compiled from their concerts in 1972 in California.

Books

Crowe, Cameron, "Light and Shade," *Led Zeppelin: The Complete Studio Recordings, 1993.*
Zalkind, Ronald, *Contemporary Music Almanac 1980/81,* Schirmer Books, 1980.

Periodicals

AP Online, March 18, 2002.
Associated Press Newswires, March 28, 2000.
Atlanta Journal and Constitution, September 2, 1988.
Billboard, December 13, 1997; April 21, 1998.
Boston Globe, August 10, 1992; January 13, 1995.
*Boston Herald,*November 14, 1993; January 13, 1995; October 21, 1999.
Buffalo News, September 19, 1993; November 18, 1994; April 24, 1998; May 12, 1998.
Calgary Herald, October 13, 2002.
Canadian Press, January 22, 2002.
Charleston Gazette, July 18, 2002.
Chicago Sun-Times, December 1, 1999.
Commercial Appeal, March 3, 1995.
Globe and Mail, May 16, 1988.
Guitar Player, February 1, 1995; February 1, 1998.
Herald, August 18, 1999.
Herald Express, October 13, 2000.
Houston Chronicle, June 5, 1988.
MX, October 17, 2001.
New Orleans Times-Picayune, March 12, 1995.
New York Times, August 15, 1975.
Plain Dealer, March 24, 1995; December 9, 1997.
Richmond News Leader, November 20, 1990.
St. Louis Post-Dispatch, June 7, 1998.
San Diego Union-Tribune, August 15, 2000.
Scottsman, February 2, 1999.
Seattle Times, March 16, 2000.
Times Union, July 9, 1998.
Toronto Star, August 27, 2002.

Turkish Daily News, March 8, 1998.
Western Mail, October 10, 2002.

Online

"Led Zeppelin," *RockinTown Bio,* http://rockintown.com/church/zeppelin.html (February 13, 2003).
"Led Zeppelin," *Rolling Stone,* http://www.rollingstone.com/artists/bio.asp?oid = 366 (February 13, 2003).
"Led Zeppelin," *VH-1.com,* http://www.vh1.com/artists/az/led_zeppelin/bio.jhtml (February 13, 2003).
"Led Zeppelin," *Yesterdayland,* http://www.yesterdayland.com/popopedia/shows/music/mu1253.php (February 13, 2003). □

Yuan Tseh Lee

Chemist Yuan Tseh Lee (born 1936) shared the 1986 Nobel Prize for Chemistry with two colleagues for the part he played in the development of chemical-reaction dynamics. Their work opened important new fields of chemistry. Remarkably, Lee developed many of the laboratory tools he employed in his research, receiving a number of patents over the years. A great educator as well as innovator, Lee would later return to his homeland to head Taiwan's top academic and research institution.

Yuan Tseh Lee was born on November 29, 1936, in Hsinchu, Taiwan. His father was a respected artist and his mother taught school. World War II had a great impact on his early life. When Lee started his elementary education, Taiwan was under Japanese occupation. His early schooling was interrupted by the war, as the Taiwanese had to move into the nearby mountains to escape the frequent bombings of the Allied Army. After the war, when Taiwan came under Chinese rule, Lee was able to continue his education as a third-grader. During his elementary school years, Lee first met Bernice Wu, who he would later marry. The marriage would produce three children: Ted, born in 1963; Sidney, born in 1966; and Charlotte, born in 1969.

During his early school years, Lee was an active student. His extracurricular activities included sports: he played baseball and was a member of a championship ping-pong team. In high school, he enjoyed tennis and played trombone in his school's marching band. Juggling schoolwork with his other interests taught Lee the value of time at a relatively youthful age. He credited this ability with his later success. "I learned how to use time productively, a skill which was very beneficial to my subsequent work," he told interviewer Ying-Yuen Hong.

Lee was an avid reader, a pursuit that helped shape his career direction. He cited a biography of Madame Curie as one of the major influences of his life. He was so impressed with Curie's passion for science and her compassion for her

fellow human beings that he decided that he, too, would become a scientist.

Studied Chemistry in College

Lee excelled as a high school student and easily qualified for college. In 1955, when he applied to the National Taiwan University, he was admitted without having to take an entrance exam. He entered with a good idea of what he wanted to study. "Before I went to college, I had already developed an interest in academic research," he told Hong.

In college, it did not take Lee long to focus on a specific career direction. At the end of his freshman year, he decided to enter the field of chemistry. Taiwan University fostered his academic and professional development: he studied under enthusiastic professors and a strong solidarity existed among the students. This helped Lee develop an innovative approach to his studies, something that would shape his later career. "After I entered the college, I knew from the experiences of others around me that if one wanted to become a laboratory scientist, one had to learn about electronic-related equipment," he told Hong. "And so I did just that. When I was researching and doing work in synthetic chemistry I needed to understand vacuums, so I studied the art of glass blowing." For his BS thesis, he worked with Professor Hua-sheng Cheng on the separation of strontium and barium using the paper electrophoresis method.

Lee began graduate work at the National Tsinghua University in 1959 and eventually received a Master's degree. His thesis involved the studies of the natural radioiso-

topes contained in hukutolite. He then stayed on at Tsinghua as a research assistant. Working with Professor C.H. Wong, Lee carried out the x-ray structure determination of tricyclopentadienyl samarium.

Relocated to the U.S.

In 1962, Lee enrolled at the University of California at Berkeley as a graduate student. His thesis involved research on chemi-ionization processes of electronically excited alkali atoms. Lee became interested in ion-molecule reactions and the dynamics of molecular scattering—particularly crossed molecular beam studies of reaction dynamics. This direction of study would eventually lead him into work that would culminate in a Nobel Prize.

Lee earned his Ph.D. in 1965 and began performing experiments involving ion molecule reactive scattering. He employed ion beam techniques that measured energy and angular distributions. Before long, he could design, build, and perform experiments with a powerful scattering apparatus. He also assembled a complete product distribution contour map. At the time, these accomplishments were considered significant achievements. They could be attributed to the innovative approach he often brought to his education. "When I got to the University of California to complete my doctorate, I also mastered machine shop skills, as I needed to know about it for my doctorate work," he related in the interview with Hong. "In my later experiments, I ended up using these practical skills. Out of all this study, I came to realize that in our society, any person with a special skill in a certain area can truly impact society. It is only in this way that progress in society can be pushed forward."

Began Work with Herschbach

At Harvard University in 1967, Lee began his association with Dudley R. Herschbach, the man with whom he would eventually share the 1986 Nobel Prize. Working as a post-doctoral fellow, Lee studied reactions of hydrogen atoms and diatomic alkali, as well as the construction of a universal crossed molecular beams apparatus. Other notable colleagues with whom Lee engaged in research included Robert Gordon, Doug McDonald, and Pierre LeBreton.

Pursuing further postdoctoral studies, Lee would experiment with and build upon the crossed molecular beam technique that Herschbach had developed. Herschbach derived his technique from elementary particle physics. It brought together molecular beams at supersonic speeds under controlled conditions, enabling researchers to closely observe how events occur during chemical reactions. Lee would bring the technology of mass spectroscopy into the technique. This allowed researchers to identify the products from chemical reactions—specifically the reactions of oxygen and fluorine atoms with complex organic compounds. By late 1967, thanks to the efforts of Lee and his colleagues, a machine was developed that was used in the first successful non alkali neutral beam experiment.

The following year, Lee entered the hugely successful academic phase of his career when he became an assistant professor in the Department of Chemistry at the James Franck Institute of the University of Chicago. Still working as a scientist, and now aided by his students, he built a new, more advanced crossed molecular beams apparatus that resulted in even more successful experiments. Lee was promoted to associate professor in 1971 and professor in 1973. He became an American citizen in 1975. That same year, he returned to Berkeley as a professor of chemistry and principal investigator at the Lawrence Berkeley Laboratory of the University of California.

Back at Berkeley, Lee would build what Richard Bernstein, professor of physical chemistry at the University of California at Los Angeles, once described as "some of the most powerful equipment in the field." As the range of Lee's work grew, his laboratory became one of the best in the world, and it attracted scientists from many countries. It contained complex molecular beams apparati designed to deal with problems associated with reaction dynamics, photochemical processes, and molecular spectroscopy.

Won Nobel Prize

Lee's association with Herschbach resulted in a share of the 1986 Nobel Prize for Chemistry, along with John C. Polanyi of the University of Toronto. The scientists were recognized for their research, performed independently, that led to the development of chemical-reaction dynamics. Their work enabled others to focus on the behavior of individual molecules in a chemical reaction, rather than just looking at the overall behavior of a large mass. According to Eric Leber of the American Chemical Society, the findings of their research presented the field with new applications that would improve the efficiency of industrial chemical reactions and the ability to burn coal and other fuels cleanly. It would also provide new information about the earth's atmosphere, such as how chemicals harm the ozone layer. At the time of his award, Lee was a chemist and University of California professor emeritus. He was also a professor emeritus of chemistry and principal investigator at the Lawrence Berkeley Laboratory.

Expanded Interests in Taiwan

Sensing that his life was becoming too complicated, Lee decided to return to Taiwan in 1987. He intended to help bring about major changes in Taiwanese society, to advance science, and to upgrade the country's leading educational institution, the Academia Sinica—and very importantly, to serve as a role model for young people. Another reason for returning was that he felt Asian scholars could make a real difference by returning to their native countries and helping them to develop.

As president of Academia Sinica, Lee would play a major role in shaping educational and scientific policy in Taiwan. He reported directly to the president of Taiwan and acted as his senior science adviser. Lee chaired Taiwan's Council of Educational Reform, advocating democratization, professionalism, and university autonomy. He also served as president of the Singapore-based Tan Kah Kee International Society, a large foundation dedicated to promoting education as a means of advancing democracy and

development. His efforts were recognized in 1998 when Lee received the Clark Kerr Award for Distinguished Leadership in Higher Education. By this time his intellectual interests extended well beyond the field of chemistry. Lee often spoke about the direction and responsibilities of higher education, the future of mankind, global warming, the futility of war, and the environment. He also embraced the idea of the world as a global village.

Online

Chandler, David L., "Harvard Chemist Awarded Nobel," *The Boston Globe,* October 16, 1986, http://www.boston.com/globe/search/stories/nobel/1986/1986j.html (February 10, 2003).

Department of Chemistry-Yuan T. Lee, *College of Chemistry-University of California Berkeley,* http://chem.berkeley.edu/people/emeriti/lee.html (February 10, 2003)

Hong, Ying-Yuen, "The Glory of the Nobel Prize—Dr. Yuan Tseh Lee," http://aries.pcsh.tpc.edu.tw/1/li.htm (February 10, 2003).

"Nobel Laureates: Yuan T. Lee 1986 Nobel Prize for Chemistry," *TEID Library Services,* 1987, http://www-library.lbl.gov/teid/tmLib/nobellaureates/LibYT_Lee.htm#bio (February 10, 2003).

"Yuan T. Lee," *Cartage,* http://www.cartage.org.lb/en/themes/Biographies/MainBiographies/L/Lee1/Lee.htm (February 10, 2003).

"Yuan T. Lee's Crossed Molecular Beam Experiment," *Office of Basic Energy Sciences,* http://aries.pcsh.tpc.edu.tw/1/li.htm (February 10, 2003).

"Yuan Tseh Lee," *Outstanding Scientists,* http://www.nstm.gov.tw/nobel/evip/evip_leeyj.htm (February 10, 2003). □

Ethel Leginska

England's Ethel Leginska (1886–1970) enjoyed an acclaimed career as a concert pianist for many years; in the 1920s she became the first woman to regularly appear as a conductor with some of the world's top orchestras. Leginska left behind a small body of musical works she wrote for the symphony and string quartet, as well as two operas. Many "were performed by major organizations at a time when women's compositions rarely received such recognition," according Leginska's profile in *Notable American Women: The Modern Period.*

Studied in Vienna

Leginska was born Ethel Liggins on April 13, 1886, in Hull, a thriving port city in northeast England. Her parents were Thomas Liggins and Annie Peck Liggins, and her innate musical talents were recognizable from an early age. With the encouragement of her parents, she began a public recital career at age six and soon became known as a child prodigy in the city. When she was in her teens, a wealthy Hull shipping family, the Wilsons, became her patrons and paid for her formal musical training on the European continent. Leginska first studied in Germany with James Kwast, a Dutch pianist, at the Hoch Conservatory in Frankfurt am Main. She then went to Vienna to study with Theodor Leschetizky for three years there. This Austrian, who enjoyed a renowned concert career in the 1840s, was inarguably the most famous piano teacher of his era. He taught Ignace Jan Paderewski, Artur Schnabel, Ossip Gabrillowitsch, and many other prominent names, and by the time Leginska came to study with him, he was one of Vienna's leading cultural icons and even friends with the Austro-Hungarian emperor.

In 1902, at the age of 16, Leginska made her solo recital debut in London. A renowned singer of the era, Lady Maud Warrender, suggested to her that she change her name to more Slavic-sounding "Leginska" to boost her professional career. At the time, Polish and Russian piano prodigies like Paderewski were very much in vogue, and Leginska soon came to be dubbed the "Paderewski of woman pianists." She studied in Berlin and made a concert tour of Europe. In 1907, she married an American, Roy Emerson Whittern, whom she had met in Vienna when he was a student of Leschetizky as well. The following year, they had a child, Cedric. In 1909 Leginska suffered what would be the first of three nervous breakdowns in her life. She separated from Whittern in 1912.

Gained Enthusiastic Following

Leginska sailed to America to make her debut at New York City's Aeolian Hall on January 20, 1913. She earned favorable reviews for the performance and decided to base herself in the city, keeping a small rehearsal studio at Carnegie Hall. Her vigorous style and fluid movements at the bench differentiated her from other concert pianists of the time, who played with a more rigid and formal demeanor. Yet Leginska believed that a more emotive technique yielded a more expressive listening experience. "Relaxation is a hobby with me," she was quoted as saying in a 1915 volume by Harriette Brower, *Piano Mastery: Talks with Master Pianists and Teachers.* "I believe in absolute freedom in every part of the arm anatomy, from the shoulder down to the finger tips. Stiffness seems to me the most reprehensible thing in piano playing, as well as the most common fault with all kinds of players."

Leginska was also somewhat daring for wearing her hair in a bobbed style and eschewing the formal, bare-shouldered evening gowns that were standard stage gear for women performers in the classical world at the time. Instead she favored an imitation of a tuxedo-a black velvet jacket, slim skirt, and white shirt. Her career began to accelerate around 1915, and she gave sold-out performances of piano works from the German canon, such as the concertos of J. S. Bach and Franz Schubert. "She was an extremely popular artist and won praise from the press for her demanding programs, her magnetism as a performer, and her innovations—for example, playing an entire Chopin program without an intermission," as noted in *Notable American Women.*

Lost Custody of Son

Leginska's husband managed her career for a time, but they were divorced by 1916. She soon took up many of the duties herself, as a *Women in World History: A Biographical Encyclopedia* essay by Neil M. Heyman noted. Heyman described her as "canny about publicity. In 1916, when she injured her finger in a door, she sent an X-ray taken of the bruised digit to a music magazine and had the satisfaction of seeing it appear in a subsequent issue." Yet a string of off-stage worries began to hinder her career. She sometimes failed to appear at scheduled engagements and entered into a bitter custody battle with Whittern over their son. She lost, though she had even offered to give up performing altogether and instead teach piano for a living. She estimated that she could earn around $300 a week—a large sum of money at the time—but the judge sided with her ex-husband.

Not surprisingly, Leginska often spoke publicly about the challenges faced by the few professional women of the time, especially regarding child care. She also urged women to move forward and break down artificial barriers. She was already doing so herself by writing her own compositions, which she began around 1914. To further her knowledge, she studied composition with Rubin Goldmark and Ernest Bloch, and the first of her works to be performed publicly was *String Quartet,* inspired by four poems by an Indian poet, which premiered in Boston in April of 1921. A symphonic poem with a title borrowed from a tale by Irish fantasy-fiction pioneer Lord Dunsany, *Beyond the Fields We Know,* made its debut in New York City the following February. The critics treated these performances of Leginska's work as somewhat of a novelty, however.

Led Europe's Top Philharmonics

Leginska decided to turn her energies to conducting. She traveled to London in 1923 to study with Eugene Gossens and later that year worked with Robert Heger, conductor of the esteemed Bavarian State Opera in Munich. Through connections realized in the classical world from her earlier stage career, she secured guest-conductor spots by agreeing to appear on the program with a piano concerto. She conducted several renowned bodies, including the Berlin Philharmonic. Soon she was able to lead orchestras in performances of her own works, beginning in December of 1924 with her *Quatre sujets barbares* suite in Munich. She made her American conducting debut on January 9, 1925, with the New York Symphony Orchestra at Carnegie Hall and appeared in a much-lauded Hollywood Bowl engagement in Los Angeles later that summer.

Leginska was still plagued by stress, however, and in 1925 and 1926 suffered two more nervous breakdowns. The 1925 episode began with a taxi trip to Carnegie Hall for a scheduled performance of hers; she vanished en route and a last-minute substitute had to be called in. Missing for four days, she was finally located in Boston. The following year, she disappeared again before a New York City engagement, leaving some 1,500 admirer's waiting for her to appear. She later claimed that her manager was supposed to have canceled the date. She also had a bad experience that same year on a tour of the Midwest. As Heyman reported in his *Women in World History* article, Leginska "abandoned a performance scheduled to take place before an audience of 4,000 in Evansville, Indiana. She had given a hint of her state of mind the previous day when she complained loudly of the city's yellow cabs, the lack of a symphony orchestra to accompany her, and the concert hall, which she described as 'an old barn.'"

Formed Groundbreaking Women's Orchestras

Consulting with doctors, Leginska was counseled to take a year off from performing and duly announced her official retirement from the concert stage as a solo pianist. She wrote her last symphonic work, *Fantasy for Piano and Orchestra,* which made its premiere on January 3, 1926, in New York. She had settled in Boston in 1925 and there founded the hundred-member Boston Philharmonic Orchestra, which was a mostly male group that offered accessible ticket prices to classical-music lovers for one short season. She then established the Women's Symphony Orchestra of Boston in 1926. It toured twice before it folded in 1930. In December of 1928 she conducted a National Opera Company performance of *Rigoletto* at the Boston Opera House. Her determination to conduct—when it was unheard of for a woman to do so at the time-ignited a media debate; detractors argued that women did not possess the intellectual rigors to handle the complexities of the job.

Leaving Boston for Europe in 1930, Leginska conducted performances of opera companies there and returned to New York City in 1931 to lead an orchestra for a Broadway revival of Franz von Suppe's *Boccaccio.* The following year, she founded another short-lived group, the National Women's Symphony Orchestra, in New York. An opera she wrote, *Gale,* made its debut at the Chicago City Opera on November 23, 1935, with Leginska at the podium. She found fewer opportunities to lead orchestras, however, and turned to teaching to support herself. Living in London and Paris in during the late 1930s, she had some notable students there, and in 1939 settled in Los Angeles. Again, she enjoyed a reputation as an esteemed instructor in her field, and her students of note from this later part of her career included James Fields, Daniel Pollack, and Bruce Sutherland. She also established a concert bureau, New Ventures in Music, with many of her students on its roster. A second opera, *The Rose and the Ring,* had its debut in Los Angeles in 1957, again with Leginska leading the orchestra. It would be the last of her works to debut before an audience.

It was not until late 1950s that women conductors began to make progress within classical circles: Leginska's true heir at the podium was American Sarah Caldwell and her Opera Company of Boston. Some years later, Caldwell became the first woman ever to conduct at the New York Metropolitan Opera House in a 1976 engagement. Leginska died in Los Angeles of a stroke on February 26, 1970, at the age of 83. Despite her pioneering forays into composition and conducting, Leginska remained devoted to her first love. "For me the piano is capable of reflecting every mood,

every feeling; all pathos, joy, sorrow—the good and the evil too—all there is in life, all that one has lived," she told Brower in the *Piano Mastery* interview. She made some recordings for the Columbia label in the mid-1920s and in 2002 these were re-issued on Ivory in the compact-disc format. Of its *Four Impromptus* by Schubert, the Chopin *Polonaise,* two Rachmaninoff *Preludes,* and Liszt's *Hungarian Rhapsody, American Record Guide* critic Harold C. Schonberg found that the tracks "reveal a superior musical mind coupled to an unerring technique."

Books

Baker's Biographical Dictionary of Musicians, Centennial Edition, edited by Nicolas Slonimsky, Schirmer, 2001.

Brower, Harriette, *Piano Mastery: Talks with Master Pianists and Teachers,* Frederick A. Stokes Company, 1915.

The New Grove Dictionary of Opera, edited by Stanley Sadie, Volume Two: E-Lom, Grove's Dictionaries of Music, 1992.

Notable American Women: The Modern Period. A Biographical Dictionary, edited by Barbara Sicherman and Carole Hurd Green, with Ilene Kantrov and Harriette Walker, Belknap/Harvard University Press, 1980.

Women in World History: A Biographical Encyclopedia, edited by Anne Commire, *Volume 9: Laa-Lyud,* Yorkin, 1999–2000.

Periodicals

American Record Guide, May/June 2001.

Los Angeles Times, March 31, 1990; August 3, 1995. □

Mike Leigh

Mike Leigh (born 1943) is a British writer and director whose works have appeared on film, television, and the stage. Leigh's unusual methodology for writing his works—working in collaboration with the actors who will would portray his characters—has resulted in such critically acclaimed films as *Naked* and *Secrets and Lies.*

Mike Leigh was born February 20, 1943, in Salford, Lancashire, England, the son of Dr. Alfred Abraham and Phyllison Pauline (Cousin) Leigh. His physician father was of Jewish descent, and the family name had been changed from Lieberman to Leigh by the time Leigh was born. Dr. Leigh's practice was in a working-class neighborhood, and Leigh attended local schools like Salford Grammar School.

A fan of films from an early age, Leigh earned a scholarship to college but chose to study acting instead and in 1960 entered London's Royal Academy of Dramatic Arts. Leigh quit two years later because of the school's stifling atmosphere, although he did direct a student production of Harold Pinter's *The Caretaker* before he left.

After leaving the Royal Academy, Leigh continued his education in a number of creative arenas. From 1963 to 1964 he attended the Camberwell School of Art and the London International School of Film Technique. The follow-

ing year he was a student at the Central School of Art and Design.

Began Career at Theater

From 1965 to 1966 Leigh was the associate director of the Midlands Art Centre for Young People, located in the industrial city of Birmingham. There he created three plays designed to be performed improv by Birmingham's inner-city youth. Leigh's first play *The Box Play* was produced in 1965, and he also directed the production. In 1966 he formed the short-lived Dramagraph production company. Before the company went bankrupt he was able to direct a production of *Little Malcolm and His Struggle against the Eunuchs,* written by David Halliwell. Leigh did not confine himself to directing and writing for the stage; he fulfilled his acting ambitions by appearing with the Victoria Theatre at Stroke-on-Kent, Staffordshire in 1966. Leigh has continued to appeared in occasional films throughout his career.

In 1967-68 Leigh worked as an assistant director of the famous Royal Shakespeare Company. While there, he directed the troupe in production of *Nenaa.* He also worked in theater-related areas, lecturing in drama at Sedgley Park and de la Salle colleges in Manchester from 1968 to 1969 and the London Film School from 1970 to 1973.

It was while working in the theater in the 1960s that Leigh devised his uncommon scriptwriting method. After he had sufficient funding for a project, he asked his actors to create characters they wished to play, then worked with each actor individually on developing that character's en-

tire life history. While Leigh had an idea of where he wanted the story to go, it was during rehearsals and improv that the whole script came together. Leigh refined this method while working in television and film later in his career. Though it sometimes was difficult to acquire funding without a finished script, Leigh eventually transcended this difficulty as producers realized that his works often gained an unusual polish and depth because of his writing method.

Made First Film

In 1972 Leigh wrote and directed his first feature-length film, *Bleak Moments,* after obtaining funding from Memorial Enterprises, a company run by actor Albert Finney, during a low point in the British film industry. *Bleak Moments* focuses on an unmarried woman, an accountant's clerk, who lives with her 29-year-old, mentally challenged sister. Although unplanned, Leigh subsequently took a break from film for 17 years, taking instead to the stage and to television, until funding once again became available for the kind of cinema projects he wished to do.

Much of Leigh's work for stage and television in the 1970s and early to mid-1980s featured themes and character types he would go on to explore in his later films. Many of his works of this period focus on the working and lower middle classes and concern unemployment and family life. Leigh did his first television drama in 1973, *Hard Labour,* a dark look at a working-class family. In 1977 he wrote and directed both a stage and television-movie version of *Abigail's Party,* about a party hostess forced to deal with a guest inconciderate enough to have a heart attack while attending Abigail's social gathering.

Other notable television movies by Leigh include *Home Sweet Home* (1982), about three postmen and their respective families, and *Nuts in May,* about a class conflict that occurs when middle- and working-class couples converge at a campsite. In 1977's *The Kiss of Death* an undertaker's apprentice discovers the fairer sex, while *Grown Ups* (1980) explores the problems in a working-class marriage which is threatened when the husband leaves his wife.

While Leigh's theater credits are not lengthy, several of his plays, such as *Babies Grow Old* (1974), *The Silent Majority* (1974), and *Smelling a Rat* (1988), explore similar themes. Produced in 1979, Leigh's *Ecstasy* is representative, focusing as it does on the way London's working-class women are abused and exploited. A number of Leigh's plays were produced in the United States after their author made a name for himself as a filmmaker.

Perhaps ironically, while Leigh often focused on left-leaning issues in his television movies and stage productions, he was not popular with British socialists and others of the political left because of his negative depiction of working-class people and their issues. Chris Savage King, in *New Statesman & Society,* praised Leigh's television work, however, writing that during the late 1970s and into the 1980s many dramatic films produced for British television subjected viewers to a lecture "on some aspect of social malaise or . . . [presented] an uncritical tour around upper-middle-class afflictions. Mike Leigh plays were special, because they were recognizable. The dramas were too close to home to be seen at any airy distance. And the characters were too insistently and pitilessly themselves to fall into a category of the oppressed.''

Returned to Cinema

In 1988 Leigh received funding for his second feature film, *High Hopes.* This quiet comedy is set in London and takes place during the regime of conservative Prime Minister Margaret Thatcher. The movie focuses on a free-spirited couple, Cyril and Shirley, who are working-class optimists by choice but with secret hopes and ambitions. The pair are forced to deal with Cyril's family: his rich sister and her husband and his problematic mother and her yuppie neighbors. While realistic, the play's naturalism is heightened for comic effect.

High Hopes received much critical praise and helped to introduce Leigh to movie audiences in the United States. Critic Jay Carr praised the film in the *Boston Globe* writing that ''Leigh is an angry, humane battler trying to keep working-class hopes and ideals alive in what he sees as an increasingly selfish and soul-crushing Thatcherian England.''

Films have remained Leigh's primary focus throughout much of his career since *High Hopes,* although he continued to venture into television and theater on occasion. In 1990, for example, he wrote the play *Greek Tragedy (an Australian Comedy)* on commission from Sydney's Belvoir Street Theatre to commemorate Australia's bicentenary. The play focuses on Greek immigrants to Australia while drawing on the history of Greek tragedies. Though Leigh's work was criticized by some in Australia, he learned much about the two cultures in the process.

In 1991 Leigh had a small hit on his hands after writing and directing the working-class family comedy *Life Is Sweet.* The story focuses on parents Wendy and Andy and their dreams. Andy, a chef, tries to start his own business selling food from a van while Wendy helps a family friend start a restaurant that soon fails. Their daughters have difficulties as well. Nicola, although intelligent, is a college dropout with an eating disorder while Natalie works as a plumber's assistant and hones her sarcastic wit on her family. *Life Is Sweet* chronicles the minutia of its characters' lives and, while there are depressing elements, Leigh shows optimism by the end.

Life Is Sweet was generally well received by critics. Vincent Canby of the *New York Times* wrote, ''Leigh's films appear to be shapeless, devoid of poetry. They are unforgiving in their portrayal of squalor. They shuffle along on tired feet, seemingly as aimless and inarticulate as their characters. Yet at some point in each of his films there comes a transforming moment when the unbearable and the hopeless fuse together to create an explosion of recognition, sometimes of high, incredible hilarity.''

Challenged Viewers with *Naked*

Leigh's next film, much darker and more bitter than *Life Is Sweet,* was 1993's *Naked.* Winning Leigh the Cannes Film Festival's award for best director, *Naked* shows its writer's conscious move away from domestic concerns.

Naked primarily focuses on one character, Johnny (played by actor David Thewlis), who rants and raves his theories as he travels the streets of his working-class London neighborhood. Arriving in London with neither money nor a place to stay, Johnny ends up sleeping at his ex-girlfriend's apartment. A dynamic character, Johnny is violent and intelligent, both a victim and a victimizer.

While *Naked* was praised by critics as thought provoking, it was better received in the United States than in Great Britain. As Canby wrote in the *New York Times,* ''*Naked* is as corrosive and sometimes as funny as anything Mr. Leigh has done to date. It's loaded with wild flights of absurd rhetoric and encounters with characters so eccentric they seem to have come directly from life. Nobody would dare imagine them.''

Secrets and Lies Garnered Broad Appeal

While *Naked* attracted a larger audience for Leigh than had his earlier works, his next movie seemed almost mainstream. *Secrets and Lies* covers the domestic front; its story focuses on a black ophthalmologist named Hortense, who finds and meets her birth mother, a white, middle-aged, working-class woman named Cynthia. Cynthia hides the revelation from her family at first, but as her brother, his wife, and one of Cynthia's daughters find out the truth, the film focuses on how it changed their lives. *Secrets and Lies* appealed to a broader audience than any other film by Leigh, earning him Academy Award nominations for best direction and best screenplay.

Leigh's next two films forged a new path for the director. His 1997 film *Career Girls* focuses on two female friends from college who meet later in their lives. The movie looks at the women's pasts and their present state, presenting a portrait that is emotionally bleak. Perhaps because of its dark nature, *Career Girls* was not as well received as Leigh's other works.

Leigh did something very different with 1999's *Topsy-Turvy,* and was much more successful. Focusing on the collaboration between 19th-century composer W. S. Gilbert and librettist Arthur Sullivan, who collaborated on such popular light operas as *The Pirates of Penzance* and *The Mikado,* Leigh's period drama begins in 1884 as the pair attempt to stage the newly completed *Mikado. Topsy-Turvy,* while very much a backstage story, nonetheless shows how Gilbert and Sullivan related to each other, as well as how their productions were staged. This film was generally well received by critics and audiences alike.

In 2002 Leigh returned to familiar territory with *All or Nothing,* which focuses on the intersecting lives of three dysfunctional working-class London families living in public housing. The couple at the center, Phil and Penny, have marital problems, and Phil cannot make enough as a cab driver to support his family. Their children are equally unhappy, but for differing reasons. Phil and Penny's neighbors include Maureen, whose teenage daughter is pregnant, and Carol, who is an alcoholic. *All or Nothing,* which takes place in one weekend, incorporated themes of despair and redemption, and of the need by humans to be loved.

Although films such as *Secrets and Lies* and *Topsy-Turvy* have made Leigh a household name in England and established a strong following in the United States, other of his films have been viewed as subversive. With each new film, each new approach, he runs the same risk of negative critical reaction, even in his native country. However, Leigh's motivation has not been fitting in with the movie mainstream. As he told Desson How of the *Washington Post,* "My ongoing preoccupation is with families, relationships, parents, children, sex, work, surviving, being born and dying. I'm totally intuitive, emotional, subjective, empirical, instinctive. I'm not an intellectual filmmaker. Primarily my films are a response to the way people are, the way things are as I experience them. In a way, they are acts of taking the temperature."

Books

Pendergast, Tom, and Sara Pendergast, editors, *International Dictionary of Films and Filmmakers,* St. James Press, 2000.

Periodicals

American Theatre, May-June, 1995.
Associated Press, October 30, 1991.
Boston Globe, March 31, 1989; January 21, 2000.
Calgary Herald, February 18, 2000.
Christian Science Monitor, September 7, 1993.
Cineaste, Fall 1996; Winter 2002.
Financial Times (London, England), October 12, 2002.
Independent (London, England), August 8, 1990; March 17, 1991; May 18, 2002; October 12, 2002.
New Statesman & Society, April 23, 1993.
New Times Los Angeles, January 13, 2000.
New York Times, September 24, 1988; February 19, 1989; April 10, 1992; December 16, 1993; September 22, 1996; November 14, 1999; October 20, 2002.
Time, September 30, 1996.
Time Out, September 25, 2002.
Washington Post, December 27, 1991; January 30, 1994. □

Lillian Leitzel

Lillian Leitzel (1892–1931), known as Queen of the Air, was an aerial performer with the Ringling Brothers and Barnum and Bailey Circus from 1915 to 1931. Leitzel astounded audiences around the world with her act, which involved a series of planges in which she rotated around like a propeller while holding onto a rope with one hand. Leitzel headlined the circus longer than any performer in history. She died after falling while performing her act.

Leitzel was born Leopoldina Altitza Pelikan in Breslau, Germany, on January 2, 1892. Her nickname, Leitzel, was a variation of her middle name and became her stage name. Leitzel's parents separated when she was young. Her father, Edward J. Eleanore, was a former Hungarian army officer who became a theatrical empresario. He raised his children as he had managed his troops, demanding obedience and physical conditioning. The willful Leitzel clashed with him frequently when she was growing up and rarely spoke of him as an adult.

Leitzel's mother, Elinor (Nellie) Pelikan, was a trapeze artist who came from a family of circus performers. Nellie's mother performed on the trapeze until age 84. An uncle, Adolph Pelikan, originated the stunt in which a clown walks with a plank balanced on his head, turns, and walks in the opposite direction with the plank in place. Nellie and two of her sisters performed around the world as the Leamy Ladies, named for their manager, Edward Leamy.

Leitzel had a brother, Arthur G. Pelikan, who became director of the Milwaukee Art Institute. Leitzel's mother was often on tour, so Leitzel and her brother lived with their maternal grandmother and attended school in Breslau. Leitzel learned to speak five languages and studied music, literature, art, and ballet. Her family and teachers considered that she may become a concert pianist, but by the age of nine, she knew she wanted to become an aerialist.

At nine, Leitzel traveled to England with her grandparents during an extended performance of the Leamy Ladies. Leitzel, who had taught herself trapeze tricks, brought a miniature trapeze to the theater one day and convinced her mother to allow her to join the act. Soon, she was upstaging her mother and aunts.

In 1911, the Leamy Ladies traveled to the United States to perform, but their act did not catch on in America. Leitzel's mother and aunts returned to Europe to perform in circuses there. Leitzel remained in the United States where she hoped to continue her career. She took a job at a New Jersey nightclub on the promise that New York producers were scouting the act. On the second of her three-night gig, Leitzel fell and landed on both knees. Her legs were sprained and bruised, but she returned the third night and completed her act to thunderous applause. The New York producers offered her jobs in vaudeville acts. She was known as "Lillian Leitzel, the World's Foremost and Most Daring Aerial Star."

In 1914, while performing in South Bend, Indiana, she was spotted by an agent for the Ringling Brothers Circus. She was offered a contract unlike any other for a new performer—$250 per week, star billing, and many other perks. She debuted with Ringling Brothers on April 17, 1915, in Chicago. When Ringling Brothers merged with the Barnum and Bailey in 1919, Leitzel was a headline performer.

Played to the Crowd

Leitzel was an aerialist, not a trapeze artist. She performer her act on movable ringing, suspended from the tent ceiling. She did not use a safety net. Theatrics was a large part of Leitzel's act and she played to the crowds who reacted wildly to her showmanship. As her act began, the lights dimmed and a lone spotlight found Leitzel in the tent's entrance. She entered the ring carried by a giant dressed as a hotel doorman. The contrast between the two accentuated Leitzel's diminutive size. She stood 4 feet, 9 inches tall and weighed 95 pounds. In the air, she looked like a fairy, but close up, her overdeveloped upper-body muscles gave her a gnome-like appearance. Leitzel's personal maid, Mabel Clemings, accompanied her into the ring and took Leitzel's robe, revealing her sequined halter, bare midriff, and trunks covered by a sheer skirt.

After playing to the crowd for a while, she kicked off her gold mules before ascending the rope web as the band played *Crimson Cradle March.* Unlike most performers who simply climbed the webbing to the apparatus, Leitzel ascended the web in a series of rollups, in which she rolled her body up and over itself while holding onto the rope. At the top of the tent, she performed a series of graceful twirls and swings on the Roman rings to the tune of *William Tell Overture.* She then glided back to the ground.

The second part of her act was Leitzel's trademark and is what made her famous. When she ascended the web again, all other circus activities stopped. Leitzel was the first person in history to gain such attention. After returning to the top of the tent, she slipped her wrist into a padded rope loop attached to a swivel and ring. She then performed a series of one-arm planges accompanied by a drumroll. A plange is a move in which Leitzel threw her body over her head, swinging around vertically like a propeller. With each turn, the cymbals clashed and the crowd counted, "33, 34, 35 . . . 89, 90 91," up to 100 or 150 turns. Her record was 249. Late in her career she performed up to 60.

Leitzel's theatrics continued to the end of her act. She often extended her act beyond its allotted time, angering the performers that followed her. Leitzel piled her long, thick blond hair atop her head and secured it in such a way that it tumbled out in sections as she spun. *Center Ring* reported that it was an unsettling sight, giving people "the idea that the act was so brutal she was flying apart at the seams, like an airplane under strain." When she returned to the floor after her act, she staggered out of the ring, swooning as if she were about to faint. The crowd ate it up.

Leitzel's mother is said to have first performed the plange, but Leitzel perfected the act. Despite Leitzel's incredible upper body strength and the ease with which she appeared to perform the act, the plange was a difficult move that took its toll on Leitzel's body. Every turn partially dislocated her shoulder, which then snapped back into place. Despite attempts to protect her wrist, the rope lacerated it with every turn and she returned to the ground bloodied. She always covered her raw, cracked wrist in public by wearing bracelets, long sleeves or a silk scarf. *Center Ring* states that when a doctor once suggested that she alternate arms when performing her act, she replied vainly, "My right arm is already ruined, but my left arm is pretty, and I'm a woman."

Adored by Fans

Outside the ring, Leitzel enjoyed the attention of her fans and the press. Her popularity rivaled that of movie stars. But her temper and her ego gave her a reputation as moody and demanding. She was the first circus performer to have her own dressing tent and a private car on the circus train. It was even equipped with a baby grand piano. During her frequent tirades, she cursed or slapped circus workers. At the same time, she adored children and tutored many of the circus employees' offspring. She bought them gifts and toys and gave them birthday parties.

Despite her volatile temper, men adored Leitzel and showered her with gifts. Railroad magnates, senators, and entertainers often visited her dressing room to meet her. Her response to them was unpredictable. When the circus played in Detroit, Henry Ford appeared at her door with a bouquet of flowers. She left him waiting before finally seeing him.

Leitzel married three times. The name of her first husband is unknown and the marriage lasted only a short time. In 1920, Leitzel married Clyde Ingalls, a side-show manager and ring announcer. Ingalls stood 6 feet tall and could not keep up with his famous wife socially or financially. He often had to ask her for money. He was jealous of the attention Leitzel continued to receive from other men. The last straw occurred when a Chicago sportsman threw Leitzel a party at the Hotel Stevens. The party featured a mermaid swimming in vintage champagne and a gold-plated statue of Leitzel. The host gave each guest a $50 bill and presented Leitzel with a diamond tiara. Ingalls filed for divorce shortly after, in 1924.

In 1928, Leitzel married the love of her life, Alfredo Codona, the "King of the Trapeze." Like Leitzel, Codona came from a family of circus performers, had begun his career as a child, and had lifted his art to a new level. Many people felt the match was predestined, but the relationship was stormy. There were frequent screaming matches, breakups, and reconciliations.

Accident Led to Death

During the Ringling Brothers off-season, Leitzel and Codona performed together and singly in vaudeville shows and circuses around the world. On Friday, February 13, 1931, Leitzel performed her act at the Valencia Music Hall in Copenhagen, Denmark. She was haunted by a nightmare that had awakened her several days earlier. In the dream, she was being hoisted to the top of the ring on a rope. Leitzel watched as the rope unraveled. Below her, her husband could not hear her cries for help. Just as the rope broke, she jolted awake.

After completing the rings portion of her act on that Friday the 13th, Leitzel began her planges. Early in the performance, the swivel ring broke as a result of repeatedly being heated from the friction of use. Leitzel fell 20 feet to the ground and landed on her shoulders and back. Although she suffered a concussion and spinal injuries, she remained conscious and attempted to continue her performance, but instead was taken to the hospital. Codona, who was performing in Berlin, rushed to her side. Leitzel convinced him that she was okay and insisted that he return to Berlin, which he did. Two days later, on February 15, 1931, Leitzel died of complications from the fall.

People were shocked at Leitzel's fall. Her husband explained that Leitzel's injuries were strangely the result of inexperience—she didn't know how to fall. The only time she'd ever fallen was long ago in the New Jersey nightclub.

Leitzel was cremated and her ashes were interred in Inglewood Park Cemetery, Inglewood, California. Codona built a memorial to his wife in the cemetery. Titled "The Spirit of Flight," it stands 12 feet high and depicts Codona, with angels' wings, and Leitzel embracing. Roman rings appear at the base of the statue.

Codona went into seclusion after Leitzel's death. He later returned to the circus and married Vera Bruce, an equestrienne member of his troupe. He became increasingly reckless in his performances and his career ended in 1933 when he injured his shoulder in a fall. He tended Bruce's horses for a while, then worked at a gas station. In 1937, Bruce filed for divorce. When Codona met her at her lawyer's office to work out a settlement, he pulled out a gun and shot and killed Bruce and himself. Codona was buried beside Leitzel's ashes at the base of the memorial statue.

Books

Notable American Woman 1607–1950: A Biographical Dictionary, Edward T. James, editor, Belknap Press, 1971.

Ogen, Tom, *Two Hundred Years of the American Circus,* Facts on File, 1993.

Taylor, Robert Lewis, *Center Ring: The People of the Circus,* Doubleday & Co., 1956.

Periodicals

American History Illustrated, July–August 1993.

Online

"Lillian Leitzel," *Ringling Bros. and Barnum & Bailey,* www.ringlingbros.com (March 11, 2003). ☐

José Arcadia Limón

José Arcadia Limón (1908–1972) is remembered as a pioneer of modern dance and choreography. He firmly established the importance of the male dancer in American modern dance through the heroes he created and the masculine movement style of his choreography for men.

Limón was born in Culiacán, Sinaloa, Mexico. His father, a musician, conductor, and pedagogue, was a widower and father of three when he married 16-year-old Francisca Traslaviña. She bore him 11 children (and another three who died at birth), of which Limón was the eldest. His mother was a devout Catholic and raised the children accordingly.

The Mexican revolution wreaked havoc in Limón's young life; at the age of five he witnessed the death by gunshot of a young uncle. His father directed various military bands during this period, and the family had to move frequently, to Cananea, Hermosilla, Nogales, and finally across the border to Tucson, Arizona, when Limón was seven. His father worked in various Arizona cities as a musician and conductor and finally settled his family in Los Angeles, California, when Limón was 12. Due to an early humiliation with English, young Limón resolved to master the language, and he continued to develop his prodigious vocabulary throughout his life. He exhibited early talent as both a musician and a visual artist. In high school he was introduced to the glories of Western art, and at about the same time began to study piano.

When Limón was 18, his mother died in childbirth, a tragedy that drove him away from the Catholic Church and his father, both of which he blamed for this devastating loss. After high school he studied painting briefly at the University of California, and then, at the urging of three "bohemian" friends, he moved to New York City in 1928 to study at the Art Students League. There he soon became disillusioned by the painting classes, believing that his classmates and teachers were merely imitating the French moderns. His vision was more influenced by El Greco, but he despaired of ever equaling his idol. By chance he attended a dance performance by German Expressionist Harald Kreutzberg and Yvonne Georgi and knew immediately that he had to dance. He enrolled in classes at the Humphrey-Weidman School, where Doris Humphrey and Charles Weidman became his artistic mentors. Pauline Lawrence, who had left Denishawn at the same time as Humphrey and Weidman, served as school registrar, tour manager, costume designer, stage manager, and accompanist for Humphrey-Weidman. These four lived communally for several years. Limón had become an earnest disciple of a revolutionary new art form, American modern dance. After very little training, he became a member of the company, performed in Broadway shows they choreographed, and began his own early choreographic efforts.

Limón's apprenticeship with Humphrey-Weidman lasted over 10 years, during which time he was increasingly featured in their concert work. His first choreographic efforts began early, and in 1930 he formed "The Little Group" with two women from the company, Eleanor King and Ernestine Henoch. The Humphrey-Weidman Company spent several summers at Bennington College, where Limón was named a Choreography Fellow in 1937. The following year he choreographed his first major work, *Danzas Mexicanas,* one of several dances he made that explored Mexican themes.

In 1940, disgusted with the triviality of commercialized Broadway dance, Limón left for the West Coast to form a duet company with former Graham dancer May O'Donnell and her husband, composer Ray Green. They developed a repertory with a commitment to contemporary American music and themes. World War II had begun in Europe, and Limón suspected he would soon be drafted. In 1941 he married Pauline Lawrence, and the following year returned to New York, disappointed with what he considered the provincialism of the San Francisco public.

In New York he resumed his association with Doris Humphrey, and created *Chaconne in D Minor,* a solo set to music by Johann Sebastian Bach, to be performed on an all-Bach program that Humphrey was producing. In April 1943, he was drafted. While in the army he was able to continue choreographing and performing in shows for the Special Services. On weekend leaves he began choreographing for a small company under Humphrey's artistic direction, which was a precursor of the José Limón Dance Company. With dancers Dorothy Bird and Beatrice Seckler, he created *Vivaldi Concerto in D Minor,* which premiered in 1945.

Humphrey had retired from dance due to a hip injury and ended her long association with Weidman; now she began to choreograph for the new company, with works that took advantage of her former protégé's exotic good looks and compelling stage presence. Among these works were *Lament for Ignacio Sánchez Mejías, Story of Mankind, Day on Earth, Night Spell, Ritmo Jondo,* and *Ruins and Visions.*

Limón invited Pauline Koner and Lucas Hoving to work with him and, returning to his Mexican heritage for inspiration, made *La Malinche* in 1949, with an original score by Norman Lloyd. The same year, with Hoving, Koner and Betty Jones, he created *The Moor's Pavane,* which John Martin, writing in the *New York Times,* called "a magnificent piece of dance theater . . . one of the major works in contemporary dance repertory." Based on the tragic story of Othello and set to music by Henry Purcell, this choreographic masterpiece has been continuously performed by ballet and modern dance companies worldwide.

In 1950 the Limón company performed in Mexico City, prompting an invitation to Limón to establish a school and company there. He created several new works for the Ballet Mexicano including *El Grito, Quatros Soles,* and *Tonantzintla* in 1951, but returned to his company in New York and a faculty position at the new Dance Department at the Juilliard School of Music, where he taught for the rest of his life.

The Limón company had been a chamber ensemble until this time, consisting of individual soloists, including Ruth Currier and Letitia Ide. His choreographic experience in Mexico and his work with Juilliard students now motivated him to explore the use of an ensemble. Working with a group of all male dancers, he created *The Traitor* (1954), *Scherzo* (1955) and *The Emperor Jones* (1956). He worked with a mixed ensemble in *Symphony for Strings* (1955), *There Is a Time* (1956), *Missa Brevis* (1958), *A Choreographic Offering* (1964), *The Winged* (1966) and *Psalm* (1967). In addition to these company works, he was creating dances almost every year for the student ensemble at Juilliard.

Limón was best known as a choreographer who made dance dramas, often based on literary or biblical themes. Hoving, lanky, blond and suave, was a striking contrast to Limón, who used him as a dramatic counterpart, particularly in *The Moor's Pavane, Dialogues, The Traitor,* and *Emperor Jones.* Tiny, quick, and dramatic, Pauline Koner was his partner in many works, and in others he used the sweetly lyric dancing of Betty Jones and Ruth Currier to represent feminine attributes. The womanly Letitia Ide had a weighted power that complemented his size. In later years he began to value greater technical virtuosity, in dancers such as Sarah Stackhouse, Jennifer Muller, Louis Falco, and Carla Maxwell, creating dances that challenged their skills while maintaining the breadth and weight of his original movement style.

Mexican themes recur throughout his work, from *Danzas Mexicanas, La Malinche, Dialogues, Tonantzintla,* and *Los Quatros Soles* to later works, *The Unsung* (1970) and *Carlota* (1972). Among his literary influences were William Shakespeare and Eugene O'Neill; religious themes appear in *The Exiles, The Visitation, The Traitor, There Is a Time,* and *Missa Brevis,* in which Limón's figure is set apart from the group, alternately appearing as a leader and a doubter.

Another important source of inspiration was the music of his favorite composers, resulting in pure movement pieces. These celebrations of the human spirit were made manifest through exultant dancing, intricate spatial designs, and sensitive musical phrasing. *A Choreographic Offering* (1964) is an outstanding example—dedicated to Doris Humphrey, its vocabulary is entirely derived from her choreography. Other notable works that were musically inspired include *Chaconne in D Minor, Vivaldi Concerto in D Minor, Mazurkas* (Chopin, 1958), and the unfinished *Beethoven Sonatas,* a full-evening work he began in 1970. He was also intrigued with silence, which he incorporated into *There Is a Time* and *The Winged* (1966), and then used in three of his last four pieces, *The Unsung,* the final section of *Dances for Isadora,* (1971) and *Carlota.*

Limón became a U.S. citizen in 1946 and a cultural ambassador for the government in 1954, when his company inaugurated the first State Department's Cultural Exchange Program with a tour of four South American cities. In 1957 the company was sent by the State Department on a five-month tour of Europe, including ''Iron Curtain'' countries Poland and Yugoslavia, which were overwhelmingly receptive. The company returned to South America in 1960, to the Far East in 1963, and to the Soviet Union in 1973 several months after Limón's death, all under State Department sponsorship. Limón was a guest at the Kennedy White House in 1962 and performed *The Moor's Pavane* at a White House state dinner in 1967 for Lyndon Johnson and his guest, King Hassan II of Morocco.

Limón was diagnosed with prostate cancer in 1967. His wife, Pauline Lawrence Limón died of cancer in 1971, and Limón died a year later, on December 2, 1972. Upon Limón's death, Clive Barnes wrote in the *New York Times:* ''As a man he was austere, grave and kindly. There was a courtliness to his every gesture, and he moved through the world like a prince. As a dancer he was an eagle. As a choreographer he was extremely gifted and fluent. He was never a particularly innovative artist, but possessed an innate understanding of that fusion of dance, drama and music that is the core of his work. He has left half a dozen ballets, at least, that should find a permanent place in the American repertory.''

Books

Cohen, Selma Jeanne, editor, *The Modern Dance: Seven Statements of Belief,* 1966.
Garafola, Lynn, editor, *José Limón: An Unfinished Memoir,* 1998.
Jowitt, Deborah, *Time and the Dancing Image,* 1988.
Koner, Pauline, *Solitary Song,* 1986.
Kriegsman, Sali Ann, *Modern Dance in America: The Bennington Years,* 1981.
Lewis, Daniel, *The Illustrated Dance Technique of José Limón,* 1984.
Lloyd, Margaret, *The Borzoi Book of Modern Dance,* 1949.
McDonagh, Don, *The Complete Guide to Modern Dance,* 1976.
Nadel, Myron Howard and Constance Gwen Nadel, editors, *The Dance Experience,* 1970.
Pollack, Barbara, and Charles Humphrey Woodford, *Dance Is a Moment: A Portrait of José Limón in Words and Pictures,* 1993.
Siegel, Marcia B., *Days on Earth: The Dance of Doris Humphrey,*1987.
Sorell, Walter, editor, *The Dance Has Many Faces,* 1966.

Periodicals

Ballet Review, 1973.
Choreography and Dance, 1992.
Current Biography, 1968.
Dance Notation Journal, Spring 1984.
Dance Observer, March 1958.
Dance Scope, Spring 1965; Spring/Summer 1973.
Impulse, 1968.
Juilliard Review, Winter 1955; Spring 1958.
Juilliard Review Annual, 1966-67.
New York Times, December, 16 1949; April 12, 1953; December 3, 1972.
The Shapes of Change: Images of American Dance, 1979. □

Horace B. Liveright

In 1916 ad agency employee Horace B. Liveright (1886–1933) and his office-mate decided to go into the book publishing business. With pooled assets of $16,500, they planned to reprint modern classics by British and European authors in inexpensive editions. Calling their venture The Modern Library of the World's Greatest Books, the two entrepreneurs eventually ranged further afield, publishing works by up-and-coming writers such as William Faulkner and Ernest Hemingway. Unfortunately, by 1930 the firm would find itself on hard times—the result of financial mismanagement and competition from other publishing houses—and Liveright was forced out. Three years later he would be dead of pneumonia.

Horace B. Liveright was born on December 10, 1886, in Osceola Mills, Pennsylvania, to Henry and Henrietta Liveright. By the time Liveright was 14 he had left school and taken a job as an office boy in Philadelphia. When he was 17 he penned the text and lyrics for a comic opera; although the opera went into rehearsal on Broadway, it never opened due to lack of a financial backer.

Entrepreneurial Aspirations

Eventually Liveright found work in New York City as a securities and bond salesman. In 1911 he married Lucile Elsas, daughter of the vice president of the International Paper Company, with whom he would have a son Herman E. Liveright in 1912. With his father-in-law's backing, Liveright started his own company to manufacture and sell toilet paper. He called his product Pick-Quick Papers.

By the end of 1915, the toilet paper venture failed, Liveright took a job at an advertising agency owned by Alfred Wallerstein. Liveright hoped to use the ad agency as a temporary base while he looked for something else to manufacture and market; his father-in-law, meanwhile, said he would back his son-in-law in only one more business venture.

Liveright's co-worker at the advertising agency was Albert Boni, who had recently run a small publishing business with his brother. After Liveright asked Boni's opinion about some of his manufacturing ideas, Boni in turn began telling his office-mate about his experience in publishing. The conversation led to a business partnership, with Liveright putting up $12,500 borrowed from his father-in-law, and Boni contributing $4,000 and the idea for the publishing business.

Boni & Liveright

By the beginning of the 20th century, most of the large publishing houses—among them Dodd, Mead & Company; E. P. Dutton; Harper & Brothers; Henry Holt; G. P. Putnam's

Early Titles

In 1917 the initial Modern Library selections included Oscar Wilde's *The Picture of Dorian Gray;* August Strindberg's *Married;* Rudyard Kipling's *Soldier's Three;* Robert Louis Stevenson's *Treasure Island;* H. G. Well's *The War in the Air;* Henrik Ibsen's *A Doll's House, The Enemy of the People,* and *Ghosts;* Anatole France's *The Red Lily;* Guy de Maupassant's *Mademoiselle Fifi;* Friedrich Nietsche's *Thus Spake Zarathustra;* and Fyodor Dostoyevsky's *Poor People.* Each book sold for 60 cents. Demand for the first set of titles was so great that Boni & Liveright immediately added six more. Boni & Liveright's publication of the works of Russian writer Leon Trotsky, Frenchman Henri Barbusse, and Hungarian Andreas Latzko would be less successful.

End of Publishing Partnership

While Boni and Liveright were temperamentally suited as business partners through their mutual sympathy for radical ideas, they frequently failed to agree on editorial matters and financial affairs. Liveright wanted to publish more unknown Greenwich Village writers as well as some writers with large followings, while Boni preferred sociopolitical works and European novelists. Eventually the two reached an impasse concerning the future direction of their firm and since neither was willing to sell out to the other, the partners decided to settle the matter over the toss of a coin. Liveright won the toss and in July 1918 became the majority owner of Boni & Liveright. Free to lead the company in whatever direction he chose, Liveright turned his attention to writers in Greenwich Village. Meanwhile, Boni departed for Europe in 1919 and eventually made his way to the Union of Soviet Socialist Republics (USSR). There he was imprisoned in 1920 on charges of spying. Upon his release, he returned to the United States where he re-entered the publishing business with his brother.

Liveright showed himself to be a quick study of book promotion and, until 1921, he handled the editorial side of the business. By 1921 the Modern Library consisted of 104 volumes, with each priced at 95 cents. It was clearly the most prestigious offering of Liveright's firm at this time. Later in the decade Liveright banked on the income from the Modern Library when, realizing the demand for books dealing with sex, he began publishing the works of psychoanalyst Sigmund Freud. Already criticized for his association with radical political works, Liveright achieved additional notoriety after he began publishing books considered outspoken in their treatment of sex.

Loved and Hated

When Liveright further expanded his publishing activities by releasing play scripts in 1924, he removed one of the walls in his office and added a false bookshelf that slid away to reveal a second room in which he hosted lavish—and not infrequently bacchanalian—parties. He gained a reputation for being alternately an exhibitionist, crude, or charming. According to Walker Gilmer in *Horace Liveright: Publisher of the Twenties,* Liveright was "tall, lean, and well-tailored with a shock of long (for the times) black hair, piercing eyes, and a John Barrymore or Mephistophelean profile." He also

Sons; and Charles Scribner's Sons were located in New York City rather than Boston, where most of the classics of the 19th century had been published. Nevertheless, in the 1910s the publishing industry was still dominated by New England Brahmins—intellectuals of the upper classes—and the opportunities in established publishing houses were few for young Jews like Liveright. As a result, many Jews established their own publishing houses. Without the contacts with established writers the older houses had, these Jewish-owned firms often took on unknown writers whose works dealt with protest or rebellion. By the 1920s several Jewish-owned publication houses—including Alfred A. Knopf; Simon & Schuster; and Viking Press—would be well on their way to commercial success.

Coincident with the startup of these new houses was the dissatisfaction among many avant-garde writers with the older publishing firms. Young writers of the time resented the power of these traditional houses, where radical or experimental ideas were routinely refused in favor of historical fiction, westerns, religious tracts, and the happy tales of contemporary life.

In the spring of 1917 Boni and Liveright announced the first titles to appear in their Modern Library. Liveright assumed the roles of president and business manager of his new publishing company, handling advertising campaigns and sales and arranging loans. Once the publication of the Modern Library classics built up a backlog of capital, Boni and Liveright planned to venture into publishing more controversial works.

acquired a reputation for treating his employees well: his staff received annual bonuses and never had to ask for raises. Liveright called his publishing house the only socialistic firm in New York, a reference to the fact that he wanted his employees to share in its profits.

Promoted Contemporary Writers

Liveright published the writings of Eugene O'Neill between 1918 and 1930 in 13 volumes, each containing one or more of O'Neill's play. He also published limited editions of the playwright's works, as well as reprints of his plays. During each year of the 1920s, except 1923, Liveright published at least one new play by the dramatist. In addition, by 1925 he had published or was about to publish works by Ernest Hemingway, William Faulkner, Roger Martin du Gard, Francois Mauriac, Hart Crane, Robinson Jeffers, and Dorothy Parker. For most of these still young writers, this would be their first publication in the United States.

Sold Modern Library

In 1925 Liveright sold the Modern Library to Bennett Cerf for $200,000. There is a story from that time that tells how Liveright's associates were furious upon learning of the sale, but that before they were able to dissuade him from going through with the deal a gunman appeared at the offices of Boni & Liveright with the intention of shooting Liveright because the publisher was having an affair with the gunman's wife. By the time the crisis had been managed, the sale had gone through. Cerf later changed the name of the Modern Library to Random House.

In 1928 Liveright's wife, Lucile, sued for divorce. However, long before this, as part of a separation agreement Liveright had agreed to repay his wife and father-in-law the large sums of money he had borrowed. Although the sale of the Modern Library averted the potential financial crisis sparked by his divorce, the loss of the Modern Library meant that the company's foundations would no longer be strong. Over the next few years, Boni & Liveright was dependent on the sales of popular best-sellers, and its fortunes eventually suffered.

In 1927 and 1928 the firm posted the highest gross profits in its history. Encouraged, in 1928 Liveright decided to change the name of the firm to Horace Liveright, Inc. Unbeknownst to Liveright at the time, more changes than the corporate name were in store for him.

Financial Collapse

By 1929 Liveright was having trouble finding new writers. The crash of the stock market that same year sent the firm into a tailspin and by the summer of 1930, Liveright had lost control of his company as a result of his continual borrowings against his majority share, and he was forced to leave.

In July 1930 Liveright left for Hollywood, after announcing that he was taking a leave of absence from the firm. His motivations were entirely financial. The firm's releases for 1929 and the first half of 1930 had not sold. There was also a book war raging among publishers in which books were sold for ridiculously low prices in at-

tempts to recapture audiences. In setting out for Hollywood, Liveright, who had also suffered major losses in the theatre and stock market, hoped to sell the movie rights to the books he still had an interest in to recoup his fortune.

In Hollywood Liveright found himself dependent on Paramount for a salary. Meanwhile he took to drinking heavily. When his contract with Paramount was not renewed in 1931, the publisher returned to New York with the intention of launching some Broadway plays, but the backing for his show-business ventures did not materialize. After he took to hanging around his old office, he was asked to leave because, he was told, it didn't look good to have him there.

In 1931 the publishing house of Horace Liveright changed its name to Liveright, Inc. Unfortunately, it never equaled its former successes, and in 1933 the company filed for bankruptcy.

On December 8, 1931, Liveright married Elise Nartlett Porter, an actress who had appeared in several Broadway plays and movies, but by 1932 the marriage was floundering. In January 1933 Liveright was hospitalized for pneumonia and later emphysema. On September 24, 1933, he died at the age of 46 of pneumonia in an apartment on West 51st Street in New York City.

In an article published after Liveright's death, colleague Cerf attributed Liveright's failure as a publisher to changes in the publishing industry that Liveright had no control of. In tribute to Liveright, writer Sherwood Anderson was quoted in *Horace Liveright: Publisher of the Twenties* as writing that "Horace was a gambler and if he believed in you would gamble on you. I have always thought, since the man's death, that too much emphasis has been put on the reckless splendor of the man rather than on his never-ending generosity and his real belief in men of talent."

Books

Dictionary of American Biography, Supplements 1 to 2: to 1940, American Council of Learned Societies, 1944–1958.
Gilmer, Walker, *Horace Liveright: Publisher of the Twenties,* David Lewis, 1970.

Periodicals

New York Times, September 25, 1933.
New Yorker, October 10, 1925.
Publishers Weekly, September 30–October 7, 1933.

Online

"Modern Library History," http://www.randomhouse.com/modernlibrary/aboutus.html (February, 2003). □

George Logan

George Logan (1753–1821) was one of the renaissance men who governed the republic in the early days of the United States. Though little known past his lifetime, he ably combined the professions of

doctor, farmer, politician, and diplomat in a career that lasted more than 40 years.

Logan was born September 9, 1753, in "Stenton," the home his grandfather had built in 1728 and to which his parents, William and Hannah Logan, and older siblings had moved from Philadelphia only four months earlier. At the time the house was located in a rural area in Philadelphia County, Pennsylvania, but it later became incorporated into the city itself. The Logans were a Quaker family; George Logan's grandfather, James, had been William Penn's secretary, who had made his fortune in fur trading. James's son, William, was a farmer who commanded the respect of the colonists and Native Americans.

Logan spent his first seven years entirely at Stenton. At age eight he attended the Friends School in Philadelphia, and in 1768 he began attending the Friends School in Worcester, England. Logan remained in Worcester for three years before returning to Stenton. This was to be the pattern for the rest of his life: no matter where his political and diplomatic careers took him, Logan always returned to his beloved Stenton.

Medical Education in Edinburgh

At this time Logan had his sights set on being a physician, but his older brother, William, had already graduated from medical school and his father thought it better that George apprentice as a merchant. Logan was temperamentally unfit for the life of business and never gave up hope of studying medicine. In 1772, William Logan, Jr., died suddenly and this, along with the coming war (Quakers being pacifists), cleared the way for Logan to study medicine at the University of Edinburgh. Ironically, Logan left for Great Britain in May 1775, a month after the Battle of Lexington and Concord; he spent the first year of the American Revolution in England, studying in preparation for entering the University of Edinburgh.

After his London stay and a tour of western England, Logan finally arrived in Edinburgh in November 1776. The following month he was selected to join the Medical Society, the prestigious student organization founded in 1734. Toward the end of his first spring term at the University of Edinburgh Logan received news that both his parents had died the previous winter. As the oldest surviving sibling he inherited Stenton but remained an absentee landlord the next three years while he pursued his medical studies. On January 27, 1779, when he was in his third and final year at the university, Logan was elected president of the Medical Society, which had only recently been granted a royal charter. He was the first American to hold the post. On June 24, 1779, having passed the rigorous oral and written examinations and published his thesis on poisons (titled *Tentamen medicum inaugurale de venenis*), Logan was awarded an M.D. from the University of Edinburgh.

By the end of June Logan had abandoned Edinburgh and gone to Paris where he visited Benjamin Franklin, then an envoy to the court of Louis XVI. Though a freshly minted doctor, Logan's political education and career were about to begin. Over the next year Logan served as courier for Franklin and John Adams delivering letters from the two Americans to their contacts in England. He returned to Stenton late in 1780.

The mansion had fallen to ruin during the war (though it had been briefly used as headquarters by both generals Washington and Howe), yet Logan still used it as a hostel for war refugees. He also practiced philanthropy in other forms, as well as the usual avocations of an eighteenth-century gentleman. He set up his medical practice in Philadelphia and began a courtship with Deborah Norris. The courtship had a touch of Romeo and Juliet; the Logan and the Norris families had been estranged for 30 years, but that ended when Logan married Norris on September 6, 1781. Not too many months later Logan decided to quit his medical practice and take up farming at Stenton as a way of reviving the ancestral home. Over the next few years, and intermittently for the rest of his life, Logan devoted himself to scientific farming. He began employing, and later improving upon, the agrarian reforms first used in England. Logan was also a charter member of the Philadelphia Society for Promoting Agriculture.

Election to the Pennsylvania Legislature

On October 11, 1785, Logan entered the political arena when he was elected to the Pennsylvania state assembly as a member of the Republican party. (Though conservative, this was not the present-day Republican party as within two years most of its members would be known as Federalists.) At that time elections were annual, and Logan served in the state assembly from 1785 to 1789; again from 1795 to 1796; and finally in 1799.

The first political crisis in which Logan became involved was over the Bank of North America, located in Philadelphia. The bank's charter had been annulled by the previous session, which was controlled by the radical Constitutionalist party (referring to the Pennsylvania state constitution). Though a Republican, Logan maintained an open mind regarding the bank's recharter, and when he finally rose to speak exerted a moderating influence over the increasingly rancorous debate. He came out in favor of rechartering the bank, but the motion was defeated when a vote was taken. Logan, though, had staked out the political middle in the state assembly. The bank was rechartered when the Republicans gained power.

In 1787 Logan, who was very much a political protégé of Benjamin Franklin, spoke out if favor of ratifying the new federal constitution that would replace the Articles of Confederation. Partly for his efforts, Pennsylvania became the second state to ratify the Constitution by a vote of 43 to 23.

The assembly's, and Logan's, next political conflict was over the reforming of the state penal code. In this Logan took a more conservative stance than most of his Quaker class by opposing the idea of incarceration as a means of reforming criminals—though Logan meant people whom, centuries later, would be classified as "career criminals." In 1788 Logan began publishing essays in the *Pennsylvania Mercury and Universal Advertiser* under the pen name Cato, in which he argued that justice was interwoven throughout the fabric of society, specifically in the relationship of rights and duties. The penal code debates marked the beginning of Logan's independent political streak. Thereafter less and less would he align himself along party and class affiliations. In the late 1780s he opposed Republican measures of protectionism in the state assembly and in his writings spoke of the dangers of the new American aristocracy. The Pennsylvania state constitution of that time forbade any member of the assembly from serving more than four consecutive terms, so with the close of the 1789 session Logan returned to Stenton to resume scientific farming full time.

Logan had been working his fields even while a legislator, but he now spent the next six years farming and working out methods to improve agriculture. These methods included crop rotation. Since 1783 he had been making notes on the best rotation for the fields, and he wrote a report for the Philadelphia Society for Promoting Agriculture. Unfortunately for Logan, the Society and the committee it set up to review his report after it had received a less than hearty welcome when he read it, were dominated by conservatives, many of whom came from the mercantile rather than the agricultural class. Though it was recommended the report be published, it was not fully supported by the Society. This led to Logan's rupture with the Society. After publishing his report and agricultural experiments in the *Independent Gazetteer* he resigned from the Society.

Logan's wariness toward the newly minted aristocracy of the mercantile class did not end there. He saw the new United States Constitution as an extension of their power in the nation. More than most, Logan keenly felt the threat to the country's agrarian lifestyle. In the early 1790s Logan's radical opposition to the new federal government—which he was able to observe firsthand since the capital had moved from New York to Philadelphia at the end of 1790—ostracized him from the Quaker community, which felt compelled to take action by issuing a "testimony" against him. Not dissuaded by this, Logan continued publishing anti-Federalist essays in the *Independent Gazetteer* (under the collective title *Letters to the Yeomanry*; they were also later published by the *National Gazette,* edited by Philip Freneau) as well as pamphlets, written under the simple byline "a farmer." These essays and letters argued against the new economic system being set in place by Secretary of State Alexander Hamilton. In this Logan had a powerful ally—Thomas Jefferson. His activity made Logan one of the leading anti-Federalists in Philadelphia and Stenton the seat of discontent in the area.

By 1793 Logan had become so anti-Federalist in outlook that no Federal policy could appease him, including the plan to build a turnpike linking the western Pennsylvania farmlands with the eastern part of the state. That same year Logan joined the Philadelphia-based *Société française des amis de la liberté et de l'égalité,* which supported the new French Republic. Following a summer which he spent in the company of none other than Citizen Genêt, Logan's political fires were temporarily tamped in the fall of 1793 by an outbreak of yellow fever in Philadelphia. He returned to his medical practice to treat the sick and also published

his ideas on treatment, which entailed a brief controversy of its own.

In January 1794 Logan joined the Democratic Society of Philadelphia, hoping it and the other Democratic societies throughout the nation would serve as a rudimentary national opposition to the Federalists. He was soon one of the firebrands of the organization—the societies were even attacked by Washington. Having thrown his lot in with the Jacobin French, Logan opposed the 1794 treaty with Britain which John Jay, minister to London and one of the authors of the *Federalist Papers,* had negotiated. In 1795 Logan again won a seat in the state assembly, but this time he was a changed man politically. He was no longer content to be seen as a moderate. He was reelected in 1796 and proved locally influential in the presidential election that year: Jefferson, around whom the national opposition had coalesced, received 13 of Pennsylvania's 15 electoral votes. However he lost the election to John Adams.

Secret Trip to France

Logan was mistrustful of Federalist policy toward France, but not even he could sway public opinion when the XYZ Affair (in which three French agents attempted to solicit a bribe and an extortionary loan from three American ministers who were sent to negotiate a commercial treaty) became common knowledge in April 1798. In the United States, as calls for war against the former ally began coming from different quarters and preparations made (these resulted in minor naval skirmishes), Logan chose a different tack. Bearing a letter from Vice President Jefferson as his credentials, Logan traveled to France in a roundabout way with the assistance of the Marquis de Lafayette.

By the time Logan reached Paris on August 7, 1798, the American ministers had all left their posts for the United States. France, they had been assured would negotiate. However France had also placed an embargo on American shipping and imprisoned a number of United States sailors. Logan met with French Foreign Minister Talleyrand and others and the result was a lifting of the embargo and the release of the imprisoned seamen. While Logan appeared to have single-handedly staved off war, the fact was the French Directory (which governed France at the time) was considering those very steps. Logan's secret diplomacy was the final and convenient evidence they considered. Logan was at once a hero and the source of embarrassment to the Federalist administration.

As a result Federalists in both houses of Congress sought revenge and they managed to exact it in a bill, since known as the Logan Act, which was passed in January 1799 and quickly signed by President Adams. The new law made it a crime for a private citizen to begin or hold "verbal or written correspondence with a foreign government . . . in relation to any disputes or controversies of the United States."

In July 1801 Logan was appointed by Governor McKean of Pennsylvania to replace Senator J.P.G. Muhlenberg, who had resigned. In December 1801 he was elected by the Pennsylvania legislature by a large majority. (Until 1913 United States senators were elected by state legislatures rather than popular vote.) By then Jefferson was president and the Republicans had gained power. Logan served as Senator until 1807, thus his term coincided with Jefferson's administration. By the end of his term Logan's early support of party policy—he had voted in favor of the Louisiana Purchase—gave way to misgivings about the path, especially the foreign policy of Jefferson and Secretary of State James Madison. Furthermore, Logan had grown weary of politics and declined to stand for reelection. When his term was up he retired to Stenton.

By 1810 Logan was again on a private diplomatic mission, in violation of the law that bore his name. He went to London to avert the ongoing crisis between the United States and Great Britain. As the War of 1812 attests, Logan was unsuccessful. However, throughout the war Logan sought out others who might play the peacemaker, including Tsar Alexander I; he wrote President Madison and Jefferson, and was politely rebuffed. His influence was nil.

Logan spent the remainder of his years at Stenton where he continued farming and writing. He died there on April 9, 1821.

Books

Logan, Deborah Norris, *Memoir of Dr. George Logan of Stenton,* The Historical Society of Pennsylvania, 1899.
Tolles, Frederick B. *George Logan of Philadelphia,* Oxford University Press, 1953.

Online

"Logan, George, 1753–1821," http://bioguide.congress.gov/scripts/biodisplay.pl?index=L000401 (February 25, 2003). □

Guy Lombardo

Canadian-born musician Guy Lombardo (1912–1977) was known for his festive approach to New Years' Eve, and his band's performance of eighteenth-century Scots poet Robert Burns's sentimental song *Auld Lang Syne* quickly became an American tradition.

In his heyday, musician Lombardo created a Big Band sound that was characterized by an exaggerated saxophone vibrato, clipped brass phrases, and a unique vocal styling that was the band leader's own. To generations of Americans, the New Year's Eve radio broadcasts by Guy Lombardo and his Royal Canadians playing "Auld Lang Syne" was an annual tradition. Lombardo's New Year's Eve Party eventually set a record as the longest-running annual special produced on radio, and between 1929 and 1952 Lombardo and the Royal Canadians charted at least one hit per year. Although Lombardo died in 1977, his theme song "Auld Lang Syne" continues to be requested by North American audiences ringing in the new year.

Beginnings

Gaetano Alberto Lombardo was born on June 19, 1902, in London, Ontario, Canada, to Gaetano and Lena Lombardo. Lombardo senior, who had immigrated to Canada from Italy, worked as a tailor, and the family lived on a small house on Queens Avenue in the town of London. Lomardo was the eldest of seven children—five boys and two girls—born between 1902 and 1924. Lombardo's parents demanded that their children not speak Italian at home, believing that they would be better able to integrate into the English-speaking culture of pre-World War I Canada if they were not burdened with a dependence on the Italian language.

Of the Lombardo children, five—Guy, Carmen, Lebert, Victor, and Rose Marie—would establish musical careers. Lombardo once said that his father wanted all his children to have a education in music, and because Guy was the eldest he was given violin lessons. Since the violin player was always the band leader, the young Lombardo was given the role he would continue to play later in life.

Early Gigs

Lombardo's band got its start in 1914 when brother Carmen, playing flute, joined Guy on violin to perform a duet for the local Mother's Club. Eventually brother Lebert joined the group, along with pianist Freddie Kreitzer. On June 22, 1919, the band was scheduled to play its first professional gig at the Lakeview Casino in Grand Bend. After the club's owner refused to give the band members an hour off for dinner—claiming that his customers paid to hear the band perform, not to watch them eat—Lombardo's father took his sons home and advised them to find another line of work. However, the affair smoothed over and within several months the Lombardo brothers had quit school and were working as full-time musicians. They got no argument on that score from their father, who had always told them that "music is a light load to carry."

In the spring of 1923 the Lombardo brothers were hired as the house band for the Hopkins Casino at Port Stanley on Lake Erie. Carmen Lombardo, who was by this time playing the saxophone with a Detroit band, quit so he could rejoin his brothers. After the band started its second season at London, Ontario's Winter Gardens, the 21-year-old Guy decided that the group was wasting its time in Canada. Within a few weeks he obtained the name of a Cleveland, Ohio, booking agent and talked his way into a one-night stand at an Ohio Elk's Club. Meanwhile, he let his friends back in London think he had booked an American vaudeville tour.

Following the band's final performance in London, Ontario, on November 24, 1923, the 10-member group was seen off at the train station by about 100 well-wishers. In spite of the lateness of the hour, many were willing to lose sleep to wish the local band good luck. By the time the band returned to Ontario in 1927 as Guy Lombardo and the Royal Canadians, Lombardo was poised for success.

Career Heated Up

In the winter of 1923, as Lombardo drove south to Ohio, the odds that his band would make it big were slim. Fiercely competitive, the U.S. music industry was particularly unforgiving of any new talent that had not established a unique, distinctive sound. Although composed of talented musicians, Lombardo's jazz band did not yet have a sound that set it apart from the competition. Recalling advice from heir father, who had urged his sons to play music that people can "sing, hum, or whistle," the three Lombardo brothers began performing dance music with pronounced melodies but without arrangement or improvisation. The music appealed to the well-to-do audiences of the late 1920s, and reportedly to even a few Prohibition-era gangsters.

Although the Lombardo brothers were convinced that, given the competition, they would never succeed by playing beat-heavy, improvisational Dixieland jazz, the other members of the band felt their creative abilities were stifled by switching to dance music. Although they were at first reluctant to go along, the Lombardos won them over. Guy Lombardo was particularly enthusiastic when he discovered that brother Carmen produced a unique tone on the saxophone that blended extremely well with the sound of the band's other two sax players. The result would be money in the bank.

Although Lombardo initially had to pay for air time on U.S. radio, it was worth it when the exposure began to attract listeners. After the band began regular live broadcasts its popularity soared. Their agent then came up with the idea of dressing the band members in Canadian Mountie uniforms, but Lombardo balked and countered with a proposal of his own: calling the band the Royal Canadians.

By the time Guy Lombardo and the Royal Canadians arrived at the Granada playhouse in Chicago in the fall of 1927, it had ceased to be a London, Ontario, group. From the Granada it went on to land an engagement at the city's Palace Theatre, a gig paying $4,000 a week. The music critic for the *Herald & Examiner* described the performance as one where he listened to "the sweetest jazzmen on any stage this side of Heaven."

In 1929 Lombardo's band made its first appearance at the Roosevelt Hotel in New York City, later to be the home of its live broadcasts on the CBS radio network. The broadcasts eventually moved, originating from New York's Waldorf-Astoria.

Although during the band's heyday rumors circulated in Canada regarding hometown concerts by the Royal Canadians, the band made only a handful of appearances in the country where it began. Lombardo never forgot his friends in Ontario, however, and when Canada's Thames River flooded in 1937 he staged a benefit for flood victims in Detroit's Fox Theatre. The band opened this engagement with a rendition of "Home Sweet Home," moving some in the audience to tears.

All in the Family

In 1942 youngest sister Rose Marie Lombardo joined the band as a song stylist. A few years later vocalist Kenny Gardner married Elaine Lombardo. Meanwhile Joseph Lombardo, one of the few siblings who had not become a musician, was hired to redecorate New York's Roosevelt Hotel, where the band wintered for 33 years. However, another member of the family made running a family business more than a challenge. Victor Lombardo, the youngest of the musical brothers, constantly provoked fights with Guy and on several occasions he left the Royal Canadians to form his own band. Guy proved long-suffering; he repeatedly took Victor back into the fold after each of the younger Lombardo's failed Big Band ventures.

Critics Notwithstanding

Despite Lombardo's popularity, not everyone was impressed with his music. By the 1950s bobbysoxers were calling the band's music "square." Popular singer Bing Crosby once commented that Lombardo and the Royal Canadians had achieved their continued success with only one single arrangement. Back in London, Ontario, some took to calling Guy "Gooey Lumbago," while others derided Lombardo as the "Schmaltz King," "Prince of Wails," and "King of Corn."

Despite perhaps more than their share of derision, Guy Lombardo and the Royal Canadians outlived most of their critics. The band continued to appeal to the large numbers of listeners who appreciated pure melody. Musicians Louis Armstrong, Louis Prima, and Ella Fitzgerald each counted themselves among Lombard's fans, and the band set a record for audience attendance at Harlem's Savoy Ballroom. Between 1929 and 1952 Lombardo's band had a minimum of one hit per year, 21 of which were number-one songs. As late as 2000, the Royal Canadians remained the only dance band in the world to sell more than 100 million records.

Although Lombardo became best known for his signature rendition of "Auld Lang Syne" and for "Boo-Hoo," he also scored major hits between 1927 and 1954 with "Charmaine," "Sweethearts on Parade," "You're Driving Me Crazy," "By the River St. Marie," "(There Ought to Be) A Moonlight Saving Time," "Too Many Tears," "Paradise", "We Just Couldn't Say Goodbye," "The Last Round-up," "Stars Fell on Alabama," "What's the Reason (I'm Not Pleasin' You)," "Red Sails in the Sunset," "Lost," "When Did You Leave Heaven?," "September in the Rain," "It Looks like Rain in Cherry Blossom Lane," "So Rare," "Penny Serenade," "The Band Played On," "It's Love-Love-Love," "Managua, Nicaragua," and "The Third Man Theme."

There is no accurate count of the number of records Guy Lombardo and the Royal Canadians sold during their career, but estimates run between 100 and 300 million. In addition to his recordings, Lombardo himself appeared in several films, including *Many Happy Returns* (1934), *Stage Door Canteen* (1943), and *No Leave, No Love* (1946). Besides his career as an entertainer, he made a number of successful business investments, and in his after hours he was an avid speedboat racer, holding the title of national champion in the late 1940s.

Several generations of Americans heard the strains of Lombardo's "Auld Lang Syne" resonating from New York's Waldorf Astoria. The band's annual New Year's Eve Party became a tradition, setting the record for the longest running annual radio special program. In 1979 the program celebrated its 50th consecutive broadcast, having first appeared on television in 1954.

End of an Era

Each year between 1929 and 1952 Lombardo managed to place at least one record on the popular music charts, and 1953 marked the first time in a quarter century years that the Royal Canadians failed to release a bestselling record. Other bad news for Lombardo came the same year, in the form of income tax problems with the Internal Revenue Service. To deal with these dual setbacks, Lombardo signed the band up for more tours, especially back home in Ontario. By 1954, the band's sun had almost set. Their recording of "Young at Heart" climbed to only number 24 on the charts. Rock 'n' roll now drove the North American music industry, eclipsing the music Lombardo specialized in.

Despite their waning fame elsewhere, Canada still had a soft spot for the band. In 1955 Guy Lombardo and the Royal Canadians performed at the London, Ontario Centennial, and the centennial organizing committee named a day in the bandleader's honor. During the next 30 years the band made nearly 20 appearances in Ontario, even as the rest of the world was embracing the Rolling Stones and the Beatles.

Mortality and Immortality

Carmen Lombardo, who created the band's signature sound, died of cancer in 1971. Carmen's death left Lombardo professionally and emotionally shattered, as Guy had been closer to Carmen than to any of his other siblings. In 1974 the Royal Canadians were stung by the first-ever unfavorable review published in their hometown paper. The band made its last appearance in London, Ontario, in June of 1977 at an event where no one on the dance floor appeared to be younger than age fifty.

On November 5, 1977, Lombardo died in Houston, Texas, having reached the age of 75. In the years since Lombardo's death "Auld Lang Syne" has remained North America's traditional musical accompaniment to the passing of each year. The last musical Lombardo brother, Victor Lombardo, passed away in 1994.

Books

Cline, Beverly Fink, *The Lombardo Story,* Musson Book Company, 1979.

Periodicals

London Free Press (London, Ontario, Canada), December 27, 1998.
Washington Post, December 31, 1970.

Online

"The Guy Lombardo Wing," *Doty Docs,* http://www.dotydocs.com/lombardo.htm (March 28, 2003). □

M

Alan Charles MacLaurin Mackerras

Charles Mackerras (born 1925) is considered one of the most dynamic conductors within modern opera. He spent 30 years at Sadler's Wells Opera during which he both presented Wolfgang Amadeus Mozart (1756–1791) operas in their intended form, but sung in English, and introduced the work of Leos Janacek, the Czech composer, to the West. He also has specialized in presenting operas from the Baroque period. He is said to have conducted more operas than any other British conductor actively working. He is equally reknown for his work with orchestral pieces.

From Oboe, Checked out Czechs as He Pursued Conducting

Alan Charles Mackerras was born on November 17, 1925, in Schenectady, New York, to Australian parents—Alan Patrick Mackerras and Catherine Brearcliffe. His father, an electrical engineer, was pursuing a scholarship at General Electric in Schenectady at the time. He and his parents returned to Australia, and Mackerras was raised and educated in Sydney. He studied oboe, piano, and composition at the New South Wales Conservatorium of Music in Sydney. He became principal oboist of the Sydney Symphony Orchestra in 1943 at the age of 21. It was during this period that he first began conducting.

Mackerras moved to Britain, where he performed with the Sadler's Wells orchestra and began studying conducting with Michael Mudie. Mackerras married Helena Judith Wilkins, a clarinet player who was also with the orchestra, in 1947. They would have two daughters. He successfully applied for a British Council Scholarship to study conducting with Vaclav Talich at the Prague in 1947.

"In those days, the only way you could study Slavonic arts or culture was to go to Czechoslovakia," Mackerras said in an interview with *Opera News*. "The Iron Curtain really was iron." He says he would have stayed, but for the fact that Communists came into power in February 1948. "[T]hey became exceedingly suspicious of foreigners. The Czechs hated anything German at that point, even Beethoven—though they still considered Mozart an 'honorary Czech' because of his love of their country and his famous opera performances in Prague."

As Stephanie Von Buchau in *Opera News* notes, "The year Mackerras spent in Czechoslovakia changed his life. He learned Czech and discovered Janacek." Mackerras told her: "Of course I knew [Antonin] Dvorak [(1841–1904)] and [Bedich] Smetana [(1824–1884)], but even in Prague in 1947, Janacek was considered an eccentric." Talich introduced him to Janacek works including *Kat'a Kabanova* and *Jenufa*. "I was determined to propagate this composer when I returned to London, and I found a willing victim in my boss at Sadler's Wells. He helped with the English translation—everything at the Wells was sung in the vernacular then—and in 1951 we produced *Kat'a Kabanova,* the first Janacek opera ever heard in Britain."

Debuted on Podium in London

Mackerras had become the conductor at Sadler's Wells Opera in 1948; he made his conducting debut with *Die*

Fledermaus. The company went on to stage Janacek's *The Makropulos Case* and *House of the Dead* as well as record other Janacek works under Mackerras's direction. As such, he is credited not only with introducing Janacek to Great Britan, but also to the West.

Mackerras learned Czech to help in this musical obsession. He became fluent in the language. He later recorded a series of these Janacek operas with the Vienna Philharmonic. Mackerras recalled, "[T]he Vienna Philharmonic was astounded when I spoke to the singers in their own language—you should have seen their faces!" Von Buchau said these recordings "have set the musicological standard since he started the series, in the early '70s."

He was a staff conductor with Sadler's Wells until 1954 and was principal conductor of the British Broadcasting Corporation Concert Orchestra during this same period, from 1954 until 1956. Mackerras became principal conductor for the English Opera Group for several of its seasons beginning in 1956. This group was founded by Benjamin Britten with the express purpose of furthering the musical form in English. With them he conducted world premieres of Britten's *Noye's Fludde* and *Ruth* by Lennox Berkeley. In 1964, Mackerras debuted at the famed Covent Garden as conductor of *Katerina Ismailova,* a work by Dmitri Shostakovich (1906–1975).

Historical Research Informed Performances

It was during his work with the English Chamber Orchestra that Mackerras decided to begin experimenting with "historically informed" performances. This requires great scholarship on the part of the conductor who must uncover and discover how the composer intended the piece to be played and how it would have been played in the era when it was written. He had begun this work in the 1950s. His 1959 recording of George Frederick Handel's (1685–1759) "Fireworks Music" with its original wind band instrumentation was the first of this type of work he had undertaken to be noticed.

"I was always interested in how things were performed in their day. And the first thing that made me really aware of it is that I used to have a recording of the Handel Water Music conducted by Sir Hamilton Harty. I knew it was an arrangement, but I had never been aware of how much of an arrangement it was," he told *Classics Today.* "But when I was a teenager I got to look at a facsimile of the score and I saw immediately that what we were hearing bore little relationship to what Handel had actually written. And with the Fireworks Music, I saw the original orchestration and I thought 'My God, I wonder what this must sound like!' You know, the original has 24 oboes, and all those bassoons and horns."

The recording was made to commemorate the Handel bicentenary. Mackerras recalled "we got every wind player in London to come for one session, in the middle of the night, and have a go at it. It was all edited and issued very quickly, in just a few days, and I must say I was a bit frightened that it would sound horrible, but of course just the opposite occurred. It sounded marvelous. I was very relieved, let me tell you! We also did the Concerti a Due Cori on the other side of the LP, and even these works hadn't been played at all since Handel's day. . . . There's still quite a lot we don't know about what really went on in those days."

Continuing with this idea, in 1965, Mackerras presented Mozart's *Le Nozze di Figaro* at Sadler's Wells Opera in England, "in English, with embellishments and appoggiaturas, those eighteenth-century expressive devices that had fallen into disuse for a century and a half," notes Stephanie Von Buchau in *Opera News.* Mackerras himself told her, "I'm sure that we went too far in that Sadler's Wells *Figaro,* exaggerating in an effort to get people's attention, but there wasn't too much opposition. The ECO was eager for fresh ideas, and the singers who performed with us on the BBC's Third Programme all wanted to learn correct style. Naturally, the BBC was also sympathetic to the cause of historical performance practice, but I think we turned the corner when I persuaded Elisabeth Schwarzkopf to sing 'Voi che sapete' in the highly ornamented version by Domenico Corri. . . . The eighteenth-century Viennese loved coloratura."

Conducted Career Around the World

Mackerras accepted an invitation to conduct the Hamburg State Opera in 1966. During his tenure as principal conductor with that company, he reportedly conducted many works for the first time, some without rehearsal. Among the critically acclaimed productions Mackerras mounted were Igor Stravinksy's (1882–1971) *The Rake's Progress, Boris Gudonov* by Modest Petrovich Mussorgsky

(1839–1881), and Richard Wagner's (1813–1883) *Der fliegende Holländer.* He held this post until 1969–1970.

Mackerras was appointed music director of Sadler's Wells, whose name was changed to English National Opera, in 1970. He held the post until either 1977 or 1978 (published accounts give varying dates). While with the company, he conducted more than 40 operas, which included some works not in the standard repertoire such as Handel's *Semele* and Gaetano Donizetti's (1797–1848) *Maria Stuarda,* the latter of which was presented as "Mary Stuart" in English. He also established himself as "a major conductor of both Verdi and Wagner," according to *International Dictionary of Opera.* In this same general time period, he was the chief guest conductor for the BBC Symphony Orchestra.

Mackerras was rarely idle. He conducted Christoph Willibald Ritter von Gluck's *Orfeo et Euridice* in his New York Metropolitan Opera debut in 1972. He returned to Australia in 1973 to christen the Sydney Opera House. He conducted both the inaugural concert and *Die Zauberflote;* Mackerras was appointed as the Sydney Symphony Orchestra's conductor in 1982, a post he held until 1985.

He has also been music/artistic director of Welsh National Opera (1987–1992), a guest conductor for the Royal Liverpool Philharmonic Orchestra, and worked with the Scottish Chamber Orchestra, San Francisco Opera, (London) Royal Philharmonic, Prague Chamber, and Czech Philharmonic orchestras.

Enjoyed Vibrant Recording Career

By virtue of his chosen profession, Mackerras has had an active recording career. His body of work includes not only operas but also orchestral pieces such as the complete Mozart symphonies and serenades. He also has recorded the complete symphonies of Brahms and Beethoven, as well as major works by composers including Handel, Dvorak, Shostakovich, Sibelius, Holst, and Haydn, among numerous others. These works have been recognized with various awards. His recording of Britten's *Gloriana,* for example was named *Gramophone Magazine*'s Best Opera Recording in 1994.

According to *International Dictionary of Opera,* Mackerras says he attempts "to hit the happy medium between being a musician and a musicologist." Yet, he does not like to be confined to any particular specialty. "Generally I prefer conducting works by unusual composers or unusual works by famous composers. I'm always interested in something new."

Mackerras also had a passion for Gilbert and Sullivan operettas in his youth which he has explored professionally. "When I was young we used to sing Gilbert and Sullivan operettas constantly in all-boys productions at school. We sang all the parts, women's too, in the same treble voices, so I got to know them all very well," he told *Classics Today.* "But I used to think how nice it would be if some of these great tunes were somehow arranged into a big symphonic suite." The result was "Pineapple Poll," which also became a ballet. "That became a tremendous success, and it was wonderful fun to do. It also opened a lot of doors for me as a

conductor because I was able to play the work all around England. Actually, my first recording with the Sadler's Wells orchestra was of 'Pineapple Poll.' I still perform it."

Continued Career, Much Lauded

In a 1995 interview with *Opera News,* Mackerras said he would take no more permanent positions. He contended to do the best possible work as a music director, one must live in that city to work closely with the orchestra. He continues to be based in London. "Today most conductors are fly-by-nighters, and if I were to take a music director's job, with all my commitments, I'd end up being a fly-by-nighter too. Besides, I don't like being a pennanent [sic] conductor. I'd much rather be freelance!"

Mackerras has received numerous honors throughout his career. He was knighted in 1979 and has been given numerous honorary degrees by universities in the United Kingdom and Czechoslovakia. Mackerras has been conductor emeritus of Welsh National Opera since 1992 and of the San Francisco Opera since 1996. He was appointed to a similar post with the Scottish Chamber Orchestra in 1995. He observed his 70th birthday with in 1995 celebrations with the San Francisco Opera, the Scottish Chamber Orchestra in Edinburgh, and the Welsh National Opera in Cardiff.

Mackerras has conducted more operas than any other active British conductor according to *International Dictionary of Opera.* This reference cites as exemplars works including Wagner's Ring Cycle, Aida and Carmen, "his Handel is vital but there has been all too little of it . . . and his Strauss is luminescent."

Books

Debrett's People of Today, Debrett's Peerage Ltd., 2002.
International Dictionary of Opera, 2 vols. St. James Press, 1993.
The New Grove Dictionary of Opera, Macmillan Press Limited, 1992.

Periodicals

Opera News, November 1995.

Online

"Sir Charles Mackerras," Telarc International website http://www.telarc.com/biography/bios.asp?aid=60 (February 28, 2003).
"A Talk With Sir Charles Mackerras," *Classics Today,* http://www.classicstoday.com/features/f1_0200.asp (February 28, 2003). □

Kunio Maekawa

Prominent among modern Japanese architects, Kunio Maekawa (1905–1986) served an apprenticeship in France during the 1930s. Well-known for his use of architectural concrete, his post-World War II

contributions included designs for prefabricated structures and high-rise apartments.

Kunio Maekawa was born in May 14, 1905, in Niigata on Northwest Honshu Island. The eldest of three children, he was well bred; the families of both of his parents were descended from the Samurai. His father, Kan'ichi Maekawa, was descended from the Ii clan of Omi. A civil engineer by profession, Kan'ichi worked in the Japanese Home Ministry, eventually becoming a high-ranking official, called *chokuninkan,* (imperial appointee). His mother, of the Tsugaru clan of Hirosaki, was a daughter of Konroku Tanaka. The family lived in a wooden house in the snow country of Niigata before moving to Tokyo's Hongo district.

Student Years

Maekawa attended elite schools and completed Tokyo First Middle School in 1918, after skipping the fifth year. In 1922 he enrolled at the First Higher School, graduating in 1925. Clearly talented, Maekawa studied architecture at Tokyo Imperial University from 1925 to 1928. There he developed into an avid reader of French architectural publications. In March 1928 Maekawa wrote his university graduation paper on the Swiss modernist architect, Charles Edouard Jeanneret, most commonly known as Le Corbusier. For his final project Maekawa submitted a futuristic design for a ten-kilowatt radio station. It was a new concept in Tokyo, where radio was a new technology that had been introduced only three years prior in 1925. This academic design of Maekawa remains in the collection of Tokyo Imperial University Architecture Department.

Immediately after his graduation ceremony on March 31, 1928, Maekawa left for Paris under an arrangement orchestrated by his mother's brother, Naotake Sato, who was a member of the Japanese foreign service. Sato was stationed in Paris at that time and opened his home to Maekawa who arrived in the city on April 17. Under the arrangement, Maekawa went to work for Le Corbusier in Paris, entering the architectural office as an unpaid draftsman, as was customary for newcomers to the prestigious firm. Already infatuated with the European modernist movement, Maekawa's association with Le Corbusier proved to be an unparalleled opportunity to work with many prominent avant-garde designers. In Paris he worked with Alfred Roth, Pierre Jeanneret, and Charlotte Perriand who was Le Corbusier's premiere interior designer at that time. Maekawa held his own intrinsic affection for many aspects of the modernist movement in his native Japanese, and this two-year sojourn in Paris fueled his interest.

As an entry-level volunteer, Maekawa learned to conform to the rigorous standards espoused at Le Corbusier's office, and in June 1928 he assisted Le Corbusier with Cité Mondiale (Mundaneum) in Geneva, a structure intended for the League of Nations. Apart from his obligations to Le Corbusier, Maekawa entered various design competitions independently. Individually he submitted a design for the Nagoya City Hall, but it was not one of his strongest works.

Some said that the entry resembled a parking garage because of the structure's prominent side wings, which indeed served as covered parking areas. Additionally he joined with two of his Paris colleagues, Ernest Weissmann and Norman Rice, in entering a competition for the design of a public office building in Zagreb, Croatia, in 1929. After his return to Japan, in the fall of 1930 four of Maekawa's independent designs were included in a Tokyo exhibition, and in December of that year, three of Maekawa's designs were featured in the Japanese publication *Kokusai kenchiku.*

Maekawa departed Paris on April 6, 1930, traveling through Moscow and arriving in Tokyo on April 16, coincidental with Le Corbusier's emergence among the architectural community of Japan. Japan during the years following World War I remained in a period known as Meiji Restoration that was characterized by a revival of traditional architectural styles. These traditional styles were tempered however by the use of updated, alternate building materials. After his arrival in Tokyo, Maekawa began to work with Bohemian architect Antonin Raymond in August 1930, according to an arrangement by Professor Riki San. This intervention by San was especially fortuitous for Maekawa because architectural commissions at that time were in great scarcity. Antonin, however, was involved in the design of the Imperial Hotel.

As a member of Raymond's firm, Maekawa served as architect-in-charge for the Viscount Soma residence. In this instance he applied an oblong, horizontal design reminiscent of a residential villa design by Le Corbusier from the 1920s. Maekawa's design for the Tokyo City Hall competition of 1932 displayed the influence of the Frenchman August Perret. From 1932 to 1934 Maekawa worked in his first independent design, for a Kimura Manufacturing research facility in Hirosaki. This research structure has since been altered and re-adapted to other uses, and the oblong housing design of Viscount Soma, enhanced by a roof garden, was seen again in the design of the Akaboshi Tetsuma housing project in 1934.

Independent Architectural Firm

Still working as a project team member for Raymond in the early 1930s, Maekawa in 1935 left that firm and established his own company out of a home office; he later moved the operation to the Ginza in Tokyo. Makoto Tanaka, Terashima Kotaro, and Kosaburo Sakitani joined Maekawa in this venture. Among their earliest projects were Hinomoto Hall of 1936 and Maekawa's 1937 design for the Memorial Hall to the Founding of the Nation competition. The use of architectural concrete, extremely large panes of glass, and cast-in-place ceramic tiles characterized much of Maekawa's work during this period. Having learned the use of these new construction materials from Raymond, Maekawa by the 1960s had matured in his use of ceramic tile work, and it had become a signature characteristic of his designs. Although a dearth of commissions characterized the decade of the 1930s, Maekawa maintained solvency, in part with the release by his father of a trust fund that was earmarked for Maekawa to purchase his first residence.

In 1937 he designed two houses for Sato, including a main residence in Tokyo and a vacation house in Karuizawa. These structures, along with a third residential design for another member of the Foreign Ministry, aspire to the modern style through the use of overlapping roof segments that create an interplay between planes, while maintaining an overall appearance in the traditional style.

Maekawa's largest single project during this pre-war period was the employee dormitories for Kako Commercial Bank in 1939. For this he opened a satellite office near the project site in Shanghai. Also ongoing from 1938 to 1941 was a project to build three technical schools for mining and manufacturing in the state of Manchuria. It was common practice that contract awards were driven largely through political clout, and designs were subject to the whims of politicians accordingly. Despite his distaste for the design limitations inherent in this system, Maekawa was nevertheless fortunate to be well connected and able to secure contracts as a result. With the expansion of World War II during the 1940s Maekawa's ability to procure contracts was limited largely to military projects. Functionality and cost constraints were the main consideration for these projects, with uninspired aesthetics that deferred to technical expertise.

After nine years of operating from an office at his home he opened an office in Yotsuda in Tokyo in 1944 and named the establishment Maekawa Institute of Design (MID) Sekkei Kenkyujo. The company was known alternately as MIDO Dojin or the MIDO colleagues. When this first Tokyo office was destroyed during an air raid in May 1945, he moved again to a headquarters in his home in Meguro. There he operated with a skeleton staff because many of his associates by that time had left for the military.

Also associated with his operation Maekawa founded the MIDO Research Institute in 1947. Under the auspices of MIDO he published Maekawa Kunio Kenchiku Jimusho sakuhin shu (the Collected Works of the Maekawa Kunio Architecture Office) that year. In the wake of losing his office, this publication had the effect for Maekawa of providing closure to the wartime and postwar eras.

Postwar Maekawa

In 1946–1947 Maekawa designed the first branch of the Kinokuniya Bookstore. Built in Shinjuku, Tokyo, it was the first of 30 projects that he would complete for that vendor. A Keio University Hospital project in Tokyo lasted from 1947 to 1948, and in 1948 he began publication of a new magazine called *Plan*. Two issues were published in all.

Having survived the difficult war years, Maekawa focused on the mass production of prefabricated structures and did considerable writing on that topic. He took his inspiration in part from Henry Ford's assembly line theories of mass production for making products accessible to the less wealthy working class. This project was spurred when a major military provider, Manchurian Aircraft Company, ceased operation after Japan's defeat in World War II. At Maekawa's suggestion the Manchurian plant at Kayama in Tottori—called San'in Manufacturing—was converted by its parent company, Nissan Heavy Industries, to a construction facility for housing components.

A new company was formed, called Prefabricated Maekawa Ono Kaoru San'in Manufacturing (PREMOS); it was named in part for Kaoru Ono, a professor at Tokyo University and a colleague of Maekawa. In 1946 under the guise of the new company the first two PREMOS units were completed. A small model was manufactured, called #7, which afforded 52 square meters of floor space, with living, dining/kitchen area, and one bedroom and toilet. The first units became a club for the soldiers in occupied Tottori. Other PREMOS units were adapted as housing for railroad workers in Shimonoseki, and one became a coffeehouse in the Ginza; some were used as private homes. Eventually an entire community was planned for the miners at Kokkaido, the site of the Kayanuma mine. The community was to be comprised of 400 PREMOS #73 structures, of which 200 were ultimately constructed.

After five years, 1,000 units had been manufactured, but the PREMOS project came to an end for lack of cost effectiveness. It was nonetheless the prototype for Japan's great third millennium prefab industry, the largest and most sophisticated industry of its type in the world.

Later Career

Among Maekawa's more significant structures, the Harumi Flats apartment project in Tokyo in 1959 represents on of the earliest high-rise apartment buildings in Japan. Harumi Flats, with its strong use of vertical lines, receding and projecting planes, and sculpted units on the roof, is based closely in a Le Corbusier design. More notable still is Maekawa's 1961 design for the Tokyo Metropolitan Festival Hall. Recognized as Maekawa's grandest and best known work, the Festival Hall has been praised for the humanism that finds expression in Maekawa's various choices of materials such as the dramatic use of marble sheeting on the interior walls. Overall the design pays tribute to rural Japan and draws inspiration from the classic *minka* (farm house) structure.

The influence of Le Corbusier on Maekawa was seen again in the roof sculptures, ramping, and pyramid forms of his design for the Gakushuin University Library building in 1964, the second of two buildings that he designed at that school, beginning in 1960. Maekawa's designs were seen in the Japanese pavilion at the World's Fair at Brussels in 1958 and again in New York City in 1954 to 1965. He contributed a number of articles to literary journals in French, English, and German during the 1960s and 1970s.

His numerous projects of the early 1980s included the Kumamoto Prefectural Concert Hall and Theater (1982), the Kunitachi College of Music Concert Hall (1983), and the Niigata Municipal museum (1985). Many of the later designs that are attributed to Maekawa were overseen largely by the younger associates of his firm.

Kunio Maekawa died on June 27, 1986, in Tokyo.

Books

Altherr, Alfred, *Three Japanese Architects: Mayekawa, Tange, Sakakura,* Arthur Niggli Ltd., 1968.

International Dictionary of Architects and Architecture, St. James Press, 1993.

Reynolds, Johanthan M., *Maekawa Kunio and the Emergence of Japanese Modernist Architectue,* Universtiy of California Press, 2001. □

Annie Turnbo Malone

Annie Turnbo Malone (1869–1957) was an African American entrepreneur and philanthropist during the early 20th century. She manufactured a line of beauty products for black women and created a unique distribution system that helped thousands of black women gain self respect and economic independence. However, her contributions to African American culture are often overlooked because her business empire collapsed from mismanagement. One of her students, Madame C.J. Walker, created a similar enterprise and is largely credited with originating the black beauty business, a feat that rightly belongs to Malone.

Malone was born Annie Minerva Turnbo born on August 9, 1869, in Metropolis, Illinois. She was the tenth of 11 children of Robert Turnbo, a poor farmer, and Isabella Cook Turnbo. Her parents died when Malone was young and an older sister raised her in nearby Peoria. Although she did attend school, frequent illness caused her to withdraw before completing high school. As a young girl, Malone enjoyed fashioning her own and her sisters' hair. She became aware of differences in hair texture and sought a way to straighten hair.

Started Hair-Care Business

During the late 19th century, African American women used soap, goose fat, and heavy oils to straighten their hair. Chemical straighteners often damaged the scalp and hair follicles. While living in Lovejoy, Illinois, around the turn of the century, Malone developed a chemical product that straightened African American hair without damage. She claimed to have studied chemistry and to have been influenced by an aunt who was trained as an herbal doctor. She expanded her hair care line to include other beauty products, including her popular Wonderful Hair Grower. Some historians also credit Malone with developing the pressing iron and comb around this time. Malone sold her products locally.

In 1902, Malone moved her business to St. Louis, Missouri, where she hired and trained three assistants. As black women, they were denied access to traditional distribution systems, so they sold the products door-to-door and provided free demonstrations. In 1903, Malone married a Mr.

Pope, but she divorced him after a short time because he tried to interfere with her business.

During the 1904 World's Fair, Malone opened a retail outlet. Visitors to St. Louis responded favorably to her products, prompting her to embark on an innovative marketing campaign aimed at distributing the product nationally. In addition to going door-to-door, she and her trained assistants traveled to black churches and community centers, providing free hair and scalp treatments. She held press conferences and advertised in black newspapers. Malone traveled throughout the South at a time of racial discrimination and violence, giving demonstrations in black churches and women's clubs. Everywhere she went, she hired and trained women to serve as local sales agents. They, in turn, recruited others. By 1910, distribution had expanded nationally.

One of her Malone's recruits was Madame C.J. Walker, a former washerwoman who eventually founded her own company with similar beauty products and distribution. She is widely regarded as the most successful black entrepreneur of the early 20th century and founder of the black beauty business in the United States. However, historians credit Malone with having developed her products and distribution system first. Walker sold her own "Wonderful Hair Straightener," which Malone called a fraudulent imitation. As a result, Malone trademarked Poro, a new name for her product and merchandising systems in 1906. (Poro is a West African word for an organization dedicated to disciplining and enhancing the body spiritually and physically.)

In 1914, Malone married Aaron Eugene Malone, an ex-teacher and Bible salesman. Her husband became the company's chief manager and president. The young couple did more than just manufacture beauty products. They also provided a way for African American women to improve themselves on many levels. At a time when few career opportunities were available, Poro offered them a chance at economic independence. Malone believed that if African American women improved their physical appearance, they would gain greater self-respect and achieve success in other areas of their lives.

Committed to Black Community

Malone was committed to community building and social welfare. To that end she built Poro College in 1918, a complex that included her business's office, manufacturing operation, and training center as well as facilities for civic, religious, and social functions. The campus was located in St. Louis's upper-middle-class black neighborhood and served as a gathering place for the city's African Americans, who were denied access to other entertainment and hospitality venues. The complex, which was valued at more than $1 million, included classrooms, barber shops, laboratories, an auditorium, dining facilities, a theater, gymnasium, chapel, and a roof garden. Many local and national organizations, including the National Negro Business League, were housed in the facility or used it for business functions. The training center provided cosmetology and sales training for women interested in joining the Poro agent network. It also taught students how to walk, talk, and behave in social situations. During the early 20th century, race improvement and positive self-image were seen as a way to increase social mobility. By teaching deportment, Malone believed she was helping African American women improve their standing in the community.

By 1926, the college employed 175 people. Franchised outlets in North and South America, Africa, and the Philippines employed some 75,000 women. Malone had become a wealthy woman. It is believed that she was worth $14 million at one point during the 1920s. Her 1924 income tax totaled nearly $40,000. However, despite her wealth, Malone lived conservatively and gave away much of her fortune to help other African Americans. She is one of America's first major black philanthropists. Malone donated large sums to countless charities. At one time, it is believed that she was supporting two full-time students in every black land-grant college in the United States. She gave $25,000 to the Howard University Medical School during the 1920s that, at the time, was the largest gift the school had ever received from an African American. She also contributed to the Tuskegee Institute. Malone was also generous with family and employees. She educated many of her nieces and nephews and bought homes for her brothers and sisters. She awarded employees with lavish gifts for attendance, punctuality, service anniversaries, and as rewards for investing in real estate.

A $25,000 donation from Malone helped build the St. Louis Colored YWCA. She also contributed to several orphanages and donated the site for the St. Louis Colored Orphans' Home. She raised most of the orphanage's construction costs and served on the home's executive board from 1919 to 1943. The home was renamed the Annie Malone Children's Home in 1946. Malone also gave generously of her time in the community. She was president of the Colored Women's Federated Clubs of St. Louis, an executive committee member of the National Negro Business League and the Commission on Interracial Cooperation, an honorary member of Zeta Phi Beta Sorority, a member of the African Methodist Episcopal Church, and a lifelong Republican.

Business Failure

Malone's generosity raised her stature in the community but contributed to the financial decline of her business. While she was spending time on civic affairs and distributing her wealth to various organizations, she left the day-to-day affairs of the business in the hands of managers, including her husband. Some of these managers were inexperienced or dishonest, eventually leading to the dismantling of her business empire.

For the six years leading up to 1927, Annie and Aaron Malone became embroiled in a power struggle over control of the Poro business. The struggle was kept quiet until 1927, when Aaron Malone filed for divorce and demanded half the business. He claimed that Poro's success was due to contacts he brought to the company. He courted black leaders and politicians who sided with him in the highly publicized divorce. Annie Malone's devotion to black women and charitable institutions led Poro workers and

church leaders to support her. She also had the support of the press and Mary McLeod Bethune, president of the National Association of Colored Women. Having the support of so powerful a woman helped Annie Malone prevail in the dispute and allowed her to keep her business. She negotiated a settlement of $200,000.

In 1930, Malone moved her business to Chicago, where its location became known as the Poro block. Her financial trouble continued when she became the target of lawsuits, including one by a former employee who claimed credit for her success. When the suit was settled in 1937, she was forced to sell the St. Louis property. Malone's business was further crippled by enormous debt to the government for unpaid real estate and excise taxes. (The federal government required a 20 percent tax on luxuries, including hair-care products during the 1920s.) In 1943, she owed almost $100,000. The government was constantly taking her to court and by 1951, it took control of Poro. Most of the property was sold to pay the taxes.

Malone's business failure tarnished her image. Her former employee, Madame C.J. Walker, often overshadows Malone because Walker's business remained successful and more widely known. Walker is often credited as the originator of the black beauty and cosmetics business and the direct distribution and sales agent system that Malone developed. Many historians believe Malone deserves more credit for her devotion to helping African Americans gain financial independence and her generous donations to educational, civic, and social causes.

Annie Turnbo Malone died of a stroke on May 10, 1957, in Chicago, Illinois. She was 87. By the time of her death, Malone had lost her national visibility and most of her money. Having no children, her estate, valued at $100,000, was left to her nieces and nephews.

Books

Contemporary Black Biography, Volume 13, Gale Research, 1996.
Notable American Women: The Modern Period, edited by Barbara Sicherman and Carol Hurd Green, Belknap Press, 1980.
Notable Black American Women, Gale Research, 1992.

Online

Peiss, Kathy L., "American Women and the Making of Modern Consumer Culture," *The Journal for MultiMedia History*, Fall 1998, http://www.albany.cdu/jmmh/vol1no1/peiss-text.html (February 5, 2003). □

Bruce McCandless

In 1984, American astronaut Bruce McCandless II (born 1937) became the first person to leave a spacecraft in space without a tether. He flew out of the payload bay of the space shuttle *Challenger* on February 7, 1984, and using a jetpack called a Manned Maneuvering Unit (MMU), flew around the

vicinity of the shuttle as an independent satellite of the Earth. Also, in 1990, flying on the space shuttle _Discovery,_ he participated in the deployment of the Hubble Space Telescope, which soon afterwards returned views of interstellar space never before seen.

Joined the Astronaut Corps from the Navy

Bruce McCandless II was born in Boston, Massachusetts, on June 8, 1937, and attended high school in Long Beach, California. After graduating from high school, he went on to the United States Naval Academy in Annapolis, Maryland. He graduated from the Naval Academy in 1958 with a bachelor of science degree.

Following his graduation from the Naval Academy (second in a class of 900), McCandless learned to pilot aircraft at the Naval Aviation Training Command based in Pensacola, Florida, and Kingsville, Texas. He received his Navy aviator wings in 1960 and went on to Key West, Florida, where he underwent aircraft carrier landing training flying F-6A Skyray aircraft.

Next McCandless was assigned to the 102nd Fighter Squadron flying Skyrays and F-4B Phantom II aircraft from the USS _Forrestal_ and the USS _Enterprise_ aircraft carriers. The latter ship participated in the United States naval blockade of Cuba in the 1960s while McCandless was serving on her.

In 1964, McCandless served as an instrument flight instructor in the 43rd Attack Squadron, based at Apollo Soucek Field at Oceana, Virginia's Naval Air Station. McCandless continued his education at Stanford University in Stanford, California, through the Naval Reserve Officer's Training Corps Unit. There, in 1965, he earned a master of science degree in electrical engineering.

During his time as a Navy aviator, McCandless became an expert pilot, gaining proficiency on almost a dozen aircraft, including jets and helicopters. He joined the National Aeronautics and Space Administration (NASA) astronaut corps in 1966, during the height of the space race in which the United States and the Soviet Union competed to be the first to send humans to the moon. In 1971, McCandless served on the support crew for _Apollo 14,_ the third mission to touch down on the surface of the moon, and two years later served on the backup crew of the United State's first mission to its first space station, Skylab. Also during this time, McCandless helped to develop the Manned Maneuvering Unit (MMU), which he was later to test fly on a space shuttle mission.

Waited 18 Years for His First Spaceflight

Eighteen years passed between the time McCandless became a member of the astronaut corps and his first flight into space. He was described by his fellow astronauts as something of a loner and appeared to be unwilling to engage in the competitive politics that many saw as a necessity for getting assigned to space missions.

A lover of the outdoors, McCandless was also an avid bird-watcher, an activity that sometimes made him the butt of jokes at the astronaut office. He proved the value of his knowledge of birds, however, after a new runway was built at the Kennedy Space Center in the middle of what had been a bird refuge. Sent to study how accidents involving birds could be avoided by NASA pilots, McCandless learned which birds were likely to nest near the runway, which birds would be frightened by aircraft noise, and in what direction they would most likely fly when startled. Armed with this knowledge, McCandless was able to advise his fellow pilots on how and at what times of the day to fly to avoid accidents with birds. Recalled moonwalking astronaut Alan Bean to Thomas O'Toole in the _Washington Post,_ NASA pilots took McCandless's suggestions "and never had an accident."

Finally, after 18 years of waiting, McCandless got his chance to fly into space. He did so by serving as mission specialist on the STS-41B space shuttle mission, which flew February 3 to 11, 1984. He was later assigned to a second space mission, STS-31, which flew April 24 to 29, 1990.

Performed the First Untethered Spacewalk

The space shuttle _Challenger_ lifted off from the Kennedy Space Center in Florida on February 3, 1984. This was the tenth space shuttle mission flown. The main tasks for this mission were the deployment of two communications satellites and to conduct the maiden flight of the MMU. McCandless accomplished this last task, flying each of the mission's two MMUs for the first time, to become the world's first free-flying spacewalker, in effect becoming an independent satellite of the earth. Helping him in this endeavor, and using the MMUs himself, was fellow astronaut Lieutenant Colonel Robert L. Stewart of the United States Army.

To fly independently of the space shuttle, McCandless and Stewart first cycled through the shuttle's airlock and made their way out into the spacecraft's payload bay. There, McCandless attached the MMU, essentially a jetpack, to his spacesuit. Next, he disengaged the MMU from its berth in the payload bay, and became, as he was quoted by Thomas O'Toole in the *Washington Post* as saying, "the smallest spaceship in history." Flying alongside the shuttle, he circled the globe at 17,500 miles per hour at an altitude of 150 miles.

After first putting the MMU through its paces in the shuttle's payload bay, McCandless got the go-ahead from mission commander Vance Brand, watching through the shuttle's windows, to take the MMU 150 feet out into space. After completing that maneuver, McCandless headed back to the shuttle, before getting the go-head to fly 300 feet from the shuttle. As he did so, he compared the sensation to flying a helicopter at 25 times the speed of sound. After returning to the shuttle's payload bay, McCandless practiced docking the MMU to docking adaptors mounted on the payload bay walls. This was to simulate similar maneuvers that would take place when docking with satellites for future repair missions. Following McCandless's lead, Stewart conducted his own MMU flight tests using the same MMU. These tests were equally successful, and the two headed back inside the shuttle.

Performed an Unscheduled Test of Rescue Procedures

Two days later, McCandless and Stewart again left the shuttle's airlock to conduct MMU tests. This time they used a second MMU along with the first. Both MMUs were mounted in the shuttle's payload bay. During this second venture outside of the spacecraft, or Extra Vehicular Activity (EVA), the two astronauts conducted an unscheduled test of the procedures that would be used to rescue an astronaut who had unintentionally floated away from the shuttle. This came about when a foot restraint that McCandless was using to secure himself while completing simulated repairs on a mockup of a satellite in the payload bay came loose. The foot restraint floated free of the payload bay, and shuttle commander Brand, following instructions radioed by McCandless, maneuvered the shuttle so that McCandless could reach out and retrieve the restraint. McCandless joked as he retrieved the restraint that his shuttle crew made pickups as well as deliveries.

After completing their second EVA of the mission, and before going back inside, McCandless and Stewart took a telephone call from President Ronald Reagan, who asked them what it was like working in space without tethers. Replied McCandless, according to Thomas O'Toole in the *Washington Post,* "The view is simply spectacular, and we're literally opening up a new frontier in what man can do in space."

Instrumental in the Development of Untethered EVAs

Forty-six years old at the time of his spacewalks, and a captain in the Navy, McCandless had been helping to develop the MMU since 1968. The device had gone through numerous design changes, and during this time McCandless had also lobbied NASA and Congress to convince them to fund it. Many decisionmakers had thought that the backpack would be too expensive and too impractical to be of use to the United States space program, but McCandless proved them wrong on his historic flight.

The first incarnation of the MMU had been flown aboard the *Gemini 9* spacecraft in 1966 and was to have been tested by astronaut Gene Cernan (who later became the last person to walk on the surface of the moon). Cernan exited *Gemini 9,* and, attached to the spacecraft with a tether, worked his way to the back of the spacecraft, where the backpack was stowed. There he found that the design of his spacesuit restricted his freedom of movement so much that he was unable to properly attach the backpack and test it.

A redesign of the backpack was finally successfully tested inside the Skylab space station in the early 1970s. By the time McCandless strapped on his MMU in 1984, the machine had been redesigned 11 times, 9 of those times at McCandless's instigation. The machine cost $60 million to design and build. McCandless himself participated materially in the design process, on one occasion inventing a way the backpack could be used to stabilize a satellite stranded in orbit. McCandless's invention prompted one of his colleagues at NASA to call him a "thorough, methodical and brilliant electronics genius," according to Thomas O'Toole in the *Washington Post.*

The successful tests of the MMUs by McCandless and Stewart on STS-41B were bright spots on what had been a disappointing mission up until that point. The shuttle's primary mission was to deploy a pair of communications satellites. The release of the satellites from the shuttle's payload bay went off without a hitch, but the booster rocket that was supposed to send the satellites into a higher orbit malfunctioned, stranding the expensive satellites in useless orbits.

After 191 hours in space, four of which he spent flying the MMUs, McCandless returned to Earth aboard the *Challenger* on February 11, 1984, touching down with his crewmates at the Kennedy Space Center's shuttle runway. It was the first time a shuttle had landed at the Space Center. In 1987, between his two space shuttle flights, McCandless earned his second masters degree, in business administration, from the University of Houston at Clear Lake.

Another Historic Space Mission

In 1990, McCandless flew on another historic shuttle flight when the shuttle *Discovery* lifted off on shuttle mission STS-31 on April 24. This mission launched the Hubble Space Telescope, the pioneering orbiting observatory that subsequently returned the clearest images of the most distant objects ever observed by human beings. This mission also set an altitude record for a space shuttle of 380 miles.

The Space Telescope almost required rescuing by Mc-Candless and fellow astronaut Kathy Sullivan. The telescope's two 20-foot solar panels failed to unfurl properly, and McCandless and Sullivan were ordered into their spacesuits and told to prepare to unfurl the solar panels manually. But, while McCandless and Sullivan waited in the shuttle's airlock for the last of the air to be pumped out so that they could venture out into the payload bay, ground controllers managed to solve the problem. McCandless and Sullivan were told to repressurize the airlock and go back inside.

After 76 orbits of the earth, during which McCandless and his crewmates spent 121 hours in space, *Discovery* touched down at the Edwards Air Force Base in California, on April 29, 1990. By the time McCandless retired from the astronaut corps (and the Navy as a captain), he had logged more than 312 hours in space on two separate missions aboard the space shuttles.

Hobbies for McCandless include, not surprising for an astronaut, flying airplanes and scuba diving, perhaps the two experiences that come closest to replicating the experiences of being in space without actually going there. He is also an electronics and photography enthusiast and enjoys cross-country skiing. An avid bird-watcher, McCandless is a past president of the Houston Audubon Society. He is married to the former Bernice Doyle, and they have two grown children.

Books

Cernan, Eugene, and Don Davis, *The Last Man on the Moon,* St. Martin's Press, 1999.

Periodicals

Aviation Week and Space Technology, February 13, 1984; April 30, 1990.
Christian Science Monitor, February 8, 1984.
New York Times, April 25, 1990.
Washington Post, February 7, 1984; February 10, 1984.

Online

"Astronaut Bio: Bruce McCandless II," *NASA,* http://www.jsc .nasa.gov (March 11, 2003). □

Joni Mitchell

In her nearly four decades as a musician and lyricist, Joni Mitchell (born 1943) has spanned the fields of folk, pop, rock, and jazz with 23 albums. Her willingness to change direction without warning has frequently left fans upset, but her free spirit has endowed her creativity. By 2002, Mitchell had achieved the stature of Bob Dylan and influenced the likes of Madonna and Prince. Even Frank Sinatra recorded one of her songs.

Joni Mitchell was born Roberta Joan Anderson on November 7, 1943, in Fort Macleod, Alberta, Canada. She was daughter of Bill Anderson, a grocer, and his wife Myrtle, a schoolteacher. Mitchell moved with her parents to North Battleford, Saskatchewan, after World War II ended. At the age of nine, she and her family would move again to Saskatoon, Saskatchewan, which Mitchell today considers her hometown.

After a friend introduced her to classical music, Mitchell asked her parents whether she could study piano. Although the seven-year-old aspiring musician did in fact start piano lessons, the lessons only lasted eighteen months. By then Mitchell had had enough of the "knuckle-rapping" school of music that was then in vogue. More importantly, she had discovered that she enjoyed creating her own music more than she did learning to do piano exercises. Also at the age of 9, Mitchell contracted polio, a disease that was often fatal at the time. Cared for by her mother, she eventually recovered. Mitchell also dates her taking up smoking to this period—a habit she continues to indulge in.

In the seventh grade, Mitchell was inspired by an English teacher who encouraged her to write about things she knew and to develop her ability to convey descriptive imagery. Mitchell would later dedicate her first record album to this teacher. Unable to afford a guitar, Mitchell purchased a baritone ukulele, which she played at parties and the local coffeehouse. After she graduated from high school, she enrolled in Calgary's Alberta College of Art. Finding the classes to be uncreative, she left after a year. Mitchell had, by this time, become a regular performer at a club in Calgary, so it was not entirely surprising that she left in June 1964 for Toronto to pursue a career as a folksinger.

False Start

Finding success in the Toronto music scene proved to be more difficult than Mitchell had imagined. Unable to afford membership in the musician's union, she was unable to get many performing jobs. Instead, she was forced to take a job in a department store. In February 1965, she gave birth to a baby girl who had been fathered by her ex-boyfriend from college. Shortly before giving birth, she had met a folk singer named Chuck Mitchell, who had offered to take care of her and the child. A few weeks after the birth of her daughter Joni and Chuck were married. Soon after, Mitchell gave her daughter up for adoption. (Mitchell kept the child a secret for 30 years, not even telling her parents. In 1995, following rumors that appeared on the Internet, Mitchell made contact with the lost daughter.) In the summer of 1965, Chuck Mitchell took Joni with him to Detroit, Michigan, where he found work. A year and a half later Joni and Chuck Mitchell had separated.

Following the 1967 divorce, Mitchell relocated to New York to pursue her musical career. Based in New York City, she acquired a reputation as an East Coast songwriter and live performer. In the fall of 1967 she met Elliot Roberts, who began managing her career. With the help of former Byrds band member David Crosby, she landed a recording contract for a solo acoustic album. In the meantime, she moved to California, where she shared a house with Crosby.

Mitchell was given very little compensation in her first recording contract. Eventually Elliot Roberts negotiated a better deal for her at Reprise, and she received total artistic control of her work. When Mitchell left Reprise, she was able to negotiate similar arrangements with Asylum Records—and later with Geffen Records—that gave her considerably more autonomy than most other recording artists enjoyed. However, disagreements over unpaid royalties would follow and relations with record boss, David Geffen, were strained.

Early Albums

Mitchell's debut album, *Joni Mitchell,* was released in March 1968. On the album she declined to record any of her songs that other artists had turned into hits. That December, Judy Collins' version of Mitchell's "Both Sides Now" would reach the top of the record charts, earning Mitchell considerable income in royalties. Instead she performed her relatively unknown folk songs. Interestingly, Mitchell's "Both Sides Now" was written when she was only 21. This fact has amazed many people who have been struck with the depth of emotion expressed in the song. But as Mitchell told *W* magazine in 2002, "When I did experience these things, I was right, so I seemed to know what I was talking about."

In April 1969, Mitchell's second album, *Clouds,* was released. It included her classics, "Chelsea Morning," "Both Sides Now," and "Tin Angel." Although Mitchell was unable to get to the 1969 Woodstock rock festival due

to excessive highway traffic, she chronicled the event with her song of the same name, which became a hit for Crosby, Stills, Nash and Young. In 1970, shortly before Reprise released her third album, *Ladies of the Canyon,* Mitchell won a Grammy for *Clouds."* In *Ladies of the Canyon,* Mitchell ventured into increasingly complex arrangements, adding woodwinds, backup singers, and a cello to her own performance. *Ladies* would become her first gold album (with 500,000 copies sold).

At this point, Mitchell decided to take a year off from performing. She began traveling through Europe, visiting France, Spain, and Greece. Her subsequent album, *Blue,* released in 1971, featured songs she had written during her travels. *Blue* was also of note because it saw Mitchell alternating between acoustic guitar- and piano-based arrangements. In "For The Roses" (1972), Mitchell used pop-rock arrangements to back up her songs about the problems with being in love and the difficulties of being an artist. The album quickly climbed the charts. Looking back, Mitchell noted that she passed through her folk period rather rapidly. Her rock 'n' roll career was equally short-lived, probably, she said, because she was never much of a "druggie."

In 1974, *Court and Spark* was released. The album found Mitchell increasingly embracing a "pop" sound, but with the addition of orchestral arrangements and jazz-inspired sounds. *Court and Spark* had the distinction of appearing when Mitchell was at the peak of her popularity. Her next offering, *Miles of Aisles* (1974), was a live rock album based on concerts she gave during the summer of 1974 at the Universal Amphitheater, backed up by the L.A. Express. *The Hissing Of Summer Lawns* (1975), although a top seller, evoked some of the first negative reviews to greet Mitchell's work. Some of her fans took particular issue with the criticisms that Mitchell levelled at society in the album. A year later, Mitchell's *Hejira* (1976) found the artist vocalizing about a spiritual journey she had made. On this album a guitar, bass, and drums accompanied her. With songs written for the most part when Mitchell was traveling by car though the U.S., the album was recorded in the summer of 1976. Many of the songs dealt with Mitchell's concerns about not having a family.

Don Juan's Reckless Daughter (1977) was followed by *Mingus* (1979). It is generally felt that in *Mingus,* which Mitchell composed with jazz great Charles Mingus shortly before his death, she failed to reach her own, and presumably Mingus's, expectations. The news was scarcely better a year later when Mitchell released *Shadows and Light* (1980), which contained live versions of songs that Mitchell had already recorded in the studio on *Miles of Aisles.* Critics called the album a disappointment.

In December 1980, Mitchell returned to Toronto for her acting debut in a film anthology entitled *Love,* about women's perceptions of love. She also contributed the title song. However, the film was never released. But there was also good news—in 1981 Mitchell was inducted into the Canadian Music Hall of Fame. She subsequently left for a six-week Caribbean vacation, during which she took time to paint.

About this time, Mitchell became embroiled in a dispute with a salmon fishing company that wanted to build a hatchery near some property she owned in Vancouver, Canada. The local newspaper sided with the hatchery, arguing that its construction would lead to more jobs, while pointing out that Mitchell was not even a full-time resident. The salmon company, for its part, claimed that Mitchell was just some Hollywood celebrity who was out to ruin its business.

The Limelight of Decline

In 1985, the all-star single, "We Are the World" was released. Mitchell, who was at the time studying yoga, later said her yoga teacher sent her to a psychic dietician who hardly allowed her to eat anything. In response, she recorded "Ethiopia" in 1985, a song about an Ethiopian who is experiencing famine. In *Dog Eat Dog* (1985), Mitchell complained angrily about increasing trends toward censorship, especially in rock 'n' roll music. The response to *Dog Eat Dog* was, as usual by this time, mostly negative, and the album ended up with only moderate sales. The disappointing reception led Mitchell to cancel her six-month 1986 tour. She instead stayed home and painted.

But there would be bright spots too. In the fall of 1990, the Los Angeles Theater Center put on a revue with five singers performing the songs of Mitchell. The show ran for three months. Then in the early part of 1991, a traveling exhibit of Mitchell's paintings made the rounds in Europe. In *Night Ride Home,* released the same year, Mitchell made do without any guest artists, and her vocals came across as deep and rich. *Turbulent Indigo* (1994) saw Mitchell return full circle in a melancholy mood to her earlier work.

In February 1996, Mitchell received the Orville H. Gibson Award for best Female Acoustic Guitar Player, even though she had by that time switched from acoustic to electric guitar. The Rock and Roll Hall of Fame inducted Mitchell in 1997. On *Taming the Tiger* (1998), Mitchell played a computerized guitar to produce a sound unlike anything she had achieved before.

Past Prime

With *Both Sides Now* (2000), Mitchell's voice came across as ravaged from her years of smoking. The album could not be salvaged even with the backup of a large orchestra conducted by Vince Mendoza. *Travelogue* (2002) once again saw Mitchell performing well past her prime. On the album, she recorded some of her old songs with the backup of the London Symphony Orchestra, Wayne Shorter, and Herbie Hancock. The album had few admirers. Part of the problem was that by 2002, Mitchell's voice no longer had the three-octave range of her youth. While her cigarette smoking had contributed, it was also as Mitchell told *W* magazine, "I don't take good care of my voice." But she added that she would rather sound gravelly like Louis Armstrong than pitch-perfect like Streisand.

Parting Shots

Following the release of *Travelogue* in 2002, Mitchell took aim at the music industry, calling it a "corrupt cess-

pool," while announcing her decision to stop recording. Mitchell also said that musicians today are made, not born. She told *W* magazine, "The artists don't have to play anything—they can cheat, buy songs and put their name on them, so they can build the illusion that they are creative. And because [the record companies] made you, they can kiss you off. Me, I don't sell that many records, but they can't kiss me off so easily." As she notes, her records have rarely sold large numbers. During her remarkable career she had only one Top 10 record ("Help Me"), and that was in 1974.

In November 1982—although the dates vary—Joni married bass player and sound engineer Larry Klein. Although they separated in 1994, they have continued to collaborate professionally. Besides her marriages to Chuck Mitchell and Larry Klein, Mitchell has been romantically linked to David Crosby, Graham Nash, James Taylor, Warren Beatty, and Jackson Browne.

Books

Fleischer, Leonore, *Joni Mitchell,* Flash Books, 1976.

Periodicals

Guardian (London, England), November 21, 2002.
New York Times, January 5, 2003.
W, December 2002.

Online

"The Joni Mitchell Homepage," Available online at http://www .jonimitchell.com/ (January 2003). ☐

Kenji Mizoguchi

Kenji Mizoguchi (1898–1956) was a Japanese film director most noted for exploring both personal and broad societal issues such as the status of women. He is, according to *The Yomiuri Shimbun* "regarded as the dean of Japanese filmmaking." Gary Arnold, writing in *The Washington Times,* called his work "a substantial but curiously fragmentary and haunted body of work." Arnold says his films extract "extraordinary eloquence and pathos from stories of human abandonment, struggle and loss."

Early Life Fraught with Sorrows

Mizoguchi's topic selection is seen as reflecting his personal life, which was filled with seemingly constant sorrow. Mizoguchi was born on May 16, 1898, in Tokyo, Japan. He was born to a roofing carpenter and the daughter of a failed herbal medicines trader, one of three children. The family, who were living in the middle-class district of Toyko known as Hongo, was devastated financially during the Russo-Japanese war by his father's attempts to sell raincoats to the Army. The business failed. The family was forced to move to Asakusa and to eventually give up their daughter for adoption. The sister's adoptive family eventually sold her into servitude in a geisha house. Mizoguchi harbored a lifelong hatred of his father.

It was after this move that Mizoguchi first had an attack of rheumatoid arthritis, a condition which ultimately affected the way he walked and persisted throughout his life. He entered elementary school in 1907, but after six years' schooling, he was sent to relatives in Morioka as apprentice to his uncle, a pharmacist. When he returned home in 1912, Mizoguchi expected to resume his education. His father refused to send him to school, however, so he went to work, though grudgingly. As noted in an essay in *World Film Directors,* "the resulting sense of inferiority about his lack of formal education stayed with him all his life."

His mother died in 1915, while Mizoguchi was still in his teens. His sister placed their father in a home and took in her brothers. These formative experiences fueled his passion for artistic expression and shaped his films. Under these freer living conditions, Mizoguchi became interested in art and theater. He moved to Kobe in 1918 to take a position as a newspaper advertising designer.

Industry Strike Provided Opportunity for Directorial Debut

Mizoguchi returned to Toyko, homesick. He moved in with a friend working at the Mukojima film studios who secured a job for Mizoguchi. Originally offered an acting job, Mizoguchi decided to become a jack of all trades—transcribing scripts and organizing sets. He was given his first opportunity to direct during a strike in 1923; he made *Aini yomigaeruhi (The Resurrection of Love).* He would make 10 more films before the Tokyo earthquake in September that same year. He was able to get equipment and film the destruction for newsreels.

Mizoguchi's life was rife with emotional episodes played out with various women. A romantic involvement in 1925 interrupted his career. Yuriko Ichijo, a call girl, attacked Mizoguchi with a razor, scarring him for life. The attendant scandal resulted in his suspension from the studio. He returned to work with a new demeanor some called "his obsessive perfectionism." Four years later, he married, but that relationship was marred with violence and frequent separations.

Arnold says it was that "history of family estrangement and bitterness on one hand and romantic turbulence and susceptibility on the other" that "conspired to create a peculiarly expressive interpreter of primal passions and misfortunes in Kenji Mizoguchi."

In 1930, Mizoguchi made his first sound film, *Furusato (Home Town),* which was also the first sound film in Japan. It was in 1935 that he and screenwriter Yoshikata Yoda first teamed for *Osaka Elegy* (1935). This creative relationship would last until Mizoguchi's death. The film was considered his first master work, but it was a financial failure.

His next major film was made in 1938, the same year his brother died. *Zangiku monogatari (The Story of the Late Chrysanthemums)* is considered by some to be represent the pinnacle of Mizoguchi's career. It is also said to be the most feminist of his films.

Made Epic *Ronin*

Mizoguchi drew from Japanese history for *Genroku Chushingura (The Loyal Forty-Seven Ronin of the Genroku Era* or *The 47 Ronin,* 1941 and 1942). Its script was written by Yoda and Kenichiro Hara. The sprawling epic was made in two parts and was the largest budget film at the time, costing 53,000 Yen. In a review of the re-release of *The 47 Ronin* in *Cineaste,* Diane Stevenson calls the film "the most beautiful movie ever made. . . . I'm not sure it's the greatest . . . but it's the most beautiful."

The film is based on a incident in Japanese history that has become legend—revenge of Lord Asano's loyal retainers following the death of their master, who was forced into *seppuku* or ritual suicide after being provoked to draw his sword in the Shogun's palace. The story has been used frequently in theater and film. Mixoguchi's version of this story delves into explorations of the samurai code, its ceremonies and obligations.

While filming the second half of the epic, Mizoguchi's wife was committed to a mental asylum. He moved in with his sister-in-law.

Stevenson and other critics wonder about Mizoguchi's choice to refrain from showing violent acts on screen in that film. "Mizoguchi has been criticized for not showing the dramatic culmination of the story, the loyal retainers finally avenging their master." In his retelling, she says, the story does not end with the successful revenge, but "the punishment for the revenge, the collective seppuku required of the forty-seven ronin in consequence of their triumph. . . . It may be said that Mizoguchi's propensity for pathos led him to emphasize the punishment rather than the triumph. But the crucial thing is ceremony. Ceremony is about social order, about social ordering. It is about hierarchy, and the story of the loyal retainers is a story about hierarchy. Like any other etiquette or courtesy, ceremony makes it possible to live with the humiliations of hierarchy. Seppuku is a ritual that makes suicide a social act."

1950s Brought Awards Streak, Acclaim

During the occupation of Japan after World War II, demand for escapist entertainment and film was at its height. Mizoguchi was depressed, thinking he was tapped and his filmmaking style outmoded. The success of Akira Kurosawa's *Rashomon* was said to have provoked him into making *The Life of Ohara* in 1952. It was considered to be ambitious and also took Mizoguchi in a new direction. The film was made without the financial support of a studio. The film shared a Silver Lion at the 1952 Venice Film Festival with John Ford's *The Quiet Man.*

Among his most enduring and popular films is *Ugetsu* (1953), a ghost story that plumbs the depths of the post-war Japanese psyche. *Time'*s Richard Corliss contrasts it with the internationally popular Gojira/Godzilla story, another postwar film classic. Corliss says *Ugetsu* "critiques . . . [Japan's] own blood-lust, most profoundly." The story follows two couples through the degradation of war, "beyond pain, beyond death . . . a horror story and a haunting masterpiece." It was awarded a Silver Lion and Italian Critics' Award.

The complexities of *Ugetsu* are explored in a comprehensive 1993 volume by the same name, edited by Keiko I. McDonald. The book contains printed materials including the film script, the two 18th-century tales on which the film was based and critical essays.

Mizoguchi had several frequent collaborators. Among them was Matsutaro Kawaguchi, a novelist whom he knew since they met in elementary school; Shuichi Hatamoto, who worked with him between 1924 and the advent of talkies in Japan; Hiroshi Mzutani, his art director from 1933 on; producer Masaichi Nagata; and screenwriter Yoshikata Yoda. With actress Kinuyo Tanaka, Mizoguchi made 11 films.

His sets were said to have been tense. Yoda observed Mizoguchi "does not have the courage to face persons, things, and ideas that assail him. The anger and resentment which he cannot deal with makes him cry hysterically." Actors were rarely given license to improvise. His concentration while working on any given film was said to have been legendary. According to *World Film Directors* "his working method tested the endurance of his collaborators, who nevertheless testify to its success as well as the affection he inspired."

Mizoguchi continued prolifically. *Sansho dayu (Sansho the Bailiff,* 1954) shared a Silver Lion with Kurosawa's *The Seven Samurai. Chikamatsu monogatari (Chikamatsu Story),* among his last films, is considered "perhaps the best-loved of all his works among his colleagues and the Japanese critics" according to *World Film Directors.*

Left Rich and Distinctive Body of Work

The resultant body of work Mizoguchi left has been studied and pondered by scholars and film buffs alike, mined for meaning and subtext. Much of his work shares similar themes. He used historic tales as well as the works of Guy de Maupassant, Tolstoy, and contemporary Japanese novelists. His work was often contrasted with that of Kurosawa during their lifetime, and continues to be simply by virtue of their both being Japanese directors.

"Like Shakespeare, Mizoguchi respected ordeal, marks of true birth (moral status), and home as the place you set out from and eventually return to, changed utterly. He knew that what we long for is undying passion and reunion with what has been lost," wrote *Village Voice* reviewer Georgia Brown in a 1996 article.

J. Hoberman, writing in the *Village Voice* in 1996, called Mizoguchi "the first universal master of Japanese cinema, a specialist in crypto-feminist-period melodrama, beloved by the critics of the French new wave for his fluid camera moves and bravura mise-en-scene." Mizoguchi drew inspiration from numerous sources, including the art of Pablo Picasso. Among the directors who inspired him

were William Wyler, John Ford, and Erich von Stroheim. One of his preferred conventions was to use long, distant camera shots. Stevenson says "The cllose-up may bring on the tear in a Hollywood movie, but it is Mizoguchi's distant camera that makes us cry." Others state they find God in his attention to those smallest details. "Mizoguchi's scenes are lit by fires of rapture, filtered through veils of an awesome sorrow," writes Brown in the *Village Voice.* "A simple tracking shot of a woman walking creates a binding spell. A couple in discussion tracked from below look like they're standing on a bridge, which, in an important sense, they are. Another bridge is an emblem of banishment; a drowning makes rings on a lake of tears. His signature crane shots look down with compassion or quiet horror. In Princess and O-hau, he shows us courage in a trailing hem."

Mizoguchi made two color films late in his career, but the experiences were not good. His final film—made in 1956—is considered the most financially successful of his work. Mizoguchi died from leukemia on August 24, 1956, while working on yet another project.

There are conflicting filmographies. Most frequently, Mizoguchi is said to have directed about 90 films between 1923 and 1956. Cinematheque Ontario and the Japan Foundation reportedly recognize 85 titles made between that same period. One obvious problem is that documentation and reels for most of his early films has been lost. Mizoguchi's own repository was destroyed in the 1923 Tokyo earthquake and then again in World War II. Then too, he was frequently dissatisfied with his work. Arnold says "Mizoguchi was hard-pressed to remember everything he had done—and content to leave the forgotten or unsatisfying projects to oblivion." Hope remains among cinephiles those prints will be found.

Books

McDonald, Keiko I., ed., *Ugetsu,* 1993.

Periodicals

Asia Africa Intelligence Wire (From *The Yomiuri Shimbun/Daily Yomiuri),* December 5, 2002.
Cineaste, Summer 2000.
Christian Science Monitor, August 25, 2000.
Japan Quarterly, October 1994.
Time International, August 23, 1999.
Village Voice, September 17, 1996; September 24, 1996.
Washington Times, February 16, 1997. □

Gilbert Murray

The Australian-born British scholar Gilbert Murray (1866–1957) first made a name for himself as an innovative scholar of Greek literature. He taught at Oxford and Glasgow Universities and translated ancient Greek texts. He applied his own unique approach to translating the works of the ancient Greek masters—including Aeschylus, Sophocles, Euripides, and Aristophanes—and in the process generated

new interest for Greek drama on the contemporary London stage. Murray was also a staunch advocate for world peace, and he gained international renown for his efforts in establishing the League of Nations and the United Nations.

Early Life and Career

The future renowned British scholar and political activist Gilbert Murray was born George Gilbert Aimé Murray on January 2, 1866, in Sydney, New South Wales, Australia. When he was 11 years old, he moved with his family to Britain. He attended Oxford University and graduated at the top of his class in 1887.

In 1888, he became a fellow at Oxford. From 1889 to 1899, he was a professor of Greek at the University of Glasgow. Only 23 years old when he started at Glasgow, he was one of the youngest professors ever at the esteemed institution. As a professor, he was noted for his enthusiasm and insight into Greek tragedy. His lectures consisted in large part of his own translations of Greek plays. These translations would later be published and presented in the London theatre. During the period between 1904 and 1912, he directed many stage productions of Greek plays. In doing so, he helped revive the Greek theatre as a vital performance art. When translating the plays, he employed rhymed verse rather than blank verse, trying to restore the rhythmic

quality that was such an important element of the ancient Greek literature. In 1908, he became Regius Professor of Greek at Oxford University. He held that position until his retirement in 1936.

Innovative Scholarship

Murray is considered one of the most important scholars of Greek history and culture. As a scholar and educator, he was noted for incorporating anthropology, then an emerging science, into his studies of Greek texts. As a result of this novel approach, he increased the academic world's understanding of the writings of Homer as well as the ancient Greek religions. A recurrent theme in his scholarly works involved the continuing importance of ancient theology and religions to modern thought. He illustrated this by recounting the many theological trends of ancient Greece.

This approach guided his writing in such scholarly works as *The Rise of the Greek Epic,* which was published in 1907, and *Five Stages of Greek Religion,* published in 1925. In the latter work, Murray described the earliest and most primitive rites as well as the classic Greek religion that included the Olympian gods and the later religion of the philosophic schools of the fourth century B.C. By outlining Greek theology in this fashion, he postulated that Christianity resulted from a cultural clash between Greek and Eastern religions. His other well-known works include *History of Ancient Greek Literature* (1897), *The Classical Tradition in Poetry* (1927), and *Hellenism and the Modern World* (1953). His *Euripides and His Age* (1918) is considered on of the best books written about its subject. Essentially, he ripped the name down from the pantheon of great Greek authors, brought the subject down to earth, and made Euripides a compelling flesh-and-blood figure, placing the writer squarely in the context of his times while emphasizing his continued relevance. "As a playwright the fate of Euripides has been strange," wrote Murray in *Euripides.* "All through a long life he was almost invariably beaten in the State competitions. He was steadily admired by some few philosophers, like Socrates; he enjoyed immense fame throughout Greece; but the official judges of poetry were against him, and his own people of Athens admired him reluctantly and with a grudge. After death, indeed, he seemed to come into his kingdom. He held the stage as no other tragedian has ever held it, and we hear of his plays being performed with popular success six hundred years after they were written, and in countries far removed from Greece."

Commenting about Greek scholarship and the value of the ancient texts, Murray once said, as quoted in *Libertystory.net,* "Between us and [ancient Greek authors], there has passed age upon age of men . . . who sought in the books that they read other things than truth and imaginative beauty, or who did not care to read books at all. Of the literature produced by the Greeks in the fifth century B.C., we possess about a twentieth part; of that produced in the seventh, sixth, fourth and third, not nearly so large a proportion. All that has reached us has passed a severe test and far from discriminating ordeal. It has secured its life by never going out of fashion for long at a time."

In another scholarly book, with subject matter more anthropological than classical, *Stoic, Christian, and Humanist,* published in 1940, Murray took a look at the world's earliest rites and religions and considered their relevance to later religions.

Became Interested in International Affairs

Murray not only made a name for himself as an important Greek scholar, he also became an important international figure as a peace advocate who was instrumental in the creation of the League of Nations and the United Nations.

In the early part of the twentieth century, Murrary's concerns grew to include world affairs. His interest began in earnest in 1914, as Europe became the center stage of World War I. Murray was stirred by Sir Edward Grey's speech before the House of Parliament on August 3, 1914, that called for Great Britain's entrance into the great conflict. Even though it meant his country was going to war, Murray recognized the "rightness" of the decision. From that point on, Murray became active in the cause of world peace. He later supported the Covenant of the League of Nations, drafted by United States President Woodrow Wilson and submitted on February 14, 1919. The document advocated the need for an international organization that could preserve peace and settle disputes by arbitration as opposed to war. The League of Nations Union itself was formed after World War I, and Murray was one of the founding members. He was appointed as a South African delegate from 1921 to 1923. From 1923 to 1938, he was chairman of the League. During World War II, he served as joint president. During this period, he published several books about international politics, including *Liberality and Civilization: Lectures Given at the Invitation of the Hibbert Trustees in the Universities of Bristol, Glasgow and Birmingham* (1938).

In 1924, while in Geneva, Switzerland, working with the League of Nations Union, Murray took part in a discussion about effective contributions to world peace. He suggested the development of an international students' group that would provide the intellectual, artistic, and social exchange of ideas among individuals of various national backgrounds. His suggestion led to the creation of the Committee of Intellectual Cooperation. Not only was he instrumental in its development, Murray served as chairman for eight years.

In 1934, Murray was one of the organizers of the famous League of Nations "Peace Ballot" of 1934–1935. More than 11 million British voters supported the ballot as well as Britain's membership in the League. Murray himself considered the ballot to be the League's greatest achievement. However, the League's efforts did little to affect the rising tide of Fascist aggression that came out of Germany and Italy during the 1930s. Murray blamed the failures on the United States' lack of participation up to that point. However, the eventual outbreak of World War II only caused Murray to be a more staunch advocate in his efforts toward world peace.

Engaged in Famine Relief

In 1942, Murray became one of the founding members of the Oxford Committee for Famine Relief, or Oxfam, as well as one of its trustees. The formation of the committee resulted from a situation in Europe directly attributable to the German invasions. In April 1941, when Greece surrendered to Germany, food and supplies belonging to the citizens were given to the German soldiers, which made a bad situation even worse. Before the invasion, the Greek people already suffered shortages due to Allied blockades intended to deplete the German army. A famine ensued and, at its peak, more than 1,500 people died a day. The situation was almost as bad in other occupied countries, including Norway, Belgium, and Poland. Not helping matters was the British government's stance on relief for the starving countries. It firmly believed that it was the duty of the occupying enemy to feed the citizens. Britain was reluctant to send relief, because it feared that any supplies offered would be given instead to German soldiers, and that could prolong the war. However, awareness of the situation—as well as their government's stance—grew among the British civilians. A movement was formed to appeal to the government to change its stance. Oxfam was part of this movement. Murray felt that in light of the deaths in Greece, the blockade was unjustifiable.

The committee first proposed a "controlled relief" program that included providing dried milk and vitamins for Greek and Belgian children. The response of the British War Cabinet was pretty much the same as before. The supplies, they believed, would inevitably be taken by the Germans and diverted to its workers in munitions factories and thus help the German war effort. British Prime Minister Winston Churchill was even bold enough to suggest that hunger might help provoke citizens of occupied countries to rise against their oppressors.

Oxfam officially came into existence on May 29, 1942. George Bell, Bishop of Chichester, a man known for his humanitarian positions, and Murray were among the members. Murray, because of his knowledge of Greece as well as the immediate Greek situation, was deemed a valuable advisor to the committee. The committee included academics and public figures. The committee's goals were to gather information about famine conditions in occupied countries and provide food relief where most needed. To support the committee, a Famine Relief Fund was established that help fund relief that the government deemed permissible. Oxfam was comprised of more than 200 local committees. However, its effect was relatively modest. The British government stuck fast to its policy on the blockade and would only allow relief to Greece. After the war, Oxfam continued its efforts on behalf of the lingering needs of European countries.

Even before Oxfam was formed, Murray had attempted to help stem the growing famine. In October of 1941, the League of Nations Union created the Committee on Starvation in Occupied Countries, and Murray and Lord Robert Cecil were appointed as joint presidents. The two men sought a meeting with the Ministry of Economic Warfare to see if anything could be done, but the government would not change its policy.

Helped Form the United Nations

In 1945, the United Nations Association was formed. It was a direct successor of the League of Nations Union. The purpose was to "help bring about a just, ordered and lasting peace, and better conditions of life for all mankind." Working out of the organization's first home office in London, Murray was integral to its creation. He was part of the early leadership that also included Viscount Cecil, C.R. Attlee, Lady Violet Bonham Carter, and Churchill. Murray would, in fact, become the first president of the general counsel of the United Nations. He would also serve as its joint president from the end of the war until his death in 1957.

Passed Away in Oxford

Murray died on May 20, 1957, in Oxford, Oxfordshire, England. After he had retired from teaching from Oxford University he always remained close to the institution. After his death, his family, friends, and fellow Oxfam supporters created a small capital fund to establish the Gilbert Murray Memorial Lecture Fund. The lectures, held every other year, feature subjects relating to international affairs, particularly relief and overseas development.

Online

"Before Oct. 5th—The Origins of Oxfam," *Oxfam.org website,* http://www.oxfam.org.uk/atwork/history/downloads/oxfam origins.rtf (March 15, 2003).

Haslett, Michael, and Isobel Haslett, "Buchan and the Classics: School and University," *John Buchan Society website,* http://216.239.33.100/search?q = cache:BGKjHqpOOmYC:www .johnbuchansociety.co.uk/classics.htm + Gilbert + Murray& =en& = UTF-8 (March 15, 2003).

"Historical Overview: 1924–Present," *iwa.org website,* http://www.iwa.org/History/history.html (March 15, 2003).

Meade, James E. "Autobiography," *Nobel e-Museum website,* http://www.nobel.se/economics/laureates/1977/meade-autobio.html (March 15, 2003).

"Murray, Gilbert," *Encyclopedia.com website,* http://www .encyclopedia.com/html/m/murray-G1i.asp (March 15, 2003).

"Murray, Gilbert," *infoplease.com website,* www.infoplease .com/ce6/people/A0834503.html (March 15, 2003).

"Murray, Gilbert," *Slider.com website,* http://www.slider.com/ enc/36000/Murray_Gilbert.htm (March 15, 2003).

Powell, Jim, "Voice for Liberty in the Ancient World," *LibertyStory.net website,* www.libertystory.net/LSARTS ANCIENTGREEKVOICES.htm (March 15, 2003). □

Pauli Murray

Pauli Murray (1910-1985), a lifelong civil rights advocate, served as a lawyer, college professor, deputy attorney general, and ordained minister. Often the first African American woman to fill the positions she occupied, Murray worked tirelessly to destroy the legal and political obstacles created by racism

and racial discrimination and fought at the same time against the Jane Crow stereotypes that limited the lives of women—especially African American women—in equally vicious ways.

Born November 20, 1910, in Baltimore, Maryland, Anna Pauline Murray was, as she noted in her autobiography *Song in a Weary Throat,* the result of "several generations of a generous intermixture of African, European, and Native American stocks." The granddaughter of a slave and the great-granddaughter of a slave owner, she was the fourth of six children born to Agnes (Fitzgerald) and William Murray, a nurse and school teacher. The family was a warm and loving one, but Murray grew up deeply conscious of the Jim Crow segregation laws that circumscribed their lives and affected every aspect of their existence. "[R]ace," she recalled, "was the atmosphere one breathed from day to day, the pervasive irritant, the chronic allergy, the vague apprehension which made one uncomfortable and jumpy. We knew the race problem was like a deadly snake coiled and ready to strike, and that one avoided its dangers only by never-ending watchfulness."

Orphaned at a Young Age

Murray's childhood happiness ended abruptly when her mother died of a cerebral hemorrhage in the summer of 1914. Her father, already weakened both mentally and physically from a nearly fatal bout of typhoid fever years before, found himself unable to care for all his children. The family was split, and Murray was sent to North Carolina, where she was raised by her mother's sisters, Pauline and Sarah Fitzgerald, and her grandparents, Robert and Cornelia (Smith) Fitzgerald. Her father's health and sanity continued to deteriorate; three years later he was sent to Crownsville State Hospital, an asylum, where he was confined until his death in 1923.

A bright and conscientious student, Murray graduated from Hillsdale High School at the top of her class in 1926. She was determined to attend college and refused to consider any of the segregated institutions in the South. She chose Hunter College, a public women's school in New York City—she first needed to remedy the second-class schooling she'd received in the South. She moved in with a cousin's family in Queens and attended Richmond Hill High School to prepare for the Regent's Exam that would allow her to enter Hunter. Studying literally around the clock, she graduated with honors a year later. The next hurdle, saving enough money to fund her studies, required Murray to work still another year, but she entered Hunter College in September of 1928.

At Hunter, her studies, particularly in anthropology, first convinced her that race and racial designations were arbitrary classifications that served only to divide people, fueling, as she wrote in her autobiography, "the poisonous notions of superior and inferior races." Her conviction that race was an artificial distinction without a biological basis would become the cornerstone of her legal and civil rights work.

Began Civil Rights Work

Murray graduated from Hunter with honors in 1933, one of four African American students out of 247. She eventually found a job with the Works Progress Administration (WPA) and taught remedial reading for a year before transferring to the WPA Workers Education Project, an effort to teach workers everything from basic English and simple math to current events and collective bargaining. The job put her in contact with a much broader group of people than she had encountered before, and the experience was enlightening. She noted in her autobiography: "I had never thought of white people as victims of oppression, but now I heard echoes of the black experience when I listened to white workers tell their personal stories of being evicted, starved out, beaten, and jailed. . . . Seeing the relationship between my personal cause and the universal cause of freedom released me from a sense of isolation, helped me to rid myself of vestiges of shame over my racial history, and gave me an unequivocal understanding that equality of treatment was my birthright and not something to be earned."

Murray's determination to fight segregation and secure her rights as an American grew, and in 1938 she applied for admission to the University of North Carolina (UNC). As a state university, however, UNC did not admit African American students. Despite the university president's liberal and sympathetic leanings and a recent Supreme Court decision requiring Missouri to admit a African American student to its state law school, UNC steadfastly rejected Murray's appli-

cation. She refused to accept defeat, writing letters to newspapers, the head of the university, and to both Franklin and Eleanor Roosevelt. She also asked the National Association for the Advancement of Colored People (NAACP) for help, and Thurgood Marshall (a future Supreme Court justice) was assigned to review the situation. Unfortunately, the NAACP decided not to take her case, saying that since she had only recently moved back to her North Carolina she could claim neither state residency nor a right to attend UNC. They wanted an open-and-shut case.

Still searching for a job that would allow her to challenge segregation laws, Murray left the WPA and began to look for other work. While traveling through the South in 1940, however, she and a friend were jailed in Petersburg, Virginia, when they refused to move to a broken seat at the back of the bus to make room for white passengers—15 years before Rosa Parks made history in the Montgomery, Alabama. Her experience with the WPA and UNC had taught Murray well, and she again contacted the NAACP, the Workers Defense League (WDL), and Mrs. Roosevelt, all of whom became involved in the case. Murray and her friend were ultimately convicted by the courts, but the publicity surrounding the case had convinced the local authorities to drop the charges of breaking segregation laws, charging the pair instead with creating a disturbance. "Although we lost the legal battle," Murray wrote later in her autobiography, "the episode convinced me that creative nonviolent resistance could be a powerful weapon in the struggle for human dignity."

Following this incident Murray joined the WDL, which had taken up the death-penalty case of Odell Waller, a African American sharecropper convicted of killing his white employer. The prosecutor charged Waller with premeditatated murder; Waller claimed self defense. Although the WDL's efforts were ultimately unsuccessful (Waller was executed in 1942), the work convinced Murray to pursue a career as a civil rights lawyer. She began her legal studies at Howard University, a black university in Washington, D.C, certain that this environment, at least, would be free from prejudice.

Discovered "Jane Crow" Discrimination

Murray discovered to her dismay that while racial bias was not a factor, sexual discrimination against women was rampant. "In my preoccupation with the brutalities of racism, I had failed until now to recognize the subtler, more ambiguous expressions of sexism," she recalled bitterly in her autobiography. "[I]n the intimate environment of a Negro law school dominated by men, . . . the factor of gender was fully exposed. . . . I soon learned that women were often the objects of ridicule disguised as a joke." This only steeled her resolve to excel.

Murray did pioneering legal work while at Howard, formulating an attack on the 1896 *Plessy v. Ferguson* Supreme Court decision mandating "separate but equal" treatment and public facilities for African Americans and whites. Murray's final paper for 1944 proposed a legal challenge to segregation based on the Fourteenth Amendment to the Constitution, which guarantees equal protection under the law to all Americans. Racial distinctions, she argued, were arbitrary classifications that could not be used to determine legal rights. In addition, segregation was a devastating psychological blow and one that clearly violated the civil rights of African American citizens. In 1951 Murray expanded this thesis into a book, *States' Laws on Race and Color.* It became the foundation of the NAACP's groundbreaking work in *Brown v. Board of Education of Topeka, Kansas,* which effectively ended segregation in public schools.

Denied Admission to Harvard

Graduating at the head of her class in 1944, Murray was the recipient of a Rosenfeld Fellowship, an honor that was usually a ticket to graduate work at Harvard. At that time, however, Harvard did not admit women—and would not for nearly 20 more years. Murray, unwilling to take "no" for an answer, lodged every possible appeal and even prevailed on her earlier acquaintance with the Roosevelts—FDR sent a letter to Harvard on her behalf—but was ultimately unable to prevail, although her appeals were enough to split the board evenly on the question of whether or not to admit her.

She went instead to the Boalt Hall of Law at the University of California in Berkeley, where she earned a master of laws degree in 1945. She worked as a Los Angeles deputy district attorney before heading back to New York a year later. In 1949, while living in Brooklyn, she made her one and only bid for public office, running for a City Council seat on the Liberal Party ticket. Although unsuccessful, she came in second, prompting her to remark in her autobiography, "Although I had no desire to run for political office again, I thought of that campaign as a harbinger of things to come when, nineteen years later, Shirley Chisholm ran . . . in the same general area of Brooklyn and was elected as the first Negro woman in Congress."

Murray chronicled her family's history in 1956 with *Proud Shoes: The Story of an American Family.* In the introduction to the 1978 edition, she recalled that writing the book "became for me the resolution of a search for identity and the exorcism of ghosts of the past. . . . I began to see myself in a new light—the product of a slowly evolving process of biological and cultural integration, a process containing the character of many cultures and many peoples, a New World experiment, fragile yet tenacious a possible hint of a stronger and freer America of the future, no longer stunted in its growth by an insidious ethnocentrism."

She went to Ghana in 1960, driven partly by a desire to learn about her African heritage. She taught constitutional law at the Ghana Law School but soon began to be perceived as a threat to President Kwame Nkrumah's drive for totalitarian power. With the political situation becoming ever more unsettled, she left the country barely more than a year later to pursue further legal studies; she earned a doctor of juridical science degree from Yale University Law School in 1965.

Worked for Women's Rights

Murray was appointed to the President's Commission on the Status of Women Committee (PCSW) in 1961, where, just as she had 1951, she surveyed state laws to compile a catalog of ways in women were kept from true legal equality. She argued that these could be overturned with a Supreme Court ruling based on the Fifth and Fourteenth Amendments to invalidate these discriminatory laws. Some of the women on the commission wanted to push for the adoption of the Equal Rights Amendment (ERA) to the Constitution (first written and proposed in 1923), but Murray firmly believed, as with race, that the Constitution—particularly the Fifth and Fourteenth Amendments already guaranteed women the rights and protections they needed. Her refusal to endorse the ERA eventually led her to part company with many feminists.

In 1964 Murray used her considerable influence to campaign for the inclusion of sex discrimination in Title VII of the Civil Rights Act. Her efforts (combined with those of others) were successful: the bill was passed by both houses of Congress and became law that year. Murray was keenly aware, however, that the statute would require active enforcement if the status of women, especially African American women, was to improve. The following year she published "Jane Crow and the Law: Sex Discrimination and Title VII" in the *George Washington Law Review,* in which she cited "ways in which the Fifth and Fourteenth amendments and the sex provisions of Title VII would be interpreted to accord women equality of rights. . . . Published . . . at a time when few authoritative legal materials on discrimination against women existed, [the] article broke new ground and was widely cited."

Helped Found NOW

A year later she joined the executive board of the American Civil Liberties Union (ACLU), beginning a seven-year collaboration with fellow ACLU board member Dorothy Kenyon, who also sought legal challenges with which to attack sex discrimination. In 1966 Murray became one of the 30 founding members of the National Organization for Women (NOW), an alliance she hoped would ensure government enforcement of Title VII. The NOW feminists were determined to push for ratification of the ERA, but Murray remained convinced that the Constitution already guaranteed women's rights. She eventually resigned from NOW's national leadership when the organization voted to push for ratification of the ERA in 1967.

In 1968 she went to Brandeis University in Waltham, Massachussetts, as a visiting professor in the school's American Civilization program. She expanded the program into a full-fledged American Studies department two years later and in 1971 was honored with the Louis Stulberg Chair in Law and Politics and a full, tenured professorship in American Studies.

Ordained an Episcopal Priest

Yet one more first remained for Pauli Murray. When she was 62, just a few years away from what many would consider retirement age, she entered the master of divinity degree program at General Theological Seminary in New York City. She became the first American black woman to become an Episcopal priest on January 8, 1977, in the National Cathedral in Washington, D.C. She celebrated her first Eucharist in Chapel Hill, North Carolina, in the little church where her grandmother, a slave, had been baptized in 1854. "All the strands of my life had come together," Murray recalled in her autobiography. "Descendent of slave and of slave owner . . . [n]ow I was empowered to minister the sacrament of One in whom there is no north or south, no black or white, no male or female—only the spirit of love and reconciliation drawing us all toward the goal of human wholeness."

Pauli Murray died in Pittsburgh, Pennsylvania, on July 1, 1985. In 1990 Orange County, North Carolina, established the Pauli Murray Human Relations Award to commemorate Murray's life and work. The annual award is given to a youth, adult, and business that, according to the county's website, "have served the community with distinction in the pursuit of equality, justice, and human rights for all citizens.

Books

Murray, Pauli, *Dark Testament and Other Poems*, Silvermine, 1970.
—, *Proud Shoes: The Story of an American Family*, Harper & Row, 1978.
—, *Song in a Weary Throat: An American Pilgrimage*, Harper & Row, 1987.
—, *States' Laws on Race and Color*, University of Georgia Press, 1997.

Periodicals

George Washington Law Review, December 1965.
Journal of Women's History, Summer 2002.
Nation, May 23, 1987.
Sarasota Herald Tribune, February 17, 1997.

Online

"Pauli Murray," North Carolina Writers' Network, http://www .ncwriters.org/pmurray.htm (February 3, 2003).
"Pauli Murray," Spartacus Educational, http://www.spartacus .schoolnet.co.uk/USAmurrayA.htm (February 3, 2003).
"Pauli Murray," Sunshine for Women, http://www.pinn.net/ ~sunshine/whm2001/p_murray.html (February 3, 2003).
"Pauli Murray, 1910–1985," Arthur and Elizabeth Schlesinger Library on the History of Women in America, Radcliffe College, Cambridge, Massachusetts, http://www.radcliffe.edu/ schles/libcolls/mssarch/findaids/Murray/MurBio.html (February 3, 2003).
"The Pauli Murray Award and the Human Relations Commission," Orange County, North Carolina, http://www.co.orange.nc.us/ hrr/pmurray (February 3, 2003).
"Respect, Contempt, and Individuality," Nancy Huntting, http://www.nancyhuntting.net/PMurray-Sem1.html (February 3, 2003).
"States' Laws on Race and Color," University of Georgia Press, http://www.ugapress.uga.edu/books/shelf/0820318833.html (February 3, 2003).
"Three Legendary Feminists," Moondance: Celebrating Creative Women, http://www.moondance.org/1998/winter98/non fiction/pauli.html (February 3, 2003).

"A Woman of Foresight, Pauli Murray," African American Registry, http://www.aaregistry.com/african_american_history/ 630/A_woman_of_foresight_Pauli_Murray (February 3, 2003). □

William Murray

William Murray, Lord Mansfield (1705–1793) established a body of rules regarding commercial transactions that became the foundation of British commercial law.

An English Chief Justice of the King's Bench for over three decades, Scottish jurist William Murray, Lord Mansfield is noted for devising the foundational rules and regulations that established equity in the British system of business law, including rules regarding bills of exchanges, promissory notes, and bank checks. Among Murray's most lasting contributions are the creation of the marine insurance system and the concept of restitution, in which an injured party is made whole through the restoration of damaged or stolen property or its equivalent.

Born into Upper Class

Murray was born March 2, 1705, at Scone, a town in the former Scottish county of Perthshire. His father, David Murray, Fifth Viscount Stormont, was a defender of the Stuart line of succession to the English throne. As the fourth son of the viscount, William Murray was not in line to inherit the family title or fortune. Fortunately, he showed an aptitude for learning. He was admitted as a king's scholar at Westminster School in 1719, then entered Christ Church, Oxford. Graduating from Oxford with a master of arts degree in June 1727, Murray embarked on a career in law under the patronage of a family friend, Lord Foley.

Murray was called to the bar in 1731. He was affiliated with the Tory party, which supported the Stuart claim to the throne and the preservation of traditional and social institutions against the expansion in parliamentary power advocated by the opposition Whig party. An educated, well-spoken young man, he took a trip to continental Europe in 1730. He traveled in social circles that included poet Alexander Pope.

Murray's legal reputation became established after his appearance in several significant Scottish appeal cases. He represented the City of Edinburgh during its legal battle following the so-called "Porteous Riot" of April 1736, during which the city's guard fired on a mob. Murray's successful defense of the city gained him public attention throughout Scotland. His reputation was cemented in England in 1737 when he gave a stirring speech before the House of Commons on behalf of a merchant who was petitioning the crown to end the widespread piracy of English trading ships by Spanish nationals. In 1738, with his law practice thriving, Murray married Lady Elizabeth Finch, daughter of the earl of Winchelsea.

Political Moderate

The England of Murray's day was experiencing the effects of the Industrial Revolution. Amid growing consumerism and prosperity were signs that society was polarizing into a working class and an affluent elite. The reign of Hanoverian King George II also saw an ever-increasing national debt due to involvement in foreign wars, as well as widespread political corruption and an increase in petty crime and lawlessness. Sir Robert Walpole, who had dominated the government under the German-speaking King George I, continued his efforts, following the succession of George II in 1727, to create the small, exclusive political group that evolved into the modern-day cabinet, while he assumed a role tantamount to prime minister and led the Whig party in the House of Lords.

In 1742, amid English involvement in the unpopular War of Austrian Succession, Walpole fell from power, although the Whig-led government continued to promote his agenda. That same year Murray was appointed to the position of solicitor-general, where he remained for 14 years while also serving as a member of the House of Commons for Boroughbridge. A political moderate despite his Tory affiliation, he gained a reputation for keeping his personal politics aside when dealing with legal issues. He led the prosecution of the Jacobite lords Balmerino (Arthur Elphinstone), Lovat (Simon Fraser), and Kilmarnock who, as supporters of the Scottish pretender prince Charles Edward Stuart, fought against England during the 1746 battle of Culloden Field. They were beheaded on London's Tower Hill. As chief spokesman for the government in the House of Commons, Murray was frequently opposed by opposition leader William Pitt the elder, an influential Whig known for his barbed oratory.

In 1754 Murray became attorney-general and for the next two years was leader of the House of Commons. When a vacancy occurred in the chief justiceship of the King's Bench in 1756, Murray was granted the post. He was also raised to a member of the cabinet and made Baron Mansfield.

As chief justice, Murray concentrated his efforts on law rather than on politics. The ruling Tory government was fast losing its supremacy. In the new Whig government, Pitt became secretary of state, propelling England into the Seven Years' War with France, a war that Murray did not support. Five years later, in 1761, Tory leader Lord Bute successfully curtailed Whig efforts to spread the war to Spain. When Pitt resigned from government, Murray returned to the political realm.

A leading member of the Tory party, Murray was a staunch advocate of moderation in his nation's foreign and domestic policies. He drew upon his vast learning and his understanding of law as the basis for his political stance. Despite this evenhanded approach to politics, in 1770 he was drawn into a hot debate on the issue of political libel and became the focus of satirical essays penned by the pseudonymous "Junius" (Sir Philip Francis). Junius accused Murray of using the law in an arbitrary fashion while overseeing a series of libel cases—one of which involved Junius himself.

Murray remained a member of the cabinet for 14 years, surviving several changes in political leadership. When asked to serve as chancellor in 1765, Murray declined.

Contributions to British Law

In his day, Murray was well known by the English public as a member of the House of Commons, but his lasting fame came from his tenure as England's chief justice. He had a distinguished career and was respected for his vast learning and his fairness and propriety. A rationalist, he reduced costly delays in the legal system, renovated outdated property laws used by courts since medieval times, and protected the right to freedom of conscience for Catholics and other non-Anglicans.

Murray's evenhandedness was notable. In one case of alleged witchcraft in which an elderly woman was accused of flying through the air, Murray ruled that the woman should be allowed to return home, and if she did so by flying, no law prevented that. In another case, Murray acquitted the leader of an anti-Catholic mob that set fire to his own house and library during the 1780 Gordon riots. Not all of his rulings gained Murray public approval. His libel ruling in favor of the government against John Wilkes, a publisher and member of Parliament, drew criticism for limiting freedom of speech.

Murray's major contributions were his development of contract theory and his creation of regulations establishing precedents for commercial case law. Before Murray's tenure as chief justice, English common law was the only source of guidance in business matters. When cases regarding trade and other commercial matters came to trial, juries had to rely on their wits. Murray established clear-cut guidelines for business litigation. Basing his work on Roman law and contemporary laws in other nations, he set forth basic principles governing business transactions that brought English law in line with international practices. His introduction of the concept of restitution, in particular, helped to make litigation between merchants and consumers more equitable.

Murray's efforts came at a crucial point in England's economic history. Industrial manufacture, particularly of textiles, was replacing agriculture as the greatest area of employment, and the increase in spending on manufactured consumer goods created a wealth of new industries throughout England. The country's newly created turnpike system allowed businessmen to expand their markets, while England's overseas colonies provided both markets and raw materials.

Murray applied the same learning and logic to other branches of English law, though with less overall success. During debates over constitutional issues, he was frequently opposed by Charles Pratt, Lord Camden, who argued for more liberal approaches to libel, warrants, and the role of juries. Pratt also fought Murray's advocacy of taxing the American colonies despite their lack of Parliamentary representation.

Murray's 1772 ruling in the case of *James Somerset vs. His Master, Mr. Stewart of Virginia* effectively ended the institution of slavery in England, if not in British colonies. "The state of slavery is . . . so odious that nothing can be suffered to support it," Murray wrote in his opinion.

Some contemporaries resented Murray's efforts as corrupting the traditions of the legal system, but more recent scholars have recognized him for his efforts to adapt these traditions to a changing society. Among jurists heavily influenced by his work was Sir William Blackstone, author of the highly influential *Commentaries on the Laws of England* (1769).

Earl of Mansfield

Although he refrained from involving himself in public office later in his life, in 1783 Murray briefly assumed the duties of speaker of the House of Lords. His term as chief justice ended with his resignation in June 1788. Murray was made earl of Mansfield in July 1792. On March 20, 1793, he died at his home in London. With no family members alive at Murray's death, the title of Lord Mansfield went to his nephew David Murray, 7th Viscount Stormont.

Books

Campbell, John Lord, *The Lives of the Chief Justices of England, from the Norman Conquest to the Death of Lord Tenterden,* Ayer Company Publishers, 1977.

Holiday, John, *The Life of William the Late Earl of Mansfield,* 1797.

Oldham, James, *The Mansfield Manuscripts and the Growth of English Law,* University of North Carolina Press, 1992.

Periodicals

International Monthly Magazine of Literature, Science, and Art, August-November 1850.

Online

"William Murray," *Significant Scots,* http://www.electricscotland.com/history/men/murray_william.htm (May 27, 2003). □

N

Bruce Nauman

Bruce Nauman (born 1941), an American artist whose prime medium was sculpture, worked in various other media including painting, video, and installation throughout his career. Constantly provocative, his work was uncomfortable even for admirers to view. "Nauman, beyond much dispute, is the most influential American artist of his generation," wrote *Time*'s Robert Hughes in 1995. "[H]ardly a corner of the mix of idioms at the end of the 1980s, from video to body pieces to process art to language games of various sorts, escaped Nauman's influence." Although critics were polarized in their response to Nauman, his work could be found in museums and private collections throughout the world.

Studied Sculpture

Nauman was born in Fort Wayne, Indiana on December 6, 1941. His father was an engineer for a utility company, and the family was often uprooted. After high school, Nauman attended the University of Wisconsin to study mathematics and music. He changed his major to art, graduating in 1964. Parallels frequently have been drawn between his initial attraction to mathematics and his means of artistic expression.

Nauman undertook graduate studies at the University of California at Davis. There he was exposed to experimental art and concentrated almost exclusively on sculpture. He graduated with a master of fine arts degree in 1966. While still in school, Nauman mounted a solo exhibit at the Nicholas Wilder Gallery in Los Angeles. The show won him praise and immediate attention.

Nauman frequently used materials such as fiberglass, neon tubing, and styrofoam in lieu of traditional sculpting materials. In 1968, he signed a contract with Leo Castelli, an influential New York art dealer. That same year, he had his first solo exhibition in Europe. One of his best-known pieces from this period is "Window or Wall Sign," a neon spiral with the words "The true artist helps the world by revealing mystic truths." About this time he began experimenting with sound in spaces and soon embarked on using holography. Gradually, Nauman built a reputation as an exciting new experimental artist.

Works Polarized Critics, Public

His first retrospective show was organized by the Los Angeles County Museum of Art in 1972. He was still in his 30s—relatively young for such a career-spanning display. The exhibit traveled throughout the United States and was shown at museums including the Whitney Museum in New York.

Throughout the 1970s, Nauman continued to make provocative art. Critics variously described his work as humorous or painful. In fact, throughout his career, his work often defied description. It was unclear whether his pieces were sexual, aggressive, conceptual, or thought-provoking. Nauman's work served as a litmus test for viewers, received either as a pop-psychology experiment or psychological torture, depending on the work and the reaction it elicited. In an interview in 1987 with Joan Simon, quoted in *Artforum International*, Nauman observed that his 1968 audio-installation work "Get Out of My Mind, Get Out of This Room" is "so angry it scares people."

Nauman's departure into even more non-traditional media, especially his use of video, made him a pioneer in postmodern art. His video pieces frequently included actors involved in bizarre, repetitive acts. Other pieces invited the viewer into oddly shaped constructed spaces in which they soon felt trapped or confined. In some of these installations, the participating viewer's panicky reaction was recorded.

Tortured Artistic Experiments

Nauman worked with a variety of materials—from bronze to video to animal parts—doing sculptures, drawings, videos, and other multifaceted installations. Amei Wallach in a 1995 *Newsday* review of Nauman's work, observed: "Bruce Nauman's subject is the human condition; his range is Shakespearean. But for most of the '60s, like other artists of his generation, he smothered any storytelling propensities in a more baldly empirical approach." His later work was informed by his own reading of accounts of political torture. His response was to build "experiments" that explored how various conditions might affect humans.

Nauman moved to a ranch near Galisteo, New Mexico. The land where he had a home and simple studio had been a Pueblo Indian village. He had, surmises Wallach, "overdosed on too much art-world attention." He spent his non-working time training horses and caring for the animals on his ranch.

In 1994, Peter Schjeldahl in *Art in America* called Nauman "a master of black humor and intellectually cunning . . . strategies . . . the best—the essential—American artist of the last quarter-century. . . . Nauman's art sets the mind on tiptoe and knocks the heart sprawling. When one has been exposed to enough of it, the effect is a sort of rapturous ennui."

Played with Video Art

As if his previous themes were not disturbing or polarizing enough for American critics, Nauman selected clowns as a metaphor in several video pieces. "Clown Torture" (1987) was a video piece featuring "the hoarse voice of Nauman, dressed as a clown, in a baggy suit of vertical stripes that slyly recalls the garb of concentration-camp prisoners, shrieking, 'No, no, no, nonono!' while writhing and jerking on the floor," wrote Hughes in *Time*.

Nauman's work was compared to earlier experimental and conceptual artists, particularly those in the Dadaist movement, such as Man Ray and Marcel Duchamp, as well as to artist Andy Warhol. Nauman, who married painter Susan Rothenberg in 1989, cited John Cage, the minimalist composer, and philosopher Ludwig Wittgenstein as important influences.

His obsession with clown imagery in the 1980s drew comparisons to author Samuel Beckett. This prompted a show in 2000 called "SAMUEL BECKETT/BRUCE NAUMAN." In his critique of the exhibition in *Artforum International*, Daniel Birnbaum said the connection between the two men was "exemplary. No other contempo-

rary artist has worked so intensively with repetitions that turn the minor absurdities of the everyday into something unendurable."

Nauman's later video installations included "Learned Helplessness in Rats," a 1988 installation featuring a Plexiglas maze and loud punk rock drumming, and "Violent Incident" (1986), in which a band of video monitors displayed a domestic squabble that ends in a double homicide.

In discussing his video work, Nauman said he was aware of the different means artists in other disciplines were using to structure time in their works. These included composers Steve Reich, La Monte Young, and John Cage; Merce Cunningham, the noted dancer and choreographer; and Warhol, particularly in his films.

"[I]t was interesting for me to have a lot of ways to think about things," he told the PBS documentary *Art21*. "And one of the things I liked about some of those people was that they thought of their works as just ongoing. And so you could come and go and the work was there. . . . you could go back and visit whenever you wanted to."

Later Work

Nauman was recognized with two art awards in 1993 and 1994, the Wolf Prize for sculpture and the Wexner Prize. The Museum of Modern Art mounted a retrospective of his work in 1994. It was Nauman's first major museum exhibition since 1972, and the critics came out swinging. "There is nothing that can be said against Nauman that hasn't already been said in his favor," wrote Perl. Hughes commented that Nauman made "art so dumb that you can't guess whether its dumbness is genuine or feigned. . . . When it is really silly, the dumbness can be disarming, as it was with Nauman's predecessor, the American Dada gagman Man Ray."

Hughes observed that "no show was ever noisier. Go in, and you hit a wall of sound, all disagreeable: moanings and groanings; the prolonged squeak of something being dragged over a hard surface, like a knife on a plate; repetitious rock drumming." He concluded that Nauman "has cut himself a different role: the artist as nuisance."

Nauman's work was called anti-art for its minimalism and the discomfort it provoked. He drew more wrath and invective than contemporaries such as Donald Judd, Mark di Suvero, and Nam June Paik. "[T]he question that ends up sticking in our minds is why people allow him to bore them on this truly staggering scale," wrote Perl.

In an interview with *Artforum International* in March 2002, Nauman explained his 2001 project called "Mapping the Studio," his first installation work in seven years: "I have all this stuff lying around the studio, leftovers from different projects and unfinished projects and notes. And I thought to myself, Why not make a map of the studio and its leftovers?" He set up a camera in seven different positions and collected six hours' worth of tape that was projected in the exhibit space. These tapes included images of the nocturnal habits of his cat and the studio mice.

Nauman also made other video pieces based on his daily life at the ranch. "Setting a Good Corner" was a later piece showing how he went about building a corner on which to stretch a fence and hang a gate. The piece was utilitarian and, Nauman contended, artistic. "I wasn't sure when I finished it if anybody would take it seriously. It turned out to be kind of interesting to watch," he said in the PBS documentary.

Art World Split

Nauman divided opinions within the art community like few other artists. "Bruce Nauman is a great artist. There is no other kind or degree of artist he could be," concluded Schjeldahl in *Art in America*. "The alternative would be to exclude Nauman from art altogether."

But Perl contended: "What's extraordinary isn't that Nauman shrieks, but that people listen. . . . He's a control freak—he hurls neon thunderbolts, builds detention chambers, shouts commands."

His work was placed in the permanent collections of the Whitney Museum and the Museum of Modern Art in New York, in the Los Angeles County Museum of Art, and in the Wallraf-Richartz-Museum in Cologne, Germany.

Books

Newsmakers 1995, Gale Research, 1995.

Periodicals

Art in America, April 1994; June 2002.
Artforum International, November 1997; March 2002; Summer 2000.
New Republic, January 23, 1995.
Newsday, March 12, 1995.
Time, April 24, 1995.

Online

"Art: 21, Bruce Nauman," *PBS,* http://www.pbs.org/art21/artists/nauman/clip1.html (February 28, 2003). □

Alice Neel

American painter Alice Neel (1900–1984) was known for her Expressionist portraits of both famous and ordinary people. Her notoriety grew later in her career with major showings and a larger following as her style came into vogue and feminists embraced her perspective.

Attended Art School

Neel was born in Merion Square, Pennsylvania, on January 28, 1900, the fourth of five children of George Washington, a department head for the Pennsylvania railway, and Alice Concross Hartley Neel. She grew up in Colwyn, Pennsylvania, a small town where she did not fit in. Though her family was middle class, they were from old, established American stock.

From an early age, Neel wanted to be a painter. To please her traditional parents, she was trained as a secretary and worked in clerical positions as a teenager. She found those jobs very stifling. To break out, Neel began taking art classes at night without anyone in her family knowing.

Telling her parents she was going to study commercial design, Neel entered the Philadelphia School of Design for Women (later known as the Moore College of Art) in 1921. She actually studied art at the school, the first college of art in the United States for women. During the summer of 1924, she attended the Chester Springs summer school at the Philadelphia Academy of Fine Arts. During her time in art school, she learned much about portraiture technique and trained to be a figure painter.

In 1925, she graduated from the Philadelphia School of Design for Women and married Carlos Enriquez, a Cuban artist. She moved with him to Havana. Living with his rich family, Neel painted portraits of poor people and exhibited with Cuban avant-garde artists. Neel and her husband had two daughters, Santillana, who soon died from diphtheria, and Isabetta.

Neel, Enriquez, and their young daughter returned to the United States in 1927, settling in New York City. Neel settled on the fringe of the avant-garde movement. She painted *Requiem* (1928) and *The Futility of Effort* (1930), inspired by her young daughter's death.

Suffered Nervous Breakdown

In 1930, Neel suffered a great personal loss when her husband took their daughter back with him to Cuba. He was supposed to get money from his wealthy family so that he, Neel, and their daughter could move to Paris and she could paint there. Instead, Enriquez left their daughter with his family and went to Paris alone. Abandoned, Neel suffered a nervous breakdown and was briefly hospitalized. She returned to Colwyn, tried to kill herself, and was hospitalized again.

After Neel recovered, her personal life continued to be difficult. In the summer of 1932, Neel saw her husband and daughter but then never saw him again and saw her daughter after that only rarely. Starting in 1932, she lived with a sailor, Kenneth Doolittle, in Greenwich Village in New York. An opium addict, he slashed 60 paintings and burned 300 watercolors in 1934 because he was jealous of her work.

She next lived with John Rothschild, who encouraged her work. Neel painted watercolors of their life together in the 1930s. Rothschild would pursue her on and off until his death in 1975. Neel eventually had two sons by different fathers—Jose Santiago, a nightclub entertainer, and Sam Brody, a Marxist filmmaker. Neel became a left-wing activist, protesting social conditions in the United States and international fascism.

Minor Initial Career

In the 1930s, Neel's career as a painter began to take off. She was funded by the Public Works of America Project in 1933 and by the Works Progress Administration from 1935 to the early 1940s. She had some minor exhibitions, including one at the Contemporary Arts Gallery in New York in 1938 and another at Pinacotheca Gallery in 1944.

Neel's painting style and subjects in this time period were not particularly in vogue. She painted people, especially her family and those who lived in her neighborhood, capturing their humor and pain. Neel also did some still lifes, landscapes, cityscapes, and narrative and genre scenes. She did much with color and interesting compositions, and her paintings had an unfinished look. At the time, however, abstract art was more in style.

A number of Neel's portraits featured people who were suffering. Since she rarely painted on commission, she had much control over her subjects. She painted them as she wanted to paint them. She also did a number of portraits of well-known people such as author Joe Gould (1922), poet Kenneth Fearing (1935), and Communist labor organizer Pat Whalen (1935).

Neel's cityscapes reflected the politics of the day. In 1933, she painted Synthesis of New York—The Great Depression, which featured people in the city with surrealist touches. In 1936, she painted Nazi Murder Jews (1936), which depicted a Communist torchlight parade with a figure carrying a sign with those three words.

Struggled as an Artist

During World War II, Neel lived in Spanish Harlem, struggling as an artist while raising her two sons. She did not exhibit much in the 1940s and 1950s and did even fewer commissions. Reflecting her sympathies for the working class, her subjects continued to be people in her neighborhood. Many were poor or suffering from illness or stress. The subject of T.B. Harlem (1940) was recovering from an operation to fix a collapsed lung brought on by tuberculosis. In 1950 and 1954, she had a major solo exhibition at the ACA Gallery and had another in 1951 at the New Playwrights Theatre.

By the late 1950s, there was revived interest in Neel's work. She began seeing a psychologist who encouraged her to be more assertive about her career. She sent out pictures for exhibitions and convinced poet Frank O'Hara to pose for her. That portrait was later redone and appeared in Art News in 1960. When her friend Muriel Bettancourt gave her an annual stipend to support her work, she was able to move out of Spanish Harlem to West 107th Street.

Neel's style changed as well. Her colors and approach became bolder, but a number of critics thought her style was still too casual and clumsy. As Grace Glueck of the New York Times wrote in 1997, "Working in a style that might be called Expressionist-realist, she laid brush to canvas in a plain, straightforward manner, using the paint not fancily but simply to convey an image."

More Favorable Notice

In the 1960s, Neel began receiving even more critical and financial support. Pop art and photorealism, which were closer to Neel's approach, were coming into style. She also received attention because of several portraits she did of famous people. They included Andy Warhol, theater producer Joseph Papp, and composer Aaron Copland. Neel often did satirical portrayals of art dealers, critics, patrons, and historians, but she remained sympathetic to the common people she painted from everyday life.

Neel was expert in getting her subjects, including John Perreault (1972), to pose nude. Neel always was very careful about details and emphasized the importance of gesture. One of her subjects, Red Grooms, told Paul Richard of the Washington Post upon her death, "She was famous for her X-ray eye, and for her cruel, biting line, that killer line that describes everything."

While Neel had a number of shows at the Graham Gallery in New York beginning in 1963 and in other chic galleries, she still favored neighborhood people in paintings like Fuller Brush Man (1965). One of her best cityscapes was 107th and Broadway depicting what she saw from her apartment in 1976. As Theodore F. Wolff wrote in the Christian Science Monitor after her death, "As an artist, Alice Neel always spoke the truth, without embellishments or evasions, and with little concern for the social amenities. Confronted by reality, she preferred to depict it as it was rather than as it should be, and to present it starkly, regardless of whose feelings were hurt or whose ideals were offended."

Higher Profile

In the 1970s, interest in Neel increased because of the women's movement. In 1974, she was the subject of a retrospective at the Whitney Museum. This exhibit brought her more of an audience and led to more exhibitions and more awards. Neel had a retrospective at the Georgia Museum of Art in Athens in 1975 and at both the University of Bridgeport, Connecticut, and Silvermind Guild of Artists in 1979. Neel was elected to the American Academy and Institute of Arts and Letters in 1976.

Neel used this higher profile in a number of ways. Because she was able to explain her art to people in an understandable fashion, she did lectures in the 1980s. Neel showed her irreverent side, often telling how she convinced her subjects to take off their clothes. At the age of 80, Neel did her own nude portrait. She also did several paintings of her two sons and their wives. Neel especially favored her daughter-in-law Nancy Neel, who worked as her assistant.

In 1981, Neel became the first living American artist to have a major retrospective exhibition in Moscow. She also painted several portraits that became covers for *Time* magazine, such as those of feminist Kate Millet (1970) and Franklin D. Roosevelt (1982). Despite the changing climate of art, Neel still did not sell many paintings since the common people who were depicted in many of them could not afford to buy them. By her death, she owned most of her work. Near the end of her life, Neel continued to paint despite illnesses including cataracts.

Neel died from cancer on October 13, 1984, in New York. Many critics believed she was underrated in her lifetime, though at the time of her passing, neo-expressionism was popular and so was she. This did not matter to Neel, who painted for her own reasons. In 1982, Neel told Enid Nemy of the *New York Times,* "I've always been interested, I've always been curious, and I've always had a profession. Painting is an obsession with me."

Books

The Dictionary of Art, Vol. 22, Grove, 1996.

Garraty, John A., and Mark C. Carnes, eds., *American National Biography,* Vol. 16, Oxford University Press, 1999.

Gaze, Delia, ed., *Dictionary of Women Artists,* Vol. 2, Fitzroy Dearborn Publishers, 1997.

Hillstrom, Laurie Collier, and Kevin Hillstrom, eds., *Contemporary Women Artists,* St. James Press, 1999.

Periodicals

Artforum International, September 2000.

Christian Science Monitor, July 11, 1985.

Feminist Studies, Summer 2002.

Newsweek, July 1, 2000.

New York Times, April 5, 1982; October 14, 1984; March 21, 1997.

Time, October 29, 1984.

Washington Post, October 16, 1984. □

E(dith) Nesbit

Best known as the author of such children's novels as ***The Railway Children*** **and** ***The Story of the Treasure-Seekers,*** **the English writer E. Nesbit (1858–1924) also authored fiction, drama, and poetry for adults. In addition she was active in political causes and together with her husband, Hubert Bland, the playwright Bernard Shaw, and others, founded the Fabian Society in England to further socialist aims.**

Early Life

Nesbit was born August 15, 1858, in London to Sarah and John Collis Nesbit, a chemist who taught at an agricultural college in south London that had been established by his father. Nesbit's earliest years appear idyllic as she and her brothers, Arthur and Harry, were free to roam and play on the expansive grounds of the school. This period came to an abrupt end, however, with the sudden death of her father at age 43 in 1862. Nesbit's mother assumed the role of providing for her family, remaining connected with the college as an administrator until the ill-health of Nesbit's elder sister Mary prompted the family to relocate to the seaside. For the remainder of her childhood Nesbit alternated between terms at boarding school and summer holidays in the country, either in England or abroad. The depiction of one-parent households and siblings spending time together away from adult supervision that characterizes her later fiction is seen to stem directly from the experiences of her own childhood. When she was nineteen years old Nesbit met Hubert Bland, a young man who shared her socialist political ideals. The two wed in April 1880, two months prior to the birth of their first child, Paul.

After their marriage, Bland developed smallpox, an illness that prevented him from working, and Nesbit undertook the financial responsibility of providing for the household. During the 1880s, a period when she gave birth to two more children, Iris in 1881 and Fabian in 1885, she began contributing short stories to magazines and writing verses for greeting cards. It was also during this time that the couple participated in the founding of the Fabian Society, a group dedicated to social justice that proposed the gradual reform of society rather than revolutionary tactics. In addition to the Blands and Shaw, the early Fabians included Sidney and Beatrice Webb, Annie Besant, H. G. Wells, and Havelock Ellis. The society remains active in British politics more than a century after its founding, with Prime Minister Tony Blair and many Cabinet ministers counted among its members.

Nesbit's liberal outlook extended even to her own domestic arrangements. Bland, who at the time of their marriage was simultaneously engaged to another woman with whom he had a child, proved to be an unfaithful husband, and Nesbit raised as her own the two children he fathered with a third woman, Alice Hoatson. According to biographers, Nesbit also entered into a series of sexual relationships outside her marriage with other writers, including Shaw, Noel Griffith, and Oswald Barron, with whom she collaborated on the short story collection *The Butler in Bohemia* (1894).

Throughout the 1880s and 1890s Nesbit produced numerous volumes of poetry, romances, horror stories, children's fiction, and several plays, and edited a series of anthologies of poetry and sketches with Robert Ellis Mack. For the most part Nesbit's works throughout this period are considered conventional by critical standards though they provided necessary financial remuneration. She and Bland, who after recovering from his illness had turned to political journalism, also collaborated on a novel, *The Prophet's Mantle*, published under the joint pseudonym Fabian Bland in 1885. In 1899 Nesbit published her first novels, the Gothic romance *The Secret of Kyriels* for adult readers and *The Story of the Treasure-Seekers*, her groundbreaking children's work.

Success as a Children's Novelist

The Story of the Treasure-Seekers was published serially, beginning in 1897, and traces the fortunes of the impoverished and motherless Bastable children, who undertake various attempts at increasing their family's income. The novel represented a significant departure from Nesbit's previous works and comprised her most notable success. The appeal of the *Treasure-Seekers* owed much to its point of view, which refrained from direct moral instruction, and to the humor stemming from its lively narrator, Oswald Bastable, considered Nesbit's most memorable character. Alison Lurie, commenting in *Writers for Children*, described Oswald as "a child much after [Nesbit's] own pattern: bold, quick-tempered, egotistic, and literary." Unlike other children's works of the era, *The Story of the Treasure-Seekers* provided a realistic rather than sentimental view of sibling relationships, including squabbling among the family and the resistance of the younger members to be dominated by the elder. Following on the success of the Bastable stories Nesbit issued two additional volumes of their adventures, *The Wouldbegoods* (1901), in which the children, now comfortably settled in a fine home, try different means of doing good for others, and *The New Treasure-Seekers* (1904), considered the most serious of the series.

Children's Fantasy Novels

At the same time that Nesbit was issuing realistic stories of childhood, she wrote a number of fantasy works, including the popular *Book of Dragons* (1900). In 1902 she published *Five Children and It,* another children's work that would bring her renown. In it she depicted a family of children—Cyril, Robert, Anthea, Jane, and their baby brother (known as "the Lamb")—who undergo a series of adventures, but in this case the adventures are magical. During their summer holidays, the children encounter a Psammead, or sand fairy, who has the power to grant them one wish per day. The wishes, including having the ability to fly or possessing great beauty, all have unforeseen, humorous consequences, and the novel has proved enduringly popular: it remains in print more than a century after its first appearance. In a sequel, *The Phoenix and the Carpet* (1904), the mythological bird hatches in their nursery fireplace and leads the children on a number of magic carpet adventures. *The Story of the Amulet* (1906) continues the story, when the children, who are staying with a relative while their parents are out of the country, rediscover the Psammead in a London pet shop, and his gratitude at being rescued leads them on a time-travel adventure to ancient Atlantis and to a utopian future based on Fabian ideals. Their quest throughout the journey is to recover the missing half of a magic amulet that will grant their heart's desire: the restoration of their family.

The Railway Children

Returning to the realistic adventure tale, Nesbit published *The Railway Children* in 1906. Her most beloved work, the novel has been adapted for stage, musical theater, cinema, and television. In the story, Roberta ("Bobbie"), Peter, and Phyllis are the children of a government worker imprisoned as a suspected spy. During her husband's absence, the children's mother moves the family from their comfortable London home into a rural cottage to reduce housekeeping expenses, and she supports the family through free-lance writing. With little else to occupy them, the children find entertainment in the nearby railway and befriend its station workers. They ultimately become known to an "Old Gentleman" who rides the train each morning and who is instrumental in clearing their father and restoring their family.

The House of Arden (1908) and Harding's Luck (1909) center on Edred and Elfrida Arden, who use magic to visit the past in hopes of finding where their family fortune is hidden. Their adventure brings them into contact with Dickie Harding, an impoverished and crippled cousin. The rightful heir to the Arden title and fortune, he chooses to remain in the seventeenth century, where he is no longer lame. In the novel Nesbit uses the device of time travel to illustrate her socialist ideals, portraying Jacobean England as an era of social harmony in stark contrast to the disparity between high society and the slum life Dickie endures in the Edwardian world.

Fiction for Adults

Despite the popularity and critical regard of her novels for children, Nesbit continued throughout her career to think of herself as primarily a writer for adults. Her most successful adult novel, The Red House (1902) concerns a young couple renovating an old country house, a plot drawn directly from her own life and the restoration of Well Hall, the Blands' home in Eltham. Among her other works for adults are The Incomplete Amorist (1906), a romance centering on an English art student in Paris, and Daphne in Fitzroy Street (1909), a fictionalized account of her relationship with Shaw. Dormant (1911) shares some elements of fantasy with her more successful children's works. In the story a scientist inherits an estate and falls in love with a woman he discovers in an enchanted sleeplike state in a secret chamber. Her final novel, The Lark (1922) is a realistic depiction of two unmarried women struggling to maintain their financial independence by operating a boarding house.

Nesbit's husband, Hubert Bland, died in April 1914. She published few new works after that time, and interest in her works declined after World War I. She married Thomas Terry Tucker, a sea captain, in 1917. Financial difficulties and illness plagued her later years, and she died May 4, 1924, in New Romney, Kent.

Reputation and Legacy

In the decades since her death, Nesbit has come to be regarded as one of the most innovative writers for children of the early twentieth century. Her importance, particularly in the development of fantasy literature for children, has prompted numerous critical appraisals. As Daria Donnelly has noted in Commonweal, "Before Nesbit, such literature fell into two types: either the entire action took place in an exotic or fantastical setting, or the child character (Dorothy or Alice) traveled from this world into a fantastical one. But in Five Children and It, a group of middle-class Edwardian children find a prehistoric, ill-tempered thing called a Psammead right in the gravel pit behind their house. And each day, corresponding to each chapter, he reluctantly grants them a wish that results in a new adventure in their very neighborhood. Locating the fantastical in everyday life was Nesbit's great and enduring innovation." Colin N. Manlove, writing in MOSAIC X/2, added that "Nesbit's fantasy is not

what one would call great literature. . . . [Her] work is fanciful rather than imaginative. But fancy has its place: and one could claim that in Nesbit's work it reaches a high point of wit and ingenuity." Nesbit's realistic stories, too, continue to please young readers, and new admirers are brought to her works through television and theatre productions of The Railway Children. Summarizing Nesbit's achievement, Claudia Nelson concluded in the Dictionary of Literary Biography that "in writing for children Nesbit proved her ability to combine humor and sympathy, the personal and the universal. Not only does her popularity in this genre continue today, she also served as a major influence upon other writers for the young, including Edward Eager and C. S. Lewis."

Books

Briggs, Julia, A Woman of Passion: The Life of E. Nesbit, 1858-1924, New Amsterdam Books, 1991.

Lurie, Alison, Writers for Children, Charles Scribner's Sons, 1988.

Moore, Doris Langley-Levy, E. Nesbit: A Biography, Rev. Ed., Chilton Books, 1966.

Nelson, Claudia, Dictionary of Literary Biography, Volume 141: British Children's Writers, 1880-1914, edited by Laura M. Zaidman and Caroline C. Hunt, The Gale Group, 1994.

Nesbit, E., Long Ago When I Was Young, Macdonald and Jane's, 1974.

Streatfeild, Noel, Magic and the Magician: E. Nesbit and Her Children's Books, Abelard Schuman, 1958.

Periodicals

Commonweal, November 5, 1999.

MOSAIC X/2, Winter 1977.

New York Review of Books, December 3, 1964.

Online

"Edith Nesbit and the Railway Children," http://www.imagix.dial.pipex.com (February 9, 2003). □

Per Nørgård

Danish composer Per Nørgård (born 1932) had a big impact on music in Denmark as he continued to pursue the study of music. His use of the metamorphosis and infinity methods were often unpopular when first presented to the public but later became classics in the history of Danish music.

Per Nørgård was born in Gentofte, Denmark, on July 13, 1932. His parents, Erhardt and Emmely, owned a wedding dress specialty shop called Eva. They lived near the shop. His aunt and grandmother lived around the corner, and he spent a lot of time with them. He also spent time with his brother, Bent, who was five years older than he was, but otherwise he did not have much contact with other children.

Artistic Skills Unfolded

Nørgård's family enjoyed music. His parents had a radio to listen to and a gramophone to play records on. His father played the accordion, and the family would sing along. A piano was purchased, and both boys took lessons, with Per beginning at age seven. Nørgård loved to draw, but he especially enjoyed developing cartoon characters, and he and his brother would provide performances with the cartoons. Nørgård would draw the characters and write the music, while Bent would create storylines and text. They called them 'Tecnics.'

Nørgård was showing a strong talent in music at a young age, and in 1942, he was admitted to the Copenhagen Municipal Choral School. The school had a strong music program, but no grammar school, so in 1944, he was sent to the Frederiksburg Grammar School. Europe was in the middle of World War II, and often this affected Nørgård. On March 1, 1945, English planes bombed the French School in error. The Frederiksberg Grammar School was also damaged.

By the time Nørgård reached his teen years, music and drawing were his main interests. However, when he was 16, his brother was called into military service. Nørgård lost interest in working on cartoons without him and began to focus on music. He was a shy young man but was comfortable playing music in front of people. By 1949, at age 17, he was certain that he wanted to become a composer, and he wrote his first piano sonata.

Began Serious Study of Music

Despite his shy disposition, he made a very bold move. He called up Vagn Holmboe, one of the most prominent Danish composers, and asked to be taken on as a student. After Holmboe reviewed some of Nørgård's work, he agreed to accept him. Nørgård received private lessons from Holmboe until 1951 when he was admitted to the Academy of Music.

The first public performance of one of Nørgård's pieces took place on March 30, 1951, when the Young Musicians Society included his Concertino No. 2 in a concert. Elvi Henrikson played his piece on the piano. The entire concert received poor reviews.

From 1952 to 1955, Nørgård studied at the Royal Danish Academy. Holmboe was again his instructor in composition. While studying, he met two other young musicians, Pelle Gudmundsen-Holmgreen and Ib Norholm. The three had very different music styles, but worked together to promote music in Denmark. They became very good friends. Nørgård began to become successful during his student years. The Royal Danish Academy was a very conservative school. Nørgård's work from this time was also conservative.

Branched Out

By 1953, Nørgård became very interested in the work of Jean Sibelius. Sibelius was not regularly accepted as a musician because of his unorthodox music, especially the concept of metamorphosis. Metamorphosis is a method of taking a common phrase or strain of music and changing it little by little, until it has become something else. This was very non-traditional and shunned by the conservatives, but Nørgård was intrigued. He sent a letter to Sibelius on July 2, 1954, assuring him that his type of music would endure. Sibelius sent him a thank you note. Nørgård later dedicated his choral work Aftonland op. 10 to Sibelius.

In April of 1955, the Erling Bloch Quartet performed Nørgård's "First String Quartet" at a concert. The work received very positive reviews. Additional good reviews were received when his "Aftonland No. 10" was performed by the Academy of Music Madrigal Choir on October 19, 1955. Nørgård was beginning to experience a string of successes.

When Nørgård completed his exams at the Academy of Music, he married Anelise Brix Thomsen. They later had two children. Jeppe was born on January 17, 1959, and Ditte was born on May 27, 1961.

On January 17, 1956, the Royal Danish Academy of Music put on a composer's evening consisting entirely of works by Nørgård. Following this debut, he left for Paris to study with Nadia Boulanger, the well-known music teacher in France. He has been recommended by Holmboe and received the Lily Boulanger Award to help to finance his stay. Nørgård and his wife lived in Paris from January 1956 to May 1957.

Began to Teach

In 1957, he became a lecturer to the Funen Academy of Music in Odense. He also began writing music critiques for a newspaper called the *Politiken.* By 1960, he also began teaching at the Royal Danish Academy of Music, leaving Odense in 1961.

Nørgård and his friends from his study days, Gudmundsen-Holmgreen and Norholm, felt there was a need for new thinking about music in Denmark. They attended the ISCM World Music Days music festival, in Cologne, Germany, together in 1960, where a large number of modern works were performed. After they returned to Denmark, they established a study circle in order to explore new techniques and ideas. They began to meet to discuss these new concepts once a week. He also began working again with his brother, Bent. Together they wrote a children's oratorio, "And It Came to Pass in Those Days." This further led to them working together to write an opera, entitled "The Labyrinth," in 1963.

Became Established as a Composer

During this time, Nørgård was working on "Constellations," a piece for strings which, at the time, was on the edge of traditional tonal relationships. In addition, in 1961, he entered his piece, "Fragment VI," for orchestra in the famous Gaudeamus Festival in Holland. He won 1st Prize for best foreign work. This accomplishment helped to establish his reputation on the international scene.

He gained further international attention in 1964 when he collaborated with Eugene Ionesco, the famous French dramatist who was looking for someone to compose music for his ballet. The Danish Broadcasting Corporation commissioned the work, and the final product was transmitted all over Europe on April 2, 1965. During the same year, Nørgård received the Danish Ballet and Music Festival Award.

Experimented with Music

Nørgård continued to struggle with the constraints of the conservatism at the Royal Danish Academy of Music. In 1965, he left to join the staff at the Jutland Academy of Music, taking his students with him. Around this same time he began experimenting more, as well as reaching out to different audiences. He moved away from writing concert music and was writing music for films and radio play.

Continuing his experimental streak, he wrote "Iris," an orchestral piece where he explored different sounds. It was commissioned by The Royal Orchestra and was initially performed May 19, 1967. A companion piece, "Luna," followed. In 1967, he also received the Harriet Cohen Medal for ballet music.

Nørgård's music became much more of an exploration of music than storytelling. He would be constantly exploring new ways of creating music. The *Economist* would later write, "The idea of continuous development has always held special fascination for Mr. Nørgård, both as it relates to his own position within the classical tradition, and in compositional terms."

One of the best-known Scandinavian compositions of the second half of the 20th century is Nørgård's "Voyage into the Golden Screen." The second movement specifically and logically unfolds the infinity series, a style that Nørgård became known for where he worked with different rhythms. It was performed for the first time in March of 1969. That same year he received the Anne Marie Nielsen and Carl Nielsen Commemorative Scholarship.

The Danish Broadcasting Corporation commissioned a piece to be used as background music for the test picture on Danish television. "Kalendermusik" (Calendar Music) was completed in 1970 and was based on the infinity series, expressing the seasons as they unfold. It premiered March 21, 1973, but only played for a few months because of complaints from viewers. His new music was not traditional enough for the common listener.

During this same period of controversy, the Academy of Opera in Stockholm had commissioned *Gilgamesh*. Nørgård completed it in 1972. The premiere was May 4, 1973, by the Jutland Operan Company. The performance was well received.

Despite his inability to sway the general public, many in the music world were impressed with his work. In 1972 the Danish Broadcasting Corporation commissioned him to write his *Third Symphony*, which he worked on until 1975. The piece was first performed on September 2, 1976. It was considered a masterpiece, although parts of it were so busy that some considered it chaotic. In 1974, Nørgård won the Nordic Council Music Award for the opera and his general work as a composer. After the *Third Symphony*, Nørgård

began exploring conflict with more depth. He struggled with ways to express conflict to his satisfaction.

In 1979, Nørgård visited an exhibit at the Louisiana Art Gallery entitled "Outsiders," which displayed work by famous artists who were mentally ill. He was particularly intrigued by the work of the schizophrenic Swiss artist, Adolf Wolfli. This led Nørgård to become more spontaneous in his composing, writing some of his most popular work, including *Wie ein Kind (Like a Child)*, in 1980; *I Ching*, in 1982; and *The Devine Circus* in 1982.

In the 1980's, Nørgård continued to produce music, providing *Between* for cello and orchestra; *Remembering Child* for viola and orchestra; and *Helle Nacht (Bright Night)* for violin and orchestra. He was the chairman of the Musical Arts Committee under the National Foundation for the Arts from 1983 to 1986. The Danish Broadcasting Corporation commissioned another Symphony in 1986. Nørgård worked on it until 1990, and the *5th Symphony* was performed in December of 1990, in a concert where works by Sibelius and Carl Nielsen were also performed, honoring Nørgård as an equal to those he had studied and admired. In 1987 he was awarded the Wilhelm Hansen Family Scholarship and then received the Henrik Steffens Award in 1988.

Gained Respect

In 1996, Nørgård won the international Leonie Sonning Music Award. This award garnered a great deal of attention and suddenly there were TV and radio shows about him, as well as coverage in the papers. In the late 1990s, Nørgård had become a legend, and some of his works, now considered classics despite the fact that the public had shunned a number of them, were now being re-recorded.

Nørgård's *Sixth Symphony* debuted on January 6th, 2000. Works from Sibelius and Carl Nielsen were also heard at the concert, and Nørgård was once again linked with his mentors.

Throughout his career, Nørgård was compelled to continue to discover and learn about music, even when it was unpopular with the public. *American Record Guide,* in the May/June 1997 edition, wrote, "He has created a sound world of his own, and no work of the last 30 years is an easy introduction to his music; but if it is the spiritual and intellectually challenging you want, then Per Nørgård's music is immensely satisifying."

Books

Beyer, Anders, *The Voice of Music,* Ashgate Publishing, 2000.

Periodicals

American Record Guide, January/February 1993; May/June 1997; September/October 1997.
Economist, August 17, 2002.

Online

"Biography," *Per Nørgård web site,* http://pernorgaard.dk (February 17, 2003). □

Marianne North

Marianne North (1830–1890) was a well-known botanical painter who traveled around the world twice in search of rare flowers and plants. Her paintings of flowers in their natural habitats gave a glimpse of plants inaccessible to most people. In 1882, a gallery of her work opened at England's Royal Botanic Gardens at Kew. The gallery, still open to the public, houses 832 paintings produced by North over 13 years.

Marianne North was born in Hastings, England, on October 24, 1830. Her father, Frederick North, was a wealthy landowner and a member of Parliament. Little is known about North's mother. North had a sister, Catherine, who was seven years younger and a brother, Charles, two years younger. North had little formal education, but the family was rich and cultured and she was exposed to well-known artists and botanists. She showed a talent for singing and took voice lessons. In 1847, the family began a three-year trip through Europe where North studied flower painting, botany, and music.

North's mother died in 1855 and North became the mistress of the family's homes in Hastings and London. She loved to sing, but when her voice gave way, she took up flower painting, which was considered a respectable hobby for a lady of leisure. Painting was never expected to be North's career, since wealthy 19th century women were not expected to work. She was also interested in botany and, through her father, knew Sir Joseph Hooker, director of the Royal Botanic Gardens at Kew.

Every summer, after Parliament closed its session, North, her father, and her sister traveled to Europe. They visited Switzerland, Austria, Spain, Italy, Greece, and the Bosphorus. As was a custom at the time, each traveled with a diary and a sketchbook. North's friends encouraged her to describe her travels. During a trip to Spain, Marianne first attempted landscape painting using watercolors.

In 1864, North's sister married. After her father lost his seat in Parliament the following year, North and her father spent even more time traveling, visiting Switzerland, the South Tirol, Egypt, and Syria. She searched out plants and painted everywhere she went. Around 1865 North learned oil painting and found that she much preferred it over watercolors. In *Visions of Eden: The Life and Work of Marianne North,* she said, "I have never done anything else since, oil-painting being a vice like dram-drinking, almost impossible to leave off once it gets possession of one."

During a trip to the Alps in 1869, Frederick North became ill and North brought him back to Hastings, where he died. North's father had doted on her throughout her life and she was devastated at the loss. She said of her father in her autobiography, "He was from first to last the one idol and friend of my life, and apart from him I had little pleasure and no secrets." Painting helped her overcome her grief.

Her large inheritance allowed her to resume her travels. She went to Sicily with her maid, but did not enjoy her companion's company. Two years later, at the age of 41, North sold the Hastings home and devoted herself to botanical painting. She began a series of trips in search of plants and flowers from all corners of the earth. "I had long had the dream of going to some tropical country to paint its peculiar vegetation on the spot in natural abundant luxuriance," North said in her autobiography.

Traveled Around the World

Her first trip, in 1871 and 1872, took her to Canada, the United States, and Jamaica. She returned to England, then went on to Brazil where she stayed for eight months and completed more than 100 paintings, working out of a hut in the jungle.

In 1875, she made plans to travel to Japan via the United States, where she visited Yosemite and other California sites. When she encountered lumberers harvesting giant redwoods, she lamented, "It broke one's heart to think of man, the civiliser, wasting treasures in a few years to which savages and animals had done no harm for centuries."

North suffered from rheumatic fever in Japan, making it difficult for her to put up with cold weather for the rest of her life. She returned to England in 1877 via Sarawak, Java, and Sri Lanka. While in Sarawak, a British colony on the island of Borneo, North discovered the largest known carnivorous pitcher plant. It became the first of five plants that were named in her honor, *Nepenthes northiana.* The others are *Northea seychellana,* a previously unreported tree in the Seychelles; *Crinum northianum,* an amaryllis; *Areca northiana,* a feather palm; and *Kniphofia northiana,* an African torch lily.

North exhibited some of her paintings in Kensington Gallery in 1877. Shortly after, she traveled to India for 15 months and produced more than 200 paintings.

Encountered Harsh Conditions

It was unusual at the time for a woman to travel alone, but that is how North preferred it. Sometimes, she started a trip with a friend or acquaintance, only to abandon them partway through the trip. In her autobiography, she claimed to prefer the company of "less civilized and more interesting people."

By less civilized, she apparently didn't mean native people, because her extensive diaries barely mention the indigenous people she must have encountered and they rarely appear in her paintings. Her diaries also gloss over the difficult conditions she endured. In the introduction to *A Vision of Eden* Anthony Huxley described how carelessly she mentions travel conditions: "Scorching sun, drenching rain, fearful road conditions, travel sickness, leeches and giant spiders, and unsalubrious accommodation are all dismissed in a few airy words," Huxley said.

North also had to deal with language barriers, a lack of doctors, and crude transportation. A typical diary entry describes how she traveled through India: "I started at four in the afternoon in a big cabin boat . . . and reached Quilon about twelve the next day . . . thence on to Nevereya, where we left the boat and crossed the boundary in a bullock cart. We went on in another canoe, hollowed out of one long tree, for twelve hours more. . . ." Much of the backcountry she visited was inaccessible by any type of vehicle, forcing her to traipse through jungles and swamps and scale cliffs and mountains, looking for botanical specimens. She was often accompanied by hired servants who carried her gear. The conditions for painting in the wild were crude and she was often forced to pack her paintings while they were still wet, then touch them up when she returned to London.

When she returned from India, she found it so tiresome to show her paintings to visitors to her London flat that she housed them in a gallery for two months so they would be accessible to the public. The show was so successful, she began to think about a permanent home for her art. She asked Sir Joseph Hooker if he would agree to building a gallery for her paintings at Royal Botanic Gardens at Kew, at her expense. He accepted her offer.

Gallery Housed Paintings

North chose the location of the gallery within the gardens. She envisioned it to be a respite for visitors where they could stop and enjoy a cup of tea or coffee. Refreshments, however, were not allowed in the gardens. North hired her friend James Fergusson, a well-known architectural historian, to design the gallery.

With planning well underway, North resumed her travels. North was a friend of Charles Darwin and shared his interest in geographical distribution of plants. In 1880-1881, North visited Australia, New Zealand, and Hawaii at Darwin's suggestion.

After returning, she spent a year arranging the gallery, which opened in 1882. The gallery features elements of Greek temple architecture. North arranged the paintings and designed and painted friezes and other architectural elements throughout the two rooms. Two hundred forty-six different types of wood that North collected in her travels are also displayed in the room. North also compiled and paid for publication of a catalog of the collection.

North used her brush as people today would use a camera. Other botanical illustrators of the time described plants and made sketches, but North's work stood out because of its vivid colors. Many of the plants she painted were barely known at the time so her work became an important part of the botanical record. Most of the plants in North's paintings are depicted in their native environment. Her interest in zoology is evident in the birds, insects, fish, and other animals that sometimes appear in her paintings. As North traveled, she met botanists around the world who led her to the specimens she sought. Sometimes, her hosts brought plants to her and these are painted in a more contrived setting. Some paintings depict a plant laying on a table or a combination of blooms arranged in a vase, like a Dutch flower painting.

In addition to flowers, birds, insects, and animals, North painted landscapes, some of which show native buildings and people. These paintings gave a glimpse of distant lands not easily accessible in her day. Shortly after the gallery opened in 1882, North went to South Africa to paint flowers on that continent. When she returned, she added the new paintings to the gallery.

By the time North traveled to Africa, she was growing weaker and suffered from nervousness and anxiety. In her diaries during the African trip, she expressed frustration that she could not paint faster. Despite failing health and increasing deafness, she traveled to the Seychelles in 1883 and Chile in 1884. In Chile, she searched for and painted *Araucaria imbricata,* known as the puzzle-monkey tree.

A Lifetime of Work Displayed

After returning from Chile, she made her last additions to the gallery, which now totaled 832 works, picturing 727 genera and 1,000 species. (In total, North completed 848 paintings in 13 years.) The paintings range in size from a few square inches to 15-by-40 inches. The paintings remain just as North arranged them: They cover the walls, with little space between them, making for a colorful visual impact when people enter the rooms.

North had devoted her life to her work and now that she had completed her gallery, she retired to a house in Gloucestershire surrounded by fields, orchards, and gardens. From 1886 until her death in 1890, she spent her time entertaining guests and transforming her home's grounds into a showcase garden filled with rare botanical treasures. She worked tirelessly on the garden, doing much of the work herself, despite poor health. Undoubtedly, North's failing health was the result of the harsh conditions she had lived in during her travels. Marianne North died on August 30, 1890, at the age of 59.

North's autobiography, *Recollections of a Happy Life,* a two-volume set compiled from her travel diaries and journals, was published in 1892. Her sister Catherine Symonds, who was a lesser-known botanical illustrator, compiled the work, as well as a third volume, *Further Recollections of a Happy Life,* published in 1893.

Books

North, Marianne, *A Vision of Eden: The Life and Work of Marianne North,* Holt, Rinehard and Winston, 1980.
Notable Women Scientists, Gale Group, 2000.
Women in World History: A Biographical Encyclopedia, Anne Commire, editor, Yorkin Publications, 1999. □

Anna Nzinga

One of the great women rulers of Africa, Queen Anna Nzinga (circa 1581–1663) of Angola fought against the slave trade and European influence in the seventeenth century. Known for being an astute diplomat and visionary military leader, she resisted Portuguese invasion and slave raids for 30 years. A skilled negotiator, she allied herself with the Dutch and pitted them against the Portuguese in an effort to wrest free of Portuguese domination. She fought for a free Angola until her death at age 82, after which weak rulers left the country open for the Portuguese to regain control.

Negotiated with Portuguese Slave Traders

In the late sixteenth century and early seventeenth century, Europeans were negotiating interests in the African slave trade. The Portuguese wanted slaves for their new colony in Brazil. Threatened by English and French interests in northeast Africa, the Portuguese moved their slave-trading activities further south to what is today the region of Congo and Angola. The name Angola comes from the Mbundu word *ngola,* or king.

Nzinga was born to Ngola Kiluanji Kia Samba sometime around 1581 in the kingdom of the Ndongo, a Mbundu-speaking people in southeastern Africa. The king had accepted limited slave trading with the Portuguese, but when the Portuguese pushed further into the country and broke boundaries set up by the king, Ndongo went to war against the Portuguese.

King Kiluanji had become a powerful and oppressive ruler, losing the support of his people and his family. In 1618, Nzinga's brother, Mbandi, overthrew and killed Kiluanji, taking the throne for himself. Just as ineffective a leader and cruel as his father, Mbandi ordered the murder of Nzinga's son in an effort to eliminate any threat to his

power. The kingdom broke apart as Mbandi fled the capital and Nzinga sought refuge in the nearby state of Matamba.

Nzinga soon had the chance to show her emerging skills as a negotiator. In an effort to restore peace, the Portuguese initiated talks with Ndongo in 1622. Nzinga was sent as Mbandi's representative to negotiate with the Portuguese governor, Corrêa de Souza, based in Luanda. She arrived resplendent in her royal clothes and retinue. A Dutch artist recorded the historical meeting in a sketch. The story is that only one chair was available at the conference—the governor's chair—a ploy to make Nzinga stand and therefore seem inferior. Nevertheless, Nzinga signaled to one of her maids who fell on her hands and knees to provide a seat for Nzinga. Now facing the governor on his level, Nzinga was able to talk as equals. Treaty negotiations were successful; Nzinga convinced the Portuguese to recognize Ndongo as an independent monarchy, while agreeing to release European captives taken by her brother.

Perhaps as more of a political move than a religious conversion, Nzinga let herself be baptized by the Catholic Church and took the Christian name Dona Anna de Souza, after the name of the governor. Using religion as a political tool, she reasoned that this would open her country to European missionaries and advanced science and technology. In 1623, she was named Governor of Luanda for the Portuguese and held the position until 1626.

Only a year after the treaty was signed, the Portuguese disregarded the terms of the treaty and resumed their slave-gathering activities. Mbandi was proving to be a weak leader. Desperately wanting to defend Ndongo and her people, Nzinga poisoned her brother and succeeded him as queen of the Ndongo kingdom in 1623.

Nzinga as Queen

An intelligent and visionary political leader, Nzinga declared all the territory of Angola a free country. She offered refuge to escaped slaves, allied herself with Dutch traders who competed against the Portuguese, and dared to encourage revolt among Africans against the Portuguese. However, when negotiations with a series of Portuguese governors failed, the Portuguese attacked, eventually deposing Nzinga and forcing her to escape to the land of the Matamba.

In 1626, the Portuguese replaced Nzinga with a puppet Ndongo ruler named Philip, who was more likely to comply with European demands. Assessing her strategy, Nzinga formed an alliance with the Imbangala or Jaga group, going so far as to marry their chief. With the Jaga behind her, Nzinga conquered the Matamba people in 1630, established the state of Matamba, and declared herself their queen. Soon though, even the Jaga chief betrayed her by attacking Matamba.

Nzinga organized a resistance army using mercenaries and Africans the Portuguese had trained. Despite being in exile, Nzinga was able to influence her people and command their respect. She hand selected soldiers who pretended to be defectors so they could infiltrate the Portuguese armies. Once inside Portuguese ranks, they attacked. This show of loyalty to Nzinga made black troops under Portuguese domination desert to the queen. Always encouraging rebellion, Nzinga had, by 1635, developed an effective anti-Portuguese coalition that virtually held the Europeans at bay for 30 years. She has been called the greatest military strategist ever to confront the armed forces of Portugal.

While Nzinga was sending ambassadors to west and central Africa to enlist fighters, she was also pursuing good relations with the Dutch, from 1641 through 1648, to help her stop Portuguese advancement, to control the slave routes, and to reclaim Ndongo. This strange alliance with the Dutch marked the first African-European alliance against another European aggressor. She was not above forming alliances with foreign powers and then pitting them against each other, all for the goal of creating an Angola free of European influence.

A setback occurred in 1648 when Portuguese reinforcements arrived from the colony of Brazil who proved to be a formidable force. The Dutch were expelled from Luanda, leaving Nzinga without her most powerful ally. Unwilling to admit defeat, Nzinga resumed peace talks with the Portuguese for the next six years. Although the Portuguese at this time were contained, it became clear that they would not be removed. Nzinga was forced to recognize Philip as king and Portugal's sovereignty over Ndongo. Nevertheless, Nzinga remained queen of independent Matamba until her death in 1663 at the age of 82.

A Dynamic Ruler

A Dutch ally reported that Queen Nzinga enjoyed fighting and sometimes dressed like a man. She survived the Portuguese by her wits and audacity. Although Nzinga was willing to ally herself to Europeans, she is remembered as an Angolan leader who never accepted Portuguese sovereignty. So influential was she, that during her life, she was responsible for holding back the Portuguese invasion into the interior of southwest Africa; after her death, the Portuguese slave trade was able to flourish in the region.

Although Nzinga handpicked her sister, Dona Barbara, to succeed her as queen and married her to the general of the army, a succession struggle ensued after Nzinga's death. All of the new rulers failed to thwart the influence of the Portuguese, who regained control of the territory in 1648. It was not until three centuries later in 1974 that a military takeover in Portugal forced the government to withdraw its troops from its African colonies.

Nzinga's rise to power was due to her personal capabilities that overcame the limitations of gender. She displayed practical maneuvers, such as her alliances with the Jaga and Dutch, as well as self-sacrifice during her exiles. Willing to fight for freedom alongside her warriors, Nzinga demonstrated bravery, intelligence, and a relentless drive to bring peace to her people.

Books

African Biography, U*X*L, 1999.

Collelo, Thomas, ed., *Angola: A Country Study,* United States Government Printing Office, 1991.

July, Robert W., *History of the African People,* Waveland Press, 1998.

Sheehan, Sean, *Cultures of the World: Angola,* Times Edition Pte., 1999.

Online

"The African Woman as Heroine: Great Black Women in History," *Sacramento Black Page website,* http://www.cwo.com/~lucumi/women.html (March 5, 2003).

"Nzingha," *Afro Centric Experience website,* http://swagga.com/queen.htm (March 5, 2003).

"Queen Nzinga," *Black History Pages website,* http://purpleplanetmedia.com/bhp/pages/nzinga/shtml (March 5, 2003).
□

O

Maruyama Okyo

One of the master painters of Japan's Edo period, Maruyama Okyo (1733–1795) was the most influential painter and teacher of the 18th century in Kyoto. Although trained in the conservative Kano School of painting, Okyo combined styles from Japanese, Chinese, and 18th century Western influences. With an eye toward realistic perspective and scientific observation, Okyo created naturalistic bird-and-flower studies and illustrated anatomy books. Broadening his range to producing large-scale screen compositions, Okyo accepted commissions from temples and the royal palace in Kyoto. Famous in his own time, he founded the Maruyama School and influenced such noted painters as Matsumura Goshun and Nagasawa Rosetsu.

Encouraged to Pursue Painting

Maruyama Okyo was born to farmers in 1733 in the Kameoka region of Tamba Province, now part of Kyoto Prefecture. Although his parents wanted him to become a monk, he showed artistic talent early in life. As a youngster he apprenticed at a clothing shop, then painted dolls for a toymaker, and then designed accessories for cosmetics shops. Although he had little formal education and was barely competent at the popular art of calligraphy, he excelled at painting.

Encouraged to pursue his talent for painting, at age 16 Okyo entered the three-century old Kano School, the official school of painters for the upper-class during the Edo period. Under master painter Ishida Yutei, Okyo copied the works of Japanese painters, learned to paint large *byobu,* or screens, practiced Chinese brush work, painted scrolls from preliminary sketches, and studied diverse painting styles favored by Yutei. For his own paintings, Okyo drew on his early life in Kyoto living among the townspeople and farmers and observing the beautiful landscapes and gorges.

Okyo eventually demonstrated more talent than his orthodox contemporaries. Although he continued to employ the monochrome brushwork he learned at Kano, the conservative school was resistant to innovation, prompting Okyo to seek new challenges. Through artist Watanabe Shiko and Okyo's own independent study, he became exposed to Western artistic influences. From Dutch prints, he learned linear perspective, modeling the human form, and a realistic approach to representation.

Blended Styles to Create His Own

In his early career up through his thirties, Okyo blended his studies of Chinese masters and the concept of perspective from Western painting to create his own style. He studied Chinese prints from Suzhou province and the works of painters in the Nagasaki School, which examined imported Chinese paintings, Western books, and copperplate etchings. Learning to present various perspectives, Okyo created *ukie* pictures which depicted a scene observed from a single viewpoint. This method was also employed for his *megane-e* (eyeglass pictures), which were painted stereographs used in an optical device that presented three-dimensional views of Chinese and Japanese landscapes.

The Western artistic styles introduced to Japan in the early 18th century included vanishing-point perspective and chiaroscuro. Through his exposure to Western style prints, copperplate engravings, and illustrated books, he designed copperplate prints for the new concept of camera oscura. Okyo produced many sketches in various forms, developing a realistic approach from sketches that used outlining brush strokes and wash. Okyo mastered both brush and ink and created a signature style that combined native techniques with Chinese and Western forms that would influence the modern Japanese style.

Despite being influenced by Western art, Okyo retained and explored his traditional Japanese roots. He adapted the decorative compositions created by fellow students of the Kano School, as well as the techniques of the native Rimpa and Tosa Schools. Okyo produced hanging scrolls that exhibited his experimentation with the naturalistic treatment of detail.

Okyo's work was at first criticized by Nanga School artists who favored literary significance in art and by the traditional Kano painters who incorporated Confucian ideas. But Okyo's simple combination of birds and flowers popularized in Chinese paintings and of European techniques created plain, easy to understand natural paintings that were appreciated by the merchant class.

After his thirties, Okyo continued to experiment with different techniques, encouraged by his friend Yujo, the abbot of the Emman'in temple in Otsu. Okyo studied and copied foreign books on surgery, used mirrors to help him visualize three-dimensional forms, studied ink paintings of the Muromachi period (1333–1568), and sketched classic Chinese-style bird-and-flower paintings. He experimented with inks, pigments, and the application of shading with a slanted brush to produce various planes. Okyo's propensity to hold a brush in whatever manner suited the creative nature of his piece, rather than holding it in the upright manner used to create calligraphy, caused controversy at the time. Nevertheless, his drive to develop his own voice propelled Okyo to become one of the most influential artists of the 18th century.

Painted from Nature

In 1774, Okyo returned to Kyoto from his studies with other masters. During the decade, he became an even more prolific painter and created works in larger formats. Okyo revived the practice of producing large-scale screen compositions. He received numerous commissions and painted some of his most important large-scale works for temples, such as Daijoji temple near the Sea of Japan, Kongoji temple in Kameoka, and the Imperial Palace in Kyoto.

Influenced by the era's boom in scientific discovery, Okyo infused his work with a combination of naturalism and stylization, as evidenced by his hanging scroll "Peacock, Hen and Peonies." His scientific interests, especially botany, spurred him to sketch directly from nature and models rather than drawing from the imagination. He advocated painting that gave a close account of nature and adopted a first-hand observation style of sketching animals and people. His earliest known sketchbooks, filled with

people and places from around Kyoto, date from the 1770s. The detailed and realistic style he used was sometimes referred to as *shaseiga* (life drawing paintings).

As explained in Okyo's entry in the *Dictionary of Art,* "Okyo's observations about painting . . . show his concern with definition of space in the picture as a whole and in the description of individual forms. His view that an artist must determine the 'bone structure' of a figure before attaching the clothing, reflected his familiarity with the Western basis of figure drawing."

During the Edo period, painters typically lacked the need to paint the natural world. Okyo, however, reveled in the flora and fauna around him and dedicated his works to capturing nature. He presented realism in his animal studies of birds and dogs that he incorporated into landscapes and featured in seasonal portrayals. He painted screens featuring blooming wisteria and misty bamboo groves in the rain on gold-foil paper and used simple brush strokes for the tree trunks. Okyo also made detailed sketchbooks of insects that are featured in the Tokyo National Museum and was known to produce medical and anatomy books.

Soon after being hired in 1790 to help restore the imperial palace in Kyoto, he contracted an eye disease. Continuing to work, he completed the 1794 piece "Waterfall and Pine Trees" for the Omote Shoin at Kotohira Shrine in Kagawa Prefecture. This piece is considered one of his best compositions.

Co-founded Maruyama-Shijo School

Okyo founded his own school for the arts in Kyoto called the Maruyama School or naturalist school. Rejecting the Kano and Tosa Schools' emphasis on tradition subjects, Maruyama School focused on a study of nature. Due to Okyo's fame during his lifetime, his school thrived and never wanted for students. His son Maruyama Ozui later succeeded him as head of the school.

Matsumura Goshun (1752–1811), who had trained in the Nanga School under Yosa no Buson (1716–1783), introduced the atmospheric landscape and bird-and-flower style of sketching called Shijo. Goshun joined Okyo and adopted Okyo's realistic style, although Goshun's work invoked a more lyrical and subtle feeling, reflecting the Nanga love of poetry.

Goshun created the Shijo division of the Maruyama School that fused Maruyama's naturalistic style with the Nanga's idealistic fashion. With its atmospheric washes, free brushwork, and sensuousness, the Shijo style was appropriate for 19th century artists. Other schools, such as Ukiyoe, adopted the style. In the late Edo period, Shiokawa Bunrin (1807–1877) combined the two schools to form the Maruyama-Shijo School, whose style remained prevalent into the 20th century. Maruyama-Shijo School technique incorporated realistic aspects based on perspective derived from Western influence and based paintings on detailed sketching from life, yet retained traditional Japanese themes.

As explained in the *Encyclopedia of Visual Arts,* Okyo pioneered or revived six painting styles that influenced his followers: dramatic decorative screens influenced by Western perspective ("Hozu Rapids"), studies of nature in relaxed brushwork ("Wisteria Screens"), unidealized genre paintings ("Seven Happinesses and Seven Misfortunes"), Chinese style portraits and bird-and-flower paintings ("Peacocks and Peonies"), displays of ink monochrome ("Dragon Screens"), and soft and misty landscapes ("Spring, Summer").

Okyo's legacy of the effects of light and shadow and his experiments with perspective influenced his followers. Many of Okyo's students became famous: Matsumura Goshun, Nagasawa Rosetsu, Komai Genki, Watanabe Nangaku, Yamaguchi Soken, Mori Tessan, and Hara Zaichu. Rosetsu excelled at a brushwork style influenced by Okyo. Tessan was inspired by Okyo's sketching from life. Zaichu adopted Okyo's spatial construction technique.

Created Master Works Featuring Nature

Okyo was a master of depicting seasonal activities, his favorite being winter and summer, the seasons least celebrated in Japanese art. The technical aspects of painting wintery snow scenes particularly challenged Okyo. To create the image of snow and snow drifts in his "Puppies among Bamboo in the Snow, Landscape in Snow" (1784), he used the *sotoguma* (outside shading) technique of applying ink and washes around areas of blank paper.

One of his finest large screen pieces is "Pine, Bamboo and Plum (Three Friends in Winter)," a pair of six-fold screens composed of ink and gold on paper. Characteristic of his bird-and-flower pieces, "Heron on a Willow Branch" was painted in the classical Japanese *yamato-e* style, using flat areas of colorful pigments set against an expansive background.

Books

Encyclopedia of Visual Arts, Grolier Education Corp., 1983.
Kodansha Encyclopedia of Japan, Kodansha, 1983.
Osborn, Harold, ed., *The Oxford Companion to Art,* Oxford University Press, 1970.
Turner, Jane, ed., *Dictionary of Art,* Macmillan Publishers, 1996.

Online

"The Manyo'an Collection of Japanese Art," Gitter-Yelen Art Study Center website, http://www.gitter-yelen.org/newsite/maruyam2.htm (March 5, 2003).
"Maruyama Okyo," The Cleveland Museum of Art website, http://www.clevelandart.org/explore/artist.asp?artistLetter = O& = 8 (March 5, 2003).
"Maruyama Okyo," The Los Angeles County Museum of Art website, http://www.lacma.org/art/perm_col/Japanese/painting/okyo.htm (March 5, 2003). □

Francisco Manuel Oller

Francisco Manuel Oller (1833–1917) was a major Puerto Rican artist whose portraits of governors and slaves and landscapes of sugar plantations and peasant shacks celebrate both the island's natural beauty and its social strife. A friend to the great French artists of the late nineteenth century, he took part in the French avant-garde movements of Realism and Impressionism. Oller is cited as the only Latin American painter to play a role in the development of Impressionism.

Although he lived for many years in France and Spain, Oller always returned to Puerto Rico. "Francisco Oller was the first painter to ponder deeply on the meaning of Puerto Rico," wrote Haydée Venegas in *Francisco Oller: Realist-Impressionist,* the catalogue of a 1983 Oller retrospective at the Ponce Art Museum in Puerto Rico. His paintings of island life convey a strong, but not uncritical, passion for his native land. Oller's work was a "profoundly moving perspective on the virtues and defects of the Puerto Rico of his era," wrote Carlos Romero-Barceló in *Francisco-Oller: Realist-Impressionist.* Oller was inducted into the Order of King Charles III of Spain and exhibited in Spain, France, Vienna, and Cuba, but much of his art was lost after his death.

Early Years

Oller was born in San Juan on June 17, 1833, the third of four children of Cayetano Juan Oller y Fromesta and María del Carmen Cestero Dávila. At age 11, he began art lessons with Juan Cleto Noa, a painter who ran an art academy in San Juan. Recognizing Oller's talent, Puerto Rico's governor, General Juan Prim, offered to send him to Rome in 1848, but his mother felt he was too young. Oller was also a gifted musician and sang with the Puerto Rican Philharmonic Society as a teenager.

From 1851 to 1853, Oller studied at the Royal Academy of Fine Arts of San Fernando in Madrid, under Federico Madrazo y Kuntz, director of the Prado Museum, and became familiar with Spanish art. On his return to Puerto Rico in 1853, he began a successful career as a portraitist, winning the Silver Medal at the Fair of San Juan in 1854 and 1855.

Acquainted with Major Artists

In 1858, Oller traveled to Paris, staying for seven years. While working as a sexton and a baritone in an opera company, he studied under Thomas Couture and the Realist artist Gustave Courbet and mingled with artists and intellectuals in the cafes. He knew Camille Pissarro, Antoine Guillemet, Claude Monet, Pierre Renoir, Paul Cézanne, and other artists who were later known as the Impressionists. "All of these artists helped to mold Oller's method and style of painting," wrote Edward J. Sullivan in *Arts Magazine.* He also enrolled in the Academie Suisse and was admitted to the official Salon. During this period, he painted "El estudiante" (The Student), using Emile Zola as model, according to Peter Bloch in *Painting and Sculpture of the Puerto Ricans.* The painting has hung in the Louvre and the Metropolitan Museum of Art.

In 1865, Oller returned to Puerto Rico, an island struggling for identity under Spanish rule. "There he used his brush, as he himself put it, 'to lash out at evil and extol the good,' " wrote Marimar Benítez in *Américas*. In 1868, Oller married Isabel Tinajero. They had two daughters, Georgina and Mercedes. Oller was part of the privileged Creole class, but he was also a nationalist and a liberal, sharply critical of colonialism and slavery. As a Realist, Oller felt art had a social, political, and religious mission to contribute to society, wrote Albert Boime in *Francisco Oller: A Realist-Impressionist.*

Oller sailed back Paris in 1873, where he painted "Orillas del Sana" (Banks of the Seine). In 1877, he moved to Madrid, producing his famous "Autorretrato" (Self-Portrait) in 1880, influenced by Spanish painters such as Diego Rodríguez Velázquez. Oller held a successful exhibit of 72 paintings at the Palace of La Correspondenciz de Espana in 1883. After a stay in Puerto Rico, he returned to Paris in 1895, embarking on his Neo-Impressionist phase, as shown in two important paintings, "Paisaje francés I y II" (French Landscapes I and II, 1895–1896). These natural scenes "capture the rich atmosphere and coloring of Neo-Impressionism," wrote Benítez.

In 1868, Oller founded the first of many art schools, the free Academy of Drawing and Painting in San Juan. Known for his interest in geometry and perspective, he wrote a popular book on perspective and drawing. Oller was "a born teacher," wrote Dr. René Taylor in *Francisco Oller: A Realist-Impressionist.* Yet his fame never translated into great wealth. "The number of private art patrons was small" in Puerto Rico, notes Bloch.

In his later years, Oller could not pay for art supplies with his small teacher's stipend. "Apparently unable to buy materials, he was reduced to painting on any surface that came to hand: stray pieces of panel, the lids of cigar and match-boxes, *yaguas* and even tambourines and smoker's pipes," wrote Taylor. He died on May 17, 1917, at the Municipal Hospital in San Juan.

After his death, many of his paintings deteriorated in Puerto Rico's tropical climate. In the early 1980s, the Ponce Art Museum launched a conservation effort to retrieve and restore his work for "Francisco Oller: A Realist-Impressionist," a retrospective commemorating the 150th anniversary of his birth. The exhibit of 73 paintings traveled around the United States, providing a new look at Oller and his contributions to the history of art and the art of Puerto Rico.

Books

Benítez, Marimar, ed., *Francisco Oller: A Realist-Impressionist,* Ponce Art Museum, 1983.
Bloch, Peter, *Painting and Sculpture of the Puerto Ricans,* Plus Ultra, 1978.

Periodicals

Américas, July/August 1985.
Artnews, April 1988.
Arts Magazine, May 1984. □

Max Ophüls

As one of the true cosmopolitan film directors of the twentieth century, Max Ophüls (1902–1957) experienced professional triumph in his native Germany, the United States, and France. He also worked in Italy and the Netherlands. Ophüls's career can be demarcated into four distinct parts—five if his nine-year theater career is included—and taken together they can be seen as the progression of an artist.

Born Max Oppenheimer in Saarbrücken, Germany, on May 6, 1902, Ophüls began his career as a journalist, but at age 19 gave it up for the theater. At this time he changed his name partly to avoid embarrassing his family—his father was a garment manufacturer—should he fail. From 1921 to 1930 Ophüls worked in Germany and Austria first as an actor, then from 1924 as a director. In 1926 he became a theatrical producer, taking creative control of the Burgtheater in Vienna. In addition to Vienna, Ophüls worked in Berlin, Frankfurt, Stuttgart, Dortmund, Wuppertal, and Breslau. Ophüls was associated with more than 200 plays during that period. By the end of the 1920s, though, Ophüls became interested in film, and he made the career change that would bring him international renown.

First French Period

Working in Germany's UFA film studios, Ophüls served a brief apprenticeship as an assistant director in charge of dialogue for Anatole Litvak on the film *Nie Wieder Liebe (No More Love).* His directorial debut came in 1930 with the film *Dann schon lieber Lebertran (I'd Rather Take Cod Liver Oil),* a film for children. Ophüls went on to direct four more films in Germany in the early 1930s before he left the country in the face of rising anti-Semitism. These early films include *Die verkaufte Braut (The Bartered Bride),* a 1932 adaptation of the Smetana opera which Ophüls coscripted, and his early masterpiece *Liebelei (Flirtation),* a love story filmed in 1932–1933 and set in Vienna. It is based on a play by Arthur Schnitzler. By the time the latter film was finished the Nazis had assumed power in Germany and their censors removed Ophüls's name from the credits. Seeing the obvious handwriting on the wall, Ophüls decamped with his family (his wife was the actress Hilde Wall while his son, Marcel, would become a noted documentary filmmaker) for France.

Ophüls's first French film, *Une Histoire d'Amour* (1933), was a French version of *Liebelei* that used most of the original footage. Other than three films, including an unfinished film he directed in 1940 in Switzerland, *L'ecole des femmes,* all of Ophüls's output between 1934 and 1940 were French productions. In 1934 Ophüls went to Italy and directed *La Signora di Tutti (Everybody's Love)* and in 1936 he filmed *Komedie om Gold (Comedy about Money)* in the Netherlands. The films he directed during his first French sojourn were profitable but are considered workmanlike by film critics and historians. In 1938 the year he acquired

French citizenship, he directed *Le Roman de Werther*, based on Goethe's classic *The Sorrows of Young Werther*. With the onset of the Second World War Ophüls was drafted into the French army and after basic training he was transferred to the radio division of the propaganda ministry. During the five-month Blitzkrieg (in which the German army swept through Belgium and France on its way to Paris) Ophüls wrote and directed German-language anti-Nazi radio broadcasts. Following the fall of Paris and the French capitulation to the Nazis in June 1940 Ophüls, who was without doubt on a "wanted" list, again decamped with his family. They first went to southern France, then Switzerland, wherein addition to the unreleased film he directed two plays, *Romeo and Juliet* and *Henry VIII and His Sixth Wife*. The Ophüls family emigrated to the safer environs of Hollywood in 1941.

The Hollywood Years

If Ophüls expected Hollywood automatically to welcome him with open arms as a refugee artist he was mistaken. For one thing the Hollywood style of filmmaking was much different than what he was used to, with a few exceptions directors were less the auteurs of the film. Another obstacle was the influx of European directors since the beginning of the war. By the time he arrived in Hollywood Ophüls was neither a novelty nor well known. Ophüls's talents went unused for more than five years. He eventually found work through the intercession of director Preston Sturges, an Ophüls admirer known for his cynical screwball comedies who was then at the height of his fame. In 1946 Sturges secured for Ophüls a position as director of the Howard Hughes film *Vendetta*. Ophüls was one of several credited directors on the film, including Sturges, Mel Ferrer, Stuart Heisler, and Hughes himself. Production of the film stopped when Hughes pulled his financial backing. *Vendetta* was not released until 1949.

Despite that setback Ophüls used his credit as director of the project (during his Hollywood stay he would be credited as Max Opuls) as a launching pad for his Hollywood career. His next film, *The Exile* (1947), was a costume drama that starred Douglas Fairbanks Jr. and was based on the exile of British king Charles II in the Netherlands. Critics were cool toward the film though they generally praised Ophüls's direction. It also faced stiff competition from other releases. As a result *The Exile* was a financial loss (though barely), but Ophüls's Hollywood career was cemented.

His next film was the best known of his Hollywood years—*Letter from an Unknown Woman* (1948), another costume drama starring Joan Fontaine and Louis Jourdan. In this film Ophüls truly brought his aesthetic to American audiences. The plot revolves around a woman's obsession with a pianist, with whom she has had a brief affair and thereby a child. Told from his female protagonist's point of view it offered a visual sensibility seldom presented in Hollywood at that time. Ophüls female characters were usually better delineated than his male characters, their struggles usually a counterpoint to the lush decors. The critic Andrew Sarris described the prototypical Ophüls woman as someone who "triumphs over reality only through a supreme act of will." In addition Ophüls used long takes (possibly a residual effect of his theater background) that resisted editing and was fond of tracking shots that made his camera fluid. Another aspect of his theater background that Ophüls carried into his filmmaking was that he shot his films in continuity, which he believed helped the actors realize the characters as well as interact with each other.

Ophüls's last two Hollywood films, *Caught,* starring James Mason, Barbara Bel Geddes, and Robert Ryan, and *The Reckless Moment,* starring Mason and Joan Bennett, are both generally thought of as films noir though that designation is problematic for *Caught,* which had also been classified as a "women's film." John Berry also directed a few scenes in Ophüls's absence. The noir aspect of the film is the psychological underpinning, which not only hints at violence but is the cause of it. Is has also been postulated that through the character of psychotic millionaire Smith Ohlrig Ophüls delivered a devastating portrait of Howard Hughes. *The Reckless Moment* (1949) is more strictly film noir but with the unmistakable Ophüls touch of having a female protagonist who, unlike most noir women, is not a femme fatale. Filled with irony and Ophüls's usual long takes and fluid camera, in nearly every respect (except for the female protagonist) it is the reverse side of *Caught.*

Though he had trouble getting work in his early years in Hollywood and he clashed with and distrusted many of his studio bosses, Ophüls essentially loved the studio system, which generally employed highly skilled people on the technical and production sides. Yet by 1950, with the studio system already in decline, Ophüls decided to return to France. Although his growth as an artist during his Hollywood period was remarkable, Ophüls literally embarked on the most creative period of his career. Ophüls never completely cut his ties with Hollywood, however. In the early 1950s European directors who had been working in Hollywood, such as Fred Zinneman and Billy Wilder, returned to Europe to make "American" films. Ophüls hoped to so the same for independent producer William Wanger, but the deal fell through. Ophüls remained in contact with Wanger and other Hollywood producers for the last five years of his life.

Second French Period

Ophüls made only four more films, but they all furthered his artistic reputation (although Ophüls admirers including film historians, critics, and the public would not become legion until after his death). Furthermore, he gave free reign to the techniques that irked his Hollywood bosses, not just the long takes and the tracking shots, but subverting of close-ups and the use of a more natural sound—Ophüls regarded Hollywood sound as "velvety."

The first of this quartet was the elegantly filmed *La Ronde* (1950), which Ophüls and Jacques Natanson based on the Arthur Schnitzler play. Starring, among others, Simone Signoret, Simone Simon, Dannielle Darrieux, and Jean-Louis Barrault, the film depicts various combinations of couples as they take and drop lovers, finally coming full circle, which is the title's meaning. Upon completing the film Ophüls debated whether or not to return to the United States, but the overwhelmingly positive reception given *La Ronde* in France decided the matter for him. In 1950 *La Ronde* won best story and screenplay at the Venice Film Festival, and in 1952 the film the honors for Best Film–Any Source at British Academy Awards.

His next film, *Le Plaisir* (1951), was based on a trio of short stories by Guy de Maupassant. Each of the film's three segments reveals a different aspect of pleasure with its attendent irony and pain. The film featured Jean Gabin and Simone Simon. In 1953 Ophüls made *Madame de . . . (The Earrings of Madame de . . .)*. In a rather convoluted plot in which a pair of diamond earrings are sold and resold many times to pay off debts and given to lovers who in turn sell them, the notion of fate is explored. While the characters seem driven less by psychological means than the usual Ophüls film, since it is the earrings that drive the plot, film historians have noted that the performances of the three featured actors—Charles Boyer, Dannielle Darrieux, and Vittorio de Sica—overcome this shortcoming.

In 1954 Ophüls returned to Germany and began directing the classics on German radio. In 1955 he was back in France directing his final film, and the one on which future film historians would pin the label of genius on Ophüls. This was *Lola Montès,* starring Peter Ustinov. Loosely based on the life of the 19th-century courtesan the film was shot in Cinemascope (wide screen), which Ophüls used to startling effect. Another technique that critics and historians alike have admired was his 360-degree pan shots. Unfortunately Ophüls, whom most contemporary critics thought frivolous, never lived to see his name in the pantheon of great film directors. He died of heart disease in Hamburg, Germany, on March 25, 1957; Ophüls was buried in the cemetery Père-Lachaise in Paris. His autobiography, *Spiel im Dasein,* was posthumously published in 1959 and in 1966 he was posthumously awarded a FIPRESCI Award at the Berlin International Film Festival.

Books

Bacher, Lutz, *Max Ophüls in the Hollywood Studios,* Rutgers University Press, 1996.

Silver, Alain, Elizabeth Ward, et al, eds., *Film Noir,* The Overlook Press, 1979.

White, Susan M., *The Cinema of Max Ophüls: Magisterial Vision and the Figure of Woman,* Columbia University Press, 1995.

Online

"Max Ophüls," http://www.imbd.com/Name?oph%FCls, +Max (January 28, 2003).

"Max Ophüls," All Movie Guide, http://www.allmovie.com/cg/avg.dll?p=avg&=B105103~C (January 28, 2003). □

William Oughtred

Anglican clergyman William Oughtred (1574–1660) is considered one of the world's great mathemati-

cians due to his writings on the subject and his invention of the logarithmic slide rule.

Although William Oughtred was by profession an Anglican clergyman, he devoted many years of his life to expanding human understanding in the areas of algebra and calculus as well as to teaching mathematics to gifted students. Oughtred was the author of several books on mathematics and has also been credited by most historians with inventing both the linear and circular slide rules. His innovations extended to the use of many unique mathematical shorthand notations, including the notation "X" for multiplication and "::" for proportion.

Raised in Academic Environment

Oughtred was born in Eton, Buckinghamshire, England, on March 5, 1574. His father, Benjamin Oughtred, was a scholar who taught writing at Eton School, and through Benjamin's connections the younger Oughtred was educated as a king's scholar at Eton. At age 15 he entered King's College of Cambridge University and became a fellow there in 1595. Oughtred went on to receive his bachelor's degree from King's College, Cambridge, in 1596, followed by a masters of arts degree four years later. Despite the fact that Oughtred's studies at Cambridge consisted predominately of philosophy and theology, as early as age 12 he had demonstrated an extraordinary interest and talent in all things mathematical. As a college student, he had built on the rudimentary mathematical study provided to him at Eton, studying late into the night after completing his required regular studies. By the time of his graduation from Cambridge, Oughtred had already completed his first work, titled *Easy Method of Mathematical Dialling.*

In 1603 the 29-year-old Oughtred was ordained an Episcopal minister, a common and well-respected career option for an educated man. Applying to the church soon afterward, he gained an appointment as vicar of Shalford in 1604. In 1610 Oughtred was promoted to a position as rector of Albury, near Guilford, Surrey, in which post he served at an annual salary of 100 pounds. During his first years at Albury Oughtred married and set about tending to his parish. Despite the fame he would eventually acquire as a well-known mathematician, he remained dedicated to his flock and held his position as rector of Albury for nearly half a century, until his death in 1660.

Although never formally trained in mathematics, Oughtred clearly had a genius for the subject. Through his writings, he quickly gained renown as a mathematician and soon began to divide the time left to him after his church duties between personal study and the instruction of others. During the 1620s he began to take on as private pupils young men interested in the study of mathematics. These students—among whom were future mathematicians Richard Delamain and John Wallis as well as Christopher Wren, the future architect of St. Paul's Cathedral—shared the home and hospitality of their teacher during their mathematical studies. Eager to impart his mathematical knowledge to these brilliant young minds, Oughtred refused payment, maintaining that he was adequately provided for by his salary as a clergyman. A small man with black hair and a quick, penetrating gaze, he became known for impatiently etching mathematical diagrams in the dust that settled on tables and floors. It was not unusual, in the Oughtred home, to find its owner dressed and awake in the middle of the night while hard at work solving a mathematical problem. On his bed he had permanently affixed an ink-horn, while on the nightstand nearby a candle and tinderbox lay in easy reach, ready for the many nights when a mathematical quandary would demand a solution before Oughtred would allow himself to sleep.

In 1628 Oughtred became math tutor to Lord William Howard, son of the earl of Arundel. Desiring a suitable text to supplement his instruction of the young aristocrat, Oughtred wrote out, in summary form, all that was currently known about arithmetic and algebra. Pleased by the mathematician's efforts on behalf of his son, the earl of Arundel became a patron of Oughtred's and encouraged the rector of Albury to publish his work. The 88-page *Arithmeticae in numeris et speciebus instituto . . . quasi clavis mathematicae est*—known more commonly as *Clavis mathematicae*—was first published in Latin in 1631. Despite its condensed format, the book quickly drew interest from Oughtred's fellow mathematicians. By the time the second edition of the work was released in 1658, its author's reputation had been cemented in the larger community of European scientists.

In his *Clavis mathematicae* Oughtred describes the Hindu-Arabic system of mathematical notation, sets forth the theory of decimal fractions, and includes a detailed discussion of algebra. Throughout the work he incorporates a number of mathematical shorthand notations he had devised as a way to denote powers, relationships, ratios, and the like. While much of Oughtred's mathematical shorthand was rejected by readers as being too complicated, two of his symbols—"X" for multiplication and "::" for proportion—have gone on to become part of universal mathematical shorthand, along with those of contemporary mathematician and scientist Thomas Harriot (circa 1530–1621). Although Oughtred utilized the notation π as one of his symbols, its use signified only the circumference of a circle, not the ratio of the circumference to the diameter as it has come to denote.

Developed Logarithmic Slide Rule

The logarithmic slide rule was designed in response to the demands of the scientific renaissance that overtook Europe during Oughtred's lifetime. The astronomical calculus that grew from the work of such men as German astronomer Johann Kepler (1571–1630) and which would appear throughout the work of English scientist Sir Isaac Newton (1624–1727) demanded a means by which the multiplication and division of both extremely small and extremely large numbers could be performed quickly. These scientific and technical calculations were performed with ease using logarithms, which raise or reduce one number to an abbreviated form through the use of exponents.

The invention of logarithms is usually credited to Scottish mathematician and inventor John Napier, baron of Merchiston (1550–1617), who described his invention in 1614 in *Logarithmorum canonis descriptio,* although Swiss watchmaker and mathematician Justus Byrgius (1552–1633) also compiled such a system of mathematical shorthand. Napier's invention was simplified by a colleague at the University of London, professor Henry Briggs (1561–1631), who suggested that the system be designed in base 10 rather than Napier's base "e." Logarithms paved the way for the expanded scientific revolution that followed, allowing that complex operations of products and quotients be completed using simpler additions and subtractions. Their use continued until the advent of the digital calculator and the electronic computer of the twentieth century.

The use of logarithms immediately suggested an instrument that could speed calculations, and that instrument was the slide rule, an analogic calculator that through its mechanism allows for the processing of the variable data represented by logarithms. In 1620 astronomer and mathematician Edmund Gunter (1581–1626) devised "Gunter's Line," a two-foot-long ruler marked with a logarithmic scale. For operations such as the multiplication or division of numbers to several places, lengths along the ruler that are equivalent to the logarithms of the relevant numbers are added and subtracted using a pair of calipers and the result converted back to numeric form through the use of the logarithmic table. Oughtred is believed to have designed the first linear slide rule after less than a year spent wrestling with Gunter's Line and its calipers. Using two rules placed parallel to one another and connected, the position of the numbers relative to each other could now be used to calculate the desired results. By discarding the calipers, Oughtred created the prototype of the modern slide rule.

In its earliest manufactured form slide rules were made of wood, ivory, and even bamboo. They also were designed in several versions: Oughtred's linear and circular versions came first, followed by a cylindrical version, each version adapted for a particular academic discipline. The slide rule quickly gained prominence as a calculating device in every field of science and technology, from astronomy to topography to chemistry to mechanical engineering. However, it was not until the end of the eighteenth century that its importance was made clear by inventor James Watt (1736–1819), who revalued it as a tool of the Industrial Revolution. Demand for slide rules became such that by 1850 they had supplanted the use of Galileo's compass of proportions, an instrument initially intended for military use. In 1850 French army officer Victor Mayer Amdée Mannheim (1831–1906) introduced a transparent slab movable cursor; other modifications and improvements continued to be introduced in the decades that followed, resulting in the slide rule of the twentieth century.

Later Career Overshadowed by Controversy

The positive reception of his *Clavis mathematicae* within the scientific community prompted Oughtred to write several other books on mathematics. His 1632 work, titled *Circles of Proportion and the Horizontal Instrument,* described both a sundial and a circular form of slide rule that operated like Oughtred's linear slide rule: it was constructed using two concentric rings, one seated inside the other and both of which were inscribed with calibrated logarithmic scales. Ironically, this concentric slide rule, which Oughtred designed for use as a navigational instrument, had been described in a book titled *Grammelogia; or, The Mathematical Ring* published in 1630 by Oughtred's former student, Richard Delamain. Credit for the invention of the circular slide rule was claimed by both teacher and pupil, resulting in an enmity that lasted for the rest of Oughtred's life. Despite the likelihood that Oughtred and Delamain each individually devised the instrument, history has ultimately granted Oughtred credit for the circular slide rule.

During the final decades of his life Oughtred published six more books, among them 1657's *Trigonometria,* which supplements its discussion of two- and three-dimensional triangles with symbolism and tables setting forth the values of trigonometric and logarithmic functions to seven places. His 1651 work, *The Solution of All Spherical Triangles,* discusses the means by which the relative measurements of three-dimensional triangles can be determined; other books by Oughtred cover such subjects as the methods by which the position of the sun can be calculated and a discussion of the art of watchmaking.

Oughtred lived during tumultuous times in England. A staunch supporter of the English crown, he was shocked by the execution of the unpopular King Charles I in January of 1649. Like many who supported the cause of Charles I's son, the Prince of Wales (later Charles II), Oughtred was viewed with suspicion by the Presbyterian-influenced government that desired to take the place of the monarchy through the will of its leader, Oliver Cromwell. During the English Civil War (1642–1646) Oughtred was sequestered and scheduled for trial before Cromwell's puritanical commissioners. Due to the quick action of the astrologer Lilly and the insistence of influential friends, however, the mathematician and teacher was spared. He remained in England throughout Cromwell's reign, despite offers from foreign rulers who had heard of his fame. Oughtred died on June 30, 1660, at the parsonage in Albury. Tradition holds that he died of joy at learning that King Charles II had returned to England from Scotland and been restored to the English throne.

Books

Biographical Dictionary of Mathematicians, Scribner's, 1991.
Notable Mathematicians, Gale, 1998.

Online

Oughtred Society website, http://www.oughtred.org (March 15, 2003). ☐

Yasujiro Ozu

Often called the most "Japanese" of Japanese directors, Yasujiro Ozu (1903–1963) created films about middle-class Japanese life and familial relationships with simplicity and austerity. Known for keeping the camera three feet off the ground in order to view the traditional Japanese sitting on the floor, Ozu presented quiet observations of parents and children caught between obligation and the modern world. Ozu, who was an acclaimed director in Japan and whose body of work reached 54 films, first began to gain notoriety in the West late in his life.

Unusual Childhood

Yasujiro Ozu was born in the Fukugawa district of Tokyo, on December 12, 1903, the son of a fertilizer salesman. Rarely seeing his father, he attended a remote school at the family's ancestral hometown where his doting mother primarily raised him. His unconventional childhood was reflected in many of his films, which invariably dealt with family life and relations between parents and their children.

An unruly youth who disliked school, Ozu favored watching the movies from Hollywood he loved so much, especially those from Charlie Chaplin, Harold Lloyd, and Rex Ingram. He worked for a few years as an assistant teacher in rural Japan and studied at Waseda University.

Ozu's break into filmmaking came in 1923 when he landed the job of assistant cameraman to director Tadamoto Okuba at Shochiku Motion Picture Company—the film company at which he would eventually spend most of his professional life. Okuba became Ozu's mentor who later influenced Ozu's own films, especially his comedies.

Directed Silent Films

Following a year of military service, Ozu returned in 1926 to become an assistant director at Shochiku. He attributed his desire to become a director to Thomas H. Ince's 1916 silent epic *Civilization*. Ozu made his first film in 1927, *Zange no yaiba (Sword of Penitence)*, an uneven silent film that showed his lack of experience. Undaunted and armed with his interest in Hollywood films, he began to adopt an American studio approach to his filmmaking.

Ozu's first major film was one of the last great silent films. The 1932 comedy/drama *Umarete wa mita keredo (I Was Born But . . .)* met with critical and financial success and was named the best Japanese film of the year in the *Kinema Jumpo* poll. In the film, as seen through the eyes of children, the world of adults is both ridiculous and painful. For this film, Ozu employed the technique that would become his trademark—unobtrusive and static camera work.

During his career, Ozu would win many awards. His 1933 *Dekigokoro (Passing Fancy)* was another *Kinema Jumpo* winner. The 1934 silent film *Ukigusa monogatari (A Story of Floating Weeds)* was one of only a few films Ozu did not make for Shochiku, but for Daiei film company. Based on an American silent film called *The Barker, Floating Weeds*, a film about the adventures of traveling players in the countryside, is considered a superior work. Still clinging to silent films, Ozu was one of the last directors to relinquish the style, wanting to explore all of the possibilities the medium had to offer, as well as waiting until sound technology was perfected. Sadly, more than half of Ozu's 30 silent films are lost.

Placed the Camera on the Floor

In the 1930s, Ozu rejected the conventions of both Japanese and Hollywood filmmaking to create his own style and themes. He experimented with camera angles, settling on a concept of simplicity. Describing his decision to limit the camera work, Ozu was quoted in Donald Richie's book *Japanese Cinema*, as having said: "For the first time, I consciously gave up the use of the fade-in and fade-out. Generally dissolves and fades are not a part of cinematic grammar. They are only attributes of the camera." The tactic worked, as Ozu became one of Japan's most popular and respected directors during the decade.

Ozu became known for his deceptively simple camera technique that used a stationary 50mm lens placed three feet off the ground. This low angle corresponded with the eye level of a person sitting on Japanese tatami mats on the floor of a traditional home. Consequently, sets on Ozu's films were built with ceilings. Observant but never intrusive,

the camera contemplated and chronicled human behavior, presenting only the bare essentials.

Rejecting the more conventional camera direction through a 180-degree space to view action, Ozu focused instead on his characters and their interactions. He rarely resorted to devices such as fades, dissolves, pans, or tracking shots. Rather, through subtle, minimal camera work, simple cuts, and measured dialogue of everyday conversation, he presented scenes that were unhurried. He often textured his films with empty rooms and uninhabited landscapes.

Focused on the Family

The thematic thread linking Ozu's films was the exploration of the human condition, specifically the domestic problems of the contemporary Japanese middle-class family. Quiet and virtually plotless, his films chronicled human behavior in ordinary situations, evoking nostalgia, duty, and Japanese sensibilities. Not spurred by the actions of heroes or villains, conflict arose from the interaction of ordinary people, usually a parent and adult child, coping with everyday challenges. Home life contrasted with work life, tradition with modern society, parental responsibility with rebellious youth.

Ozu often used repetition in his films to evoke the familiar and the dependable. He would refer back to an outside shot of a building or a pond or leave the camera on a principal character. For example, in the 1956 film *Soshun (Early Spring)*, he chaptered scenes with a repeated view of early morning in the suburbs. Many of the same actors returned again and again in Ozu's films to play similar characters. Ozu's favorite actor was Chishu Ryu, who most often played the father of an adult child he does not understand.

A writer as well as a director, Ozu perpetuated his fondness for repetition, as evidenced in his series of films titled with the seasons. *Early Spring*, 1956; *Banshun (Late Spring)*, 1949; *Bakushu (Early Summer)*, 1951; *Kohayagawa-ke no aki (Autumn for the Kohayagawa Family)*, 1961; and *Akibiyori (Late Autumn)*, 1960, suggest a circular round of life as well as the figurative spring or autumn of his characters' lives. He also directed the series *Daigaku wa deta keredo (I Graduated But . . .)*, 1929; *Rakudai wa shita keredo (I Flunked But . . .)*, 1930; and *I Was Born But. . . ,* 1932.

Attained Success after the War

At first, Ozu did not fare well with talking pictures. His first two films *Hitori musuko (The Only Son)*, 1936, a story about maternal love, and *Shukujo wa nani o wasureta ka (What Did the Lady Forget?)* 1937, about a bossy wife, were described as dull and badly paced.

When World War II loomed, Ozu was drafted and sent to China, and in 1945 he was confined for six months in a British POW camp. He made only two films between 1937 and 1948, continuing to focus on his usual humanist values rather than addressing the war. The 1941 film *Todake no kyodai (The Brothers and Sisters of the Toda Clan)*, about a mother and daughter, was Ozu's first box-office hit garnering critical acclaim. The film was made in collaboration with Yuharu Atsuta, who would become Ozu's regular cameraman. The other film, *Chichi ariki (There Was a Father)*, 1942, concerned the obligatory conflict between parents and children and virtually ignored the war.

After World War II, Ozu reached the pinnacle of his talent making what many critics propound as some of his finest films. Roger Greenspun of the *New York Times* called Ozu's 1949 film *Late Spring* the most beautiful Ozu movie he knew. The study of a widowed father and his adult daughter both considering marriage was also one of the director's own favorite films.

Directed the Masterpiece *Tokyo Story*

Ozu's most acclaimed film was the 1953 masterpiece *Tokyo monogatari (Tokyo Story)* about an elderly couple from a small town who visit their married children in Tokyo. With their children too caught up in the frenzy of modern life to pay them appropriate attention, the couple is packed off to one house after another. They receive kindness only from the widow of their dead son. Soon after the elderly couple returns home, the wife dies. *Tokyo Story* appeared in the top 10 films of all time in *Sight and Sound's* poll of international film critics.

In his trademark style, Ozu left the camera a few feet off the ground, unmoving. This technique limited the field of vision, yet allowed the camera to observe the interaction of the characters. No actor was to dominate a scene; the camera commanded the attention of all. With regular actor Chishu Ryu playing the father, the film condemned none of the characters. While the children are not portrayed as evil, they are uncaring and unresponsive to anything but their own desires. The movie advocated a certain resigned sadness to the way things have become.

Ozu, as well as his characters, adopted this gentle resignation and acceptance which culminated in the face of the corrupting influence of postwar society on family traditions. This *mono no aware* outlook on life is a belief that the world will go on despite the uncertainty surrounding you. Live in the present, acknowledge that the past is gone, sympathize but don't complain, face your life with serenity and calm.

The scope of Ozu's films were black comedies, satires, social criticism, melodramas, and even a gangster film, the 1933 *Hijosen no onna ("Dragnet Girl")*. The last film Ozu made in black and white was the 1957 *Tokyo boshoku (Twilight in Tokyo)*, perhaps his darkest and most pessimistic portrayal of the disintegration of the family. Embracing color for the 1958 *Higanbana (Equinox Flower)*, Ozu employed a newly developed Japanese color-film process to tell the story of the younger generation, this time with Shin Saburi as the father reconciling with his errant daughter.

Late in Ozu's career, the new wave of Japanese artists criticized him for his rigid style and refusal to address current social issues. Undeterred, he made *Sanma no aji (An Autumn Afternoon)*, 1962, which would be his last film. A story about loneliness, the movie was influenced by the death, during filming, of his mother. Chishu Ryu returned as a widower who had married off his only daughter and occupied the rest of his days drinking.

Influenced Filmmakers Around the World

Ozu, who lived with his mother until her death in 1962, died of cancer on December 11, 1963, just shy of his 60th birthday.

The West was slow to embrace Ozu's films, which did not appear in foreign theaters or film festivals until the 1960s, shortly before his death. Japanese distributors feared that his work was too subtle for Western audiences who were more familiar with the adventures from Akira Kurosawa and Kenji Mizoguchi, who were winning awards abroad. Nevertheless, Ozu's simplicity of presentation fortunately gave his films international appeal and a universal desire for family, affection, and security.

Ozu himself has been an influence on such diverse Western directors as Jim Jarmusch, Paul Schrader, and Martin Scorsese. He inspired a documentary by Wim Wenders and was frequently the subject of books by Donald Richie, a scholar of Japanese cinema.

In 1983, Ozu's devoted assistant Kazuo Inoue produced a documentary profile of the director, called *I Lived But . . . The Life and Works of Yasujiro Ozu* that featured interviews with Ozu's production crew and recurring actors, plus excerpts from newsreels, home movies, and clips from two dozen of Ozu's films. Ozu's cameraman Yuharu Atsuta shot the film, and his long-time production company Shochiku produced it.

On December 12, 2003, in honor of the 100th anniversary of Ozu's birth, the Berlin International Film Festival, in collaboration with Shochiku Co. Ltd., will present a retrospective on the Japanese director. The retrospective will go on to screen at festivals in Hong Kong and New York.

Books

Garbicz, Adam and Jacek Klinowski, *Cinema, The Magic Vehicle: A Guide to Its Achievement*, Scarecrow Press, 1975.

Richie, Donald., *Japanese Cinema: Film Style & National Character*, Anchor Books, 1971.

Shipman, David, *The Story of Cinema*, St. Martin's Press, 1982.

Thomson, David, *Biographical Dictionary of Film*, Alfred A. Knopf Co., 1996.

Online

Malcolm, Derek, "Yasujiro Ozu: Tokyo Story," *The Guardian*, http://film.guardian.co.uk/Century_Of_Films/Story/0,4135,217142,00.html (February 3, 2003).

"Ozu: Poet of the Everyday," *Harvard Film Archive website*, http://www.harvardfilmarchive.org/calendars/99sep/ozu.htm (February 3, 2003).

"Yasujiro Ozu," *Malaspina Great Books*, http://www.malespina.com/site/person_906.asp (February 3, 2003).

"Yasujiro Ozu," *World Cinema: Directors*, http://www.geocities.com/Paris/Metro/9384/directors/ozu.htm (February 3, 2003).

"Yasujiro Ozu," *Yahoo Movies*, http://movies.yahoo.com (February 3, 2003). □

P

Georg Wilhelm Pabst

Though many of his films became merely historical curiosities, G.W. Pabst (1885–1967) was one of Germany's leading early film directors. A master of silent realist cinema, Pabst explored various genres, and his post-World War I films show a marked concern with the evils of Nazism and anti-Semitism.

Background in Theater

Georg Wilhelm Pabst was born on August 27, 1885, in what was then Raudnice in Bohemia, a province of the Austro-Hungarian Empire, which dissolved following the defeat of Austria-Hungary in the First World War. Later spelled Roudnice, the city is now located in the Czech Republic. Pabst attended school in Vienna, where the family had moved when he was a child. He studied engineering until 1902, when he began studying at Vienna's Academy of Decorative Arts. In 1904 Pabst began working as an actor, and the following year he moved to Zürich, Switzerland. Over the next four years he traveled to the European cities of Salzburg, St. Gallen, and Danzig. In 1910 he traveled to New York to direct and act in German-language plays.

Pabst was in France when World War I broke out, and he was arrested and held as an enemy alien in a prisoner-of-war camp near Brest. He remained in that camp for the duration of the war, but nevertheless managed to organize a theater company and direct French-language plays. Pabst returned to Vienna after the Armistice was signed on November 11, 1918, and fit right in with the avant-garde theater of the era. He directed Expressionist theater in Prague, including two plays by Frank Wedekind, *König Nikolo* and *Erdgeist (Earth Spirit)*. In 1919 Pabst became head of the *Neuen Wiener Bühne* (New Vienna Stage). But he soon had doubts about the artistic future of theater; film was the obvious next step.

Early Films

In 1920 Pabst relocated to Berlin, where for the next two years he served as a protégé of director Carl Froelich. In 1921 he acted in Froelich's film, *Im Banne der Krolle,* and in 1922 Pabst was Froelich's assistant and scenarist for *Der Taugenichts* and *Luise Millerin.* Pabst directed his first film, *Der Schatz (The Treasure),* in 1923. The film, about a buried treasure that tears apart a blissful family, was Pabst's only true Expressionist film. Critics and film historians have tended to downplay the effort. Furthermore, it was not a commercial success. Froelich, who had helped fund *Der Schatz,* once again came to Pabst's rescue when his protégé could not find work. Because of his own busy schedule he recommended Pabst direct *Gräfin Donelli (Countess Donelli)* in 1924. A less than ordinary melodrama, the film proved to be a commercial success. In fact, the producers tried to entice Pabst to do more work in that vein, but he did not want to fall into the rut of churning out commercial fluff. That year, 1924, Pabst married Gertrude Henning.

In 1925 Pabst directed his first major film *Die Freudlose Gasse (The Joyless Street),* which starred Greta Garbo and Asta Nielsen. It was his first attempt at cinematic realism, and in it he expressed the cynicism and resignation that gripped a defeated Germany during the years of the Weimar Republic. The film's opening title card quoted from Dante's *Inferno,* "Abandon hope all ye who enter here," suggesting the despair that gripped everyday life in Germany. While this was Pabst's initial move toward the realism that would define his career, the film included melodrama and, to a far lesser degree, Expressionism. Yet this film, whose story included murder, prostitution, starvation, and economic misfortune, was a far less sentimental evocation of the urban environment than most of its contemporaries, especially D.W. Griffith's *Isn't Life Wonderful?*, which was filmed in Germany in 1924. Griffith's location shots are considered superior to Pabst's, who employed sets much of the time, but otherwise Pabst was eclipsing the cinema pioneer.

Die Freudlose Gasse was a highly successful film, though censors everywhere made cuts in it, so that in different countries different aspects of the film were emphasized. It was originally ten reels long, but after its premiere it became "a mere shell of a film," as Lee Atwell wrote in the book *G.W. Pabst*. Despite this, Pabst's artistic vision still shone through. This is the film that really launched Garbo's career. Though she had previously acted in a few unknown Swedish films and in Pabst's earlier film, Garbo's performance in *Die Freudlose Gasse* caught the attention of Hollywood moguls.

In his next film Pabst, who was an admirer of Sigmund Freud, turned to psychological drama and the surreal. Through various connections he managed to base *Geheimnisse einer Seele (Secrets of the Soul)* (1926) on an actual case history. It's a film about sexual anxiety and impotence, complete with hypnosis and dream sequences and possibly the first overtly psychological use of dreams in German cinema. Although the film is marred by a sentimental ending, it was successful with critics, audiences, and the censors, who found very little to condemn in it.

Pabst's next major film was 1927's *Die Liebe der Jeanne Ney (The Love of Jeanne Ney)*, based on the novel of the same name by Russian author Ilya Ehrenburg. The subject matter reflects Pabst's growing sympathy with the Left: he was involved with a German film worker's syndicate named *Dacho* and in 1928 joined the organization Volksverband der Filmkunst (Popular Association for Film Art). The Ehrenburg novel is set partially in Russia during the time of the Bolshevik Revolution, all the more remarkable since UFA, the German studio conglomerate that produced the film, was at first run by military men and bankers, two notoriously politically conservative groups. At about the time of the filming of *Die Liebe der Jeanne Ney*, ownership of UFA was transferring to the equally conservative Hugenberg Press. The film was another artistic leap forward for Pabst in that he used fewer title cards for character exposition, letting the camera reveal the characters. In *Geheimnisse einer Seele* the camera had played the primary role in revealing the protagonist's psychological dilemma; now Pabst employed it in a more subtle manner.

Pandora's Box

For his next film Pabst returned to the work of Frank Wedekind, conflating the Swiss-German dramatist's two "Lulu plays," *Erdgeist*, written in 1895, and *Die Büesche der Pandora (Pandora's Box)*, written in 1905. These were two Expressionistic plays that transformed the Greek myth of Pandora into the modernist Lulu, whose sexual desire consumes

men. In Pabst's hands the Expressionism was toned down by a naturalism that, ironically, Wedekind had revolted against but which Pabst used to magnificent advantage. The resulting film, *Die Büesche der Pandora*, made in 1928, is generally considered Pabst's masterpiece. Pabst's use of American actress Louise Brooks in the title role produced a Lulu who was at once a predator and an innocent: Lulu seduces and abandons men and women and even commits murder, yet she remains loyal to her love, nearly falls victim to a white slave trader, and in the end (in the film's classically Expressionist scenes) prostitutes herself and falls victim to the notorious London rapist Jack the Ripper. Brooks makes all of this believable. Pabst had originally thought of casting Marlene Dietrich in the role of Lulu, but her screen persona lacked the innocence of the unknown Brooks.

Critics were cool toward *Die Büesche der Pandora*, dismayed that Pabst had turned away from the social themes that marked *Die Freudlose Gasse* and *Die Liebe der Jeanne Ney*. The film's sexual explicitness was decimated by censors or banned altogether. Still, Pabst's mythic vision of feminine desire has been preserved by cineastes in France and Switzerland who managed to assemble a complete film from existing prints, using Pabst's shooting script as a guide. The result is one of the greatest films of the silent era.

Pabst's other film starring Brooks was *Das Tagebuch einer Verlorenen (Diary of a Lost Girl)*, filmed in 1929. Prior to that, also in 1929, he had made *Die Weisse Hölle vom Pitz-Palü*, a rather melodramatic film whose plot centers around a mountain climbing tragedy. The film features Leni Riefenstahl, who would gain fame as the most prominent Nazi film documentarian.

Das Tagebuch einer Verlorenen was Pabst's final silent film. This time he carried the eroticism of *Die Büesche der Pandora* into the realm of social realism, answering his critics, while he indicted the decadence of Weimar Germany. Brooks plays an innocent caught in society's sexual hypocrisy: a young woman made pregnant but unable to marry her seducer because her dowry is inadequate. She is forced to give up her child (who dies), is sent away to a reformatory from which she escapes, and ultimately ends up in a brothel. Where *Die Büesche der Pandora* employed Expressionist techniques to reveal gloom and death in counterpoint to the vital naturalism of Lulu, in *Das Tagebuch einer Verlorenen* Pabst maintained an unremitting realism throughout the film. The critics were again unkind to Pabst, who made an alternate ending for domestic German distribution that was devoid of irony and turned the protagonist into a high-society heroine who denounces the cruelty of the reformatory.

The "Social Trilogy"

Pabst's first "talkies" were what Atwood has termed his "social trilogy." These films include the antiwar *Westfront 1918* (1930), *Die Dreigroschenoper (The Threepenny Opera,* 1931), and *Kameradschaft (Comradeship,* 1932). In 1930 he also made *Skandal um Eva (Scandalous Eva)*. Of the social trilogy films, *Die Dreigroschenoper* is the best known but the weakest in terms of the realism on which Pabst's reputation rests. *Westfront 1918*, released the same year as another antiwar classic, *All Quiet on the Western Front*, is a tale of four German soldiers in the trenches during the final months of the World War I, living a life of horror framed by boredom. Since *Westfront 1918* was Pabst's first sound film, he wanted to express the aesthetic possibilities of the new medium, and most film historians have judged his attempt a success.

Kameradschaft, the final film of the trilogy, is an attempt to portray the friendship between the French and German peoples. The story is about a mine disaster on the border of France and Germany, in the province of Lorraine. Significantly, Pabst used French and German actors, each speaking their own language, to heighten the tension and the realism. In 1958, more than twenty-five years after it premiered, *Kameradschaft* was chosen by film critics as one of the thirty most important films. When the film was released in 1932 the German press criticized its leftist radicalism, though its artistic quality was beyond rebuke, while the French government awarded Pabst the Order of the Legion of Honor.

In between *Westfront 1918* and *Kameradschaft* was *Die Dreigroschenoper.* The strangest thing about Pabst's filming of the Bertolt Brecht/Kurt Weill opera was that he did it twice, in German and in French. The well-known story of the London underworld of beggars and thieves and the infamous Mack the Knife (Mackie Messer) featured Lotte Lenya in the German version in the role of Jenny Toler, which she had already made famous. The film relies less on realism than the other two in the social trilogy and employs a kind of Victorian romanticism and some scenes of Expressionism. A success upon its release, it is probably the second most viewed of Pabst's films.

On the day Adolf Hitler assumed power in Germany as chancellor, Pabst left for France. He remained there for eight years, with a brief interlude in the United States, making six films. One of these, *Don Quichotte (Don Quixote),* (1933) featured Russian basso Fyodor Chaliapin in the title role. In 1934 Pabst made *A Modern Hero* for Warner Brothers. The film flopped so badly that Pabst wanted to remove it from his filmography. Pabst was totally unfit for the Hollywood system and left for New York in 1935 to plan a film version of Charles Gounod's *Faust,* but this never materialized. He then returned to France.

The War Years and Afterward

In 1939, five months before the onset of World War II, Pabst returned to Austria, now under Nazi control. He stayed in Germany throughout the war and directed three wartime films. His widow later went public with a story about how the Pabst family was trapped by a series of circumstances in Austria when the war broke out. Others refute her assertions, and the truth regarding Pabst's motives for staying in Nazi Austria has been lost.

The first of three wartime, semipropagandistic films he directed was *Komodianten (Comedians,* 1941), for which he won the gold medal for best direction at the Venice Film Festival. In 1943 he directed *Paracelsus,* a story about the 16th-century metaphysician, and in 1944 he directed *Der Fall Molander (The Case of Molander),* filmed in German-controlled Prague but left unfinished when the Soviet army liberated the city.

In 1947 Pabst made *Der Prozess (The Trial),* and he again won the gold medal for direction at the Venice Film Festival. The film is a sharp indictment of anti-Semitism and in it Pabst vented his feelings toward Nazism. Pabst made seven more films in Germany, Austria, and Italy, including two more anti-Nazi films: *Der Letze Akt (The Last Ten Days,* 1955) and *Es geschah am 20 Juli (It Happened on July 20,* 1955). Considered Pabst's last masterpiece, *Der Letze Akt* depicts the final downfall of the Nazi regime. *Es geschah am 20 Juli,* about an attempt by German army officers to assassinate Hitler, suffers from being hurried. Pabst directed two films in 1956 and then retired.

Pabst was essentially an invalid for the last decade of his life. For years he had suffered from diabetes, and that was complicated when, in 1957, he was diagnosed with Parkinson's disease. He also suffered from cerebral arteriosclerosis. Pabst died in Vienna on May 29, 1967, from a liver infection.

Books

Atwell, Lee, *G.W. Pabst,* Twayne Publishers, 1977.

Manvell, Roger and Heinrich Fraenkel, *The German Cinema,* Praeger Publishers, 1971.

Rentschler, Eric, ed., *The Films of G.W. Pabst: An Extraterritorial Cinema,* Rutgers University Press, 1990.

Online

"Biography for Georg Wilhelm Pabst," http://us.imbd.com/Bio?Pabst,%20Georg%20Wilhelm (February 4, 2003).

"Films by G.W. Pabst," http://riverlightspictures.com/toe/pabst.html (February 4, 2003).

"Georg Wilhelm Pabst," *All Movie Guide,* http://www.allmovie.com/cg/avg.dll?p = avg& = B105326~C (February 4, 2003). □

Al Pacino

Al Pacino (born 1940) has been called one of the best actors in film history. He established himself as a Hollywood icon when he burst onto the scene in *The Godfather* and followed that critically acclaimed performance with eight Academy Award nominations and more than 20 movies over 30 years. Through it all, Pacino stayed grounded in his first love: theater. But despite three decades of fame and success, the man behind the actor, who cherished his privacy, remained something of a mystery.

The Young Actor

Pacino was born April 25, 1940, in New York City to Salvatore and Rose Pacino. Pacino's father left the family when Al was a baby and although Pacino visited his father in East Harlem, he was raised by his mother

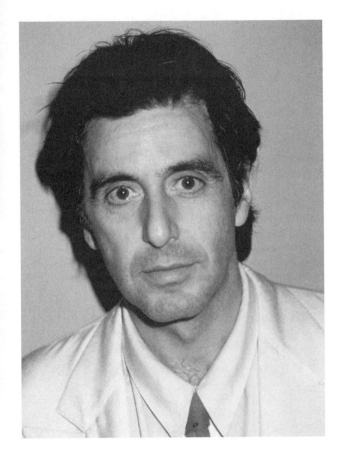

and maternal grandparents in a bilingual Italian American three-room household. Rose Pacino was ill throughout his childhood, as well as mentally troubled and poor, and died of a heart attack when Pacino was 22. He was under strict rule at home but had a happy, sheltered childhood. He was bored and unmotivated in school. He found his place in school plays and dreamed of a career in acting.

Pacino's first acting lessons were at the Dover Theater, where he would go with his mother or grandmother to watch movies. After imitating the action on the screen for his grandmother, he was often asked to do the "looking for the bottle scene" from *The Lost Weekend*. Pacino found he could get positive attention with his acting antics. He won admission into Manhattan's prestigious High School of the Performing Arts but dropped out at age 17. As a teenager, Pacino took acting lessons from Charlie Laughton, who became a friend. Pacino held odd jobs to support the family.

Broadway

Pacino moved to Greenwich Village and started to audition. Once on the theater scene, Pacino entered a period of depression and poverty. There were days when he could not afford bus fare or even lunch. He lived for awhile off the pay of his soap-opera-actor girlfriend and future movie star, Jill Clayburgh. He found work where he could, in a coffeehouse, a workshop, a mailroom, a theater, and elsewhere.

Finally, in 1966, he entered the prestigious Actors Studio and studied under Lee Strasberg, known for his

Method Approach to acting. In 1967, Pacino won an Obie for his performance in *The Indian Wants the Bronx,* an off-Broadway, one-act play that ran for 204 performances. In 1969, he won the Antoinette Perry (Tony) Award for the Broadway play *Does the Tiger Wear a Necktie?* The play had only a brief run, but Pacino's work in *Tiger* got him noticed by film director Dominick Dunne.

Hit It Big with *Godfather*

In 1969 Pacino debuted on screen in *Me, Natalie.* But he felt awkward away from the stage and had such a bad experience that he did not return to film for a couple of years. He said to Jimmy Breslin of *Esquire,* "I was used to working on a tightrope onstage. A movie is just a line painted on the floor." In 1971 he played a junkie in *Panic in Needle Park,* directed by Dunne.

In the early 1970s, such actors as Robert Redford, Warren Beatty, Jack Nicholson, and Robert De Niro sought the role of Michael Corleone in Francis Ford Coppola's *The Godfather.* But Coppola wanted Pacino, who had given solid performances in *Panic in Needle Park* and on Broadway. After a series of disastrous screen tests, no one—from the producers to fellow actors—wanted Pacino in the film, except for Coppola. Coppola stuck to his guns, and Pacino earned his first Academy Award nomination.

Pacino decided not to ride a wave of Hollywood success into lightweight blockbusters. Instead, he took a series of difficult, important film roles that highlighted his genuine acting abilities. 1973's *Serpico* was a crime drama spotlighting the mental struggles of a New York cop. Pacino was nominated for an Oscar for *Serpico* and for his portrayal of Michael Corleone in *The Godfather II* in 1974. In 1975, Pacino was nominated for an Oscar for his role in *Dog Day Afternoon,* the story of a man trying to get money for his gay lover's sex change operation by holding up a bank and taking hostages. In 1977, *Bobby Deerfield* foreshadowed a downturn in his career, but Pacino received another Oscar nomination for best actor for the hard-hitting legal drama *. . . And Justice for All.*

A Decade Without a Blockbuster

Pacino's career turned south with the controversial *Cruising,* a look at the gay netherworld, in 1980, and *Author! Author!* in 1982. 1983's *Scarface* met with some criticism, partially for Pacino's Cuban accent and incessant cursing, but it would later become a cult classic.

Revolution—an epic war movie on the Revolutionary War released in 1985—has been called by some critics the worst film of all time. Pacino was in the starring role. *Revolution* had a cursed shoot full of rewrites, Pacino became sick with pneumonia, and upon release the film was savagely attacked by critics. They were Pacino's first truly awful reviews, and he was criticized again for his accent. He stayed out of Hollywood for the next several years.

Caught the Limelight Again

Pacino's return to Hollywood came in the film *Sea of Love* in 1989, an erotic-romantic film that cast him as a hard-drinking cop. In 1990, Pacino reprised his role of

Michael Corleone in *The Godfather: Part III,* earning praise for his acting amid mixed reviews for the film. *Dick Tracy* was also released in 1990, and Pacino got rave reviews for his comedic spoof on a gangster, a type of character he usually played seriously. He was nominated for another Oscar for best supporting actor for *Dick Tracy.*

Pacino teamed up with Michelle Pfieffer for a romantic role in *Frankie and Johnny* in 1991. Two years later, Pacino was nominated for Oscars for two roles: a shark-like real estate agent in *Glengary Glen Ross* and a bitter, blind former army colonel in *Scent of a Woman.* Pacino was awarded a best actor Oscar for *Scent of a Woman.* In subsequent years, Pacino turned out many films that were box-office successes. Between 1993 and 2003, Pacino appeared in such hits as *Carlito's Way, Heat, City Hall, Donnie Brasco, Devil's Advocate, The Insider, Any Given Sunday, Insomnia,* and *The Recruit.* As of 2002, his average salary was $10 million a picture.

Theatre Always His First Love

Even as Pacino's star was rising in Hollywood, he continued to act in the theater. In 1970 he appeared in *Camino Real,* and in 1972 he began playing the lead in *The Basic Training of Pavlo Hummel* in Boston. That story of a Vietnam War recruit began a stint in New York in 1977, with Pacino in the lead, and he won his second Tony.

During his self-imposed exile from film in the 1980s, Pacino immersed himself in theater. According to Breslin, "He stepped back and went to where he always felt at home—three flights up in a drafty place where they can put down enough chairs to call it a theater." He performed in *Julius Caesar* and gave readings at colleges and small theaters. He directed *The Local Stigmatic* and filmed it starring himself. It remains unreleased to the public. *Stigmatic* is a movie adaptation of a Heathcote Williams play that Pacino performed during his early days on the stage in 1968. In the 1990s, Pacino produced, directed, and starred in *Looking for Richard,* a marriage of theater (William Shakespeare's *Richard III*) and film documentary that Pacino devoted himself and his money to for over four years. More than one reporter noted that while Pacino remained characteristically tight-lipped about most of his movies and his private life, he would enthusiastically talk about *Looking for Richard.*

Pacino often turned down potential hit movies to do theater, he took long breaks between films, and he was constantly involved in independent ventures. Breslin points out, "There is no other recorded case like this in the history of American movie stars. Sure, some big movie actor or actress will occasionally find a spare week or two to throw at Shakespeare. . . . But no movie star has ever created his own work of artistic obsession, let alone two of them. Only this guy." In 2000, he became involved in the Actors Studio in New York's *Oedipus Rex.* In 2002, Pacino was off-Broadway with *The Resistible Rise of Arturo Ui* and in Oscar Wilde's *Salome* opposite Marissa Tomei.

The Personal Pacino

Pacino was an enduring bachelor, one of the few Hollywood men never to marry despite romances with Diane Keaton and other high-profile actresses. Despite his aversion to matrimony, Pacino had a daughter, Julie Marie, by acting teacher Jan Tarrant, and a set of twins–Anton and Olivia–with long-time girlfriend Beverly D'Angelo. Breslin wrote, "Pacino is famous mostly because of his extreme, unique, and undeniable talents as an actor and movie star during the past twenty-five of his fifty-five years. But he is also well-known for being hard to figure. . . . He is reluctant to talk to reporters, for example." Pacino has never been comfortable with fame.

When he attained fame in his early 30s, he was unequipped to handle it. He started drinking heavily and became reclusive and unstable. But his friends convinced him to join Alcoholics Anonymous, and in two years he quit both drinking and smoking.

Pacino is a living legend. He "can play small as rivetingly as he can play big. . . . he can implode as well as explode," according to Jeff Giles in *Newsweek.* Pacino told Bronwen Hruska of *Entertainment Weekly,* "For me it's always been the character—'the play's the thing'—not my personality. When one overshadows the other, you become more a celebrity than an actor. I hope the perception is that I'm an act."

Books

American Decades, Gale Research, 1998.
Complete Marquis Who's Who, Marquis Who's Who, 2001.
Contemporary Theatre, Film and Television, Volume 23, Gale Group, 1999.
International Dictionary of Films and Filmmakers, Volume 3: *Actors and Actresses,* St. James Press, 1996.
Newsmakers 1993, Issue 4, Gale Research, 1993.
St. James Encyclopedia of Popular Culture, St. James Press, 2000.

Periodicals

Daily Variety, October 30, 2002; January 8, 2003.
Entertainment Weekly, November 12, 1993.
Esquire, February 1996.
Newsweek, June 3, 2002.
Rolling Stone, February 2, 1984.
US Weekly, January 29, 2001.

Online

"Pacino's Biography," http://www.fortunecity.com/lavender/exorcist/665/biography.htm. (February 10, 2003). □

Camille Paglia

Social critic and educator Camille Paglia (born 1947) has outraged or befuddled countless readers with her defiantly iconoclastic writings. She has, for example, argued that pornography constitutes sexual reality, that prostitutes enjoy their work, that bisexuality should be an accepted norm, and that all drugs should be legalized. But as anyone willing to read her books and essays soon discovers, her state-

ments are more often than not well-reasoned conclusions that cannot be dismissed out-of-hand.

Camille Paglia was born on April 2, 1947, in Endi-
cott, New York, to Pasquale and Lydia Paglia, who
had immigrated to the United States from Italy. Her
father was a professor of Romance languages at LeMoyne
College in Syracuse, New York, while his wife, Lydia,
worked at home sewing wedding dresses until their daughter was three; after that she worked as a bank teller.

Encouraged in Art of Debate

Paglia's family had little money when she was growing
up; by way of compensation her parents encouraged her to
engage her intellectual curiosity. Paglia would later tell an
interviewer for *Playboy:* "I was silent as a child. But it's true
that my father was very opinionated, and he trained me in
my earliest years to be an individual thinker. Italian culture
is like Chinese culture. There is respect for elders. You never
raise your voice to elders. There are no explosions. My
father was totally in control."

Among Paglia's earliest memories, dating to the age of
two and a half, is an episode of rage she experienced when
she was not allowed to attend a film because she could not
yet read. Rage is an emotion that would serve her well many
years later when she became one of America's leading
social critics.

Within a few years of the film brouhaha, Paglia had
become something of a tomboy, frequently getting into
scuffles with her male cohorts. It must have come as a relief
to her father when she finally became interested in ancient
Egypt. But by then she was just as much a devotee of Hollywood popular culture as of antiquity. Paglia recalled a
lecture she received from her father regarding 18th-century
Swiss writer Voltaire's poor opinion of actors that came just
about the time she started collecting pictures of actress
Elizabeth Taylor.

Paglia experienced the rebellious 1960s as a high
school student. Because she was attracted to women in high
school, she assumed she was a lesbian, but, as she told
Playboy, "it wasn't possible for me to do anything about my
attraction to women. Lesbianism didn't exist in that time, as
far as I knew. . . . I always felt frustrated and excluded,
looking in from a distance." This stance marked the beginning of her own rebellion against social norms. In later years
she would find that lesbians disliked her because of her
belief that most women are bisexual. Her relationships with
men, on the other hand, continued to be compromised by
her lack of patience and unwillingness to assume the role of
nurturer.

Although feeling excluded socially, Paglia excelled academically and in college graduated valedictorian at the
State University of New York at Binghamton in 1968. She
went on to spent four years at Yale University, earning her
Ph.D. in English before taking a teaching position at Bennington College in Vermont.

Became College Teacher

Paglia's seven years at Bennington were unsatisfying,
to say the least. As she told *Playboy,* "I would go to a faculty
meeting and be aware that everyone hated me. The men
were appalled by a strong, loud woman. . . . [T]he men at
the college were terrified because they are eunuchs, and I
threatened every . . . one of them." Her interactions even
became physical: in one case Paglia left an obnoxious male
student sprawled on the cafeteria floor. After several such
incidents, Bennington reportedly asked her to leave, but
with legal intervention she managed to stay on until 1979.
After Bennington College she landed a low-paying faculty
position as professor of humanities at the Philadelphia College of Performing Arts (now the University of the Arts).

"Hurricane Camille"

In 1990 Paglia earned the sobriquet "Hurricane
Camille" after publishing the 700-page tome on sex, art,
and literature titled *Sexual Personae: Art and Decadence
from Nefertiti to Emily Dickinson.* The book, which was
nominated for a National Book Critics Circle award, became a bestseller and propelled Paglia to celebrity status.
This success did not come without persistence on Paglia's
part, however. After she completed the manuscript in 1981,
she submitted it to seven publishers, all of whom rejected it;
she finally found a publisher, Yale University Press, to accept it nine years later.

Appropriately for a work that rivals the Bible in thick-
ness, *Sexual Personae* opens with the lines: "In the begin-

ning was nature. The background from which and against which our ideas of God were formed, nature remains the supreme moral problem. We cannot hope to understand sex and gender until we clarify our attitude toward nature. Sex is a subset to nature. Sex is the natural in man." She wastes no time in making her point: on the first page she writes, "Feminists grossly oversimplify the problem of sex when they reduce it to a matter of social convention: readjust society, eliminate sexual inequality, purify sex roles, and happiness and harmony will reign."

Martha Duffy, reviewing *Sexual Personae* for *Time,* attributed the book's popularity to an emergent backlash among those who had become fed up with feminism. According to Duffy, "Paglia articulates positions that many people of both genders seem to want to hear. . . . To them feminism has gone quite far enough, and they like *Personae*'s neoconservative cultural message: Men have done the work of civilization and can take credit for most of its glories. Women are powerful too, but as the inchoate forces of nature are powerful. Religion and marriage are historically the best defenses against chaos."

After setting forth her views in *Sexual Personae,* Paglia went on to author more essays dealing with feminist issues. Published in 1992, *Sex, Art, and American Culture* takes on the testimony of Anita Hill, who accused a soon-to-be Supreme Court Justice of sexual harassment, the so-called "beauty myth" coined by feminist author Naomi Wolf, and the decline of education in America while offering personal commentary on Paglia's own career in journalism and academia. Ann Oakley, writing in *Sociology,* dubbed the work "essentially an autobiographical record of Paglia's professional life to date as she sees it." The 1994 collection *Vamps and Tramps: New Essays* deals with the arts, gay activism, and such celebrity figures as Bill and Hillary Clinton. Mimi Udovitch, writing in *Artforum International,* found this collection to be Paglia's "most enjoyable work to date" and praised it for demonstrating that the author has a joie de vivre that can effectively counterbalance "her excesses." Paglia is also the author of *The Birds,* a study of Alfred Hitchcock's movie of the same name.

Iconoclast par Excellence

By the mid-1990s Paglia was a celebrity considered among the most well-known social philosophers in the United States. With a popular image that the *Playboy* interviewer described as "antifeminist feminist, antigay lesbian and antiliberal liberal," she had acquired a reputation as an academic attack dog. For her part, Paglia told the interviewer that she considered herself a feminist, but added that other feminists disliked her because she had criticized the women's movement. Unlike most mainstream feminists, she believes feminism has betrayed women by replacing dialogue between the sexes with political correctness. Given the sacrifices that so-called sexual liberation entails, Paglia maintained that, in the end, it was the children—by way of neglect—who suffered most from the women's movement.

She has also faulted the movement for the division it has caused between the sexes and traces much of the on-

going confusion about gender identity to the sexual revolution of the 1960s. As she told *Playboy,* "After the sixties there was a collapse in almost everything we believed in. . . . It all unraveled in the seventies. AIDS, appearing in the early eighties, was the period at the end of the sentence. AIDS forced most people to wake up to the fact that the sexual revolution had failed." Still, she has remained optimistic about social progress. "Social change is evolutionary, not revolutionary," Paglia explained. "Deep social change takes time. And slowly the culture is changing."

Found Appreciative Readership

While considered to be at once a humorist, pedant, iconoclast, egotist, and exhibitionist, Paglia and her essays on art, politics, and society were taken seriously by readers frustrated by the false humility characteristic of the late 20th century, and she has continued to inspire others to reconsider society. From the left, Paglia's writings have provoked animosity, contempt, and outrage. As First Lady of feminism Betty Friedan told the *Playboy* interviewer: "How can you take [Paglia] seriously? She is an exhibitionist, and she takes the most extreme elements of the women's movement and tries to make the whole movement antisexual, antilife, antijoy. And neither I nor most of the women I know are that way." Paglia, for her part, prefers to compare herself to conservative radio talk-show hosts Rush Limbaugh and Howard Stern, viewing herself as a champion of unbridled discussion.

Books

Feminist Writers, St. James Press, 1996.
Paglia, Camille, *Sex, Art, and American Culture: Essays,* Vintage, 1992.
Paglia, Camille, *Sexual Personae: Art and Decadence from Nefertiti to Emily Dickinson,* Yale University Press, 1990.
Paglia, Camille, *Vamps and Tramps: New Essays,* Vintage, 1994.

Periodicals

Artforum International, Summer 1995.
Publishers Weekly, November 28, 1994.
Sociology, November 1994.
Time, January 13, 1992.

Online

"Interview with Camille Paglia," *Playboy Web site,* http://privat .ub.uib.no/BUBSY/playboy.htm. □

Phoebe Worrall Palmer

Phoebe Worrall Palmer (1807–1874) was an evangelist and religious writer involved with the "Holiness" movement. Raised as a Methodist, Palmer became one of the most influential female religious leaders in the latter part of the nineteenth century. At a time when most evangelists were men, Palmer converted thousands of people in the United

States, Canada, Great Britain, and Europe, and she did much to advance the role of women in religion.

Early Life

Phoebe Worrall Palmer was born in New York City on December 18, 1807, one of two daughters of Henry Worrall and Dorothea Blanche Wade. Her father was born in Yorkshire, England, and came to America in his early 20s. Her mother was born in America.

Palmer and her sister Sarah were raised in a strict religious household. Their parents were active members of the Methodist Episcopal Church in New York City. They instilled in their children strict Methodist values and they conducted twice-daily in-house family worship services. Palmer received catechism lessons from Nathan Bangs, a well-known Methodist leader. Palmer was a pious child, and by the time she was 11 she was writing religious material that expressed her strong commitment to Jesus, including a poem she wrote inside her copy of the New Testament that read: "This revelation—holy, just, and true/Though oft I read, it seems forever new/While light from heaven upon its pages rest/I feel its power, and with it I am blessed."

Palmer was 19 when she married Dr. Walter Palmer, a respected homeopathic physician. They would have four children, but only one survived past infancy. That child, Phoebe Knapp, became a well-known religious composer.

As husband and wife, the Palmers shared deep religious convictions, they were both involved in the Methodist Episcopal Church, and they were both raised in strict Methodist homes. Like his wife's parents, Dr. Palmer's parents, Miles and Deborah Clarke Palmer, were committed Methodists. For years, they held "class meetings" in their home, a Methodist practice that was started by John Wesley in 1742 and later taken up by Walter and Phoebe Palmer as their religious commitment deepened.

Family Tragedies and Spiritual Struggles

At the outset of the marriage, it appeared that Palmer's life would be centered around the church and raising a family. However, great personal tragedy profoundly influenced the direction her life would take. Indeed, her strong religiosity and subsequent evangelism appear to be, in great part, a reaction to intense grief and overwhelming guilt. In the first ten years of their marriage, the Palmers lost three of their four children. Rather than embittering her and turning her away from religion, the deaths caused Palmer to lean more heavily on her Methodist faith. The tragedies caused her to question her motives and the strength of her religious convictions. She wondered if her love for her children diminished her faith and devotion to God.

Her first two children died soon after they were born. The first, a son named Alexander, was born the day after the Palmers celebrated their first wedding anniversary in September 1828 and died nine months later. Palmer had delayed the child's baptism so she could finish sewing his special baptismal outfit. After her child died, she feared that God had judged her negatively because she had spent so much time on the clothing rather than proceeding with the ritual. Her second child, another son, was born in 1830. Palmer first looked upon the birth as a blessing, believing that God was replacing her first child. But the child lived only seven weeks. Again, she believed the loss resulted from her lack of devotion. Essentially, this was God's way of punishing her, she felt. Her response was to increase her religious pursuits. Thus, she and her husband became more actively involved in their home church. This was part of Palmer's efforts to achieve a more spiritually satisfying life—a search that, at first, left her unfulfilled.

The Palmers had two more children. The first of these survived, but the fourth was killed in 1835 when gauze curtains near the cradle accidentally caught fire. That child's death caused Palmer to resign herself totally to God.

While the deaths of her three children and Palmer's emotional and spiritual response certainly contributed to her eventual evangelism, there were other motivating factors. Starting well before her marriage, Palmer endured a protracted spiritual struggle as she wrestled with the Methodist belief that an individual's spiritual conversion should be a highly emotional and powerful experience. Such a conversion would lead to an individual's "Christian Perfection," a Methodist tenet that referred to purity of heart resulting from a cleansing by the blood of Christ. Yet Palmer felt her own conversion had been more low-key and gradual. In fact, she could point to no single defining moment of conversion, and this caused her to question her standing in the eyes of God and the promise of her salvation. In other words, she feared she was unworthy of heaven.

Emerged as a Methodist Leader

The significant step toward the resolution of her spiritual struggle—as well as toward her emergence as an important female religious figure—occurred when Palmer's sister, Sarah Lankford, came to live with her in 1831. Lankford, who had experienced the required emotional Methodist conversion, helped Palmer understand that belief in God was enough to assure her salvation. This understanding formed the basis of the "Holiness" doctrine that Palmer would later preach. By 1837, Palmer was able to claim that her devotion to God and her freedom from sin was complete.

Lankford also inspired her sister to assume more of a leadership role in Methodist prayer meetings for women. Beginning in 1835, Palmer conducted regular women's prayer meetings at her home. These meetings would become a major part of the "Holiness movement toward Christian perfection." At first, Lankford led these Tuesday "meetings for the promotion of holiness." Palmer took them over only after her sister moved away. From that point, Palmer became a pivotal figure in the movement, basing her teachings on her own experiences on the path to "Christian perfection." Her basic message was that people should place every part of themselves on the altar of God to ensure that they would become perfect in love and, thus, holy. Attendance at the meetings grew from a small group to hundreds, forcing Palmer and her husband to build extra rooms.

By 1839, the meetings became open to evangelicals of both sexes. Soon, the meetings attracted people from other religious demoninations. Attendees included bishops and pastors as well as professors and laypeople.

As her influence grew, Palmer expanded her activities to include "protracted meetings," another established Methodist practice that had been introduced by revivalist Charles Finney. By this time, Palmer had become a skillful and articulate speaker, and the protracted meetings provided her with a forum where she began her preaching. With her husband, she soon began preaching at Methodist camp meetings and Holiness revivals in other parts of the country. By 1850, the couple traveled throughout the eastern United States and Canada, preaching at camp meetings and other venues.

Wrote Several Books

Palmer became a regular contributor to the *Guide to Holiness,* the leading publication of the perfectionist movement. She also wrote several books including *The Way of Holiness* (1843), her best-known book and the one that established her as a leader of the perfectionist movement. She also wrote *Entire Devotion to God* (1845) and *Faith and its Effects* (1848).

In 1847, she refined and further developed the concept of "altar theology," which explained the idea of the "second blessing," or immediate sanctification. As a basis for this concept, she drew on the Apostle Paul, who had advanced the idea of placing oneself as a "living sacrifice" on the altar of God to represent complete consecration. This "altar theology" simplified sanctification into a three-step process that included consecration, faith, and testimony. This concept, as well as her central theme of holiness of heart and life, gained popularity with Methodists, but it was not widely accepted in the Methodist Episcopal Church. Opponents challenged her, finding her theology less sound than that of church founder John Wesley. Even Bangs, who taught Palmer her catechism when she was a child, disagreed with her. He complained that she was turning sanctification into a simplistic and mechanical process.

Activities Increased

In 1850 she headed the Methodist Ladies' Home Missionary Society and established a mission in the squalid Five Points neighborhood in New York City. The mission grew out of her belief that holiness was best demonstrated by human service. It also stemmed from her conviction that people needed food, clothing, and shelter to be able to best respond to God. Palmer administered care for the sick and needy within the dangerous slum. She also worked as a corresponding secretary for the New York Female Assistance Society for the Relief and Religious Instruction of the Sick Poor. As far as social issues were concerned, Palmer was a moderate in her stance, but she spoke out against slavery and alcohol, and she advocated more freedom for women in church and society.

By the end of the 1850s, Palmer had reached the high point of her preaching career, as both men and women viewed her as a leader. She not only brought the sexes together in worship, she also advanced the role of female preachers. She had become a prominent religious figure at a time when very few women rose to positions of power in America. Other women involved in leadership roles performed their services in their homes. Palmer was one of the few who took her message on the road and in the process became the recognized spokesperson for the Holiness movement.

Part of her success was attributable to her power as a speaker. She converted thousands of people in the United States, and by the end of the decade she and her husband were preaching in England as well. But she also happened to be in the right place at the right time. Many of her converts had been seeking an alternative to the message of the traditional church. Also, at this point in American history, the revivalist or evangelical approach to religion perfectly suited the temper of the times and the "Manifest Destiny" vision of the United States.

Later Years

By 1862, Palmer's husband bought the *Guide to Holiness,* the leading publication of the Holiness movement, and Palmer became the publication's editor, a position she held for the rest of her life. In 1865, she wrote *Four Years in the Old World,* a book that chronicled her experiences in England.

After the Civil War, she served as a leader of the National Camp Meeting Association for the Promotion of Holiness. Also, the international reach of her mission extended beyond Canada and Great Britain and into other areas in Europe. In 1867, she and her husband established the National Association for the Promotion of Holiness, which encompassed much of her evangelical work. She also continued holding her Tuesday meetings right up until she died in New York City on November 2, 1874. She was buried in Greenwood Cemetery in Brooklyn. After her death, the new editors of the *Guide to Holiness* continued printing previously unpublished articles she had written as well as some of her letters and diary entries.

Online

Flory, Barbara, "A Passion For Souls!" *Holiness Digest,* http://www.messiah.edu/whwc/Articles/article8.htm (March 15, 2003).

Howie, Barbara A., "Phoebe Palmer, 1807–1874," *West Virginia University.edu,* http://are.as.wvu.edu/phebe.htm (March 15, 2003).

McEllhenney, John G., "Phoebe Palmer: A Woman Who Proclaimed a 'Shorter Way' to Holiness 1807–1874," *BulletinInserts.com,* http://www.gcah.org/BulletinInserts/BI_Palmer.htm (March 15, 2003).

"Palmer, Phoebe Worrall," *Women in American History,* http://search.eb.com/women/articles/Palmer_Phoebe_Worrall.html (March 15, 2003).

White, Charles Edward, "What the Holy Spirit Can and Cannot Do: The Ambiguities of Phoebe Palmer's Theology of Experience," *Wesley Center Online,* http://wesley.nnu.edu/WesleyanTheology/theojrnl/16-20/20-08.htm (March 15, 2003). □

Charles Fox Parham

Charles Fox Parham (1873–1929) is often referred to as the "Father of Modern Day Pentecostalism." Rising from a nineteenth century frontier background, he emerged as the early leader of a major religious revivalist movement. He emphasized the role of the Holy Spirit and the restoration of apostolic faith. With his evangelistic zeal, he also advanced the concept of "speaking in tongues." Though his influence in the movement diminished later in life, his enormous impact on the development of Pentecostal faith was widely recognized.

Early Life

Charles Fox Parham was born June 4, 1873, in Muscatine, Iowa, the third son of William and Ann Parham. He lived the American frontier experience, reared on the tenets of populism. In 1878, William Parham packed his family into a covered wagon and moved to Anness, Kansas, where they lived comfortably on a profitable 160-acre farm.

Parham was a sickly youth, suffering from encephalitis and tapeworms. Making matters worse, when he was nine years old, he caught rheumatic fever, which weakened his heart, a condition that troubled him throughout his life.

His parents adhered to no particular religious faith but they were God-fearing people. Parham embarked on his own theological journey, first joining the Methodist faith in 1886 after he was converted during an evangelistic meeting. An intelligent youth and avid reader, Parham taught Methodist Sunday school and then, when he was only 15, he became a minister.

Parham's religious beliefs and the later teachings of his ministry were greatly influenced by two deeply spiritual experiences he had as a youth. The first occurred, he claimed, when he was 13 years old, when he became bathed in a bright light while performing a repentance prayer ritual. The second event, which he claimed took place when he was 18, involved a miraculous cure of his rheumatic fever and resulting heart condition. Though Parham would continue having heart troubles, he came to see himself on a mission to provide the same healing experience for others.

Beginning in 1890, he attended Southwest Kansas College in Winfield, studying religion and then medicine. After he suffered a recurrence of rheumatic fever that nearly killed him, he returned to his evangelistic pursuits. He earned a minister's license from the Southwest Kansas Conference of the Methodist Episcopal Church, and when he was 20 he became a temporary pastor at the Eudora Methodist Church near Lawrence, Kansas. But Parham was often at odds with his Methodist superiors. Conflicts arose because Parham's theology veered in the direction of the Holiness movement, a revivalist offshoot of Methodist theology with tenets that included sanctification, baptism by the Holy Spirit, and divine healing.

Started Own Ministry

By 1895, Parham broke with Methodism—in fact, all denominationalism—for good. He started his own independent evangelical ministry in Kansas, where he held revival meetings that emphasized personal salvation. He also advocated a return to the fundamental teachings of the scriptures, or "primitive Christianity."

In 1886, he married Sarah Thistlethwaite, the daughter of Quaker parents. A year later they had a son. In 1898, as his ministry grew, Parham moved his family to Topeka, Kansas, where he established his base of operations. His other activities included running a rescue mission for the poor and sinners, an employment agency, and an orphanage service and publishing the *Apostolic Faith,* a Holiness periodical.

For much of this period, Parham took his evangelistic mission through parts of the United States and Canada. When his efforts met with little success, he became discouraged. But his sense of mission was revitalized in 1890 when he studied with Frank Sandford, a well-known member of the Holiness Movement who had started the the Holy Ghost and Us Bible School in Shiloh, Maine. Parham's visit to Shiloh strengthened his beliefs about baptism of the Holy Spirit. Taking that belief a step further, Parham started to believe that the Holy Spirit would enable converts to spontaneously speak foreign languages. This he termed "missionary tongues," because it would enable the new believers to go out and convert people all over the world. This ability eventually became widely known as "speaking in tongues."

Parham first heard someone imbued with the power to speak in tongues at Shiloh. However, Sandford placed less significance on it than Parham, believing it to be something that only occasionally happened during intense prayer. But Parham felt that converts could use the ability to evangelize the world.

Credited with Starting Pentecostalism

Now revitalized, Parham returned to Kansas and started his own Bible school in October 1900. Calling it the Bethel Healing Home, he modeled it in part after Sandford's school, and he taught college-age students the need for a restoration of New Testament Christianity, or a return to "primitive Christianity." Biblical truth, Parham preached, could be gained only by returning to the teachings of the Apostles and following the words found in the Book of Acts. That part of the Bible, Parham believed, was where the true word of God was found. Parham eventually expanded his theology to include the laying of hands on others during prayer, speaking in tongues, and baptism of the Holy Spirit, which led to purification of the soul. Religious historians regard the opening of Parham's Bible school as the birth of modern Pentecostalism.

Parham had about 40 students. In late December 1900, Parham left the school for several days to fulfill some outside preaching engagements. He told his students to pray and study while he was gone. During Parham's absence, the students participated in intense collective prayer sessions, allowing themselves to be overwhelmed by a spiritual fervor. The students believed they were in the "last days," as Parham had predicted the world would end in 1925. When Parham returned, he was told that one of his students, Agnes Ozman, spontaneously had gained the ability to speak in tongues during a prayer session.

Apparently, on the last day of 1900, Ozman began speaking Chinese, despite the fact that she never had studied the language. This led Parham to deduce that the baptism of the Holy Spirit would be accompanied by the ability to speak in tongues, a novel conclusion at the time. In Pentecostal historical chronicles, Ozman's experience is regarded as a significant event, and she is cited as being the first Bible student of modern times to undergo apostolic baptism of the Holy Spirit accompanied by speaking in tongues. According to accounts, within a few days, Parham and about half the students also underwent the same experience. Parham maintained that this sudden collective ability was directly attributable to God. Parham termed the ability to speak in tongues as "xenoglossae," which means "foreign tongues" in Greek. The reason God provided this gift, he said, was to allow true believers to go out into all parts of the world and save souls without having to learn a foreign language. In the wake of this collective experience, Parham founded a new movement called the "Apostolic Faith."

In 1901, Parham closed his school and took some of his students on the road, holding evangelistic services throughout the Midwest. But his efforts met with only middling success. Around this time, Parham endured other troubles. His beliefs were drawing criticism and even ridicule from newspapers and local citizens. Also, his one-year-old son died.

Expanded his Ministry

By 1903, it was being noticed that none of the followers of Parham were leaving the heartland of America to go overseas and envangelize the world. Still, his Apostolic Faith movement entered a period of strong growth. He held a hugely successful revival in Galena, Kansas, which lasted for months and resulted in 800 conversions. Participants also reported hundreds of Holy Spirit baptisms accompanied by the speaking of tongues as well as 1,000 testimonies of healing. Buoyed by this success, Parham decided to expand his ministry into the Southwest.

In 1905, he was invited to preach in Orchard, Texas, on Easter Sunday. His message was well received and it soon spread throughout the state. In the fall, he conducted a huge revival in Galveston, Texas. In December, he opened the Bible Training School in Houston.

In Houston, Parham met William Joseph Seymour, an African American Baptist minister who wanted to join Parham's school. Despite his own segregationist beliefs, Parham allowed Seymour to attend. Seymour was poor and uneducated. But he would have a huge impact on the development of Pentecostalism. Seymour went to Los Ange-

les in 1906 and, using the preaching credentials he earned from Parham, he opened a mission in an old warehouse located on Azusa Street.

Meanwhile, Parham traveled to Illinois, where he was well received. His missionaries were beginning to travel to places such as India and Africa. It seemed as if he was finally realizing his vision of an international mission.

In Los Angeles thousands of people were soon attracted to Seymour's mission, where services were held three times daily, seven days per week. Over the next several years, Pentecostal missionaries who had received the baptism in the Holy Spirit at Seymour's mission were going across the world, setting up other missionaries.

The huge success of the Azusa Street mission was a big surprise. During the enthusiastic services, participants reportedly spoke in tongues and engaged in fervent prayer. The mission also gained a reputation as a setting for wild scenes. The meetings began to be filled with fringe figures such as spiritualist mediums, hypnotists, and others who had a deep interest in the occult. Newspapers reported hearing "weird babbling" emanating from the structure. Soon the mission attracted the curious, who had no desire to be saved but merely wanted to witness the events.

Despite the controversy it generated and the curiosity it aroused, the mission also attracted true believers. Hundreds were saved and set out on evangelistic missions. In fact, almost all of the major Pentecostal associations that sprung up in subsequent years could trace their origins back to Azusa Street.

Diminished Influence

By 1907, nearly 13,000 people reportedly had accepted Parham's Pentecostalism. However, at this point, the movement began to slip away from him, take on a life of its own and move in other directions. The great success of the Azusa mission created an irreparable rift between Parham and Seymour. Parham visited the mission once and was reportedly aghast at the racial integration and the extreme emotionalism demonstrated. Parham tried to exercise some control over the proceedings, but Seymour discouraged his efforts.

Parham's inability to exercise his influence over the mission marked the start of his decline as a leader. Parham not only alienated Seymour, but others became disenchanted with his judgmental attitude as well as some of his theological concepts. After 1906 and the emergence of the Azusa Street mission, Parham's name turns up less frequently in the history of Pentecostalism.

Also, in 1907 Parham encountered some legal difficulties that did terrible harm to his reputation. He was arrested in Texas for alleged sexual misconduct involving young boys. However, charges were dropped as no one came forward to testify. Today, it is generally regarded that the charges were without merit and most likely resulted from a conspiratorial campaign to discredit him initiated by anti-Pentecostal religious leaders. Nevertheless, the accusation was enough to do substantial damage, and he subsequently lost much of his credibility with the neo-Pentecostal movement.

Many of Parham's most loyal followers began rejecting some of his concepts, including his beliefs about salvation and the coming "Rapture" or end of the world. They also started revising his notions about speaking in tongues. The new Pentecostals reviewed the Bible to gain more understanding of this mysterious phenomenon, and they believed it was an intense and personal spiritual experience that resulted from prayer, but they rejected Parham's idea that it could be useful in establishing international missions. Many had even less tolerance for his more bizarre ideas. Indeed, some of his beliefs later made him an embarrassment to the movement, particularly his belief in Anglo-Israelism, which claimed that Anglo-Saxons were descended from the ten lost tribes of Israel. The concept was closely tied with the so-called "two seed theory of Christian Identity," which had racist and anti-Semitic overtones.

The Movement Splintered

By the end of 1913 independent Pentecostal organizations began forming within the movement, including the Church of God in Christ, the Assemblies of God, the United Pentecostal Church, and the Pentecostal Church of God. As Parham watched his influence slip away, he became embittered and resentful. In 1919 Charles Shumway of Boston University published a dissertation, *A Critical History of Glossolalia,* that was highly critical of Parham and maintained that speaking in tongues was a psychological phenomenon rather than a spiritual one.

In retrospect, religious historians recognized Parham's importance to the development of Pentecostalism. Many of the individuals who would become leading figures in the movement received their baptism and education in Parham's ministry. Loyal followers, who remained staunch in their support, downplayed his alleged anti-Semitism by pointing to the love he demonstrated later in his life for Israel and the Jewish people. In 1927, two years before he died, Parham even made a trip to Palestine.

Parham died in his home in Baxter Springs, Kansas, sometime in 1929. The date of his death is not certain. After his death, the Charles F. Parham Center for Pentecostal-Charismatic Studies, an independent research facility at South Texas Bible Institute in Houston, was established. The Center maintains an extensive special library, conducts research projects, and presents public symposiums and other events. Just as Parham was throughout his ministry, the center is non-demoninational and strives to serve all churches.

Online

"Charles Fox Parham," *History and Times of the Kingdom,* http://www.fwselijah.com/Parham.htm (March 15, 2003).

"Charles Fox Parham," *World Shakers,* http://www.prophetic resources.web.id/Revivalist/WorldShakers/Charles FoxParham.htm (March 15, 2003).

Longman, Robert, "Azusa Street Timeline," *Spirithome.com,* www.spirithome.com/histpen1.html (March 15, 2003).

McGee, Gary B., "Tongues, the Bible Evidence: The Revival Legacy of Charles F. Parham," *Assemblies of God USA,* http://www.ag.org/enrichmentjournal/199903/068_tongues .cfm (March 15, 2003).

Olsen, Ted, "American Pentecost," *Christian History,* www .christianityonline.com/christianhistory/58H/58H010.html (March 15, 2003).

"Parham Center," *South Texas Bible Institute,* http://www.stbi .edu/cfp_intro.html (March 15, 2003).

"Sins of the Father—Charles F. Parham," *Seek God,* http://www .seekgod.ca/fatherparham.htm (March 15, 2003).

Trillin, Tricia, "The New Thing," *Cross + Word,* http://www .banner.org.uk/res/newthingappx.html (March 15, 2003). □

Lucy González Parsons

A multidimensional pioneer, Lucy González Parsons (1853–1942) not only was one of the first minority activists to associate openly with left radical social movements, she emerged as a leader in organizations primarily composed of white males. In her associations with anarchist, socialist, and communist organizations, González Parsons took up the causes of workers, women, and minorities, as well as the homeless and unemployed.

González Parsons's origins are shrouded in mystery. Much of the mystery is due to her own conflicting accounts of her place of birth, name, date of marriage, and national origins. The best record dating her birth indicates sometime in March of 1853, and her birthplace was probably on a plantation in Hill County, Texas. She publicly denied her African ancestry and claimed only a Native American and Mexican mixed heritage. According to Carolyn Ashbaugh in *Lucy Parsons, American Revolutionary,* however, there is a very strong probability that she was born a slave, and there is historical evidence that she lived with a former slave of African descent, Oliver Gathing, before her union with Albert Parsons in 1871.

Albert Parsons, a confederate soldier in his youth, was a radical Republican and was the subject of violent mob attacks both as a result of his politics and his marriage to a woman of darker hue. (Albert Parsons was white.) Texas's hostile environment as a Ku Klux Klan stronghold made the couple's departure imperative, and in 1873 they took up residence in Chicago.

Experienced Chicago Labor Unrest

Albert and Lucy Parsons arrived in Chicago during a period stamped by an economic crisis and intense labor unrest. The clashes between workers, whose material conditions had eroded drastically, and capitalists, who had enlisted armed support, were daily public encounters. Albert Parsons was a printer by trade, and the couple made their home in a poor working class community. Living among Chicago's impoverished yet militant workers was the catalyst for the Parsons' political transformation from radical Republicanism to radical labor movement activism. The Parsons had two children: Albert Richard, born in 1879, and Lula Eda, born in 1881. Lula Eda died in 1889 from lympodenomia.

Their initial association with the political left was through the Social Democratic Party and the First International, founded by Karl Marx and Frederick Engels. It was through this contact that the Parsons became aware of the socialist ideology of Marxism. Their ties to these groups, however, were short-lived, since both organizations were disbanded in 1876, the year the Parsons became affiliated. In the wake of the dissolution of the Social Democratic Party and the First International, they joined the Workingmen's Party of the United States.

Minority Socialists Emerged

The Chicago chapter of the Workingmen's Party (WPUSA) held many of its meetings in the Parsons' home. Albert, as a representative of the WPUSA, vied in the 1877 local elections for ward alderman. The year 1877 was a crucial turning point in the history of the United States. It marked the end of the Reconstruction era and the start of the first general strike ever witnessed in this country, the great railroad strike of 1877. While the WPUSA did not start the strike, it was the most active political party to lend organized support to it. It attempted to infuse the strike with socialist propaganda. Out of the strike and the political womb of the WPUSA were born the first minority socialists in the United States, Lucy González Parsons and Peter H. Clark. Clark had joined the Workingmen's Party in March of 1877 and was affiliated with the Cincinnati branch.

While the party's work around the strike had considerably enhanced its visibility and membership roll, a political division resulted in the formation of a new party in December of 1877, the Socialistic Labor Party (SLP). (In 1892, the name became the Socialist Labor Party.) The SLP organ, the *Socialist*, became a means for González Parsons to express her views on the struggles of the working class. In addition to poems, she penned articles denouncing the capitalist class and describing the plight of the workers. González Parsons combined writing for the *Socialist*, speaking for the Working Women's Union, and motherhood. The Working Women's Union, founded some time in the mid-1870s, pressed women's issues before the SLP and demanded women's suffrage as a party platform item, as well as equal pay for men and women.

By the early 1880s, both González Parsons and Peter H. Clark had left the SLP. Clark departed due to the neglect of a specific program addressing the issue of black people, while González Parsons left to join the International Working People's Association (IWPA). The IWPA was an anarchist organization; it called for the abolition of the state, cooperative production, and autonomy of workers through voluntary association. The foremost problem of the SLP, in González Parsons's view, was its reformism; that is, its peaceful approach to transforming capitalist social relations.

Advocated Violent Overthrow of Capitalism

The IWPA was open to all methods that would lead to the overthrow of capitalism. According to Carolyn Ashbaugh, González Parsons stated: "Let every dirty, lousy tramp arm himself with a revolver or knife on the steps of the palace of the rich and stab or shoot their owners as they come out. Let us kill them without mercy, and let it be a war of extermination and without pity." González Parsons had no illusions about the peaceful transfer of power, nor any belief in the peaceful coexistence of capitalism and labor. However, she did cling to one of the SLP's illusions, that racism would immediately be eradicated in class struggle. The SLP believed further that the origin of racist violence was not in racism, but in the dependency of minorities as workers.

Though González Parsons belittled the complexity of the relationship of racism to capitalism, she, unlike most minority leaders in 1886, called for armed resistance. According to Foner, she made the point, "You are not absolutely defenseless. For the torch of the incendiary, which has been known with impunity, cannot be wrested from you."

This statement is most revolutionary and radical, especially when placed in the context of minority political leadership. For example, the year 1886 was the high tide of Booker T. Washington's accommodationist posture. On May 1, 1886, González Parsons was a key leader in the strike at Haymarket Square, Chicago, for an eight-hour work day. The strike ultimately resulted in a bombing and the arrest of Albert Parsons and seven other activists. Lucy González Parsons attempted to rally a defense of the "Haymarket Eight" and made over 40 speeches in a tour of 17 states as part of this effort. In 1887, however, Albert Parsons was executed, along with three of his comrades.

González Parsons Founded Newspaper

The added tragedy of the death of her daughter shortly following her husband's execution did not discourage González Parsons's involvement in radical politics. In 1892 she started her paper, *Freedom*, which covered such issues as lynching and peonage of black sharecroppers. By 1905, she became a founding member of the Industrial Workers of the World (IWW). The IWW's political line espoused the independence of trade unions and their control of the wealth and power. González Parsons insisted that women, Mexican migrant workers, other minorities, and even the unemployed, be full and equal members of the IWW. She also worked closely with William "Big Bill" Haywood and Elizabeth "The Rebel Girl" Gurly Flynn, both of whom later joined the Communist Party.

Organizing the homeless and unemployed, González Parsons led significant battles in San Francisco in 1914 and Chicago in 1915. The cause of political prisoners became a central focus for her in the 1920s and she joined the International Defense Fund. She was involved in the cases of Tom Mooney, the trade unionist, the "Scottsboro Boys," and Angelo Herndon. She was elected to serve on the national committee of the ILD in 1927. In 1939, she became a member of the Communist Party.

In 1942 González Parsons died in a fire in her home, which was subsequently ransacked by government authorities. Papers, books, and other sources that captured the long life of a veteran of the political movements of the left were removed. Lucy González Parsons's legacy was preserved, however, by the younger members of the Communist Party, for whom she had been a source of knowledge, experience, and political wisdom.

Books

Ashbaugh, Carolyn, *Lucy Parsons, American Revolutionary,* Charles H. Kerr Publishing Company, 1976.

Foner, Philip S., *American Socialism and Black Americans,* Greenwood Press, 1977.

Hine, Darlene Clark, ed., *Black Women in America,* Carlson Publishing, 1993.

Katz, William L., *The Black West,* Open Hand Publishing, 1987.

Parsons, Lucy, ed., *Famous Speeches of the Eight Chicago Anarchists,* Arno Press and the New York Times, 1969.

Salem, Dorothy, ed., *African American Women: A Biographical Dictionary,* Garland, 1993. □

Arvo Pärt

Arvo Pärt (born 1935) was a prolific modern composer whose works were noted for their minimalism and deep spirituality. He composed works for full orchestra and chamber groups as well as choral and keyboard pieces. His work was performed in concert halls and incorporated into religious observances.

Began Career in Radio

Pärt was born on September 11, 1935, in Paide, Estonia, and was raised in Tallinn, the Estonian capital. He worked for Estonian Radio in Tallinn from 1957 until 1967 as a sound director. He also composed music for film and television for the Estonian network. His radio work had an unexpected influence on his approach to composition. In a 1998 interview in the Estonian newspaper *Postimees,* Pärt said: "The high end of audio techniques, which comes from having a high quality apparatus, drove me to the opposite extreme. To music's being, because audio cosmetics do not speak of substance. Music's substance is the interaction between two, three or four notes. The first steps, the changes which occur between these notes. For this you don't need sound techniques, you don't require a Steinway. This comes from the human voice, it begins with the most primitive instrument. I am not against the progress of audio techniques but you shouldn't overestimate their importance."

While at the Tallinn Conservatory, he studied composition with Heino Eller. He graduated in 1963. Pärt won first prizes in the 1962 All-Union Young Composers' Competi-

tion in Moscow for a children's cantata and an oratoria. He also worked with twelve-tone structure and other experimental forms.

Interest in Early Music

Pärt was first associated with mainstream modernist and avant-garde composition. He particularly explored serial composition, in works such as the orchestral piece "Nekrolog" (1960–1961) and many others up through "Credo" (1968).

Pärt interrupted his career for several years in the 1970s, choosing to study medieval and Renaissance music rather than to focus on his own music. In particular, he examined early chants and polyphony. About this same time, he converted to the Russian Orthodox faith. The only two pieces he wrote during this period were Symphony No. 3, written in 1971, and a cantata composed in 1972.

Pärt resumed composing in 1976. *Opera News* observed that after his hiatus, "his work has reflected that study, combining elements of early music, Eastern Orthodox spirituality and a search for unity through pristine beauty and simplicity." Because his music was so experimental and his newer works were concerned with religious ideas, his music was "not recommended" for performance during the 1970s by officials of the Soviet Union, of which Estonia was a member. Estonian student musicians and professionals continued performing Pärt's works in secret. In 1980, Pärt and his wife left Estonia, first moving to Israel and then to Austria, where he became a naturalized citizen.

"Holy Minimalism"

Pärt was most frequently compared to his contemporaries Henryk Gorecki, a Polish composer of works such as Third Symphony, Op. 36, "Symphony of Sorrowful Songs" (1976), and John Tavener, a British composer. Their genre was dubbed "holy minimalism." Terry Teachout wrote in *Commentary* in 1995: "There is no commonly accepted term for this style, though it is sometimes referred to as 'European mysticism' or 'holy minimalism.' ... All three men are intensely religious, are associated with orthodox faiths, and write both secular scores and music intended for liturgical usage; all three use repetition in a manner broadly reminiscent of the American minimalists."

Pärt's music was built on the successes of popular avant-garde minimalist composers such as Philip Glass and Steve Reich. Teachout said "the long road away from Schoenberg and Cage to Henryk Gorecki was paved in part by the easy-on-the-ear minimalism of Philip Glass and his contemporaries, as well as by the accessible avant-gardism of George Crumb.... It took classical music a full half-century to escape the cul de sac of hermetic modernism and reclaim the usable past of tonality."

Pärt called his musical approach tintinnabuli. Jeffers Engelhardt, writing in *Notes* in 2001, explained it as "an onomatopoeic term recalling liturgical bells. As a musical language, tintinnabuli is concerned with three essential elements: the triad, the linear melodic line, and silence. As a compositional process, tintinnabuli unites these elements with a sacred text in a manner that is at once systematic and deeply symbolic. . . . What emerges is a constellation of word and tone ranging from the austere to the playful.'' According to Engelhardt, the best examples of such works by Pärt were ''Zwei slawische Psalmen (1984),'' a piece using Psalms 117 and 131, sung in Church Slavonic, and ''Te Deum'' (1984–1985; rev. 1992).

The Sound of Silence

Another telling characteristic of Pärt's work was his use of silence within music. In a 1998 interview with Daniel Zwerdling on National Public Radio, Pärt, through an interpreter, referred to those silences as ''intervals,'' which he said ''take up a life of their own when the whole piece is being played in a cathedral. In my music, there is no difference concerning the importance between the musical parts and the parts with the silences. I would even go as far as to say that the silences become a very special life and a very special importance of their own. The score is written in a way that makes it necessary to have the silences for the overtones to create a new layer that vibrates during the silence parts.''

Pärt was usually silent himself, rarely submitting to interviews. And when he did, he seemed evasive, even shy, in answering questions about his works and their meaning. He said he disliked talking and preferred silence. During a press conference, Brian Hunt of the *Daily Telegraph* said he came to see Pärt's seeming evasiveness as ''a complete misunderstanding. He does not want to say anything without meaning; he does not want to manufacture answers simply to satisfy a questioner; he does not want words to obscure truths which only music can express.''

Pärt said in the 1998 interview in *Postimees* that it was difficult to use language to describe his music: ''There are as many different ways of perception as there are listeners and all of them are justified. From the perception to the words, however, there is a great loss when music is being written about. . . . You can write about your impressions, the music's structure, its form and perhaps something else. It is much more difficult to put music itself into words. I think that this truth, that exists in art and music, causes a resonance in a person somewhere deep and secret. When they themselves have a need to feel the truth and a gift for the cognition of the truth. Music remains music and a word is still a word. They can very freely and peaceably coexist.''

Pärt frequently based his work on passages from the Bible such as the Psalms or New Testament, while other pieces used religious texts such as the prayers of St. John Chrysostom or church liturgies such as the Russian Orthodox Canon of Repentance. Examples of the latter include ''Memento'' (1994) and ''Kanon Pokajonen'' (1997). Many of Pärt's works were recorded by the Estonian Philharmonic Chamber Choir and the Tallinn Chamber Orchestra.

Difficulty in Simplicity

Tom Manoff, music critic for the National Public Radio program ''All Things Considered,'' observed that Pärt was a ''kind, often funny man. Pärt can communicate the most profound sentiment without solemnity. . . . Pärt's music may strike the listener as sometimes sparse, but this apparent simplicity does not make for easy performance. His often transparent collage of sound in which an instrument or a voice may suddenly enter and then disappear makes his music difficult to perform.''

Pärt said the act of composition is different for each artist, but it is always difficult. He said in the *Postimees* interview: ''I believe that a true artist [is] always faced with the situation of making a sacrificial choice. . . . Behind the sacrifice is love. Universal love.'' In the same interview, Pärt said his commercial compositions helped him only in ''getting money for a sandwich. It doesn't help me in any other way.''

Critics Divided

Though many contemporary critics found Pärt's compositions accessible, others thought his work too minimal. In a 2000 *Opera News* review of Pärt's ''I Am the True Vine,'' a piece originally commissioned for the nine hundredth anniversary of the Norwich Cathedral, the anonymous reviewer wrote: ''I appreciate this music, respect it and am even moved at times by its plain beauty and its holy treatment of its ancient liturgical texts; I understand how it differs from minimalism and from New Age. Still, in the end, stasis is stasis is stasis.''

''The music of Arvo Pärt can be somewhat polarizing,'' observed Rick Anderson in a 2002 review in *Notes* about Pärt's ''Johannes-Passion,'' a recording of a choral piece based on the Passion According to St. John. ''While many find the emotional intensity and spirituality of his compositions inspiring and uplifting, others react with less enthusiasm to the relatively static harmonic movement and lack of thematic development that typify his work.''

Will Hermes flippantly pointed out in a 1998 *Entertainment Weekly* review of ''Kanon Pokajanen'' that Pärt was ''championed by Bjork, Michael Stipe, and discerning candle merchants worldwide'' but called the recording ''a landmark a cappella choral work of brooding majesty based on the Russian Orthodox canon of repentance. Ambient-music fans may be a bit overwhelmed. But enter its exquisite polyphony and Christian pathology, and you will be utterly transported.''

Pärt contended in the 1998 interview that he had no favorite composition: ''All the compositions are like my own children. It is not necessarily so that the healthiest or most beautiful child is the most precious. Some piece which has not succeeded and which may never be finished may still be the closest to one's heart.''

Books

Baker's Biographical Dictionary of Musicians, Centennial Edition, Schirmer, 2001.
The New Grove Dictionary of Music and Musicians, Grove Press, 1980.

Periodicals

Commentary, April 1995.
The Daily Telegraph, November 1, 1997.
Entertainment Weekly, September 11, 1998.
Notes, June 2001; March 2002.

Opera News, July 2000.
Washington Post, May 12, 2000.

Other

"All Things Considered," National Public Radio, July 6, 1994; December 13, 1998.
David Pinkerton's Arvo Pärt Information Archive, http://www .arvopart.org (February 28, 2003). □

Paul V

Pope Paul V (1550–1621) served as leader of the Roman Catholic Church for almost 16 years (1605–1621). Educated as a lawyer, he was a renowned expert on canon law. As pope, he often mediated political conflicts and sometimes was at the center of disputes, such as one with Venice in 1606 that almost escalated into a war. One of his major accomplishments was completing the construction of the Vatican. He was most famous for clashing with Galileo, forbidding him to publicly support the Copernican theory of the universe.

Early Life and Career

Pope Paul V was born as Camillo Borghese in Rome, Italy, on September 17, 1550. He was a descendent of an influential noble family of Siena. Family members claimed they were related to Saint Catherine, the great mystic. Paul V studied philosophy and law at Perugia and Padua and became an expert canon lawyer. In 1588 he was sent by Pope Sixtus V to Bologna as vice-legate.

His rise through the ecclesiastical ranks was slow but steady. In 1596, he was made cardinal and vicar of Rome by Pope Clement VIII. Paul V became known for showing no favoritism to any particular faction. Politically, that was a liability.

Assumed Papacy

When Pope Leo XI died on May 8, 1605, Borghese was one of several candidates to succeed him. The others included Cardinals Baronius and Robert Bellarmine. Paul V's neutral stance toward the Church and society seemed to make him the logical choice. Still, some cardinals favored Cardinal Toschi of Modena. However, Cardinal Baronius said Toschi's lack of education and eloquence would be detrimental to the church. Thirty-two cardinals declared for Baronius. However, Paul V's neutrality made him more acceptable, and he was named Pope on May 16, 1605, becoming Pope Paul V when he was 55 years old.

When he took the reins of the church, he was under no obligation to anyone, and he refused to dispense any special favors. In one of his first acts, he ordered all bishops in Rome to return to their dioceses. He also saw it as his duty to ensure that every right earned by his predecessors was not violated. When he became pope, he immediately sought to restore any such privileges that had been taken away.

The new pope was described as vigorous and youthful for his age. His tall, commanding presence and his dignified bearing made him a charismatic figure, and he gained the respect and admiration of the people. But Paul was criticized for nepotism. It was said that he dispensed favors on his relatives and that he made the Borghese family wealthy while he was pope. However, many popes before him had done similar things.

Paul's reign as pope lasted nearly 16 years. He served from May 16, 1605, until his death on January 28, 1621. During his reign, he canonized St. Charles Borromeo and St. Frances of Rome. He also beatified Sts. Ignatius Loyola, Francis Xavier, Philip Neri, Theresa the Carmelite, Louis Bertrand, Thomas of Villanova, and Isidore of Madrid. Beatification is the last step toward canonization.

Uncompromising Leader

As in his previous positions, Paul V proved to be uncompromising. He enforced rules strictly, contributing to a number of disputes with various states. The dispute with the city of Venice in 1606 was the most serious, almost leading to a war throughout Europe. The controversy involved matters of ecclesiastical jurisdiction and relations between church and state.

There were two major issues. First, Venice defied church law that forbade the erection of new church buildings. Second, it arrested two clerics: Scipio Saraceni, canon of Vicenza, and Brandolino Valmarino, abbot of Narvesa. The oligarchs of the city wanted to put the clerics on trial in a secular rather than an ecclesiastical court. The two men were accused of crimes that included rape and homicide. When they were tried and imprisoned without notification to the Roman court, Paul protested. A staunch defender of ecclesiastical immunities, Pope Paul ordered his nephew, Horace Mattis, to secure the release of the imprisoned clerics. Paul intervened himself on their behalf with the Venetian ambassador in Rome. However, Venice denied the request, refusing to excuse the clerics from the jurisdiction of the civil courts.

Paul then demanded that Venice repeal its anti-clerical ordinances and further insisted the clerics be released from prison and given over to the ecclesiastical court. Venice refused to acknowledge his authority in the matter and Paul responded by placing the city under interdict that forbade services. The Venetian government defied the interdict by ordering priests to go ahead with church services. Some clerics refused, and they were expelled from the city. However, many other clerics sided with the city. Venice countered by expelling any papal representatives who tried to enforce Paul's ruling.

The dispute grew quite harsh and almost developed into a war. Paul even tried to raise an army, but he backed down when England and Holland threatened to intervene on behalf of Venice. The dispute then became a war of words. Cardinals Baronius and Bellarmine stated the case for the church, while Paolo Sarpi, a Servite who was a sworn enemy of the Roman Court, attacked the pope.

Finally, in 1607, King Henry IV of France mediated and settled the matter peacefully. However, it turned out to be a victory for Venice. The city ceded very little and the Pope released it from censure. Still, Paul was extremely grateful to Henry IV for his intervention, and he would develop affection for the king. When Henry IV was assassinated in May of 1610 by a fanatic, Paul was deeply saddened and experienced a period of intense depression.

Paul V also had a dispute with King James of England. At issue was a new oath of allegiance required by the king. Paul felt the oath contained some clauses that would be impossible for Catholics, in good conscience, to accept. Paul wrote a friendly letter to the king in July of 1606, first congratulating him on his accession to the throne and then asking him to revise the oath. (Essentially the oath required that Catholics be loyal to the king above all else.) Paul condemned the oath twice in written briefs, first in September 1606 and then in August 1607. The matter was serious enough to create division among Catholics in England.

Sometimes, during his reign, Paul himself was called upon to act as a mediator. The best example is when he helped establish a pace between France and Spain. He also settled disputes involving the Emperor Rudolph II and the Archduke Matthias.

Opposed Galileo's Theories

Perhaps Paul's most historically significant dispute involved a matter of science rather than the affairs of nations.

At issue were beliefs advanced by the famous scientist Galileo. Paul opposed Galileo's opinions about the Copernican theory of the universe, which clerics tended to view as heresy.

In the late 15th century, Galileo came to accept the Copernican model of the universe, which states that the Sun is the center of the universe and that the earth experiences annual motion. In the early 16th century, he began experimenting with telescopes and made some important discoveries that supported the theory, including the moons of Jupiter, Saturn's rings, and the phases of Venus. He also began observing sunspots. In 1611, Cardinal Bellarmine asked Jesuit mathematicians to confirm Galileo's discoveries. Even though they did, they offered different interpretations for the discoveries. In 1613, clerics started attacking the Copernican theory. Two years later, Cardinal Bellarmine told contemporary scientists to treat Copernican views only as a theory. Meanwhile, a Dominican friar, Niccolo Lorini, who had earlier criticized Galileo's view in private conversations, filed a written complaint with the Roman Inquisition against Galileo's views. Galileo wrote to Rome to defend his beliefs about the Copernican theory.

In 1616, a committee of advisors to the Roman Inquisition declared that the Copernican model of the universe was heresy. Galileo would even visit Roman to defend the theory. About Galileo's visits, Guicciardini, ambassador from the Grand Duke of Tuscany, wrote that, "Galileo insisted on obtaining from the pope and the Holy Office a declaration that the system of Copernicus was founded on the Scriptures. He haunted the antechambers of the court and the palaces of the cardinals; he composed memorial after memorial. Galileo thought more of his own opinions than of those of his friends. After having persecuted and wearied many other cardinals, he at length won over Cardinal Orsini. The latter, with more warmth than prudence, urged His Holiness to favor the wishes of Galileo. The pope, tiring of the conversation, broke it off. Galileo carried into all these proceedings an extreme heat, which he had neither the strength nor the prudence to control. He might throw us all into great embarrassment, and I cannot see what he is likely to gain by a longer stay here."

Paul then told Cardinal Bellarmine to order Galileo not to advocate the Copernican theory. Specifically, the cardinal told the scientist not to hold, teach, or defend the theory. At the same time, however, both the pope and cardinal assured Galileo that he would not be put on trial or condemned by the Roman Inquisition. But, in 1633 Galileo was interrogated by the Inquisition for 18 days. In April of that year, he admitted that he might have stated his case too strongly. He even offered to refute the theory in a book. Paul was not impressed with either the admittance or the offer; he decided that Galileo should be imprisoned for an indefinite period of time. The Inquisition sentenced him to prison and religious penances. Later, at a ceremony at the church of Santa Maria Sofia Minerva, Galileo disavowed his acceptance of his previous beliefs, and he was placed in house arrest in Sienna, where he remained until 1642. (More than 300 years later, in 1983, the Church finally admitted that Galileo might have been right.)

Completing the Vactican

During his papacy, Paul V demonstrated a great love of art. A patron of artists, he commissioned Carlo Maderna to finalize the construction of the Vatican. The Basilica, which had been initiated by Julius II, was not yet complete. As part of the completion project, Paul ordered the construction of some chapels, the choir, the lower portico, a church, and the upper portico for the papal benediction.

During his Papacy, Paul also ordered new institutes for education and charity. He claimed that the increased construction provided two advantages: not only did it improve Rome, it also provided employment for artists and craftsmen who needed the work.

Died in Rome

Paul V died of a stroke on January 28, 1621, in Rome. He was 70 years old. He was pope for fifteen years, seven months, and thirteen days. He was succeeded by Pope Gregory XV. His remains were interred in the Vatican, in the Borghese chapel in St. Mary Major's, where his monument was erected.

Online

"Paul V," *The Columbia Encyclopedia,* Columbia University Press, http://www.bartleby.com/65/pa/Paul5.html (March 15, 2003).

"Paul V," *Defending the Faith,* http://www.cfpeople.org/Books/Pope/POPEp231.htm (March 15, 2003).

"Paul V," *The Papal Library,* http://papal-library.saint-mike.org/PaulV/Biography.html (March 15, 2003).

"Pope Paul V," *New Advent,* http://www.newadvent.org/cathen/11581b.htm (March 15, 2003).

"Pope Paul V," *Slider.com,* http://www.slider.com/enc/40000/Paul_V_pope.htm (March 15, 2003).

"Pope Paul V," *Wikipedia, the Free Encyclopedia,* http://www.wikipedia.org/wiki/Pope_Paul_V (March 15, 2003).

"The Trial of Galileo," *Famous Trials,* http://www.law.umkc.edu/faculty/projects/ftrials/galileo/galileochronology.html (March 15, 2003).

Wudka, Jose, "Galileo and the Inquisition," *Phyun5.edu,* http://phyun5.ucr.edu/~wudka/Physics7/Notes_www/node52.html (March 15, 2003). □

Paco Peña

Spanish guitarist Paco Peña (born 1942) is known for his continued contributions to and explorations of flamenco music. He has recorded frequently, but appears to be in his element when performing in front of an audience, which could be anywhere throughout the world.

*A*coustic Guitar noted in a 2002 interview that Peña "is known all over the world for the depth and intelligence of his music and for the breadth of his work as a collaborator, composer, and producer. His primary vehicle has always been the flamenco cuadro, a small ensemble including guitar, singers and dancers and his primary focus has always been on flamenco puro, pure flamenco. . . . However, he has never treated flamenco as something to be kept sacrosanct and separate from other forms of music and has shared the bill with everyone from Jimi Hendrix to Joe Pass to Leo Kottke."

Childhood Devoted to Learning Guitar

Peña was born in Cordóba, Spain, in 1942 and grew up in Andalucía. He was one of nine children, one brother and seven sisters included. Peña recalled in that same *Acoustic Guitar* interview that his "mother had a vegetable stall in the market. We lived in a Casa de Vecinos, a house shared by about ten families. We had one very small room upstairs, and one room downstairs. The families lived in various bits of the house and we all shared one toilet and one kitchen," he said. "In that situation, people made their own entertainment, and the kind of entertainment they made was a kind of flamenco or whatever was going on in the popular music of the time. The inclination of any young child was to join in."

Peña explained this music to the *UCLA Daily Bruin,* "Flamenco is similar to the blues. . . . It has a tinge of sadness, an element of fight and rebellion. It is pain and suffering with explosions of great happiness. It is a symbol of Spain."

Peña's brother had begun playing guitar, which prompted him to start playing as well. Peña was not formally tutored in the art of guitar; he learned from his brother or friends and neighbors. He joined in with whomever was playing or singing in the neighborhood for fun. Peña was inspired by other musicians he heard on the radio, namely Elvis Presley and Paul Anka. His desire was to emulate them and other successful musicians.

His only musical education came at age nine, when he joined a rondalla, or folk ensemble. He contends his future successes were directly correlated to his desire and talent, which made others in the community invite him to play or participate in concerts. Peña was playing guitar whenever he could with whomever would ask him to play or accompany them.

Peña told *Acoustic Guitar,* "the thing was to just join in and make mistakes. That's the way you learn flamenco. I don't want to sound sad or dramatic, but I didn't have any money for lessons. I had a friend, about my age, who played guitar in the market square. He had a teacher. He was learning bits from his teacher and I was learning bits from him. You try to absorb what you can."

By some accounts, Peña began his professional career at the age of 12. He was involved in a government program designed to keep the traditions of various folk music and dances in Spain alive. It was during tours throughout Spain, as a part of this program, that he was hired to tour with a flamenco company. Peña was still attending school, but two years later, he was forced to leave school to help the family. He worked for a notary and in a hardware store while continuing to play.

Knowing that he wanted to pursue a career as a flamenco guitarist, he left for Madrid, then played clubs in the Costa Brava. Performers playing in the Costa Brava had a relatively easy life which consisted of playing guitar each night for about an hour-and-a-half. Days were spent meeting women at the beach and eating good food, but that was not enough.

Embarked on Career as Soloist

During a tour, he had been asked to perform a solo, which was atypical within the Spanish flamenco tradition. Peña began to wonder about the possibility of becoming a successful solo performer. In retrospect, he told the *UCLA Daily Bruin* in 1996 that his experience as part of a company left him "disillusioned." He says he "expected people to be perfect, which was stupid, and when I saw that some people were not seeking artistic endeavors, I felt I was wasting my time and decided to play on my own." As for the transition to performing solo, he says it was "all quite by accident."

Peña ultimately moved to London with a flamenco company at the age of 24. Recalling his only solo appearance, the guitarist was tentative about performing alone, but says everything fell into place quickly. "I had a job waiting for me when I arrived. I was the main attraction at Restaurante Antonio in Covent Garden in London. Of course, my intention was to push on. Eventually, a manager saw me and one thing led to another," he told *Acoustic Guitar*. "I was fascinated with the idea of being a professional, of being able to convince [an audience] with what I was doing."

One of his first big performances was at a "guitar in" at London's Royal Festival Hall. Jimi Hendrix was the headlining performer. Peña made his solo debut at Wigmore Hall, also in London. Of that performance, Peña told *Mixdown Monthly* that he was "quite unprepared for the experience of that event. It was very dramatic, because I was quite young, and in a way quite innocent about showbiz and all that."

About this same time, he began learning technique from other guitarists, both classical and flamenco. He ultimately decided he needed to change his playing technique dramatically in order to improve his playing. Among the other players whom he credits as inspiration include Niño Ricardo, Ramón Montoya—who had been long dead, but whose recordings were an important learning tool—, and Sabicas. "I didn't learn directly from them, but everything I played was in a way touched by their music. But it was always trying to be my music," he told *Acoustic Guitar*. "I studied their music, listening to their recordings. I discovered a lot about their personalities through their music, what motivated them, and I fell in love, even more strongly, with their contribution."

Attained Notoriety Abroad and at Home

In 1970, he organized his first flamenco touring company named Flamenco Puro. Since, he has been continually active in creating learning and performing opportunities for those interested in flamenco. He is the founder of a course leading to a degree in flamenco guitar at the Conservatory of

Rotterdam, in which he is still actively involved. Peña founded the International Guitar Festival in Cordóba in 1980. His newest troupe, Paco Peña Flamenco Dance Company has toured throughout the world in various productions, each of which seems to generate critical acclaim for their dance and music fusion.

The Connecticut Classical Guitar Society in announcing a performance called Peña not simply a guitarist and composer, but also "dramatist, producer and artistic mentor" who "embodies both authenticity and innovation in flamenco." For five consecutive years, readers of *American Guitar* magazine voted Peña as "Best Flamenco Guitarist of the Year."

In a 1994 review in *American Record Guide,* William Ellis called Peña "simply the finest flamenco guitarist of his generation: breath-taking technique, passion to spare, and an ear for compositional improvisation few peers can match." Ellis also wrote that although "Paco De Lucia may have the name from his cross-over forays into jazz and pop . . . Peña is the real deal, committed to the purity of cante flamenco." Ironically, it was Peña who was named one of *Billboard* magazine's Top 10 Crossover Artists of 1988.

Peña composes almost all the music he plays. Perhaps his best known work to date is *Misa Flamenco,* a flamenco-styled mass commissioned for a festival of religious music held in Poland. The piece was performed in collaboration with other flamenco artists as well as the renown Choir of the Academy of St. Martin in the Fields, a renowned British choral group, in 1991. It was later seen at the 1992 EXPO in Seville, Spain, then in worldwide performances. In 1997 Peña was given the Oficial de la Cruz de la Orden del Merito Civil by Spain's King Juan Carlos.

Remained True to Flamenco

In a 2002 review of his Paco Peña Dance Company's Voces y Ecos or Voices and Echoes, UK reviewer Nadine Meisner wrote in the *Independent* that the production is "a perfect fusion of flamenco connoisseurship and stage know-how." Of this same show, Sanjoy Roy wrote in *The Guardian* that it "is no picture-postcard tour of gypsy exotica. . . . Instead, it realises Peža's open vision of flamenco's diversity while remaining true to its soul."

Reviewers have also noted with performances such as these by Paco Peña, "the dark soul of flamenco . . . is not just safe but vibrantly alive," Jenny Gilbert commented in the *Independent.* "Despite appearances—the man is small, quiet, and cuts an almost absurdly modest figure hunched over his instrument on stage—the Cordóba-born musician knows just where to locate the [essence] of his native art form."

Peña told *Mixdown Magazine* in 1999 he owns about 20 guitars "because through the years I have gone buying guitars, hoping to find something really good." The one he plays most is a Spanish guitar built by Gerundino that he plays "endlessly, and still enjoy[s] it the most." Many of his instruments are custom-made. Peña prefers an instrument that combines the best of the flamenco style guitar and classical guitar. These have very different sounds and construction. "It's sort of intimate and difficult to explain, but fundamentally what is important is the sound." He goes on to say, "some guitars sing to you, and some may sound very loud but don't have the sweet quality that you want to express."

Life-Long Loves: Musical Collaboration, Travel

Peña has been very frank about his life-long love for playing—or, as he calls it, "linking"—with other performers. He says this linking is a creative recharging and learning process. He has played with a variety of other individuals and groups from a wide variety of backgrounds and musical traditions, including Inti-Illimani, a Chilean group; John Williams; and Peter Gabriel.

Peña makes his home in London, but still has family in Córdoba, where he keeps a second home. He told the *UCLA Daily Bruin* he enjoys touring. "Traveling exposes you to different people from whom you can learn. My travel experiences come back to my music. In fact, everything inspires my musical compositions. Flamenco deals with serious emotions of mankind, and I feel I am in tune with my music in that sense."

Periodicals

American Record Guide, May-June 1994.
Europe Intelligence Wire (From *The Guardian*), October 22, 2002.
Europe Intelligence Wire (From *The Independent*), October 21, 2002.

Online

"Interview with Paco Peña," reposted from *Acoustic Guitar,* May 2000, http://www.mojacarflamenco.com/pacopena.html (January 22, 2003).
"MUSIC: Mixed music and dance troupe to captivate audiences at Wadsworth," *UCLA Daily Bruin,* November 15, 1996, http://www.dailybruin.ucla.edu/db/issues/96/11.15/ae.pena .html (January 27, 2003).
"Paco Peña: Beyond the Frets of Mortal Man," *Mixdown Monthly,* October 6, 1999, http://www.users.bigpond.com/ apertout/Pe%F1a2.htm (January 27, 2003).
"Paco Peña Brings Flamenco Troupe Here," Northwestern University News Release, November 18, 2002, http://www .northwestern.edu/univ-relations/media_relations/releases/ 11_2002/pacopena_text (January 21, 2003).
"Paco Peña Flamenco Dance Company: Paco Peña—Guitarist," Connecticut Classical Guitar Society, http://www.ccgs.org/ concerts02/paco.html (January 27, 2003).
"Paco Peña," Flamenco World website, http://www.flamenco-world.com/autores/resena.sql?idautor=244 (January 21, 2003).
"Well, at least it sounds good. . . ," *Independent UK,* October 20, 2002 http://enjoyment.independent.co.uk/theatre/ reviews/story.jsp?story=344684 (January 27, 2003). □

Arno Allen Penzias

At various times—and sometimes all at once—German-born American scientist Arno Penzias (born 1933) has been a researcher, educator, and busi-

nessman. Because of that, he has often been called a "renaissance man," someone who excels and exerts significant influence in a variety of areas. His most notable accomplishments were scientific—particularly in the field of astronomy—and his pioneering research resulted in him receiving the Nobel Prize in Physics. Working from the home base of Bell Laboratories, where he was employed for 37 years, Penzias would make scientific discoveries that provided new knowledge about the origin of the universe. He also was a prolific author, lecturer, and innovative businessman. As a high-ranking corporate executive, his innovative—indeed revolutionary—management strategies help create new paradigms that greatly influenced the direction of the corporate world in the late 20th and early 21st centuries. He has also been described as an engineer, philosopher, and humanitarian.

Early Life

Arno Allen Penzias was born April 26, 1933, in Munich, Germany, the eldest son of Karl and Justine Eisenreich Penzias. He had one brother, Gunther. His father was a self-employed leather broker. The close-knit, middle-class family lived a rather comfortable life in Adolf Hitler's pre-World War II Germany. However, in 1938, when Penzias was six years old, the Nazis deported Jews of Polish origin, including the Penzias family, to that country. (Penzias's grandfather was born in Poland, so the Nazis refused to recognize the family's German citizenship.) When the family arrived at the border, they were told that that Poland's deadline for accepting immigrants had transpired. The Penzias family was sent back to Germany, a circumstance that most likely saved their lives. According to Penzias, the Polish Jews who had arrived on time were placed in an open enclosure where more than half froze to death.

Once back in Munich, Karl Penzias sought ways to get his family safely out of the country and, hopefully, into the United States. In the first step of their journey, they made it to England. The British government accepted 10,000 Jewish children, including Arno and Gunther, on humanitarian grounds and Penzias's parents later acquired the necessary paperwork to enter the country. Finally, in 1939, the family obtained passage to the United States, leaving on an ocean liner. They arrived in New York City in January 1940.

Growing Up in the United States

Penzias attended public schools in the Bronx. His father found employment as an apartment building superintendent, which provided the family with rent-free housing. Later Karl Penzias worked in a carpenter shop at the Metropolitan Museum of Art while his wife worked in a coat factory, which provided the family with a much-needed second income. As a teenager, Penzias attended Brooklyn Technical High School. After graduation, he attended City College of New York, where he majored in chemical engineering. He graduated in the top 10 percent of his class in 1954. Also during this period, Penzias met and married his wife, Anne. After graduation, Penzias served for two years as a radar officer in the U.S. Army Signal Corps at Fort Devens, Massachusetts. After the army, he applied to Columbia University in the fall of 1956 and got a research assistantship in the Columbia University Radiation Laboratory, which was then involved with microwave physics.

Began Relationship with Bell Labs

In 1956, Penzias enrolled as a graduate student. For his thesis, he was assigned to build a maser amplifier in a radio-astronomy, a device he could then employ in an experiment of his choice. He studied under Charles Townes, a Bell Labs consultant who would later receive the 1964 Nobel Prize in Physics for his invention of the maser and its later advancement, the laser. When Penzias completed his thesis in 1961, he got a temporary job at Bell Labs. Thus began a fruitful association that would last for 37 years. Later, he became a full-time member of the technical staff, conducting research in radio communications (radio astronomy, radio transmission, satellite communications, and radio reception). Employment at the labs provided him with the invaluable opportunity to participate in the groundbreaking, historic Echo and Telstar communications satellite experiments.

The "Big Bang" and Nobel Prize

It was at Bell Labs that Penzias established what would turn out to be a historically significant relationship with Bob Wilson, who was hired as a second radio astronomer by the company in 1963. Together, Penzias and Wilson were soon conducting research in radio astronomy and satellite communications, employing the company's extremely sensitive radio astronomy antenna. In 1965, using this highly sensitive receiving system to study radio emissions from the Milky Way, they discovered a faint signal—a low-level noise—that seemed to permeate all space. When they first discovered the signal, they attributed it to a number of sources including the Milky Way, the sun, the antenna itself, and even pigeon droppings. After eliminating these possibilities, they found—to their astonishment—that it seemed to emanate from outside the Galaxy. Then they realized the source was the entire universe itself. Later, Penzias had an opportunity to discuss the perplexing phenomena with Princeton physicist Robert H. Dicke, who was developing the Big Bang Theory of the universe. When Dicke went to Bell Labs to see for himself, he helped confirm Penzias and Wilson's discovery. Further, and more significantly, Dicke concluded that the two young researchers discovered what he had already predicted in his theory, that a background radiation at 3-degree Kelvin left over from the initial Big Bang would exist throughout the universe.

The existence of this microwave background radiation confirmed Dicke's theory about the creation of the universe. It not only answered the "how" but the "when:" 15 billion years ago. Penzias and Wilson's discovery, scientists would later say, was one of the most important in the history of the world. It was a major breakthrough in understanding the origin of the universe. In 1978, Penzias and Wilson would receive a Nobel Prize in Physics for their discovery.

Career Advancement at Bell Labs

In addition to his astronomical research, Penzias actively engaged in communications work at Bell Labs. In 1972 he became the head of the Radio Physics Research Department. His duties also grew to include administrative responsibilities. In 1976, he was named director of the Radio Research Laboratory.

His research continued producing scientific landmarks. In 1973, Penzias, Wilson, and co-worker Keith Jefferts discovered the existence of deuterium (heavy hydrogen) in outer space, which provided even more information about the birth of the universe. In 1976, he became the first American to receive an honorary doctorate degree in from the Paris Observatory, a 309-year-old institution founded by King Louis XIV. Penzias eventually would receive more than 20 honorary degrees for the work he did during the 1970s. He was often cited for his groundbreaking research in interstellar chemistry—efforts that would result in the discovery of key chemicals existing among the stars. In this research, he employed his own techniques to observe millimeter-wave radio spectra emanating from space, enabling him and his associates to identify carbon monoxide and other simple molecules in the clouds present in the spaces between stars. Their findings included the nuclear composition of the constituent atoms of these molecules, which proved to be remnants of burned-out stars and the raw materials for new ones. The impact these discoveries had on the field of astronomy was enormous.

In 1979, in addition to his other functions, he became head of Bell Labs' Communications Sciences Research Division. Penzias would attribute his enormous success to Bell Labs, which gave him a great deal of freedom as a researcher.

Research Phase of Career Ended

In 1981, his career as a research scientist came to a sudden and unexpected end, thanks to a legal decision. AT&T and the U.S. Department of Justice settled a large antitrust suit by breaking up the Bell System. Because of the situation, Penzias was promoted to Vice-President of Research for the reorganized AT&T, a position he would hold for 15 years. As a result, his interest in astrophysics was soon replaced by an interest in the underlying principles of the creation and effective use of technology in society. This interest resulted in a book, *Ideas and Information,* published in 1989. Essentially, Penzias's message in his book was that computers made wonderful tools but awful role models; that is, if a worker did not want to get replaced by a machine, then they should not act like one.

In 1995, he became vice president and chief scientist of AT&T Bell Laboratories. A year later, in 1996, Bell Labs split from AT&T and became part of Lucent. Despite the merger, Penzias retained his position. In 1997, he retired from Bell after 37 years. After retirement, he continued working as a senior technology advisor and spokesperson for Lucent. In addition, he became involved with the burgeoning venture capital community in California's Silicon Valley, serving as an advisor and board member for several new small and mid-sized companies.

Gained Fame as Writer

Besides his research and business activities, Penzias was a prolific author during his career. He wrote more than 100 scientific papers, two books, two science fiction stories, and many technical and business articles. Because of his two books, he was inducted into the New Jersey Institute of Technology's Literary Hall of Fame. His first book, *Ideas and Information,* received wide acclaim and was translated into most major foreign languages. His second book, *Digital Harmony: Business, Technology and Life After Paperwork,* looked at how new technologies were changing how people worked and lived, and it described how machines could work well together and with their human users.

Innovated Management Strategies

Penzias became almost as well known for his unique research and development management strategies as he did for his scientific discoveries. He would design strategic uses for information systems, and he helped the business world better understand the applications and impact of emerging technologies.

During the managerial phase of his career, he developed new and innovative business strategies that were em-

braced throughout the corporate world. In his later years with Bell Labs, he helped restructure that company and, in the process, developed new business models that helped other companies restructure their own organizations to be more efficient and profitable. Penzias's managerial vision focused on integrating new technologies as well as freeing businesses from the traditional vertically integrated hierarchy. The vision also included increased product development and a stronger focus on customer satisfaction.

He also filed a number of patents including ones for a computer-based transportation system, a doubly-encrypted identity verification system, a participant tracking system for telephone conferences, and fraud prevention techniques for calling cards.

After retiring from the East Coast-based Bell Labs, Penzias relocated to California, offering his technical managerial knowledge to emerging technology-based companies in Silicon Valley. In 1997, he joined New Enterprise Associates, a venture-capital firm that specialized in early-stage investments in information technology and medical-and life-science companies.

Activities

Throughout his long and illustrious career, Penzias became affiliated with more than 25 organizations and academic institutions, including Harvard University, Princeton University, the California Institute of Technology, the University of Pennsylvania, and the State University of New York at Stony Brook. He was elected into many major organizations including memberships in the National Academy of Sciences, the International Union of Radio Science, the National Academy of Engineering, and the International Astronomical Union and fellowships in the American Academy of Arts and Sciences and the American Physical Society. He served on the board of directors for Home Wireless Networks, Fibex Technologies, A.D. Little, Duracell, and Warpspeed Communications. His academic activities also included a visiting membership with the Astrophysical Sciences Department at Princeton University from 1972 to 1982. He also became vice chairman of the Committee of Concerned Scientists, a national organization devoted to working for the political freedom of scientists in politically repressive countries.

Online

"Arno Penzias," *New Enterprise Associates,* http://www.nea.com/Partners/Bios/Menlo/APenziasBio (February 10, 2003).

"Arno Penzias Profile," *Arno Penzias' Homepage,* http://www.bell-labs.com/user/apenzias/profile1.html (February 10, 2003).

"Arno Penzias-Venture Partner," *Fast Company,* http://www.fastcompany.com/ftalk/sanfran/penzias.html (February 10, 2003).

Bishop, Gordon, "Nobel Laureate Arno Penzias Retires After 37 Years at Bell Labs," *Lucent Technologies,* http://www.bell-labs.com/user/feature/archives/penzias (February 10, 2003).

E. Kim, Eugene, "Arno Penzias Gives Keynote," *Dr. Dobb's Journal,* http://www.ddj.com/documents/s = 893/ddj9950d/9950d.htm (February 10, 2003).

Penzias, Arno, "Arno Penzias-Autobiography," *Nobel e-Museum,* http://www.nobel.se/physics/laureates/1978/penzias-autobio.html (February 10, 2003).

"Penzias and Wilson's Discovery is One of the Century's Key Advances," *Lucent Technologies,* http://www.bell-labs.com/project/feature/archives/cosmology (February 10, 2003). □

Oscar Peterson

One of the most admired, though sometimes controversial, pianists in jazz, Oscar Peterson (born 1925) in the post-war era claimed the same sort of status as earlier greats such as James P. Anderson, Art Tatum, Teddy Wilson, Fats Waller, Thelonious Monk, Bud Powell, and Bill Evans. Possibly the most successful artist produced by Canada, he has appeared on well over 200 albums spanning six decades and has won numerous awards, including eight Grammys. During his career he has performed and recorded with, among others, Louis Armstrong, Count Basie, Ella Fitzgerald, Dizzy Gillespie, Duke Ellington, and Charlie Parker.

Peterson came of age during the bebop and swing years of the 1940s. A brute force on the piano, Peterson, similar to his idol Art Tatum, seems to play without strain and with a great command of his instrument. "Oscar told me," said younger pianist Billy Green to Don Heckman of the *Los Angeles Times,* "that the first thing he does when he sits down at the piano is to gauge the key drop—how far the keys on an individual instrument need to be depressed before the hammer hits the strings. He says—and he makes it sound so simple—that once he scopes that out, then he's in complete control of the piano. For the rest of us, of course, there are a lot more steps involved."

However, Peterson's abilities proved both a blessing and a curse. His tendency to play at high speeds and overuse of harmonic complexities have led critics to call his technique too overwhelming at times. Furthermore, according to music historians, Peterson's playing sometimes drowned out expression, leaving the intended musical statement uncommunicated. But perhaps, as many loyalists claim, Peterson just may be too good. And his durability and accomplishments have certainly validated his importance in the history of jazz.

Born with Talent

Oscar Peterson was born on August 15, 1925, in the Canadian city of Montreal, acquiring the musical confidence he exhibits today at an early age. Born with a naturally perfect pitch, he learned to play classical piano from his older sister Daisy, who also taught piano to Montreal pianist Oliver Jones. However, Peterson credits his father with first instilling in him the importance of music. Daniel Peterson, a West-Indian born Canadian Pacific Railroad

porter and amateur musician himself, insisted that each of his five children develop musical skills. In particular, he wanted them to be exposed to music outside the values of the family, unlike the hymns that Peterson's mother (Kathleen Olivia John), a cook and a housekeeper, sang at home.

In 1930, at the age of five, Peterson began on the trumpet and piano, concentrating on the piano alone by seven years of age after a bout with tuberculosis. Although his father was a strict disciplinarian and expected perfection from his children, Peterson says that he remained always his biggest supporter. "He told me, 'If you're going to go out there and be a piano player, don't just be another one be the best.' He always had the belief in me, for which I'm grateful," as quoted by *Maclean's* contributor Nicholas Jennings. Deriving a sense of dedication from his father, Peterson thus practiced from morning until night, taking breaks only for lunch and dinner.

Later, at the age of 14, Peterson studied with Paul de Marky, a renowned Hungarian-born classical pianist. He discovered through de Markey, who, according to Peterson, could mimic Art Tatum exactly, an interest in jazz. Another teacher, Lou Hooper, led Peterson to recognize the importance of the classics, teaching his students to communicate in phrases such as "I have always felt Chopin was looking at a lovely landscape at the time he composed this piece because everything about it is so lush and green-like," recalled Peterson, as quoted by Gene Santoro for the *New York Times.*

Began Professional Career

Also at the age of 14, Peterson's determination as a child resulted in his winning a Canadian Broadcasting Company radio show competition, and before long he was making regular appearances. Then, in 1942, he accepted an invitation to join the Johnny Holmes Orchestra, a popular Canadian jazz ensemble. Afterwards, in the mid-1940s, he formed his first jazz trio and landed a recording contract with the RCA Victor Canada label. By now, he was already known for his masterful, fluid playing technique. Those that visited the Alberta Lounge in Montreal to witness Peterson and his trio perform included Count Basie, Ella Fitzgerald, and other now-legendary figures in jazz.

On one particular night at the club in 1949, American jazz impresario Norman Granz was so impressed with Peterson that he asked the pianist to come to New York City with him as a surprise guest for his Jazz at the Philharmonic (J.A.T.P.) events at Carnegie Hall. At the performance, Peterson shared the stage with the likes of Charlie Parker, Lester Young, and Coleman Hawkins, setting the young musician's international career in motion. Thereafter, he spent much of the early-1950s touring with Philharmonic ensemble, traveling to 41 cities in North America in addition to appearing in Japan, Hong Kong, Australia, and the Philippines. Meanwhile, Granz became one of Peterson's closest friends and manager. His record companies recorded a number of Peterson's recordings, usually teaming the pianist with established artists like Fitzgerald.

The Classic Peterson

For most fans, the classic Oscar Peterson remains his trio organized in 1953, featuring bassist Ray Brown and guitarist Herb Ellis. Although drummerless, Peterson's percussive style left little room for one anyway. The trio's recordings together include 1955's *At Zardis,* 1956's *At the Stratford Shakespearean Festival,* and 1957's *At Concertgebouw.* His next trio, in place by the late-1950s, included Brown and drummer Ed Thigpen, who remained with Peterson until 1965.

When Thigpen replaced Ellis, the group shifted from one in which any instrument could provide melody and harmony to the more standard piano, bass, and drums format. From here forward, Peterson would most often record in a standard trio setting. Some departures include *Oscar Peterson Trio + 1,* with flugelhornist Clark Terry, and the solo outing *Tracks,* both recorded in 1971.

Beginning in the early 1970s, Peterson embarked on a prolific touring and recording career, mostly for the Pablo Records label. Returning briefly to the drummerless trio, he recorded in 1973 *Tracks* and *The Good Life,* both featuring bassist Niels-Henning Orsted Pedersen and guitarist Joe Pass. He also recorded in a number of other settings, from duets with Dizzy Gillespie and Terry to symphony orchestra appearances. Meanwhile, Peterson was growing increasingly popular for his solo concerts, and he was recording during the 1970s and 1980s up to six albums per year.

Other Interests

During the 1990s, Peterson spent less time touring and recording in order to focus more on composing. However, in 1990, he reunited with Brown, Ellis, and drummer Martin Drew for an engagement at New York's Blue Note, which yielded four releases. In these performances, critics praised Peterson's emotional depth and softer playing style.

In 1993, Peterson suffered a stroke that diminished his ability to use his left hand. However, Peterson resolved not to give up performing and recording, initially spending hours in therapy to regain flexibility and control. And, as is often associated with strokes, he had to deal with the psychological trauma. "I still can't do some of the things I used to be able to do with my left hand," he said to Don Heckman for the *Los Angeles Times.* "But I've learned to do more things with my right hand. And I've also moved in a direction that has always been important to me, toward concentrating on sound, toward making sure that each note counts."

In addition to his output on record, Peterson had been the subject of a 1995 video titled *Oscar Peterson: Music in the Key of Oscar,* featuring footage of various concerts, and a 1996 documentary called *Oscar Peterson: The Life of a Legend.* In 2002, the book *A Jazz Odyssey: The Life of Oscar Peterson,* written by the pianist in collaboration with literary scholar and jazz journalist Richard Palmer, was issued. Two years earlier, in July of 2000, Peterson was the subject of an exhibition at the National Library of Canada called "Oscar Peterson: A Jazz Sensation."

Positions held by Peterson, who has 12 honorary degrees, include chancellor at York University, from 1991 until 1994. He also founded the Advanced School of Contemporary Music in Toronto. Peterson lives outside the city with his fourth wife, Celine, and continues his career as a concert pianist, though he knows he will one day make a final performance. "When that happens, there's going to be no fanfare," he told Jennings. "I'm just going to get up from the piano, take my bows, thank my group, and say, 'This is it.' Then I'll close the piano and that will be the last time I play publicly."

Books

Almanac of Famous People, 6th edition, Gale Research, 1998.
Complete Marquis Who's Who, Marquis Who's Who, 2001.
Contemporary Musicians, Volume 11, Gale Research, 1994.

Periodicals

Atlanta Journal-Constitution, October 24, 1997.
Billboard, December 12, 1992; September 7, 1996; April 7, 2001.
Booklist, February 15, 1999; July 2002.
Boston Globe, March 12, 1987.
Commentary, October 2002
Chicago Tribune, August 7, 1994; June 6, 1999; June 14, 1999; September 30, 2002.
Down Beat, March 1993; August 1993; December 1994; August 1995; September 1995; October 1995; July 1996; February 1997; May 1997; September 1997; January 1998; February 1998; March 1998; September 1998; July 1999; September 1999; February 2000; March 2001; February 2002.

Guitar Player, February 1996.
Jet, July 17, 1995.
Library Journal, July 2002.
Los Angeles Times, November 16, 1986; January 6, 1995; June 18, 1995; April 15, 1997; February 27, 1998; August 6, 1998; August 21, 1998; March 21, 1999; August 24, 2001; November 24, 2002.
Maclean's, November 2, 1992; December 28, 1992; June 16, 1997; September 13, 1999; July 24, 2000; September 4, 2000; September 2, 2002.
New York Times, June 29, 1999; July 30, 2001; July 14, 2002.
People, June 23, 1997.
Performing Arts, Autumn 2000.
Publishers Weekly, June 10, 2002.
Saturday Night, September 1995.
USA Today, November 13, 1990.
Wall Street Journal, January 11, 1995.
Washington Post, November 1, 2001. □

Sándor Petöfi

Sándor Petöfi (1823–1849) was the foremost 19th century Hungarian lyricist. He was a master of the Magyar language, the native language of Hungary. His poems celebrated nature, life's joys and sorrows, the Hungarian people, married love, and later in his life, political freedom. Petöfi was a leader in the 1848–1849 Hungarian War of Independence. He died in battle.

Sándor Petöfi was born on January 1, 1823, in the rural community of Kiskörös, Hungary. His father, István Petrovics, was an innkeeper and butcher and his mother Mária Hruz, was the daughter of artisans and peasants. Petöfi had a brother, István, who was two years younger. The family moved to Fâlegyháza when Petöfi was a child and he always considered that city to be his birthplace.

Petöfi was born during a time of renewed national pride in Hungary. By the early 19th century Hungary had endured nearly two centuries of warfare. Its native people, the Magyars, were oppressed and living in poverty under the control of the ruling family of Austria, the Hapsburgs. But a wave of national consciousness swept through the country during the first half of the century. This native pride brought a renewal of the Magyar language, in lieu of Latin and Germany. In the Lowlands where Petöfi grew up, he learned to love the Magyar language and the country's landscape. The poetry for which he became known vividly describes the landscape, villages, animals, birds, and people of the Hungarian Lowlands.

The Petöfi family was considered well-to-do, but when Petöfi was 15, his father's business failed following a flood and an attempt to expand the enterprise. Subsequent business ventures were never as successful as the inn had been.

Petöfi's talent for writing poetry emerged when he was a teenager and at the age of 15, he won first prize for a poem

written in hexameters. From his earliest works, Petöfi's poems were noted for their honesty. In *Hungarian Writers and Literature,* Joseph Remânyi said, ''While it is somewhat difficult to apply strict literary judgment to his first versifying attempts, the honesty of expression was apparent in his formative years. He knew that creative sincerity must be blended with human sincerity.''

Despite his literary talent, Petöfi performed poorly in school, which frustrated his father. Petöfi attended eight schools by the time he was 16. At one point, he attempted to become an actor. Petöfi's father disowned him in 1839, when he was 16, because of his disinterest in school. The rift did not diminish Petöfi's lifelong love for his parents.

Out of frustration, Petöfi enlisted in the Army. He hoped to go to Italy but instead was sent to Graz, Austria, and then to Karlavoc, Croatia. While serving in the Army, Petöfi became ill and was hospitalized. When he was discharged from the Army, he was thin and frail. Petöfi moved to Pest (later a part of Budapest), where he took minor jobs in the National Theater and acted in provincial theaters. These were difficult years for Petöfi who traveled on foot and sometimes slept on park benches.

In 1842, Petöfi submitted four poems to a leading literary periodical *Athenaeum.* Three of the poems were rejected. A fourth, ''Borozó'' (The Wine Bibber), was published. This was a turning point in Petöfi's literary career since it was the first time his poetry earned serious recognition. He continued to struggle as a writer and actor for the next two years. In 1844, at the age of 21, Petöfi was destitute. He's quoted in *Five Hungarian Writers,* by Mervyn Jones: "After a week's painful wandering I reached Pest. I did not know to whom to turn. . . . A desperate courage seized me and I went to one of Hungary's greatest men, with the feeling of a card-player staking all he had left, for life or death. The great man read through my poems; on his enthusiastic recommendation the Circle published them, and I had money and a name."

The great man Petőfi visited was well-known romantic poet Mihály Vörösmarty. He recognized Petőfi's talent and helped him publish a book of poems in 1844. The same year, Vörösmarty helped Petőfi secure a job as assistant editor of a popular periodical, *Pesti Divatlap,* where he translated foreign fiction. He worked for editor Imre Vahot. The work was routine, but it provided a steady income. Shortly after taking this job, he met 15-year-old Csap Etelke. He was very attracted to her and therefore was deeply affected when she died two months later. Feeling depressed and restless, he resigned his assistant editorship, gave Vahot exclusive right to publish his poems, and traveled to northern Hungary. The poems written during the next 12 weeks indicate that the sojourn helped him overcome his despair.

He returned to Pest, where he fell in love with another young woman, Mednyanszky Berta, the daughter of an estate manager. She inspired Petőfi to write a new series of love poems. Petőfi asked Berta's father for her hand in marriage, but he refused. Berta, in fact was not in love with Petőfi. During the next year and a half, Petőfi traveled back and forth between northern Hungary and Pest.

This was one of Petőfi's most prolific periods. He produced a poem almost every other day and his writing matured. His early works included a large proportion of drinking songs. The next period reflected the bitterness he felt. In 1846, his poetry became political; freedom was a frequent theme. In December of 1846, he published a poem in which he associated a struggle for freedom with his own death.

In 1846, Petőfi met Julia Szendrey, the daughter of a member of the landed gentry. They were married a year later, when he was 24 and she was 18. Szendrey's family's opposed the marriage and her father did not attend the wedding. Petőfi's love for his wife inspired many poems about married happiness and love.

A complete edition of Petőfi's poems appeared in 1847. The book sold out almost immediately and his fame grew. He read his poems on stage at the National Theater, where he had once run errands.

For the next year and a half, Petőfi wrote some of his best poems. He also wrote newspaper articles on timely topics, unsuccessfully ran for the National Assembly, and became involved in the Hungarian revolutionary movement. The Hungarian people had been dominated politically, economically, socially, culturally, and demographically in their own country for many years. Encouraged by nationalist revolutions sweeping Europe, Hungarians demanded control of their homeland.

Petőfi became the intellectual leader of the revolutionaries who wanted Hungary to be free from imperialist Austria. In March 1848, Petőfi wrote "National Song," in which he implored Hungarians to rise up for freedom. The poem began:

"Up, Hungarian, your country is calling! Here is the time, now or never! Shall we be slaves or free? This is the question, answer! By the God of the Hungarians we swear, we swear to be slaves no more!"

On March 15, Petőfi read a list of demands of behalf of the revolutionaries and recited "National Song," also known as "Talpra Magyar" or "Rise, Magyar" at a Pest cafâ. Participants seized a printing press and duplicated and distributed the list of demands and the poem. One of the demands was for a free press and "National Song" was the first document printed in Hungary without censorship. Surrounded by a swelling crowd of students, artisans, and peasants, Petőfi stood on the steps of the National Museum and recited his poem, which helped awaken Hungarians to their rights. Initially, it appeared that the revolution would be peaceful, but the Austrians urged the minority groups in Hungary to take up arms against the Magyars. "Rise, Magyar" became the Hungarian's rallying cry during the War of Independence that followed.

With the free press, Petőfi published many previously censored poems in which he lashed out at the monarchy. Petőfi witnessed much of the misery and social injustice that Hungarians endured and the poems he wrote during the revolution are filled with anger. Although his political poems were inspired by the Hungarian fight for independence, they have a universal perspective and are appreciated by all people fighting for freedom. When the war advanced, Petőfi volunteered for the military. Shortly after he enlisted, Julia gave birth to a son, Zoltán.

Petőfi served as a major in the National Army in Debrecen and later in Transylvania. In Transylvania, he was an aide-de-camp to General Ben, who tried to keep Petőfi away from danger zones. Ben also attempted to buffer the clashes Petőfi had with the higher military authorities. At one point, Petőfi resigned after being punished for insubordination. In 1849, a typhus epidemic killed Petőfi's parents.

Petőfi fought in several battles against the Russians, who allied with the Austrians. In July 1849, General Bem attempted a surprise attack on the much larger Russian forces near Segesvár. Petőfi died in this unsuccessful battle. He was last seen alive on July 31, 1849. It's believed that he is buried in a mass grave along with other Hungarian soldiers who died in the battle. He was 26 years old.

Russian intervention helped the Austrians defeat the Hungarians. They continued to struggle for liberty and in 1867, the Austro-Hungarian Compromise granted them limited self-rule. The continued conflicts between ethnic groups in Hungary eventually contributed to World War I, after which Hungary became a part of the Soviet bloc.

Petőfi's poetry continued to gain popularity after his death. By the turn of the century, a million copies of his poems had been sold. No Hungarian poet had ever gained such a following. His lyric poems celebrated nature, everyday life, married love, family life, and patriotism. Petőfi also published narrative and epic poems.

Statues of Petöfi were built throughout Hungary. He was recognized internationally as well. A bust of Petöfi appears in the Cleveland (Ohio) Public Library and in a public garden in Buffalo, New York. In Rimini, Italy, there is a Petöfi street.

Petöfi's poems have been translated into countless languages. He is the subject of numerous books and critical essays by Hungarian writers and scholars. Thirty booklets about Petöfi's life and work were published and titled *Petöfi Könyvtár (Petöfi Library).* In 1896 a complete edition of his works in six volumes was published. Many of his poems have been put to music, resulting in some 510 compositions by 184 composers, including Franz Liszt.

His role in the War of Independence is remembered in Hungary. The events of March 15 are a source of pride and are celebrated every year as a national holiday.

Books

Jones, D. Mervyn, *Five Hungarian Writers,* Clarendon Press, 1966.
Reményi, Joseph, *Hungarian Writers and Literature,* Rutgers University Press, 1964. □

Mark Plotkin

Ethnobotanist Mark Plotkin (born 1955) has, since the 1980s, scoured the tropical rain forests of Central and South America in search of plants with the power to heal. In his quest Plotkin has enlisted the help of the powerful shamans, or witch doctors, of the Amazon region. For Plotkin, the search has been a race against time, as more and more of the rich resources of the tropical rain forest fall to the bulldozers and land-clearing crews feverishly making way for the inexorable march of civilization.

Throughout the world, during the 20th century man's destruction of the tropical rain forest advanced at a frightening pace. According to ethnobotanist Mark Plotkin, 90 percent of the original forest cover was gone on the island of Madagascar by 2000. Matters were even worse in eastern Brazil where 98 percent of the tropical rain forest was destroyed. One area that has remained relatively untouched has been the northeastern corner of the Amazon region, in and around Surinam, and it is there that Plotkin has done much of his research. At the urging of his mentor, the late Richard Evan Schultes, a pioneer ethnobotanist and professor of botany at Harvard University, Plotkin first traveled to the northeastern Amazon in 1977. "I came down to Surinam actually as a gofer," he told an interviewer on the online *Shaman's Apprentice,* "just following around some other biologists, trying to get the lay of the land, and figuring out if this is really for me." To Plotkin, whose research has depended on close cooperation with the native peoples of the rain forest, one of the most alarming phenomena has been the disappearance of the rain forest cultures, which have dropped from sight even faster than the forests themselves.

Intrigued by Dinosaurs as a Boy

Plotkin was born in New Orleans, Louisiana, on May 21, 1955. One of two sons of George (a shoe store owner) and teacher Helene (Tatar) Plotkin, he attended Newman High School, graduating in 1973. Fascinated by nature as a child, he spent most of his free time crawling through nearby swamps, collecting snakes and other wildlife. Like a lot of boys his age, Plotkin was also intrigued by dinosaurs, and credits the discovery that dinosaurs had become extinct with his decision to become an environmentalist.

After graduating from high school, Plotkin enrolled at the University of Pennsylvania in Philadelphia to study biology. Disappointed by the preoccupation with molecular and cellular biology at the school's science department, he dropped out but soon found himself in Cambridge, Massachusetts, working with the herpetology collection at Harvard University's Museum of Comparative Zoology. One of the perks of Plotkin's job at the museum was free tuition for night classes at Harvard. His decision to enroll in a class called "The Botany and Chemistry of Hallucinogenic Plants," taught by Schultes, quite simply changed his life. On the very first night of class, Schultes showed students some slides he had taken on one of his many trips to the Amazon. One slide in particular fascinated Plotkin. It showed three men wearing grass skirts and bark masks. Schultes described the photo's subjects as Yukuna Indians performing a sacred dance under the influence of a hallucinogenic potion, pointing out that the man on the left in the photo had a Harvard degree. "That one slide did it," Plotkin told an interviewer for *Life.* "First of all, the rain forest in the background looked just like the pictures in my old dinosaur books. Second, it was wonderful to think of this straight-laced professor down in the jungle, wildly hallucinating on an Indian psychedelic. Third, I wanted to save the world, and I realized that reptiles couldn't save the world, but plants could."

Determined to become an ethnobotanist, Plotkin threw himself into his studies at Harvard's extension school, earning his bachelor's degree in 1979. Two years later he received a master's degree from Yale University's School of Forestry, then got his Ph.D. from Tufts University in 1989. During his student years Plotkin traveled to the Amazon region and other tropical forests in the Americas whenever he could get away. On one such journey he met Costa Rican conservationist Liliana Madrigal, whom he later married and with whom he has two daughters, Gabrielle and Ann Lauren. The topic of Plotkin's doctoral dissertation was the use of plant-based medicinals among the Tirio tribesmen of Surinam, and he found the rain forests of the country an ideal location for his research due to the presence of not only native tribes but also of "maroons" of African descent as well as several ethnic groups from tropical Asia.

Sought Plants with Medicinal Potential

Since plants had played a vital role in the development of about one-quarter of all existing prescription drugs, Plotkin hoped that with the help of the Amazonian shamans he might be able to uncover still more tropical plants with medicinal potential. He told Christopher Hallowell of *Time* about a 1987 trip to the Venezuelan rain forest to learn more about a hallucinogen he thought might have some medicinal benefits. Deep in the Venezuelan rain forest, an ancient shaman blew a bit of hallucinogenic powder into Plotkin's left nostril. The ethnobotanist reacted immediately, he told Hallowell, feeling as though he "had been hit with a war club." He saw tiny men dancing before his eyes. When he asked the shaman who they were, the old wise man replied, "They are the hekuri, the spirits of the forest." Subsequent research by French scientists has indicated that one of that powder's ingredients—sap from a nutmeg tree—has the potential to fight fungal infections.

On an earlier visit to Surinam in 1982, Plotkin found himself suffering from an annoying fungal infection on both of his elbows. He showed the rash to a Tirio shaman, his host at a tiny village deep in the Amazon rain forest. Without a word, the shaman walked over to a nearby tree and slashed it with a knife. Out oozed a brilliant orange sap, which the shaman smeared on Plotkin's elbows. Within two days the infection had disappeared. It was a pivotal moment for Plotkin. "I had always heard that there were things in the jungle that worked, but I had never experienced them," he told a *People* contributor. "I was stunned and excited." By the early 1990s Plotkin had catalogued more than 300 plants used by Amazonian shamans to treat viruses, skin disease, coughs, colds, and even diabetes. "Rain forests are immense libraries of future drugs and medicines," he explained, pointing out that only 94 plant species are currently being exploited for medicinal purposes. Among the better known plant-derived drugs are quinine, used to treat malaria; digitalis, taken by those with heart conditions; and vinblastine, which has proven useful in the treatment of Hodgkin's disease and Kaposi's sarcoma.

In the late 1980s Plotkin joined the World Wildlife Fund to become its director of plant conservation, a position he held for four years. In 1993 he became a research associate at Harvard's Botanical Museum and also joined Conservation International as vice president for plant conservation. In 1995 Plotkin, along with his wife and Canadian environmentalist Adrian Forsyth, co-founded the Amazon Conservation Team (ACT), an organization dedicated to the preservation of the biological and cultural integrity of the Amazon rain forest. Plotkin serves ACT as its president and also serves as research associate for the Smithsonian Institution's Department of Botany.

Called Attention to Amazonia's Plight

To call the public's attention to the growing plight of Amazonia as well as to the region's treasures, Plotkin wrote several books, the first of which, *Sustainable Harvest and Marketing of Rain Forest Products*, published in 1991, received little notice outside scholarly circles. Two years later, he published the very popular *Tales of a Shaman's Appren-*

tice: An Ethnobotanist Searches for New Medicines in the Amazon Rain Forest. This book, which went through numerous printings, was also published in Dutch, German, Italian, Japanese, and Spanish. Working with illustrator and co-author Lynne Cherry, author of *The Great Kapok Tree,* Plotkin in 1997 turned out a children's version of the best seller. *The Shaman's Apprentice: A Tale of the Amazon Rain Forest* was hailed by *Smithsonian* magazine as an outstanding environmental and natural history title. More recently, Plotkin coauthored *The Killers Within* with *Vanity Fair* staff writer Michael Shnayerson. This 2002 work calls attention to the threats posed by drug-resistant bacteria.

Interviewed by Eleanor Imster for *Earth & Sky.com,* Plotkin was asked to explain the controversy surrounding the search for medicinal plants in the tropical rain forests. "The whole issue of intellectual property rights has come to the fore, as well it should," he noted. "Ethnobotany, or really any type of research in the tropics, was really a 'rape and run' operation. They had information we wanted. They had plants we wanted . . . everything from pineapples to curare. We took advantage of the stuff, and the local people never really benefitted in a big way. So there's been a huge hue and cry about the need to make sure local peoples—and I'm talking about both the indigenous peoples and local governments—would benefit from this type of development of plant resources—as well it should."

Campaigned for Reciprocity

Plotkin remains outspoken in support of measures he believes will ensure that indigenous peoples are compensated for the ways their know-how and native plant species advance the cause of medicine and science. In an interview for *AccessExcellence.org,* he discussed some of the barriers he has experienced in seeking reciprocity for native peoples. "If I go to the pharmaceutical company that is making $100 million per year from rosy periwinkle alkaloids (used for cancer treatment) and say, 'that came from Madagascar, one of the poorest countries in the world, how about giving 1 percent of the proceeds back to Madagascar?,' they will tell me to take a hike. However, if I go to the big pharmaceutical company and say, 'Hey, the market for antivirals is going through the roof, we are looking at hundreds of millions per year. If you will put up some money to help the natives of the Northeast Amazon, money to train local scientists, money for equipment to upgrade labs, and if you will promise a percentage of profits for a trust fund the local people, we can do some great research,' then the company will be more receptive." He pointed out that a number of large pharmaceutical companies have begun doing just that, based on the reciprocity model established by a small company called Shaman Pharmaceuticals.

In the third decade of his career, Plotkin's work goes on. He continues to travel to the rain forests frequently, combing the region's depths in search of plants that hold the promise of a cure. Asked by *Earth & Sky.com* about the importance of preserving our natural environment, Plotkin was passionate in his reply. "People need to learn that the environment is way too important to be left to environmentalists. We all need clear air. We all need clean water. We all need medicines when we get sick. It doesn't matter if you're a Republican or a Democrat or whatever. Everyone everywhere needs these things. Environmentalism is about life on Earth and making it better for everyone.''

Books

Almanac of Famous People, 6th edition, Gale, 1998.
Newsmakers 1994, Issue 4, Gale, 1994.
Notable Scientists: From 1900 to the Present, Gale, 2001.

Periodicals

People, December 6, 1993.
Time, December 14, 1998.
Washington Post Book World, August 25, 2002.

Online

''A Conversation with Mark Plotkin,'' http://www.theshamans apprentice.com/shaminterview1.html (February 16, 2003).
''Earth Day: Ethnobotanist Mark Plotkin,'' *Time.com,* http://www .time.com/time/community/transcripts/2000/042000plotkin .html (April 20, 2000).
''Scientist Profile: Mark J. Plotkin, Ethnobotanist,'' http://www .earthsky.com/edge/profiles/plotkin.html (October, 2002).
''*The Shaman's Apprentice:* Mark Plotkin Talks about Rain Forest Medicines,'' http://www.accessexcellence.org/WN/NM/ plotkin1.html (1996).
Time Warner Bookmark, http://www.twbookmark.com/authors/ 58/2533/ (February 15, 2003). □

Roman Polanski

Polish film director Roman Polanski (born 1933) inundates cinema with black humor, alienated and isolated characters, violence, and suspense. Plagued, yet motivated by a lifetime of personal tragedy, Polanski is a director sympathetic to individuals caught in desperate circumstances, an inherent theme throughout his work. The most significant films of his lengthy and unpredictable career are: *Rosemary's Baby, Repulsion, Chinatown, Tess,* and *The Pianist.*

Holocaust Survivor

Horrific experiences have shaped Polanski's life and worldview. Many of Polanski's films may have been influenced by his intense and tragic childhood experiences during the Nazi Holocaust. Polanski was born in Paris on August 18, 1933. His father was a Jewish man from Poland who married a Russian immigrant, and the family moved back to Poland when Polanski was three.

The Nazis invaded Kraków's Jewish ghetto when Polanski was six years old; his father and a Polish policeman helped him escape before both of his parents were sent to concentration camps. His mother died at Auschwitz, but his father survived at a different camp. Polanski made it through

World War II by hiding with Catholic peasant families and occasionally fending for himself. This did not prevent him from being used once for target practice by the Nazis and from being seriously injured in a war-related explosion. Often he hid in movie theaters to escape attention and seeing all those films under conditions of severe stress shaped his later thinking about the meaning and purpose of cinema. After the war, his father returned and remarried, and Polanski survived another near-tragedy when a serial killer almost made him his next victim, beating him over the head with a rock.

Polanski left home to go to a technical school and then an art school, where he studied film. He began acting in radio and plays in Kraków and made his screen debut with a small part in Andrezj Wajda's *Pokolonie (A Generation),* in 1954. He was accepted that year into the select directors' course at the prestigious Łódź Film School. There, he learned to make stripped-down films with a hand-held camera and few other resources. This training gave his films a spare, simple power.

Polanski was almost expelled from the state-sponsored film school for staging and filming *Rozbijemy Zabawe (Break Up the Dance),* in which he paid hoodlums to crash and disrupt a student party. A similar brand of absurdist humor attracted critics attention in his next short film, *Two Men and a Wardrobe,* which won five international awards. After graduating, Polanski moved to Paris and made another short film, *La Gros et el Maigre,* a dark comic view of a sado-masochistic relationship.

Breakthrough and First Exile

Polanski's first feature film, *Knife in the Water,* a stark psychological thriller about a couple who invite a young hitchhiker about a sailboat and spar with him, won a British Academy Award as the best film of 1962. During the shooting, the lead actress was so unresponsive that Polanski fired a pistol near her ear to get her to react. It's the only feature film Polanski made in Poland. But it was denounced by the ruling Communist Party for showing too many negative features of Polish life.

His funding cut off by the Polish government, Polanski relocated to England after several abortive attempts to escape from behind the Iron Curtain by hiding in the false ceiling of a railcar rest room. His brief marriage to actress Barbara Kwiatkowska (also known as Barbara Lass) in 1959 had already ended in divorce. In England he wrote and directed his classic thriller, *Repulsion,* starring Catherine Deneuve as a woman forced into contemplating murder. Reviews compared it to the work of Alfred Hitchcock, and the film brought Polanski to the attention of critics worldwide as a masterful young maverick. The film was Polanski's personal favorite.

Polanski usually wrote his own screenplays or at least collaborated on them. That was the case on his second film in England, *Cul-de-Sac,* another story about people trapped in doomed relationships. His next effort, *The Fearless Vampire Killers,* or *Pardon Me but Your Teeth Are in My Neck,* was a comic vampire film with dark overtones. It failed to make much of an impact.

Hollywood Success and Tragedy

After establishing himself as an European auteur, Polanski moved to Hollywood. There he made his most popular feature, *Rosemary's Baby,* a classic horror film that paved the way for many cheap imitations in subsequent years by other directors mining the vein of Satanism. Polanski was nominated for an Academy Award for best adapted screenplay for the film, which managed to make mass audiences cringe and critics rave. In this and other films, Polanski made fear and terror palpable mostly through his use of brooding psychological techniques; his films were slow and deliberate, though spiked with sudden outbursts of violence, and he never indulged in cheap shocks.

With the success of *Rosemary's Baby* and his marriage to young actress Sharon Tate, Polanski at age 35 seemed to have the world at his fingertips. Then another tragedy struck. In 1969, Tate, who was pregnant, and three friends were brutally murdered by Charles Manson and his followers in a sensational crime publicized worldwide. Through it all, Polanski somehow continued to work. His next feature, *Macbeth,* released in 1971, was a faithful adaptation of Shakespeare's play, but Polanski drenched the climactic scenes in blood, in an obvious reflection of his own torment over his wife's death.

Polanski continued to take small acting parts, and he usually appeared somewhere in his own movies. In his masterful noir suspense drama, *Chinatown,* released in 1974, Polanski has a cameo as a thug who slices the nose of Jack Nicholson's protagonist, Jake Gittes. The character, a private investigator trying to puzzle out a web of criminal intrigue connected with a political scandal, spends the rest of the film with his nose in a bandage, adding to his absurdity. The nose injury was one of many Polanski touches that helped elevate the celebrated Robert Towne screenplay to a masterpiece. Polanski made the climax of the film more brutal and hopeless than Towne had scripted it. *Chinatown,* which earned Polanski his second Oscar nomination, this time for best director, showcases a mature director at the height of his powers, weaving a spellbinding tale and coaxing great performances out of Nicholson, Faye Dunaway, and John Huston. The film won a British Academy Award and propelled Polanski once again to the front ranks of directors.

Permanent Exile

But again, just as he was at the pinnacle of success, personal troubles would topple Polanski. His follow-up to *Chinatown* disappointed many critics. It was the dour and frightening psychological thriller *The Tenant,* in which the director-writer cast himself in the lead role of a paranoid, nearly insane man whose face looks haunted and guilt-ridden. Bizarre, overwrought, and complete with a gruesome, outrageous ending, *The Tenant,* shot in the same neighborhood where Polanski had lived in Paris, seemed to show that Polanski had not purged himself of his personal demons. Like many of his films, it features a misfit who seems to be losing his moorings.

In 1977, Polanski's Hollywood career imploded when he was arrested for statutory rape. He fled the country rather than face jail time after pleading guilty to charges of having sex with a 13-year-old girl. The famous director entered a long exile, returning to France. There, he suddenly abandoned his customary themes of fear, terror, and alienation and directed a lustrous, serene, intoxicating, old-fashioned love story, *Tess,* based on the Thomas Hardy novel *Tess of the d'Urbervilles.* It starred his newest lover, 17-year-old Nastassia Kinski, but was dedicated to Tate. A critical success though hardly a commercial blockbuster, the 170-minute period romance was the most expensive film ever made to date in France, and it netted Polanski another directorial Oscar nomination.

After *Tess,* however, Polanski found it difficult to get his movie ideas funded and produced. He grew increasingly active as an opera producer, theater director, and actor all over Europe. He directed and starred in an adaptation of *Amadeus* in Warsaw in 1981 and took the show to Paris in 1982. In 1988, he played the lead role in a Paris production of Kafka's *Metamorphosis.* In 1997, Polanski's musical *Dance of the Vampires,* an adaptation of his movie *The Fearless Vampire Killers,* opened in Vienna.

His movie career proceeded in fits and starts. Following the release of *Tess,* seven years passed before he wrote and directed another movie, and that was the uncharacteristically lightweight spoof *Pirates,* a swashbuckling satire starring Walter Matthau in a role Polanski had intended for Nicholson. The film went nowhere and was one of his biggest flops. Next, he directed Harrison Ford in the Hitchcock-like thriller *Frantic,* about a man trapped in an impossible situation in a foreign land—just as Polanski was. It also was disappointing at the box office and among critics.

In 1989, Polanski was in his mid-50s when he married actress Emmanuelle Seigner, who was in her early 20s. Seigner had appeared in *Frantic.* The two had a daughter, Morgane, in 1992.

Polanski, now a permanent exile from Hollywood, continued to take acting roles, mostly in French films, and in 1992 directed *Bitter Moon,* an erotic suspense film that introduced Hugh Grant and included Seigner. Polanski fared a little better among critics, but no better at the box office, with his 1994 film *Death and the Maiden,* an adaptation of an Ariel Dorfman play starring Ben Kingsley and Sigourney Weaver. *Los Angeles Magazine*'s Ivor Davis called it "an intriguing and ambitious tale of torture, brainwashing, revenge and possible false memory."

In 1996, Polanski directed the experimental short film *Gli Angeli,* based on a music album by Vaco Rossi, then returned to mainstream territory with the thriller *The Ninth Gate* in 1999. That film, based on a best-selling Spanish novel about a book collector hunting for an obscure Satanic text, starred Johnny Depp and Seigner. Around the time of the release of *The Ninth Gate,* Polanski told Gary Arnold of the *Washington Times,* "There are stacks of great books I would have loved to film" but added that the circumstances were rarely right. "Sometimes I think I am always living in the wrong time," he concluded.

Repeated attempts to resolve Polanski's legal situation in the United States proved unsuccessful, even though his victim, Samantha Geimer, had gotten what she wanted in a civil suit reportedly settled for $225,000 and said she felt he should be able to return. "I have suffered enough," Polanski told Ivor. And he told the *New Yorker:* "I'd like to be able to return . . . to just be able to work in a normal fashion. I miss the logic and efficiencies of the Hollywood system."

Coming Full Circle

Polanski was in his late 60s when for the first time he made a feature film about the event that had shaped his whole life—the Holocaust. Polanski had toyed with the idea of making a movie about his own experiences, and he had advised Stephen Spielberg on the script for his Holocaust film *Schlinder's List* and even had turned down an offer to direct that film. *The Pianist,* released in 2002 and starring Adrien Brody, won critical acclaim worldwide. The story of a Jewish concert pianist who somehow escapes destruction while the world falls apart around him in Warsaw during World War II, the film has obvious autobiographical overtones even though it is based on pianist Wladyslaw Szpilman's memoirs.

The Pianist, which received the Palm d'Or at the 2002 Cannes Film Festival, marked a triumphant comeback for Polanski. At Cannes, Polanski said he had wanted to make "a neutral, low-key movie about events that speak for themselves," and said the memoirs "helped me recreate the events without talking about myself or people around me." Polanski was nominated for his fifth Academy Award with a best director nomination for *The Pianist* for the 2003 Oscars. Polanski won the Oscar but due to his exile was unable to accept the award in person. Two additional Academy Awards were given for work on *The Pianist:* Brody was recognized as Best Actor and Ronald Harwood won the Oscar for Writing (Adapted Screenplay).

Assessing Polanski's body of work is ultimately a daunting task. Many of his films are demanding, and some are puzzling. But they are almost always intriguing. D. Keith Mano of *People* described Polanski's directorial career as "a hard-to-pigeonhole mixture of obsession, brilliant self-indulgence and honest commercial pragmatism." J.P. Telotte and John McCarty, in an essay in *The St. James Film Directors Encyclopedia,* conclude: "Roman Polanski's importance as a filmmaker hinges upon a uniquely unsettling point of view. All his characters try continually, however clumsily, to connect with other human beings, to break out of their isolation and to free themselves of their alienation." His films, in other words, are a reflection of the struggles of his own difficult life.

Books

Sarris, Andrew, *The St. James Film Directors Encyclopedia,* Visible Ink Press, 1998.
Thomson, David, *A Biographical Dictionary of Film,* Alfred A. Knopf, 1994.

Periodicals

Asia Africa Intelligence Wire, October 21, 2002.
Daily Variety, May 30, 2002; December 19, 2002.
Entertainment Weekly, September 18, 1992; February 3, 1995; April 4, 2003.
Europe Intelligence Wire, October 7, 2002; January 13, 2003.
Los Angeles Magazine, January 1995.
People Weekly, March 5, 1984.
Time, October 13, 1997.
Variety, June 3, 2002.
Washington Times, March 11, 2000; January 3, 2003.

Online

"Roman Polanski," *All Movie Guide,* http://www.allmovie.com (February 7, 2003). □

Sigmar Polke

German artist Sigmar Polke (born 1941) has boldly ventured to creative realms where few have dared to tread. As a result, he has had a great influence on young American artists, especially in the 1980s. With an ironic, mocking sense of humor, he parodied artistic movements early in his career and even created his own style called "Capitalist Realism," which commented on German culture and society. A trailblazer in more ways than one, Polke revolutionized painting in the second half of his career by using non-art materials and chemical sub-

stances to "paint" canvases. These magical and mutable pieces earned Polke the title of "alchemical artist."

Polke was born in Oels, Germany, on February 13, 1941. As a 12-year-old boy, Polke escaped from East to West Berlin in 1953 by faking sleep on a subway car. The formative experience of crossing the border would have a major impact on the content and style of his art in later years. After apprenticing as a glass painter for a brief time, he went on to study at the Dusseldorf Art Academy from 1961 to 1967, where he became deeply influenced by his teacher Joseph Beuys. As Robert Hughes wrote in *Time*, "He seems to have got two big things from Beuys: first, the ides of the artist as clown, shaman and alchemist; second, a healthy reluctance to believe in the final value of categories of style. Hence his early parodies of the sacred modes of Modernism." Polke and two fellow students, Gerhard Richter and Konrad Fischer-Leug, formed a movement of artistic style called "Capitalism Realism," a term they used ironically to refer to the modern art of the West.

1960s: Capitalist Realism and Artistic Parody

Capitalist Realism was the merging of Pop Art style with images emblematic of a postwar German consumer society. Polke, although aware of American Pop art, was not interested in the conventions of graphic design. Rather than trans-

lating graphic advertising images into painted forms, Polke's, Capitalist Realism "was about objects of desire, seen from a distance," as Hughes put it. The artist's main focus in the early years was to portray these objects of desire, and he did so in a flat somewhat unappealing way. The mundane, and often trite objects portrayed in Polke's paintings of the era—cakes, plastic tubs, liverwurst—were represented in a less flashy way than the substance of American Pop, but they possessed a political significance relating to the historical context in which Polke was situated. These objects, common in Polke's current world, were symbolic of the split between East and West Germany, and their presence on canvas called attention to their absence on the Eastern side of the Berlin Wall. Hughes wrote, "The split between East and West, for ordinary Germans, lay along the ruts of consumption rather than the peaks of rhetoric." Works like *Plastik Wannen (Tubs, 1964)*, which uses the plastic wash basins and food containers that were hard to get at the time in Eastern bloc countries as its subject, pokes fun at consumerism, while revealing the reality of a culture still suffering from the deprivations of war. These early works mark a break with the abstract expressionist style that was prevalent in prior years. Polke's paintings mirror life as it is directly experienced through human consciousness.

Whereas Polke's mid-'60s paintings were concerned with plain, immediate, ordinary subjects found in the everyday world, his paintings from the latter part of the decade take up art as their theme, often in a humorous way. Polke responded with a certain sense of irony to American Pop art. His huge raster grids were inspired by Roy Lichenstein's bold Benday dots and Andy Warhol's early use of photographic transfer made its way into his work. Polke's mysterious juxtaposition of disparate images came from James Rosenquist, while Francis Pacabia's late paintings acted as important influences. Polke made fun of conceptual art in *Solutions*, 1967, and he satirized geometric abstraction in *Modern Art*, 1968. The same year, he produced *Higher Beings Command: Paint an Angle!*, a simple "L" drawn in black ink on a piece of notebook paper with the title typed below. His sense of humor is present in this work, for he did it "at a time when art circles in Germany, and the U.S. too, were still given to overheated 'spiritual' rhetoric about the transcendent powers of all sorts of abstract art. . . . As an art joke, it gets close to the mustache on Mona Lisa," Hughes wrote in a 1999 article in *Time*. Polke even suggested the silliness of his work in an installation called *The Fifties*, 1969, for which he placed 12 of his previous pieces over colored trelliswork. The idea was that even his own art had been tritely stylized to fit the times.

Conveyed Layers of Consciousness

In the '70s and '80s Polke brought disparate images together, reflecting poetic and bizarre movements of the mind. The mental states being conveyed were often drug-induced, and the artist masterfully brought the experience of such consciousness to his viewers. Polke took up Francis Picabia's technique of layering images one on top of another, and American artists like David Salle and Julian Schnabel sought to imitate him, while looking to breathe new life into their painting in the midst of Conceptualism.

In pieces like *Alice in Wonderland,* 1971, Polke's work overtly suggests altered states of consciousness and an awareness affected by marijuana. He has painted the scene from Lewis Carroll's story in which Alice talks to the hookah-smoking caterpillar, there are loud printed fabrics on the sides, over which he has painted a phantom white basketball player. As John Caldwell wrote in *Sigmar Polke,* "The artist has succeeded in creating a precise visual analogue of drugged consciousness, just as he did for the consumer goods that fixated much of the 1950s and early 1960s. The painting depicts the experience of watching sports on television after consuming a drug. . . ." Caldwell also said, "Polke's discovery of a way to depict several layers of consciousness at the same time by means of superimposing one or more figural motifs over a ground of printed fabric was one that he would return to repeatedly during the years to come." Again, in 1983 with *Hallucinogen,* Polke gave his viewers a direct experience of the human mind, not by portraying consumer items like cakes and wash bins, but by making on-lookers feel as if they are truly on psychedelic drugs. The artist's process of allowing chance reactions between his compositional materials to determine the look of the painting suggests a great deal about the effect of the art on the viewer. The uncontrolled randomness of the painting, with its patches of deep purple and clouds of dark, unidentifiable matter makes it both a groundbreaking piece of artwork, as well as an intense sensory experience for viewers.

Focused on Germany's Past

In the early '80s and '90s Polke's subject matter dealt primarily with Germany's Nazi past as well as the reality of people's lives during the country's split between East and West. The canvases became courageous testaments to the horror of the Holocaust, and Polke's entry into the use of non-art materials turned them into powerful experimental works with a life of their own. *Lager (Camp)* 1982, for example, portrays a concentration camp with its barbed wire fencing and electric lights, painted partially with embers. The canvas bears the burn holes that prove the existence of fire and convince us that the camp and its terror are real. This painting is also an example of Polke's signature ability to merge abstraction with form in one work. The iridescent purples, both paint and fabric, act as vaporous clouds that sometimes shroud forms and sometimes reveal them. Similarly, depending on the distances from which the piece is viewed, different visual information is given and various figural representations become apparent or disappear. Thus, a lamp assumes the form of a helmet, seen from one perspective.

Before the fall of the Berlin Wall, Polke continued working with a favored subject, Germany's East/West split and its relationship to consumerism. In his 1987–1988 *Watchtower with Geese,* the menacing border guard tower acts as a symbol of the country's internal division. It is placed on one side of the canvas, while on the other is a piece of black fabric patterned with "kitsch emblems of leisure—beach umbrellas, sunglasses, deck chairs—and in between the two a gaggle of outlined geese, with no clue as to whether they are citizens of West or East," wrote Hughes.

The overwhelmingly large scale of the *Hochsitz (Watch tower)* series from the mid-'80s is both terrifying and arresting, especially because viewers are placed in the position of feeling like they are in the camps, hunted prey. Polke used his trademark technique of placing fabric swatches with gaudy patterns as the backdrop for pop culture images and overlaid drawings. As Dorothy Valakos mentioned in a biographical sketch of Polke, "[They] suggest the frightening, mechanized impersonality of fascism and dictatorship, and the social conformity and complicity that permits them to exist." Their gold and black colors created by silver bromide, iodine, and chloride, are connected to some of his later abstract works, which are made of alchemical mixtures of silver nitrate, resins, meteor particles, and unstable pigments, among other non-art materials. The stuff of these paintings suggests both the poisons of industrial by-products and the magic of alchemical change.

Alchemical Art

"In the early 1980s Polke embarked upon a series of experiments that continue down to the present, which have often been termed alchemical and in which the paintings themselves, as real, physical objects, effectively serve as his laboratory and at the same time the objects of his experiments," wrote Caldwell. *The Spirits that Lend Strength are Invisible,* 1988, is a series of five risky pieces, created for the Carnegie International exhibition in Pittsburgh. The title fittingly comes from a Native American saying, while the paintings pay tribute to the New World by containing materials from the Americas, rather than Europe. Polke attached unconventional materials and objects to the canvases— pure tellurium blown onto artificial resin, ground meteor particles, layers of nickel and silver nitrate, as well as Neolithic tools—thus creating another set of paintings that were not exactly painted. They are toxic in their constitution, but refer abstractly to nature without having a specific, identifiable subject matter. In his description of the series, Caldwell noted, "We are in a strangely empty, yet magical landscape, in which the dust of meteors and of obscure chemical elements is moved about by silent, unfelt winds."

Another series of six paintings from this time period, *Speigelbilder (Mirror Images, 1986),* "present images of cosmic forces interacting, erupting, exploding. From galactic detritus to vaporous congealing lacquer surfaces, these paintings 'mirror' processes of abstraction's spiritual essence . . . By employing complicated, alchemical mixtures of resins, violet pigments and silver nitrate, Polke's surfaces trap, conduct and model light in refractive, elusive ways," wrote David Moos in *Art/Text.*

From 1982 on, the artist continually created pieces that transformed themselves based on the passage of time or on their surroundings. Works like *Lager* and *Watchtower II* reveal various images based on the angle the viewer takes. In the latter painting, the guard tower vanishes and reappears as the onlooker shifts positions. In addition, the painting's very color alters as the external conditions of temperature and humidity shift around it. In Pittsburgh, the piece had a purple hue, while in Los Angeles it turned green. In 1986, Polke's big wall painting in the German Pavilion at the

Venice Bienale changed its appearance based on humidity, his 1988 mural in Paris responded to temperature, and a series of canvases including *The Spirits that Lend Strength Are Invisible IV,* 1988, revealed little or nothing at first, but then gradually began displaying images, as if painted in invisible ink. Aside from disturbing the viewer's sense of logic, these mutable paintings play an important role in creating art forms that are irreproducible—unique and almost supernatural in their inability to be pinned down by photography. In that sense, they move counter to art in the modern world, which can lose its magic, in a sense, due to its ability to be copied. Polke's shifting canvases are truly original works, acting as living creatures that have the potential to react to their environment.

Although it was primarily his early works that were exhibited in the foremost United States museums in the '90s, in 1999, *Art News* dubbed Polke one of "Ten Most Important Living Artists." The same year, New York City's Museum of Modern Art showed *Works on Paper: 1963–1974,* which included *The Ride on the Eight of Infinity,* four overwhelmingly large pieces that suggested the non-linear streams of consciousness and collaging of images that were to come in the next 20 years. In Los Angeles and Minneapolis Polke exhibited some of his manipulated photographs, paintings from the '80s and early '90s, and collaged images. In Germany, however, museums across the country exhibited a thorough, retrospective show called *Three Lies of Painting.*

Polke's approach through the '90s was a continuation and deepening of the anti-art, alchemical technique he had begun to experiment with decades before. His work included the use of resins, enamel-like coats of color, and other man-made chemical and metallic combinations applied to layers of see-through polyester fabrics. This time, though, the artist's subject, rather than being stimulated by Pop culture was inspired by literature, mythology, and history, along with the under-current of social and political commentary that infused his earlier work. Still, he employed the raster dot patterns he became known for in his early days. In 2002, Polke's artistic lifetime achievements earned him the distinguished honor of receiving the Japan Art Association's 14th Praemium Imperiale Award for painting. Along with his diploma and medal, he was presented with $125,000 for his contribution to international arts and culture.

Although Polke's art has been called one of appropriation, it is much more than that. True, his installations, paintings, drawings, collages, and photography do grab images from sources belonging to both high and low culture— from William Blake to comic books and silly advertisements. Often, there is no linear narrative and the artist leaps from one visual to the next, creating a free-spirited and mad dance for the eyes. It is important to remember, though, that Polke creates entirely new art forms and particular states of consciousness with his work. It transcends art as viewers have traditionally been trained to think of it and blasts them into a mystical world of abstract, unidentifiable substances and concrete images—masterfully combining form and formlessness.

Books

Pendergast, Sara and Tom, editors, *Contemporary Artists, Fifth Edition,* St. James Press, 2002.
Polke, Sigmar, *Sigmar Polke,* San Francisco Museum of Modern Art, 1990.

Periodicals

Art/Text, Fall 1998.
Time, December 9, 1991; May 31, 1999. □

Judith Graham Pool

Judith Graham Pool (1919–1975) was a researcher who made an important discovery in the treatment of hemophilia. In 1964, she developed cryoprecipitation, a way to produce concentrated amounts of antihemophilic factor, or AHF, a blood component necessary for clotting. The discovery of cryo revolutionized the treatment of hemophilia, making it easier and safer.

Early Interest in Science

Pool was born Judith Graham on June 1, 1919, in Queens, a borough of New York City. Graham was the oldest of three children of Leon Wilfred and Nellie Baron Graham. Nellie Graham was a teacher. Leon Graham was a native of England who worked as a stockbroker. Pool earned good grades in high school and especially loved science. She majored in biochemistry at the University of Chicago, where she was a member of Phi Beta Kappa and Sigma Xi.

While at the University of Chicago, Pool married political science student Ithiel de Sola Pool. She graduated with a bachelor of science degree in 1939 and pursued graduate studies while working as an assistant in physiology at the university.

In 1942, the Pools moved to Geneva, New York, where Ithiel Pool got a job as a political science professor at Hobart and William Smith Colleges. Pool began teaching physics at the same institutions. The Pools had two sons, Jonathon, born in 1942, and Jeremy, born in 1945. The couple divorced in 1953.

Overlooked in Frog Research

While working and caring for her young family, Pool worked toward her Ph.D. in physiology. Her dissertation was on the electrophysiology of muscle fibers. She worked in the laboratory of neurophysiologist Ralph Waldo Gerard at Hobart College. In 1942, Pool, Gerard, and another researcher published a paper in which they described the use of a microelectrode to record electromagnetic impulses in frog muscle fibers. Gerard furthered the research and was nominated for a Nobel Prize in 1950 for his work. Pool's contribution was largely overlooked, according to the book *Women of Science: Righting the Record.*

Pool received her Ph.D. from the University of Chicago in 1946. The Pools returned to Chicago when Ithiel Pool developed tuberculosis and began a long hospital stay. Pool worked a variety of jobs, including as a secretary, an English and physics teacher, a cancer researcher, and a teacher in a school for mentally handicapped children.

Ithiel Pool eventually recovered and moved the family to California when he was hired at Stanford University's Hoover Institution on War, Revolution and Peace. Pool became a researcher at the Stanford Research Institute. In 1953, she joined the staff at Stanford University's School of Medicine as a research fellow supported by a grant of the Bank of America-Giannini Foundation. With the exception of a year in Oslo, Norway, as a Fulbright research fellow, she spent the rest of her career at Stanford Medical School.

Breakthrough in Hemophilia Treatment

When Pool came to Stanford, her research focus changed from muscle physiology to blood physiology, an area she had no experience in. Nonetheless, the results of her research greatly improved the way hemophilia was treated. Until that time, hemophiliacs were treated with transfusions of plasma. Because the plasma contained low concentrations of antihemophilic factor (AHF), the component that aided blood clotting, the patients needed huge quantities of mostly useless fluid in order to receive adequate quantities of AHF. These massive transfusions carried a risk of circulatory overload and congestive heart failure.

Pool discovered a way to separate AHF from plasma so patients could get greater quantities of it. Pool discovered that when fresh frozen plasma is slowly thawed, it separates into layers. The bottom layer has heavy concentrations of AHF, ten times more than fresh plasma. Pool removed this layer and refroze it. The concentrated residue was called cryoprecipitate, or cryo for short, because it was precipitated by extreme cold.

Pool and her colleagues first published the procedure in the journal *Nature* in 1964. She co-wrote a similar article for the *New England Journal of Medicine* in 1965. The procedure quickly became the standard in blood banks for treating hemophiliacs. Cryo had many advantages over previous treatments. It was more convenient and safer for patients, it could be refrozen and stored for a year, and it was relatively inexpensive and easy to prepare.

As a result of Pool's discovery, she was recognized as a leader in hemophilia research. She was awarded the Murray Thelin Award of the National Hemophilia Foundation in 1968 and the Elizabeth Blackwell Award from Hobart and William Smith Colleges in 1973. She delivered several lectures, including the Paul M. Anggeler Memorial Lecture in 1974. Pool became a member of the national scientific advisory committee of the National Institutes of Health and the American Red Cross Blood Program. In 1975, the University of Chicago gave her its Professional Achievement Award. After her death, the National Hemophilia Founda-

tion changed the name of its grants to the Judith Graham Pool Research Fellowships.

In *Journey,* a book about hemophilia, Pool modestly said of her discovery, "I had no greater insight than anyone else. I just happened to be there at the right moment." Pool remained a senior research associate at Stanford until 1970, when she became a senior scientist. In 1972, when many academic institutions promoted women because of affirmative action, she was named a full professor, without having been in the lower professorial ranks.

Continued Recognition

Pool continued her research in blood coagulation for the remainder of her life. She devoted the later years of her career to advancing opportunities for women scientists. She was elected co-president of the Association of Women in Science in 1971. She was first chairwoman of the Professional Women of Stanford University Medical Center.

When she was 44, Pool gave birth to a daughter, Lorna. In 1972, Pool married Maurice Sokolow, professor of medicine and hematology, but the marriage lasted only three years.

Pool died of a brain tumor on July 13, 1975, in Stanford, California, at the age of 56. The book *Notable American Women: The Modern Period* reports that after Pool was diagnosed, she said, "The last few years of my life have been, I think, very unusual in that they have amounted to an experience for me of feeling overrewarded, overrecognized, overgratified beyond what anyone could expect, so there is no possibility of feeling cheated or regretful about what I will not have had as a result of dying earlier than expected. Quite the converse; it has almost been embarrassing in the other extreme."

An international medical journal published a tribute to Pool in 1988. It said, "One of the greatest contributions to the treatment of classic hemophilia was made by Dr. Judith Pool and her associates in 1964 and 1965. Dr. Pool's name will always be associated with greatness in the hemophilic and blood coagulation community for this discovery. Her place in the history of the treatment of hemophilia is secure and deservedly so."

Books

Kass-Simon, G. and Patricia Farnes, *Women of Science: Righting the Record,* Indiana University Press, 1990.

Massie, Robert and Suzanne Massie, *Journey,* Alfred A. Knopf, 1975.

Notable Women Scientists, Gale Group, 2000.

Ogilvie, Marilyn and Joy Harvey, editors, *Biographical Dictionary of Women in Science,* Routledge, 2000.

Sicherman, Barbara and Carol Hurd Green, *Notable American Women: The Modern Period,* Belknap Press, 1980.

Online

"Five Key People in Hemophilia History," http://www.hemo philiagalaxy.com (February 17, 2003). □

Charley Frank Pride

Charley Pride (born 1938) was country music's first African American star. For the past 25 years, Pride has been ranked among the top 15 best-selling recording artists of all time. During his career, he has had 36 number-one hit singles, and he has sold over 25 million albums. He has had 31 gold albums, 4 platinum albums, and 1 quadruple platinum album. Pride was elected to the Country Music Hall of Fame in 2000, the highest honor a country musician can receive. As an RCA Records recording artist, Pride is second in sales only to Elvis Presley.

Mississippi Delta Childhood

Charl (mistakenly changed to "Charley" on his birth certificate) Frank Pride was born on March 18, 1938, in Sledge, Mississippi. Like many other Mississippi Delta towns, Sledge consisted only of little more than a "grocery store, a barber shop, a hardware and farm supply store, a general merchandise store, a café, and a gas station." In the pre-civil rights era that coincided with Pride's childhood, life for African Americans in the Mississippi Delta was strictly regulated by enforced codes of segregation that governed who could use rest rooms, attend schools, and purchase housing.

The fourth of eleven children—eight boys and three girls—Pride grew up in a family headed by Mack and Tessie B. Stewart Pride. Pride's parents worked as sharecroppers and picked cotton. The family shared a three-room tin and cracked-wood "shotgun" house, so named because a person could "fire a shotgun through the front door and out the back without hitting anything."

Although the Pride family was poor, Pride's mother insisted there were people with a lot more money who would give millions for what her son had. She pointed out to him, as an example, that he had all of his fingers and both eyes.

Pride and his siblings suffered frequent beatings at the hands of their father, a stern disciplinarian. Said Pride, "He showed concern for his children by using the strap to keep us on a straight and narrow path and he showed tenderness by protecting us and caring for us. We all survived the hardships of our youth and turned out to be reasonably solid citizens."

Charley's father, Mack Pride, was a deacon in the Baptist church, but Pride later said that it was his mother who seemed the more spiritual of his parents. In his autobiography, *Pride: The Charley Pride Story,* Pride said that he grew up not liking his father very much. "I loved him and there was a lot about him that I admired but I didn't like him," he wrote. Elsewhere in the book, Pride added, "Over time, I have come to realize that Daddy was not unfeeling; he was just unable to express his emotions in the normal way." But he went still further, saying, "However I account for him in my own mind, it doesn't change one thing—how much I regret that there was no warmth or tenderness between us."

As a young boy, Pride had little choice in how he spent his time and was made to pick cotton. In his autobiography, Pride recalled telling his father. "I just don't want to be a cotton picker, Daddy." His father reportedly replied, "You don't want to pick cotton? Well. What do you think you're going to do?"

Pride grew up listening to country music on the radio and learning the songs of Hank Williams and Roy Acuff. From the age of six, Pride became a devotee of the Grand Ole Opry radio broadcasts. A neighbor began calling Charley "Mocking Bird" when the boy showed a reluctance to do much besides sing and play baseball. Although Pride dreamed of being a country music star, he was actually planning on becoming a baseball player.

At the age of 14, Pride bought a guitar from the Sears, Roebuck catalog after saving for most of year to buy it. He then began teaching himself to play a few chords. He eventually began mimicking songs on the radio, using his index finger as a capo and playing open bar chords. After he accidentally left his guitar outside one night in a heavy rain, he was forced to tinker with make-shift instruments, including a comb, for a while.

Between Baseball and Country Music

Pride's mother died in 1956. After her death, Pride's ties to Sledge, Mississippi, were largely severed. By his late teens, Pride had left home and traveled to Memphis. At 17, one day after entering a talent contest at Lave's Grand Theater in Memphis, Pride left for baseball training camp. He recalls having to walk seven miles to pitch nine innings, and then having to walk the seven miles back home again.

About this time, one of Pride's teammates asked him why he was not pursuing a career as a singer, and Pride told him, "I want to go to the major leagues. Years from now, when they ask who hit the most home runs, I don't want the answer to be Babe Ruth, I want it to be Charley Pride." Jackie Robinson had broken the color barrier in the major leagues in 1947, and by the mid-1950s every major league team had two or three black players on its roster.

In 1955, Pride joined the American Negro League, playing for Detroit, Michigan; Memphis, Tennessee; and Birmingham, Alabama. Pride met his wife Rozene, a cosmetologist from Oxford, Mississippi, while playing baseball in Memphis. The couple later had three children, Kraig, Dion, and Angela. Meanwhile, Pride's baseball career was interrupted by a two-year hitch in the service.

The Mighty Casey

In 1958, Pride resumed his career with the American Negro League, now playing for the Birmingham Black Barons. After Pride was cut from the Memphis team in 1959, he decided to go to Montana where he ended up taking a job at the Zinc Smelting Manning Company and playing semi-professional baseball at night. He also sang in a nightclub two nights a week.

Pride later said of his time in Montana, "Montana wasn't just geographically far removed from the South, but the thinking was pretty isolated too. When the sit-ins and boycotts and protest marches began in the south, guys I worked with would ask things like, 'What's going on with y'all down there.'"

By 1960, Pride had abandoned semi-professional baseball and the American Negro League for a Major League C-team. After rejections from the Angels, Pride tried the Mets, whose coach, the legendary Casey Stengel, told him, "We ain't running no damn tryout camp down here." Stengel went on to suggest that Pride go out in a cow pasture where someone else could look at him. Pride decided to give up a baseball career following that episode.

RCA Recording Contract

Returning home from the debacle with Casey Stengel, Pride auditioned for songwriter and record producer Jack Clement in Memphis. Chet Atkins, then vice-president of RCA recording in Nashville, was sufficiently impressed with Pride that he offered him an RCA recording contract.

In 1966, Pride was named best country and western male vocalist after having recorded 13 songs. By 1975, he released 22 records, and had 12 gold singles. Among his most popular recordings were "Snakes Crawl at Night" and "Just Between You and Me."

Medical Problems

In 1968, Pride was hospitalized following a USO tour with symptoms of manic depression that included an inability to sleep, delusions, and hyper-activity. Told that he would need to take medication for the rest of his life, Pride refused. After the symptoms recurred in 1982 though, Pride began taking lithium carbonate to control his manic swings. He then stopped taking the medication after he developed a skin rash that he thought was a lithium side-effect, but after another episode in 1989, he finally came to terms with his need to take the medication. Pride explained in his autobiography, "I've taken lithium regularly for the past few years and have had no further bouts with manic depression. I've always been a hyper person, one who needed to be doing something physical all the time. I had difficulty sitting through business meetings or any other sedentary activity. I'm still that way, but I run on an even keel—no wild highs, no migraines, and no imagining things that aren't there. And I sleep very well."

On Top

In 1969, Pride scored his first number one single with the release of "All I Have to Offer You (Is Me)." Over the next 15 years, he would go on to top the charts with more than 36 number one country singles, bringing him within close range of becoming Billboard magazine's all-time record holder in that category.

Some of Pride's songs, like "Kiss an Angel Good Morning," are now considered classics. Other big hits have included "Is Anybody Goin' to San Antone?," "I'm So Afraid of Losing You Again," "Mississippi Cotton Picking Delta Town," "Someone Loves You Honey," "When I Stop Leaving I'll Be Gone," "Burgers and Fries," "Mountain of Love," and "You're So Good When You're Bad." "Kiss An Angel Good Morning" helped Pride capture Country Music Association's awards as Entertainer of the Year (1971) and Top Male Vocalist (1971, 1972).

Businessman

By the 1980s, Pride was dividing his time between his careers as musician and businessman. His business activities then included banking, broadcasting, and real estate. He holds the most shares in Texas's largest minority owned bank and has real estate holdings across the country. He also owns a music publishing company and a production company.

Career Achievements

On May 1, 1993, Pride was inducted into the Grand Ole Opry, where he had first performed 26 years earlier. Pride received the Academy of Country Music's Pioneer Award in 1994, the same year he released his autobiography, *Pride: The Charley Pride Story*. Pride opened the 2000-seat Charley Pride Theatre in Branson, Missouri, in June 1994. He performed there for four years, doing approximately 200 shows a year.

Pride received the Trumpet Award from Turner Broadcasting in January 1996 in recognition of his outstanding achievement as an African American. The state of Mississippi adopted his "Roll On Mississippi" as its official song and named a stretch of highway in the state for him. Also that year, he performed in a special Christmas program at the White House for President and Mrs. Clinton. In 2000, he was elected to the Country Music Hall of Fame.

Pride still works out each year with the Texas Rangers baseball team, fulfilling a boyhood aspiration. He also enjoys playing golf when he is not on tour or recording.

Besides the U.S., Pride has performed in Europe, Australia, New Zealand, Japan, Fiji, and Canada. He frequently appears on USO tours, entertaining military personnel stationed overseas. Once during a USO tour, after being heckled by black soldiers for singing country music, Pride told the mixed race audience, "I'm singing for my brothers on this side of the room, and for my brothers on this side. I told you in the beginning. I'm not James Browne. I'm not Sam Cooke. I'm Charley Pride, country singer. I'm just me and that's what you get."

Pride currently splits his time between his homes in Dallas, Texas, and Branson, Missouri.

Books

Pride, Charley, (with Jim Henderson), *Pride: The Charley Pride Story*, William Morrow and Company, 1994.

Online

"Charley Pride," http://www.charleypride.com/ (January 2003).
"Charley Pride," http://www.topblacks.com/entertainment/charlie-pride.htm (January 2003). □

Thomas Pringle

Scottish writer Thomas Pringle (1789–1834) is considered the father of South African poetry. He lived in South Africa for six years, during which time he established a family settlement in the Eastern Cape. Unable to make a living as a writer in South Africa, he moved to London where he worked for the abolition of slavery. Pringle is recognized in South Africa as the first successful poet to publish in English. His poems and narratives describe South Africa's landscape, native people, and social conditions.

Pringle was the third of seven children of Robert and Catherine Haitlie Pringle. He was born January 5, 1789, in Kelso, Linton, Roxburghshire, Scotland. Tragically, his mother died in 1795, when Thomas was six years old, leaving his father to remarry.

When Pringle was three months old, his nanny accidentally dropped him, dislocating his hip. The nanny was afraid to admit her mistake, with the result that Pringle not given medical care until it was too late to correct the damage. Consequently, he walked using crutches throughout his entire life. Perhaps out of guilt, the nanny lavished attention on him, allowing him to become headstrong and unmanageable.

Because he was lame, Pringle was unable to participate in athletics and did not follow his family into farming. To prepare for a profession, his father sent Pringle to Kelso Grammar School and Edinburgh University where he became interested in writing. He wrote every day, producing letters, journal entries, poems, and essays.

Began Writing Career

Pringle left Edinburgh University without earning a degree and took a job in the General Register Office, where he worked as a clerk from 1808 to 1817. He continued to write and in 1811 published, with Robert Story, "The Institute," a satire on the Edinburgh Philamanthic Society, a literary group. The first of his poems to gain attention, "Autumnal Excursion," was published in 1816. The poem celebrates the Scottish land where Pringle grew up and includes vignettes from his childhood. Among those who read the poem was noted novelist Sir Walter Scott. Pringle and Scott soon formed a friendship that lasted until Scott's death in 1832.

In 1817 Pringle became joint editor of the *Edinburgh Monthly* but resigned after a disagreement with the magazine's publisher, William Blackwood. He later edited both *The Star*, a newspaper, and *Edinburgh Magazine*. Also in 1817 Pringle married Margaret Brown, a woman nine years older than Pringle, and two years later he published his first volume of verse, *The Autumnal Excursion and Other Poems*.

Affected by Economic Downturn

Unable to make a living as a writer, Pringle returned to the register office for a short time. His family, like many throughout Scotland during the early 1800s, was encountering financial difficulties; a decline in agriculture had forced Robert Pringle to move south to a farm in England.

In addition to agricultural problems, Great Britain and most of Europe were suffering economic difficulties as a result of the political restructuring following the Napoleonic wars. The British government now offered thousands of its residents the opportunity to resettle in South Africa, promising free land and inexpensive supplies for those willing to make the trip to colonize this new addition to the British Empire, recently purchased from the Dutch. Pringle pursued this opportunity and in 1820, through his friendship with Scott, obtained free passage for himself and his extended family to travel to the eastern cape of South Africa.

Settled in South Africa

The Pringles sailed for 75 days, then traveled inland for another month before arriving at their new home in Glen Lynden, located in the upper valley of South Africa's Baavians River. The location proved to be a good choice, as colonists who settled closer to the coast experienced difficult weather conditions that proved disastrous for farming.

It took two years for Pringle, his father, and the rest of the family to establish the family homestead, which eventually comprised 20,000 acres of land. As he had done prior to the family's traveling to South Africa, Pringle served as the family spokesperson and conferred with government and military officials. His influence helped the family succeed in South Africa whereas many other immigrants did not. After his family was settled Pringle himself moved to Cape Town, where he worked in the newly created South African Public Library and pursued his writing career.

To supplement his small income from the library, the enterprising Pringle opened a school with a friend from Scotland, John Fairbairn. In 1823 he also started a newspaper, the *South African Journal,* and a magazine, the *South African Commercial Advertiser,* in which he and his staff published editorials advocating reforms of the British colonial system. After both publications were censored by the government Pringle resigned. After his reformist views also led to the failure of his academy, he resigned from the library and in 1824 returned to his family's settlement. For the rest of his time in South Africa Pringle continued to fight for freedom of the press and improvement in the position of the native people.

Most of the poetry and prose Pringle published while living in South Africa deals with local matters. It contains images of the land and its native people and is imbued with its author's passion for promoting independence and spreading Christianity. Published in 1824, Pringle's *Some Account of the Present State of the English Settlers in Albany, South Africa* describes the landscape, the housing, and the experiences Scots settlers encountered in South Africa. Unlike the Pringle family, many settlers did not find life to be that which they had been promised. Their crops failed and inclement weather destroyed most of what they had. Pringle concluded that, despite all, Scots immigrants should remain in South Africa, and he began efforts to appeal to Britain for humanitarian aid.

Ultimately, the harsh conditions in South Africa took their toll, and the idealistic Pringle and his wife were forced to leave his father and returned to London in 1826, financially ruined. A recently published article about slavery in South Africa had attracted the attention of the British Anti-Slavery Society, which now offered Pringle a job as secretary. The job suited Pringle perfectly: his craving for independence extended to blacks as well as Scots, and he had firsthand knowledge of the conditions of Native Africans. He worked with noted abolitionists William Wilberforce, Thomas Clarkson, Zachary Macaulay, and Sir Foxwell Buxton, his anti-slavery writings earning him recognition around the world.

Pringle earned a modest living through the Society that he supplemented by working as editor of an annual literary publication. He continued to write poetry based on his South African experiences and in 1828 published *Ephemerides; or, Occasional Poems, written in Scotland and South Africa.* The South African poems in particular proved very popular, placing him in the ranks of Britain's favorite poets shared by William Wordsworth, Samuel Taylor Coleridge, George Byron, Percy Shelley, and John Keats.

As the first poet from South Africa to write in English, Pringle had a captive audience that consumed everything he wrote, including his 1834 work *Narrative of a Residence in South Africa.* A travel adventure about the land, animals, and the native people of South Africa, *Narrative of a Residence in South Africa* is considered his greatest work. It stands out because it was written from the perspective of a man who, although a native Scot, considered South Africa to be his homeland. Traveling to places where few non-Africans visited, Pringle shared his observations with his readers, along with his love for the land and its people.

Life's Work Completed

Pringle's work with the Anti-Slavery Society ended when Parliament abolished slavery on August 23, 1833. Emancipation came after a decree signed by Pringle was published on June 27, 1834. The next day, Pringle showed the first signs of an illness, which was later diagnosed as tuberculosis. Doctors recommended a milder climate, and Pringle prepared to return to South Africa. Unfortunately, the disease advanced rapidly and on December 5, 1834, he died in London at age forty-five.

Pringle died having reached many of his life goals. He had published a book of poems that he hoped would establish his place in South African literature. He had published a narrative about his adopted homeland. And his work with the Anti-Slavery Society had succeeded. Decades after his death, his poems continued to attract attention. Though generally considered to be a minor poet, he is credited with beginning the modern South African literary tradition. His best-known poem is "Afar in the Desert," which was originally published in the *South African Journal* in 1824. The magazine's circulation was very limited and the poem attracted little initial attention, but when it was included in George Thompson's *Travels in Southern Africa* Samuel Taylor Coleridge read the poem and wrote to Pringle. As quoted in John Robert Doyle, Jr.'s biography *Thomas Pringle,* Coleridge exclaimed of the poem: "I do not hesitate to declare it, among the two or three most perfect lyric poems in our language."

Books

Doyle, John Robert Jr., *Thomas Pringle,* Twayne Publishers, 1972.

Kunitz, Stanley J., editor, *British Authors of the Nineteenth Century,* H. W. Wilson, 1936. □

Stanley Ben Prusiner

Stanley Prusiner (born 1942) won the Nobel Prize in Physiology for Medicine in 1997 for his discovery of the prion, originally described as a disease-producing agent in animals and humans that, unlike any other known pathogen, contains no RNA or DNA. The prize was widely seen as a vindication of Prusiner's research and methods.

Grew Up in Midwest

Prusiner was born on May 28, 1942, in Des Moines, Iowa, to Lawrence and Miriam Prusiner and named for his father's younger brother who died of Hodgkin's disease at age 24. In those World War II years, his father was drafted into the Navy shortly after Prusiner was born. The family moved to Boston so his father could attend officer training school. When he left for the South Pacific, his wife and son moved to Cincinnati, Ohio, to live near her mother. In his autobiography for the Nobel Foundation, Prusiner wrote fondly of his maternal grandmother and paternal grandfather, Ben Prusiner, who as a child immigrated to the United States from Moscow in 1896 and grew up in Sioux City, Iowa. At the end of the war, the reunited Prusiner family moved back to Des Moines.

In 1952, the family moved back to Cincinnati, where Prusiner's father worked as an architect for the next 25 years. Prusiner attended Walnut Street High School and studied Latin for five years. "I found high school rather uninteresting," he wrote in his autobiography for the Nobel Prize committee. He felt, however, that college was a different matter. "The intellectual environment of the University of Pennsylvania was extraordinary," he said, recalling how surprisingly willing the faculty members were to take time for undergraduates. He studied science, philosophy, history of architecture, economics, and Russian history. In the summer of 1963, he began a research project with Sidney Wolfson that continued through Prusiner's senior year, and he

decided to stay at the university for medical school "largely because of the wonderful experience of doing research with Sidney Wolfson." Prusiner received his bachelor's degree in 1964.

Chose Biomedical Research Career

In his second year of medical school, Prusiner began a study of fluorescence and brown fat that led to spending much of his fourth year at the Wenner-Gren Institute in Stockholm working on a related topic. That "exciting time" helped him choose to pursue a career in biomedical research.

In 1968 Prusiner returned to Philadelphia and received his M.D. He began a medical internship at the University of California, San Francisco (UCSF), as a prerequisite to a post in the U.S. Public Health Service at the National Institutes of Health (NIH). While in San Francisco, he met and married Sandy Turk, a high school math teacher. They subsequently had two children, Helen and Leah.

Once at the NIH, Prusiner spent three years studying glutaminases in *E. coli*. He called the period "critical in my scientific education" and said, "I learned an immense amount about the research process." Following the NIH post, he chose a residency in neurology rather than postdoctoral fellowships in neurobiology as "a better route to developing a rewarding career in research."

Began to Study Slow Viruses

A key event in his career came about in September 1972, while he was serving his residency in neurology at UCSF. He admitted a patient dying from Creutzfeldt-Jacob disease (CJD), a rare, fatal condition in which the brain deteriorates. Prusiner learned that CJD did not elicit the body's usual immune response and behaved in ways uncharacteristic of viral pathogens. He was fascinated and over the next two years read "every paper that I could find" on the CJD family of diseases, known then as "slow virus" diseases because they appeared relatively late in life.

In 1974, as an assistant professor of neurology at UCSF, Prusiner set up a lab to study scrapie, the "slow virus" disease that affects sheep. He secured funds for the project from the Howard Hughes Medical Institute (HHMI) and eventually the NIH. A temporary career crisis arose when (1) his research into scrapie failed to yield the viral pathogen he expected, (2) the HHMI ended its funding, and (3) UCSF denied him tenure. The crisis was short-lived. He streamlined some of his methods and found two new funding organizations, R. J. Reynolds Company and Sherman Fairchild Foundation, which he credits with buying the enormous number of mice and hamsters he used. His tenure denial was also reversed. NIH funding continued, amounting to $56 million between 1975 and 1997, according to one source.

Over the next eight years, Prusiner pursued the pathogen responsible for the so-called slow virus diseases and also became a professor of neurology and biochemistry at UCSF. In the spring of 1982, *Science* magazine published his first article on his research, which, in Prusiner's words, "set off a firestorm." He broke with scientific orthodoxy, announcing that his years of work had identified not a virus but a protein as the agent causing a set of diseases known as transmissible spongiform encephalopathies (TSEs) (the same group formerly known as the "slow viruses"). He also coined the term "prion," derived from "proteinaceous infectious particle," for his discovery. (Gary Taubes, writing in *Discover* magazine, says Prusiner tinkered with the spelling of his coinage for euphony's sake. Prion rhymes with Leon.)

The TSEs include Bovine Spongiform Encephalopathy (BSE), also known as Mad Cow Disease because of the way infected cattle behave; scrapie, documented in the eighteenth century in Iceland and in the 1940s in Scotland, where shepherds named it for the way infected sheep scrape their wool against fence posts; several other forms affecting animals; and the forms found in humans, including CJD, Gerstmann-Straussler-Scheinker (GSS) disease and fatal familial insomnia, each of which affects a very small number of related individuals, and kuru, a disease of indigenous people on New Guinea and now virtually extinct. All are fatal. All end in degeneration of brain tissue into a mass riddled with holes, like a sponge-accounting for the "spongiform" part of their collective name. The ones affecting humans threaten only a very small number of people, perhaps one in one million (the number in the United States with CJD has been put at some 225), but in the 1980s and 1990s, a new threat arose when BSE "broke the species barrier": Infected cattle apparently transmitted something that caused a form of CJD in humans who ate infected beef. Some 100 people, mostly in the United Kingdom, were thought to have contracted the disease in this fashion, and at least 130,000 British cattle were affected. Many were destroyed to avoid further spread of the disease. The specter of an unchecked spread panicked Europeans who consumed British beef.

Theory Described Novel Protein Behavior

Prusiner's work sparked controversy immediately. "His findings go against the central dogma of biology, which is that you can transmit information only with DNA and RNA," said Michael Shelanski, chairman of the department of pathology at Columbia-Presbyterian Medical Center. Infectious agents recognized in orthodox science include bacteria, viruses, fungi, and parasites, all of which contain DNA or RNA. While efforts to prove and disprove Prusiner's prion theory are ongoing, it has achieved a wide acceptance, especially the idea that prion proteins are involved in some way in the diseases like CJD. The theory itself has evolved since 1982. Regardless of the theory that achieves consensus in the end, Prusiner's work and the work of his critics have enriched the science associated with these diseases. In 2001, for example, WebMD reported that Prusiner's lab had identified at least two drugs, chlorpromazine and quinacrine, that may be effective against CJD contracted from BSE-infected beef.

Based on his work with mice and hamsters infected with scrapie, Prusiner concluded that prion protein (PrP) occurs naturally in white blood cells and brain cells. Its function is not understood, but ordinarily it is harmless. PrPs

can be altered, however, so that their normal helical, or spiral, shape becomes flat and rigid. Collections of these flat, rigid prions form rods that group together into sheets or plaques that kill nerve cells, producing porous, spongy brain texture, dementia, and death.

The agent causing normal prions to change conformation is novel: As Prusiner explained to Rae Frey of Australian Radio National, "the abnormal protein is capable of recruiting the normal one into the abnormal form. . . . [O]nce the abnormal form of the prion protein is in the body, it then grabs on to the normal form and co-opts it and turns it into a rogue, or an abnormal form. . . . It becomes a chain reaction and more and more of the abnormal form accumulates . . . and eventually kills the host." The process is very slow. Prusiner says experiments in his lab confirmed the ability of scrapie-infected prion protein (PrPSc) to cause normal, helical PrP to change conformation.

Prion diseases arise in three ways: by infection (1 percent of human cases), by heredity (5-15 percent), and by no known cause, said to be sporadic (all the rest). Sporadic cases are thought to be genetic. The particular gene that carries the instructions for the amino acid sequence that makes up the prion protein has been pinpointed, and Prusiner has found a mutation that produces the "rogue" protein—provided the mutant gene is present on both "halves" of its chromosome.

Several Areas Drew Criticism

Prusiner concluded the "villain" in scrapie and the other prion diseases was not viral but protein on the basis of several pieces of evidence. For instance, procedures that normally kill viruses did not destroy the ability of the material he extracted from infected laboratory animals to infect others in turn; the agent works very slowly-behavior uncharacteristic of viruses; it does not trigger the immune system to produce antibodies (a virus does); enzymes that destroy nucleic acids (the building blocks of DNA and RNA, which all viruses contain) do not kill it; and scientists have been unable to find a viral agent in more than thirty years of searching. Several other pieces of evidence support Prusiner's claim of a protein agent: Protein-destroying enzymes destroy its infectivity, and when the gene that encodes the prion protein is removed from laboratory animals, exposure to PrPSc does not lead to the disease; no PrP means no possibility of PrPSc, so therefore PrP must be present for the disease to occur.

Prusiner's theory is controversial not only because it is unorthodox, scientists have also accused him of claiming his lab work proves things it does not (perhaps the stunning degree to which the best-trained scientific minds can disagree on the design, conduct, and interpretation of scientific experiments reflects how very complicated the area is) and of failing to credit earlier workers, for instance researcher Pat Merz, who identified rigid protein plaques in the brains of mice with scrapie in 1978 and published her findings in 1981. Prusiner is said to have ignored her work in his 1982 paper, in which he claimed to have discovered prion rods. Others have alleged Prusiner rushed to the press early on with the suggestion that Alzheimer's and other diseases of brain-riddling amyloid protein plaque might be related to prion diseases. "It is an astounding finding," Prusiner told the *New York Times* in 1983 that, "we never would have dreamed that amyloid and prions are the same. The implications of the findings may be enormous." Alzheimer's expert George Glenner said there was no proof at the time that Alzheimer's amyloids and scrapie proteins were the same (and their difference has since been confirmed). Glenner explained in *Discover*, "I have the greatest respect for Stanley, but he wanted to get in the press fast. I do not think it should have been released at all." Prusiner as recently as 1999 still expressed optimism that his discoveries would link up with Alzheimer's, which affects far more people than does CJD and related diseases and therefore attracts more research dollars. He told an interviewer in Australia that once drugs for treating prion diseases are discovered, "The blueprint for going after drugs, for producing drugs that will stop Alzheimer's Disease, will stop Parkinson's Disease will be laid out. . . . Once you have one success, then many other successes will follow much more quickly."

Nobel Award Deviated from Norm

Prusiner's Nobel Prize was unusual in several ways. First, the annual prize in physiology or medicine is usually shared by more than one person. Prusiner was the first single winner in ten years and one of only six singletons in the preceding 40 years. Moreover, the Nobel is usually awarded after major controversies have been resolved, but one member of the Nobel award committee, Dr. Lars Edstrom, suggested the committee may have taken a side. In a *New York Times* article, Dr. Edstrom noted: "There are still people who don't believe that a protein can cause these diseases, but we believe it." Prusiner's prize was also unusual because he was the second person to win for work on TSEs. Dr. Carleton Gajdusek won in 1976 for his work with kuru. With two awards in the area, the committee would be unlikely to award a third, which could dampen the enthusiasm of other researchers in the area; the clout, the glory, and the $1 million that go with the Nobel are mighty incentives in science.

Lately it seems that prions alone may not explain how PrPSc forces PrP (or PrPC, the normal, "cellular" PrP) to trim rigid, clump together, and kill brain cells after all. In his research summary on his UCSF Web page, Prusiner says an additional agent now seems to be involved. He calls it "an as yet to be identified factor that we have provisionally designated protein X." Protein X "binds to PrPC. The PrPC/protein X complex then binds PrPSc; by an unknown process, PrPC is transformed into a second molecule of PrPSc. We are attempting to isolate protein X."

One or two of Prusiner's critics have suggested his protein X sounds suspiciously like a viral agent proposed in the 1970s by three scientists of the British Neuropathogenesis Unit in Edinburgh, Scotland. They were trying to isolate the agent causing scrapie and hypothesized it was "a small piece of nucleic acid protected by a protein made by genes in the host, rather than genes in the agent." They called it a "virino." Will it turn out to be Prusiner's protein X, or will protein X reveal itself as virus X? The end of the story has yet to be written. Perhaps some words of Francis Bacon are apt to the issue. "He that will not apply new remedies must expect new evils; for time is the greatest innovator."

Periodicals

Chemistry and Industry, October 2, 2000.
JAMA, November 12, 1997.
Lancet, June 10, 2000.
New York Times, October 7, 1997; October 12, 1997.
Science, October 10, 1997; October 22, 1999.

Online

Barclay, Laurie, "Hope for Mad Cow Disease," WebMDHealth, http://my.webmd.com/ (February 9, 2003).
Bolton, David C., "Do Prions Exist?" NOVA Online, http://www.pbs.org/wgbh/nova/madcow/prions.html (February 9, 2003).
Levine, Joseph S., "When Science Faces the Unknown," NOVA Online, http://www.pbs.org/wgbh/nova/madcow/faces.html (February 9, 2003).
Nobel Assembly at the Karolinska Institute, "Press Release: The 1997 Nobel Prize in Physiology or Medicine," http://www.nobel.se/medicine/laureates/1997/html (February 10, 2003).
"Prions," Radio National the health report with Rae Fry, http://www.abc.net.au/rn/talks/8.30/helthrpt/stories/s44356.htm (February 9, 2003).
Prusiner, Stanley B., "Autobiography," Nobel e-Museum, http://www.nobel.se/medicine/laureates/1997/prusiner-autobio.html (January 21, 2003).
Prusiner, Stanley B., "Curriculum Vitae," Nobel e-Museum, http://www.nobel.se/medicine/laureates/1997/prusiner-cv.html (January 21, 2003).
Prusiner, Stanley B., "The Prion Diseases," *Scientific American.com,* http://www.sciam.com/ (February 10, 2003).
Prusiner, Stanley, "Research Summary," UCSF Neuroscience, http://www.ucsf.edu/neurosc/faculty/neuro_prusiner.html (January 21, 2003).
"Prusiner Wins Horwitz and Nobel Prizes," *Columbia University Record,* http://www.columbia.edu/cu/record/archives/vol23/vol23_iss7/18.html (February 9, 2003).
Somerville, Robert A., "Do Prions Exist?" NOVA Online, http://www.pbs.org/wgbh/nova/madcow/prions.html (February 9, 2003).
Taubes, Gary, "The game of the name is fame. But is it science?" *Discover,* http://web6.infotrac.galegroup.com/ (January 23, 2003). □

R

Bernard Rands

Bernard Rands (born 1934) is a major composer and conductor in contemporary music, publishing more than 100 works in a wide range of performance genres. Born in England but now an American citizen, Rands studied in Italy under Luciano Berio, Luigi Dallapiccola, and Roman Vlad. His distinguished academic career included professorships at York University, Oxford University, and the University of California San Diego. His composition "Canti del Sole" won the 1984 Pulitzer Prize in Music, and his orchestral suites "Le Tambourin" won the 1986 John F. Kennedy Center Friedheim Award. Rands has been called one of the most important musical voices of our time.

Career in Composition and Academia

Rands was born March 2, 1934, in Sheffield, England. He studied music and English literature at the University College of Wales, Bangor, earning a bachelor's degree in music in 1956 and a master's degree in 1958. After completing his academic degrees, he traveled around Italy for two years to study composition and conducting under Roman Vlad in Rome, Luigi Dallapiccola in Florence, and Bruno Maderna. Rands's most influential teacher in Italy was Luciano Berio from Milan. From 1961 to 1964 he attended the summer courses of Boulez at Darmstadt.

Rands's early compositions in the 1960s explored new instrumental techniques. He employed a mature style that was lyrical, dynamic, and sensitive. He superimposed original timbres on an intuitively derived chromatic pitch content. His writings for voice accompaniment for orchestra and chamber ensemble were treated with elegance.

Rands demonstrated an impressive academic career and held fellowships at numerous universities. He was a guest lecturer at the University of Wales from 1963 to 1967, and in 1966 acted as composer-in-residence and visiting fellow at Princeton University and composer-in-resident at the University of Illinois until 1970. He was a member of the faculty in music and Granada fellow of creative arts at York University from 1968 to 1975. From 1972 to 1975, Rands was a fellow in creative arts and professor of music at Brasenose College at Oxford University.

In 1975 he emigrated to the United States and became professor of music at the University of California at San Diego. In 1983, Rands became a US citizen. Eventually traversing the country, he served as professor of composition at Boston University and simultaneously as a faculty member of Juilliard School of Music in New York City. He was also composer-in-residence at Aspen, Colorado, and Tanglewood, Massachusetts, festivals. From 1989 to 1996 he was composer-in-residence for the Philadelphia Orchestra.

Rands also had a career as a conductor with ensembles and orchestras around the world. Composers, performers, audiences, and critics praised him for his performances of a large and diverse repertoire of contemporary music. An impressive list of fellow conductors led orchestras in Rands's music, such as Pierre Boulez, Luciano Berio, Bruno Maderna, Neville Marriner, Zubin Mehta, Riccardo Muti, Seiji Ozawa, Helmuth Rilling, Esa-Pekka Salonen,

Wolfgang Sawallisch, Gunther Schuller, Giuseppe Sinopoli, Leonard Slatkin, Christoph von Dohnanyi, and David Zinman.

Affiliations and Awards

Some of his many organization affiliations include membership in the American Society of University Composers and a seat on the advisor board of the Boston Modern Orchestra Project. He has been chosen as the Walter Bigelow Rosen Professor of Music at Harvard University and serves as the Walter Channing Cabot Fellow also at Harvard.

The beginning of Rands's long record of honors and awards was his receipt of the 1966 Harkness International Fellowship of the Commonwealth Fund of New York. Starting in 1977, Rands received a total of three National Endowment for the Arts grants and earned an American Academy of Arts and Letters award. He received the 1978 California Arts Council Award and earned a 1982 Guggenheim Fellowship. He was also honored by the Fromm and Koussevitzky Foundations, Pew Trust, and Carey Trust.

With his musical voice demanding to be spoken, Rands has shined in the past two decades. His compositions have won prestigious awards, such as the 1984 Pulitzer Prize in Music for "Canti del Sole," which Rands wrote for tenor and orchestra and which was premiered by Paul Sperry and the New York Philharmonic, conducted by Zubin Mehta. In 1986, Rands won the John F. Kennedy Center's prestigious Friedheim Award for his orchestral suites "Le Tambourin."

Received Commissions from Around the World

Over the years, Rands has been perused for commissions from major ensembles, orchestras, and festivals around the world. International commissions have come from the Suntory Concert Hall in Tokyo, the BBC Symphony Orchestra in London, the Israel Philharmonic, and the Internationale Bach Akademie in Stuttgart. Commissions in the U.S. were awarded from the Boston Symphony Orchestra, the Choral Arts Society of Philadelphia, Los Angeles Philharmonic, Chicago Symphony, and the Eastman Wind Ensemble.

Rands wrote a piece for the New York Philharmonic's 100th anniversary, a cello concerto for the Rostropovitch celebration of this 70th birthday, and a piece for a consortium of orchestras and soloists for Meet the Composer. Recently he wrote for the Cleveland Chamber Symphony, the Dale Warland Singers, and the Mendelssohn String Quartet, which has performed a world premiere of his string quartet.

Rands received two commissions from the Serge Koussevitzky Music Foundation in the Library of Congress. The first was in 1983 for his "Suite No. 2–Le Tambourin." The second was presented in 1994 by The Serge Koussevitzky Music Foundation and the Koussevitzky Music Foundation, Inc. to Rands and to the Philadelphia Orchestra, where he was composer-in-residence. The new work was premiered in May 1995, under the direction of music director Wolfgang Sawallisch.

The San Francisco-based Chanticleer vocal chamber ensemble commissioned a set of pieces from Rands for inclusion in its 1991 *Colors of Love* album. Rands wrote "Canti d'Amor," a set of fifteen poems from James Joyce's *Chamber Music,* a volume of verse published in 1907. Chanticleer selected seven of Rands's pieces, including "Winds of May that dance on the sea" and "Silently she's combing her long hair," that evoked complex harmonies for a warm and sensuous experience. *Colors of Love* won the Grammy award for Best Small Ensemble Performance. Rands's commission of "Canti d'Amor" was paid for by a grant from the Meet the Composer/*Reader's Digest* Commissioning Program, in partnership with the National Endowment for the Arts and the Lila Wallace/*Reader's Digest* Fund.

Influenced Performers and Conductors

Rands is known for composing for a wide range of performance genres. He expresses an original and distinctive style that has been described as "plangent lyricism" with "dramatic intensity." His music drew parallels between text and musical structure in his compositions.

Rands developed his elegant technical mastery from his studies in Italy. Berio had a lasting musical influence on Rand's music, evidenced by Rands's early compositions, the 1971 "Metalepsis II" and the 1980 "Canti Lunatici," for the way Rands approached word settings and his choice of multi-lingual libretto. Influenced most conspicuously by his teacher Berio, Rands infused his music with his enjoyment of solo virtuosity and in his approach to verbal language.

Rands himself influenced the next generation of performers. He was the main composition teacher of British modernist singer and composer Vic Hoyland, who attended York University in the late 1960s. Rands's enthusiasm for the Italian approach to music and composition imparted an impression on Hoyland.

Rands's 1998 album *The Works of Bernard Rands,* performed by the Cleveland Chamber Symphony, features three works connected with Rands's teacher Luciano Berio. "Metalepsis II," dedicated to Bruno Maderna, was conducted by Berio. The five short movements of "Madrigali" were inspired by Berio's "Il Combattimento." The final piece was the world premiere of Rands's "Triple Concert," dedicated to Berio and commissioned by the Core Ensemble. Reviewer Hubert Culot wrote of the album, "This wonderful release undoubtedly provides for a thought-provoking survey of Bernard Rands' musical journey and also a good introduction to his often beautiful sound world and his honest and serious musical thinking."

Rands's 2000 album featuring his piece "Ceremonial for Symphonic Wind Band" is a collection of new-band music. A send up of "Bolero," "Ceremonial" presents a single repeated melody that becomes progressively elaborate generating its own harmony. In his review of the composition in *Fanfare* magazine, Robert Carl noted that the effect was like a grave processional, gathering in substance throughout the piece. "What could in other hands be a great aesthetic miscalculation instead sounds imaginative and personal, proving that a good idea can continue to live in new guises," Carl said.

Concerts and Guest Appearances

In demand all over world, Rands has been guest composer at many international festivals and was the featured topic at the Rands Symposium held at Brigham Young University in November 1994. Also in 1994, the Aspen (Colorado) Music Festival commissioned Rands to write a piece for its 50th anniversary. For the festival, Rands wrote his first chamber opera, "Belladonna," 1 of 160 new works that premiered at Aspen. Japanese mezzo-contralto Makiko Narumi, a Juilliard Opera Center performer, sang the role of Agatha Liu in the world premiere of "Belladonna."

Rands was one of 50 composers featured at the 35th National Conference of the Society of Composers, Inc. hosted by Syracuse University's Setnor Auditorium and performed by the Center for New Music at the University of Iowa. The three-day marathon in March 2001 highlighted works by live composers from around the country. Rands's selected piece "Concertino for Oboe and Ensemble," commissioned by the Philadelphia Network for New Music in 1998, displayed imagination, originality, and technical mastery.

In November 2001, the Colorado College's Great Performances and Ideas Series presented a concert of Rands's solo and chamber works, performed by the college's Lanner Faculty artists, the Da Vinci Quartet, and the Italian Contemporary Players. In December 2001, the concert group The Ensemble Sospeso in New York presented the world premiere of a newly commissioned work by Rands. Sospeso's oboist Jacqueline Leclair performed the piece.

Rands's works are a popular source of music for various organizational events, such as the 2001 Netherlands-America Foundation (NAF) fundraiser concert by the NAF Fellows and NAF beneficiaries. Rands's "Memo" for solo soprano was presented at Southeast Alaska's CrossSounds 2002 music festival.

Books

Griffiths, Paul, Ed., *Thames & Hudson Encyclopedia of 20th Century Music,* Thames & Hudson, 1986.
Hitchcock, H. Wiley and Stanley Sadie, eds., *New Grove Dictionary of American Music,* Macmillan Press, 1986.
Morton, Brian and Pamela Collins, *Contemporary Composers,* St. James Press, 1992.
Who's Who in American Music, Read Publishing, 2nd edition, 1985.

Online

Bernard Rands website, http://www.bernardrands.com (March 5, 2003).
"Bernard Rands," European American Music Distributors website, http://www.eamdc.com/08.html (March 5, 2003).
"Bernard Rands," Music Web, http://www.musicweb.uk.net/classrev/2002/Oct02/Rands.htm (March 5, 2003).
"Bernard Rands, Concertino for oboe and ensemble," University of Iowa School of Music website, http://www.uiowa.edu/~cnm/35.010329.html (March 5, 2003).
"Commissioned Works Artist: Bernard Rands," Chanticleer website, http://www.chanticleer.org/brands.htm (March 5, 2003).
"Koussevitzky Commissions Awarded to Seven Composers," Library of Congress website, http://www.loc.gov/today/pr/1994/94-104 (March 5, 2003).
"Rands Ceremonial," eConcertBand, http://www.econcertband.com/fanfare/jan-00.html (March 5, 2003). □

Razia

A descendant of the Moslems of Turkish extraction who invaded India in the eleventh century, Razia (died 1240) was the only woman ever crowned in the Delhi sultanate, which ruled parts of India from 1210 to 1526. Razia reigned for approximately three and a half years (1236–1240), and although she made important reforms in government, she was ultimately unable to reconcile her Muslim nobility to her ruling as a woman.

The Delhi Sultanate

I n 1192 A.D., the Turkish leader, Muhammad of Ghur, defeated the Rajputs at the second battle of Tarain, gaining control of the Kingdom of Delhi. After establishing his reign, Ghur returned to Afghanistan, leaving his conquest in the hands of his trusted slave, Qutb-ud-din Aibak.

When Ghur died in 1206 without leaving an heir, Qutb-ud-din declared himself Sultan of Delhi. Qutb-ud-din's reign marked the beginning of the Delhi sultanate under the Slave dynasty—so named because many of the sultans of this time were former slaves. Qutb-ud-din is best remembered for his destruction of Hindu and Jain temples and for building mosques.

Iltutmish

Although Qutb-ud-din's son Aram Baksh inherited the throne in 1210 following the death of his father, he quickly proved himself to be incompetent. Following an abbreviated reign, Qutb-ud-din's son-in-law, Shamsuddin Iltutmish, assumed power.

Iltutmish had come to Delhi as a slave. After gaining the confidence of his master, Qutb-ud-din, he rose to become a provincial governor. Upon Qutb-ud-din's death, Iltutmish had the backing of the Amirs—the Turkish nobility—to succeed Qutb-ud-din as sultan.

At the time of Iltutmish's death in 1236, he had been in power for 26 years. As sultan, he had consolidated Turkish control of northern India and his empire extended from Prashar in the northwest to the Brahmaputra River in Bengal and Gujurat and Orissa in the south. Iltutmish had introduced important reforms to the Delhi sultanate—including a monarchy, a ruling class, and coinage—and had left a legacy as a patron of the arts.

Razia Sultana

Iltutmish became the first sultan to appoint a woman as his successor when he designated his daughter Razia as his heir apparent. (According to one source, Iltumish's eldest son had initially been groomed as his successor, but had died prematurely.) But the Muslim nobility had no intention of acceding to Iltutmish's disregard of tradition in appointing a woman as heir, and after the sultan died on April 29, 1236, Razia's brother, Ruknuddin Feroze Shah, was elevated to the throne instead.

Ruknuddin's reign was short. With Iltutmish's widow Shah Turkaan for all practical purposes running the government, Ruknuddin abandoned himself to the pursuit of personal pleasure and debauchery, to the considerable outrage of the citizenry. On November 9, 1236, both Ruknuddin and his mother Shah Turkaan were put to death—after only six months in power.

With reluctance, the nobility next agreed to allow Razia to reign as sultana of Delhi. As a child and adolescent, Razia had had little contact with the women of the harem, so she had had little opportunity to learn the customary behavior of women in the Muslim society that she was born into. Even before she became queen—during her father's reign—she was reportedly preoccupied with the affairs of state. As sultana, Razia adopted men's dress; and contrary to custom, she would later show her face when she later rode an elephant into battle at the head of her army.

A shrewd politician, Razia managed to keep the nobles in check, while enlisting the support of the army and the populace. Her greatest accomplishment on the political front was to manipulate rebel factions into opposing each other. At that point, Razia seemed destined to become one of the most powerful rulers of the Delhi sultanate.

But the sultana miscounted the consequences that a special relationship with one of her Assyrian slaves, Jamal Uddin Yaqut, would have for her reign. According to some accounts, Razia and Yaqut were lovers; other sources simply identify them as close confidants. In any case, before long she had aroused the jealousy of the Muslim nobility by the favoritism she displayed toward Yaqut. Eventually, the governor of Bhatinda, a childhood friend named Malik Ikhtiar-ud-din Altunia, rebelled, refusing any longer to accept Razia's authority.

A battle between Razia and Altunia ensued, with the result that Yaqut was killed and Razia taken prisoner. To escape death, Razia agreed to marry Altunia. Meanwhile, Razia's brother, Muiuddin Bahram Shah, had usurped the throne. After Altunia and Razia undertook to take back the sultanate from Bahram through battle, both Razia and her husband—neither one more than 30 years of age—were both killed on October 14, 1240 (some sources say October 13). Bahram, for his part, would later be dethroned for incompetence.

End of the Delhi Sultanate

The Slave dynasty would come to an end some fifty years after the death of Razia. The most memorable of her successors was Balban (1266–1287), who succeeded in establishing a strong, central government and saw the position of sultan elevated to divine status. Following his death in 1287, the Slave dynasty would continue three more years under the competing rule of his inept grandsons.

Under other dynasties, however, the Delhi sultanate would persist until 1525, achieving its maximum physical extent under the reign of Muhammad ibn Tughluk in the first half of the fourteenth century, when most of the subcontinent was under the sultan's dominion. But in 1398, Timur the Lame (Tamurlane) plundered Delhi. By the early fifteenth century, the sultanate consisted only of Delhi and immediately adjacent lands. Although the Delhi sultanate regained control of most of northern India in the early sixteenth century, it was finally destroyed by Babur, founder of the Mughal empire, in 1526.

Early Sources

The Tabakat-I-Nasiri is a generalized history of Delhi that ends at about 1259, about twenty years after the death of Razia. The work's author, Minhajus Seraj, served Iltumish, Razia, and Balban. Although Minhaj's history of the times is considered to be among the most reliable sources of information about Razia, Mihaj spent the last years of his life in the service of Balban, who had brought an end to Razia's rule.

Minhaj's point of view is therefore suspect given that he was unlikely to have included details in his account that would have brought embarrassment to his patron. Every other chronicle of the times is based on Minhaj's history.

Rafiq Zakaria, writing in his book, *Razia Warrior Queen of India,* quotes Minhaj on Razia as follows, ''[She was] a great sovereign, sagacious, just, beneficent, the patron of the learned, a dispenser of justice, the cherisher of her subjects and of warlike talent, and was endowed with all the admirable attributes and qualifications necessary for kings. . . . She was endowed with all the qualities befitting a king, but she was not born of the right sex and so in the estimation of men all these virtues were worthless.''

In his research, Zakaria consulted early sources to put together a work of historical fiction based on the life of the sultana. In Zakaria's portrayal, Razia was essentially hamstrung by her emotions. Zakaria believes that Altunia was deeply in love with Razia, but that he was repeatedly rebuffed by her aloofness. Zakaria speculates that the queen may have been too preoccupied with the affairs of state or may have been psychologically blocked—possibly from her upbringing—to have given sway to her emotions.

Zakaria argues that besides the prejudice Razia would have faced because of her sex, she would also have been targeted for her racial tolerances. On one hand, she met criticism from the Turkish Amirs, who were the royal multi-tribal leaders, and the Maliks, who led the small communities, for the favoritism she showed toward her Abyssinian slave, Jamaluddin Yaqut. Whether Yaqut was Razia's lover has been debated for centuries, but even if he was not, Zakaria feels that the fact that he continued getting promotions to higher ranks would have elicited the envy of the Maliks. (Casting a new slant on the historical debate, Zakaria points out that Altunia would probably not have married Razia if he had been convinced she had had an affair with her slave Yaqut.) In any case, Razia aroused the jealousy of the nobility, and some have held this jealousy to have been a major factor in her dethronement.

Razia's marriage to Altunia was apparently endorsed by their followers, and it proved central to the revolt against those who had dethroned her at Delhi. Razia's popularity with her subjects must have further aroused the envy of the Amirs and Maliks, setting the nobles against her on yet another score. According to Zakaria, it was because Minhaj shared the attitude of the nobles and of his patron Balban that he portrayed her in his writings as a coward—for example, saying that she met her death hiding in a corner where she was killed by Hindu robbers—in the final battle with Balban that claimed her life.

Besides Minhaj, there are two other contemporary chroniclers of Razia's life: Fakhr-I-Mudabbir and Sadruddin Hasan Nizami. But their accounts have never achieved the authority of Minhaj's. Two later historians, Isami and Barani, attempted to reconstruct the facts from family accounts (Isami) or independent analysis (Barani). Isami's history is noteworthy for its contradiction of Minhaj's account of Razia's death; in Isami's telling, the sultana fought along with Altunia in two battles before she was finally killed. Other sources, while providing valuable details about the time that Razia lived, attribute little significance to her life.

Razia's Legacy

As sultana, Razia reportedly sought to abolish the tax on non-Muslims but met opposition from the nobility. By way of response, Razia is said to have pointed out that the spirit of religion was more important than its parts, and that even the Muslim Prophet spoke against overburdening the non-Muslims. On another occasion, Razia reportedly tried to appoint an Indian Muslim convert from Hinduism to an official position but again ran into opposition from the nobles. In this case she yielded, having concluded that the bonds of Islam were weaker than old prejudices.

Razia was reportedly devoted to the cause of her empire and to her subjects. There is no record that she made any attempt to remain aloof from her subjects, rather it appears she preferred to mingle among them. Her tolerance of Hinduism would later bring her criticism from Muslim historians.

Razia established schools, academies, centers for research, and public libraries that included the works of ancient philosophers along with the Koran and the Traditions of the Prophet. Hindu works in the sciences, philosophy, astronomy, and literature were reportedly studied in schools and colleges.

Razia's Tomb

Today Razia's unpretentious tomb lies among the narrow lanes of Old Delhi in Northern India. Crumbling and covered by dust and grime, the tomb has clearly suffered the ravages of time. The grave is surrounded on all sides by unattractive residential buildings. Meanwhile modern-day encroachers have placed plastic sheets around the tomb and started to live in it, turning it into an urban ghetto.

In the thirteenth century, the site of the tomb was a jungle, and no one knows how Razia's body ended up where it lies today. Though a second grave accompanies Razia's, the identity of the occupant is unknown. Some of the local residents have turned the tomb into a place of worship, where prayers are conducted five times each day.

Books

Olsen, Kirstin, *Chronology of Women's History,* Greenwood Press, 1994.

Zakaria, Rafiq, *Razia Queen of India,* Oxford University Press, 1966.

Online

''The Delhi Sultanate,'' Historytoday.com, http://www.history today.com/index.cfm?articleid=1371 (February 2003).

''History of Razia Sultana,'' http://www.angelfire.com/ga/files girl/history.html (February 2003).

Santwana Bhattacharya, ''Old Delhi walks all over Razia Sultan's tomb,'' *Indian Express,* http://www.indianexpress.com/ie/daily/20000208/ina08051.html (February 2003).

''The Slave Dynasty,'' History of India, http://www.historyofindia.com/hist_text/slave.html (February 2003).

''The Slave Dynasty,'' Delhi123, http://www.delhi123.com/history/slave.php3 (February 2003).

''Sultana Razia of Delhi,'' http://www.crescentlife.com/thisthat/razia.htm (February 2003).

Swapna Khanna, "She lies among the untrodden ways," *The Rediff Special,* http://www.rediff.com/news/2000/mar/27razia.htm (February 2003).

"The Turkish Invasions," History of India, http://www.historyofindia.com/hist_text/turks.html (February 2003). □

Sumner Murray Redstone

Sumner Redstone (born 1923) built a multi-billion-dollar media empire starting with a string of movie theatres in the Boston area. After fighting successfully for ownership of a little-known cable TV company, Viacom, in 1987, Redstone went on to build Viacom into a personal kingdom that controlled MTV, Nickelodeon, VH1, TV Land, Comedy Central, UPN, TNN, Country Music Television, Showtime/TMC, CBS, Paramount Pictures, Simon & Schuster, Blockbuster, Infinity Broadcasting, and Paramount Parks. In 2002, Redstone's personal fortune was valued at $9 billion.

Early Interests

S umner Murray Redstone was born on May 27, 1923, to Max and Belle Rothstein in Boston, Massachusetts. Redstone's father got his start selling newspapers on the streets of Boston, then became a linoleum salesman and eventually got into the nightclub business, buying Boston's Latin Quarter from Lou Walters, the father of Barbara Walters. Max Rothstein, who later changed the family name to Redstone, opened the third drive-in theater in the United States, on New York's Long Island, and built a small chain of drive-ins that did well in the years after World War II. But Redstone insisted the real driving force in the family was his mother, who used to turn the clock back when he was practicing piano to make him work a little bit longer.

After spending his early years in a tenement which had a bathroom shared with other tenants, Redstone attended the Boston Latin School. There he headed the debating team and graduated at the top of his class. Redstone pursued undergraduate studies at Harvard. During World War II, with classes interrupted, he worked with his professor of Japanese, Edwin Reischauer, on a project aimed at deciphering Japanese military code. After the war, he attended Harvard Law School.

In 1951 Redstone became a partner in the Washington, D.C. law firm of Ford, Bergson, Adams, Borkland & Redstone. But in 1954 he abandoned law and returned to Boston to work with his father in the movie theater business.

National Amusements

At that time his father's company, National Amusements, was able to attract only second-run movies from Hollywood. But after Redstone brought a lawsuit against the

Hollywood studios, National Amusements acquired access to Hollywood's best films. Under Redstone's direction, National Amusements would grow from 59 screens in 1964 to 129 in 1974.

In 1972, Redstone, by then reasonably wealthy, served as co-chairman of Senator Edmund Muskie's presidential campaign. A liberal Democrat, Redstone also became a friend and supporter of Senator Edward M. Kennedy.

During a screening of *Star Wars* in 1977 Redstone reportedly rushed out of the theatre to place an order for 25,000 shares of stock in Twentieth Century Fox. The investment would bring him $20 million when he sold the stock in 1981. He picked up another $40 million by buying and selling stock in Columbia Pictures and MGM/UA.

Trial By Fire

In 1979, the 55-year-old Redstone checked into Boston's Copely Plaza Hotel, where he planned to attend a party for a Warner Brothers Pictures branch manager. Sometime after midnight, Redstone awoke to the smell of smoke. After opening the door to his room, he found himself engulfed in flames. Making his way to the window, he climbed out on a tiny ledge and hung on until a hook-and-ladder fire truck rescued him. He suffered third-degree burns on over 45 percent of his body.

Doctors initially feared for his life, then said he'd never walk again, and later expressed concern that he might lose an arm to infection. After five operations, lasting a total of sixty hours, one of his doctors told him, according to an article in *Broadcasting,* "Listen, everything we know is on your body. Bone grafts, skin grafts, and the reason you're alive is you."

In 2001, Redstone wrote in his autobiography, *A Passion to Win,* "The most exciting things that have happened to me in my professional life have occurred after the fire but not because of it. It doesn't take near death to bring you to life. Life begins whenever you want it to begin." He eventually recovered fully except for a right arm that hung limply from his shoulder and a purplish cast to the skin on his hand.

Viacom Acquisition

In 1987, at the age of 63, Redstone set out to buy Viacom, which at that time operated the tenth-largest cable system in the country and owned several cable networks, including MTV, Nickelodeon, and The Movie Channel. Although Redstone had no experience with cable television or rock videos, he saw them as competitors to movie theaters. He was also astute enough to realize that the home entertainment market was poised for tremendous growth.

Acquiring Viacom was easier said than done. Redstone was forced to raise his offer for the cable company three times in a bitter takeover war with Viacom executives before he finally seized control.

Paramount Merger

By 1993, Redstone's original stake in Viacom was worth $5.5 billion, and he had set his sights on acquiring Paramount Communications, which owned Paramount Pictures, the Paramount television production unit, and a library of nearly 900 films. Also held by Paramount was the publisher Simon & Schuster, which owned Prentice-Hall, Macmillan, Scribner, and Pocket Books; Madison Square Garden; the National Hockey League's New York Rangers; the National Basketball Association's New York Knicks; and cable's MSG Networks. Redstone's stated goal in acquiring Paramount was to create the leading software-driven media company in the world.

But when Paramount indicated it was willing to be acquired by Viacom, Redstone wondered why. He concluded that Paramount's CEO Martin Davis trusted and had a genuine affection for him and that Davis preferred to do business with him rather than with others who were also trying to take over Paramount. But Redstone also gave Davis credit for recognizing the combined strength of the company that a merger would create. When Redstone announced Viacom's acquisition of Paramount and the creation of Paramount Viacom International on September 12, 1993, he said "This is a deal only a nuclear war will tear asunder."

But with the merger Redstone had on his hands an unwieldy giant burdened by debt. However, by selling off Madison Square Garden and some cable systems and radio stations and a video game company, Redstone slashed his debts from $11 billion to less than half that. He also scored a coup with his sale of Simon & Schuster's educational division to Pearson for $4.6 billion, far more than industry analysts expected him to get.

New Directions

In the late 1990s, with Viacom's Blockbuster Video in trouble, it appeared that Redstone's fortunes would diminish along with those of his company. But Redstone hung on, redesigning Blockbuster's business mode, patching up marketing and distribution problems, and bringing in a new chief executive. As a result, new life was pumped into the video subsidiary.

Redstone, meanwhile, required that Paramount make movies developed by its Viacom cousins, MTV and Nickelodeon, against initial opposition from the reluctant partners. But the arrangement worked, and Paramount and MTV made a string of profitable movies, while Nickelodeon did very well with its *Rugrats* movies.

Making movies was the most difficult side of Viacom's business. Its bread was buttered by its cable networks and their strong brands, low overhead, and high profit margins. Nickelodeon ranked at the top in children's viewing; MTV received top billing for those between 12 and 24; and VH1 gained popularity among baby boomers with its music offerings. There was also growing interest in TV Land and Comedy Central.

MTV and Nickelodeon began reversing losses overseas as Redstone looked abroad for Viacom's future. He told *Fortune* in 1999, "Anybody who ignores the fact that 96% of the world's eyeballs are outside the U.S. is going to pay for it."

On September 7, 1999, Viacom and CBS announced the merger of the two companies, with Viacom purchasing the television network for $37.3 billion. Although Redstone until that time had shown no interest in purchasing a major television network, he was attracted by CBS's assets, which included production houses and radio stations. Redstone later wrote in his autobiography, "Bigger is not necessarily better, although it is certainly true that bigger is better than smaller. But this merger was not about bigness; it was about putting together two groups of assets that would produce an extraordinary company."

About the time the merger between CBS and Viacom was falling into place, Redstone's wife decided to divorce him after 52 years of marriage. According to Redstone, the divorce hit him "like a bullet," even though he claimed the marriage had been troubled for a long time.

Proving Critics Wrong

Redstone met success through relentless persistence, not by marketing a new technology or selling a personal vision. He reportedly viewed his company's stock price as a public scorecard. And rather than wearing him down, work seemed to rejuvenate the entertainment mogul. For the tightly focused Redstone, there was reportedly no life outside his company. He told *Fortune* magazine, "Viacom is me . . . I'm Viacom. That marriage is eternal, forever."

Redstone encountered plenty of naysayers along his path to success. Initially dismissed as a "two-bit theater operator from Boston" by the Viacom old guard, he was later called "the foolish boss of a bloated empire" after the troubles at Blockbuster surfaced.

But Redstone always enjoyed proving his critics wrong. And he did not seem to hold a lot of grudges; he even suggested future business deals with those who opposed him in the past. He told *Fortune,* "It's a mistake, if you want to run your company right, to let history get in the way of the future." The much-maligned Paramount merger paid off. Redstone told *Fortune,* "The deal from hell has become a helluva deal!"

Simple Tastes

Redstone reportedly had no designated heir apparent waiting to take over upon his departure. He assured investors that neither his son Brent, a Denver attorney, nor his daughter Shari, who presides over National Amusements, would assume the Viacom reins when he left.

Although Redstone made more money from the entertainment industry than any other human being, he spent most of his life out of the glare of publicity. Part of the reason is that Viacom lacked the romantic appeal of Disney or AOL Time Warner. But in his trademark cheap suits, Redstone also lacked the charisma of Ted Turner.

Redstone kept an apartment in New York's Pierre Hotel, but he still lived in the same home in the Boston suburbs that he bought for $43,000. His wants seemed simple, his aspirations without bound. He told *Fortune* magazine, "To me, staying in a bungalow at the Beverly Hills Hotel, walking out and being surrounded by flowers, and then going down the path to play tennis—that's the height of my material aspirations . . . Then I get in the car to go to the studio."

Books

Redstone, Sumner, with Peter Knobler, *A Passion to Win,* Simon & Schuster, 2001.

Periodicals

Broadcasting, November 14, 1988.
Electronic Media, April 26, 1999.
Forbes, October 17, 1994.
Fortune, April 26, 1999.
Time, September 27, 1993. ☐

Ishmael Reed

A novelist, journalist, and playwright, American writer Ishmael Reed (born 1938) has been cited by critics as among the greatest contemporary African American literary figures of his generation.

According to Lee Hubbard in *American Visions,* Ishmael Reed is "an unorthodox writer who has taken on the media, the writing establishment, feminists, politicians, blacks, whites and [the] American institution of higher learning." Reed's satire has been controversial, to say the least, but he has nonetheless joined

novelists Toni Morrison and Samuel Delany as among the most important forces in the distinct African American culture that developed during the 20th century.

Early Years in New York

Reed was born in Chattanooga, Tennessee, but grew up in Buffalo, New York, in a working-class neighborhood. He graduated from Buffalo public schools in 1956 and enrolled as a night student at Millard Fillmore College. While there, Reed wrote a short story about a young African American man and showed it to his English professor. Impressed with Reed's abilities, the professor aided Reed in enrolling for day school at the University of Buffalo, where he attended classes from 1956 to 1960. Financially unable to remain in college, however, Reed dropped out before graduating but continued to write. While in Buffalo he wrote a jazz column for the *Empire Star Weekly,* an African American community newspaper, and co-hosted a Buffalo radio program that was canceled after Reed interviewed controversial black leader Malcolm X.

Reed moved to New York City in 1962, where he worked as an editor for a Newark, New Jersey, weekly and organized the American Festival of Negro Art. Reed established himself as a founder of the *East Village Other,* a respected underground newspaper, and as a member of the Umbra Writers Workshop. The workshop, in the words of Robert Elliot Fox in *The Oxford Companion to African-American Literature,* was "one of the organizations instrumental in the creation of the Black Arts movement and its efforts to establish a Black Aesthetic." The goals of the workshop—especially the establishment of a black aesthetic—would stay with Reed for the rest of his career. While in New York City, Reed befriended Langston Hughes, a major influence in African American poetry who became a major influence in Reed's work. Hughes was also instrumental in getting Reed's first novel published.

Established Neohoodism

Unhappy with the African American literary movement on the east coast, Reed relocated to Oakland, California, where he settled permanently, living at least part of the time in the city's so-called black ghetto. That same year, 1967, his first novel, *The Freelance Pallbearers,* was published. With his first novel, Reed established the various themes and styles that would become his trademark. *The Freelance Pallbearers* was a satire heavily critical of the Western European Christian tradition, the formal literature of that tradition, and African Americans within different black communities. It was Reed's second novel, *Yellow Back Radio Broke Down,* published in 1969, that established his usage of "HooDoo" and folklore.

"Neohoodism is the name Reed gave to the philosophy and aesthetic processes he employs to take care of business on behalf of the maligned and mishandled," explained Fox. This African American version of voodoo appealed to Reed because of its mystery and especially its eclectic nature. It became a way for Reed to avoid using Western literary traditions while creating a new multi-ethnic voice. Reed respects voodoo as a world view due to its ease of adaptation, its flexibility, and its way of eating and dissolving into itself other ways of living. His written work is known for satirizing and challenging existing social and literary conventions, According to Hubbard, Reed is a "self-proclaimed multiculturalist who consistently incorporates different aspects of other people's cultures into his work."

Multi-faceted Career in Oakland

With his stints in Buffalo and New York City in radio, his editing work, and the publication of his first novel, Reed set his sights on building a multifaceted career. He has since become known not just for his novels, but for his extensive collections of essays, his poetry, his journalism, his editing, publishing, play-writing, song-writing, television producing, lecturing, teaching, and founding of various organizations. In most of these fields, Reed has been honored for his accomplishments and talents, making him a one-man *tour de force.*

In 1970 Reed's first collection of poetry, *Catechism of D Neoamerican HooDoo Church,* was published. Around this time he also started teaching at the University of California in Berkeley, where he remained on staff for upwards of 20 years (even without tenure). In 1971 Reed started the Yardbird Publishing Co., which published, among other things, the magazine *Y'Bird.*

Reed's *Mumbo Jumbo,* a novel published in 1972, was his first book to achieve widespread notoriety. It has also been considered by many to be his best work, along with *Neo-HooDoo Manifesto,* a collection of essays published

the same year. *Manifesto* was nominated for a National Book Award along with *Conjure: Selected Poems, 1963-1970,* also published in 1972. In 1973 Reed published another collection titled *Chattanooga: Poems.* Meanwhile, he co-founded another publishing enterprise, Reed, Cannon & Johnson Communications. This new publishing company published *Quilt* magazine, which was designed for students, minorities, and writers living and working on the West Coast of the United States.

A Voice for Many Causes

The year 1974 saw the publication of another novel by Reed, *The Last Days of Louisiana Red.* In 1976 the novel *Flight to Canada* was published to critical acclaim and was praised as among his best works. Also in 1976, Reed co-founded the Before Columbus Foundation, a multiethnic organization promoting a cross-cultural America. The Before Columbus Foundation has often been cited as Reed's most important contribution to U.S. society.

In 1978 Reed published a volume of poetry titled *Secretary to the Spirits* as well as a volume of essays titled *Shrovetide in Old New Orleans.* By 1980 he was involved in the world of theater and wrote and produced the play *The Ace Boons.* He published two more plays in 1982: *Hell Hath No Fury* and *Mother Hubbard.*

The novel *Reckless Eyeballing,* published in 1986, reveals Reed's feelings about slavery in the United States and the Jim Crow era that followed abolition. In the novel the practice of "reckless eyeballing"—a black man looking at a white woman—is dealt with directly in Reed's satire. *Reckless Eyeballing* was followed by *New and Collected Poetry* and the 1988 essay collection *Writin' Is Fightin': Thirty-seven Years of Boxing on Paper.* In 1989 Reed published a sequel to his 1982 novel *The Terrible Twos* titled *The Terrible Threes,* a criticism of throwaway pop culture. He also edited the *Before Columbus Foundation Fiction Anthology: Selections from the American Book Awards 1980–1990.*

In 1990 Reed published *Tell My Horse: Voodoo and Life in Haiti and Jamaica,* in which he presents an account of Haiti as the country of origination for Voodoo. Reed also notes that Voodoo—or Hoodoo—because of its flexible qualities, has existed throughout history in many subversive forms. He told Reginald Martin in a *Review of Contemporary Fiction* interview: "I've decided that gospel music is just a front for Voodoo. . . . I think when they're praising Jesus, they're really singing about Legba or something like that."

Battled Mainstream Media

In 1992 Reed organized a boycott of major television networks that was led by the Oakland chapter of the international writers' organization PEN. The boycott was only one step in the author's ongoing battle against mainstream media. Reed has claimed that the media systematically undermines and unfavorably portrays minorities in the United States, and these inaccurate portrayals have been detrimental to the production of a healthy, multiethnic society and a healthy African American self-view. He spent years monitoring the media's portrayal of people and wrote letters whenever necessary. He has also attacked the media in his essays, novels, and poems. "The state of American journalism in its portrayal of minorities is horrible," Reed commented to Holland, and further expanded on his views of the media in his 1993 essay collection *Airing Dirty Laundry.*

In 1993 Reed published the novel *Japanese by Spring* and four years later edited the anthology *MultiAmerica: Essays on Cultural Wars and Cultural Peace,* which showcases writers communicating about race relations in the United States.

Life and Time of Reed

Besides having taught at the University of California at Berkeley since the late 1960s, Reed has held visiting appointments at such places as Harvard University, Yale University, and Dartmouth College. In Germany and Switzerland he has lectured to standing-room-only crowds. Among his continuing projects is a musical titled *Gethsemane Park* and a novel about the O. J. Simpson trial. He has received a Pulitzer Prize nomination to accompany his two National Book Award nominations, as well as many other awards, grants, and fellowships. He founded I. Reed Books as well as the journal *Konch* and wrote a libretto for the San Francisco Opera Company. Reed is married to Carla Blank, a dancer and choreographer. The couple has one daughter, Tennessee, and Reed has another daughter from a previous marriage.

Hubbard called Reed "the establishment agitator who has been called a conservative, a radical, a black nationalist, a sexist and a crazed fool;" he has also been called America's best satirist since Mark Twain. Reed's work, known for its principle of collage and cited as having its roots in the Yoruba tradition of West Africa, has been criticized for incoherence. It has also been praised for its multicultural-ness, revolutionary-ness, and Reed's awareness of mythic archetypes. In his own defense against such criticism, Reed told Martin, "I don't think there is any standard English. I think there is such a thing as protocol English." Reed writes with neither. His English is a "HooDoo" English, full of an awareness of multiethnicity and concerned with a multi-race—and a distinctly African American race—of writers.

Books

Oxford Companion to African-American Literature, Oxford University Press, 1997.

Periodicals

American Visions, April-May, 1998.
Callaloo, Fall 1994.
Review of Contemporary Fiction, Summer 1984.

Online

"Ishmael Reed," http://www.math.buffalo.edu/~sww/reed/reed_ishmael_bio.html (February 10, 2003).
"Ishmael Reed," http://www.poets.org/poets/poets.cfm?prmID=769 (February 10, 2003).

Martin, Reginald, "An Interview with Ishmael Reed," http://www.centerforbookculture.org/interviews/interview_reed.htm l (February 10, 2003). □

Alain Resnais

French film director Alain Resnais (born 1922) was one of the most noted innovators in the history of twentieth-century film. His many film credits include *Night and Fog, Hiroshima, Mon Amour,* and *Marienbad.*

After paying his dues as an actor, editor, screenwriter, and assistant director in the 1940s and 1950s, Resnais emerged as a leading member of the French cinema's New Wave. His themes, which frequently involve memory, history, and time, revolutionized film conventions. Resnais's films typically involve characters who, though their outward appearances seem conventional, inevitably find themselves caught up in existential dilemmas. In the course of his career Resnais has collaborated with many top writers, among them Marguerite Duras, Alain Robbe-Grillet, Jean Gruault, Jorge Semprun, and Jean Cayrol. As one of the foremost proponents European art cinema, Resnais has profoundly influenced other film makers, if only by forcing them to examine their own assumptions about their craft.

Early Life

Resnais was born on June 3, 1922, in Vannes, Morbihan, Bretagne, France. Like his hero, French novelist Marcel Proust, the young Resnais was educated at home because he suffered from asthma. By most accounts Resnais became interested in film-making at an early age, and his first work, titled "Fantomas," was filmed with the help of friends when he was 14. The 8mm film, which runs only three minutes, employed several cinematic "tricks" designed to vary the appearance of the characters.

Despite this early effort, Resnais had no youthful aspirations toward a career in cinema. As he told Joan Dupont in *Interview:* "I never had any special appetite for filmmaking, but you have to make a living and it is miraculous to earn a living working in film. My father and grandfather were pharmacists, but I couldn't become one because you needed the baccalaureate [high school diploma] and because my health was bad, I failed." In any case, after finishing his preparatory studies, Resnais entered the Institut des Hautes Etudes Cinématographiques in Paris, where he became thoroughly immersed in the world of film.

Resnais's early films, which were shot in black and white on 16mm film, are short documentaries dealing with art and artists. In 1948, for example, he made the film *Van Gogh,* which was followed by another filmed in 1950 and titled *Gauguin.* During the 1950s he also shot and edited scenes for other directors. Resnais's own early films foreshadow certain themes that the filmmaker would take up in

the 1960s: including time, memory, post-capitalist imperialism, and the role of the artist. He remained concerned with the role of the artist in society throughout much of his career.

Three Masterpieces

In 1955 Resnais made the 30-minute documentary-style film *Night and Fog (Nuit et brouillard),* which presents a riveting look at German concentration camps. The film juxtaposes grainy black-and-white historical footage of the Nazi-run concentration camps during operation with color footage of the same camps as they appeared a decade after they were abandoned. Archival footage from Bergen Belsen, Buchenwald, Auschwitz, and Einstanz Grüppe was used by Resnais to create this collage of atrocities, and the film's script was written by poet and former prison-camp inmate Jean Cayrol. In *Night and Fog,* Resnais explores the ambiguities between cinematic and real time, as well as between memory and conscience. The film expresses the message that although individual people would like to evade responsibility, ultimately it is collective humanity that must bear the responsibility for the Nazi horrors.

Discussing *Night and Fog,* Resnais told Dupont that with "little money and few documents, we had nothing. So I used formal techniques to make the film more perceptive emotionally. For the first time, I used a mix of black and white with color In the editing room, I asked myself, 'What are you doing manipulating corpses this way?' It was repugnant, but it was the only way to communicate."

American film director Errol Morris commented in *Filmmaker* that many people's beliefs about the Holocaust were influenced by *Night and Fog.* According to Morris, although the film was successful in bringing the Nazi atrocities into popular consciousness, it also had the effect of muddling history. For example, Morris noted that there is no mention in the film of the role French gendarmes played in the Holocaust. According to James Monaco, writing in his *Alain Resnais,* in the original film a French gendarme is clearly visible in one of the photographs. Because this version was unacceptable to French censors, the gendarme's uniform was edited out of the film before it was screened publically.

Resnais followed *Night and Fog* with *Le Chant du styrene* (1958), in which he attempts to capture a plastics factory in cinematographic poetry. The film traces the manufacture of polystyrene from the finished product back through the industrial pipelines to the raw starting materials. Monaco dubbed *Le Chant due styrene* the most remarkable "industrial" film ever made.

In 1959 Renais filmed the full-length 35mm black-and-white feature *Hiroshima, Mon Amour,* based on a script by novelist Marguerite Duras. The film, which explores the relationship between history and memory, was awarded the Cannes Film Festival's International Critics Prize. In the film a French actress on assignment in Japan and a Japanese architect have a brief, adulterous affair. The actress is haunted by her past in occupied France, where she had an affair with a German soldier, and the architect is haunted by his family's sufferings during the atomic bomb attack on Hiroshima. In *Hiroshima, Mon Amour* Resnais uses the medium of film to break down the linearity that encapsulates time and memory and creates a dream state. The clean, modern lines of the hotel where the affair takes place are contrasted in the film with the natural curves of the lovers, the rivers that wind through the town, and the memories in the protagonists' pasts.

In discussing *Hiroshima, Mon Amour* with Dupont, Resnais explained that he and Duras "had this idea of working in two tenses: The present and the past coexist, but the past shouldn't be in flashback. The heroine's memory, her affair with the German soldier, was the past, but the sound was in the present; we hear the sounds of Tokyo." Film critic John Francis Kreidl, writing in *Alain Resnais,* agreed with Monaco that the film ultimately turns out to be about the impossibility of making a documentary about Hiroshima.

In Resnais's 1961 work *Last Year at Marienbad,* a man and woman meet in a palatial home. The man insists that the two have met before and, further, that they had an affair the year before at a spa in Marienbad. Resnais uses the couple's encounter to examine memory, imagination, desire, and fulfillment. Of *Last Year in Marienbad* Resnais told Dupont, "I never thought of Proust; I thought of Andre Breton. [The film's screenwriter] Alain Robbe-Grillet and I were very impressed by surrealism. . . . Most of what happens is in the characters' imaginations, so the memory of silent film was a big influence." Monaco found the film to be essentially a story about storytelling.

Of Time and Remembrance

Resnais's next film, *Muriel* (1963), concerns a middle-aged woman who invites an old lover to visit her and her stepson, who has just returned from the war in the Algiers. The soldier is troubled by memories of a young girl who had been tortured to death in his presence, while the two former lovers suffer from their own painful memories. In the film Resnais uses time to explore the ways the past influences present experiences. Relating also to the historical present, *Muriel* captures the constraints placed on freedom in France by the Algerian war in 1962, and the mood associated with that period. To the director's disappointment, many critics disliked this film.

After creating what are considered to be Resnais's three masterpieces—*Night and Fog, Hiroshima, Mon Amour,* and *Marienbad*—Resnais gained a reputation as one of the leading New Wave film directors. However, as he later explained to Dupont, Resnais did not consider himself "part of the New Wave, but thanks to [the impact made by its directors], I made movies. . . . Before, you had to be an assistant on nine films, and you couldn't just go from making a short to a feature. Finally, a producer asked me to make a feature, and I made three in a row, but after *Muriel,* which wasn't a success, I stopped for a while."

When he returned to his position behind the camera, Resnais again chose to dwell on time and remembrance. His richly emotional 1966 work *La Guerre est finie* concerns an aging Leftist, while *Stavisky* (1974) tells the story of a Russian-Jewish swindler in 1930s France. *Providence,* filmed in 1977 and Resnais's first English-language effort, deals with a dying novelist.

In *Mon Oncle d'Amerique* (1980) Resnais examines the interconnections in the lives of three individuals and interprets these connections using the biochemical theories of French biologist Henri Laborit about the workings of the human brain. In the film contrasts—distance and emotion, surrealism and the natural—are used to force the audience to an awareness of new possibilities. By playing disparate moods, tones, and styles off against each other, Resnais attempted to draw the viewer into a closer relationship with the film's characters.

On one level, 1983's *Life Is a Bed of Roses* tells the story of a wealthy count who constructs his "temple of happiness" during the 1920s. On another level, it presents a symposium on alternative education held at the site of the former temple.

Resnais's later films, which have not always been as well received by critics as were his work of the late 1950s and early 1960s, include *L'Amour e mort* (1984), *Melo* (1986), *I Want to Go Home* (1989), and *Smoking and No Smoking* (1993). In 1992 he directed a one-hour tribute to U.S. composer George Gershwin.

Looking Back

It has been reported that Resnais refuses to view any of his early films. "I don't think about them and can't stand seeing them again," he told Dupont. "It's painful, either because the people onscreen have died, or because I don't think the direction is good. There's always something." The films of other directors are a different matter, however. "When I was twelve, the passage from silent film to the talkies had an impact on me—I still watch silent films. I don't think that there is any such thing as an old film; you don't say, 'I read an old book by Flaubert,' or 'I saw an old play by Moliere.' "

Resnais's obsession with time and memory reflects a French tradition that goes back to Henri Bergson and Proust. In *Night and Fog,* for example, he attempts to recapture the past through a combination of archival film footage and poetry, while in *Hiroshima, Mon Amour* he adopts an imitation documentary format to examine the repercussions of the atomic bomb attack on Japan. In *Last Year at Marienbad* the film's characters attempt to rewrite their own history at a European spa.

Resnais told Luc Honorez of *Le Soir* that his life could be summarized by listing the names of some of the most influential individuals of the twentieth century: Sigmund Freud, Pablo Picasso, Gershwin, Hergé, and Franz Kafka. Still, he added, in spite of his advanced age he wanted to move on to other passions. The director insists that becoming fixated on any one of his many influences would be equivalent to signing up to die. The introduction of video and DVD technologies has allowed Resnais to study the films of fellow directors Fritz Lang, Alfred Hitchcock, Clint Eastwood, Victor Minnelli, F. W. Murnau, Jean Renoir, Tati, Charles Laughton, and Martin Scorsese.

According to Resnais, of all the arts only cinema is an absolute mystery because of the juxtaposition of objects, the attitudes of the actors, and the use of music. However, he views much of modern cinematography as a failure because the promotion of a film has become more important than what the film ultimately is. His own approach to his art has been determined by memories, including loves and sorrows, many of which originated in films, books, or songs. Regarding the power of twentieth-century cinema, Resnais has cited that the most effective films are those able to connect with those instinctive emotions people attempt to mask in order to appear less "animal-like."

Books

Kreidl, John Francis, *Alain Resnais,* Twayne, 1977.
Monaco, James, *Alain Resnais,* Oxford University Press, 1979.

Periodicals

Filmmaker, Spring 2000.
Interview, November 1999.
Le Soir, May 21, 2002. ☐

Condoleezza Rice

Condoleezza Rice (born 1954) is a classic overachiever. Growing up in segregated Birmingham, Alabama, Rice refused to let the boundaries set by society limit her. She has become a close adviser to

President George W. Bush, involved in decisions that shape the future of the United States of America.

Rice Groomed For Success

Condoleezza Rice was born in Birmingham, Alabama, on November 14, 1954. Her father, John Wesley Rice, was a school guidance counselor during the week and a Presbyterian minister on the weekends. Her mother, Angelena, was a schoolteacher. The family lived in a middle-class, black community called Titusville, where education was a high priority for children who were expected to succeed regardless of any prejudices or boundaries.

John and Angelena Rice tried to give everything possible to their young daughter, providing intangible support by developing her sense of pride, faith, and responsibility. "They wanted the world," Connie Rice (a second cousin to Rice) said in a biography by Antonia Felix entitled *Condi: The Condoleezza Rice Story.* "They wanted Rice to be free of any kind of shackles, mentally or physically, and they wanted her to own the world. And to give a child that kind of entitlement, you have to love her to death and make her believe that she can fly." John Rice coached football and taught his daughter everything he could about tactics and strategy. Rice grew to love the game and would follow football wherever she went.

Terror in Birmingham

In the early 1960s, the civil rights movement landed in Birmingham. Schoolchildren were encouraged to participate in marches and other demonstrations. The Rice family did not join in but sometimes went down to watch history unfold. "My father was not a march-in-the street preacher," Rice said in the biography. "He saw no reason to put children at risk. He would never put his own child at risk." Unfortunately, sometimes the police would use fire hoses to spray the children, or dogs would chase the children. Some of the young adults arrested were John Rice's students. Television cameras caught it all on tape for the nation to see.

Events that were stirring the emotions of the nation were occurring right in Birmingham when Rice was only eight years old. Vigilantes bombed the home of a family friend, Arthur Shores, twice in the fall of 1963. On September 15, 1963, the 16th Street Baptist Church was bombed, killing four young girls attending Sunday school. One of the girls, Denise Nair, was Rice's friend from school. Rice had heard the explosion and felt the shudder of the blast. She remembers her father and the other men from the neighborhood organizing to patrol the streets at night with shotguns. She was growing up with terrorism. The Rice family watched on television when President Lyndon Johnson signed the Civil Rights Act on July 2, 1964. Not long after, the family went to dinner at a previously all-white restaurant in Birmingham.

Rice was a bright student and skipped both first and seventh grade. Her parents encouraged her to do well in everything she tried, and they provided lessons in piano, ballet, violin, French, and skating, and instruction in dress, grooming, and manners. In 1965, she was the first black student to attend music classes at Birmingham Southern Conservatory of Music.

When Rice was 11 years old, her father accepted a position in Tuscaloosa, Alabama, as a college administrator. Two years after that, he accepted a position as vice chancellor at the University of Denver in Colorado. For the first time, Rice attended integrated school at St. Mary's Academy, a private Catholic school. During her first year, a school counselor advised her that she was not college material, despite her excellent grades and musical and athletic accomplishments. "Condi was stunned, but her parents—immune to talk of limitation or failure—didn't flinch," stated Felix in the biography. "They assured her that the assessment was wrong and that she should just ignore it."

Became Interested in Politics

At age 15, Rice graduated from high school and started attending the University of Denver, hoping to become a concert pianist. She won a young artist's competition and was invited to play Mozart's Piano Concerto in D Minor with the Denver Symphony Orchestra. Although she was a talented performer, she knew that the competition for professional performers was stiff. Partway through college, she decided she would never become a concert pianist. She took a course called "Introduction to International Politics." Her professor, Dr. Josef Korbel, a Soviet specialist and the father of Madeleine Albright (who later became secretary of state under President Bill Clinton), inspired her. She changed her major to political science. Rice was an avid student, and in 1974, she earned her bachelor's degree in political science (cum laude and Phi Beta Kappa) at age 19. She was awarded the Political Science Honors Award for "outstanding accomplishment and promise in the field of political science." She went on to get her Master's degree in government and international studies at Notre Dame University in just one year. She returned to Denver, unsure of what to do next.

"I thought I had a job as executive assistant to a vice president of Honeywell," she told Nicholas Lemann in the *New Yorker.* "Before I could go to work, they reorganized, and I lost the job." She taught piano lessons and applied to law school. Then, when she was down at the university, Dr. Korbel recommended that she take some classes. By 1981, she had received her Ph.D. in international studies from the University of Denver.

She was awarded a fellowship at Stanford's Center for International Security and Arms Control. It was the first time the Center had ever admitted a woman. The fellowship was supposed to be for one year, but Rice made a big impression and was offered a job as an assistant professor of political science at Stanford University, which she accepted. In her classes, Rice often used football analogies in her lectures, comparing war to football. Her classes were popular and attracted many athletes.

To Washington

In 1984, Rice attended a faculty seminar where Brent Scowcroft, then head of President Reagan's Commission of Strategic Forces, spoke on arms control. During the dinner following the seminar, Rice asked Scowcroft some challenging questions. Scowcroft was impressed. "I thought, This is somebody I need to get to know. It's an intimidating subject. Here's this young girl, and she's not at all intimidated," he told the *New Yorker*'s Lemann. Scowcroft began arranging for her to attend seminars and conferences. In 1986, she was appointed as the special assistant to the Director-Joint Chiefs of Staff position at the Pentagon through a Council on Foreign Relations Fellowship. Then, in 1989, when Scowcroft became National Security Advisor, he appointed Rice to the National Security Council as the chief authority on the Soviet Union. She was involved in forming the American reaction to the fall of the Berlin Wall, the dissolution of the Warsaw Pact, and the demise of what was then considered the Soviet Union.

During this time period, Rice had been doing a lot of writing. In 1984, she published *Uncertain Allegiance: The Soviet Union and the Czechoslovak Army 1948-1963.* She also wrote *The Gorbachev Era* with Alexander Dallin in 1986. Rice joined the Board of Directors of the Stanford Mid-Peninsula Urban Coalition in 1986. The organization provided vocational and academic assistance to minority students at high risk of dropping out of high school.

Rice returned to Stanford in 1991. She was appointed to the board of directors of Chevron. She apparently served them well, as they named a tanker after her in 1993, and she went to Rio de Janeiro to christen it. She also served on the boards for TransAmerica Corporation and Hewlett Packard.

Rice Chosen as Provost

During meetings to help select a new president for Stanford, Rice impressed the man who was given the job, Gerhard Casper. He appointed her to the number-two position of provost. She entered the position during a difficult time. There were large deficits in the budget and cuts were necessary. Rice took on the job with her usual efficiency. *Forbes* reported, "In her first year, Rice, 39, balanced the university's $410 million unrestricted budget without dipping into reserves for the first time in six years." When she stepped down, six years later, the $40 million deficit had become a surplus.

In 1995, she and Philip Zelikow co-authored, *Germany Unified and Europe Transformed: A Study in Statecraft.* The book was awarded the Akira Iriye International History Book Award for 1994-1995.

Rice and President George W. Bush

In July of 1999, she took a leave of absence from her provost position to become the foreign policy advisor for Texas Governor George W. Bush's presidential campaign. When Bush won the election, he tapped Rice for the position of National Security Advisor. As National Security Adviser, Rice has to balance some strong personalities and viewpoints and pull all of the information together for the president. Evan Thomas of *Newsweek* reported, "By law, the secretary of state is the president's chief foreign-policy advisor; the national security adviser runs no department and commands no troops. But he or she (Rice was the first-ever woman to get the job) is usually the first to see the president in the morning and the last at night."

On September 11, 2001, Rice immediately recognized the planes striking the World Trade Center as a terrorist attack. She called a meeting of the National Security Council. When a plane hit the Pentagon, they were ordered to evacuate the White House and take shelter in an underground bunker. She made calls throughout the day to heads of state throughout the world, assuring them that the United States government was up and running. She was suddenly thrust into the spotlight, as the Bush administration evaluated their next steps.

Rice works very hard not to reveal her own views, but instead to gather the information provided and present it to the president. *Newsweek*'s Thomas stated, "She has often said that she is 'determined to leave this town' without anyone outside Bush's tight inner circle ever figuring out where she stands on major issues. She claims that she 'rarely' tells the president her private opinions, and if she does, she never shares her advice to the president, not even with her closest aides."

Rice is very dedicated to her physical fitness and gets up at 5 a.m. to exercise. She has never married, has no brothers or sisters, and her parents have passed away. Her job is the main focus in her life, and she regularly works 15-16 hour days. She relaxes by playing the piano. She enjoys shopping, and *Newsweek*'s Thomas reported that Saks Fifth

Avenue has been known to open up for her after hours. Her aides affectionately refer to her as the "Warrior Princess," according to Thomas. Her faith is strong, and she prays every night and sometimes during the day as well. She is passionate about football and often states that she would someday like to become the commissioner of the National Football League.

Newsweek's Thomas summed it up when he stated in an article on September 9, 2002, "At an early age, she drove right through the boundaries of race and chased excellence and accomplishment all the way to the northwest corner office of the West Wing."

Books

Felix, Antonia, *Condi: The Condoleezza Rice Story,* Newmarket Press, 2002.

Periodicals

Forbes, October 24, 1994.
National Review, August 30, 1999.
Newsweek, September 9, 2002; December 16, 2002.
New Yorker, October 14, 2002.

Online

"Biography of Dr. Condoleezza Rice: National Security Advisor," *The White House,* http://www.whitehouse.gov/nsc/ricebio.html (January 15, 2003).
"Condoleezza Rice: U.S. national security adviser," CNN.com, http://www.cnn.com (January 15, 2003). □

Gerhard Richter

German artist Gerhard Richter (born 1932) is considered one of the most significant and challenging artists of the last quarter-century. His diverse paintings cover a range of artistic genres, from Realism and Naturalism to Impressionism, Pop Art, Conceptualism, and Post-Abstract Expressionism. Richter often painted from photographs, either clipped from newspapers and various other sources or shot by the artist himself, and worked mainly in groups of paintings numbered sequentially.

In Richter's portrayals, one always senses a sense of faith coupled with cruelty. For instance, nature to Richter is at once sublime but indifferent to the human condition, and popular culture transforms people who would otherwise think as individuals into submissive followers. His works furthermore contain a darkness and reveal a mistrust of any sort of dogma. However, faith and beauty remain underlying elements. Indeed, Richter sees art as the highest form of hope. "I constantly despair at my own incapacity, at the impossibility of ever accomplishing anything, of painting a valid, true picture or of even knowing what such a thing ought to look like," Richter once wrote, as quoted in the *New York Times.* "But then I always have the hope that, if I persevere, it might one day happen."

Childhood Experiences

Born in Dresden, Germany, on February 9, 1932, and raised in the outlying villages of Reichenau and Waltersdorf, Richter grew during a tumultuous and horrific period in world history, coming of age just after World War II. Undoubtedly, Richter's early experiences—including the teachings and beliefs of his parents and living his first 13 years under the Nazis—impacted his development both artistically and intellectually, leading him to later depict subjects as varied as a Nazi uncle, fighter planes, religion, landscapes, gangs of young German terrorists, and his own wife and child.

By comparison, Richter's parents seemed ill-matched for one another. His father, a conventional-minded schoolteacher, embraced Nazism and fought for the regime on the Eastern and Western fronts. He died, as did Richter's uncles, during the war. Richter also had a mentally disabled aunt who perished in a Nazi euthanasia program. Richter's mother, in contrast, was raised in a cultured and at one time wealthy family. The daughter of a talented pianist and bookseller, she exposed Richter to literature, philosophy, and music, and encouraged his interest in painting and drawing.

Following the collapse of the Third Reich, Richter lived for another 16 years under the oppressive hand of East Germany. But he would later recall that by the age of 17, "my fundamental aversion to all beliefs and ideologies was fully developed," as quoted by Jay Tolson for *U.S. News and World Report*. Richter left grammar school at 15 years of age, taking a series of temporary jobs like assisting a local photographer, decorating banners for the East German communist regime, and painting sets for a theater located in the small town of Zittau.

School of Socialist Realism

Intent on studying art more formally, Richter, in 1952, after failing to gain acceptance on the first try, won admittance into the Hochscule für Bildende Kunste in Dresden. At the art academy, where he trained until 1957, Richter gained a thorough knowledge of the masters and studied extensively with Heinz Lothmar, a former Surrealist and supporter of communism who headed the mural painting department. Ironically, this department allowed students the greatest degree of freedom of self-expression, due largely to the fact that the strict enforcers of the state-sanctioned Socialist Realist aesthetic considered the painting of murals as merely "decorative."

Upon graduation, Richter obtained work painting murals. His first official commission, a mural of bathers for the German Hygeine Museum, was executed in the approved bombastic style. Soon thereafter, Richter was attracting recognition as well as a steady income, allowing him the opportunity to travel outside East Germany.

Confronted by Western Art

On one excursion to the West in 1959, Richter received permission to visit Documenta 2 in Kassel, West Germany, discovering for the first time Abstract painting. Today, the Documenta exhibition takes place every five years and has evolved into a major site for experiencing contemporary art on the worldwide circuit. But at the event's inception in 1955, the exhibition held an immense political and cultural significance for art in Germany. By surveying international modern and contemporary art, the sponsors of Documenta hoped to fill the void in German cultural history that had occurred during the 12-year period of domination by the Nazis, who had stigmatized modern art as degenerate. Consequently Germany, through Documenta, intended to reaccept into the culture what it had in the past sought to destroy.

Attending Documenta was a turning point in Richter's career, and he began to feel an internal pressure to engage in the dialogues of modern art. Many of the artists represented at the event were completely unknown to Richter at the time. Lucio Fontana and Jackson Pollock, among others, impressed him most of all. Thus, in 1961, shortly before the erection of the Berlin Wall, Richter fled Dresden for West Berlin.

A Second Education

Upon the advice of a friend who had already made the move to West Germany, Richter promptly enrolled in art school in Düsseldorf at the Staatliche Kunstakademie. In many ways, Richter, before graduating in 1964, unlearned everything he had been taught at the conservative school in Dresden. At Düsseldorf, he studied with Art Informel or gesture painter Karl Otto Gotz and also worked for a brief period in an aggressive style influenced by Alberto Burri, Jean Dubuffet, Jean Fautrier, and Fontana. The same year Richter entered the school, Joseph Beuys, who would become the most famous artist of the post-war era, was named professor of monumental sculpture. Richter kept his distance from Beuys throughout his years as a student. But the two became faculty colleagues when the Richter himself was appointed professor at the academy in 1971.

At school, Richter also met German trendsetters Sigmar Polke and Blinky Palermo (also refugees from the East), as well as Konrad Lueg (who later changed his name to Konrad Fischer). Along with Lueg and Polke, Richter developed an interest in the burgeoning Pop Art scene. They particularly enjoyed the work of Andy Warhol, Roy Lechtenstein, and Claes Oldenburg. Another area of intrigue for Richter and his friends was the group Fluxus, an international art movement influenced by Marcel Duchamp and John Cage, which held "events" that could either resemble to chaotic Pop Art "happenings" or remain quite simple and subdued.

Photorealism

In 1963, Lueg and Richter traveled to Paris, introducing themselves to art dealer/gallery owner Iileana Sonnabend as German Pop artists because they did not view the movement as strictly an American or British domain. Returning home unsuccessful yet undeterred, they mounted one year later two exhibitions/demonstrations of their own work. These events provided the first occasions for Richter to show his photo-based paintings. One of his earliest works is the modest 1962 painting "Table." A depiction of an ordinary, institutional-style metal table, the canvas is split horizontally with a dark gray floor beneath a lighter gray wall. On the painting's surface is an aggressive brush of gray paint in looping arcs, forcing the viewer to look through the scribbles to see the room.

Richter continued for the next several years to concentrate on the blurred but precise photographic style that became his trademark. Unlike other artists who employ photographs only as a reference aid, Richter uses photographs—either found or taken by the painter himself—as if they were reality. And although he cares about what the images are of, he often chooses a subject that he has no independent experience of, such as, for example, a clipping from a newspaper. In transferring the subjects, Richter first traces meticulously onto canvas the details of the photographic image, then introduces any number of distortions. In effect, when looking at a photorealist painting by Richter, one is simultaneously seeing but not seeing.

Uncovering a new way of looking at the relationship between photographs and painting was an exciting moment for Richter. "I was surprised by photography, which we all use so massively everyday," he told Michael Kimmelman in an interview for the *New York Times Magazine*. "Suddenly, I saw it in a new way, as a picture that offered me a new view, free of all the conventional criteria I had always associated with art. It had no style, no comparison, not judgment. It freed me from personal experience. For the first time, there was nothing to it: it was pure picture. That's why I wanted to have it, to show it—not to use it as a means of painting, but use painting as a means to photography."

Beyond Photo-based Paintings

In the mid-1960s, Richter turned to painting his series "Color Charts," similar to the paint charts found in stores but larger and with the colors situated in no certain order. They were actually, according to Richter, picked at random. For Richter, the group appeared to serve as a renouncement of the clichâs of Abstract art. The paintings contained elements of Pop Art and Minimalism, though they were neither. Furthermore, they were not classifiable as simply Conceptual.

From the color chart pieces, Richter in the late-1960s turned to art inspired by the works of Carl Andre, Sol Lewitt, Robert Ryman, and Dan Flavin, as well as the techniques of Conceptualism. His paintings of this period are minimal landscapes and seascapes, exemplified in the monochromatic series "Gray Pictures." In the early-1970s, Richter moved to an impressive photo-based series of figurative works entitled "48 Portraits" (also known as "Achtundvierzig Portaits").

Richter also exhibited for the first time "Atlas," an ongoing massive inventory of every source used in his paintings. It includes thousands of new photos, snapshots, postcards, and drawings. Richter next focused on the series "Abstract Paintings," featuring an array of incongruous stylistic gestures. These paintings signified yet another departure for Richter from his figurative work, naturalistic paintings, and non-figurative charts.

Throughout his career, however, Richter repeatedly took a different course that what others expected or desired, received critical opinion as suspect, and refused to let postmodernists label him as any sort of specified artist. "My works are not just rhetorical, except in the sense that all art is rhetorical," Richter said to Kimmelman. "I believe in beauty."

In the 1980s, Richter, after beginning a series of "Candle Paintings," returned to photorealism with what is considered one of the most significant series in this domain with "October 18, 1977," also known as the Baader-Meinhof paintings. The group consists of 15 modestly sized, mostly black pictures of individual figures, crowd scenes, jail cells, and buildings. With this series, Richter succeeded in making the larger issues surrounding the subject matter more important that the subject matter itself. One does not have to know the story of the Red Army Faction—led by street hustler Andreas Baader and radical journalist Ulrike Meinhof, and responsible for a string of robberies, shootings, and bombings of American Army bases—to understand the meaning of the paintings. "They set a new standard for me," expressed Richter, quoted by *Village Voice* contributor Jerry Saltz.

Forty Years of Painting

Since the late-1960s, Richter's work has been the subject of numerous monographs, exhibitions, and retrospectives, and is represented in permanent collections throughout Germany and the Guggenheim Museum in New York. The first major retrospective in the United States opened in February of 2002 at New York's Museum of Modern Art. "Gerhard Richter: 40 Years of Painting" featured a vast collection of paintings covering the artist's prolific, 40-year career.

Richter married three times and divorced twice, first in 1957 to Marienne (Ema) Eufinger, with whom he had a daughter named Betty; then to artist Isa Genzken in 1982; and finally in 1995 to Sabine Moritz, with whom he had a son named Moritz and a daughter named Ella. He lives and works—in a studio in front of his home—in a suburb outside Cologne, Germany.

Books

Complete Marquis Who's Who, Marquis Who's Who, 2001.
Contemporary Artists, St. James Press, 1996.
Newsmakers 1997, Issue 4, Gale Research, 1997.

Periodicals

Art in America, September 1993; January 1994; September 1994; November 1996; January 2002.
Art Journal, Spring 2002.
Artforum, Summer 2002.
Artforum International, March 1993; September 1993; January 1994; February 1999; November 2002.
Atlanta Journal-Constitution, March 24, 2002.
Chicago Tribune, September 25, 1988; December 22, 1988; June 30, 2002.
Christian Science Monitor, June 2, 1997.
Europe, May 2002.
Interview, September 2001.
Los Angeles Times, March 26, 1989; January 14, 1990; April 6, 2002.
Nation, May 13, 2002.
New Republic, April 1, 2002.
New Statesman, May 6, 2002.
New York Times, October 5, 2001; February 15, 2002; February 22, 2002; May 16, 2002.
New York Times Magazine, January 27, 2002.
Newsweek, March 25, 2002.
Salmagundi, Winter/Spring 2002.
Time, May 6, 2002.
U.S. News & World Report, February 11, 2002.
Village Voice, March 5, 2002.
Wall Street Journal, November 22, 1988.
Washington Post, December 11, 1988; January 12, 1989. □

Eslanda Goode Robeson

A distinguished cultural anthropologist in her own right, Eslanda Goode Robeson (1896–1965) is remembered also as the wife and long-time business manager of singer/actor Paul Robeson Sr. Highly educated and cultured, she traveled widely in pursuit of her own career and that of her husband until the couple was effectively grounded by a passport revocation in the mid-1950s. They resumed their travels only

after a Supreme Court decision in 1958 upheld the unconstitutionality of the unfounded restrictions.

Robeson was born Eslanda Cardozo Goode in Washington, D.C., on December 15, 1896. Known as "Essie" to her family and friends, Robeson was the youngest of three children and was the only daughter of Eslanda (Cardozo), a one-time schoolteacher, and John J. Goode, a U.S. War Department clerk who died when his daughter was four. Robeson's father was a mixture of Native American, English, and Scotch. Her mother was descended from a wealthy Spanish-Jewish immigrant who, against all social taboos, had boldly married an octoroon (someone of one eighth black ancestry) slave. Thus, although she was a Negro, Robeson was very light-skinned in appearance. After the death of her father, she and her brothers were raised by their mother who brought them to New York where she operated a beauty shop in order to support them. The next move was to Chicago in 1912.

Highly confident and intelligent, Robeson was raised in a cultured environment. She possessed a particularly pleasing singing voice and at the urging of her high school music teacher, Theresa Armitage, took private singing lessons for approximately one year. After graduating from high school at age 16, Robeson enrolled in a domestic science program at the University of Illinois on a full scholarship. She soon lost interest however in both her curriculum and in the school environment and transferred instead to Teachers College of Columbia University in New York City. There she undertook a more challenging program in the physical sciences and graduated with a Bachelor of Science in chemistry in 1920. According to some accounts, Robeson earned a chemistry degree from the University of Illinois in 1917, although United States Federal Bureau of Investigation (FBI) files, which were opened on Robeson during the 1940s, suggest that the prior is true.

Married Paul Robeson

She met her future husband, Paul Robeson, in 1920 at Presbyterian Hospital where she had secured a student job in the surgical pathological laboratory. Also a student at Columbia, Paul Robeson was enrolled in the law school and was hospitalized with a football injury when they met. The two were married on August 17, 1921, and she continued to work at the hospital until 1925. In 1920, largely at his wife's insistence, Paul Robeson accepted the title role in a Harlem YMCA production of *Simon the Cyrenian.* He later appeared in *Taboo* and performed in London when the play went on the road in 1922. In the years immediately following her marriage, Robeson's life revolved largely around her husband's career when, after completing his law degree and working briefly at the law firm of a friend, he turned permanently to a career in performance as both an actor and a singer. Robeson then assumed the role of his manager and handled the family finances. When her husband gained international renown, she followed him in his travels across Europe.

Due to complications from appendix surgery, Robeson had been unable to travel with her husband on his first trip to England in 1922, but she accompanied him in 1925 when he returned to star in Eugene O'Neill's *Emperor Jones.* The couple set up housekeeping in Chelsea, and after the play closed in early October they moved to Villefranche-sur-Mer at the foot of the Alps and remained there until December of that year. Robeson was deeply in love with her husband at that time and was happy with her life in general. She later wrote in *Paul Robeson, Negro* of the small French Riviera town where they lived on Cap Ferrat, calling it, "One of the most beautiful harbors in the world." Likewise of her singer-husband she wrote, "I've married the most beautiful Voice I've ever heard."

Upon her return to the United States, she felt an urgent desire to conceive and bear a child, although her husband remained ambivalent to the notion of parenting, citing her past frail health as the reason for his reluctance. Robeson's determination prevailed, and she became pregnant. Their son and only child, Paul Robeson Jr., was born in New York City on November 2, 1927. Paul Sr. at the time of the birth was performing in Paris, France. Robeson rejoined him five moths later, in May of 1928, in London. After they settled early on in Hampstead, Robeson sent for her mother and son in the United States to join her and her husband. She remained in England until October of 1929 and returned on December 28, 1931.

In the late 1920s Robeson had begun work on her first published manuscript, which was a biography of her husband. After numerous rewrites, the book entitled *Paul Robeson, Negro* was published by Harper in 1930. Also in 1930, she starred with her husband in a relatively obscure silent film drama called *Borderline.* Written and directed by Kenneth MacPherson, the movie presents the story of an adulterous relationship between a black woman Adah, played by Robeson, and a white man named Thorne.

Personal Career Success

Two years later, Robeson informally separated from her husband. She enrolled in graduate school at London University from 1933 to 1935, specializing in anthropology with a focus on the colonized black people of the world, who were commonly called Negroes in the context of the times. She graduated in 1937 from the London School of Economics.

During these years as a student in England, she made her first trip to Africa, in 1936, in realization of a life-long dream, but only after considerable difficulty in obtaining a visa. Such a visa clearance to Africa, as she learned in the process, was rarely given to a Negro. Despite bureaucratic obstacles, she obtained the necessary papers after citing her academic curriculum as the purpose behind her visit. Accompanied by her young son, then eight years old, she embarked on a three-month junket, with an itinerary extending from Cape Town, South Africa, to Cairo. In her second full-length writing, *African Journey,* published by Day in 1945, she provided a diary-formatted chronicle of the 1936 excursion. Among her observations in the book, Robeson reported on the superior political awareness that she perceived among black Africans in comparison to black Americans. The book went into a second printing soon after publication, and Greenwood Press reprinted the volume in 1972.

After anthropological visits to Costa Rica and Honduras in 1940, the Robesons moved from New York City to Enfield, Connecticut, where they purchased an estate, called The Beeches, in 1941. In Enfield, they were the only family of color in the entire town, with the exception of migrant tobacco farmers. Paul Jr. was sent to high school in Springfield, Massachusetts.

World War II

Always socially aware, Robeson's community involvement accelerated during the years of World War II. She was heard widely in her lectures on race relations and worked professionally with Pearl Buck. In 1949 the two co-authored a book, *An American Argument,* published by Day. Also during the 1940s Robeson enrolled at the Hartford Seminary in Connecticut where she earned a Ph.D. in 1945.

With her marriage seriously fractured by 1945 she remained active on other fronts. Working from her home base in Enfield, she maintained a high visibility through community involvement, participating in the Red Cross Motor Corps and keeping active as a writer. She held a seat on the staff of the Council of African Affairs (CAA) and traveled to San Francisco in the capacity of CAA observer to the formation of the Untied Nations. She made a visit to India during which she struck up a friendship with the Indian National Congress leader, Jawaharlal Nehru. After her return she maintained a friendship with him by mail and later entertained his nieces, the Pandit sisters, in her Enfield home when they attended college at Harvard's Wellesley College.

Robeson returned to Africa in 1946, where she visited the Congo, French Equatorial Africa, and Ruanda-Burundi (now Rwanda). During this visit she noted a growing sympathy for socialism among black Africans. Robeson had traveled to the Soviet Union in 1934 while on tour with her husband, and both of her brothers had emigrated from the United States and lived there for many years. Yet she had come to regard that nation with skepticism, in part based on feedback from her brothers.

Persecution under McCarthyism

Political sympathies notwithstanding, during the 1950s, Robeson and her husband were caught up in the phenomenon known as McCarthyism, by which a large number of Americans—many of them prominent entertainers—were investigated by the U.S. government and placed under suspicion of conducting un-American activities. Many of these individuals were blacklisted in their professions and had their careers ruined, including Paul Robeson.

The FBI opened a file on the Robesons in the early 1940s. On July 7, 1953, Robeson was subpoened by the United States Senate and asked if she was a member of the Communist Party. Although she was known to subscribe to the *Daily Worker,* she had never held party membership. Regardless she refused to give testimony, citing her Consti-

tutional rights under the Fifth Amendment. She offered instead unsolicited statements and accused the Senate committee of pursuing a racially biased agenda. "I am Negro, and this is a very white committee . . ." she said, as quoted in *Contemporary Black Biography.* Her passport was revoked as was her husband's, but the pair made use of the confinement, which lasted until 1958, and joined the vanguard of the growing U.S. civil rights movement.

Without a passport, Robeson was nonetheless able to participate with a group from the United Nations that traveled to Trinidad in the spring of 1958. The trip, in conjunction with a celebration of the independence of the British West Indies, was for anthropological purposes. Robeson joined the tour in the capacity of correspondent for the *New World Review.* In the course of the two-week trip, which lasted from April 17 through April 30, she lectured on race relations in Africa and the United States and also visited Port-au-Prince and Jamaica.

Her passport was restored only as a result of a Supreme Court decision of June 16, 1958, prohibiting the FBI from revoking passports by reason of a person's Communist Party affiliations. Less than one month later, having secured the return of their passports, Robeson and her husband departed for Europe on July 10, 1958, with plans to live in London. They continued on to the Soviet Union, and from there she made a third trip to Africa, to attend a conference in Ghana, which had recently attained independence.

Robeson remained in the Soviet Union until 1963. At that time, suffering from breast cancer, she returned with her husband to the United States, stopping en route to East Germany where she was honored with the German Peace Medal and the Clara Zetkin Medal. She died at Beth Israel Hospital in New York City on December 13, 1965.

Robeson's avocations included many sports, among them basketball, swimming, and bowling. She was also a talented photographer, and her pictures—in particular from her African travels—were very well received by the public.

Books

Contemporary Black Biography, Volume 13, Gale Research, 1996.
Robeson, Eslanda Goode, *Paul Robeson, Negro,* Harper & Brothers, 1930.

Other

Department of Justice, "Federal Bureau of Investigation File: Paul and Eslanda Robeson," 1940–60. □

Randall Robinson

Randall Robinson (born 1941) is an internationally recognized author and foreign policy activist. In 1977, he founded TransAfrica—a lobbying group dedicated to promoting "enlightened and progressive" U.S. foreign policy toward countries in Africa

and the Caribbean. As president of TransAfrica, Robinson led the U.S. campaign to bring democracy to South Africa, putting an end to that county's apartheid policies.

Beginnings

Randall Robinson, the son of Maxie Robinson and his wife Doris, was born on July 6, 1941, in Richmond, Virginia. He spent the first 15 years of his life in a ground-floor flat in the African American section of Richmond. Maxie Robinson taught history by day and coached athletics in the evening, while Doris was a full-time homemaker. Robinson's parents were both college graduates. 26-year-old Maxie Robinson and 18-year-old Doris Jones had met in Richmond, Virginia, at Virginia Union University. Doris was attending the school as preparation for a teaching career. Maxie was a star athlete. They married on August 31, 1936.

Robinson states in his autobiography, *Defending the Spirit: A Black Life in America,* that his grandmother raised his father to be "a highly principled teetotaler, unaccustomed to the social domesticities of family life and with small gift for intimacy." Robinson's paternal grandparents had married in Richmond, Virginia, when they were still adolescents. They divorced shortly after Maxie was born. Maxie's father subsequently left for Baltimore where he

remarried and lost contact with his son. Robinson's grandmother, meanwhile, remarried a recovered alcoholic who worked for the railroad.

According to Robinson, his mother, born Doris Alma Jones, was raised in Portsmouth, Virginia, in a large, white two-story house. She was the first of seven children born to Nathan and Jeanie Jones. Robinson wrote of his family heritage in *Defending the Spirit,* "Mama's family was deep and eternal. Daddy's was small and patched."

Childhood

One of four children born to Maxie and Doris Robinson, Robinson was surrounded by books when he was growing up. His older sister, Jewell, was an excellent student and eventually won a scholarship that allowed her to become the first African American student to attend Goucher College. Robinson's brother, Maxie Jr., who won an even more lucrative scholarship, became the nation's first African American news anchor on ABC's *World News Tonight.* Robinson, however, was more of a late bloomer and headed off for Norfolk State College on a basketball scholarship, later transferring to Virginia Union University. His younger sister, Jeanie, would eventually become an elementary school teacher in Washington, D.C.

On May 17, 1954, 13-year-old Robinson was sitting in his science class when his teacher announced that the Supreme Court had just ruled that public school segregation violated the U.S. Constitution. Robinson later said he never expected the ruling—but in any case, he later pointed out, forty-three years after the decision was handed down, Richmond's schools were still as segregated as they were in 1954.

Robinson claims he never met a white person until he was drafted into the Army in 1963. Following his discharge from the service—which came just as the United States was beginning to build up its forces in Vietnam—he re-enrolled in Virginia Union University.

Harvard Law School

In the fall of 1967, following his graduation from Virginia Union, Robinson was admitted to Harvard University Law School. But after one year of Harvard, Robinson says he knew he would never practice law. He would nevertheless go on to pass the Massachusetts bar exam.

In late summer 1970, Robinson left for Tanzania. By then his first marriage was severely strained, and, though it would continue for another seventeen years, Robinson traces its eventual disintegration to his marrying before he really knew himself. Meanwhile, in Tanazania, he found a country riddled with problems. He concluded, "I could best serve Africa by going home to America, for America had become a substantial contributor to Africa's problems. . . . The United States was doing Africa a terrible disservice and African-Americans, in general, were none the wiser," Robinson later wrote in *Defending the Spirit.*

In 1971, Robinson was hired by the Boston Legal Assistance Project (BLAP) to provide legal representation in civil and juvenile court matters to the poor. But after he made the tactical mistake of demanding that the BLAP bring in African American leadership, he was fired. Robinson wrote in *Defending the Spirit,* "My legal career, after less than a year, had mercifully come to an end."

From 1972 to 1974, Robinson worked for the Roxbury Multi-Service Center as a community organizer. Among his first assignments was to put together a campaign against Gulf Oil in protest of that company's support of Portuguese presence in Africa. In the campaign, Robinson targeted Harvard University for its holdings of Gulf Oil stock.

TransAfrica

Robinson worked as an administrative assistant to Congressman Charles C. Diggs from 1976 until Diggs was forced to resign from Congress prior to being sent to prison for graft in 1978. Shortly thereafter, in 1977, Robinson opened an office for an organization he called TransAfrica in a made-over apartment in Washington, D.C. TransAfrica's two-person staff consisted of Robinson as executive director and Dolores Clemons as his assistant.

TransAfrica's immediate agenda was to change American policy toward South Africa. The United States was at the time still sympathetic to white rule in South Africa. Robinson wrote in his autobiography, "Americans had to be made aware of all the needless hurt that had been caused in their name. African-Americans had to be made to understand that this American policy affront to Africa was an insult to them as well." Toward this end, Robinson testified before Congress and even joined Senator George McGovern in a debate with two U.S. senators over U.S. policy in South Africa.

Robinson faced criticism from some U.S. African Americans that there were domestic racial problems that needed to be addressed before America looked to correct apartheid abuses overseas. But Robinson countered that domestic and foreign policy issues need not be addressed separately.

In 1981, a disgruntled employee of the U.S. State Department handed over to Robinson a sheaf of classified documents outlying U.S. support of white-ruled South Africa. Robinson in turn turned the documents over to a writer for the *Washington Post.* On May 29, 1981, the story hit the front pages of that newspaper. A year later, Robinson leaked to the *Washington Post* a classified State Department memo describing South Africa's intention to obtain a new loan from the International Monetary Fund.

Robinson met his second—and current—wife, Hazel, about this time. She was an international banking analyst who had moved to Washington to volunteer her knowledge of economic affairs in the Caribbean to TransAfrica. They were married in 1987.

By 1989, with the election of F. W. deKlerk as South Africa's leader and the release of Nelson Mandela from prison the next year, Robinson was allowing himself to believe that democracy would ultimately prevail in South Africa. Wrote Robinson in *Defending the Spirit,* "I had marched, testified, written, orated, debated, petitioned, proselytized, and committed repeated acts of civil disobedi-

ence. . . . We had done everything seemly and imaginable in our efforts to turn the United States onto a humane course and keep it there."

Ironically, after coming to power, South Africa's black African National Congress (ANC) virtually cut off all ties to TransAfrica. According to Robinson, the ANC has preferred to work with "the American Establishment and its multinational corporations." Robinson feels this policy may ultimately be self-defeating, given that American political parties come in and out of power with unpredictable frequency.

More recently, Robinson undertook a twenty-seven-day hunger strike in support of democratic reforms in Haiti and in opposition to U.S. policy against accepting Haitian refugees. Partly as a result, the U.S. in 1994 organized a multinational campaign to return Haiti's first democratically elected government to power, after it had been overthrown. Robinson also went on record as opposing the Mengistu government in Ethiopia and corruption in Nigeria. He also fought attempts by the U.S. to end Caribbean access to Europe's banana markets.

The Debt

In *The Debt: What America Owes to Blacks* (2000), Robinson argued that the United States owes major reparations to the descendants of African American slaves. He told *Black Issues in Higher Education* in 2001, "It is not complicated and difficult to argue that when you expropriate the value of a people's labor for 246 years of slavery, and follow that with a century of formal discrimination based on race with government involvement that those who were in the beneficiary group stood to gain from the expropriation of the value of that labor. And those who had the value of their hire stolen from them stood to suffer, hence this enormous economic gap yawning still and static, separating blacks from whites in the United States and throughout the world."

Robinson believes the reason that most Americans, whether they be black or white, oppose reparations is that they are uninformed. And for Robinson, that is the crux of the matter. He feels that the American citizenry is in a state of denial about the suffering that the United States has caused to people in the U.S. and in other parts of the world.

When *Black Issues in Higher Education* asked Robinson in 2001 how optimistic he was about the prospects of the reparations movement, he replied, "I'm very optimistic. I put no clock on these things, you see. I don't know [if] it will happen in my lifetime in the same way I didn't know if apartheid would end in my lifetime. . . . But you fight prepared to go the long term, and if your life won't cover the term of the struggle, then you hand off your progress to the next generation. Seen in that light, I'm extremely optimistic (reparations) will happen."

Recognition

Robinson has been awarded nineteen honorary doctorates. His contributions to altering U.S. foreign policy have been recognized by the United Nations, the Congressional Black Caucus, Harvard University, the Essence Magazine Awards Show, the Martin Luther King Center for Non-

Violent Change, the NAACP, and the Ebony Magazine Awards Show. He has also been named ABC-News Person of the Week. Robinson has appeared on ABC's *Nightline,* CBS's *60 Minutes,* NBC's *Today Show,* CNN, C-Span, and other American television programs.

Robinson is the author of three books, *Defending the Spirit, The Debt: What America Owes to Blacks,* and *The Reckoning: What Blacks Owe to Each Other.* He has begun work on a fourth book, about the past and ongoing impact of U.S. foreign policy on English-speaking nations in the Caribbean. He makes his home on the Caribbean island of St. Kitts with his wife and daughter.

Books

Robinson, Randall, *Defending the Spirit: A Black Life in America,* Dutton, 1998.

Periodicals

"Fighting the good fight," *Black Issues in Higher Education,* November 8, 2001.
"Randall and Hazel Robinson: what's love got to do with it?" *Essence,* February 1991. □

Lola Rodríguez de Tío

Lola Rodríguez de Tío (1843–1924) is a revered figure in both Cuban and Puerto Rican history. She is considered to be Puerto Rico's premier nineteenth century lyric poet and one of Latin America's most important early feminists.

Rodríguez de Tío was born September 14, 1843, in San Germain, Puerto Rico. Born into the island's ruling class, she was the daughter of Don Sebastian Rodríguez de Astudillo, Dean of the Magistracy of Puerto Rico, and Doña Carmen Ponce de León, a descendant of Ponce de León, the explorer and first governor of the colony. Rodríguez de Tío was a bright child who showed early promise as a poet. Her education in religious schools and by private tutors was guided by her mother, who was described in the *Enciclopedia Puertorriqueña Ilustrada* as "an educated, well-read woman with a fine spirit and the wide-awake intelligence of a child." It was rare for women to be educated in Puerto Rico; most women, especially poor women, were illiterate. It was rarer still for a woman to be an intellectual, but Rodríguez de Tío was supported and encouraged in her progress as a poet by poet Ursula Cardona de Quinones. Her understanding of the disparity of opportunity for women made her one of Latin America's most influential early feminists.

Became Revolutionary Poet and Patriot

Rodríguez de Tío married at age 20; her husband, Bonacio Tío Segarra, was a respected and influential journalist and poet. Partners in life and politics, the couple were a thorn in the side of the government. As a colony,

Puerto Rico had been long abused, suffering corruption and brutality under Spain's colonial governors. Puerto Rico's visionary patriot Eugenio María de Hostos was an important influence on Rodríguez de Tío. Hostos spent most of his life in exile. His eloquent writings inspired many others to call for independence from Spain. Rodríguez de Tío's home in Mayaguez became a salon where the leading intellectuals, including Hostos, discussed politics and called for revolution. Forthright in her opposition, she boldly challenged the government.

The work for which Rodríguez de Tío is best known, and which caused her to be deported, was "La Borinquena." In 1868, she composed a fiery lyric for a traditional melody; she read it aloud at a literary gathering at her home to immediate acclaim. It begins: "Awake, Borinquenos, for they've given the signal!/Awake from your sleep, for it's time to fight!" "La Borinquena" became Puerto Rico's national anthem, but Rodríguez de Tío's lyrics were later replaced with the more sentimental lyrics of Manuel Fernandez Juncos. The Lares Uprising of 1868 brought about a repressive response from the government—Rodríguez de Tío and her husband were given hours to leave the island. They went into exile in Caracas, Venezuela, where Hostos was already living. They grew closer to Hostos during their time in Venezuela; Rodríguez de Tío was a bridesmaid at his wedding in 1878.

Finally, the family was allowed to return to Puerto Rico in 1885, but once again, Rodríguez de Tío's writing infuriated the government. "Nochebuena," a tribute to political prisoners, was published in 1887, the "terrible year" of the "Componte." Rodríguez de Tío and her family were exiled in 1889 to Cuba, never again to live in Puerto Rico. However, she devoted the rest of her life to achieving independence for both her homeland and Cuba.

Found a Second Homeland

Their political activity for Cuban independence caused Rodríguez de Tío and her husband to be expelled from Havana in 1892. They joined a group of Cuban exiles in New York City, where Rodríguez de Tío met José Martí, the legendary Cuban patriot and poet. This period in her life was one of intense political activity—the group of political exiles created the Cuban Revolutionary Party in 1895. Martí regarded Rodríguez de Tío as an equal in art and in politics. When Martí was killed in Cuba in 1895, the exiles carried on their efforts through political clubs. Rodríguez de Tío was elected president of "Rius Rivera" in 1896, and secretary of another club, "Caridad," in 1897. She and her family returned to Cuba in 1899 after the Spanish-American War, and she devoted the rest of her life to social justice and the betterment of the condition of women in Cuba.

Rodríguez de Tío is considered a leading literary figure and a national hero: she was named to the Cuban Academy of Arts and Letters in 1910 and Patron of the Galician Beneficent Society in 1911. She continued to be active in politics and served as inspector general of the private schools in Havana, as well as in the Ministry of Education. Like many other feminists of her time, Rodríguez de Tío also sought to reform women's fashions. Federico Ribes Tovar described her attire in *Enciclopedia Puertorriqueña Ilustrada:* "This strange woman with her radical thoughts, wore a skirt of a very peculiar design, like an Amazon's, and wore a blouse with a high neckline and a wide bow tie, and her hair was cut like a man's." He also reported that she was considered to be devout, a fine wife and mother, and an "exemplary friend."

Referred to as "Daughter of the Isles"

Rodríguez de Tío's importance as a poet is a matter of dispute among literary critics, but her place in Puerto Rican letters is not. Referred to in the *Encyclopedia of Latin American Literature* as that country's "most distinguished 19th-century lyric poet," her style is sometimes dismissed as derivative, but her verses are well known and very influential. No less an authority than Ruben Dario, considered Spanish America's greatest modern poet, praised Rodríguez de Tío, calling her "the Daughter of the Isles."

As a disciple of Romanticism, Rodríguez de Tío was influenced by Spanish Golden Age poets and the traditional stanza. She published three books: *Mis Cantares,* in 1876 (*My Songs*); *Claros y Nieblas,* in 1885 (*Bright Intervals and Mist*); and *Mi Libro de Cuba,* in 1893 (*My Book on Cuba*). One of her most famous verses, "Cuba and Puerto Rico," was quoted by Fidel Castro in a 1966 speech: "Cuba and Puerto Rico are/of one bird, the two wings;/they receive flowers and bullets/in the same heart." However, he mistakenly attributed it to Jose Marti. Rodríguez de Tío's poem does capture her affection for both Puerto Rico and

her adopted homeland: it concludes: "What a lot if in the illusion/that glows red in a thousand tones,/ Lola's muse dreams/ with fervent fantasy/ of making one single homeland/ of this land and of mine." She died on November 10, 1924, in Havana, Cuba, at the age of 81.

Books

Babin, Maria Teresa, and Stan Steiner, *Borinquen: An Anthology of Puerto Rican Literature,* Vintage Books, 1974.

Marques, Rene, *The Docile Puerto Rican,* Temple University Press, 1976.

Smith, Verity, ed., "Puerto Rico," *Encyclopedia of Latin American Literature,* Fitzroy Dearborn, 1997.

Tío, Carlos F. Mendoza, *Contribución al Estudio de la Obra Poetica de Lola Rodríguez de Tío,* 1974.

—, "Lola Rodríguez de Tío," *Investigaciónes Literarias,* 1974.

Tovar, Federico Ribes, "Lola Rodríguez de Tío," *Enciclopedia Puertorriquena Ilustrada,* Plus Ultra Educational Publications, Inc., 1970. □

Charlemae Hill Rollins

Charlemae Hill Rollins (1897–1979) was a Chicago librarian and author who was dedicated to improving the image of African Americans in children's literature. She served as an advisor to authors, teachers, and publishers, encouraging them to disregard negative stereotypes and honestly portray black culture and history. Rollins taught two generations of children to love books and appreciate their ethnic heritage.

Charlemae Hill Rollins was born October 21, 1897, in the small farming community of Yazoo City, Mississippi. She was the oldest child of Allen G. Hill, a farmer, and Birdie Tucker Hill, a teacher. The family was poor, but Rollins remembered a childhood rich in family life, the result of growing up among a large extended family. Her grandmother, a former slave, was a wonderful storyteller who shared her book collection with her grandchildren. Rollins recalled her grandmother's influence in *More Books by More People; Interviews with 65 Authors of Books for Children:* "She gave us all the books that belonged to her master who was the father of her children, one of whom was my father. We enjoyed the books in his library, even though most of them were medical books. But I would read anything and everything."

The Hill family moved to the Indian Territory—now Oklahoma—when Rollins was still a child. She attended a school for African Americans founded by her family, and her mother was one of the first black teachers in the territory. As Rollins grew older few educational opportunities existed for blacks nearby, so she enrolled in black secondary schools in Missouri, Mississippi, and Kansas. She graduated from a segregated boarding school in Quindoro, Kansas, in 1916.

After graduating, Rollins taught briefly in Beggs, Oklahoma, before enrolling in Howard University in Washington, D.C. After a year at Howard she returned to Oklahoma where she married Joseph Walter Rollins in 1918. The couple had a son, Joseph Walter Rollins Jr., in 1920. They moved to Chicago, where Joseph Sr. worked for the Young Men's Christian Association.

Began Career as Librarian

In 1927 Rollins combined her love of books and teaching by taking a job as a children's librarian at the Harding Square Branch of the Chicago Public Library. When the George Cleveland Hall Branch Library opened in 1923 she was named head of the children's department there. This branch was the first to be located in the city's black neighborhoods and it served a diverse population representing all socioeconomic levels.

The library system helped Rollins continue her education. She enrolled in library training at Columbia College of the University of Chicago and remained a children's department librarian at Hall Library for 36 years. Serving the community in a caring, imaginative way, she guided two generations of young patrons to discover and love books and reading. Rollins organized events to draw people into the library and was dedicated to educating patrons on the contributions of black people. Storytelling sessions were a major part of her work, as she explained to an *Illinois Libraries* contributor: "Storytelling is a wonderful way of breaking down barriers, or getting acquainted with new people, and drawing groups and individuals together. Hearing a wonderful story well told, can bring escape from hunger, from drab surroundings, from hate and rejection, and escape from injustices of all kinds."

Advised Publishers

Rollins believed that children's programs could only be effective if the adults in the children's lives also took an interest. Encouraging and teaching parents and teachers to become involved with children and books, she organized a reading guidance clinic for families and maintained close contact with Patent-Teacher Association groups. Rollins's library programs often centered on black history. She felt a strong need to teach children about their heritage, but she was frustrated by the lack of books available on the topic during the 1930s. She found that when children asked for her help with a school paper about a black person, there were no appropriate books in the library. "For many years books about Negro children followed a stereotyped pattern," Rollins was quoted as remarking on the University of Mississippi Library web site. "The characters portrayed were the barefoot menial, or the red-lipped clown. Rarely did the Negro character in a story where there were other children ever take part in the story as equals. Illustrators, it seemed, could not resist presenting the quaint 'pickaninny' type."

Rollins wanted her young patrons to read books that honestly portrayed African Americans in all phases of life. "Children as they are growing up need special interpretations of the lives of other peoples," she maintained, "[and] must be helped to an understanding and tolerance. They cannot develop these qualities through contacts with others, if those closest to them are prejudiced and unsympathetic with other races and groups. Tolerance and understanding can be gained through reading the right books."

Rollins made it her mission to improve the image of blacks in children's books and to teach her young patrons about their heritage. She formed a Negro history club and a series of appreciation hours in which she taught children about the contributions of blacks. She researched and collected materials for her programs and made publishers aware of the need for books about African American culture and history. "I got to be quite a nuisance for the publishers, writing them letters on top of letters for more information," she told a contributor to *American Libraries*.

Her interest in African American books led Rollins to complete a research paper on the topic of blacks in children's books for one of her library classes at the University of Chicago. She became recognized as an evaluator of children's literature and became a member of the Chicago Public Library's advisory committee on book selection. Rollins transformed her research paper into a mimeographed list of books relating to blacks that was used by children's librarians. This list evolved into one of the first significant publications on African American literature for children. Published in 1941 by the National Council of Teachers of English as *We Build Together, A Reader's Guide to Negro Life and Literature for Elementary and High School Use,* the pamphlet includes introductory text about how to write and select books about blacks and an annotated bibliography of recommended books. *We Build Together* raised the level of consciousness among librarians, teachers, and publishers to the need for more honest portrayals of African Americans in children's literature. The landmark publication was revised in 1948 and 1967.

Earned National Recognition

Her 1941 publication earned Rollins a national reputation as an authority on African American children's books. Publishers, becoming aware of the stereotypes they presented in their books, began seeking Rollins's and other black librarians' and teachers' advice. Many publishers and authors sent manuscripts to Rollins for evaluation, and she was asked to serve on the editorial advisory boards of *World Book Encyclopedia, American Educator,* and *Bulletin of the Center for Children's Books.* She chaired the Jane Addams Book Award committee for the Women's International League for Peace and Justice in 1964–1965 and in 1962 traveled to Oslo, Norway, to present the award to Aimee Sommerfelt, author of *The Road to Agra.*

Many universities and professional associations invited Rollins to teach, write, and lecture on African American books. She contributed articles to many journals, including *American Childhood, Illinois Libraries* and *Junior Libraries.* She lectured at Fisk University, Morgan State College, the University of Mississippi, Rosary College, San Francisco State College, and the University of Chicago, and taught a class in children's literature at Roosevelt University in Chicago.

Rollins also became involved in professional associations. She was active in the Illinois State Library Association, the Catholic Library Association, and the American Library Association (ALA). She worked on many ALA committees and became the association's first black president in 1957. In 1972 she was the first African American to receive an honorary lifetime membership in the ALA.

Rollins retired in August 1963 at the age of 66. She had been involved with books her entire life and had met many authors in her role as a children's librarian. In retirement she began writing books of her own, among them juvenile biographies of black men and women. Among her books are *They Showed the Way,* 1964; *Famous American Negro Poets for Children,* 1965; *Famous Negro Entertainers of Stage and Screen,* 1967; and *Black Troubadour, Langston Hughes,* 1971. Her biography on Hughes was inspired by her own friendship with Hughes, whom she had met during the 1930s at a Works Project Administration-sponsored writer's project hosted by her library.

In 1963 Rollins wrote *Christmas Gif': An Anthology of Christmas Poems, Songs, and Stories Written by and about Negroes.* The title, *Christmas Gif',* was based on a holiday tradition celebrated by her family that originated in the days of slavery. The book includes selections from Hughes, Paul Laurence Dunbar, Booker T. Washington, and Pulitzer Prize-winning poet Gwendolyn Brooks, who had been a patron at the George Cleveland Hall Branch Library as a child.

Received Many Awards

Rollins's role in elevating the status of African Americans in children's books earned her many awards from library, education, and humanitarian organizations. She received the American Brotherhood Award from the National Conference of Christians and Jews in 1952, the Library Letter Award from the ALA in 1953, and the Grolier Foundation Award from the ALA in 1955. She also received the Good American Award of the Chicago Committee of One Hundred in 1962, the Children's Reading Round Table award in 1963, and the New Jersey Library and Media Association's Coretta Scott King Award in 1971. In 1974 Columbia College, Chicago awarded Rollins a doctorate of humane letters, and three years later the Chicago Public Library dedicated a room in her name at the Carter G. Woodson Regional Library.

Rollins died in Chicago on February 3, 1979. She was 81 years old. In her memory, the School of Library and Information Science at North Carolina Central University presents the biennial Charlemae Hill Rollins Colloquium, while the ALA's Library Service to Children division presents the Charlemae Rollins President's Program at its annual summer conferences.

The research Rollins conducted in her lifetime included studies of Head Start, African American bibliography, and segregation. Her papers and journals are housed at the African-American Resources Program at the School of Library and Information Sciences, North Carolina Central University.

Books

Contemporary Black Biography, Volume 27, Gale, 2001.
Notable Black American Women, Gale, 1992.

Periodicals

American Libraries, September, 1973.
Public Libraries, Fall 1982.

Online

"The Black Experience in Children's Literature," http://www.lib .usm.edu/~degrum/blackexperience/homepage.html (February 19, 2003). □

Samuel Romilly

English lawyer and law reformer Sir Samuel Romilly (1757–1818) divided his time between the law and public service. He served as chancellor of Durham from 1805 to 1815 and was a member of Parliament beginning in 1806. A supporter of the social and political views of the Swiss Enlightenment philosopher Jean-Jacques Rousseau, Romilly devoted his life to advocating on behalf of the lower classes and worked to reform England's criminal law by abolishing capital punishment for minor crimes.

Inspired by French Ancestry

Born in London, England, on March 1, 1757, Romilly was the second son born to Peter and Margaret (Garnault) Romilly. Both of Romilly's parents hailed from French families whose members had fled France for England after the revocation of the Edict of Nantes by French King Louis XIV in 1685. The wealth of the Garnault family allowed Margaret Romilly and her family, now newly of London, to live in comfort while her husband established a business as a watchmaker and jeweler.

In addition to gaining a basic education, Romilly worked in his father's shop where he began to learn the watchmaker's trade. A good student of the classics, he also excelled at the study of French literature, and when he inherited a legacy of 2,000 pounds from a French relative, he left his father's shop and went to work in a London law office. There Romilly determined to become a clerk in the Court of Chancery—a judicial body presided over by the Lord Chancellor wherein litigants could directly petition the king for justice. To this end he set about training himself and saving up sufficient funds to purchase the office. In 1778, however, the 21-year-old law clerk, determined to go to the bar, had entered himself at Gray's Inn, one of the four inns of court that conferred the rank of barrister.

In 1781 Romilly traveled abroad and visited Geneva, where he met Pierre Etienne Louis Dumont (1759–1829), a Swiss democrat who had been a protegé of politician and orator the Compte de Mirabeau during the French Revolution. The influence of the Enlightenment that inspired Dumont and Mirabeau would also inspire Romilly, and he eventually came to know *Encyclopédie* collaborators Denis Diderot and Jean d'Alembert.

Called to the bar in 1783, Romilly appeared briefly in circuit courts but spent most of his time working in the Court of Chancery. A reading of Martin Madan's *Thoughts on Executive Justice with Respect to Our Criminal Laws* inspired him to contemplate the issue of capital punishment and resulted in Romilly's first published book in 1786, the *Observations of a Late Publication, intitled, Thoughts on Executive Justice.* During work on his response to Madan, Romilly was introduced to Mirabeau himself and spent much time with the French politician.

While Romilly busied himself in the Court of Chancery, across the English Channel France was in the throes of political upheaval. In 1789 economic and class anxieties came to a head as King Louis XVI and his wife, Marie Antoinette, were imprisoned and political power fell to a new body, the Estates-General. Due to his influence, Mirabeau quickly gained power in the Estates-General, and he turned to Romilly for help in acquiring a procedural manual of the English House of Commons for use as a model. Intrigued by the revolution and its ideals of equality and brotherhood, Romilly visited Paris and in 1790 published a pamphlet titled *Thoughts on the Probable Influence of the Late Revolution in France upon Great Britain.* His larger work, *Letters Containing an Account of the Late Revolution in France,* more fully expressed the alignment of his political sympathies with those of the revolutionary leadership, albeit the theoretical aspects rather than the terrifying reality of bloody revolution.

During the next decade Romilly's practice at the Court of Chancery flourished, and in 1800 he was honored by the government. In 1798 he married Anne Garbett of Herefordshire. In 1805 he was appointed chancellor of the county court of Durham. Due to his philosophical leanings, Romilly had become known to many in the Whig party. In 1806, on the succession of the Whigs to power under Lord Grenville, he was knighted and appointed to the position of solicitor-general. Because Romilly would not qualify for the post unless he was a member of Parliament, it was arranged that the newly knighted Romilly stand for Queensborough in the House of Commons.

Throughout his tenure as solicitor-general, Romilly began the legal reform that would occupy the rest of his life. In keeping with his position, he instituted several changes in England's bankruptcy procedures. Although Romilly lost the post of solicitor-general when the Tories regained control of the government, he kept his seat in the House of Commons where he sat for Horsham, Wareham, and Arundel. During his tenure in Parliament, he became a strong advocate of social reform, using his skills as an orator, his firm grounding in the law, and his belief in democracy and equality for the benefit of the English people.

Active in Social Reform

Despite a growing public outcry to abolish the institution of slavery in England and its colonies, the issue of slavery had been politically controversial for several years. By 1804 however, the slavery question began to attract renewed interest, in part due to the influx of new Irish members, who tended as a whole to be abolitionists. Noted abolitionist and member of Parliament William Wilberforce (1759–1833) first introduced his Abolition Bill in 1804 and then 1805, both times without success. In 1806 Wilberforce published an influential pamphlet advocating Abolition and drumming up enough interest to force the issue once again to a Parliamentary vote. With sufficient support from the Whigs, the Abolition Bill passed on February 23, 1807, by an overwhelming majority of votes. One of the bill's staunchest advocates, Romilly added his voice to support of the bill, praising Wilberforce for his efforts and receiving a standing ovation from the House of Commons. Abolition would be the first of many social issues that would benefit from the new member of Parliament's support.

Reform of England's Penal Code

At the turn of the 19th century the social and economic landscape of England was in a state of flux due to the effects of the Industrial Revolution. The widening rift between poorer working classes and the wealthy elite had created tensions that the unfolding French Revolution continued to fuel. Police and guard details found themselves constantly short-handed when faced with ever-increasing crimes, riots, outbreaks of mob violence, and other types of social disorder. Larger cities often relied on English troops to reestablish order, while smaller towns called on their local militias when needed.

As a practicing attorney confronted with the burgeoning cases brought to trial each year, Romilly had become aware of the many inequities in England's criminal justice system. Often ill-conceived and frequently cruel, the nation's statutory laws governing criminal activity doled out the death penalty as a punishment for 220 crimes, many of them minor infractions that did not warrant it. Children as well as adults were subject to these outdated laws, many dating back to the more brutal age of Queen Elizabeth I and some applying to minimal crimes—among them pickpocketing, pulling down turnpike gates, stealing fish from ponds, and highway robbery when the goods taken were valued greater than a penny. Because the execution of all those men, women, and children whose crimes demanded death according to the statutes was infeasible, the death penalty eventually began to be enforced randomly. Many of the condemned—including children, who would remain subject to the death penalty until 1908–were given a less-harsh sentence after their initial condemnation; of course, there were others who received the prescribed penalty because of the personal whims of the judge or some other arbitrary reason.

Romilly believed that it was the certainty of punishment rather than the severity of punishment that was the true deterrent to crime. He gathered statistics showing that despite the increasing use of the death penalty during the 18th century, the number of crimes had not decreased, in fact, crime had increased. In 1808 he managed to begin the process of repeal in the case of an Elizabethan statute which made petty theft a capital offence. Unfortunately, his success in this instance resulted in opposition from the House of Lords in the person of Lord Ellenborough, and three other pieces of reform legislation were discarded. Romilly continued to fight for reform, but ultimately waged a losing battle. Success came in 1812, when he requested the repeal of an even more unjust statute that declared it a capital offence for an English soldier to beg without written permission from his commanding officer. In 1813, after attempting to introduce a bill before the House of Commons that would repeal the law, making it a capital offence to steal goods of a minimal value from a store or warehouse, he watched the bill pass by a two-to-one margin in the House of Commons on March 26 and then be thrown out of the House of Lords scarcely a week later.

For the remainder of his career in Parliament, Romilly continued his efforts at penal reform and during the same period he saw little legislative progress. However, his well-articulated arguments for change did not fall on deaf ears, for he wisely published them in widely read periodicals such as the *Edinburgh Review* and the changes he envisioned were eventually enacted.

Romilly soon became famous throughout Europe, where his 1810 work *Observations on the Criminal Law of England* was widely known. Other writings by the legal reformer would be published posthumously, among them a collection of his speeches published in 1820 and a version of his memoirs, edited by his sons and published in 1840.

Tragically, Romilly's long career of public service ended too soon. On the Isle of Wight on November 2, 1818, three days after his wife died following a long illness, he descended into a grief so great that he took his own life. Following his death at age 61, Romilly's work to reform England's penal codes was continued by Sir James MacIntosh, who in early March of 1819 succeeded in establishing a Parliamentary committee to review the uses of the death penalty. Many of Romilly's proposed changes in English law were made later in the 19th century during the reign of Queen Victoria. Romilly's second son, John, Baron Romilly, followed in his father's footsteps, becoming solicitor general in 1848 at age 46 and attorney-general in 1850.

Books

Collins, W. J., *Life and Work of Sir Samuel Romilly*, Huguenot Society, 1908.

Romilly, Samuel, *Thoughts on the Criminal Law of England as It Relates to Capital Punishments, and on the Mode in Which It Is Administered*, T. Cadell & W. Davies, 1810.

—, *The speeches of Sir Samuel Romilly in the House of Commons*, 2 volumes, James Ridgway & Sons, 1820.

—, *Memoirs of the Life of Sir Samuel Romilly*, 3 volumes, [London, England], 1840.

The Speeches of Sir Samuel Romilly in the House of Commons, 2 volumes [London, England], 1820.

Periodicals

United States Magazine and Democratic Review, Volume 27, 1851.

Online

Reading Romilly Association Web site, http://www.rdg.ac.uk/romilly/Aboutus/sirsromilly.htm (May 27, 2003). □

Patrick Roy

Over the course of his 18–year professional career, Canadian hockey player Patrick Roy (born 1965) proved to himself and hockey fans everywhere his outstanding skills and instincts as a goaltender. His heroic actions to defend his team, even when ill or suffering from appendicitis, in addition to his outstanding skill in front of the net made him a popular icon. When he retired from professional hockey in 2003, he left as the National Hockey League's (NHL's) all-time career leader in victories and games played as a goaltender. In addition, his playoff performances are marked by records as the goaltender with the most playoff wins, games played, minutes played, shutouts, and consecutive wins in the post season.

Patrick Roy was born on October 5, 1965, in Quebec City, in the province of Quebec in Canada. His parents lived in the nearby suburb of Sainte Foy. He came from athletic stock: his mother was a nationally ranked synchronized swimmer and his father was an accomplished tennis player and amateur baseball player. Roy grew up cheering for his home-province team, the Quebec Nordiques.

The Early Years

Roy began playing hockey at age six. He did not start out at the goal, but when one of the neighborhood kids was injured he stepped into the net and never left. When he was seven he strapped pillows to his legs with his dad's belts to create goalie pads. He eventually played goalie for local midget and junior leagues.

Roy's family was highly respected within their community, and the young hockey fan's father held high-ranking government positions. While his brother and sister both attended school in English, Roy continued his education in French and concentrated on hockey and goaltending. Most children from his neighborhood went on to college and professional careers, but in 1982 Roy dropped out of school in the eleventh grade and, with the support of his parents, played hockey for the Granby Bisons of the Quebec junior league. The team did not do well, winning only 16 of 44 games. "It was tough playing [for the Granby Bisons,]" the competitive Roy later recalled in *A Breed Apart: An Illus-*

trated History of Goaltending. "But I got a lot of work and it was a good experience. I learned to deal with the frustrations of losing and now I appreciate more the enjoyment of winning." Despite his team's record, Roy was named the Quebec Junior League's top goaltender.

Skated with the Pros

In 1984 the Montreal Canadiens chose Roy as their fourth-round pick in the 1985 National Hockey League (NHL) draft. Then 19 years old, Roy was the 51st draft pick overall. The Canadiens sent Roy to play for their American League affiliate, the Sherbrooke Canadiens, where he watched the game as a third-string goaltender. Then, during the American League playoffs, opportunity knocked on Roy's door after Sherbrooke's regular starter, Paul Pageau, took time off for the birth of his a child at the same time that the team's second-string goalie had trouble with some of his equipment. Roy joined the team on the ice in front of the net. He stayed there, winning 10 out of 13 playoff games, and Sherbrooke won the Calder Cup championship. The next fall Roy was called up to the Canadiens. "It was a dream come true, to be playing in my province and for Canada's team," he told an interviewer for *Sports Illustrated for Kids.*

During Roy's 1985–1986 rookie season, the Canadiens won their 23rd Stanley Cup championship. Roy had an awesome average of 1.92 goals per game during the playoffs, was voted Most Valuable Player, and won the Conn Smythe Trophy. Despite his professional performance, he still acted like a kid, playing street hockey, living in a basement apartment, and subsisting on a diet of hamburgers, French fries, and potato chips. Eventually his team brought in a nutrition expert to teach Roy to use food to fuel his body in order for him to have enough energy to last throughout the game. This may have led to Roy's routine of eating spaghetti and water at 1 p.m. on game days.

Quirks and Superstitions

Very superstitious, Roy adopted many routines that fans came to recognize. Before each game he skated out to the blue line and stared at his net, beaming thoughts to his goal posts. "I talk to my posts," he admitted in *A Breed Apart*. "It's a superstition. The forwards talk to each other. The defense is always close, but the goaltender is alone." He would also not skate on the blue or red lines. He wrote the names of his children on his sticks before each game and kept a puck from every shutout during the season in his locker.

Roy earned an eight-game suspension at the beginning of the 1987–1988 season for slashing the leg of Minnesota's Warren Babe. However, as soon as he was back, he impressed the crowd by shutting out Chicago 3–0. During the 1988–1989 season he won the Vezina Trophy, an award given to the goaltender playing the most games on the team with the most Goals against Average. Roy became his team's main goalie during the 1989–1990 season and played more than 50 games. He won another Vezina Trophy that year and was named to the All-Star team.

The Building of a Legend

During the early 1990s Roy slowly climbed his way back into the public's favor. By the time the 1992–1993 playoffs rolled around he recorded the most wins of any goaltender—16 of 20 games—and the lowest goals against average—2.13. He set a record with ten straight sudden-death wins, gaining immortality in Canadein lore. During game four of the Stanley Cup finals against the Los Angeles Kings, the score was tied and Tomas Sandstrom was taking multiple shots on Roy. Partway through the third period Sandstom stormed the net attempting a rebound, but Roy smothered the puck. Roy looked up at Sandstrom and winked. The TV cameras caught the wink and played it repeatedly, and it became one of the lasting pictures of the playoffs. "I knew Sandstrom was taking lots of shots, but not getting anything," Roy told a *Saturday Night* interviewer. "And I knew he wasn't going to beat me." Roy led the team to another Stanley Cup win and again walked away with the Conn Smythe. Montreal rewarded him with a new four-year contract for $16 million.

During the 1994 playoffs Roy became even more of a legend. He was diagnosed with appendicitis and hospitalized, but convinced his doctors to let him out of the hospital without surgery. Loaded up on antibiotics, he played in game four, stopping 39 shots and helping Montreal win 5–2. He then returned to the hospital for the surgery and was back on the ice a few days later. Roy's position on the Canadiens seemed secure.

Tantrum Led to Trade

Unfortunately for Roy, things are not always as they seem. On December 2, 1995, he became irritated with Canadiens coach Mario Tremblay after Montreal star Vincent Damphousse was allowed to play despite the fact that he showed up only minutes before warm-ups. Roy made his feelings known to Tremblay before the game. Out on the ice the Canadiens took a beating from the Detroit Red Wings, and Tremblay let Roy simmer in the net for nine goals before pulling him out late in the second period. Furious, Roy went over to Canadiens president Ronald Corey, who was seated behind the Montreal bench, and declared publicly that he had played his last game for Montreal. "The only thing I regret is raising my hands" in mock salute to fans, who had cheered sarcastically after a save, Roy explained in *Sports Illustrated*. "They'd been great to me. It showed a short memory on my part." His tantrum and obvious insubordination ended his career with Montreal, and he was traded to the Colorado Avalanche within four days. Roy worked well with the Avalanche, which coincidentally used to be his childhood favorite Quebec Nordiques. A few weeks after the trade the Avalanche played against the Canadiens and won. After the game Roy flipped a puck at Tremblay. "It made me feel so good. It was a mistake, but I don't regret it," Roy was quoted as saying according to *Hockey's Greatest Stars*. "I'm an emotional person. I let my emotions go. I know sometimes it gets me in trouble, but I know it sometimes helps me to play better too."

Six months later the Avalanche went to the 1996 Stanley Cup to play against the Florida Panthers. That year the Panther fans had taken to throwing plastic rats out onto the ice when their team scored. During the first two games, Roy only let one goal in each game. But in the third game, the Panthers scored two goals quickly, and the ice was showered with plastic rats. As the maintenance crew picked them up, Roy skated over to the Avalanche bench and told his teammates, "No more rats," according to *Hockey's Greatest Stars*. There was not another goal scored against Roy during the rest of the series, and the Avalanche won the cup in a triple-overtime shutout in game four.

Unique Style Proved Effective

Roy's signature style, known as the butterfly, where he kneeled on the ice with his legs at right angles to his body, is physically impossible for most mortals. His flexibility enabled him to cover the entire bottom of the net with his goalpads, reducing the number of goals scored against him. In October of 2000 Roy's technique helped him beat Terry Sawchuk's record of 447 regular-season wins to result in an all-time high. He was so entrenched in the Avalanche success story that a ceremony honoring him was held at the Pepsi Center in Denver, Colorado. The mayor announced he had named a street after Roy, and the state's governor proclaimed Patrick Roy Week. Team owner Stan Kroenke displayed a bronze bust of Roy. Perhaps the attention was too much for Roy; just 24 hours later the police were called to his home where he had lost his temper and was ripping doors off their hinges. He spent six hours in custody on charges of misdemeanor criminal mischief in connection with domestic violence. Roy was quickly back out on the ice minding the net, and in 2001 he won another Stanley Cup with the Avalanche as well as another Conn Smythe Trophy.

In May 2003 Roy retired from the NHL. He made the decision to leave the game while still playing at the top of his game. Indeed, he left the NHL with impressive records in both regular season and playoff games. His regular season records include being the goaltender with the most victories (551) and games played (1,029), and his post-season play is marked by his records as the goaltender with the most playoff wins (151), games played (247), minutes played (15,209), shutouts (23), and consecutive wins in the post season (11 in 1993).

Despite his inability to control his emotions outside the game, Roy's personality quirks seemed to help him on the ice. "His teams have always fed off his energy," Stars center Mike Modano told a contributor to *Sporting News.* "He's like the guy at the carnival dunking booth, daring you to dunk him. But very few can." Perhaps it all started with another of Roy's rituals: that of leading his teammates through an elaborate stick-and-glove tapping ritual before the opening face-off of every game.

Books

Hunter, Douglas, *A Breed Apart: An Illustrated History of Goal-tending,* Benchmark Press, 1995.
McDonnell, Chris, *Hockey's Greatest Stars,* Firefly Books, 1999.
The Top 100 Hockey Players of All Time, edited by Steve Dryden, Transcontinental Sports Publications, 1997.

Periodicals

Hockey Digest, May 2002.
Rocky Mountain News, October 29, 2000.
Saturday Night, March, 1995.
Sporting News, October 23, 2000.
Sports Illustrated, October 23, 2000.
Sports Illustrated for Kids, April 1995.

Online

"Patrick Roy #33," *All Sports.com,* http://www.allsports.com/nhl/players/Patrick-Roy.html (February 17, 2003).
"Patrick Roy Announces His Retirement," *Colorado Avalanche.com,* http://www.coloradoavalanche.com/features/feature103427152126.html (June 4, 2003). ☐

Donald Harold Rumsfeld

Donald Rumsfeld (born 1932) became the United States 21st Secretary of Defense on January 20, 2001. Before assuming that position, he was a Navy pilot, President Gerald Ford's Secretary of Defense, President Ford's White House Chief of Staff, U.S. Ambassador to NATO under President Richard Nixon, a U.S. Congressman from Illinois, and chief executive officer at two Fortune 500 companies.

Beginnings

Donald Harold Rumsfeld was born in Chicago on July 9, 1932, the son of George Donald Rumsfeld, a real estate salesman, and Jeannette Huster Rumsfeld. He was raised in Winnetka, Illinois, a wealthy suburb on Chicago's North Shore. At New Trier High School, Rumsfeld was a champion wrestler in the 145-pound class. He would marry his high school sweetheart in 1954.

Following his graduation from high school, Rumsfeld attended Princeton University on an academic and NROTC scholarship and became captain of the football and wrestling teams. There is a legend about Rumsfeld during his college days that says he would do one-armed push-ups for money. Rumsfeld admitted years later that he did not have much money in college, and that he did the push-ups because he needed to scrape together some cash. In any case he graduated from Princeton with an A.B. degree in 1954 with a major in political science.

In 1954, he began three years of service in the U.S. Navy as an aviator and flight instructor. In 1957, he transferred to the Ready Reserve. As a member of the reserve, he continued his flying and administrative assignments during drills until 1975. (Upon becoming Secretary of Defense in 1975, he would transfer to the Standby Reserve. In 1989, he was re-assigned to the Retired Reserve with the rank of captain.)

Washington Bound

In 1957, Rumsfeld moved to Washington to serve as administrative assistant to a congressman. Two years later, he became a congressional staff assistant. Rumsfeld left Washington from 1960 to 1962 to serve as a representative of the Chicago investment banking firm, A.G. Becker and Company. But in 1962, at the age of 30, Rumsfeld won election to the U.S. House of Representatives from Illinois. He would also go to win re-election in 1964, 1966, and 1968. But in 1969, he gave up his seat in Congress to join the Nixon administration as director of the Office of Economic Opportunity, assistant to the president, and member of the president's cabinet.

In 1971, Rumsfeld was named counselor to the president and director of the Economic Stabilization Program, while continuing in his role as a member of the president's cabinet. Two years later, he was appointed U.S. ambassador to the North Atlantic Treaty Organization (NATO) in Brussels, Belgium. Rumsfeld returned to Washington in 1974 to serve as chairman of President Gerald R. Ford's transition team, and stayed on as President Ford's White House chief of staff and member of Ford's cabinet.

Thirteenth Secretary of Defense

On November 11, 1975, the U.S. Senate confirmed Rumsfeld's appointment as the 13th Secretary of Defense. Taking office nine days later, he became the youngest person, at 43, to serve as defense secretary in the nation's history. His tenure would continue until January 20, 1977, when the Carter administration took office. In 1977, Rumsfeld was awarded the Presidential Medal of Freedom, the highest award that can be given to a U.S. citizen.

CEO

The change of administrations resulted in a time-out in Rumsfeld's political career. Between 1977 and 1985, he served as president and chief executive officer of the multinational pharmaceutical company, G.D. Searle & Co. At Searle, Rumsfeld increased profits on such mundane products as Metamucil by introducing orange and lemon flavors. His greatest success, however, was bringing NutraSweet to market. Rumsfeld's achievements at Searle brought him awards as the Outstanding Chief Executive Officer in the Pharmaceutical Industry from the *Wall Street Transcript* (1980) and *Financial World* (1981). On June 1, 1985, he became the first person in the company's history who was not a member of the Searle family to serve as chairman of the board.

While still with Searle, Rumsfeld also found time to serve the Reagan administration as a member of the President's General Advisory Committee on Arms Control (1982–1986); special envoy on the Law of the Sea Treaty (1982–1983); special envoy to the Middle East (1982–1984); senior advisor to the President's Panel on Strategic Systems (1983–1984); and member of the U.S. Joint Advisory Commission on U.S.-Japan Relations.

Rumsfeld's resume shows him to have been in private business from 1985 to 1990. On May 30, 1986, the *Wall Street Journal* announced that he planned to seek the Republican nomination for president for the 1988 election. But by March 2, 1987, he had apparently changed his mind and announced that he would not seek the presidency after all. From 1987 to 1990, Rumsfeld was a member of the National Commission for Public Service. He served on the National Economic Commission from 1988 to 1989 and as a member of the Board of Visitors of the National Defense University from 1988 to 1992.

In 1990, he joined the General Instrument Corporation, a leader in broadband transmission, distribution, and access control technologies, as chairman and chief executive officer. He remained at General Instrument until 1993. From 1992 to 1993, he also served on the U.S. Federal Communication Commission's High Definition Television Advisory Committee.

Rumsfeld remained in private business after 1993, becoming chairman of the board of directors of Gilead Sciences, Inc., and a member of the boards of Asea Brown Boveri, Ltd., Amylin Pharmaceuticals, and the Tribune Company. He also served as chairman of the Salomon Smith Barney International Advisory Board and an advisor to a number of companies, including Investor AB of Sweden. In the public sector, he served as chairman of the U.S. Commission to Assess National Security Space Management and Organization.

Political Ties

Rumsfeld continued to maintain alliances with Republican causes and commissions while pursuing his business career. In 1996, he worked with Bob Dole's presidential campaign in an attempt to unseat incumbent Bill Clinton. From 1998 to 1999, he served as chairman of the Commission to Assess the Ballistic Missile Threat to the United States. From 1999 to 2000, he was a member of the U.S. Trade Deficit Review Commission and in 2000 served as chairman of the Commission to Assess United States National Security Space Management and Organization.

Twenty-first Secretary of Defense

Rumsfeld became the 21st Secretary of Defense on January 20, 2001. When Rumsfeld took office, he was initially faced with the task of whittling down the Pentagon's $300 billion budget. At that time, he attempted to portray himself as a champion of the taxpayers who was trying to keep money from being wasted on political and military boondoggles. But in a war with the Pentagon in which his mission was to reduce military waste, most Washington insiders were betting that Rumsfeld would fail. The military, finding itself left out of planning Rumsfeld's reforms, began taking potshots at him in press conferences. Before the terrorist attacks of September 11, 2001, Rumsfeld seemed to be headed toward marginalization, a fate often reserved for politicians who have no further ambition. But after September 11, Rumsfeld found himself confronted with prosecuting a war instead of fighting Pentagon bureaucracy.

Rumsfeld began revamping Department of Defense strategy and reworking the model used to assess the country's military manpower needs. With presidential authorization, he undertook to reorganize the United States' worldwide command structure (into the U.S. Northern Command and the U.S. Strategic Command). Rumsfeld also looked at the nation's military capabilities in space and developed a model of strategic deterrence that reduces nuclear weapons. He also beefed up missile defense research and testing.

With the declaration of the war on terrorism, many of Rumsfeld's deficits seemed to turn into assets, including his marked tendency toward arrogance. Jeffrey Krames, writing in *The Rumsfeld Way,* quotes from Rumsfeld's speech to members of the U.S. Armed Forces on the day after the September 11 terrorist attack, "Great crises are marked by their memorable moments. At the height of peril to his own nation, Winston Churchill spoke of their finest hour. Yesterday, America and the cause of human freedom came under attack, and the great crisis of America's twenty-first century was suddenly upon us." Krames wondered whether Rumsfeld really meant to imply that he was up to dealing with the hand of destiny.

In the war against the Taliban in Afghanistan in 2001, shortly after the September 11 attacks, Rumsfeld initially seemed bent on taking personal control of the war. He urged the Central Command to put more ground troops on the battlefield, after the commanding general failed to achieve any progress with bombing raids. But he eventually decided that the best way to win a war is to let the senior military run it—winning him more than a few points with the Pentagon.

Also during the Afghanistan war, Rumsfeld acquired a reputation of speaking in plain English at press conferences, instead of using the military speak many reporters had become used to. Criticism of Rumsfeld initially remained sparse following the September 11 attacks, if only because there was a fear of being branded a traitor if one did not sign up to his cut-and-dry agenda.

But by 2003, when the war on terrorism had transformed itself into a "showdown with Saddam Hussein," Rumsfeld's reputation as a plain speaker seemed to be unraveling, and dissenters were finding their voice. Mike Moore, senior editor of the *Bulletin of the Atomic Scientists,* accused Rumsfeld of deliberately distorting the difference between a preventive and pre-emptive war in his public statements. Citing the Department of Defense's own Dictionary of Military Terms, Moore pointed out that a pre-emptive war is one "initiated on the basis of incontrovertible evidence that an enemy attack is imminent," while a preventive war is "initiated in the belief that military conflict, while not imminent, is inevitable, and that to delay would involve greater risk." Moore argued that while a pre-emptive war may be morally and legally justified, a preventive war is unworthy of any law-abiding nation and a violation of international law.

In 2001, *U.S. News and World Report* quoted Henry Kissinger as saying, "Rumsfeld afforded me a close-up look at a special Washington phenomenon: the skilled full-time politician bureaucrat in whom ambition, ability, and substance fuse seamlessly."

Private Citizen

Rumsfeld's civic activities have included service on the Boards of Trustees of the Chicago Historical Society, Eisenhower Exchange Fellowships, the Hoover Institution at Stanford University, the Rand Corporation, and the National Park Foundation.

Among honors that have come to Rumsfeld are the Distinguished Eagle Scout Award (1975), the George Catlett Marshall Award (1984), the Woodrow Wilson Award (1985), the Dwight Eisenhower Medal (1993), and many honorary degrees. In 1977, he was awarded the nation's highest civilian award, the Presidential Medal of Freedom.

Rumsfeld married Joyce Pierson in 1954. They have three children and several grandchildren. Rumsfeld has a ranch in Taos, New Mexico, where he skis and sometimes ropes cattle.

Books

Krames, Jeffrey A., *The Rumsfeld Way,* McGraw-Hill, 2002.

Periodicals

Bulletin of the Atomic Scientists, January-February 2003.
U.S. News & World Report, December 17, 2001.

Online

"The Honorable Donald Rumsfeld, Secretary of Defense," http://www.defenselink.mil/bios/rumsfeld.html (January 2003).

"The Honorable Donald Rumsfeld," http://www.ustdrc.gov/members/rumsfeld.html (January 2003). □

S

Edith Sampson

Edith Sampson (c. 1901–1979) became America's first African American female judge after succeeding as a social worker, a lawyer, and an international advocate for democracy and free market trade. As a representative of the State Department during the Cold War, Sampson traveled around the world, defending the United States against Soviet propaganda. As a judge, she was known as a compassionate, efficient, and powerful mediator.

Trained as Social Worker

Sampson was born Edith Spurlock in Pittsburgh, Pennsylvania, on October 13, but the exact year is unknown. It was probably earlier than 1901, because some sources say her younger brother was born in 1900. She was one of eight children born to Louis Spurlock and Elizabeth McGruder Spurlock. Louis Spurlock was a shipping clerk in a cleaning and dying business. Elizabeth Spurlock worked at home making buckram hat frames and switches of false hair. The family worked hard, owned its own home, attended church, and obeyed the law. Sampson told *Readers Digest,* "I suppose we were poor, but we never knew it. We wore hand-me-down clothes, and we all worked."

At age 14, Sampson left school and got her first full-time job, cleaning and deboning fish in a fish market. She eventually resumed her education, earned good grades, and graduated from Peabody High School.

After Sampson graduated, her Sunday school teacher helped her get a job with Associated Charities, a New York social work organization. Associated Charities arranged for her to attend the New York School of Social Work. There, she excelled in a criminology class taught by George W. Kirchwey of Columbia University School of Law. He told her she would make a good attorney and advised her to enroll in law school. Instead, Sampson completed her social work degree.

Excelled in Law School

After she graduated from college, Sampson married Rufus Sampson, a field agent for the Tuskegee Institute, and the couple moved to Chicago. Sampson worked with the Illinois Children's Home and Aid Society and the Young Women's Christian Association (YWCA). She worked with neglected and abused children, placing them in foster and adoptive homes. When Kirchwey passed through Chicago to deliver a speech, her former instructor again encouraged her to pursue a law career. This time, she followed his advice and enrolled in the John Marshall Law School, attending classes at night while working full-time as a social worker. She excelled in law school and received a special dean's commendation for ranking highest among the 95 students in her jurisprudence class.

Eventually, her marriage to Rufus Sampson ended in divorce, but she retained his name throughout her life. She never had children of her own but raised her sister's two children after her sister died.

Sampson received her bachelor of law degree in 1925 and took the bar exam but failed. She attributed the failure to overconfidence and later said failing the exam was the best thing that could have happened because it motivated her to work harder. She enrolled at Loyola University law

school and in 1927 became the first woman to earn a master of law degree from that university. That same year, she passed the bar exam and was admitted to the Illinois bar.

While in graduate school at Loyola, Sampson had worked as a probation officer. In 1927, she opened her own law firm on the south side of Chicago while also working as a referee for the Juvenile Court of Cook County. She said working with the court taught her the practical side of law. Her law firm specialized in criminal law and domestic relations, offering legal advice to many poor, African American people who could not otherwise afford it.

In 1934, Sampson was admitted to practice before the U.S. Supreme Court. She was one of the first African American women to earn this distinction. In 1938, she and Georgia Jones Ellis became the first African Americans to join the Chicago chapter of the National Association of Women Lawyers. Sampson joined many other professional and civic organizations, including the League of Women Voters, the National Association for the Advancement of Colored People (NAACP), and the National Council of Negro Women. In 1947, Sampson was appointed assistant state's attorney of Cook County.

In 1934, Sampson married attorney Joseph Clayton. The couple worked as law partners for more than ten years. Clayton died in 1957.

Anti-Communist Spokeswoman

During the late 1940s, when Sampson was serving as chairwoman of the executive committee of the National Council of Negro Women, she was selected to represent the group in a 72-day world lecture tour. The tour included representatives of various American groups who spoke out on current problems in radio broadcasts called "America's Town Meeting of the Air." Its purpose was to promote American democracy, countering Soviet Cold War propaganda.

Sampson overcame stage fright during the tour and spoke eloquently about democracy. She was often confronted with difficult questions about U.S. civil rights. The Soviet Union used America's record of racial discrimination as a tool against the United States. Sampson countered many misconceptions about African American people in America. She later commented that people seemed to think that African Americans were living behind barbed wire. Sampson pointed out the progress African Americans had made since emancipation and emphasized that she was a powerful example of a successful, educated African American.

When people criticized the United States for its civil rights record, she acknowledged problems, but defended democracy for what it offered African Americans. The *New York Times* reported that at one stop she quieted a heckler when she said, "You ask, do we get fair treatment? My answer is no. Just the same, I'd rather be a Negro in America than a citizen of any other country. In the past century we have made more progress than dark-skinned people anywhere else in the world."

During a speech Sampson made in Pakistan, the prime minister's wife collected $5,000 to offset Sampson's tour costs. Sampson graciously accepted the gift, then promptly donated it to the League of Pakistani Women for charitable work.

When the tour ended in 1950, the World Town Hall Seminar became a permanent organization to promote democracy around the world, and Sampson was named its president. The trip changed her life. Although she still practiced law, it was no longer the sole focus of her career. She devoted herself to promoting peace and world unity.

Worked With United Nations

Sampson's work with the World Town Hall Seminar caught the attention of President Harry S. Truman, who appointed her an alternate delegate to the fifth regular session of the General Assembly of the United Nations. She was the first African American woman to be named an official American representative to the U.N. She served on the U.N.'s Social, Humanitarian and Cultural Committee, which worked for land reform, reparation of prisoners, repatriation of Greek children, and efforts to stop governments' jamming of radio broadcasts. She was reappointed alternate delegate in 1952 and later was named member-at-large of the U.S. Commission for United Nations Educational, Scientific and Cultural Organization (UNESCO) during President Dwight Eisenhower's administration.

Sampson served as a spokesperson for the State Department throughout the 1950s. She visited Europe, the Middle East, and South America, addressing the status of African Americans. *Ebony* magazine called her "one of the country's most potent weapons against Communist distortion of the Negro's status in the U.S." Sampson strongly criticized Soviet distortions of the lives of African Americans. She once told Soviet U.N. delegate Andrei Vyshinsky, "We Negroes aren't interested in communism. We were slaves too long for that."

Sampson acknowledged racial discrimination in her speeches, but she chose to emphasize the positive aspects of democracy for African American people. She described a 1950 trip to Austria with *Ebony* magazine: "There were times when I had to bow my head in shame when talking about how some Negroes have been treated in the United States. . . . But I could truthfully point out that these cases, bad as they are, are the exceptions—the Negro got justice for every one where justice was denied. I could tell them that Negroes have a greater opportunity in America to work out their salvation than anywhere else in the world."

In 1961 and 1962, Sampson was appointed to serve on the United States Citizens Commission on the North Atlantic Treaty Organization (NATO). In 1964 and 1965, she was a member of the U.S. Advisory Committee on Private Enterprise in Foreign Aid.

Pioneered as Judge

Sampson was a friend and supporter of Chicago Mayor Richard Daley. This relationship helped her when she ran for a judgeship and Chicago African American leader William Dawson opposed her. In 1962, Sampson became the first African American female judge in the United States when she was elected associate to the Municipal Court of Chicago. She handled divorce, custody, and other domestic disputes. She was known as a mediator who tried at all times to preserve families.

In 1966, Sampson was elected to a seat on the Circuit Court of Cook County, where she heard landlord-tenant disputes. She was the first African American woman to hold this position. She served poor neighborhoods of Chicago and quickly moved to clear up a huge backlog on the court docket, hearing as many as 10,000 cases a year. Although she handled cases quickly, she took an interest in the parties, offering social services referrals when needed. She tried to avoid evicting tenants if it was clear that they could not afford to pay their rent.

Some civil rights leaders criticized Sampson, saying that she downplayed the barriers African Americans faced and did not sufficiently support the country's civil rights movement. Sampson described her philosophy in *Reader's Digest:* "Don't tear down the old homestead until you have a clear idea of what you'll build in its place. Just because you are impatient with moving at only five mile an hour, it doesn't follow that accelerating to 150 will solve your problems. We are beginning to move. We haven't reached cruising speed yet; but we are moving toward a better America at an ever-increasing pace."

Sampson received several honorary degrees, including a doctor of law degree from the John Marshall Law School. She retired from the bench in 1978. Her favorite pastimes included interior decorating, playing canasta, canning preserves, and making jelly. Although she had no children, she was very close to her nieces and nephews. Two of her nephews became judges: Oliver Spurlock of Chicago and Charles T. Spurlock of Boston. Sampson died on October 8, 1979, in Chicago.

Books

Contemporary Black Biography, Volume 13, Gale Research, 1996.
Notable Black American Women, Gale Research, 1992.
Women in World History: A Biographical Encyclopedia, edited by Anne Commire, Yorkin Publications, 1999.

Periodicals

New York Times, October 11, 1979.

Online

Gordon, Kathleen E., "Edith S. Sampson," www.stanford.edu/group/WLHP/papers/edith.html (February 11, 2003). □

Sanapia

Sanapia (1895–1979) was a Comanche medicine woman whose healing practices were documented by graduate student David E. Jones in the early 1970s. Sanapia did not begin practicing as a doctor until after she reached menopause. She had received her training from her mother and maternal uncle while still a young girl.

Powerful Forebearers

Although it is impossible to trace the origin of the Comanche tribe, there are indications that it first emerged in present-day Wyoming, between Yellowstone and Platte Rivers. According to legend, two groups of the tribe disagreed about how to divide up a slain animal and decided to separate. One group went north, where it became known as the Shoshone. The other turned east and south and became the Comanche.

Sanapia, whose Christian name was Mary Poafpybitty, was born in the spring of 1895 in a tepee pitched near Fort Sill, Oklahoma. Her family had travelled to Fort Sill to obtain rations. Because she was unsure of the actual date of her birth, Sanapia later adopted an arbitrary date of May 20, 1895. The sixth of eleven children born to her Comanche father David Poafpybitty and Comanche-Arapaho mother Chappy Poafpybitty, Sanapia grew up with five older brothers, three younger brothers, and two younger sisters.

Among the Comanche, it was believed that religious power could be obtained from a supernatural being through dreams. Sanapia's mother and maternal uncle were both Comanche shamans or eagle doctors. Sanapia's maternal uncle was also active in the Comanche peyote cult. Her paternal grandfather was a Comanche chief, and her mother's brother was an Arapaho chief.

Sanapia's mother refused to accept white culture and would not even speak English in a white man's presence. Sanapia's father, however, became a Christian. After he embraced Christianity, he turned his back on his Comanche heritage, and although he never directly attacked the old Comanche beliefs, he ignored or withdrew from them. But Sanapia did not recall any instances of her father interfering with her mother's Indian healing or peyote practices.

Sanapia was also raised with the help of her maternal grandmother, who made sure Sanapia learned the old ways and old stories. As a result, Sanapia was exposed to the Christian ideas of her father, her uncle's peyote practices, and her mother's vision quests as an eagle doctor.

Eagle doctors identified the eagle as their source of power. According to Sanapia's account of the origin of eagle doctors, a stingy old woman's grandson turned himself into an eagle after his grandmother refused to give him food. He then flew into the sky and dropped a feather with the promise that whoever found it would have his help whenever he or she needed it to help other people.

Training as Eagle Doctor

At the age of seven, Sanapia began attending Cache Creek Mission School in southern Oklahoma. Her attendance at the school marked her first prolonged contact with white society. During her summer vacations, she learned to identify herbal medicines as part of her training to become a medicine woman.

At the age of 14, Sanapia left school. She spent the next three years studying with her mother and uncle, acquiring the knowledge of an eagle doctor. Sanapia also learned the rituals associated with the collection of certain plants and methods for turning the plants into usable medicine. She was taught to administer the medicines and to diagnose and treat illnesses. She also had long talks with her mother and uncle about the proper deportment of a doctor. By the time she was 17, she had all the skills, knowledge, and supernatural powers she would need to become a medicine woman.

During her training, Sanapia was watched over by her mother, her maternal uncle, her grandmother, and her paternal grandfather. Each of these individuals had to give Sanapia his or her blessing before she would be allowed to practice. While her mother assumed responsibility for Sanapia's training as a doctor, her maternal grandmother and paternal grandfather taught her the proper system of values, morals, and ethics.

Transmission of Power

The eagle doctor's powers were believed to be concentrated in the doctor's hands and mouth. In the first phase of power transmission, Sanapia's mother transferred live coals into her daughters' hand without burning her. Then her mother drew two eagle feathers across Sanipia's mouth. In the second phase, her mother inserted an "eagle egg" into Sanapia's stomach. In the next phase, Sanapia acquired her medicine song. The culmination of Sanapia's training as an eagle doctor was her participation in a vision quest—four days and nights of solitary meditation.

After Sanapia's mother explained to her what was involved in the vision quest, including encounters with supernatural spirits, Sanapia was too frightened to go through with it. Although she spent the days of the quest sitting on the hill where her mother had sent her, she returned to her house at night and slept under the front porch. In the morning, she would go back to the hill without her mother or uncle knowing what she had done. Sanapia later attributed her suffering as a young woman to this deception.

Shortly after the vision quest, Sanapia's mother gave up doctoring, convinced that she had transmitted her skills and powers to her daughter. Sanapia was not expected to become a doctor for many more years, however, until she had reached menopause.

Marriages and Troubles

Having completed her training, Sanapia was considered ready for marriage. Her husband, a friend of her brother, was picked out by her mother. While Sanapia had no objections to the marriage, she was not in love with her spouse. After giving birth to a son, Sanapia left her husband at the urging of her mother. Within a year she was married again, to a husband she stayed with her until his death in the 1930s. Her second marriage produced a son and daughter.

Following the death of her second husband, Sanapia drank excessively, engaged in promiscuous sex, and exhibited violent tantrums. She also acquired a taste for gambling. Informants attributed Sanapia's behavior at this time to her grief at the loss of her husband. Sanapia later referred to this time as her "roughing-it-out" period. During this phase of her life, one of Sanapia's sisters asked her to heal her sick child. The child recovered, and Sanapia took the recovery as a sign that she should begin doctoring.

Eagle Doctor

Some time around 1945, Sanapia married for the third time. She abandoned her problematic behavior and began doctoring seriously. Doctors were expected to lead exemplary lives, and any bad behavior was thought to bring disgrace on the doctor and on her medicine; in the worst case, it could even cause the doctor's death.

The doctor was expected to be always accessible and was not permitted to refuse to treat anyone. The doctor was not supposed to boast of her powers; to do so would be to deny that the doctor's power was a gift. The doctor was not allowed to approach a patient with the offer of a cure but was to wait for the patient to come to her. The amount of payment for services rendered was always left up to the patient.

After Sanapia began her healing practice, she began to have "real" dreams, which she distinguished from ordinary dreams by their power to change her behavior. These dreams frequently dealt with the peyote ritual. But Sanapia considered the power of peyote subordinate to the power possessed by the spirits of her mother and uncle. She considered peyote a gift of the Christian God to the Indian people.

Ghost Sickness

Sanapia felt that ghosts were probably the spirits of evil persons who had died and who were destined to wander the earth forever. The ghosts were believed to be jealous of the living. (The spirits of good people who had died were believed to reside in another realm.) According to Comanche beliefs, ghosts had the power to deform their victims by causing facial contractions or hand and arm paralysis. Ghosts were believed to attack people when the victims were outside and alone at night. According to Sanapia, ghost sickness was called "stroke" by white people, but she nevertheless made a distinction between the two ailments and would not treat a stroke victim.

According to David E. Jones, writing in *Sanapia, Comanche Medicine Woman,* a more closely drawn analysis suggests that ghost sickness actually corresponds to Bell's palsy, a paralysis of the muscles on one side of the face. Bell's palsy, which results from an inflammation of the facial nerve, has a sudden onset that typically occurs at the time of awakening. The modern treatment may involve facial massage. Although Bell's palsy is the most common cause of facial paralysis, its cause is unknown.

In treating ghost sickness, Sanapia initially had her patient bathe in a stream. Following prayers in which she asked the eagle to help heal her patient, Sanapia "smoked" the patient with cedar smoke. She then chewed recumbent milkweed and applied it to the parts of the patient's body that exhibited the ghost sickness. She then began sucking on the contorted part of the patient's face to draw out the sickness.

If the patient had not responded to three treatments by the end of the first day, Sanapia called a peyote meeting, and the patient was given a tea made from the peyote plant. The tea was also applied to the patient's face, head, and hands. Applications of sweet sage and charcoal from the peyote drum followed.

Sanapia's last resort was to invoke the intercession of the medicine eagle. To do so, she sang her medicine song repeatedly until she felt the spirits had come to her. At that point, she returned to the patient and continued doctoring, using only her medicine feather and smoke. She did not touch the patient at this point, for fear that she might kill him. By this time, the treatment would have lasted three days.

Sanapia's Pharmacopoeia

Sanapia's medicine kit consisted of both botanical and non-botanical medicines. Botanical cures included red cedar to dispel the influence of ghosts; sneezeweed to treat heart palpitations, low blood pressure and congestion; mescal bean for ear problems; rye grass for the treatment of cataracts; prickly ash to treat fever; iris for colds, upset stomachs and sore throats; gray sage for insect bites; sweet sage for use in the sucking ceremony; recumbent milkweed for ghost sickness, broken bones, and menstrual cramps; and broomweed for treatment of skin rashes. Peyote was Sanapia's medicine of general use; it was employed in the treatment of any type of illness, and she kept several peyote buttons with her at all times.

Non-botanical medicines included crow feathers to protect against ghosts; slivers of glass to make incisions; a piece of cow horn used in sucking sickness from the bodies of her patients; charcoal from a peyote drum to retard the spread of pain and swelling; white otter fur and porcupine quills to treat infants; fossilized bone to treat wounds and infections; a Bible to help in her quest for power; a medicine feather from a golden eagle to fan her patients; beef fat to treat burns; mouth wash to kill poisons that entered her mouth while sucking, and red paint for treating ghost sickness.

According to the doctoring tradition of her people, the medicine power needed to be transferred to someone willing and worthy of the responsibility. It is unclear whether or not Sanapia forwarded her power to a successor. Perhaps out of a concern that she would be unable to pass her power on to the next generation, Sanapia allowed anthropologist David E. Jones to record the details of her life and the medicine tradition beginning in 1967. The result was several articles and a book (*Sanapia, Comanche Medicine Woman*). Sanapia died in 1984 in Oklahoma and was buried in the Comanche Indian cemetery near Chandler Creek, Oklahoma.

Books

Jones, David E., *Sanapia, Comanche Medicine Woman,* Waveland Press, 1972.
Margolis, Simeon, ed., *Johns Hopkins Symptoms and Remedies,* Rebus, 1995.

Online

"Artists' Biography: Eleanor McDaniel," *Native American Store Online,* http://www.nativeamericanstoreonline.com/ab4 .html (January 2003). □

Alexander Schindler

Rabbi Alexander Schindler (1925–2000) thought he was going to be an engineer. But when he saw Jews emerging from Dachau in Germany—a concentration camp—at the end of World War II, his plans changed. He returned to the United States to a lifelong pursuit of religion and social studies, becoming one of the most prominent Jewish figures of the century. He became a creating force in Reform Judaism—leading the movement for over a quarter of a century—and innovatively offered Judaism to whoever might be interested.

Growing Up

Schindler was born on October 4, 1925, in Munich, Germany, to a Hasidic, Yiddish poet, Eliezer Schindler, and his wife, Sali. When Schindler was 12 years old, the boy and his family fled Germany and the Nazi regime and settled in New York City around 1937.

Schindler studied engineering until he enrolled as a United States soldier in World War II. He found his way into the Alpine Patrol ski troops in Europe as a corporal and said at the National Museum of American Jewish History website, "We fought our way through the Apennines." Schindler distinguished himself in war with three combat ribbons for bravery, a Purple Heart, and a Bronze Star.

Life Changed

Schindler was overseas near the Yugoslav border when the war ended. A forward observer for the artillery, he borrowed a jeep from his captain and went to Germany to observe what had happened. Curious about his relatives in Germany, he traveled to Munich to find them. He ended up in Dachau, where the concentration camp was just releasing many of the Jewish prisoners. Schindler said at the Jewish History website, "It subconsciously had a great impact on my life's development."

When Schindler returned to the United States, he dropped his engineering studies to pursue social studies and social sciences as well as Jewish studies, Jewish history, Yiddish, and Hebrew. He entered City College (College of the City of New York) and graduated in 1949. Meanwhile, he involved himself at the Jewish Theological Seminary, Hebrew Union College—the Reform Judaism movement's seminary—and the New School. He was studying society and Judaism "in [an] . . . effort, I suppose, to find out why [the Holocaust] happened," Schindler shared at the Jewish History website.

Early Career

In 1953, Schindler graduated from Hebrew Union College's Jewish Institute of Religion in Cincinnati, Ohio, with a Masters in Hebrew Letters and a rabbinical ordination. He took on his first congregation in 1953—Temple Emanuel in Worcester, Massachusetts—and spent six years there honing his Reform convictions. Schindler met 24-year-old Rhea Rosenblum during his appointment in Worcester. He proposed marriage to her the day that they met, but she left, as previously planned, for Israel soon after. Upon her return, Schindler and Rosenblum married on September 29, 1956.

The Schindlers moved to Boston in 1959, where Schindler founded the New England Coalition of Reform Synogoues, propelling him into leadership in the national Reform Movement. Soon after relocation to New York, Schindler was appointed director of the Union of American Hebrew Congregations (UAHC) New England regional office. By 1963, Schindler was the national director of education for the UAHC in Manhattan; by 1967, he was the vice president of the UAHC; and by 1973, he was the president. Schindler would serve in this position for more than 20 years and use it as a springboard to reach many Americans and many Jews worldwide.

Controversial Reforms

The Interfaith Family website noted, Schindler "[viewed] Judaism as a dynamic faith that evolved through its dialogue with tradition." Schindler was a pioneer for justice and equality both inside and outside of the Jewish community. He helped carve a place for Reform Jews in the Jewish communities both in the United States and worldwide. He helped imbue Reform Judaism with respectability with his friend-winning personality, while at the same time making reforms that were often controversial and anti-mainstream.

Schindler fought for the equal treatment of Jewish gays and lesbians, helping secure a place for them in Reform Judaism temples. He worked hard for women's rights in the temple, as well. Early during his time of leadership with the UAHC, the first woman rabbi was ordained. Schindler also fought for women's rights outside the Jewish faith. He had a passion for people with physical handicaps and worked to have hearing assistance devices installed in temples, as well as other modifications to aid the physically handicapped. Schindler also worked for the causes of the poor and those inhibited by racism.

Most importantly, Schindler helped to enlarge the sphere of Jewish outreach, not only through his work with the gay and lesbian communities, but through outreach to traditionally shunned members of the "Jewish family." In 1978, Schindler enacted the "Outreach" program which targeted spouses of Jews, aiming to have them accepted—and their Jewish spouses restored—to the Jewish faith. This move, along with others, reversed more-than-500-year-old traditions against proselytizing. Schindler was known to welcome any honest soul into the Jewish way of life. One of Schindler's most controversial actions was to reach out to patrilineal descendants of Jews. Traditionally, only matrilineal descendency was accepted as true Jewishness, but

Schindler would embrace any child of a Jew who was given a proper Jewish education.

An online Interfaith Family article claimed that "Schindler built the [Reform Judaism] movement into one of the most vigorous forces in American religious life. He was renowned for his unrelenting commitment to issues of peace, social justice, and equality." Juli Cragg Hilliard quoted Schindler in *Sarasota Herald Tribune* as having said, "Social activism is part of God's mandate to congregations." Schindler certainly took his own advice seriously and ended up changing the face of Judaism in America.

Other Accomplishments

In the political arena, Schindler was deeply involved. He said to Hilliard, "Religion and politics are inextricable." In the late 1970s he served as Chairman of the Conference of Presidents of Major Jewish Organizations. The coalition led Jewish bodies to act as a liaison between the United States and Israeli governments. Schindler also became a confidant of Israeli Prime Minister Menachem Begin. His work with the Isreali peace process led him to be awarded the Bublick Prize of Hebrew University. Schindler also worked to get Switzerland and other countries to return property stolen from Jews during the holocaust. Schindler claimed that the displaced Jews needed restoration as a matter of principle but also to rectify the fact that many of them were living lives of "destitution." Begin was quoted on the Interfaith Family website calling Schindler one "who has written his name into the pages of the Jewish people's story of freedom, dignity, and strength."

Schindler authored and oversaw the publication of the first Torah commentary in the Reform tradition, *The Torah: A Modern Commentary*. He also served on various committees and organizations, including president of the International Memorial Foundation for Jewish Culture, vice president of the World Jewish Congress, Co-Chairman on the Commission on East-West Relations for the World Jewish Congress, representative for various sects of Judaism regarding peace in the Middle East, and lay leader for the Memorial Foundation. He also acted to further the work of Reform Judaism's social program and the Reform Judaism Reform Action Center in Washington, D.C. His work for Jewish equal rights culminated in the founding of the Association of Reform Zionists of America (ARZA). A Jewish National Fund forest of 500,000 trees in Israel bears his name. Schindler retired from many of his committee duties in the 1990s—including the presidency of the UAHC in 1996—but maintained an involved schedule. He said to Hilliard, "Retirement, I think, is a problem only for people who have forgotten how to start anew."

Schindler had a history of plaguing cardiac complaints and suffered two heart attacks, one in the 1960s and one in the 1980s while visiting Masada, Isreal. He died at his Westport, Connecticut, home on November 15, 2000, from a coronary arrest in his sleep. He died before waking. Schindler had recently celebrated his 75th birthday and was still serving as president of the Memorial Foundation for Jewish Culture and vice president of the World Jewish Congress. He left behind him his wife of 44 years, Rhea Rosenblum Schindler; children Elisa Ruth, Debra Lee, Jonathan David, Joshua Michael, and Rabbi Judith Rachel Schindler; and 9 grandchildren.

Periodicals

Sarasota Herald Tribune, January 17, 1997.

Online

"Interfaith Family" http://www.interfaithfamily.com/article/issue49/schindler.phtml (February 10, 2003).
"Jewish Bulletin News," http://www.jewishsf.com/bk001117/obschindler.shtml (February 10, 2003).
"National Museum of American Jewish History," http://www.nmajh.org/exhibitions/galut/schindler.htm (February 10, 2003).
"Rabbi Alexander Schindler, 1925-2000," http://www.obits.com/schindleralex.html (February 10, 2003).
"To the Memory: Rabbiner Alexander Schindler," http://www.beth-shalom.de/2000/12/schindler.htm (February 10, 2003). □

Olive Schreiner

Author of what most consider the first great novel— *The Story of an African Farm*—to come out of South Africa, Olive Schreiner (1855–1920) is perhaps equally well remembered as an eloquent spokesman for feminist and pacifist causes. Plagued by asthma and severe bouts of depression throughout her life, Schreiner campaigned vigorously against the more predatory aspects of Cecil Rhodes's imperialist philosophy and the British role in the Anglo-Boer War of 1892–1902. Schreiner also set herself apart with her brazen rejection of the prevailing code of Victorian decorum, particularly as it applied to the women of her time.

L argely self-educated, Schreiner read voraciously and was particularly influenced by the writings of naturalist Charles Darwin and philosophers Herbert Spencer and John Stuart Mill. Adopting a progressive outlook on life, she rejected the generally accepted gender roles of her era and advocated "an equality of shared labor between men and women," according to Ruth First and Ann Scott, coauthors of *Olive Schreiner*. Although Schreiner first gained attention as a novelist, most of the writings published during her lifetime consisted of social and political essays, including her controversial feminist credo, as outlined in *Women and Labour*.

Experienced Difficult Childhood

Schreiner was born Olive Emilie Albertina Schreiner at Wittenbergen Mission Station in the South African territory of Basutoland (now the country of Lesotho) on March 24, 1855. The ninth of 12 children born into an impoverished missionary family, she had an unsettled childhood of great hardship. Traveling with her family from post to post, Schreiner experienced little permanency in her early years. The family's difficulties worsened when her father, Gottlieb, a Boer, was expelled from the London Missionary Society for supplementing his meager missionary salary with income from private trading transactions. Schreiner's mother, English-born Rebecca Lyndall, was also a missionary. Because their father was hard-pressed to support his large family, 11-year-old Olive and her 9-year-old brother Will were sent to live in Cradock, a town in South Africa's Cape Colony. There they lived with their older brother, Theo, who was the headmaster of a school in Cradock. It was just the first stop for Shreiner, who spent the next several years boarding with family and friends.

Although she received no formal education to speak of, Schreiner read extensively, happily digesting the contents of every book she could find. At the age of 15, already depressed by the sudden death of a younger sister, Schreiner rejected the strict religious principles of her parents. By 1872, the 17-year-old Schreiner had found an informal position as a governess for a family in Dordrecht, a village in South Africa's Eastern Cape. While working in Dordrecht, Schreiner experienced her first love affair—a brief dalliance with Swiss businessman Julius Gau. She ended the affair and once again moved in with brother Theo, who had since relocated to South Africa's diamond fields. Shortly thereafter, Schreiner began working full time as a governess for wealthy Boer families in the Cape Colony. During her free time, she wrote. During 1874 and 1875, Schreiner largely completed work on three novels, *Undine,* which was published posthumously in 1929; *The Story of an African Farm,* published in London in 1883; and *Man to Man,* also published posthumously in 1924.

First Novel Published in England

In 1881, Schreiner left South Africa for England, where she hoped to become a nurse and get her novels published. She was forced to give up her dream of becoming a nurse when an asthmatic condition from her days in the diamond fields became chronic not long after she relocated. She did, however, continue her search for a publisher that might be interested in her writing. In 1882, Schreiner's semi-autobiographical *The Story of an African Farm* was accepted for publication by Chapman and Hall of London with the proviso that it appear under the pseudonym, Ralph Irons, to overcome the prevailing bias of the era against women authors. Although the novel, first published in 1883, stirred considerable controversy with its liberal views on marriage and religion, it was widely acclaimed as the first realistic description of life in South Africa. It was eight years before the true identity of the book's author could be revealed when a second edition was published in 1891.

Schreiner's novel examines in detail the lives of two orphaned cousins. One, Em, is a fairly traditional young woman, who feels her happiness will be complete when she has found a husband and become a mother. The other, Lyndall (the character thought to represent Schreiner) is an outspoken, sometimes stubborn embodiment of the "New Woman" ideal who refuses to marry her lover after

he impregnates her. Although Lyndall and her child eventually die, the rebellious cousin's hopes for the future remain intact. "In the future ... perhaps," Schreiner wrote, "perhaps, to be born a woman will not be to be born branded."

Joined London's Inner Circles

Although the true identity of the novel's author was kept from the public until 1891, Schreiner's accomplishment was well known to a small group of England's prominent, young socialists, who quickly welcomed the South African author into their inner circle. Members of this exclusive group included Edward Carpenter, George Bernard Shaw, W.E. Gladstone, and Eleanor Marx. Another close associate of Schreiner during her years in England was noted "sexologist" Havelock Ellis, with whom Schreiner had a brief love affair. Although the affair was over almost before it began, Ellis and Schreiner remained lifelong friends. In 1885 Schreiner was invited to join the Men's and Women's Club, an exclusive discussion group headed by Karl Pearson, a one-time attorney who had taken up a second career as a professor of mathematics. Smitten by Pearson, Schreiner tried unsuccessfully to take their friendship to a higher level. Frustrated by Pearson's lack of response, she set off on a tour of England, France, Germany, and Italy. During her travels she began work on *From Man to Man,* a novel she never was able to finish. In 1889 a brief romantic relationship with novelist-poet Amy Levy ended in tragedy when Levy committed suicide.

Increasingly troubled by her asthmatic condition, Schreiner in 1889 returned to South Africa, settling in the country's pollution-free central high plateau known as the Karoo. Through her brother, William, who was then attorney general in the Cape Colony government of Cecil Rhodes, she met and developed a close friendship with the controversial prime minister. The friendship was to last only a few years, ending in 1892 when the two became locked in a bitter dispute over the future direction of South Africa's political and social development.

Married Ostrich Farmer

Less than two years after her split with Rhodes, Schreiner married ostrich farmer Samuel "Cron" Cron wright, who shared many of her convictions and was extremely supportive of her writing career. Although Schreiner retained her maiden name, her husband took the joint surname Cronwright-Schreiner, perhaps hoping to trade on his wife's growing fame as an author. Cronwright worked at a variety of jobs—including farmer, estate agent, and land dealer—before being elected in 1902 to a seat in the parliament of the Cape Colony. In April 1895, Schreiner gave birth to a daughter, who died only 16 hours later, setting off a deep depression in the author. In 1897, Schreiner published *Trooper Peter Halkett of Mashonaland,* an anti-war allegory extremely critical of Britain's imperialism and racism in South Africa. Convinced that Rhodes was likely to push South Africa into war, Schreiner wrote *An English South African's View of the Situation,* an impassioned plea to head off a conflict between the majority Afrikaners and the British. But her plea fell on deaf ears. The Anglo–Boer War of 1899–1902 was a difficult period for Schreiner. For her outspoken support of the Afrikaner cause, she was interned by the British for more than a year. Even more devastating was the burning of her house, in which were stored all her manuscripts, including the notes for her feminist credo *Women and Labour.*

Released from detention by the British at the end of the war, Schreiner feverishly struggled to reconstruct her notes for *Women and Labour.* When the book was finally published in 1911, it quickly developed into the "bible" of the early-20th-century feminist movement. Although Schreiner expressed some disappointment with her final product, the book was widely acclaimed as an important statement of feminist aspirations. In the book, Schreiner, a strong supporter of universal suffrage who in 1908 founded the Women's Enfranchisement League in Cape Town, argued that the vote was "a weapon, by which the weak may be able to defend themselves against the strong, the poor against the weak." In making her case that there was essentially no difference between the productive potential of men and women, Schreiner wrote: "When all the branches of productive labor be considered, the value of the labor of the two halves of humanity will be found so identical and so closely to balance that no superiority can possibly be asserted to either as the result of the closest analysis."

Develolped a Heart Condition

The asthma that had plagued Schreiner for years eventually led her to develop a heart condition. In 1914 she made plans to visit Italy for treatment but was forced at the last minute to divert to England after war was declared. She remained in England for the entirety of World War I, working on a new book that examined pacifism within a feminist and socialist moral framework. During the war she also championed the rights of conscientious objectors. In the early fall of 1920, convinced that death was near, Schreiner returned to South Africa, where she suffered a heart attack and died on December 11, 1920. Before her death, she had requested that her remains, along with those of her infant daughter and longtime pet dog, be entombed on a mountain in the Karoo, not far from Cradock. Schreiner's husband, Samuel Cronwright, saw that this wish was carried out.

Cronwright, Schreiner's sole heir and the executor of her will, was, however, less faithful in discharging some of his late wife's other requests. In her will, Schreiner had insisted that only a select few of her unpublished works be submitted for publication. Specifically, she expressed the wish that only *The Child's Day* and a series of essays under the general title of *Stray Thoughts on South Africa* be published. Cronwright, from whom Schreiner had long been estranged though never divorced, decided instead to submit a number of her other works to publishers, hoping that he might continue to profit from his wife's celebrity. Under his direction, Schreiner's *From Man to Man, or Perhaps Only* was published in 1926. The book, a collection of essays outlining Schreiner's political and sociological philosophies, dealt with a wide variety of subjects, including the exploitation of women in prostitution and marriage, the promise of sisterhood, the importance of death within the context of life, and the moral obligation of whites to promote anti-racism in their dealings with blacks. Potentially even more damaging to Schreiner's legacy was the publication in 1928, authorized by Cronwright, of *Undine,* the unfinished first novel written by the author.

Despite Cronwright's callous disregard of Schreiner's last wishes, the author's reputation appears to have survived untarnished. She will be long remembered not only for her writing but for her unwavering commitment to feminist and pacifist causes. Schreiner's ultimate goal is perhaps expressed best through the voice of Lyndall, the author's heroine in *The Story of an African Farm,* who argued that "the world will never come right, till . . . the female element of the race makes its influence felt."

Books

Contemporary Authors, Gale Group, 2000.
Encyclopaedia Britannica 2003, Encyclopedia Britannica Inc., 2002.
Feminist Writers, St. James Press, 1996.
First, Ruth, and Ann Scott, *Olive Schreiner,* Schoken Books, 1980.
Merriam-Webster's Biographical Dictionary, Merriam-Webster Inc., 1995.

Online

"Creative Quotations from Olive Schreiner," *Creative Quotations for Creative Thinking,* http://www.creativequotations.com/one/998.htm (February 11, 2003).
"Olive Emilie Albertina Schreiner," *InsaneTree Promotions,* http://www.insanetree.com/olive.htm (February 11, 2003).
"Olive Schreiner," *Spartacus Educational,* http://www.spartacus.schoolnet.co.uk/TUschreiner.htm (February 11, 2003).
"Olive Schreiner," *Washington State University,* http://www.wsu.edu:8080/~dee/Schreiner.html (February 11, 2003).
"Olive Schreiner (1855-1920)," *Drew University,* http://www.depts.drew.edu/wmst/corecourses/wmst111/timeline_bios/OSchreiner.htm (February 11, 2003).
"Olive Schreiner: Biographical Overview," *Emory University,* http://www.emory.edu/ENGLISH/Bahri/Schreiner.html (February 11, 2003). □

Charlotte Angas Scott

British-born Charlotte Angas Scott (1858–1931) was pivotal in the development of mathematics education in the United States. She was among the first faculty members at Bryn Mawr College and the school's first head mathematics teacher. She devised the curriculum at the college and standardized minimum mathematics requirements nationally through the College Entrance Examination Board. She also helped organize the American Mathematical Society.

Uphill Battle to Learn Math

Scott was born on June 8, 1858, in Lincoln, England. She was the daughter of the Reverend Caleb and Eliza Ann Exley Scott. Her father was president of Lancashire College, located near Manchester, England. He was also a Congregationalist minister. Her grandfather was also an educator. Both men were social reformers and presidents of Congregational Church colleges. Scott, one of seven children, was tutored in mathematics beginning at age seven by students from her father's school.

In that era, women were not encouraged to seek anything beyond a basic education. The prevailing wisdom was that intellectual pursuits would damage a young woman's health and marital prospects. Despite this, her family wanted Scott to have a university education and encouraged her academically from a young age.

Scott was awarded a scholarship to Hitchin College (now Girton College, the women's division of Cambridge University). There were only ten other women in her class, and they were forced to sit behind a screen that separated them from the male students and obscured their view of the blackboard. Unescorted women found on the school grounds could be carted to the Spinning House, a prison for prostitutes.

But during Scott's stay at the university, conditions were changing. Starting in 1872, undergraduate women were allowed to take the 50-hour-long oral examinations for third-year students in mathematics on an informal basis. Scott took the examination in January 1880 and placed eighth among all students. University policy was not to reveal the results, but word of her accomplishment spread. Scott was not recognized at the awards ceremony, save by a few young men who shouted "Scott of Girton!" when her name should have been read. Women were not permitted to be at the commencement exercises, but Scott was reportedly "crowned with laurels" in a private ceremony.

"Her spectacular achievement in a 'man's field' sparked a movement that culminated in a resolution enabling all resident women to take Cambridge examinations and to have their names publicly announced with those of men," wrote Patricia C. Kenschaft in *The College Mathematics Journal* in 1987. Cambridge allowed women to take examinations with the male students beginning in February 1881.

Earned Pioneering Degree

Scott continued her studies at the University of London under Arthur Cayley, her doctoral adviser and mentor. Scott began attending his lectures in 1880. "Students had to pay extra to attend university lectures," noted Kenschaft, quoting from a Girton administrator, "and as the daughter of a Congregationalist minister, she was probably poor, but she could go as a chaperone to students without paying."

Scott received her bachelor of science degree in mathematics from the University of London in 1882. She attended Cambridge for nine years, but Cambridge did not award degrees to women until 1948. She also lectured at Girton until 1894. Her studies concentrated on algebraic geometry, specifically, analyzing singularities in algebraic curves. Scott was the first British woman and the second woman in the world to be awarded a doctoral degree in this field.

Started Bryn Mawr Career

Scott left England for the United States in 1885. That year, the Society of Friends opened Bryn Mawr College in Pennsylvania. It was the first women's college to offer graduate degrees. Cayley's recommendation helped Scott get a teaching appointment. The college's executive committee noted in its discussion of hiring Scott that Cayley had given her "a high recommendation for her attainments and her capacity for original work. [The] Mistress of Girton College testifies to C.A. Scott's popularity as a teacher, her success in organizing the mathematical department of the College, and her personal courtesy and friendliness to students." The report added that she "has two defects—she is decidedly hard of hearing, and is in delicate health. Yet neither of these has thus far proved a bar to her being a really able teacher."

Scott joined the faculty as an associate professor of mathematics, the only woman on the six-person faculty when the college opened. She soon became instrumental in beefing up the school's admissions criteria. Scott pushed for entering students to have basic competency in mathematics, including courses in arithmetic, algebra—including studies of quadratic equations and geometrical progressions—and plane geometry. Those students unable to pass admissions examinations in solid geometry and trigonometry were required to pass classes on these subjects prior to graduation.

Scott became a professor of mathematics in 1888. In 1891, she became an active member of the New York Mathematical Society (later the American Mathematical Society).

In a letter she wrote to the president of Bryn Mawr in 1918, her conservative upbringing was apparent: "Now I object very much to smoking by women. . . . But also I hold a strong objection to any discrimination between members of the teaching staff as men or women. . . . I grant that the example is bad for the students; but I am not convinced that the boils that may arise from this discrimination are not fully as serious. May I add that I think fully as undesirable an example is set to the students by certain foolish young women on our teaching staff whose 'make up' is so conspicuous? I certainly was taken aback the other day to see one of these, in our Faculty Cloakroom, renewing the make-up of the face between two classes."

Scott founded the College Entrance Examination Board and was its chief examiner from 1902 to 1903. The policies she established have changed little since their adoption. Scott received Bryn Mawr's first endowed chair in 1909.

Key Contributions to Mathematics

Scott published *An Introductory Account of Certain Modern Ideas and Methods in Plane Analytical Geometry* in 1894. This textbook was very important in its field. As Kenschaft explained, the book covered "such then recent concepts as groups, subgroups, invariants and covariants, and her treatment of projective geometry. . . . Since analytic geometry played a far more important role in the college curriculum then than now, the book had enormous impact. . . . Scott's smaller book on 'school' geometry, which appeared in 1907, was not as successful because its innovations were not adopted by the mathematical public."

She also contributed heavily to the then-new field of algebraic geometry through her work on singularities in algebraic curves. "Her specialty was interpreting all possible geometric manifestations of particular algebraic expressions of degree higher than two; that is, describing plane curves that were neither linear nor conics," wrote Kenschaft.

Scott was named co-editor of the American Journal of Mathematics in 1899. She held the post until two years after her retirement. She also served on the Council of the American Mathematical Society and was its vice-president in 1905. Scott was active in various European mathematical societies including the London Mathematical Society and Deutsche Mathematiker-Vereinigung.

Throughout her career, Scott had an impressive amount of published articles, including eight papers published in European journals between 1896 and 1906. Her work was also cited frequently. Among Scott's most notable achievements was her paper "A Proof of Noether's Fundamental Theorem," published in 1900 in a European mathematics journal.

Scott's development of the mathematics program at Bryn Mawr into one that enjoyed a worldwide reputation was among her leading achievements. She was reportedly an excellent teacher who "had the rare gift of lucid explanation combined with an intuitive perception of just what the student could grasp," according to Isabel Maddison, one of her students, quoted in *Notable American Women, 1607–1950.* "Nor did she spare any effort to help a stupid student who really tried, though she was ruthless with the lazy or casual." Scott's reputation attracted other female mathematicians to the school, including Emmy Noether and Anna Pell Wheeler. In one poll, her peers ranked her 14th among the world's leading mathematicians.

Personal Life

Little is known about Scott outside her professional life. According to *Notable Scientists: From 1900 to the Present,* her "own personal life was . . . circumspect, clouded further by the fact that all her personal correspondence was apparently disposed of or lost."

At first, she lived on the Bryn Mawr campus in a small apartment lined with her collection of books. Scott, who never married, eventually rented a house from the college, where she lived for 31 years. Her cousin Eliza Nevin stayed with her as a housekeeper and companion.

Despite Scott's role as a trailblazer for women in colleges, she was not a staunch feminist. She believed men would give credit as due to intelligent women and did not want women's education to differ from men's.

"A friendship of peoples is the outcome of personal relations. A life's work such as that of Professor Charlotte Angas Scott is worth more to the world than many anxious efforts of diplomatists," said Alfred North Whitehead, the renowned English philosopher, speaking in 1922 at a meeting of the American Mathematical Society held in Scott's honor at Bryn Mawr. An estimated 70 former students and an equal number of members of the American Mathematical Society gathered for the event. It was Whitehead's first appearance in the United States, and he had reportedly turned down requests to speak at Columbia and Harvard during his visit, saying that he did not want to detract from the celebration for Scott. Whitehead said Scott "is a great example of the universal brotherhood of civilisations."

Returned to England

Scott retired from her teaching career in 1925. After her retirement, she stayed on until her last doctoral student graduated. That student, Marguerite Lehr, succeeded Scott on the staff. Scott then spent her time traveling, visiting family and colleagues, and mentoring young women mathematicians. Eventually she returned to England.

Rheumatoid arthritis caused some health problems for Scott, as did a worsening deafness. When her doctor advised her to take up gardening to improve her health, Scott cultivated a new species of chrysanthemum. She also started playing golf.

Scott died on November 10, 1931, in Cambridge, England, at the age of 73. She was buried in a family plot in St.

Giles's Churchyard next to Nevin, who had died in 1928. Her textbook on analytical geometry was reissued in 1961 as *Projective Methods in Plane Analytical Geometry.*

Books

A to Z of Women in Science and Math, Facts on File, 1999.
Contemporary Authors Online, The Gale Group, 2000.
Encyclopedia of World Biography, 2nd ed. Gale Research, 1998.
Notable American Women, 1607–1950, Belknap Press, 1971.
Notable Scientists: From 1900 to the Present, Gale Group, 2001.
Women in Science: Antiquity through the Nineteenth Century, MIT Press, 1986.

Periodicals

College Mathematics Journal, March 1987.

Online

"Charlotte Angas Scott (1858–1931)," *European Women in Mathematics Newsletter, Number 3,* http://www.math .helsinki.fi/EWM/newsletter/No3/No3.html#charlotte (March 7, 2003).
"References for Charlotte A. Scott," *School of Mathematics and Statistics, University of St. Andrews, Scotland,* http://www-history.mcs.st-andrews.ac.uk/history/References/Scott.html (February 28, 2003). □

Ntozake Shange

When African American writer Ntozake Shange's (born 1948) *for colored girls who have considered suicide/when the rainbow is enuf: a choreopoem* **appeared on the theater scene in New York City in 1975, it achieved immense popularity. Ten years later, it was still being produced in various theaters throughout the United States. With this "choreopoem"—a performance piece made up of a combination of poems and dance—Shange introduced various themes and concerns that continue to characterize her writings and performances. Her works are often angry diatribes against social forces that contribute to the oppression of black women in the United States combined with a celebration of women's self-fulfillment and spiritual survival.**

Ntozake Shange was born Paulette Williams, the oldest of Paul and Eloise Owens Williams's four children, on October 18, 1948, in Trenton, New Jersey. Shange experienced what Sandra L. Richards described in *African American Writers* as a "childhood blessed with material security and loving parents who traveled widely, maintained an international set of friends, and transmitted a pride in African and African American cultures." Shange explained her parents' influence to Claudia Tate: "My parents have always been especially involved in all kinds of Third World culture. We used to go to hear Latin

music, jazz and symphonies, to see ballets. . . . I was always aware that there were different kinds of black people all over the world. . . . So I knew I wasn't on this planet by myself. I had some connections with other people."

The family moved to St. Louis, Missouri, in 1953 when Shange was five years old, and she was one of the first children to integrate the public school system. However, the young Shange rebelled at an early age against her parents' middle-class complacency, identifying with the live-in domestic help who took care of her when she was a child. In 1961 the Williams family moved to Lawrenceville, New Jersey. At Morristown High School, Shange wrote poetry centered on black themes and subjects. Although she was published in the school magazine, her choice of subject matter was criticized, and she began to realize her need for black women role models. As she told Michele Wallace in the *Village Voice,* "There was nothing to aspire to, no one to honor. [Nineteenth-century civil rights advocate] Sojourner Truth wasn't a big enough role model for me. I couldn't go around abolishing slavery."

In 1966 Shange enrolled at Barnard College and separated from her husband, a law student. She attempted suicide several times, frustrated by what Richards termed "a society that penalized intelligent, purposeful women." Nonetheless, she graduated with honors in American Studies in 1970 and entered the University of Southern California at Los Angeles, where she earned a master's degree in American Studies in 1973.

In 1971 Shange adopted her Zulu name: Ntozake means "she who comes with her own things," and Shange translates as "one who walks with lions." She explained to Allan Wallach in *Newsday* that the name change was due, in part, to her belief that she was "living a lie:" "[I was] living in a world that defied reality as most black people, or most white people, understood it—in other words, feeling that there was something that I could do, and then realizing that nobody was expecting me to do anything because I was colored and I was also female, which was not very easy to deal with."

Feminist Persceptive

Moving to California put Shange in touch with a feminist perspective. She related to Claudia Tate in *Black Women Writers at Work* that she didn't "start out to write feminist tracts." She continued, "I was writing what I had to write, and the people who wanted to hear what I was writing were women." She soon joined a Third World Women's Cooperative, which she explained to Tate was "supportive and instrumental" in her development: "I didn't really do anything about integrating feminism and black consciousness. We met together in groups by ourselves: black, white, Asian, and Native-American women. We did our work for our own people, and all of my work just grew from there."

While living in California and teaching humanities and women's studies courses at Mills College in Oakland, the University of California Extension, and Sonoma State College, Shange began to associate with poets, teachers, performers, and black and white feminist writers who nurtured her talents. Lesbian poet Judy Grahn's 1973 *The Common Woman* provided the model for Shange's work *for colored girls.* Shange also discovered other women poets who were exploring the "implications of liberation movements as they affected the lives of women of color" and "rejecting the claims of patriarchy," observed Richards in *African American Writers.* Shange and her friends began to perform their poetry, music, and dance in bars and coffeehouses in the San Francisco area, and feminist presses like Shameless Hussy and the Oakland Women's Press Collective began to publish women's writings.

Theater

Shange's first experience with women's theater also occurred while she was in California. Because of her exposure to New World African religions, choreographer Halifu Osumare cast Shange as a priestess in *The Evolution of Black Dance,* a dance-drama performed in Oakland and Berkeley public schools in 1973 and 1974. Richards remarked that Shange "became imbued with Osumare's confidence in the legitimacy of their own women-centered/African-centered vision." When she left the company, Shange began to collaborate on poems, dance, and music that would form the basis of *for colored girls.*

for colored girls who have considered suicide/when the rainbow is enuf is a mixture of genres—poems, narratives, dialogues, dance—dramatized through the voices of and interaction among the seven women characters who represent the black woman "[who has] been dead so long/closed in silence so long/she doesn't know the sound/of her own voice/her infinite beauty." "The collage of danced poems," a choreopoem, according to Richards, "is a gift or a song calculated to restore [the black woman] to life. . . . Because the women play multiple unnamed characters, what emerges is not an individual protagonist but an essential Everywoman." As one of the characters says, we want to "sing a black girl's song. . . . Sing a song of life, she's been dead so long."

Remaining in New York until 1982, Shange produced several plays, including *Spell #7: A Geechee Quick Magic Trance Manual,* which received some positive reviews. In this production, Shange returns to the choreopoem structure, building the play on a series of poetry and dance vignettes that contemplate what it is like to be black in the United States. The main icon of the play is a black minstrel mask that dominates the set, providing what Richards referred to in *African American Writers* as "a specific historical context and a temporally undifferentiated psychic terrain . . . a hideous representation of blacks in the American popular imagination." At the turning point of the play, the characters begin to rip off their masks and to journey to a land behind the masks where, Richards observed, "blacks are free to create identities unfettered by white assumptions." In this "exorcised space," Richards continued, "the actors explore a complexity seldom accorded black characters."

Began Writing Fiction

During her New York years, Shange also began writing fiction. *Sassafras: A Novella* was published in 1977 and was expanded into her first novel, *Sassafras, Cypress & Indigo,* in 1982. Her second novel, *Betsey Brown,* was published three years later. In *Betsey Brown,* the writer shifts her focus to more autobiographical settings and themes. Betsey, the thirteen-year-old heroine, is a black girl growing up in St. Louis in 1959. Like Shange herself, Betsey is involved in the integration of public schools and is forced to ride three different buses "to learn the same things with white children that she'd been learning with colored children." Betsey asks, "Why didn't the white children come to her school?" Like many other young black heroines in coming-of-age stories, Betsey must ultimately learn to reconcile her cultural heritage with the white environment she becomes a part of through integration.

Just as in her theater pieces and novels, Shange's collections of poetry, such as *Nappy Edges* (1978), *A Daughter's Geography* (1983), and *Riding the Moon in Texas* (1987), push the limits of generic conventions. She uses nonstandard spelling, punctuation, and line breaks to convey her concerns with what she has called the "slow erosion of our humanity" and to capture the rhythms and sounds of vernacular black speech patterns. Shange told Tate in *Black Women Writers at Work* that she "really [resents] having to meet somebody else's standards or needs, or having to justify their reasons for living."

Shange cites LeRoi Jones (Imamu Baraka) and Ismael Reed among her models for her use of "lower-case letters, slashes, and spelling" in her poetry and explained to Tate that she is interested in the way poetry looks on the page. The writer further offered that she likes letters and words that "dance" on the page because they stimulate visually and encourage the readers to become "rigorous" participants. Her irregular spellings, she told Tate, "reflect the language as I hear it."

Shange has many awards to her credit. *for colored girls* won the 1977 Obie, Outer Critics Circle, Audelco, and Mademoiselle awards and received Tony, Grammy, and Emmy nominations. In 1981 she won an Obie for her adaptation of Brecht's *Mother Courage and Her Children* and earned a Guggenheim fellowship. Shange is a member of the New York State Council of the Arts and is an artist-in-residence at Houston's Equinox Theater.

In 1977 Shange married musician David Murray—whom she later divorced—and their daughter, Savannah Thulani Eloisa, was born in 1981. She left New York two years later to become a Mellon Distinguished Professor of Literature at Rice University in Houston for the spring semester and an associate professor of drama in the Creative Writing Program at the University of Houston. Shange returned East in 1989 to be closer to the New York arts scene, an environment that *African American Writers'* Richards suspected "allows for greater artistic experimentation."

In 1993 Shange directed Ina Cesaire's *Fire's Daughters* for the Ubu Repertory Theater. *Fire's Daughters* takes place on the eve of the 1870 rebellion by former slaves against French colonialism on the island of Martinique. A mother and two daughters conceal a wounded rebel in their home, a man in whom their neighbor, Sister Smoke, is interested.

In 1994 Shange's third novel, *Liliane: The Resurrection of the Daughter,* was published. *Liliane* is set in Mississippi during the last days of legal segregation and in the Bronx, New York, in the midst of conflict within the African American community. Many voices are interwoven into the novel: the main character's childhood friends and current lovers, her own artistic visions, and her dialogue with her analyst. By coming to terms with her past experiences, Liliane pieces together a "landscape of her future."

Subsequent writings include a children's book and a collection of essays. *Whitewash* (1997) is the story of a young African American girl who is traumatized when a gang attacks her and her brother on their way home from school and spray-paints her face white. *If I Can Cook You Know God Can* (1998) is a series of conversational essays about the culinary habits of African Americans, Nicaraguans, Londoners, Barbadoans, Brazilians, and Africans. Recipes range from the traditional, like collard greens, to the exotic, like turtle eggs and feijoada. As *Booklist* notes, the recipes are interwoven with a "fervent, richly impassioned chronicle of African American experience" that examines political turmoil and relates "how connections are made beyond issues of class or skin color."

In 2002, Shange's works *Float Like a Butterfly* and *Daddy Says* were published. *Float Like a Butterfly,* a biography of Muhammad Ali, is a picture book piece that explores the forces that shaped Ali in his ascent to the top of the sports world, including his childhood in the segregated South and the influence of his parents' support on his future success. The African American rodeo scene is the backdrop of Shange's young adult novel *Daddy Says.* Shange weaves a tale around adolescent sisters Lucie-Marie and Annie Sharon and their father, Cowboy "Tie-Down," as they work through the death of their mother, Tie-Down's wife.

Books

Betsko, Kathleen, and Rachel Koenig, editors, *Interviews With Contemporary Women Playwrights,* Beech Tree Books, 1987.

Brown-Gillory, Elizabeth, *Their Place on the Stage: Black Women Playwrights in America,* Greenwood Press, 1988.

Christ, Carol P., *Diving Deep and Surfacing: Women Writers on Spiritual Quest,* Beacon Press, 1980.

Christian, Barbara, *Black Feminist Criticism: Perspectives on Black Women Writers,* Pergamon Press, 1985.

Geis, Deborah R., *Feminine Focus: The New Women Playwrights,* edited by Enoch Brater, Oxford University Press, 1989.

Richards, Sandra L., *African American Writers,* edited by Valerie Smith, Scribner's, 1991.

Tate, Claudia, editor, *Black Women Writers at Work,* Continuum, 1983.

Periodicals

Booklist, January 1, 1998.

Los Angeles Times Book Review, August 22, 1982; January 8, 1984; July 29, 1984.

Mother Jones, June 1985.

Ms., September 1976.

Newsday, August 22, 1976.

New York Post, September 16, 1976.

New York Times, December 22, 1977; July 22, 1979; May 14, 1980; June 15, 1980; October 20, 1993.

New York Times Book Review, October 21, 1979.; September 12, 1982.; May 12, 1985.

The Progressive, January 1983.

Publisher's Weekly, September 16, 2002; November 25, 2002.

Village Voice, August 16, 1976.

Washington Post Book World, October 15, 1978; August 22, 1982. □

Paul Signac

French painter Paul Signac (1863–1935) was one of the leading figures of Neo-Impressionism, the school of painters that followed the Impressionists. The extraordinary quality and quantity of his artistic work, which included oils, watercolors, etchings, lithographs, and pen-and-ink pointillism, was matched by the breadth of his interests as a writer and, toward the end of his life, his deep opposition to fascism.

Paul Victor-Jules Signac was born in Paris on November 11, 1863. His father, Jules Jean-Baptiste Signac, was a harness and saddle maker, as was his grandfather. Signac's mother was Héloïse Anaïs-Eugénie (Deudon) Signac. The Signac family lived above the shop run by his

father. As a child Signac was described as delicate and high strung by his father. During the Franco-Prussian War (1870–1871) he was sent to northern France to live with his maternal grandmother and her second husband. By 1877 Signac was enrolled at the Collège Rollin in Montmartre (now the Lycée Jacques Decour); he remained a student there until 1880, the year his father died of tuberculosis. Soon after his father's death the family business was sold, thus releasing Signac from having to maintain it.

The year 1880 was pivotal for Signac. In April he visited the fifth Impressionist exhibit and began making sketches after a painting by Edgar Degas. Gauguin, no less, spotted him and threw the 16-year-old Signac out of the building. Later that year, with the urging of his mother and grandfather, he reentered the Collège Rollin to study mathematics, but withdrew after the first term. By the end of the year he had begun painting and also taken up what became a lifelong hobby: boating. (During his lifetime Signac would own 32 sailing crafts.) Almost a year later Signac, along with six or seven others, formed an informal literary society, which they named Les Harengs Saurs Épileptiques Baudelairiens et Anti-Philistins ("The Epileptic, Baudelarian, Antiphilistine Smoked Herrings").

The next year, 1882, proved a busy one for Signac. In February and March he published two essays in the journal *Le Chat Noir,* and that summer he began his habit of escaping Paris for the countryside or the sea to paint. His first such trip was to his maternal grandmother's home at Guise where he painted *The Haystack.* Signac later designated this

as his "first picture." Most important, Signac met Berthe Roblès, a distant cousin of artist Camille Pissarro (1830–1903). They became lovers and were married in 1892. Roblès's first appearance in Signac's work was in "The Red Stocking," which Signac painted in 1883. Also in 1883 Signac began studying with painter Émile Bin (1825–1897). Among his influences at this time was Claude Monet (1840–1926).

Société des Artistes Indépendants

Over the next few years Signac came into his own as an artist. In 1884 he became involved with the French literary symbolists and cultivated their friendship. Among this group was journalist Felix Fénéon (1861–1944), who became one of Signac's staunchest allies. He also began selling his paintings that year. In May 1884 Signac met Monet in Paris and soon after met Georges Seurat (1856–1891), with whom he had a close friendship. On June 11, 1884 Signac, Seurat, Charles Angrand (1854–1926), and Henri Edmond Cross (1856–1910) formed the Société des Artistes Indépendants and from mid-December 1884, through January 17, 1885, the group held its first exhibition in Paris to benefit cholera victims.

Another important figure in fostering Signac's career was Pissarro, whom he met in early 1885. The next year the Pissarro connection came through when Signac was invited to exhibit in New York City at an exhibition titled "Works in Oil and Pastel by the Impressionsts of Paris," although none of his six paintings sold. By then Signac had painted "The Junction at bois-Colombes, The Gas Tanks at Clichy," and "Passage de Puits-Bertin, Clichy," all in the divisionist style, in which dots of contrasting color are placed side-by-side to create a luminous visual effect. In the spring of 1886 Signac exhibited at the eighth and final Impressionist exhibition, though his and Seurat's presence in the exhibition caused something of a controversy that was only smoothed over through Pissarro's intercession. On September 19, 1886, the term "néo-impressioniste" was used for the first time in a review by Fénéon of the second exhibition of the Independents. However the term did not come into general use until 1892. Signac was on the exhibition's hanging committee and exhibited ten paintings.

In 1887 Signac met Vincent Van Gogh (1853–1890) in Paris. The two not only became friends but painted together in April and May 1887. By the end of that year Signac, Seurat, and Van Gogh had exhibited together.

In late January 1888 Signac traveled to Brussels to exhibit at the Salon des XX. He also wrote a review of the exhibition using the pen name Neo that was published in *Le Cri du People.* By this time the exhibitions of the Société des Artistes Indépendants were well-established annual events thanks to Signac's efforts as an organizer. Although Seurat was given first place among the Neo-Impressionists, critics had begun to appreciate Signac's contribution to the movement.

Leader of Neo-Impressionists

On March 29, 1891, Seurat died suddenly in Paris. The death of his friend thrust Signac into a primary position within the Neo-Impressionist movement. Pissarro, however, predicted the end of pointillism without Seurat. Indeed, Signac abandoned the technique in the early 20th century. Soon after Seurat's death Signac anonymously published an article titled "Impressionistes et révolutionnaires" in the literary supplement of *La Révolte*. That summer he sailed in several regattas off the coast of Brittany, and in 1892 had seven paintings exhibited in the eighth exhibition held by the Neo-Impressionists. Later that year he exhibited his work in Antwerp and in December showed seven paintings in the first Neo-Impressionist exhibit, among them "Portrait of My Mother," "The Dining Room," and "Woman Arranging Her Hair." Signac also made the first of many trips to Saint-Tropez to paint and relax.

At the end of 1893 the Neo-Impressionist Boutique was opened in Paris and in 1894 Signac had an exhibition there of 40 of his watercolors. He exhibited widely in the late 1890s and early years of the 20th century in Paris, Brussels, Provence, Berlin, Hamburg, the Hague, Venice, and elsewhere. In the 1890s he became more involved with writing, working on a journal he had begun in 1894. In 1896 the anarchist journal *Les Temps nouveaux* published a black-and-white lithograph by Signac titled "The Wreckers." Politically, Signac was, and had been for some time, squarely in the anarchist camp: in 1898 he signed a collective statement supporting Emile Zola's position in the infamous Dreyfus Affair and in 1906 placed an antimilitary drawing in *Le Courier européen*.

In 1896 Signac began working on his study of Delacroix and in mid-1899 published *D'Eugéne Delacroix au néo-impressionnisme,* excerpts of which had already appeared in French and German journals. In 1903 the German edition was published.

In 1909 Signac exhibited three pieces at the International Exhibition, better known as the Odessa Salon: "Traghetto Lantern," "Diablerets," and "Port Decorated with Flags, Saint-Tropez." After Odessa the exhibition went to Kiev, Saint Petersburg, and Riga. Beginning in 1910 Signac slowed his output from the incredible pace he had maintained for more than 20 years. His sole painting that year was "The Channel, Marseilles," and in 1911 he painted only "Towers, Antibes." From there his output increased to nine paintings in 1912–1913, but he never again painted at his earlier, youthful pace.

Signac and his wife, Berthe, permanently separated in 1913, but they never divorced. The separation was amicable and the pair remained in contact with each other, Signac providing his wife with financial support. Signac then began living with his lover Jeanne Selmersheim-Desgrange, who gave birth to their daughter, Ginette-Laure-Anaïs on October 2, 1913. Less than a year later, in August 1914, World War I began. Signac was deeply affected by the war and painted very little—in 1917 he acknowledged that he had only painted seven pictures in three years—despite the fact that in 1915 he was named as a painter to the department of the navy. The annual exhibitions held by the Société des Artistes Indépendants were suspended, Signac himself rejecting a call to resume the exhibitions during wartime. By the time the war ended Signac was involved in taking care of his finances, specifically the welfare of Selmersheim-Desgrange and their daughter. In December 1919 he entered into an agreement with three art dealers, turning over his artistic output to them at the rate of 21 oil paintings per year. The contract was renewed annually until 1928, when it was renegotiated.

Elder Statesman of French Art

In early 1920 the Société des Artistes Indépendants renewed their annual exhibition (their 31st that year) though Signac was too ill to fully participate. However he recovered sufficiently by spring to assume the post of commissioner of the French Pavillion at the Venice Biennale, where he mounted a special Cézanne exhibit. All 17 of Signac's works exhibited at the Biennale were sold within a month. Long acknowledged in the communities of artists and collectors, his fame was further cemented in 1922 when he was the subject of a monograph by Lucie Cousturier. In 1927 Signac published a monograph of his own devoted to the painter Johan Barthold Jongkind. In late 1928 he accepted a commission to paint the ports of France in watercolors. He began with the eastern Mediterranean port of Sète in January 1929 and worked his way south, then west, and then northward. He continued working on the series until April 1931. Politics and finances occupied Signac in the last years of his life, which coincided with the Great Depression. In December 1931 Signac he met with Mahatma Gandhi (1869–1948) in Paris. Despite his close friendship with Marcel Cachin, director of the French Communist Party daily newspaper, *L'Humanité,* Signac refused to join the party. He did, however, lend his support in 1932 to the Bureau of the World Committee against War and often attended meetings of the Vigilance Committee of Anti-Fascist Intellectuals.

In January 1933 Signac testified on behalf of Henri Guilbeaux, who had been sentenced to death in absentia for high treason in 1919. Guilbeaux ultimately returned from the Soviet Union and was acquitted. At the end of 1933 Signac was made a commander of the Legion of Honor. In failing health by 1934 he prepared for the 50th anniversary of the Société des Artistes Indépendants and its 45th exhibition. In February he published an attack on the École des Beaux-Arts in *Monde*. Signac's health generally deteriorated as the year wore on, and on November 7, 1934, he resigned as president of the Société and was succeeded by Maximilien Luce.

In January 1935 Signac participated in the 46th exhibition of the Société des Artistes Indépendants; it was his final one. That March he was invited to tour the USSR but declined for health reasons. In May 1935 the Société named Signac its honorary president. The following month he took to his bed with what turned out to be his final illness. Signac lingered for most of the summer but died in Paris on August 15, 1935. In 1947 fragments of his journal, edited by George Besson, were published in *Arts de France*.

Books

Ferretti-Bocquillon, Marina, and others, *Signac, 1863–1935,* Metropolitan Museum of Art, 2001.

Online

"Paul Signac (1863–1935)," *Olga's Gallery,* http://www.abc
gallery.com/S/signac/signacbio.html (February 28, 2003).
"Paul Signac: French Neo-Impressionist Painter, 1863–1935,"
http://renoirauction.com/biography/signac.htm (February 28,
2003). □

Pauline Smith

South African writer Pauline Smith (1882–1959) is remembered for works of realistic fiction chronicling life among Afrikaner settlers in the western cape region of South Africa. Her best-known volume, the short story collection *The Little Karoo* (1925), was praised by the South African novelist Alan Paton in the *New York Herald Tribune Book Review* in 1959 as "one of the most remarkable collections of Afrikaner stories ever written."

Childhood on Two Continents

Smith was born in Oudtshoorn, South Africa, on April 2, 1882, the daughter of physician Herbert Urmson Smith and his wife, Jessy (Milne) Smith, a nurse. Her parents had immigrated to South Africa from England during the 1870s in hopes of relieving symptoms of ill health that plagued Herbert Smith. He was the first trained doctor to settle in the area and he traveled widely to treat his patients. Smith accompanied her father, learning a great deal about the landscape and the people who farmed, herded goats, or raised ostrich in the fertile region.

The Dutch-speaking Afrikaners, also known as Boers, were descendants of Dutch colonists who were the first European settlers in the area. They subscribed to a strict interpretation of Christian doctrine and valued hard work. Their society was characterized by racial prejudice and gender inequality: one of Smith's stories, for example, concerns a father who sells his daughter in order to keep his farm.

Smith and her sister, Dorothy, enjoyed a happy though isolated childhood and were educated at home until 1895, when they were sent to school in Scotland. In a 1947 letter recalling this period and quoted by biographer Sheila Roberts in the *Dictionary of Literary Biography,* Smith wrote: "In my own case, and my sister's, we lost far more than we gained by being sent to 'boarding school in England' 6,000 miles away from our parents—and the loss was our parents' too—I look back upon that break in our happy childhood as a tragedy for us all. . . ."

Smith's father died in 1899, and she left school soon afterward, in poor health and grieving for her father. During this period she began to write. She later noted in the essay "Why and How I Became an Author," which first appeared in the journal *English Studies in Africa,* that she hoped through her stories "to set down for [her] own comfort the memories of . . . happier days."

Smith's first published story, "A Tenantry Dinner," was published in the Aberdeen *Evening Gazette and Weekly Free Press* in 1902 under the pseudonym Janet Tamson, and she continued to contribute sketches and poetry, often with Scottish subjects, to the *Gazette* over the next two years. In 1905 she returned to Oudtshoorn for a visit and recorded her impressions of the region in what became known as her "1905 Diary."

Smith returned to Europe and began working on a novel and a series of stories for children. While vacationing in Switzerland in 1908 Smith met the English novelist Arnold Bennett, and he took an interest in her writing. Rather than flatter her with praise, Bennett offered honest assessments of weaknesses and strengths in her work and identified the unique value of her writings about Afrikaner life. Of this encounter she wrote in "Why and How I Became an Author," "The 'damning' of my novel brought me an astonishing sense of relief, and established my faith in the critic's judgment as no praise would have done. . . . I began to work, with a clearer purpose, for this self-appointed master."

The Little Karoo

Smith returned to Oudtshoorn for a year and worked on a new set of stories set in a region called the Little Karoo. Among these was "The Sisters," published in the *New Statesman* in 1915, and her first significant success, "The Pain," published by John Middleton Murry in the *Adelphi.* These stories and others, including "The Sinners," "The Miller," and "Ludovitje," were later collected in the volume *The Little Karoo,* which initially drew attention for documenting a passing era in a little-known colonial region. Bennett supplied an introduction for the volume in which he characterized his protégé's writing as a "strange, austere, tender and ruthless talent."

Among the best-known stories in *The Little Karoo* is "The Pain," a portrait of aging *bywoners,* or sharecroppers. In the story, an elderly couple—tenant farmers whose rustic, isolated existence has consisted of working relentlessly for their simplest needs—are thrust into the world of modern medicine in a regional hospital and cannot endure the pain of being separated by the regulations of the institution. Commenting on "The Pain," a contemporary review in the *Cape Times,* reprinted in *Twentieth-Century Literary Criticism,* asserted, "No lovelier tale of old age has ever been written, and it reveals at once the chief secret of the writer's power. She has a rare gift of insight."

Other stories in *The Little Karoo* treat themes of isolation, loss, injustice, oppression, suffering, and religious obsession, presenting an unrelenting tragic picture of life. In "The Miller," the title character waits too long to offer a gesture of tenderness to the wife he has treated cruelly, dying in her arms unable to articulate his remorse and repentance. In "The Schoolmaster," the teacher's stifled emotion, stemming from his desire for a female student, Engela, erupts during a drive with his pupils, when he wildly assaults the cart mules that will not cross a stream and gouges out their eyes. He leaves and later is found drowned in the same stream. "The Sisters" chronicles the dealings of two rival farmers, one of whom is driven to madness by his desire to extend his property. In his blind desire to acquire water rights from his neighbor, Burgert de Jager offers his daughter Marta to Jan Redlinghuis, who owns the land de Jager wants. Marta's sister, Sukey, is rebuked by Redlinghuis when she offers herself in place of her delicate sister. Eventually, Marta is humiliated by Redlinghuis who treats her as property, and she dies, with Sukey left trying to comprehend the situation in terms of the Christian meaning of sin and redemption.

In addition to the poignancy of its subjects and themes, the collection has been praised for rendering in English the rhythms and speech patterns of Afrikaans, but, with the exception of "Ludovitje," it fails to treat the important subject of race relations. In that story, a young boy who is not highly valued by members of his own family has a deep spiritual impact on the African laborers who serve as gravediggers in the area. One worker is so moved by the boy's spirituality that when the boy dies the worker converts to Christianity and offers to prepare a special grave for the child. He is rewarded by the boy's family with a place to stay and the promise of favorable treatment.

Reviewing the volume in the *Saturday Review of Literature*, critic Brooks Shepard wrote that Smith "has succeeded overwhelmingly in breathing life into the Karoo, with its remote farms and hamlets, its laborious journeyings in a rumbling ox cart, its stern, sober, simple, shrewd men and women, its utter detachment from the world and civilization . . . ; but she has succeeded also in picturing the man and woman in each of us, so that the people and the country of which she writes with strange brooding pity seem only incidental to her brooding upon mankind." When the collection was reprinted in 1990, Sybil Steinberg, writing in *Publishers Weekly*, commented that "the stories still ring true in their empathetic yet clear-eyed portrayal of a stern, obstinate tribe of white settlers at war with an unforgiving God."

The Beadle

A more extended examination of Afrikaner life, Smith's novel *The Beadle* was published in 1926. Set in the late 19th Century, the story centers on Andrina, an Afrikaner teenager who is the illegitimate child of a woman now dead and Aalst Vlokman, a minor church official, who has never admitted his paternity. Raised by her mother's sisters, Andrina is seduced by a visiting Englishman and flees the community when she discovers that she is pregnant. Through her predicament, Vlokman gains the courage to publicly admit that he is her father and to go in search of her. Ultimately, the birth of Andrina's own illegitimate child brings reconciliation with her father.

Because of its setting within a pious, isolated community, "The Beadle" is often compared with Nathaniel Hawthorne's *The Scarlet Letter.* George Dale, writing in *Crux,* asserted that the novel "ranks a high place in any company, for its theme is universally valid and the characterization

convincing." South African novelist and critic Nadine Gordimer praised the simplicity and unity of the novel in a 1963 review in the *New York Times Book Review,* declaring, "This is one of the great novels that should never be allowed to go out of print. It will always be rediscovered with astonishment and admiration."

Later Career and Legacy

Smith's volume of children's fiction and poetry, *Platkops Children,* was published in 1935. Later considered interesting primarily for their autobiographical elements, the stories offer character sketches and scenic descriptions in a rhythmic language heavily influenced by Smith's early reading of the Old Testament. Critic Sheila Scholten commented in the book *Pauline Smith,* edited by Dorothy Driver, that the ballads "although not literary . . . are delightfully evocative," and she concluded that "[i]n the poems as well as the stories of *Platkops* . . . Smith has achieved an authentic picture of life in a small Karoo town at the turn of the century."

Smith wrote little after the death of her mentor Arnold Bennett in 1931, though she did publish a memoir of their friendship, *A. B. " . . . A Minor Marginal Note, (memoir)"* in 1933.

In an article published in 1945 in the journal *South African Opinion* and reprinted in *Twentieth-Century Literary Criticism,* the South African poet and novelist Herman Charles Bosman concluded: "Smith's stories are . . . for ever a part of South African literature. They depict South African life with a truth and a beauty which no writer has so far achieved in the short story form written in Afrikaans." However, Smith was not widely known when she died in Broadstone, England, on January 29, 1959. A revival of Smith's works coincided with the centenary of her birth in 1982, and after that various editions and collections were published with regularity. Her minor writings appeared in such volumes as *The Unknown Pauline Smith: Unpublished and Out-of-Print Stories, Diaries and Other Prose Writings* (1993) and *Secret Fire: The 1913–14 South African Journal of Pauline Smith* (1997), a result of continuing academic interest in Smith's body of work.

Books

Driver, Dorothy, ed., *Pauline Smith,* McGraw-Hill Book Co., 1983.

Roberts, Sheila, *Dictionary of Literary Biography, Volume 226: South African Writers,* Gale Group, 2000.

Twentieth-Century Literary Criticism, Vol. 25, Gale Group, 1988.

Periodicals

Crux, February 1979.

English Studies in Africa, September 1963.

New York Herald Tribune Book Review, October 18, 1959.

Publishers Weekly, August 10, 1990. □

Catherine Helen Spence

Among the more prolific writers of nineteenth century colonial Australia, Catherine Helen Spence (1825–1910) provided valuable insights to life in South Australia through her various novels, magazine articles, and lectures. A dauntless social activist, she dedicated much of her life and times to the education of girls and toward improving conditions for poor children. Near the turn of the twentieth century Spence became increasingly involved with the struggle for women's suffrage and contributed to the success of that movement in her adopted homeland.

Catherine Helen Spence was born in Melrose, Scotland, on October 31, 1825. She was the daughter of David S., an attorney, and Helen (Brodie) Spence. The fifth of eight siblings, Catherine Spence was well educated as her parents were well to do. The family moved to Adelaide, South Australia, for a fresh start in November 1839, after their father lost a sizeable fortune as a result of untimely speculation in the wheat market. The South Australian territory at that time was a newly established British colony on the verge of a gold rush that peaked from 1850 to 1860.

Pioneer of the Australian Novel

Spence, who never married, went to work as a governess at age 17. As an advocate for destitute children during the course of her lifetime she opened her home to three separate families of orphaned siblings and devoted much of her effort to the education of girls. Over time her concern for children led her to open her own school.

Encouraged by relatives and teachers, she entertained a notion also of pursuing a career as a writer. After authoring articles for local publications, her first piece of fiction was published anonymously in 1854 through J. W. Parker of London. *Clara Morison, A Tale of South Australian Gold Fever,* is widely regarded as her best work. It was the first of seven novels written by Spence and was the first novel to be published about Australia by an Australian writer. The story, which she had written in her spare time over a period of years, has been likened to a Cinderella tale. Described as a domestic novel by the author, the book offers a quasi-autobiographical point-of-view in the supporting character of Margaret Elliott who charms the reader by means of her self-satisfaction. Elliott's ability to maintain a strong sense of self—despite her status as an unmarried woman—provided a provocative and incongruous notion to Spence's contemporaries.

After expenses, Spence received a sum of 30 pounds sterling for the book, which was republished by Rigby in 1971 and again in 1986, during a two-decade long revival of Spence's works related in part to the Australian bicentennial. Additionally, *Clara Morison* was included in the

Queensland University Press Portable Australian Anthology, as part of an author-specific volume on Spence.

Spence's second novel, *Tender and True: A Colonial Tale,* was published in two volumes by Smith & Elder of London in 1856. She received a payment of 30 pounds sterling for the manuscript, which like *Clara Morison* was published anonymously. A second edition of *Tender and True* was published in 1862 and was printed as a single volume. An 1867 novel, *Hugh Lindsay's Guest,* appeared in serial form in the Adelaide *Observer,* and Bentley published the work in book form under the title *The Author's Daughter.* Although she sometimes hid her identity as a female and abandoned fiction altogether during her final years, Spence is regarded highly among the genre novelists of the Australian gold rush era.

Activist Calling

From the 1850s onward, the parliaments of the six Australian colonies were voted by the populace. Although a variety of electoral methods prevailed, each permitted victory by a simple one-vote margin. In the late 1850s Spence espoused the political theories of Thomas Hare regarding proportional representation in government and strengthened her resolve to bring about social reform in this arena. Her awareness of the need for a more egalitarian government soon permeated her writing. Hare's promise of pure democracy became a foundation of Spence's political beliefs throughout her lifetime. Among her early political writings, an 1861 pamphlet, entitled *A Plea for Pure Democracy,* touted the Hare system of proportional representation. Although South Australia would not convert to a preferential voting system until 1929, other colonies converted earlier, beginning with Queensland in 1892.

Also high on Spence's political agenda was the need for gender equality. In 1859 she began to work as a correspondent for the Adelaide *Argus,* but she was forced to assume the identity of her brother, John Brodie Spence, or risk certain exclusion from assignments over the issue of her gender. Overall publishers feared that her notions were too extreme to gain acceptance and frequently greeted her radical ideas regarding feminism and egalitarian government with apprehension. Several of her works could not be sold during her lifetime because publishers viewed them as too extreme.

In her serialized novel, ''Uphill Work,'' Spence deals directly with the issue of gender discrimination and with poor working conditions and wages among middle-class women. The installments were published in the Adelaide *Weekly Mail* in 1863 and 1864, for which she received 50 pounds sterling altogether in payment. A book-length manuscript was published in three volumes as *Mr. Hogarth's Will,* by Bentley of London in 1865. Spence received one-half of the profits for the publication of the novel, with her share totaling 35 pounds sterling. It was the first of her fiction works to be published under her true name. The editor of *Argus* prior to his death acknowledged that the novel by Spence served as a motivation behind his gift of 5,000 pounds sterling per year—left in his will—to Melbourne charities. He left an additional sum to Victoria causes.

Feminist on the Early Lecturer Circuit

Spence on an 1865–1866 lecture trip to Britain included a return visit to Scotland for the first time since her early childhood. Over the next two decades her public presence increased, beginning in 1868 when she became the first woman ever to receive an invitation to read papers at the South Australian Institute. Having earlier converted from her traditional Scottish Presbyterian religious beliefs to Unitarian, she became a preacher in her newly adopted faith. Some years later, in 1884 she penned a memoir-like chronicle of her *Journey through Conversion.* The manuscript was published by Williams and Norgate of London. In 1904 she published *Each in His Own Tongue: Two Sermons* through Vardon & Pritchard.

As her writing grew more political in orientation, in 1878 she advanced her theories of social reforms through a collection of articles that she had published in the *Melbourne Review.* The causes that she endorsed included child welfare, parliamentary reform, and tax reform. Also among these articles were essays about the lives and works of her contemporaries, including George Eliot (Mary Ann Evans) who was a personal friend of Spence's. Coincidentally with her contributions to that journal, in 1878 she secured a position as a regular outside contributor to *The Register.* She penned word games, wrote book reviews, and proffered views on a wide variety of social topics, from children's issues to industrialization and electoral reform. Her articles included such as "Some Social Aspects of South Australian Life" (1878), "A Literary Calling" (1880), and "The Australian in Literature" (1902).

In 1879, in association with the South Australian Minister of Education, she wrote a text for children, entitled *The Laws We Live Under, With Some Chapters on Elementary Political Economy and the Duties of Citizens.* The manuscript was published by the Government Printing Office in Adelaide in 1880 and was adopted by the South Australian Schools as a civics/social studies text in 1881.

Spence's futuristic novel, *Handfasted,* was completed in 1879, but the manuscript failed to win recognition when submitted to a competition sponsored by the *Sydney Mail.* Radical in tone and theme, *Handfasted* in fact remained unpublished until 1984, long after the author's death. In the book, Spence describes a utopian society in an American valley called Columba. The story, which advocates a revision of social standards, espouses enlightened humanism. The term handfasting refers to a legendary custom of trial marriage.

Her 1881 novel *Gathered In* is seen as one of her best works, second only to *Clara Morison.* Although her efforts to find a publisher in 1878 went unrewarded, the tale appeared in serialized form in the *Observer, Brisbane Courier,* and *Queenslander.* Publication of the manuscript in book form, however, was delayed for nearly 100 years, until 1977.

"A Week in the Future," believed to be Spence's final work of fiction, was serialized in *Centennial* in 1889. This science fiction piece relates a tale of a utopian London in the year 1988. The first book-length publication of "A Week in the Future" was delayed until 1987 when it was published in anticipation of the 1988 setting in which the story takes place.

From the 1890s until her death she devoted her efforts almost exclusively to the furtherance of social reform programs. She joined the South Australian Women's Suffrage League in 1891, and as vice president of that organization she helped to bring about the women's right to vote in state elections and the women's right to stand for the state parliament. These measures were accepted in South Australia in 1894, at which time the women of that colony distinguished themselves as one of the first communities in the world to enfranchise women. Spence was instrumental also in founding the Effective Voting League in 1895. She worked toward establishing a South Australia chapter of the National Council of Women and continued to fight for women's suffrage in other sections of Australia. In part through the efforts of Spence, the women of Western Australia earned the franchise in 1899 as did the women of New South Wales in 1902.

In 1893 Spence went to the United States as a representative of the South Australian State Children's Council at the International Conference on Charities and Correction. At the end of that conference, which was scheduled in conjunction with the Chicago World's Fair, she extended her tour, traveling throughout the United States and Canada. In the course of her travels she presented lectures on a number of political issues, not the least of which was women's suffrage. She toured England and Scotland the following year and in 1897 made an historical run for office, becoming at that time the first Australian woman to place her name in candidacy for the federal convention elections. The significance of the event was not diminished by her loss in the election.

In 1907 Spence published *State Children in Australia: A History of Boarding Out and Its Developments,* in support of her ideas that orphaned children should be migrated from public institutions into private foster homes. At the time of her death, on April 3, 1910, in Adelaide, Australia, she was involved in writing her autobiography. The book, published as *Catherine Helen Spence: An Autobiography,* was completed by Jeanne F. Young, a close friend of Spence.

Books

Blain, Virginia, Patricia Clements, and Isobel Grundy, *The Feminist Companion to Literature in English: Women Writers from the Middle Ages to the Present,* Yale University Press, 1990.

Buck, Clair (ed.), *The Bloomsbury Guide to Women's Literature,* Prentice Hall General reference, 1992.

Samuels, Selina (ed.), *Dictionary of Literary Biography: Australian Literature, 1788–1914,* The Gale Group, 2001.

Wilde, William H., Joy Hooton, and Barry Andres, *The Oxford Companion to Australian Literature,* Oxford University Press, 1985. □

Mark Spitz

American swimmer Mark Spitz (born 1950) is considered to have been the fastest swimmer in history. For six years, beginning in 1966, he dominated the sport, winning a world record seven gold medals in the 1972 Olympics held in Munich, West Germany. This was the most gold medals won by anyone in a single Olympiad, and each of his medal-winning performances broke a world swimming record. Spitz was also named World Swimmer of the Year in 1969, 1971, and 1972.

Encouraged in Competitive Swimming by His Father

Spitz was born on February 10, 1960, in Modesto, California, to Arnold and Lenore Spitz. Spitz's family relocated to Hawaii when Spitz was two years old. There Spitz's father taught Spitz how to swim. When Spitz was six years old, the family moved back to California, settling this time in Sacramento. At the Sacramento YMCA, Spitz began to train in competitive swimming for the first time. Sensing that Spitz had surpassed the training available at the YMCA, Arnold Spitz took his son to the Arden Hills

Swim Club, where he began to train under Sherm Chavoor, a well-known swim instructor. Chavoor was to remain a mentor to Spitz throughout his career.

Spitz's father was a driving force behind Spitz's swimming career, drilling into his son the maxim, as reported by M. B. Roberts on ESPN.com, "Swimming isn't everything; winning is." Spitz took his father's advice to heart; by the time he was ten years old, he held 17 national swimming records for his age group and one world record. He also earned the title of the world's top swimmer in the 10-and-under age group.

When Spitz was 14 years old, Spitz's father realized that his son was ready for a new level in his training. He decided to move the family to Santa Clara so that Spitz could train under a new coach, George Haines, who was based at the famous Santa Clara Swim Club. This move increased Spitz's father's commute to work to 80 miles each way, but he wanted more than anything else for his son to become the best swimmer he could.

The move paid off. Spitz continued to reach new levels of excellence in swimming, including in the butterfly stroke. This stroke, considered by many to be the most difficult stroke in swimming, became Spitz's favorite. When Spitz was 16 years old, he won the 100-meter butterfly title at the National Amateur Athletic Union (AAU) Championships. It was the only the first of 24 AAU titles he would win during his career.

Entered His First Olympics in 1968

The year 1967 saw Spitz's rise to international prominence. That year he won no less than five gold metals at the Pan-American Games, held in Winnipeg, Canada. These were for the 100-meter butterfly, the 200-meter butterfly, the 400-meter freestyle relay, the 800-meter freestyle relay, and the 400-meter medley relay.

Spitz seemed perfectly poised to sweep the 1968 Olympics, held that year in Mexico City. He boasted that he would win six gold metals there. While he did shine at the Olympics, he fell short of the goals that he had set for himself, winning two gold medals in team events—for the 4 x 100 and 4 x 200-meter freestyle relay events. He also won two metals for individual events—a silver metal for the 100-meter butterfly and a bronze for the 100-meter freestyle event.

Spitz was disappointed in his showing at the Olympics, and he vowed to try harder. He knew that physically he had what it took to win gold at the Olympics; what he needed to work on was his mental preparation. He began to develop a cool demeanor, an attitude of relaxed concentration that was in marked contrast to the boastful air he had assumed in the 1968 Olympics. Following the 1968 Olympics, Spitz entered college at Indiana University, there to train with famous swimming coach Doc Counsilman. Counsilman had been Spitz's coach in Mexico City, and it was at his instigation that he went to Indiana University.

At Indiana, Spitz began a pre-dental program while continuing to swim competitively. In his freshman year, he won the 200-meter and the 500-meter freestyle, as well as the 100-meter butterfly competition at the NCAA swimming championships. He also won the 100-meter butterfly competition at the NCAA championships the following year. The year after that, 1971, he again won the NCAA championship in the 100-meter butterfly, as well as the 200-meter butterfly. His achievements earned him the Sullivan Award in 1971 for being the best amateur athlete in the United States. He was also awarded the title of World Swimmer of the Year in 1969, 1971, and 1972.

Won Seven Olympic Gold Medals in 1972

Spitz graduated from Indiana University in 1972, just in time for the 1972 Olympics, held in Munich, West Germany. This time, he vowed to take home no less than seven gold medals. And he did. Spitz swept the swimming events exactly as he promised to do, collecting his seventh gold medal on September 4, 1972. No other athlete had ever taken home that many gold medals at a single Olympics. He won gold metals for four individual events and three team events. His first win was for the 200-meter butterfly. Next, he won the 200-meter freestyle, followed by the 100-meter butterfly. This last event was Spitz's favorite, and he won it by a full body length, reaching the finish in just 54.27 seconds. Spitz's final gold metal-winning performance in individual competition was for the 100-meter freestyle event.

In addition to his four individual gold medals, Spitz also won three gold medals for relay races. These were for the 4 x 100-meter freestyle relay, the 4 x 200-meter freestyle relay, and the 4 x 100-meter medley relay. With each gold metal-winning performance Spitz, then just 22, set a new world record for performance. He won all of his gold medals over a period of eight days.

Spitz's euphoria over his record seven gold metals was marred by tragedy. In the early morning hours of September 5, members of a Palestinian terrorist organization invaded the dormitory where the Olympic athletes were sleeping. They killed two Israelis and kidnapped nine others. The terrorists passed over Spitz and his American teammates, who were sound asleep not far away.

The crime rattled Spitz, who is Jewish. He made a brief statement to the press that day, saying, as reported by M. B. Roberts on ESPN.com, "I think the murders in the village are very tragic. I have no further comment." He immediately left Germany for London, without waiting to attend the Olympics' closing ceremonies. Meanwhile, the nine hostages were all killed during a botched rescue attempt.

Returned to the U.S. a Hero

In spite of the tragedy overshadowing Spitz's unprecedented achievements at the Olympics, he returned home to the United States a major celebrity, comparable in stature to Charles Lindbergh, the first person to fly nonstop across the Atlantic Ocean. He was also called by some the second most recognized person in the United States, after then-president Richard Nixon. Spitz cancelled his plans to become a dentist and looked forward to making a career as a corporate spokesperson.

Soon after his return to the U.S., Spitz landed several lucrative corporate endorsement contracts. He earned about $7 million in a two-year period, and, helped by his photogenic looks, established himself as a well-known corporate spokesperson. Companies and organizations for which he endorsed products included the Schick Company, the California Milk Advisory Board, Adidas, Speedo, and many more. A photograph of Spitz wearing a swimsuit and his seven gold medals was made into a poster, and it quickly became a best seller.

Also during the year following the 1972 Olympics, Spitz courted and married Suzy Weiner, the daughter of one of his father's business associates. At the time Weiner was a theater student at the University of California at Los Angeles (UCLA) and also a model.

Spitz's bid to become a Hollywood star was less successful than either his swimming career or his career as a corporate spokesperson; viewers were highly critical of his performances in television commercials and shows, which included a Bob Hope special, the Sonny & Cher show, and the Johnny Carson show. He managed to maintain a presence as a sports commentator for a few years, but after that he largely dropped out of the public eye.

Still, Spitz and his wife now had plenty of money, and he took up sailing as a hobby. Eventually he started a real estate agency in Beverly Hills, California. The business proved successful and it gave a thriving new career to the former swimming champion.

As the 1980s drew to a close, Spitz decided to come out of retirement and become an Olympic swimmer for the first time since 1972. In 1989, now 39 years old, Spitz began to train for the 1992 Olympic Trials. This decision was not completely out of the blue; in 1984 he had raced against Rowdy Gaines, who at the time held the world record time for the 100-meter butterfly—and beat him. After two years of training, Spitz was ready to attempt to qualify for the 1992 Olympics. In 1991 he raced against Tom Jager and Matt Biondi, both Olympic swimmers. The races, two separate 50-meter butterfly races, were televised on ABC's "Wide World of Sports." Unfortunately, Spitz lost both races. He also fell just over two seconds short of the qualifying time of 55:59 he needed to rejoin the U.S. Olympic swim team.

Mark Spitz settled in Los Angeles, where he continues to live with his family. Spitz enjoys to sail and has added traveling to his list of hobbies. No longer in the real estate business, he has involved himself in various other business ventures. He has also returned to his role as a spokesperson for prominent companies and organizations, including the U.S. Olympic Committee. He was found to have abnormally high cholesterol levels in 1995. He cut those levels in half through a program of diet, exercise, and medication, and then embarked on a national campaign to educate people about the risk of heart disease brought about by high cholesterol.

Spitz has not lost his competitive spirit. His backyard contains a swimming pool, but he has vowed never to race his sons in that pool. As he told Martin Fennelly in 2000 in the *Tampa Tribune*, "I never race them. I never race. Because I've taught them that when I swim against somebody, I don't care if you're my son, I'm going to kick your butt."

Periodicals

Independent, September 6, 1998.
Tampa Tribune, June 16, 2000.
Times-Picayune, September 26, 1999.

Online

"Laureus World Sports Awards—Mark Spitz," *WorldSport.com,* http://www.worldsport.com (March 11, 2003).
"Spitz Lived Up to Enormous Expectations," *ESPN.com,* http://www.espn.go.com (March 11, 2003). □

Christina Stead

Australian-born novelist Christina Stead (1902–1983) is best remembered as the author of *The Man Who Loved Children* (1940), a depiction of dysfunctional family life based to a significant extent on her own childhood in suburban Sydney. Living the greater part of her life outside Australia, Stead employed a variety of settings in her fiction, including London, Paris, and Washington, D.C., and often used her fiction to highlight such political and economic issues as the oppression of workers and the parallels between paternalistic colonial authority and gender inequality.

Early Life

Stead was born in Rockdale, near Sydney, on July 17, 1902, the daughter of David George and Ellen Butters Stead. Her father was a marine biologist who worked for the government and supported socialist ideals. Her mother died when Stead was two years old, and her father remarried in 1907. With his new wife, David Stead had six more children, and the ensuing dissatisfaction of their domestic life provided the basis for Stead's best-known novel, *The Man Who Loved Children.* Stead was educated in Sydney and enrolled in Sydney Teachers' College in 1920. She began teaching in 1923, working as a demonstrator and lecturer in psychology at the college, but it proved a short-lived career, and she turned to clerical work while writing children's stories in her free time.

In 1928 Stead left Australia for England, following Keith Duncan, a graduate student with whom she had begun an affair in Australia. She took a job in London as a secretary in a grain company, where she met William Blech (later Blake), a Marxist economist and a married man who was to become her life partner. She moved to Paris with Blake in 1929, where he took a position in an investment bank, but they did not marry until 1952 when he finally obtained a divorce from his wife. During the early 1930s Stead worked

as a bank clerk in Paris while seeking a publisher for her novel *Seven Poor Men of Sydney* and for the short story collection *The Salzburg Tales,* both of which were published in 1934.

Early Works

Seven Poor Men of Sydney offers an impressionistic portrait of seven working-class men (and one woman) and through them, Stead examines issues of class oppression and colonialism in Australia during the opening decades of the twentieth century. Among the central characters, Michael is a shell-shocked veteran of World War I who commits suicide by jumping off a cliff into Fisherman's Bay, and his sister, Catherine, is a woman so marginalized by the male-dominated political and economic structures that she spirals downward through society and ends in an asylum for the mentally ill. One character espouses Communist ideals as a means of transforming society, while another immigrates to the United States in pursuit of a better life. None of the seven is able to achieve a satisfying, economically secure life in Australia.

During the mid-1930s Stead also became involved in various leftist causes and attended the First International Congress of Writers for the Defense of Culture in Paris in June 1935. She later produced "The Writers Take Sides," an account of the proceedings, published in the periodical *Left Review.* She and Blake traveled to Spain in 1936 on the eve of the Spanish Civil War. That same year her novel *The Beauties and Furies,* a chronicle of a disappointing love affair, was published. After briefly returning to London, Blake and Stead moved to the United States, where they remained until 1946. In America she was associated with leftist journals and for a time worked in Hollywood as a scriptwriter for Metro-Goldwyn-Mayer (MGM).

In Stead's next novel, *House of All Nations* (1938), which is significantly named after an infamous Parisian brothel, she presented an epic fictional treatment of the world of international finance that also provided a Marxist critique of global capitalism. Focusing on the fictitious Banque Mercure, headquartered in Paris and based on the bank in which Stead and Blake worked during the 1930s, the novel depicts the cunning schemes and illicit deals that lie beneath the surface of international monetary operations. Biographer R. G. Geering, quoted in *Contemporarty Authors* judged *House of All Nations* as "Stead's greatest intellectual achievement—its knowledge of the workings of international finance and its revelation of the greed, the ruthlessness, the energy, the sheer luck, and the genius that go into money-making, are by any standards remarkable."

The Man Who Loved Children

The Man Who Loved Children, which was described by Pearl K. Bell in the *New Republic* as a "profoundly original triumph of imagination and memory," is an ironically titled work that describes a dysfunctional family whose life together is characterized by bitterness, violent outbursts, and gender inequities. Though the story is set in the United States, the novel is based Stead's own experiences growing up in Australia. Sam Pollitt, modeled on her father, David Stead, is a tyrannical, self-centered civil servant whose escalating quarrels with his embittered wife, Henny, spark murderous thoughts in their adolescent daughter, Louisa. In the end Henny commits suicide, and Louisa, like Stead, leaves home to start life abroad. Bell concluded that its achievement earned "this remarkable writer a permanent place in the pantheon of literature."

In a work that extends themes introduced in *The Man Who Loved Children, For Love Alone* (1944) focuses on a young woman whose background is similar to Louisa. In this novel, Teresa Hawkins emigrates from Australia to England, where she hopes to escape her domineering father and the stifling atmosphere of provincial political and economic life. She succeeds in London, where she falls in love and embarks on a literary career. *For Love Alone* was closely followed by *Letty Fox: Her Luck* (1946), a satirical novel set among the intellectual Left in New York.

Following World War II, Stead and Blake returned to Europe but established no permanent home until 1953 when they settled in London. During these years Stead continued writing, but her works found little favor with publishers, and only *A Little Tea, a Little Chat* (1948) and *The People with the Dogs* (1952) were published. Set in New York during the war, *A Little Tea, a Little Chat* comprises a piercing character study of a scoundrel told largely through his own self-serving monologues. However, the novel was faulted at the time as overlong, and later critics have relegated it to minor status. *The People with the Dogs* fared better with critics. Centering on Edward Massine, a wealthy

New Yorker with a country retreat in the Catskills, it was praised for its insightful examination of American manners and its sharp presentation of character. According to Bill Greenwell in *New Statesman, The People with the Dogs* is "an astonishing novel, one which sprawls, ripples and explodes beneath the fingers. . . . *The People with the Dogs* is genius on the loose."

Career Revival in the 1960s

Coinciding with the Cold War years in international politics, the blacklisting of Communist writers, and the general turn away from Marxist influence in literature, Stead had difficulty securing publication of her works. She and Blake wrote journalism and worked as researchers in an effort to meet the barest financial needs. This situation was at last relieved when *The Man Who Loved Children* was reissued in the United States in 1965 with a highly approbatory introduction by the American poet Randall Jarrell. Stead's financial woes were somewhat alleviated by literary prizes and, rediscovered by the academic world, she became a fixture in the late-twentieth-century canon of feminist literature.

In 1966 she produced *Dark Places of the Heart* (also published as *Cotter's England),* an examination of English society in the postwar era, when working-class empowerment gave currency to socialist ideals. Focusing on the Cotter family, particularly on Nellie Cotter Cook, a writer married to a labor organizer, and her philandering brother Tom, the novel presents a bleak assessment of contemporary British culture and politics. According to Louise Yelin in *British Writers:* "Left-wing political theory, like political action, reaches a dead end in *Cotter's England,"* and Nellie effectively represents "the rage and despair that characterized Stead's life during the Cold war years, when she wandered from one European city to another and struggled to support herself by writing." A lesser work, the novella collection *The Puzzleheaded Girl* was published in 1967. In the four short works included in the volume, Stead followed four American, female protagonists navigating the changing social and sexual landscape of the postwar era.

Later Career and Reputation

In 1974 Stead drew on her travel experiences in Europe for the novel *The Little Hotel,* and in *Miss Herbert* (1976) she traced the career of an English beauty from her youthful pursuit of conventional happiness through marriage and motherhood to maturity. According to Helen Yglesias in a review in the *New York Times Book Review, Miss Herbert* is a "supremely English novel, infused with the troubled, cocky and half-defeated spirit of contemporary England." She concluded, "Stead has created a stunning addition to her stunning body of work."

Blake died in 1968 and shortly afterward Stead visited Australia for the first time in forty years. In 1974 Stead returned to live in Australia and remained there until she died, in Sydney on March 31, 1983. Since her death Stead has been elevated in critical circles to the position of a beloved, major writer, particularly in Australia where her works were not even published until the mid-1960s. In response to growing interest in Stead, several new collections of her fiction have been issued as well as reprint editions of her works. Her writings remain a fertile source for academic research. Yglesias commented in the *New York Times Book Review* that "Stead novels are great to read-long rich, funny, moving, utterly surprising in their rambles through a marvelously rendered and varied scene, the whole built solidly on ground chosen and controlled by a master." And the English novelist Angela Carter concurred in the *London Review of Books* in 1982, writing, "To open a book, any book, by Christina Stead and read a few pages is to be at once aware that one is in the presence of greatness."

Books

Contemporary Authors, Gale Group, 2000.
Geering, R. G., *Christina Stead,* Twayne, 1969.
Gribble, Jennifer, *Christina Stead,* Oxford University Press, 1994.
Lidoff, Joan, *Christina Stead,* Ungar, 1992.
Rooney, Brigid, *Dictionary of Literary Biography, Volume 260: Australian Writers, 1915–1950,* edited by Selina Samuels, The Gale Group, 2002.
Rowley, Hazel, *Christina Stead: A Biography,* Holt, 1994.
Yelin, Louise, *British Writers, Supplement 4,* Charles Scribner's Sons, 1997.

Periodicals

London Review of Books, September 16, 1982.
New Statesman, August 21, 1931.
New Republic, September 8, 1986.
New York Times Book Review, June 13, 1976. □

Jakob Steiner

Swiss mathematician Jakob Steiner (1796–1863) made groundbreaking intellectual contributions to the field of mathematics in the area of geometry.

Beginning his education at the age of 18, Steiner attended universities in both Berlin and Heidelberg, then worked at a Prussian school while developing the mathematical theories that caused him to be hailed by many as the most eminent geometer since Apollonius of Perga (250–220 B.C.), whose study of conic sections earned him the title "the Great Geometer." He developed the Steiner surface and the Steiner theorem, the building blocks of what we now know as projective, or modern geometry, and ended his career as an esteemed professor of mathematics at the University of Berlin.

Demonstrated Skill with Sums

The eighth child born to farmer Niklaus Steiner and his wife, Anna, Steiner quickly found that his apptitude for mathematical calculations was useful. Born in Utzendorf, a farming village near Bern, Switzerland, on March 18, 1796, he was the youngest child in a family where hard work won out over formal education. At the age of 14 he learned to write, and the mastery of this skill Steiner saw as a way to escape the harsh life of a farmer. Despite his parents' objec-

tions, in 1814 the 18-year-old farmer's son left home and traveled to Yverdon, where educational reformer Johann Heinrich Pestalozzi (1746–1827) had established a school.

Highly influenced by the theories of Swiss enlightenment philosopher Jean Jacques Rousseau outlined in Rousseau's 1762 novel *Émile* Pestalozzi was an adherent of the philosophy that the state of nature is the best teacher. Dedicating himself to the education of the poor, he used his school to put a number of his educational theories to the test, in 1805 opening a secondary school at Yverdon. Steiner was a willing subject. His methodology, which has since become a foundation of elementary educational theory, takes into account the unique needs and talents of each student; traditional classroom repetition and memorization are replaced by hands-on learning and the resulting development of critical-thinking skills. Steiner shared the naturalistic approach to education promoted by his teacher and flourished under Pestalozzi's tutelage. Within a year and a half he was teaching math to other students and had adopted an innovative approach to his subject. Although he left Yverdon at age 22, he continued to draw on Pestalozzi's approach. With his innovative, open-minded approach to mathematics, Steiner excelled as a researcher, and during his tenure as a university professor, he also encouraged his students to think "outside the box."

University Career in Germany

In the fall of 1818 Steiner left his native Switzerland and moved to Germany to attend the University of Heidelberg, where he fell into the company of other mathematicians, such as Norwegian-born Niels Henrik Abel (1802–1829) and German mathematician Carl Gustav Jacobi (1804–1851), both of whom independently derived elliptical functions. His teaching experience at Yverdon was sufficient to allow him to fund his education by working as a tutor, and his days were divided between attending lectures in algebra, combinatorial analysis, and differential and integral calculus by such renowned mathematicians as Ferdinand Schweins and fulfilling his own teaching duties. Three years later, in the early spring of 1821, he followed the suggestion of a friend and moved to the Prussian capital city of Berlin in hopes of finding a teaching post and then enrolling at the city's prestigious university.

The lack of a formal, structured education came back to haunt Steiner in Berlin. In order to be allowed to teach in the cosmopolitan Prussian capital, teachers were expected to be well-rounded in their education, and examinations in a variety of subjects were required. Although his ability at math was great, Steiner was less adept at history and literature, and his stubbornness, belligerent nature, and unwillingness to work out with licensing officials a way to overcome any academic deficiencies made things worse. He was only able to earn a partial teaching license, and the best job he could find was a teaching post at a *gymnasium,* the German version of the North American high school. Although he was dismissed within a few months due to his unconventional teaching methods, the resourceful young man managed to replace this job with work as a tutor, and by November of 1822 Steiner was enrolled at the University of Berlin.

Leaving the university in August of 1824, Steiner found a post at a Berlin technical school and spent the next decade teaching mathematics there, first as assistant master and after 1929 as senior master. Although his role as educator to younger students relegated him teaching basic mathematical concepts, he challenged his intellect outside the classroom with theoretical work and published some of his most significant findings beginning in 1826 with his most notable work, "Einige geometrische Betrachtungen," which appeared in a periodical published by his friend, A. L. Crelle, the *Journal für die reine und angewandte Mathematik* (Journal for Pure and Complex Mathematics).

Developed Projective Geometry

During the course of his career, Steiner contributed over 60 articles to Crelle's *Journal für die reine und angewandte Mathematik* as he continued his research in geometry. These articles combine with his book-length works *Systematische Entwicklung der Abhangigkeit geometrischer Gestalten voneinander* (1832), the two-volume *Vorlesungen über synthetische Geometrie* (1867), and *Allgemeine Theorie über das Berühren und Schneiden der Kreise und der Kugeln* (1931) to encompass Steiner's foundational work in the area of what has since become the discipline of projective, or pure geometry.

Steiner was convinced, as Euclid had been, in what he termed the "organic unity of all the objects of mathematics": that there are interrelationships between what were then considered to be unrelated geometric theorems. He desired to uncover these interrelationships, thereby allowing mathematicians to deduce such theorems by means of logical deduction. "Here the main thing is neither the synthetic nor the analytic method," he wrote in *Systematische Entwicklung,* "but the discovery of the mutual dependence of the figures and of the way in which their properties are carried over from the simplest to the more complex ones." Steiner's work developed from a single principle: the stereographic projection of the plane onto the sphere.

The principle underlying Steiner's projective geometry is the principle of duality, an algebraic concept that holds that if A equals B, then what holds for A holds as well for B. Algebra is the area of mathematics that uses letters or other symbols to describe the properties and relationships among complex numbers and other abstract entities. In contrast, geometry developed from ancient man's desire to measure the earth, a goal impossible to accomplish except by abstract means. Where algebra concerns itself with numerical abstractions, geometry concerns itself with the study of the properties of constant entities, such as angles, points, lines, and one- and multi-dimensional surfaces. Steiner reasoned that what held for complex numbers should hold also for complex shapes, and through his work he proved that if two geometric operations are interchangeable or dual, then whatever results are true for one are also true for the other.

Following from his original work, Steiner derived other mathematical theorems and relationships. The Steiner ellipse is an ellipse that passes through the vertices of a triangle with points A, B, and C and also shares the centroid of those points as well as a fourth point, called the Steiner point. The Steiner surface contains an infinity of conic sections; the Steiner theorem states that the points of intersection of corresponding lines of two sets of geometric objects form a conic section. The Steiner problem relates to triangle geometry: Given a plane containing three straight lines {l, m, n} and three points {P, Q, R}, construct a triangle ABC such that the vertices A, B, and C lie on lines l, m, n and sides BC, CA, and AB pass through points P, Q, and R.

Steiner also extrapolated the work of his colleague, French geometer Jean Poncelet (1788–1837), a military engineer and professor of mechanics at the University of Paris. Like Poncelet, Steiner believed that geometry was a tool that encouraged creative thinking while algebra merely reiterated existing numerical complexities. In an example of the ability of geometry to create new relationships, the Poncelet-Steiner theorem proves that a single given circle with its center and a straight edge are needed for any Euclidian construction.

A Dedicated Educator

Through the efforts of Jacobi as well as other noted German intellectuals, on October 8, 1834, the 38-year-old mathematician was honored by the University of Berlin, which established a chair of geometry for him. Steiner remained an extraordinary professor at the university until his death 29 years later. He never married, but dedicated much of his adult life to his students. A blunt and somewhat coarse manner combined with surprisingly liberal social attitudes to make Steiner a unique and memorable individual, particularly to students used to seeing his impassioned lectures on mathematical subjects. He was known for both the startling nature of his lectures and the originality of his research, and influenced many of his students, including the noted mathematician Georg Friedrich Bernhard Riemann. Inspired by Steiner, Riemann (1826–1866) went on to become professor of mathematics at Göttingen and developed the system of elliptical space that Albert Einstein would one day draw on in his formulation of the Theory of Relativity.

Over the course of a long career, many honors came his way. Again through the influence of Jacobi, an honorary doctorate from the University of Königsberg was conferred upon Steiner in 1833, and the following year he was elected a fellow of the Prussian Academy of Science. He also became a corresponding member of the French Acadmie Royale des Sciences after a winter of lecturing in Paris in 1844 and 1845, and held membership in the Accademia dei Lincei as well.

A successful career as a teacher and lecturer combined with the frugal nature developed during childhood to provide Steiner with a comfortable income throughout his adult lifetime. Living conservatively, he amassed a significant estate which at his death was valued at 90,000 Swiss francs. In his will Steiner bequeathed a third of his fortune to the Berlin Academy to establish the Steiner Prize. In addition, he directed that an endowment of 750 francs be presented to the public school in his native village of Utzensdorf to establish prizes for students adept at mathematics. To his death, he never forgot the value of education, nor the bitter memory of the lack of it in his own youth.

Steiner left Germany in the final ten years of his life, with a kidney ailment confining him to his home in Switzerland for much of the year. He returned to German to lecture during the winters until he became bedridden. Steiner died at age 67 in Bern, Switzerland, on April 1, 1863, mourned by students and colleagues who revered him as both a brilliant mathematician and a dedicated and inspiring teacher. Steiner's articles and books were eventually collected and published in the two-volume *Gesammelte Werke* in 1881–1882, while many of his problems and theorems continue to be included in modern texts, providing challenges for future mathematicians.

Books

Burckhardt, *Dictionary of Scientific Biography,* edited by Charles Coulston Gillispie, Charles Scribner's Sons, 1980.

Dörrie, Heinrich, *One Hundred Great Problems of Elementary Mathematics, Their History and Solution,* translated from the German by David Antin, Dover, 1965.

Kollros, Louis, *Jakob Steiner,* Birkhauser, 1947.

Notable Mathematicians, Gale, 1998.

Stark, Marion Elizabeth, and Raymond Clare Archibald, *Jacob Steiner's Geometrical Constructions with a Ruler, Given a Fixed Circle with Its Center,* Scripta Mathematica, Yeshiva University, 1970.

Steiner, Jakob, *Gesammelte Werke,* two volumes, Prussian Academy of Sciences, 1881–82, reprinted, Chelsea House, 1971.

Online

Jakob Steiner (1796-1863) Geometer, http://faculty.evansville.edu/ck6/bstud/steiner.html (February 12, 2003). □

Juanita Kidd Stout

Juanita Kidd Stout (1919–1998) aspired to be a lawyer when few African Americans and few women were in the profession. When Stout was elected judge of the Court of Common Pleas in Philadelphia, Pennsylvania, she became the first African American woman to be elected to the bench. Almost 30 years later, Judge Stout became the first African American woman to serve on a state supreme court, when she was sworn in as an associate justice in Pennsylvania.

Early Life

Stout was born Juanita Kidd on March 7, 1919, in Wewoka, Oklahoma, the only child of two schoolteachers, Henry and Mary (Chandler) Kidd. From an early age, the value of an education and the importance of achievement were instilled in the little girl. She could read by the time she was three, and when she began school at the age of six, she started school in the third grade. She also began to study piano at the age of five.

Stout was a top student in both grade school and high school. However after graduating high school at the age of 16, she had to leave Oklahoma to find an accredited college that would admit an African American woman. She moved to Missouri and for two years attended Lincoln University in Jefferson City. She later transferred to the University of Iowa where she earned a bachelor of arts degree in music in 1939.

Became a Teacher

At only the age of 20, Stout began her teaching career in Seminole, Oklahoma. She taught grade school and also taught music at the Booker T. Washington High School. She remained in Seminole for two years. Her next teaching assignment was near Tulsa, Oklahoma, in the town of Sand Springs. It was there that she met her future husband, Charles Otis Stout, who was also a teacher and the boys' counselor.

As the daughter of two teachers, Stout believed that in order for learning to occur, there had to be rules and discipline; the students needed to know she was in charge. However, many of Stout's students were bigger than she was, and she sometimes had problems. She started to send her "problem" students to her future husband, and soon, the problem students were few.

Over time, the relationship between the two teachers grew. They spent a lot of their spare time together. However, after a year of teaching together, World War II broke out.

Charles Stout went into the Army, and Juanita Stout decided to go to Washington, D.C. with another teacher.

Settled in Washington, D.C.

The two young women found Washington, D.C. more exciting than Oklahoma, and they decided to stay there and find jobs. Stout found employment as a secretary. However, she soon observed that others were given opportunities that she was not. She quit her job, but a promising job lead quickly followed. She learned that the prominent law firm of Houston, Houston, and Hastie was seeking an additional secretary. Since Stout was excellent in typing and shorthand and had a genuine interest in the law, she was hired. She worked directly with Charles Hamilton Houston.

Marriage and Law School

When Juanita Stout and Charles Stout left Sand Springs and went their separate ways, there was no discussion about the future or marriage. However, her future husband tracked her down through their former high school principal. On his first leave from the Army, he went to Washington, D.C. to renew the relationship. The couple married on June 23, 1942. They had no children.

In many interviews Stout gave throughout her life, she reflected that she had wanted to be a lawyer from an early age. Although Stout had "never even seen a woman lawyer, never mind a black woman lawyer," she stated in a 1990 telephone interview with Emery Wimbish, Jr., "it was my dream." In an interview with *Ebony,* Stout recalled that her husband's response to her dream of becoming a lawyer was "selfless and swift." He used his Army GI educational funds to put her through law school.

Although Stout began her legal studies at Howard University in Washington, D.C., she soon transferred to Indiana University, where her husband was working on his doctorate degree. She earned her law degree from Indiana in 1948 and a graduate law degree in 1954. In 1966, her alma mater presented her with an honorary graduate law degree.

Began Law Career

Stout returned to Washington, D.C., and it was here that her law career truly began. According to *Contemporary Black Biography,* Stout took a job as secretary to William Hastie, a prominent African American lawyer, in 1950. Hastie was soon appointed by U.S. President Harry S. Truman to the U.S. Court of Appeals in Philadelphia. He was first African American appellate court judge in U.S. history. Hastie asked Stout to accompany him to Philadelphia, and there she continued to serve as his administrative secretary.

In 1954, Stout passed the Pennsylvania bar exam and began a private law practice. Two years later, she accepted a position as assistant district attorney for the city of Philadelphia. A few years later, Stout was promoted to chief of appeals, pardons, and paroles division of the district attorney's office, but still maintained her private practice.

In September of 1959, Pennsylvania Governor David L. Lawrence appointed Stout to fill a vacancy on the municipal court, making her the first African American woman to sit on the bench in Philadelphia. Two months later, she was elected to a ten-year term, beating her opponent by a two-to-one margin. Stout had made history, becoming the first elected African American female judge in the United States. She would serve a ten-year term on the municipal court and was then elected to two ten-year terms on the court of common pleas.

"Tell It to the Judge"

Stout quickly developed a reputation as a tough but fair judge. "She was a strong proponent of education," a colleague shared with writer Sufiya Abdur-Rahman of the *Philadelphia Inquirer.* "She was outspoken against gang violence, deadbeat dads, the exclusion of blacks from juries—and bad grammar." Attorney John F. Street (who was elected mayor of Philadelphia in 1999), added, "I tried cases in her courtroom, and she was a very, very stern taskmaster. You left that courtroom a better lawyer, a better person, and a better citizen."

During the mid-1960s, Stout received national attention for her tough sentencing of juvenile offenders and gang members. She was featured in a 1965 issue of *Life* magazine, in an article entitled "Her Honor Bops the Hoodlums." That same year, the National Association of Women Lawyers named Stout the outstanding woman lawyer of the year. The Philadelphia Bar Association noted that she "was a mentor for younger attorneys and an example for all lawyers." However, not everyone was a fan of the judge. She received death threats from gang members and was criticized by some groups, including the American Civil Liberties Union.

However, the judge knew she was making a difference. In a 1989 interview with *Ebony* magazine, she recalled passing down an 18-month sentence on a young gang member in the 1970s. "He was the best little gang leader in Philadelphia," Stout recalled. "He was bright but had gotten mixed up with the wrong crowd."

Three years later, the young man came to her office, to thank her for being tough on him. The young man told her, "The day you sentenced me, I said if I ever got out, I would make something of myself." The young man went on to graduate from college and law school, "and the next time he appeared in Stout's courtroom, it was as her law clerk." The young man eventually established a successful law practice in Philadelphia.

Contemporary Black Biography recounted a similar story about Judge Stout. One day, a woman Stout did not know stopped her on the street. The woman explained that she had been inspired to switch careers after serving on a jury in Stout's courtroom. The woman shared that had returned to college, finished law school, and passed the bar exam.

Many believe that Stout's success is due to her genuine love of the law. She once shared with the *Philadelphia Tribune,* "I cannot understand how a person can work eight hours a day or more at a job that they do not like. I love my job. I just love the law. I enjoy it." When she received the Henry G. Bennett Distinguished Service Award in 1980, she was described as a "tireless and relentless public servant . . . a champion of justice."

Appointed to State Supreme Court

In January of 1988, Stout made history a second time. Governor Robert P. Casey appointed her to the Pennsylvania Supreme Court. When she was sworn in as an associate justice, she became the first African American woman to serve on a state supreme court. That same year, the National Association of Women Judges named Stout the justice of the year. Despite these professional accomplishments, Stout also experienced a personal loss. Her husband passed away in August of that year.

With her achievements, Stout was quick to recall those her influenced her along the way. In *Notable Black American Women,* Stout remembered her parents, "who taught her the value of education and moral living," and acknowledged "the unswerving support of her husband." Perhaps they inspired Stout's famous quote: "A person educated in mind and not in morals is a menace to society."

A Lifetime of Honors

In 1989, Justice Stout reached the state supreme court's mandatory retirement age of 70 and was forced to step down. She returned to the court of common pleas as a senior judge in the homicide division. She served on this court until her death.

During her career Stout was active in many professional and service organizations and received many honors. Her memberships included the American Bar Association, the Pennsylvania Bar Association, the Philadelphia Bar Association, the National Association of Women Lawyers, and the American Judges Association. She also served on the boards of Rockford College, Saint Augustine's College, and the Medical College of Pennsylvania, the first medical school that was established for women. Her abilities and contributions have been recognized by eleven colleges and universities, which have awarded her honorary degrees.

In 1981, a very special event occurred. Her home state of Oklahoma, the place she was forced to leave in order to get her college education, inducted her into its Hall of Fame. Two years later, she was inducted into the Oklahoma Women's Hall of Fame. In 1988, Stout received the Gimbel Award for Humanitarian Services by the Medical College of Pennsylvania and was named a Distinguished Daughter of Pennsylvania by the governor.

Her alma maters also remembered her. The University of Iowa named her a distinguished alumnus in June of 1974, and in 1992 Indiana University presented her with the Distinguished Alumni Service Award.

On August 21, 1998, Stout died of leukemia in Philadelphia. Although she had not heard cases for several months, she had planned to be back on the bench in the fall. Posthumous honors followed. In December of 1998, Stout received the Oklahoma Human Rights Award, and in 2002, as it celebrated its 200th year, the Philadelphia Bar Association named Stout as a "legend of the law."

Shortly after her death, writer John Shelley reflected on the impact Stout made during her career. He wrote, "We'll miss this lady. . . . Particularly the swift and sure justice she handed out to criminals, regardless of race. . . . The nation could use thousands more like her."

Books

Notable Black American Women, Book 1, Gale Research, 1992.
Phelps, Shirelle, editor, *Contemporary Black Biography, Volume 24,* Gale Group, 2000.
Smith, Jessie Carney, editor, *Epic Lives: One Hundred Black Women Who Made a Difference,* Visible Ink Press, 1993.
Who's Who Among African Americans, 14th ed., Gale Group, 2001.

Periodicals

Ebony, February 1989.
Jet, September 7, 1998.
Legal Intelligencer, January 9, 2002.
Life, July 9, 1965.
New York Times, August 24, 1998.
Philadelphia Inquirer, March 7, 1988; October 30 1989; August 22, 1998; June 30, 2000.
Philadelphia Tribune, October 14, 1994; August 25, 1998.
Time, April 16, 1965.

Online

"4 Thoughts of the Week," *Netastic!* http://www.netastic.com/4tow/ (January 18, 2003).
"Association Goverance: Urging that the Criminal Justice Center be Renamed the 'Juanita Kidd Stout Center for Criminal Justice,' " *Philadelphia Bar Association,* http://www.philabar.org/member/governance/resolutions/resolution.asp?pubid=1653552222000 (March 17, 2003).
"Different Viewpoints," *John Shelley's Journal,* http://www.gdnctr.com/aug_28_98.htm (January 18, 2003).
"First Female Black Judge Died," *newsnet5.com,* http://www.newsnet5.com/news/stories/news-980822-155758.html (January 18, 2003).
"Human Rights Day—15th Annual Human Rights Day Awards Ceremonies," *OneNet Oklahoma's Official Telecommunications and Information Network,* http://www.onenet.net/~ohrc2/Human_Rights_Day.htm (January 18, 2003).
"Juanita Kidd Stout," *blackseek.com,* http://www.blackseek.com (January 18, 2003).
"Judge Juanita Kidd Stout," *Oklahoma State University Library website,* http://www.library.okstate.edu/about/awards/winners/stout.htm (January 18, 2003).
"Today in History," *A.C.H.A.—African Canadian Heritage Association website,* http://www.achaonline.org/1todayhis.htm (January 18, 2003). □

Meryl Louise Streep

A versatile screen actress known for immersing herself in her characters, Meryl Streep (born 1949) distinguished herself with two Academy Awards and has been nominated 13 times, more than any other actor in history. Intelligent, commanding, and unafraid to play unglamorous and difficult women,

Streep embodied an increasing realism for female characters in major studio films.

Standout Thespian

Streep was born in Summit, New Jersey, on June 22, 1949, to wealthy parents. Her mother was a commercial artist and her father a pharmaceutical executive. She has two younger brothers. Raised in Bernardsville, New Jersey, she took operatic voice lessons as a child and started acting at Bernards High School. She was also a varsity cheerleader, Homecoming Queen, and an academic stalwart.

Though her ambition was to be an interpreter for the United Nations, Streep continued her theater work at Vassar, where she was the star of the drama department. She spent one semester at Dartmouth and then enrolled in the prestigious Yale Drama School. There she appeared in more than three dozen productions with the Yale Repertory Theater and became well-known for her astounding range and the intensity of her performances.

Streep went directly from Yale to the New York theater scene. She appeared at the Public Theater—its impresario Joseph Papp was her mentor—in the musical *Alice in Concert.* Soon Streep arrived on Broadway, and she was nominated for a Tony Award in 1977 for Tennessee Williams's *27 Wagons Full of Cotton.*

While playing a lead role in a Shakespeare in the Park production of *Measure for Measure,* she met and fell in love with actor John Cazale, with whom she would work in *The Deer Hunter.* They never married, but she cared for him until he died of cancer in 1978. A few months later, she married sculptor Don Gummer.

A Woman of Substance

In 1977, Streep made her debut on the small screen in the made-for-TV movie *The Deadliest Season* and on the big screen in *Julia.* In 1978, she won an Emmy Award for playing a Jewish woman persecuted by the Nazis in the TV miniseries *Holocaust.* Also that year, Streep was nominated for the first time for an Academy Award for a small but stirring role in *The Deer Hunter* as a woman in love with two men during the Vietnam conflict.

The Deer Hunter made many Hollywood directors eager to work with Streep. The first to grab her was Woody Allen, who cast her as his hostile ex-wife in *Manhattan.* In that role and in others to come, Streep demonstrated she was comfortable portraying an unlikable character.

In fact, Streep was perfectly suited to play the new roles that were opening up because of the feminist movement. Though Streep was a blonde with elegant features, she was rarely glamorous, and she could easily suppress her beauty and look ordinary. Playing a woman conflicted about divorcing her husband in *Kramer vs. Kramer* in 1979, Streep embodied the difficult choices facing millions of women. "In 1979, nobody was talking about depression," Streep later told *Entertainment Weekly*'s Mark Harris, "but this woman probably thought about killing herself once or twice a day." One of the first movies to treat divorce from an egalitarian standpoint, *Kramer vs. Kramer* was a cultural landmark in American film. Streep's portrayal merited an Academy Award for Best Supporting Actress and made her a household name.

Also in 1979, Streep showed her versatility by portraying a sexy attorney who snares a politician in *The Seduction of Joe Tynan.* Two years later, she was nominated again for an Academy Award for a supporting role, playing two characters (the mistress of a Victorian gentleman and a modern actress playing her) in *The French Lieutenant's Woman.* Critics and the public, especially female moviegoers, embraced her. Already hailed as the greatest actress of her time, she won the Academy Award as Best Actress for *Sophie's Choice* in 1982. In that film, she adopted a convincing Polish accent after enrolling in a Berlitz course.

Oscar's Favorite

What was unusual about Streep was not just her willingness to take on difficult roles, but her ability to utterly disappear into her characters. A thorough researcher, she could adopt a different era, nationality, accent, or personality. Some critics, however, most notably Pauline Kael of the *New Yorker,* criticized her work as too stylized. To such detractors, Streep came off as a masterful technician who lacked warmth and genuine emotion. Reacting to this common criticism, Streep, in an interview in the *Washington Times* in 2002, said that she approached her roles instinctually rather than analytically: "I like to think I am the opposite of technical. I only worked once with a voice coach, and it was a disaster."

However she had accomplished it, in five years Streep had gone from a virtual unknown to the pinnacle of Hollywood stardom. In the noir thriller *Still of the Night,* Streep again attempted a seductive character, but did not fare well. "I didn't know what I was doing in that!" she told *Entertainment Weekly*'s Harris. "I didn't know who my character was. I hate noir. It's not about playing a person, but a representation."

Able to pick and choose her roles, she next took on an openly political character, playing a nuclear power industry whistleblower in the biographical picture *Silkwood.* To this role she brought a convincing recklessness and courage, and once again she was among the Best Actress nominees on Oscar night.

Again switching gears, Streep followed up with a romantic role opposite Robert DeNiro in the film *Falling in Love,* which flopped despite featuring the biggest male and female stars of the day—possibly because audiences could not picture either of them in a romantic pairing. Streep returned to serious drama in 1985 with *Plenty,* playing a woman in the French Resistance who has trouble piecing her life back together after World War II. The next year, in *Out of Africa,* Streep gave another Oscar-nominated performance as a Danish woman having an affair in Kenya. Her next picture was the comic romance *Heartburn,* which was filmed while she was pregnant.

Streep got her by-now-customary Best Actress nominations in 1987 and 1988 for *Ironweed,* in which she played a Depression-era alcoholic, and for *A Cry in the Dark,* in which she took on the thankless role of a much-reviled Australian woman accused of murdering her own child. She later told Liz Smith in an interview in *Good Housekeeping* that this was her favorite role, explaining: "I'm drawn to disagreeable women. . . . I loved trying to put somebody out there that you wouldn't normally look at or care about." Ty Burr, in a 1996 *Entertainment Weekly* article that named Streep number 37 among the 100 greatest movie stars, opined: "She's the movie star as medicine: good for you, but not much fun. . . . She inhabits her roles with a craft that can occasionally seem academic. "

Ranged Far and Wide

With her career direction in question, Streep decided to try comedy. She gave her voice to a character in the animated television sitcom *The Simpsons.* Streep shocked almost everyone by appearing opposite comic Roseanne Barr in *She-Devil,* a notable flop. Next, she played Carrie Fisher's alter ego in Fisher's semi-autobiographical *Postcards from the Edge*—the first movie she made in Hollywood. It netted her another Oscar nomination. She followed that with a starring role in Richard Brooks' comedy *Defending Your Life.* None of these comic roles attracted much attention, but Streep was funny in the over-the-top satire *Death Becomes Her,* playing a zombie-like character opposite Goldie Hawn.

Having proven she could act in comedies, Streep returned to drama in the harrowing *The House of the Spirits,* in which her ten-year-old daughter Mamie appeared. She decided to show her children she could be adventurous by doing her own whitewater rafting in her next film, *The River Wild,* a harrowing tale about a family expedition that goes wrong.

Streep had to cry for entire days during the filming of the tear-jerking romantic drama *The Bridges of Madison County,* a guaranteed box-office success because it adapted one of the decade's most popular novels. For this part, playing an Iowa farm wife wooed by a photographer, she put on weight and shed makeup. After a five-year absence from Oscar night, the role earned her a tenth Academy Award nomination.

In 1996, Streep played the mother of a teenage boy accused of murder in *Before and After.* The same year, she appeared in *Marvin's Room,* playing the mother of Leonardo DiCaprio. During her career, Streep also played the real-life role of mother on a secluded 89-acre estate in rural Connecticut with Gummer and their four children: Henry, Mary Wills (Mamie), Grace, and Louisa. She turned down theater roles because they would take her away at night, and she tried to maintain a normal family life as much as possible, guarding her children's privacy. In 1998, she told Smith in the *Good Housekeeping* interview: "I always feel like my life is straining at the seams. . . . Basically I've now decided I can do one movie a year."

Discussing her daughters and how they influenced her acting choices, Streep told Dana Kennedy of *Entertainment Weekly:* "I want them to see not just examples of beautiful young women, I want them to see that women are beautiful throughout their lives and important and formidable and exciting, because I think those fantasies are what you build your dreams on. I know I did when I was a kid." Kennedy observed that "by sheer strength of personality," Streep "could probably command the U.S. armed forces in addition to tending to her acting career, her husband, and her four children."

Second Wind

By the mid-1990s, Streep's flirtation with comedy was over, and she had returned to playing the kind of drama that had made her so famous, and with an assured maturity. She played a terminally ill wife and mother in *One True Thing,* garnering another Oscar nomination, and added an Irish brogue to her linguistic repertoire in *Dancing at Lughnasa.* She played an inner-city violin teacher in *Music of the Heart,* netting her a 12th Academy Award nomination.

After lending her voice talents to a role in *A.I.: Artificial Intelligence* in 2001, Streep returned to the stage to star in a Broadway adaptation of *The Seagull,* directed by Mike Nichols. *Newsweek*'s Cathleen McGuigan said "Streep commands the stage—but never steals scenes—in a wonderfully funny, wrenching performance."

Having turned 50, Streep was determined not to fade away as too many great actresses do in middle age. In 2002, she returned to the forefront with two critically acclaimed performances. In the offbeat comedy *Adaptation,* she played *New Yorker* columnist Susan Orlean, who falls for the subject of her article and book, a scraggly gap-toothed orchid thief in Florida. She won a Golden Globe as a supporting actress and also landed a Golden Globe nomination for her standout performance in *The Hours,* in which she played a New York book editor throwing a party for a longtime friend dying of AIDS. About that portrayal, David Ansen of *Newsweek* raved: "Few actresses can express their inner lives without a line of dialogue as eloquently as Streep: her warm, flustered performance allows us to become mind readers." Her Academy Award nomination for Best Supporting Actress for *Adaptation* allowed her to pass Katherine Hepburn as the most Oscar-nominated actor in movie history. Director Alan Pakula said: "If there's a heaven for directors, it would be to direct Meryl Streep your whole life."

For her part, Streep told *Daily Variety* that she was proud of the integrity of her career, of "this eccentric, quirky collection of movies I've done, all with their idiosyncratic pleasures. They've never said about my movies, 'What's the sequel?' and 'Can we merchandise this?' "

Utterly rejecting the idea that she approached acting mechanically, Streep said in the *Washington Times* interview: "We need art like food. I'm not religious but I think of my work—this is so pretentious—a bit like going to the altar. Like going to God. . . . You can't get ready for it, I believe. Acting is surrender. All you really have to do is listen."

Books

Thomson, David, *A Biographical Dictionary of Film,* Alfred A. Knopf, 1994.

Periodicals

Daily Variety, November 18, 2002; January 8, 2003.
Entertainment Weekly, February 11, 1994; Fall 1996; March 24, 2000.
Good Housekeeping, September 1998.
Knight Ridder/Tribune News Service (Orlando Sentinel), January 16, 2003.
Newsweek, August 20, 2001.
People Weekly, June 26, 1995; January 27, 1997.
Washington Times, February 20, 2002;

Online

"Meryl Streep," *All Movie Guide,* http://www.allmovie.com (February 7, 2003). □

T

Tamara

The Kingdom of Georgia in Asia Minor, located on the easternmost fringes of the thirteenth-century Christian world, reached the pinnacle of its political power during the reign of Queen Tamara (1169–1212), who reigned from 1184 to 1212. Tamara ruled over the largest territory ever to come under the control of Georgia; during her reign, the kingdom stretched from Azerbaijan, north of present-day Iran, to the borders of Cherkessia, in the North Caucasus.

With an official title of "Tamar Bagrationi, by the will of our Lord, Queen of the Abkhazians, Kartvels, Rans, Kakhs and the Armenians, Shirvan-Shah and Shah-in-Shah and ruler of all East and West," Tamara successfully defended her kingdom against multiple incursions by hostile forces. But within 20 years of her death, Mongol invasions would destroy the governmental and military foundations of the country.

Historical Context

Although the trans-Caucasian state of Georgia in Asia Minor first emerged as an independent state in the first millennium B.C., its Golden Age did not begin until the reign of David Aghmashenebeli (1089–1125), also known as David the Builder. At a time that coincided with the Christian Crusades, David drove the Seljuk Turks from the boundaries of his kingdom. Encouraged by his early success, he then refused to pay tribute to the Turks and urged Georgians to return to their homes from their places of refuge in the mountains. Having gained control of the rural areas of Georgia, David next set out to defeat the Turks in their strongholds in the cities. Finally, on August 12, 1121, David and his Armenian, Kipchak, Ossetian, and Shirvan allies defeated Sultan Mahmud of Iraq at Didgori. In the following year (1122), David took Tbilisi.

By the time of David's death in 1125, Tbilisi was the capital of an empire that stretched from the Black Sea in the east to the Caspian Sea in the west. But David's immediate successors were too embroiled in dispute with each other to be effective rulers, and Georgia would not flourish again until the reign of David's great-granddaughter, Tamara.

Tamara

In 1177 or 1178, David's grandson, King Georgi III, crowned his 19-year-old daughter by the celebrated beauty Bourduhan, Tamara, co-ruler of Georgia. He also named her as his successor as part of his plan for instituting an orderly succession upon his death, which would take place six years later.

Upon assuming the throne in 1184, the 25-year-old Tamara initially was made a guardian of her paternal aunt, Rusudani. The nobility, anxious to have an heir to the throne, quickly arranged a marriage for the queen. Tamara would marry twice—first in 1187 to a Russian-born prince by the name of George Bobolybski (also known as Georgi Rusi or Prince Yuri) who fell out of the Queen's favor after he sent troops off to fight the Muslims and Persians while he stayed home in debauchery. Within two years the marriage had ended, and Tamara exiled Bobolybski. In 1189, Tamara married again—this time to an Ossetian prince named David Sosland who had been raised in the Georgian court. She would bear David Sosland two children—a son and a daughter; both would later ascend to the throne of Georgia.

Following his exile, Bobolybski attacked Georgia with the aid of Russian troops. Meeting two defeats, Bobolybski fled in exile to the south where he allied himself with Turkish forces. He once more attacked Georgia, but was once again defeated. In May 1204, after Tamara led her troops to victory over the Turks at the Battle of Basiani, she was proclaimed "Our King Tamara." Following her victory over the Turks at Basiani, she won another major victory at Kars in 1205.

During her reign, Tamara tried to play off various factions within the nobility by giving political appointments to generals and nobles. About the time that her son was born in 1194—followed by her daughter one year later—Tamara successfully quelled a rebellion in the mountainous regions of her kingdom. After Byzantium was taken by the Christians during the Fourth Crusade, she sent troops in support of her relative, Alexios Comnenus, who would become the Byzantine emperor in 1205. She maintained firm control over her Muslim semi-protectorates and exacted tribute from some of the provinces in southern Russia.

Several years later, in 1209, the Emir of Ardabil attacked Georgia, killing 12,000 Georgians. Tamara responded by attacking the Emir's forces, killing him and 12,000 of his followers, and taking many others captive as slaves during raids into Persia. Tamara then proceeded with her army into North Persia and neighboring regions.

Queen Tamara of Georgia died on January 18, 1212. Medieval chronicles indicate that some of her subjects offered to die in her place when the queen was on her deathbed. Tamara left her kingdom to her son, Georgi IV Lasha (1212–1223).

Upon learning of the Christian Crusades to Palestine, Georgi Lasha initially made plans to join the campaign. A Mongol attack on Armenia in 1220, however, followed by incursions to the north into Georgia changed his mind, and he instead chose to engage the invaders in battle. But Georgi Lasha and his 90,000 mounted soldiers proved no match for the Mongols, and he died in battle in 1223. Upon his death, Georgi Lasha's sister, Rusudan, became queen. After the Mongols attacked Tbilisi in 1236, Queen Rusudan sought refuge in Kutaisi as the Mongol hordes swept through the country. Following their victory, the Mongols dominated Georgia for more than a century.

It would not be until the fourteenth century that Georgia would finally obtain relief from Mongol rule. Under Georgi V (1314–1346), the country would stop paying tribute to its Mongol overlords and would finally succeed in casting off its oppressors. Under Georgi V, Georgia would once again enjoy some of the prosperity it had experienced under Queen Tamara.

Gender Issues

Although some have argued that Tamara's gender was irrelevant to her reign, there clearly were instances where it played a role. Tamara was by some accounts forced by the nobility into her disastrous first marriage by the Georgian nobility, which was anxious to have an heir to the throne in place. The nobles also hoped to find in Tamara's husband a military leader. In still another example, in 1205, the Seljuk

ruler Rukn ad-Din gave as the reason for his decision to invade Georgia that fact that Tamara was a woman—a common perception of the time being that women rulers weakened the authority and military power of a kingdom.

According to a source cited by Antony Eastmond, writing in an essay entitled "Gender and Orientalism in Georgia in the Age of Queen Tamar" in *Women, Men and Eunuchs: Gender in Byzantium,* there are indications that men actually when out of their minds after falling in love with Tamara. One is even said to have pined to death.

In the mid-nineteenth century, Mikhail Lermontov wrote a poem entitled "Tamara" that raised even deeper questions about the role of Tamara's gender on her kingdom. In Lermontov's interpretation, Tamara was a slave to her sexual desires and was reduced to seducing a different lover every night to satisfy her lusts. Wrote Lermontov, "That tower on the desperate Terek/Belonged to Tamara, the Queen;/Her beautiful face was angelic,/Her spirit demonic and mean."

But at almost the same time that Lermontov was writing his poem, engravings intended for mass audiences depicting the Queen as passive, gentle, and saintly were in circulation. The inspiration for these engravings was thought to have been a thirteenth-century wall painting of Tamara that had recently been uncovered. The wall painting, which was restored, appeared to have originally shown Tamara to have been a classical Persian beauty, with an oval face, pale coloring, and eyes like pearls. Under restoration, Tamara's face showed more European features with almost virginal beauty.

According to Antony Eastmond, "All accounts of Tamar's reign rely in the end on the assessment of the society from which she came and its attitudes towards women. To Lermontov, Georgia was an exotic, 'oriental,' society with all the attraction and excitement associated with those terms. . . . This orientalist view was adopted by many other nineteenth-century writers."

Today Lermontov's portrayal of Tamara scarcely registers serious comment among historians who attempt to reconstruct her life. But the engravings, which were based on the reconstructed wall painting, are probably equally misleading in their coloring of the Queen by sentimental yearnings. As a result, Tamara has tended to be portrayed by history as either a siren or a saint.

Legacy

During the reign of Queen Tamara, the Kingdom of Georgia experienced a burst of activity in architecture and literature. The kingdom also enjoyed advancements in science and agriculture. Under Tamara's rule, palaces and churches were built throughout Georgia. Construction of the Metechi Church was completed after she was enthroned and even the minor churches in the kingdom were adorned with frescoes. Shota Rustaveli wrote his epic "The Knight in the Panther Skin" as an ode to the Queen. Book illumination reached new levels and metalworking thrived.

During Tamara's reign, Tbilisi occupied an important position along the trade routes. Traders traveling east and west passed through the city, as did merchants from the mountains in the north and the lands to the south. A variety of languages must have filled the streets as merchants haggled over the prices of such exotic goods as spices and carpets. Buffer states paid tribute to the queen. During his travels through the country some years after Tamara's reign, Marco Polo (1254–1324) reportedly called Georgia "a handsome city, around which are settlements and many fortified posts."

Under Tamara's rule, Georgia acquired a parliament; this achievement came approximately 25 years before the Magna Carta was signed in England (1215). It was reportedly at the parliament's direction that Tamara divorced her first husband.

Antony Eastmond quotes from a text that is reputed to date from the early thirteenth century which mourns Tamara's passing: "In those times we had nothing but the name of Tamar[a] on our lips; acrostics in honor of the queen were written on the walls of houses; rings; knives and pilgrims' staves were adorned with her praises. Every man's tongue strove to utter something worthy of Tamar[a]'s name; ploughmen sang verses to her as they tilled the soil; musicians coming to Iraq celebrated her fame with music; Franks and Greeks hummed her praises as they sailed the seas in fair weather. The whole earth was filled with her praise, she was celebrated in every language wherever her name was known."

The Russian Orthodox Church added Tamara to its roster of saints in recognition of her good works, among which the Church enumerated concern for the poor, widows, and orphans and contributions to the Church.

Books

Eastmond, Antony, "Gender and Orientalism in Georgia in the Age of Queen Tamar," in Liz James, editor, *Women, Men and Eunuchs: Gender in Byzantium,* Routledge, 1997.
Olsen, Kirstin, *Chronology of Women's History,* Greenwood Press, 1994.

Online

"Georgian History," Edisher.com, http://www.edisher.com/history.asp (February 2003).
"History of Georgia," http://members.tripod.com/ggdavid/georgia/history.htm (February 2003).
"Saint Tamara, Queen of Georgia," http://www.fatheralexander.org/booklets/english/saints/tamara_georgia.htm (February 2003).
"Tbilisi, the Golden Age (1100–1300)," http://www.georgian-art.com/articles/jwright/golden.html (February 2003).
"Women in Power, 1150–1200," http://www.guide2women leaders.com/womeninpower/Womeninpower1150.htm (February 2003). □

Helen Tamiris

Helen Tamiris (1903–1966) was one of the founders of modern dance in the United States. Trained in ballet and influenced by social issues of the 1920s and 1930s, she developed the concert dance form of modern dance. A white woman, Tamiris choreographed eight dances that were known as the *Negro Spirituals* between 1928 and 1941, which rank among her finest and most often restaged works. Later in her career, she entered musical theater and choreographed Broadway plays such as *Annie Get Your Gun* and *Showboat.* She received the Antoinette Perry Award in 1949 for best choreography for *Touch and Go.* After co-founding the Tamiris-Nagrin Dance Company with her husband, Daniel Nagrin, in 1960, Tamiris continued to teach and dance until her death in 1966.

Studied Rigid Ballet Techniques

Born Helen Becker on April 24, 1903, in New York City to parents who emigrated from Russia, Tamiris grew up on the Lower East Side of New York City. At the age of eight, she began studying dance with Irene Lewisohn at the Henry Street Settlement then studied with the children's chorus of the Metropolitan Opera Company and later learned Italian ballet techniques at the Met. From 1918 to 1920 she studied modern dance at the Neighborhood Playhouse before the Playhouse began to teach the style of Louis Horst.

Tamiris also studied natural dancing at an Isadora Duncan studio but disliked its emphasis on personal expression and lyrical movements. Restless at the studio, she soon left to develop her own approach to dance, a quest that would make her one of the pioneers in modern dance. She spent a couple of years as a specialty dancer playing in stage shows of movie houses and making nightclub appearances.

In 1922, Bracale Opera Company borrowed Tamiris from the Met to dance lead solo ballet in its productions that toured South America. Traveling outside the United States exposed her to international dance forms. When she returned to New York, she resigned from the Met and abandoned the rigid Italian ballet style she had been taught. For the next year she studied Russian ballet techniques with Mikhail Fokine and danced with his company in Gilbert Miller's production of *Casanova.*

At this time, Tamiris chose the stage name Tamiris (later calling herself Helen Tamiris) to project an exotic appeal. In 1924 and 1925, she was a principal dancer in John Murray Anderson's *Music Box Revue.* The next year, she toured the country as a soloist in moving picture presentation units under Anderson.

Concert Debut in 1927

Disappointed at not finding what she wanted to do with dance, Tamiris took a year off to develop her own techniques and voice. Rejecting such dance elements as mimed stories, theatricality, and technical tricks, she turned to concert dance. During the 1920s and 1930s, she became a leader in concert dance, choreographing solos or shared programs for herself and for small groups of female dancers.

On October 9, 1927, Tamiris made her concert debut at the Little Theatre in New York. With Horst playing piano, Tamiris performed a program of solos, including her pieces *Florentine, Portrait of a Lady, Impressions of the Bullring,* and *Circus Sketches.*

Tamiris's concert career lasted from 1927 to 1944, during which time she created works for herself and her contemporaries, such as Martha Graham, Doris Humphrey, and the choreographers of the New Dance League and Group, of which Sophie Maslow, Lily Mehlman, and Anna Sokolow were members.

Tamiris was establishing herself as a choreographer who searched for flow and ease of movement in her pieces. She had a striking appearance and buoyant personality. Her dances expressed her central concern for human dignity, clear expression, range, and economy. For a program book, she declared, "Dancing is simply movement with a personal conception of rhythm," according to the *International Encyclopedia of Dance.*

Viewing life as a conflict, she expressed herself verbally and artistically, preparing works that were vigorous and exuberant. In her choreography, she infused her dances with unique accompaniment to reflect social commentary. In her dances, she complemented urban life with sirens, evoked an aura of Ernest Hemingway with flashing colors, and made a statement on sex with frank voluptuousness. Her dancers also used kettle drums, carried instruments, beat their elbows on drums, and played triangles and cymbals.

The Negro Spirituals

With a penchant for exploring traditional American themes and believing that American dance must use indigenous sources, Tamiris was probably best known for choreographing a series of eight pieces under the umbrella title *Negro Spirituals* between 1928 and 1941. Dance critic Margaret Lloyd said, "The *Negro Spirituals* were the musts of her programs. Every new one was hailed with hurrahs. This was the thing she could really do, this was what she did best," according to *Black Tradition in American Dance.*

Tamiris, who was white, blended her sympathy for oppressed human beings with her uninhibited nature and love of the unpremeditated. She reveled in the emotional energy of black music and dance and incorporated black themes and movement styles into her work, which was influenced by the jazz, Harlem, and African ceremonial dances of the time. The *Negro Spirituals* were simple in design and execution, displaying slicing or staccato arms anchored in a deeply weighted body. For her spirituals she also used arrangements of J. Rosamond Johnson and Lawrence Brown. Not only did she produce such dances, but she broke though color barriers by choosing black performers as well. Tamiris was instrumental in introducing African American dancer Pearl Primus to the public.

Her second solo concert in 1928 featured two *Negro Spirituals,* "Nobody Knows de Trouble I See" and "Joshua Fit de Battle ob Jericho." They were very successful, and she went on to perform them in Paris and Berlin. In April 1929, she added a version of "Swing Low, Sweet Chariot" to her program in New York. By 1932, she had danced six *Negro Spirituals,* her latest being "Gris-Gris Ceremonial," which included percussive gourds shaken in a West African tradition. In 1933, she appeared in Lewisohn Stadium, in the outdoor concert season of the Philharmonic Orchestra, performing that piece with the Bahama Negro Dancers.

Her 1937 *How Long, Brethren?,* one of her best known concert pieces, was danced to songs of protest. Dramatized in dance from Lawrence Gellert's "Negro Songs of Protest" and sung by a black chorus, the piece depicted the despair of unemployed Southern blacks.

Founded Dance Companies

In 1930, Tamiris was a major organizer of the Dance Repertory Theatre. Modern choreographers such as Martha Graham, Doris Humphrey, and Charles Weidman joined together to create a place where they could produce and perform their individual works. Tamiris was president of the company during its first two years. At the same time she worked for the American Dance Association and the Works Progress Administration's Federal Dance Project, where she encouraged the inclusion of dance and served as principal choreographer from 1937 to 1939. From 1930 to 1945, Tamiris was director and teacher of the School of American Dance.

Tamiris and her company of dancers called Her Group excelled in modern dance in the mid-1930s. Dances took on social issues, made statements on freedom and decadence, denounced war, and highlighted the schism between the haves and have-nots. Tamiris created one of the best compositions of her career with her 1934 *Walt Whitman Suite,* a set of six related dances based on themes from Whitman, set to music by Genevieve Pitot. This project, which contained three solos, demonstrated the maturity of the work by Tamiris and her troupe.

For the next few years, she had a satisfactory extended tour with her group; was one of the primary organizers of the weeklong First National Dance Congress and Festival in 1936; and choreographed the Dance Project in New York from 1937 to 1939. In 1938, she presented some of her solo dances at the Salzburg Festival, and in 1939 she produced the first big modern ballet, *Adelante,* a 75-minute, all-dance work on Loyalist Spain. From 1930 to 1945, she taught extensively outside her own school, including body movement for actors and directors, while continuing to perform and produce.

Choreographed for Broadway

In addition to her concert work, Tamiris had a successful Broadway choreography career. From 1943 to 1957 she choreographed modern dances in 18 musical comedies and worked with Nagrin as her assistant on six musicals. Her first theatrical works were created for experimental groups and were staged for the Provincetown players, the Group Theater, and the Federal Theatre Project.

As noted in the *International Encyclopedia of Dance,* "Rather than using chorus lines or technical displays to advance the script or to enhance the music, Tamiris integrated dance into such theater pieces as *Up in Central Park* (1945), *Annie Get Your Gun* (1946), *Inside USA* (1948), and *Plain and Fancy* (1955)." She also choreographed *Park Avenue* (1946) and *Showboat* (1946). Her choreography for *Touch and Go* (1949) won the Antoinette Perry Award. Some of the Broadway shows she worked on toured in Europe.

In her productions, she strove to create clever characterizations and evoke the spirit of America's regions and periods. She integrated her dance numbers with acting, song, and stage pictorialisms. Also noteworthy was the caliber of dancers in her shows, such as Lidija Franklyn, Joseph Gifford, George Bockman, Dorothy Bird, J.C. McCord, Pearl Lang, Valeri Bettis, Rod Alexander, Claude Marchant, Talley Beatty, and Pearl Primus.

Tamiris continued to dance and teach later in her life. In 1951, she performed in Donald McKayle's *Games* that premiered at Hunter College. She performed the modern dances *Pioneer Memories* (1957), *Dance for Walt Whitman* (1958), and *Memoir* (1959).

She taught at Perry-Mansfield School of Theatre and Dance in Colorado and Maine in 1956 and taught stage movement for directors at the American Dance Festival in Connecticut. In 1960, she co-founded the Tamiris-Nagrin Dance Company with her husband and worked on *Women's Song* (1960) and *Once Upon a Time* (1961). In 1962, she conducted summer workshops with Nagrin at C. W. Post College of Long Island University.

On August 4, 1966, Tamiris died of cancer in New York City. In 1996, she posthumously received the Scripps/American Dance Festival award with Pearl Primus. Nagrin accepted the award in her memory.

Remembered and Recreated

Tamiris's works were rarely choreographed for other companies, and her philosophy was that each dance must create its own expressive means and focus on bringing out what was unique about each dancer. Consequently, it was difficult to bequeath a "Tamiris" style or technique to her followers.

In the late 20th Century, there were attempts to reconstruct some of her most important works, such as the *Negro Spiritual* series (1928–1942), *How Long, Brethren?* (1937–1942), and sections of the *Walt Whitman Suite* (1934), especially "Salut au Monde" and "I Sing the Body Electric." As early as 1965, the *Negro Spirituals* were restaged at the School of the Performing Arts in New York City, and they were recorded in 1967.

In 1986, Arizona State University in Tempe published *The Tamiris Conference,* edited by Nagrin. Nagrin is also the author of *Helen Tamiris and the Dance Historians: Why Has She Been Neglected by Contemporary Historians?,* parts of which were presented at the Society of Dance History Scholars Conference held at the university in 1989. Portions of the *Negro Spirituals* were restaged at Emory College, and the University of Utah restaged her "Dance for Walt Whitman." Dianne McIntyre re-created the *Negro Spirituals,* which were performed in the 1990s by the Scripps/American Dance Festival.

Books

Chujoy, Anatole & P.W. Manchester, *Dance Encyclopedia,* Simon & Schuster, 1967.
Cohen, Selma Jeanne, ed., *International Encyclopedia of Dance,* Oxford University Press, 1998.
Cohen-Stratyner, Barbara, *Biographical Dictionary of Dance,* Macmillan, 1982.
Lloyd, Margaret, *Borzoi Book of Modern Dance,* Dance Horizons, 1949.
Long, Richard, *Black Tradition in American Dance,* Rizzoli International Publishers, 1989.
Martin, John, *America Dancing,* Dance Horizons, 1968.

Online

"Helen Tamiris," *Women in American History by Encyclopedia Britannica,* http://search.eb.com/women/articles/Tamiris_Helen.html (March 5, 2003). □

Andrei Arsenyevich Tarkovsky

Russian film director Andrei Tarkovsky (1932–1986) was, arguably, the greatest filmmaker of his nation. While perhaps not the innovator that fellow Russian Sergei Eisenstein was, Tarkovsky nevertheless imbued each of his films with a poetry that embraced life and sought to reveal the myriad ways in which humanity manifests itself.

Andrei Arsenyevich Tarkovsky was born on April 4, 1932, in the Russian town of Zavrazhye, located on the Volga River, about 500 kilometers northeast of Moscow in the Kostroma Region. Members of the Tarkovsky family were members of the Russian intelligentsia. His father, Arseny, was a poet and a translator while Tarkovsky's mother, Maria Ivanovna, was primarily an editor at the First State Publishing House in Moscow and also an actress. Tarkovsky also had a younger sister, Marina, who became a philologist. Tarkovsky was four years old when his parents separated; they ultimately divorced. His father remarried twice, but his mother never married again. Their separation evoked a deep crisis in Tarkovsky that he later explored in his autobiographical film *The Mirror.* Tarkovsky and his sister lived with his mother and his grandmother and much has been made of the feminine sensibility that influenced Tarkovsky as a child. In their book *The Films of Andrei Tarkovsky: A Visual Fugue* Vida T. Johnson and Graham Petrie revealed that, in contrast with the "official" version of his youth, Tarkovsky spent a good deal of time rebelling against this sensibility, especially during his teenage years. During World War II—called the Great Patriotic War in his

native Russia—Tarkovsky and his family lived in the town of Yuryevets, but returned to Moscow at the war's end.

Like all parents of her class, Maria Ivanovna sought to instill a love and vocation for the arts and the intellect in her children. Tarkovsky initially studied painting, literature, and music; initially enamored of the classic Russian composers, he later came to love the Germans, especially Bach. As a youth he carried on his person the poems his father wrote, which poems were unpublished at the time. Though their meetings were infrequent, Tarkovsky felt a great affinity for his father that fueled his natural rebellion against the parental authority wielded by his mother.

Film School

After graduating from high school in 1951 Tarkovsky entered the Institute for Oriental Studies in Moscow where he studied Arabic, but left during his second year. Various reason have been cited for his leaving, ranging from poor health to lack of interest. Whatever his motives, after leaving school Tarkovsky spent time in Siberia working on a geological expedition, and while there he decided his career direction. When he returned to Moscow he entered the Soviet State Film School where he became 1 of 15 students from a pool of 500 applicants selected to study under noted film director Mikhail Romm. In 1957 Tarkovsky married Irma Rausch, a classmate who was also studying directing, but switched to acting. The couple's son Arseny was born in 1962.

As a student Tarkovsky was involved in two collaborative films: *Ubiytsy (The Killers,* based on the short story by Ernest Hemingway) and *Segodnya uvolneniya ne budet (There Will Be No Leave Today),* a docudrama airing on Soviet television in 1959. The first film for which he took full directorial credit was his 1960 diploma film, *Katok i skripka (The Steamroller and the Violin),* for which he received high marks. It is a fairly conventional film in the Soviet-Realist tradition—although at 46 minutes longer than the usual student film of that period—about the relationship between a young boy who is studying the violin and a steamroller driver who protects the boy from bullies and guides him toward manhood. Tarkovsky tried to enlist the services of internationally renowned cameraman Sergei Urusevsky, among whose credits is *The Cranes Are Flying,* but failed. However Urusevsky's cinematographer, Vadim Yusov, would work often with Tarkovsky. Overall, the Russian press lauded Tarkovsky's first solo effort.

Built on Early Success

Tarkovsky's first feature film was *Ivanovo detstvo,* released in the United States as *My Name Is Ivan.* Completed in 1962, it immediately brought Tarkovsky international fame. The film tells the story of a 12-year-old boy whose mother (played by Tarkovsky's wife, Irma Rausch) is murdered by the invading Germans during World War II and who subsequently serves as a scout for the Soviet army. Ivan's lost childhood, shown in idyllic dream sequences, is contrasted with the stark devastation caused by the war. The filmmaker's former teacher, Romm, not only gave the film his exuberant stamp of approval, but praised Tarkovsky to the audience and critics at the film's first official showing. Internationally *Ivanovo detstvo* was also a success, sharing the coveted Golden Lion at the Venice Film Festival with *Cronaca familiare.* Overnight Tarkovsky's name became known to cineastes around the world.

After this success Tarkovsky chose as his second feature the epic film *Andrei Rublev,* having submitted the proposal for the film to the Mosfilm studio in 1961, even before completing *Ivanovo detstvo.* This was to become his general working procedure while in the Soviet Union. Tarkovsky and scenarist Andrei Mikhalkov-Konchalovsky— Tarkovsky's friend since his VGIK days and also a well-known director—worked on the script for two years before filming began. Nominally about the struggles of medieval Russian monk and icon painter Andrei Rublev, the film is also about the triumph of art in the face of barbarism; the function of art as an aspect of humanity's spiritual nature as personified by Rublev's spiritual journey; and the idea of art being integrated deeply into the lives of common people. The Soviet government did not fail to notice the allegorical critique that lay just below the film's surface, and *Andrei Rublev* was not released in the Soviet Union (or the USSR: Union of Soviet Socialist Republics) until 1971. Meanwhile, critics hailed it as a masterpiece: in 1969 it was shown out of competition at the Cannes Film Festival and awarded the Federation Internationale de la Presse Cinematographique (FIPRESCI) award, and two years later it was named best foreign film by the French Syndicate of Cinema Critics. In the film Tarkovsky made use of both black-and-white and color stock, the latter at the end of the film as the camera slowly pans on actual icons painted by Rublev in the 15th century. Grounding the film in reality provides a powerful ending to a dramatic story that reconnects art—and the film itself as a work of art—to its own spiritual beginnings.

While working on *Andrei Rublev* Tarkovsky separated from his wife, who played the part of the holy fool in the film, and began living with actress Larissa Pavlovna Yegorkina. Tarkovsky and Yegorkina were married in 1970, the year their son Andrei was born.

Science Fiction and Autobiography

During his five-year battle with the Soviet bureaucracy, Tarkovsky began working on his next film, *Solaris,* based on the science-fiction novel of the same name by Polish writer Stanislaw Lem. While *Solaris* is not the director's only science-fiction film, it is unique in the Tarkovsky oeuvre in that it features a love story, though it is slanted to reflect Tarkovsky's personal take on the subject. Set on a space station orbiting the planet Solaris, the film focuses on scientist Kris Kelvin, who has arrived to study the possibility of shutting down the station and returning its three inhabitants to earth. However one of the men, Kelvin's friend, has died and the other two are struggling with a force emanating from the planet that tests their sanity, as it will soon test Kelvin's. Solaris has the power to summon into actuality those who populate the memories—or perhaps the imaginations—of Kelvin and his fellow cosmonauts. In Kelvin's case it is his wife, who years earlier had committed suicide. Kelvin and his faux wife—he had been estranged from his real wife at the time of her death—renew their love in a manner that while physically gratifying is in reality an illusion. By the end of the film, through Tarkovsky's manipulation of time and narrative structure the camera pulls back to reveal that more than love is an illusion. In 1972 *Solaris* won both the jury Grand Prize and the FIPRESCI Award at Cannes.

Tarkovsky next embarked on his most personal film. In *Zerkalo (The Mirror,* 1975), he relives his own childhood and the dissolution of his family. Here the filmmaker goes beyond simply using color and black-and-white stock, incorporating other film clips to tell his story. *Zerkalo* actually begins with "found" footage showing a psychologist examining a young boy with a speech impediment who resorts to hypnotism to cure him. As the film continues, the filmmaker's subconscious seems to become unblocked and his filmic voice recounts the turmoil endured by a young boy old enough to be affected by the events of separation, family dissolution, and war. *Zerkalo* is intensely personal and few feature-length films have approached it in that respect, its subject matter and nonnarrative stream-of-consciousness structure more commonly the purview of experimental filmmakers. In a bit of Freudian revelation, the actress who plays the mother as a young woman also plays the narrator's wife. Tarkovsky adds to the film's subjectivity—which critics have noted verges on being almost too personal and cloying but is never completely so—by having his own mother play the elderly mother in the film. Tarkovsky's father is also in the film: he reads his poetry as a counterpoint to the actual narrator. Tarkovsky also cast his second wife and step-

daughter in the film. Not surprisingly, *Zarkalo* was another of Tarkovsky's films that ran afoul of the Soviet bureaucracy.

In 1977 Tarkovsky took a break from film directing to stage a version of Shakespeare's *Hamlet* that was poorly received by Moscow critics. This setback had little effect on his career, and he was soon immersed in his next film, 1979's *Stalker.* Based on the science-fiction novel *Roadside Picnic,* by Boris and Arkady Strugatsky, *Stalker* proved to be Tarkovsky's most problematic film from a production standpoint and the finished film required no cuts from Soviet censors. In the film a stalker—a person licensed to enter a mysterious "zone" which is devoid of life and in which the physics of reality are reshaped—agrees to lead two other men, a skeptical professor and a cynical writer, into the zone. After journeying into the zone the trio reach a room at the area's heart but decline to enter, instead retreating to their more comfortable worlds.

Numerous complications dogged filming of *Stalker,* not the least of which was that in April of 1978 Tarkovsky suffered a heart attack. Furthermore, he was unhappy with his shooting script; worse still was the revelation that more than halfway through the shooting it was discovered that the film stock was defective. Tarkovsky received permission to reshoot everything and the Strugatsky brothers rewrote the script to suit him. Their efforts were worth it; *Stalker* won the Ecumenical Jury prize at Cannes in 1980.

Asylum in Western Europe

In 1979 Tarkovsky worked in Italy directing the television film *Tempo di Viaggio (Time of Travel).* He also met with his friend, screenwriter Tonino Guerra, a colleague of Italian director Michelangelo Antonioni. Tarkovsky and Guerra had been planning a film for years, but little had come of it; now the two began planning what was to become the film *Nostalghia (Nostalgia,* 1983). New trouble with Soviet authorities arose when he applied for an exit visa for himself and his family to work in Italy: he and his wife were allowed to go but their son, Andrei, was denied a visa on the assumption that if they were together abroad the Tarkovskys would then apply for asylum. Nevertheless Tarkovsky would direct *Nostalghia* and when it was completed he did indeed decide to remain in Western Europe. Another battle with Soviet authorities ensued as he attempted to claim his son.

Nostalghia, cowritten by Guerra and Tarkovsky, is a personal film, though less intentionally so than *The Mirror.* The protagonist—also named Andrei—is a Russian poet living in the northern Italian province of Tuscany who is researching a biography of Russian composer and expatriate Pavel Sosnovsky. (The model for the fictional Sosnovsky was Maximillian Beryozovsky, an 18th-century Ukrainian composer.) Andrei, like Tarkovsky himself, finds that he is caught between two worlds: his homeland and his adopted land. Aside from *Andrei Rublev, Nostalghia* is considered Tarkovsky's most poetic film. At Cannes it was awarded the Ecumenical Jury prize and the FIPRESCI award, while Tarkovsky shared best director honors with Robert Bresson, director of *L'Argent.*

After *Nostalghia* Tarkovsky remained in Western Europe. He shot what would be his final film *Offret (The Sacrifice,* 1986), in Sweden with cinematographer Sven Nyquist. *Offret* revolves around a man's sacrifice to avert a nuclear holocaust, but Tarkovsky again plays with dreams and reality to keep the viewer off balance. At Cannes in 1986 *Offret* won the Ecumenical Jury prize, the Jury grand prize, and the FIPRESCI award, and went on to win a British Academy award for best foreign film two years later. Tarkovsky became ill during the filming of *Offret,* but it was not until after filming had been completed that he was diagnosed with lung cancer. Chemotherapy and other procedures failed to stem the disease, and, sensing the filmmaker's imminent death, Soviet authorities finally allowed his son an exit visa. Tarkovsky died in Paris on December 28, 1986, just a few weeks after his son rejoined him. He was posthumously awarded the Lenin Prize in 1990.

Tarkovsky's small body of work ranks among the world's greatest films, his greatest talent the ability to blend the natural into the unreal and vice versa. In many of his films Tarkovsky integrated classical art into the scene. In addition to the iconic art of *Rublev,* he filmed works by Breughel (in *Solaris*) and Jan Van Eyck's Ghent alterpiece (in *Stalker*). In *Nostalghia* Piero della Francesca's *Madonna of Childbirth* is seen in the opening sequence.

Tarkovsky has been described often as a poet of nature for his ability to capture the beauty and sometimes the horror to be found in the landscape and often employed the natural elements as visual metaphors. But if there is a single recognizable metaphor that runs through every one of his films it is water: Rivers, lakes, oceans, puddles, dripping water, rain—especially rain—in sudden torrents that seem to catch the characters by surprise. No filmmaker has been able to capture the movement—or the stillness—of water like Tarkovsky, and certainly none has used it so artistically throughout his career.

Books

Johnson, Vida T., and Graham Petrie, *The Films of Andrei Tarkovsky: A Visual Fugue,* Indiana University Press, 1994.
Tarkovsy, Andrey, *Time within Time: The Diaries 1970-1986,* translated by Kitty Hunter-Blair, Verso, 1993.

Online

"Andrei Tarkovsky," http://www.senseofcinema.com/contents/directors/02/tarkovsky.html (January 28, 2003). □

Kateri Tekakwitha

Kateri Tekakwitha (1656–1680) is the first Native American to be venerated by the Roman Catholic church. As a Christian convert, in an Iroquois community that possessed a longstanding hostility to all things French, Tekakwitha became an outcast in her village and was forced to flee to a mission near Montreal, where she died at the age of 24. Some-

times called "the Lily of the Mohawk," she was beatified by Pope John Paul II in 1980.

Caught Between Two Cultures

Tekakwitha was born in 1656 in Ossernenon, near what is modern Auriesville, New York. Her father, Kenneronkwa, was a Mohawk and member of its Turtle clan. Her mother, Kahenta, was Algonquin and hailed from a village near Trois Rivieres, Quebec. Kahenta had been converted to Christianity by early missionaries to the area. The Algonquin were one of first Native American populaces to ally with French traders but were bitter foes of the Mohawk. The Mohawk were part of the mighty Iroquois League, a confederation of Mohawk, Oneida, Onondaga, Cayuga, and Seneca nations. Politically organized and known as fierce belligerents, the Iroquois began trading with the Dutch and obtained firearms from them and used the weapons to renew hostilities with their neighbors beginning with a 1649 attack on the Huron. Several other communities were dispersed, among them the Algonquin to which Tekakwitha's mother belonged.

War had decimated the Iroquois ranks, however, and it became standard practice to take their defeated as prisoners and subsume them into the population of their Five Nations. Tekakwitha's mother had been captured by the Mohawk around 1653 and became part of a community in this way. Her union with Kenneronkwa resulted in a son and daughter, Tekakwitha. In 1660, when Tekakwitha was four years old, a smallpox epidemic decimated the community, and both her parents as well as her brother died. She survived the outbreak, though it left her face scarred and her vision impaired. She was taken in by her uncle, a village chief, who was a great foe of the Roman Catholic missionaries from France in the area. When Tekakwitha was ten years old the French emerged victorious over the Iroquois League, and the peace treaty permitted the determined order of Jesuit priests, whom the Native Americans called "Black Robes," access to Mohawk villages in order to convert the residents to Christianity.

Refused an Arranged Marriage

Tekakwitha's uncle was forced to be hospitable to three Jesuits fathers named Fremin, Bruyas, and Pierron, and assigned the 11-year-old Tekakwitha to look after them. She was reportedly impressed by their exemplary manners and conduct, and though she likely knew her mother was Christian, this may have been her first genuine introduction to Christianity. Eventually the Jesuits established St. Peter's Mission in 1670 and consecrated a chapel inside one of the traditional Iroquois longhouse dwellings. Two missionaries who took over noted that as a teen Tekakwitha became increasingly devout and rejected her family's attempts to arrange a marriage. They grew increasingly angry at her behavior and sometimes denied her food for her obstinacy.

It is likely that Tekakwitha had heard about a community of unwed women in Quebec who lived together in devotion to their Roman Catholic faith, as the Jesuits did; these women were called the Ursuline sisters. There was also some history of virgins and voluntary chastity in the Iroquois nation. However, Europeans had reportedly given these women alcohol and their behavior had brought shame on the Iroquois; such professions of celibacy had subsequently been prohibited. Tekakwitha's determination to remain unmarried was helped by the arrival of the Jesuit James de Lamberville in 1674 at St. Peter's. Tekakwitha confided in him that she wished to fully convert, and he encouraged her in that goal. After catechism classes, she was baptized on Easter Sunday of 1676 and given the name "Catherine," or Kateri.

Shunned by Community

Immediately Tekakwitha became a pariah in her village. "Her new religion angered her relatives and the villagers, who saw her conversion as a traitorous embracing of the white man's religion and a rejection of their own customs," noted *America* writer George M. Anderson. She remained there six months and was forbidden food on Sundays and Christian holidays because she refused to work in accordance with Christian doctrine. Her relatives and the other villagers increased their harassment campaign and even accused her of attempting to seduce other women's husbands at the remote prayer site she liked to visit.

To rescue her, Lamberville sent Tekakwitha to the Jesuit mission of Saint Francis Xavier, at Kanawake, Quebec, on the Sault Saint Louis straits. She made the 200-mile trip in 1677 with the help of other converted Native Americans, at a time

when her vision was worsening. Her relatives were furious and sent a search party after her, but she was able to hide in tall grasses and elude them with the help of her traveling companions. The Saint Francis Xavier mission had several Christian Native Americans in residency, about 150 families, and Tekakwitha found a sympathetic spiritual mentor in Anastasie Tegonhatsiongo, who had known her mother. Tegonhatsiongo, however, agreed with Tekakwitha's family and believed it would be best if she married.

Known for Her Piety

Tekakwitha was still determined to become a nun, however, and at one point made a trip to Montreal and met the sisters of the Hotel-Dieu hospital there. She had gone with two other Native American women, and the three resolved to form their own religious community back at Kanawake. Tegonhatsiongo requested the intervention of one Father Cholenic, who consulted his superiors on the matter; all agreed that it was far too early for an exclusively Native American cloister, but Tekakwitha was finally granted her wish and allowed to take her vow of chastity on March 25, 1679, the Feast of Annunciation.

Tekakwitha's devotion to her religion was legendary. Her "penances," wrote Anderson in *America*, "went far beyond such standard practices as fasting and vigils. Walking barefoot in snow and whipping herself with reeds until her back bled were among the milder ones." She ate little, and sometimes mixed what she did with ashes first. She stood for hours barefoot in the snow before the cross, praying the rosary, and spent more hours inside the mission's unheated chapel on bare knees on the stone floor. She reportedly slept on a bed of thorns for three nights and even arranged to be flagellated. Such ascetic practices were the hallmarks of the truly devout Catholic saints, but they also had some precedence in Iroquois spirituality as well. Its system of belief held great store in dreams, which were termed "the language of the soul." To not dream, the Iroquois believed, was unhealthy, and so for those that could not attain or remember their dreams, there were means to induce a trance—either via a sweat-bath, fasting, chanting, or even acts of self-mutilation. The mixing of food and ashes that Tekakwitha tried also had its origins in these practices.

In the end, Tekakwitha's punishing penances were debilitating, and she died at the age of 24 on April 17, 1680. According the Jesuits who prayed over her body afterward, the smallpox scars on her face miraculously disappeared some 15 minutes after she died. On this account she was beatified by Pope John Paul II on June 30, 1980. A petition for her canonization was submitted to the Vatican in 1884, and her sainthood requires proof of one more miracle. There are quarterlies in her honor, among them *Lily of the Mohawks*, and Native American Catholics consider her an important historical and spiritual figure. She is also the patroness of the environment and ecology.

Books

Catholic Encyclopedia, Volume XIV, Robert Appleton Company, 1912, Online Edition, 2003.
Notable Native Americans, Gale, 1995.

Periodicals

America, October 1, 2001; December 2, 2002.
Daily News (Los Angeles, CA), September 12, 1999.
National Catholic Reporter, February 16, 1996. ☐

Mary Church Terrell

For 70 years, Mary Church Terrell (1863–1954) was a prominent advocate of African American and women's rights. She traveled around the world speaking about the achievements of African Americans and raising awareness of the conditions in which they lived.

Mary Eliza Church was born in Memphis, Tennessee, on September 23, 1863, to two recently emancipated slaves. Her father, Robert Reed Church, was the son of a white river boat captain and a black house servant. After settling in Memphis, Robert Church operated a saloon. Mary's mother, Louisa Ayers Church, had been a house servant who was well educated and well treated before her emancipation.

Robert and Louisa Church were both light-skinned African American blacks who lived a comfortable life in a white neighborhood outside Memphis where Louisa operated a successful hair salon. Mary, known as Mollie, had a brother four years younger. She grew up with white friends and knew little about the condition in which most African American people lived until she was about five years old. When her maternal grandmother, a former house slave, told her stories about the brutality of slave owners, Terrell began to understand the history of African Americans. In her autobiography, *A Colored Woman in a White World,* Terrell described how she cried when she heard her grandmother's stories and her grandmother comforted her, saying, "Never mind, honey. Gramma ain't a slave no more."

Robert and Louisa Church divorced when Mary was very young and Louisa moved north to New York where she opened another, equally successful, hair salon. Because educational opportunities for African American children were poor in Memphis, Terrell was sent north to live with her mother when she was six years old. Terrell was one of only a handful of African American children in the school she now attended, and she was sometimes ridiculed because of her race. When studying the Emancipation Proclamation, a fellow student made a rude remark to Terrell. In her autobiography she described her reaction: "I resolved that so far as this descendant of slaves was concerned, she would show those white girls and boys whose forefathers had always been free that she was their equal in every respect. . . . I felt I must hold high the banner of my race."

Terrell eventually attended Oberlin High School in Oberlin, Ohio, and from there enrolled at Oberlin College where she earned a bachelor of arts degree in 1884. After graduating she returned to Memphis, where her father had remarried. By this time, Robert Church had become very wealthy. In 1879 Memphis experienced a yellow fever epidemic, causing residents to evacuate the city in a panic, selling their property for next to nothing as they fled. Robert Church invested all of his money in real estate during the evacuation and within a few years he was a millionaire.

Began Teaching Career

Robert Church was opposed to his daughter working; he wished her to remain in Memphis and marry. But Terrell was restless; she had been looking forward to a teaching career and promoting the welfare of her race. After a year in Memphis she returned to the Midwest, taking a teaching job at Wilberforce University, near Xenia, Ohio. Her father was incensed that she had defied his wishes and for a time he refused to communicate with her.

In 1887 Terrell moved to Washington, D.C. where she taught Latin at the M Street Colored High School. After a year, her father, with whom she had by now reconciled, sent her to study in Europe. She spent two years traveling in France, Germany, and Italy, countries free from racial discrimination. She considered staying in Europe, but said in her autobiography, "I knew I would be much happier trying to promote the welfare of my race in my native land, working under certain hard conditions, than I would be living in a foreign land where I could enjoy freedom from prejudice, but where I would make no effort to do the work which I then believed it was my duty to do."

Terrell returned to the M Street School, where she was reunited with her supervisor, Robert Heberton Terrell. Robert Terrell was one of the first African Americans to graduate from Harvard University, and he had paid court to Terrell before her trip to Europe. In 1891 the two were married, and they made their new home in Washington, D.C. Marriage marked the end of Terrell's teaching career, since married women did not work. Robert Terrell attended law school at night and left teaching to work as an attorney and eventually became the first African American municipal judge in the nation's capitol city.

The first few years of the Terrells' marriage were marked by illness and disappointment. Mary Terrell was often sick and within five years had lost three babies shortly after their birth. Her fourth child, a girl named Phyllis, was born healthy in 1898. The couple adopted Mary's ten-year-old niece, also named Mary, in 1905.

Raised Awareness of Discrimination

Terrell devoted her life to improving the lives of African Americans and especially women. Her public service began when she was appointed to the Washington, D.C. school board. The first African American woman on the board, she served from 1895 to 1901 and again from 1906 to 1911.

Terrell and her husband were both advocates of women's suffrage. Terrell often marched for women's rights in front of the White House and Capitol Hill. At meetings of the National American Woman Suffrage Association, a group led by suffragist Susan B. Anthony, Terrell encouraged the group to include African American women in their agenda. In 1898 Anthony invited Terrell to address the group on "The Progress and Problems of Colored Women." A few years later she spoke again, this time without regard to race, on "The Justice of Woman Suffrage." Terrell soon earned a reputation as an effective speaker and activist.

After passage of the 19th Amendment to the U.S. Constitution giving women the right to vote, the Republican Party named Terrell director of Colored Women of the East. She organized efforts in eastern states encouraging women to use their right to vote.

Advocating on behalf of African American women led Terrell to found the National Association of Colored Women in 1896. She served two terms as the group's president and then was named honorary president for life. She was also a charter member of the National Association for the Advancement of Colored People (NAACP).

Terrell's oratory skills earned her a position as a professional lecturer for Slayton Lyceum Bureau. She traveled throughout the south and east speaking of the achievements of African American women and advocating for justice and education for African Americans and people of color around the world. Terrell was surprised at how little white people knew about the conditions in which African Americans lived, and she worked to raise awareness of discrimination, disenfranchisement, and lynching. She also wrote numerous magazine and newspaper articles highlighting civil rights issues.

On The Road

It was not easy or safe for a African American woman to travel alone in the South during the early 20th century. Terrell was light skinned and was sometimes mistaken for a white person. Although she did not advocate African American people crossing "the color line" and living as white, she did not draw attention to her race if she could get away with using white accommodations. When she was recognized as African American, she was prohibited from eating in restaurants, traveling in Pullman cars, or staying in most hotels. She described many examples of such discrimination in her autobiography.

Despite her political activism, Terrell was devoted to her children and never left home for more then three weeks at a time. Her mother lived with her family for 15 years and cared for the children when Terrell was away. Daughters Phyllis and Mary both graduated from college and became teachers. Daughter Mary was a musician as well.

Terrell's speaking engagements took her abroad for the first time in 1904, when she spoke at the International Congress of Women in Berlin, Germany. Her speech raised awareness in Europe of the race problem in America. She spoke at the International Congress of Women again following World War I in 1919. Although the conference included women from around the world, Terrell was the only woman of color in attendance. She felt that she represented not only the United States, but all the non-white countries of the world. In her speech she emphasized the importance of justice and fairness for people of color, stressing that a lasting peace will never come to pass while inequality exists among the races.

Elderly Activist

Robert Terrell suffered a stroke in 1921 and died four years later. Terrell was 62 years old when she was widowed. Six years later she fell in love again, but because the man was married the relationship ended. In 1937, when Terrell was aged 73, her brother died, leaving her to raise her ten-year-old nephew, Thomas Church.

In 1940 the 77-year-old activist's autobiography, *A Colored Woman in a White World,* was published. The book describes Terell's childhood, education, and her years of travel and advocacy on behalf of African American rights. Terrell described the prejudice she encountered in restaurants, hotels, theaters, education, employment, while buying a home—virtually every aspect of her life. She described times when, weak with hunger, she had to pass by restaurants in Washington, D.C. because they did not serve African American people. She recounted how she was offered jobs or club memberships, only to have the offers revoked when it was discovered that she was African American. While Terrell intended the book to be a forthright account of the prejudice she had experienced, the autobiography described events in polite terms and was less critical of American society than she perhaps intended. In contrast, her diaries reveal a more emotional response to the treatment she had endured.

As she aged Terrell became more forceful in her fight for civil rights. She appeared before the U.S. Congress to urge passage of an anti-lynching bill. In 1946 she applied for membership in the American Association of University Women. When her application was rejected, she appealed and after three years the board finally voted to admit African American women.

In 1949, when she was 86 years old, Terrell was invited to be honorary chairperson of the coordinating committee for the Enforcement of the D.C. Anti-Discrimination Law in Washington, D.C. The District of Columbia had on its books 1872 and 1873 laws prohibiting exclusion of African American people from restaurants, theaters, and other public places, although these statutes had never been enforced. In fact, they had been illegally deleted from the District Code in the 1890s. Terrell, not satisfied with being honorary chair, became the group's working chairperson. She presided over meetings, spoke at rallies, and on January 7, 1950, led a group of four African American people to Thompson's cafeteria, located two blocks from the White House. Terrell and her companions put soup on their trays and sat down to eat. They were asked to leave, prompting the committee to file a lawsuit charging the restaurant with violating their civil rights.

While the suit dragged through the courts, Terrell and her group met with restaurant and store owners trying to convince them to open their lunch counters to everyone. Some businesses complied, but many more remained closed to African Americans. Terrell encouraged boycotts and picketed the holdouts. For two years Terrell, now aged and stooped, led the picket line day after day, in all kinds of weather. In *Black Foremothers: Three Lives,* a younger picketer is quoted as recalling: "When my feet hurt I wasn't going to let a women fifty years older than I do what I couldn't do. I kept on picketing." One by one, the restaurants gave in and on June 8, 1953, the U.S. Supreme Court ruled in Terrell's favor.

Terrell continued to fight battles on behalf of her race until her death. Her 90th birthday was marked by a party for 700 people and included a White House reception. Addressing the gathering, she pledged to see an end to racial discrimination within Washington, D.C. by the time she reached 100 years of age. Her wish would not be granted, however; a few months later, on July 24, 1954, Terrell died of cancer at her summer home in Highland Beach, Maryland. Her body lay in state in the headquarters building of the National Association of Colored Women, which she had co-founded nearly 60 years earlier. Thousands paid their respects.

Books

Notable American Women: The Modern Period, edited by Barbara Sicherman and Carol Hurd Green, Belknap Press, 1980.

Sterling, Dorothy, *Black Foremothers: Three Lives,* Feminist Press, 1988.

Terrell, Mary Church, *A Colored Woman in a White World,* Ransdell Inc., 1940.

Women in World History: A Biographical Encyclopedia, Anne Commire, editor, Yorkin Publications, 1999. □

Theano

Theano (born c. 546 B.C.), the wife of the Greek mathematician and philosopher Pythagoras, ran the Pythagorean school in southern Italy in the late sixth century B.C. following her husband's death. She is credited with having written treatises on mathematics, physics, medicine, and child psychology. Her most important work is said to have been an elucidation of the principle of the Golden Mean.

Theano's husband, Pythagoras (c. 582–500 B.C.), was inspired one of the most influential sects in the ancient world. Best known for devising the Pythagorean Theorem—which states that the sum of the squares of the sides of a right triangle is equal to the square of the hypotenuse—Pythagoras was considered the greatest scientist of antiquity by classical Greek scholars and is considered to have been the first mathematician. However, given that Pythagoras lived seven generations before Plato, most of the information about him comes from fairly late sources—a few as late as the third century A.D. Another problem is that some of these sources are of doubtful reliability. However, references to Pythagoras's ideas can be found in earlier writings, including those of Empedocles, Heraclitus, Herodotus, Plato, and Aristotle.

Influenced by Her Husband

Theano's husband is believed to have been born on the large island of Samos, just off the coast of Asia Minor. Pythagoras reportedly left the island when he was 18 and began traveling throughout the Mediterranean world to study with a variety of teachers, including Thales in Miletus. According to some accounts, he also spent time in Egypt, Babylon, Crete, and Sparta. He is believed to have moved to the Greek colony of Croton in southern Italy around 531 B.C., at the age of about fifty-six.

In Croton Pythagoras established a quasi-religious society dedicated to mathematical and philosophical speculations about the nature of the universe. He is reported to have taught purification of the spirit through study and proper diet and to have urged self-control and self-awareness through meditative techniques. However, because the Pythagorean community swore its members to secrecy very little about the society was made public during Pythagoras's lifetime.

There is, however, evidence that Pythagoras's academy accepted men and women on an equal basis. By some accounts there were at least 28 women teachers and students in the school, which is said to have eventually numbered some 300 adherents. Concerned with the quasi-religious, quasi-political study of mathematics and philosophy, the academy's religious ideas tended to be mystical, while its approach to natural philosophy was entirely rational.

Theano

Peter Gorman, writing in *Pythagoras: A Life,* cited Porphyry's account of Pythagoras's arrival in Croton. According to Porphyry, Pythagoras was at that time "tall," with "great charm and elegance in his voice." The mathematician reportedly spoke to the council of elders at Croton "with many fine words" and later addressed the school children and, finally, the women. Porphyry added: "One of the women is especially famous, Theano by name."

According to Gorman, Theano was the daughter of the Orphic disciple Brontinus. The Orphics were members of a religious group that centered its beliefs around the death and resurrection symbolism in the Egyptian deity Osiris. The Orphics further believed in reincarnation and an afterlife spent with the gods. Like the Orphics, the Pythagoreans owed many of their beliefs to Egyptian mythologies, so it is not surprising that Brontinus eventually became a disciple of Pythagoras. More significantly for the historical record, he would eventually become Pythagoras's father-in-law.

Brontinus's daughter—and Pythagoras's future wife—Theano also became Pythagoras's student. Pythagoras was reportedly Theano's senior by 36 years. According to Gorman, Theano would later bear Pythagoras a daughter named Damo and a son named Telauges. By other accounts, Pythagoras and Theano had three daughters, Damo, Myria, and Arignote, and two sons.

Theano is said to have eventually become a teacher of mathematics at the school in Croton. Legend has it that Pythagoras ran his school without discrimination based on gender. If true, this policy would have set him apart from his contemporaries, who granted no educational or political rights to women. In Pythagoras's time, women were usually considered property and relegated at best to the roles of housekeeper or spouse.

According to some of Pythagoras's earliest biographers, the philosopher and mathematician had other female students besides Theano. One source identifies a woman by the name of Aristoclea as a member of the early community. A third-century A.D. source lists 16 women who belonged to Pythagoras's school. Some historians have argued that the survival of these womens' names so long after Pythagoras's lifetime attests to the importance of women scholars in his school.

Death of Pythagoras

After Pythagoras's academy gained control of the local government of Croton, the local populace grew to resent the Pythagorean aristocracy and destroyed the school. The teachers and students were reportedly either killed or exiled. By some accounts Pythagoras himself was killed during this uprising.

Surviving the attack, Theano reportedly ran the dispersed Pythagorean School following her husband's death with the assistance of two of her daughters; in fact, one source says that Theano's daughter Damo was responsible for safeguarding her father's writings following his death. Theano has been credited with writing treatises on mathematics, physics, medicine, and child psychology, and there

are reportedly references to her work in the writings of Athenaeus, Suidas, Diogenes Laertius, and Iamblichus.

Theano and her daughters acquired reputations as excellent physicians. According to the Pythagoreans, the human body is a miniature copy of the universe as a whole. In a debate with the physician Euryphon on the nature of fetal development, Theano and her daughters reportedly prevailed with their argument that the fetus is viable after the seventh month.

Offshoots of the Pythagorean academy continued for some 200 years after its founder's death. In the fifth century B.C. there were reportedly still several prominent women members of the Pythagorean school.

Theano's Writings

There were reportedly many individuals—both teachers and students—living communally at Pythagoras's school. Because all writings were published under Pythagoras's name, it is difficult to determine who was actually responsible for which work. However, given that Theano was a member of the Pythagorean academy, certain facts of her existence can be taken for granted.

There are no surviving written works by any of the Pythagoreans; all that is known of them comes from the writings of others, including Plato and Herodotus. Whenever one refers to the writings of Pythagoras or his students, one is in fact referencing a body of work that was done between approximately 585 B.C. and 400 B.C. The discoveries of the Pythagoreans were considered to be the common property of all members of the school, which was organized along the lines of a brotherhood or secret society.

According to one source, Theano's principal works included a *Life of Pythagoras,* a *Cosmology, The Theorem of the Golden Mean, The Theory of Numbers, The Construction of the Universe,* and a work titled *On Virtue.* None of the primary sources that remain, however, reveals anything of her personality.

Theano's most important work is said to have been the principle of the Golden Mean. Like the geometrical constant pi, the Golden Mean is an irrational number that shows up in many relationships in nature. Its decimal value is approximately 1.6180. In geometry, a "golden" rectangle is one whose sides are related by the Golden Mean ratio, for example 13:8. Both the ancient Greeks and Egyptians designed buildings and monuments with proportions based on the Golden Mean. It is now known that some growth patterns observed in nature occur in accordance with the Golden Mean, examples being the spirals in the nautilus shell and the ratio of clockwise to counterclockwise spirals in a sunflower.

In a treatise on the construction of the universe attributed to Theano, she reportedly argues that the universe consists of ten concentric spheres: the Sun, the Moon, Saturn, Jupiter, Mars, Venus, Mercury, Earth, Counter-Earth, and the stars. The Sun, Moon, Saturn, Jupiter, Mars, Venus, and Mercury move in orbit about a central fire. The stars are fixed and are not considered to move. In Theano's theory, the distances between the spheres and the central fire are in the same arithmetic proportion as the intervals in the musical scales.

The Pythagorean mathematical investigations into the relation between numerical ratios and musical intervals reportedly extended to other areas as well. According to one tradition Pythagoras could cure ailing psyches with his music.

In the Pythagorean school, matter was held to be discontinuous. According to Aristotle, the Pythagoreans believed numbers to be the ultimate component of material objects. Because astronomy and music are ultimately reduced to arithmetic and geometry in the Pythagorean framework, even those disciplines were considered to be mathematical subjects. Thus numbers for the Pythagoreans played much the same role that atoms do in modern scientific theory. Significantly, the Pythagorean cosmology, with later modifications by Plato, Eudoxus, and Aristotle, formed the basis of natural philosophy during the Middle Ages.

A Second Theano

The confusion surrounding Theano's life is compounded by the existence of a second Pythagorean woman of the same name who reportedly lived in the fourth century B.C. According to a tenth-century source known as the "Suda," this Theano was a Pythagorean woman from Metapontum, a town along the coast of southern Italy not far from Croton.

Based on this Theano's surviving writings, it would appear that women were still influential participants in the Pythagorean school in the fourth century. In fact, a literature directed to female readership had evolved by then. Some historians have speculated, however, that the writings attributed to this Theano were actually written by men, using the name of Pythagoras's wife as a pseudonym.

Books

Alic, Margaret, *Hypatia's Heritage: A History of Women in Science from Antiquity to the Late Nineteenth Century,* Women's Press, 1986.

Gorman, Peter, *Pythagoras: A Life,* Routledge & Kegan Paul, 1979.

Kline, Morris, *Mathematical Thought from Ancient to Modern Times,* Oxford University Press, 1972.

Olsen, Kirstin, *Chronology of Women's History,* Greenwood Press, 1994.

Snyder, Jane McIntosh, *The Woman and the Lyre: Woman Writers in Classical Greece and Rome,* Southern Illinois University Press, 1989. □

Alma Woodsey Thomas

Abstract painter Alma Woodsey Thomas (1891–1978) devoted her life to the youth of Washington and other local communities, both as a teacher and as an organizer of cultural events. In 1924 she became the first graduate of Howard University's School of Fine Arts. She possessed a natural sense of genius for color and form and upon retiring from teaching at age 68 embarked on a successful career as a professional artist.

Born Alma Woodsey Thomas on September 22, 1891, in Columbus, Georgia, she was the eldest of four daughters of John Maurice Harris, a teacher, and Amelia (Cantey) Thomas. Highly cultured and socially involved, the Thomas family owned a large Victorian home on 21st Street in Columbus's Rose Hill district, where Thomas was born and lived until the age of 15. As children, Thomas and her sisters enjoyed memorable visits to the home of their maternal grandparents, on a plantation near Fort Mitchell, Alabama. In her youth, she displayed a fondness for nature and the outdoors and enjoyed molding teacups and other pottery from the plentiful red Georgia clay.

The Thomas family remained in Georgia until the idyllic pace of life was disturbed by a period of racially motivated rioting in the fall of 1906. Unnerved by the violence, Thomas's parents took the family to Washington, D.C., arriving on July 31, 1907, after traveling by train from Georgia. They set up housekeeping at a new residence at 1530 15th Street NW, where Thomas was to live most of her life for the next 71 years, until her death in 1978.

Washington, like many of the southern United States, remained segregated in the early 1900s. Regardless, the Thomases anticipated better educational opportunities for their four children and greater cultural exposure for the family as a whole. Opportunities for employment were more plentiful too, for John Thomas as well as for his wife, who as a dress designer catered in her craft to the affluent women of Washington.

Talented in math and possessing an artistic bent, Thomas attended Armstrong Manual Training High School from 1907 to 1911, where she excelled in architectural drawing. For two years after high school she specialized in early child development at Miner Normal School, obtaining a teaching certificate in 1913. She took her first teaching job with the Princess Anne, Maryland, school district.

Two years later, in 1915 Thomas moved to Wilmington, Delaware, to the Thomas Garrett Settlement House. There she lived and worked at the community-operated school for resident children, teaching arts and crafts. She also devoted her time to making costumes for various school productions and to community arts productions.

Art Educator

In 1921 Thomas entered Howard University, initially contemplating a career in costume design. With that goal in mind she enrolled in a home economics program but changed paths by the end of her first semester, enrolling instead in the school's newly launched fine arts program at the urging of professor James V. Herring who recognized her talent and became her mentor.

Thomas's artwork during her years at Howard was founded almost exclusively in realism. In addition to many costume sketches and designs, she painted with oils and sculpted in ceramics. Also among her many three-dimensional works is the plaster "Bust of a Young Girl," completed around 1923, which is believed to be constructed in the image of her youngest sister, Fannie Cantey Thomas, then deceased. Among Thomas's most recognized works as a student is a still life done in oils in 1923. It is an untitled study depicting a vase with flowers; the bust of a woman appears to the right of the vase, in front of a draped background. Some experts believe that Thomas personally endowed the bust with the specific features and head covering that impart its distinctively African appearance and that the original model did not appear that way.

Thomas received a bachelor of fine arts degree in 1924, becoming the first ever to graduate from the Howard program. She moved briefly to Pennsylvania to teach at the Cheyney Training School for Teachers, returning to Washington after one term, to join the teaching staff at Shaw Junior High School. On February 2, 1925, she began teaching at Shaw, and in the process opened the door to a 35-year career at that school.

At Shaw, Thomas immersed herself totally in her life choices both as an educator and artist. She spent her summers in New York, at Teacher's College, Columbia University, where in 1934 she received a master's degree in fine arts education. In 1935 she summered in New York City as a student of England's premiere marionette maker, Tony Sarg. Thereafter she worked in collaboration with a Washington-based painter, Lois Mailou Jones, creating colorful string-operated puppets together. With Thomas contributing the design and fashioning the pieces of the puppets from balsa wood, Jones gave the toys a personality, using watercolors to paint faces on the wooden heads. Together the women created entire puppet troupes and sponsored performances at local venues such as the Phillis Wheatley Young Women's Christian Association and Howard University's Gallery of Art. Thomas produced popular children's classics—such as *Alice in Wonderland*—as puppet shows and wrote assorted scripts of her own. The need for these cultural events was especially acute because it came at a time in U.S. history when African American children were denied access to similar programs at the National Theater.

In 1936 she organized the Washington School Arts League. This program, also geared toward children of African American descent, was devised to sponsor and encourage tours, lectures, and other presentations at cultural venues such as museums and colleges. In 1938 she conceived of a program to create art galleries within the Washington schools. Beginning with a temporary exhibit at Shaw, she borrowed selected art works from the Howard Gallery and expanded the program from that starting point.

Community Arts Patron

Thomas with her cultural influence made deep inroads into the Washington community, extending well beyond the youth programs with which she is most frequently associated. In 1943 she contributed to the efforts of two Howard professors, Herring and Alonzo J. Aden, to found the Barnett Aden Gallery at their residence at 126 Randolph Street NW. The gallery quickly found its niche in the Washington cul-

tural scene and became a popular gathering place for local society. Barnett Aden attracted patrons from diverse social, political, and artistic backgrounds within the national capital. Near the end of the decade, Jones and Céline Tabary opened a more casual space, called "The Little Paris Studio," at Jones's 1220 Quincy Street NE residence. There, too, Thomas could be found frequently, not only with her students, but also relaxing in private.

As the Washington artistic community experienced major growth throughout the 1940s, Thomas in 1950, at age 59, enrolled at American University to continue her education and expand her study of art. A subsequent metamorphosis from full-time educator to full-time artist ensued. Her works from this early period are characterized as somber and heavy, both in color and mood. Blues and browns predominate, with rough, dense shapes. Among her many oils on canvas, she painted "Grandfather's House" in 1952, evoking the natural serenity of the Cantey homestead in Alabama. The complacent emotion of the plantation is represented predominantly in blues with heavy brown trees and foliage. The painting hangs at the Columbus Museum in Georgia.

The artist's evolution toward color and abstraction can be traced through the progression of her impressionist still life paintings. "Joe Summerford's Still Life Study," also dated 1952, is heavy with detail; dark shadows and olive tones are used freely. Her migration toward abstraction is foreshadowed only in the reflective surfaces such as the face of a clock and the glassy bulb of an empty vase. The objects appear on a table of brown wood, and the exposed background wall is brown also and significantly darker.

"Still Life with Chrysanthemums," from 1954, retains a sense of realism in the foreground objects while fading to abstraction with allusions to sun and foliage in the backdrop. By 1958, with "Blue and Brown Still Life," Thomas's reality fades into coherent blocks of color, while allowing for specific images such as the cat tossing yarn and the appearance of vessels in the background. The environment overall is noncommittal, in shades of browns and blues.

Emergence of Color and Abstraction

After spending the summer in Europe in 1958, Thomas's work underwent a gradual migration toward vivid color as she abandoned the use of oils, deferring to watercolor. The browns were colorfully split apart to reveal the reds and yellows as seen in "City Lights" and "Yellow and Blue," both from 1959. Increasing levels of activity in the paintings are depicted by black brush strokes in the foreground, as reds emerge and sometimes overpower the backgrounds. This style is seen prominently in "Macy's Parade" and "Untitled Study" in red and green, both from 1960. Having retired on January 31 of that year, Thomas held a solo exhibition at Washington's Dupont Theatre Art Gallery from September through December. By 1961 her move toward abstraction and geometric form was all but complete with "Blue Abstraction."

Yet the total abandonment of impressionism was yet to be accomplished by Thomas. Her devotion to realism is vividly evident in "March on Washington," completed in 1964.

The painting, with its infusion of a socio-political backdrop, employs the new reds and yellows of her 1960s period, while reprising her moody blues from the 1950s. Thomas in fact participated in the August 28 March on Washington in 1963, and this work serves as her commentary.

Maturity of Style

Thomas in her signature style of later years employs an abundance of square stripes of acrylic color that flow about the canvas. Aerial views and bird's eye representations of trees, leaves, rivers, and brooks typify this period. Primary colors break forth from muted backgrounds, as in her 1969 "Azaleas." Also during these years she produced her Earth and Space series, including "Light Blue Nursery" and "The Eclipse," in 1968 and 1970, respectively.

Working from her first floor quarters in the same 15th Street NW home of her adolescence, Thomas was inspired most distinctively by a holly tree that grew within the view of a bay window in the living area. There, by means of the holly tree, the indoor world was insulated from the rush of traffic on the busy street outside, and her impressions of the holly tree surface repeatedly in the imagery of her brush-stroke patterns.

By the 1970s Thomas worked with increasing frequency on very large canvases of 72 by 52 inches, sometimes combining two or three of these large panels into a single image. Often she tied a strip of elastic around the frame as she painted, to guide the movement of the color. "Wind and Crepe Myrtle Concerto" and the paneled "Elysian Fields" from 1973 are typical of this phase of her art. A sense of movement characterizes her work from this time and is evident especially in the progression between the panels of "Red Azaleas Singing and Dancing Rock and Roll Music" in 1976. News of Thomas's work, ripe with personal caché, seeped into the cosmopolitan art world in 1972 when the Whitney Museum in New York held a solo exhibit of her paintings. The Corcoran Gallery in Washington held a retrospective of her work that year, and in 1973 the Martha Jackson Gallery featured her work also as a solo exhibit.

Suffering from arthritis and having tripped and broken her hip at home in 1974, she was inactive for two years while convalescing. She resumed painting in 1976. A second exhibit at the Martha Jackson Gallery opened on October 23, 1976, and was in retrospect Thomas's final solo exhibition prior to her death in 1978. In all she was featured in 16 solo exhibitions from 1959 to 1976.

On February 24, 1978, she died at Howard University Hospital in Washington, D.C., after emergency surgery to repair a damaged artery. She had carried her paint box and drawing pad with her to the hospital, where she arrived by ambulance. The luminous "Rainbow" of 1978 is her last known work.

Thomas defined both abstraction and impressionism on her own terms in the mid-twentieth century. She was a contemporary of those artists who comprised the Washington Color School of painting—including Gene Davis and Kenneth Noland—yet she rejected the practice of staining her canvases to create the void of relief that typifies that movement. Thomas's paintings in contrast forced texture to

the forefront and her layered acrylics exhort the feel of the colors.

Books

Alma W. Thomas: A Retrospective of the Paintings, Fort Wayne Museum of Art, 1998.
Foresta, Merry A., *A Life in Art: Alma Thomas 1891–1978,* Smithsonian Institution Press, 1981.

Periodicals

Art in America, January 2002.
New York Times Biographical Edition, May 1972.
New York Times Biographical Service, February 1978. □

Bertel Thorvaldsen

During the early 19th century, Danish artist Bertel Thorvaldsen (1770–1848) was considered the greatest sculptor in Europe. A student of classical art, he incorporated the styles of ancient Greece and Rome into his own work. In doing so, he became one of the leaders of the Neoclassical movement, which spanned the 18th and 19th centuries.

Born in Denmark

Bertel Thorvaldsen was born in Copenhagen, Denmark, on November 13, 1770. He was the son of Gottskalk Thorvaldsen, an Icelandic woodcarver, and Karen Dagnes (Grønlund). His father was something of a failed artist and he drank heavily. However, Gottskalk's habits or lack of success did not have a negative impact on the young Bertel. Determined to avoid the fate of his father, Thorvaldsen decided that he would become a great sculptor.

Pursuing his ambition, Thorvaldsen gained entrance into the finest art schools of his time. His formal artistic training began at the Royal Danish Academy of Fine Arts School, where he studied freehand drawing. In 1796 he entered the Copenhagen Academy of Fine Arts, and a year later went to Rome, Italy, on a scholarship. The move would have enormous impact on his life, as Italy provided the kind of academic environment that spurred his growth as an artist. He soon began developing his own style, basing it on classical sculpture, which proved to be his greatest inspiration.

Influenced by Ancient Artists

Thorvaldsen remained in Rome until 1838, then returned to his homeland to teach for intermittent periods. Although he would never marry, while residing in Rome Thorvaldsen fathered two children with Anna Maria Magnani: a son, Carlo Alberto (1806–1811) and a daughter, Elisa (1813–1846). In his early years in that city, Thorvaldsen was able to study examples of classical art up

these works by copying the ancient artists' styles and subject matter. Like these artists, neoclassical-inspired sculptors strived for a purity of form, creating idealized figures in white marble that possessed a severity of structure and clear, hard contours.

The Neoclassical movement lasted from the mid-18th century to the mid-19th century. At first, Canova was the leading neoclassical sculptor, but Thorvaldsen would eventually emerge as Canova's recognized peer. By 1808 the Danish sculptor began to receive recognition as a great artist, and after Canova's death he became recognized as the greatest living sculptor in Europe and the pre-eminent neoclassical artist.

Like other neoclassical artists, Thorvaldsen produced most of his works in white marble. These included relief sculptures, monuments, and portrait busts. His fidelity to the classical style was revealed in his early works, including his *Jason* (1802–1823), depicting the adventurous figure of Greek mythology who traveled the seas with his Argonauts, and *Janus* (1803), the Roman god of gates and doors who possessed two faces looking in either direction. These works provided Thorvaldsen's artistic breakthrough and brought him international fame. The choice of subjects for one of his best-known works, *Hebe,* especially reflects his intent. In mythology Hebe was an attendant to Venus, the goddess of beauty, and she served as the cup bearer for the gods. Because she possessed pure beauty as well as everlasting youth, she proved an appropriate subject for Thorvaldsen. His most famous works are allegorical reliefs and statues of classical subjects. Other famous works include *Venus with the Apple* (1806) and *Amor and Psiquis in the Sky* (1807).

Opened a Workshop

It was Thorvaldsen's fame and demand for his work that helped advance Neoclassicism as a movement. As demand increased from around the world, he fulfilled many international commissions for clients who specifically asked for a work of art that exemplified the Neoclassical style. Many of the commissioned artworks he created included busts and statues of famous Europeans.

Thorvaldsen's artistic output during his lifetime was huge. He produced 550 sculptures, reliefs, and portrait busts. In 1797, with demand growing and his workload increasing, he felt compelled to establish an efficient studio workshop which employed the services of his pupils and assistants.

During this period, he produced works for his home country, including the decorative scheme of marble statues and reliefs for the new Church of Our Lady in Copenhagen that features a striking Christ figure. Thorvaldsen himself created the figures of Christ and St. Paul; the rest were made by his assistants from Thorvaldsen's models. Thorvaldsen also created works for clients throughout Europe. These include historical portrait sculptures of Pope Pius VII and Conradin, last of the Hohenstaufen, as well as the design for the world-famous memorial sculpture *Lion of Lucerne* (1819–1821) erected in Switzerland. This much-celebrated allegorical sculpture was created on the wall of what had once been a mine. It commemorates the destruction of the

close. Influenced by the ancient works as well as by the contemporary neoclassicists, he came to hold the ancient Greco-Roman sculptors in high regard, believing that they were the only sculptors who had achieved purity of formal beauty without respect to content. Like these artists he took many of his subjects from ancient literature and mythology; also like them he attempted to recreate the human form in sculpture with clear outlines, smooth surfaces, pleasing proportions, and idealized facial features. He believed that imitation of ancient classical works of art was the best way to become a great artist. The strategy worked for Thorvaldsen; he soon joined Italian sculptor Antonio Canova as of the major artists of the Neoclassical movement.

Neoclassical Movement

The Neoclassical art movement embraced the values of the art of ancient Greece and Rome, and its emergence was a reaction to the previous, more fanciful Rococo and Baroque styles. It was part of the larger, overall movement that revived neoclassical thought and included writing, painting, and philosophy. Influential German art historian Johann J. Winckelmann helped initiate the art movement when he identified the most important elements of classical works: the noble stillness and simplicity and the calm grandeur. Neoclassical sculptors were also inspired by the excavation of the ancient cities of Pompeii and Herculaneum in Rome, which began in 1748 and provided the world with the opportunity to rediscover classical works. Neoclassical artists sought to capture the quality of

Swiss Guard during the storming of the Tuileries in Paris in 1792, near the close of the French Revolution. The fallen Swiss are memorialized as a dying lion. The most remarkable element of the *Lion of Lucerne* is the sad expression on the lion's face; American writer Samuel Clemens (Mark Twain), when visiting Europe and observing the sculpture, remarked that it was "the saddest and most moving piece of rock in the world." Thorvaldsen's students performed the actual carving of the stone.

Thorvaldsen was also greatly admired in Russia. For the Russian czar's court he created sculptures of Countess Elizabeth Ostermann-Tolstaya (1815) and Czar Alexander I (1820).

Thorvaldsen's artistic activities were not restricted to sculpture. He would also perform restorations, believing along with his contemporaries that restoration projects provided a rewarding creative process. One of his most famous projects involved restoring ancient Aeginetan marbles, a task he performed for Prince Louis of Bavaria.

By 1820 Thorvaldsen employed 40 assistants to help complete the commissions, and his workshop was a fascinating place, bustling with activity. When producing a sculpture, Thorvaldsen began with a plaster model. After the finished artwork was delivered to a client, this plastic model remained in the workshop. Thus, the facility was filled with many stunning figures, the number of which grew over the years. Eventually, the sculpture envisioned the creation of a museum where his work could be viewed by the public. This seed of an idea would eventually grow to fruition.

Returned to Denmark

Although Thorvaldsen spent most of his life in Rome where he lived from 1797 to 1838, he was also active in Copenhagen. He became professor at the Royal Danish Academy of Fine Arts in 1805 and directed the Academy from 1833 to 1844. He also served as a professor at Rome's St. Luca Academy in 1812, eventually becoming vice president (1826) and president (1827–1828) there.

When he returned permanently to Copenhagen to live in 1838, Thorvaldsen was welcomed home with great enthusiasm. By that time he was considered the greatest sculptor in Europe, and his countrymen regarded him as a national hero. In fact, his fame was so great that several of the era's most well-known painters chose him as a portrait subject, including Russian painter Orest Kiprensky, whose 1833 portrait of Thorvaldsen hangs in the museum in St. Petersburg, Russia. His renown spread across the sea as well, and many American sculptors traveled to Europe to study with Thorvaldsen.

Donated Works for Museum

Thorvaldsen's will bequeathed a large collection of his works—as well as collected works of other artists—to the city of Copenhagen. In 1839 the city began building a museum—appropriately designed in the neoclassical style—to house the aging sculptor's valuable collection.

Thorvaldsen had first broached the idea of the remarkable bestowment in 1827, in a letter to Danish Crown Prince Christian Frederik (eventually King Christian VIII). The idea was then taken to King Frederik VI, who was asked if Denmark would be willing to build a museum for the collections if Thorvaldsen decided to donate. The king took the idea to the people and, later, initiated a fundraising campaign. The idea moved forward in 1830, when Thorvaldsen drew up his first will, a document that bestowed parts of his collections to Denmark.

A national appeal for money was started in 1837, to raise money for the museum construction. The Danish people responded enthusiastically and their support funded the project. A year later, when Thorvaldsen returned to Copenhagen after living in Rome, King Frederik VI designated a site for the envisioned museum adjacent to the Christiansborg Palace. The Royal Coach House, which stood on the proposed site, was to be rebuilt to accommodate Thorvaldsen's collections. A building committee was appointed, which included four architects who designed the basic elements of the reconstruction, and work began in 1839. Architect Michael Gottlieb Bindesbøll was appointed to lead the project, which took almost a decade to complete. The Thorvaldsen's Museum finally opened on September 18, 1848, the first museum to be built in Denmark.

The museum includes the original plaster models of Thorvaldsen's sculptures, the original design sketches, and many original pieces of his artwork, including his *Self Portrait* (1839). It also includes many priceless items that Thorvaldsen amassed over the years, including his extensive collection of paintings, drawings, engravings, antiques, and books.

Died in Birth City

Thorvaldsen passed away in Copenhagen on March 24, 1848, reportedly while attending the theater. He died only a week after his museum opened, at age 68. His funeral was held in the Cathedral Church of Our Lady in Copenhagen, and his coffin was eventually interred in the inner courtyard of the Thorvaldsen Museum.

During his lifetime, Thorvaldsen was a member of a large number of academies of fine arts, societies, and associations throughout Europe, Russia, and the United States. He became a member of the Danish Royal Academy of Fine Arts in 1805 and the St. Luca Academy in 1808. He also was named a Citizen of Honor in Mainz in 1835, in Copenhagen in 1838, and in Stuttgart in 1841.

Books

Plon, Eugene, *Thorvaldsen: His Life and Works,* R. Bently & Son, 1874.

Thiel, Just Mathias, *Thorvaldsen and His Works,* J. G. Unnevehr, 1869.

Online

"Bertel Thorvaldsen, Danish Sculptor," http://arthistory1.school .dk/frame_Thorvaldsen.htm (December 27, 2002).

"'Hebe' by Thorvaldseon," http://www.eleganza.com/detailed/ hebe.html (February 10, 2003).

"Thorvaldsen—Life and Work," http://www.thorvaldsens museum.dk/shownewslist.asp?ID=17 (February 10, 2003).

□

Samuel Chao Chung Ting

Nuclear physicist Samuel C. C. Ting (born 1936) shared the 1976 Nobel Prize for physics with Burton Richter for discovering the existence of a new particle called j/psi.

Samuel Chao Chung Ting's study of the physics of electron-positron pairs produced during a nuclear reaction led to the discovery of a new particle. This particle, j/psi, supplied nuclear theorists with the key to a suspected fourth quark and opened research into a fourth type of subatomic particle whose existence had until then been speculative. Ting's work during the latter decades of the twentieth century found him involved in what was dubbed "Big Science," experimentation requiring financing by top-notch teams of scientists, expensive state-of-the art equipment, governing boards, and an international approach. Ting was especially suited for work in such a high-pressure environment. An *Economist* contributor noted in profiling the American physicist that he "is determined to get authoritative results, and demands that his associates be similarly single-minded. An experiment run by Dr. Ting is not a casual affair; to say that he is strict is . . . an understatement. He can be charming. He can also be ruthless."

Raised in War-torn China

Ting was born January 27, 1936, in Ann Arbor, Michigan. His parents, Kuan Hai Ting, an engineering professor, and Tsun-Ying Wang, a psychology professor, were graduate students at the University of Michigan; while they had intended to return to their native China before Tsun-Ying gave birth, the infant was born two months early. He was the first of three children born to the Tings.

Two months after Ting's birth, his parents returned to mainland China, where he was raised by his parents and maternal grandmother. Because of the disruption caused by the Japanese invasion of China during World War II, Ting was not able to enter school until he was 12. His early education fell to his family, especially to his maternal grandmother, a independent-minded widow and teacher who raised her daughter and put both herself and Ting's mother through college during a time when women in China were not usually so self-reliant. Both his parents worked throughout Ting's childhood, and through their affiliation with academics from several Chinese universities they instilled in their son an interest in learning. As Ting noted in his autobiography for the online *Nobel e-Museum*, "Perhaps because of this early influence, I have always had the desire to be associated with university life."

During his teens he and his family moved to Taiwan, where his father taught engineering at the National Taiwan

University. Accepted at one of Taipei's most acclaimed senior high schools, Ting excelled in chemistry, physics, mathematics, and history.

Encouraged by his parents to attend their alma mater, Ting was accepted to the University of Michigan. On December 6, 1956, he arrived at Detroit's Metropolitan Airport with a hundred dollars and only a few words of English. Fortunately, the dean of the university's engineering school was a friend of Ting's father, and he and his family opened their home to the 20-year-old student. While his inability to communicate with his fellow students caused Ting difficulty as a college freshman at Michigan, he quickly gained skill in English and was relatively fluent by his sophomore year.

Little Money, Large Goals

Ting was determined to excel in his studies. He was able to obtain enough scholarship and grant money to fund his degree, and after switching from the School of Engineering to the School of Science, he earned his B.S. in engineering mathematics and physics in 1959. Ting earned his M.A. the following year and by 1962 received his Ph.D. in physics, a remarkable feat considering that Ting had only a weak grasp of English six years previously.

Ting courted a young architect named Kay Louise Kuhne; they married in 1960 and had two daughters, Jeanne and Amy, before their eventual divorce. With his Ph.D. completed, in 1963 Ting and his family moved to Geneva, Switzerland, where he served as a Ford Foundation post-doctoral scholar at the European Organization for Nuclear

Research. There, Ting worked alongside Italian physicist Guisseppe Cocconi on a new type of particle accelerator called the Proton Synchrotron, emulating the Italian physicist's exacting methodology.

Returning to the United States the following spring, Ting joined the faculty at Columbia University, where he worked with a number of well-known physicists and became interested in the physics of electron-positron pair production. Electrons and positrons are similiar subatomic particles, with electrons negatively charged and positrons positively charged. In the process of atomic decay, electron-positron pairs are produced.

During Ting's second year at Columbia, he heard about an interesting experiment using Harvard University's Electron Accelerator, with results seemingly in violation of accepted predictions of quantum electrodynamics (the interaction of matter with electromagnetic radiation). In the Harvard experiment, photons collided with a nuclear target, creating electron-positron pairs.

Perplexed by the Harvard results, in March 1966 Ting took a leave of absence from Columbia and went to the Deutsches Elektronen-Synchrotron installation in Hamburg, Germany, to see if he could duplicate the Harvard experiment. With a team of colleagues, he constructed a double-arm spectrometer, an instrument capable of verifying that the quantum electrodynamics description of particle emissions is correct to distances as small as one hundred-trillionth of a centimeter. Using this spectrometer, Ting was able to study the physics of electron pairs, particularly the way such pairs are created during the decay of photon-like particles. The instrument also allowed Ting to view the angles of particulate deflection from the beam of radiation, facilitating calculations of particulate mass and allowing scientists to view the relationships between specific particles.

In 1967 Ting returned to the United States and joined the physics faculty as an assistant professor at the Massachusetts Institute of Technology; he became a full professor two years later. In early 1972, Ting led his research team in a follow-up experiment at the Brookhaven National Laboratory on Long Island, New York. To aid his research into the production of electron-positron pairs, Ting designed a more advanced version of the double-arm spectrometer. This new version, using a higher-energy proton beam, was able to increase the beam's energy in small increments and monitor the effect of those incremental changes on particle pair production. Ting hoped that the change would create a heavier particle that would decay into electron-positron pairs. The new spectrometer proved effective, and Ting's reputation among his colleagues was greatly enhanced by his demanding quest for irrefutable findings while at Brookhaven.

The J Particle

In August 1974 the experiment at Brookhaven produced a surprising reading, a spike in the production of electron-positron pairs at 3.1 billion electron volts. This reading diverged from then-current atomic theory. Believing the reading to denote the presence of a yet-unknown high-mass particle, Ting analyzed the experimental data for months, reporting his finding to colleague Giorgio Bellet-

tini, director of Italy's Frascati Laboratory. Bellettini confirmed Ting's discovery, and in November the physicists jointly presented their findings in papers published in *Physical Review Letters.* Ting had discovered a new elementary particle three times heavier than a proton, with a narrow range of energy states, and with a longer life span than anything known in physics. Since Ting's work involved electromagnetic currents bearing the symbol "j," and because the Chinese character representing the word "Ting" is similar in form to the letter "J," he called his discovery the "J particle."

Shortly after Ting's announcement, Stanford University's Linear Accelerator Center director Wolfgang Panofsky notified Ting that Stanford University physicist Burton Richter had also recently demonstrated the existence of a new particle, dubbed the "psi particle," by forcing collisions between electrons and positrons in Sanford's accelerator. When the two physicists met and compared their results, they realized the particles they had each discovered were the same. The dual discovery by Ting and Richter of what is now called the "j/psi particle" sparked research by other physics laboratories, providing nuclear theorists with the first experimental evidence of the existence of a fourth fundamental subatomic particle or "quark," dubbed "charm," whose existence some nuclear theorists had predicted as early as 1970. It was speculated that charm unified electromagnetic forces with other, weaker forces, balancing such forces at high energy.

Nobel Prize

In 1976 the 40-year-old Ting joined Richter in sharing the Nobel Prize in physics for their discovery of a heavy elementary particle of a new kind. Because less than two years had passed since the announcement of their dual discoveries, the two physicists set a record for the briefest period between discovery to Nobel recognition in the award's history. Although the speed with which the award was bestowed concerned some members of the scientific community, Ting and Richter's discovery has stood the test of time. Earning the Nobel Prize solidified the reputation of both physicists. Ting was hailed as a daring, precise experimentalist who approached his work with great insight and attention to detail.

Other kudos quickly followed. Immediately following his Nobel win, Ting was presented with the Ernest Orlando Lawrence Memorial Award for Physics from the U.S. Energy Research and Development Agency, followed by the Eringen medal in 1977 and the Forum Engelberg prize in 1996. In 1978 the University of Michigan honored its esteemed graduate with a Doctoris Honoris Causa. Other honorary degrees came from the Chinese University in Hong Kong in 1987, the University of Bologna in 1988, Columbia University and China's University of Science and Technology in 1990, Moscow State University in 1991, and the University of Bucharest in Romania in 1993.

Research into Atomic Construction

After his Nobel win, Ting continued to involve himself in large-scale, expensive experiments in his continued search for new subatomic particles. In 1979 he worked with researchers at China's University of Science and Technology to verify the existence of gluon, which transmits energy between quarks. In the late 1980s he became active in the scientific community's advocacy of a proposed superconducting super collider, a $8-plus billion particle collider supported by President Ronald Reagan. In 1990 Ting and his team were one of three groups competing for the contract to build the giant particle detector required for use with the Texas-based super-collider. Ting's proposed detector was not chosen for the project.

In 1989 Ting led a team of physicists in an experiment based in France that attempted to prove the existence of yet another subatomic particle, the "Higgs boson," a force recognized as a key to understanding the origins of mass—the quality that causes objects to have inertia and requires the application of some degree of force in order to move them. In 1996 Ting joined a group of astrophysicists in positioning an antimatter detector called the Alpha Magnetic Spectrometer on a NASA space shuttle.

As well as serving on the MIT faculty, in 1977 Ting was named MIT's first Thomas Dudley Cabot Institute Professor, and he has traveled to Beijing Normal College, Jiatong University in Shanghai, and the University of Bologna to serve as honorary professor to advanced physics students at those institutions. He was made a fellow of the American Academy for Arts and Sciences, the Pakistani Academy of Science, Academia Sinica, the Russian Academy of Science, the Hungarian Academy of Science, the Deutsche Academie Naturforscher Leopoldina, and the National Academy of Sciences. Ting also belongs to physical societies in both the United States and Europe.

In April 1985 Ting married his second wife, educator Susan Carol Marks, with whom he had a son, Christopher. A soft-spoken yet authoritarian person with well-known ambition, Ting was as meticulous in his experimentation and analysis as in his dress. Noted for his uniform of a dark suit and tie, he retained the same drive to uncover new facets of the physical world as he did as a young student on his way to America in pursuit of knowledge.

Books

Notable Asian Americans, Gale, 1995.
Notable Scientists: From 1900 to the Present, Gale, 2001.

Periodicals

Discover, April 1996.
Economist, May 25, 1991.
Omni, July 1981.
Science, April 8, 1988; December 21, 1990; January 4, 1991; November 27, 1992.
Smithsonian, March 1989.
Washington Post, December 30, 2000.

Online

"Samuel C. C. Ting—Autobiography," *Nobel e-Museum,* http://www.nobel.se/physics/laureates/1976/ting-autobio.html (August 8, 2002). □

Jean Toomer

Refusing to be labeled black or white, writer Jean Toomer (1894–1967) was first exalted, then criticized, ignored, and forgotten. However, during the Harlem Renaissance of the 1960s and 1970s, Toomer was not only rediscovered but also "hailed as one of America's finest African American writers," noted the University of North Carolina's (UNC) website dedicated to English studies. Thus, he became "something he wouldn't have liked"—labeled. Toomer believed that "my racial composition and my position in the world are realities which I alone may determine," quoted the *Southern Literary Journal.*

Raised Both Black and White

Born Nathan Eugene Pinchback Toomer on December 26, 1894, in Washington D.C., Toomer, until the age of 18, was perceived by others and lived alternatively as a black and as a white young man. After his father abandoned the family when Toomer was only one year old, he and his mother, Nina, moved in with her father, Pinckney Benton Stewart Pinchback, the first United States governor of African American descent.

While living with his grandfather in Washington D.C., Toomer attended an all-black elementary school, but lived in an affluent white neighborhood. However, when his mother remarried and moved her new family to New York, Toomer's life turned 180 degrees. In New York, he entered an all-white high school but lived in an all-black neighborhood. In 1909, after his mother's death, Toomer's life once again turned 180 degrees. He moved back into his grandfather's home in Washington D.C. and graduated from an all-black high school.

Living in both black and white worlds affected Toomer greatly. He saw that the world—both the black world and white world—had labeled him based on his appearance. Being a "fair-skinned, straight-nosed, straight-haired" African American, as UNC online described him, allowed Toomer acceptable entrance into the white world. However, by not looking absolutely "passable" white also allowed him entrance into the black world. This dual-entrance ability "added to his sense of isolation from any group identity," noted *Black Issues Book Review.* As a result, Toomer, by 1914, began rejecting all attempts to be classified by anyone in any world as "black" or "white." Toomer became the only label he would never refuse, "American."

Prepared to Be a Writer

Throughout the mid-1900s, Toomer continued his education by attending a variety of colleges including the University of Wisconsin and the City College of New York. He also studied many subjects such as agriculture, psychology,

and literature. Yet, he never earned a degree. Unbeknownst to even himself, Toomer was not preparing for one career, but for his life as a seeker of knowledge and for his life as a writer.

Toomer began his life as a writer in 1918; for the next few years, he wrote many short stories and poems. Most reflected Toomer's steadfast idea that there was not a black or white race, but a "new race, that I was one of the first conscious members of this race . . . American," quoted Darwin Turner in *The Wayward and the Seeking*. However, these short stories and poems were not widely accepted or read by a popular audience. Unaffected, Toomer continued to write but abruptly stopped just two years later.

Adopted New Philosophy

In 1920, Toomer met writer Waldo Frank. Frank believed that a writer's or artist's duty and responsibility was to "[shape] American culture and society," stated *Black Issues Book Review*. Since Toomer had proclaimed that he was of no race but American, he adopted Frank's philosophy that as an American he should use his writing to "[set] the cultural agenda in a way that legislation or political activism could not."

Shortly after adopting Frank's beliefs, Toomer discovered a new philosophy—the philosophy of idealism. In order to delve into this new philosophy, Toomer stopped writing. Seeking knowledge, he began to study idealism which led him to believe that "in life nothing is only physical. There is also the symbolical. White and Black . . . In

general, the great contrasts. The pair of opposites," further quoted Turner in *The Wayward and the Seeking*. Toomer's role in this philosophy was not so much that of a writer, but as a "reconciler" between the great contrasts of black and white.

To further his role as a "reconciler," Toomer sought out other writers who believed in and who demonstrated this idealistic philosophy in their work. He found the Imagist poetics or Symbolists: Charles Baudelaire and Walt Whitman. These writers, with "their insistence on fresh vision and on the perfect clean economical line was just what I had been looking for," commented Toomer in *The Wayward and the Seeking*. Yet, it was not only these writers or this new philosophy which would result in Toomer's most praised and most criticized novel. It was another geographical move—this time to the South.

Published a Literary Masterpiece

In 1921, Toomer began working and living in Sparta, Georgia. During this time in American history, the segregation of the races could be most blatantly seen in the rural South. No longer could Toomer remain focused on being only a "reconciler," a seeker of knowledge, or believe in one race, American. In the South, race could not be ignored. This indisputable fact forced Toomer to confront his own personal views on what others had labeled him—both black and white. How he did so was by writing *Cane*.

Like Toomer's own three-part identity—black, white, American—the structure of *Cane* is segregated into three sections. The first focuses on African American life in the South. By detailing the lives of six African American women, Toomer, in this section creates "the idealization of rural African Americans" noted the *Southern Literary Journal*. In section two, Toomer presents the opposite identity from section one—the urban North. He portrays this urban North as "a place of shallow, materialistic and antimystical striving," further noted the *Southern Literary Journal*. The third section once again shifts identities this time back to the rural South. However, Toomer focuses on an artist plagued by what role he should play in the world—should he represent the African American race or strive to become unidentified with any race.

Hailed by many critics of the time as a literary masterpiece, *Cane* nevertheless faded into obscurity. However, the ending of the book has provided clues as to why Toomer never again specifically focused on the black and white races as separate identities and how these identities can be harmoniously blended. *Cane* ends with the plagued artist watching a sunrise. As the sun rises, he theorizes that a bridge between races is not possible, yet a "bridge between himself and the universe" is, noted the *Southern Literary Journal*. Toomer's subsequent writings emphasized this philosophy.

Challenged Others to Think

Over the next 27 years, Toomer, unlike *Cane,* did not fade into obscurity. He married twice, became a father, and continued to challenge himself and others to think about their perception of the world. His belief that there is no black or white race, only American, never wavered; yet, how people should discover this belief changed with each new philosophy Toomer studied. For example, in 1938, Toomer traveled to India where he began writing about spiritual enlightenment. However, he struggled with India's "a life of withdrawal from the world," noted biographers Cynthia Kerman and Richard Eldridge in *The Lives of Jean Toomer: A Hunger for Wholeness.*

During the 1940s, Toomer continued to struggle to connect his understanding of idealism to another religion: Quakerism. He tried to work through this struggle by organizing a living space called the Mill House. The Mill House welcomed both Quakers and laymen and offered an opportunity for both to dismiss all separations of religions and cultures. One member of Mill House praised Toomer for the "opened doors we were ready to walk through," quoted *BANC!.* Toomer wrote many essays and lectured frequently about Mill House; however, unlike *Cane,* they were not widely read. By 1950, Toomer stopped writing altogether, slowly withdrew from public life, and on March 30, 1967, in Doylestown, Pennsylvania, he died.

Rediscovered Masterpiece and Writer

Why Toomer remained forgotten until the Harlem Renaissance has been widely debated. One popular theory is that Toomer was "frustrated by his inability to market much of his work," noted *African American Review.* Therefore, because of the time in which Toomer had been writing, he had been labeled a black writer. And, the white society had been taught not to read a novel, an essay, a poem, or other others works by a writer identified as "black."

The *Southern Literary Journal* has offered another popular theory as to why Toomer was forgotten. Toomer created his own obscurity by showing two faces—the "good" Toomer and the "bad" Toomer. The good Toomer "briefly and tactfully uses race to contain literary ambiguity [in *Cane*], but the bad Toomer jettisons both race and literary ambiguity." In other words, Toomer was seen as a race traitor because he "challenged his culture's demand for absolute distinctions between white and black," noted *African American Review.* Consequently, because Toomer maintained his belief that he was no race but American, he pushed himself into obscurity.

However, this view changed during the 1960s and 1970s. Toomer was no longer seen as "bad" or a "race traitor." During this time of the Harlem Renaissance, "Toomer's rejection of race sounded, more importantly, like a rejection of white cultural hegemony," stated *Black Issues Book Review.* Therefore, Toomer became a cultural African American icon who, like civil rights activist Malcolm X, promoted the African American race as a separate identity.

Yet, by the 1990s, another theory would once again reemphasize that Toomer was not rejecting the white race or the black race. He accepted and truly believed that there is only one race, American. Integrating Roland Bartres classic 1956 essay *Myth Today,* Charles Harmon in the *Southern Literary Journal* offered his own interpretation of *Cane* using the philosophy of "neither/norism."

This philosophy, Bartres defined as "stating two opposites and balancing the one by the other so as to reject them both," Harmon quoted. Thus, Toomer, in *Cane,* which had presented both the black viewpoint and white viewpoint while ultimately rejecting both, had done just what Bartres defined. Therefore, Toomer should not be seen as "good" or "bad," rejecting the white hegemony, or as a race traitor—or in effect, a two-faced writer. What Toomer should be seen as is a writer who courageously challenged a belief by writing a masterpiece.

Ultimately, Toomer has been remembered as a significant writer—a significant African American writer. Although still labeled, Toomer's own words live on to reject that label. As quoted by the *African American Review,* Toomer never worried about how others saw him. He had always "simply gone and lived here and there. I have been what I am." And, as he further commented on racial identity, he urged people to realize that "both white and colored people share the same stupidity." However, it is Toomer's message to writers and artists that may truly silence his critics and his labelers: "Art . . . embraces all life . . . [its] noblest function . . . is to expand, elevate, and enrich that life."

Books

Kerman, Cynthia and Richard Elrigde, *The Lives of Jean Toomer: A Hunger for Wholeness,* 1987.
Turner, Darwin, editor, *The Wayward and the Seeking,* 1980.

Periodicals

African American Review, Fall 1998.
BANC! 2, 1972.
Black Issues Book Review, January/February 2001.
Southern Literary Journal, Spring 2000.

Online

Jean Toomer (1894–1967), University of North Carolina online, http://www.inc.edu/courses/eng81br1/toomer/html (February 28, 2003). □

Joseph Burr Tyrrell

Canadian geologist Joseph Burr Tyrrell (1858–1957) inadvertently made one of the most important discoveries of dinosaur bones in North America in 1884. The skull and skeleton he dug up by accident in a remote part of Alberta proved to be the *Albertosaurus sarcophagus,* a slightly smaller cousin of *Tyrannosaurus rex* and the first of its genus found anywhere in the world. Tyrrell's findings aroused international interest and brought hordes of paleontologists to dig in this unpopulated part of western Canada. Tyrrell was one of Canada's most famed geologists and explorers and mapped out vast stretches of its northern lands.

Avoided Career in Law

Tyrrell was born on November 1, 1858, in Weston, Ontario, a town his father had founded. It later became part of metropolitan Toronto. His father's family was an esteemed Irish clan that hailed from Castle Grange in County Kildare. The elder Tyrrell emigrated to Canada and made a fortune as a stonemason in Ontario before marrying Elizabeth Burr, whose family roots in the New World dated back to 1682. In Weston, the Tyrrell family lived in an immense 24-room stone house. As a child, Tyrrell suffered a bout with scarlet fever that left him partially deaf; his vision was impaired as well, but he wore glasses to correct it. He studied at Upper Canada College as a teen and went on to an arts course at the University of Toronto.

The senior Tyrrell steered his son into a career in law, but Tyrrell was fascinated by the natural world and studied biology, botany, and other branches of science in his spare time. He even conducted research on his own with a microscope and published a paper in the *Ottawa Field Naturalist* on mites that cause feline ailments. Professors introduced him to associates of the Geological Survey of Canada (GSC), the government agency formed in the 1840s with a mandate to search out coal fields and other potential sources of revenue for what was then the province of Quebec and Ontario. The agency and its staff expanded considerably over the next few decades as Canada became a full-fledged confederacy.

After Tyrrell finished at the University of Toronto in 1880, he began studying for the bar and working at a local firm, as was the custom in the era before law schools became commonplace, but he was still weak from a bout with pneumonia a few years earlier. His physician suggested that outdoor work would restore him to health, so Tyrrell found a temporary post as an assistant at the GSC, which was moving its offices from Montreal to Ottawa and needed additional staff. His first task was to unpack and sort through hundreds of specimens of Canadian rocks.

Ventured into Rough Terrain

One of the GSC's leading names was George Mercer Dawson, a member of the International Boundary Commission. While surveying lands along the 49th Parallel, Dawson discovered the first dinosaur bones in southern Saskatchewan and Alberta in 1874. Such fossil finds were a relatively recent development. In 1770 in Holland, the first ancient skeleton of what was thought to be an immense marine lizard was unearthed. In 1800, the first ancient specimen uncovered by Europeans in North America was a set of fossilized dinosaur tracks in Connecticut.

Dawson, impressed by Tyrrell's dedication to his job, invited him to accompany a GSC survey that was planned to help the Canadian Pacific railroad determine its westward route through the foothills of the Rockies in 1883. Tyrrell eagerly accepted. After having spent his life in Toronto and Ottawa, he found the Canadian West a lawless but exciting place, where horses were stolen if camps were not guarded

well enough. The trip was an arduous one, both for the surveying work itself—which involved counting the number of steps taken and taking compass measurements—but also for the terrain. "Black flies without number from six a.m. till noon," Tyrrell wrote in his journal, according to Alex Inglis's biography, *Northern Vagabond: The Life and Career of J. B. Tyrell, the Man Who Conquered the Canadian North.* "At eight o'clock the bull-dog flies came to their assistance and made the horses' lives a burden to them until evening. There was a short respite, then the mosquitoes arrived to prevent any rest for the night."

Discovered Immense Dinosaur Fossil

In 1884, at the age of 26, Tyrrell was given his own field party to lead. He and his assistants traveled by canoe to an area north of the Bow River in southwestern Alberta. On a mission to search for coal deposits in the Red Deer River valley, on June 9 Tyrrell and his party instead found a giant skull in the area. Digging further, he unearthed a large cache of bones and arranged to have them taken to Fort Calgary. The load was so heavy that it broke the axle of the wagon. From there they were shipped to Philadelphia for verification, and Professor E.D. Cope termed the skeleton *Laelaps incrassatus* and dated it as 70 million years old. It was later reclassified as an *Albertosaurus sarcophagus* by American Museum of Natural History scholar Henry Fairfield Osborne in 1905. It was the first of its genus ever discovered and confirmed as a smaller cousin of *Tyrannosaurus rex*.

News of the find sparked what became known as the Great Canadian Dinosaur Rush in the Red Deer River valley, and many more important discoveries were made. Yet Tyrrell was not a paleontologist and was far more interested in the bituminous coal deposits that were found in the area. The area where he found *Albertosaurus sarcophagus* soon became the large mining center of Drumheller, which thrived well into the 20th Century.

Canada's Forbidding "Barren Lands"

Tyrrell lived in an Ottawa boarding house during the winter months when not traveling on behalf of the GSC. Despite the hardships of his job, he enjoyed the work very much. "My idea of peace and comfort was a tent by a clear brook anywhere north of 50 degrees of North Latitude," he wrote in his log, "a ground-sheet and blankets enough, a side of salt pork and a bag of flour. . . . For glory I had the stars and the Northern Lights." His nomadic lifestyle presented certain challenges for his bride, Mary Edith Carey, the daughter of an Ottawa Baptist minister, whom he wed in 1894. The couple were often separated for long periods of time. At other times, he brought along his brothers Grattan or James to serve as his assistants.

Tyrrell's next major assignment was a lengthy GSC expedition of what was known as the Barren Lands, the area west of the Hudson Bay and north of Winnipeg. His trip beginning in 1893 would secure his place in Canadian history, for the area had only recently come under Canadian sovereignty. It was formerly held by the Hudson's Bay Company, a fur-trading enterprise, and there were very few settlers there. To prepare for his trip, Tyrrell read the journals of David Thompson, the Hudson's Bay surveyor who measured much of the Canadian wilderness in the 1780s and 1790s.

Sometimes Presumed Missing

Over the course of the next four years Tyrrell and his party of seven made lengthy trips that brought back a wealth of information about the region. It was an arduous journey, marked by bitterly cold temperatures and supported by a bare minimum of food supplies. They traveled by canoe, dog sled, and snowshoe, meeting many communities of Athapascan Indians and Inuit along the way. At times they camped with the indigenous people and shared native delicacies such as fried moose. Tyrrell thought it interesting that when he offered an Athapascan a job as a guide, it was the man's wife who decided if he should take it. Nearly half of the thousands of square miles Tyrrell and his party covered had been utterly unknown territory and had not even been surveyed by the Hudson's Bay Company.

At times, Tyrrell's party was delayed by weather or other mishaps, and rumors spread that they had perished. Based on his explorations, Tyrrell became intrigued by glaciation, a relatively new field of study at the time. In 1897, he delivered a paper before the British Association for the Advancement of Science in which he agreed with Swiss-American geologist Louis Agassiz, whose 1840 *tude sur les glaciers* posited that the continents were formed by movements of glaciers during the various ice ages. Supporting Agassiz's theory, Tyrrell wrote that he had found scratches in the Manitoba granite that showed glacier movement; furthermore, he noted, it was not a single movement but rather a series. He argued that the glaciers had moved south and west to the valleys of the Ohio and Mississippi rivers. Tyrrell also asserted that underneath the Barren Lands were large swaths of Precambrian rock, which later proved true when the entire Canadian Shield was mapped.

Established Lucrative Business

Tyrrell had gone to the Klondike area, a region of the Yukon Territory just east of Alaska, in 1898 to take part in its famous "Gold Rush" that year. Though he did not become rich, he saw how easy it was for fortunes to grow overnight, and he vowed to change careers. In January 1896, Tyrrell and his wife had become parents, and the expanded household strained their finances. Over the years, he had often struggled to make ends meet, for he failed to earn what he thought was an appropriate salary at the GSC despite his renown. The ostensible reason was that he lacked the academic credentials, but there was some backbiting within the agency and others seemed resentful of his fame.

Realizing that one of the little nuggets he saw panned by others was equal to his month's salary, Tyrrell resigned from the GSC effective January 1, 1899, and went back to the Yukon later that month. In Dawson City he opened a mining consulting business, though he had little actual experience save for his vast knowledge of the area's geography. The business proved quite successful in investigating possible claims. He moved his firm to Toronto in 1907 to be closer to his family and take advantage of the cobalt and silver rush taking place in northern Ontario. In 1924, he made a wise investment in the Kirkland Lake gold mine in eastern Ontario, and it made him a millionaire.

In the later years of his life, Tyrrell edited the journals of Thompson for publication by the Champlain Society. He settled on a farm and orchard outside of Toronto, which was later subsumed by the city zoo. He died on August 26, 1957, in Toronto, Ontario, at the age of 98. The Drumheller, Alberta, museum near where he made his *Albertosaurus sarcophagus* discovery housed the skeleton and was named the Royal Tyrrell Museum of Paleontology.

Books

Inglis, Alex, *Northern Vagabond: The Life and Career of J. B. Tyrell, the Man Who Conquered the Canadian North*, McClelland & Stewart, 1978. □

U

Mitsuko Uchida

In a career that has spanned almost 30 years, Mitsuko Uchida (born 1948) has earned her title as one of the greatest classical pianists of the 20th century. She is most readily associated with her ability and recordings of Mozart's piano works and is a sought-after concert pianist worldwide.

Mitsuko Uchida was born in Tokyo, Japan, on December 20, 1948. She was the third child of Fukito Uchida, a diplomat, and Tasuko Uchida, a homemaker. Before Uchida was born her father had served in Europe in the Japanese diplomatic corps during World War II.

Uchida began her piano lessons when she was three years old as part of a traditional Japanese education. She quickly developed a love for classical music, especially Mozart, as she listened to her father's collection of European composers' recordings. She told the *Detroit Free Press,* "as a small child I remember vividly listening to Mozart again and again." Mozart would prove to be her life's passion at the piano. Although her parents probably never envisioned their daughter becoming one of the most important pianists of her generation, her gift was instantly recognizable from early on. Her father would proudly ask her to play for anyone who would listen. But as she told a group of students at Johns Hopkins once, "My parents wanted me to be an ordinary Japanese housewife. They gave me piano lessons so that I could make them proud. . . ." Little did they know that she would go on to become one of the great treasures of current classical music and considered one of the best interpreters of Mozart.

Uchida was an inquisitive youth with questions not only about her music but also about life in general. Her curiosity remained unfulfilled while living in Japan. In addition, the Japanese approach to teaching also seemed stifling to Uchida. "There is a tradition in Japanese society that one is not to question," she explained to the *New York Times.* The customary technique to music education in Japan focused more on the mechanical aspect of training, but Uchida sensed the need for a more interpretive training. Without the background of the Western music tradition, Japanese teachers taught the pure mechanics of the instrument instead of its musicality. She resented the endless rules about notes and formulas because she just wanted to be able to feel and play the music.

At the age of 12, Uchida and her family moved to Vienna, Austria, where her father was a member of the Japanese diplomatic mission. It was in Vienna that Uchida's eagerness for Western music could be satiated. Though the culture was accessible to her, she still did not seem to find what she was searching for musically. While she learned German and began her musical studies in the Viennese school of music under Richard Hauser at the Vienna Academy of Music, she still felt restricted by her instructors. As she related to the *New York Times,* it was "full of fixed ideas. There are masses of do's and don'ts, and 'music should be played this way.' So I had to get out of that."

London Gave Uchida Her Freedom

Once she came to this realization, Uchida moved to London and ended her formal education at age 22. Enticed by London's independent musical atmosphere, it was there that English became her third "first" language and where she still makes her home. In London Uchida was finally free to explore music on her own terms. For the next several

years, Uchida taught herself. She spent all her time studying and listening to music, especially the recordings of the celebrated pianists and conductors of the 20th century. She was especially drawn to Fritz Busch's recordings of Mozart, and her music seemed to go in a new direction. Busch's tasteful liberties with Mozart influenced Uchida to concentrate on the immortal composer's music with great detail, especially the sonatas and piano concertos.

It was playing Mozart's music that gave Uchida her first taste of success. Though she placed first in Vienna's Beethoven Competition in 1969 and second in both Britain's Leeds International and the Warsaw Chopin Competition, these competitions did little to advance or even begin her career. This was acceptable to Uchida, however, who held the belief that a career could and should unfold slowly and at the one's own pace. As she told to *Ovation*, "My life has been built very slowly and securely. If the career goes ahead of you, there will be one day when you fall off of it."

Broke into Music World with Style

Clearly to Uchida the music is more important than the public image. But the public, once they heard Uchida's mastery, applauded her as one of her profession's finest. It was in 1982 when she gave a series of concerts of the complete Mozart sonatas when listeners in great numbers sat up and took notice of her talent for the first time. Though clearly regarded as one of the finest composers, Mozart's piano sonatas have sometimes been dubbed simplistic. This simply was not so under the careful study and performance

of Uchida, who captivated spectators with her thoughtful and intense interpretation of the pieces.

Her reviewers of this series had nothing but radiant praise to bestow upon her. *Biography Today* quoted a London *Times* critic who noted: "She does not sing the music; she exists in it." The interviewer had an astute observation; Uchida feels strongly about her interpretation of the music she plays and the relationship she has with the composer. She also has a humble opinion of her ability. From an interview that she had with Catherine Pate of the London Symphony Orchestra Uchida confided, "All I want is that the people will pick up the beauty of Mozart. I don't care if they forget it was me playing it as long as they feel the music!"

A few years after her innovative performances of Mozart's sonatas, she presented all 21 piano concertos in a series of concerts with the English Chamber Orchestra. She conducted these concertos from the piano over the 1985–1986 concert season. Again both audiences and critics were smitten by her ability and expression. She had made the music of Mozart her own while still keeping his intent in the forefront of the music in a way that few performers had been able to achieve. As she revealed in *Time,* Mozart's music is a "kind of world in itself . . . so complete that you can forget about the rest. Then you come out, and you are blinded."

The series of sonata and concerto concerts propelled Uchida into the worldwide spotlight. Soon she was performing in concert halls all over the world and recording award-winning CDs. She has recorded her performances of Mozart's piano concertos and sonatas, as well as pieces by Beethoven, Chopin, Debussey, and Schubert, just to name a few. Her 2001 recording of the Schoenberg Piano Concerto has won four awards including a Gramophone Award for the best concerto recording.

In preparation for her career and indeed, her mastery of any piece that she chooses to perform, Uchida undertakes the task with intricate deliberation. Not only does she study the music and writings of the composer, but she also searches for insight into what the composer was thinking and how his ideas came about. It was this knowledge of music she craved as a youth in Japan but could not find. Now on her own she was free to discover it. She does this in part by examining music theory with Heinrich Schenker, a theorist, editor, and pianist who is known for his revolutionary method of musical analysis. He has been a great influence on her as she told a group of students she spoke to in 1998 at Johns Hopkins University. "I have found his analysis fascinating. . . ."

Uchida brings this knowledge and careful preparation to her performances, where audiences and critics alike are privy to it. Critics have praised her incessantly. *Time* wrote that she "plays . . . with a remarkable combination of energy and tenderness, a considerable rhythmic freedom and a lovely tone." In the *American Record Guide* Shirley Fleming wrote "Her range of touch is extraordinary. . . . Perhaps her overriding characteristic is lyrical flow, captured in . . . complete elegance of phrasing." Louis Gerber identified her as an artist with "refreshing interpretations of Beethoven's works and clear and pure playing." Uchida has absolutely earned her reputation as one of the world's supreme concert pianists.

By most standards, Uchida is conservative in how many concerts she will give in a year. She tries to keep the number between 50 and 60 a year, though she has done 70 once. She told the *New York Times,* "It was excessively hard for me. If you stick to two piano concertos plus one recital program, you can play 100 concerts. But I like to play different things. The repertory is so vast." In addition to wanting to play a more varied concert program, she is careful to restrict her numbers to ward off burnout. Even so, she is incredibly busy as an artist. In 1998 she was named the first woman director of the Ojai Music Festival in California. At the same time, she was acting as co-director of the Marlboro Festival in Vermont. She was also an Artist-in-Residence at the Cleveland Orchestra.

Undaunted by the bias the profession has for younger musicians, Uchida has already made plans to perform a series of concerts in 2018. According to *Biography Today,* "She is already preparing for a series of concerts she plans to give . . . when she turns 70. That year, she plans to perform Bach's Goldberg Variations and all 48 of his Preludes and Fugues." The music will take her years to prepare, but she is looking forward to it. It is still a joy for her to play the instrument after so many years.

Life outside of performing for Uchida is still consumed with the piano and music. She is a confirmed Londoner and lives in a house there with a separate studio that houses her five pianos. She has never married and has never had children, believing, according to *Biography Today,* that her career would not have been possible if she had had a child. Because of the travel required, as well as preparation, both children and her work would have suffered greatly. In this way, though she enjoys other activities such as reading and theater, she has little time for much else other than music and it is a positive choice that Uchida has made. As she told Catherine Pate in an interview, "I have no other passions. I like other things, but I only have enough room for one real passion, and that is music."

Books

Harris, Laurie Lanzen, *Biography Today,* Omnigraphics, Inc., 1999.

Periodicals

American Record Guide, March–April 1996.
The Detroit Free Press, November 28, 1984.
The New York Times, February 23, 1988; October 16, 1988.
Ovation, October 1988.
Time, March 25, 1991.

Online

"Interview-Mitsuko Uchida," *The London Symphony Orchestra website,* http://www.lso.co.uk/newsfeatures/uchida.html (January 30, 2003).
"Mitsuko Uchida," Biography Resource Center Online, Gale Group, 1989.
"Mitsuko Uchida Biography," *Arts Management Group, Inc. website,* http://artsmg.com/uchida.htm (January 30, 2003).

"Uchida Speaks at Peabody," *Johns Hopkins University website,* http://www.jhu.edu/~newslett/03-03-98/Arts/5.html (January 30, 2003). □

Al Unser

Although Al Unser (born 1939) may not be ranked as the greatest race-car driver of all time, he is the most successful racer in the history of the Indianapolis 500 Motor Speedway. During his three-decade career Unser had four first-place finishes, three second-place finishes, four third-place finishes, one fourth-place finish, one fifth-place finish, and two other top-ten finishes in the race.

Alfred Unser was born on May 29, 1939, in Albuquerque, New Mexico. The youngest of four brothers, he grew up in a racing family. His father Jerry and uncles Louis and Joe were or had been race car drivers, and although they never made it to the Indianapolis 500 they were annual competitors in Colorado's Pikes Peak International Hill Climb starting in 1926. Joe Unser was the first member of the Unser family to lose his life racing, dying in 1929 following an accident in Colorado while test-driving a FWD Coleman Special.

A Family Affair

Unser's eldest brother, Jerry, a rising star in the racing world, was the reigning national stock car champion in 1956. Jerry Unser became the first family member to compete in the Indianapolis 500 in 1958, finishing 31st. A year later, he lost his life following a fiery crash during a practice run, leaving other family members to compete in his stead. By 2002 six Unsers had competed in the Indy 500: brothers Al and Bobby, as well as Al's son, Al Jr., with a combined nine victories, had walked away with over a quarter of all Indy first-place wins. Bobby Unser (born 1934) made his first appearance in the Indy 500 in 1963 and won the race in 1968, 1975, and 1981. Al Unser, Jr. (born 1962) went on to become the first second-generation Indy 500 champion. Besides Al Jr., other Indy competitors in the Unser family include Jerry's son Johnny and Bobby's son Robby.

The Indy 500

The first Indianapolis 500 was held on Memorial Day 1911, at the Indianapolis, Indiana Motor Speedway. Built in 1909 as a testing ground for Indiana's then rapidly expanding automobile industry, the Indianapolis Motor Speedway was originally used to promote automobile sales. Affectionately known as "The Brickyard," the track was originally surfaced with paving bricks. Although the modern track is covered by asphalt, most of the original paving bricks are still in place under the asphalt surface. Running 2.5 miles in length, the track has four turns linked by two long straight sections and two short straight sections. Today, billed as the Greatest Spectacle in Racing, the 500-mile competition is

America's premier automobile race, pitting drivers against each other as they travel at average speeds well in excess of 150 miles per hour (mph).

In 1957 18-year-old Unser began driving modified roadsters in Albuquerque. He first drove in the Pike's Peak Hill Climb in 1960, taking second in that race to his older brother Bobby's first. He also won the dirt track "Hoosier Hundred" four years in a row. In 1964 Unser made his Indy car debut in Milwaukee, Wisconsin. Later the same year he won the Pikes Peak Hill Climb, putting an end to his brother Bobby's six-year winning streak. During this time he also raced sprints and midgets.

In 1965 Unser entered his first Indy 500, finishing ninth after starting in the last row. That same year he also captured his first "champ car" victory at Pikes Peak. In 1967 he came in second in the Indy 500, finishing behind A. J. Foyt, and claimed his first lead position by posting the fastest qualifying speed. Racing United States Auto Club stock cars, Unser was named Rookie of the Year, and in 1968 won five consecutive races and took five poles—the pole, or lead starting, position is awarded to the car with the fastest qualifying time. He was unable to compete in the 1969 Indy 500 due to a broken leg, but the year nevertheless saw him win five races in 19 starts.

"Everything Went Right"

In 1970 Unser drove his Johnny Lightning Special to an Indy 500 victory after leading for all but ten of the 200 laps and maintaining an average speed of 155.749 mph. Among his competitors in the race was his brother Bobby. Aided by a pit crew able to provide the driver with lightning-quick pit stops, Unser went on to accumulate a total of ten victories on oval road and dirt tracks during the 1970 season, earning him the United States Auto Club national championship. In the same year, he took eight poles, including at Indianapolis. Unser would later tell *ESPN.com:* "Everything went right that year. Everything. The car was right. The mechanics. I was right. You find that very seldom. I was almost unbeatable."

In 1971 Unser repeated his previous year's Indy 500 victory, averaging 157.735 mph to become one of only four back-to-back winners. He has maintained that the biggest difference in his two victories was that, after the second one, he did not have any trouble finding the victory lane. There was a near tragedy during the 1971 race, however, when Unser's brother Bobby was involved in a two-car crash. Unser, though he saw the accident, didn't find out whether his brother was alright until the next lap, when he saw Bobby standing beside the track waving at him.

Life in the Slow Lane

Following his 1971 repeat Indy 500 win, Unser went four years with only a single major racing victory. In 1972 he just missed his bid to become the first person to win the Indy 500 three times in a row after he finished second to Mark Donohue. In 1973 Unser joined the Penske racing team, posting ten top-five finishes and claiming a second PPG Industries championship.

In 1977 Unser won races at Pocono, Milwaukee, and Phoenix. He also came in second in Indy-car points—points are awarded to the fastest qualifier and to the driver leading by the most laps in a race—and won the International Race of Champions (IROC) championship. The following year he took racing's Triple Crown by winning at Indianapolis, Pocono, and Ontario. He also recaptured the IROC championship.

A Long Shot

Entering the 1978 Indianapolis 500 in a FNCTC Chaparral Lola, Unser was considered a long shot in that year's race. Then, during the 75th lap, he took the lead. With less than a third of the race remaining, his closest competitor blew an engine and Unser went on to win the race with an average speed of 161.363 mph. Unser's combined victories at Indianapolis, Pocono, and the California 500's in 1978 made him the first driver to clinch what were quickly dubbed "Triple Crown" honors.

In 1983 Unser became the first driver to race against his son, Al Jr., in the Indy 500, then went on to capture the Championship Auto Racing Teams (CART) championship series. Two years later, at the age of 46, he became the oldest ranking Indy car-CART champion after defeating Al Unser, Jr. by one point.

The Old Man

The year 1987 marked Unser's most exciting Indy 500 victory. That year car owner Roger Penske dropped the 48-year-old Unser from his racing team in favor of a younger driver named Danny Ongais. After Ongais crashed his car into a wall during practice shortly before qualifications, both the driver and Penske's car were out of commission. The Penske team quickly began readying a used 1986 March that had been sitting in a hotel lobby in Pennsylvania and installed a Cosworth DFX engine in the March after they were unable to find a preferred Chevy engine for it. Penske asked Unser to race the car at Indy.

Accepting Penske's offer, Unser took his first practice laps in the March only three days before the second weekend of Indy 500 qualifications. On race day, after starting in the 20th position, Unser took the lead during the 183rd lap and sped to victory with an average speed of 162.175 mph. The win—Unser's fourth—tied him with A. J. Foyt for the most wins in the Indy 500. At the same time, Unser also broke his brother Bobby's record as the oldest Indy 500 winner. A year later, in 1988, Unser became the record holder for the most laps led—625—at the Indy 500.

Retirement and Legacy

Unser announced his retirement on May 17, 1994, a day after the 54-year-old race-car driver attempted to qualify for his 28th Indy 500 race. As Unser told ESPN.com, "I always said if the day came when I wasn't producing the right way, if I wasn't happy, I'd get out. . . . The time has come. A driver has to produce 100 percent. You can't just come in and strap one of these cars on and expect to give answers to the team that they need. I finally realized that it just wasn't there, and I wasn't producing like I should."

At his retirement Unser ranked first in points earned at the Indianapolis 500; second in miles driven and total money won; and—a tie—in total number of Indy 500 starts. In a racing career lasting from 1964 to 1994 he won the Indianapolis 500 four times—in 1970, 1971, 1978, and 1987—and earned victories in 35 other races. By the time he called it quits, Unser's 39 career CART victories placed him third behind A. J. Foyt's 67 and Mario Andretti's 52 wins. Before retiring in 1994, Unser had won over $6 million on the Indy car circuit. He also achieved distinction as one of only three drivers to win on paved ovals, road courses, and dirt tracks in a single season, a feat he accomplished three years running (1968, 1969, and 1970). Unser was inducted in the Motorsports Hall of Fame in 1991. Andretti, in an interview with *ESPN.com,* praised Unser as one of the top five racers who had ever lived.

Books

Keyser, Michael, *The Speed Merchants: The Drivers, the Cars, the Tracks: A Journey through the World of Motor Racing, 1969–1972,* R. Bentley, 1998.

Online

"Al Unser," *Motorsports Hall of Fame,* http://www.motorsports halloffame.com/halloffame/1998/Al_Unser_Sr_main.htm (January 20, 2003).

"Al Unser, Sr. Had Race Savvy," *ESPN.com,* http://espn.go.com/classic/biography/s/Unser_al.html (January 20. 2003).

"Al, You're My Hero," *World of Racing Web site,* http://www.bjwor.com/2k1210.html (January 17, 2002).

"Carving the Unser Name into Racing Legend," *Barnes Dyer Marketing Web site,* http://www.trainingforum.com/Speakers/aunser.html (January 20, 2003).

"History of the Indianapolis 500," http://ims.brickyard.com/history.php (January 20, 2003). □

Urraca

Queen Urraca (c. 1078–1126), who ruled the Kingdom of Leon-Castilla (also known as Castille-Leon) in northern Spain from 1109 to 1126, was the only woman during the Spanish medieval era to rule in her own right. The failure of her political marriage, which had been designed to unite the kingdoms of Leon-Castilla and Aragon, ultimately led to a civil war.

Background

Between 985 and 1002, the armies of the Muslim Caliphate of Cordoba repeatedly defeated the Christian armies of northern Spain. But with the death of the Muslim dictator's son and successor in 1008, the Cordoban caliphate began to collapse. With the fall of the caliphate, the dynasties of northern Spain began to rebuild themselves.

But fighting ensued between the Spanish provinces of Leon, Castilla, and Navarra. The Navarrese king eventually took control of both Castilla and Leon—the largest of the northern Christian states—giving rise to a new kingdom under the rule of the king of Navarra. When King Fernando I died in 1065, he divided his empire between his three sons. Fratricidal fighting followed, with Fernando's eldest son, Alfonso VI, becoming king.

Urraca

Urraca was the daughter of King Alfonso VI and Queen Constance of Burgundy. Constance was the second of the king's wives, both of them French, a reflection of the monarch's wish to strengthen his territorial claims.

Urraca's first husband, Count Raymond of Burgundy, came to Spain around 1086. Evidence suggests that he was almost immediately betrothed, and possibly married, to Urraca, who was then no more than eight years of age. Although canon law set a minimum age for marriage at twelve years for women, exceptions occurred. Records indicate that the marriage of Raymond and Urraca was formalized by 1090, when Alfonso VI issued a charter to the church of Palencia in their name.

In late September 1107, following Count Raymond's death, Urraca succeeded her husband as ruler of Galicia, the Zamora district, and lands to the southeast. As the wife of Raymond, Urraca was familiar with the politics of the royal court. She was about 27 years old, with two children. Her first child, Sancha, was born sometime before 1095. Her son, Alfonso Raimundez, who would later become Alfonso VII, was born on March 1, 1105. There may have been as many as seven other conceptions that ended in miscarriages, stillbirths, or childhood deaths during the marriage of Urraca and Raymond.

Political Marriage

Before Alfonso VI died, he arranged to have Urraca marry her relative, Alfonso I of Aragon. When the king died on June 30, 1109, Urraca ascended to the throne and, in accord with her father's wishes, married Alfonso I around October 1109. The alliance meant that Leon-Castilla would be governed by a male warrior who was related to Urraca by blood but who stood above local divisions within the kingdom. Alfonso I was about 36 at the time of the marriage, Urraca about 29. For Alfonso the match held political advantage and promise, while for Urraca it meant a loss of the power she had held since 1107.

The marriage agreement between Urraca and Alfonso I stipulated that if either party left the other against the other person's will, he or she would forfeit the loyalty of his or her followers. Alfonso had to promise not to leave Urraca for reasons of blood relationship or excommunication. If Alfonso were to have a son by Urraca, the child would inherit his territories in Aragon jointly with Urraca following Alfonso's death. If no child was conceived, Urraca and her heirs would be the inheritors. If Urraca died first, Alfonso would be entitled to the profits from her lands until he died; following his death the lands would fall to her son by her first marriage, Alfonso Raimundez.

Although Alfonso I would become the greatest warrior of his time—in 1118, he would defeat the great taifa of Zaragoza—he proved too weak to compel acceptance of the alliance with Leon-Castilla. He also failed to father a child with Urraca as quickly as expected. Urraca accused him of physical abuse. Finally, after the Church condemned the marriage on the grounds of consanguinity, there was no way the marriage could continue.

Marital Discord and Civil War

The Muslims threatened to occupy Aragon in the summer of 1109, but Alfonso, accompanied by Urraca, defeated the Muslim forces on January 24, 1110. The following summer, Urraca and Alfonso separated. Two years later, Urraca led her forces against those of Alfonso in an attempt to retake Castilla, which had been seized by her husband. By 1113, Alfonso laid claim to Toledo, Leon, Castilla, and Aragon. The marriage between Urraca and Alfonso was annulled in 1114.

With continued fighting between Urraca and Alfonso I, Urraca made her son by Count Raymond, Alfonso Raimundez, her co-ruler and heir. By the winter of 1116, Urraca had reclaimed most of Castilla from her ex-husband. By that time, Alfonso I was planning on laying siege to the Muslim stronghold of Zaragoza. To free his hand, Alfonso agreed to negotiate a truce with Urraca. The truce would hold until Urraca's death nine years later. And so, in 1117, Urraca chose to hold Castilla at the expense of giving up Zaragoza.

Alfonso I captured Zaragoza from the Moors in 1118. He spent the next five years consolidating that victory, capturing Calatayud in 1120, and many other towns after that. In 1125 he raided Andalusia, raising Christian morale, while encouraging Christians in Muslim lands to settle in his domain. Meanwhile, Urraca focused her attention on securing Toledo.

In 1120, Urraca made the tactical mistake of briefly seizing the prelate Bishop Gelmirez, who had served her father but favored a faction surrounding her son following the death of Alfonso VI. The act placed her at risk of excommunication and could have led to her deposition and replacement by her son. But by appealing directly to the pope, she was able to counter her enemies at home.

Death of Urraca

Urraca died on March 8, 1126, at Saldana on the Rio Carrion in the Tierra de Campos. (Some sources the give the date of her death as March 9.) It is not known whether she died of an extended illness.

Some writers have stated that Urraca took as lovers Count Gomez of Candespina and Count Pedro Gonzalez of Lara. It has also been speculated that Urraca used her relationships with suitors as a weapon to achieve political gains,

since there is no record that she was ever dominated by any of her reputed paramours. In speeches attributed to Urraca, the queen referred to herself as a lone, poor, weak woman, but her motivation for making these statements is not clear. Possibly they were only meant to appeal to sympathetic listeners.

Uracca's son and heir Alfonso VII was initially refused the crown in favor of Urraca's consort, Count Pedro Gonzalez of Lara and his brother, Rodrigo Gonzalez, Count Astururias de Santillana. But with the support of his allies, Urraca's son ascended to the throne as Alfonso VII in fairly short order, inheriting a kingdom internally at peace. He then set about to recover lands that had been lost to Alfonso I. In 1134, he defeated Alfonso I, who was killed in the battle. Urraca's daughter, Sancha, who never married, played no further role in the monarchy.

Urraca's Legacy

Of Urraca's seventeen years on the throne, only four did not involve a military campaign. Still, Urraca was probably fortunate because the Muslim threat to Leon-Castilla reached its peak at the end of the reign of her father.

During her reign, Urraca made four major policy decisions: to end her Aragonese marriage in 1110–1112; to associate her son with herself in governing her kingdom in 1111 and 1116; to make a truce with Aragon in 1117; and to seize the Archbishop Gelmirez in 1120.

Urraca left 118 known charters. Urraca's administration appears to have been successful, given the paucity of surviving documents. Her society was chiefly agricultural, with a limited exchange of goods locally. Her government would have been expected to arbitrate disputes rather than establish social directions. A number of coins from Urraca's reign survive, some bearing her likeness.

In the 12th century, the Church was involved at every level of political, social, economic, and religious dispute. The bishops of Leon-Castilla opposed Urraca's marriage with Alfonso I, supported her son, and organized military expeditions in defense of her kingdom against the Aragonese in the east and the Muslims in the south. Urraca was able to secure papal support to achieve her own purposes. She avoided excommunication in 1110–1111 over her marriage and persuaded the Church to bless her truce with Alfonso I in 1117.

Books

Reilly, Bernard F., *The Kingdom of Leon-Castilla under Queen Urraca, 1109–1126,* Princeton University Press, 1982.

Online

"Urraca of Castile and Leon," http://www.goldenfrog.com/jeffman/genealogy/html/d0001/I4493.html (February 2003). □

V

Theodore Newton Vail

Theodore Newton Vail (1845–1920) was an American entrepreneur who made his fortune in the telephone and mining business and became the first president of the Bell Telephone Company (later American Telegraph and Telephone or AT&T). President of the company for two separate tenures, he was instrumental in establishing telephone service, both local and long distance. A true visionary when it came to running a corporation, Vail oversaw the building of the first U.S. coast-to-coast telephone system, and it was his dedication to basic science that initiated a new research arm for AT&T's Bell Laboratories.

Vail was born on July 16, 1845, near the town of Minerva, Ohio. His family was rich and influential, its members descended from John Vail, a Quaker preacher who settled in New Jersey in 1710.

Strong Family Heritage

Affluence was not the Vail family's only attribute. There was a strong tradition of mechanical innovation, business acumen, and foresight. Vail's relatives were builders, inventors, and engineers. His grandfather, Lewis Vail, was a civil engineer who moved to Ohio and made his name building canals and highways, relatively new infrastructures at that point in American history. One of his uncles, Stephen Vail, was founder of the Speedwell Iron Works, near Morristown, New Jersey. The Speedwell company built a great deal of

the mechanical technology that went into the first steamship that crossed the Atlantic Ocean.

Appropriately enough, other relatives were involved in communications. Vail's uncle Stephen, together with Stephen's sons George and Alfred Vail, funded inventor Samuel F. B. Morse with the money for his wireless transmitter. Cousin Alfred Vail invented the dot-and-dash alphabet utilized by Morse's telegraph. In 1848 Vail himself learned to operate this telegraph when he moved to New Jersey and worked as a clerk in a drugstore. By the time he turned 19, he was working at the Western Union Telegraph Company in New York City.

Married, Vail had one adopted daughter, Katherine, who was actually the daughter of his brother, William Alonzo Vail. She would become one of the founders of Bennington College in Bennington, Vermont.

In 1866 Vail moved his family to Iowa. Three years later, he joined the U.S. Post Office, working in the postal railway service. Like family members before him, he proved to have a knack for innovation. He started the "Fast Mail," the first mail-only train service, which in 1875 began operations between New York City and Chicago. In 1876 Vail became general superintendent of this railway mail service.

Besides being an innovator, Vail was also an investor and entrepreneur. However, not all of his investments flourished. In 1889 he lost a great deal of money when an enterprise he was involved in, the Boston Heating Company, went out of business.

Joined Bell Telephone

In 1878 Vail left the Postal Office to become general manager of the recently established American Bell Telephone Company, which was started on July 9, 1877. The company had been organized by Gardiner G. Hubbard,

419

creative and effective research and development branch of the company. This division essentially changed the way the people of the world electronically communicated with each other. Also, he helped establish the Western Electric Company, a division of Bell Telephone that built telephone equipment.

Vail proved to be an appropriate choice to head the company, as he introduced business practices than facilitated the almost unparalleled growth of Bell Telephone. At first, however, he might have often questioned his own decision. As a new invention, the telephone was viewed as little more than a "toy," and the public was at first slow to accept the instrument. During Vail's first tenure with the company, less than ten percent of the population had embraced the telephone. Vail also had to deal with legal opposition from communications rival Western Union Telegraph Company. However, after years of legal battles the phone company prevailed in court.

Eventually Vail left Bell following a dispute with the company's board of directors. Board members wanted higher dividends; Vail wanted to put more money back into the company.

Vail played a large part in the success of Bell Telephone due to his strong business sense and his forward-looking vision. He has been credited with seeing the company as more than just a communications business. He recognized early on that the overriding concern was customer service. Vail stated as much to his management staff and brought them all in line with that vision. Later, when he returned from retirement to head the company a second time, he clarified this notion as "universality of service." The strength of the Bell System, he wrote in the company's annual report to shareholders in 1907, resided in its universality, which "carries with it the obligation to occupy and develop the whole field."

Retirement and Return

Vail retired from the Bell Telephone Company in 1889. True to his entrepreneurial spirit, he then involved himself with investments in mining, waterpower plants, and railway systems in Argentina. When not in South America, he reportedly lived a peaceful life on his Vermont farm. However, the company would eventually come calling again, and Vail was lured out of retirement in 1909.

Vail was 62 years when he went back to work, lured by financier J. P. Morgan, who now controlled the company. By this time the Bell Telephone Company had become American Telephone & Telegraph (AT&T). Vail's mission was to save the troubled organization, which had gotten into trouble because its phone patents had expired and other smaller companies were coming into the telephone communications business.

Vail was repositioned in his previous job but faced a situation and territory that had changed substantially. AT&T now faced competition. When Bell's telephone patents expired in 1893 and 1894 many independent telephone companies entered the game. By 1900 almost 6,000 new companies provided service to nearly 600,000 customers. Vail confronted this new problem with three workable solu-

father-in-law of Alexander Graham Bell. It was Hubbard who lured Vail from the postal service to the new company. Hubbard became familiar with Vail when he was involved in congressional investigations into Post Office methods of payment for mail transportation. Hubbard recognized in Vail the qualities that would be necessary to head a new and technologically innovative company. For his part, Vail recognized the viability of the new invention and realized its potential applications. Though his friends and family advised him against the move, Vail accepted the position.

At Bell, Alexander Graham Bell, inventor of the telephone, became the company's "electrician," earning a nominal salary of $3,000 annually. Bell's assistant, Thomas A. Watson, recipient of the world's first-ever phone call, was named superintendent in charge of research and manufacturing, while Vail held the managerial position until 1887. Years later, Vail would come out of retirement to lead the company a second time.

During his first tenure, Vail demonstrated both a knack for anticipating technical developments and the vision for combining technologies. One of his major accomplishments was directing the expansion of local telephone exchanges. In 1881 he directed the first long-distance phone system, which extended from Boston, Massachusetts, to Providence, Rhode Island. In addition, he organized the financing and business structure of the system. By 1885 Vail had created a vertically integrated supply division as well as a network of affiliates licensed by the parent company. Perhaps even more significantly, he had created a highly tions. First and most importantly, he decided AT&T should offer the best phone system possible. To this end he focused the company on establishing a long-distance phone network that would encompass all of the United States. To accomplish this ambitious aim, Vail knew he would have to commit large-scale investments into the area of scientific research. This commitment resulted in the creation of the company's own research branch, Bell Laboratories.

Vail's most significant accomplishment in the direction was establishing a connection with all existing phone companies into the AT&T system. This resulted in the creation and implementation of the envisioned long-distance system. On January 25, 1915, the first transcontinental phone line was up and running. Vail himself was part of this first transmission that connected Alexander Graham Bell in New York to Thomas Watson in San Francisco. The connection would also include President Woodrow Wilson in Washington, D.C. Only a year later, long-distance phone service was established to Europe.

Vail's second solution involved cooperation with competitors and leasing them use of his company's phone lines. Third, and perhaps most tricky, he convinced the U.S. government that the best possible phone service—his concept of "universal service"—could best be accomplished through a monopoly. At first the government had balked at the idea. Federal regulators were unhappy with what it felt was the ruthless behavior the company demonstrated during the interim between Vail's two leadership tenures. In addition to prohibiting smaller companies the use of its network, AT&T also held a stranglehold on long-distance circuits. The smaller companies, lacking the funds to battle a giant like AT&T, were swallowed up by the larger company. In fact, not only was the government unhappy with AT&T; the public was, too.

To counter the government's resistance, Vail advanced a rather interesting argument: that telephone service essentially amounted to a natural monopoly, like postal service, and that everyone was best served by such a monopoly. The government saw the merits in this notion. In 1913 the legal department of President Woodrow Wilson's administration granted AT&T a phone monopoly in exchange for certain concessions. For one thing, AT&T had to agree to allow independent companies to connect to its network. This agreement was known as the Kingsbury Commitment, as it was initiated by AT&T Vice President Nathan C. Kingsbury, who understood that such an agreement would diminish the perception that his company was a bullying giant. The agreement was concluded without the public's knowledge, and it would stand for decades until the deregulation that came late in the 20th century.

Benevolent Monopoly

The company's monopoly served both the company and customers well, and AT&T grew both financially and technologically. In the ensuing decades it became the most advanced and reliable phone system in the world. In the process, the telephone—in the hands of AT&T—had a profound effect on society and business. Indeed, as early as 1934 telecommunications had become so firmly en-

trenched that Congress felt compelled to create the Federal Communications Commission.

A great part of the great transformation wrought by the industry is directly attributable to Vail's vision as a leader. When he combined the engineering departments of AT&T and Western Electric he created a research department—Bell Laboratories—that produced innovations that would have far-reaching implications, such as the transistor, touch-tone telephones, data networking, and optical and digital technologies. Through the years Bell Labs and its researchers would be honored with six Nobel Prizes, nine U.S. Medals of Science, six Medals of Technology, and many other awards.

Second Retirement

Vail retired a second time in 1919. He joined the company's board of directors, but died a year later on April 16, 1920, in New York state. He was survived by his adopted daughter, Katherine Hurd; two sons, Theodore N. V. and Andrew C.; 14 grandchildren; and nine great-grandchildren.

After his death, the Vail Award was established to honor his memory. It is awarded to individuals who perform above and beyond the call of duty on their jobs or who display unusual bravery or heroism during emergencies.

Periodicals

Fortune, September 18, 2001.

Online

"History and Regulation of the Telephone Industry," *The International Engineering Consortium Web site,* http://www.scte .org/chapters/newengland/reference/Telephony/topic 01.htm (March 15, 2003).

"Theodore N. Vail," *District Energy Biographies,* http://www .energy.rochester.edu/bio/vail/ (March 15, 2003).

Theodore Newton Vail, Biography.com, http://search.biography .com/print_record.pl?id=20292 (March 20, 2003).

"Theodore Newton Vail," *GeneExchange.org,* http://www .genexchange.org/bioreg2.cfm?state=nj&=8916 (March 15, 2003).

"Theodore Newton Vail," *Transistorized,* http://www.pbs.org/ transistor/album1/addlbios/vail.html (March 15, 2003). □

Luisa Valenzuela

Luisa Valenzuela (born 1938) is an Argentine writer of both fiction and journalistic works. She is among her nation's most significant writers, best known for the style of writing that blends magical and fantastic elements into prose known as magical realism, a style often associated with Latin-American writers such as Gabriel García Marquez and Julio Cortazar. Valenzuela is also one of the most widely translated female South American writers. As Naomi Lindstrom wrote in *World Literature Today,* Valenzuela "has

created numerous narratives in which authoritarian rule in society is mirrored by patriarchal domination in relations between men and women."

Luisa Valenzuela was born November 26, 1938, in Buenos Aires, Argentina, to parents Pablo Francisco Valenzuela, a physician, and Luisa Mercedes Levinson, a writer of note in Argentina. Valenzuela, an insatiable reader since childhood, attended a British school in her youth.

Began Journalism Career as a Teen

Given her parents' place in society and the family's connections with academics, Valenzuela was able to meet writers such as as Jorge Luis Borges, Ernesto Sabato, and Peyrou in her youth. Her parents were a formative influence: "As a child I thought writing was dreary, drab, but they loved it," recalled Valenzuela in *Americas.* "They could be quite obnoxious but funny. That impressed me that writing was more lively than one would think." While she originally hoped to become a painter or a mathematician, writing eventually won out over those early career aspirations.

Valenzuela's first journalistic work appeared in magazines including *Esto Es, Atlantida, Quince Abriles,* and *El Hogar* while she was still in her teens. Her first short story, "Ese Canto," was published in 1956. Valenzuela also worked for a time at the Biblioteca Nacional, where Borges

was the library's director. She went on to earn a bachelor of arts degree from the University of Buenos Aires.

In 1958 Valenzuela married Theodore Marjak, a French merchant marine and moved with her husband to Normandy, where her daughter, Anna-Lisa, was born. It was while living in France that Valenzuela wrote her first novel, published in 1966 as *Hay que sonreir* (published in English as *Clara),* which she wrote while her daughter was napping. In a review of the book, a reviewer for *Publishers Weekly* called the tale a chronicle of "the bizarre, brutal existence of characters on the fringes" and a "harsh, provoking yet graceful tale of exploitation."

Divorcing her husband after five years of marriage, Valenzuela moved to Paris and began working as a writer for Radio Television Française. She returned to Buenos Aires in 1961 and worked as an editor at *La Nacion,* the Buenos Aires newspaper, as editor of the Sunday supplement from 1964 to 1972. "I learned a lot from journalism because when I began to work for the supplement to *La Nacion* I stayed there for nine years," Valenzuela commented in an interview with *Matrix.* "I had a boss, Ambrosio Vecino, who was a literary man and was very keen on style. He taught me how to express ideas in a very concise way." Journalism "allows for a horizontal view of facts, as opposed to the vertical, in-depth, literary vision," she went on, adding: "I still appreciate journalism because I'm so interested in the world, and there are many issues that make me want to express an opinion, so I still use journalism as a tool and write columns and keep my fiction free of 'messages.'"

Fellowship and Grant Allowed for Travel

A collection of short stories titled *Los hereticos* was published in 1967. Valenzuela was subsequently awarded a Fulbright grant in 1969 that allowed her to participate in the International Writers Program at the University of Iowa. The result of this fellowship award was the novel *El gato eficaz,* which was published in 1972 and translated as *Cat-o-Nine-Deaths.*

Valenzuela began her freelance journalism career and started lecturing about writing in 1970. Over the course of the next two years she traveled to Barcelona, Paris, and Mexico on a grant from the National Arts Foundation of Argentina. Her journalistic work appeared in publications in the United States, Mexico, France, and Spain, as well as in various publications based in Buenos Aires. These publications included *La Nacion, New York Review of Books, Vogue,* and the New York-based *Village Voice.*

Left Argentina

Returning to Buenos Aires in 1974, Valenzuela discovered that the political situation in Argentina following the death of Juan Peron had degenerated into a paramilitary dictatorship rife with violence and repression. Between 1976 and 1983 some 20,000 Argentine citizens "disappeared." Continuing to work as an editor, Valenzuela also found fictional inspiration in the political regime under which she now found herself living, resulting in another short story collection, *Aqui pasan cosas raras,* published in 1975. Valenzuela had been teaching at Columbia

University periodically since 1973; in 1979 she was offered a writer-in-residence position and decided to move to the United States to escape the political repression. "I decided to leave in order not to fall into self-censorship," she told a contributor to *Belles Lettres.* "Exile may be devastating, but perspective and separation sharpen the aim." At Columbia University she became a teacher in the school's writing division from 1980 to 1983, the year she was awarded a Guggenheim fellowship.

Her fellowship allowed Valenzuela to move across town to New York University, where she was appointed visiting professor in 1985. She held that post until 1990, traveled frequently to lecture, and was a guest speaker at writing conferences in locations throughout the world, including the Americas, Israel, and Australia.

Political Repression Informed Fiction

Valenzuela became a fellow at the New York Institute for the Humanities in 1982 and belonged to the Freedom to Write committee of PEN's American Center. Her concerns with human rights issues prompted her to join Amnesty International.

As an essayist noted in the *Dictionary of Hispanic Biography,* Valenzuela's work continues to revolve around themes of politics and women's issues. Also rooted within her work is the violence and suffering experienced in many Latin American countries under authoritarian regimes. In her novel *Cola de lagartija*—translated as *The Lizard's Tail*—the protagonist, a cruel sorcerer, is based on Jose Lopez Rega, Isabel Peron's Minister of Social Welfare.

Z. Nelly Martinez, writing in *World Literature Today,* observed that Valenzuela's "main pre-occupation throughout the years has been the repressive character of our primarily masculinist Western culture. Thus the fate of women ... as well as that of all marginalized peoples, is at the center of the fictional realms she creates." Martinez maintained that through the power of language Valenzuela "has obsessively defied the established order," be it masculine, political, or religious, "with her own fictional practice."

"Another salient feature of Valenzuela's style is her approach to language as not only the means of conveying a theme, but also as the object of the story," added an essayist in *Feminist Writers.* For Valenzuela, "Language is supple and malleable, its purpose can be different for different people, and the denial of access to its multiple ranges of applications is seen as another form of oppression. Valenzuela contends that, as a writer, she is always discovering new meanings to words and that she hopes to unlock their secrets each time she endeavors to write something new."

Eventual Return to Argentina

With democracy restored to Argentina in April of 1989 Valenzuela returned to Buenos Aires. Returning on occasion to New York City, she continued to write prolifically, as evidenced by the publication of the novels *Novela negra con argentinos*—translated as *Black Novel (with Argentines)*—and *La travesia* as well as the 1990 short-story collection *Realidad nacional desde la cama (Bedside Manners).* A *Publishers Weekly* contributor, in a review of *Black*

Novel (with Argentines), dubbed the work "powerful, unusual and unsettling." Reviewing 2001's *La travesia,* Lindstrom described the novel as, while "not the most strikingly innovative of Valenzuela's fictions," nonetheless a book with "a good dose of social satire, a tricky and fast-paced plot whose diverse strands are well coordinated, and a cast of memorably weird secondary characters."

Valenzuela's works have been translated into English and have appeared in anthologies. Among the published collections to appear in translation is *Strange Things Happen Here: Twenty-Six Short Stories and a Novel* (1979), which includes the novel *Como en la guerra (He Who Searches)* as well as stories from *Aqui pasan cosas raras.* Among her best known works in translation are *Other Weapons, The Lizard's Tail, Black Novel (with Argentines),* and *Bedside Manners.* Much of her work has been published in translation outside the Americas, including Japan, and her books can be found in French, German, and Portuguese translations, leading to her acclaim as the most widely translated of the South American female authors.

"Valenzuela could be placed into the post-boom generation of Latin American writers, following on the heals [sic] of the explosion of popularity of authors who enjoyed a widely translated readership in Europe and North America," concluded the *Feminist Writers* essayist. "She is emphatic, however, that the Latin American boom was a sexist phenomenon, since all the writers recognized within that group were men, and since women whose writing was of comparable quality were virtually ignored."

Books

Dictionary of Hispanic Biography, Gale, 1996.
Feminist Writers, St. James Press, 1996.

Periodicals

Americas, January-February, 1995.
Belles Lettres, January, 1996.
Knight Ridder/Tribune News Service, August 10, 1994.
Publishers Weekly, March 9, 1992; November 21, 1994; December 20, 1999.
World Literature Today, Winter 1984; Autumn 1995; Spring 2002.

Online

"Interview with Luisa Valenzuela," *Matrix,* http://alcor .concordia.ca/~matrix/excerpt3.html (February 28, 2003). □

Gregorio Vázquez Arce y Ceballos

South American artist Gregorio Vázquez de Arce y Ceballos (1638-1711) was the most important painter of the Spanish Colonial era in Columbia. He worked during an era dominated by the Hispano-American Baroque style that flourished from 1650 to 1750. Vázquez has come to be regarded as the great-

est painter to come from Colombia. Most of his paintings are religious in nature, with subjects that include the life of Christ and of the Virgin, the saints, and scenes of the New Testament.

Gregorio Vázquez de Arce y Ceballos was born May 9, 1638, in Bogota, Columbia. Raised in that city, he grew up in the Creole society that first settled there in 1630. He was descended from a family of Andalusian ancestry, his family emigrating from Seville, Spain, settling in South America in the late 16th century.

The area where Vázquez grew up possessed a vibrant and artistic culture. This greatly influenced the young artist, providing him with an environment that fostered his artistic ambition. Still, Vázquez had to work long and hard to develop his artistic talents. To accomplish this, he often copied the styles and techniques of famous European artists.

Vázquez received his early education in a Jesuit seminary. When he was 15 years old, his father, Bartholomew Vázquez, recognized in his son an artistic talent that needed nurturing, and he encouraged the boy to paint. Through his father's efforts, Vázquez was able to study under Balthasar de Figueroa, one of the most famous artists of the day and a member of an artistic family. Even though his education with Figueroa did not last long, Vázquez learned a great deal and was inspired to begin producing works on linen cloth. One of his first works was painted for the convent of

Santa Clara de Tunja in 1657, when the artist was only 19 years old.

Diverse Artistic Influences

In addition to his studies as a disciple of Figueroa, Vázquez was inspired by European drawings and engravings as well as by the major works of art produced by European masters. His main inspirations included the Spanish artist Juan de Valdés Leal (1622–1690), who painted in the baroque style. Other influences included Italian Painters Sassoferrato (1609–1685) and Guido Reni (1575–1642), Flemish Painter Peter Paul Rubens (1577–1640), and Bartoleme Murillo (1617–1682), another Spanish painter, all of whose works found their way to Columbia. It is believed that Vázquez met Murillo's oldest son, who lived in Bogota from 1678 to 1700, and was able to see up close the works of the Spanish master.

Painted in the Baroque Style

Because of his technique and his use of color, Vázquez is considered a baroque painter. The baroque painting style emerged as a movement in Europe around the beginning of the 17th century as a reaction against the Mannerist style which dominated the late Renaissance period with its intricate and formulaic technique. The baroque style developed in Italy and then spread throughout Europe and into the Latin-American colonies. Baroque artists strove for a simpler, more realistic approach that would be emotionally engaging, and the movement was encouraged by the Catholic Church, then a major patron of the arts. Members of the Church regarded the baroque style as more traditional and spiritual. In this way, baroque painting demonstrates an influence of the ancient Greek and Roman art through its use of idealized human figures. The greatest artists of the baroque movement were Caravaggio, Peter Paul Rubens, Rembrandt, Gian Lorenzo Bernini, and Jan Vermeer.

More specifically, Vázquez belonged to the School of Colonial Painting, which combined Spanish baroque with the influence of the Italian, Flemish, and French schools and which is sometimes called "Creole art." What drove the development of colonial painting was the encouragement of the ecclesiastical powers, such as the Catholic Church, who saw art as a way to interpret religious beliefs for natives. In general, Spanish colonial art is very ornate, rich in color, and features strong delineation. The earliest of the Creole painters were Gaspar, de Figueroa, and Vázquez himself. The style flourished in the 1600s before declining in the early 18th century.

Even though Vázquez is generally regarded as the most outstanding Creole painter of his generation, his work has often drawn criticism. His style was said to lack a "dynamic impulse," though his forms were elegant, and he personalized his paintings with a series of signature gestures that identified his work. His work is viewed as lacking originality of composition, as he often copied European masters, but he remains a painter of note due to his skillful and compelling use colors.

It has been said of Vázquez that, like many other artists of his era, he largely ignored the world around him. For one thing, there seemed to be no recognition of the rich racial mosaic that surrounded him in Bogota, as his works mainly depicted Caucasians and Creoles. Also, his works display no great interest in the surrounding landscape, either in urban or rural settings, and reveal very little about Bogota in the 17th century. Even though he lived in a tropical landscape with lush foliage, he rarely depicted the local vegetation. When he painted fruits or flowers he usually used those that existed in Europe and America. Little, if anything, is seen of indigent tropical fruits such as mangoes or pineapples.

Became a Prolific Artist

Vázquez was said to have been a prolific artist and, unlike other artists of his era, he left behind a great number of drawings. He operated a studio located in the Candelmas district, where he trained many of his students. Here he kept busy completing commissioned works. Working with him at the studio were his wife Bernal, who often served as his model, his brother Juan Baptist, his son Bartholomew Luis, and his beloved daughter Feliciano. At this studio, he produced a great many works of varying subjects and sizes which he painted on linen canvases. His works were later displayed in temples and convents as well as in houses around Bogota.

At his studio Vázquez also taught students, among whom it is believed were Camargo and Francisco de Sandoval, two other artists who became well known. As a result of Vázquez's teaching and commissions, a great output of work came from this studio. Unfortunately, it has often been hard to distinguish his original paintings from the works of his students, who copied his style. However, there are a number of his works whose titles and dates of origin are known. One of the oldest, signed in 1657 is "Huida a Egipto," or "Escape from Egypt."

During the mid-1600s the painter spent almost 20 years producing little original work, instead copying the works of other artists. Around 1669 he copied the work of Murillo in "Vision de S. Antonio" and the work of Sassoferrato in "Virgen Modestissima." His "Virgen de los Angeles" is dated to 1670 and follows the style of Reni, though Vázquez only employed the vaguest of associations. The next year he created "La Anunsacion" for the Convent of Mongui. Ten paintings produced by Vázquez can be found at this famous Franciscan convent, and it is believed that he spent a good deal of time there. In 1674 he produced his highly regarded "Jucio Final" for the Church of Saint Francisco in Bogota. For this work he was most likely inspired by the anatomical drawings of Juan Valverde and Hamusco. When he was 32, he painted his first-large scale work on linen, "Purgatorio," for the parochial temple of Funza.

In 1680 Vázquez entered a very significant period in his career and was at his most prolific, producing many works for the convents in Bogota. This also was the period when he produced his "Self Portrait" (1685), which appeared in the cathedral of Bogota. During this time Vázquez was also commissioned to produce a series of works for the Church of the Shrine in Bogota. In this major project he was once again influenced by European models, after the founder of this church, his friend and patron Gomez de

Sandoval, brought back from a trip to Spain a series of stamps by Rubens.

During this period also he painted "S. Ingacio" for the Jesuits, completing this work in 1686. In 1698 he completed "Calvario" and "Predicacion de S. Francisco Javier," two more of his best-known works. Many of the paintings produced during this period of intense activity are now at the Museum of Colonial Art in Bogota, which contains 76 oils and 106 drawings by the artist. The museum was originally constructed by Jesuits who arrived in Colombia in the 17th century.

Later Life

The start of the 18th century marked the beginning of what would be a very difficult period in Vázquez's life. In the a short span of time his wife died and his daughter was seduced away from her father's home and went on to lead a life of hardship. Friend and patron Gomez de Sandoval also passed away. In addition to personal troubles, the painter endured financial difficulties and was briefly confined in prison. Still, Vázquez found the inspiration to paint even in confinement and produced six large works on linen cloth that eventually decorated the arches of the Chapel of the Shrine. Toward the end of 1710, only months before his death, Vázquez produced his final work, "Concepcion." Vázquez died in 1711 in Bogato, Colombia.

Online

"Art of the Americas," *New Orleans Museum of Art Web site,* http://www.noma.org/html_docs/amer_la.html (March 15, 2003).

"Gregorio Vázquez de Arce y Ceballos," *CanalSocial.com,* http://www.canalsocial.com/biografia/pintura/ceballos.htm (March 15, 2003). □

Yvonne Vera

Yvonne Vera (born 1964), one of Africa's most esteemed writers, has been showered with awards and her work has landed on feminist and African studies curriculums at universities across the world. Vera was born and raised against the backdrop of faltering colonialism and vicious guerilla warfare in 1970's Rhodesia, Southern Africa. Her childhood was spent watching men go off to war, many never to return, and watching women struggle to survive in a society where being a woman meant being a second-class citizen at best, ignored and abused at worst. Vera was just 15 when the guerilla armies triumphed over the colonialists, and Zimbabwe, declaring its independence, was born.

A s Vera finished her secondary studies, Zimbabwe was fitfully learning how to be a post-colonial nation. Though the country's white oppressors had been shaken off and black men were enjoying new free-doms, black women were learning that freedom would not yet be theirs. Traditional culture kept them down, in the kitchen, in the fields, in the bedroom, quiet and submissive. Paraphrasing the title of Vera's 1997 book, Zimbabwean women were expected to keep things "under the tongue," to suffer in silence. These oppressions—colonialism, racism, war, and sexism—have fueled Vera's writing.

Educated Amidst Revolution and Sexism

Vera was born in Bulawayo, Zimbabwe's second largest city, on September 19, 1964. Her mother was a school-teacher and her father, unlike many Zimbabwean men, supported his daughter's education. Even as a schoolgirl, Vera showed the promise of the future writer she would become. According to literature professor Charles R. Larson writing in *The World and I*, "A love of books was established before [Vera] began attending primary school (she could read and write before her formal education). Perhaps more important, she began writing when she was still a child. She remembers leaving notes and poems she often wrote for her mother. In school, other students identified her as 'the writer.'"

Of her early education Vera told *The World and I*, "I had an idyllic education in the sense of landscape. I was first educated in the rural schools of Matabeleland. It was marvelous. We ate, played, slept, and read under the moon. We had wild fruit and smoke from fires. Then I came back to the city and attended school in the townships of Luveve and Mzilikazi." Vera continued, "This offered a contrast and introduced me more fully to the urban African milieu, with all its contradictions and spontaneity. This was in the seventies, and all the rumblings of an armed struggle were about." This contrast between the beauty of the land and the horror of war has also become a dominant theme in Vera's writing.

Became a Writer in Canada

Following her secondary education in Zimbabwe, Vera traveled to Europe and encountered Western art and culture. Art galleries and the cosmopolitan lifestyle of the cities impressed her. This experience helped motivate her to apply to York University in Toronto, Canada. There she majored in film criticism and literature eventually earning a bachelor's degree, a master's, and a doctorate. She also penned her first work, 1992's *Why Don't You Carve Other Animals?*, a collection of short stories. Of her segue into the role of writer she told *The World and I*, "Writing crept upon me and surprised me, then I discovered that I loved the process and art of writing. It came by degrees, through my fingers to my body. . . . I wanted to be a writer and could answer at airports and immigration points and borders that I was a writer."

Vera was still living in Toronto when she wrote her first novel, *Nehanda*, a historical novel based on Mbuya Nehanda's struggle to lead Zimbabwe out of the clutches of colonialism. Brinda Bose wrote in *World Literature Today* that *Nehanda* "speaks to both post-colonialism and feminism in the historical context of Zimbabwe. *Nehanda*

[embodies] the essences of both the hope and the despair that mark the story of Zimbabwean."

Unlike her first work, which was published by a Toronto company, *Nehanda* was published by Baobab Books, a Zimbabwean publisher based in Harare. This collaboration marked the beginning of a very close relationship between Vera and Baobab Books. The company has since published all her works. Though the loyalty of this relationship has allowed Vera to truly explore her themes, some critics noted that this same relationship may have been what has kept Vera from the international literary radar for so long. Regardless, the literary awards that have been heaped upon her work have declared Vera one of the top African female writers. *Nehanda* received Second Prize for the Zimbabwean Publishers Literary Award for Fiction in English and special mention for the Commonwealth Writers Prize for Africa Region.

Spoke the Unspoken

With the 1994 publication of *Without a Name*, Vera began to explore darker themes, such as the tragedies that effect women. *Without a Name* details one woman's struggle during the tumultuous war of pre-independence Zimbabwe. A victim of rape caught between the ruthless, racist regime of the colonialists and the violent uprisings of guerilla fighters, she sees escape and a new beginning far from her rural home in the city of Harare. However, even worse consequences await her there and in desperation she kills her newborn child and returns to mourn in her hometown. This novel was short-listed for the Commonwealth Writers' Prize.

In her third novel, *Under the Tongue* (1996), Vera tackled another taboo subject that gnaws at the hearts of women—incest and rape. As in her previous novel, Zimbabwe's war for independence is a major character in the novel. *Under the Tongue* won first prize in the Zimbabwe Publishers' Literary Awards, was awarded the 1997 Commonwealth Writers' Prize (Africa region), and two years later won the prestigious Swedish literary award "The Voice of Africa."

Butterfly Burning was published in 1998 and set in a black township of Southern Rhodesia in the late 1940s. It is a bittersweet love story between a young girl and her much older lover. As he spends more and more time away on construction projects, she begins to follow her own life and is selected to train as one of the first black nurses in the country. When an unwanted pregnancy jeopardizes her training, she retreats alone to the harsh land and, with the long thorn of a bush, performs her own abortion.

Of the recurrence of normally private, painful themes in her novels, Vera told *The World and I*, "The position of women needs to be reexamined with greater determination and a forceful idea for change. In Zimbabwe, as perhaps elsewhere in the world, there is limited understanding of each moment of a woman's worst tragedy or her personal journey. Women have been expected to be the custodians of our society as well as its worst victims, carrying on no matter how hemmed in they feel and how abandoned in their need." By bringing the shameful, hidden tragedies that mar women's lives to the surface, Vera demanded that her culture change.

Became Director of Art Gallery

During these prolific years, Vera moved back to Bulawayo. She told *The World and I,* "I spent eight years in Toronto trying to grow up. I finally realized the necessity of my return to Zimbabwe and my hometown. I have never regretted it." In 1997 she was appointed Director of the National Gallery in Bulawayo. Voicing the challenges of running a gallery in her hometown, Vera told Radio Netherlands, "There is no word for gallery in Ndebele, the local language of Bulawayo. The building used to be a huge, half empty room with paintings. In a country where as many as 17 people have to live together in one room, which is maybe 3 meters by 3 meters, all that space was senseless." With that in mind, Vera has focused on making the gallery relevant to the community and to the townships. She has installed local folk and fine art and instituted workshops for women and children.

The Stone Virgins was published in early 2003. In it Vera tells the story of two sisters, Thenjiwe and Nonceba, living in the rural village of Kezi following the independence of Zimbabwe from Britain in the early 1980s. A soldier murders Thenjiwe and then rapes and multilates Nonceba. Vera once again calls to the forefront the terror of war and the heavy price that women in her culture have paid in the process.

Periodicals

Library Journal, September 15, 2000.
Publishers Weekly, February 17, 2003.
Village Voice, Literary Supplement, September 2000.
The World and I, June 1, 1999.
World Literature Today, January 1, 1995; June 1, 1996; Spring 1999.

Online

Brown University, www.landow.stg.brown.edu/post/Zimbabwe/vera.html.
Radio Netherlands, www.rnw.nl/culture/html/zimbulawayo 991217.html.
Universitat Bremen, http://www.fb10.uni-bremen.de/anglistik/kerkhoff/AfrWomenWriters/Vera/VeraIntro.html.
University of Australia, www.arts.uwa.edu.au/AFLIT/VeraEN.html. □

Vigilius

Pope Vigilius (died 555), whose pontificate lasted from 537 to 555, schemed as a deacon to become pope, only to suffer more pains for his ambitions than personal rewards. His pontificate was almost entirely dedicated to resolving a dispute with the Emperor Justinian of Constantinople over a question of Church dogma.

The argument between the pope and the emperor concerned certain writings that had been endorsed by the Council of Chalcedon in the fifth century. A sect of Christians known as the Monophysites objected to these writings. The Monophysites, who were numerous in the eastern part of the Roman empire, had the support of the emperor, who wished to see them brought into the Church.

Vigilius spent the last eight years of his life as a house prisoner of Justinian in Constantinople because of his refusal to condemn the disputed writings. Although Vigilius eventually agreed to censure the writings, he also attempted to reconcile his condemnation with the decisions made at the Council of Chalcedon. With the emperor satisfied, Vigilius was allowed to depart from Constantinople. He died shortly thereafter en route to Rome.

The Monophysite Dispute

The Council of Chalcedon, which first convened in 451, endorsed several writings that seemed to suggest that Jesus Christ had two distinct natures, one human and one divine, with the two natures united in one person. This idea had been advanced by the Patriarch Nestorius in the fifth century. The writings seemed to be given legitimacy in 519, when the Emperor Justin I enforced the Chalcedonian definition of faith.

By the sixth century, the Monophysites, who held that Jesus had a single divine nature, and not two as held by the Nestorians, constituted a large Christian sect in the eastern half of the Roman empire. Unable to reconcile their belief with the rulings of the Council of Chalcedon, the Monophysites remained outside the Church.

In 544, hoping to reconcile the Monophysites to the Church, the Emperor Justinian issued an edict that condemned Nestorian writings endorsed by the Council of Chalcedon on the grounds that they contained unorthodox ideas. This edict, known as the Three Chapters, was a list of condemnations of the writings of three authors: Theodore of Mopsuestia, Theodoret, and Ibas. Since the Council of Chalcedon had already cleared these authors of any heresy, Justinian's edict was interpreted as a slight to the council and an encouragement to the Monophysites.

The edict confused many members of the Church because parts of the condemned writings were in fact considered orthodox. The Second Council of Constantinople in 553 would also condemn the writings but would uphold the Chalcedonian canons. The Nestorian interpretation of Christ's dual nature was promulgated outside the Roman Empire in the sixth century by missionaries in Arabia, China, and India. By the 14th Century, however, the idea had begun to disappear.

Papal Ambitions

Pope Vigilius, who reigned as pope from 537 to 555, was descended from a Roman family of distinction. Vigilius's father, Johannes, had received the title of consul from the emperor, and the pope's brother, Repartus, was a Roman senator.

In 531, Vigilius was made a deacon of the Church. That year, a decree was issued allowing the pope to select his successor. Pope Boniface II (530–532) selected Vigilius to succeed him. But the clergy at St. Peter's opposed the idea. Boniface retracted his choice and destroyed the decree that allowed him to name a successor.

Representative to Constantinople

Boniface's eventual successor, Pope Agapetus I (535–536), made Vigilius a papal representative to Constantinople. There, the actress, theologian, and empress Theodora attempted to enlist Vigilius's help in gaining support for the Monophysites, including the Monophysite Patriarch Anthimus who had been deposed by Agapetus, in exchange for her help in making Vigilius pope and reportedly some seven hundred pounds of gold. Vigilius is said to have agreed to intervene on behalf of the Monophysites.

Following the death of Agapetus in April 536, Vigilius returned to Rome with letters from the Court of Constantinople and the money the empress had given him. But by then Silverius had already been made pope, with the help of the King of the Goths. A short time later, the Byzantine commander Belisarius stationed troops in Rome, which was facing a siege by the Goths.

The Empress Theodora wrote to Belisarius, asking him to pressure Silverius into restoring Anthimus as patriarch of Constantinople. Belisarius summoned Silverius to his headquarters and falsely accused him of scheming to help the Goths gain entry to Rome. The Byzantine commander demanded that Silverius reinstate Anthimus and lend his support to the Monophysites. Following Silverius' refusal, the pope was seized and officially deposed.

Elevated to Pope

Under pressure from Belisarius, Vigilius was elevated to pope, being consecrated and enthroned on March 29, 537. Meanwhile the falsely maligned Silverius was kept in Vigilius's custody, where he soon died from the harsh treatment he received.

With the enthronement of a pope sympathetic to the Monophysite cause, all should have been well between Rome and Constantinople. But the Empress Theodora soon discovered that Vigilius was just as much opposed to the Monophysites as his predecessor Agapetus had been. Although a letter that has been attributed to Vigilius expresses the pope's sympathies for the Monophysites, some feel it is a forgery. In any case, Vigilius did not restore Anthimus to his former position as patriarch.

In 540, Vigilius wrote two letters to Constantinople outlining his position on Monophysitism, one addressed to the Emperor Justinian and the other to the Patriarch Menas. In them, Vigilius supported the rulings of the Council of Chalcedon and approved the deposition of Anthimus.

Other letters from the first years of Vigilius's reign have survived that shed further light on his pontificate. In March 538, for example, he wrote to the Bishop of Arles about the Austrasian King Theodobert's marriage to his brother's widow. Also in 538, he sent a letter to the Bishop of Braga about Church discipline.

Disputes over Dogma

Meanwhile, fundamental disagreements over Church dogma were developing with Constantinople. In 543, the Emperor Justinian published a decree that condemned the heresies of Origen and sent copies to the patriarchs and to Vigilius. In an attempt to refocus Justinian's interventions, the Bishop of Caesarea pointed out that condemnation of Nestorianism would make it easier to bring the Monophysites into the Church.

Justinian had wanted to placate the Monophysites. But he also had a preoccupation with questions of dogma. After he was told that a condemnation of three fifth century ecclesiastics who had exhibited Nestorian tendencies—but had been endorsed by the Council of Chalcedon—would placate the Monophysites, Justinian issued an edict toward that end. Vigilius refused to accept Justinian's edict. In response, the emperor called the pope to Constantinople to resolve the matter.

Called to Constantinople

Vigilius was celebrating the feast of St. Cecilia when he was called away from the service and ordered by an imperial official to depart at once for Constantinople. The pope was taken to a ship. Meanwhile, the Goths under Totila were laying siege to Rome, causing tremendous misery to the populace. As the ship taking Vigilius to the eastern capital departed, stones were thrown at it and the pope cursed. The ship reportedly left on November 22, 545, and arrived in Constantinople around the end of that year. Although Vigilius sent ships laden with grain back to Rome, they were apparently captured en route.

In Constantinople, Vigilius tried to persuade Justinian to provide assistance to the Romans and Italians under siege by the Goths, but Justinian was preoccupied with his edict. Especially in the West, the Three Chapters had raised opposition because they seemed to condemn men who had long ago died in good standing with the Church and because the condemnation was seen as an insult to the Council of Chalcedon. It was also felt that the emperor had no business making Church doctrine. Nevertheless, there was nothing unorthodox about the Three Chapters.

Justinian pressured Vigilius into supporting the edict. Caught between the emperor's demands that he support the Three Chapters, and the western Church's insistence that he reject them, Vigilius wavered and then initially agreed to support Justinian's edict.

Facing the opposition of his own retinue of western bishops, Vigilius next retracted his support for the edict, prompting Justinian to make him a house prisoner. After Vigilius escaped, fleeing from a window by a suspended rope, the emperor persuaded him to return by proposing a general council.

The Council of Constantinople

Justinian called for the council to be in Constantinople. Vigilius preferred it to be held in Sicily or Italy so that more western bishops could attend. Nevertheless, it assembled in Constantinople on May 5, 553, at Hagia Sophia Cathedral, with the Patriarch of Constantinople presiding. Vigilius boycotted the council because the eastern bishops outnumbered those from the west. While the council was approving the Three Chapters, Vigilius condemned them.

On May 14, 553, Vigilius issued his Constitution, which rejected 60 propositions of Theodore of Mopsuestia. Vigilius's Constitution also refused to condemn either Theodoret or Ibas because the testimony of the Council of Chalcedon had removed all suspicion of heresy against them. But on June 2, 553, the council once again condemned the disputed writings, siding with Justinian.

After thinking over the matter for six months, Vigilius decided that ending the persecutions of the emperor against his clergy would be well worth the cost of his endorsement of the council. So in December 553, after a residence of eight years in Constantinople, Vigilius reached an understanding with the emperor in which Vigilius agreed to censure the disputed writings while endorsing the canons of the Council of Chalcedon. Once again, his decision brought criticism in the west.

Justinian allowed Vigilius to depart for Rome with the promise that the pope would share temporal power there. Vigilius began his journey home in 555. But before reaching Rome, he died en route at Syracuse on June 7, 555, leaving a troubled legacy to his successors. His body was taken to Rome and buried in the Basilica of Sylvester.

Books

Brusher, Joseph S., *Popes through the Ages,* Neff-Kane, 1980.

Online

"The Council of Constantinople," *Eternal Word Television Network,* http://www.ewtn.com/library/COUNCILS/CONSTAN2.HTM (February 2003).
"Pope Vigilius," *Catholic Encyclopedia,* http://www.newadvent.org/cathen/15427b.htm (February 2003). □

Jean Vigo

Film director Jean Vigo (1905–1934) had a brief career encompassing only four films, all of which were shot during the beginning of the sound era, but only one of which was full-length. Yet the critical acclimation of the poetic beauty of his work, which came posthumously, has been nearly unanimous.

Vigo was born Jean Bonaventure de Vigo in Paris on April 26, 1905, the son of anarchists Emily Clâro and Miguel Almereyda (real name: Eugêne Bonaventure de Vigo). In the early 1900s Almereyda was arrested numerous times and in 1901, at age 18, was sentenced to a year in prison for the manufacture of a bomb that failed to explode. He served nearly his entire sentence in solitary confinement. In 1904 Almereyda attended an antimilitarist congress in Amsterdam out of which sprang the *Association Internationale Antimilitariste* (AIA). Almereyda became one of the leaders of the French AIA. As such he was arrested and sentenced to prison in December 1905. He was released on an amnesty in June 1906. That same year he cofounded a weekly newspaper, *La Guerre Sociale (The Social War).*

Thus the tone was set for Vigo's early life. The anarchism and plotting were broken only by his father's jail sentences. In 1908 Almereyda was given a two-year prison sentence for praising a mutiny in the pages of *La Guerre Sociale.* He was released in August 1909. In 1913 Almereyda left *La Guerre Sociale* and cofounded the weekly, *Le Bonnet Rouge,* which became a daily the following year. Almereyda was named editor-in-chief. When war broke out in August 1914 Almereyda slowly began to inveigh against the military in the pages of his paper. Eventually the militarists who had maintained the upper hand in French politics had enough and he was arrested on August 6, 1917. He died in his cell under mysterious circumstances a week later. There is little doubt that Almereyda was murdered, though he was extremely ill with a ruptured appendix and peritonitis. Jean Vigo was 12 years old at the time.

Poor Health and Boarding Schools

Throughout his childhood Vigo was plagued by poor health, which worsened in the year after his father's death. Furthermore Vigo's mother shunted him off to relatives and boarding schools. Since his father's name was still notorious in France, Vigo was often forced to enroll under an assumed name-Jean Salles. Beginning in 1919, though, he spent two weeks with his mother in Paris every September. In the early 1920s he was in contact with his father's friends, who related to him facts about Almereyda's life and personality. In 1922 Vigo began attending Lycâe Marceau, a boarding school in Chartres. His studies concentrated on Latin and science, but more importantly he was near his mother, with whom he spent his vacations and occasional weekends. Enough time had elapsed since his father's death that he was able to enroll under his own name. In his late teens Vigo's health improved and he not only participated in sports at Lycâe Marceau, but he excelled in the 100-meter dash and football, where he was a goalkeeper. This almost semi-idyllic period in his life was to come to a sudden end, and the result was Vigo's estrangement from his mother.

Vigo was well versed in his father's work and legend, but the facts of Almereyda's death had always been glossed over, especially his mother's role in the legal drama that occurred afterward. From reading *Le Mystêre de Fresnes* (Fresnes was the prison where Almereyda died), by Albert Monniot, Vigo discovered that his mother—in order to win a lawsuit that would ensure Vigo's interests—consented to the lawyer's hypothesis that Almereyda's murder had been ordered by his own accomplices in order to stave off treachery to the cause. In 1924 the 19-year-old Vigo spent his summer vacation assembling a file that (he intended) would prove his father innocent of treachery.

Met Lydou at a Sanatorium

In June 1925 Vigo left Lycâe Marceau. His original plan was to enroll in a university, thereby extending his military deferment. Already Vigo, imbued with his father's antimilitarism, had managed to have his military physical postponed from December 1924. In late 1925 Vigo took some courses at the Sorbonne. It has been conjectured that it was at this time that Vigo decided to embark on a career in cinema. In early 1926 he fell ill once again and went to southern France to recuperate—first with his relatives, the Aubês (who had taken him in after Almereyda's death), then at a sanitorium, Font-Romeu, near Andorra, by the Spanish border. Because of his illness Vigo had to forgo the possibility of working on Abel Gance's film, *Napolâon,* but upon recovering and returning to Paris at the end of 1926 he set about using whatever contacts he had to gain entrée into the French film industry. Within a few months Vigo had a relapse of his illness and was back at Font-Romeu. To make matters worse, his continually deteriorating relationship with his mother left Vigo weakened and depressed. On and off he remained in such a state for more than a year, despite assistance from many friends (which at times left Vigo feeling guilty).

In 1928 his life and outlook began to take a positive turn. It was at the sanitorium that year where he met 19-year-old Elsiabeth Lozinska, known as Lydou. She was the daughter of a Polish industrialist who had been studying in Switzerland. If anything Lydou's condition was worse than Vigo's, as she was bedridden for most of her first year at Font-Romeu. In November 1928 the two were well enough

to return to Paris and announce their engagement. They were married on January 24, 1929.

Vigo soon had his first job in film, assisting the cameraman on a film titled *Vénus.* When the film ended, though, he was out of work and the couple relied on Lydou's father to help them financially. With the money his father-in-law sent Vigo purchased a secondhand Debrie film camera with which he set about filming the animals in the zoo. This first attempt ended in disaster and Vigo never worked as cameraman on any of his other films. However, he was undismayed and began planning a script centered on the city of Nice, where he and Lydou had traveled. Unfortunately before he could begin production of his film his health, and that of Lydou's, took another bad turn. The couple returned to Paris for medical consultations. By then Vigo had met Boris Kaufman, possibly the youngest brother of the pioneering Soviet filmmakers Dziga Vertov (real name Denis Kaufman) and Mikhail Kaufman. Kaufman would eventually serve as cameraman on all of Vigo's films. After Vigo's death, he immigrated to Hollywood where he worked on such films as *On the Waterfront, Twelve Angry Men,* and *The Pawnbroker.*

Directed *A Propos de Nice*

With Kaufman behind the camera, the young director saw that most of his sketchy film plan would not translate well to the screen, thus prompting him to create a serious outline for his project. The film that resulted was the short "documentary" *A Propos de Nice.* Vigo's anarchist politics and his sense of satire are both strong elements of the film, which contrasts the wealthy and the poor in the city of Nice. It has often been compared to two other "city films" of the period: *Berlin, The Symphony of a Great City,* directed by Walter Ruttmann and Vertov's *The Man with a Movie Camera,* which was set in Moscow.

However *A Propos de Nice* differs from those films in an important way; it is less reliant on temporal chronology in its structure. Thus while Ruttmann and Vertov both shaped a narrative around a "day in the life" (of Berlin or Moscow), Vigo opened his film with fireworks at night. Secondly, Vigo used toys as symbols for people and juxtaposed seemingly unrelated scenes. These elements moved the film away from being solely a documentary. In fact *A Propos de Nice,* with a running time of approximately 20 minutes, is at once a highly subjective critique of the city and a documentary of the gap between the rich and the poor. Filmed in 1929, *A Propos de Nice* debuted in Paris on May 28, 1930.

Vigo's next film is the least known and shortest of his quartet, and, likewise, the least appreciated. *Taris* (also known as *Taris, roi de l'eau* and *Taris, champion de natation),* filmed in 1931, is a short film featuring French swimming champion Jean Taris. The film included voice-over by Taris describing swimming trechniques, but the outstanding aspect is how Vigo once again turned the genre of documentary inside out, though *Taris* is neither as subjective nor as anarchistic as *A Propos de Nice.* When discussing *Taris* critics and film historians generally focus on the film's underwater shots and by extension the silence that engulfs the film. Both of these elements give *Taris* a dreamlike quality that is enhanced by the ending in which Taris is seen walking on water.

Zero de Conduite

Critics and film historians continue to debate which of Vigo's films is his masterpiece with many acknowledging that the title belongs to his third film, the 41-minute-long *Zero de conduite (Zero for Conduct)*. Others consider Vigo's last film, *L'Atalante*, his masterpiece. *Zero de conduite*, shot in 1933, was Vigo's first film that had a narrative structure in the usual sense, though in the filmic sense the story was far more poetic than realist. The film's plot revolves around the children of a boarding school who decide to revolt against the strict rules of behavior. The film highlights the child's world from beginning to end: it opens with two boys delighting each other on a train with tricks and games as they return to school after a vacation. These tricks reveal their own awakening sexuality and imitation of adulthood. They, along with a third boy, will become the chief plotters in the revolt after having been given a "zero for conduct." *Zero de conduite* was banned in France until 1946, but thereafter became an inspiration for many French New Wave filmmakers, especially Francois Truffaut who directed his own film about children, *The 400 Blows*.

Depsite the fact that *Zero de conduite* was banned Vigo managed to secure studio backing for his next project, *L'Atalante* (1934). It was Vigo's final film and the only one he directed that was feature length. *L'Atalante* is the story of two newlyweds who sail France's waterways on a barge, named L'Atalante. When the wife grows tired of barge life she abandons her husband for Paris, but the city overwhelms her. The husband sets out to find her, but in the end it is the half-crazy bargeman (portrayed by Michel Simon) who discovers her and returns with her to the barge.

The film was first shown in Paris in April 1934, and its first public performance was in September 1934 under the title *Le Chaland qui passâ*. Less than a month later Vigo finally succumbed to the tuberculosis from which he had suffered for years. He died in Paris on October 5, 1934. At the time of his death Vigo had left behind more than two dozen unrealized projects, including scripts by himself, Claude Aveline, and Blaise Cendrars. *L'Atalante*, which had been reedited and retitled during his final illness, was eventually restored and the world would come to recognize Vigo's genius.

Books

Salles Gomes, P.E., *Jean Vigo*, University of California Press, 1971.
Simon, William G. *The Films of Jean Vigo*, UMI Research Press, 1981.

Online

"Jean Vigo," *The Internet Movie Database*, http://us.imbd.com/Name?Vigo, + Jean (February 19, 2003).
"Jean Vigo," *Senses of Cinema*, http://www.senseofcinema.com/contents/directors/02/vigo.html (February 19, 2003). □

W

Mary Edwards Walker

Mary Edwards Walker (1932–1919) was a dress-reform advocate and women's rights activist who served as a physician for the Union army during the Civil War. She challenged the social and cultural mores of the Victorian-era middle class to their limits and in the process "out-raged the sensibilities even of those who believed themselves tolerant and progressive," as Elizabeth D. Leonard points out in her book *Yankee Women: Gender Battles in the Civil War.* Yet Walker refused to back off from her lifelong insistence that women deserved nothing less than full equality with men.

Mary Edwards Walker was born on November 26, 1832, in Oswego, New York. She was the youngest daughter of Alvah Walker, a farmer, teacher, and self-taught physician, and Vesta Whitcomb Walker, who was also a teacher. Influenced by reform movements advocating abolition and sexual equality that swept through their part of the state during the 1820s and 1830s, the Walkers were very liberal thinkers by the standards of the time. They supported the idea of equal education for boys and girls and urged all of their children—five daughters and a son—to aspire to professional careers and personal independence.

As a child, Walker attended a local school run by her parents. Later, she continued her education at a seminary in Fulton, New York, but left there in 1852 to teach. Within two years, however, Walker had made up her mind to become a doctor instead, challenging society's belief that teaching was the only appropriate job for a woman. She enrolled in Syracuse Medical College (one of the few institutions that admitted women) in 1853 and graduated two years later, then practiced briefly in Columbus, Ohio, before relocating to Rome, New York. There she married a fellow physician named Albert Miller, and together they set up a medical practice. But most people were not ready to accept the idea of a woman doctor, and the practice soon failed. So, too, did the marriage; Walker and Miller separated in 1859 and divorced ten years later.

Several years earlier, Walker had enthusiastically embraced the tenets of the emerging reform movement in the United States. One of the first and most symbolic confrontations with the establishment was over women's clothing, which at the time featured tight corsets and awkward, ankle-length hoop skirts. Walker had always felt constrained by such attire and resented having to conform to what society deemed acceptable for a proper lady of the middle class. Thus, when the "bloomer dress" (invented by feminist and temperance activist Amelia Bloomer) became a political statement for radical women's rights advocates during the early 1850s, Walker was among the first to hem her skirt to just below the knee and replace her petticoats with a pair of long, full trousers that eventually came to be known as "bloomers."

Walker's activities on behalf of the dress-reform movement claimed ever-increasing amounts of her time during the rest of the decade. Beginning in January of 1857, she became a regular contributor to the group's newspaper, *The Sibyl: A Review of the Tastes, Errors, and Fashions of Society,* and later that same year, she attended a convention of dress-reform supporters held in Middletown, New York. By the end of 1857, she had made a name for herself as a writer

and lecturer on the topic, and in 1860, she was elected to serve as one of the vice-presidents of the National Dress Reform Association. Meanwhile, she also began to turn her attention to other controversial issues in the women's rights movement, speaking out on subjects such as education, marriage, abortion, and the concept of equal pay for equal work.

Shortly after the Civil War broke out, Walker headed to Washington, D.C., where she tried to obtain an official commission to serve as a surgeon in the U.S. Army. When that was not forthcoming, she resolved to stay in the nation's capital and keep trying to persuade the War Department of her qualifications and willingness to serve. In the meantime, she volunteered her services to the Indiana Hospital, a makeshift facility that had been set up in a crowded section of the U.S. Patent Office to treat wounded and sick troops from Indiana.

However, Walker could not afford to work without pay indefinitely, so in early 1862, she left Washington to take some classes at New York Hygeio-Therapeutic College in the hope that the additional schooling would enhance her medical credentials. During the fall of that same year, she moved one step closer to her goal when she began working in an unofficial capacity as a contract surgeon at a couple of field hospitals in Virginia.

Once again, however, Walker soon found herself in need of a more dependable source of income, so she turned her attention to providing other kinds of assistance. One of her first projects was organizing the Women's Relief Associ-

ation, a group that helped female visitors to Washington find a safe place to stay. Walker raised funds from local suffrage groups to rent a house and turned it into a women's lodging facility. In exchange for her services, she was allowed to live there free of charge. The enterprising Walker also started a service that helped women locate their loved ones in the various hospitals around Washington. But her attempts to set up and run a private medical practice during this same period were not as successful. Nevertheless, she enjoyed a reputation around the capital as someone who was genuinely interested in the welfare of soldiers and their families.

In late 1863, Walker headed to Tennessee on her own to provide medical aid to the survivors of the Battle of Chickamauga, one of the bloodiest confrontations of the war. Denied permission to work as a doctor, she served instead as a nurse until early 1864, when her persistence, combined with the army's desperate need for medical personnel, finally paid off. In late January, over the objections of male army doctors who were openly hostile to the idea of a woman practicing medicine, Walker received a long-awaited official appointment to the post of assistant army surgeon with the rank of lieutenant—a first for a woman.

By the time Walker obtained her commission, however, the troops of her regiment were in relatively good health. The same could not be said of the civilian population living in the communities around the camp. So Walker routinely crossed over into Confederate territory to deliver babies, treat various diseases, pull teeth, and perform all-around medical care for the war-weary local citizens. Many people believe that she may have also worked as a Union spy while behind enemy lines, although there is no solid evidence to back up that claim.

It was also around this time that Walker quit wearing women's clothes entirely and donned exclusively male attire, a practice she observed for the rest of her life. She made slight modifications to a typical officer's uniform and wore that instead to make it easier to move around and work under difficult conditions in field hospitals.

As far as Walker was concerned, such clothes were far more sanitary and practical than long skirts that dragged through the dirt and hindered natural body movements. Society did not see it quite that way, however, and she was arrested numerous times for disturbing the peace or "masquerading in men's clothes" as she strolled around in pants—a matter of great pride for the defiantly nonconformist physician.

On April 10, 1864, Walker was captured when she rode alone and unarmed deep into Confederate territory. She was held in Richmond, Virginia, until being released on August 12, at which time she made her way back to Washington. Accepting the somewhat ambiguous post of "surgeon-in-charge," she served first as head of a hospital for female Confederate prisoners in Louisville, Kentucky, where her constant run-ins with a resentful and uncooperative staff eventually led her to request a transfer in March 1865. Walker then spent the final weeks of the war running a home for orphans and refugees in Clarksville, Tennessee. She ended up leaving government service altogether in June of that year and several months later was awarded the Medal of Honor for "meritorious services," making her the only woman ever to receive the nation's highest military decoration for bravery in combat.

After the war, Walker tried to secure a commission as a peacetime army surgeon, setting her sights on a position as a medical inspector with the new Bureau of Refugees and Freedmen, but her request was turned down in late 1865. Following a brief stint as a journalist with a New York newspaper, she headed back to Washington. She then tried to open a medical practice but instead found herself becoming involved again in both the women's movement and the dress-reform movement. She also petitioned Congress to secure military pensions for Civil War nurses and proposed that they deserved the right to vote in light of their service to the country.

In 1867, following a lengthy visit to England, where she delivered speeches on temperance, dress reform, and her Civil War experiences, Walker stepped up her efforts on behalf of the crusade for women's suffrage. She lectured on the topic throughout New England, the Midwest, and the South and even testified before Congress. But she could not support the suffragists' call for the adoption of a special amendment to the Constitution granting the vote to women. Her position on the amendment certainly did not spring from any belief that women shouldn't have the right to vote; according to Walker's interpretation of the Constitution, women *already* had the right to vote. Therefore, she insisted, the suffragists' actions were pointless. By refusing to budge on this issue, Walker drove a wedge between herself and more mainstream activists such as Elizabeth Cady Stanton and Susan B. Anthony, who feared her extremism would paint the movement in a negative light and jeopardize its goals.

As the years went by, Walker grew increasingly eccentric in both dress and personal behavior, which only managed to alienate more moderate reformers and make her a target of abuse and mockery. Finding a steady means of support was also a nagging problem. Walker's efforts to obtain compensation for her wartime service were only partly successful; she drew a pension from the government that amounted to only half of what men of her rank received. Repeated attempts to establish her own medical practice failed because male doctors continually questioned her credentials and dismissed her as a quack. A brief stint working for the government in the Pension Office mailroom ended in 1883 when she was fired for insubordination. The next few years were especially difficult; beginning in 1887, Walker resorted to talking about her Civil War experiences in a traveling show known as a "museum" to earn a little extra money.

In 1890, Walker returned to the family homestead in New York. She remained there for the rest of her life and ran the farm. She also continued to work on behalf of women's rights and pursued a somewhat more militant agenda that included founding a commune for women in 1897 named "Adamless Eve." In addition, she ran a sanatorium near Oswego for tuberculosis patients.

During a visit to Washington in 1917, the same year her Medal of Honor was revoked for lack of proper War Department documentation (it was restored sixty years later by President Jimmy Carter), Walker fell on the Capitol steps and suffered injuries from which she never fully recovered. She died two years later at her home in Oswego at the age of 86, alone and virtually penniless, remembered more for her peculiarities than for her brave and honorable wartime service to her country.

Books

Leonard, Elizabeth D., *Yankee Women: Gender Battles in the Civil War,* Norton, 1994.
Snyder, C.M., *Dr. Mary Walker: The Little Lady in Pants,* Vantage Press, 1962.

Periodicals

American Heritage, December 1977.
Smithsonian, March 1977. □

Jeff Wall

Art, a form of self-expression, can create or reflect reality. Canadian artist Jeff Wall (born 1946) expresses himself by recreating paintings as photographic panoramas and by reflecting a natural but staged reality. His work is "clearly the work of a man with a deft visual sense and an interestingly complicated mind," noted Jed Perl in the *New Republic*.

Jeff Wall was born in 1946 in Canada. Growing up in Vancouver, British Columbia, Wall pursued his artistic talent with support from his family. Yet, his decision to attend the University of British Columbia and not an art school surprised his relatives. This would be only one decision that seemed out of character for an artist. Wall earned a master's degree in art and continued his doctoral education at the Courtauld Institute in London. However, "feeling that he had acquired enough learning to serve his creative purposes," commented Lee Robbins in *ARTnews,* Wall left the Institute and began a career, not as an artist, but as a teacher.

Throughout the 1970s and 1980s, Wall taught art history at the Nova Scotia College of Art and Design and at Simon Fraser University. By 1987, Wall accepted a position at his alma mater, the University of British Columbia, where he remains a member of the faculty. Other personal information Wall has kept private. He believes that "this information is [not] relevant to an understanding of his art," reported Robbins in *ARTnews.* However, the public has learned that Wall is married and has maintained a close relationship to his family—they have appeared as models in his photographs.

Recreated Old Masters into Photographs

Wall's journey as an artist began in the 1960s. During this time of dropping out, establishment rejection, and free love, Wall discovered that "the best tool for expressing his own conceptual ideas [was photography] and taught himself how to use a camera," Robbins stated in *ARTnews*. By the early 1970s, Wall had successfully revealed his artistic ideas by blending both written text and photographs to create a documentary of everyday life.

By the late 1970s, Wall had tired of creating documentaries. He wanted to "move back toward pictorial art," *ARTnews* further affirmed. He wanted to create powerful images that represented, and not just documented, life but was unsure of how to do so. Inspiration struck when Wall noticed how lighted advertisements on city streets captured his attention. "I thought immediately that the medium although it was used for advertising—in fact did not belong to advertising in any essential sense," he told *ARTnews*. "It was a free medium, one inherent to photography and film."

Wall explored this new, free medium by recreating legendary paintings as photographic backlit transparencies. For example, in 1978, Wall reflected the past with his work, *The Destroyed Room*. Taking the theme of hidden violence within the home from Delacroix's 1827 work *Death of Sardanapalus, The Destroyed Room* offered its own depiction of modern life. Wall connected the two works by restaging "compositional elements . . . in contemporary urban settings, tempering them with an aura of 20th-century banality," noted *ARTnews*.

For the next 10 years, Wall continued recreating paintings into photographs. In 1979, he even "metaphorically [placed himself] in the role of Manet's obtrusive male customer-spectator" in his recreation of that artist's *Picture for Women* noted Reed Johnson in the *Daily News*. Wall's reasoning for these recreations are "not out to bury art in worshipful attitudes, but to grapple with its most exacting standards."

Art critics praised Wall for his ingenuity in using backlight for his photography and for his honorable attempts to bring masterful paintings new life through pictures. More praise was to come because Wall's true self-expression had not yet been explored. His true self was not a recreative photographer. As the *Times* (London) stated, Wall's true self was much more theatrical: "Wall has the hands and the eyes of a photographer, but in his veins the blood of a cinematographer flows."

Turned Photography into Film-Making

During the 1990s, Wall began seeing photography as a medium to connect film and literature to art. To create such a connection, Wall first redesigned his studio, modeling it after "cinematic film production-miniaturized," stated *ARTnews*. Next, he began shooting his photographs much like a Hollywood movie; he built and dressed large sets, gathered costumes, and hired models. The resulting photographs were a representation of the natural world. However, Wall had not simply happened upon a scene and clicked a picture. He artificially recreated the natural scene where he controlled the image.

This control of the image dominated much of Wall's future works. *Art in America* writer Richard Vine noticed that in these works the "forced stillness, irreal lighting and blatantly artificial composition" question their reality. For example, in his 1995 photograph *Man on the Street,* Wall juxtaposes one man sitting on a bench, his gaze downward, smiling with that of the same man walking down the street, his gaze still downward, frowning. The viewer recognizes that the scene is staged, but by "blatantly devising his shots, he induces us [viewers] to ask exactly what is we ordinarily read as "natural"—and why," Vine further commented.

Wall's artification of the natural world drove him to search everywhere for subjects and themes for his work. He told Robbins in *ARTnews* that "a subject can emerge from anything at all. . . . Reading something, meeting a person whose appearance sets something off, a place. . . ." In 1997, a place inspired Wall to create his next work, but this time his work would not be a backlit photograph, but a "photograph in iron," quoted Daniel Birnbaum in *Artforum*.

Discovered New Media

Commissioned by the Dutch government to create a monument for Rotterdam's Whilhelmina pier, Wall leapt into a new medium for his art-iron. And, he actually gathered trash—ropes, luggage, crates—and used them as pieces of the monument. "These discarded possessions bear witness to a specific moment," Birnbaum noted in *Artforum*. The intended effect of this specific moment was that he wanted people walking down the pier to "find themselves inside a completely artificial world, reminiscent of a stage set." And, once inside this world, they would be able to feel that they've discovered "some quite ordinary things that have been forgotten and the complex experience of relating to things from the past."

Also in the late 1990s, Wall, still maintaining his love for recreating reality through artification, stepped away from that artificial world and stepped into landscape photography. This photography became a "more personal . . . artistic adventure. . ." stated the *Times* (London). However, Wall's "devious intention" of making his landscapes look like snapshots continued his theme of artification even in these photographs. "I am interested in getting these pictures to look like they could have been snapshots, partly because that is the way photographs are expected to look," Wall told the *Times* (London). "Moreover, most very beautiful and successful photographs have looked that way."

Critically Praised and Rewarded

In 2002, Wall enjoyed critical success when he was awarded the Hassleblad Foundation International Award in Photography. With this recognition, the world was reminded that photography—whether it recreates history or reflects nature in a staged reality—is an important art medium. And, Wall's ability to "marry his high intentions with the easy accessibility of his chosen format . . . is real genius," hailed the *Independent*. However, Wall's technological genius is not the only quality that sets his photography apart from other art. As *Time Canada* writer Deborah Solomon suggested, it is his ability, his self-expression through his photography that makes it "hard to think of another living photographer whose work leaves us with so potent a record of how actual life actually feels."

Periodicals

Art in America, April 1996.
Artforum, May 1997.
ARTnews, November 1995.
Daily News, July 28, 1997.
*Independent,*March 19, 1996.
*New Republic,*April 28, 1997.
*Time Canada,*March 1, 1999.
Times (London), December 10, 2002. □

Nancy Ward

Nancy Ward (1738–1822), a mixed-blood Cherokee woman who lived during the eighteenth century, was the Cherokee nation's last "Beloved Woman." At a time that the Cherokee nation was frequently at battle with American troops and white settlers who had occupied their traditional lands, Ward made repeated attempts to establish peace between the various parties.

Early Life

Nancy Ward is believed to have been born around 1738 in the Cherokee village of Chota, in what is today Monroe County, Tennessee. Chota, the Cherokee capital, was known as a "City of Refuge," meaning that it was a place where those in distress could seek asylum.

When Ward was growing up, Cherokee lands were bordered by the Ohio River in the north and the Tennessee River in the south. They extended to the headwaters of the Coosa, the Chattahoochee, the Savannah, the Saluda, and the Tugaloo Rivers. Today the traditional Cherokee lands correspond to the area where the states of Tennessee, Georgia, South Carolina, and North Carolina come together, at the edge of the Great Smoky Mountains.

As a child Nancy Ward was known as "Tsituna-Gus-Ke" (Wild Rose). Her mother, Tame Doe, was a member of the Wolf clan and the sister of Attakullacull (another source says she was the sister of Oconostota), a Cherokee chief. Although there is separate tradition that Ward's father was a member of a Delaware tribe, most sources seem to agree that she was the daughter of Francis Ward, the son of Sir Francis Ward of Ireland. According to some sources, Francis Ward married Tame Doe after settling in the Tyger River area of present-day Spartanburg County, South Carolina. There is also a tradition that Francis Ward was eventually

banished from the Cherokee nation. According to Harold W. Felton, writing in *Nancy Ward, Cherokee,* Ward learned both the Cherokee and English languages from her mother.

Early in her life, Ward is said to have had a vision of spirits helping her find her way home after she had become lost. After that time she became known as "Nanye'hi," which means "One who is with the Spirit People." She subsequently married a Cherokee warrior by the name of Kingfisher, a member of the Deer Clan. Felton says they had two children, a boy named Fivekiller and a girl named Catharine.

Tribal Warfare

In the early 1760s, the Cherokee nation was committed to helping the American colonists in the French and Indian War in exchange for protection for their families from hostile Creeks and Choctaws. But, colonial assistance also brought interference with Cherokee affairs in the form of frontier posts and military garrisons. The frontier posts were soon accompanied by settlers hungry for Cherokee land.

An incident in West Virginia in which some Virginia frontiersmen robbed and killed a group of Cherokees on their way back from helping the British take Fort Duquesne resulted in the revenge killing of more than 20 settlers by the Native Americans. This was the beginning of a conflict that would last more than two years, in which the Cherokees, under Chief Oconostota, defeated the British forces and captured Fort Loudon.

Following a truce, an army of Carolina Rangers, British light infantry, Royal Scots, and Native American troops ravaged Cherokee territory, burning crops and towns. War weary and hungry, the insurgent Cherokees agreed to give up large portions of their eastern lands.

Beloved Woman

In an intertribal conflict known as the Battle of Taliwa, which took place in 1775, the Creeks fought the Cherokees. According to Felton, Ward assisted her warrior husband during the battle by "chewing his bullets." After her husband was mortally wounded, Ward reportedly took up his rifle and joined the fight. In recognition of her valor, the Cherokee Nation gave her the name "Ghihau," meaning Beloved Woman or Mother. The title made Ward a member of the tribal council of chiefs.

Still in her teens, the widowed mother of two children was also made the leader of the Women's Council of Clan Representatives. As a member of the tribal council of chiefs, she served as a peace negotiator and ambassador for the Cherokee people. Ward achieved a reputation as an unflinching advocate of human rights and peace.

Revolutionary War

During the Revolutionary War, the Cherokees were divided on the issues of helping the British and whether force should be used to expel American settlers on Cherokee land. Nancy's cousin, Dragging Canoe, the son of Attakullaculla, wanted to side with the British against the white settlers. Ward, however, spoke up in favor of supporting the American settlers.

In May 1775, a delegation of Shawnee, Delaware, and Mohawk emissaries traveled south to help the British win the support of the Cherokees and other tribes. That July, the Chickamauga Cherokee band of the Tennessee River Valley led by Dragging Canoe began attacking white settlements and forts in the Appalachians and in isolated areas of Virginia, the Carolinas, and Georgia. In retaliation, state militias destroyed Cherokee villages and crops. By 1777, the militias would force the Cherokee to give up some of their land.

In July 1776, Ward warned white settlers on the Holston River and on the Virginia border that the Cherokees were planning an attack. Later, she saved the life of a captured white woman who was about to be executed. The white woman's husband was William Bean, reportedly a friend of Daniel Boone and a captain in the colonial militia. Ward and Mrs. Bean developed a friendship during the time that Mrs. Bean remained with the Cherokees, and Ward learned about dairy farming from her. Apparently out of gratitude, Ward's village was spared from being razed when the frontier militia made its way through Cherokee lands.

Meanwhile, Dragging Canoe and his band continued to attack American settlements with arms supplied by the British. Finally, in 1778, Colonel Evan Shelby and 600 men invaded Dragging Canoe's territory. The result was that Cherokee resistance from that point forward was limited to minor conflict.

In 1780, Ward provided American soldiers with advanced warning of a another Cherokee attack, and tried to prevent retribution against the Cherokees by the whites. According to Felton, Ward even arranged to have a herd of her own cattle sent to the hungry militia. Nevertheless, the North Carolina militia would again invade Cherokee territory, destroying villages and demanding further land cessions. In the ensuing battle, which Ward had tried in vain to stop, she and her family were captured by the Americans; she was eventually released and allowed to return to her home in Chota.

In July 1781, Ward helped negotiate a peace treaty between the Cherokees and the Americans. The signing of the treaty freed the Americans to move a detachment of troops to fight with George Washington's army against the British General Cornwallis in the final battle of the American Revolution.

During the negotiation of the Treaty of Hopewell (1785), Ward attempted to promote mutual friendship between the whites and the Cherokees. She argued for the adoption of farming and dairy production by the Cherokees and became the first Cherokee dairy farmer. Much later, she urged her tribe not to sell tribal land to the whites, but she failed to exert influence on this score. When the Cherokee council met in 1817 to discuss the idea of moving west, Ward, too ill to attend, sent a letter in which she wrote, "[D]on't part with any more of our lands but continue on it and enlarge your farms and cultivate and raise corn and cotton and we, your mothers and sisters, will make clothing for you. . . . It was our desire to forewarn you all not to part

with our lands," according to Felton. The tribal lands north of the Hiwassee River were sold in 1819, however, obliging Ward to relocate.

Opened an Inn

After the death of her husband Kingfisher, Ward had married her cousin Bryant Ward. Bryant Ward was the nephew of Francis Ward, Nancy's father. The couple had a son, Little Fellow, and a daughter, Elizabeth, before Bryant Ward left the area.

As indicated by documentation on the RootsWeb website, Ward is said to have once written to the President of the United States, saying: "Our people would have more hoes, plows, seed, cotton carding and looms for weaving. They would learn your way of cultivation. If you would send these things we will put them to good use." The president reportedly agreed to help and sent government agents to help the Cherokees.

Ward later opened an inn in southeastern Tennessee on the Ocoee River, at a place called Woman Killer Ford, near present-day Benton. She died in that place in 1822 (some sources say 1824). Over the years that followed, she became the subject of many tales and legends. She is reportedly mentioned in Teddy Roosevelt's *Book on The West, The Virginia State Papers, The South Carolina State Papers, Mooney's Book,* and *The Draper Collection.* A chapter of The American Daughters Of the Revolution in Tennessee has been named after her. There is also a Descendants of Nancy Ward Association in Oklahoma.

Near the end of her life, Nancy Ward reportedly had a vision in which she saw a "great line of our people marching on foot. Mothers with babies in their arms. Fathers with small children on their back. Grandmothers and Grandfathers with large bundles on their backs. They were marching West and the 'Unaka' (White Soldiers) were behind them. They left a trail of corpses the weak, the sick who could not survive the journey." The vision was to prove prophetic.

The Trail of Tears

In the years following Ward's death, the state of Georgia, with the support of President Andrew Jackson, began taking Cherokee lands for extremely low compensation and promises of land in the west. Cherokee property was also taken by greedy settlers. Using the Cherokees' resistance as an excuse, the Georgia militia moved in to Chota and destroyed the printing press used there in the publication of the tribe's newspaper.

Although a few Cherokees managed to escape the ensuing round-up of Native Americans by taking refuge in the mountains of North Carolina (where some of their descendants still live today), most of the members of the Cherokee nation were destined to enforced exile. Beginning in the spring of 1838, the dispossessed Native Americans were made to travel through rain and mud, and then snow and ice, to lands west of the Mississippi. About 4,000 Cherokees died during the 800-mile exodus that would eventually become known among them as the "Nunna-da-ult-sun-yi" (The Trail of Tears).

Books

Felton, Harold W., *Nancy Ward, Cherokee,* Dodd, Mead & Company, 1975.

Waldman, Carl, *Atlas of the North American Indian,* Facts on File, 1985.

Online

Bataille, Gretchen M., ed., *Native American Women: A Biographical Dictionary,* Garland Publishing, 1993, http://www .pinn.net/~sunshine/whm2002/ward.html (January 2003).

RootsWeb.com, http://www.rootsweb.com/~scsparta/spb_scot .htm. See also RootsWeb Archives, http://archiver.rootsweb .com/th/read/OK-RECORDS/2000-10/0971600639 (January 2003). □

Ellen Gould Harmon White

When Ellen Gould Harmon White (1827–1915) was 17, she received a message from God in the form of a vision. It was the first of some 2,000 visions White experienced in her lifetime. The visions formed the basic teachings of the Seventh Day Adventist Church, which White and her husband co-founded in 1863. White served as the church's spiritual leader throughout her life. She wrote 26 books based on her visions, led a health reform movement, and established schools and sanitariums.

White and her twin sister Elizabeth were the youngest of eight children born to Robert and Eunice Harmon. When the twins were born on November 26, 1827, the family lived on a farm near Gorham, Maine. A few years later, Robert Harmon gave up farming and moved the family to Portland, where he worked out of his home making hats. The whole family, including young Ellen, helped in the hat-making enterprise.

An unfortunate incident occurred when White was nine years old. While walking home from school, a classmate threw a rock at White, hitting her in the face and knocking her unconscious for three weeks. White was left disfigured and for the rest of her life she suffered from recurring health problems, including nervousness, tremors, and dizziness. The symptoms made it impossible for her to complete her schoolwork and she was forced to withdraw from school. White considered this incident to be a defining moment in her life; her ill health caused her to become withdrawn and she became deeply interested in religion.

The Harmons were Methodists and in 1840, when White was 12, she attended a church camp meeting where she devoted her life to God, received baptism, and became a member of the Methodist Church. White was devoted to the church, but she feared that she was not worthy of salvation.

During the early 1840s, the Harmon family attended Adventist meetings. The Adventist church was a Christian denomination that believed that the coming of Christ, or advent, was imminent. The Harmons were especially taken with the views of William Miller who predicted Christ's return on October 22, 1844. The conflict between the Methodist and Millerite beliefs resulted in the Harmon family's removal from the Methodist Church in 1843.

October 22, 1844, passed without Christ's return. The event, called the Great Disappointment, caused many Adventists to waver in their faith. White remained earnest and tried to make sense of the failed prediction. In December 1944, while praying with four other women, White experienced the first of many visions she had during her life. The vision showed her that Adventists had misunderstood the significance of October 22. It was the beginning of a special time of preparation that would culminate in the coming of Christ.

When White revealed her vision to others, they accepted it as a gift from God. White had subsequent visions and she began to travel, sharing her visions with other Adventists. She believed that God had selected her as a prophet through whom God would communicate to the world and prepare for Christ's second coming. She helped rally Adventists, who had become scattered after the Great Disappointment.

White was only 17 when she began her mission as God's messenger. She experienced some 2,000 visions in her lifetime. Without warning, she would go into a trance, which began when she shouted "Glory!" three times. If no one caught her, she then swooned to the floor. The trances lasted from a few minutes to several hours, during which time her eyes were open and her heart and respiration rate slowed to an almost imperceptible level. Sometimes she exhibited extraordinary physical strength during the trance. When she came out of it, she sometimes remained blind for a few days. In later years, White's daytime trances stopped and her visions occurred in nighttime dreams.

Skeptics offered various explanations for White's visions. Some believed they were the result of hypnotism. Others thought she suffered from hysteria or other mental disorder. But most Adventist followers accepted her as a prophet who received messages from God. White believed it was her mission to relay the messages she received, although she was somewhat uncomfortable with the responsibility. Although she was young and frail, suffering from breathing difficulties, fatigue, and fainting spells, she traveled to churches and camp meetings, where she was accepted as a messenger of God.

Married James White

In her travels, White met James White, a Millerite minister, whom she married in 1846. Like his wife, James had lifelong health problems. The couple traveled throughout the eastern states preaching their message and living off the charity of Adventists they visited along the way. When their children, Henry and James Edson were born, the parents left them in the care of friends so they could continue their mission. Being separated from her children distressed White, but she felt God was calling her to preach.

James White encouraged his wife to write down the messages received in visions and in 1849 the couple began publishing her teachings. *The Present Truth* was an eight-page semimonthly newspaper containing Ellen White's prophetic views. Later, they published the *Review and Herald* and *Youth's Instructor*. White's first book, *A Sketch of the Christian Experience and Views of Ellen G. White,* was published in 1854. James White was the driving force behind his wife's publishing.

In 1852, the Whites stopped traveling and the impoverished family settled down in Rochester, New York. In 1854, their third child, Willie, was born. White gave birth to her fourth son, Herbert, in 1860. He died three months later.

In 1853, the family moved to Battle Creek, Michigan, where Adventist believers built them a headquarters for their Review and Herald Publishing Company. The following years were spent writing and publishing messages from White's visions, which became the basis of the church's teachings. In 1858, White wrote her most important book, *The Great Controversy Between Christ and His Angels and Satan and His Angels*. The book was based on a vision and described the war between good and evil and the second coming of Christ. It was the first of four volumes published under the title, *Spiritual Gifts.*

Up until this time, the Adventists were a scattered, unorganized group of believers. In 1863, the movement that White led was formally organized as the Seventh Day Adventist Church. The name came from the belief, from a vision, that the Sabbath should be observed on Saturday, the seventh day of the week. James White took on much of the church's administrative duties, although he turned down the opportunity to serve as president. Ellen White was the church's spiritual leader.

Led Health Reform Movement

Shortly after establishing the church, White had a vision that showed the connection between physical health and spirituality. She published a series of pamphlets titled *Health, or How to Live* that described her guidelines for healthy living. Thus began a lifelong crusade for health reform.

White advocated a strict vegetarian diet that included whole grains and only two meals a day. Butter, tea, and coffee were strictly forbidden as were medicine, tobacco, and alcohol. Hydratherapy, the use of water baths and wraps, was used as a treatment for disease. These were not unique ideas in the mid-nineteenth century. Before the Civil War, preachers and medical doctors advocated fresh air, vegetarianism, and abstinence from tobacco and alcohol as alternatives to traditional medical treatments such as blood letting, blistering, and purging. Medical clinics, called water cures, opened across the country before the Civil War. These health reform ideas were readily available in publications and some people suggested that White took her ideas from medical doctors who had previously published articles on the topic. White claimed that she never read their articles before writing down the ideas she received in visions.

In 1865, a vision inspired White to establish the church's first health institute to care for the sick and to teach preventive medicine in an atmosphere of Adventist spirituality. The Western Health Reform Institute (later the Battle Creek Sanitarium) was established in Battle Creek in 1866. It operated under the direction of John Harvey Kellogg, who later invented Cornflake breakfast cereal and founded the Kellogg Company. The institute attracted patients from around the world. The sanitarium left the control of the church in 1906 following a dispute between White and Kellogg.

Continued Preaching and Publishing

Despite the fact that health reform was a defining characteristic of the church, the White family continued to suffer health problems throughout their lives. Henry White died of pneumonia at the age of 16 in 1863.

During the 1870s, the Whites traveled extensively on behalf of the church. Much of their work was in the west, where they established Pacific Press Publishing Association. White spoke at camp meetings, churches, conferences, in town squares, and even prisons. Temperence was a frequent topic and in 1877 it was reported that White spoke on that topic to an audience of 20,000 people in Groveland, Massachusetts.

The Whites also established schools, beginning with Battle Creek College (later Andrews University) in 1874. The church's membership increased five-fold between 1863 and 1880.

James White's health deteriorated in the late 1870s and he died on August 6, 1881. White became even more involved in the church and her son Willie took on more responsibilities. In the 1880s, White began spreading the Adventist message worldwide. She traveled to Europe in 1885–1889 and lived in Australia for nine years beginning in 1891. White established a bible school and a sanitarium in Australia.

When she returned to the United States at the age of 71, she moved to Elmshaven, a rural town in northern California, from which she traveled throughout the South preaching to African Americans. She founded Oakwood College, a school for African Americans, in Huntsville, Alabama, and established the Southern Publishing Association in Nashville, Tennessee.

White spearheaded a reorganization of the church in 1901. In 1903, she moved its headquarters from Battle Creek to suburban Washington, D.C. She also established medical schools to train doctors for the church's health facilities. In 1909, she founded the College of Medical Evangelists at Loma Linda, California, which is now Loma Linda University and Medical Center. White continued writing, completing a number of books and articles between 1910 and 1915. In total, White wrote 26 books and numerous articles and pamphlets. Together with her diaries and other writings, she produced more than 100,000 pages in her lifetime.

In February 1915, White broke her hip in a fall. She was confined to a wheelchair and died five months later, on July 16, 1915, in Elmshaven, California, at the age of 87. She was buried beside her husband and sons in Battle Creek, Michigan.

After White's death, the Seventh Day Adventist Church continued to grow and draw inspiration from her teachings. Church membership increased from 135,000 in 1915 to more than 12.3 million in 2001. The church's network of schools and hospitals has also expanded.

White's books are still considered a major source of inspiration in the church. They've been translated into 320 languages. All are still in print and are available and searchable on the official website of the Ellen G. White Estate, a corporation established in her will, at www.whiteestate .com.

Books

Numbers, Ronald L., *Prophetess of Health: A Study of Ellen G. White,* Harper & Row, 1976.

Women in World History: A Biographical Encyclopedia, Anne Commire, editor, Yorkin Publications, 1999.

Online

"139th Annual Statistical Report-2001," General Conference of Seventh-day Adventists, www.adventist.org (February 21, 2003).

American Decades CD-ROM, Gale Research, 1998.

White, Arthur L., "Ellen G. White: A Brief Biography," The Ellen G. White Estate Inc. web site, www.whiteestate.org (February 20, 2003). □

Mary Watson Whitney

Astronomer and educator Mary Watson Whitney (1847–1921) is most noted as the successor to Maria Mitchell, professor and director of the Vassar College Observatory. Like Mitchell and other women professionals working in the academic fields of science and mathematics in the late 1800s, Whitney worked diligently on her own career and also fought to advance women's educational and professional opportunities.

The daughter of Mary Watson Crehore and Samuel Buttrick Whitney, Mary Watson Whitney was born on September 11, 1847, in Waltham, Massachusetts. The family was among New England's oldest settlers and were able to trace their roots to 1635. Whitney was the second of five children. Her father was a real estate broker, and his professional success and encouragement of intellectual pursuits enabled her and her four siblings access to a good education. This was unusual, for women were typically discouraged from attaining any education during this era.

Educated Despite Gender Obstacles

Whitney reportedly loved to study and excelled in mathematics. Graduating from high school in 1864, she became interested in a college for women that was to be opened in New York's Hudson Valley by Matthew Vassar. Whitney spent a year waiting for the women's college to open, during which time she attended a Swedenborgian school located in Waltham, registering there as a private student. When Vassar College opened its doors in Poughkeepsie, New York, in September of 1865, Whitney attended with her father's blessing. She was given advanced standing upon her entrance to the college. Eager to embark on her education in astronomy, she studied with Maria Mitchell, the preeminent American woman astronomer of her day.

"Her superiority and interest endeared her to the older woman and she became one of her most cherished pupils," explained Caroline E. Furness, Whitney's eventual successor, in an essay published in the *Dictionary of American Biography.* "Whitney was much admired by her fellow students and recognized as a leader. Several times she served as president of their newly formed organizations. Her fine presence, good judgment and impartiality made her an excellent presiding officer, while her modesty and kindness of heart won their devoted affection." Mitchell, as a perceptive judge of people, "must have recognized very quickly the superior ability and earnest purpose of this gifted young woman," Furness added in *Popular Astronomy,* going on to note of Mitchell that, "In later years, she frequently said she did not know which was her greatest feat: to discover the comet which made her famous or to find Mary Whitney."

Continued Studies in Astronomy, Mathematics

Whitney graduated from Vassar in 1868 after completing her astronomy degree in three years' time. Second in her class, she graduated with distinction in the fields of both astronomy and physical science. Rather than continue her astronomy studies, she was forced to return home because, with the deaths of both her father and older brother, her mother now needed her. Whitney briefly taught school in Auburndale, Massachusetts, to help support her family and continued spending as much time as possible furthering her studies of mathematics and astronomy.

In August of 1869 Whitney was invited to join Mitchell and her students to view a total solar eclipse in Iowa. Whitney took with her on this trip a three-inch telescope which was reportedly made especially for this occasion. Observations she and Mitchell made appeared in the Nautical Almanac Office official report. She also worked with Mitchell in 1872 on a project designed to accurately determine the latitude of the Vassar College observatory.

Mitchell was able to convince noted Harvard mathematician Benjamin Peirce to allow Whitney to audit his course on quaternions. At that time the Harvard University campus was not open to women; Peirce had to physically escort Whitney between the classroom and the college gates for each and every lecture. She later was able to participate in a graduate-level astronomy course on celestial mechanics and began working with Truman H. Safford at the Dearborn Observatory of the University of Chicago in 1870.

Professor Ormand Stone was a private pupil studying with Safford when he met Whitney with Mitchell's other charges in Safford's home. "As a young woman Miss Whitney was attractive and handsome, gentle and refined, affable but dignified," he was quoted as writing by Furness in *Popular Astronomy*. "In after life I had only glimpses of her at scientific gatherings, but she always seemed to retain the beauty of feature, manner and character that she had in those earlier days, the only difference being that beauty of maturity replaced beauty of youth."

Whitney was awarded her master's degree from Vassar in 1872. A year later, when her sister entered medical school in Zurich, Switzerland, the family accompanied her. Whitney was able to study mathematics and celestial mechanics at the University of Zurich for three years.

Frustrated by Search for Work

When she returned to the United States in 1876 Whitney was unable to find a job teaching university-level courses—or any job, for that matter, in which she could use her knowledge and advanced education. She was a woman, and women who taught were expected to do so in women's colleges. Whitney opted to teach at her high school alma mater, a job broken by periodic requests by Mitchell to help perform various research tasks. According to Furness, these years of frustration were "perhaps the least satisfactory" to Whitney, as "Her forward looking student days were over." With limited options, "she chafed at the blank wall of prejudice that faced her and came to use a homely expression which often fell from her lips in later years. 'I hope that when I get to heaven I shall not find the women playing second fiddle.'"

Replaced Mitchell at Vassar

Whitney ultimately returned to Vassar as Mitchell's private assistant in 1881, as Mitchell was in failing health. Whitney was initially responsible for establishing research programs, while Mitchell continued to teach and focused on getting additional equipment for the school. Whitney succeeded Mitchell as professor of astronomy and director of the observatory when Mitchell retired in 1888, having been specifically requested as Mitchell's replacement.

Whitney's sister became an invalid just as Whitney took her post at Vassar, and Whitney cared for her in her new home at the observatory. Despite this, Whitney flourished in her position, developing a reputation as an excellent teacher as well as a patient and inspirational mentor. She was made a full professor of astronomy in 1889 and by 1906 there were 160 students enrolled in eight different astronomy courses. Vassar was one of the first institutions to teach subjects including astrophysics and variable stars to its undergraduate students, and Whitney also created a fine reputation for the school's observatory, particularly for the caliber and accuracy of research conducted there. Althogh her sister and mother died during her tenure, she went on with her work.

Whitney employed her mathematics skills in her observations of comets and asteroids, then calculated their orbits, publishing her findings in the *Astronomical Journal*. With information from Vassar's observatory as well as data from the newly opened Smith College Observatory, she was able to study double and variable stars, the latter being those stars whose brightness changes over a fixed period. Whitney was among the most important researchers on the topic at this time and her work was favorably and frequently acknowledged by her peers in the field.

Research Led to Numerous Published Papers

With the development of technology that enabled accurate measurements of stars to be recorded on photographic plates, Whitney was able to conduct research on plates from other observatories. She subsequently arranged with Columbia University to study and measure their photographic plates made by Lewis Rutherford of star clusters in 1896.

In 1894 Whitney hired Caroline Furness as her teaching and research assistant, paying the younger astronomer with her own money. Once students had completed their use of the equipment in the observatory, typically about 10 p.m., Whitney and Furness used the gear for their own work into the early morning hours. By 1905 she and Furness had published a catalog containing all stars located within two degrees of the North Pole. Whitney charted positions of comets and asteroids as well and eventually concentrated on studying variable stars, novae, and photometry. All together, Whitney published more than 70 papers on various astronomy topics in journals in both the United States and Germany. "Her research work was marked by accuracy and thoroughness," recalled Furness. "As a teacher she was noted for her clearness in explaining difficult mathematical points and for the vividness and elegance with which she presented the more descriptive topics. Many students elected her courses merely to come in contact with her personality. As a member of the faculty, she was highly esteemed for her soundness of judgment and her progressive ideas. As a scholar she was a constant stimulus to her younger colleagues. She read extensively on political and philosophical topics, and had highly developed tastes in literature and music."

Varied Interests Outside Career

Throughout her life Whitney continually strove to better educational opportunities for women. One of her goals was to demonstrate women's capabilities in the fields of scientific research, and at Vassar she cultivated those students with the potential to achieve professional success in positions at observatories throughout the United States. She was active in a variety of organizations, including the Vassar Alumnae Association and the Association for the Advancement of Women, and was a charter member of the American Astronomical Society and several other organizations devoted to science education. Whitney was also a fellow of the American Academy for the Advancement of Science and president of the Maria Mitchell Association of Nantucket.

Among her hobbies were nature study, especially bird watching. Whitney reportedly was also interested in poetry, particularly American poets. She also wrote verse for her own enjoyment or when pressed to do so by her companions. Not surprisingly, her favorite writers included Ralph Waldo Emerson, Henry David Thoreau, and William Wordsworth as well as Shakespeare. She reportedly liked to take turns reading aloud with friends while sewing. She also read philosophical and religious works such as sermons.

Whitney retired from her post at Vassar in 1910 following a stroke that spring that left her paralyzed and in a semi-invalid condition and died of pneumonia in her hometown of Waltham, Massachusetts, on January 21, 1921. Furness succeeded her in her position at Vassar.

Books

American Women in Science: A Biographical Dictionary, ABC-CLIO, 1994.
Dictionary of American Biography, American Council of Learned Societies, 1928–1936.
Notable Women Scientists, Gale, 2000.
Women in Science: Antiquity through the Nineteenth Century, MIT Press, 1986.

Periodicals

Popular Astronomy, January 1922; January 1923.

Online

Whitney Research Group Web site, http://www.whitneygen.org/ (February 28, 2003). □

Andrew J. Wiles

In 1993 Princeton University professor Andrew J. Wiles (born 1953) announced that he had solved one of the most legendary challenges in mathematics. Fermat's Last Theorem was an elegantly simple problem in need of a proof, and it had confounded mathematicians both professional and amateur for some 350 years. Wiles's successful cracking of the necessary code caused a stir in the math community and even landed him on the front page of the *New York Times* for solving what *Science* writer Barry Cipra asserted was "one of the unconquered peaks of mathematics."

Andrew J. Wiles was born April 11, 1953, in Cambridge, England, where his father was professor of theology at the famed medieval university there. In the Cambridge library the ten-year-old Wiles first came across Fermat's Last Theorem, and it intrigued him. He worked on it in his teens before realizing it was far more complex a challenge than he had originally assumed. After earning an undergraduate degree from Oxford University in 1974, Wiles went on to earn graduate degrees in math from Clare College, Cambridge, and specialized in elliptical curves, a relatively new field of higher math. In 1982, two years after he earned his Ph.D., he began teaching at Princeton University in New Jersey.

Boyhood Fascination Rekindled

Although Wiles was still intrigued by Fermat's Last Theorem, he knew it would be foolish to devote time and energy to it. Many, many minds before him had failed. The most successful had been Ernst Eduard Kummer, whose development of algebraic number theory led to some notable advances in solving the puzzle in the 1870s. As Wiles told *Sciences* writer Peter G. Brown, he had given up on it himself by graduate school. "I think I also must have realized that it was not a good idea, for the reason that not much new theory had been developed to deal with the problem since Kummer. . . . You don't want to waste your whole life as a mathematician trying to find some bizarre, ephemeral proof."

The Missing Proof

Fermat's Last Theorem dates back to 1637. "What makes the theorem so tantalizing is that for all its fiendish difficulty to prove, it is almost absurdly simple to state," noted *Time* contributor Michael D. Lemonick. Pierre Fermat was a brilliant self-taught mathematician and lawyer living in France. Before his 1665 death he made several important advances in probability theory and analytic geometry theory. The theorem that bears his name had its origins in a note he scribbled, as was his habit, in the margin of a copy of Diophantus's *Arithmetic,* a treatise dating from third-century Greece. In short, Fermat asserted that "a to the nth power + b to the nth power = c to the nth power" can never be true when the exponent "n" is greater than two. In a way, it is similar to the well-known Pythagorean theorem, which holds that the square of the longest side of a right triangle is equal to the sum of the squares of the other two sides. Fermat, explained *Guardian* writer Simon Singh, "created the equation [x to the nth power + y to the nth power = z to the nth power], where "n" represents any number bigger than 2. Fermat came to the extraordinary conclusion that this new equation had no solutions—among the infinity of numbers, none existed that fitted his equation."

Fermat did not leave behind a "proof," or solution, proving his assertion, noting instead that he had found one that was very simple, but the margin of the book was too small for him to write it down. That boast incited a 350-year-quest to find it, which would end with Wiles's historic solution. As Wiles explained to Singh: "Pure mathematicians just love a challenge. They love unsolved problems. Most deceptive are the problems which look easy, and yet they turn out to be extremely intricate. Fermat is the most beautiful example of this. It just looked as though it ought to have a simple proof and, of course, it's very special because Fermat said that he had a proof."

Lured the Learned, the Daft

Proving Fermat's theorem had confounded generations of Wiles's predecessors. In 1780 Leonhard Euler found that an exponent of three would not work, and others found that exponents of 5, 7, and 13 cannot be true either. The maddening problem so intrigued German industrialist Paul Wolfskehl that he offered a large cash prize to anyone who could solve it. His announcement in 1907 sent a flood of solutions to a special prize commission office established at the University of Göttingen, every single submission required being checked. There were a dwindling number of entries each decade, but a few still came in every month as the 100th-anniversary deadline to solve it—September 13, 2007—neared. In some cases the submissions were from qualified researchers, noted Singh, adding that, in other cases, "manuscripts bore clear signs of schizophrenia." Some respected names in the field began to theorize that the proof Fermat mentioned never existed, or that he recognized its serious flaws and destroyed it. Writing in *Sciences,* Brown described Fermat's Last Theorem as "a siren call for the unwary since the seventeenth century. Amateur and professional mathematicians alike have been lured into its quicksand, many to give up, after years of effort, in frustration and disgust."

With the dawn of the computer age, programmers ran calculations in an attempt to solve Fermat's Last Theorem up to the number 4,000,000, but little real advancement was made. In 1984 a panel of number theorists declared it would never be proved or disproved. Characteristically, the final solution was linked to Wiles's chosen discipline. "One newish branch of algebraic geometry deals with a group of shapes known as elliptical curves, most of which look like a wiggly hump with an egg on top," explained an *Economist* contributor. "It is by manipulating such curves that mathe-maticians now find they can infer various things about statements such as Fermat's last theorem."

Solution Buried in Another Riddle

In the mid-1950s Yutaka Taniyama, a Japanese mathematician, asserted that an elliptic curve has modular form; this idea was picked up in 1971 by another Japanese mathematician, Goro Shimura and came to be called the Taniyama-Shimura conjecture. A conjecture is an intriguing but unproven theory. Little else came out of this idea until the early 1980s, when an academic in Saarbrucken, Germany, named Gerhard Frey issued a paper asserting the key to proving Fermat's Last Theorem was in the Taniyama-Shimura conjecture. Frey stated that an elliptical curve could represent all the solutions to Fermat's equation; in other words, if Fermat's Last Theorem were false, there would be elliptic curves that violated the Taniyama-Shimura conjecture. A University of California at Berkeley mathematician, Kenneth Ribet, agreed with this idea. In 1986 "Ribet showed that if Fermat's theorem is wrong, then some elliptic curves should exist that could not be constructed according to Taniyama's conjecture," explained *Discover* writer Tim Folger.

Upon learning of Ribet's announcement, Wiles set out to prove that such curves exist. He went back to work on solving Fermat's Last Theorem that same day, telling no one save for his wife and one trusted colleague. He spent seven years working on it in the attic office of his home in Princeton, leaving only to spend time with his family, which includes two daughters, and to teach classes. He abandoned all of his other work to concentrate on it, and was rarely seen at professional conferences. In an interview with *Science* contributor Cipra, he likened the process to "entering a darkened mansion. You enter a room, and you stumble months, even years, bumping into the furniture. Slowly you learn where all the pieces of furniture are, and you're looking for the light switch. You turn it on, and the whole room is illuminated. Then you go on to the next room and repeat the process."

Historic Announcement Made

In 1991, after five years of concentrating how to find the solution, Wiles made the breakthrough that set him on the right path. He reduced the theorem to a calculation that had been used unsuccessfully by others and, as he told Cipra, became convinced that "the proof was just around the corner . . . but the corner was a bit longer than I anticipated." In May of 1993 he felt that he had the proof nearly complete, save for one part. At that point he came across a paper from Harvard mathematician Barry Mazur that described one type of mathematical construction, and Wiles used it to get through the final roadblock. This last step took him just six weeks.

Wiles decided to announce his finding at a series of lectures held at Cambridge University. Their title, "Modular Forms, Elliptic Curves, and Galois Representations," did not give any hint of the historic revelation he was about to make, but Wiles had been out of sight for so long that rumors abounded days before his lecture series. On the first day Wiles recounted the first five years of his work on the Taniyama-Shimura conjecture. The second day he presented his findings from the 1991 to 1993 period. On the final day he summed up, with copious blackboard notations, his last six weeks of work. On that day, June 23, 1993, he concluded by telling the assembled mathematicians that he had proven the Taniyama-Shimura conjecture, and noted, in a casual aside, that it meant Fermat's Last Theorem was also proven to be true. The audience burst into tremendous applause, and news quickly circulated throughout the scientific community.

Yet Wiles refused to immediately release his 200-page proof to his international colleagues for verification, and rumors arose that there was a flaw near the end of it. In December of 1993 he announced that there was indeed a problem, but that he planned to solve it himself. "The problem occurred in Wiles's construction of a mathematical object known as an Euler system, which is a relatively new and largely unexplored idea," explained Cipra. "Wiles's Euler system was intended to prove a sizable chunk of the Taniyama-Shimura conjecture . . . but the system he had come up with turned out not to work in quite the right way."

After 90 Years Prize Awarded

On September 19, 1994, Wiles had a eureka moment and closed the theoretical gap. "It was so simple and elegant that at first it seemed too good to be true," he recalled to *Science* interviewer Cipra. A month later he finished and announced his corrections; the findings were published in the May 1995 issue of *Annals of Mathematics*. As befitting the historic nature of the proof, an entire issue was devoted to it, one part containing Wiles's paper for the original 1993 theory and a shorter one written by his former student, Richard Taylor, explaining how the flaw was overcome. As Brown remarked in *Sciences*, "in Wiles's proof Fermat's last theorem . . . tumbles out of a massive and intricate mathematical machine as a mere corollary, the consequence of a result that lies at the confluence of virtually every major stream of modern mathematics."

It took another two years to firmly double-check Wiles's proof of Fermat's Last Theorem—in part because there is a limited number of mathematicians who could grasp its complexities—before the Wolfskehl committee finally granted him the long-awaited prize. He received a number of other honors in his field and returned to Princeton where he continued teaching courses in number theory.

Books

Math and Mathematicians: The History of Math Discoveries around the World, U*X*L, 1999.
Notable Mathematicians, Gale, 1998.
Notable Scientists: From 1900 to the Present, Gale, 2001.
Singh, Simon, *Fermat's Enigma: The Epic Quest to Solve the World's Greatest Mathematical Problem,* Walker, 1997.

Periodicals

Discover, January 1994.
Economist, July 3, 1993.
Guardian (London, England), June 26, 1997; July 22, 1999.
Science, December 24, 1993; November 4, 1994; May 26, 1995.

Science News, November 5, 1994.
Sciences, September-October 1993.
Time, July 5, 1993. □

Mary Lou Williams

Pianist, composer, and arranger Mary Lou Williams (1910–1981) is often referred to as the First Lady of Jazz in the annals of American music history. Williams was a highly respected musician in her day whose repertoire spanned several seminal jazz styles, from boogie-woogie to bebop, and she was an integral member of what became known as the Kansas City big-band sound during the 1930s. In her later years she wrote jazz-inflected liturgical works for Roman Catholic masses and taught at Duke University. Williams, remarked *Denver Post* writer Glenn Giffin, "was the first, for a long time the only, and many claim the most significant, woman in jazz between the era of the '20s and her death in 1981."

Learned at Mother's Knee

Williams was born on May 10, 1910, in Atlanta, Georgia, as Mary Elfreda Winn. She did not meet her biological father until she was in her twenties, and her early years were rough. Her mother was a drinker and took in laundry to support Williams and an older sister. Her mother also liked to play the reed organ and kept the infant Williams on her lap when she practiced. According to an unpublished biography, Williams recalled that one day, she reportedly reached out and picked out the notes her mother had just played. "I must have frightened her so that she dropped me then and there, and I started to cry," she recalled, according to an article in *World and I* by David Conrads. "It must have really shaken my mother. She actually dropped me and ran out to get the neighbors to listen to me."

Soon Williams was playing by ear the African American slave spirituals and ragtime that her mother knew, and her mother "wouldn't consent to my having music lessons, for she feared I might end up as she had done—unable to play except from paper," Williams later recalled in a 1954 *Melody Maker* interview. Around 1914 or 1915, the family moved to Pittsburgh, which offered a thriving musical environment in its African American community. Around the East Liberty neighborhood where they lived, Williams soon emerged as a child musical prodigy, with perfect pitch and a remarkable musical memory. Her new stepfather, Fletcher Burley, bought a player piano for the home, and here Williams first learned the works of Jelly Roll Morton and other early jazz pioneers. "As a stepfather he was the greatest," Williams later said of Burley in the *Melody Maker* interview, "and he loved the blues. Fletcher taught me the first blues I

ever knew by singing them over and over to me." Burley also smuggled the young Williams into the bars where he liked to gamble, and she sometimes earned $20 in tips by playing the piano there.

Started in Black Vaudeville

Williams was soon known around all of Pittsburgh as "The Little Piano Girl" and once even played for a party at the home of the city's leading family, the Mellons. She made her formal debut with a band in 1922 at the age of 12, when an African American vaudeville review came to town and one of its musicians fell ill. Managers learned of William's prowess, and impresario "Buzzin" Harris visited the home—Williams recalls that she was playing hopscotch outside that day—and convinced her parents to let her tour with them. Her mother found a friend to go along to chaperone her, and Williams earned a lucrative $30 a week for gigs that took her to Detroit, Chicago, Cincinnati, and as far west as St. Louis.

Williams left Pittsburgh's Westinghouse High School in 1926 at the age of 16 and joined the Seymour and Jeanette Show, another popular black vaudeville act. That same year she married its bandleader, John Williams, who was also a talented saxophone player. She made her first recordings accompanying him on the piano as part of the "John Williams Synco Jazzers" for the Paramount, Gennett, and Champion labels. A woman playing with a jazz act was a relative rarity at the time and word of Williams's talents soon spread to New York City. On tour stops there, she met

and played for such greats as Morton and Fats Waller and once even sat in with Duke Ellington's Washingtonians at the Lincoln Theater for a week-long engagement.

The Kansas City Sound

For a time in the late 1920s Williams lived in Memphis, her husband's home town, but soon followed him out to Oklahoma City when he was offered a new gig. That band became Andy Kirk and the Twelve Clouds of Joy, and Williams soon joined it herself as its second pianist. Taking the act and settling in Kansas City, Kirk pioneered the new blues-based style of jazz that became synonymous with the booming and somewhat lawless Plains town, rich from newly discovered oil in the region. It was a lively scene, even when Prohibition was still in force. "Kansas City in the Thirties was jumping harder than ever," Williams recalled in the *Melody Maker* interview. "The 'Heart of America' was at that time one of the nerve centres of jazz, and I could write about it for a month and never do justice to the half of it. . . . Of course, we didn't have any closing hours in these spots. We could play all morning and half through the day if we wished to, and in fact we often did. The music was so good that I seldom got to bed before midday."

It was Kirk who helped Williams with some of her first forays into formal musical notation when she began arranging songs for his band. She quickly grew tired of having Kirk transcribe what she wanted and began to learn to notate herself. In Kansas City, Kirk's Twelve Clouds enjoyed tremendous success, fueled in part by Williams's arrangements and her compelling piano solos. She was also somewhat of a novelty, she admitted in a 1979 interview with *Books & Arts* writer Catherine O'Neill, for there were few women in jazz in the day except for vocalists. "In St. Louis once, I was sitting on the stand waiting for the band to come in, and I heard someone say, 'Get that little girl off the stage so the band can start up.' But I just stayed there, and when the band came in and I started playing, the house went into an uproar, cheering and laughing."

Gained Fame as Arranger

Williams cut her first solo record in Chicago in 1930, with two of her own compositions, "Drag 'Em" and "Night Life." She was never paid for them, however, and later had to threaten a lawsuit to have them taken off the market. For the rest of the decade she attained widespread recognition and was in great demand as both a pianist and an arranger. She arranged songs for Ellington, Earl "Fatha" Hines, Louis Armstrong, Tommie Dorsey, Benny Goodman, and Cab Calloway, among others. Her best-known works remain "Camel Hop" and "Roll 'Em" for Goodman and "What's Your Story Morning Glory," a song that helped make her longtime friend Jimmie Lunceford's band a success.

Williams divorced her husband in 1940 and remained with the Kirk band until 1942. By then, a new style of jazz called bebop was emerging in New York City, and Williams headed there. She came to know its principals—Charlie "Bird" Parker, Dizzie Gillespie, Max Roach, Bud Powell, and Thelonious Monk—and many liked to gather in her Harlem apartment for impromptu sessions. Drummer Art

Blakey encouraged her to form her own combo, which she did with the man who would become her second husband, trumpeter Harold "Shorty" Baker. It was a short-lived union, however, and the combo was as well. She signed on with Ellington's band as its arranger, and the highlight of this period of her career was her arrangement of "Blue Skies (Trumpet No End)," a classic Ellington song from 1946.

Dropped Out for a Time

In 1943, Williams began a regular engagement at the Café Society in Greenwich Village, New York City's first racially integrated jazz club. The nightspot was such a success that a second venue soon opened uptown, and Williams played there after 1948, to crowds that often included prominent artists, writers, and film stars of the day. In 1946 her first large-scale composition, *Zodiac Suite,* made its debut with the New York Philharmonic Orchestra at Carnegie Hall. Each of its parts delivers a jazzy piano interpretation of the 12 signs of the zodiac, with " 'Leo' a growling march," noted *Down Beat* critic Jim Macnie of its recorded version some years later, while "the seesaw agitation of 'Gemini' comes neatly balanced." Macnie asserted that "it's hard to imagine Williams' intricate miniatures not raising the eyebrows of all who heard them at the time. Almost instantly memorable, their clever construction beguiled listeners by revamping the functions of theme and variation."

Around this time Williams began hosting her own radio show, the *Mary Lou Williams Piano Workshop,* but she was beginning to weary of the musician's lifestyle. She moved to Europe in the early 1950s, where she enjoyed regular work as a jazz pianist at London and Paris nightclubs, but one day in 1954 walked off a Paris stage and went back to New York. She announced her official retirement from performing and delved into charity work in Harlem. She also underwent a religious awakening and converted from her Southern Baptist roots to Roman Catholicism. In 1957, she established the Bel Canto Foundation to help New York-area musicians with substance abuse problems, and she personally ran the thrift shop that funded it.

Wrote Jazz Mass

Encouraged by others, Williams returned to stage in 1957 with Dizzy Gillespie at the Newport Jazz Festival. She founded a trio, as well as her own record company—the first established by a woman—called Mary Records, but she also began writing liturgical music. Her 1962 cantata, "Black Christ of the Andes," honored Saint Martin de Porres, the first African-heritage saint in the Roman Catholic Church who had been canonized by Pope John XXIII that same year. Williams's most famous work from this era, however, remains *Music for Peace,* commissioned by the Vatican in 1969 and sometimes referred to as "Mary Lou's Mass." It was adapted for ballet and staged by the Alvin Ailey American Dance Theater in 1971, and a performance of it was given at St. Patrick's Cathedral in Manhattan in 1975, which made history as the first jazz Mass ever held there.

Williams made an important recording in 1970 titled *The History of Jazz.* A solo piano performance and lecture, Williams gave a first-person account of her years in jazz and demonstrated its changing rhythms and styles on the keyboard. She became a purist about jazz in her later years, voicing a strong dislike for modernist and rock influences on the form. She did, however, perform with avant-garde pianist Cecil Taylor in 1977 at Carnegie Hall. That same year she took a post as artist-in-residence at Duke University in North Carolina, where she taught a new generation of jazz and piano students. It was also the first regular paycheck of her life. She was diagnosed with cancer in 1979 and gave her last performance in Tallahassee, Florida, in 1980. Later that year she was also involved in a performance of one of her masses at Sacred Heart Cathedral in Raleigh, North Carolina, though she was by then debilitated from radiation treatments. She died just a few weeks after her 71st birthday on May 28, 1981, in Durham, North Carolina. She was inducted into *Down Beat* magazine's Hall of Fame in 1990 as the first female instrumentalist ever to earn that honor. A "Mary Lou Williams Women in Jazz" festival at the John F. Kennedy Center for the Performing Arts in Washington, D.C. has been held annually since 1996.

Books

Contemporary Black Biography, Volume 15, Gale, 1997.
Notable Black American Women, Book 1, Gale, 1992.
Scribner Encyclopedia of American Lives, Volume 1: 1981–
    1985, Charles Scribner's Sons, 1998.

Periodicals

Books and Arts, December 7, 1979.
Denver Post, September 8, 2000.
Down Beat, April 1996.
Melody Maker, April-June 1954.
World and I, June 2000.
Washington Post, March 26, 1999. □

Kenneth Geddes Wilson

Kenneth Geddes Wilson (born 1936) won the Nobel Prize in physics in 1982 for his work applying renormalization group analysis to previously unsolved problem in theoretical physics concerning critical points and phase transitions. Affiliated with Cornell University for a number of years, Wilson was also involved with getting government support for supercomputers on campuses. He later was a physics professor at Ohio State University, again doing research in physics and becoming involved in education reform.

Wilson was born on June 8, 1936, in Waltham, Massachusetts. He was the first of six children born to Edgar Bright Wilson, Jr., and his wife

Emily Fisher (nee Buckingham). Wilson was born into an academic family. His father was a professor of chemistry at Harvard University and an expert on microwave spectroscopy. His maternal grandfather had taught mechanical engineering at the Massachusetts Institute of Technology. Wilson's mother had done some graduate work in physics. All five of his siblings also became either academics or scientists.

Wilson himself was an exceptional student from an early age. His grandfather taught him how to do math in his head, and while waiting for the bus a young Wilson would do cube roots. He was given an education at private schools in his home state, in cities such as Wellesley and Woods Hole, Massachusetts, and the Shady Hill School in Cambridge, Massachusetts. While still a teenager, Wilson also attended Magdalen College School at Oxford University in Oxford, England, for a year.

Entered Harvard University

When Wilson graduated in 1952 from The George School (a Quaker school) in Pennsylvania, he was only 16 years old. He then entered Harvard University, where he studied mathematics and physics. Wilson was not, however, just an academic. He was also a member of the track team, where he won a varsity letter as a mile runner. He graduated from Harvard with his B.A. in physics in 1956.

After graduating from Harvard, Wilson entered graduate school at the California Institute of Technology. There he studied physics, primarily quantum field theory with Murray Gell-Mann as his advisor. Wilson's thesis was entitled *An Investigation of the Low Equation and the Chew-Mandelshtam Equations*. It concerned renormalization group analysis, an area of work that would eventually win Wilson the Nobel prize.

Renormalization group analysis was a mathematical process that was developed to address certain kinds of problems in the area of quantum electrodynamics, related to the mathematical representation of aspects of this theory when applied elsewhere. In his thesis, Wilson solved a problem dealing with K-mesons or kaons. Wilson used these mathematical methods to create a knowledge of the magnetic properties of atoms.

Earned Ph.D.

Wilson earned his Ph.D. from Cal Tech in 1961. In this time period, he was given two postdoctoral fellowships. The first was at Harvard, where he was a Junior Fellow at the Harvard Society of Fellows from 1959 to 1963. From 1962 to 1963, Wilson worked on a Ford Foundation Fellowship at the European Organization for Nuclear Research (CERN) in Geneva, Switzerland. After Wilson completed the fellowship at CERN, he was hired for a tenure track position in the physics department at Cornell University, where he would spend the next 25 years.

Wilson's Theory

In Wilson's early theoretical work at Cornell, he continued to study renormalization groups, but this time, he applied them to critical phenomena and phase changes and transitions such as when liquids change to gases and in alloys. With critical phenomena, materials behave differently under defined environmental conditions. They experience changes that are very different. The conditions under which these changes happen are known as the critical point. Near this point, the complexities of what happens with critical phenomena, in terms of short-range actions and bigger connection between the whole body of the material, including the various ranges and scales of interaction, were nearly unmanageable. Wilson was one of many scientists trying to address the problem by reducing the complexity while keeping the theory being addressed valid.

Wilson successfully solved this problem by applying renormalization group analysis to it. The way Wilson proposed using renormalization group analysis involved computers and using an averaging procedure on the broken-down parts of the system. Wilson applied the analysis to properties of the material near the critical point. He used a lattice-like network of first smaller blocks on a smaller scale, then with each step, larger-scale system fluctuations, before the entire system was addressed. These small blocks made the problems easier to solve and removed infinities from the equation.

During the course of his work, Wilson learned that near critical points, a number of systems could be universally defined by a limited number of parameters. His theory was later expanded and applied elsewhere. Thus Wilson's method became a general theory which allowed observations about individual atoms to predict the properties of a systems of many interacting atoms.

Much of this work was published in two articles in *Physical Review* in 1971. Many scientists believed that Wilson's work answered some of the biggest unsolved problem in theoretical physics. He later tried to apply his renormalization theory to quarks (that is, what makes up protons, neutrons, and other subatomic particles) in the mid-1970s.

Won Nobel Prize

In 1982, Wilson was award the Nobel Prize in Physics for this work, applying renormalization group analysis to previously unsolved problem in theoretical physics concerning critical points and phase transitions. The prize was not unexpected. Wilson's father told Bayard Webster of *New York Times,* "Of course I'm very happy for him. People in physics have been telling me for a long time that it was going to happen. It is nice when it really does happen."

In his acceptance speech, published at the Nobel e-museum, Wilson emphasized the importance of supporting science research. He said, "The scientist's inquiry into the causes of things is providing an ever more extensive understanding of nature. In consequence, science is more important than ever for industrial technology. Industry now should become a full partner of government in supporting long-range basic research."

While Wilson was working on his Nobel Prize-winning theory, he continued to have a strong academic career. In 1970, Wilson was given a full professorship at Cornell. Four years later, he was named to an endowed chair, the James

A. Weeks Chair. It was the combination of academics and research that influenced his next area of research.

Promoted Building of Supercomputers

After 1976, much of Wilson's theoretical work was concerned with computer simulations and modeling. He promoted the idea of building supercomputer centers for scientists so they would have access to the greatest amount of technology because of the limits of computer technology of the time. His goal was to continue to improve the scientific community as well as the computer industry.

Beginning in 1981, he was part of a group of leading scientists that worked to get federal funding to get supercomputers on college campuses. Wilson did less research and honed his public speaking skills as he lobbied Congress, federal officials, and executives of corporations. Wilson gave about a speech a week to promote this cause. People would listen to him more than other scientists, it seemed, because he had won the Nobel Prize. In his speeches, Wilson claimed that without national supercomputers, the United States would not continue to be the leader in this technology.

In 1985, Wilson got his wish when the National Science Foundation gave $200 million over five years to four universities to create four supercomputer centers on their campuses, including Wilson's home university of Cornell. (The other supercomputer centers were located at Princeton, University of Illinois, and University of California.) Later, the federal government via the National Science Foundation did not provide the funding at the rate promised. In 1985, before the funding failed to be delivered, he served as the director of the Center for Theory and Simulation in Science and Engineering.

Moved to Ohio State University

In 1988, Wilson left Cornell to become a professor at Ohio State University. He did this in part because of his wife, Alison Brown, whom he married in 1982. She was a computer specialist and had been the associate director for advanced computing and networking at Cornell's Theory Center. She was hired to be the associate director of a new entity at Ohio State, the Ohio Supercomputer Center, as well as the associate director of research computing.

As for Wilson, he had reached his goal of getting the Theory Center off the ground and wanted to return to doing his own research. At Ohio State, he was named the Hazel C. Youngberg Trustees Distinguished Professor of Physics. His research continued to be related to computers, focusing on computer simulations and the modeling of physical phenomena.

Wilson also had interests outside of physics. He became especially concerned with education and education curriculum. After 1990, Wilson was involved in national policy for science. He was involved in the National Academy of Science's Committee on Physical Science, Mathematics and Applications as well as Committee on the Federal Role in Educational Research. In 1992, he was named the co-leader in Project Discovery, a five-year project funded by the National Science Foundation. It was to develop new techniques of teaching science and math. By 1993, Wilson was the chair of Ohio Model Science Curriculum Advisory Committee for the Ohio Department of Education.

With co-author Bennett Daviss, Wilson published a book on the subject, *Redesigning Education* (1994). It outlines Wilson's ideas for reforming America's educational process. After the end of Project Discovery, in 1996, Wilson was named co-director of Learning by Redesign. He continued to be involved in education reform into the 2000s.

Books

McGrath, Kimberly, ed., *World of Scientific Discovery,* Gale, 1999.

Muir, Hazel, ed., *Larousse Dictionary of Scientists,* Larousse, 1994.

Narins, Brigham, ed., *Notable Scientists: From 1900 to the Present,* Volume 5, Gale, 2001.

Wasson, Tyler, ed., *Nobel Prize Winners: An H.W. Wilson Biographical Dictionary,* H.W. Wilson Company, 1987.

Weber, Robert L., *Pioneers of Science: Nobel Prize Winners in Physics,* Adam Hilger, 1988.

Periodicals

Houston Chronicle, October 28, 1992.
New York Times, October 19, 1982; March 16, 1985.
Plain Dealer, February 21, 1993.
Science, April 1, 1988.

Online

"Kenneth G. Wilson-Banquet Speech," http://www.nobel.se/physics/laureates/1982/wilson-speech.html (March 24, 2003).

"Kenneth Wilson Curriculum Vitae," http://www.physics.ohio-state.edu/~kgw/kgwcv.html (March 24, 2003).

"Profile of Kenneth Wilson," http://www.physics.ohio-state.edu/~kgw/kgw.html (March 24, 2003).

"Redesign Education Home page," http://www.physics.ohio-state.edu/~kgw/RE.html (March 24, 2003).

"Redesigning Education-Kirkus Reviews," http://www.physics.ohio-state.edu/~kgw/kirkus.html (March 24, 2003). □

Y

Jeana Yeager

In December of 1986 Jeana Yeager (born 1952) became the first woman to fly an airplane nonstop around the world without refueling. She and fellow pilot Dick Rutan made history when their specially built aircraft, *Voyager,* became the first airplane to completely circle the globe on one load of fuel. The journey took nine days.

Jeana Yeager was born on May 18, 1952, in Fort Worth, Texas. Despite her last name, she bears no relation to fellow aviation pioneer Chuck Yeager, who was the first to fly faster than the speed of sound. She grew up in a small town near Dallas, Texas, where one of her parents worked as a school teacher. Early hobbies for Yeager included horseback riding and running track, but she also developed an early interest in helicopters. Yeager studied drafting in high school, a skill that would prove extremely valuable in her later project to design the first-round-the-world aircraft. When Yeager was 19, she married a police officer, but the two were divorced after five years of marriage.

Retained Childhood Fascination with 'Copters

In 1977 Yeager left her failing marriage and settled in Santa Rosa, California. There she worked as a draftsman and surveyor for an energy company specializing in geothermal energy. In 1978, at age 26, she earned her private pilot's license, her ultimate goal being to learn to fly helicopters.

Yeager first became involved in the world of experimental aerospace design when she met Bob Truax at about the same time that she received her pilot's license. Truax was a rocket scientist who was attempting to develop a fully reusable spacecraft—something that had never been accomplished—at a company called Project Private Enterprise. Truax hired Yeager to work at his company as a draftswoman.

Conceived of a Pioneering Voyage

While attending an air show in Chino, California, in 1980 Yeager met fellow pilot Dick Rutan along with Rutan's brother, Burt Rutan, an aircraft designer. Dick Rutan, who had flown combat missions in the Vietnam war and was 14 years older than Yeager, was a featured acrobatic flyer at the show. At the time he held the title of chief test pilot for Burt Rutan's aircraft company, based in California's Mojave desert. Yeager and Dick Rutan fell in love, and in the early 1980s Yeager moved to the desert to work as a pilot for Burt Rutan's company, Flying Rutan aircraft, There she set new speed records for a woman pilot.

One day while dining at a restaurant, Yeager and the Rutan brothers conceived a plan to make the first nonstop airplane flight around the world without refueling. Burt Rutan mentioned that the lightweight composite materials out of which he built his planes could easily break distance records. Yeager and Dick Rutan suggested that they try to break the then-current record, which stood at 12,500 miles and had been set by a B-52 bomber in the early 1960s. Burt Rutan said he was confident that he could build a plane that could cover twice that distance, which happened to be about the distance around the world.

Yeager and the Rutans began their project in earnest in 1981. Deciding to make the first-round-the world, nonstop airplane flight was one thing; getting the funds with which to do it was another. Yeager and the Rutans formed the Voy-

feet—longer than that of a Boeing 727 airliner—and a cockpit no bigger than a telephone booth. Loaded with all the fuel needed to make the round-the-world flight, it was inherently unsafe, referred to even by its designers as a flying bomb. It was also extremely difficult to fly. Unstable in the air, it required constant attention to keep it aloft. It was powered by two engines, one in front to pull the aircraft forward in flight, and the other in the back to push. Built of a graphite composite known by the brand name Magnamite, the plane's only metal was contained in its engines and a few nuts and bolts.

Before *Voyager* could take off, however, it had to be loaded with enough fuel to travel around the world nonstop: more than 1,200 gallons. This feat was made possible because of the advanced structural materials—very strong and very light—with which the plane had been built.

Record-breaking Flight

Voyager took off from Edwards Air Force base in California on December 14, 1986. The plane was so heavy on takeoff that its wings scraped the ground as it gathered sufficient speed for take-off. The wing tips were damaged, but not enough to abort the flight.

Yeager, then 34 years old, had undergone extensive training in ocean navigation and communications before the trip, and she acted as the copilot and main navigator, flying the plane while Dick Rutan slept. Other preparations Yeager made for the flight included taking an Air Force water-survival training course. She was one of the first civilians to complete this extremely difficult course. She also qualified for a commercial pilot's license, as well as multi-engine and instrument ratings.

Voyager traveled at an average speed of 115.8 miles per hour. Its flight path took it from California across the Pacific and Indian oceans, across Africa, and on across the Atlantic before crossing the United States to its point of take-off. The flight was not without its perils. At one point, storms became so severe that Yeager and Rutan seriously considered abandoning their round-the-world attempt and landing. Forced to run both engines to avoid a typhoon four days into the journey, the pilots feared they had used up too much fuel to make it all the way around the world.

Near the end of the flight, the rear engine suddenly quit. Because the front engine had been turned off to save fuel, the plane dropped quickly from 8,500 to 5,000 feet before the front engine could be restarted. The failure of the rear engine was later attributed to air pockets in the fuel lines that fed the engine from the plane's 17 fuel tanks.

Loud engine noise was Yeager and Rutan's constant companion, and Yeager ended the flight with permanent hearing damage. The pair slept very little, managing only 3 1/2 hours or so of sleep each night. Other dangers included oxygen deprivation and the constant battering the pilots took as the plane's uneven flight tossed them against the sides of the cockpit.

ager project for this purpose, but it was not until Yeager started a fundraising program that money started to come in. In fact that program was the major source of funding for Voyager. The project received no funding from the U.S. government, and Yeager, on speaking tours after her historic flight, cited the project as an example of what is possible with enough determination.

It was Yeager who named the project and the airplane that would result: Voyager. She also drafted the plane's engineering drawings. She ran the business operation that kept the project afloat financially. Turning down sponsorship offered by a tobacco company—Yeager and Rutan are both opposed to smoking—and from a Japanese company because they felt the project should remain entirely American, Yeager and the Voyager team subsisted largely on donations from private individuals in the early days.

Gave Birth to *Voyager*

The project to design, fund, build, and test-fly the round-the-world aircraft *Voyager* took five years. Two of those years were required to build the craft after it had been designed. The project also required two million dollars in funding. The plane was hand-built by a team of volunteers, who collectively put in 22,000 hours of effort. Some materials and equipment were donated by various aircraft systems manufacturers.

At the end of it, the plane was built that could do the job. The experiment known as *Voyager* was able to carry several times its weight in fuel, had a wingspan of 110

Landed in History Books after Nine Days

Nine days after it had taken off—a total of 116 hours in the air—*Voyager* landed at Edwards Air Force base the morning of December 23, 1986. Yeager and Rutan had traveled 28,000 miles, landing them solidly in the record books with eight gallons of fuel to spare, enough to have taken them only another 100 miles. By flying around the world *Voyager* almost doubled the previous endurance record, which had been set in 1962. "It's the last 'first' in aviation," Rutan radioed as his and Yeager's flight neared its end, according to Michael Specter in the *Washington Post*. "I have to admit there have been times during the flight when I didn't think it was possible."

After *Voyager* landed, the first person to approach the craft was a representative from the National Aeronautics Association (NAA). The representative checked seals and other devices on the cockpit and landing gear to verify that the plane had not touched down since its takeoff nine days earlier. The NAA subsequently certified that the plane had, in fact, broken the world record for a nonstop flight.

Thousands of spectators greeted Yeager and Rutan after they landed, and the two exhausted pilots sat atop the craft's fuselage and answered questions. They then climbed into separate ambulances so that they could be taken to a hospital at the Air Force base for medical evaluation.

President Ronald Reagan reacted to news of the flight with enthusiasm and invited Yeager and Rutan to meet him in Los Angeles the following week. At their meeting, Reagan presented Yeager and Rutan with the Presidential Citizen's Metal in recognition of their feat. Yeager and Rutan, along with their colleagues on the Voyager project, were later awarded the prestigious Collier Trophy for aviation.

Rebuilt Lives after Historic Flight

Voyager had reached the end of its own endurance; while the plane was being flown from the landing field at Edwards Air Force Base back to its hanger in Mojave, California, the seal for its coolant system became permanently damaged. The craft was eventually donated to the Smithsonian Air and Space Museum in Washington, D.C., where it was put on display along with other pioneering air and spacecraft, including Charles Lindbergh's *Spirit of St. Louis* and the Apollo 11 command module that took the first astronauts to the moon.

Following their flight, Yeager and Rutan traveled around the world again, this time at a more leisurely pace as they spoke about their experience. These appearances helped them raise money to pay back the debts they had incurred in connection with their pioneering flight. These debts were estimated to be in the neighborhood of $250,000.

Yeager and Rutan's relationship disintegrated in the aftermath of their historic flight. Yeager would later trace the erosion of their relationship to the very thing that had brought them together: their shared love of flight. Each intensely motivated and driven by their dreams, they competed for control not only of the aircraft they flew together, but of their relationship.

Speaking of life after *Voyager* to John May of the *Guardian*, Yeager said she was ready to take on new challenges, including developing a science museum and thriving "on doing things that are new and exciting for me. I enjoy learning and finding out, figuring out, planning, organizing. For me that is fun."

Periodicals

Christian Science Monitor, December 30, 1986.
Guardian, March 2, 1988.
New York Times, December 24, 1986.
St. Louis Post-Dispatch, April 11, 1991.
Toronto Star, December 28, 1986.
Washington Post, December 24, 1986.

Online

"Jeana Yeager," *Edwards Air Force Base Web site,* http://www.edwards.af.mil (March 17, 2003).
"Jeana Yeager," *Smithsonian National Air and Space Museum,* http://www.nasm.edu (March 17, 2003).
"Voyager Aircraft Return from Non-stop Trip around the World," *National Air and Space Administration Web site,* http://www.dfrc.nasa.gov (March 17, 2003). □

Steve Yzerman

Longtime captain of the National Hockey League's Detroit Red Wings, Steve Yzerman (born 1965) was the key player on three Stanley Cup champion teams and the linchpin of Detroit's hockey dynasty in the late 1990s and early 2000s.

Young Hockey Sensation

Yzerman was born in Cranbrook, British Columbia, on May 9, 1965. By Canadian hockey standards, he was a bit of a late bloomer, not picking up the game until he was seven. But once bitten by the hockey bug, Yzerman spent all his free time on the ice. When he was nine, the family moved to Nepean, Ontario, a suburb of Ottawa. Yzerman became a member of the Nepean Raiders, the local peewee hockey team. Asked by *Ottawa Sun* reporter Bruce Garroch if Yzerman's potential was evident at that early age, former Raiders coach Elwood Johnson replied: "Was he a great player? I'll give you a hint: We had Dave Lowry [now with the Calgary Flames] playing left wing on a line with Steve Yzerman in 1978, and we finished with a 78-2 record, and we won nine straight tournaments. We won the Ontario peewee championship because we had Steve Yzerman. We had a lot of other great players, but he was the guy that everything was built around. He was a guy who could get the job done."

In 1981, at the age of 16, Yzerman joined the Peterborough Petes of the Ontario Hockey League. In his debut 1981–1982 season with the Petes, he compiled 21 goals and 43 assists. The following season, Yzerman doubled his

total goals to 42 and posted 49 assists. After two years in the juniors, he was selected by the Red Wings in the first round of the 1983 National Hockey League entry draft.

On October 5, 1983, Yzerman made his NHL debut in a game against the Winnipeg Jets, posting a goal and an assist. For the season, he put up a total of 87 points and 48 assists, more than any other rookie that year. His 39 goals for the season were second only to the 40 scored by Sylvain Turgeon of the Hartford Whalers. At season's end, Yzerman was named Rookie of the Year by the *Sporting News* and was runner-up for the Calder Trophy as Rookie of the Year. Most significantly for the Red Wings, Yzerman's dazzling play propelled the team into the playoffs for the first time in six years. In post-season play, the Red Wings center scored three goals and six points.

Red Wings Stalwart

In 1984–1985, his second season with the Red Wings, Yzerman played in all 80 games of the regular season and finished tied with Ron Duguay with 89 points. He led the Wings in assists with 59. Yzerman's brilliant play once again helped carry the Wings into the playoffs, where he scored two goals in three games. Sidelined with a broken collarbone for the last third of the regular season in 1985–1986, Yzerman nevertheless managed to score points in 27 of the 51 games he played. However, without its star center at full strength, the Red Wings failed to make the playoffs.

In recognition of his leadership abilities, Yzerman in 1986 was named captain of the Red Wings, becoming at age 21 the youngest captain in franchise history. Once again back at full strength, he played in all 80 games of the regular 1986–1987 season, posting points in 53 of those games. For the season, Yzerman scored 31 goals and 59 assists. A knee injury on March 1, 1988, cut short Yzerman's season in 1987–1988. Although he played in only 64 games, he still managed to lead the team in goals (50), assists (52), and points (102). He missed 16 regular season games and 13 playoff games before returning on May 7, 1988, to play in the Campbell Conference Finals against Edmonton.

During the 1988–1989 season Yzerman scored a career-high 65 goals and 90 assists. He also led the Red Wings in power play goals with 17. Yzerman scored points in 70 of his 80 regular season games. In the playoffs, he led the Red Wings in goals (5) and points (10). For his impressive performance, Yzerman was rewarded with the Lester B. Pearson Award as the NHL's top performer in balloting by the National Hockey League Players Association. Also impressed were hockey fans, who voted Yzerman Player of the Year in a fan poll conducted by *Hockey News*.

Yzerman turned in an almost equally impressive performance in 1989–1990, scoring 62 goals and 65 assists. He was only the sixth NHL player in history to post successive 60-goal seasons. In 1990–1991, Yzerman managed 51 goals and 57 assists, posting his fourth consecutive season with more than 100 points. He repeated this feat in 1991–1992 with a total of 103 points and in 1992–1993 with 137 points, the second-highest point total of his career.

A herniated disk kept Yzerman out of action for 26 games during the early months of the 1993–1994 season, but he nevertheless managed to score 24 goals and 58 assists for a total of 82 points. Between December 27, 1993, and January 19, 1994, he scored in 11 straight games. In late February 1994, Yzerman won Player of the Week honors after scoring 10 points in only four games. By season's end the Red Wings, with 46 wins, had captured the NHL's Central Division title. Once again, Yzerman performed brilliantly in the playoffs, scoring four points in three games. After the playoffs, he underwent surgery to remove the herniated disk from his neck.

In the 1994–1995 season, shortened to 48 games by a lengthy lockout and strike, Yzerman scored 38 points in 47 games, leading Detroit to the President's Trophy championship. Scoring 15 points in 12 playoff games, Yzerman helped the Red Wings win the Clarence Campbell Bowl in the Western Conference finals before falling to the New Jersey Devils in the conference finals. The following season, he captained the Red Wings to the team's second straight President's Trophy championship with a league record of 62 wins. On January 1996, Yzerman reached a career landmark, scoring his 500th goal. In the playoffs, he scored 20 points in 18 games.

Stanley Cup Champions

One of the most important achievements of Yzerman's hockey career came in 1996–1997 when he led the Red Wings to their first Stanley Cup championship in more than four decades. In the 20 games he played during the post-season, Yzerman scored 13 points. The following season, the Red Wings finished the regular season in second place in the Central Division but managed once again to fight their way to the Stanley Cup. In the regular season, Yzerman led the Red Wings with 45 assists and 69 points. He was selected the most valuable player in the playoffs, winning the coveted Conn Smythe Trophy.

With 74 points and 13 power play goals, Yzerman led Detroit to another Central Division title in 1998–1999. He was selected to start in the mid-season All-Star Game but was forced to miss the game because of an injury. Scoring nine goals in 10 games, he led his team into the second round of the playoffs. In 1999–2000 Yzerman once again led the Red Wings with 79 points and 15 power play goals. He scored his 600th career goal on November 26, 1999. In the post-season, Yzerman contributed four assists in eight playoff games. The following season, he led the Wings to their sixth division title in 10 years.

By far the most remarkable performance of Yzerman's career came in 2001–2002, when he led the Red Wings to their third Stanley Cup championship during his tenure as captain. Over the years the veteran center's knees had taken a beating, and an MRI taken after he played for Canada's hockey team in the 2002 Winter Olympics revealed there was virtually no cartilage left in his right knee. For the remainder of the regular season and into the playoffs, Yzerman was forced to play with severe pain. Of Yzerman's ability to play through that pain, Red Wings trainer John Wharton told *ESPN* magazine: "His pain tolerance—I cannot fathom it. I wonder if his nervous system is different than the rest of us."

Never Considered Retirement

On August 2, 2002, less than two months after leading the Red Wings to their third Stanley Cup title in six years, Yzerman underwent an osteotomy, or realignment of the knee. The operation was designed to remedy the acute arthritic condition of his right knee, a condition rarely seen in someone so young. Even Yzerman's knee surgeon, Pete Fowler of London, Ontario, was astounded at the hockey player's rebound from surgery. "I don't know of a pro athlete who has had an osteotomy," Fowler told Ryan Pyette, sports reporter for the *London Free Press*. "I certainly don't know of a pro athlete who has had an osteotomy while they were still a pro athlete. We didn't do it (the surgery) so Steve could return to hockey. We did it so Steve could return to walking without pain and for day-to-day activities."

But, amazingly, Yzerman came back. Although Yzerman limited his time on the ice after his return to the

game in late February 2003, just having him back with the team lifted the morale of his Red Wings teammates. Most importantly, Yzerman's comeback meant a return to the tough practice sessions he'd instituted as team captain. On February 20, 2003, Red Wings coach Dave Lewis handed the team over to Yzerman at the end of the Wings' regular practice session. Although Yzerman could have let the team rest up for the next night's game, he decided instead to subject his teammates to a sprint session. As Lewis told Jason La Canfora of the *Washington Post,* "We had already had a full practice, but Stevie skated them hard, and we ended up having pretty good success the next night. That's just one little example of what Stevie Yzerman means to this team. He demands and commands as much of his team as he commands and demands of himself. And Stevie has pretty high standards."

Yzerman never really considered retirement as an option. More than two decades in professional hockey had not dulled his enthusiasm for the game. He told La Canfora: "It never really occurred to me. . . . I'm just not ready to retire. Whether it's due to my knee condition or one day I just lose the desire to play, I'll know that then, but I don't have that now. I definitely haven't lost any desire to play. Until I get out there and know that I can't play anymore, then I'll stop."

Yzerman's unprecedented rebound from surgery confounded just about everybody around him, particularly the sports writers who were prepared to write the final chapter to his brilliant career.

Periodicals

ESPN, June 14, 2002.
London (Ontario) Free Press, February 27, 2003.
Ottawa Sun, August 25, 2002.
Washington Post, February 22, 2003.

Online

"No. 19, Steve Yzerman, C," *CBS.SportsLine.com,* http://cbs.sportsline.com/u/hockey/nhl/players/19035.htm (March 1, 2003).
"Players Bio: Steve Yzerman," *NHLPA.com,* http://www.nhlpa.com/Content/The_Players/player_bio1.asp?ID = 6091 (March 2, 2003).
"Steve Yzerman," *Detroit Red Wings.com,* http://www.detroitredwings.com/players/player_bio_career.asp?sw = 19 (March 1, 2003).
"Steve Yzerman, Center," *LetsGoWings.com,* http://www.letsgowings.com/players/yzerman_steve.html (March 1, 2003).
"Steve Yzerman: Vital Statistics," *The Steve Yzerman Page,* http://www.geocities.com/Colosseum/7198/zvital.htm (March 1, 2003). □

HOW TO USE THE *SUPPLEMENT* INDEX

The *Encyclopedia of World Biography Supplement (EWB)* Index is designed to serve several purposes. First, it is a cumulative listing of biographies included in the entire second edition of *EWB* and its supplements (volumes 1–23). Second, it locates information on specific topics mentioned in volume 23 of the encyclopedia—persons, places, events, organizations, institutions, ideas, titles of works, inventions, as well as artistic schools, styles, and movements. Third, it classifies the subjects of *Supplement* articles according to shared characteristics. Vocational categories are the most numerous—for example, artists, authors, military leaders, philosophers, scientists, statesmen. Other groupings bring together disparate people who share a common characteristic.

The structure of the *Supplement* Index is quite simple. The biographical entries are cumulative and often provide enough information to meet immediate reference needs. Thus, people mentioned in the *Supplement* Index are identified and their life dates, when known, are given. Because this is an index to a *biographical* encyclopedia, every reference includes the *name* of the article to which the reader is directed as well as the volume and page numbers. Below are a few points that will make the *Supplement* Index easy to use.

Typography. All main entries are set in boldface type. Entries that are also the titles of articles in *EWB* are set entirely in capitals; other main entries are set in initial capitals and lowercase letters. Where a main entry is followed by a great many references, these are organized by subentries in alphabetical sequence. In certain cases—for example, the names of countries for which there are many references—a special class of subentries, set in small capitals and preceded by boldface dots, is used to mark significant divisions.

Alphabetization. The Index is alphabetized word by word. For example, all entries beginning with *New* as a separate word (*New Jersey, New York*) come be-

fore *Newark.* Commas in inverted entries are treated as full stops (*Berlin; Berlin, Congress of; Berlin, University of; Berlin Academy of Sciences*). Other commas are ignored in filing. When words are identical, persons come first and subsequent entries are alphabetized by their parenthetical qualifiers (such as *book, city, painting*).

Titled persons may be alphabetized by family name or by title. The more familiar form is used—for example, *Disraeli, Benjamin* rather than *Beaconsfield, Earl of.* Cross-references are provided from alternative forms and spellings of names. Identical names of the same nationality are filed chronologically.

Titles of books, plays, poems, paintings, and other works of art beginning with an article are filed on the following word (*Bard, The*). Titles beginning with a preposition are filed on the preposition (*In Autumn*). In subentries, however, prepositions are ignored; thus *influenced by* would precede the subentry *in* literature.

Literary characters are filed on the last name. Acronyms, such as UNESCO, are treated as single words. Abbreviations, such as *Mr., Mrs.,* and *St.,* are alphabetized as though they were spelled out.

Occupational categories are alphabetical by national qualifier. Thus, *Authors, Scottish* comes before *Authors, Spanish,* and the reader interested in Spanish poets will find the subentry *poets* under *Authors, Spanish.*

Cross-references. The term *see* is used in references throughout the *Supplement* Index. The *see* references appear both as main entries and as subentries. They most often direct the reader from an alternative name spelling or form to the main entry listing.

This introduction to the *Supplement* Index is necessarily brief. The reader will soon find, however, that the *Supplement* Index provides ready reference to both highly specific subjects and broad areas of information contained in volume 23 and a cumulative listing of those included in the entire set.

INDEX

A

AALTO, HUGO ALVAR HENRIK (born 1898), Finnish architect, designer, and town planner **1** 1-2

AARON, HENRY LOUIS (Hank; born 1934), American baseball player **1** 2-3

ABBA ARIKA (circa 175-circa 247), Babylonian rabbi **1** 3-4

ABBAS I (1571-1629), Safavid shah of Persia 1588-1629 **1** 4-6

ABBAS, FERHAT (born 1899), Algerian statesman **1** 6-7

ABBOTT, BERENICE (1898-1991), American artist and photographer **1** 7-9

ABBOTT, GRACE (1878-1939), American social worker and agency administrator **1** 9-10

ABBOTT, LYMAN (1835-1922), American Congregationalist clergyman, author, and editor **1** 10-11

ABBOUD, EL FERIK IBRAHIM (1900-1983), Sudanese general, prime minister, 1958-1964 **1** 11-12

ABD AL-MALIK (646-705), Umayyad caliph 685-705 **1** 12-13

ABD AL-MUMIN (circa 1094-1163), Almohad caliph 1133-63 **1** 13

ABD AL-RAHMAN I (731-788), Umayyad emir in Spain 756-88 **1** 13-14

ABD AL-RAHMAN III (891-961), Umayyad caliph of Spain **1** 14

ABD EL-KADIR (1807-1883), Algerian political and religious leader **1** 15

ABD EL-KRIM EL-KHATABI, MOHAMED BEN (circa 1882-1963), Moroccan Berber leader **1** 15-16

ABDUH IBN HASAN KHAYR ALLAH, MUHAMMAD (1849-1905), Egyptian nationalist and theologian **1** 16-17

ABDUL RAHMAN, TUNKU (1903-1990), Former prime minister of Malaysia **18** 340-341

ABDUL-BAHA (Abbas Effendi; 1844-1921), Persian leader of the Baha'i Muslim sect **22** 3-5

ABDUL-HAMID II (1842-1918), Ottoman sultan 1876-1909 **1** 17-18

ABDULLAH II (Abdullah bin al Hussein II; born 1962), king of Jordan **22** 5-7

'ABDULLAH AL-SALIM AL-SABAH, SHAYKH (1895-1965), Amir of Kuwait (1950-1965) **1** 18-19

ABDULLAH IBN HUSEIN (1882-1951), king of Jordan 1949-1951, of Transjordan 1946-49 **1** 19-20

ABDULLAH IBN YASIN (died 1059), North African founder of the Almoravid movement **1** 20

ABDULLAH, MOHAMMAD (Lion of Kashmir; 1905-1982), Indian political leader who worked for an independent Kashmir **22** 7-9

ABE, KOBO (born Kimifusa Abe; also transliterated as Abe Kobo; 1924-1993), Japanese writer, theater director, photographer **1** 20-22

ABEL, IORWITH WILBER (1908-1987), United States labor organizer **1** 22-23

ABEL, NIELS (1802-1829), Norwegian mathematician **20** 1-2

ABELARD, PETER (1079-1142), French philosopher and theologian **1** 23-25

ABERCROMBY, RALPH (1734-1801), British military leader **20** 2-4

ABERDEEN, 4TH EARL OF (George Hamilton Gordon; 1784-1860), British statesman, prime minister 1852-55 **1** 25-26

ABERHART, WILLIAM (1878-1943), Canadian statesman and educator **1** 26-27

ABERNATHY, RALPH DAVID (born 1926), United States minister and civil rights leader **1** 27-28

ABIOLA, MOSHOOD (1937-1998), Nigerian politician, philanthropist, and businessman **19** 1-3

Abolitionists, English
Pringle, Thomas **23** 319-320

ABRAHAM (Abraham of the Chaldrrs; Father Abraham; c. 1996 BCE - c. 1821 BCE), considered the "father of the world's three largest monotheistic religions **23** 1-3

ABRAHAMS, ISRAEL (1858-1925), British scholar **1** 29

ABRAMOVITZ, MAX (born 1908), American architect **18** 1-3

ABRAMS, CREIGHTON W. (1914-1974), United States Army commander in World War II and Vietnam **1** 29-31

ABRAVANEL, ISAAC BEN JUDAH (1437-1508), Jewish philosopher and statesman **1** 31

ABU BAKR (circa 573-634), Moslem leader, first caliph of Islam **1** 31-32

ABU MUSA (born Said Musa Maragha circa 1930), a leader of the Palestinian Liberation Organization **1** 32-33

ABU NUWAS (al-Hasan ibn-Hani; circa 756-813), Arab poet **1** 33-34

ABU-L-ALA AL-MAARRI (973-1058), Arab poet and philosopher **1** 32

ABZUG, BELLA STAVISKY (1920-1998), lawyer, politician, and congresswoman **1** 34-35

ACHEBE, CHINUA (born 1930), Nigerian novelist **1** 35-37

457

ACHESON, DEAN GOODERHAM
(1893-1971), American statesman **1**
37-38

Acquired immune deficiency syndrome
(AIDS)
Ho, David Da-I **23** 145-148

**ACTION, JOHN EMERICH EDWARD
DALBERG** (1834-1902), English
historian and philosopher **1** 38

Activists
Australian
Spence, Catherine Helen **23**
374-375
British
Jex-Blake, Sophia **23** 168-170
Chilean
Arrau, Claudio **23** 17-18
Cuban
Rodríguez de Tío, Lola **23** 345-346
Puerto Rican
Rodríguez de Tío, Lola **23** 345-346

Activists, American
civil rights
Height, Dorothy Irene **23** 139-141
Murray, Pauli **23** 253-256
Terrell, Mary Church **23** 397-399
dress reform
Walker, Mary Edwards **23** 432-434
education
Whitney, Mary Watson **23** 440-442
environmental
Plotkin, Mark J. **23** 308-310
Native American rights
Austin, Mary Hunter **23** 23-25
Burlin, Natalie Curtis **23** 50-52
peace
Sampson, Edith **23** 356-358
social reform
Height, Dorothy Irene **23** 139-141
Paglia, Camille **23** 286-288
women's rights
Murray, Pauli **23** 253-256
women's suffrage
Terrell, Mary Church **23** 397-399

Actors and entertainers, American
aerialists
Leitzel, Lillian **23** 225-227
choreographers
Humphrey, Doris **23** 157-159
Limón, José Arcadia **23** 227-229
Tamiris, Helen **23** 390-392
dancers
Humphrey, Doris **23** 157-159
Limón, José Arcadia **23** 227-229
Tamiris, Helen **23** 390-392
filmmakers/directors
Brooks, Mel **23** 48-50
Deren, Maya **23** 95-97
Geffen, David Lawrence **23** 119-122
Hanks, Tom **23** 135-137
Polanski, Roman **23** 310-312
film stars
Farrar, Geraldine **23** 106-108
Hanks, Tom **23** 135-137
Pacino, Al **23** 284-286
Streep, Meryl Louise **23** 384-387
film writers
Burnett, Carol **23** 52-55

opera singers
Joyner, Matilda Sissieretta **23**
179-181
singers
Bailey, Mildred **23** 28-30
stage directors
Brooks, Mel **23** 48-50
stage performers
Pacino, Al **23** 284-286
Shange, Ntozake **23** 367-369
television
Burnett, Carol **23** 52-55

Actors and entertainers, Australian
Campion, Jane **23** 58-60

Actors and entertainers, Canadian
band leaders
Lombardo, Guy **23** 234-236

Actors and entertainers, European
• GREAT BRITAIN
filmmakers/directors
Glyn, Elinor **23** 126-128
Leigh, Mike **23** 222-225
stage directors
Leigh, Mike **23** 222-225
• THE CONTINENT
aerialists
Leitzel, Lillian **23** 225-227
band leaders
Cugat, Xavier **23** 81-82
filmmakers/directors
Almodóvar, Pedro **23** 6-9
Deren, Maya **23** 95-97
Ophüls, Max **23** 275-277
Pabst, G. W. **23** 282-284
Polanski, Roman **23** 310-312
Resnais, Alain **23** 333-335
Tarkovsky, Andrei **23** 392-395
Vigo, Jean **23** 429-431
stage directors
Ophüls, Max **23** 275-277

Actors and entertainers, Japanese
Kobayashi, Masaki **23** 199-201
Mizoguchi, Kenji **23** 248-250
Ozu, Yasujiro **23** 279-281

ADAM, JAMES (1730-1794), British
architect **1** 38-40

ADAM, ROBERT (1728-1792), British
architect **1** 38-40

ADAMS, ABIGAIL (Abigail Smith; 1744-
1818), American first lady **18** 3-7

ADAMS, ANSEL (1902-1984), landscape
photographer and conservationist **1**
40-41

ADAMS, CHARLES FRANCIS (1807-
1886), American diplomat and
politician **1** 41-42

ADAMS, GERALD (born 1948), president
of the Sinn Fein Irish political party **1**
42-44

ADAMS, HANK (born 1944), Native
American activist **1** 45

ADAMS, HENRY BROOKS (1838-1918),
American historian and author **1** 45-47

ADAMS, HERBERT BAXTER (1850-1901),
American historian and teacher **1** 47

ADAMS, JAMES LUTHER (1901-1994),
American social ethicist, theologian,
and defender of religious and political
liberalism **1** 47-48

ADAMS, JOHN (1735-1826), American
statesman and diplomat, president
1797-1801 **1** 48-51

ADAMS, JOHN COUCH (1819-1892),
English mathematical astronomer **1**
51-52

ADAMS, JOHN QUINCY (1767-1848),
American statesman and diplomat,
president 1825-29 **1** 52-54

ADAMS, PETER CHARDON BROOKS
(1848-1927), American historian **1** 54

ADAMS, SAMUEL (1722-1803),
American colonial leader and
propagandist **1** 55-56

ADAMSON, JOY (Friederike Victoria
Gessner; 1910-1980), Austrian
naturalist and painter **18** 7-9

ADDAMS, JANE (1860-1935), American
social worker, reformer, and pacifist **1**
56-57

ADDISON, JOSEPH (1672-1719), English
essayist and politician **1** 57-58

ADDISON, THOMAS (1793-1860),
English physician **1** 58-59

ADENAUER, KONRAD (1876-1967),
German statesman, chancellor of the
Federal Republic 1949-63 **1** 59-61

ADLER, ALFRED (1870-1937), Austrian
psychiatrist **1** 61-63

ADLER, FELIX (1851-1933), American
educator and Ethical Culture leader **1**
63-64

ADLER, MORTIMER JEROME (1902-
2001), American philosopher and
educator **22** 9-11

ADONIS ('Ali Ahmad Said; born 1930),
Lebanese poet **1** 64-65

ADORNO, THEODOR W. (1903-1969),
German philosopher and leader of the
Frankfurt School **1** 65-67

ADRIAN, EDGAR DOUGLAS (1st Baron
Adrian of Cambridge; 1889-1977),
English neurophysiologist **1** 67-69

Adventurers
Bird, Isabella **23** 41-42

ADZHUBEI, ALEKSEI IVANOVICH
(1924-1993), Russian journalist and
editor **18** 9-11

AELFRIC (955-circa 1012), Anglo-Saxon
monk, scholar, and writer **1** 69-70

AESCHYLUS (524-456 B.C.), Greek playwright **1** 70-72

AFFONSO I (1460?-1545), king of Kongo **1** 72

AFINOGENOV, ALEKSANDR NIKOLAEVICH (1904-1941), Russian dramatist **1** 72-73

'AFLAQ, MICHEL (born 1910), Syrian founder and spiritual leader of the Ba'th party **1** 73-74

African American art
see African American history (United States)

African American history (United States)
• POLITICIANS
cabinet officials
Rice, Condoleezza **23** 335-338
• SOCIETY and CULTURE
art
Burlin, Natalie Curtis **23** 50-52
Fuller, Meta Warrick **23** 112-114
Thomas, Alma Woodsey **23** 401-403
business leaders
Graves, Earl Gilbert, Jr. **23** 130-132
Malone, Annie Turnbo **23** 242-243
education
Malone, Annie Turnbo **23** 242-243
law
Sampson, Edith **23** 356-358
Stout, Juanita Kidd **23** 382-384
literature (20th century)
Reed, Ishmael Scott **23** 331-333
Rollins, Charlemae Hill **23** 346-348
Shange, Ntozake **23** 367-369
Toomer, Jean **23** 408-410
music
Armstrong, Lillian Hardin **23** 15-17
Hooker, John Lee **23** 155-157
Hunter, Alberta **23** 160-162
Johnson, Robert **23** 172-174
Joyner, Matilda Sissieretta **23** 179-181
Leadbelly **23** 208-211
Pride, Charley Frank **23** 317-319
Williams, Mary Lou **23** 444-446
photography
Johnston, Frances Benjamin **23** 174-177
publishing
Graves, Earl Gilbert, Jr. **23** 130-132

African Americans
see African American history (United States)

AGA KHAN (title), chief commander of Moslem Nizari Ismailis **1** 74-76

AGAOGLU, ADALET (Adalet Agoglu; born 1929), Turkish playwright, author, and human rights activist **22** 11-13

AGASSIZ, JEAN LOUIS RODOLPHE (1807-1873), Swiss-American naturalist and anatomist **1** 76-78

AGEE, JAMES (1909-1955), American poet, journalist, novelist, and screenwriter **1** 78-79

AGESILAUS II (circa 444-360 B.C.), king of Sparta circa 399-360 B.C. **1** 79-80

AGHA MOHAMMAD KHAN (circa 1742-1797), shah of Persia **1** 80-81

AGIS IV (circa 262-241 B.C.), king of Sparta **1** 81-82

AGNELLI, GIOVANNI (1920-2003), Italian industrialist **1** 82-83

AGNESI, MARIA (1718-1799), Italian mathematician, physicist, and philosopher **20** 4-5

AGNEW, SPIRO THEODORE (1918-1996), Republican United States vice president under Richard Nixon **1** 83-85

AGNODICE (born ca. 300 BC), Greek physician **20** 5-5

AGNON, SHMUEL YOSEPH (1888-1970), author **1** 85-86

AGOSTINO (1557-1602) **1** 86

AGOSTINO DI DUCCIO (1418-1481?), Italian sculptor **1** 86

AGRICOLA, GEORGIUS (1494-1555), German mineralogist and writer **1** 86-87

AGRIPPINA THE YOUNGER (Julia Agrippina; 15-59), wife of Claudius I, Emperor of Rome, and mother of Nero **20** 5-8

AGUINALDO, EMILIO (1869-1964), Philippine revolutionary leader **1** 88

AHAD HAAM (pseudonym of Asher T. Ginsberg, 1856-1927), Russian-born author **1** 88-89

AHERN, BERTIE (Bartholomew Ahern; born 1951), Irish Prime Minister **18** 11-13

AHIDJO, AHMADOU (1924-1989), first president of the Federal Republic of Cameroon **1** 89-90

AIDOO, AMA ATA (Christina Ama Aidoo; born 1942), Ghanaian writer and educator **20** 8-10

AIKEN, CONRAD (1889-1973), American poet, essayist, novelist, and critic **1** 90-91

AIKEN, HOWARD (1900-1973), American physicist, computer scientist, and inventor **20** 10-12

AILEY, ALVIN (1931-1989), African American dancer and choreographer **1** 91-94

AILLY, PIERRE D' (1350-1420), French scholar and cardinal **1** 94

Air pioneers
see Aviators

Aircraft (aeronautics)
pilots
Yeager, Jeana **23** 449-451

AITKEN, WILLIAM MAXWELL (Lord Beaverbrook; 1879-1964), Canadian businessman and politician **1** 94-96

AKBAR, JALAL-UD-DIN MOHAMMED (1542-1605), Mogul emperor of India 1556-1605 **1** 96

AKHMATOVA, ANNA (pseudonym of Anna A. Gorenko, 1889-1966), Russian poet **1** 96-97

AKIBA BEN JOSEPH (circa 50-circa 135), Palestinian founder of rabbinic Judaism **1** 97-98

AKIHITO (born 1933), 125th emperor of Japan **1** 98-99

AKUTAGAWA, RYUNOSUKE (Ryunosuke Niihara; 1892-1927), Japanese author **22** 13-14

ALAMÁN, LUCAS (1792-1853), Mexican statesman **1** 99-100

ALARCÓN, PEDRO ANTONIO DE (1833-1891), Spanish writer and politician **1** 100-101

ALARCÓN Y MENDOZA, JUAN RUIZ DE (1581?-1639), Spanish playwright **1** 101

ALARIC (circa 370-410), Visigothic leader **1** 101-102

ALA-UD-DIN (died 1316), Khalji sultan of Delhi **1** 102-103

ALAUNGPAYA (1715-1760), king of Burma 1752-1760 **1** 103

ALBA, DUKE OF (Fernando Álvarez de Toledo; 1507-1582), Spanish general and statesman **1** 103-104

Albania (nation, Southeastern Europe)
Kastrioti-Skanderbeg, Gjergj **23** 187-189

AL-BANNA, HASSAN (1906-1949), Egyptian religious leader and founder of the Muslim Brotherhood **1** 104-106

ALBEE, EDWARD FRANKLIN, III (born 1928), American playwright **1** 106-108

ALBÉNIZ, ISAAC (1860-1909), Spanish composer and pianist **1** 108-109

ALBERDI, JUAN BAUTISTA (1810-1884), Argentine political theorist **1** 109-110

ALBERS, JOSEPH (1888-1976), American artist and art and design teacher **1** 110

ALBERT (1819-1861), Prince Consort of Great Britain **1** 110-112

ALBERT I (1875-1934), king of the Belgians 1909-1934 **1** 112

ALBERT II (born 1934), sixth king of the Belgians **1** 112-113

ALBERTI, LEON BATTISTA (1404-1472), Italian writer, humanist, and architect **1** 113-115

ALBERTI, RAFAEL (born 1902), Spanish poet and painter **18** 13-15

ALBERTUS MAGNUS, ST. (circa 1193-1280), German philosopher and theologian **1** 115-116

ALBRIGHT, MADELEINE KORBEL (born 1937), United States secretary of state **1** 116-118

ALBRIGHT, TENLEY EMMA (born 1935), American figure skater **23** 3-6

ALBRIGHT, WILLIAM (1891-1971), American archaeologist **21** 1-3

ALBUQUERQUE, AFONSO DE (circa 1460-1515), Portuguese viceroy to India **1** 118-119

ALCIBIADES (circa 450-404 B.C.), Athenian general and politician **1** 119-120

ALCORN, JAMES LUSK (1816-1894), American lawyer and politician **1** 120-121

ALCOTT, AMOS BRONSON (1799-1888), American educator **1** 121

ALCOTT, LOUISA MAY (1832-1888), American author and reformer **1** 122

ALCUIN OF YORK (730?-804), English educator, statesman, and liturgist **1** 122-123

ALDRICH, NELSON WILMARTH (1841-1915), American statesman and financier **1** 123-124

ALDRIN, EDWIN EUGENE, JR. (Buzz Aldrin; born 1930), American astronaut **18** 15-17

ALDUS MANUTIUS (Teobaldo Manuzio; 1450?-1515), Italian scholar and printer **21** 3-5

ALEICHEM, SHOLOM (Sholom Rabinowitz; 1859-1916), writer of literature relating to Russian Jews **1** 124-125

ALEIJADINHO, O (Antônio Francisco Lisbôa; 1738-1814), Brazilian architect and sculptor **1** 125-126

ALEMÁN, MATEO (1547-after 1615), Spanish novelist **1** 126

ALEMÁN VALDÉS, MIGUEL (1902-1983), Mexican statesman, president 1946-1952 **1** 126-127

ALEMBERT, JEAN LE ROND D' (1717-1783), French mathematician and physicist **1** 127-128

ALESSANDRI PALMA, ARTURO (1868-1950), Chilean statesman, president 1920-1925 and 1932-1938 **1** 128-129

ALESSANDRI RODRIGUEZ, JORGE (born 1896), Chilean statesman, president 1958-1964 **1** 129-130

ALEXANDER I (1777-1825), czar of Russia 1801-1825 **1** 130-132

ALEXANDER II (1818-1881), czar of Russia 1855-1881 **1** 132-133

ALEXANDER III (1845-1894), emperor of Russia 1881-1894 **1** 133-134

ALEXANDER VI (Rodrigo Borgia; 1431-1503), pope 1492-1503 **1** 134-135

ALEXANDER, SAMUEL (1859-1938), British philosopher **1** 141

ALEXANDER OF TUNIS, 1ST EARL (Harold Rupert Leofric George Alexander; born 1891), British field marshal **1** 135-136

ALEXANDER OF YUGOSLAVIA (1888-1934), king of the Serbs, Croats, and Slovenes 1921-1929 and of Yugoslavia, 1929-1934 **1** 136-137

ALEXANDER THE GREAT (356-323 B.C.), king of Macedon **1** 137-141

ALEXIE, SHERMAN (born 1966), Native American writer, poet, and translator **1** 141-142

ALEXIS MIKHAILOVICH ROMANOV (1629-1676), czar of Russia 1645-1676 **1** 142-143

ALEXIUS I (circa 1048-1118), Byzantine emperor 1081-1118 **1** 143-144

ALFARO, JOSÉ ELOY (1842-1912), Ecuadorian revolutionary, president 1895-1901 and 1906-1911 **1** 144-145

ALFIERI, CONTE VITTORIA (1749-1803), Italian playwright **1** 145-146

ALFONSÍN, RAUL RICARDO (born 1927), politician and president of Argentina (1983-) **1** 146-148

ALFONSO I (Henriques; 1109?-1185), king of Portugal 1139-1185 **1** 148

ALFONSO III (1210-1279), king of Portugal 1248-1279 **1** 148-149

ALFONSO VI (1040-1109), king of León, 1065-1109, and of Castile, 1072-1109 **1** 149
Urraca **23** 417-418

ALFONSO X (1221-1284), king of Castile and León 1252-1284 **1** 150-151

ALFONSO XIII (1886-1941), king of Spain 1886-1931 **1** 151

ALFRED (849-899), Anglo-Saxon king of Wessex 871-899 **1** 151-153

Algebra (mathematics)
algebraic geometry
  Scott, Charlotte Angas **23** 364-367
development (9th-16th century)
  Oughtred, William **23** 277-279
equations
  Harriot, Thomas **23** 137-139

ALGER, HORATIO (1832-1899), American author **1** 153-154

ALGREN, NELSON (Abraham; 1909-1981), American author **1** 154-155

ALI (circa 600-661), fourth caliph of the Islamic Empire **1** 155-156

ALI, AHMED (1908-1998), Pakistani scholar, poet, author, and diplomat **22** 16-18

ALI, MUHAMMAD (Cassius Clay; born 1942), American boxer **1** 156-158

ALI, SUNNI (died 1492), king of Gao, founder of the Songhay empire **1** 158-159

ALIA, RAMIZ (born 1925), president of Albania (1985-) **1** 159

ALINSKY, SAUL DAVID (1909-1972), U.S. organizer of neighborhood citizen reform groups **1** 161-162

All About My Mother (film)
Almodovar, Pedro **23** 6-9

ALLAL AL-FASSI, MOHAMED (1910-1974), Moroccan nationalist leader **1** 162

Allegory (literature)
prose
  Gambaro, Griselda **23** 115-117

ALLEN, ETHAN (1738-1789), American Revolutionary War soldier **1** 163-164

ALLEN, FLORENCE ELLINWOOD (1884-1966), American lawyer, judge, and women's rights activist **1** 164-165

ALLEN, GRACIE (1906-1964), American actress and comedian **22** 18-20

ALLEN, PAULA GUNN (born 1939), Native American writer, poet, literary critic; women's rights, environmental, and antiwar activist **1** 165-167

ALLEN, RICHARD (1760-1831), African American bishop **1** 168

ALLEN, STEVE (1921-2000), American comedian, author, and composer **22** 20-22

ALLEN, WOODY (born Allen Stewart Konigsberg; born 1935), American actor, director, filmmaker, author, comedian **1** 169-171

ALLENBY, EDMUND HENRY HYNMAN (1861-1936), English field marshal **1** 171-172

ALLENDE, ISABEL (born 1942), Chilean novelist, journalist, dramatist **1** 172-174

ALLENDE GOSSENS, SALVADOR (1908-1973), socialist president of Chile (1970-1973) **1** 174-176

ALLSTON, WASHINGTON (1779-1843), American painter **1** 176-177

ALMAGRO, DIEGO DE (circa 1474-1538), Spanish conquistador and explorer **1** 177-178

ALMODOVAR, PEDRO (Calmodovar, Caballero, Pedro; born 1949), Spanish film director and screenwriter **23** 6-9

ALP ARSLAN (1026/32-1072), Seljuk sultan of Persia and Iraq **1** 178-179

ALTAMIRA Y CREVEA, RAFAEL (1866-1951), Spanish critic, historian, and jurist **1** 179

ALTDORFER, ALBRECHT (circa 1480-1538), German painter, printmaker, and architect **1** 179-180

ALTGELD, JOHN PETER (1847-1902), American jurist and politician **1** 180-182

ALTHUSSER, LOUIS (1918-1990), French Communist philosopher **1** 182-183

ALTIZER, THOMAS J. J. (born 1927), American theologian **1** 183-184

ALTMAN, ROBERT (born 1925), American filmmaker **20** 12-14

ALTMAN, SIDNEY (born 1939), Canadian American molecular biologist **23** 9-11

ÁLVAREZ, JUAN (1780-1867), Mexican soldier and statesman, president 1855 **1** 184-185

ALVAREZ, JULIA (born 1950), Hispanic American novelist, poet **1** 185-187

ALVAREZ, LUIS W. (1911-1988), American physicist **1** 187-189

AMADO, JORGE (born 1912), Brazilian novelist **1** 189-190

Amazon River (South America)
Plotkin, Mark J. **23** 308-310

AMBEDKAR, BHIMRAO RAMJI (1891-1956), Indian social reformer and politician **1** 190-191

AMBLER, ERIC (born 1909), English novelist **1** 191-192

AMBROSE, ST. (339-397), Italian bishop **1** 192-193

AMENEMHET I (ruled 1991-1962 B.C.), pharaoh of Egypt **1** 193-194

AMENHOTEP III (ruled 1417-1379 B.C.) pharaoh of Egypt **1** 194-195

American architecture
Guastoavino tile arch system
Guastavino, Rafael **23** 132-134

American art
abstract
Thomas, Alma Woodsey **23** 401-403
African American
Fuller, Meta Warrick **23** 112-114
cartoons
Hokinson, Helen Elna **23** 150-152
experimental films
Nauman, Bruce **23** 259-261
expressionism
Neel, Alice **23** 261-263
Native American
Gorman, R.C. **23** 128-130
naturalism
Huntington, Anna Hyatt **23** 162-164
performance art
Nauman, Bruce **23** 259-261
photography
Karsh, Yousuf **23** 184-187
portraiture (18th-19th century)
Gorman, R.C. **23** 128-130
portraiture (20th century)
Neel, Alice **23** 261-263
sculpture (20th century)
Deren, Maya **23** 95-97
Fuller, Meta Warrick **23** 112-114
Hoffman, Malvina Cornell **23** 148-150
Nauman, Bruce **23** 259-261
social realism
Fuller, Meta Warrick **23** 112-114

AMERICAN HORSE (aka Iron Shield; 1840?-1876), Sioux leader **1** 195-198

American literature
African American fiction and drama
Reed, Ishmael Scott **23** 331-333
Shange, Ntozake **23** 367-369
Toomer, Jean **23** 408-410
biography
Beveridge, Albert Jeremiah **23** 39-41
feminist writings
Atherton, Gertrude **23** 21-23
humor
Brooks, Mel **23** 48-50
Native American
Erdrich, Louise **23** 102-105
political commentary
Robinson, Randall **23** 342-345
religious literature
White, Ellen Gould **23** 438-440
satire
Reed, Ishmael Scott **23** 331-333
social commentary
Atherton, Gertrude **23** 21-23
Kincaid, Jamaica **23** 196-199
Paglia, Camille **23** 286-288
Robinson, Randall **23** 342-345

American music
20th century
blues
Hooker, John Lee **23** 155-157
Hunter, Alberta **23** 160-162
classical
Rands, Bernard **23** 324-326
contemporary
Rands, Bernard **23** 324-326
country and western
Pride, Charley Frank **23** 317-319
folk and national themes
Leadbelly **23** 208-211
Mitchell, Joni **23** 246-248
jazz and blues
Armstrong, Lillian Hardin **23** 15-17
Burlin, Natalie Curtis **23** 50-52
Johnson, Robert **23** 172-174
Mitchell, Joni **23** 246-248
Williams, Mary Lou **23** 444-446
orchestral music
Beach, Amy **23** 30-32
popular and show music
Joyner, Matilda Sissieretta **23** 179-181
rock and roll
Geffen, David Lawrence **23** 119-122
Hooker, John Lee **23** 155-157
Mitchell, Joni **23** 246-248
sacred music
Beach, Amy **23** 30-32
Burlin, Natalie Curtis **23** 50-52

American Telephone and Telegraph Co.
Vail, Theodore Newton **23** 419-421

AMES, ADELBERT (1835-1933), American politician **1** 198

AMES, FISHER (1758-1808), American statesman **1** 199-200

AMHERST, JEFFERY (1717-1797), English general and statesman **1** 200-201

AMIET, CUNO (1868-1961), Swiss Postimpressionist painter **1** 201-202

AMIN DADA, IDI (born circa 1926), president of Uganda (1971-1979) **1** 202-204

AMINA OF ZARIA (Amina Sarauniya Zazzau; c. 1533-c. 1610), Nigerian monarch and warrior **21** 5-7

AMORSOLO, FERNANDO (1892-1972), Philippine painter **1** 204

AMOS (flourished 8th century B.C.), Biblical prophet **1** 205

AMPÈRE, ANDRÉ MARIE (1775-1836), French physicist **1** 205-206

AMUNDSEN, ROALD (1872-1928), Norwegian explorer **1** 206-207

AN LU-SHAN (703-757), Chinese rebel leader **1** 239-240

Analytic geometry
see Geometry—analytic

ANAN BEN DAVID (flourished 8th century), Jewish Karaite leader in Babylonia **1** 207-208

Anarchism (political philosophy) Haymarket Riot Parsons, Lucy González **23** 293-295

ANAXAGORAS (circa 500-circa 428 B.C.), Greek philosopher **1** 208-209

ANAXIMANDER (circa 610-circa 546 B.C.), Greek philosopher and astronomer **1** 209-210

ANAXIMENES (flourished 546 B.C.), Greek philosopher **1** 210

ANCHIETA, JOSÉ DE (1534-1597), Portuguese Jesuit missionary **1** 210-211

ANDERSEN, DOROTHY (1901-1963), American physician and pathologist **1** 212

ANDERSEN, HANS CHRISTIAN (1805-1875), Danish author **1** 212-214

ANDERSON, CARL DAVID (1905-1991), American physicist **1** 214-215

ANDERSON, JUDITH (1898-1992), American stage and film actress **1** 215-216

ANDERSON, JUNE (born 1953), American opera singer **1** 216-218

ANDERSON, MARIAN (1902-1993), African American singer **1** 218-219

ANDERSON, MAXWELL (1888-1959), American playwright **1** 219-220

ANDERSON, SHERWOOD (1876-1941), American writer **1** 220-221

ANDO, TADAO (born 1941), Japanese architect **18** 17-19

ANDRADA E SILVA, JOSÉ BONIFÁCIO DE (1763-1838), Brazilian-born statesman and scientist **1** 221-222

ANDRÁSSY, COUNT JULIUS (1823-1890), Hungarian statesman, prime minister 1867-1871 **1** 222-223

ANDREA DEL CASTAGNO (1421-1457), Italian painter **1** 223-224

ANDREA DEL SARTO (1486-1530), Italian painter **1** 224-225

ANDREA PISANO (circa 1290/95-1348), Italian sculptor and architect **1** 225-226

ANDRÉE, SALOMON AUGUST (1854-1897), Swedish engineer and Arctic balloonist **1** 226

ANDREESSEN, MARC (born 1972), American computer programmer who developed Netscape Navigator **19** 3-5

Andrei Rublev (film) Tarkovsky, Andrei **23** 392-395

ANDREOTTI, GIULIO (born 1919), leader of Italy's Christian Democratic party **1** 226-228

ANDRETTI, MARIO (born 1940), Italian/ American race car driver **1** 228-230

ANDREW, JOHN ALBION (1818-1867), American politician **1** 230-231

ANDREWS, CHARLES McLEAN (1863-1943), American historian **1** 231

ANDREWS, FANNIE FERN PHILLIPS (1867-1950), American educator, reformer, pacifist **1** 231-232

ANDREWS, ROY CHAPMAN (1884-1960), American naturalist and explorer **1** 232-233

ANDROPOV, IURY VLADIMIROVICH (1914-1984), head of the Soviet secret police and ruler of the Soviet Union (1982-1984) **1** 233-234

ANDROS, SIR EDMUND (1637-1714), English colonial governor in America **1** 234-235

ANDRUS, ETHEL (1884-1976), American educator and founder of the American Association of Retired Persons **19** 5-7

ANGELICO, FRA (circa 1400-1455), Italian painter **1** 235-236

ANGELL, JAMES ROWLAND (1869-1949), psychologist and leader in higher education **1** 236-237

ANGELOU, MAYA (Marguerite Johnson; born 1928), American author, poet, playwright, stage and screen performer, and director **1** 238-239

Angola (West Africa) Nzinga, Anna **23** 270-271

ANGUISSOLA, SOFONISBA (Sofonisba Anguisciola; c. 1535-1625), Italian artist **22** 22-24

ANNA IVANOVNA (1693-1740), empress of Russia 1730-1740 **1** 240-241

ANNAN, KOFI (born 1938), Ghanaian secretary-general of the United Nations **18** 19-21

ANNE (1665-1714), queen of England 1702-1714 and of Great Britain 1707-1714 **1** 241-242

Annie Get Your Gun (musical) Tamiris, Helen **23** 390-392

ANNING, MARY (1799-1847), British fossil collector **20** 14-16

ANOKYE, OKOMFO (Kwame Frimpon Anokye; flourished late 17th century), Ashanti priest and statesman **1** 242-243

ANOUILH, JEAN (1910-1987), French playwright **1** 243-244

ANSELM OF CANTERBURY, ST. (1033-1109), Italian archbishop and theologian **1** 244-245

ANTHONY, ST. (circa 250-356), Egyptian hermit and monastic founder **1** 246-248

ANTHONY, SUSAN BROWNELL (1820-1906), American leader of suffrage movement **1** 246-248

ANTHONY OF PADUA, SAINT (Fernando de Boullion; 1195-1231), Portuguese theologian and priest **21** 7-9

ANTIGONUS I (382-301 B.C.), king of Macedon 306-301 B.C. **1** 248-249

ANTIOCHUS III (241-187 B.C.), king of Syria 223-187 B.C. **1** 249-250

ANTIOCHUS IV (circa 215-163 B.C.), king of Syria 175-163 B.C. **1** 250

Antislavery movement (Great Britain) Pringle, Thomas **23** 319-320

ANTISTHENES (circa 450-360 B.C.), Greek philosopher **1** 250-251

ANTONELLO DA MESSINA (circa 1430-1479), Italian painter **1** 251-252

ANTONIONI, MICHELANGELO (born 1912), Italian film director **1** 252-253

ANTONY, MARK (circa 82-30 B.C.), Roman politician and general **1** 253-254

ANZA, JUAN BAUTISTA DE (1735-1788), Spanish explorer **1** 254-255

AOUN, MICHEL (born 1935), Christian Lebanese military leader and prime minister **1** 255-257

Apartheid (South Africa) opponents Robinson, Randall **23** 342-345

APELLES (flourished after 350 B.C.), Greek painter **1** 257

APESS, WILLIAM (1798-1839), Native American religious leader, author, and activist **20** 16-18

APGAR, VIRGINIA (1909-1974), American medical educator, researcher **1** 257-259

APITHY, SOUROU MIGAN (1913-1989), Dahomean political leader **1** 259-260

APOLLINAIRE, GUILLAUME (1880-1918), French lyric poet **1** 260

APOLLODORUS (flourished circa 408 B.C.), Greek painter **1** 261

APOLLONIUS OF PERGA (flourished 210 B.C.), Greek mathematician **1** 261-262

APPELFELD, AHARON (born 1932), Israeli who wrote about anti-Semitism and the Holocaust **1** 262-263

APPERT, NICOLAS (1749-1941), French chef and inventor of canning of foods **20** 18-19

APPIA, ADOLPHE (1862-1928), Swiss stage director **1** 263-264

APPLEGATE, JESSE (1811-1888), American surveyor, pioneer, and rancher **1** 264-265

APPLETON, SIR EDWARD VICTOR (1892-1965), British pioneer in radio physics **1** 265-266

APPLETON, NATHAN (1779-1861), American merchant and manufacturer **1** 266-267

APULEIUS, LUCIUS (c. 124-170), Roman author, philosopher, and orator **20** 19-21

Aquafuertes portenas (column) Arlt, Roberto **23** 11-13

AQUINO, BENIGNO ("Nino"; 1933-1983), Filipino activist murdered upon his return from exile **1** 267-268

AQUINO, CORAZON COJOANGCO (born 1933), first woman president of the Republic of the Philippines **1** 268-270

ARAFAT, YASSER (also spelled Yasir; born 1929), chairman of the Palestinian Liberation Organization **1** 270-271

ARAGON, LOUIS (1897-1982), French surrealist author **1** 271-272

ARANHA, OSVALDO (1894-1960), Brazilian political leader **1** 272-273

ARATUS (271-213 B.C.), Greek statesman and general **1** 273-274

ARBENZ GUZMÁN, JACOBO (1913-1971), president of Guatemala (1951-1954) **1** 274-276

ARBUS, DIANE NEMEROV (1923-1971), American photographer **1** 276-277

ARCHIMEDES (circa 287-212 B.C.), Greek mathematician **1** 277-280

ARCHIPENKO, ALEXANDER (1887-1964), Russian-American sculptor and teacher **1** 280-281

Architecture Maekawa, Kunio **23** 239-242

Arctic exploration Canadian Bernier, Joseph E. **23** 35-37

ARDEN, ELIZABETH (Florence Nightingale Graham; 1878?-1966), American businesswoman **1** 281-282

ARENDT, HANNAH (1906-1975), Jewish philosopher **1** 282-284

ARENS, MOSHE (born 1925), aeronautical engineer who became a leading Israeli statesman **1** 284-285

ARÉVALO, JUAN JOSÉ (1904-1951), Guatemalan statesman, president 1944-1951 **1** 285-286

Argentine literature fiction Gambaro, Griselda **23** 115-117 magical realism Valenzuela, Luisa **23** 421-423 poetry Gambaro, Griselda **23** 115-117 social criticism Arlt, Roberto **23** 11-13

ARIAS, ARNULFO (1901-1988), thrice elected president of Panama **1** 286-287

ARIAS SANCHEZ, OSCAR (born 1941), Costa Rican politician, social activist, president, and Nobel Peace Laureate (1987) **1** 287-289

ARIOSTO, LUDOVICO (1474-1533), Italian poet and playwright **1** 289-290

ARISTARCHUS OF SAMOS (circa 310-230 B.C.), Greek astronomer **1** 290-291

ARISTIDE, JEAN-BERTRAND (born 1953), president of Haiti (1990-91 and 1994-95); deposed by a military coup in 1991; restored to power in 1994 **1** 291-293

ARISTOPHANES (450/445-after 385 B.C.), Greek playwright **1** 293-294

ARISTOTLE (384-322 B.C.), Greek philosopher and scientist **1** 295-296

ARIUS (died circa 336), Libyan theologian and heresiarch **1** 297-298

ARKWRIGHT, SIR RICHARD (1732-1792), English inventor and industrialist **1** 298

ARLEN, HAROLD (born Hyman Arluck; 1905-1986), American jazz pianist, composer, and arranger **19** 7-9

ARLT, ROBERTO (Roberto Godofredo Christophersen Arlt; 1900-1942), Argentine author and journalist **23** 11-13

ARMANI, GIORGIO (1935-1997), Italian fashion designer **1** 299-301

ARMINIUS, JACOBUS (1560-1609), Dutch theologian **1** 301-302

ARMOUR, PHILIP DANFORTH (1832-1901), American industrialist **1** 302

ARMSTRONG, EDWIN HOWARD (1890-1954), American electrical engineer and radio inventor **1** 302-303

ARMSTRONG, HENRY (Henry Jackson, Jr.; 1912-1988), American boxer and minister **21** 9-11

ARMSTRONG, LANCE (born 1971), American cyclist **23** 13-15

ARMSTRONG, LILLIAN HARDIN (1898-1971), African American musician **23** 15-17

ARMSTRONG, LOUIS DANIEL (1900-1971), African American jazz musician **1** 303-304 Armstrong, Lillian **23** 15-17

ARMSTRONG, NEIL ALDEN (born 1930), American astronaut **1** 304-306

ARMSTRONG, SAMUEL CHAPMAN (1839-1893), American educator **1** 306-307

ARNAZ, DESI (Desiderio Alberto Arnaz y De Acha; 1917-1986), American musician and actor **21** 12-14

ARNE, THOMAS AUGUSTINE (1710-1778), English composer **1** 307-308

ARNIM, ACHIM VON (Ludwig Joachim von Achim; 1781-1831), German writer **1** 308-309

ARNOLD, GEN. BENEDICT (1741-1801), American general and traitor **1** 309-310

ARNOLD, HENRY HARLEY (Hap; 1886-1950), American general **1** 310-311

ARNOLD, MATTHEW (1822-1888), English poet and critic **1** 311-313

ARNOLD, THOMAS (1795-1842), English educator **1** 313-314

ARNOLD, THURMAN WESLEY (1891-1969), American statesman **1** 314

ARNOLD OF BRESCIA (circa 1100-1155), Italian religious reformer **1** 314-315

ARNOLFO DI CAMBIO (1245?-1302), Italian sculptor and architect **1** 315-316

ARON, RAYMOND (1905-1983), academic scholar, teacher, and journalist **1** 316-317

ARP, JEAN (Hans Arp; 1887-1966), French sculptor and painter **1** 317-318

ARRAU, CLAUDIO (1903-1991), Chilean American pianist **23** 17-18

ARRHENIUS, SVANTE AUGUST (1859-1927), Swedish chemist and physicist **1** 318-320

Art of War, The (treatise) Jomini, Antoine Henri **23** 177-179

ARTAUD, ANTONIN (1896-1948), developed the theory of the Theater of Cruelty **1** 320-321

ARTHUR, CHESTER ALAN (1830-1886), American statesman, president 1881-1885 **1** 321-323

ARTIGAS, JOSÉ GERVASIO (1764-1850), Uruguayan patriot **1** 323

Artists, American
architects (19th-20th century)
Guastavino, Rafael **23** 132-134
cartoonists
Hokinson, Helen Elna **23** 150-152
fashion designers
Herrera, Carolina **23** 141-143
painters (20th century)
Gorman, R.C. **23** 128-130
Neel, Alice **23** 261-263
Thomas, Alma Woodsey **23** 401-403
photographers
Johnston, Frances Benjamin **23** 174-177
printmakers
Neel, Alice **23** 261-263
sculptors (19th-20th century)
Hoffman, Malvina Cornell **23** 148-150
sculptors (20th century)
Fuller, Meta Warrick **23** 112-114
Huntington, Anna Hyatt **23** 162-164
Nauman, Bruce **23** 259-261

Artists, Canadian
photographers
Karsh, Yousuf **23** 184-187
Wall, Jeff **23** 434-436

Artists, Colombian
Vázquez Arce Y Ceballos, Gregorio **23** 423-425

Artists, Danish
Thorvaldsen, Bertel **23** 403-406

Artists, English
painters (19th century)
North, Marianne **23** 268-270

Artists, French
painters (19th-20th century)
Signac, Paul **23** 369-372

Artists, German
painters (20th century)
Polke, Sigmar **23** 312-315
Richter, Gerhard **23** 338-340
photographers
Polke, Sigmar **23** 312-315

Artists, Japanese
architects
Maekawa, Kunio **23** 239-242
painters (17th-19th century)
Okyo, Maruyama **23** 272-274

Artists, Puerto Rican
Oller, Francisco Manuel **23** 274-275

Artists, Russian
illustrators
Kabakov, Ilya **23** 182-184
painters (20th century)
Kabakov, Ilya **23** 182-184

Artists, Venezuelan
Herrera, Carolina **23** 141-143

ASAM, COSMAS DAMIAN (1686-1739), German artist **1** 323-324

ASAM, EGID QUIRIN (1692-1750), German artist **1** 323-324

ASBURY, FRANCIS (1745-1816), English-born American Methodist bishop **1** 324-325

ASCH, SHALOM (1880-1957), Polish-born playwright and novelist **1** 325-326

ASH, MARY KAY WAGNER (born circa 1916), cosmetics tycoon **1** 326-327

ASHARI, ABU AL- HASAN ALI AL- (873/883-935), Moslem theologian **1** 327-328

ASHCROFT, JOHN (born 1942), American statesman and attorney general **23** 18-21

ASHE, ARTHUR ROBERT, JR. (1943-1993), world champion athlete, social activist, teacher, and charity worker **1** 328-330

ASHIKAGA TAKAUJI (1305-1358), Japanese shogun **1** 330-332

ASHKENAZY, VLADIMIR (born 1937), Russian musician **22** 24-26

ASHLEY, LAURA (Mountney; 1925-1985), British designer of women's clothes and home furnishings **1** 332-333

ASHLEY, WILLIAM HENRY (circa 1778-1838), American businessman, fur trader, and explorer **1** 333-334

ASHMORE, HARRY SCOTT (1916-1998), American journalist **1** 334-335

ASHMUN, JEHUDI (1794-1828), American governor of Liberia Colony **1** 335-336

ASHRAWI, HANAN MIKHAIL (born 1946), Palestinian spokesperson **1** 336-338

ASHURBANIPAL (died circa 630 B.C.), Assyrian king 669-ca. 630 **1** 338

ASIMOV, ISAAC (1920-1992), American author **1** 338-341

ASOKA (ruled circa 273-232 B.C.), Indian emperor of the Maurya dynasty **1** 341-342

ASPASIA (ca. 470-410 BC), Milesian courtesan and rhetorician **22** 26-28

ASPIN, LES (1938-1995), United States congressman and secretary of defense **1** 342-344

ASPLUND, ERIC GUNNAR (1885-1945), Swedish architect **1** 344

ASQUITH, HERBERT HENRY (1st Earl of Oxford and Asquith; 1852-1928), English statesman, prime minister 1908-1916 **1** 344-346

ASSAD, HAFIZ (born 1930), president of Syria **1** 346-348

ASTAIRE, FRED (Frederick Austerlitz; 1899-1987), dancer and choreographer **1** 348-350

ASTON, FRANCIS WILLIAM (1877-1945), English chemist and physicist **1** 350-351

ASTOR, JOHN JACOB (1763-1848), American fur trader, merchant, and capitalist **1** 351-352

ASTOR, NANCY LANGHORNE (1879-1964), first woman to serve as a member of the British Parliament (1919-1945) **1** 352-354

Astronauts
McCandless, Bruce, II **23** 243-246

Astronomy
sunspots
Harriot, Thomas **23** 137-139

Astronomy (science)
big bang theory
Penzias, Arno Allen **23** 301-304
double stars
Whitney, Mary Watson **23** 440-442
galaxies
Leavitt, Henrietta Swan **23** 211-213
star catalogs
Leavitt, Henrietta Swan **23** 211-213
Whitney, Mary Watson **23** 440-442

ASTURIAS, MIGUEL ANGEL (born 1899), Guatemalan novelist and poet **1** 354-355

ATAHUALPA (circa 1502-1533), Inca emperor of Peru 1532-1533 **1** 355-356

Atalante, L' (film)
Vigo, Jean **23** 429-431

ATANASOFF, JOHN (1903-1995), American physicist **20** 21-22

ATATÜRK, GHAZI MUSTAPHA KEMAL (1881-1938), Turkish nationalist, president 1923-1938 **1** 356-357

ATCHISON, DAVID RICE (1807-1886), American lawyer and politician **1** 357-358

ATHANASIUS, ST. (circa 296-373), Christian theologian, bishop of Alexandria **1** 358-359

ATHERTON, GERTRUDE (Gertrude Franklin Horn Atherton; 1857-1948), American author **23** 21-23

Athletes
Canadian
Roy, Patrick **23** 351-353
Yzerman, Steve **23** 451-453

Finnish
Kekkonen, Urho Kaleva **23** 189-191

Athletes, American
cyclists
Armstrong, Lance **23** 13-15
football players
Elway, John **23** 98-100
race car drivers
Unser, Al, Sr. **23** 415-417
skaters
Albright, Tenley Emma **23** 3-6
Blair, Bonnie **23** 42-44
Button, Dick **23** 55-57
swimmers
Spitz, Mark **23** 376-378

ATKINS, CHET (Chester Burton Atkins; 1924-2000), American musician **22** 28-30

ATKINSON, LOUISA (Louisa Warning Atkinson; 1834-1872), Australian author **22** 30-33

ATLAS, CHARLES (Angelo Siciliano; 1893-1972), American body builder **21** 14-15

Atomism (philosophy)
Cavendish, Margaret Lucas **23** 66-67

ATTAR, FARID ED-DIN (circa 1140-circa 1234), Persian poet **1** 359-360

ATTENBOROUGH, RICHARD SAMUEL (born 1923), English actor and filmmaker **18** 21-23

ATTILA (died 453), Hun chieftain **1** 360

ATTLEE, CLEMENT RICHARD (1st Earl Attlee; 1883-1967), English statesman, prime minister 1945-1951 **1** 361-362

Attorneys general
see statesmen, American

ATWOOD, MARGARET ELEANOR (born 1939), Canadian novelist, poet, critic, and politically committed cultural activist **1** 362-364

AUBERT DE GASPÉ, PHILIPPE (1786-1871), French-Canadian author **1** 364

AUDEN, WYSTAN HUGH (1907-1973), English-born American poet **1** 364-366

AUDUBON, JOHN JAMES (1785-1851), American artist and ornithologist **1** 366-367

AUER, LEOPOLD (1845-1930), Hungarian violinist and conductor **20** 22-24

AUGUSTINE, ST. (354-430), Christian philosopher and theologian **1** 367-370

AUGUSTINE OF CANTERBURY, ST. (died circa 606), Roman monk, archbishop of Canterbury **1** 370-371

AUGUSTUS (Octavian; 63 B.C.-A.D. 14), Roman emperor 27 B.C.-A.D. 14 **1** 371-373

AUGUSTUS II (1670-1733), king of Poland and elector of Saxony **1** 373-374

AULARD, ALPHONSE FRANÇOIS VICTOR ALPHONSE (1849-1928), French historian **1** 374

Auld Lang Syne (song)
Lombardo, Guy **23** 234-236

AUNG SAN (1915-1947), Burmese politician **1** 374-375

AUNG SAN SUU KYI (born 1945), leader of movement toward democracy in Burma (Myanmar) and Nobel Peace Prize winner **1** 375-376

AURANGZEB (1618-1707), Mogul emperor of India 1658-1707 **1** 377

AUSTEN, JANE (1775-1817), English novelist **1** 377-379

AUSTIN, JOHN (1790-1859), English jurist and author **22** 33-35

AUSTIN, JOHN LANGSHAW (1911-1960), English philosopher **1** 379-380

AUSTIN, MARY HUNTER (1868-1934), American author **23** 23-25

AUSTIN, STEPHEN FULLER (1793-1836), American pioneer **1** 380-381

Australia, Commonwealth of (island continent)
social reforms
Spence, Catherine Helen **23** 374-375

Australian literature
Campion, Jane **23** 58-60
Kendall, Thomas Henry **23** 191-194
Spence, Catherine Helen **23** 374-375
Stead, Christina Ellen **23** 378-380

Authors, American
African American fiction and drama
Toomer, Jean **23** 408-410
biographers (19th-20th century)
Atherton, Gertrude **23** 21-23
biographers (20th century)
Beveridge, Albert Jeremiah **23** 39-41
essayists (19th-20th century)
Austin, Mary Hunter **23** 23-25
essayists (20th century)
Kincaid, Jamaica **23** 196-199
Reed, Ishmael Scott **23** 331-333
nonfiction writers
Penzias, Arno Allen **23** 301-304
novelists (19th-20th century)
Atherton, Gertrude **23** 21-23
Austin, Mary Hunter **23** 23-25
novelists (20th century)
Erdrich, Louise **23** 102-105
Kincaid, Jamaica **23** 196-199
Reed, Ishmael Scott **23** 331-333
Toomer, Jean **23** 408-410
playwrights (20th century)
Shange, Ntozake **23** 367-369
poets (20th century)
Erdrich, Louise **23** 102-105

religious writers
Palmer, Phoebe Worrall **23** 288-290
White, Ellen Gould **23** 438-440
satirists
Reed, Ishmael Scott **23** 331-333
scriptwriters (20th century)
Brooks, Mel **23** 48-50
Burnett, Carol **23** 52-55
short-story writers (19th-20th century)
Austin, Mary Hunter **23** 23-25
short-story writers (20th century)
Kincaid, Jamaica **23** 196-199
social critics
Paglia, Camille **23** 286-288
Parsons, Lucy González **23** 293-295
Robinson, Randall **23** 342-345

Authors, Argentine
novelists
Arlt, Roberto **23** 11-13
Gambaro, Griselda **23** 115-117
Valenzuela, Luisa **23** 421-423
playwrights
Arlt, Roberto **23** 11-13
Gambaro, Griselda **23** 115-117
short-story writers
Arlt, Roberto **23** 11-13
Gambaro, Griselda **23** 115-117
Valenzuela, Luisa **23** 421-423

Authors, Australian
novelists
Spence, Catherine Helen **23** 374-375
Stead, Christina Ellen **23** 378-380
poets
Kendall, Thomas Henry **23** 191-194
screenwriters
Campion, Jane **23** 58-60

Authors, Canadian
autobiographers
Karsh, Yousuf **23** 184-187

Authors, Caribbean
Kincaid, Jamaica **23** 196-199

Authors, Cuban
Rodríguez de Tío, Lola **23** 345-346

Authors, Danish
Brandes, Georg **23** 45-47
Holberg, Ludvig **23** 152-155

Authors, Dutch
Cats, Jacob **23** 64-66

Authors, English
autobiographies
Cavendish, Margaret Lucas **23** 66-67
children's-story writers
Nesbit, E(dith) **23** 263-265
lyricists
Campion, Thomas **23** 60-62
novelists (19th-20th century)
Nesbit, E(dith) **23** 263-265
novelists (20th century)
Glyn, Elinor **23** 126-128
poets (16th-17th century)
Campion, Thomas **23** 60-62
poets (19th century)
Pringle, Thomas **23** 319-320
scientific writers
Cavendish, Margaret Lucas **23** 66-67

screenwriters
    Glyn, Elinor **23** 126-128
    Leigh, Mike **23** 222-225
translators
    Murray, Gilbert **23** 250-253
travel writers
    Bird, Isabella **23** 41-42

Authors, French
biographers
    Signac, Paul **23** 369-372
essayists (16th-18th century)
    de Gournay, Marie le Jars **23** 88-90
playwrights (18th century)
    de Gouges, Marie Olympe **23** 85-88
poets (16th-17th century)
    de Gournay, Marie le Jars **23** 88-90

Authors, Hungarian
Petöfi, Sándor **23** 306-308

Authors, Japanese
novelists
    Enchi, Fumiko Ueda **23** 100-102
playwrights
    Chikamatsu, Monzaemon **23** 70-72
translators
    Enchi, Fumiko Ueda **23** 100-102

Authors, Norwegian
Holberg, Ludvig **23** 152-155

Authors, Puerto Rican
Rodríguez de Tío, Lola **23** 345-346

Authors, Romanian
Caragiale, Ion Luca **23** 62-64

Authors, Scottish
poets
    Pringle, Thomas **23** 319-320

Authors, South African
Pringle, Thomas **23** 319-320
Schreiner, Olive **23** 362-364
Smith, Pauline **23** 372-373

Authors, Zimbabwean (expatriate)
Vera, Yvonne **23** 425-427

Automobile racing
Unser, Al, Sr. **23** 415-417

AVEDON, RICHARD (born 1923),
American fashion photographer **1**
381-382

AVERROËS (1126-1198), Spanish-Arabian
philosopher **1** 382-383

AVERY, OSWALD THEODORE (1877-
1955), Canadian/American biologist
and bacteriologist **1** 384-386

Aviators
American
    Yeager, Jeana **23** 449-451

AVICENNA (circa 980-1037), Arabian
physician and philosopher **1** 386-387

ÁVILA CAMACHO, GEN. MANUEL
(1897-1955), Mexican president 1940-
1946 **1** 387-388

**AVOGADRO, LORENZO ROMANO
AMEDO CARLO** (Conte di Quaregna e

di Cerreto; 1776-1865), Italian
physicist and chemist **1** 388-389

AWOLOWO, CHIEF OBAFEMI (born
1909), Nigerian nationalist and
politician **1** 389-390

AX, EMANUEL (born 1949), American
pianist **1** 391

AYCKBOURN, ALAN (born 1939), British
playwright **18** 23-25

AYER, ALFRED JULES (1910-1989),
English philosopher **1** 391-393

AYLWIN AZÓCAR, PATRICIO (born
1918), leader of the Chilean Christian
Democratic party and president of
Chile **1** 393-395

AYUB KHAN, MOHAMMED (1907-
1989), Pakistani statesman **1** 395-396

AZAÑA DIAZ, MANUEL (1880-1940),
Spanish statesman, president 1936-
1939 **1** 396-397

AZARA, FÉLIX DE (1746-1821), Spanish
explorer and naturalist **1** 397-398

AZCONA HOYO, JOSÉ (born 1927),
president of Honduras (1986-1990) **1**
398-399

AZHARI, SAYYID ISMAIL AL- (1898-
1969), Sudanese president 1965-1968
1 399-401

AZIKIWE, NNAMDI (born 1904),
Nigerian nationalist, president 1963-
1966 **1** 401-402

AZUELA, MARIANO (1873-1952),
Mexican novelist **1** 402

B

BA MAW (1893-1977), Burmese
statesman **1** 480-481

BAADER and MEINHOF (1967-1976),
founders of the West German "Red
Army Faction" **1** 403-404

BAAL SHEM TOV (circa 1700-circa
1760), founder of modern Hasidism **1**
404-405

BABAR THE CONQUEROR (aka Zahir-
ud-din Muhammad Babur; 1483-
1530), Mogul emperor of India 1526-
1530 **1** 405-407

BABBAGE, CHARLES (1791-1871),
English inventor and mathematician **1**
407-408

BABBITT, BRUCE EDWARD (born 1938),
governor of Arizona (1978-1987) and
United States secretary of the interior **1**
408-410

BABBITT, IRVING (1865-1933),
American critic and educator **22** 36-37

BABBITT, MILTON (born 1916),
American composer **1** 410

BABCOCK, STEPHEN MOULTON (1843-
1931), American agricultural chemist **1**
410-411

BABEL, ISAAC EMMANUELOVICH
(1894-1941), Russian writer **1** 411-412

BABEUF, FRANÇOIS NOEL ("Caius
Gracchus"; 1760-1797), French
revolutionist and writer **1** 412

BACA-BARRAGÁN, POLLY (born 1943),
Hispanic American politician **1**
412-414

BACH, CARL PHILIPP EMANUEL (1714-
1788), German composer **1** 414-415

BACH, JOHANN CHRISTIAN (1735-
1782), German composer **1** 415-416

BACH, JOHANN SEBASTIAN (1685-
1750), German composer and organist
1 416-419

BACHARACH, BURT (born 1928),
American composer **22** 38-39

BACHE, ALEXANDER DALLAS (1806-
1867), American educator and scientist
1 420

BACKUS, ISAAC (1724-1806), American
Baptist leader **1** 420-421

BACON, SIR FRANCIS (1561-1626),
English philosopher, statesman, and
author **1** 422-424

BACON, FRANCIS (1909-1992), English
artist **1** 421-422

BACON, NATHANIEL (1647-1676),
American colonial leader **1** 424-425

BACON, ROGER (circa 1214-1294),
English philosopher **1** 425-427

BAD HEART BULL, AMOS (1869-1913),
Oglala Lakota Sioux tribal historian
and artist **1** 427-428

BADEN-POWELL, ROBERT (1857-1941),
English military officer and founder of
the Boy Scout Association **21** 16-18

BADINGS, HENK (Hendrik Herman
Badings; 1907-1987), Dutch composer
23 26-28

BADOGLIO, PIETRO (1871-1956),
Italian general and statesman **1**
428-429

BAECK, LEO (1873-1956), rabbi, teacher,
hero of the concentration camps, and
Jewish leader **1** 429-430

BAEKELAND, LEO HENDRIK (1863-
1944), American chemist **1** 430-431

BAER, GEORGE FREDERICK (1842-
1914), American businessman **22**
39-41

BAER, KARL ERNST VON (1792-1876), Estonian anatomist and embryologist **1** 431-432

BAEZ, BUENAVENTURA (1812-1884), Dominican statesman, five time president **1** 432-433

BAEZ, JOAN (born 1941), American folk singer and human rights activist **1** 433-435

BAFFIN, WILLIAM (circa 1584-1622), English navigator and explorer **1** 435-436

BAGEHOT, WALTER (1826-1877), English economist **1** 436-437

BAGLEY, WILLIAM CHANDLER (1874-1946), educator and theorist of educational "essentialism" **1** 437-438

BAHR, EGON (born 1922), West German politician **1** 438-440

BAIKIE, WILLIAM BALFOUR (1825-1864), Scottish explorer and scientist **1** 440

BAILEY, F. LEE (born 1933), American defense attorney and author **1** 441-443

BAILEY, FLORENCE MERRIAM (1863-1948), American ornithologist and author **1** 443-444

BAILEY, GAMALIEL (1807-1859), American editor and politician **1** 444-445

BAILEY, MILDRED (Mildred Rinker, 1907-1951), American jazz singer **23** 28-30

BAILLIE, D(ONALD) M(ACPHERSON) (1887-1954), Scottish theologian **1** 445

BAILLIE, JOHN (1886-1960), Scottish theologian and ecumenical churchman **1** 445-447

BAKER, ELLA JOSEPHINE (1903-1986), African American human and civil rights activist **18** 26-28

BAKER, HOWARD HENRY, JR. (born 1925), U.S. senator and White House chief of staff **18** 28-30

BAKER, JAMES ADDISON III (born 1930), Republican party campaign leader **1** 447-448

BAKER, JOSEPHINE (1906-1975) Parisian dancer and singer from America **1** 448-451

BAKER, NEWTON DIEHL (1871-1937), American statesman **1** 451

BAKER, RAY STANNARD (1870-1946), American author **1** 451-452

BAKER, RUSSELL (born 1925), American writer of personal-political essays **1** 452-454

BAKER, SIR SAMUEL WHITE (1821-1893), English explorer and administrator **1** 454-455

BAKER, SARA JOSEPHINE (1873-1945), American physician **1** 455-456

BAKHTIN, MIKHAIL MIKHAILOVICH (1895-1975), Russian philosopher and literary critic **1** 456-458

BAKUNIN, MIKHAIL ALEKSANDROVICH (1814-1876), Russian anarchist **1** 458-460

BALAGUER Y RICARDO, JOAQUÍN (1907-2002), Dominican statesman **1** 460-461

BALANCHINE, GEORGE (1904-1983), Russian-born American choreographer **1** 461-462

BALBOA, VASCO NÚÑEZ DE (circa 1475-1519), Spanish explorer **1** 462-463

BALBULUS, NOTKER (circa 840-912), Swiss poet-musician and monk **11** 434-435

BALCH, EMILY GREENE (1867-1961), American pacifist and social reformer **1** 463-464

BALDWIN I (1058-1118), Norman king of Jerusalem 1100-1118 **1** 464-465

BALDWIN, JAMES ARTHUR (1924-1987), African American author, poet, and dramatist **1** 465-466

BALDWIN, ROBERT (1804-1858), Canadian politician **1** 466-468

BALDWIN, STANLEY (1st Earl Baldwin of Bewdley; 1867-1947), English statesman, three times prime minister **1** 468-469

BALFOUR, ARTHUR JAMES (1st Earl of Balfour; 1848-1930), British statesman and philosopher **1** 469-470

BALL, GEORGE (1909-1994), American politician and supporter of an economically united Europe **1** 470-471

BALL, LUCILLE (Lucille Desiree Hunt; 1911-1989), American comedienne **1** 472-473

BALLA, GIACOMO (1871-1958), Italian painter **1** 473-474

BALLADUR, EDOUARD (born 1929), premier of the French Government **1** 474-475

BALLARD, ROBERT (born 1942), American oceanographer **19** 10-12

Ballet (dance)
Limón, José Arcadia **23** 227-229

Ballet (music)
Nørgård, Per **23** 265-267

BALLIVIÁN, JOSÉ (1805-1852), Bolivian president 1841-1847 **1** 475

BALMACEDA FERNÁNDEZ, JOSÉ MANUEL (1840-1891), Chilean president 1886-1891 **1** 475-476

BALTHUS (Balthasar Klossowski; born 1908), European painter and stage designer **1** 476-477

BALTIMORE, DAVID (born 1938), American virologist **1** 477-478

BALZAC, HONORÉ DE (1799-1850), French novelist **1** 478-480

BAMBA, AMADOU (1850-1927), Senegalese religious leader **1** 481-482

BAMBARA, TONI CADE (1939-1995), African American writer and editor **1** 482-483

BANCROFT, GEORGE (1800-1891), American historian and statesman **1** 483-484

BANCROFT, HUBERT HOWE (1832-1918), American historian **1** 484-485

BANDA, HASTINGS KAMUZU (1905-1997), Malawi statesman **1** 485-486

BANDARANAIKE, SIRIMAVO (also Sirima) RATWATTE DIAS (born 1916), first woman prime minister in the world as head of the Sri Lankan Freedom party government (1960-1965, 1970-1976) **1** 486-488

BANERJEE, SURENDRANATH (1848-1925), Indian nationalist **1** 488

BANKS, DENNIS J. (born 1932), Native American leader, teacher, activist, and author **1** 488-489

BANKS, SIR JOSEPH (1743-1820), English naturalist **1** 489-490

BANNEKER, BENJAMIN (1731-1806), African American mathematician **1** 490-491

BANNISTER, EDWARD MITCHELL (1828-1901), African American landscape painter **1** 491-493

BANNISTER, ROGER (born 1929), English runner **21** 18-20

BANTING, FREDERICK GRANT (1891-1941), Canadian physiolgist **1** 493-494

BANZER SUÁREZ, HUGO (1926-2002), Bolivian president (1971-1979) **1** 494-496

BAO DAI (born 1913), emperor of Vietnam 1932-1945 and 1949-1955 **1** 496-497

BAR KOCHBA, SIMEON (died 135), Jewish commander of revolt against Romans **2** 5

BARAK, EHUD (born 1942), Israeli prime minister **1** 497-498

BARAKA, IMAMU AMIRI (Everett LeRoi Jones; born 1934), African American poet and playwright **1** 498-499

BARANOV, ALEKSANDR ANDREIEVICH (1747-1819), Russian explorer **1** 499-500

BARBER, SAMUEL (1910-1981), American composer **1** 500-501

BARBIE, KLAUS (Klaus Altmann; 1913-1991), Nazi leader in Vichy France **1** 501-503

BARBONCITO (1820-1871), Native American leader of the Navajos **20** 25-27

BARBOSA, RUY (1849-1923), Brazilian journalist and politician **1** 503-504

BARDEEN, JOHN (1908-1991), American Nobel physicist **2** 1-3

BARENBOIM, DANIEL (born 1942), Israeli pianist and conductor **2** 3-4

BARENTS, WILLEM (died 1597), Dutch navigator and explorer **2** 4-5

BARING, FRANCIS (1740-1810), English banker **21** 20-22

BARLACH, ERNST (1870-1938), German sculptor **2** 5-6

BARLOW, JOEL (1754-1812), American poet **2** 6-7

BARNARD, CHRISTIAAN N. (1922-2001), South African heart transplant surgeon **2** 7-8

BARNARD, EDWARD EMERSON (1857-1923), American astronomer **2** 8-9

BARNARD, FREDERICK AUGUSTUS PORTER (1809-1889), American educator and mathematician **2** 9-10

BARNARD, HENRY (1811-1900), American educator **2** 10

BARNES, DJUNA (a.k.a. Lydia Steptoe; 1892-1982), American author **2** 11-13

BARNETT, MARGUERITE ROSS (1942-1992), American educator **21** 22-24

BARNUM, PHINEAS TAYLOR (1810-1891), American showman **2** 13-15

BAROJA Y NESSI, PÍO (1872-1956), Spanish novelist **2** 15-16

BARON, SALO WITTMAYER (1895-1989), Austrian-American educator and Jewish historian **2** 16-17

Baroque painting (Spanish)
genre
Vázquez Arce Y Ceballos, Gregorio **23** 423-425

BARRAGÁN, LUIS (1902-1988), Mexican architect and landscape architect **2** 17-19

BARRAS, VICOMTE DE (Paul François Jean Nicolas; 1755-1829), French statesman and revolutionist **2** 19

BARRE, RAYMOND (1924-1981), prime minister of France (1976-1981) **2** 19-20

BARRÈS, AUGUSTE MAURICE (1862-1923), French writer and politician **2** 20-21

BARRIE, SIR JAMES MATTHEW (1860-1937), British dramatist and novelist **2** 21-22

BARRIENTOS ORTUÑO, RENÉ (1919-1969), populist Bolivian president (1966-1969) **2** 22-23

BARRIOS, JUSTO RUFINO (1835-1885), Guatemalan general, president 1873-1885 **2** 23-24

Barristers
see Jurists, English

BARRY, JOHN (1745-1803), American naval officer **2** 24-25

BARRY, MARION SHEPILOV, JR. (born 1936), African American mayor and civil rights activist **2** 25-28

BARRYMORES, American theatrical dynasty **2** 28-30

BARTH, HEINRICH (1821-1865), German explorer **2** 30-31

BARTH, KARL (1886-1968), Swiss Protestant theologian **2** 31-32

BARTHÉ, RICHMOND (1901-1989), African American sculptor **2** 33-34

BARTHOLOMAEUS ANGLICUS (Bartholomew the Englishman; Bartholomew de Glanville; flourished 1220-1240), English theologian and encyclopedist **21** 24-25

BARTLETT, SIR FREDERIC CHARLES (1886-1969), British psychologist **2** 34-35

BARTÓK, BÉLA (1881-1945), Hungarian composer and pianist **2** 35-36

BARTON, BRUCE (1886-1967), American advertising business executive and congressman **2** 36-37

BARTON, CLARA (1821-1912), American humanitarian **2** 37-39

BARTON, SIR EDMUND (1849-1920), Australian statesman and jurist **2** 39-40

BARTRAM, JOHN (1699-1777), American botanist **2** 40-41

BARTRAM, WILLIAM (1739-1823), American naturalist **2** 41-42

BARUCH, BERNARD MANNES (1870-1965), American statesman and financier **2** 42-43

BARYSHNIKOV, MIKHAIL (born 1948), ballet dancer **2** 43-44

BASCOM, FLORENCE (1862-1945), American geologist **22** 42-43

BASEDOW, JOHANN BERNHARD (1724-1790), German educator and reformer **2** 44-45

BASHO, MATSUO (1644-1694), Japanese poet **2** 45-48

BASIE, COUNT (William Basie; 1904-1984), pianist and jazz band leader **2** 48-49

BASIL I (circa 812-886), Byzantine emperor 867-886 **2** 49-50

BASIL II (circa 958-1025), Byzantine emperor 963-1025 **2** 50-51

BASIL THE GREAT, ST. (329-379), theologian and bishop of Caesarea **2** 51-52

BASKIN, LEONARD (1922-2000), American artist and publisher **22** 43-46

BASS, SAUL (1920-1996), American designer of film advertising **21** 25-27

BASSI, LAURA (1711-1778), Italian physicist **20** 27-29

BATES, DAISY MAE (née O'Dwyer; 1861-1951), Irish-born Australian social worker **2** 52-53

BATES, HENRY WALTER (1825-1892), English explorer and naturalist **2** 53-54

BATES, KATHARINE LEE (1859-1929), American poet and educator **2** 54-55

BATESON, WILLIAM (1861-1926), English biologist concerned with evolution **2** 55-57

BATISTA Y ZALDÍVAR, FULGENCIO (1901-1973), Cuban political and military leader **2** 57-58

BATLLE Y ORDÓÑEZ, JOSÉ (1856-1929), Uruguayan statesman and journalist **2** 58-59

BATTLE, KATHLEEN (born 1948), American opera and concert singer **2** 59-60

BATU KHAN (died 1255), Mongol leader **2** 60-61

BAUDELAIRE, CHARLES PIERRE (1821-1867), French poet and art critic **2** 61-63

BAUER, EDDIE (1899-1986), American businessman **19** 13-14

BAULIEU, ÉTIENNE-ÉMILE (Étienne Blum; born 1926), French physician and biochemist who developed RU 486 **2** 63-66

BAUM, HERBERT (1912-1942), German human/civil rights activist **2** 66-73

BAUM, L. FRANK (1856-1919), author of the Wizard of Oz books **2** 73-74

BAUR, FERDINAND CHRISTIAN (1792-1860), German theologian **2** 74-75

BAUSCH, PINA (born 1940), a controversial German dancer/choreographer **2** 75-76

Bavarian art
see German art

BAXTER, RICHARD (1615-1691), English theologian **2** 76-77

BAYLE, PIERRE (1647-1706), French philosopher **2** 77-78

BAYNTON, BARBARA (1857-1929), Australian author **22** 46-48

BEA, AUGUSTINUS (1881-1968), German cardinal **2** 79

BEACH, AMY (born Amy Marcy Cheney; 1867-1944), American musician **23** 30-32

BEACH, MOSES YALE (1800-1868), American inventor and newspaperman **2** 79-80

BEADLE, GEORGE WELLS (1903-1989), American scientist, educator, and administrator **2** 80-81

BEALE, DOROTHEA (1831-1906), British educator **2** 81-83

BEAN, ALAN (born 1932), American astronaut and artist **22** 48-50

BEAN, LEON LEONWOOD (L.L. Bean; 1872-1967), American businessman **19** 14-16

BEARD, CHARLES AUSTIN (1874-1948), American historian **2** 84

BEARD, MARY RITTER (1876-1958), American author and activist **2** 85-86

BEARDEN, ROMARE HOWARD (1914-1988), African American painter-collagist **2** 86-88

BEARDSLEY, AUBREY VINCENT (1872-1898), English illustrator **2** 88-89

BEATLES, THE (1957-1971), British rock and roll band **2** 89-92

BEATRIX, WILHELMINA VON AMSBERG, QUEEN (born 1938), queen of Netherlands (1980-) **2** 92-93

BEAUCHAMPS, PIERRE (1636-1705), French dancer and choreographer **21** 27-29

BEAUFORT, MARGARET (1443-1509), queen dowager of England **20** 29-31

BEAUJOYEULX, BALTHASAR DE (Balthasar de Beaujoyeux; Baldassare de Belgiojoso; 1535-1587), Italian choreographer and composer **21** 29-30

BEAUMARCHAIS, PIERRE AUGUST CARON DE (1732-1799), French playwright **2** 93-94

BEAUMONT, FRANCIS (1584/1585-1616), English playwright **2** 95

BEAUMONT, WILLIAM (1785-1853), American surgeon **2** 95-96

BEAUREGARD, PIERRE GUSTAVE TOUTANT (1818-1893), Confederate general **2** 96-97

BECARRIA, MARCHESE DI (1738-1794), Italian jurist and economist **2** 97-98

BECHET, SIDNEY (1897-1959), American jazz musician **22** 50-52

BECHTEL, STEPHEN DAVISON (1900-1989), American construction engineer and business executive **2** 98-99

BECK, LUDWIG AUGUST THEODOR (1880-1944), German general **2** 99-100

BECKER, CARL LOTUS (1873-1945), American historian **2** 100-101

BECKET, ST. THOMAS (1128?-1170), English prelate **2** 101-102

BECKETT, SAMUEL (1906-1989), Irish novelist, playwright, and poet **2** 102-104

BECKMANN, MAX (1884-1950), German painter **2** 104-105

BECKNELL, WILLIAM (circa 1797-1865), American soldier and politician **2** 105-106

BECKWOURTH, JIM (James P. Beckwourth; c. 1800-1866), African American fur trapper and explorer **2** 106-107

BÉCQUER, GUSTAVO ADOLFO DOMINGUEZ (1836-1870), Spanish lyric poet **2** 107-108

BECQUEREL, ANTOINE HENRI (1852-1908), French physicist **2** 108-109

BEDE, ST. (672/673-735), English theologian **2** 109-110

BEDELL SMITH, WALTER (1895-1961), U.S. Army general, ambassador, and CIA director **18** 30-33

BEEBE, WILLIAM (1877-1962), American naturalist, oceanographer, and ornithologist **22** 52-54

BEECHER, CATHARINE (1800-1878), American author and educator **2** 110-112

BEECHER, HENRY WARD (1813-1887), American Congregationalist clergyman **2** 112-113

BEECHER, LYMAN (1775-1863), Presbyterian clergyman **2** 113

BEERBOHM, MAX (Henry Maximilian Beerbohm; 1872-1956), English author and critic **19** 16-18

BEETHOVEN, LUDWIG VAN (1770-1827), German composer **2** 114-117

BEGAY, HARRISON (born 1917), Native American artist **2** 117-118

BEGIN, MENACHEM (1913-1992), Israel's first non-Socialist prime minister (1977-1983) **2** 118-120

BEHAIM, MARTIN (Martinus de Bohemia; 1459?-1507), German cartographer **21** 30-32

BEHN, APHRA (1640?-1689), British author **18** 33-34

BEHRENS, HILDEGARD (born 1937), German soprano **2** 120-121

BEHRENS, PETER (1868-1940), German architect, painter, and designer **2** 121-122

BEHRING, EMIL ADOLPH VON (1854-1917), German hygienist and physician **2** 122-123

BEHZAD (died circa 1530), Persian painter **2** 123

BEISSEL, JOHANN CONRAD (1690-1768), German-American pietist **2** 123-124

BELAFONTE, HARRY (Harold George Belafonte, Jr.; born 1927), African American singer and actor **20** 31-32

BELASCO, DAVID (1853-1931), American playwright and director-producer **2** 124-125

BELAÚNDE TERRY, FERNANDO (1912-2002), president of Peru (1963-1968, 1980-1985) **2** 125-126

BELGRANO, MANUEL (1770-1820), Argentine general and politician **2** 126-127

BELINSKY, GRIGORIEVICH (1811-1848), Russian literary critic **2** 128

BELISARIUS (circa 506-565), Byzantine general **2** 128-129

BELL, ALEXANDER GRAHAM (1847-1922), Scottish-born American inventor **2** 129-131

BELL, ANDREW (1753-1832), Scottish educator **2** 131-132

BELL, DANIEL (Bolotsky; born 1919), American sociologist **2** 132-133

BELL, GERTRUDE (1868-1926), British archaeologist, traveler, and advisor on the Middle East **22** 54-55

BELL BURNELL, SUSAN JOCELYN (born 1943), English radio astronomer **2** 133-134

Bell Telephone Co.
Vail, Theodore Newton **23** 419-421

Bell Telephone Laboratories (research organization)
Penzias, Arno Allen **23** 301-304

BELLAMY, EDWARD (1850-1898), American novelist, propagandist, and reformer **2** 134-135

BELLARMINE, ST. ROBERT (1542-1621), Italian theologian and cardinal **2** 135-136

BELLECOURT, CLYDE (born 1939), Native American activist **2** 136-137

BELLINI, GIOVANNI (circa 1435-1516), Itlaian painter **2** 137-138

BELLINI, VINCENZO (1801-1835), Italian composer **2** 138-139

BELLO, ALHAJI SIR AHMADU (1909-1966), Nigerian politician **2** 139-140

BELLO Y LÓPEZ, ANDRÉS (1781-1865), Venezuelan humanist **2** 140-141

BELLOC, JOSEPH HILAIRE PIERRE (1870-1953), French-born English author and historian **2** 141

BELLOW, SAUL (born 1915), American novelist and Nobel Prize winner **2** 141-143

BELLOWS, GEORGE WESLEY (1882-1925), American painter **2** 143

BELLOWS, HENRY WHITNEY (1814-1882), American Unitarian minister **2** 143-144

BELMONT, AUGUST (1816-1890), German-American banker, diplomat, and horse racer **22** 56-57

BEMBO, PIETRO (1470-1547), Italian humanist, poet, and historian **2** 144-145

BEN AND JERRY ice cream company founders **18** 35-37

BEN BADIS, ABD AL-HAMID (1889-1940), leader of the Islamic Reform Movement in Algeria between the two world wars **2** 147-148

BEN BELLA, AHMED (born 1918), first president of the Algerian Republic **2** 148-149

BENDIX, VINCENT (1881-1945), American inventor, engineer, and industrialist **19** 18-20

BEN-GURION, DAVID (born 1886), Russian-born Israeli statesman **2** 160-161

BEN-HAIM, PAUL (Frankenburger; 1897-1984), Israeli composer **2** 161-162

BEN YEHUDA, ELIEZER (1858-1922), Hebrew lexicographer and editor **2** 181-182

BENALCÁZAR, SEBASTIÁN DE (died 1551), Spanish conquistador **2** 145-146

BENAVENTE Y MARTINEZ, JACINTO (1866-1954), Spanish dramatist **2** 146-147

BENCHLEY, ROBERT (1889-1945), American humorist **2** 150-151

BENDA, JULIEN (1867-1956), French cultural critic and novelist **2** 151-152

BENEDICT XIV (Prospero Lorenzo Lambertini; 1675-1758), Italian pope **23** 32-35

BENEDICT XV (Giacomo della Chiesa; 1854-1922), pope, 1914-1922 **2** 153-154

BENEDICT, RUTH FULTON (1887-1948), American cultural anthropologist **2** 154-155

BENEDICT, ST. (circa 480-547), Italian founder of the Benedictines **2** 154-155

BENEŠ, EDWARD (1884-1948), Czechoslovak president 1935-1938 and 1940-1948 **2** 155-157

BENÉT, STEPHEN VINCENT (1898-1943), American poet and novelist **2** 157-158

BENETTON, Italian family (Luciano, Giuliana, Gilberto, Carlo and Mauro) who organized a world-wide chain of colorful knitwear stores **2** 158-159

BENEZET, ANTHONY (1713-1784), American philanthropist and educator **2** 159-160

BENJAMIN, ASHER (1773-1845), American architect **2** 162-163

BENJAMIN, JUDAH PHILIP (1811-1884), American statesman **2** 163-164

BENJAMIN, WALTER (1892-1940), German philosopher and literary critic **20** 32-34

BENN, GOTTFRIED (1886-1956), German author **2** 164

BENN, TONY (Anthony Neil Wedgewood Benn; born 1925), British Labour party politician **2** 164-166

BENNETT, ALAN (born 1934), British playwright **2** 166-167

BENNETT, ENOCH ARNOLD (1867-1931), English novelist and dramatist **2** 167-168

BENNETT, JAMES GORDON (1795-1872), Scottish-born American journalist and publisher **2** 168-169

BENNETT, JAMES GORDON, JR. (1841-1918), American newspaper owner and editor **2** 169-170

BENNETT, JOHN COLEMAN (1902-1995), American theologian **2** 170-171

BENNETT, RICHARD BEDFORD (1870-1947), Canadian statesman, prime minister 1930-1935 **2** 171-172

BENNETT, RICHARD RODNEY (born 1936), English composer **2** 172

BENNETT, ROBERT RUSSELL (1894-1981), American arranger, composer, and conductor **21** 32-34

BENNETT, WILLIAM JOHN (born 1943), American teacher and scholar and secretary of the Department of Education (1985-1988) **2** 172-174

BENNY, JACK (Benjamin Kubelsky; 1894-1974), American comedian and a star of radio, television, and stage **2** 174-176

BENTHAM, JEREMY (1748-1832), English philosopher, political theorist, and jurist **2** 176-178

BENTLEY, ARTHUR F. (1870-1957), American philosopher and political scientist **2** 178

BENTON, SEN. THOMAS HART (1782-1858), American statesman **2** 178-179

BENTON, THOMAS HART (1889-1975), American regionalist painter **2** 178-179

BENTSEN, LLOYD MILLARD (born 1921), senior United States senator from Texas and Democratic vice-presidential candidate in 1988 **2** 180-181

BENZ, CARL (1844-1929), German inventor **2** 182-183

BERCHTOLD, COUNT LEOPOLD VON (1863-1942), Austro-Hungarian statesman **2** 183-184

BERDYAEV, NICHOLAS ALEXANDROVICH (1874-1948), Russian philosopher **2** 184-185

BERELSON, BERNARD (1912-1979), American behavioral scientist **2** 185-186

BERENSON, BERNARD (1865-1959), American art critic and historian **20** 34-35

BERG, ALBAN (1885-1935), Austrian composer 2 186-187

BERG, PAUL (born 1926), American chemist 2 187-189

BERGER, VICTOR LOUIS (1860-1929), American politician 2 189-190

BERGMAN, (ERNST) INGMAR (born 1918); Swedish film and stage director 2 190-191

BERGMAN, INGRID (1917-1982), Swedish actress 20 35-37

BERGSON, HENRI (1859-1941), French philosopher 2 191-192

BERIA, LAVRENTY PAVLOVICH (1899-1953), Soviet secret-police chief and politician 2 192-193

BERING, VITUS (1681-1741), Danish navigator in Russian employ 2 193-194

BERIO, LUCIANO (1925-2003), Italian composer 2 194-195
Rands, Bernard 23 324-326

BERISHA, SALI (born 1944), president of the Republic of Albania (1992-) 2 195-197

BERKELEY, BUSBY (William Berkeley Enos; 1895-1976), American filmmaker 20 38-39

BERKELEY, GEORGE (1685-1753), Anglo-Irish philosopher and Anglican bishop 2 197-198

BERKELEY, SIR WILLIAM (1606-1677), English royal governor of Virginia 2 198-199

BERLE, ADOLF AUGUSTUS, JR. (1895-1971), American educator 2 199-200

BERLE, MILTON (1908-2002), American entertainer and actor 18 37-39

BERLIN, IRVING (1888-1989), American composer 2 200-201

BERLIN, ISAIAH (1909-1997), British philosopher 2 201-203

Berlin, University of
mathematics
Steiner, Jakob 23 380-382

BERLINER, ÉMILE (1851-1929), American inventor 20 39-41

BERLIOZ, LOUIS HECTOR (1803-1869), French composer, conductor, and critic 2 203-205

BERMEJO, BARTOLOMÉ (Bartolomé de Cárdenas; flourished 1474-1498), Spanish painter 2 205

BERNADETTE OF LOURDES, SAINT (Marie Bernarde Soubirous; 1844-1879), French nun and Roman Catholic saint 21 34-36

BERNANOS, GEORGES (1888-1948), French novelist and essayist 2 206-207

BERNARD, CLAUDE (1813-1878), French physiologist 2 208-210

BERNARD OF CLAIRVAUX, ST. (1090-1153), French theologian, Doctor of the Church 2 207-208

BERNARDIN, CARDINAL JOSEPH (1928-1996), Roman Catholic Cardinal and American activist 2 210-211

BERNAYS, EDWARD L. (1891-1995), American public relations consultant 2 211-212

BERNBACH, WILLIAM (1911-1982), American advertising executive 19 20-22

BERNERS-LEE, TIM (born 1955), English computer scientist and creator of the World Wide Web 20 41-43

BERNHARDT, SARAH (Henriette-Rosine Bernard; 1844-1923), French actress 2 212-214

BERNIER, JOSEPH E. (Joseph-Elzéan Bernier; 1852-1934), Canadian explorer 23 35-37

BERNINI, GIAN LORENZO (1598-1680), Italian artist 2 214-216

BERNOULLI, DANIEL (1700-1782), Swiss mathematician and physicist 2 216

BERNOULLI, JAKOB (Jacques or James Bernoulli; 1654-1705), Swiss mathematician 23 37-39

BERNSTEIN, DOROTHY LEWIS (born 1914), American mathematician 2 217

BERNSTEIN, EDUARD (1850-1932), German socialist 2 218

BERNSTEIN, LEONARD (1918-1990), American composer, conductor, and pianist 2 218-219

BERRI, NABIH (born 1939), leader of the Shi'ite Muslims in Lebanon 2 220-222

BERRIGAN, DANIEL J. (born 1921), activist American Catholic priest 2 222-223

BERRUGUETE, ALONSO (1486/90-1561), Spanish sculptor 2 223-224

BERRY, CHUCK (born 1926), African American performer 2 224-226

BERRY, MARY FRANCES (born 1938), African American human/civil rights activist and official 2 226-229

BERRYMAN, JOHN (John Allyn Smith, Jr.; 1914-1972), American poet and biographer 19 22-25

BERTHIER, LOUIS ALEXANDRE (1753-1815), French soldier and cartographer 20 43-44

BERTHOLLET, CLAUDE LOUIS (1748-1822), French chemist 2 229-230

BERTILLON, ALPHONSE (1853-1914), French criminologist 2 230-231

BERTOLUCCI, BERNARDO (born 1940), Italian film director 18 39-41

BERZELIUS, JÖNS JACOB (1779-1848), Swedish chemist 2 231-233

BESANT, ANNIE WOOD (1847-1933), British social reformer and theosophist 2 233-234

BESSEL, FRIEDRICH WILHELM (1784-1846), German astronomer 2 234-235

BESSEMER, SIR HENRY (1813-1898), English inventor 2 235-236

BEST, CHARLES HERBERT (1899-1978), Canadian physiologist 2 236-237

BETANCOURT, RÓMULO (1908-1990), Venezuelan statesman 2 237-238

BETHE, HANS ALBRECHT (born 1906), Alsatian-American physicist 2 238-239

BETHMANN HOLLWEG, THEOBALD VON (1856-1921), German statesman 2 239-240

BETHUNE, HENRY NORMAN (1890-1939), Canadian humanitarian physician 2 240-241

BETHUNE, MARY MCLEOD (1875-1955), African American educator 2 241-242

BETI, MONGO (Alexandre Biyidi; born 1932), Cameroonian novelist 2 242-243

BETJEMAN, JOHN (1906-1984), Poet Laureate of Britain 1972-1984 2 243-245

BETTELHEIM, BRUNO (1903-1990), Austrian-born American psychoanalyst and educational psychologist 2 245-246

BETTI, UGO (1892-1953), Italian playwright 2 246

BEUYS, JOSEPH (1921-1986), German artist and sculptor 2 246-248

BEVAN, ANEURIN (1897-1960), Labour minister responsible for the creation of the British National Health Service 2 248-249

BEVEL, JAMES LUTHER (born 1936), American civil rights activist of the 1960s 2 250-251

BEVERIDGE, ALBERT JEREMIAH (1862-1927), American statesman 23 39-41

BEVERIDGE, WILLIAM HENRY (1st Baron Beveridge of Tuccal; 1879-1963), English economist and social reformer **2** 251-252

BEVERLEY, ROBERT (circa 1673-1722), colonial American historian **2** 252

BEVIN, ERNEST (1881-1951), English trade union leader and politician **2** 252-253

BHABHA, HOMI JEHANGIR (1909-1966), Indian atomic physicist **2** 253-254

BHAKTIVEDANTA PRABHUPADA (Abhay Charan De; 1896-1977), Hindu religious teacher who founded the International Society for Krishna Consciousness **2** 254-255

BHASHANI, MAULANA ABDUL HAMID KHAN (1880-1976), Muslim leader who promoted nationalism in Assam, Bengal, and Bangladesh **2** 255-257

BHAVE, VINOBA (born 1895), Indian nationalist and social reformer **2** 257-258

BHUMIBOL ADULYADEJ (born 1927), king of Thailand (1946-) representing the Chakri Dynasty **2** 258-259

BHUTTO, BENAZIR (born 1953), prime minister of Pakistan (1988-1990) **2** 259-261

BHUTTO, ZULFIKAR ALI (1928-1979), Pakistan's president and later prime minister (1971-1979) **2** 261-262

BIALIK, HAYYIM NAHMAN (1873-1934), Russian-born Hebrew poet **2** 262-263

Bible (book)
• OLD TESTAMENT
  prophets
    Abraham **23** 1-3

Biblical studies
see Bible

BICHAT, MARIE FRANÇOIS XAVIER (1771-1802), French anatomist, pathologist, and physiologist **2** 263-264

BIDDLE, NICHOLAS (1786-1844), American financier **2** 264-265

BIDWELL, JOHN (1819-1900), American pioneer and agriculturist **2** 265

BIEBER, OWEN (born 1929), American union executive **2** 266-268

BIENVILLE, SIEUR DE (Jean Baptiste Le Moyne; 1680-1768), French colonizer and administrator **2** 268-269

BIERCE, AMBROSE GWINETT (1842-1914?), American journalist and author **2** 269-270

BIERSTADT, ALBERT (1830-1902), American painter **2** 270-271

BIGELOW, JOHN (1817-1911), American journalist, editor, and diplomat **2** 271-272

BIGGE, JOHN THOMAS (1780-1843), English judge and royal commissioner **2** 272

BIGGS, HERMANN MICHAEL (1859-1923), American physician **2** 272-273

BIKILA, ABEBE (1932-1973), Ethiopian marathon runner **20** 44-46

BIKO, STEVE (Stephen Bantu Biko; 1946-1977), political activist and writer and father of the Black Consciousness movement in the Union of South Africa **2** 273-274

BILLINGS, JOHN SHAW (1838-1913), American physician and librarian **22** 57-60

BILLINGS, WILLIAM (1746-1800), American composer **2** 274-275

BILLINGTON, JAMES HADLEY (born 1929), American scholar and author **2** 275-276

BILLY THE KID (W.H. Bonney; 1859-1881), American frontiersman and outlaw **2** 277

BIN LADEN, OSAMA (born 1957), Saudi terrorist **22** 60-62

BINET, ALFRED (1857-1911), French psychologist **2** 277-278

BINGHAM, GEORGE CALEB (1811-1879), American painter **2** 278-279

BINGHAM, HIRAM (1875-1956), American explorer **20** 46-48

Biochemistry (science)
immunochemistry
  Prusiner, Stanley Ben **23** 320-323
plant photosynthesis
  Deisenhofer, Johann **23** 90-93

Biology (science)
molecular
  Altman, Sidney **23** 9-11
  Cech, Thomas Robert **23** 68-70
  Gilbert, Walter **23** 122-124
  Ho, David Da-I **23** 145-148

Biophysics (science)
  Deisenhofer, Johann **23** 90-93

Biotechnology
  Gilbert, Walter **23** 122-124

BIRD, ISABELLA (Isabella Bird Bishop; 1831-1904), English explorer and author **23** 41-42

BIRD, LARRY (born 1956), American basketball player **2** 279-281

BIRD, ROBERT MONTGOMERY (1806-1854), American dramatist and novelist **2** 281-282

BIRDSEYE, CLARENCE (1886-1956), American naturalist, inventor, and businessman **19** 25-27

BIRENDRA (Bir Bikram Shah Dev; 1945-2001), King of Nepal (1972-) **2** 282-283

BIRINGUCCIO, VANNOCCIO (1480-1539), Italian mining engineer and metallurgist **2** 283

BIRNEY, JAMES GILLESPIE (1792-1857), American lawyer and abolitionist **2** 283-284

BIRUNI, ABU RAYHAN AL- (973-circa 1050), Arabian scientist and historian **2** 284-285

BIRYUKOVA, ALEKSANDRA PAVLOVNA (1929-1990), a secretary of the Central Committee of the Communist party of the Soviet Union and a deputy prime minister (1986-1990) **2** 285-287

BISHARA, ABDULLAH YACCOUB (born 1936), Kuwaiti statesman and first secretary-general of the Gulf Cooperative Council **2** 287-288

BISHOP, BRIDGET (died 1692), Salem, Massachusetts, witch trial defendant **2** 288-290

BISHOP, ELIZABETH (1911-1979), American poet **2** 290-292

BISHOP, ISABEL (1902-1988), American artist **22** 64-67

BISHOP, MAURICE (1944-1983), leader of the New Jewel Movement and prime minister of Grenada (1979-1983) **2** 292-293

BISMARCK, OTTO EDUARD LEOPOLD VON (1815-1898), German statesman **2** 294-296

BITRUJI, NUR AL-DIN ABU ISHAQ AL (circa 1150-1200), Spanish Moslem astronomer **2** 296

BITZER, BILLY (George William Bitzer; 1872-1944), American cinematographer **21** 36-38

BIYA, PAUL (born 1933), president of Cameroon **18** 41-43

BIZET, GEORGES (1838-1875), French composer **2** 296-297

BJELKE-PETERSEN, JOHANNES ("Joh;" born 1911), Australian politician **2** 297-299

BJERKNES, VILHELM (1862-1951), Norwegian meteorologist **20** 48-50

BJØRNSON, BJØRNSTJERNE (1832-1910), Norwegian author **2** 299-300

BLACK, CONRAD MOFFAT (born 1944), Canadian-born international press baron **2** 300-301

BLACK, HUGO LAFAYETTE (1886-1971), American jurist **2** 301-303

BLACK, JOSEPH (1728-1799), British chemist **2** 303

Black Patti's Troubadours (musical group)
Joyner, Matilda Sissieretta **23** 179-181

BLACK, SHIRLEY TEMPLE (born 1928), American actress and public servant **2** 303-305

BLACK ELK, NICHOLAS (1863-1950), Oglala Sioux medicine man **2** 305-306

Black Enterprise (magazine)
Graves, Earl Gilbert, Jr. **23** 130-132

BLACK HAWK (1767-1838), Native American war chief **2** 308

BLACKBEARD (Edward Teach; 1680-1718), English pirate **21** 38-41

Blackbody radiation
see Radioactivity

BLACKBURN, ELIZABETH HELEN (born 1948), Australian biologist **18** 43-45

BLACKETT, PATRICK M.S. (1897-1974), British physicist **2** 306-307

BLACKMUN, HARRY (1908-1999), United States Supreme Court justice **2** 309-310

Blacks
see African American history (United States); Africa

BLACKSTONE, SIR WILLIAM (1723-1780), English jurist **2** 310-311

BLACKWELL, ANTOINETTE BROWN (1825-1921), American minister and suffragette **21** 41-43

BLACKWELL, ELIZABETH (1821-1910), American physician **2** 311-312

BLACKWELL, EMILY (1826-1910), American physician and educator **19** 27-29

BLAINE, JAMES GILLESPIE (1830-1893), American statesman **2** 312-313

BLAIR, BONNIE (born 1964), American athlete **23** 42-44

BLAIR, FRANCIS PRESTON (1791-1876), American journalist and politician **2** 313-315

BLAIR, JAMES (1655-1743), British educator and Anglican missionary **2** 315-316

BLAIR, TONY (born 1953), British prime minister **18** 45-47

BLAKE, WILLIAM (1757-1827), English poet, engraver, and painter **2** 316-318

BLAKELOCK, RALPH ALBERT (1847-1919), American painter **2** 318

BLANC, LOUIS (1811-1882), French journalist, historian, and politician **2** 318-319

BLANC, MEL (1908-1989), American creator of and voice of cartoon characters **2** 319-320

BLANCHARD, FELIX ("Doc" Blanchard; born 1924), American football player and military pilot **21** 43-45

BLANCHE OF CASTILE (1188-1252), French queen **21** 45-47

BLANCO, ANTONIO GUZMÁN (1829-1899), Venezuelan politician, three-times president **2** 320-321

BLANDIANA, ANA (born Otilia-Valeria Coman, 1942), Romanian poet **2** 321-322

BLANDING, SARAH GIBSON (1898-1985), American educator **2** 322-323

BLANKERS-KOEN, FANNY (Francina Elsja Blankers-Koen; born 1918), Dutch track and field athlete **20** 50-52

BLANQUI, LOUIS AUGUSTE (1805-1881), French revolutionary **2** 323-324

BLAVATSKY, HELENA PETROVNA (Helena Hahn; 1831-1891), Russian theosophist **22** 67-69

BLEDSOE, ALBERT TAYLOR (1809-1877), American lawyer, educator, and Confederate apologist **2** 324-325

BLEULER, EUGEN (1857-1939), Swiss psychiatrist **2** 325

BLIGH, WILLIAM (1754-1817), English naval officer and colonial governor **2** 325-326

BLOCH, ERNEST (1880-1959), Swiss-born American composer and teacher **2** 326-327

BLOCH, ERNST (1885-1977), German humanistic interpreter of Marxist thought **2** 327-328

BLOCH, FELIX (1905-1983), Swiss/American physicist **2** 328-330

BLOCH, KONRAD (born 1912), American biochemist **2** 330-332

BLOCH, MARC (1886-1944), French historian **2** 332-333

BLOCK, HERBERT (Herblock; 1909-2001), American newspaper cartoonist **2** 333-334

BLOK, ALEKSANDR ALEKSANDROVICH (1880-1921), Russian poet **2** 335

Blood (human)
clotting
Pool, Judith Graham **23** 315-316

BLOOM, ALLAN DAVID (1930-1992), American political philosopher, professor, and author **2** 335-337

BLOOMER, AMELIA JENKS (1818-1894), American reformer and suffrage advocate **2** 337

BLOOMFIELD, LEONARD (1887-1949), American linguist **2** 338

BLOOR, ELLA REEVE ("Mother Bloor"; 1862-1951), American labor organizer and social activist **2** 338-340

BLÜCHER, GEBHARD LEBERECHT VON (Prince of Wahlstatt; 1742-1819), Prussian field marshal **2** 340-341

Blues (music)
Hooker, John Lee **23** 155-157
Hunter, Alberta **23** 160-162
Johnson, Robert **23** 172-174

BLUFORD, GUION STEWART, JR. (born 1942), African American aerospace engineer, pilot, and astronaut **2** 341-343

BLUM, LÉON (1872-1950), French statesman **2** 343-344

BLUME, JUDY (born Judy Sussman; born 1938), American fiction author **2** 344-345

BLUMENTHAL, WERNER MICHAEL (born 1926), American businessman and treasury secretary **2** 345-346

BLY, NELLIE (born Elizabeth Cochrane Seaman; 1864-1922), American journalist and reformer **2** 346-348

BLYDEN, EDWARD WILMOT (1832-1912), Liberian statesman **2** 348-349

BOAS, FRANZ (1858-1942), German-born American anthropologist **2** 349-351

BOCCACCIO, GIOVANNI (1313-1375), Italian author **2** 351-353

BOCCIONI, UMBERTO (1882-1916), Italian artist **2** 353-354

BÖCKLIN, ARNOLD (1827-1901), Swiss painter **2** 354-355

BODE, BOYD HENRY (1873-1953), American philosopher and educator **2** 355-356

BODIN, JEAN (1529/30-1596), French political philosopher **2** 356-357

BOEHME, JACOB (1575-1624), German mystic **2** 357

BOEING, WILLIAM EDWARD (1881-1956), American businessman **2** 357-358

BOERHAAVE, HERMANN (1668-1738), Dutch physician and chemist **2** 358-359

BOESAK, ALLAN AUBREY (born 1945), opponent of apartheid in South Africa and founder of the United Democratic Front **2** 359-360

BOETHIUS, ANICIUS MANLIUS SEVERINUS (480?-524/525), Roman logician and theologian **2** 360-361

BOFF, LEONARDO (Leonardo Genezio Darci Boff; born 1938), Brazilian priest **22** 69-71

BOFFRAND, GABRIEL GERMAIN (1667-1754), French architect and decorator **2** 361

BOFILL, RICARDO (born 1939), post-modern Spanish architect **2** 362-363

BOGART, HUMPHREY (1899-1957), American stage and screen actor **2** 363-364

BOHEMUND I (of Tarantò; circa 1055-1111), Norman Crusader **2** 364

BOHLEN, CHARLES (CHIP) EUSTIS (1904-1973), United States ambassador to the Soviet Union, interpreter, and presidential adviser **2** 364-366

BÖHM-BAWERK, EUGEN VON (1851-1914), Austrian economist **2** 366

BOHR, NIELS HENRIK DAVID (1885-1962), Danish physicist **2** 366-368

BOIARDO, MATTEO MARIA (Conte di Scandiano; 1440/41-1494), Italian poet **2** 369

BOILEAU-DESPRÉAUX, NICHOLAS (1636?-1711), French critic and writer **2** 369-371

BOK, DEREK CURTIS (born 1930), dean of the Harvard Law School and president of Harvard University **2** 371-372

BOK, EDWARD WILLIAM (1863-1930), American editor and publisher **22** 71-73

BOK, SISSELA ANN (born 1934), American moral philosopher **2** 372-374

BOLEYN, ANNE (1504?-1536), second wife of Henry VIII **18** 47-49

BOLINGBROKE, VISCOUNT (Henry St. John; 1678-1751), English statesman **2** 374-375

BOLÍVAR, SIMÓN (1783-1830), South American general and statesman **2** 375-377

BOLKIAH, HASSANAL (Muda Hassanal Bolkiah Mu'izzaddin Waddaulah; born 1946), Sultan of Brunei **18** 49-51

BÖLL, HEINRICH (1917-1985), German writer and translator **2** 377-378

BOLTWOOD, BERTRAM BORDEN (1870-1927), American radiochemist **2** 378-379

BOLTZMANN, LUDWIG (1844-1906), Austrian physicist **2** 379-380

BOMBAL, MARÍA LUISA (1910-1980), Chilean novelist and story writer **2** 380-381

BONAPARTE, JOSEPH (1768-1844), French statesman, king of Naples 1806-1808 and of Spain 1808-1813 **2** 381-382

BONAPARTE, LOUIS (1778-1846), French statesman, king of Holland 1806-1810 **2** 382-383

BONAVENTURE, ST. (1217-1274), Italian theologian and philosopher **2** 383-384

BOND, HORACE MANN (1904-1972), African American educator **2** 384-386

BOND, JULIAN (born 1940), civil rights leader elected to the Georgia House of Representatives **2** 386-387

BONDFIELD, MARGARET GRACE (1873-1953), British union official and political leader **2** 388-389

BONDI, HERMANN (born 1919), English mathematician and cosmologist **18** 51-52

Bonham, John (1949-1980), British drummer
Led Zeppelin **23** 216-218

BONHOEFFER, DIETRICH (1906-1945), German theologian **2** 389-391

BONHEUR, ROSA (Marie Rosalie Bonheur; 1822-1899), French artist **19** 29-31

BONIFACE, ST. (circa 672-754), English monk **2** 391

BONIFACE VIII (Benedetto Caetani; 1235?-1303), pope 1294-1303 **2** 392-393

BONIFACIO, ANDRES (1863-1897), Filipino revolutionary hero **2** 393-394

BONINGTON, RICHARD PARKES (1802-1828), English painter **2** 394-395

BONNARD, PIERRE (1867-1947), French painter **2** 395-396

BONNIN, GERTRUDE SIMMONS (Zitkala-Sa; Red Bird; 1876-1938), Native American author and activist **18** 52-54

BONO, SONNY (Salvatore Bono; 1935-1998), American entertainer and U.S. Congressman **18** 54-56

BONTEMPS, ARNA (Arnaud Wendell Bontempsl 1902-1973), American author and educator **21** 47-50

BONVALOT, PIERRE GABRIEL ÉDOUARD (1853-1933), French explorer and author **2** 396

BOOLE, GEORGE (1815-1864), English mathematician **2** 396-397

BOONE, DANIEL (1734-1820), American frontiersman and explorer **2** 397-398

BOORSTIN, DANIEL J. (born 1914), American historian **2** 398-400

BOOTH, CHARLES (1840-1916), English social scientist **2** 400-401

BOOTH, EDWIN (1833-1893), American actor **2** 401-402

BOOTH, EVANGELINE CORY (1865-1950), British/American humanist **2** 402-403

BOOTH, HUBERT CECIL (1871-1955), English inventor of the vacuum cleaner **21** 50-52

BOOTH, JOHN WILKES (1838-1865), American actor **2** 404

BOOTH, JOSEPH (1851-1932), English missionary in Africa **2** 404-405

BOOTH, WILLIAM (1829-1912), English evangelist, Salvation Army founder **2** 405-406

BOOTHROYD, BETTY (born 1929), first woman speaker in Great Britain's House of Commons **2** 406-407

BORAH, WILLIAM EDGAR (1865-1940), American statesman **2** 408

BORDEN, GAIL (1801-1874), American pioneer and inventor of food-processing techniques **2** 409

BORDEN, SIR ROBERT LAIRD (1854-1937), Canadian prime minister, 1911-1920 **2** 409-411

BORGES, JORGE LUIS (1899-1986), Argentine author and critic **2** 411-412

BORGIA, CESARE (1475-1507), Italian cardinal, general, and administrator **2** 412-413

BORGIA, LUCREZIA (1480-1519), Italian duchess of Ferrara **2** 413-416

BORGLUM, JOHN GUTZON DE LA MOTHE (1867-1941), American sculptor and engineer **2** 416-417
Hoffman, Malvina Cornell **23** 148-150

BORI, LUCREZIA (Lucrezia Gonzá de Riancho; 1887-1960), Spanish American opera singer **23** 44-45

Borinquén
see Puerto Rico

BORJA CEVALLOS, RODRIGO (born 1935), a founder of Ecuador's Democratic Left (Izquierda Democratica) party and president of Ecuador (1988-) **2** 417-418

BORLAUG, NORMAN ERNEST (born 1914), American biochemist who developed high yield cereal grains **2** 418-420

BORN, MAX (1882-1970), German physicist **2** 420-421

BOROCHOV, DOV BER (1881-1917), early Zionist thinker who reconciled Judaism and Marxism **2** 421-422

BORODIN, ALEKSANDR PROFIREVICH (1833-1887), Russian composer **2** 422-423

BORROMEO, ST. CHARLES (1538-1584), Italian cardinal and reformer **2** 423-424

BORROMINI, FRANCESCO (1599-1667), Italian architect **2** 424-425

BOSANQUET, BERNARD (1848-1923), English philosopher **2** 425-426

BOSCH, HIERONYMUS (1453-1516), Netherlandish painter **2** 426-428

BOSCH, JUAN (born 1909), Dominican writer, president, 1963 **2** 428-429

BOSE, SATYENDRANATH (1894-1974), Indian physicist **20** 52-54

BOSE, SIR JAGADIS CHANDRA (1858-1937), Indian physicist and plant physiologist **2** 430-431

BOSE, SUBHAS CHANDRA (1897-1945), Indian nationalist **2** 430-431

BOSOMWORTH, MARY MUSGROVE (Cousaponokeesa;1700-1765), Native American/American interpreter, diplomat, and businessperson **20** 54-56

BOSSUET, JACQUES BÉNIGNE (1627-1704), French bishop and author **2** 431-432

BOSWELL, JAMES (1740-1795), Scottish biographer and diarist **2** 432-434

BOTHA, LOUIS (1862-1919), South African soldier and statesman **2** 434-436

BOTHA, PIETER WILLEM (born 1916), prime minister (1978-1984) and first executive state president of the Republic of South Africa **2** 436-438

BOTHE, WALTHER (1891-1957), German physicist **2** 438-439

BOTTICELLI, SANDRO (1444-1510), Italian painter **2** 439-440

BOUCHER, FRANÇOIS (1703-1770), French painter **2** 440-442

BOUCICAULT, DION (1820-1890), Irish-American playwright and actor **2** 442-443

BOUDICCA (Boadicea; died 61 A.D.), Iceni queen **18** 56-58

BOUDINOT, ELIAS (Buck Watie; Galagina; 1803-1839), Cherokee leader and author **21** 52-54

BOUGAINVILLE, LOUIS ANTOINE DE (1729-1811), French soldier and explorer **2** 443-444

BOULANGER, NADIA (1887-1979), French pianist and music teacher **20** 56-58

BOULEZ, PIERRE (born 1925), French composer, conductor, and teacher **2** 444-445

BOUMEDIENE, HOUARI (born 1932), Algerian revolutionary, military leader, and president **2** 445-446

BOURASSA, JOSEPH-HENRI-NAPOLEON (1868-1952), French-Canadian nationalist and editor **2** 446-447

BOURASSA, ROBERT (born 1933), premier of the province of Quebec (1970-1976 and 1985-) **2** 447-449

BOURDELLE, EMILE-ANTOINE (1861-1929), French sculptor **2** 449-450

BOURGEOIS, LÉON (1851-1925), French premier 1895-1896 **2** 450-451

BOURGEOIS, LOUISE (born 1911), American sculptor **2** 451-452

BOURGEOYS, BLESSED MARGUERITE (1620-1700), French educator and religious founder **2** 452-453

BOURGUIBA, HABIB (1903-2000), Tunisian statesman **2** 453-455

BOURKE-WHITE, MARGARET (1904-1971), American photographer and photojournalist **2** 455-456

BOURNE, RANDOLPH SILLIMAN (1886-1918), American pacifist and cultural critic **2** 456-457

BOUTROS-GHALI, BOUTROS (born 1922), Egyptian diplomat and sixth secretary-general of the United Nations (1991-) **2** 457-458

BOUTS, DIRK (1415/20-1475), Dutch painter **2** 458-459

BOWDITCH, HENRY INGERSOLL (1808-1892), American physician **2** 459-460

BOWDITCH, NATHANIEL (1773-1838), American navigator and mathematician **2** 460-461

BOWDOIN, JAMES (1726-1790), American merchant and politician **2** 461-462

BOWEN, ELIZABETH (1899-1973), British novelist **2** 462-463

BOWERS, CLAUDE GERNADE (1878-1958), American journalist, historian, and diplomat **2** 463

BOWIE, DAVID (David Robert Jones; born 1947), English singer, songwriter, and actor **18** 58-60

BOWLES, PAUL (1910-1999), American author, musical composer, and translator **19** 31-34

BOWLES, SAMUEL (1826-1878), American newspaper publisher **2** 464

BOWMAN, ISAIAH (1878-1950), American geographer **2** 464-465

BOXER, BARBARA (born 1940), U.S. Senator from California **2** 465-468

BOYD, LOUISE ARNER (1887-1972), American explorer **22** 73-74

BOYER, JEAN PIERRE (1776-1850), Haitian president 1818-1845 **2** 468-469

BOYLE, ROBERT (1627-1691), British chemist and physicist **2** 469-471

BOYLSTON, ZABDIEL (1679-1766), American physician **2** 471

BOZEMAN, JOHN M. (1837-1867), American pioneer **2** 471-472

BRACKENRIDGE, HUGH HENRY (1749-1816), American lawyer and writer **2** 472-473

BRACTON, HENRY (Henry of Bratton; c. 1210-1268), English jurist **21** 54-55

BRADBURY, RAY (born 1920), American fantasy and science fiction writer **2** 473-474

BRADDOCK, EDWARD (1695-1755), British commander in North America **2** 474-475

BRADFORD, WILLIAM (1590-1657), leader of Plymouth Colony **2** 475-476

BRADFORD, WILLIAM (1663-1752), American printer **2** 476-477

BRADFORD, WILLIAM (1722-1791), American journalist **2** 477

BRADLAUGH, CHARLES (1833-1891), English freethinker and political agitator **2** 478

BRADLEY, ED (born 1941), African American broadcast journalist **2** 478-481

BRADLEY, FRANCIS HERBERT (1846-1924), English philosopher **2** 481-482

BRADLEY, JAMES (1693-1762), English astronomer **2** 482-483

BRADLEY, JOSEPH P. (1813-1892), American Supreme Court justice **22** 74-77

BRADLEY, MARION ZIMMER (born 1930), American author **18** 60-62

BRADLEY, OMAR NELSON (1893-1981), American general **2** 483-484

BRADLEY, TOM (1917-1998), first African American mayor of Los Angeles **2** 484-485

BRADMAN, SIR DONALD GEORGE (born 1908), Australian cricketer **2** 485-486

BRADSTREET, ANNE DUDLEY (circa 1612-1672), English-born American poet **2** 486-487

BRADY, MATHEW B. (circa 1823-1896), American photographer **2** 487-488

BRAGG, SIR WILLIAM HENRY (1862-1942), English physicist **2** 488-489

BRAHE, TYCHO (1546-1601), Danish astronomer **2** 489-490

BRAHMS, JOHANNES (1833-1897), German composer **2** 490-492

BRAILLE, LOUIS (1809-1852), French teacher and creator of braille system **2** 492-493

BRAMAH, JOSEPH (Joe Bremmer; 1749-1814), English engineer and inventor **20** 58-59

BRAMANTE, DONATO (1444-1514), Italian architect and painter **2** 493-494

BRANCUSI, CONSTANTIN (1876-1957), Romanian sculptor in France **2** 494-496

BRANDEIS, LOUIS DEMBITZ (1856-1941), American jurist **2** 496-497

BRANDES, GEORG (Georg Morris Cohen Brandes; 1842-1927), Danish literary critic **23** 45-47

BRANDO, MARLON (born 1924), American actor **2** 497-499

BRANDT, WILLY (Herbert Frahm Brandt; 1913-1992), German statesman, chancellor of West Germany **2** 499-500

BRANSON, RICHARD (born 1950), British entrepreneur **19** 34-36

BRANT, JOSEPH (1742-1807), Mohawk Indian chief **2** 500-501

BRANT, MARY (1736-1796), Native American who guided the Iroquois to a British alliance **2** 501-503

BRANT, SEBASTIAN (1457-1521), German author **2** 503-504

BRAQUE, GEORGES (1882-1967), French painter **2** 504-505

BRATTAIN, WALTER H. (1902-1987), American physicist and co-inventor of the transistor **2** 505-507

BRAUDEL, FERNAND (1902-1985), leading exponent of the *Annales* school of history **2** 507-508

BRAUN, FERDINAND (1850-1918), German recipient of the Nobel Prize in Physics for work on wireless telegraphy **2** 508-509

BRAY, JOHN RANDOLPH (1879-1978), American animator and cartoonist **21** 55-57

BRAZZA, PIERRE PAUL FRANÇOIS CAMILLE SAVORGNAN DE (1852-1905), Italian-born French explorer **2** 509-510

BREASTED, JAMES HENRY (1865-1935), American Egyptologist and archeologist **2** 510-511

BRÉBEUF, JEAN DE (1593-1649), French Jesuit missionary **2** 511-512

BRECHT, BERTOLT (1898-1956), German playwright **2** 512-514

BRECKINRIDGE, JOHN CABELL (1821-1875), American statesman and military leader **22** 77-79

BRENDAN, SAINT (Brenainn; Brandon; Brendan of Clonfert; c. 486- c. 578), Irish Abbott and explorer **22** 79-80

BRENNAN, WILLIAM J., JR. (born 1906), United States Supreme Court justice **2** 514-515

BRENTANO, CLEMENS (1778-1842), German poet and novelist **2** 515-516

BRENTANO, FRANZ CLEMENS (1838-1917), German philosopher **2** 516-517

BRESHKOVSKY, CATHERINE (1844-1934), Russian revolutionary **2** 517-519

BRETON, ANDRÉ (1896-1966), French author **2** 519-520

BREUER, MARCEL (1902-1981), Hungarian-born American architect **2** 520-521

BREUIL, HENRI EDOUARD PROSPER (1877-1961), French archeologist **2** 521-522

BREWSTER, KINGMAN, JR. (1919-1988), president of Yale University (1963-1977) **2** 522-523

BREWSTER, WILLIAM (circa 1566-1644), English-born Pilgrim leader **2** 523-524

BREYER, STEPHEN (born 1938), U.S. Supreme Court justice **2** 524-527

BREZHNEV, LEONID ILICH (1906-1982), general secretary of the Communist party of the Union of Soviet Socialist Republics (1964-1982) and president of the Union of Soviet Socialist Republics (1977-1982) **2** 527-528

BRIAN BORU (940?-1014), Irish king **18** 62-64

BRIAND, ARISTIDE (1862-1932), French statesman **2** 528-529

BRICE, FANNY (1891-1951), vaudeville, Broadway, film, and radio singer and comedienne **3** 1-2

BRIDGER, JAMES (1804-1881), American fur trader and scout **3** 2-3

BRIDGES, HARRY A.R. (1901-1990), radical American labor leader **3** 3-5

BRIDGMAN, PERCY WILLIAMS (1882-1961), American physicist **3** 5-6

BRIGHT, JOHN (1811-1889), English politician **3** 6-7

BRIGHT, RICHARD (1789-1858), English physician **3** 7-8

BRIGHTMAN, EDGAR SHEFFIELD (1884-1953), philosopher of religion and exponent of American Personalism **3** 8-9

BRINK, ANDRE PHILIPPUS (born 1935), South African author **22** 80-83

BRISBANE, ALBERT (1809-1890), American social theorist **3** 9

BRISTOW, BENJAMIN HELM (1832-1896), American lawyer and Federal official **3** 9-10

BRITTEN, BENJAMIN (1913-1976), English composer **3** 10-11

BROAD, CHARLIE DUNBAR (1887-1971), English philosopher **3** 12

BROCK, SIR ISAAC (1769-1812), British general **3** 12-13

BRODSKY, JOSEPH (Iosif Alexandrovich Brodsky, 1940-1996), Russian-born Nobel Prize winner and fifth United States poet laureate **3** 13-15

BRONTË, CHARLOTTE (1816-1855), English novelist **3** 17-18

BRONTË, EMILY (1818-1848), English novelist **3** 18-19

BRONZINO (1503-1572), Italian painter **3** 19

BROOK, PETER (born 1925), world-renowned theater director **3** 19-21

BROOKE, ALAN FRANCIS (Viscount Alanbrooke; 1883-1963), Irish military leader **20** 59-61

BROOKE, SIR JAMES (1803-1868), British governor in Borneo **3** 21-22

BROOKE, RUPERT (1887-1915), English poet **3** 22-23

BROOKNER, ANITA (born 1928), British art historian and novelist **3** 23-24

BROOKS, GWENDOLYN (born 1917), first African American author to receive the Pulitzer Prize for Literature **3** 24-26

BROOKS, MEL (Melvin Kaminsky; born 1926), American actor, playwright, and film and theatre producer/director **23** 48-50

BROOKS, PHILLIPS (1835-1893), American Episcopalian bishop **3** 26

BROTHERS, JOYCE (Joyce Diane Bauer; born 1927), American psychologist who pioneered radio phone-in questions for professional psychological advice **3** 26-28

BROUDY, HARRY SAMUEL (born 1905), American philosopher, teacher, and author **3** 28-29

BROUGHAM, HENRY PETER (Baron Brougham and Vaux; 1778-1868), Scottish jurist **22** 83-85

BROUWER, ADRIAEN (1605/06-1638), Flemish painter **3** 29-30

BROWDER, EARL RUSSELL (1891-1973), American Communist leader **3** 30-31

BROWN, ALEXANDER (1764-1834), American merchant and banker **3** 31-32

BROWN, BENJAMIN GRATZ (1826-1885), American politician **3** 32-33

BROWN, CHARLES BROCKDEN (1771-1810), American novelist **3** 33

BROWN, CHARLOTTE EUGENIA HAWKINS (born Lottie Hawkins; 1882-1961), African American educator and humanitarian **3** 34

BROWN, GEORGE (1818-1880), Canadian politician **3** 35-36

BROWN, HELEN GURLEY (born 1922), American author and editor **3** 36-37

BROWN, JAMES (born 1928), African American singer **3** 37-39

BROWN, JOHN (1800-1859), American abolitionist **3** 39-41

BROWN, JOSEPH EMERSON (1821-1894), American lawyer and politician **3** 41-42

BROWN, LES (Leslie Calvin Brown; born 1945), American motivational speaker, author, and television host **19** 36-39

BROWN, MOSES (1738-1836), American manufacturer and merchant **3** 42-43

BROWN, RACHEL FULLER (1898-1980), American biochemist **3** 43-44

BROWN, ROBERT (1773-1858), Scottish botanist **20** 61-63

BROWN, RONALD H. (1941-1996), African American politician, cabinet official **3** 44-47

BROWN, TINA (Christina Hambly Brown; born 1953), British editor who transformed the English magazine *Tatler*, then the United States magazines *Vanity Fair* and the *New Yorker* **3** 47-48

BROWN, WILLIAM WELLS (1815/16-1884), African American author and abolitionist **3** 48-49

Brown v. Board of Education of Topeka (1954) Murray, Pauli **23** 253-256

BROWNE, SIR THOMAS (1605-1682), English author **3** 49-50

BROWNE, THOMAS ALEXANDER (Rolf Bolderwood; 1826-1915), Australian author **22** 85-87

BROWNER, CAROL M. (born 1955), U.S. Environmental Protection Agency administrator **3** 50-52

BROWNING, ELIZABETH BARRETT (1806-1861), English poet **3** 52-53

BROWNING, ROBERT (1812-1889), English poet **3** 53-55

BROWNLOW, WILLIAM GANNAWAY (1805-1877), American journalist and politician **3** 55-56

BROWNMILLER, SUSAN (born 1935), American activist, journalist, and novelist **3** 56-57

BROWNSON, ORESTES AUGUSTUS (1803-1876), American clergyman and transcendentalist **3** 57-58

BRUBACHER, JOHN SEILER (1898-1988), American historian and educator **3** 58-59

BRUBECK, DAVE (born 1920), American pianist, composer, and bandleader **3** 59-61

BRUCE, BLANCHE KELSO (1841-1898), African American politician **3** 62-63

BRUCE, DAVID (1855-1931), Australian parasitologist **3** 63

BRUCE, JAMES (1730-1794), Scottish explorer **3** 63-64

BRUCE, LENNY (Leonard Alfred Schneider; 1925-1966), American comedian **19** 39-41

BRUCE OF MELBOURNE, 1ST VISCOUNT (Stanley Melbourne Bruce; 1883-1967), Australian statesman **3** 61-62

BRUCKNER, JOSEPH ANTON (1824-1896), Austrian composer **3** 64-65

BRUEGEL, PIETER, THE ELDER (1525/30-1569), Netherlandish painter **3** 65-67

BRÛLÉ, ÉTIENNE (circa 1592-1633), French explorer in North America **3** 67-68

BRUNDTLAND, GRO HARLEM (1939-1989), Norwegian prime minister and chair of the United Nations World Commission for Environment and Development **3** 68-69

BRUNEL, ISAMBARD KINGDOM (1806-1859), English civil engineer **3** 69-70

BRUNELLESCHI, FILIPPO (1377-1446), Italian architect and sculptor **3** 70-72

BRUNER, JEROME SEYMOUR (born 1915), American psychologist **3** 72-73

BRUNHOFF, JEAN de (1899-1937), French author and illustrator **19** 41-42

BRUNNER, ALOIS (born 1912), Nazi German officer who helped engineer the destruction of European Jews **3** 73-74

BRUNNER, EMIL (1889-1966), Swiss Reformed theologian **3** 74-75

BRUNO, GIORDANO (1548-1600), Italian philosopher and poet **3** 75-76

BRUTON, JOHN GERARD (born 1947), prime minister of Ireland **3** 76-77

BRUTUS, DENNIS (born 1924), exiled South African poet and political activist opposed to apartheid **3** 77-78

BRUTUS, MARCUS JUNIUS (circa 85-42 B.C.), Roman statesman **3** 79-80

BRYAN, WILLIAM JENNINGS (1860-1925), American lawyer and politician **3** 80-82

BRYANT, PAUL (''Bear;'' 1919-1983), American college football coach **3** 82-83

BRYANT, WILLIAM CULLEN (1794-1878), American poet and editor **3** 83-85

BRYCE, JAMES (1838-1922), British historian, jurist, and statesman **3** 85

Bryn Mawr College (Pennsylvania)
Scott, Charlotte Angas **23** 364-367

BRZEZINSKI, ZBIGNIEW (1928-1980),
assistant to President Carter for
national security affairs (1977-1980) **3**
85-87

BUBER, MARTIN (1878-1965), Austrian-
born Jewish theologian and
philosopher **3** 87-89

BUCHALTER, LEPKE (Louis Bachalter;
1897-1944), American gangster **19**
42-44

BUCHANAN, JAMES (1791-1868),
American statesman, president 1857-
1861 **3** 89-90

BUCHANAN, PATRICK JOSEPH (born
1938), commentator, journalist, and
presidential candidate **3** 90-91

Büchse der Pandora, Die (Pandora's Box;
film)
Pabst, G. W. **23** 282-284

BUCK, PEARL SYDENSTRICKER (1892-
1973), American novelist **3** 91-93

BUCKINGHAM, 1ST DUKE OF (George
Villiers; 1592-1628), English courtier
and military leader **3** 93-94

BUCKINGHAM, 2D DUKE OF (George
Villiers; 1628-1687), English statesman
3 94-95

BUCKLE, HENRY THOMAS (1821-1862),
English historian **3** 95-96

BUCKLEY, WILLIAM F., JR. (born 1925),
conservative American author, editor,
and political activist **3** 96-97

BUDDHA (circa 560-480 B.C.), Indian
founder of Buddhism **3** 97-101

BUDDHADĀSA BHIKKHU (Nguam
Phanich; born 1906), founder of Wat
Suan Mokkhabalārama in southern
Thailand and interpreter of Theravāda
Buddhism **3** 101-102

BUDÉ, GUILLAUME (1467-1540),
French humanist **3** 102-103

BUDGE, DON (J. Donald Budge; born
1915), American tennis player **21**
57-59

BUECHNER, FREDERICK (born 1926),
American novelist and theologian **3**
103-105

BUEL, JESSE (1778-1839), American
agriculturalist and journalist **3** 105

BUFFALO BILL (William Frederick Cody;
1846-1917), American scout and
publicist **3** 105-106

BUFFETT, WARREN (born 1930),
American investment salesman **3**
106-109

BUFFON, COMTE DE (Georges Louis
Leclerc; 1707-1788), French naturalist
3 109-111

**BUGEAUD DE LA PICCONNERIE,
THOMAS ROBERT** (1784-1849), Duke
of Isly and marshal of France **3** 111

BUICK, DAVID (1854-1929), American
inventor and businessman **19** 44-45

**BUKHARI, MUHAMMAD IBN ISMAIL
AL-** (810-870), Arab scholar and
Moslem saint **3** 111-112

BUKHARIN, NIKOLAI IVANOVICH
(1858-1938), Russian politician **3**
112-113

BUKOWSKI, CHARLES (1920-1994),
American writer and poet **3** 113-115

BULATOVIC, MOMIR (born 1956),
president of Montenegro (1990-1992)
and of the new Federal Republic of
Yugoslavia (1992-) **3** 115-116

BULFINCH, CHARLES (1763-1844),
American colonial architect **3** 116-117

BULGAKOV, MIKHAIL AFANASIEVICH
(1891-1940), Russian novelist and
playwright **3** 117

BULGANIN, NIKOLAI (1885-1975),
chairman of the Soviet Council of
Ministers (1955-1958) **3** 118-119

BULOSAN, CARLOS (1911-1956),
American author and poet **21** 59-61

BULTMANN, RUDOLF KARL (1884-
1976), German theologian **3** 119-120

BULWER-LYTTON, EDWARD (1st Baron
Lytton of Knebworth; 1803-1873),
English novelist **22** 87-88

BUNAU-VARILLA, PHILIPPE JEAN
(1859-1940), French engineer and
soldier **3** 120-121

BUNCHE, RALPH JOHNSON (1904-
1971), African American diplomat **3**
121-122

BUNDY, McGEORGE (born 1919),
national security adviser to two
presidents **3** 122-124

BUNIN, IVAN ALEKSEEVICH (1870-
1953), Russian poet and novelist **3** 124

BUNSEN, ROBERT WILHELM (1811-
1899), German chemist and physicist **3**
124-125

BUNSHAFT, GORDON (1909-1990),
American architect **3** 125-127

BUÑUEL, LUIS (1900-1983), Spanish
film director **3** 127-128

BUNYAN, JOHN (1628-1688), English
author and Baptist preacher **3** 128-129

BURBANK, LUTHER (1849-1926),
American plant breeder **3** 129-131

BURCHFIELD, CHARLES (1893-1967),
American painter **3** 131-132

BURCKHARDT, JACOB CHRISTOPH
(1818-1897), Swiss historian **3**
132-133

BURCKHARDT, JOHANN LUDWIG
(1784-1817), Swiss-born explorer **3**
133

BURGER, WARREN E. (1907-1986),
Chief Justice of the United States
Supreme Court (1969-1986) **3** 133-136

BURGESS, ANTHONY (John Anthony
Burgess Wilson; 1917-1993), English
author **3** 136-137

BURGOYNE, JOHN (1723-1792), British
general and statesman **3** 137-138

BURKE, EDMUND (1729-1797), British
statesman, political theorist, and
philosopher **3** 138-141

BURKE, KENNETH (born 1897),
American literary theorist and critic **3**
141-142

BURKE, ROBERT O'HARA (1820-1861),
Irish-born Australian policeman and
explorer **3** 142-143

BURKE, SELMA (1900-1995), African
American sculptor **3** 143-144

BURLIN, NATALIE CURTIS (Natalie
Curtis; 1875-1921), American
ethnomusicologist **23** 50-52

BURLINGAME, ANSON (1820-1870),
American diplomat **3** 144-145

BURNE-JONES, SIR EDWARD COLEY
(1833-1898), English painter and
designer **3** 145-146

BURNET, SIR FRANK MACFARLANE
(1899-1985), Australian virologist **3**
146-147

BURNET, GILBERT (1643-1715), British
bishop and historian **3** 147

BURNETT, CAROL (born 1933),
American television entertainer **23**
52-55

BURNETT, FRANCES HODGSON
(Frances Eliza Hodgson Burnett; 1849-
1924), English-born American author
18 64-67

BURNETT, LEO (1891-1971), American
advertising executive **19** 45-47

BURNEY, FRANCES "FANNY" (1752-
1840), English novelist and diarist **3**
147-148

BURNHAM, DANIEL HUDSON (1846-
1912), American architect and city
planner **3** 148-149

BURNHAM, FORBES (1923-1985),
leader of the independence movement

in British Guiana and Guyana's first prime minister **3** 149-151

BURNS, ANTHONY (1834-1862), African American slave **3** 151

BURNS, ARTHUR (1904-1987), American economic statesman **3** 151-153

BURNS, GEORGE (born Nathan Birnbaum; 1896-1996), American comedian and actor **3** 153-155

BURNS, KEN (Kenneth Lauren Burns; born 1953), American documentary filmmaker **20** 63-65

BURNS, ROBERT (1759-1796), Scottish poet **3** 155-156

BURR, AARON (1756-1836), American politician, vice president 1801-1805 **3** 156-159

BURRI, ALBERTO (1915-1995), Italian painter **3** 159-160

BURRITT, ELIHU (1810-1879), American pacifist, author, and linguist **3** 160

BURROUGHS, EDGAR RICE (1875-1950), American author **18** 67-68

BURROUGHS, JOHN (1837-1921), American naturalist and essayist **3** 160-161

BURROUGHS, WILLIAM S. (1914-1997), American writer **3** 162-163

BURTON, RICHARD (Richard Jenkins; 1925-1984), British actor **3** 163-164

BURTON, SIR RICHARD FRANCIS (1821-1890), English explorer, author, and diplomat **3** 164-166

BURTON, ROBERT (1577-1640), English author and clergyman **3** 166-167

BUSCH, ADOLPHUS (1839-1913), American brewer and businessman **19** 47-49

BUSH, GEORGE (George Herbert Walker Bush; born 1924), United States vice president (1981-1989) and president (1989-1993) **3** 167-169

BUSH, GEORGE WALKER (born 1946), United States president (2001-) **21** 61-64
  Ashcroft, John **23** 18-21
  Rice, Condoleezza **23** 335-338
  Rumsfeld, Donald Harold **23** 353-355

BUSH, VANNEVAR (1890-1974), American scientist and engineer **3** 169-171

BUSHNELL, DAVID (1742-1824), American inventor **21** 64-65

BUSHNELL, HORACE (1802-1876), American Congregational clergyman **3** 171-172

BUSIA, KOFI ABREFA (1914-1978), Ghanaian premier and sociologist **3** 172-173

Business and industrial leaders
  South Korean
    Chung, Ju Yung **23** 72-74

Business and industrial leaders, American
  communications industry
    Vail, Theodore Newton **23** 419-421
  computer industry
    Dell, Michael Saul **23** 93-95
  cosmetics and beauty aids industry
    Malone, Annie Turnbo **23** 242-243
  entertainment industry
    Geffen, David Lawrence **23** 119-122
    Redstone, Sumner Murray **23** 329-331
  fashion industry
    Herrera, Carolina **23** 141-143
  oil industry
    Geffen, David Lawrence **23** 119-122
  pharmaceutical industry
    Rumsfeld, Donald Harold **23** 353-355
  printing industry
    Graves, Earl Gilbert, Jr. **23** 130-132

BUSONI, FERRUCCIO BENVENUTO (1866-1924) Italian musician **3** 173-174

BUSSOTTI, SYLVANO (born 1931) Italian composer **3** 174-175

BUSTAMANTE, WILLIAM ALEXANDER (1884-1977), Jamaican labor leader and first prime minister (1962-1967) **3** 175-177

BUTE, 3D EARL OF (John Stuart; 1713-1792), British statesman, prime minister 1762-1763 **3** 177-178

BUTHELEZI, MANGOSUTHU GATSHA (born 1928), chief of the Zulu "homeland" and an important figure in the struggle to end apartheid in South Africa **3** 178-179

BUTLER, BENJAMIN FRANKLIN (1818-1893), American politician and military leader **21** 65-67

BUTLER, JOHN (1728-1796), British Indian agent and Loyalist leader **3** 180

BUTLER, JOSEPH (1692-1752), English philosopher and theologian **3** 180-181

BUTLER, NICHOLAS MURRAY (1862-1947), American educator **3** 181

BUTLER, OCTAVIA E. (born 1947), African American novelist and essayist **3** 182-183

BUTLER, SAMUEL (1613-1680) English poet **3** 183-184

BUTLER, SAMUEL (1835-1902), English novelist and essayist **3** 183

BUTTERFIELD, JOHN (1801-1869), American financier and politician **3** 184-185

BUTTON, DICK (Richard Totten Button; born 1929), American figure skater and sports commentator **23** 55-57

BUXTEHUDE, DIETRICH (1637-1707), Danish composer and organist **3** 185-186

BYRD, RICHARD EVELYN (1888-1957), American admiral and polar explorer **3** 186-187

BYRD, WILLIAM (1543?-1623), English composer **3** 187-188

BYRD, WILLIAM (1652-1704), English colonial planter and merchant **3** 188-189

BYRD, WILLIAM II (1674-1744), American diarist and government official **3** 189-190

BYRNE, JANE (born 1934), first woman mayor of Chicago **3** 190-191

BYRNES, JAMES FRANCIS (1879-1972), American public official **3** 191-192

BYRON, GEORGE GORDON NOEL (6th Baron Byron; 1788-1824), English poet **3** 193-194

C

CABELL, JAMES BRANCH (1879-1958), American essayist and novelist **3** 195-196

CABET, ÉTIENNE (1788-1856), French political radical **3** 196

CABEZA DE VACA, ÁLVAR NÚÑEZ (circa 1490-circa 1557), Spanish explorer **3** 197

CABEZÓN, ANTONIO (1510-1566), Spanish composer **3** 197-198

CABLE, GEORGE WASHINGTON (1844-1925), American novelist **3** 198-199

CABOT, JOHN (flourished 1471-1498), Italian explorer in English service **3** 199-200

CABOT, RICHARD CLARKE (1868-1939), American physician **3** 200

CABOT, SEBASTIAN (circa 1482-1557), Italian-born explorer for England and Spain **3** 200-201

CABRAL, AMÍLCAR LOPES (1924-1973), father of modern African nationalism in Guinea-Bissau and the Cape Verde Islands **3** 202-203

CABRAL, PEDRO ÁLVARES (1467/68-1520), Portuguese navigator **3** 203-204

CABRILLO, JUAN RODRÍGUEZ (died 1543), Portuguese explorer for Spain **3** 204-205

CABRINI, ST. FRANCES XAVIER (1850-1917), Italian-born founder of the Missionary Sisters of the Sacred Heart **3** 205

CACCINI, GIULIO (circa 1545-1618), Italian singer and composer **3** 205-206

CADAMOSTO, ALVISE DA (circa 1428-1483), Italian explorer **3** 206-207

CAEDMON (650-c.680), English Christian poet **20** 66-67

CADILLAC, ANTOINE DE LAMOTHE (1658-1730), French explorer and colonial administrator **18** 69-71

CAESAR, (GAIUS) JULIUS (100-44 B.C.), Roman general and statesman **3** 207-210

CAESAR, SHIRLEY (born 1938), African American singer **3** 210-211

CAGE, JOHN (1912-1992), American composer **3** 211-214

CAGNEY, JAMES (1899-1986), American actor **21** 68-71

CAHAN, ABRAHAM (1860-1951), Lithuanian-American Jewish author **3** 214

CAILLIÉ, AUGUSTE RENÉ (1799-1838), French explorer **3** 214-215

CAIN, JAMES (1892-1977), American journalist and author **19** 50-52

CAJETAN, ST. (1480-1547), Italian reformer; cofounder of the Theatines **3** 215-216

CALAMITY JANE (Martha Jane Cannary; 1852-1903), American frontier woman **3** 216

Calculus (mathematics)
of probability
Bernoulli, Jakob **23** 37-39

CALDECOTT, RANDOLPH (1846-1886), English artist and illustrator **19** 52-55

CALDER, ALEXANDER (1898-1976), American sculptor **3** 216-218

CALDERA RODRÍGUEZ, RAFAEL (born 1916), president of Venezuela (1969-1974) **3** 218-219

CALDERÓN, ALBERTO P. (1920-1998), Hispanic American mathematician **3** 219-220

CALDERÓN, PEDRO (1600-1681), Spanish poet and playwright **3** 221-222

CALDERÓN FOURNIER, RAFAEL (born 1949), president of Costa Rica (1990-) **3** 222-223

CALDICOTT, HELEN BROINOWSKI (born 1938), Australian physician and activist **18** 71-73

CALDWELL, ERSKINE (1903-1987), American novelist **3** 223-224

CALDWELL, SARAH (born 1924), long-time artistic director, conductor, and founder of the Opera Company of Boston **3** 224-226

CALHOUN, JOHN CALDWELL (1782-1850), American statesman **3** 226-228

CALIGULA (12-41), Roman emperor 37-41 **3** 228-229

CALLAGHAN, EDWARD MORLEY (1903-1990), Canadian novelist **3** 229-230

CALLAGHAN, LEONARD JAMES (born 1912), Labor member of the British Parliament and prime minister, 1976-1979 **3** 230-231

CALLAHAN, DANIEL (born 1930), American philosopher who focused on biomedical ethics **3** 231-233

CALLAHAN, HARRY (1912-1999), American photographer **20** 67-69

CALLAS, MARIA (Cecilia Sophia Anna Maria Kalogeropoulos; 1923-1977), American opera soprano **18** 73-75

CALLEJAS ROMERO, RAFAEL LEONARDO (born 1943), president of Honduras (1990-) **3** 233-234

CALLENDER, CLIVE ORVILLE (born 1936), African American surgeon **18** 75-77

CALLES, PLUTARCO ELÍAS (1877-1945), Mexican revolutionary leader **3** 234-235

CALLIMACHUS (circa 310-240 B.C.), Greek poet **3** 235-236

CALLOWAY, CAB (1907-1994) American singer, songwriter, and bandleader **3** 236-238

CALVERT, CHARLES (3rd Baron Baltimore; 1637-1715), English proprietor of colonial Maryland **3** 238

CALVERT, GEORGE (1st Baron Baltimore; circa 1580-1632), English statesman, founder of Maryland colony **3** 238-239

CALVIN, JOHN (1509-1564), French Protestant reformer **3** 239-242

CALVIN, MELVIN (1911-1986), American chemist **3** 242-243

Calvinism (religion)
influence of
Cats, Jacob **23** 64-66

CALVINO, ITALO (1923-1985), Italian author **3** 243-244

CAMDESSUS, MICHEL (born 1933), French civil servant and managing director of the International Monetary Fund **3** 244-246

CAMERON, JULIA MARGARET (1815-1879), British photographer **20** 69-71

CAMERON, SIMON (1799-1889), American politician **3** 246-247

CAMOËNS, LUIS VAZ DE (1524-1580), Portuguese poet **3** 247-249

CAMPANELLA, ROY (1921-1993), American baseball player **19** 55-57

CAMPANELLA, TOMMASO (Giovanni Domenico Campanella; 1568-1639), Italian philosopher, political theorist, and poet **3** 249

CAMPBELL, ALEXANDER (1788-1866), Irish-born American clergyman **3** 249-250

CAMPBELL, AVRIL PHAEDRA DOUGLAS (KIM) (born 1947), Canada's first woman prime minister **3** 250-252

CAMPBELL, BEN NIGHTHORSE (born 1933), Native American United States senator from Colorado **3** 252-253

CAMPBELL, COLIN (Baron Clyde; 1792-1863), English army officer **20** 71-73

CAMPBELL, JOSEPH (1904-1987), American editor and popularizer of comparative mythology **3** 253-255

CAMPIN, ROBERT (circa 1375/80-1444), Flemish painter **3** 255

CAMPION, JANE (born 1954), Australian film director and screenwriter **23** 58-60

CAMPION, THOMAS (Thomas Campian; 1567-1620), English poet and musician **23** 60-62

CAMPOS, ROBERTO OLIVEIRA (1917-2001), Brazilian economist and diplomat **18** 77-79

CAMUS, ALBERT (1913-1960), French novelist, essayist, and playwright **3** 255-257

Canada (nation, North America)
exploration
Bernier, Joseph E. **23** 35-37
Tyrrell, Joseph Burr **23** 410-412

Canadian art
photography
Karsh, Yousuf **23** 184-187
Wall, Jeff **23** 434-436

Canadian literature
children's books
Johnson, Pauline **23** 170-172

Canadian music
Lombardo, Guy **23** 234-236
Peterson, Oscar Emanuel **23** 304-306

CANALETTO (1697-1768), Italian painter **3** 257-258

Cancer victims
Armstrong, Lance **23** 13-15

Cane (book)
Toomer, Jean **23** 408-410

CANISIUS, ST. PETER (1521-1597), Dutch Jesuit **3** 258

CANNING, GEORGE (1770-1827), English orator and statesman **3** 258-260

CANNON, ANNIE JUMP (1863-1941), American astronomer **3** 260-261

CANNON, JOSEPH GURNEY (1836-1926), American politican **3** 261-262

Canon law (Roman Catholic)
Benedict XIV **23** 32-35

CANOT, THEODORE (1804-1860), French-Italian adventurer and slave trader **3** 262-263

CANOVA, ANTONIO (1757-1822), Italian sculptor **3** 263-264

CANTOR, EDDIE (Isador Iskowitz; 1892-1964), American singer and comedian **3** 264-265

CANTOR, GEORG FERDINAND LUDWIG PHILIPP (1845-1918), German mathematician **3** 265-266

CANUTE I THE GREAT (c. 995-1035), Viking king of England and Denmark **3** 266-269

CANUTT, YAKIMA (Enos Edward Canutt; 1896-1986), American rodeo performer, actor, stuntman, and film director **21** 71-72

CAPA, ROBERT (Endre Friedmann; 1913-1954), Hungarian-American war photographer and photojournalist **3** 269-271

ČAPEK, KAREL (1890-1938), Czech novelist, playwright, and essayist **3** 271-272

CAPETILLO, LUISA (1879-1922), Puerto Rican labor leader and activist **20** 73-74

Capital punishment (criminology)
Romilly, Samuel **23** 348-351

CAPONE, AL (Alphonso Caponi, a.k.a. "Scarface;" 1899-1947), American gangster **3** 272-273

CAPOTE, TRUMAN (born Truman Streckfus Persons; 1924-1984), American author **3** 273-275

CAPP, AL (Alfred Gerald Capp; 1909-1979), American cartoonist and satirist **3** 275-276

CAPRA, FRANK (1897-1991), American film director **3** 276-278

CAPRIATI, JENNIFER (born 1976), American tennis player **3** 278-281

CAPTAIN JACK (Kientpoos; circa 1837-1873), American tribal leader **21** 72-74

CARACALLA (188-217), Roman emperor **3** 281-282

CARAGIALE, ION LUCA (1852-1912), Romanian author **23** 62-64

CARAVAGGIO (1573-1610), Italian painter **3** 282-284

CARAWAY, HATTIE WYATT (1878-1950), first woman elected to the United States Senate in her own right **3** 284-285

CARDANO, GERONIMO (1501-1576), Italian mathematician, astronomer, and physician **3** 285-286

CARDENAL, ERNESTO (born 1925), Nicaraguan priest, poet, and revolutionary **19** 57-59

CÁRDENAS, LÁZARO (1895-1970), Mexican revolutionary president 1934-1940 **3** 286-287

CÁRDENAS SOLORZANO, CUAUHTÉMOC (born 1934), Mexican politician **3** 287-288

CARDIN, PIERRE (born 1922), French fashion designer **18** 79-81

CARDOSO, FERNANDO HENRIQUE (born 1931), sociologist and president of Brazil **18** 81-83

CARDOZO, BENJAMIN NATHAN (1870-1938), American jurist and legal philosopher **3** 288-290

CARDUCCI, GIOSUÈ (1835-1907), Italian poet **3** 290-291

CAREW, ROD (born 1945), Panamanian baseball player **3** 291-292

CAREY, GEORGE LEONARD (born 1935), archbishop of Canterbury **3** 293-294

CAREY, HENRY CHARLES (1793-1879), American writer on economics **3** 294-295

CAREY, PETER (born 1943), Australian author **3** 295-297

CAREY, WILLIAM (1761-1834), English Baptist missionary **3** 297

CAREY THOMAS, MARTHA (1857-1935), American educator **3** 297-298

CARÍAS ANDINO, TIBURCIO (1876-1969), Honduran dictator (1932-1949) **3** 298-299

CARISSIMI, GIACOMO (1605-1674), Italian composer **3** 299-300

CARLETON, GUY (1st Baron Dorchester; 1724-1808), British general and statesman **3** 300-301

CARLIN, GEORGE (born 1937), American comedian **3** 301-303

CARLSON, CHESTER F. (1906-1968), American inventor of the process of xerography **3** 303-304

CARLYLE, THOMAS (1795-1881), Scottish essayist and historian **3** 304-305

Carmen (film)
Farrar, Geraldine **23** 106-108

CARMICHAEL, STOKELY (1941-1998), African American civil rights activist **3** 305-308

CARNAP, RUDOLF (1891-1970), German-American philosopher **3** 308-309

CARNEADES (circa 213-circa 128 B.C.), Greek philosopher **3** 309

CARNEGIE, ANDREW (1835-1919), American industrialist and philanthropist **3** 309-312

CARNEGIE, HATTIE (born Henrietta Kanengeiser; 1889-1956), American fashion designer **3** 313

Carnegie Hall (New York City)
Guastavino, Rafael **23** 132-134

CARNOT, LAZARE NICOLAS MARGUERITE (1753-1823), French engineer, general, and statesman **3** 313-314

CARNOT, NICHOLAS LÉONARD SADI (1796-1832), French physicist **3** 315

CARO, ANTHONY (born 1924), English sculptor **3** 316

CARO, JOSEPH BEN EPHRAIM (1488-1575), Jewish Talmudic scholar **3** 316-317

CAROTHERS, WALLACE HUME (1896-1937), American chemist **3** 317-318

CARPEAUX, JEAN BAPTISTE (1827-1875), French sculptor and painter **3** 318-319

CARR, EMILY (1871-1945), Canadian painter and writer **3** 319

CARR, EMMA PERRY (1880-1972), American chemist and educator **22** 89-91

CARR-SAUNDERS, SIR ALEXANDER MORRIS (1886-1966), English demographer and sociologist **3** 333-334

CARRANZA, VENUSTIANO (1859-1920), Mexican revolutionary, president 1914-1920 **3** 321-322

CARREL, ALEXIS (1873-1944), French-American surgeon **3** 322-323

CARRERA, JOSÉ MIGUEL (1785-1821), Chilean revolutionary **3** 323-324

CARRERA, JOSÉ RAFAEL (1814-1865), Guatemalan statesman, president 1851-1865 **3** 324-325

CARRERAS, JOSE MARIA (born 1946), Spanish opera singer **22** 91-93

CARRIER, WILLS (1876-1950), American inventer who was the ''father of air conditioning'' **3** 325-326

CARRINGTON, BARON (born 1919), British politician and secretary-general of the North Atlantic Treaty Organization (1984-1988) **3** 326-327

CARROLL, ANNA ELLA (1815-1893), American political writer and presidential aide **3** 327-331

CARROLL, JOHN (1735-1815), American Catholic bishop **3** 331-332

CARROLL, LEWIS (pseudonym of Charles Lutwidge Dodgson; 1832-1898), English cleric and author **3** 332-333

CARSON, BEN (born 1951), African American surgeon **18** 83-85

CARSON, CHRISTOPHER "KIT" (1809-1868), American frontiersman **3** 334-335

CARSON, JOHNNY (born 1925), American television host and comedian **3** 335-337

CARSON, RACHEL LOUISE (1907-1964), American biologist and author **3** 337-338

CARTER, ELLIOTT COOK, JR. (born 1908), American composer **3** 338-339

CARTER, HOWARD (1874-1939), English archaeologist and artist **20** 74-76

CARTER, JAMES EARL (''Jimmy'' Carter; born 1924), United States president (1977-1981) **3** 339-342

CARTIER, SIR GEORGE-ÉTIENNE (1814-1873), Canadian statesman **3** 342-343

CARTIER, JACQUES (1491-1557), French explorer and navigator **3** 343-344

CARTIER-BRESSON, HENRI (born 1908), French photographer and painter **19** 59-61

CARTWRIGHT, ALEXANDER (1820-1898), baseball pioneer **21** 74-77

CARTWRIGHT, PETER (1785-1872), American Methodist preacher **3** 344-345

CARUSO, ENRICO (1873-1921), Italian operatic tenor **3** 345

CARVER, GEORGE WASHINGTON (1864-1943), African American agricultural chemist **3** 346-347

CARVER, JONATHAN (1710-1780), American explorer and writer **3** 347-348

CASALS, PABLO (born Pau Carlos Salvador Casals y Defill; 1876-1973), Spanish cellist, conductor, and composer **3** 348-350

CASANOVA, GIACOMO JACOPO GIROLAMO, CHEVALIER DE SEINGLAT (1725-1798), Italian adventurer **3** 350-351

CASE, STEVE (born 1958), American businessman **19** 61-64

CASEMENT, ROGER (1864-1916), Irish diplomat and nationalist **20** 76-78

CASEY, WILLIAM J. (1913-1987), American director of the Central Intelligence Agency (CIA) **3** 351-353

CASH, JOHNNY (born 1932), American singer and songwriter **3** 353-355

CASH, W. J. (Joseph Wilbur Cash; 1900-1914), American journalist and author **22** 93-95

CASS, LEWIS (1782-1866), American statesman **3** 355-356

CASSATT, MARY (1845-1926), American painter **3** 356-357

CASSAVETES, JOHN (1929-1989), American filmmaker **22** 96-98

CASSIODORUS, FLAVIUS MAGNUS AURELIUS, SENATOR (circa 480-circa 575), Roman statesman and author **3** 357-358

CASSIRER, ERNST (1874-1945), German philosopher **3** 358-359

CASTELO BRANCO, HUMBERTO (1900-1967), Brazilian general, president 1964-1966 **3** 359-360

CASTIGLIONE, BALDASSARE (1478-1529), Italian author and diplomat **3** 360-361

CASTILLA, RAMÓN (1797-1867), Peruvian military leader and president **3** 361

CASTLE, IRENE and VERNON (1910-1918), ballroom dancers **3** 361-363

CASTLEREAGH, VISCOUNT (Robert Stewart; 1769-1822), British statesman **3** 363-364

CASTRO ALVES, ANTÔNIO DE (1847-1871), Brazilian poet **3** 364-365

CASTRO RUZ, FIDEL (born 1926), Cuban prime minister **3** 365-368

CATHER, WILLA SIBERT (1873-1947), American writer **3** 368-369

CATHERINE OF ARAGON (1485-1536), Spanish princess, first queen consort of Henry VIII of England **18** 85-88

CATHERINE OF SIENA, ST. (1347-1380), Italian mystic **3** 369-370

CATHERINE THE GREAT (1729-1796), Russian empress 1762-1796 **3** 370-372

Catholic Church
see Roman Catholic Church

CATILINE (Lucius Sergius Catilina; circa 108-62 B.C.), Roman politician and revolutionary **3** 372-373

CATLIN, GEORGE (1796-1872), American painter **3** 373-374

CATO, MARCUS PORCIUS, THE ELDER (234-149 B.C.), Roman soldier, statesman, and historian **3** 375

CATO THE YOUNGER (Marcus Porcius Cato Uticensis; 95-46 B.C.), Roman politician **3** 374-375

CATS, JACOB (1577-1660), Dutch poet, moralist, and statesman **23** 64-66

CATT, CARRIE CHAPMAN (1859-1947), American reformer **3** 375-376

CATTELL, JAMES McKEEN (1860-1944), American psychologist and editor **3** 376-377

CATULLUS, GAIUS VALERIUS (circa 84-circa 54 B.C.), Roman poet **3** 377-378

CAUCHY, AUGUSTIN LOUIS (1789-1857), French mathematician **3** 378-380

CAVAFY, CONSTANTINE P. (Konstantinos P. Kabaphēs; 1863-1933), first modernist Greek poet **3** 381-382

CAVALCANTI, GUIDO (circa 1255-1300), Italian poet **3** 382

CAVALLI, PIETRO FRANCESCO (1602-1676), Italian composer **3** 382-383

CAVENDISH, HENRY (1731-1810), English physicist and chemist **3** 383-384

CAVENDISH, MARGARET LUCAS (1623-1673), English natural philosopher **23** 66-67

CAVOUR, CONTE DI (Camillo Benso; 1810-1861), Italian statesman **3** 385-386

CAXIAS, DUQUE DE (Luiz Alves de Lima e Silva; 1803-1880), Brazilian general and statesman **3** 386

CAXTON, WILLIAM (1422-1491), English printer **3** 386-387

CEAUSESCU, NICOLAE (1918-1989), Romanian statesman **3** 387-388

CECH, THOMAS ROBERT (born 1947), American biochemist **23** 68-70
Altman, Sidney **23** 9-11

CECIL OF CHELWOOD, VISCOUNT (Edgar Algernon Robert Cecil; 1864-1958), English statesman **3** 388-389

CELA Y TRULOCK, CAMILO JOSÉ (1916-2002), Spanish author **3** 389-390

CÉLINE, LOUIS FERDINAND (pen name of Ferdinand Destouches; 1894-1961), French novelist **3** 390-391

CELLINI, BENVENUTO (1500-1571), Italian goldsmith and sculptor **3** 391-392

CELSIUS, ANDERS (1701-1744), Swedish astronomer **3** 392

CELSUS, AULUS CORNELIUS (circa 25 B.C.-A.D. 45?), Roman medical author **3** 393

CEREZO AREVALO, MARCO VINICIO (born 1942), president of Guatemala (1986-1991) **3** 393-395

CERF, BENNETT (1898-1971), American editor, publisher, author, and television performer **22** 98-100
Liveright, Horace B. **23** 229-231

CERNAN, GENE (Eugene Andrew Cernan; born 1934), American astronaut **22** 100-102

CERVANTES, MIGUEL DE SAAVEDRA (1547-1616), Spanish novelist **3** 395-398

CÉSPEDES, CARLOS MANUEL DE (1819-1874), Cuban lawyer and revolutionary **3** 398-399

CESTI, PIETRO (Marc'Antonio Cesti; 1623-1669), Italian composer **3** 399-400

CETSHWAYO (Cetewayo; circa 1826-1884), king of Zululand 1873-1879 **3** 400

CÉZANNE, PAUL (1839-1906), French painter **3** 400-402

CHADLI BENJEDID (born 1929), president of the Algerian Republic (1979-) **3** 402-404

CHADWICK, FLORENCE (1918-1995), American swimmer **19** 64-66

CHADWICK, SIR EDWIN (1800-1890), English utilitarian reformer **3** 404-405

CHADWICK, SIR JAMES (1891-1974), English physicist **3** 405-406

CHADWICK, LYNN RUSSELL (1914-2003), English sculptor **18** 88-90

CHAGALL, MARC (1887-1985), Russian painter **3** 406-407

CHAI LING (born 1966), Chinese student protest leader **19** 67-68

CHAIN, ERNST BORIS (1906-1979), German-born English biochemist **3** 407-408

Chalcedon, Council of (451)
Vigilius **23** 427-429

CHALMERS, THOMAS (1780-1847), Scottish reformer and theologian **3** 408-409

CHAMBERLAIN, ARTHUR NEVILLE (1869-1940), English statesman **3** 409-411

CHAMBERLAIN, HOUSTON STEWART (1855-1927), English-born German writer **3** 411

CHAMBERLAIN, JOSEPH (1836-1914), English politician **3** 411-413

CHAMBERLAIN, WILT (born 1936), American basketball player **3** 413-415

CHAMBERLIN, THOMAS CHROWDER (1843-1928), American geologist **3** 415-416

CHAMBERS, WHITTAKER (Jay Vivian; 1901-1961), magazine editor who helped organize a Communist spy ring in the United States government **3** 416-417

CHAMORRO, VIOLETA BARRIOS DE (born 1930), newspaper magnate, publicist, and first woman president of Nicaragua (1990) **3** 417-419

CHAMPLAIN, SAMUEL DE (circa 1570-1635), French geographer and explorer **3** 419-421

CHAMPOLLION, JEAN FRANÇOIS (1790-1832), French Egyptologist **3** 421

CHANCELLOR, RICHARD (died 1556), English navigator **3** 422

CHANDLER, ALFRED DU PONT, JR. (born 1918), American historian of American business **3** 422-423

CHANDLER, RAYMOND, JR. (1888-1959), American author of crime fiction **3** 423-425

CHANDLER, ZACHARIAH (1813-1879), American politician **3** 425-426

CHANDRAGUPTA MAURYA (died circa 298 B.C.), emperor of India 322?-298 **3** 426

CHANDRASEKHAR, SUBRAHMANYAN (1910-1995), Indian-born American physicist **3** 426-429

CHANEL, COCO (born Gabrielle Chanel; 1882-1971), French fashion designer **3** 429

CHANEY, LON (Alonzo Chaney; 1883-1930), American actor **19** 68-70

CHANG CHIEN (1853-1926), Chinese industrialist and social reformer **3** 429-430

CHANG CHIH-TUNG (1837-1909), Chinese official and reformer **3** 430-431

CHANG CHÜ-CHENG (1525-1582), Chinese statesman **3** 431-432

CHANG CHÜEH (died 184), Chinese religious and revolutionary leader **3** 432-433

CHANG HSÜEH-CH'ENG (1738-1801), Chinese scholar and historian **3** 433

CHANG PO-GO (died 846), Korean adventurer and merchant prince **3** 433-434

CHANG TSO-LIN (1873-1928), Chinese warlord **3** 434-435

CHANNING, EDWARD (1856-1931), American historian **3** 435

CHANNING, WILLIAM ELLERY (1780-1842), Unitarian minister and theologian **3** 435-436

CHAO MENG-FU (1254-1322), Chinese painter **3** 436-437

CHAPIN, F(RANCIS) STUART (1888-1974), American sociologist **3** 437-438

CHAPLIN, CHARLES SPENCER (1889-1977), American film actor, director, and writer **3** 438-440

CHAPMAN, GEORGE (1559/60-1634), English poet, dramatist, and translator **3** 440-441

CHAPMAN, JOHN (Johnny Appleseed; c. 1775-1847), American horticulturist and missionary **21** 77-78

CHAPMAN, SYDNEY (1888-1970), English geophysicist **3** 441

CHARCOT, JEAN MARTIN (1825-1893), French psychiatrist **3** 442

CHARDIN, JEAN BAPTISTE SIMÉON (1699-1779), French painter **3** 442-443

CHARGAFF, ERWIN (1905-2002), American biochemist who worked with DNA **3** 444-445

CHARLEMAGNE (742-814), king of the Franks, 768-814, and emperor of the West, 800-814 **3** 445-447

CHARLES (born 1948), Prince of Wales and heir apparent to the British throne **3** 448-450

CHARLES I (1600-1649), king of England 1625-1649 **3** 450-452

CHARLES II (1630-1685), king of England, Scotland, and Ireland 1660-1685 **3** 452-454

CHARLES II (1661-1700), king of Spain 1665-1700 **3** 454

CHARLES III (1716-1788), king of Spain 1759-1788 **3** 454-455

CHARLES IV (1316-1378), Holy Roman emperor 1346-1378 **3** 455-456

CHARLES IV (1748-1819), king of Spain 1788-1808 **3** 456-457

CHARLES V (1337-1380), king of France 1364-1380 **3** 459-460

CHARLES V (1500-1558), Holy Roman emperor 1519-1556 **3** 457-459

CHARLES VI (1368-1422), king of France 1380-1422 **3** 460-461

CHARLES VII (1403-1461), king of France 1422-1461 **3** 461-462

CHARLES VIII (1470-1498), king of France 1483-1498 **3** 462-463

CHARLES X (1757-1836), king of France 1824-1830 **3** 463-464

CHARLES XII (1682-1718), king of Sweden 1697-1718 **3** 464-466

CHARLES XIV JOHN (1763-1844), king of Sweden 1818-1844 **2** 205-206

CHARLES, RAY (Robinson; born 1932), American jazz musician–singer, pianist, and composer **3** 469-470

CHARLES ALBERT (1798-1849), king of Sardinia 1831-1849 **3** 466

CHARLES EDWARD LOUIS PHILIP CASIMIR STUART (1720-1788), Scottish claimant to English and Scottish thrones **3** 466-467

CHARLES THE BOLD (1433-1477), duke of Burgundy 1467-1477 **3** 467-469

CHARNISAY, CHARLES DE MENOU (Seigneur d'Aulnay; circa 1604-1650), French governor of Acadia **3** 470-471

CHARONTON, ENGUERRAND (circa 1410/15-after 1466), French painter **3** 471

CHARPENTIER, MARC ANTOINE (1634-1704), French composer **3** 471-472

CHARRON, PIERRE (1541-1603), French philosopher and theologian **3** 472

CHASE, PHILANDER (1775-1852), American Episcopalian bishop and missionary **3** 472-473

CHASE, SALMON PORTLAND (1808-1873), American statesman and jurist **3** 473-475

CHASE, SAMUEL (1741-1811), American politician and jurist **3** 475-476

CHASE, WILLIAM MERRITT (1849-1916), American painter **3** 476-477

CHATEAUBRIAND, VICOMTE DE (1768-1848), French author **3** 477-479

CHATELET, GABRIELLE-EMILIE (1706-1749), French physicist and chemist **22** 102-103

CHATICHAI CHOONHAVAN (1922-1998), prime minister of Thailand (1988-1990) **3** 479-480

CHATTERJI, BANKIMCHANDRA (1838-1894), Bengali novelist **3** 480-481

CHATTERTON, THOMAS (1752-1770), English poet **3** 481-482

CHAUCER, GEOFFREY (circa 1345-1400), English poet **3** 482-485

CHAUNCY, CHARLES (1705-1787), American Calvinist clergyman and theologian **3** 485-486

CHÁVEZ, CARLOS (1899-1978), Mexican conductor and composer **3** 486

CHAVEZ, CESAR (1927-1993), American labor leader **3** 486-487

CHÁVEZ, DENNIS (1888-1962), Hispanic American politician **3** 488-489

CHAVEZ, LINDA (born 1947), Hispanic American civil rights activists **3** 489-491

CHAVIS, BENJAMIN (born 1948), African American religious leader, civil rights activist, labor organizer, and author **3** 491-493

CHEEVER, JOHN (1912-1982), American short-story writer **3** 493-494

CHEKHOV, ANTON PAVLOVICH (1860-1904), Russian author **3** 494-497

CHELMSFORD, 1st VISCOUNT (Frederic John Napier Thesigner Chelmsford; 1868-1933), English statesman **3** 497

Chemistry (science)
chemical reactions
Fukui, Kenichi **23** 111-112
Lee, Yuan Tseh **23** 218-220

CH'EN TU-HSIU (1879-1942), Chinese statesman and editor **3** 501-502

CHENEY, RICHARD B(RUCE) (born 1941), U.S. secretary of defense under George Bush **3** 497-499

CHENG HO (1371-circa 1433), Chinese admiral **3** 500

CHÉNIER, ANDRÉ MARIE (1762-1794), French poet **3** 500-501

CHERENKOV, PAVEL ALEKSEEVICH (1904-1990), Russian physicist **3** 502-503

CHERNENKO, KONSTANTIN USTINOVICH (1911-1985), the Soviet Union general secretary from February 1984 to March 1985 **3** 503-504

CHERNYSHEVSKY, NIKOLAI GAVRILOVICH (1828-1889), Russian journalist, critic, and social theorist **3** 504-505

Cherokee Indians (North America)
raids and wars
Ward, Nancy **23** 436-438

CHERUBINI, LUIGI CARLO ZANOBI SALVATORE MARIA (1760-1842), Italian-born French composer **3** 505-506

CHESNUT, MARY BOYKIN (1823-1886), Civil War diarist **3** 506-508

CHESNUTT, CHARLES WADDELL (1858-1932), African American author and lawyer **20** 78-82

CHESTERTON, GILBERT KEITH (1874-1936), English author and artist **3** 508-509

CHEVROLET, LOUIS (1878-1941), auto racer and entrepreneur **20** 82-84

CH'I PAI-SHIH (1863-1957), Chinese painter and poet **3** 526-527

CHIA SSU-TAO (1213-1275), Chinese statesman **3** 514-515

CHIANG CHING-KUO (1910-1988), chairman of the Nationalist party and president of the Republic of China in Taiwan (1978-1988) **3** 509-510

CHIANG KAI-SHEK (1887-1975), Chinese nationalist leader and president **3** 510-513

CHIARI, ROBERTO (born 1905), president of Panama (1960-1964) **3** 513-514

Chicago (city, Illinois)
public library
Rollins, Charlemae Hill **23** 346-348

CHICAGO, JUDY (Judith Cohen; born 1939), American artist and activist **3** 515-516

CHICHERIN, GEORGI VASILYEVICH (1872-1936), Russian statesman **3** 516-517

CHIEN-LUNG (Hung-li; 1711-1799), Chinese emperor (1735-1799) **21** 78-79

CHIEPE, GAOSITWE KEAGAKWA TIBE (born 1926), intellectual, educator, diplomat, politician, and cabinet minister of external affairs of Botswana **3** 517

CHIFLEY, JOSEPH BENEDICT (1885-1951), Australian statesman **3** 518

CHIH-I (Chih-k'ai, 538-597), Chinese Buddhist monk **3** 518-519

CHIKAMATSU, MONZAEMON (1653-1725), Japanese playwright **23** 70-72

Chikamatsu Story (film) Mizoguchi, Kenji **23** 248-250

CHILD, JULIA McWILLIAMS (born 1912), chef, author, and television personality **3** 519-520

CHILD, LYDIA MARIA FRANCIS (1802-1880), American author and abolitionist **3** 520-521

CHILDE, VERE GORDON (1892-1957), Australian prehistorian and archeologist **3** 521-522

Children's literature *see* Literature for children

CHILDRESS, ALICE (1920-1994), African American dramatist, author, and poet **3** 522-524

CH'IN KUEI (1090-1155), Chinese official **3** 524-525

Chinatown (film) Polanski, Roman **23** 310-312

CHINN, MAY EDWARD (1896-1980), African American physician **3** 525-526

CHIPPENDALE, THOMAS (1718-1779), English cabinetmaker **4** 1-2

CHIRAC, JACQUES (born 1932), French prime minister **4** 2-3

CHIRICO, GIORGIO DE (1888-1978), Italian painter **4** 4

CHISHOLM, CAROLINE (1808-1877), British author and philantropist **4** 4- 7

CHISHOLM, SHIRLEY ANITA ST. HILL (born 1924), first African American woman to serve in the United States Congress **4** 7-9

CHISSANO, JOAQUIM ALBERTO (born 1939), a leader of Mozambique's war for independence and later president of Mozambique (1986-) **4** 9-11

CHISUM, JOHN SIMPSON (1824-1884), American rancher **4** 11

CH'I-YING (circa 1786-1858), Chinese statesman and diplomat **4** 12

CHMIELNICKI, BOGDAN (1595-1657), Cossack leader of Ukrainian revolt **4** 12-13

CHOATE, JOSEPH HODGES (1832-1917), American lawyer and diplomat **22** 103-106

CHOATE, RUFUS (1799-1859), American lawyer and statesman **22** 106-107

CH'OE CH'UNG-HON (1149-1219), Korean general **4** 13

CHOMSKY, NOAM AVRAM (born 1928), American linguist and philosopher **4** 13-15

CHONG CHUNG-BU (1106-1179), Korean general **4** 15

CHONGJO (1752-1800), king of Korea **4** 15-16

CHOPIN, FRÉDÉRIC FRANÇOIS (1810-1849), Polish-French composer and pianist **4** 16-18

CHOPIN, KATHERINE ("Kate"; born Katherine O'Flaherty; 1851-1904), American writer, poet, and essayist **4** 18-20

CHOPRA, DEEPAK (born 1946), Indian physician, author, and educator **20** 84-86

CHOU EN-LAI (1898-1976), Chinese Communist premier **4** 20-22

CHOU KUNG (flourished circa 1116 B.C.), Chinese statesman **4** 22-23

CHRESTIEN DE TROYES (flourished 12th century), French poet **4** 23-24

CHRÉTIEN, JOSEPH-JACQUES-JEAN "JEAN" (born 1934), French Canadian politician and Canada's 20th prime minister **4** 24-25

CHRISTIAN IV (1577-1648), king of Denmark and Norway 1588-1648 **20** 86-89

Christianity (religion) expansion (Roman Empire) Clement I **23** 78-81 foundation and doctrine Abraham **23** 1-3

CHRISTIE, AGATHA (Agatha Mary Clarissa Miller; 1890-1976), best selling mystery author **4** 25-26

CHRISTINA OF SWEDEN (1626-1689), queen of Sweden 1632-1654 **4** 26-29

CHRISTINE DE PISAN (1364/65-circa 1430), French author **4** 29-30

CHRISTO (Christo Vladimiroff Javacheff; born 1935), Bulgarian-born sculptor

noted for large-scale environmental artworks **4** 30-31

CHRISTOPHE, HENRI (1767-1820), Haitian patriot and king **4** 32

CHRISTOPHER, WARREN MINOR (born 1925), United States secretary of state **4** 32-33

CHRISTUS, PETRUS (circa 1410-1472/73), Flemish painter **4** 33-34

CHRISTY, EDWIN P. (1815-1862), American minstrel **4** 34-35

CHRYSIPPUS (circa 280-circa 206 B.C.), Greek Stoic philosopher **4** 35-36

CHRYSLER, WALTER PERCY (1875-1940), American manufacturer **4** 36-37

CHU YUAN-CHANG (Hongwu; T'ai Tsu; Kao-ti; 1328-1398), Chinese emperor (1368-1398) **21** 79-81

CHU, PAUL CHING-WU (born 1941), Chinese-American experimentalist in solid-state physics **4** 37-39

CHU HSI (Chu Fu-tzu; 1130-1200), Chinese scholar and philosopher **4** 40-43

CHU TEH (1886-1976), Chinese Communist military leader **4** 54-55

CHULALONGKORN (Rama V; 1853-1910), king of Thailand 1868-1910 **4** 43-45

CHUN DOO HWAN (born 1931), army general turned politician and president of the Republic of Korea (South Korea); 1981-1988 **4** 45-47

CHUNG, CONNIE (born 1946), American correspondent and resporter **4** 47-48

CHUNG, JU YUNG (1915-2001), Korean businessman **23** 72-74

CHUNG, KYUNG WHA (born 1948), Korean violinist **23** 74-76

CHUNG-SHU, TUNG (circa 179-104 B.C.), Chinese man of letters **4** 48-49

CHURCH, FREDERICK EDWIN (1826-1900), American painter **4** 49-50

Church law *see* Canon law

Church of Rome *see* Roman Catholic Church

CHURCHILL, WINSTON (1871-1947), American novelist **4** 50-51

CHURCHILL, SIR WINSTON LEONARD SPENCER (1874-1965), English statesman **4** 51-53

CHURRIGUERA, JOSÉ BENITO DE (1665-1725), Spanish architect and sculptor **4** 53-54

CICERO, MARCUS TULLIUS (106-43 B.C.), Roman orator and writer **4** 55-58

CID, THE (Cid Campeador; 1043-1099), Spanish medieval warrior **4** 58-59

CILLER, TANSU (born 1946), prime minister of Turkey (1993-) **4** 59-60

CIMABUE (flourished late 13th century), Italian painter **4** 60-61

CIMAROSA, DOMENICO (1749-1801), Italian opera composer **4** 61-62

CINQUE, JOSEPH (circa 1813-circa 1879), West African slave leader **4** 62

CISNEROS, HENRY G. (born 1947), first Hispanic mayor in Texas **4** 62-64

CISNEROS, SANDRA (born 1954), Hispanic American short story writer and poet **4** 64-65

CISSÉ, SOULEYMANE (born 1940), Malian filmmaker **4** 65-66

CITROËN, ANDRÉ-GUSTAVE (1878-1935), French automobile manufacturer **4** 66-68

Civil rights movement (United States) crises and protests
        Height, Dorothy Irene **23** 139-141

CLAIBORNE, LIZ (Elizabeth Claiborne Ortenberg; born 1929), American businesswoman and clothing designer **4** 68-69

CLANCY, TOM (born 1947), American author **4** 70-71

CLAPHAM, SIR JOHN HAROLD (1873-1946), English economic historian **4** 71

CLAPP, MARGARET ANTOINETTE (1910-1974), American author, educator, and president of Wellesley College (1949-1966) **4** 71-72

CLAPPERTON, HUGH (1788-1827), Scottish explorer of Africa **4** 72-73

CLAPTON, ERIC (born 1945), English guitarist, singer, and songwriter **18** 90-92

CLARENDON, 1ST EARL OF (Edward Hyde; 1609-1674), English statesman and historian **4** 73-75

CLARE OF ASSISI, SAINT (Chiara Offreduccio di Favorrone; 1194-1253), Italian relisious leader **23** 76-78

CLARK, GEORGE ROGERS (1752-1818), American Revolutionary War soldier **4** 75-76

CLARK, JOHN BATES (1847-1938), American economist **4** 76-77

CLARK, JOHN MAURICE (1884-1963), American economist **4** 77-78

CLARK, KENNETH B. (born 1914), American social psychologist **4** 78-79

CLARK, KENNETH M. (Lord; 1903-1983), English art historian **4** 79-80

CLARK, MARK WAYNE (1896-1984), American general **4** 80-81

CLARK, TOM CAMPBELL (1899-1977), President Harry S. Truman's attorney general and Supreme Court justice **4** 81-82

CLARK, WILLIAM (1770-1838), American explorer and soldier **4** 82-83

CLARK, WILLIAM ANDREWS (1839-1925), American copper entrepreneur and politician **4** 83-85

CLARKE, ARTHUR CHARLES (born 1917), English author **18** 92-94

CLARKE, KENNETH HARRY (born 1940), Conservative politician and Great Britain's chancellor of the exchequer (1993-) **4** 85-87

CLARKE, MARCUS ANDREW HISLOP (1846-1881), English-born Australian journalist and author **4** 87-88

CLARKE, SAMUEL (1675-1729), English theologian and philosopher **4** 88

Classicism (music)
        Uchida, Mitsuko **23** 413-415

CLAUDE LORRAIN (1600-1682), French painter, draftsman, and etcher **4** 89-90

CLAUDEL, CAMILLE (1864-1943), French sculptor **22** 107-110

CLAUDEL, PAUL LOUIS CHARLES (1868-1955), French author and diplomat **4** 90-91

CLAUDIUS GERMANICUS, TIBERIUS (Claudius I; 10 B.C. -A.D. 54), emperor of Rome 41-54 **4** 91-92

CLAUSEWITZ, KARL VON (Karl Philipp Gottlieb von Clausewitz; 1780-1831), Prussian military strategist **20** 89-91

CLAUSIUS, RUDOLF JULIUS EMANUEL (1822-1888), German physicist **4** 92-94

CLAVER, ST. PETER (1580-1654), Spanish Jesuit missionary **4** 94

CLAY, HENRY (1777-1852), American lawyer and statesman **4** 94-96

CLAYTON, JOHN MIDDLETON (1796-1856), American lawyer and statesman **4** 96-97

CLEARY, BEVERLY (nee Beverly Bunn; born 1916), American author of children's books **22** 110-112

CLEAVER, LEROY ELDRIDGE (1935-1998), American writer and Black Panther leader **4** 97-98

CLEISTHENES (flourished 6th century B.C.), Athenian statesman **4** 98-99

CLEMENCEAU, GEORGES (1841-1929), French statesman **4** 99-101

CLEMENS NON PAPA, JACOBUS (circa 1510-circa 1556), Flemish composer **4** 101

CLEMENT I (died c. 100 A.D.), Bishop of Rome, pope **23** 78-81

CLEMENT V (1264-1314), pope 1304-1314 **4** 101-102

CLEMENT VII (Giulia de Medici; 1478-1534), pope (1523-1534) **21** 81-83

CLEMENT OF ALEXANDRIA (circa 150-circa 215), Christian theologian **4** 102-103

CLEMENTE, ROBERTO (1934-1972), Hispanic American baseball player **19** 70-72

CLEOMENES I (flourished circa 520-490 B.C.), Spartan king **4** 103

CLEOMENES III (circa 260-219 B.C.), king of Sparta 235-219 **4** 103-104

CLEON (circa 475-422 B.C.), Athenian political leader **4** 104-105

CLEOPATRA (69-30 B.C.), queen of Egypt **4** 105-106

CLEVELAND, JAMES (1932-1991), African American singer, songwriter, and pianist **4** 106-108

CLEVELAND, STEPHEN GROVER (1837-1908), American statesman, twice president **4** 108-110

CLINE, PATSY (born Virginia Patterson Hensley; 1932-1963), American singer **4** 110-112

CLINTON, DeWITT (1769-1828), American lawyer and statesman **4** 112-113

CLINTON, GEORGE (1739-1812), American patriot and statesman **4** 113-114

CLINTON, SIR HENRY (1738?-1795), British commander in chief during the American Revolution **4** 114-115

CLINTON, HILLARY RODHAM (born 1947), American politician and first lady **4** 115-117

CLINTON, WILLIAM JEFFERSON ("Bill" Clinton; born 1946), 42nd president of the United States **4** 117-119

CLIVE, ROBERT (Baron Clive of Plassey; 1725-1774), English soldier and statesman **4** 119-120

CLODION (1738-1814), French sculptor **4** 121

CLODIUS PULCHER, PUBLIUS (died 52 B.C.), Roman politician **4** 121-122

Clothing industry
Herrera, Carolina **23** 141-143

CLOUET, FRANÇOIS (circa 1516-circa 1572), French portrait painter **4** 122-123

CLOUET, JEAN (circa 1485-circa 1541), French portrait painter **4** 122-123

CLOUGH, ARTHUR HUGH (1819-1861), English poet **4** 123-124

CLOVIS I (465-511), Frankish king **4** 124

COBB, JEWEL PLUMMER (born 1924), African American scientist and activist **22** 112-114

COBB, TYRUS RAYMOND (1886-1961), baseball player **4** 124-126

COBBETT, WILLIAM (1763-1835), English journalist and politician **4** 126-127

COBDEN, RICHARD (1804-1865), English politician **4** 127-128

COCHISE (circa 1825-1874), American Chiricahua Apache Indian chief **4** 128

COCHRAN, JACQUELINE (Jackie Cochran; 1910-1980), American aviator and businesswoman **18** 94-96

COCHRAN, JOHNNIE (born 1937), African American lawyer **4** 128-131

COCHRANE, THOMAS (Earl of Dundonald; 1775-1860), British naval officer **20** 91-93

COCKCROFT, JOHN DOUGLAS (1897-1967), English physicist **4** 131-132

COCTEAU, JEAN (1889-1963), French writer **4** 132-133

COE, SEBASTIAN (born 1956), English track athlete **20** 93-95

COEN, JAN PIETERSZOON (circa 1586-1629), Dutch governor general of Batavia **4** 133

COETZEE, J(OHN) M. (born 1940), white South African novelist **4** 133-135

COFFIN, LEVI (1789-1877), American antislavery reformer **4** 135

COFFIN, WILLIAM SLOANE, JR. (born 1924), Yale University chaplain who spoke out against the Vietnam War **4** 135-137

COHAN, GEORGE MICHAEL (1878-1942), American actor and playwright **4** 137-138

COHEN, HERMANN (1842-1918), Jewish-German philosopher **4** 138-139

COHEN, MORRIS RAPHAEL (1880-1947), American philosopher and teacher **4** 139-140

COHEN, WILLIAM S. (born 1940), American secretary of defense **18** 96-98

COHN, FERDINAND (1829-1898), German botanist **20** 95-97

COHN-BENDIT, DANIEL (born 1946), led "new left" student protests in France in 1968 **4** 140-141

COKE, SIR EDWARD (1552-1634), English jurist and parliamentarian **4** 141-142

COLBERT, JEAN BAPTISTE (1619-1683), French statesman **4** 142-143

COLBY, WILLIAM E. (1920-1996), American director of the Central Intelligence Agency (CIA) **4** 143-145

Cold War (international politics) propogandists
Sampson, Edith **23** 356-358

COLDEN, CADWALLADER (1688-1776), American botanist and politician **4** 145-146

COLE, GEORGE DOUGLAS HOWARD (1889-1959), English historian and economist **4** 146-147

COLE, JOHNNETTA (born 1936), African American scholar and educator **4** 147-149

COLE, NAT (a.k.a. Nat "King" Cole, born Nathaniel Adams Coles; 1919-1965), American jazz musician **4** 149-151

COLE, THOMAS (1801-1848), American painter **4** 151-152

COLEMAN, BESSIE (1892-1926), first African American to earn an international pilot's license **4** 152-154

COLERIDGE, SAMUEL TAYLOR (1772-1834), English poet and critic **4** 154-156

COLES, ROBERT MARTIN (born 1929), American social psychiatrist, social critic, and humanist **4** 156-157

COLET, JOHN (circa 1446-1519), English theologian **4** 157-158

COLETTE, SIDONIE GABRIELLE (1873-1954), French author **4** 158-159

COLIGNY, GASPARD DE (1519-1572), French admiral and statesman **4** 159-160

College Entrance Examination Board (established 1906)
Scott, Charlotte Angas **23** 364-367

COLLIER, JOHN (1884-1968), American proponent of Native American culture **4** 160-162

COLLINGWOOD, ROBIN GEORGE (1889-1943), English historian and philosopher **4** 162

COLLINS, EDWARD KNIGHT (1802-1878), American businessman and shipowner **4** 162-163

COLLINS, EILEEN (born 1956), American astronaut **4** 163-165

COLLINS, MARVA (born Marva Deloise Nettles; born 1936), African American educator **4** 165-167

COLLINS, MICHAEL (1890-1922), Irish revolutionary leader and soldier **4** 167-168

COLLINS, WILLIAM (1721-1759), English lyric poet **4** 168-169

COLLINS, WILLIAM WILKIE (1824-1889), English novelist **4** 169-170

COLLOR DE MELLO, FERNANDO (born 1949), businessman who became president of Brazil in 1990 **4** 170-172

Colombian art
Vázquez Arce Y Ceballos, Gregorio **23** 423-425

Color vision (physiology)
Ladd-Franklin, Christine **23** 202-204

COLT, SAMUEL (1814-1862), American inventor and manufacturer **4** 172-173

COLTRANE, JOHN (1926-1967), African American jazz saxophonist **4** 173-174

COLUM, PADRAIC (1881-1972), Irish-American poet and playwright **4** 174-175

COLUMBA, ST. (circa 521-597), Irish monk and missionary **4** 175-176

COLUMBAN, ST. (circa 543-615), Irish missionary **4** 176

COLUMBUS, CHRISTOPHER (1451-1506), Italian navigator, discoverer of America **4** 176-179

COLWELL, RITA R. (born 1934), American marine microbiologist **4** 179-180

Comanche Indians (North America)
Sanapia **23** 358-360

COMANECI, NADIA (Nadia Conner; born 1961), Romanian gymnast **18** 98-100

COMENIUS, JOHN AMOS (1592-1670), Moravian theologian and educational reformer **4** 180-181

COMINES, PHILIPPE DE (circa 1445-1511), French chronicler **4** 181

COMMAGER, HENRY STEELE (1902-1998), American historian, textbook author, and editor **4** 181-183

COMMONER, BARRY (born 1917), American biologist and environmental activist **4** 183-185

COMMONS, JOHN ROGERS (1862-1945), American historian **4** 185

COMNENA, ANNA (1083-1148), Byzantine princess and historian **4** 185-186

COMPTON, ARTHUR HOLLY (1892-1962), American physicist **4** 186-188

COMSTOCK, ANNA BOTSFORD (1854-1930), American artist and natural science educator **20** 97-99

COMSTOCK, ANTHONY (1844-1915), American antivice crusader **4** 188-189

COMSTOCK, HENRY TOMPKINS PAIGE (1820-1870), American gold prospector **4** 189

COMTE, AUGUSTE (1798-1857), French philosopher **4** 189-191

CONABLE, BARBER B., JR. (born 1922), head of the World Bank (1986-1991) **4** 191-192

CONANT, JAMES BRYANT (1893-1978), American chemist and educator **4** 192-193

Concerto (musical form)
for violin
Chung, Kyung Wha **23** 74-76

CONDÉ, PRINCE DE (Louis II de Bourbon 1621-1686), French general **4** 193-194

CONDILLAC, ÉTIENNE BONNOT DE (1715-1780), French philosopher and educator **4** 194-195

CONDORCET, MARQUIS DE (Marie Jean Antoine Nicolas Caritat; 1743-1794), French philosopher and mathematician **4** 195-196

CONE, JAMES HALL (born 1938), American theologian **4** 196-197

CONFUCIUS (551-479 B.C.), Chinese teacher and philosopher **4** 197-200

Congressional Medal of Honor (United States)
Walker, Mary Edwards **23** 432-434

Congressmen
see Statesmen, American–legislative

CONGREVE, WILLIAM (1670-1729), English dramatist **4** 200-201

CONKLING, ROSCOE (1829-1888), American politician **4** 201-202

CONNALLY, JOHN BOWDEN, JR. (born 1917), Texas governor, political

adviser, and confidant to presidents **4** 202-204

CONNERY, SEAN (Thomas Connery; born 1930), Scottish actor **18** 100-102

CONNOLLY, CYRIL (1903-1974), British novelist and literary and social critic **4** 204-205

CONNOLLY, MAUREEN (1934-1969), American tennis player **19** 72-74

CONRAD, JOSEPH (1857-1924), Polish-born English novelist **4** 205-207

CONRAD, PETE (Charles "Pete" Conrad, Jr.; 1930-1999), American astronaut and businessman **22** 114-116

CONSTABLE, JOHN (1776-1837), English landscape painter **4** 208-209

CONSTANTINE I (circa 274-337), Roman emperor 306-337 **4** 209-211

CONSTANTINE XI (Palaeologus; 1405-1453), Byzantine emperor 1448-1453 **4** 211-212

Constitution of the United States (1787) ratification (Middle Colonies; for)
Logan, George **23** 231-234

CONTI, NICCOLÒ DE' (circa 1396-1469), Venetian merchant-adventurer **4** 212-213

CONWAY, JILL KATHRYN KER (born 1934), historian interested in the role of women and president of Smith College **4** 213-214

COOGAN, JACKIE (John Leslie Coogan, Jr.; 1914-1984), American actor **21** 83-85

COOK, JAMES (1728-1779), English explorer, navigator, and cartographer **4** 214-215

COOKE, JAY (1821-1905), American merchant banker **4** 215-216

COOLEY, CHARLES HORTON (1864-1929), American social psychologist, sociologist, and educator **4** 216-217

COOLEY, THOMAS MCINTYRE (1824-1898), American jurist and public servant **22** 116-119

COOLIDGE, JOHN CALVIN (1872-1933), president of the United States 1923-1929 **4** 217-219

COOMBS, HERBERT COLE (Nugget; born 1906), Australian economist **4** 219-220

COONEY, JOAN GANZ (born 1929), American television program producer and publicist **19** 74-76

COOPER, ANNIE (Anna Julia Cooper; 1858-1964), African American

educator, author, and activist **22** 119-121

COOPER, GARY (Frank James Cooper; 1901-1961), American motion picture actor **21** 85-87

COOPER, JAMES FENIMORE (1789-1851), American novelist and social critic **4** 220-223

COOPER, PETER (1791-1883), American inventor and manufacturer **4** 223-224

COOPER, THOMAS (1759-1839), English-born American scientist and educator **4** 224

COORS, ADOLPH (Adolph Herrman Kohrs; 1847-1929), American brewer and businessman **19** 76-78

COPEAU, JACQUES (1879-1949), French dramatic theorist, director, and actor who established the Vieux Colombier **4** 225

COPERNICUS, NICOLAUS (1473-1543), Polish astronomer **4** 226-227

COPLAND, AARON (1900-1990), American composer **4** 227-228

COPLEY, JOHN SINGLETON (1738-1815), American portrait painter **4** 228-230

COPPOLA, FRANCIS FORD (born 1939), American filmmaker and author **18** 102-104

CORDOBA, GONZALO FERNANDEZ DE (1453-1515), Spanish military leader **20** 99-100

CORELLI, ARCANGELO (1653-1713), Italian composer and violinist **4** 230-231

CORI, GERTY T. (born Gerty Theresa Radnitz; 1896-1957), American biochemist **4** 231-234

CORINTH, LOVIS (1838-1925), German artist **4** 234

Corinthians, Letters to the (New Testament book)
Clement I **23** 78-81

CORMAN, ROGER (born 1926), American film director and producer **21** 87-89

CORNEILLE, PIERRE (1606-1684), French playwright **4** 234-236

CORNELL, EZRA (1807-1874), American financier and philanthropist **4** 236-237

CORNELL, JOSEPH (1903-1972), American artist **4** 237-238

Cornell University (Ithaca, New York State)
physics
Wilson, Kenneth Geddes **23** 446-448

CORNING, ERASTUS (1794-1872), American merchant and financier **4** 238-239

CORNPLANTER (c. 1732-1836), Seneca village leader **4** 239-241

CORNWALLIS, CHARLES (1st Marquess Cornwallis; 1738-1805), British soldier and statesman **4** 241-243

CORONA, BERT (born 1918), Hispanic American union organizer **4** 243-247

CORONADO, FRANCISCO VÁSQUEZ DE (1510-1554), Spanish explorer and colonial official **4** 247

COROT, JEAN BAPTISTE CAMILLE (1796-1875), French painter **4** 247-249

CORREGGIO (circa 1494-1534), Italian painter **4** 249-251

CORRIGAN, MICHAEL AUGUSTINE (1839-1902), American Catholic archbishop **4** 253

CORRIGAN and WILLIAMS founders of the women's peace movement in Northern Ireland **4** 251-253

CORT, HENRY (1740-1800), English ironmaster **4** 254

CORTE REÁL, GASPAR AND MIGUEL, Portuguese explorers **4** 254-255

CORTÉS, HERNÁN (1485?-1547), Spanish conquistador **4** 255-256

CORTONA, PIETRO DA (1596-1669), Italian painter and architect **4** 256

COSBY, WILLIAM HENRY, JR. ("Bill" Cosby; born 1937), American entertainer **4** 257-258

COSGRAVE, LIAM (born 1920), Irish foreign minister and prime minister (1973-1977) **4** 258-260

COSIO VILLEGAS, DANIEL (1898-1976), Mexican teacher, civil servant, and author of studies of Mexican history **4** 260-261

Cosmetic industry
Malone, Annie Turnbo **23** 242-243

COTTEN, ELIZABETH ("Libba"; born Elizabeth Nevills; 1892-1987), African American musician **4** 261-263

COTTON, JOHN (1584-1652), American Congregationalist clergyman **4** 263-265

COUBERTIN, PIERRE DE (Pierre Fredy, Baron de Coubertin; 1863-1937), French organizer of the modern Olympic Games **21** 89-92

COUGHLIN, CHARLES EDWARD (1891-1979), Canadian-American priest and politician **4** 265-266

COULOMB, CHARLES AUGUSTIN DE (1736-1806), French physicist **4** 266-267

COULTON, GEORGE GORDON (1858-1947), English historian **4** 267

Country Music Hall of Fame
Pride, Charley Frank **23** 317-319

COUNTS, GEORGE S(YLVESTER) (1889-1974), American educator and educational sociologist **4** 267-269

COUPER, ARCHIBALD SCOTT (1831-1892), British chemist **4** 269-270

COUPER, JAMES HAMILTON (1794-1866), American agriculturist **4** 270

COUPERIN, FRANÇOIS (1668-1733), French composer, organist, and harpsichordist **4** 270-271

COURBET, JEAN DESIRÉ GUSTAVE (1819-1877), French painter **4** 271-273

COURLANDER, HAROLD (1908-1996), American folklorist and author **19** 78-80

COURNOT, ANTOINE AUGUSTIN (1801-1877), French mathematician, philosopher, and economist **4** 273

COUSIN, VICTOR (1792-1867), French educator and philosopher **4** 273-274

COUSINS, NORMAN (1912-1990), editor-in-chief of the *Saturday Review* and advocate for world peace **4** 274-276

COUSTEAU, JACQUES-YVES (1910-1997), undersea explorer, photographer, inventor, writer, television producer, and filmmaker **4** 276-277

COUSY, BOB (Robert Joseph Cousy; born 1928), American basketball player and coach **21** 92-94

COUZENS, JAMES (James Joseph Couzins, Jr.; 1872-1936), American industrialist, politician, and philanthropist **22** 121-125

COVERDALE, MILES (1488-1568), English Puritan **4** 278

COVILHÃO, PEDRO DE (circa 1455-circa 1530), Portuguese explorer and diplomat **4** 278-279

COWARD, NOEL (1899-1973), English playwright, actor, and composer **4** 279-280

COWELL, HENRY DIXON (1897-1965), American composer and pianist **4** 280-281

COWLEY, ABRAHAM (1618-1667), English writer **4** 281-282

COWPER, WILLIAM (1731-1800), English poet **4** 282

COX, ARCHIBALD (born 1912), American lawyer, educator, author, labor arbitrator, and public servant **4** 283-284

COX, HARVEY (born 1929), American theologian and author **4** 284-285

COXE, TENCH (1755-1824), American political economist and businessman **4** 285-286

COXEY, JACOB SECHLER (1854-1951), American reformer and businessman **4** 286-287

COYSEVOX, ANTOINE (1640-1720), French sculptor **4** 287-288

CRABBE, GEORGE (1754-1832), English poet **4** 288

CRAFT, ELLEN (ca. 1826-1897), African American activist **22** 125-127

CRAIG, EDWARD GORDON (1872-1966), European actor, designer, director, and theoretician **4** 288-289

CRANACH, LUCAS, THE ELDER (1472-1553), German painter, engraver, and designer of woodcuts **4** 289-290

CRANDALL, PRUDENCE (1803-1890), American educator **4** 291

CRANE, HART (1899-1932), American poet **4** 291-293

CRANE, STEPHEN (1871-1900), American writer and poet **4** 293-295

CRANMER, THOMAS (1489-1556), English reformer, archbishop of Canterbury **4** 295-296

CRASHAW, RICHARD (1612/1613-49), English poet **4** 296

CRASSUS DIVES, MARCUS LICINIUS (circa 115-53 B.C.), Roman financier and politician **4** 296-297

CRAVEIRINHA, JOSÉ (born 1922), Mozambican journalist and lyric poet **4** 297-299

CRAWFORD, JOAN (Lucille Fay LeSueur; 1906-1977), American actress **19** 80-82

CRAWFORD, WILLIAM HARRIS (1772-1834), American politician **4** 299-300

CRAXI, BETTINO (1934-2000), statesman and prime minister of the Italian republic (1983-1987) **4** 300-301

CRAY, SEYMOUR (1925-1996), American computer engineer **4** 301-303

CRAZY HORSE (circa 1842-1877), American Indian, Oglala Sioux war chief **4** 303-304

CREEL, GEORGE (1876-1953), American writer and journalist **4** 304-305

CRÉMAZIE, OCTAVE (1827-1879), Canadian poet **4** 305-306

CRERAR, THOMAS ALEXANDER (1876-1975), Canadian political leader **4** 306

CRESSON, EDITH (born 1934), first woman prime minister of France **4** 306-307

CRÈVECOEUR, ST. JOHN DE (1735-1813), French-American farmer and writer **4** 307-308

CRICHTON, (JOHN) MICHAEL (a.k.a. Michael Douglas, Jeffrey Hudson, and John Lange; born 1942), American novelist, screenwriter, and director **4** 308-310

CRICK, FRANCIS HARRY CROMPTON (born 1916), English molecular biologist **4** 310

Criminal law
England
Romilly, Samuel **23** 348-351

CRISPI, FRANCESCO (1819-1901), Italian statesman **4** 310-311

CRISTIANI, ALFREDO ("Fredy" Cristiani; born 1947), president of El Salvador (1989-) **4** 311-313

CRISTOFORI, BARTOLOMEO (1655-1731), Italian musician and inventor of the piano **21** 94-96

CROCE, BENEDETTO (1866-1952), Italian philosopher, critic and educator **4** 313-314

CROCKETT, DAVID (1786-1836), American frontiersman **4** 314-316

CROGHAN, GEORGE (ca. 1720-1782), American Indian agent and trader **22** 127-129

CROLY, HERBERT DAVID (1869-1930), American editor and author **4** 316-317

CROLY, JANE (Jennie June; 1829-1901), American journalist **21** 96-96

CROMER, 1ST EARL OF (Evelyn Baring; 1841-1907), English statesman **4** 317

CROMWELL, OLIVER (1599-1658), English statesman and general **4** 317-320

CROMWELL, THOMAS (Earl of Essex; circa 1485-1540), English statesman 1532-1540 **4** 320-321

CRONKITE, WALTER LELAND, JR. (born 1916), American journalist and radio and television news broadcaster **4** 321-322

CROOK, GEORGE (1828-1890), American general and frontiersman **4** 322-323

CROOKES, SIR WILLIAM (1832-1919), English chemist and physicist **4** 323-324

CROSBY, HARRY LILLIS (Bing; 1903-1977), American singer and radio and television personality **4** 324-326

CROWLEY, ALEISTER (1875-1947), English author and magician **18** 107-109

CROWTHER, SAMUEL ADJAI (circa 1806-1891), Nigerian Anglican bishop **4** 326

CRUMB, GEORGE (born 1929), American composer and teacher **4** 326-328

CRUZ, OSWALDO GONÇALVES (1872-1917), Brazilian microbiologist and epidemiologist **4** 328-329

CUAUHTEMOC (circa 1496-1525), Aztec ruler **4** 329

Cuban music
Lecuona, Ernesto **23** 213-216

CUBBERLEY, ELLWOOD PATTERSON (1868-1941), American educator and university dean **4** 329-331

CUDWORTH, RALPH (1617-1688), English philosopher and theologian **4** 331

CUFFE, PAUL (1759-1817), African American ship captain and merchant **4** 331-332

CUGAT, XAVIER (1900-1990), Spanish musician **23** 81-82

CUGOANO, OTTOBAH (circa 1757-after 1803), African abolitionist in England **4** 332-333

CUKOR, GEORGE (1899-1983), American film director **19** 82-84

CULLEN, COUNTEE (1903-1946), African American poet **4** 333-334

CULLEN, MAURICE GALBRAITH (1866-1934), Canadian painter **4** 334

CULLEN, PAUL (1803-1879), Irish cardinal **20** 100-103

Cultural anthropology (social science)
African studies
Robeson, Eslanda Goode **23** 340-342

CUMMINGS, EDWARD ESTLIN (1894-1962), American poet **4** 334-336

CUNHA, EUCLIDES RODRIGUES PIMENTA DA (1866-1909), Brazilian writer **4** 336-337

CUNNINGHAM, GLENN (1909-1988), American track and field athlete **21** 96-99

CUNNINGHAM, IMOGEN (1883-1976), American photographer **19** 84-86

CUNNINGHAM, MERCE (born 1919), American dancer and choreographer **4** 337-338

CUOMO, MARIO MATTHEW (born 1932), Democratic New York state governor **4** 338-339

CURIE, ÈVE (Eve Curie Labouisse; born 1904), French musician, author and diplomat **18** 109-111

CURIE, MARIE SKLODOWSKA (1867-1934), Polish-born French physicist **4** 339-341
Gleditsch, Ellen **23** 124-126

CURIE, PIERRE (1859-1906), French physicist **4** 341-344

CURLEY, JAMES MICHAEL (1874-1958), American politician **4** 344-345

CURRIE, SIR ARTHUR WILLIAM (1875-1933), Canadian general **4** 345

CURRIER AND IVES (1857-1907), American lithographic firm **4** 345-346

CURRY, JABEZ LAMAR MONROE (1815-1903), American politician **4** 346-347

CURTIN, ANDREW GREGG (1815-1894), American politician **4** 347-348

CURTIN, JOHN JOSEPH (1885-1945), Australian statesman, prime minister **4** 348-349

CURTIS, BENJAMIN ROBBINS (1809-1874), American jurist, United States Supreme Court justice **4** 349

CURTIS, CHARLES BRENT (1860-1936), American vice president (1929-1932) and legislator **21** 99-100

CURTIS, GEORGE WILLIAM (1824-1892), American writer and reformer **4** 349-350

CURTISS, GLENN HAMMOND (1878-1930), American aviation pioneer **4** 350-351

CURZON, GEORGE NATHANIEL (1st Marquess Curzon of Kedleston; 1859-1925), English statesman **4** 351-352

CUSA, NICHOLAS OF (1401-1464), German prelate and humanist **4** 352-353

CUSHING, HARVEY WILLIAMS (1869-1939), American neurosurgeon **4** 353-354

CUSHMAN, CHARLOTTE (1816-1876), American actress **4** 354-355

CUSTER, GEORGE ARMSTRONG (1839-1876), American general **4** 355-356

CUTLER, MANASSEH (1742-1823), American clergyman, scientist, and politician **4** 356-357

CUVIER, BARON GEORGES LÉOPOLD (1769-1832), French zoologist and biologist **4** 357-359

CUVILLIÉS, FRANÇOIS (1695-1768), Flemish architect and designer **4** 359-360

CUYP, AELBERT (1620-1691), Dutch painter **4** 360-361

CYNEWULF (8th or 9th century), Anglo-Saxon poet **20** 103-104

CYPRIANUS, THASCIUS CAECILIANUS (died 258), Roman bishop of Carthage **4** 361-362

CYRIL (OF ALEXANDRIA), ST. (died 444), Egyptian bishop, Doctor of the Church **4** 362

CYRIL, ST. (827-869), Apostle to the Slavs **4** 362

CYRUS THE GREAT (ruled 550-530 B.C.), founder of the Persian Empire **4** 363-364

D

DA PONTE, LORENZO (Emanuele Conegliano; 1749-1838), Italian librettist and poet **20** 105-106

DAGUERRE, LOUIS JACQUES MANDÉ (1787-1851), French painter and stage designer **4** 365-366

DAHL, ROALD (1916-1990), Welsh-born English author **4** 366-367

DAIGO II (1288-1339), Japanese emperor **4** 367-368

DAIMLER, GOTTLIEB (1834-1900), German mechanical engineer **4** 368

DALADIER, ÉDOUARD (1884-1970), French statesman **4** 369

DALAI LAMA (Lhamo Thondup; born 1935), 14th in a line of Buddhist spiritual and temporal leaders of Tibet **4** 369-371

DALE, SIR HENRY HALLETT (1875-1968), English pharmacologist and neurophysiologist **4** 371-373

DALEY, RICHARD J. (1902-1976), Democratic mayor of Chicago (1955-1976) **4** 373-375

DALHOUSIE, 1ST MARQUESS OF (James Andrew Broun Ramsay; 1812-1860), British statesman **4** 375-376

DALI, SALVADOR (1904-1989), Spanish painter **4** 376-377

DALLAPICCOLA, LUIGI (1904-1975), Italian composer **4** 377-378

DALTON, JOHN (1766-1844), English chemist **4** 378-379

DALY, MARCUS (1841-1900), American miner and politician **4** 379-380

DALY, MARY (born 1928), American feminist theoretician and philosopher **4** 380-381

DALZEL, ARCHIBALD (or Dalziel; 1740-1811), Scottish slave trader **4** 381-382

DAM, CARL PETER HENRIK (1895-1976), Danish biochemist **4** 382-383

DAMIEN, FATHER (1840-1889), Belgian missionary **4** 383

DAMPIER, WILLIAM (1652-1715), English privateer, author, and explorer **4** 384

DANA, CHARLES ANDERSON (1819-1897), American journalist **4** 384-385

DANA, RICHARD HENRY, JR. (1815-1882), American author and lawyer **4** 385-386

DANDOLO, ENRICO (circa 1107-1205), Venetian doge 1192-1205 **4** 386-387

DANDRIDGE, DOROTHY (1922-1965), African American actress and singer **18** 112-114

DANIELS, JOSEPHUS (1862-1948), American journalist and statesman **4** 387

Danish literature and culture
see Denmark–culture

D'ANNUNZIO, GABRIELE (1863-1938), Italian poet and patriot **4** 388

DANQUAH, JOSEPH B. (1895-1965), Ghanaian nationalist and politician **4** 388-389

DANTE ALIGHIERI (1265-1321), Italian poet **4** 389-391

DANTON, GEORGES JACQUES (1759-1794), French revolutionary leader **4** 391-393

DARBY, ABRAHAM (1677-1717), English iron manufacturer **20** 106-107

DARÍO, RUBÉN (1867-1916), Nicaraguan poet **4** 393-394

DARIUS I (the Great; ruled 522-486 B.C.), king of Persia **4** 394-395

DARROW, CLARENCE SEWARD (1857-1938), American lawyer **4** 396-397

DARWIN, CHARLES ROBERT (1809-1882), English naturalist **4** 397-399

DARWIN, ERASMUS (1731-1802), English physician, author, botanist and inventor **18** 114-116

DARWISH, MAHMUD (born 1942), Palestinian poet **4** 399-401

DAS, CHITTA RANJAN (1870-1925), Indian lawyer, poet, and nationalist **4** 401-402

DATSOLALEE (Dabuda; Wide Hips; 1835-1925), Native American weaver **22** 130-131

DAUBIGNY, CHARLES FRANÇOIS (1817-1878), French painter and etcher **4** 402

DAUDET, ALPHONSE (1840-1897), French novelist and dramatist **4** 402-403

DAUMIER, HONORÉ VICTORIN (1808-1879), French lithographer, painter, and sculptor **4** 403-405

DAVENPORT, JOHN (1597-1670), English Puritan clergyman **4** 405-406

DAVID (ruled circa 1010-circa 970 B.C.), Israelite king **4** 406-407

DAVID, JACQUES LOUIS (1748-1825), French painter **4** 407-409

DAVID, SAINT (Dewi; 520-601), Welsh monk and evangelist **23** 83-85

DAVID I (1084-1153), king of Scotland **4** 407

DAVIES, ARTHUR BOWEN (1862-1928), American painter **4** 409-410

DAVIES, RUPERT (1917-1976), British actor **18** 116-117

DAVIES, WILLIAM ROBERTSON (1913-1995), Canadian author **18** 117-119

DAVIGNON, VISCOUNT (ETIENNE) (born 1932), an architect of European integration and unity through the Commission of the European Communities **4** 410-411

DAVIS, ALEXANDER JACKSON (1803-1892), American architect **4** 411

DAVIS, ANGELA (Angela Yvonne Davis; born 1944), African American scholar and activist **4** 412-413

DAVIS, ARTHUR VINING (1867-1962), general manager of the Aluminum Company of America (ALCOA) **4** 413-414

DAVIS, BENJAMIN O., SR. (1877-1970), first African American general in the regular United States Armed Services **4** 414-415

DAVIS, BETTE (1908-1989), American actress **18** 119-121

DAVIS, COLIN REX (born 1927), British conductor **22** 131-133

DAVIS, ELMER HOLMES (1890-1958), American journalist and radio commentator **22** 133-136

DAVIS, GLENN (born 1925), American football player **21** 101-103

DAVIS, HENRY WINTER (1817-1865), American lawyer and politician **4** 415-416

DAVIS, JEFFERSON (1808-1889), American statesman, president of the Confederacy 1862-1865 **4** 416-418

DAVIS, JOHN (circa 1550-1605), English navigator **4** 419

DAVIS, MILES (1926-1991), jazz trumpeter, composer, and small-band leader **4** 419-421

DAVIS, OSSIE (born 1917), African American playwright, actor, and director **4** 421-422

DAVIS, RICHARD HARDING (1864-1916), American journalist, novelist, and dramatist **4** 422-423

DAVIS, SAMMY, JR. (1925-1990), African American singer, dancer, and actor **4** 423-424

DAVIS, STUART (1894-1964), American cubist painter **4** 424-425

DAVIS, WILLIAM MORRIS (1850-1934), American geographer and geologist **4** 425-426

DAVY, SIR HUMPHRY (1778-1829), English chemist and natural philosopher **4** 426-427

DAWES, HENRY LAURENS (1816-1903), American politician **4** 427

DAWSON, WILLIAM LEVI (1899-1990), African American composer, performer, and music educator **4** 427-428

DAY, DOROTHY (1897-1980), a founder of the Catholic Worker Movement **4** 428-429

DAYAN, MOSHE (1915-1981), Israeli general and statesman **4** 429-431

DAYANANDA SARASWATI (1824-1883), Indian religious leader **4** 431

DE ANDRADE, MARIO (Mario Coelho Pinto Andrade; born 1928), Angolan poet, critic, and political activist **4** 434-435

DE BEAUVOIR, SIMONE (1908-1986), French writer and leader of the modern feminist movement **4** 440-441

DE BOW, JAMES DUNWOODY BROWNSON (1820-1867), American editor and statistician **4** 441-442

DE BROGLIE, LOUIS VICTOR PIERRE RAYMOND (1892-1987), French physicist **4** 442-444

DE FOREST, LEE (1873-1961), American inventor **4** 459-460

DE GASPERI, ALCIDE (1881-1954), Italian statesman, premier 1945-1953 **4** 462-463

DE GAULLE, CHARLES ANDRÉ JOSEPH MARIE (1890-1970), French general, president 1958-1969 **4** 463-465

DE GOUGES, MARIE OLYMPE (born Marie Gouzes; 1748-1793), French author **23** 85-88

DE GOURNAY, MARIE LE JARS (1565-1645), French author **23** 88-90

DE KLERK, FREDRIK WILLEM (born 1936), state president of South Africa (1989-) **4** 466-468

DE KOONING, WILLEM (1904-1997), Dutch-born American painter **4** 468-469

DE LA MADRID HURTADO, MIGUEL (born 1934), president of Mexico (1982-1988) **4** 471-472

DE LA ROCHE, MAZO LOUISE (1879-1961), Canadian author **4** 474-475

DE LEON, DANIEL (1852-1914), American Socialist theoretician and politician **4** 479-480

DE L'ORME, PHILIBERT (1510-1570), French architect **9** 519

DE MILLE, AGNES (1905-1993), American dancer, choreographer, and author **4** 486-488

DE NIRO, ROBERT (born 1943), American actor and film producer **21** 103-106

DE SANCTIS, FRANCESCO (1817-1883), Italian critic, educator, and legislator **4** 505

DE SICA, VITTORIO (1902-1974), Italian filmmaker **21** 106-108

DE SMET, PIERRE JEAN (1801-1873), Belgian Jesuit missionary **4** 509-510

DE SOTO, HERNANDO (1500-1542), Spanish conqueror and explorer **4** 510-511

DE VALERA, EAMON (1882-1975), American-born Irish revolutionary leader and statesman **4** 514-515

DE VRIES, HUGO (1848-1935), Belgian botanist in the fields of heredity and the origin of species **4** 516-518

DE WOLFE, ELSIE (1865-1950), American interior decorator **20** 107-108

DEÁK, FRANCIS (1803-1876), Hungarian statesman **4** 431-432

DEAKIN, ALFRED (1856-1919), Australian statesman **4** 432-433

DEAN, JAMES (James Byron Dean; 1931-1955), American actor and cult figure **4** 433-434

DEANE, SILAS (1737-1789), American merchant lawyer and diplomat **4** 435-437

DEB, RADHAKANT (1783-1867), Bengali reformer and cultural nationalist **4** 437

DEBAKEY, MICHAEL ELLIS (born 1908), American surgeon **4** 437-438

DEBARTOLO, EDWARD JOHN, SR. and JR., real estate developers who specialized in large regional malls **4** 438-440

DEBS, EUGENE VICTOR (1855-1926), American union organizer **4** 444-445

DEBUSSY, (ACHILLE) CLAUDE (1862-1918), French composer **4** 445-447

DEBYE, PETER JOSEPH WILLIAM (1884-1966), Dutch-born American physical chemist **4** 447-448

DECATUR, STEPHEN (1779-1820), American naval officer **4** 448-449

DEE, RUBY (born Ruby Ann Wallace; born 1924), African American actor **4** 449-452

DEER, ADA E. (born 1935), Native American social worker, activist, and director of Bureau of Indian Affairs **4** 452-454

Deer Hunter, The (film)
Streep, Meryl Louise **23** 384-387

DEERE, JOHN (1804-1886), American inventor and manufacturer **4** 455

DEERING, WILLIAM (1826-1913), American manufacturer **4** 455-456

DEES, MORRIS S., JR. (born 1936), American civil rights attorney **4** 456-457

DEFOE, DANIEL (1660-1731), English novelist, journalist, and poet **4** 457-459

DEGANAWIDA (also DeKanahwidah; c. 1550-c. 1600), Native American prophet, leader, and statesman **4** 460-461
Hiawatha **23** 143-145

DEGAS, (HILAIRE GERMAIN) EDGAR (1834-1917), French painter and sculptor **4** 461-462

DEISENHOFER, JOHANN (born 1943), German biochemist and biophysicist **23** 90-93

DEKKER, THOMAS (circa 1572-circa 1632), English playwright and pamphleteer **4** 465-466

DELACROIX, (FERDINAND VICTOR) EUGÈNE (1798-1863), French painter **4** 469-471
influence of (France)
Signac, Paul **23** 369-372

DELANCEY, STEPHEN (1663-1741), American merchant and politician **4** 473

DELANY, MARTIN ROBINSON (1812-1885), African American army officer, politician, and judge **4** 473-474

DELAUNAY, ROBERT (1885-1941), French abstract painter **4** 475-476

DELBRÜCK, MAX (1906-1981), German-born American molecular biologist **4** 476-478

DELCASSÉ, THÉOPHILE (1852-1923), French statesman **4** 478-479

Dell Computer corporation
Dell, Michael Saul **23** 93-95

DELL, MICHAEL SAUL (born 1965), American businessman **23** 93-95

DELLINGER, DAVID (born 1915), American pacifist **4** 480-481

DELORIA, ELLA CLARA (1889-1971), Native American ethnologist, linguist, and author **22** 136-138

DELORIA, VINE, JR. (born 1933), Native American author, poet, and activist **4** 481-484

DELORS, JACQUES (born 1925), French president of the European Commission and chief architect of Western Europe's drive toward market unity by 1992 **4** 484-486

DEL PILAR, MARCELO H. (1850-1896), Philippine revolutionary propagandist and satirist **4** 486

DEMILLE, CECIL BLOUNT (1881-1959), American film director and producer **4** 488-490

DEMIREL, SÜLEYMAN (born 1924), Turkish politician, prime minister, and leader of the Justice party **4** 490-493

DEMOCRITUS (circa 494-circa 404 B.C.), Greek natural philosopher **4** 493-494

DEMOIVRE, ABRAHAM (1667-1754), Franco-English mathematician **4** 494-495

DEMOSTHENES (384-322 B.C.), Greek orator **4** 495-496

DEMPSEY, JACK (William Harrison Dempsey; 1895-1983), American boxer **4** 496-497

DEMUTH, CHARLES (1883-1935), American painter **4** 497-498

DENG XIAOPING (Teng Hsiao-p'ing; 1904-1997), leader in the People's Republic of China (PRC) in the 1970s **4** 498-500

DENIKIN, ANTON (1872-1947), Russian soldier **20** 108-111

DENKTASH, RAUF (born 1924), president of the Turkish Republic of Northern Cyprus (1985-) **4** 500-502

Denmark (kingdom, Europe)
culture (art)
Thorvaldsen, Bertel **23** 403-406
culture (literature)
Brandes, Georg **23** 45-47
Holberg, Ludvig **23** 152-155
culture (music)
Nørgård, Per **23** 265-267

DENNING, ALFRED THOMPSON (Tom Denning' 1899-1999), British judge and author **22** 138-140

DEODORO DA FONSECA, MANOEL (1827-1892), Brazilian statesman, president 1890-1891 **4** 502

DERAIN, ANDRÉ (1880-1954), French painter **4** 503

DEREN, MAYA (Eleanora Solomonovna Derenkovskaya; 1917-1961), Ukrainian American author and filmaker **23** 95-97

DERRICOTTE, JULIETTE ALINE (1897-1931), African American educator **22** 140-141

DERRIDA, JACQUES (born 1930), French philosopher **4** 503-505

DESCARTES, RENÉ (1596-1650), French philosopher and mathematician **4** 505-508

DESSALINES, JEAN JACQUES (1758-1806), Haitian nationalist and politician **4** 511-512

Detroit Red Wings (hockey team)
Yzerman, Steve **23** 451-453

DETT, ROBERT NATHANIEL (1882-1943), African American composer, conductor, and music educator **4** 512

DEUTSCH, KARL WOLFGANG (1912-1992), American political scientist **4** 512-514

DEVLIN, BERNADETTE (McAliskey; born 1947), youngest woman ever elected to the British Parliament **4** 515-516

DEVRIES, WILLIAM CASTLE (born 1943), American heart surgeon **4** 518-519

DEW, THOMAS RODERICK (1802-1846), American political economist **4** 519

DEWEY, GEORGE (1837-1917), American naval officer **4** 520

DEWEY, JOHN (1859-1952), American philosopher and educator **4** 520-523

DEWEY, MELVIL (1851-1931), American librarian and reformer **4** 523-524

DEWEY, THOMAS EDMUND (1902-1971), American lawyer and politician **4** 524

DEWSON, MARY WILLIAMS (Molly; 1874-1962), American reformer, government official, and organizer of women for the Democratic party **4** 525

DIAGHILEV, SERGEI (1872-1929), Russian who inspired artists, musicians, and dancers to take ballet to new heights of public enjoyment **4** 525-527

DIAGNE, BLAISE (1872-1934), Senegalese political leader **4** 527

DIAMOND, DAVID (born 1915), American composer and teacher **4** 527-529

DIANA, PRINCESS OF WALES (born Diana Frances Spencer; 1961-1997), member of British royal family **4** 529-533

DIAS DE NOVAIS, BARTOLOMEU (died 1500), Portuguese explorer **4** 533-534

DÍAZ, PORFIRIO (José de la Cruz Porfirio Díaz; 1830-1915), Mexican general and politician **4** 534-536

DÍAZ DEL CASTILLO, BERNAL (circa 1496-circa 1584), Spanish soldier and historian **4** 536-537

DÍAZ ORDAZ, GUSTAVO (1911-1979), president of Mexico (1964-1970) **4** 537-538

DICKENS, CHARLES JOHN HUFFAM (1812-1870), English author **4** 538-541

DICKEY, JAMES (1923-1997), American poet **19** 87-89

DICKINSON, EMILY (1830-1886), American poet **4** 541-543

DICKINSON, JOHN (1732-1808), American lawyer, pamphleteer, and politician **4** 543-544

DICKSON, LAURIE (William Kennedy Laurie Dickson; 1860-1935), British inventor and filmmaker **20** 112-113

DIDEROT, DENIS (1713-1784), French philosopher, playwright, and encyclopedist **5** 1-2

DIDION, JOAN (born 1934), American author **20** 113-116

DIEBENKORN, RICHARD (born 1922), American abstract expressionist painter **5** 2-4

DIEFENBAKER, JOHN GEORGE (1895-1979), Canadian statesman **5** 4-5

DIELS, (OTTO PAUL) HERMANN (1876-1954), German organic chemist **5** 5-6

DIEM, NGO DINH (1901-1963), South Vietnamese president 1955-1963 **5** 6-7

DIESEL, RUDOLF (1858-1913), German mechanical engineer **5** 7

DIKE, KENNETH (Kenneth Onwuka Dike; 1917-1983), African historian who set up the Nigerian National Archives **5** 7-8

DILLINGER, JOHN (1903-1934), American criminal **5** 9

DILTHEY, WILHELM CHRISTIAN LUDWIG (1833-1911), German historian and philosopher **5** 10

DIMAGGIO, JOE (born Giuseppe Paolo DiMaggio, Jr.; 1914-1999), American baseball player **5** 10-11

DIMITROV, GEORGI (1882-1949), head of the Communist International (1935-1943) and prime minister of Bulgaria (1944-1949) **5** 11-13

DINESEN BLIXEN-FINECKE, KAREN (a.k.a. Isak Dinesen; 1885-1962), Danish author **5** 13-14

DINGANE (circa 1795-1840), Zulu king **5** 14-15

DINKINS, DAVID (born 1927), African American politician and mayor of New York City **5** 15-18

Dinosaur (extinct reptile) Tyrrell, Joseph Burr **23** 410-412

DINWIDDIE, ROBERT (1693-1770), Scottish merchant and colonial governor **5** 18-19

DIOCLETIAN (Gaius Aurelius Valerius Diocletianus; 245-circa 313), Roman emperor 284-305 **5** 19-20

DIOGENES (circa 400-325 B.C.), Greek philosopher **5** 20-21

DIOP, CHEIKH ANTA (1923-1986), African historian **5** 21-22

DIOR, CHRISTIAN (1905-1957), French fashion designer **5** 22

Diplomats
Mexican
García Robles, Alfonso **23** 117-119

Diplomats, American
20th century (to NATO)
Rumsfeld, Donald Harold **23** 353-355

DIRAC, PAUL ADRIEN MAURICE (1902-1984), English physicist **5** 23-24

DIRKSEN, EVERETT McKINLEY (1896-1969), Republican congressman and senator from Illinois **5** 24-26

DISNEY, WALTER ELIAS (1901-1966), American film maker and entrepreneur **5** 26-27

DISRAELI, BENJAMIN (1st Earl of Beaconsfield; 1804-1881), English statesman, prime minister 1868 and 1874-1880 **5** 27-29

District of Columbia
see Washington, D.C.

DIVINE, FATHER (born George Baker?; c. 1877-1965), African American religious leader **5** 29-32

DIX, DOROTHEA LYNDE (1802-1887), American reformer **5** 32-33

DIX, OTTO (1891-1969), German painter and graphic artist **5** 33-34

DJILAS, MILOVAN (1911-1995), Yugoslavian writer **5** 34

DO MUOI (born 1917), prime minister of the Socialist Republic of Vietnam (1988-) **5** 53-55

DOBELL, SIR WILLIAM (1899-1970), Australian artist **5** 34-35

DOBZHANSKY, THEODOSIUS (1900-1975), Russian-American biologist who studied natural selection **5** 35-37

DOCTOROW, EDGAR LAURENCE (born 1931), American author **19** 89-91

DODGE, GRACE HOADLEY (1856-1914), American feminist, philanthropist, and social worker **5** 37-38

DODGE, GRENVILLE MELLEN (1831-1916), American army officer and civil engineer **22** 142-145

DODGE, JOHN FRANCIS (1864-1920) AND HORACE ELGIN (1868-1920), American automobile manufacturers **18** 121-123

DOE, SAMUEL KANYON (1951-1990), Liberian statesman **5** 38-39

DOENITZ, KARL (1891-1980), German naval officer **20** 116-117

DOI TAKAKO (born 1928), chairperson of the Japan Socialist party **5** 39-41

DOLE, ELIZABETH HANFORD (born 1936), American lawyer, politician, and first female United States secretary of transportation **5** 41-43

DOLE, ROBERT J. (born 1923), Republican Senator **5** 43-46

DOLE, SANFORD BALLARD (1844-1926), American statesman **5** 46

DOLLFUSS, ENGELBERT (1892-1934), Austrian statesman **5** 47

DÖLLINGER, JOSEF IGNAZ VON (1799-1890), German historian and theologian **5** 47-48

DOMAGK, GERHARD JOHANNES PAUL (1895-1964), German bacteriologist **5** 48-50

DOMINGO, PLACIDO (born 1941), Spanish-born lyric-dramatic tenor **5** 50-51

DOMINIC, ST. (circa 1170-1221), Spanish Dominican founder **5** 51-52

DOMINO, FATS (Antoine Domino, Jr.; born 1928), African American singer, pianist, and composer **22** 145-147

DOMITIAN (Titus Flavius Domitianus Augustus; 51-96), Roman emperor 81-96 **5** 52-53

DONATELLO (Donato di Niccolò Bardi; 1386-1466), Italian sculptor **5** 55-56

DONATUS (died circa 355), schismatic bishop of Carthage **5** 56-57

DONG, PHAM VAN (born 1906), premier first of the Democratic Republic of Vietnam (DRV) and after 1976 of the Socialist Republic of Vietnam (SRV) **5** 57-59

DONIZETTI, GAETANA (1797-1848), Italian opera composer **5** 59-60

DONLEAVY, JAMES PATRICK (born 1926), Irish author and playwright **19** 91-93

DONNE, JOHN (1572-1631), English metaphysical poet **5** 60-61

DONNELLY, IGNATIUS (1831-1901), American politician and author **5** 62

DONNER, GEORG RAPHAEL (1693-1741), Austrian sculptor **5** 63

DONOSO, JOSÉ (1924-1996), Chilean writer **5** 63-65

DONOVAN, WILLIAM JOSEPH (1883-1959), American lawyer and public servant **22** 147-149

DOOLITTLE, HILDA (1886-1961), American poet and novelist **5** 65-66

DOOLITTLE, JAMES HAROLD (1896-1993), American transcontinental pilot **5** 66-68

DORIA, ANDREA (1466-1560), Italian admiral and politician **18** 123-125

DORR, RHETA CHILDE (1868-1948), American journalist **5** 68-69

DORSEY, JIMMY (James Dorsey; 1904-1957), American musician and bandleader **19** 93-95

DORSEY, THOMAS ANDREW (1900-1993), African American gospel singer and composer **22** 149-151

DOS PASSOS, RODERIGO (1896-1970), American novelist **5** 69-71

DOS SANTOS, JOSÉ EDUARDO (born 1942), leader of the Popular Movement for the Liberation of Angola and president of Angola **5** 71-72

DOS SANTOS, MARCELINO (born 1929), Mozambican nationalist insurgent, statesman, and intellectual **5** 72-74

DOSTOEVSKY, FYODOR (1821-1881), Russian novelist **5** 74-77

DOUGLAS, DONALD WILLS (1892-1981), American aeronautical engineer **5** 77

DOUGLAS, GAVIN (circa 1475-1522), Scottish poet, prelate, and courtier **5** 77-78

DOUGLAS, SIR JAMES (1286?-1330), Scottish patriot **5** 80-82

DOUGLAS, MARY TEW (born 1921), British anthropologist and social thinker **5** 79-80

DOUGLAS, STEPHEN ARNOLD (1813-1861), American politician **5** 80-82

DOUGLAS, THOMAS CLEMENT (1904-1986), Canadian clergyman and politician, premier of Saskatchewan (1944-1961), and member of Parliament (1962-1979) **5** 82-83

DOUGLAS, WILLIAM ORVILLE (1898-1980), American jurist **5** 83-85

DOUGLAS-HOME, ALEC (Alexander Frederick Home; 1903-1995), Scottish politician **20** 117-119

DOUGLASS, FREDERICK (circa 1817-1895), African American leader and abolitionist **5** 85-86

DOUHET, GIULIO (1869-1930), Italian military leader **22** 151-152

DOVE, ARTHUR GARFIELD (1880-1946), American painter **5** 86-87

DOVE, RITA FRANCES (born 1952), United States poet laureate **5** 87-89

DOW, CHARLES (1851-1902), American journalist **19** 95-97

DOW, NEAL (1804-1897), American temperance reformer **5** 89-90

DOWLAND, JOHN (1562-1626), British composer and lutenist **5** 90

DOWNING, ANDREW JACKSON (1815-1852), American horticulturist and landscape architect **5** 90-91

DOYLE, SIR ARTHUR CONAN (1859-1930), British author **5** 91-92

DRAGO, LUIS MARÍA (1859-1921), Argentine international jurist and diplomat **5** 92-93

DRAKE, DANIEL (1785-1852), American physician **5** 93-94

DRAKE, EDWIN (1819-1880), American oil well driller and speculator **21** 108-110

DRAKE, SIR FRANCIS (circa 1541-1596), English navigator **5** 94-96

DRAPER, JOHN WILLIAM (1811-1882), Anglo-American scientist and historian **5** 96-97

DRAYTON, MICHAEL (1563-1631), English poet **5** 97-98

DreamWorks (movie studio) Geffen, David Lawrence **23** 119-122

DREISER, (HERMAN) THEODORE (1871-1945), American novelist **5** 98-100

DREW, CHARLES RICHARD (1904-1950), African American surgeon **5** 100-101

DREW, DANIEL (1797-1879), American stock manipulator **5** 101-102

DREXEL, KATHERINE (1858-1955), founded a Catholic order, the Sisters of the Blessed Sacrament **5** 102-103

DREXLER, KIM ERIC (born 1955), American scientist and author **20** 119-121

DREYER, CARL THEODOR (1889-1968), Danish film director **22** 152-155

DREYFUS, ALFRED (1859-1935), French army officer **5** 103-105

DRIESCH, HANS ADOLF EDUARD (1867-1941), German biologist and philosopher **5** 105

DRUCKER, PETER (born 1909), American author and business consultant **21** 110-112

DRUSUS, MARCUS LIVIUS (circa 124-91 B.C.), Roman statesman **5** 105-106

DRYDEN, JOHN (1631-1700), English poet, critic, and dramatist **5** 106-107

DRYSDALE, SIR GEORGE RUSSELL (1912-1981), Australian painter **5** 107-109

DUANE, WILLIAM (1760-1835), American journalist **5** 109

DUARTE, JOSÉ NAPOLEÓN (1926-1990), civilian reformer elected president of El Salvador in 1984 **5** 109-111

DUBČEK, ALEXANDER (1921-1992), Czechoslovak politician **5** 112-113

DUBE, JOHN LANGALIBALELE (1870-1949), South African writer and Zulu propagandist **5** 113

DU BELLAY, JOACHIM (circa 1522-1560), French poet **5** 113-114

DUBINSKY, DAVID (1892-1982), American trade union official **5** 114-115

DUBNOV, SIMON (1860-1941), Jewish historian, journalist, and political activist **5** 115-116

DU BOIS, WILLIAM EDWARD BURGHARDT (1868-1963), African American educator, pan-Africanist, and protest leader **5** 116-118

DU BOIS-REYMOND, EMIL (1818-1896), German physiologist **5** 118-119

DUBOS, RENÉ JULES (1901-1982), French-born American microbiologist **5** 119

DUBUFFET, JEAN PHILLIPE ARTHUR (born 1901), French painter **5** 119-120

DUCCIO DI BUONINSEGNA (1255/60-1318/19), Italian painter **5** 121-122

DUCHAMP, MARCEL (1887-1968), French painter **5** 122-123

DUCHAMP-VILLON, RAYMOND (1876-1918), French sculptor **5** 123

DUDLEY, BARBARA (born 1947), American director of Greenpeace **5** 123-124

DUDLEY, THOMAS (1576-1653), American colonial governor and Puritan leader **5** 124-125

DUFAY, GUILLAUME (circa 1400-1474), Netherlandish composer **5** 125-126

DUFF, ALEXANDER (1806-1878), Scottish Presbyterian missionary **5** 126-127

DUGAN, ALAN (born 1923), American poet **5** 127-128

DUGDALE, RICHARD LOUIS (1841-1883), English-born American sociologist **5** 128-129

DUHEM, PIERRE MAURICE MARIE (1861-1916), French physicist, chemist, and historian of science **5** 129

DUKAKIS, MICHAEL (born 1933), American governor of Massachusetts **5** 130-133

DUKE, JAMES BUCHANAN (1856-1925), American industrialist and philanthropist **5** 133-134

DULL KNIFE (born Morning Star; c. 1810-1883), Northern Cheyenne tribal leader **5** 135-136

DULLES, JOHN FOSTER (1888-1959), American statesman and diplomat **5** 134-135

DUMAS, ALEXANDRE (1803-1870), French playwright and novelist **5** 136-138

DUMAS, JEAN BAPTISTE ANDRÉ (1800-1884), French Chemist **5** 138-139

DU MAURIER, DAPHNE (Lady Browning; 1907-1989), English author **18** 125-127

DUNANT, JEAN HENRI (1828-1910), Swiss philanthropist **5** 139-141

DUNBAR, PAUL LAURENCE (1872-1906), African American poet and novelist **5** 141-142

DUNBAR, WILLIAM (circa 1460-circa 1520), Scottish poet and courtier **5** 142-143

DUNBAR, WILLIAM (1749-1810), Scottish-born American scientist and planter **5** 143-144

DUNCAN, ISADORA (1878-1927), American dancer **5** 144-145

DUNHAM, KATHERINE (born 1910), African American dancer, choreographer, and anthropologist **5** 145-146

DUNMORE, 4TH EARL OF (John Murray; 1732-1809), British colonial governor **5** 147

DUNNE, FINLEY PETER (1867-1936), American journalist **5** 147-148

DUNNING, WILLIAM ARCHIBALD (1857-1922), American historian **5** 148-149

DUNS SCOTUS, JOHN (1265/66-1308), Scottish philosopher and theologian **5** 149-150

DUNSTABLE, JOHN (circa 1390-1453), English composer **5** 150-151

DUNSTAN, ST. (circa 909-988), English monk and archbishop **5** 151-152

DUNSTER, HENRY (circa 1609-1659), English-born American clergyman **5** 152-153

DUONG VAN MINH (born 1916), Vietnamese general and politician **18** 285-287

DUPLEIX, MARQUIS (Joseph François; 1697-1763), French colonial administrator **5** 153

DU PONT, ÉLEUTHÈRE IRÉNÉE (1771-1834), French-born American manufacturer **5** 154

DU PONT, PIERRE SAMUEL (1870-1954), American industrialist **5** 154-155

DU PONT DE NEMOURS, PIERRE SAMUEL (1739-1817), French political economist **5** 155-156

DURAND, ASHER BROWN (1796-1886), American painter and engraver **5** 156-157

DURANT, THOMAS CLARK (1820-1885), American railroad executive **5** 157-158

DURANT, WILLIAM CRAPO (1861-1947), American industrialist **5** 158

DÜRER, ALBRECHT (1471-1528), German painter and graphic artist **5** 159-161

DURHAM, 1ST EARL OF (John George Lambton; 1792-1840), English statesman **5** 161-162

DURKHEIM, ÉMILE (1858-1917), French philosopher and sociologist **5** 162-163

DURRELL, LAWRENCE (1912-1990), British author of novels, poetry, plays, short stories, and travel books **5** 163-164

DÜRRENMATT, FRIEDRICH (1921-1990), Swiss playwright **5** 164-165

Dutch literature
Cats, Jacob **23** 64-66

Dutch music
Romantic modern
Badings, Henk **23** 26-28

DUVALIER, FRANÇOIS (Papa Doc; 1907-1971), Haitian president 1957-1971 **5** 165-166

DUVALIER, JEAN CLAUDE (Baby Doc; born 1949), president of Haiti (1971-1986) **5** 166-168

DVOŘÁK, ANTONIN (1841-1904), Czech composer **5** 168-169

DWIGHT, TIMOTHY (1752-1817), American educator and Congregational minister **5** 169

DYLAN, BOB (born Robert Allen Zimmerman; born 1941), American singer, songwriter, and guitarist **5** 170-171

DYSON, FREEMAN JOHN (born 1923), British-American physicist **5** 171-173

DZERZHINSKY, FELIX EDMUNDOVICH (1877-1926), Soviet politician and revolutionary **5** 173-174

E

EADS, JAMES BUCHANAN (1820-1887), American engineer and inventor **5** 175-176

EAKINS, THOMAS (1844-1916), American painter **5** 176-177

EARHART, AMELIA MARY (1897-1937), American aviator **5** 177-179

EARL, RALPH (1751-1801), American painter **5** 179

EARLE, SYLVIA A. (born Sylvia Alice Reade; born 1935), American marine biologist and oceanographer **5** 180-181

EARNHARDT, DALE (1951-2001), American race car driver **22** 156-158

EARP, WYATT BARRY STEPP (1848-1929), gun-fighting marshal of the American West **5** 181-182

EAST, EDWARD MURRAY (1879-1938), American plant geneticist **5** 182-183

EASTMAN, CHARLES A. (1858-1939), Native American author **5** 183-185

EASTMAN, GEORGE (1854-1932), American inventor and industrialist **5** 186

EASTMAN, MAX (Max Forrester Eastman; 1883-1969), American poet, radical editor, translator, and author **5** 187-188

EASTWOOD, ALICE (1859-1953), American botanist **22** 158-160

EASTWOOD, CLINT (born 1930), American movie star and director **5** 188-190

EATON, DORMAN BRIDGMAN (1823-1899), American lawyer and author **5** 190-191

EBAN, ABBA (Abba Solomon Eban; 1915-2002), Israeli statesman, diplomat, and scholar **5** 191-192

EBB, FRED (born 1935), American lyricist **21** 113-115

EBBERS, BERNIE (born 1941), American businessman **20** 122-124

EBBINGHAUS, HERMANN (1850-1909) German psychologist **5** 192-193

EBERT, FRIEDRICH (1871-1925), German president 1919-1925 **5** 193-194

EBOUÉ, ADOLPHE FELIX SYLVESTRE (1885-1944), African statesman, governor of French Equatorial Africa **5** 194

ECCLES, MARRINER STODDARD (1890-1977), American banker **22** 160-162

ECCLES, SIR JOHN CAREW (1903-1997), Australian neurophysiologist **5** 195-196

ECEVIT, BÜLENT (born 1925), Turkish statesman and prime minister **5** 196-197

ECHEVERRÍA, JOSÉ ESTÉBAN (1805-1851), Argentine author and political theorist **5** 197-198

ECHEVERRIA ALVAREZ, LUIS (born 1922), president of Mexico (1970-1976) **5** 198-200

ECK, JOHANN MAIER VON (1486-1543), German theologian **5** 200

ECKERT, JOHN PRESPER (1919-1995), American computer engineer **20** 124-126

ECKHART, (JOHANN) MEISTER (circa 1260-circa 1327), German Dominican theologian **5** 200-201

ECO, UMBERTO (born 1932), Italian scholar and novelist **18** 128-130

EDDINGTON, SIR ARTHUR STANLEY (1882-1944), English astronomer **5** 201-202

EDDY, MARY BAKER (1821-1910), American founder of the Christian Science Church **5** 202

EDELMAN, MARIAN WRIGHT (born 1939), lobbyist, lawyer, civil rights activist, and founder of the Children's Defense Fund **5** 202-204

EDEN, ANTHONY (1897-1977), English statesman, prime minister 1955-1957 **5** 204-205

EDERLE, GERTRUDE (born 1906), American swimmer **19** 98-100

EDGEWORTH, MARIA (1767-1849), British author **5** 205-206

EDINGER, TILLY (Johanna Gabriella Ottelie Edinger; 1897-1967), American paleontologist **22** 163-164

EDISON, THOMAS ALVA (1847-1931), American inventor **5** 206-208

Editors
English
de Gournay, Marie le Jars **23** 88-90

Education (Asia)
Lee, Yuan Tseh **23** 218-220

Education (Australia)
Spence, Catherine Helen **23** 374-375

Education (Europe)
England
Jex-Blake, Sophia **23** 168-170

Education (United States)
art and music
Thomas, Alma Woodsey **23** 401-403
in law
Langdell, Christopher Columbus **23** 204-206
mathematics
Scott, Charlotte Angas **23** 364-367

EDWARD I (1239-1307), king of England 1272-1307 **5** 208-210

EDWARD II (Edward of Carnarvon; 1284-1327), king of England 1307-27 **5** 210

EDWARD III (1312-1377), king of England 1327-77 **5** 211-212

EDWARD IV (1442-1483), king of England 1461-70 **5** 212-213

EDWARD VI (1537-1553), king of England and Ireland 1547-53 **5** 213-214

EDWARD VII (1841-1910), king of Great Britian and Ireland 1901-10 **5** 214-215

EDWARD VIII (1894-1972), King of England (1936) and Duke of Windsor after abdicating his throne **5** 215-217

EDWARD THE BLACK PRINCE (1330-1376), English soldier-statesman **5** 217-218

EDWARD THE CONFESSOR (died 1066, last king of the house of Wessex, reigned 1042-1066) **5** 218-219

EDWARD THE ELDER (died 924), king of England 899-924 **5** 219-220

EDWARDS, JONATHAN (1703-1758), American Puritan theologian **5** 220-222

EDWARDS, MELVIN (born 1937), African-American sculptor **5** 222-223

EGGLESTON, EDWARD (1837-1902), American Methodist minister and historian **5** 223-224

EHRENBURG, ILYA GRIGORIEVICH (1891-1967), Russian author **5** 224-225

EHRLICH, PAUL (1854-1915), German bacteriologist **5** 225-226

EICHMANN, ADOLF (1906-1962), German Nazi war criminal **5** 226-227

EIFFEL, ALEXANDRE GUSTAVE (1832-1923), French engineer **5** 227-228

EIJKMAN, CHRISTIAN (1858-1930), Dutch physician and biologist **5** 228

EINHORN, DAVID RUBIN (1809-1879), German theolgian **22** 164-166

EINSTEIN, ALBERT (1879-1955), German-born American physicist **5** 228-231

EISAI (1141-1215), Japanese Buddhist monk **5** 231-232

EISELEY, LOREN COREY (1907-1977), American interpreter of science for the layman **5** 232-233

EISENHOWER, DWIGHT DAVID (1890-1969), American general and statesman, president 1953-61 **5** 233-236

EISENHOWER, MAMIE DOUD (1896-1979), American First Lady **5** 236-237

EISENHOWER, MILTON (Milton Stover Esisenhower; 1899-1985), American adviser to U.S. presidents and college president **5** 237-238

EISENMAN, PETER D. (born 1932), American architect **5** 239-240

EISENSTAEDT, ALFRED (1898-1995), American photographer and photojournalist **19** 100-102

EISENSTEIN, SERGEI MIKHAILOVICH (1898-1948), Russian film director and cinema theoretician **5** 240-242

EISNER, MICHAEL (born 1942), American businessman **19** 102-104

EITOKU, KANO (1543-1590), Japanese painter of the Momoyama period **5** 242

EKWENSI, CYPRIAN (born 1921), Nigerian writer **5** 242-243

ELDERS, JOYCELYN (born 1933), first African American and second woman U.S. surgeon general **5** 243-246

ELEANOR OF AQUITAINE (circa 1122-1204), queen of France 1137-52, and of England 1154-1204 **5** 246-247

Electronic music
Badings, Henk **23** 26-28

ELGAR, SIR EDWARD (1857-1934), English composer **5** 247-248

ELGIN, 8TH EARL OF (James Bruce; 1811-63), English governor general of Canada **5** 248-249

ELIADE, MIRCEA (1907-1986), Rumanian-born historian of religions and novelist **5** 249-250

ELIAS, TASLIM OLAWALE (1914-1991), Nigerian academic and jurist and president of the International Court of Justice **5** 250-251

ELIJAH BEN SOLOMON (1720-1797), Jewish scholar **5** 251-252

ELION, GERTRUDE B. (1918-1999), American biochemist and Nobel Prize winner **5** 252-254

ELIOT, CHARLES WILLIAM (1834-1926), American educator **5** 254
Langdell, Christopher Columbus **23** 204-206

ELIOT, GEORGE (pen name of Mary Ann Evans; 1819-80), English novelist **5** 254-256

ELIOT, JOHN (1604-1690), English-born missionary to the Massachusetts Indians **5** 256-258

ELIOT, THOMAS STEARNS (1888-1965), American-English poet, critic, and playwright **5** 258-261

ELIZABETH (Elizabeth Petrovna; 1709-61), empress of Russia 1741-61 **5** 261-263

ELIZABETH I (1533-1603), queen of England and Ireland 1558-1603 **5** 263-266

ELIZABETH II (born 1926), queen of Great Britain and Ireland **5** 266-269

ELIZABETH BAGAAYA NYABONGO OF TORO (born 1940), Ugandan ambassador **5** 269-271

ELIZABETH BOWES-LYON (Elizabeth Angela Marguerite Bowes-Lyon; 1900-2002), queen of Great Britain and Ireland (1936-1952) and Queen Mother after 1952 **5** 261-263

ELIZABETH OF HUNGARY (1207-1231), saint and humanitarian **5** 271-272

ELLINGTON, "DUKE" EDWARD KENNEDY (born 1899), American jazz composer **5** 273-274

ELLIS, HAVELOCK (Henry Havelock Ellis; 1959-1939), British psychologist and author **20** 126-128

ELLISON, RALPH WALDO (1914-1994), African American author and spokesperson for racial identity **5** 274-275

ELLSBERG, DANIEL (born 1931), U.S. government official and Vietnam peace activist **5** 275-277

ELLSWORTH, LINCOLN (1880-1951), American adventurer and polar explorer **5** 277

ELLSWORTH, OLIVER (1745-1807), American senator and Supreme Court Chief Justice **21** 115-117

ELSASSER, WALTER MAURICE (1904-1991), American physicist **5** 277-278

ELWAY, JOHN (born 1960), American football player **23** 98-100

ELY, RICHARD (1854-1943), American economist and social reformer **21** 117-120

EMERSON, RALPH WALDO (1803-1882), American poet, essayist, and philosopher **5** 278-280

EMINESCU, MIHAIL (1850-1889), Romanian poet **5** 280-281

EMMET, ROBERT (1778-1803), Irish nationalist and revolutionary **5** 281-282

EMPEDOCLES (circa 493-circa 444 B.C.), Greek philosopher, poet, and scientist **5** 282

ENCHI, FUMIKO UEDA (1905-1986), Japanese author **23** 100-102

ENCINA, JUAN DEL (1468-1529?), Spanish author and composer **5** 283

ENDARA, GUILLERMO (born 1936), installed as president of Panama by the U.S. Government in 1989 **5** 283-284

ENDECOTT, JOHN (1588-1655), English colonial governor of Massachusetts **5** 284-285

ENDERS, JOHN FRANKLIN (1897-1985), American virologist **5** 285-286

ENGELS, FRIEDRICH (1820-1895), German revolutionist and social theorist **5** 286-288

ENGLAND, JOHN (1786-1842), Irish Catholic bishop in America **5** 288

English art and architecture
botanical painting
North, Marianne **23** 268-270

English literature
biography
Cavendish, Margaret Lucas **23** 66-67
children's literature
Nesbit, E(dith) **23** 263-265
fantasy
Nesbit, E(dith) **23** 263-265
Latin
Campion, Thomas **23** 60-62
modern (novel)
Glyn, Elinor **23** 126-128
romance
Glyn, Elinor **23** 126-128
social protest
Pringle, Thomas **23** 319-320
travel
Bird, Isabella **23** 41-42

English music
heavy metal
Led Zeppelin **23** 216-218

ENNIN (794-864), Japanese Buddhist monk **5** 288-289

ENNIUS, QUINTUS (239-169 B.C.) Roman poet **5** 289

ENSOR, JAMES (1860-1949), Belgian painter and graphic artist **5** 289-290

Environmental activists (United States)
Plotkin, Mark J. **23** 308-310

EPAMINONDAS (c. 425-362 B.C.), Theban general and statesman **5** 291-292

EPÉE, CHARLES-MICHEL DE L' (1712-1789), French sign language developer **21** 120-122

EPHRON, NORA (born 1941), American author, screenwriter and film director **18** 130-132

EPICTETUS (circa 50-circa 135), Greek philosopher **5** 292

EPICURUS (circa 342-270 B.C.), Greek philosopher, founder of Epicureanism **5** 292-294

EPSTEIN, ABRAHAM (1892-1945), Russian-born American economist **5** 294-295

EPSTEIN, SIR JACOB (1880-1959), American-born English sculptor **5** 295-296

EQUIANO, OLAUDAH (1745-circa 1801), African author and former slave **5** 296-297

ERASISTRATUS (c. 304 B.C.- c. 250 B.C.), Greek physician and anantomist **5** 297-298

ERASMUS, DESIDERIUS (1466-1536), Dutch author, scholar, and humanist **5** 298-300

ERASMUS, GEORGES HENRY (born 1948), Canadian Indian leader **5** 300-301

ERATOSTHENES OF CYRENE (circa 284-circa 205 B.C.), Greek mathematician, geographer, and astronomer **5** 301-302

ERCILLA Y ZÚÑIGA, ALONSO DE (1533-1594), Spanish poet, soldier, and diplomat **5** 302

ERDOS, PAUL (1913-1996), Hungarian mathematician **22** 166-168

ERDRICH, LOUISE (Karen Louise Erdrich; born 1954), Native American author **23** 102-105

ERHARD, LUDWIG (1897-1977), German statesman, West German chancellor 1963-66 **5** 302-304

ERIC THE RED (Eric Thorvaldsson; flourished late 10th century), Norwegian explorer **5** 304

ERICKSON, ARTHUR CHARLES (born 1924), Canadian architect and landscape architect **5** 304-306

ERICSON, LEIF (971-circa 1015), Norse mariner and adventurer **5** 306-307

ERICSSON, JOHN (1803-1889), Swedish-born American engineer and inventor **5** 307-308

ERIGENA, JOHN SCOTUS (circa 810-circa 877), Irish scholastic philosopher **5** 308-309

ERIKSON, ERIK HOMBURGER (1902-1994), German-born American psychoanalyst and educator **5** 309-310

ERLANGER, JOSEPH (1874-1965), American physiologist **5** 310-311

ERNST, MAX (born 1891), German painter **5** 311-312

ERSHAD, HUSSAIN MOHAMMAD (born 1930), Bengali military leader and president of Bangladesh (1982-1990) **5** 312-314

ERSKINE, THOMAS (1750-1823), British lawyer **22** 168-170

ERTÉ (Romain de Tirtoff; 1892-1990), Russian fashion illustrator and stage set designer **5** 314-316

ERVIN, SAM J., JR. (1896-1985), lawyer, judge, U.S. senator, and chairman of the Senate Watergate Committee **5** 316-317

ERVING, JULIUS WINFIELD (a.k.a. Dr. J.; born 1950), African American basketball player **5** 317-319

ERZBERGER, MATTHIAS (1875-1921), German statesman **5** 319-320

ESCALANTE, JAIME (born 1930), Hispanic American educator **5** 320-321

ESCHER, MAURITS CORNELIS (M.C. Escher; 1898-1972), Dutch graphic artist **18** 132-134

ESCOFFIER, AUGUSTE (Georges Auguste Escoffier; 1846-1935), French chef **21** 122-124

ESENIN, SERGEI ALEKSANDROVICH (1895-1925), Russian poet **5** 321

ESSEX, 2D EARL OF (Robert Devereux; 1567-1601), English courtier **5** 321-322

ESTES, RICHARD (born 1932), American realist painter **5** 322-323

ESTEVAN (a.k.a. Estabanico, Estevanico the Black; c. 1500-1539), Moroccan explorer **5** 324-325

ESTRADA CABRERA, MANUEL (1857-1924), Guatemalan president 1898-1920 **5** 325-326

ESTRADA PALMA, TOMÁS (1835-1908), Cuban president 1902-1906 **5** 326-327

ETHELRED THE UNREADY (968?-1016), Anglo-Saxon king of England 978-1016 **5** 327

Ethics (philosophy)
values
Cats, Jacob **23** 64-66

EUCLID (flourished 300 B.C.), Greek mathematician **5** 327-329

EUDOXUS OF CNIDUS (circa 408-circa 355 B.C.), Greek astronomer, mathematician, and physician **5** 329-330

EUGENE OF SAVOY (1663-1736), French-born Austrian general and diplomat **5** 330-331

EULER, LEONARD (1707-1783), Swiss mathematician **5** 331-332

EURIPIDES (480-406 B.C.), Greek playwright **5** 332-334

EUTROPIUS (fl. 4th century), Roman historian and official **20** 128-130

EUTYCHES (circa 380-455), Byzantine monk **5** 335

Evangelism (religion)
missionaries
Palmer, Phoebe Worrall **23** 288-290
pentecostal
Parham, Charles Fox **23** 291-293

EVANS, ALICE (1881-1975), American bacteriologist **19** 104-106

EVANS, SIR ARTHUR JOHN (1851-1941), English archeologist **5** 335-336

EVANS, EDITH (1888-1976), English actress who portrayed comic characters **5** 336-337

EVANS, GEORGE HENRY (1805-1856), American labor and agrarian reformer **5** 337-338

EVANS, OLIVER (1755-1819), American inventor **5** 338

EVANS, WALKER (1903-1975), American photographer of American life between the world wars **5** 339

EVANS-PRITCHARD, SIR EDWARD EVAN (1902-1973), English social anthropologist **5** 340

EVARTS, WILLIAM MAXWELL (1818-1901), American lawyer and statesman **5** 340-341

EVATT, HERBERT VERE (1894-1965), Australian statesman and jurist **5** 341-343

EVELYN, JOHN (1620-1706), English author **5** 343-344

EVERETT, EDWARD (1794-1865), American statesman and orator **5** 344

EVERGOOD, PHILIP (1901-1973), American painter **5** 345

EVERS, MEDGAR (1925-1963), African American civil rights leader **5** 345-348

EVERS-WILLIAMS, MYRLIE (born Myrlie Louise Beasley; born 1933), civil rights leader, lecturer, and writer **5** 348-350

EWING, WILLIAM MAURICE (1906-1974), American oceanographer **5** 350-351

EWONWU, BENEDICT CHUKA (born 1921), Nigerian sculptor and painter **5** 351-352

Explorers, American
of space
McCandless, Bruce, II **23** 243-246

Explorers, Canadian
Bernier, Joseph E. **23** 35-37
Tyrrell, Joseph Burr **23** 410-412

Explorers, English
of North America
Harriot, Thomas **23** 137-139

EYCK, HUBERT VAN (died 1426), Flemish painter **5** 352-354

EYCK, JAN VAN (circa 1390-1441), Flemish painter **5** 352-354

EYRE, EDWARD JOHN (1815-1901), English explorer of Australia **5** 354

EZANA (flourished 4th century), Ethiopian king **5** 354-355

EZEKIEL (flourished 6th century B.C.), Hebrew priest and prophet **5** 355-356

EZRA (flourished 5th century B.C.), Hebrew priest, scribe, and reformer **5** 356-357

F

FABERGÉ, CARL (Peter Carl Fabergé; Karl Gustavovich Fabergé; 1846-1920), Russian jeweler and goldsmith **21** 125-127

Fabian Society (England)
members
Nesbit, E(dith) **23** 263-265

FABIUS, LAURENT (born 1946), prime minister of France in the 1980s **5** 358-359

FACKENHEIM, EMIL LUDWIG (born 1916), liberal post-World War II Jewish theologian **5** 359-361

FADIL AL-JAMALI, MUHAMMAD (born 1903), Iraqi educator, writer, diplomat, and politician **5** 361-362

FADLALLAH, SAYYID MUHAMMAD HUSAYN (born 1935), Shi'i Muslim cleric and Lebanese political leader **5** 362-364

FAHD IBN ABDUL AZIZ AL-SAUD (born 1920), son of the founder of modern Saudi Arabia and king **5** 364-366

FAHRENHEIT, GABRIEL DANIEL (1686-1736), German physicist **5** 366

FAIDHERBE, LOUIS LÉON CÉSAR (1818-1889), French colonial governor **5** 366-367

Fair, A. A.
see Gardner, Erle Stanley

FAIR, JAMES RUTHERFORD, JR. (born 1920), American chemical engineer and educator **20** 131-131

FAIRBANKS, DOUGLAS (Douglas Elton Ulman; 1883-1939), American actor and producer **19** 107-108

FAIRCLOUGH, ELLEN LOUKS (born 1905), Canadian Cabinet minister **5** 367-368

FAIRUZ (née Nuhad Haddad; born 1933), Arabic singer **5** 368-369

FAISAL I (1883-1933), king of Iraq 1921-33 **5** 370-371

FAISAL II (1935-1958), king of Iraq, 1953-1958 **20** 132-132

FAISAL IBN ABD AL AZIZ IBN SAUD (1904-1975), Saudi Arabian king and prominent Arab leader **5** 371-372
Khalid Bin Abdul Aziz Al-Saud **23** 194-196

FALCONET, ÉTIENNE MAURICE (1716-1791), French sculptor **5** 372

FALLA, MANUEL DE (1876-1946), Spanish composer **5** 372-373

FALLETTA, JOANN (born 1954), American conductor **5** 373-375

FALWELL, JERRY (born 1933), fundamentalist religious leader who also promoted right-wing political causes **5** 375-376

FAN CHUNG-YEN (989-1052), Chinese statesman **5** 376-377

FANEUIL, PETER (1700-1743), American colonial merchant and philanthropist **5** 377

FANFANI, AMINTORE (1908-1999), Italian prime minister **5** 378-379

FANON, FRANTZ (1925-1961), Algerian political theorist and psychiatrist **5** 379-380

FARABI, AL- (Abou Nasr Mohammed ibn Tarkaw; 870-950), Turkish scholar and philosopher **22** 14-16

FARADAY, MICHAEL (1791-1867), English physicist and chemist **5** 380

FARGO, WILLIAM GEORGE (1818-1881), American businessman **5** 380-381

FARLEY, JAMES A. (1888-1976), Democratic Party organizer and political strategist **5** 381-383

FARMER, FANNIE MERRITT (1857-1915), American authority on cookery **5** 383

FARMER, JAMES (1920-1999), American civil rights activist who helped organize the 1960s "freedom rides" **5** 383-385

FARMER, MOSES GERRISH (1820-1893), American inventor and manufacturer **5** 385

FARNESE, ALESSANDRO (Duke of Parma; 1545-1592), Italian general and diplomat **20** 132-135

FARNSWORTH, PHILO T. (1906-1971), American inventor of the television **5** 386-387

FAROUK I (1920-1965), king of Egypt 1937-1952 **5** 387-388

FARRAGUT, DAVID GLASGOW (1801-1870), American naval officer **5** 388-389

FARRAKHAN, LOUIS (Louis Eugene Walcott, born 1933), a leader of one branch of the Nation of Islam popularly known as Black Muslims and militant spokesman for Black Nationalism **5** 389-390

FARRAR, GERALDINE (1882-1967), American opera singer **23** 106-108

FARRELL, JAMES THOMAS (1904-1979), American novelist and social and literary critic **5** 390-391

FARRELL, SUZANNE (née Roberta Sue Ficker; born 1945), American classical ballerina **5** 391-393

"Father of..."
see Nicknames

Fathers of the Church
see Religious leaders, Christian—Fathers

FAULKNER, BRIAN (1921-1977), prime minister of Northern Ireland (1971-1972) **5** 393-395

FAULKNER, WILLIAM (1897-1962), American novelist **5** 395-397
Liveright, Horace B. **23** 229-231

FAURÉ, GABRIEL URBAIN (1845-1924), French composer **5** 397-398

FAUSET, JESSIE REDMON (1882-1961), African American writer and editor **20** 135-138

FAWCETT, MILLICENT GARRETT (1847-1929), British feminist **5** 398-400

FAYE, SAFI (born 1943), Senegalese filmmaker and ethnologist **5** 400-401

FECHNER, GUSTAV THEODOR (1801-1887), German experimental psychologist **5** 401-402

FEE, JOHN GREGG (1816-1901), American abolitionist and clergyman **5** 402-403

FEIFFER, JULES RALPH (born 1929), American satirical cartoonist and playwright and novelist **5** 403-404

FEIGENBAUM, MITCHELL JAY (born 1944), American physicist **5** 404-405

FEIGL, HERBERT (born 1902), American philosopher **18** 135-137

FEIJÓ, DIOGO ANTÔNIO (1784-1843), Brazilian priest and statesman **5** 405-406

FEININGER, LYONEL (1871-1956), American painter **5** 406-407

FEINSTEIN, DIANNE (Goldman; born 1933), politician, public official, and San Francisco's first female mayor **5** 407-408

FELA (Fela Anikulapo Kuti; 1938-1997), Nigerian musician and activist **21** 127-129

FELICIANO, JOSÉ (born 1945), Hispanic American singer and guitarist **19** 109-110

FELLER, BOB (Robert William Andrew Feller; born 1918), American baseball player **21** 129-131

FELLINI, FEDERICO (1920-1993), Italian film director **5** 408-409

FELTRE, VITTORINO DA (1378-1446), Italian humanist and teacher **5** 409-410

Feminist movement
see Women's rights

Feminists
American
Johnston, Frances Benjamin **23** 174-177
Shange, Ntozake **23** 367-369
Walker, Mary Edwards **23** 432-434
Australian
Spence, Catherine Helen **23** 374-375
French
de Gouges, Marie Olympe **23** 85-88
de Gournay, Marie le Jars **23** 88-90
Japanese
Enchi, Fumiko Ueda **23** 100-102
Latin American
Rodríguez de Tío, Lola **23** 345-346
South African
Schreiner, Olive **23** 362-364
Zimbabwean
Vera, Yvonne **23** 425-427

FÉNELON, FRANÇOIS DE SALIGNAC DE LA MOTHE (1651-1715), French archbishop and theologian **5** 410-411

FENG KUEI-FEN (1809-1874), Chinese scholar and official **5** 411-412

FENG YÜ-HSIANG (1882-1948), Chinese warlord **5** 412-413

FERBER, EDNA (1887-1968), American author **5** 413

FERDINAND (1865-1927), king of Romania 1914-1927 **5** 413-414

FERDINAND I (1503-1564), Holy Roman emperor 1555-1564, king of Hungary and Bohemia 1526-64 and of Germany 1531-1564 **5** 414-415

FERDINAND II (1578-1637), Holy Roman emperor 1619-1637, king of Bohemia 1617-1637 and of Hungary 1618-1637 **5** 415

FERDINAND II (1810-1859), king of the Two Sicilies 1830-1859 **5** 415-416

FERDINAND III (1608-1657), Holy Roman emperor 1637-1657, king of Hungary 1626-1657 and of Bohemia 1627-1657 **5** 416-417

FERDINAND V (1452-1516), king of Castile 1474-1504, of Sicily 1468-1516, and of Aragon 1479-1516 **5** 417-418

FERDINAND VII (1784-1833), king of Spain 1808 and 1814-1833 **5** 418-420

FERGUSON, ADAM (1723-1816), Scottish philosopher, moralist, and historian **5** 420-421

FERGUSON, HOWARD (1908-1999), Irish musician and composer **18** 137-138

FERMAT, PIERRE DE (1601-1665), French mathematician **5** 421-422
Wiles, Andrew J. **23** 442-444

FERMI, ENRICO (1901-1954), Italian-American physicist **5** 422-424

FERNÁNDEZ DE LIZARDI, JOSÉ JOAQUIN (1776-1827), Mexican journalist and novelist **5** 424-425

FERNEL, JEAN FRANÇOIS (circa 1497-1558), French physician **5** 425-426

FERRARO, GERALDINE (born 1935), first woman candidate for the vice presidency of a major U.S. political party **5** 426-428

FERRER, GABRIEL MIRÓ (1879-1930), Spanish author **5** 428

FERRER, JOSÉ FIGUÉRES (born 1906), Costa Rican politician **5** 428-429

FERRERO, GUGLIELMO (1871-1942), Italian journalist and historian **5** 429-430

FERRY, JULES FRANÇOIS CAMILLE (1832-1893), French statesman **5** 430

FEUCHTWANGER, LION (1884-1958), post-World War I German literary figure **5** 430-432

FEUERBACH, LUDWIG ANDREAS (1804-1872), German philosopher **5** 432

FEYNMAN, RICHARD PHILLIPS (1918-1988), American physicist **5** 432-434

FIBIGER, JOHANNES (Johannes Andreas Grib Fibiger; 1867-1928), Danish bacteriologist and pathologist **21** 131-133

FIBONACCI, LEONARDO (circa 1180-circa 1250), Italian mathematician **5** 434-435

FICHTE, JOHANN GOTTLIEB (1762-1814), German philosopher **5** 435-436

FICINO, MARSILIO (1433-1499), Italian philosopher and humanist **5** 436-437

FIEDLER, ARTHUR (1894-1979), American conductor of the Boston Pops **5** 437-438

FIELD, CYRUS WEST (1819-1892), American merchant **5** 438-439

FIELD, DAVID DUDLEY (1805-1894), American jurist **5** 439-440

FIELD, MARSHALL (1834-1906), American merchant **5** 440-441

Field Museum of Natural History
Hoffman, Malvina Cornell **23** 148-150

FIELD, STEPHEN JOHNSON (1816-1899), American jurist **5** 441-442

FIELDING, HENRY (1707-1754), English novelist **5** 442-444

FIELDS, W. C. (stage name of William Claude Dukenfield; 1879-1946), American comedian **5** 444

FIGUEIREDO, JOÃO BATISTA DE OLIVEIRA (born 1918), Brazilian army general and president (1979-1985) **5** 445-446

Figure skating (sport)
Albright, Tenley Emma **23** 3-6
Button, Dick **23** 55-57

FILLMORE, MILLARD (1800-1874), American statesman, president 1850-1853 **5** 447-448

FILMER, SIR ROBERT (died 1653), English political theorist **5** 448

FINK, ALBERT (1827-1897), American railroad engineer and economist **21** 133-135

FINKELSTEIN, RABBI LOUIS (born 1895), American scholar and leader of Conservative Judaism **5** 448-450

Finland, Republic of (nation; Northern Europe)
Kekkonen, Urho Kaleva **23** 189-191

FINLAY, CARLOS JUAN (1833-1915), Cuban biologist and physician **5** 450

FINNEY, CHARLES GRANDISON (1792-1875), American theologian and educator **5** 450-451

FIRDAUSI (934-1020), Persian poet **5** 451-452

FIRESTONE, HARVEY SAMUEL (1868-1938), American industrialist **5** 452-453

FIRST, RUTH (1925-1982), South African socialist, anti-apartheid activist, and scholar **5** 453-454

FISCHER, BOBBY (born 1943), American chess player **5** 454-456

FISCHER, EMIL (1852-1919), German organic chemist **5** 456-457

FISCHER, HANS (1881-1945), German organic chemist **5** 457-459

FISCHER VON ERLACH, JOHANN BERNHARD (1656-1723), Austrian architect **5** 459-461

FISH, HAMILTON (1808-1893), American statesman **5** 461-462

FISHER, ANDREW (1862-1928), Australian statesman and labor leader **5** 462

FISHER, IRVING (1867-1947), American economist **5** 462-463

FISHER, JOHN ARBUTHNOT (Baron Fisher of Kilverstone; 1841-1920), British admiral **22** 171-173

FISHER, SIR RONALD AYLMER (1890-1962), English statistician **5** 463-464

FISK, JAMES (1834-1872), American financial speculator **5** 464-465

FISKE, JOHN (1842-1901), American philosopher and historian **5** 465-466

FISKE, MINNIE MADDERN (Mary Augusta Davey; 1865-1932), American "realistic" actress who portrayed Ibsen heroines **5** 466-467

FITCH, JOHN (1743-1798), American mechanic and inventor **5** 467-468

FITZGERALD, ELLA (1918-1996), American jazz singer **5** 468-469

FITZGERALD, FRANCES (born 1940), American author **5** 469-470

FITZGERALD, FRANCIS SCOTT KEY (1896-1940), American author **5** 470-472

FITZGERALD, GARRET (born 1926), Irish prime minister (1981-1987) **5** 472-474

FITZHUGH, GEORGE (1806-1881), American polemicist and sociologist **5** 474

FITZPATRICK, THOMAS (1799-1854), American trapper, guide, and Indian agent **5** 474-475

FIZEAU, HIPPOLYTE ARMAND LOUIS (1819-1896), French physicist **5** 475

FLAGLER, HENRY (1830-1913), American industrialist **21** 135-137

FLAHERTY, ROBERT (1884-1951), American documentary filmmaker **5** 476-477

Flamenco (music)
Peña, Paco **23** 299-301

FLAMININUS, TITUS QUINCTIUS (circa 228-174 B.C.), Roman general and diplomat **5** 477

FLAMSTEED, JOHN (1646-1719), English astronomer **5** 477-478

FLANAGAN, HALLIE (1890-1969), American director, playwright, and educator **5** 478-479

FLANNAGAN, JOHN BERNARD (1895-1942), American sculptor **5** 480

FLAUBERT, GUSTAVE (1821-1880), French novelist **5** 480-482

FLEISCHER, MAX (1883-1972), American animator, cartoonist, and inventor **22** 173-175

FLEISCHMANN, GISI (1894-1944), Czechoslovakian leader who rescued many Jews from the Nazi Holocaust **5** 482-483

FLEMING, SIR ALEXANDER (1881-1955), Scottish bacteriologist **5** 485-486

FLEMING, SIR SANDFORD (1827-1915), Scottish-born Canadian railway engineer **5** 485-486

FLEMING, WILLIAMINA (1857-1911), American astronomer **22** 175-176

FLETCHER, ALICE CUNNINGHAM (1838-1923), American anthropologist **5** 486-487

FLETCHER, JOHN (1579-1625), English playwright **5** 487

FLETCHER, JOSEPH FRANCIS (1905-1991), American philosopher who was the father of modern biomedical ethics **5** 488-489

FLEXNER, ABRAHAM (1866-1959), American educational reformer **5** 489-490

FLINDERS, MATTHEW (1774-1814), English naval captain and hydrographer **5** 490

FLORES, CARLOS ROBERTO (Carlos Roberto Flores Facussé;born 1950), Honduran politician **18** 138-140

FLORES, JUAN JOSÉ (1801-1864), South American general, president of Ecuador **5** 491

FLOREY, HOWARD WALTER (Baron Florey of Adelaide; 1898-1968), Australian pathologist **5** 491-492

FLORY, PAUL (1910-1985), American chemist and educator **5** 492-494

FLOYD, CARLISLE (born 1926), American composer of operas **5** 494-496

FLYNN, ELIZABETH GURLEY (1890-1964), American labor organizer **5** 496-497

FLYNN, JOHN (1880-1951), founder and superintendent of the Australian Inland Mission **5** 497-498

FO, DARIO (born 1926), Italian playwright and actor **18** 140-143

FOCH, FERDINAND (1851-1929), French marshal **5** 498-499

FOLEY, TOM (born 1929), Democratic representative from the state of Washington and Speaker of the U.S. House of Representatives (1989-1995) **5** 499-501

Folk music
Spain
Peña, Paco **23** 299-301

FOLKMAN, JUDAH (Moses Judah Folkman; born 1933), American physician and medical researcher **22** 176-179

FOLKS, HOMER (1867-1963), American social reformer **21** 137-140

FONDA, HENRY (1905-1982), American actor and producer **20** 138-140

FONDA, JANE (born 1937), actress whose career included films, television, exercise videocassettes, and writing **5** 501-502

FONG, HIRAM LEONG (born 1907), American politician and businessman **18** 143-144

FONSECA, RUBEM (born 1925), Brazilian author **5** 502-504

FONTANA, LAVINIA (1552-1614), Italian artist **22** 179-180

FONTANE, THEODOR (1819-1898), German author **5** 504

FONTEYN, DAME MARGOT (Margaret "Peggy" Hookham; 1919-1991), classical ballerina who devoted her career to the Royal Ballet in England **5** 504-505

FOOT, MICHAEL (born 1913), left-wing journalist and British Labour Party member of Parliament **5** 505-507

Football (sport)
Elway, John **23** 98-100

FOOTE, HENRY STUART (1804-1880), American politician **18** 144-146

FOOTE, SHELBY (born 1916), American author **18** 146-148

for colored girls who have considered suicide/when the rainbow is enuf (choreopoem)
Shange, Ntozake **23** 367-369

FORBES, JOHN (1710-1759), British general **5** 507-508

FORBES, MALCOLM (1919-1990), American businessman and publisher **5** 508-509

FORBES, ROBERT BENNET (1804-1889), American merchant and shipowner **5** 509-510

FORD, BETTY (nee Elizabeth Ann Bloomer; born 1921), American first lady **20** 140-142

FORD, BILL (William Clay Ford, Jr.; born 1957), American businessman **19** 110-113

FORD, EDSEL BRYANT (1893-1943), American auto designer and industrialist **18** 148-150

FORD, EILEEN (Eileen Otte; born 1922), American businesswoman and author **19** 113-115

FORD, FORD MADOX (1873-1939), English author and editor **6** 1-2

FORD, GERALD (Leslie Lynch King, Junior; born 1913), U.S. Republican vice president (1973) and president (1974-1976) **6** 2-5
Rumsfeld, Donald Harold **23** 353-355

FORD, HENRY (1863-1947), American industrialist **6** 5-6

FORD, HENRY, II (born 1917), American industrialist **6** 6-7

FORD, JOHN (1586-1639?), English playwright **6** 7-8

FORD, JOHN SEAN O'FEENEY (circa 1890-1973), American film director **6** 8-9

FORD, PAUL LEICESTER (1865-1902), American bibliographer and novelist **6** 9-10

FORMAN, JAMES (born 1928), writer, journalist, political philosopher, and leader of the Student Nonviolent Coordinating Committee **6** 10-11

FORMAN, MILOS (Tomas Jan Forman, born 1932), American screenwriter and film director **20** 143-145

FORREST, EDWIN (1806-1872), American actor **6** 11-12

Forrest Gump (film) Hanks, Tom **23** 135-137

FORREST, JOHN (1st Baron Forrest of Bunbury; 1847-1918), Australian explorer and politician **6** 12-13

FORREST, NATHAN BEDFORD (1821-1877), American Confederate general **6** 13-14

FORRESTAL, JAMES VINCENT (1892-1949), American statesman **6** 14

FORSSMANN, WERNER (1904-1979), German physician **21** 140-141

FORSTER, EDWARD MORGAN (1879-1970), English novelist and essayist **6** 14-16

FORTAS, ABE (1910-1982), noted civil libertarian who served four years on the Supreme Court (1965-1969) **6** 16-17

FORTEN, JAMES (1766-1842), African American abolitionist and inventor **6** 17-18

FORTUNE, DION (Violet Mary Firth; 1890-1946), British author and occultist **22** 180-182

FORTUNE, TIMOTHY THOMAS (1856-1928), African American journalist **6** 18-21

FOSCOLO, UGO (1778-1827), Italian author, poet, and patriot **6** 21

FOSDICK, HARRY EMERSON (1878-1969), American Presbyterian minister **6** 21-22

FOSSE, BOB (1927-1987), American director, choreographer, and dancer **6** 22-23

FOSSEY, DIAN (1932-1985), world's leading authority on the mountain gorilla **6** 23-24

FOSTER, ABIGAIL KELLEY (1810-1887), American reformer **6** 25

FOSTER, NORMAN (born 1935), British architect **19** 115-117

FOSTER, STEPHEN COLLINS (1826-1864), American composer **6** 25-27

FOSTER, WILLIAM ZEBULON (1881-1961), American Communist party leader **6** 27-28

FOUCAULT, JEAN BERNARD LÉON (1819-1868), French physicist **6** 28-29

FOUCAULT, MICHEL (1926-1984), French philosopher, critic, and historian **6** 29-30

FOUCHÉ, JOSEPH (1759-1820), French statesman **6** 30-31

FOUQUET, JEAN (ca. 1420- ca. 1480), French painter **6** 31

FOURIER, FRANÇOIS CHARLES MARIE (1772-1837), French socialist writer **6** 31-32

FOURIER, BARON JEAN BAPTISTE JOSEPH (1768-1830), French mathematical physicist **6** 32-33

FOWLES, JOHN (born 1926), English novelist **6** 33-35

FOX, CHARLES JAMES (1749-1806), English parliamentarian **6** 35-37

FOX, GEORGE (1624-1691), English spiritual reformer **6** 37-38

FOX, VICENTE (born 1942), Mexican president **21** 142-143

FOX, WILLIAM (1879-1952), American film producer **21** 143-144

FRACASTORO, GIROLAMO (Hieronymus Fracastorius; c. 1478-1553), Italian physician, poet, astronomer, and logician **21** 144-147

FRAENKEL, ABRAHAM ADOLF (Abraham Halevi Fraenkel; 1891-1965), Israeli mathematician **23** 109-111

FRAGONARD, JEAN HONORÉ (1732-1806), French painter **6** 38-39

FRANCE, ANATOLE (1844-1924), French novelist **6** 39-40

FRANCIS I (1494-1547), king of France 1515-1547 **6** 40-43

FRANCIS II (1768-1835), Holy Roman emperor 1792-1806 and emperor of Austria 1804-1835 **6** 43-44

FRANCIS FERDINAND (1863-1914), archduke of Austria **6** 44

FRANCIS JOSEPH (1830-1916), emperor of Austria 1868-1916 and king of Hungary 1867-1916 **6** 45-46

FRANCIS OF ASSISI, SAINT (1182-1226), Italian mystic and religious founder **6** 46-47 Clare of Assisi, Saint **23** 76-78

FRANCIS OF SALES, SAINT (1567-1622), French bishop **6** 47

FRANCIS XAVIER, SAINT (1506-1552), Spanish Jesuit missionary **6** 48

FRANCK, CÉSAR (1822-1890), French composer **6** 48-49

FRANCK, JAMES (1882-1964), German physicist **6** 49-52

FRANCO BAHAMONDE, FRANCISCO (1892-1975), Spanish general and dictator **6** 52-54

FRANCO OF COLOGNE (Franco of Paris; flourished circa 1250-1260), French music theorist **6** 52

FRANK, ANNE (1929-1945), 16-year-old holocaust victim who kept a famous diary **6** 54-56

FRANKENHEIMER, JOHN (1930-2002), American filmmaker **22** 182-185

FRANKENTHALER, HELEN (born 1928), American painter **6** 56-57

FRANKFURTER, FELIX (1882-1965), American jurist **6** 57

FRANKLIN, ARETHA (born 1942), African American singer and songwriter **6** 58-60

FRANKLIN, BENJAMIN (1706-1790), American statesman, diplomat, and inventor **6** 60-64

FRANKLIN, SIR JOHN (1786-1847), English explorer **6** 68-69

FRANKLIN, JOHN HOPE (born 1915), pioneer African American historian **6** 65-67

FRANKLIN, MILES (1879-1954), Australian novelist **6** 68-69

FRANKLIN, ROSALIND ELSIE (1920-1958), British physical chemist and molecular biologist **6** 67-68

FRANKLIN, WILLIAM (circa 1731-1813), American colonial administrator **6** 69-70

FRASER (PINTER), LADY ANTONIA (born 1932), popular British biographer, historian, and mystery novelist **6** 70-71

FRASER, MALCOLM (born 1930), prime minister of Australia (1975-1983) **6** 71-73

FRASER, PETER (1884-1950), New Zealand prime minister 1940-49 **6** 73-74

FRASER, SIMON (1776-1862), Canadian explorer and fur trader **6** 74-75

FRASER-REID, BERT (born 1934), Jamaican chemist **20** 145-146

FRAUNHOFER, JOSEPH VON (1787-1826), German physicist **6** 75-76

FRAZER, SIR JAMES GEORGE (1854-1941), Scottish classicist and anthropologist **6** 76

FRAZIER, EDWARD FRANKLIN (1894-1962), African American sociologist **6** 77

FRÉCHETTE, LOUIS-HONORÉ (1839-1908), French-Canadian poet **6** 77-78

FREDEGUND (Fredegunda, Fredegond; c. 550-597), Frankish queen **20** 146-149

FREDERICK I (1123-1190), Holy Roman emperor 1152-1190 **6** 78-79

FREDERICK II (1194-1250), Holy Roman emperor 1215-1250 **6** 79
and papacy
Innocent IV **23** 165-167

FREDERICK II (1712-1786), king of Prussia 1740-1786 **6** 81-84

FREDERICK III (1415-1493), Holy Roman emperor and German king 1440-1493 **6** 84-85

FREDERICK WILLIAM (1620-1688), elector of Brandenburg 1640-1688 **6** 85-86

FREDERICK WILLIAM I (1688-1740), king of Prussia 1713-1740 **6** 86-87

FREDERICK WILLIAM III (1770-1840), king of Prussia 1797-1840 **6** 87

FREDERICK WILLIAM IV (1795-1861), king of Prussia 1840-1861 **6** 87-88

FREED, JAMES INGO (born 1930), American architect **6** 88-90

FREEH, LOUIS J. (born 1950), director of the Federal Bureau of Investigation (FBI) **6** 90-91

FREEMAN, DOUGLAS SOUTHALL (1886-1953), American journalist **6** 91-92

FREEMAN, ROLAND L. (born 1936), American photographer of rural and urban African Americans **6** 92-93

FREGE, GOTTLOB (1848-1925), German mathematician and philosopher **6** 93-94

FREI MONTALVA, EDUARDO (born 1911), Chilean statesman **6** 94-95

FREIRE, PAULO (born 1921), Brazilian philosopher and educator **6** 95-96

FRELINGHUYSEN, THEODORUS JACOBUS (1691-circa 1748), Dutch Reformed clergyman and revivalist **6** 96-97

FRÉMONT, JOHN CHARLES (1813-1890), American explorer and politician **6** 97-98

FRENCH, DANIEL CHESTER (1850-1931), American sculptor **6** 98-99

French art
art cinema
Resnais, Alain **23** 333-335
neo-impressionism
Signac, Paul **23** 369-372

French literature
criticism
de Gournay, Marie le Jars **23** 88-90
drama (17th-18th century)
de Gouges, Marie Olympe **23** 85-88
essays
de Gournay, Marie le Jars **23** 88-90

French Revolution (1789-1799)
• 1792-1795 (1ST REPUBLIC)
Terror victims
de Gouges, Marie Olympe **23** 85-88

FRENEAU, PHILIP MORIN (1752-1832), American poet and journalist **6** 99-100

FRERE, SIR HENRY BARTLE EDWARD (1815-1884), English colonial administrator **6** 100-101

FRESCOBALDI, GIROLAMO (1583-1643), Italian composer and organist **6** 101-102

FRESNEL, AUGUSTIN JEAN (1788-1827), French physicist **6** 102-103

FREUD, ANNA (1895-1982), British psychoanalyst **18** 150-153

FREUD, LUCIAN (born 1922), British painter **20** 149-151

FREUD, SIGMUND (1856-1939), Viennese psychiatrist, founder of psychoanalysis **6** 103-106

FREYRE, GILBERTO (1900-1987), Brazilian sociologist and writer **6** 106-107

FREYTAG, GUSTAV (1816-1895), German novelist, dramatist, and critic **6** 107-108

FRICK, HENRY CLAY (1849-1919), American industrialist and financier **6** 108-109

FRIEDAN, BETTY (Betty Naomi Goldstein; born 1921), women's rights activist and author **6** 109-111

FRIEDMAN, MILTON (born 1912), American economist **6** 111-112

FRIEDRICH, CARL JOACHIM (1901-1984), German-born educator who became a leading American political theorist **6** 113-114

FRIEDRICH, CASPAR DAVID (1774-1840), German romantic painter **6** 114-115

FRIEL, BERNARD PATRICK (born 1929), author, teacher, and playwright from Northern Ireland **6** 115-116

FRIES, JAKOB FRIEDRICH (1773-1843), German philosopher **6** 116-117

FRISCH, KARL VON (1886-1982), Austrian zoologist **6** 117-118

FRISCH, MAX (born 1911), Swiss novelist and dramatist **6** 118-119

FRISCH, OTTO ROBERT (1904-1979), Austrian-British nuclear physicist **6** 119-120

FROBERGER, JOHANN JAKOB (1616-1667), German composer and organist **6** 120-121

FROBISHER, SIR MARTIN (circa 1538-1594), English explorer **6** 121-122

FROEBEL, FRIEDRICH WILHELM AUGUST (1782-1852), German educator and psychologist **6** 122-123

FROHMAN, CHARLES (1860-1915), American theatrical producer **6** 123-124

FROISSART, JEAN (circa 1337-after 1404), French priest, poet, and chronicler **6** 124-125

FROMM, ERICH (1900-1980), German writer in the fields of psychoanalysis, psychology, and social philosophy **6** 125-127

FRONDIZI, ARTURO (1908-1995), leader of the Argentine Radical Party and Argentine president (1958-1962) **6** 127-128

FRONTENAC ET PALLUAU, COMTE DE (Louis de Buade; 1622-1698), French colonial governor **6** 128-130

FRONTINUS, SEXTUS JULIUS (circa 35-circa 104), Roman magistrate, soldier, and writer **6** 130

FROST, ROBERT LEE (1874-1963), American poet **6** 130-133

FROUDE, JAMES ANTHONY (1818-1894), English historian **6** 133-134

FRUNZE, MIKHAIL VASILIEVICH (1885-1925), Soviet military leader **6** 134

FRY, ELIZABETH (1780-1845), British reformer **6** 134-136

FRY, WILLIAM HENRY (1813-1864), American composer **6** 136-137

FRYE, NORTHROP (Herman Northrop Frye; born 1912), Canadian literary scholar **6** 137-139

FUAD I (1868-1936), king of Egypt 1922-1936 **6** 139

FUCHS, LEONHARD (1501-1566), German botanist **20** 152-152

FUCHS, SIR VIVIAN (1908-1999), English explorer and geologist **6** 140

FUENTES, CARLOS (born 1928), Mexican author and political activist **6** 141-142

FUGARD, ATHOL (born 1932), South African playwright **6** 142-143

FUGGER, JAKOB (Jacob Fugger; 1459-1525), German banker **21** 147-149

FUJIMORI, ALBERTO KEINYA (born 1938), president of Peru **6** 143-145

FUJIWARA KAMATARI (614-669), Japanese imperial official **6** 145

FUJIWARA MICHINAGA (966-1027), Japanese statesman **6** 145-146

FUKUI, KENICHI (born 1918), Japanese chemist **23** 111-112

FUKUYAMA, FRANCIS (born 1952), American philosopher and foreign policy expert **6** 146-147

FULBRIGHT, JAMES WILLIAM (1905-1995), American statesman **6** 147-149

FULLER, ALFRED (1885-1973), American businessman and inventor **19** 117-118

FULLER, JOHN FREDERICK CHARLES (1878-1966), British soldier and author **22** 185-186

FULLER, META WARRICK (1877-1968), American sculpter **23** 112-114

FULLER, MILLARD (born 1935), American lawyer and social activist **18** 153-155

FULLER, RICHARD BUCKMINISTER (born 1895), American architect and engineer **6** 149-150

FULLER, SARAH MARGARET (1810-1850), American feminist **6** 150-151

FULTON, ROBERT (1765-1815), American inventor, engineer, and artist **6** 151-152

FUNK, CASIMIR (1884-1967), Polish-American biochemist **22** 187-189

FURPHY, JOSEPH (1843-1912), Australian novelist **6** 152-153

FÜRÜZAN (Fürüzan Selçuk; born 1935), Turkish author and director **22** 189-190

FUSELI, HENRY (1741-1825), Swiss painter **6** 153-155

FUSTEL DE COULANGES, NUMA DENIS (1830-1889), French historian **6** 155

FUX, JOHANN JOSEPH (1660-1741), Austrian composer, conductor, and theoretician **6** 155-156

G

GABLE, WILLIAM CLARK (1901-1960), American film actor **6** 157-158

GABO, NAUM (1890-1977), Russian sculptor and designer **6** 158-159

GABOR, DENNIS (1900-1979), Hungarian-British physicist who invented holographic photography **6** 159-160

GABRIEL, ANGE JACQUES (1698-1782), French architect **6** 160-161

GABRIELI, GIOVANNI (circa 1557-1612), Italian composer **6** 161-162

GADAMER, HANS-GEORG (1900-2002), German philosopher, classicist, and interpretation theorist **6** 162-163

GADDAFI, MUAMMAR AL- (born 1942), head of the revolution that set up the Libyan Republic in 1969 **6** 163-165

GADSDEN, JAMES (1788-1858), American soldier and diplomat **6** 165-166

GAGARIN, YURI ALEXEIVICH (1934-1968), Russian cosmonaut **6** 166-167

GAGE, MATILDA JOSLYN (1826-1898), American reformer and suffragist **6** 167-169

GAGE, THOMAS (1719/20-1787), English general **6** 169-170

GAGNÉ, ROBERT MILLS (born 1916), American educator **6** 170

GAINSBOROUGH, THOMAS (1727-1788), English painter **6** 170-172

GAISERIC (died 477), king of the Vandals 428-477 **6** 172

GAITÁN, JORGE ELIÉCER (1898-1948), Colombian politician **6** 172-173

GAITSKELL, HUGH (1906-1963), British chancellor of the exchequer (1950-1951) and leader of the Labour Party (1955-1963) **6** 173-174

GALBRAITH, JOHN KENNETH (born 1908), economist and scholar of the American Institutionalist school **6** 174-177

GALDÓS, BENITO PÉREZ (1843-1920), Spanish novelist and dramatist **6** 177-178

GALEN (130-200), Greek physician **6** 178-180

GALILEO GALILEI (1564-1642), Italian astronomer and physicist **6** 180-183 Church condemns Paul V **23** 297-299

GALLATIN, ALBERT (1761-1849), Swiss-born American statesman, banker, and diplomat **6** 183-184

GALLAUDET, THOMAS HOPKINS (1787-1851), American educator **6** 185

GALLEGOS FREIRE, RÓMULO (1884-1969), Venezuelan novelist, president 1948 **6** 185-186

GALLO, ROBERT CHARLES (born 1937), American virologist **22** 191-193

GALLOWAY, JOSEPH (circa 1731-1803), American politician **6** 186-187

GALLUP, GEORGE (1901-1984), pioneer in the field of public opinion polling and a proponent of educational reform **6** 187-189

GALSWORTHY, JOHN (1867-1933), English novelist and playwright **6** 189-190

GALT, SIR ALEXANDER TILLOCH (1817-1893), Canadian politician **6** 190-191

GALT, JOHN (1779-1839), Scottish novelist **18** 156-158

GALTIERI, LEOPOLDO FORTUNATO (1926-2002), president of Argentina (1981-1982) **6** 191-193

GALTON, SIR FRANCIS (1822-1911), English scientist, biometrician, and explorer **6** 193-194

GALVANI, LUIGI (1737-1798), Italian physiologist **6** 194-195

GÁLVEZ, BERNARDO DE (1746-1786), Spanish colonial administrator **6** 195-196

GÁLVEZ, JOSÉ DE (1720-1787), Spanish statesman in Mexico **6** 196

GALWAY, JAMES (born 1939), Irish flutist **18** 158-160

GAMA, VASCO DA (circa 1460-1524), Portuguese navigator **6** 196-198

GAMBARO, GRISELDA (born 1928), Argentine author **23** 115-117

GAMBETTA, LÉON (1838-1882), French premier 1881-1882 **6** 198-199

GAMOW, GEORGE (1904-1968), Russian-American nuclear physicist, astrophysicist, biologist, and author of books popularizing science **6** 199-200

GANDHI, INDIRA PRIYADARSHINI (1917-1984), Indian political leader **6** 200-201

GANDHI, MOHANDAS KARAMCHAND (1869-1948), Indian political and religious leader **6** 201-204

GANDHI, RAJIV (1944-1991), Indian member of Parliament and prime minister **6** 204-205

GARBO, GRETA (1905-1990), Swedish-born American film star **6** 205-207

GARCIA, CARLOS P. (1896-1971), Philippine statesman, president 1957-61 **6** 207-208

GARCIA, JERRY (Jerome John Garcia; 1942-1995), American musician **21** 150-152

GARCÍA MÁRQUEZ, GABRIEL (born 1928), Colombian author **6** 208-209

GARCÍA MORENO, GABRIEL (1821-1875), Ecuadorian politician, president 1861-1865 and 1869-1875 **6** 209-210

GARCÍA ROBLES, ALFONSO (1911-1991), Mexican diplomat **23** 117-119

GARCILASO DE LA VEGA, INCA (1539-1616), Peruvian chronicler **6** 210-211

GARDINER, SAMUEL RAWSON (1829-1902), English historian **6** 211

GARDNER, ERLE STANLEY (1889-1970), American mystery writer **22** 193-195

GARDNER, ISABELLA STEWART (1840-1924), American art patron and socialite **21** 152-155

GARDNER, JOHN W. (1912-2002), American educator, public official, and political reformer **6** 211-213

GARFIELD, JAMES ABRAM (1831-1881), American general, president 1881 **6** 213-214

GARIBALDI, GIUSEPPE (1807-1882), Italian patriot **6** 215-217

GARLAND, HANNIBAL HAMLIN (1860-1940), American author **6** 217-218

GARLAND, JUDY (1922-1969), super star of films, musicals, and concert stage **6** 218-219

GARNEAU, FRANÇOIS-XAVIER (1809-1866), French-Canadian historian **6** 219-220

GARNER, JOHN NANCE ("Cactus Jack" Garner; 1868-1967), American vice president (1933-1941) **21** 155-157

GARNIER, FRANCIS (Marie Joseph François Garnier; 1839-1873), French naval officer **6** 220-221

GARNIER, JEAN LOUIS CHARLES (1825-1898), French architect **6** 221-222

GARRETT, JOHN WORK (1820-1884), American railroad magnate **6** 225

GARRETT, THOMAS (1789-1871), American abolitionist **6** 225-226

GARRETT (ANDERSON), ELIZABETH (1836-1917), English physician and women's rights advocate **6** 222-225

GARRISON, WILLIAM LLOYD (1805-1879), American editor and abolitionist **6** 226-228

GARVEY, MARCUS MOSIAH (1887-1940), Jamaican leader and African nationalist **6** 228-229

GARY, ELBERT HENRY (1846-1927), American lawyer and industrialist **6** 229-230

GASCA, PEDRO DE LA (circa 1496-1567), Spanish priest and statesman **6** 230-231

GASKELL, ELIZABETH (1810-1865), English novelist **6** 231-232

GATES, WILLIAM HENRY, III ("Bill"; born 1955), computer software company co-founder and executive **6** 232-234

GATLING, RICHARD JORDAN (1818-1903), American inventor of multiple-firing guns **6** 234-235

GAUDÍ I CORNET, ANTONI (1852-1926), Catalan architect and designer **6** 235-236

GAUGUIN, PAUL (1848-1903), French painter and sculptor **6** 236-238

GAULLI, GIOVANNI BATTISTA (1639-1709), Italian painter **6** 238-239

GAULTIER, JEAN PAUL (born 1952), French avant-garde designer **6** 239-240

GAUSS, KARL FRIEDRICH (1777-1855), German mathematician and astronomer **6** 240-242

GAVIRIA TRUJILLO, CESAR AUGUSTO (born 1947), president of Colombia **6** 242-243

GAY, JOHN (1685-1732), English playwright and poet **6** 243-244

GAYLE, HELENE DORIS (born 1955), African American epidemiologist and pediatrician **6** 244-245

GAY-LUSSAC, JOSEPH LOUIS (1778-1850), French chemist and physicist **6** 245-246

GEDDES, SIR PATRICK (1854-1932), Scottish sociologist and biologist **6** 246-247

GEERTGEN TOT SINT JANS (Geertgen van Haarlem; circa 1460/65-1490/95), Netherlandish painter **6** 248

GEERTZ, CLIFFORD (born 1926), American cultural anthropologist **6** 248-249

GEFFEN, DAVID LAWRENCE (born 1943), American record and film producer **23** 119-122

GEHRIG, LOU (Henry Louis Gehrig; 1903-1941), American baseball player **19** 119-121

GEHRY, FRANK O. (née Goldberg; born 1929), American architect **6** 250-251

GEIGER, HANS (born Johannes Wilhelm Geiger; 1882-1945), German physicist **6** 251-253

GEISEL, ERNESTO (1908-1996), Brazilian army general, president of Brazil's national oil company (Petrobras), and president of the republic (1974-1979) **6** 253-255

GEISEL, THEODOR (a.k.a. Dr. Seuss; 1904-1991), American author of children's books **6** 255-256

GELLER, MARGARET JOAN (born 1947), American astronomer **6** 256-257

GELL-MANN, MURRAY (born 1929), American physicist **6** 257-258

GEMAYEL, AMIN (born 1942), Lebanese nationalist and Christian political leader; president of the Republic of Lebanon (1982-1988) **6** 258-259

GEMAYEL, PIERRE (1905-1984), leader of the Lebanese Phalangist Party **6** 259-261

Gene (biology)
see Genetics

GENET, EDMOND CHARLES (1763-1834), French diplomat **6** 261-262

GENET, JEAN (1910-1986), French novelist and playwright **6** 262-263

Genetics (biology)
DNA
Altman, Sidney **23** 9-11
Cech, Thomas Robert **23** 68-70
engineering
Gilbert, Walter **23** 122-124
gene mapping
Gilbert, Walter **23** 122-124

GENGHIS KHAN (1167-1227), Mongol chief, creator of the Mongol empire **6** 263-265

GENSCHER, HANS-DIETRICH (born 1927), leader of West Germany's liberal party (the FDP) and foreign minister **6** 265-266

GENTILE, GIOVANNI (1875-1944), Italian philosopher and politician **6** 267

GENTILE DA FABRIANO (Gentile di Niccolò di Giovanni di Massio; circa 1370-1427), Italian painter **6** 266-267

GENTILESCHI, ARTEMISIA (1593-1652), Italian painter **22** 195-196

GEOFFREY OF MONMOUTH (circa 1100-1155), English pseudohistorian **6** 268

Geological Survey (Canada)
Tyrrell, Joseph Burr **23** 410-412

Geometry (mathematics)
golden mean
Theano **23** 399-401
plane
Scott, Charlotte Angas **23** 364-367
projective
Steiner, Jakob **23** 380-382

GEORGE I (1660-1727), king of Great
Britain and Ireland 1714-1727 **6**
268-269

GEORGE II (1683-1760), king of Great
Britain and Ireland and elector of
Hanover 1727-1760 **6** 269-270

GEORGE III (1738-1820), king of Great
Britain and Ireland 1760-1820 **6**
270-272

GEORGE IV (1762-1830), king of Great
Britain and Ireland 1820-1830 **6**
272-273

GEORGE V (1865-1936), king of Great
Britain and Northern Ireland and
emperor of India 1910-1936 **6**
273-275

GEORGE VI (1895-1952), king of Great
Britain and Northern Ireland 1936-
1952 **6** 275

GEORGE, DAN (1899-1981), Native
American actor **22** 196-198

GEORGE, HENRY (1839-1897),
American economist and social
reformer **6** 276

GEORGE, JAMES ZACHARIAH (1826-
1897), American politician and jurist **6**
276-277

GEORGE, STEFAN (1868-1933), German
symbolist poet **6** 277-278

Georgia (ancient Iberia; now Georgian
Soviet Socialist Republic)
Tamara **23** 388-390

GEPHARDT, RICHARD ANDREW (born
1941), Democratic majority leader in
the House of Representatives **6**
278-280

**GÉRICAULT, JEAN LOIS ANDRÉ
THÉODORE** (1791-1824), French
painter **6** 280-281

GERMAIN, SOPHIE (Marie-Sophie
Germain; 1776-1831), French
mathematician **21** 157-158

German art
capitalist realism
Polke, Sigmar **23** 312-315
photography
Polke, Sigmar **23** 312-315
photorealism
Richter, Gerhard **23** 338-340
social realism
Richter, Gerhard **23** 338-340

GERONIMO (1829-1909), American
Apache Indian warrior **6** 281-282

GERRY, ELBRIDGE (1744-1814),
American patriot and statesman **6**
282-283

GERSHOM BEN JUDAH (circa 950-
1028), German rabbi, scholar, and
poet **6** 283-284

GERSHWIN, GEORGE (1898-1937),
American composer **6** 284-285

GERSHWIN, IRA (Israel Gershvin; 1896-
1983), American lyricist **20** 153-155

GERSON, JOHN (1363-1429), French
theologian **6** 285-286

GERSTNER, LOU (Louis Vincent
Gerstner, Jr.; born 1942), American
businessman **19** 121-124

GESELL, ARNOLD LUCIUS (1880-1961),
American psychologist and
pediatrician **6** 286-287

GESNER, KONRAD VON (1516-1565),
Swiss naturalist **6** 287

GESUALDO, DON CARLO (Prince of
Venosa; circa 1560-1613), Italian
composer **6** 287-288

GETTY, JEAN PAUL (1892-1976),
billionaire independent oil producer **6**
288-290

**GHAZALI, ABU HAMID MUHAMMAD
AL-** (1058-1111), Arab philosopher
and Islamic theologian **6** 290-291

GHIBERTI, LORENZO (circa 1381-1455),
Italian sculptor, goldsmith, and painter
6 291-292

GHIRLANDAIO, DOMENICO (1449-
1494), Italian painter **6** 292-293

GHOSE, AUROBINDO (1872-1950),
Indian nationalist and philosopher **6**
293-294

GIACOMETTI, ALBERTO (1901-1966),
Swiss sculptor and painter **6** 294-295

GIANNINI, A. P. (Amadeo Peter; 1870-
1949), Italian-American financier and
banker **6** 295-297

GIAP, VO NGUYEN (born 1912),
Vietnamese Communist general and
statesman **6** 297-299

GIBBON, EDWARD (1737-1794),
English historian **6** 299-300

GIBBONS, CEDRIC (1893-1960),
American film production designer **21**
158-159

GIBBONS, JAMES (1834-1921),
American Roman Catholic cardinal **6**
300-301

GIBBS, JAMES (1682-1754), British
architect **6** 301-302

GIBBS, JOSIAH WILLARD (1839-1903),
American mathematical physicist **6**
302-303

GIBRAN, KAHLIL (1883-1931), Lebanese
writer and artist **6** 303-305

GIBSON, ALTHEA (born 1927), African
American tennis player **6** 305-306

GIBSON, BOB (Robert Gibson; born
1935), American baseball player **21**
159-162

GIBSON, WILLIAM (born 1914),
American author **6** 306-307

GIDDINGS, FRANKLIN HENRY (1855-
1931), American sociologist **6** 307-308

GIDE, ANDRÉ (1869-1951), French
author **6** 308-309

GIELGUD, JOHN (born 1904), English
Shakespearean actor **6** 310-311

GIERKE, OTTO VON (1841-1921),
German jurist **6** 311-312

GIGLI, ROMEO (born 1949), Italian
designer **6** 312

GILBERT, SIR HUMPHREY (circa 1537-
1583), English soldier and colonizer **6**
313

GILBERT, WALTER (born 1932),
American molecular biologist **23**
122-124

GILBERT, WILLIAM (1544-1603), English
physician and physicist **6** 313-314

GILBERT, SIR WILLIAM SCHWENCK
(1836-1911), English playwright and
poet **6** 314-315

GILBRETH, FRANK (1868-1924),
American engineer and management
expert **21** 162-163

GILBRETH, LILLIAN (born Lillian Evelyn
Moller; 1878-1972), American
psychologist and industrial
management consultant **6** 315-317

GILES, ERNEST (1835-1897), Australian
explorer **6** 317-318

GILKEY, LANGDON BROWN (born
1919), American ecumenical Protestant
theologian **6** 318-319

GILLESPIE, DIZZY (born John Birks
Gillespie; 1917-1993), African
American jazz trumpeter, composer,
and band leader **6** 320-322

GILLETTE, KING CAMP (1855-1932),
American businessman and inventor
21 163-166

GILLIAM, SAM (born 1933), American
artist **6** 322-323

GILMAN, CHARLOTTE ANNA PERKINS
(1860-1935), American writer and
lecturer **6** 323-325

GILMAN, DANIEL COIT (1831-1908), educator and pioneer in the American university movement **6** 325-326

GILPIN, LAURA (1891-1979), American photographer **6** 326-327

GILSON, ÉTIENNE HENRY (1884-1978), French Catholic philosopher **6** 327-328

GINASTERA, ALBERTO EVARISTO (1916-1983), Argentine composer **6** 328-329

GINGRICH, NEWT (born 1943), Republican congressman from Georgia **6** 329-332

GINSBERG, ALLEN (1926-1997), American poet **6** 332-333

GINSBURG, RUTH BADER (born 1933), second woman appointed to the United States Supreme Court **6** 333-336

GINZBERG, ASHER (Ahad Ha-Am; means "one of the people;" 1856-1927), Jewish intellectual leader **6** 336-337

GINZBERG, LOUIS (1873-1953), Lithuanian-American Talmudic scholar **6** 337-338

GINZBURG, NATALIA LEVI (1916-1991), Italian novelist, essayist, playwright, and translator **6** 338-339

GIOLITTI, GIOVANNI (1842-1928), Italian statesman **6** 339-340

GIORGIONE (1477-1510), Italian painter **6** 340-341

GIOTTO (circa 1267-1337), Italian painter, architect, and sculptor **6** 342-345

GIOVANNI, YOLANDE CORNELIA, JR. (born 1943), African American poet **6** 346-347

GIOVANNI DA BOLOGNA (1529-1608), Italian sculptor **6** 345-346

GIPP, GEORGE (1895-1920), American football player **19** 124-126

GIRARD, STEPHEN (1750-1831), American merchant and philanthropist **6** 347-348

GIRARDON, FRANÇOIS (1628-1715), French sculptor **6** 348-349

GIRAUDOUX, JEAN (1882-1944), French novelist, playwright, and diplomat **6** 349-350

GIRTY, SIMON (1741-1818), American frontiersman **6** 350

GISCARD D'ESTAING, VALÉRY (born 1926), third president of the French Fifth Republic **6** 350-352

GISH, LILLIAN (1896-1993), American actress **20** 155-158

GIST, CHRISTOPHER (circa 1706-1759), American frontiersman **6** 352-353

GIULIANI, RUDOLPH WILLIAM (born 1944), mayor of New York City **6** 353-355

GLACKENS, WILLIAM (1870-1938), American painter **6** 355-356

GLADDEN, WASHINGTON (1836-1918), American clergyman **6** 356-357

GLADSTONE, WILLIAM EWART (1809-1898), English statesman **6** 357-360

GLASGOW, ELLEN (1873-1945), American novelist **6** 360-361

GLASHOW, SHELDON LEE (born 1932), American Nobel Prize winner in physics **6** 361-362

GLASS, PHILIP (born 1937), American composer of minimalist music **6** 362-364

GLASSE, HANNAH (Hannah Allgood; 1708-1770), English cookbook author **21** 166-167

GLEDITSCH, ELLEN (1879-1968), Norwegian chemist **23** 124-126

GLENDOWER, OWEN (1359?-1415?), Welsh national leader **6** 364-365

GLENN, JOHN HERSCHEL, JR. (born 1921), military test pilot, astronaut, businessman, and United States senator from Ohio **6** 365-367

GLIDDEN, JOSEPH (1813-1906), American businessman and inventor **21** 167-170

GLIGOROV, KIRO (born 1917), first president of the Republic of Macedonia **6** 367-369

GLINKA, MIKHAIL IVANOVICH (1804-1857), Russian composer **6** 369-370

GLOUCESTER, DUKE OF (1391-1447), English statesman **6** 370-371

GLUBB, SIR JOHN BAGOT (1897-1986), British commander of the Arab Legion 1939-56 **6** 371-372

GLUCK, CHRISTOPH WILLIBALD (1714-1787), Austrian composer and opera reformer **6** 372-374

GLUCKMAN, MAX (1911-1975), British anthropologist **6** 374-375

GLYN, ELINOR (born Elinor Sutherland; 1864-1943), British author and filmmaker **23** 126-128

GOBINEAU, COMTE DE (Joseph Arthur Gobineau; 1816-1882), French diplomat **6** 375-376

GODARD, JEAN-LUC (born 1930), French actor, film director, and screenwriter **19** 126-128

GODDARD, ROBERT HUTCHINGS (1882-1945), American pioneer in rocketry **6** 376-377

GÖDEL, KURT (1906-1978), Austrian-American mathematician **6** 377-379

GODFREY OF BOUILLON (circa 1060-1100), French lay leader of First Crusade **6** 379

GODKIN, EDWIN LAWRENCE (1831-1902), British-born American journalist **6** 380

GODOLPHIN, SIDNEY (1st Earl of Godolphin; 1645-1712), English statesman **6** 380-381

GODOY Y ÁLVAREZ DE FARIA, MANUEL DE (1767-1851), Spanish statesman **6** 381-382

GODUNOV, BORIS FEODOROVICH (circa 1551-1605), czar of Russia 1598-1605 **6** 382-383

GODWIN, WILLIAM (1756-1836), English political theorist and writer **6** 383-384

GOEBBELS, JOSEPH PAUL (1897-1945), German politician and Nazi propagandist **6** 384-385

GOEPPERT-MAYER, MARIA (1906-1972), American physicist **6** 385-387

GOETHALS, GEORGE WASHINGTON (1858-1928), American Army officer and engineer **6** 387-388

GOETHE, JOHANN WOLFGANG VON (1749-1832), German poet **6** 388-391

GOGOL, NIKOLAI (1809-1852), Russian author **6** 391-393

GOH CHOK TONG (born 1941), leader of the People's Action Party and Singapore's prime minister **6** 393-395

GOIZUETA, ROBERTO (1931-1997), Cuban American businessman and philanthropist **18** 160-162

GÖKALP, MEHMET ZIYA (1875/76-1924), Turkish publicist and sociologist **6** 395-396

GOKHALE, GOPAL KRISHNA (1866-1915), Indian nationalist leader **6** 396

GOLD, THOMAS (born 1920), American astronomer and physicist **18** 162-164

GOLDBERG, ARTHUR JOSEPH (1908-1990), U.S. secretary of labor, ambassador to the United Nations, and activist justice of the U.S. Supreme Court **6** 397-398

GOLDBERG, WHOOPI (born Caryn E. Johnson; born 1949), African American actress **6** 398-402

GOLDEN, HARRY (1902-1981), Jewish-American humorist, writer, and publisher **6** 402-403

GOLDIE, SIR GEORGE DASHWOOD TAUBMAN (1846-1925), British trader and empire builder **6** 404

GOLDING, WILLIAM (1911-1993), English novelist and essayist **6** 404-406

GOLDMAN, EMMA (1869-1940), Lithuanian-born American anarchist **6** 406-407

GOLDMARK, JOSEPHINE (1877-1950), advocate of government assistance in improving the lot of women and children **6** 407-408

GOLDMARK, PETER CARL (1906-1977), American engineer and inventor **21** 170-172

GOLDONI, CARLO (1707-1793), Italian dramatist, poet, and librettist **6** 408-409

GOLDSMITH, JAMES MICHAEL (1933-1997), British-French industrialist and financier **6** 409-411

GOLDSMITH, OLIVER (1730-1774), British poet, dramatist, and novelist **6** 411-413

GOLDSMITH, OLIVER (1794-1861), Canadian poet **6** 411

GOLDWATER, BARRY (1909-1998), conservative Republican U.S. senator from Arizona (1952-1987) **6** 413-415

GOLDWYN, SAMUEL (1882-1974), Polish-born American film producer **6** 416

GOMBERT, NICOLAS (circa 1500-1556/57), Franco-Flemish composer **6** 416-417

GÓMEZ, JUAN VICENTE (1857-1935), Venezuelan dictator **6** 417-418

GÓMEZ, MÁXIMO (1836-1905), Dominican-born Cuban general and independence hero **6** 418-419

GÓMEZ CASTRO, LAUREANO ELEUTERIO (1889-1965), Colombian statesman, president **6** 419-420

GOMPERS, SAMUEL (1850-1924), American labor leader **6** 420-422

GOMULKA, WLADISLAW (1905-1982), Polish politician **6** 422-424

GONCHAROV, IVAN ALEKSANDROVICH (1812-1891), Russian novelist **6** 424

GONCHAROVA, NATALIA (1881-1962), Russian painter and theatrical scenery designer **6** 424-426

GONCOURT BROTHERS (19th-century French writers) **6** 426-427

GÓNGORA Y ARGOTE, LUIS DE (1561-1627), Spanish poet **6** 427-428

GONNE, MAUD (c. 1866-1953), Irish nationalist **20** 158-160

GONZÁLEZ, JULIO (1876-1942), Spanish sculptor **6** 428-429

GONZÁLEZ MARQUEZ, FELIPE (born 1942), Socialist leader of Spain **6** 429-431

GONZÁLEZ PRADA, MANUEL (1848-1918), Peruvian essayist and poet **6** 431

GONZALO DE BERCEO (circa 1195-after 1252), Spanish author **6** 431-432

GOOCH, GEORGE PEABODY (1873-1968), British historian and political journalist **6** 432-433

GOODALL, JANE (born 1934), British scientist who studied primates **6** 433-434

GOODLAD, JOHN INKSTER (born 1917), American education researcher and prophet **6** 434-436

GOODMAN, BENNY (Benjamin David Goodman; 1909-1986), jazz clarinetist and big band leader (1935-1945) **6** 436-438

GOODMAN, ELLEN HOLTZ (born 1941), American journalist **6** 438-439

GOODNIGHT, CHARLES (1836-1926), American cattleman **6** 439

GOODPASTER, ANDREW JACKSON (born 1915), American Army officer active in organizing NATO forces in Europe and adviser to three presidents **6** 439-441

GOODYEAR, CHARLES (1800-1860), American inventor **6** 441

GORBACHEV, MIKHAIL SERGEEVICH (born 1931), former president of the Union of Soviet Socialist Republics. **6** 441-444

GORBACHEV, RAISA MAXIMOVNA (née Titorenko; 1932-1999), first lady of the Soviet Union **6** 444-446

GORDEEVA, EKATERINA (born 1971), Russian ice skater and author **18** 164-166

GORDIMER, NADINE (born 1923), South African author of short stories and novels **6** 446-447

GORDON, AARON DAVID (1856-1922), Russian-born Palestinian Zionist **6** 447-448

GORDON, CHARLES GEORGE (1833-1885), English soldier and adventurer **6** 448-449

GORDON, JOHN BROWN (1832-1904), American businessman and politician **6** 449-450

GORDON, PAMELA (born 1955), Bermudan politician **18** 166-167

GORDY, BERRY, JR. (born 1929), founder of the Motown Sound **6** 450-451

GORE, ALBERT, JR. (born 1948), Democratic U.S. representative, senator, and 45th vice president of the United States **6** 452-453

GORGAS, JOSIAH (1818-1883), American soldier and educator **6** 453-454

GORGAS, WILLIAM CRAWFORD (1854-1920), American general and sanitarian **6** 454-455

GORGES, SIR FERDINANDO (1568-1647), English colonizer and soldier **6** 455-456

GORGIAS (circa 480-circa 376 B.C.), Greek sophist philosopher and rhetorician **6** 456

GÖRING, HERMANN WILHELM (1893-1946), German politician and air force commander **6** 457-458

GORKY, ARSHILE (1905-1948), American painter **6** 458

GORKY, MAXIM (1868-1936), Russian author **6** 458-460

GORMAN, R.C. (Rudolph Carl Gorman; born 1931), Native American artist **23** 128-130

GORRIE, JOHN (1803-1855), American physician and inventor **21** 172-174

GORTON, SAMUELL (circa 1592-1677), English colonizer **6** 460

GOSHIRAKAWA (1127-1192), Japanese emperor **6** 460-461

GOSHO, HEINOSUKE (1902-1981), Japanese filmmaker **22** 199-200

GOTTFRIED VON STRASSBURG (circa 1165-circa 1215), German poet and romancer **6** 461-462

GOTTLIEB, ADOLPH (1903-1974), American Abstract Expressionist painter **6** 462-463

GOTTSCHALK, LOUIS MOREAU (1829-1869), American composer **6** 463-464

GOTTWALD, KLEMENT (1896-1953), first Communist president of Czechoslovakia (1948-1953) **6** 464-466

GOUDIMEL, CLAUDE (circa 1514-1572), French composer **6** 466

GOUJON, JEAN (circa 1510-1568), French sculptor **6** 466-467

GOULART, JOÃO (1918-1976), Brazilian statesman **6** 467-469

GOULD, GLENN (1932-1982), Canadian musician **6** 469-470

GOULD, JAY (1836-1892), American financier and railroad builder **6** 470-472

GOULD, STEPHEN JAY (1941-2002), American paleontologist **6** 472-473

GOUNOD, CHARLES FRANÇOIS (1818-1893), French composer **6** 473-474

GOURLAY, ROBERT (1778-1863), British reformer in Canada **6** 474

GOURMONT, REMY DE (1858-1915), French author, critic, and essayist **6** 475

GOWER, JOHN (circa 1330-1408), English poet **6** 475-476

GOYA Y LUCIENTES, FRANCISCO DE PAULA JOSÉ DE (1746-1828), Spanish painter and printmaker **6** 476-478

GOYEN, JAN VAN (1596-1656), Dutch painter **6** 478-479

GRACCHUS, GAIUS SEMPRONIUS (ca. 154-121 B.C.) member of a Roman plebeian family referred to as the Gracchi; flourished 3rd-2nd century B.C. **6** 479-480

GRACCHUS, TIBERIUS SEMPRONIUS (ca. 163-133 B.C.) member of a Roman plebeian family referred to as the Gracchi; flourished 3rd-2nd century B.C. **6** 479-480

GRACE, WILLIAM RUSSELL (1832-1904), Irish-born American entrepreneur and politician **6** 480-481

GRACIÁN Y MORALES, BALTASAR JERÓNIMO (1601-1658), Spanish writer **6** 481-482

GRADY, HENRY WOODFIN (1850-1889), American editor and orator **6** 482-483

GRAETZ, HEINRICH HIRSCH (1817-1891), German historian and biblical exegete **6** 483

GRAHAM, KATHARINE MEYER (1917-2001), publisher who managed *The Washington Post* **6** 483-485

GRAHAM, MARTHA (1894-1991), American dancer and choreographer **6** 485-486

GRAHAM, OTTO (born 1921), American football player and coach **21** 174-176

GRAHAM, SYLVESTER (1794-1851), American reformer and temperance minister **6** 486-487

GRAHAM, WILLIAM FRANKLIN, JR. ("Billy"; born 1918), American evangelist **6** 487-488

GRAMSCI, ANTONIO (1891-1937), Italian writer and Communist leader **6** 488-489

GRANADOS, ENRIQUE (1867-1916), Spanish composer and pianist **6** 489-490

GRANGE, RED (Harold Edward Grange; 1903-1991), American football player **19** 128-130

GRANT, CARY (born Archibald Alexander Leach; 1904-1986), English actor **6** 490-492

GRANT, ULYSSES SIMPSON (1822-1885), American general, president 1869-1877 **6** 492-494

GRANVILLE, EVELYN BOYD (born 1924), African American mathematician **6** 494-496

GRASS, GÜNTER (born 1927), German novelist, playwright, and poet **6** 496-497

GRASSELLI, CAESAR AUGUSTIN (1850-1927), third generation to head the Grasselli Chemical Company **6** 497-498

GRATIAN (died circa 1155), Italian scholar, father of canon law **6** 498-499

GRATTAN, HENRY (1746-1820), Irish statesman and orator **6** 499

GRAU SAN MARTIN, RAMÓN (1887-1969), Cuban statesman and physician **6** 499-500

GRAUNT, JOHN (1620-1674), English merchant and civil servant **21** 176-178

GRAVES, EARL GILBERT, JR. (born 1935), African American publisher **23** 130-132

GRAVES, MICHAEL (born 1934), American Post-Modernist architect **6** 500-502

GRAVES, NANCY STEVENSON (1940-1995), American sculptor **6** 502-504

GRAVES, ROBERT RANKE (1895-1985), English author **6** 504-506

GRAY, ASA (1810-1888), American botanist **6** 506-507

GRAY, HANNAH HOLBORN (born 1930), university administrator **6** 507-508

GRAY, ROBERT (1755-1806), American explorer **6** 508-509

GRAY, THOMAS (1716-1771), English poet **6** 509-510

GRAY, WILLIAM H., III (born 1941), first African American to be elected House Whip for the U.S. House of Representatives **6** 510-511

Great Britain (United Kingdom of Great Britain and Northern Ireland; island kingdom; northwestern Europe)
• 1714-1901 (HANOVER)
1760-1820 (George III)
Murray, WIlliam **23** 256-258

GRECO, EL (1541-1614), Greek-born Spanish painter **6** 511-514

Greek literature (classical)
translations of
Murray, Gilbert **23** 250-253

GREELEY, ANDREW M. (born 1928), American Catholic priest, sociologist, and author **6** 514-515

GREELEY, HORACE (1811-1872), American editor and reformer **6** 515-517

GREELY, ADOLPHUS WASHINGTON (1844-1935), American soldier, explorer, and writer **6** 517-518

GREEN, CONSTANCE MCLAUGHLIN (1897-1975), American author and historian **6** 518-519

GREEN, EDITH STARRETT (1910-1987), United States congresswoman from Oregon (1954-1974) **6** 519-520

GREEN, THOMAS HILL (1836-1882), British philosopher **6** 520-521

GREEN, WILLIAM R. (1872-1952), American labor union leader **6** 521

GREENAWAY, KATE (Catherine; 1846-1901), English author and illustrator **18** 168-169

GREENBERG, CLEMENT (1909-1994), American art critic **6** 521-523

GREENE, CATHERINE LITTLEFIELD (1755-1814), American inventor **22** 200-203

GREENE, GRAHAM (born 1904), English novelist and dramatist **6** 523-524

GREENE, GRAHAM (born ca. 1952), Canadian-Native American actor **6** 524-525

GREENE, NATHANAEL (1742-1786), American Revolutionary War general **6** 525-526

GREENSPAN, ALAN (born 1926), American economist **6** 526-528

GREER, GERMAINE (born 1939), author and authoritative commentator on women's liberation and sexuality **6** 528-530

GREGG, JOHN ROBERT (1867-1948), American inventor of system of shorthand writing **21** 178-180

GREGG, WILLIAM (1800-1867), American manufacturer **6** 530-531

GREGORY I, SAINT (circa 540-604), pope 590-604 **6** 531-532

GREGORY VII (circa 1020-1085), pope 1073-85 **6** 532-534

GREGORY IX (Ugo [Ugolino] di Segni; 1145-1241), Roman Catholic pope (1227-1241) **21** 180-183

GREGORY XII (Angelo Corrario; c. 1327-1417), pope 1406-1415 **18** 169-171

GREGORY XIII (1502-1585), pope 1572-1585 **6** 534

GREGORY, LADY AUGUSTA (1852-1932), Irish dramatist **6** 535-536

GREGORY, DICK (Richard Claxton Gregory; born 1932), comedian and civil rights and world peace activist **6** 536-537

GREGORY OF TOURS, SAINT (538-594), Frankish bishop and historian **6** 534-535

GRETZKY, WAYNE (born 1961), Canadian hockey star **6** 537-539

GREUZE, JEAN BAPTISTE (1725-1805), French painter **6** 539

GREY, CHARLES (2nd Earl Grey; 1764-1845), English statesman, prime minister 1830-1834 **6** 539-540

GREY, SIR GEORGE (1812-1898), English explorer and colonial governor **6** 540-541

GREY, ZANE (Pearl Zane Gray; 1872-1939), American author **20** 160-162

GRIBEAUVAL, JEAN BAPTISTE VAQUETTE DE (1715-1789), French army officer **20** 162-163

GRIEG, EDVARD HAGERUP (1843-1907), Norwegian composer **6** 541-542

GRIERSON, JOHN (1898-1972), Canadian and British filmmaker **6** 542-543

GRIFFES, CHARLES TOMLINSON (1884-1920), American composer **6** 543-544

GRIFFITH, DAVID WARK (1875-1948), American film maker **6** 544-545

GRIFFITH, SIR SAMUEL WALKER (1845-1920), Australian statesman and jurist **6** 545-546

GRIFFITH JOYNER, FLORENCE (1959-1998), American athlete **19** 130-133

GRILLPARZER, FRANZ (1791-1872), Austrian playwright **6** 546-547

GRIMKÉ, ANGELINA EMILY (1805-1879) AND SARAH MOORE (1792-1873), American abolitionists and women's rights agitators **7** 1-2

GRIMKÉ, ARCHIBALD HENRY (1849-1930), American editor, author, and diplomat **7** 1-2

GRIMM, JAKOB KARL (1785-1863) AND WILHELM KARL (1786-1859), German scholars, linguists, and authors **7** 3-4

GRIMMELSHAUSEN, HANS JAKOB CHRISTOFFEL VON (1621/22-1676), German author **7** 4-5

GRIS, JUAN (1887-1927), Spanish painter **7** 5-6

GRISHAM, JOHN (born 1955), American author and attorney **7** 6-8

GROMYKO, ANDREI ANDREEVICH (1909-1988), minister of foreign affairs and president of the Union of Soviet Socialist Republic (1985-1988) **7** 9-11

GROOMS, RED (born 1937), American artist **7** 11-12

GROOTE, GERARD (1340-1384), Dutch evangelical preacher **7** 12-13

GROPIUS, WALTER (1883-1969), German-American architect, educator, and designer **7** 13-14

GROS, BARON (Antoine Jean Gros; 1771-1835), French romantic painter **7** 14-15

GROSS, SAMUEL DAVID (1805-1884), American surgeon, author, and educator **21** 183-185

GROSSETESTE, ROBERT (1175-1253), English bishop and statesman **7** 15

GROSSINGER, JENNIE (1892-1972), American hotel executive and philanthropist **7** 15-17

GROSZ, GEORGE (1893-1959), German-American painter and graphic artist **7** 17-18

GROTIUS, HUGO (1583-1645), Dutch jurist, statesman, and historian **7** 18-19

GROTOWSKI, JERZY (born 1933), founder of the experimental Laboratory Theatre in Wroclaw, Poland **7** 19-20

GROVE, ANDREW (András Gróf; born 1936), American businessman **18** 171-174

GROVE, FREDERICK PHILIP (circa 1871-1948), Canadian novelist and essayist **7** 20-21

GROVES, LESLIE (1896-1970), military director of the Manhattan Project (atom bomb) during World War II **7** 21-22

GRÜNEWALD, MATTHIAS (circa 1475-1528), German painter **7** 23-24

GUARDI, FRANCESCO (1712-1793), Italian painter **7** 24-25

GUARINI, GUARINO (1624-1683), Italian architect, priest, and philosopher **7** 25-26

GUASTAVINO, RAFAEL (Rafael Guastavino Morano; 1842-1908), Spanish-American architect **23** 132-134

GUCCIONE, BOB, JR. (born ca. 1956), American publisher **7** 26

GUDERIAN, HEINZ (1888-1953), German military leader **20** 163-165

GÜEMES, MARTÍN (1785-1821), Argentine independence fighter **7** 26-27

GUERCINO (Giovanni Francesco Barbieri; 1591-1666), Italian painter **7** 27

GUERICKE, OTTO VON (1602-1686), German physicist **7** 27-28

GUERIN, VERONICA (1959-1996), Irish investigative reporter and journalist **18** 174-176

GUERRERO, VICENTE (1783-1831), Mexican independence fighter, president 1829 **7** 28-30

GUEVARA, ERNESTO ("Che"; 1924-1967) Argentine revolutionary and guerrilla theoretician **7** 30-31

GUEYE, LAMINE (1891-1968), Senegalese statesman **7** 31

GUGGENHEIM, DANIEL (1856-1930), American industrialist and philanthropist **21** 185-187

GUGGENHEIM, MEYER (1828-1905), Swiss-born American industrialist **7** 31-32

GUICCIARDINI, FRANCESCO (1483-1540), Italian historian and statesman **7** 32-33

GUIDO D'AREZZO (circa 995-circa 1050), Italian music theorist **7** 33

GUILLAUME DE LORRIS (circa 1210-1237), French poet **7** 33-34

GUILLÉN, NICOLÁS (born 1902), Cuban author 7 34-35

GUILLÉN Y ALVAREZ, JORGE (1893-1984), Spanish poet 7 35-36

GUINIZZELLI, GUIDO (1230/40-1276), Italian poet 7 36-37

GUINNESS, ALEC (born 1914), British actor of the stage, films, and television 7 37-38

GÜIRÁLDEZ, RICARDO (1886-1927), Argentine poet and novelist 7 38-39

GUISCARD, ROBERT (1016-1085), Norman adventurer 7 39-40

GUISEWITE, CATHY (born 1950), American cartoonist and author 18 176-177

GUIZOT, FRANÇOIS PIERRE GUILLAUME (1787-1874), French statesman and historian 7 40-41

GUMPLOWICZ, LUDWIG (1838-1909), Polish-Austrian sociologist and political theorist 7 41

GUNN, THOM (born 1929), English poet 18 177-178

GÜNTHER, IGNAZ (1725-1775), German sculptor 7 41-42

GUSTAVUS I (Gustavus Eriksson; 1496-1560), king of Sweden 1523-1560 7 42-43

GUSTAVUS II (Gustavus Adolphus; 1594-1632), king of Sweden 1611-1632 7 43-45

GUSTAVUS III (1746-1792), king of Sweden 1771-1792 7 45-46

GUSTON, PHILIP (1913-1980), American painter and a key member of the New York School 7 47-48

GUTENBERG, JOHANN (circa 1398-1468), German inventor and printer 7 48-49

GUTHRIE, EDWIN RAY (1886-1959), American psychologist 7 49-50

GUTHRIE, TYRONE (1900-1971), English theater director 7 50-51

GUTHRIE, WOODROW WILSON ("Woody"; 1912-1967), writer and performer of folk songs 7 51-52 Leadbelly 23 208-211

GUTIÉRRÉZ, GUSTAVO (born 1928), Peruvian who was the father of liberation theology 7 52-53

GUY DE CHAULIAC (circa 1295-1368), French surgeon 7 54

H

HABASH, GEORGE (born 1926), founder of the Arab Nationalists' Movement (1952) and of the Popular Front for the Liberation of Palestine (PFLP; 1967) 7 55-56

HABER, FRITZ (1868-1934), German chemist 7 56-58

HABERMAS, JÜRGEN (born 1929), German philosopher and sociologist 7 58-60

HABIBIE, BACHARUDDIN JUSUF (born 1936), president of Indonesia 19 134-136

HADRIAN (76-138), Roman emperor 117-138 7 60-61

HAECKEL, ERNST HEINRICH PHILIPP AUGUST (1834-1919), German biologist and natural philosopher 7 61-62

HAFIZ, SHAMS AL-DIN (circa 1320-1390), Persian mystical poet and Koranic exegete 7 63

HAGEN, UTA THYRA (born 1919), American actress 18 179-180

HAGEN, WALTER (1892-1969), American golfer 21 188-190

HAGUE, FRANK (1876-1956), American politician 7 63-64

HAHN, OTTO (1879-1968), German chemist 7 64-65

HAHNEMANN, SAMUEL (Christian Friedrich Samuel Hahnemann; 1755-1843), German physician and chemist 21 190-193

HAIDAR ALI (1721/22-1782), Indian prince, ruler of Mysore 1759-1782 7 65-66

HAIG, ALEXANDER M., JR. (born 1924), American military leader, diplomat, secretary of state, and presidential adviser 7 66-67

HAIG, DOUGLAS (1st Earl Haig; 1861-1928), British field marshal 7 67-68

HAILE SELASSIE (1892-1975), emperor of Ethiopia 7 68-70

HAKLUYT, RICHARD (1552/53-1616), English geographer and author 7 70

HALBERSTAM, DAVID (born 1934), American journalist, author and social historian 18 180-183

HALDANE, JOHN BURDON SANDERSON (1892-1964), English biologist 7 70-71

HALE, CLARA (nee Clara McBride; 1905-1992), American humanitarian and social reformer 20 166-168

HALE, EDWARD EVERETT (1822-1909), American Unitarian minister and author 7 71-72

HALE, GEORGE ELLERY (1868-1938), American astronomer 7 72-74

HALE, SARAH JOSEPHA (née Buell; 1788-1879), American editor 7 74-75

HALES, STEPHEN (1677-1761), English scientist and clergyman 7 75

HALÉVY, ÉLIE (1870-1937), French philosopher and historian 7 76

HALEY, ALEX (1921-1992), African American journalist and author 7 76-78

HALEY, MARGARET A. (1861-1939), American educator and labor activist 7 78-79

HALFFTER, CHRISTÓBAL (born 1930), Spanish composer 7 79-80

HALIBURTON, THOMAS CHANDLER (1796-1865), Canadian judge and author 7 80

HALIDE EDIP ADIVAR (1884-1964), Turkish woman writer, scholar, and public figure 7 80-82

HALIFAX, 1ST EARL OF (Edward Frederick Lindley Wood; 1881-1959), English statesman 7 82-83

HALL, ASAPH (1829-1907), American astronomer 7 83-84

HALL, DONALD (born 1928), New England memoirist, short story writer, essayist, dramatist, critic, and anthologist as well as poet 7 84-85

HALL, EDWARD MARSHALL (1858-1927), British attorney 22 204-205

HALL, GRANVILLE STANLEY (1844-1924), American psychologist and educator 7 85-86

HALL, RADCLYFFE (Marguerite Radclyffe Hall; 1880-1943), British author 20 168-170

HALLAJ, AL-HUSAYN IBN MANSUR AL (857-922), Persian Moslem mystic and martyr 7 86-87

HALLAM, LEWIS, SR. AND JR. (Lewis Sr. ca. 1705-1755; Lewis Jr. 1740-1808), American actors and theatrical managers 7 87

HALLECK, HENRY WAGER (1815-1872), American military strategist 22 205-207

HALLER, ALBRECHT VON (1708-1777), Swiss physician 7 87-88

HALLEY, EDMUND (1656-1742), English astronomer 7 88-89

HALS, FRANS (1581/85-1666), Dutch painter **7** 89-91

HALSEY, WILLIAM FREDERICK (1882-1959), American admiral **7** 91-92

HALSTED, WILLIAM STEWART (1852-1922), American surgeon **22** 207-209

HAMANN, JOHANN GEORG (1730-1788), German philosopher **7** 92

HAMER, FANNIE LOU (born Townsend; 1917-1977), American civil rights activist **7** 93-94

HAMILCAR BARCA (circa 285-229/228 B.C.), Carthaginian general and statesman **7** 94-95

HAMILTON, ALEXANDER (1755-1804), American statesman **7** 95-98

HAMILTON, ALICE (1869-1970), American physician **7** 98-99

HAMILTON, EDITH (1867-1963), American educator and author **22** 209-211

HAMILTON, SIR WILLIAM ROWAN (1805-1865), Irish mathematical physicist **7** 99-100

HAMMARSKJÖLD, DAG (1905-1961), Swedish diplomat **7** 100-101

HAMM-BRÜCHER, HILDEGARD (born 1921), Free Democratic Party's candidate for the German presidency in 1994 **7** 101-103

HAMMER, ARMAND (1898-1990), American entrepreneur and art collector **7** 103-104

HAMMERSTEIN, OSCAR CLENDENNING II (1895-1960), lyricist and librettist of the American theater **7** 104-106

HAMMETT, (SAMUEL) DASHIELL (1894-1961), American author **7** 106-108

HAMMOND, JAMES HENRY (1807-1864), American statesman **7** 108-109

HAMMOND, JOHN LAWRENCE LE BRETON (1872-1952), English historian **7** 108-109

HAMMOND, LUCY BARBARA (1873-1961), English historian **7** 109

HAMMURABI (1792-1750 B.C.), king of Babylonia **7** 109-110

HAMPDEN, JOHN (1594-1643), English statesman **7** 110-111

HAMPTON, LIONEL (1908-2002), African American jazz musician **22** 211-213

HAMPTON, WADE (circa 1751-1835), American planter **7** 111-112

HAMPTON, WADE III (1818-1902), American statesman and Confederate general **7** 112

Hampton Institute (Virginia) Johnston, Frances Benjamin **23** 174-177

Hampton Normal and Industrial Institution see Hampton Institute

HAMSUN, KNUT (1859-1952), Norwegian novelist **7** 113-114

HAN FEI TZU (circa 280-233 B.C.), Chinese statesman and philosopher **7** 124-125

HAN WU-TI (157-87 B.C.), Chinese emperor **7** 136

HAN YÜ (768-824), Chinese author **7** 136-137

HANAFI, HASSAN (born 1935), Egyptian philosopher **7** 114

HANCOCK, JOHN (1737-1793), American statesman **7** 114-116

HAND, BILLINGS LEARNED (1872-1961), American jurist **7** 116

HANDEL, GEORGE FREDERICK (1685-1759), German-born English composer and organist **7** 116-119

HANDKE, PETER (born 1942), Austrian playwright, novelist, screenwriter, essayist, and poet **7** 119-121

HANDLIN, OSCAR (born 1915), American historian **7** 121-122

HANDSOME LAKE (a.k.a. Hadawa' Ko; ca. 1735-1815), Seneca spiritual leader **7** 122-123

HANDY, WILLIAM CHRISTOPHER (1873-1958), African American songwriter **7** 123-124

HANKS, NANCY (1927-1983), called the "mother of a million artists" for her work in building federal financial support for the arts and artists **7** 126-127

HANKS, TOM (Thomas Jeffrey Hanks; born 1956), American actor **23** 135-137

HANNA, MARCUS ALONZO (1837-1904), American businessman and politician **7** 127-128

HANNIBAL BARCA (247-183 B.C.), Carthaginian general **7** 128-130

Hanover dynasty (Great Britain) see Great Britain–1714-1901 (Hanover)

HANSBERRY, LORRAINE VIVIAN (1930-1965), American writer and a major figure on Broadway **7** 130-131

HANSEN, ALVIN (1887-1975), American economist **7** 131-132

HANSEN, JULIA BUTLER (1907-1988), American politician **7** 132-133

HANSON, DUANE (1925-1990), American super-realist sculptor **7** 133-135

HANSON, HOWARD (1896-1981), American composer and educator **7** 135-136

HAPGOOD, NORMAN (1868-1937), American author and editor **7** 137-138

HARA, KEI (1856-1921), Japanese statesman and prime minister 1918-1921 **7** 138

HARAND, IRENE (born Irene Wedl; 1900-1975), Austrian political and human rights activist **7** 139-145

HARAWI, ILYAS AL- (Elias Harawi; born 1930), president of Lebanon **7** 145-146

HARDENBERG, PRINCE KARL AUGUST VON (1750-1822), Prussian statesman **7** 146-147

HARDIE, JAMES KEIR (1856-1915), Scottish politician **7** 147-148

HARDING, WARREN GAMALIEL (1865-1923), American statesman, president 1921-1923 **7** 148-149

HARDY, HARRIET (1905-1993), American pathologist **7** 150

HARDY, THOMAS (1840-1928), English novelist, poet, and dramatist **7** 150-152

HARE, ROBERT (1781-1858), American chemist **7** 152-153

HARGRAVES, EDWARD HAMMOND (1816-1891), Australian publicist **7** 153-154

HARING, KEITH (1958-1990), American artist tied to New York graffiti art of the 1980s **7** 154-155

HARINGTON, JOHN (1560-1612), English author and courtier **21** 193-195

HARJO, SUZAN SHOWN (born 1945), Native American activist **18** 183-185

HARKNESS, GEORGIA (1891-1974), American Methodist and ecumenical theologian **7** 155-156

HARLAN, JOHN MARSHALL (1833-1911), American jurist **7** 156-157

HARLAN, JOHN MARSHALL (1899-1971), U.S. Supreme Court justice **7** 157-159

Harlem renaissance (American literature) Hunter, Alberta **23** 160-162 Toomer, Jean **23** 408-410

HARLEY, ROBERT (1st Earl of Oxford and Earl Mortimer; 1661-1724), English statesman **7** 159-160

HARNACK, ADOLF VON (1851-1930), German theologian **7** 160

HARNETT, WILLIAM MICHAEL (1848-1892), American painter **7** 160-161

HAROLD I (circa 840-933), king of Norway 860-930 **7** 161-162

HAROLD II (Harold Godwinson; died 1066), Anglo-Saxon king of England of 1066 **7** 162

HAROLD III (1015-1066), king of Norway 1047-1066 **7** 163

HARPER, FRANCES (Frances Ellen Watkins Harper; 1825-1911), African American author, abolitionist and women's rights activist **18** 185-187

HARPER, JAMES (1795-1869), American publisher **22** 213-216

HARPER, WILLIAM RAINEY (1856-1906), American educator and biblical scholar **7** 163-164

HARPUR, CHARLES (1813-1866), Australian poet and author **22** 216-218

HARRIMAN, EDWARD HENRY (1848-1909), American railroad executive **7** 164-165

HARRIMAN, PAMELA (1920-1997), American ambassador and patrician **18** 187-189

HARRIMAN, W. AVERELL (1891-1986), American industrialist, financier, and diplomat **7** 165-166

HARRINGTON, JAMES (1611-1677), English political theorist **7** 166-167

HARRINGTON, MICHAEL (1928-1989), American political activist and educator **7** 167-169

HARRIOT, THOMAS (1560-1621), English scientist and mathematician **23** 137-139

HARRIS, ABRAM LINCOLN, JR. (1899-1963), African American economist **7** 169-171

HARRIS, BARBARA CLEMENTINE (born 1930), African American activist and Anglican bishop **7** 171-172

HARRIS, FRANK (1856-1931), Irish-American author and editor **7** 172-173

HARRIS, JOEL CHANDLER (1848-1908), American writer **7** 173-174

HARRIS, LADONNA (born 1931), Native American activist **18** 189-191

HARRIS, PATRICIA ROBERTS (1924-1985), first African American woman in the U.S. Cabinet **7** 174-175

HARRIS, ROY (1898-1979), American composer **7** 175-176

HARRIS, TOWNSEND (1804-1878), American merchant and diplomat **7** 176-177

HARRIS, WILLIAM TORREY (1835-1909), American educator and philosopher **7** 177-178

HARRISON, BENJAMIN (1833-1901), American statesman, president 1889-1893 **7** 178-179

HARRISON, PETER (1716-1775), American architect and merchant **7** 179-180

HARRISON, WILLIAM HENRY (1773-1841), American statesman, president 1841 **7** 180-181

HARSHA (Harshavardhana; circa 590-647), king of Northern India 606-612 **7** 181-182

HART, GARY W. (born 1936), American political campaign organizer, U.S. senator, and presidential candidate **7** 182-184

HART, HERBERT LIONEL ADOLPHUS (1907-1992), British legal philosopher **22** 218-219

HARTE, FRANCIS BRET (1837-1902), American poet and fiction writer **7** 184-185

HARTLEY, DAVID (1705-1757), British physician and philosopher **7** 185

HARTLEY, MARSDEN (1877-1943), American painter **7** 186

HARTSHORNE, CHARLES (born 1897), American theologian **7** 186-187

HARUN AL-RASHID (766-809), Abbasid caliph of Baghdad 786-809 **7** 188

HARUNOBU, SUZUKI (ca. 1725-1770), Japanese painter and printmaker **7** 188-189

HARVARD, JOHN (1607-1638), English philanthropist **21** 195-197

Harvard College
see Harvard University

Harvard University (Cambridge, Massachusetts)
Law School
Langdell, Christopher Columbus **23** 204-206

HARVEY, WILLIAM (1578-1657), English physician **7** 189-190

HASAN, IBN AL-HAYTHAM (ca. 966-1039), Arab physicist, astronomer, and mathematician **7** 190-191

HASKINS, CHARLES HOMER (1870-1937), American historian **7** 191-192

HASSAM, FREDERICK CHILDE (1859-1935), American impressionist painter **7** 192

HASSAN, MOULEY (King Hassan II; 1929-1999), inherited the throne of Morocco in 1961 **7** 194-195

HASSAN, MUHAMMAD ABDILLE (1864-1920), Somali politico-religious leader and poet **7** 194-195

HASTINGS, PATRICK GARDINER (1880-1952), British lawyer and politician **22** 219-221

HASTINGS, WARREN (1732-1818), English statesman **7** 195-196

HATCH, WILLIAM HENRY (1833-1896), American reformer and politician **7** 196

HATSHEPSUT (ruled 1503-1482 B.C.), Egyptian queen **7** 196-197

HATTA, MOHAMMAD (1902-1980), a leader of the Indonesian nationalist movement (1920s-1945) and a champion of non-alignment and of socialism grounded in Islam **7** 197-199

HAUPTMANN, GERHART JOHANN ROBERT (1862-1946), German dramatist and novelist **7** 199-201

HAUSHOFER, KARL (1869-1946), German general and geopolitician **7** 201

HAUSSMANN, BARON GEORGES EUGÈNE (1809-1891), French prefect of the Seine **7** 201-202

HAVEL, VACLAV (born 1936), playwright and human rights activist who became the president of Czechoslovakia **7** 202-205

HAVEMEYER, HENRY OSBORNE (1847-1907), American businessman **22** 222-224

HAWES, HARRIET ANN BOYD (1871-1945), American archeologist **22** 224-225

HAWKE, ROBERT JAMES LEE (born 1929), Australian Labor prime minister **7** 205-206

HAWKING, STEPHEN WILLIAM (born 1942), British physicist and mathematician **7** 206-208

HAWKINS, COLEMAN (1904-1969), American jazz musician **7** 208-210

HAWKINS, SIR JOHN (1532-1595), English naval commander **7** 210-211

HAWKS, HOWARD WINCHESTER (1896-1977), American film director **22** 225-226

HAWKSMOOR, NICHOLAS (1661-1736), English architect **7** 211-212

HAWTHORNE, NATHANIEL (1804-1864), American novelist **7** 212-215

HAY, JOHN (1838-1905), American statesman **7** 215-216

HAYA DE LA TORRE, VICTOR RAUL (born 1895), Peruvian political leader and theorist **7** 216-217

HAYDEN, FERDINAND VANDIVEER (1829-1887), American geologist and explorer **22** 227-229

HAYDEN, ROBERT EARL (1913-1980), African American poet **22** 229-231

HAYDEN, THOMAS EMMET (born 1939), American writer and political activist **7** 217-219

HAYDN, FRANZ JOSEPH (1732-1809), Austrian composer **7** 219-221

HAYEK, FRIEDRICH A. VON (1899-1992), Austrian-born British free market economist, social philosopher, and Nobel Laureate **7** 221-223

HAYES, HELEN (1900-1993), American actress **7** 223-224

HAYES, CARDINAL PATRICK JOSEPH (1867-1938), American cardinal **7** 224-225

HAYES, ROLAND (1887-1977), African American classical singer **7** 225-227

HAYES, RUTHERFORD BIRCHARD (1822-1893), American statesman, president 1877-1881 **7** 227-228

HAYFORD, J. E. CASELY (1866-1903), Gold Coast politician, journalist, and educator **7** 228-230

HAYKAL, MUHAMMAD HUSAIN (born 1923), Egyptian journalist and editor of *al-Ahram*(1957-1974) **7** 230-231

Haymarket Riot (Chicago; 1886) Parsons, Lucy González **23** 293-295

HAYNE, ROBERT YOUNG (1791-1839), American politician **7** 231-232

HAYNES, ELWOOD (1857-1925), American inventor and businessman **22** 231-234

HAYS, WILL (William Harrison Hays; 1879-1954), American film censor **21** 197-199

HAYWOOD, WILLIAM DUDLEY (1869-1928), American labor leader **7** 232-233

HAYWORTH, RITA (born Margarita Carmen Cansino; 1918-1987), American actress **7** 233-235

HAZLITT, WILLIAM (1778-1830), English literary and social critic **7** 235-236

HEAD, EDITH (1898-1981), American costume designer **18** 191-193

HEADE, MARTIN JOHNSON (1819-1904), American painter **7** 236

HEALY, BERNADINE (born 1944) American physician and administrator **7** 237-238

HEANEY, SEAMUS JUSTIN (born 1939), Irish poet, author, and editor **7** 238-240

HEARN, LAFCADIO (1850-1904), European-born American author **7** 240

HEARNE, SAMUEL (1745-1792), English explorer **7** 241-242

HEARST, GEORGE (1820-1891), American publisher and politician **7** 242

HEARST, PATRICIA (born 1954), kidnapped heiress who became a bank robber **7** 242-243

HEARST, WILLIAM RANDOLPH (1863-1951), American publisher and politician **7** 243-244

HEATH, EDWARD RICHARD GEORGE (born 1916), prime minister of Great Britain (1970-1974) **7** 244-246

HEAVYSEGE, CHARLES (1816-1876), Canadian poet and dramatist **7** 246

HEBBEL, FRIEDRICH (1813-1863), German poet and playwright **7** 247

HEBERT, JACQUES RENÉ (1757-1794), French journalist and revolutionist **7** 247-248

HECHT, BEN (1894-1964), American journalist, playwright, and Hollywood scriptwriter **7** 248-250

HECKER, ISAAC THOMAS (1819-1888), American Catholic religious founder **7** 250-251

HECKLER, MARGARET MARY O'SHAUGHNESSY (born 1931), American attorney, congressional representative, secretary of health and human services, and ambassador **7** 251-252

HEDIN, SVEN ANDERS (1865-1952), Swedish explorer and geographer **7** 252-253

HEFNER, HUGH (born 1926), founder and publisher of Playboy magazine **7** 253-254

HEGEL, GEORG WILHELM FRIEDRICH (1770-1831), German philosopher and educator **7** 254-256

HEIDEGGER, MARTIN (1889-1976), German philosopher **7** 257-258

HEIDENSTAM, CARL GUSTAF VERNER VON (1859-1940), Swedish author **7** 258-259

HEIFETZ, JASCHA (1901-1987), American violinist **20** 170-172

HEIGHT, DOROTHY IRENE (born 1912), civil and human rights activist **23** 139-141

HEINE, HEINRICH (1797-1856), German poet and essayist **7** 259-260

HEINRICH, ANTHONY PHILIP (1781-1861), American composer **7** 261

HEINZ, HENRY JOHN (H.J. Heinz; 1844-1919), American businessman **19** 136-138

HEISENBERG, WERNER KARL (born 1901), German physicist **7** 261-263

HELLER, JOSEPH (1923-1999), American author **7** 263-265

HELLER, WALTER (1915-1987), chairman of the Council of Economic Advisors (1961-1964) and chief spokesman of the "New Economics" **7** 265-266

HELLMAN, LILLIAN FLORENCE (born 1905), American playwright **7** 267-268

HELMHOLTZ, HERMANN LUDWIG FERDINAND VON (1821-1894), German physicist and physiologist **7** 268-269

HELMONT, JAN BAPTISTA VAN (1579-1644), Flemish chemist and physician **7** 269-271

HELMS, JESSE (born 1921), United States Senator from North Carolina **7** 271-272

HELPER, HINTON ROWAN (1829-1909), American author and railroad promoter **7** 272-273

HELVÉTIUS, CLAUDE ADRIEN (1715-1771), French philosopher **7** 273-274

HEMINGWAY, ERNEST MILLER (1898-1961), American novelist and journalist **7** 274-277 publishers of Liveright, Horace B. **23** 229-231

HÉMON, LOUIS (1880-1913), French-Canadian novelist **7** 277

Hemophilia (medicine) Pool, Judith Graham **23** 315-316

HEMPHILL, JOHN (1803-1862), American jurist and statesman **22** 234-236

HENDERSON, ARTHUR (1863-1935), British statesman **7** 277-278

HENDERSON, DONALD AINSLIE (D.A.; born 1928), American public health official **22** 236-238

HENDERSON, RICHARD (1735-1785), American jurist and land speculator **7** 278-279

HENDRIX, JIMI (born Johnny Allen Hendrix; 1942-1970), African American guitarist, singer, and composer **7** 279-283

HENG SAMRIN (born 1934), Cambodian Communist leader who became president of the People's Republic of Kampuchea (PRK) in 1979 **7** 283-285

HENIE, SONJA (1912-1969), Norwegian figure skater **20** 172-173

HENRI, ROBERT (Robert Henry Cozad; 1865-1929), American painter **22** 238-240

HENRY I (876-936), king of Germany 919-936 **7** 285-286

HENRY I (1068-1135), king of England 1100-1135 **7** 286-287

HENRY II (1133-1189), king of England 1154-1189 **7** 287-289

HENRY III (1017-1056), Holy Roman emperor and king of Germany 1039-1056 **7** 290

HENRY III (1207-1272), king of England 1216-1272 **7** 290-292

HENRY IV (1050-1106), Holy Roman emperor and king of Germany 1056-1106 **7** 292

HENRY IV (1367-1413), king of England 1399-1413 **7** 292-293

HENRY IV (1553-1610), king of France 1589-1610 **7** 293-295

HENRY V (1081-1125), Holy Roman emperor and king of Germany 1106-1125 **7** 295-296

HENRY V (1387-1422), king of England 1413-1422 **7** 296-297

HENRY VI (1421-1471), king of England 1422-61 and 1470-1471 **7** 298-299

HENRY VII (1274-1313), Holy Roman emperor and king of Germany 1308-1313 **7** 299-300

HENRY VII (1457-1509), king of England 1485-1509 **7** 300-302

HENRY VIII (1491-1547), king of England 1509-1547 **7** 302-305

HENRY, AARON (born 1922), African American civil rights activist **7** 306-307

HENRY, JOSEPH (1797-1878), American physicist and electrical experimenter **7** 307-308

HENRY, MARGUERITE (Margurite Breithaupt; 1902-1997), American author **19** 138-140

HENRY, O. (pseudonym of William Sydney Porter; 1862-1910), American short-story writer **7** 308-309

HENRY, PATRICK (1736-1799), American orator and revolutionary **7** 309-311

HENRY THE NAVIGATOR (1394-1460), Portuguese prince **7** 305-306

HENSON, JIM (James Maury Henson, 1936-1990), American puppeteer, screenwriter, and producer **19** 140-142

HENSON, JOSIAH (1789-1883), African American preacher and former slave **7** 311-312

HENSON, MATTHEW A. (1866-1955), African American Arctic explorer **7** 312-314

HENZE, HANS WERNER (born 1926), German composer **7** 314

HEPBURN, AUDREY (born Edda Van Heemstra Hepburn-Ruston; 1929-1993), Swiss actress and humanitarian **7** 314-316

HEPBURN, KATHARINE (born 1907), American actress on the stage and on the screen **7** 316-317

HEPPLEWHITE, GEORGE (died 1786), English furniture designer **7** 317-318

HEPWORTH, BARBARA (1903-1975), English sculptor **7** 318-319

HERACLIDES OF PONTUS (circa 388-310 B.C.), Greek philosopher **7** 319-320

HERACLITUS (flourished 500 B.C.), Greek philosopher **7** 320

HERACLIUS (circa 575-641), Byzantine emperor 610-641 **7** 320-321

HERBART, JOHANN FRIEDRICH (1776-1841), German philosopher-psychologist and educator **7** 321-322

HERBERG, WILL (1906-1977), Jewish theologian, social thinker, and biblical exegete **7** 322-323

HERBERT, EDWARD (1st Baron Herbert of Cherbury; 1583-1648), English philosopher, poet, diplomat, and historian **7** 324

HERBERT, GEORGE (1593-1633), English metaphysical poet and Anglican priest **7** 324-326

HERDER, JOHANN GOTTFRIED VON (1744-1803), German philosopher, theologian, and critic **7** 327-328

HERMAN, JERRY (born 1931), American composer and lyricist **20** 173-175

HERNÁNDEZ, JOSÉ (1834-1886), Argentine poet **7** 328-329

HERNÁNDEZ COLÓN, RAFAEL (born 1936), Puerto Rican governor **7** 329-330

HEROD THE GREAT (circa 73-4 B.C.), king of Judea **7** 333-334

HERODOTUS (circa 484-circa 425 B.C.), Greek historian **7** 330-333

HERON OF ALEXANDRIA (flourished circa 60), Greek engineer, mathematician, and inventor **7** 334-335

HERRERA, CAROLINA (Maria Carolina Josefina Pacanins y Nino; born 1939), Venezuelan designer **23** 141-143

HERRERA, JUAN DE (circa 1530-1597), Spanish architect **7** 335

HERRERA LANE, FELIPE (1922-1996), Chilean banker and economist **7** 336

HERRICK, ROBERT (1591-1674), English poet and Anglican parson **7** 336-339

HERRIOT, ÉDOUARD (1872-1957), French statesman and author **7** 339-340

HERRMANN, BERNARD (Benny Herrmann; 1911-1975), American composer **21** 199-202

HERSCHEL, CAROLINE (1750-1848), German/English astronomer and mathematician **20** 175-176

HERSCHEL, SIR JOHN FREDERICK WILLIAM (1792-1871), English astronomer **7** 340-341

HERSCHEL, SIR WILLIAM (1738-1822), German-born English astronomer **7** 341-343

HERSHEY, ALFRED DAY (1908-1997), American microbiologist **7** 343-345

HERSHEY, MILTON (1857-1945), American businessman and philanthropist **19** 142-144

HERSKOVITS, MELVILLE JEAN (1895-1963), American anthropologist **7** 345

HERTZ, HEINRICH RUDOLF (1857-1894), German physicist **7** 346-347

HERTZOG, JAMES BARRY MUNNIK (1866-1942), South African prime minister 1924-39 **7** 347-348

HERUY WÄLDÄ-SELLASÉ (1878-1938), Ethiopian writer and government press director **7** 348-349

HERZBERG, GERHARD (born 1904), German-born Canadian chemist/physicist **7** 349-350

HERZEN, ALEKSANDR IVANOVICH (1812-1870), Russian author and political agitator **7** 351-352

HERZL, THEODOR (1860-1904), Hungarian-born Austrian Zionist author **7** 352-354

HERZOG, CHAIM (1918-1997), president of the State of Israel **7** 354-355

HERZOG, ROMAN (born 1934), president of the German Federal Constitutional Court (1987-1994) and president of Germany **7** 355-357

HESBURGH, THEODORE MARTIN (born 1917), activist American Catholic priest who was president of Notre Dame (1952-1987) **7** 357-358

HESCHEL, ABRAHAM JOSHUA (1907-1972), Polish-American Jewish theologian **7** 358-359

HESELTINE, MICHAEL (born 1933), British Conservative politician **7** 359-361

HESIOD (flourished circa 700 B.C.), Greek poet **7** 361-362

HESS, VICTOR FRANCIS (1883-1964), Austrian-American physicist **7** 362-363

HESS, WALTER RICHARD RUDOLF (1894-1987), deputy reichsführer for Adolf Hitler (1933-1941) **7** 363-365

HESS, WALTER RUDOLF (1881-1973), Swiss neurophysiologist **7** 365

HESSE, EVA (1936-1970), American sculptor **7** 365-367

HESSE, HERMANN (1877-1962), German novelist **7** 367-369

HESSE, MARY B. (born 1924), British philosopher **7** 369-371

HEVESY, GEORGE CHARLES DE (1885-1966), Hungarian chemist **7** 371

HEWITT, ABRAM STEVENS (1822-1903), American politician and manufacturer **7** 371-372

HEYDRICH, REINHARD (1904-1942), German architect of the Holocaust **20** 176-178

HEYERDAHL, THOR (1914-2002), Norwegian explorer, anthropologist and author **18** 194-196

HEYSE, PAUL JOHANN LUDWIG (1830-1914), German author **7** 372-373

HEYWOOD, THOMAS (1573/1574-1641), English playwright **7** 373-374

HIAWATHA (c. 1450), Native American Leader **23** 143-145

HICKOK, JAMES BUTLER ("Wild Bill"; 1837-1876), American gunfighter, scout, and spy **7** 374-375

HICKS, EDWARD (1780-1849), American folk painter **7** 375

HIDALGO Y COSTILLA, MIGUEL (1753-1811), Mexican revolutionary priest **7** 375-377

HIDAYAT, SADIQ (1903-1951), Persian author **7** 377-378

HIGGINS, MARGUERITE (1920-1966), American journalist **7** 378-380

HIGGINSON, THOMAS WENTWORTH (1823-1911), American reformer and editor **7** 380

HILDEBRANDT, JOHANN LUCAS VON (1663-1745), Austrian architect **7** 380-381

HILDRETH, RICHARD (1807-1865), American historian and political theorist **7** 382

HILFIGER, TOMMY (born 1952), American fashion designer **19** 144-146

HILL, ANITA (born 1956), African American lawyer and professor **7** 382-385

HILL, ARCHIBALD VIVIAN (1886-1977), English physiologist **7** 385-386

HILL, BENJAMIN HARVEY (1823-1882), American politician **7** 386-387

HILL, HERBERT (born 1924), American scholar and civil rights activist **7** 387-388

HILL, JAMES JEROME (1838-1916), American railroad builder **7** 388-389

HILL, ROWLAND (1795-1879), British educator, postal reformer, and administrator **21** 202-204

HILLARY, EDMUND (born 1919), New Zealander explorer and mountaineer **7** 389-390

HILLEL I (circa 60 B.C. -circa 10 A.D.), Jewish scholar and teacher **7** 390-391

HILLIARD, NICHOLAS (circa 1547-1619), English painter **7** 391-392

HILLMAN, SIDNEY (1887-1946), Lithuanian-born American labor leader **7** 392-393

HILLQUIT, MORRIS (1869-1933), Russian-born American lawyer and author **7** 393-394

HILLS, CARLA ANDERSON (born 1934), Republican who served three presidents as lawyer, cabinet member, and U.S. trade representative **7** 394-396

HILTON, BARRON (William Barron Hilton; born 1927), American businessman **19** 146-148

HILTON, CONRAD (1887-1979), American hotelier **20** 178-180

HIMES, CHESTER BOMAR (1909-1984), American author **22** 242-244

HIMMELFARB, GERTRUDE (born 1922), American professor, writer, and scholar **7** 396-398

HIMMLER, HEINRICH (1900-1945), German Nazi leader **7** 398-399

HINDEMITH, PAUL (1895-1963), German composer **7** 399-400

HINDENBURG, PAUL LUDWIG HANS VON BENECKENDORFF UND VON (1847-1934), German field marshal, president 1925-1934 **7** 400-401

HINES, GREGORY OLIVER (born 1946), American dancer and actor **7** 401-403

HINOJOSA, ROLANDO (born 1929), Hispanic-American author **7** 403-405

HINSHELWOOD, SIR CYRIL NORMAN (1897-1967), English chemist **7** 405-406

HINTON, SUSAN ELOISE (born 1950), American novelist and screenwriter **7** 406-407

HIPPARCHUS (flourished 162-126 B.C.), Greek astronomer **7** 407-408

HIPPOCRATES (circa 460-circa 377 B.C.), Greek physician **7** 408-410

HIROHITO (1901-1989), emperor of Japan **7** 410-412

HIROSHIGE, ANDO (1797-1858), Japanese painter and printmaker **7** 412-413

Hiroshima, Mon Amour (film) Resnais, Alain **23** 333-335

HISS, ALGER (1904-1996), U.S. State Department official convicted of having provided classified documents to an admitted Communist **7** 413-415

HITCHCOCK, ALFRED (1899-1980), English-born film director **7** 415-416

HITCHCOCK, GILBERT MONELL (1859-1934), American publisher and politician **7** 416-417

HITLER, ADOLF (1889-1945), German dictator, chancellor-president 1933-1945 **7** 417-420

HO, DAVID DA-I (born 1952), American AIDS researcher **23** 145-148

HO CHI MINH (1890-1969), Vietnamese revolutionary and statesman **7** 426-428

HOBART, JOHN HENRY (1775-1830), American Episcopal bishop **7** 420-421

HOBBES, THOMAS (1588-1679), English philosopher and political theorist **7** 421-423

HOBBY, OVETA CULP (1905-1995), American government official and businesswoman **7** 423-425

HOBHOUSE, LEONARD TRELAWNY (1864-1929), English sociologist and philosopher **7** 425-426

HOBSON, WILLIAM (1793-1842), British naval commander and colonial governor **7** 426

Hockey (sport)
Roy, Patrick **23** 351-353
Yzerman, Steve **23** 451-453

HOCKING, WILLIAM ERNEST (1873-1966), American philosopher **7** 428-429

HOCKNEY, DAVID (born 1937), English photographer and artist **7** 429-431

HODGKIN, ALAN LLOYD (born 1914), English physiologist **7** 431-432

HODGKIN, DOROTHY CROWFOOT (1910-1964), English chemist **7** 432-434

HODLER, FERDINAND (1853-1918), Swiss painter **7** 434-435

HOE, RICHARD MARCH (1812-1886), American inventor and manufacturer **7** 435-436

HOFFA, JAMES R. (''Jimmy''; 1913-1975) American union leader **7** 436-437

HOFFMAN, ABBIE (1936-1989), American writer, activist, and leader of the Youth International Party **7** 437-439

HOFFMANN, ERNST THEODOR AMADEUS (1776-1822), German author, composer, and artist **7** 439-440

HOFFMANN, JOSEF (1870-1956), Austrian architect and decorator **7** 440-441

HOFFMAN, MALVINA CORNELL (1885-1966), American sculptor **23** 148-150

HOFHAIMER, PAUL (1459-1537), Austrian composer, and organist **7** 441

HOFMANN, AUGUST WILHELM VON (1818-1892), German organic chemist **7** 441-442

HOFMANN, HANS (1880-1966), German-American painter **7** 442-443

HOFMANNSTHAL, HUGO VON (1874-1929), Austrian poet and dramatist **7** 443-444

HOFSTADTER, RICHARD (1916-1970), American historian **7** 444-445

HOGAN, BEN (1912-1997), American golfer **19** 148-150

HOGARTH, WILLIAM (1697-1764), English painter and engraver **7** 446-447

HOGG, HELEN BATTLES SAWYER (1905-1993), Canadian astronomer **22** 244-247

HOKINSON, HELEN ELNA (1893-1949), American cartoonist **23** 150-152

HOKUSAI, KATSUSHIKA (1760-1849), Japanese painter and printmaker **7** 447-448

HOLBACH, BARON D' (Paul Henri Thiry; 1723-1789), German-born French encyclopedist and philosopher **7** 448-449

HOLBEIN, HANS, THE YOUNGER (1497/98-1543), German painter and graphic artist **7** 449-450

HOLBERG, LUDVIG (Hans Mikkelsen; 1684-1754), Scandinavian author **23** 152-155

HOLBROOK, JOSIAH (1788-1854), American educator **7** 450-451

HÖLDERLIN, JOHANN CHRISTIAN FRIEDRICH (1770-1843), German poet **7** 451-452

HOLIDAY, BILLIE (1915-1959), American jazz vocalist **7** 452-453

HOLLAND, JOHN PHILIP (1840-1914), Irish-American inventor **7** 453-454

HOLLERITH, HERMAN (1860-1929), American inventor and businessman **19** 151-152

HOLLY, BUDDY (Charles Hardin Holley; 1936-1959), American singer, songwriter, and bandleader **22** 247-249

HOLM, HANYA (née Johanna Eckert; born 1893), German-American dancer and teacher **7** 454-455

HOLMES, ARTHUR (1890-1965), English geologist and petrologist **7** 455-456

HOLMES, JOHN HAYNES (1879-1964), American Unitarian clergyman **7** 456-457

HOLMES, OLIVER WENDELL (1809-1894), American physician and author **7** 457-458

HOLMES, OLIVER WENDELL, JR. (1841-1935), American jurist **7** 458-459

Holocaust
films about
Resnais, Alain **23** 333-335

HOLST, GUSTAV (1874-1934), English composer **7** 459-460

Holy Roman Empire
1138-1254 (Hohenstaufen dynasty)
Innocent IV **23** 165-167

HOLYOAKE, KEITH JACKA (1904-1983), New Zealand prime minister and leader of the National Party **7** 460-462

HOLZER, JENNY (born 1950), American Neo-Conceptualist artist **7** 462-463

HOMANS, GEORGE CASPAR (1910-1989), American sociologist **7** 463-465

HOMER (ancient Greek epic poet) **7** 468-469

HOMER, WINSLOW (1836-1910), American painter **7** 468-469

HONDA, SOICHIRO (1906-1991), Japanese automaker **7** 469-470

HONECKER, ERICH (1912-1994), German Communist Party leader and head of the German Democratic Republic (1971-80s) **7** 471-472

HONEGGER, ARTHUR (1892-1955), Swiss composer identified with France **7** 472-473

HONEN (1133-1212), Japanese Buddhist monk **7** 473

HOOCH, PIETER DE (1629-after 1684), Dutch artist **7** 473-474

HOOK, SIDNEY (1902-1989), American philosopher and exponent of classical American pragmatism **7** 474-475

HOOKE, ROBERT (1635-1703), English physicist **7** 475

HOOKER, JOHN LEE (1917-2001), African American musician **23** 155-157

HOOKER, RICHARD (1554-1600), English theologian and Church of England clergyman **7** 475-476

HOOKER, THOMAS (1586-1647), English Puritan theologian, founder of Connecticut Colony **7** 476-477

HOOKS, BELL (born Gloria Jean Watkins, born 1952) African American social activist, feminist, and author **7** 477-481

HOOKS, BENJAMIN LAWSON (born 1925), executive director of the NAACP and first African American commissioner of the FCC **7** 481-483

HOOVER, HERBERT CLARK (1874-1964), American statesman, president 1929-1933 **7** 483-485

HOOVER, JOHN EDGAR (1895-1972), American lawyer, criminologist, and FBI director **7** 485-487

HOPE, BOB (born Leslie Townes Hope; born 1903), entertainer in vaudeville, radio, television, and movies **7** 487-489

HOPE, JOHN (1868-1936), African American educator and religious leader **7** 489-490

HOPKINS, ANTHONY (Philip Anthony Hopkins; born 1937), Welsh actor **18** 196-198

HOPKINS, ESEK (1718-1802), American Revolutionary patriot **7** 490-491

HOPKINS, SIR FREDERICK GOWLAND (1861-1947), English biochemist **7** 496

HOPKINS, GERARD MANLEY (1844-1889), English Jesuit poet **7** 492-494

HOPKINS, HARRY LLOYD (1890-1946), American statesman **7** 494-495

HOPKINS, MARK (1802-1887), American educator **7** 495-496

HOPKINS, SAMUEL (1721-1803), American clergyman and theologian **7** 496

HOPKINSON, FRANCIS (1737-1791), American politician, writer, and composer **7** 496-497

HOPPER, EDWARD (1882-1967), American realist painter **7** 497-498

HOPPER, GRACE (born Grace Brewster Murray; 1906-1992), American computer scientist **7** 498-500

HORACE (Quintus Horatius Flaccus; 65-8 B.C.), Roman poet and satirist **7** 500-503

HORNE, HERMAN HARRELL (1874-1946), American philosopher and educator **7** 503-504

HORNE, LENA (born 1917), popular entertainer **7** 504-506

HORNER, MATINA SOURETIS (born 1939), American scholar and administrator **7** 506-508

HORNEY, KAREN DANIELSEN (1885-1952), German-born American psychoanalyst **7** 508-509

HORNSBY, ROGERS (1896-1963), American baseball player and manager **21** 204-206

HOROWITZ, VLADIMIR (1904-1989), American pianist **7** 509-510

HORTHY DE NAGYBÁNYA, NICHOLAS (1868-1957), Hungarian admiral and statesman, regent 1920-1944 **7** 510-512

HOSEA (flourished 750-722 B.C.), Hebrew prophet of the kingdom of Israel **7** 512

HO-SHEN (1750-1799), Manchu official in China **7** 512-513

HOSTOS, EUGENIO MARÍA DE (1839-1903), Puerto Rican philosopher, educator, and writer **7** 513-514

HOUDINI, HARRY (born Erich Weiss; 1874-1926), American magician and illusionist **7** 514-516

HOUDON, ANTOINE (1741-1828), French sculptor **7** 516-517

HOUNSFIELD, GODFREY (born 1919), English biomedical engineer **7** 517-519

HOUPHOUËT-BOIGNY, FELIX (1905-1993), Ivorian statesman 1960 **7** 519-520

HOUSE, EDWARD MANDELL (1858-1938), American diplomat **7** 520-521

House of Representatives, U.S.
see U.S. House of Representatives

HOUSMAN, ALFRED EDWARD (1859-1936), English poet **7** 521-522

HOUSSAY, BERNARDO ALBERTO (1887-1971), Argentine physiologist **7** 522-523

HOUSTON, CHARLES HAMILTON (1895-1950), African American lawyer and civil rights leader **7** 523-526

HOUSTON, SAMUEL (1793-1863), American statesman and soldier **7** 526-527

HOUSTON, WHITNEY (born 1963), American singer and actress **19** 152-155

HOVLAND, CARL I. (1912-1961), American psychologist **7** 527-528

HOWARD, JOHN WINSTON (born 1939), Australian prime minister **18** 198-200

HOWARD, OLIVER OTIS (1830-1909), American Union general **7** 528-529

HOWARD, RON (born 1954), American actor, director, and producer **19** 155-158

HOWE, EDGAR WATSON (1853-1937), American author and editor **7** 529

HOWE, ELIAS (1819-1867), American inventor **7** 529-530

HOWE, FLORENCE ROSENFELD (born 1929), feminist American author, publisher, literary scholar, and historian **7** 530-531

HOWE, GEOFFREY (Richard Edward; born 1926), British foreign secretary **7** 531-532

HOWE, GORDIE (born 1928), Canadian hockey player **7** 532-534

HOWE, JOSEPH (1804-1873), Canadian journalist, reformer, and politician **7** 534-535

HOWE, JULIA WARD (1819-1910), American author and reformer **7** 535-536

HOWE, RICHARD (Earl Howe; 1726-1799), English admiral **7** 536-537

HOWE, SAMUEL GRIDLEY (1801-1876), American physician and reformer **7** 537

HOWE, WILLIAM (5th Viscount Howe; 1729-1814), British general **7** 538-539

HOWELLS, WILLIAM DEAN (1837-1920), American writer **7** 539-541

HOWELLS, WILLIAM WHITE (born 1908), American anthropologist **7** 541-542

HOXHA, ENVER (1908-1985), leader of the Communist Party of Albania from its formation in 1941 until his death **8** 1-3

HOYLE, EDMOND (1672-1769), English authority on card games **21** 206-208

HOYLE, FRED (born 1915), English astronomer and author **18** 200-202

HRDLIČKA, ALEŠ (1869-1943), American physical anthropologist **8** 3-4

HSIA KUEI (flourished 1190-1225), Chinese painter **8** 4-5

HSIEH LING-YÜN (385-433), duke of K'ang-lo, Chinese poet **8** 5-6

HSÜAN TSANG (circa 602-664), Chinese Buddhist in India **8** 6-7

HSÜAN-TSUNG, T'ANG (685-762), Chinese emperor **8** 7-8

HSÜN-TZU (Hsün Ch'ing; circa 312-circa 235 B.C.), Chinese philosopher **8** 8

HU SHIH (1891-1962), Chinese philosopher **8** 63-65

HUANG CH'AO (died 884), Chinese rebel leader **8** 8-9

HUANG TSUNG-HSI (1610-1695), Chinese scholar and philosopher **8** 9-10

HUBBARD, L. RON (1911-1986), American author and founder of Scientology **18** 202-204

HUBBLE, EDWIN POWELL (1889-1953), American astronomer **8** 10-11

HUBLEY, JOHN (1914-1977), American animator and filmmaker **21** 208-210

HUCH, RICARDA (1864-1947), German novelist, poet, and historian **8** 11-12

HUDSON, HENRY (flourished 1607-1611), English navigator **8** 12-13

Hudson Bay (Canada)
Bernier, Joseph E. **23** 35-37

HUERTA, DOLORES (born 1930),
Hispanic American labor activist **18**
204-207

HUERTA, VICTORIANO (1854-1916),
Mexican general and politician **8**
13-14

HUGGINS, SIR WILLIAM (1824-1910),
English astronomer **8** 14-15

HUGHES, CHARLES EVANS (1862-
1948), American jurist and statesman **8**
15-16

HUGHES, HOWARD ROBARD (1905-
1976), flamboyant American
entrepreneur **8** 16-17

HUGHES, JOHN JOSEPH (1797-1864),
Irish-American Catholic archbishop **8**
17-18

HUGHES, LANGSTON (1902-1967),
African American author **8** 18-19

HUGHES, RICHARD (1900-1976),
English author **19** 158-160

HUGHES, TED (1930-1998), English poet
laureate **8** 19-21

HUGHES, WILLIAM MORRIS (1864-
1952), Australian prime minister 1915-
1923 **8** 21-22

HUGO, VICOMTE VICTOR MARIE
(1802-1885), French author **8** 22-25

HUI-TSUNG (1082-1135), Chinese
emperor and artist **8** 25

HUI-YÜAN (334-416), Chinese Buddhist
monk **8** 25-26

HUIZINGA, JOHAN (1872-1945), Dutch
historian **8** 26-27

HULAGU KHAN (Hüle'ü; circa 1216-
1265), Mongol ruler in Persia **8** 27-28

HULL, BOBBY (Robert Marvin Hull; born
1939), Canadian hockey player **20**
181-183

HULL, CLARK LEONARD (1884-1952),
American psychologist **8** 28

HULL, CORDELL (1871-1955), American
statesman **8** 28-29

HULL, WILLIAM (1753-1825), American
military commander **8** 29-30

Human Condition, The (Ningen no
joken; film)
Kobayashi, Masaki **23** 199-201

HUMAYUN (1508-1556), Mogul
emperor 1530-1556 **20** 183-185

**HUMBOLDT, BARON FRIEDRICH
HEINRICH ALEXANDER VON** (1769-
1859), German naturalist and explorer
8 30-31

HUMBOLDT, BARON WILHELM VON
(1767-1835), German statesman and
philologist **8** 31

HUME, BASIL CARDINAL (George
Haliburton Hume; 1923-1999), English
clergyman and theologian **22** 249-250

HUME, DAVID (1711-1776), Scottish
philosopher **8** 31-34

HUMPHREY, DORIS (Doris Batcheller
Humphrey; 1895-1959), American
dancer and choreographer **23** 157-159
Limón, José Arcadia **23** 227-229

HUMPHREY, HUBERT HORATIO, JR.
(1911-1978), mayor of Minneapolis,
U.S. senator from Minnesota, and vice-
president of the U.S. **8** 34-36

HUN SEN (born 1951), Cambodian
prime minister **8** 39-42

HUNDERTWASSER, FRIEDENSREICH
(Friedrich Stowasser; 1928-2000),
Austrian-born visionary painter and
spiritualist **8** 36-37

HUNG HSIU-CH'ÜAN (1814-1864),
Chinese religious leader, founder of
Taiping sect **8** 37-38

Hungarian revolution (1848)
Petöfi, Sándor **23** 306-308

HUNG-WU (1328-1398), Chinese Ming
emperor 1368-98 **8** 38-39

HUNT, H. L. (1889-1974), American
entrepreneur **8** 42-44

HUNT, RICHARD MORRIS (1827-1895),
American architect **8** 44

HUNT, WALTER (1796-1859), American
inventor **21** 210-212

HUNT, WILLIAM HOLMAN (1827-
1910), English painter **8** 44-45

HUNTER, ALBERTA (1895-1984), African
American blues singer **23** 160-162

HUNTER, FLOYD (born 1912), American
social worker and administrator,
community worker, professor, and
author **8** 45-46

HUNTER, MADELINE CHEEK (1916-
1994), American educator **8** 47-48

HUNTER, WILLIAM (1718-1783),
Scottish anatomist **8** 48-49

HUNTINGTON, ANNA HYATT (Anna
Vaughn Hyatt; 1876-1973), American
sculptor and philanthropist **23** 162-164

HUNTINGTON, COLLIS POTTER (1821-
1900), American railroad builder **8** 49

HUNTLEY AND BRINKLEY (1956-1970),
American journalists and radio and
television news team **8** 49-51

HUNYADI, JOHN (1385-1456),
Hungarian military leader, regent
1446-1452 **8** 51-52

HURD, DOUGLAS (born 1930), English
Conservative Party politician and
foreign secretary **8** 52-55

HURSTON, ZORA NEALE (1903-1960),
African American folklorist and
novelist **8** 55-56

HUS, JAN (a.k.a. John Hus; ca.1369-
1415), Bohemian religious reformer **8**
56-59

HUSÁK, GUSTÁV (born 1913), president
of the Czechoslovak Socialist Republic
(1975-1987) **8** 59-61

HUSAYN, TAHA (1889-1973), Egyptian
author, educator, and statesman **8**
61-62

HUSAYNI, AL-HAJJ AMIN AL- (1895-
1974), Moslem scholar/leader and
mufti of Jerusalem (1922-1948) **8**
62-63

HUSEIN IBN ALI (circa 1854-1931),
Arab nationalist, king of Hejaz 1916-
1924 **8** 63

HUSSEIN IBN TALAL (1935-1999), king
of the Hashemite Kingdom of Jordan
(1953-80s) **8** 65-67

HUSSEINI, FAISAL (1940-2001),
Palestinian political leader **19** 160-162

HUSSERL, EDMUND (1859-1938),
German philosopher **8** 67-68

HUSTON, JOHN MARCELLUS (1906-
1987), American film director,
scriptwriter, and actor **22** 250-252

HUTCHINS, ROBERT MAYNARD (1899-
1977), American educator **8** 68-69

HUTCHINSON, ANNE MARBURY
(1591-1643), English-born American
religious leader **8** 69-71

HUTCHINSON, THOMAS (1711-1780),
American colonial governor **8** 71-72

HUTTEN, ULRICH VON (1488-1523),
German humanist **8** 72-73

HUTTON, JAMES (1726-1797), Scottish
geologist **8** 73-74

HUXLEY, ALDOUS LEONARD (1894-
1963), English novelist and essayist **8**
74-75

HUXLEY, JULIAN (1887-1975), English
biologist and author **8** 75-77

HUXLEY, THOMAS HENRY (1825-1895),
English biologist **8** 77-79

HUYGENS, CHRISTIAAN (1629-1695),
Dutch mathematician, astronomer, and
physicist **8** 79-81

HUYSMANS, JORIS KARL (1848-1907), French novelist **8** 81-82

HYDE, DOUGLAS (1860-1949), Irish author, president 1938-45 **8** 82-83

HYDE, IDA HENRIETTA (1857-1945), American physiologist and educator **22** 252-254

HYMAN, LIBBIE HENRIETTA (1888-1969), American zoologist **8** 83-84

HYPATIA OF ALEXANDRIA (370-415), Greek mathematician and philosopher **8** 85

Hyundai Group
Chung, Ju Yung **23** 72-74

I

IACOCCA, LIDO (LEE) ANTHONY (born 1924), American automobile magnate **8** 86-88

IBÁÑEZ DEL CAMPO, CARLOS (1877-1960), Chilean general and president **8** 88

ÍBARRURI GÓMEZ, DOLORES (1895-1989), voice of the Republican cause in the Spanish Civil War **8** 88-90

IBERVILLE, SIEUR D' (Pierre le Moyne; 1661-1706), Canadian soldier, naval captain, and adventurer **8** 90-91

IBN AL-ARABI, MUHYI AL-DIN (1165-1240), Spanish-born Moslem poet, philosopher, and mystic **8** 91

IBN BATTUTA, MUHAMMAD (1304-1368/69), Moslem traveler and author **8** 91-92

IBN GABIROL, SOLOMON BEN JUDAH (circa 1021-circa 1058), Spanish Hebrew poet and philosopher **8** 92

IBN HAZM, ABU MUHAMMAD ALI (994-1064), Spanish-born Arab theologian and jurist **8** 93

IBN KHALDUN, ABD AL-RAHMAN IBN MUHAMMAD (1332-1406), Arab historian, philosopher, and statesman **8** 93-94

IBN SAUD, ABD AL-AZIZ (1880-1953), Arab politician, founder of Saudi Arabia **8** 94-95

IBN TASHUFIN, YUSUF (died 1106), North African Almoravid ruler **8** 95-96

IBN TUFAYL, ABU BAKR MUHAMMAD (circa 1110-1185), Spanish Moslem philosopher and physician **8** 96

IBN TUMART, MUHAMMAD (circa 1080-1130), North African Islamic theologian **8** 96-97

IBRAHIM PASHA (1789-1848), Turkish military and administrative leader **8** 97-98

IBSEN, HENRIK (1828-1906), Norwegian playwright **8** 98-100

ICKES, HAROLD LECLAIRE (1874-1952), American statesman **8** 100-101

ICTINUS (flourished 2nd half of 5th century B.C.), Greek architect **8** 101

IDRIS I (1889-1983), king of Libya 1950-69 **8** 102

IDRISI, MUHAMMAD IBN MUHAMMAD AL- (1100-1165?), Arab geographer **8** 102-103

IGLESIAS, ENRIQUE V. (born 1930), Uruguayan economist, banker, and public official **8** 106-107

IGNATIUS OF ANTIOCH, SAINT (died circa 115), Early Christian bishop and theologian **8** 107-108

IGNATIUS OF LOYOLA, SAINT (1491-1556), Spanish soldier, founder of Jesuits **8** 108-109

IKEDA, DAISAKU (born 1928), Japanese Buddhist writer and religious leader **8** 109-110

IKHNATON (ruled 1379-1362 B.C.), pharaoh of Egypt **8** 110-111

ILIESCU, ION (born 1930), president of Romania (1990-) **8** 111-112

ILITCH, MIKE (born 1929), American businessman **19** 163-165

ILLICH, IVAN (1926-2002), theologian, educator, and social critic **8** 112-114

IMAI, TADASHI (1912-1991), Japanese film director **22** 255-257

IMAM, ALHADJI ABUBAKAR (1911-1981), Nigerian writer and teacher **8** 114-115

IMAOKA, SHINICHIRO (1881-1988), progressive and liberal religious leader in Japan **8** 115

IMHOTEP (ca. 3000 B.C. - ca. 2950 B.C.), Egyptian vizier, architect, priest, astronomer, and magician-physician **8** 116-117

Impressionism (art)
Puerto Rico
Oller, Francisco Manuel **23** 274-275
United States
Thomas, Alma Woodsey **23** 401-403

In a Glass Darkly (collection of horror stories)
Le Fanu, Joseph Sheridan **23** 206-208

INCE, THOMAS (1882-1924), American film producer and director **21** 213-215

India, Republic of (nation, southern Asia)
• CA 1000-1600 (MOSLEM)
Delhi Sultanate (1192-1398)
Razia **23** 326-329

Industrial Workers of the World (established 1905)
Parsons, Lucy González **23** 293-295

INGE, WILLIAM RALPH (1860-1954), Church of England clergyman, scholar, social critic, and writer **8** 118-119

INGENHOUSZ, JAN (1730-1799), Dutch physician, chemist, and engineer **8** 119-120

INGERSOLL, ROBERT GREEN (1833-1899), American lawyer and lecturer **8** 120-121

INGRES, JEAN AUGUSTE DOMINIQUE (1780-1867), French painter **8** 121-123

INNESS, GEORGE (1825-1894), American painter **8** 123-124

INNIS, HAROLD ADAMS (1894-1952), Canadian political economist **8** 124-125

INNOCENT III (Lothar of Segni; 1160/1161-1216), pope 1198-1216 **8** 125-127

INNOCENT IV (Sinibaldo de' Fieschi; died 1254), pope 1243-1254 **23** 165-167

INÖNÜ, ISMET (1884-1973), Turkish military man, statesman, and second president **8** 127-129

INSULL, SAMUEL (1859-1938), English-born American entrepreneur **8** 130

INUKAI, TSUYOSHI (1855-1932), Japanese journalist and statesman **8** 130-131

IONESCO, EUGÈNE (1912-1994), Franco-Romanian author **8** 131-132

IQBAL, MUHAMMAD (1877?-1938), Indian Moslem poet and philosopher **8** 132-133

IRELAND, JOHN (1838-1918), American Catholic archbishop **8** 133-134

IRELAND, PATRICIA (born 1945), president of the National Organization for Women (NOW) **8** 134-135

IRENE OF ATHENS (ca. 752-803), Byzantine empress 797-802 **8** 135-138

IRIGOYEN, HIPÓLITO (circa 1850-1933), Argentine statesman, twice president **8** 139-140

Irish literature
ghost stories
Le Fanu, Joseph Sheridan **23** 206-208

Irons, Ralph
see Schreiner, Olive

IRVING, JOHN WINSLOW (John Wallace Blunt Jr.; born 1942), American author **22** 257-259

IRVING, KENNETH COLIN (''K. C.''; 1899-1992), Canadian industrialist, the ''Paul Bunyan of New Brunswick'' **8** 140-141

IRVING, WASHINGTON (1783-1859), American author and journalist **8** 141-143

IRWIN, JAMES BENSON (1930-1991), American astronaut **22** 259-261

ISAAC, HEINRICH (circa 1450-1517), Flemish composer **8** 143-144

ISAACS, JORGE (1837-1895), Colombian novelist **8** 144

ISABELLA I (1451-1504), queen of Castile 1474-1504 **8** 144-145

ISABELLA II (1830-1904), queen of Spain 1833-1868 **8** 145-146

ISAIAH (flourished circa 740-701 B.C.), Hebrew prophet **8** 146-147

ISHERWOOD, CHRISTOPHER (1904-1986), British-born American writer of fiction, drama, film, travel, and autobiography **8** 147-149

ISHI (ca. 1860-1961), Native American aboriginal **22** 261-263

ISIDORE OF SEVILLE, SAINT (560-636), Spanish cleric and encyclopedist **8** 149-150

Islam (religion)
• DOCTRINE
foundation
Abraham **23** 1-3

ISMAIL PASHA (1830-1895), khedive of Egypt 1863-1879 **8** 150-151

ISOCRATES (436-338 B.C.), Athenian orator **8** 151

ISOZAKI, ARATA (born 1931), Japanese architect **8** 152-153

Israel, State of (nation; southwestern Asia)
peace process
Schindler, Alexander Moshe **23** 360-362

ITAMI, JUZO (Ichizo itami; Ichizo Atami; born Ikeuchi Yoshihiro; 1933-1997), Japanese film director, actor and author **22** 263-265

ITO, HIROBUMI (1841-1909), Japanese statesman **8** 153-155

ITURBIDE, AGUSTÍN DE (1783-1824), Mexican military leader **8** 155-156

IVAN III (1440-1505), grand duke of Moscow 1462-1505 **8** 156-157

IVAN IV (1530-1584), grand duke of Moscow, czar of Russia 1547-1584 **8** 157-159

IVES, CHARLES EDWARD (1874-1954), American composer **8** 159-160

IVORY, JAMES (born 1928), American film director and producer **20** 186-188

IWAKURA, TOMOMI (1825-1883), Japanese statesman **8** 160-161

IWW
see Industrial Workers of the World

IZETBEGOVIC, ALIJA (born 1926), president of the eight-member presidency of the Republic of Bosnia-Herzegovina **8** 161-163

J

JA JA OF OPOBO (ca. 1820-1891), Nigerian politician **8** 201-204

JABBAR, KAREEM ABDUL (Ferdinand Lewis Alcinor, Junior; born 1947), American basketball player **8** 164-165

JABER AL-SABAH, JABER AL-AHMAD AL- (born 1926), amir of Kuwait **8** 166-167

JABIR IBN HAYYAN (flourished latter 8th century), Arab scholar and alchemist **8** 167

JABOTINSKY, VLADIMIR EVGENEVICH (1880-1940), Russian Zionist **8** 167-168

JACKSON, ANDREW (1767-1845), American president 1829-1837 **8** 168-172

JACKSON, HELEN HUNT (1830-1885), American novelist **8** 172

JACKSON, HENRY MARTIN (Scoop; 1912-1983), United States senator and proponent of anti-Soviet foreign policy **8** 172-174

JACKSON, JESSE LOUIS (born 1941), U.S. civil rights leader and presidential candidate **8** 174-176

JACKSON, MAHALIA (1911-1972), American singer **19** 166-168

JACKSON, MAYNARD HOLBROOK, JR. (born 1938), first African American mayor of Atlanta, Georgia (1973-81 and 1989-1993) **8** 176-178

JACKSON, MICHAEL JOE (born 1958), one of the most popular singers in history **8** 178-180

JACKSON, REGINALD ''REGGIE'' MARTINEZ (born 1946), African American baseball player **8** 180-182

JACKSON, ROBERT HOUGHWOUT (1892-1954), American jurist **8** 182-183

JACKSON, SHIRLEY ANN (born 1946), African American physicist **8** 183-184

JACKSON, THOMAS JONATHAN (''Stonewall''; 1824-1863), American Confederate general **8** 184-185

JACOB, JOHN EDWARD (born 1934), African American activist and president of the National Urban League **8** 185-188

JACOBI, ABRAHAM (1830-1919), American physician **8** 188-189

JACOBI, DEREK (born 1938), British actor **19** 168-170

JACOBI, FRIEDRICH HEINRICH (1743-1819), German philosopher **8** 189-190

JACOBI, MARY PUTNAM (1834-1906), American physician **8** 188-189

JACOBS, HARRIET A. (1813-1897), runaway slave and abolitionist **8** 190-193

JACOBSEN, JENS PETER (1847-1885), Danish author **8** 193-194

JACOBSON, DAN (born 1929), South African author **22** 266-268

JACOPONE DA TODI (circa 1236-1306), Italian poet and mystic **8** 194

JACQUARD, JOSEPH MARIE (1752-1834), French inventor **21** 216-218

JAGGER, MICHAEL PHILIP (''Mick''; born 1944), lead singer for the Rolling Stones **8** 194-196

JAHANGIR (1569-1627), fourth Mughal emperor of India **8** 196-199

JAHN, HELMUT (born 1940), German-American architect **8** 199-201

JAMES I (1394-1437), king of Scotland 1406-1437 **8** 206-207

JAMES I (James VI of Scotland; 1566-1625), king of England 1603-1625 **8** 204-206

JAMES II (1633-1701), king of England, Scotland, and Ireland 1685-1688 **8** 207-208

JAMES III (1451-1488), king of Scotland 1460-1488 **8** 208-209

JAMES, DANIEL, JR. (''Chappie''; 1920-1978), first African American man in the U.S. to become a four star general **8** 209-211

JAMES, HENRY (1843-1916), American novelist **8** 211-212

JAMES, JESSE WOODSON (1847-1882), American outlaw **8** 212-213

JAMES, P. D. (born 1920), British crime novelist **8** 213-215

JAMES, WILLIAM (1842-1910), American philosopher and psychologist **8** 215-217

JAMESON, SIR LEANDER STARR (1853-1917), British colonial administrator **8** 218

JAMI (Maulana Nur al-Din Abd al-Rahman; 1414-1492), Persian poet **8** 218-219

JANÁČEK, LEOŠ (1854-1928), Czech composer **8** 219
Mackerras, Alan Charles **23** 237-239

JANET, PIERRE MARIE FÉLIX (1859-1947), French psychologist **8** 220

JANSEN, CORNELIS (1585-1638), Dutch Roman Catholic theologian **8** 220-221

Japanese architecture
Maekawa, Kunio **23** 239-242

Japanese art
Maruyama school
Okyo, Maruyama **23** 272-274
naturalists
Okyo, Maruyama **23** 272-274

JAQUES-DALCROZE, EMILE (1865-1950), Swiss teacher and composer who developed eurhythmics **8** 221-222

JARRELL, RANDALL (1914-1965), American poet and critic **8** 222-223

JARUZELSKI, WOJCIECH WITOLD (born 1923), career soldier who became Poland's head of state (1981-1990) **8** 223-225

JASPERS, KARL (1883-1969), German philosopher **8** 225-226

JAURÈS, JEAN (1859-1914), French Socialist and politician **8** 226-227

JAWARA, SIR DAUDA KAIRABA (born 1924), Gambian statesman **8** 227-228

JAWLENSKY, ALEXEJ VON (1864-1941), Russian Expressionist painter **8** 228-229

JAWORSKI, LEON (1905-1982), American lawyer and independent prosecutor of Watergate **8** 229-230

JAY, JOHN (1745-1829), American diplomat and jurist **8** 230-232

JAY, WILLIAM (1789-1858), American reformer **8** 232-233

JAYEWARDENE, JUNIUS RICHARD (JR; 1906-1996), leader of the nationalist movement in Ceylon and president of Sri Lanka **8** 233-234

Jazz (music)
Armstrong, Lillian Hardin **23** 15-17
Bailey, Mildred **23** 28-30
Peterson, Oscar Emanuel **23** 304-306
Williams, Mary Lou **23** 444-446

JEAN DE MEUN (circa 1240-1305), French author **8** 234-235

JEANS, SIR JAMES HOPWOOD (1877-1946), English mathematician, physicist, and astronomer **8** 235-236

JEFFERS, JOHN ROBINSON (1887-1962), American poet **8** 236-237

JEFFERSON, JOSEPH (1829-1905), American actor **8** 237

JEFFERSON, THOMAS (1743-1826), American philosopher and statesman, president 1801-1809 **8** 238-241

JEFFREYS, SIR HAROLD (1891-1989), English mathematician, astronomer, and philosopher **8** 241-242

JELLICOE, JOHN RUSHWORTH (1859-1935), English admiral **8** 242-243

JEMISON, MAE C. (born 1956), African American physician and astronaut **8** 243-244

JENKINS, ROY HARRIS (born 1920), British Labour politician and author **8** 244-245

JENNER, BRUCE (born 1949), American track and field athlete and motivational speaker **21** 218-221

JENNER, EDWARD (1749-1823), English physician **8** 245-246

JENNEY, WILLIAM LE BARON (1832-1907), American architect and engineer **21** 221-223

JENNINGS, ROBERT YEWDALL (born 1913), British judge who was president of the International Court of Justice **8** 246-247

JEREMIAH (flourished late 7th-early 6th century B.C.), Hebrew priest and prophet **8** 247-248

JEROBOAM I (ruled circa 931-circa 910 B.C.), king of the northern kingdom of Israel **8** 248-249

JEROME, ST. (circa 345-420), Early Christian biblical scholar **8** 249

JESSEL, GEORGE (1898-1981), American screen, stage, radio, and television actor and comedian and film director, composer, and screenwriter **8** 249-251

JESUS BEN SIRA (Sirach; flourished circa 170 B.C.), Jewish sage and author **8** 251

JESUS OF NAZARETH (circa 4 B.C. - 29/30A.D.), founder of the Christian faith **8** 251-255

JEVONS, WILLIAM STANLEY (1835-1882), English economist, logician, and statistician **8** 255-256

JEWETT, SARAH ORNE (1849-1909), American novelist **8** 256

JEX-BLAKE, SOPHIA (1840-1912), British physician and women's rights advocate **23** 168-170

JHABVALA, RUTH PRAWER (born 1927), English screenwriter and novelist **18** 208-210

JIANG QING (Madame Mao Zedong; 1914-1991), Chinese revolutionary and leader of the Great Proletarian Cultural Revolution **8** 256-260

JIANG ZEMIN (born 1927), general secretary of the Chinese Communist Party Central Committee **8** 260-261

JIMÉNEZ, JUAN RAMÓN (1881-1958), Spanish symbolist poet **8** 261-262

JIMÉNEZ DE QUESADA, GONZALO (1509-1579), Spanish conquistador **12** 509-510

JINNAH, MOHAMMAD ALI (1876-1948), Pakistani governor general 1947-1948 **8** 262-263

JOACHIM OF FIORE (circa 1132-1202), Italian mystic **8** 263-264

JOAN OF ARC (1412?-1431), French national heroine **8** 264-265

JOBS, STEVEN (born 1955), American computer designer and co-founder of Apple Computers **8** 265-267

JODL, ALFRED (1892?-1946), German general **18** 210-212

JOFFRE, JOSEPH JACQUES CÉSAIRE (1852-1931), French marshal **8** 267-268

JOFFREY, ROBERT (born Abdullah Jaffa Anver Bey Khan; 1930-1988), American dancer and choreographer **8** 268-270

JOGUES, ST. ISAAC (1607-1646), French Jesuit missionary and martyr **8** 270-271

JOHANAN BEN ZAKKAI (flourished circa 70 A.D.), Jewish teacher **8** 271-272

JOHANNES IV (1836-1889), Ethiopian emperor 1872-1889 **8** 272-273

JOHN (1167-1216), king of England 1199-1216 **8** 274-275

JOHN II (1319-1364), king of France 1350-1364 **8** 275-276

JOHN II (1455-1495), king of Portugal 1481-1495 **21** 223-225

JOHN III (John Sobieski; 1629-1696), king of Poland **8** 276-277

JOHN XXIII (Angelo Giuseppe Roncalli; 1881-1963), pope 1958-1963 **8** 277-280

JOHN, AUGUSTUS EDWIN (1878-1961), Welsh painter **8** 291

JOHN, ELTON HERCULES (Reginald Kenneth Dwight; born 1947), English singer, songwriter and humanitarian **18** 212-214

JOHN, ST. (flourished 1st century A.D.), Christian Apostle and Evangelist **8** 273-274

JOHN CHRYSOSTOM, ST. (circa 347-407), bishop of Constantinople **8** 280-281

JOHN MAURICE OF NASSAU (1604-1679), Dutch governor general of Netherlands Brazil **8** 281-282

JOHN OF AUSTRIA (1547-1578), Spanish general **20** 189-192

JOHN OF DAMASCUS, ST. (circa 680-750), Syrian theologian **8** 282

JOHN OF GAUNT (5th Duke of Lancaster; 1340-1399), English soldier-statesman **8** 282-283

JOHN OF LEIDEN (1509-1536), Dutch Anabaptist **8** 283

JOHN OF PIANO CARPINI (circa 1180-1252), Italian Franciscan monk **8** 284

JOHN OF SALISBURY (1115/20-1180), English bishop and humanist **8** 284-285

JOHN OF THE CROSS, ST. (1542-1591), Spanish Carmelite mystic **8** 285

JOHN PAUL I (Albino Luciani; 1912-1978), Roman Catholic pope (August 26-September 28, 1978) **8** 286-287

JOHN PAUL II (Karol Wojtyla; born 1920), cardinal of Krakow, Poland, and later Roman Catholic pope **8** 287-290

JOHN THE BAPTIST, ST. (flourished circa 29 A.D.), New Testament figure, forerunner of Jesus of Nazareth **8** 290

JOHNS, JASPER (born 1930), American painter and sculptor **8** 291-293

JOHNSON, ALVIN SAUNDERS (1874-1971), American economist and editor **8** 293-294

JOHNSON, ANDREW (1808-1875), American statesman, president 1865-1869 **8** 294-295

JOHNSON, BETSEY (born 1941?), American fashion designer **8** 295-296

JOHNSON, CHARLES SPURGEON (1893-1956), African American educator and sociologist **8** 296-297

JOHNSON, EARVIN, JR. ("Magic"; born 1959), popular African American star of the Los Angeles Lakers basketball team **8** 297-299

JOHNSON, GUY BENTON (1901-1991), sociologist, social anthropologist, and archaeologist who was a student of African American culture and an advocate of racial equality **8** 299-300

JOHNSON, HIRAM WARREN (1866-1945), American politician **8** 300-301

JOHNSON, JACK (1878-1946), African American boxer **8** 301-304

JOHNSON, JAMES WELDON (1871-1938), African American author and lawyer **8** 304-305

JOHNSON, SIR JOHN (1742-1830), American loyalist in the American Revolution **8** 305-306

JOHNSON, JOHN HAROLD (born 1918), American entrepreneur and founder of the Johnson Publishing Company **8** 306-308

JOHNSON, JONATHAN EASTMAN (1824-1906), American painter **8** 308

JOHNSON, LYNDON BAINES (1908-1973), American statesman, president 1963-1969 **8** 308-312

JOHNSON, MARIETTA LOUISE PIERCE (1864-1938), founder and 30-year teacher of an Alabama experimental school **8** 312-313

JOHNSON, PAULINE (Emily Pauline Johnson; Tekahionwake 1861-1913), Canadian poet **23** 170-172

JOHNSON, PHILIP (born 1906), American architect, critic, and historian **8** 313-314

JOHNSON, RAFER (born 1935), American decathlete and goodwill ambassador **21** 225-227

JOHNSON, ROBERT (1911-1938), African American musician **23** 172-174

JOHNSON, SAMUEL (1696-1772), American clergyman and educator **8** 314-315

JOHNSON, SAMUEL (1709-1784), English author and lexicographer **8** 315-317

JOHNSON, TOM LOFTIN (1854-1911), American entrepreneur and politician **8** 317

JOHNSON, VIRGINIA E. (born 1925), American psychologist and sex therapist **8** 317-319

JOHNSON, WALTER ("Big Train"; 1887-1946), American baseball player and manager **21** 228-230

JOHNSON, SIR WILLIAM (1715-1774), British colonial administrator **8** 319-320

JOHNSON, WILLIAM (1771-1834), American jurist **22** 268-270

JOHNSON, WILLIAM H. (1901-1970), African American painter of the Black experience **8** 320-322

JOHNSTON, FRANCES BENJAMIN (1864-1952), American photographer **23** 174-177

JOHNSTON, HENRY HAMILTON (Sir Harry Johnston; 1858-1927), English administrator, explorer, and author **8** 322-323

JOHNSTON, JOSEPH EGGLESTON (1807-1891), American Confederate general **8** 323

JOHNSTON, JOSHUA (a.k.a. Joshua Johnson; ca. 1765 - ca 1830), African American portrait artist **8** 323-325

JOHNSTON, LYNN (born 1947), Canadian cartoonist and artist **18** 214-216

JOINVILLE, JEAN DE (1224/25-1317), French author **8** 325

JOLIOT-CURIE, IRÈNE (1897-1956), French chemist and physicist **8** 325-327

JOLIOT-CURIE, JEAN FRÉDÉRIC (1900-1958), French physicist **8** 327-328

JOLLIET, LOUIS (1645-1700), French-Canadian explorer, hydrographer, and fur trader **8** 328-329

JOLSON, AL (Asa Yoelson; 1886-1950), American vaudeville, theater, and radio singing performer and film actor **8** 329-330

JOMINI, ANTOINE HENRI (1779-1869), Swiss military strategist **23** 177-179

JONATHAN, CHIEF JOSEPH LEABUA (1914-1987), Lesothoan statesman **8** 330-331

JONES, ERNEST ALFRED (1879-1958), British psychologist **8** 331-332

JONES, FAY (born 1921), American architect **8** 332-333

JONES, FREDERICK MCKINLEY (1893(?)-1961), African American inventor **20** 192-194

JONES, INIGO (1573-1652), English architect and designer **8** 333-334

JONES, JAMES EARL (born 1931), African American actor **8** 334-337

JONES, JOHN PAUL (1747-1792), American Revolutionary War naval officer **8** 337-338

Jones, John Paul (John Baldwin; born 1946), British musician Led Zeppelin **23** 216-218

JONES, LOIS MAILOU (1905-1998), African American artist **20** 194-196

JONES, MARY HARRIS ("Mother"; 1830-1930), Irish immigrant who devoted her life to improving conditions of the working class **8** 338-339

JONES, QUINCY DELIGHT, JR. (born 1933), African American musician-composer-arranger-producer-film and television executive **8** 339-341

JONES, ROBERT EDMOND (1887-1954), American designer of scenes for the theater **8** 341-342

JONES, ROBERT TYRE (Bobby; 1902-1971), American golf great **8** 342

JONES, SAMUEL MILTON (1846-1904), American manufacturer and political reformer **8** 342-343

JONG, ERICA (born 1942), American author **18** 216-219

JONSON, BEN (1572-1637), English playwright and poet **8** 343-345

JOPLIN, SCOTT (1868-1917), African American composer and instrumental musician **8** 345-347

JORDAENS, JACOB (1593-1678), Flemish painter **8** 347-349

JORDAN, BARBARA CHARLINE (1936-1996), attorney and U.S. congresswoman from Texas **8** 349-350

JORDAN, DAVID STARR (1851-1931), American scientist and educator **8** 350-351

JORDAN, JUNE (1936-2002), Jamaican American poet and activist **8** 351-353

JORDAN, LOUIS (1908-1975), African American bandleader, singer, and instrumentalist **8** 353-355

JORDAN, MICHAEL (born 1963), African American basketball superstar of the Chicago Bulls **8** 355-357

JORDAN, VERNON (born 1935), American civil rights leader **8** 357-358

JOSEPH (circa 1840-1904), American Nez Percé Indian chief **8** 358-359

JOSEPH II (1741-1790), Holy Roman emperor 1765-1790 **8** 359-360

JOSEPHUS FLAVIUS (circa 37-100), Jewish historian, diplomat, and military leader **8** 360-361

JOSQUIN DES PREZ (circa 1440-1521), Franco-Flemish composer **8** 361-363

JOULE, JAMES PRESCOTT (1818-1889), English physicist **8** 363-364

Journalists
    Argentine
        Arlt, Roberto **23** 11-13
        Valenzuela, Luisa **23** 421-423

JOWETT, BENJAMIN (1817-1893), English educator and Greek scholar **8** 364-365

JOYCE, JAMES (1882-1941), Irish author **8** 365-367

JOYNER, MATILDA SISSIERETTA (Sissieretta Jones; 1869-1933), African American singer **23** 179-181

JOYNER-KERSEE, JACKIE (born 1962), American track and field athlete **19** 170-173

JUAN CARLOS I (born 1938), king of Spain **8** 368-369

JUANA INÉS DE LA CRUZ, SISTER (1651-1695), Mexican nun, poet, and savant **8** 367-368

JUÁREZ, BENITO (1806-1872), Mexican statesman, president 1857-1872 **8** 369-372

JUDAEUS, PHILO (circa 20 B.C. -circa A.D. 45), Hellenistic Jewish philosopher **12** 282-283

JUDAH I (circa 135-circa 220), Jewish scholar **8** 372-373

JUDAH, THEODORE DEHONE (1826-1863), American engineer and railroad promoter **8** 373-374

JUDAH HALEVI (circa 1085-circa 1150), Spanish Hebrew poet **8** 373

Judaism (religion)
    reform
        Schindler, Alexander Moshe **23** 360-362
    United States
        Schindler, Alexander Moshe **23** 360-362

JUDAS MACCABEUS (died 160 B.C.), Jewish patriot and revolutionary **8** 374-375

JUDD, CHARLES HUBBARD (1873-1946), psychologist and education reformer **8** 375-376

JUDD, DONALD (1928-1994), American sculptor and art writer **8** 376-377

JUDSON, ADONIRAM (1788-1850), American Baptist missionary in Burma **8** 377-378

JULIA, RAUL (Julia y Arcelay, Raul Rafael Carlos; 1940-1994), American acotr and humanitarian **21** 230-232

JULIAN (The Apostate; Flavius Claudius Julianus; 331-363), Roman emperor 361-363 **8** 378-379

JULIAN, PERCY LAVON (1899-1975), African American chemist and civil rights activist **18** 219-221

JULIAN OF NORWICH (1342-after 1416), English mystic **8** 381

JULIANA (born 1909), queen of the Netherlands (1948-1980) **8** 379-380

JULIAS OF ROME, THE (Julia Domna, ca. 169-ca. 217; Julia Maesa, ca. 164-225; Julia Soamias, died 222; and Julia Mammaea, died 234), empresses of the so-called Severan Dynasty of Rome **8** 381-384

JULIUS II (Giuliano della Rovere; 1443-1513), pope 1503-1513 **8** 384-386

JUMBLATT, KAMAL (1917-1977), Lebanese ideologue and Druze leader **8** 386-387

JUNAYD, ABU AL-QASIM IBN MUHAMMAD AL (circa 830-910), Islamic mystic **8** 388

JUNG, CARL GUSTAV (1875-1961), Swiss psychologist and psychiatrist **8** 388-389

JUNG, LEO (1892-1987), American Orthodox Jewish Rabbi **8** 390-391

JÜNGER, ERNST (1895-1998), German author **8** 391-392

Jurists
    English
        Romilly, Samuel **23** 348-351
    Scottish
        Murray, William **23** 256-258

Jurists, American
    • JUDGES
        county courts
            Sampson, Edith **23** 356-358
        state courts
            Stout, Juanita Kidd **23** 382-384
    • LAWYERS
        19th century
            Langdell, Christopher Columbus **23** 204-206

JUST, ERNEST (1883-1941), American marine biologist **8** 392-393

JUSTIN MARTYR, (circa 100-circa 165), Early Christian apologist **8** 395-396

JUSTINIAN I (circa 482-565), Byzantine emperor 527-565 **8** 393-395
    and the Catholic church
        Vigilius **23** 427-429

JUSTO, AGUSTIN PEDRO (1876-1943), Argentine general, president 1932-1938 **8** 396

JUVARA, FILIPPO (1678-1736), Italian architect and designer **8** 396-397

JUVENAL (Decimus Junius Juvenalis; died after 127), Roman satirist **8** 397-399

Juvenile literature
see Literature for children

K

KABAKOV, ILYA (born 1933), Russian artist **23** 182-184

KABALEVSKY, DMITRI (1904-1987), Soviet composer, pianist, and conductor **8** 400-401

KABILA, LAURENT (born 1939), Congolese revolutionary and president **18** 222-224

KADALIE, CLEMENTS (circa 1896-1951), South Africa's first Black national trade union leader **8** 401-402

KÁDÁR, JÁNOS (born 1912), Hungarian statesman **8** 402-403

KAFKA, FRANZ (1883-1924), Czech-born German novelist and short-story writer **8** 403-406

KAHANAMOKU, DUKE (1890-1968), Hawaiian swimmer **20** 197-199

KAHLO, FRIDA (1907-1954), Mexican painter **8** 406-407

KAHN, ALBERT (1869-1942), American architect **8** 407-408

KAHN, LOUIS I. (1901-1974), American architect **8** 408-410

KAIFU TOSHIKI (born 1931), Japanese prime minister (1989-1991) **8** 410-411

KAISER, GEORG (1878-1945), German playwright **8** 411-412

KAISER, HENRY JOHN (1882-1967), American industrialist **8** 412-413

KALAKAUA, DAVID (1836-1891), king of Hawaiian Islands 1874-1891 **8** 413-414

KALIDASA (flourished 4th-5th century), Indian poet and dramatist **8** 414-415

KALMUS, NATALIE (Natalie Mabelle Dunfee; 1883?-1965), American inventor and cinematographer **21** 233-235

KAMARAJ, KUMARASWAMI (1903-1975), Indian political leader **8** 415

KAMEHAMEHA I (circa 1758-1819), king of the Hawaiian Islands 1795-1819 **8** 416

KAMEHAMEHA III (circa 1814-1854), king of the Hawaiian Islands 1825-1854 **8** 416-417

KAMENEV, LEV BORISOVICH (1883-1936), Russian politician **8** 417-418

KAMERLINGH ONNES, HEIKE (1853-1926), Dutch physicist **8** 418-420

KAMMU (737-806), Japanese emperor 781-806 **8** 420

KANDER, JOHN (born 1927), American composer and lyricist **21** 235-237

KANDINSKY, WASSILY (1866-1944), Russian painter **8** 420-422

KANE, JOHN (1860-1934), Scottish-born American primitive painter **8** 422

KANE, PAUL (1810-1871), Canadian painter and writer **8** 422-423

K'ANG YU-WEI (1858-1927), Chinese scholar and philosopher **8** 426-428

K'ANG-HSI (1654-1722), Chinese emperor 1661-1722 **8** 423-426

KANISHKA (ca. 78- ca. 103), Kashan ruler **8** 428-429

KANT, IMMANUEL (1724-1804), German philosopher **8** 430-432

KAO-TSUNG (1107-1187), Chinese emperor **8** 433

KAPITSA, PYOTR LEONIDOVICH (born 1894), Soviet physicist **8** 433-435

KAPLAN, MORDECAI MENAHEM (1881-1983), American Jewish theologian and educator **8** 435-436

KAPP, WOLFGANG (1858-1922), German nationalist politician **8** 436

KAPTEYN, JACOBUS CORNELIS (1851-1922), Dutch astronomer **8** 436-437

KARADZIC, RADOVAN (born 1945), leader of the Serbian Republic **8** 437-440

KARAMANLIS, CONSTANTINE (1907-1998), Greek member of parliament, prime minister (1955-1963; 1974-1980), and president (1980-1985) **8** 440-441

KARAMZIN, NIKOLAI MIKHAILOVICH (1766-1826), Russian historian and author **8** 441-442

KARAN, DONNA (born 1948), American fashion designer and businesswoman **8** 442-444

KARENGA, MAULANA (born Ronald McKinley Everett; born 1941), African American author, educator, and proponent of black culturalism **8** 444-447

KARIM KHAN ZAND (died 1779), Iranian ruler, founder of Zand dynasty **8** 447

KARLE, ISABELLA (born 1921), American chemist and physicist **8** 447-449

KARLSTADT, ANDREAS BODENHEIM VON (circa 1480-1541), German Protestant reformer **8** 449

KARMAL, BABRAK (born 1929), Afghan Marxist and Soviet puppet ruler of the Democratic Republic of Afghanistan (1979-1986) **8** 449-451

KÁRMÁN, THEODORE VON (1881-1963), Hungarian-born American physicist **8** 451-452

KARSH, YOUSUF (1908-2002), Canadian photographer **23** 184-187

KARUME, SHEIKH ABEID AMANI (1905-1972), Tanzanian political leader **8** 452-453

KASAVUBU, JOSEPH (circa 1913-1969), Congolese statesman **8** 453-455

KASSEBAUM, NANCY (born 1932), Republican senator from Kansas **8** 455-457

KASTRIOTI-SKANDERBEG, GJERGJ (1405-1468), Albanian military leader **23** 187-189

KATAYAMA, SEN (1860-1933), Japanese labor and Socialist leader **8** 457

KAUFMAN, GEORGE S. (1889-1961), American playwright **8** 457-458

KAUFMAN, GERALD BERNARD (born 1930), foreign policy spokesman of the British Labour Party **8** 458-460

KAUFMANN, EZEKIEL (1889-1963), Jewish philosopher and scholar **8** 460

KAUNDA, KENNETH DAVID (born 1924), Zambian statesman **8** 460-461

KAUTILYA (4th century B.C.), Indian statesman and author **8** 462

KAUTSKY, KARL JOHANN (1854-1938), German Austrian Socialist **8** 462-463

KAWABATA, YASUNARI (1899-1972), Japanese novelist **8** 463-464

KAWAWA, RASHIDI MFAUME (born 1929), Tanzanian political leader **8** 464-465

KAZAN, ELIA (born 1909), American film and stage director **8** 465-466

KAZANTZAKIS, NIKOS (1883-1957), Greek author, journalist, and statesman **8** 466-468

KEAN, EDMUND (1789-1833), English actor **21** 237-239

KEARNEY, DENIS (1847-1907), Irish-born American labor agitator **8** 468

KEARNY, STEPHEN WATTS (1794-1848), American general **8** 468-469

KEATING, PAUL JOHN (born 1944), federal treasurer of Australia (1983-1991) **8** 469-470

KEATON, BUSTER (Joseph Frank Keaton; 1895-1966), American comedian **20** 199-201

KEATS, JOHN (1795-1821), English poet **8** 470-472

KEFAUVER, CAREY ESTES (1903-1963), U.S. senator and influential Tennessee Democrat **8** 472-474

KEILLOR, GARRISON (Gary Edward Keillor, born 1942), American humorist, radio host, and author **22** 271-273

KEITA, MODIBO (1915-1977), Malian statesman **8** 474-475

KEITEL, WILHELM (1882-1946), German general **18** 224-226

KEITH, SIR ARTHUR (1866-1955), British anatomist and physical anthropologist **8** 475-476

KEITH, MINOR COOPER (1848-1929), American entrepreneur **8** 476-477

KEKKONEN, URHO KALEVA (1900-1986), Finnish athlete and politician **23** 189-191

KEKULÉ, FRIEDRICH AUGUST (1829-1896), German chemist **8** 477-478

KELLER, GOTTFRIED (1819-1890), Swiss short-story writer, novelist, and poet **8** 478-479

KELLER, HELEN ADAMS (1880-1968), American lecturer and author **8** 479-480

KELLEY, FLORENCE (1859-1932), American social worker and reformer **8** 483-484

KELLEY, HALL JACKSON (1790-1874), American promoter **8** 480

KELLEY, OLIVER HUDSON (1826-1913), American agriculturalist **8** 480-481

KELLOGG, FRANK BILLINGS (1856-1937), American statesman **8** 481

KELLOGG, JOHN HARVEY (1852-1943), American health propagandist and cereal manufacturer **21** 239-242
White, Ellen Gould **23** 438-440

KELLOR, FRANCES (1873-1952), American activist and politician **8** 481-482

KELLY, ELLSWORTH (born 1923), American artist **8** 482-483

KELLY, GENE (born Eugene Curran Kelly; 1912-1996), American actor, dancer, and choreographer **8** 484-486

KELLY, GRACE (Grace, Princess; 1929-1982), princess of Monaco **19** 174-176

KELLY, PATRICK (1954-1990), African American fashion designer **22** 273-275

KELLY, PETRA (born 1947), West German pacifist and politician **8** 486-487

KELLY, WALT (Walter Crawford Kelly; 1913-1973), American Cartoonist **22** 275-278

KELLY, WILLIAM (1811-1888), American iron manufacturer **8** 487-488

KELSEY, HENRY (circa 1667-1724), English-born Canadian explorer **8** 488

KELVIN OF LARGS, BARON (William Thomson; 1824-1907), Scottish physicist **8** 488-489

KEMAL, YASHAR (born 1922), Turkish novelist **8** 489-491

KEMBLE, FRANCES ANNE (Fanny Kemble; 1809-1893), English actress **8** 491

KEMP, JACK FRENCH, JR. (born 1935), Republican congressman from New York and secretary of housing and urban development **8** 491-493

KEMPIS, THOMAS À (circa 1380-1471), German monk and spiritual writer **8** 493-494

KENDALL, AMOS (1789-1869), American journalist **8** 494

KENDALL, EDWARD CALVIN (1886-1972), American biochemist **8** 495

KENDALL, THOMAS HENRY (Henry Clarence Kendall; 1839-1882), Australian poet **23** 191-194

Kendrake, Carleton
see Gardner, Erle Stanley

KENDREW, JOHN C. (1917-1997), English chemist and Nobel Prize winner **8** 495-496

KENEALLY, THOMAS MICHAEL (born 1935), Australian author **18** 226-228

KENNAN, GEORGE F. (born 1904), American diplomat, author, and scholar **8** 496-498

KENNEDY, ANTHONY M. (born 1936), United States Supreme Court justice **8** 498-500

KENNEDY, EDWARD M. (Ted; born 1932), U.S. senator from Massachusetts **8** 500-502

KENNEDY, JOHN FITZGERALD (1917-1963), American statesman, president 1960-1963 **8** 502-506

KENNEDY, JOHN PENDLETON (1795-1870), American author and politician **8** 506-507

KENNEDY, JOHN STEWART (1830-1909), American financier and philanthropist **8** 507-508

KENNEDY, JOSEPH (1888-1969), American financier, ambassador, and movie producer **19** 176-178

KENNEDY, ROBERT FRANCIS (1925-1968), American statesman **8** 508-509

KENNEDY, WILLIAM (born 1928), American author **19** 178-180

Kenny, Charles J.
see Gardner, Erle Stanley

KENNY, ELIZABETH (Sister Kenny; 1886-1952), Australian nursing sister **8** 509-510

KENT, JAMES (1763-1847), American jurist **8** 510-511

KENT, ROCKWELL (1882-1971), American painter and illustrator **8** 511

KENYATTA, JOMO (circa 1890-1978), Kenyan statesman **8** 512-514

KEOHANE, NANNERL OVERHOLSER (born 1940), American feminist activist and university chancellor **18** 229-230

KEPLER, JOHANNES (1571-1630), German astronomer **8** 514-516

KERENSKY, ALEKSANDR FEDOROVICH (1881-1970), Russian revolutionary and politician **8** 516-517

KERN, JEROME DAVID (1885-1945), American composer **8** 517-518

KEROUAC, JEAN-LOUIS LEBRIS DE (Jack; 1922-69), American writer of autobiographical fiction **8** 518-519

KERR, CLARK (born 1911), American economist, labor/management expert, and university president **8** 519-521

KERREY, J. ROBERT (born 1943), Democratic senator from Nebraska and 1992 presidential candidate **8** 521-522

KESSELRING, ALBERT (1885-1960), German field marshal **8** 522-523

KESSLER, DAVID A. (born 1951), commissioner of the Food and Drug Administration **8** 523-524

KETTERING, CHARLES F. (1876-1958), American engineer, industrial pioneer, and apostle of progress **8** 524-525

KEVORKIAN, JACK (born 1928), American pathologist who practiced assisted suicide **19** 180-182

Kew Gardens
see Royal Botanical Gardens

KEY, FRANCIS SCOTT (1779-1843), American poet and attorney **8** 525-527

KEY, VLADIMIR ORLANDO, JR. (1908-1963), American political scientist **8** 527-528

KEYNES, JOHN MAYNARD (1st Baron Keynes of Tilton; 1883-1946), English economist **8** 528-530

KHACHATURIAN, ARAM ILICH (or Khachaturov; 1903-1978), Russian composer **8** 530-531

KHALID BIN ABDUL AZIZ AL-SAUD (1912-1982), Saudi king and prime minister **23** 194-196

KHALIL, SAYYID ABDULLAH (1892-1970), Sudanese general, prime minister 1956-1958 **8** 531-532

KHAMA, SIR SERETSE M. (born 1921), Botswana political leader **8** 532-533

KHAMENEI, AYATOLLAH SAYYID ALI (born 1939), supreme spiritual and political leader of the Islamic Republic of Iran **8** 533-535

KHOMEINI, AYATOLLAH RUHOLLAH MUSAVI (born 1902), founder and supreme leader of the Islamic Republic of Iran **8** 535-537

KHORANA, HAR GOBIND (born 1922), Indian organic chemist **8** 537-538

KHOSROW I (died 579), Sassanid king of Persia 531-576 **8** 538-539

KHRUSHCHEV, NIKITA SERGEEVICH (1894-1971), Soviet political leader **8** 539-540

KHUFU (ruled 2590-2568 B.C.), Egyptian king **8** 540-541

KHWARIZMI, MUHAMMAD IBN MUSA AL- (died circa 850), Arab mathematician, astronomer, and geographer **8** 541

KIDD, WILLIAM (c. 1645-1701), Scottish pirate **21** 242-244

KIDDER, ALFRED VINCENT (1885-1963), American archeologist **8** 541-542

KIDMAN, SIDNEY (1857-1935), ''The Cattle King'' of Australia **8** 542-544

KIEFER, ANSELM (born 1945), German artist **8** 544-546

KIENHOLZ, EDWARD (born 1927), American Pop artist **8** 546-547

KIERKEGAARD, SØREN AABYE (1813-1855), Danish philosopher **8** 547-549
Brandes, Georg **23** 45-47

KILPATRICK, WILLIAM H. (1871-1965), American educator, college president, and philosopher of education **9** 1-3

KIM DAE-JUNG (born 1925), worked for the restoration of democracy and human rights in South Korea after 1971 **9** 3-4

KIM IL-SUNG (born 1912), North Korean political leader **9** 4-6

KIM JONG IL (born 1941), heir-apparent of Kim Il-sung, the founder and leader of the Democratic People's Republic of Korea **9** 6-7

KIM OK-KYUN (1851-1894), Korean politician **9** 7-8

KIM PUSIK (1075-1151), Korean statesman, historian, and general **9** 8-9

KIM YOUNG SAM (born 1927), South Korean statesman **9** 9-10

KINCAID, JAMAICA (Elaine Potter Richardson; born 1949), African American author **23** 196-199

KINDI, ABU-YUSUF YAQUB IBN-ISHAQ AL- (died 873), Arab philosopher **9** 10-11

KING, B. B. (born Riley B. King; born 1925), African American blues musician, singer, and songwriter **9** 11-14

KING, BILLIE JEAN (born 1943), international tennis star **9** 14-15

KING, CLARENCE (1842-1901), American geologist and mining engineer **9** 15-16

KING, CORETTA SCOTT (born 1929), American advocate of civil rights, nonviolence, international peace, full employment, and equal rights for women **9** 16-17

KING, ERNEST JOSEPH (1878-1956), American admiral **9** 17-18

KING, FREDERIC TRUBY (1858-1938), New Zealand doctor and founder of the Plunket Society **9** 18-19

KING, MARTIN LUTHER, JR. (1929-1968), African American minister and civil rights leader **9** 20-22

KING, MARY-CLAIRE (born 1946), American geneticist **19** 182-183

KING, RUFUS (1755-1827), American statesman and diplomat **9** 22-23

KING, STEPHEN (a.k.a. Richard Bachman and John Swithen; born 1947), American horror novelist **9** 23-25

KING, WILLIAM LYON MACKENZIE (1874-1950), Canadian statesman **9** 25-26

KINGSFORD SMITH, SIR CHARLES (''Smithy''; 1897-1935), Australian long-distance aviator **9** 26-28

KINGSLEY, CHARLES (1819-1875), English author and Anglican clergyman **9** 28

KINGSLEY, HENRY (1830-1867), British author **22** 278-280

KINGSLEY, MARY (1862-1900), English explorer and author **20** 201-204

KINGSTON, MAXINE HONG (Maxine Ting Ting Hong; born 1940), Asian-American feminist author **18** 231-232

KINNOCK, NEIL (born 1942), British Labour Party politician **9** 29-30

KINO, EUSEBIO FRANCISCO (1645-1711), Spanish missionary, explorer, and cartographer **9** 30-31

KINSEY, ALFRED C. (1894-1956), American zoologist **9** 31-32

KIPLING, JOSEPH RUDYARD (1865-1936), British poet and short-story writer **9** 32-33

KIRCH, MARIA WINCKELMANN (1670-1720), German astronomer **20** 204-205

KIRCHHOFF, GUSTAV ROBERT (1824-1887), German physicist **9** 33-34

KIRCHNER, ERNST LUDWIG (1880-1938), German expressionist painter **9** 34-35

KIRKLAND, JOSEPH LANE (1922-1999), American labor union movement leader **9** 35-37

KIRKLAND, SAMUEL (1741-1808), American Congregationalist missionary **9** 37

KIRKPATRICK, JEANE J. (born 1926), professor and first woman U.S. ambassador to the United Nations **9** 37-39

KIRSTEIN, LINCOLN (1906-1996), a founder and director of the New York City Ballet **9** 39-41

KISHI, NOBUSUKE (1896-1987), Japanese politician **9** 41-43

Kiss an Angel Good Morning (song)
Pride, Charley Frank **23** 317-319

KISSINGER, HENRY ALFRED (born 1923), U.S. secretary of state and co-winner of the Nobel Peace prize **9** 43-45

KITCHENER, HORATIO HERBERT (1850-1916), British field marshal and statesman **9** 45-46

KIWANUKA, BENEDICTO KAGIMA MUGUMBA (1922-1972), Ugandan politician **9** 46-47

KLEE, PAUL (1879-1940), Swiss painter and graphic artist **9** 47-49

KLEIN, A. M. (1909-1972), Canadian journalist, lawyer, novelist, and poet **9** 49-50

KLEIN, CALVIN (born 1942), American fashion designer 9 50-52

KLEIN, MELANIE (1882-1960), Austrian psychotherapist 9 52

KLEIST, HEINRICH VON (1777-1811), German author 9 52-53

KLEMPERER, OTTO (1885-1973), German conductor 20 205-207

KLIMA, VIKTOR (born 1947), Austrian chancellor 18 232-234

KLIMT, GUSTAV (1862-1918), controversial Austrian painter 9 53-55

KLINE, FRANZ (1910-1962), American painter 9 55

KLOPSTOCK, FRIEDRICH GOTTLIEB (1724-1803), German poet 9 55-56

KLUCKHOHN, CLYDE (1905-1960), American anthropologist 9 56-57

KLYUCHEVSKY, VASILY OSIPOVICH (1841-1911), Russian historian 9 57-58

KNAPP, SEAMAN ASAHEL (1833-1911), American educator and agricultural pioneer 9 58

KNIGHT, FRANK HYNEMAN (1885-1972), American economist 9 58-59

KNIGHT, PHIL (born 1938), American businessman 19 183-186

KNIPLING, EDWARD FRED (1909-2000), American entomologist 9 59-60

KNOPF, ALFRED A. (1892-1984), American publisher 9 60-61

KNOPF, BLANCHE WOLF (1894-1966), American publisher 9 61-62

KNOWLES, MALCOLM SHEPHERD (1913-1997), American adult education theorist and planner 9 62-64

KNOX, HENRY (1750-1806), American Revolutionary War general 9 64

KNOX, JOHN (circa 1505-1572), Scottish religious reformer 9 65-66

KNOX, PHILANDER CHASE (1853-1921), American statesman 9 66-67

KNUDSEN, WILLIAM S. (1879-1948), American auto industry leader 9 67-68

KOBAYASHI, MASAKI (1916-1996), Japanese film director 23 199-201

KOCH, EDWARD I. (born 1924), New York City mayor 9 68-69

KOCH, ROBERT HEINRICH HERMANN (1843-1910), German physician and bacteriologist 9 69-70

KODÁLY, ZOLTÁN (1882-1967), Hungarian composer 9 71

KOESTLER, ARTHUR (1905-1983), author of political novels 9 71-73

KOHL, HELMUT (born 1930), chancellor of West Germany (1982-1990) and first chancellor of a united Germany since World War II 9 73-74

KOJONG (1852-1919), Korean king 9 74-75

KOKOSCHKA, OSKAR (1886-1980), Austrian painter, graphic artist, and author 9 75-76

KOLAKOWSKI, LESZEK (born 1927), philosopher who wrote on broad themes of ethics, metaphysics, and religion 9 76-77

KOLCHAK, ALEKSANDR VASILIEVICH (1873-1920), Russian admiral 9 77-78

KOLLONTAI, ALEKSANDRA MIKHAILOVNA (1872-1952), Soviet diplomat 9 79

KOLLWITZ, KÄTHE (1867-1945), German expressionist graphic artist and sculptor 9 79-81

KONEV, IVAN STEFANOVICH (1897-1973), Soviet marshal 9 81-82

KONOE, PRINCE FUMIMARO (or Konoye; 1891-1945), Japanese premier 1937-1939 and 1940-1941 9 82-83

KOONS, JEFF (born 1955), American artist 9 83-84

KOOP, C. EVERETT (born 1916), American surgeon general 18 235-237

KÖPRÜLÜ, AHMED (Köprülüzade Fazil Ahmed Pasha; 1635-1676), Turkish statesman and general 9 84-85

KORNBERG, ARTHUR (born 1918), Americna biochemist 9 85-87

KORNILOV, LAVR GEORGIEVICH (1870-1918), Russian general 9 87-88

KOSCIUSZKO, TADEUSZ ANDRZEJ BONAWENTURA (1746-1817), Polish patriot, hero in the American Revolution 9 88

KOSSUTH, LOUIS (1802-1894), Hungarian statesman 9 88-90

KOSYGIN, ALEKSEI NIKOLAEVICH (1904-1980), chairman of the U.S.S.R. Council of Ministers and head of the Soviet government (1964-1980) 9 90-91

KOTZEBUE, OTTO VON (1787-1846), Russian explorer 9 91-92

KOUFAX, SANDY (Sanford Braun; born 1945), American baseball player 20 208-210

KOVACS, ERNIE (1919-1962), American comedian 19 186-188

KOVALEVSKY, SOPHIA VASILEVNA (Sonya Kovalevsky; 1850-1891), Russian mathematician 22 280-282

KOZYREV, ANDREI VLADIMIROVICH (born 1951), Russian minister of foreign affairs and a liberal, pro-Western figure in Boris Yeltsin's cabinet 9 92-93

KRAMER, LARRY (born 1935), American AIDS activist and author 20 210-212

KRASNER, LEE (Lenore; 1908-1984), American painter and collage artist 9 93-94

KRAVCHUK, LEONID MAKAROVYCH (born 1934), president of the Ukraine (1991-1994) 9 94-95

KREBS, SIR HANS ADOLF (1900-1981), German British biochemist 9 95-97

KREISKY, BRUNO (1911-1983), chancellor of Austria (1970-1983) 9 97-98

KRENEK, ERNST (born 1900), Austrian composer 9 98-99

KREPS, JUANITA MORRIS (born 1921), economist, university professor, United States secretary of commerce (1977-1979), and author 9 99-101

KRIEGHOFF, CORNELIUS (1815-1872), Dutch-born Canadian painter 9 101

KRISHNAMURTI, JIDDU (1895-1986), Indian mystic and philosopher 9 101-103

KROC, RAYMOND ALBERT (1902-1984), creator of the McDonald's chain 9 103-104

KROCHMAL, NACHMAN KOHEN (1785-1840), Austrian Jewish historian 9 104-105

KROEBER, ALFRED LOUIS (1876-1960), American anthropologist 9 105-106

KROGH, SCHACK AUGUST STEENBERG (1874-1949), Danish physiologist 9 106

KROPOTKIN, PETER ALEKSEEVICH (1842-1921), Russian prince, scientist, and anarchist 9 107-108

KRUGER, STEPHANUS JOHANNES PAULUS ("Paul"; 1825-1904), South African statesman 9 108-109

KRUPP FAMILY (19th-20th century), German industrialists 9 109-111

KU CHIEH-KANG (born 1893), Chinese historian 9 120-121

KU K'AI-CHIH (circa 345-circa 406), Chinese painter 9 125-126

KUANG-HSÜ (1871-1908), emperor of China 1875-1908 9 111-112

KUANG-WU-TI (6 B.C. - 57 A.D.), Chinese emperor ca. 25-57 **9** 112-113

KUBITSCHEK DE OLIVEIRA, JUSCELINO (1902-1976), president of Brazil 1956-1961 **9** 113-115

KUBLAI KHAN (1215-1294), Mongol emperor **9** 115-118

KÜBLER-ROSS, ELISABETH (born 1926), Swiss-born American psychiatrist **9** 118-120

KUBRICK, STANLEY (1928-1999), American filmmaker **18** 237-239

KUCAN, MILAN (born 1941), President of the Republic of Slovenia **18** 239-242

KUHN, MAGGIE (1905-1995), American activist and founder of the Gray Panthers **19** 188-190

KUHN, THOMAS SAMUEL (1922-1996), American historian and philosopher of science **9** 121-123

KUK, ABRAHAM ISAAC (1865-1935), Russian-born Jewish scholar **9** 123-124

KUKAI (774-835), Japanese Buddhist monk **9** 124-125

KUKRIT PRAMOJ, MOMRAJAWONG (M.R.; born 1911), literary figure and prime minister of Thailand (1975-1976) **9** 126-127

KUMARAJIVA (344/350-409/413), Indian Buddhist monk **9** 127

KUNDERA, MILAN (born 1929), Czech-born author **9** 128-129

KÜNG, HANS (born 1928), Swiss-born Roman Catholic theologian **9** 129-130

KUNIN, MADELEINE MAY (born 1933), first woman governor of Vermont **9** 130-131

KUNITZ, STANLEY JASSPON (born 1905), American poet laureate **22** 282-284

KUNSTLER, WILLIAM M. (1919-1995), American civil rights attorney and author **9** 131-133

KUO MO-JO (born 1892), Chinese author **9** 133-134

KUPKA, FRANTISEK (Frank; 1871-1957), Czech painter and illustrator **9** 134-135

KUROSAWA, AKIRA (1910-1998), Japanese film director **9** 135-137

KUTUZOV, MIKHAIL ILARIONOVICH (1745-1813), Russian field marshal **9** 137-138

KUZNETS, SIMON (1901-1985), American economist, researcher, and author **9** 138-139

KWANGGAET'O (375-413), Korean statesman, king of Koguryo **9** 139-140

KWANGJONG (925-975), Korean statesman, king of Koryo **9** 140

KYD, THOMAS (1558-1594), English dramatist **9** 140-141

KYPRIANOU, SPYROS (born 1932), president of the Republic of Cyprus **9** 141-143

L

LA BRUYÈRE, JEAN DE (1645-1696), French man of letters and moralist **9** 145

LA FARGE, JOHN (1835-1910), American artist and writer **9** 149-150

LA FAYETTE, COMTESSE DE (Marie Madeleine Pioche de la Vergne; 1634-93), French novelist **9** 150-151

LA FLESCHE, FRANCIS (1857-1932), Native American ethnologist **9** 152-154

LA FLESCHE, SUSETTE (1854-1903), Native American activist and reformer **9** 152-154

LA FOLLETTE, ROBERT MARION (1855-1925), American statesman **9** 155-156

LA FONTAINE, JEAN DE (1621-1695), French poet **9** 156-157

LA GUARDIA, FIORELLO HENRY (1882-1947), American politician, New York City mayor **9** 166-167

LA METTRIE, JULIEN OFFRAY DE (1709-1751), French physician and philosopher **9** 179-180

LA ROCHEFOUCAULD, FRANÇOIS, DUC DE (1613-1680), French moralist **9** 208-209

LA SALLE, SIEUR DE (René Robert Cavelier; 1643-1687), French explorer and colonizer **9** 210-211

LA TOUR, GEORGE DE (1593-1652), French painter **9** 222

LA VERENDRYE, SIEUR DE (Pierre Gaultier de Varennes; 1685-1749), French-Canadian soldier, explorer, and fur trader **9** 239-240

LABROUSTE, PIERRE FRANÇOIS HENRI (1801-1875), French architect-engineer **9** 144

LACAN, JACQUES (1901-1981), French psychoanalyst **9** 145-147

LACHAISE, GASTON (1882-1935), French-born American sculptor **9** 147

LACHAPELLE, MARIE (1769-1821), French obstetrician and teacher **21** 245-247

LACOMBE, ALBERT (1827-1916), Canadian missionary priest **9** 147-148

LACORDAIRE, JEAN BAPTISTE HENRI (1802-1861), French Dominican preacher **9** 148

LADD, WILLIAM (1778-1841), American pacifist **9** 149

LADD-FRANKLIN, CHRISTINE (1847-1930), American logician and psychologist **23** 202-204

LAENNEC, RENÉ (René-Théophile-Hyacinthe Laënnec; 1781-1826), French physician and inventor **21** 247-249

LAFAYETTE, MARQUIS DE (Marie Joseph Paul Yves Roch Gilbert du Motier; 1757-1834), French general and statesman **9** 151-152

LAFONTAINE, SIR LOUIS-HIPPOLYTE (1807-1864), Canadian politician **9** 157-158

LAFONTAINE, OSKAR (born 1943), German politician **9** 158-160

LAFORGUE, JULES (1860-1887), French poet **9** 160-161

LAGERFELD, KARL (born 1938), German-French designer of high fashion **9** 161-162

LAGERKVIST, PÄR FABIAN (born 1891), Swedish author **9** 162-163

LAGERLÖF, SELMA OTTILIANA LOVISA (1858-1940), Swedish author **9** 163-164

LAGRANGE, JOSEPH LOUIS (1736-1813), Italian-born French mathematician **9** 164-166

LAHR, BERT (Irving Lahrheim; 1895-1967), performer and comedian in burlesque, vaudeville, musical comedy, film, and television **9** 167-168

LAIRD, MELVIN R. (born 1922), U.S. congressman and secretary of defense **9** 168-170

LAKSHMIBAI (Laksmi Bai; Rani of Jhansi; c.1835-1857), Indian queen and national hero **22** 41-42

LALIBELA (ruled circa 1181-circa 1221), Ethiopian king and saint **9** 170

LAMAR, LUCIUS QUINTUS CINCINNATUS (1825-1893), American politician and jurist **9** 170-171

LAMARCK, CHEVALIER DE (Jean Baptiste Pierre Antoine de Monet;

1744-1829), French naturalist **9** 171-173

LAMARTINE, ALPHONSE MARIE LOUIS DE (1790-1869), French poet and diplomat **9** 173-175

LAMAS, CARLOS SAAVEDRA (1878-1959), Argentine scholar, statesman, and diplomat **9** 175-176

LAMB, CHARLES (1775-1834), English author, critic, and minor poet **9** 176-177

LAMBSDORFF, OTTO GRAF (born 1926), West German minister of economics **9** 177-179

LAMENNAIS, HUGUES FÉLICITÉ ROBERT DE (1782-1854), French priest and political writer **9** 179

L'AMOUR, LOUIS (Louis Dearborn LaMoore; 1908-1988), American author of westerns **20** 213-215

LAMPMAN, ARCHIBALD (1861-1899), Canadian poet **9** 180-181

LAMPRECHT, KARL (1856-1915), German historian **9** 181

LAMY, JEAN BAPTISTE (1814-1888), French archbishop in the United States **9** 181-182

LANCASTER, BURT (Burton Stephen Lancaster; 1913-1994), American actor **20** 215-218

LANCASTER, JOSEPH (1778-1838), English educator **9** 182-183

LAND, EDWIN HERBERT (1909-1991), American physicist, inventor, and manufacturer **9** 183-184

LANDAU, LEV DAVIDOVICH (1908-1968), Soviet theoretical physicist **9** 184-185

LANDINI, FRANCESCO (circa 1335-1397), Italian composer and poet **9** 185-186

LANDIS, KENESAW MOUNTAIN (1866-1944), American baseball commissioner **22** 285-287

LANDOR, WALTER SAVAGE (1775-1864), English poet, essayist and critic **9** 186-187

LANDOWSKI, MARCEL (born 1915), French composer of lyric works **9** 187-188

LANDRY, TOM (Thomas Wade Landry; 1924-2000), American football coach **22** 290-292

LANDSTEINER, KARL (1868-1943), Austrian-born American immunologist **9** 188-189

LANE, FITZ HUGH (1804-1865), American marine painter **9** 189

LANFRANC (circa 1010-1089), Italian theologian, archbishop of Canterbury **9** 189-190

LANG, FRITZ (1890-1976), film director **9** 190-192

LANG, JOHN THOMAS (1876-1975), Australian politician **9** 192-193

LANGDELL, CHRISTOPHER COLUMBUS (1826-1906), American lawyer **23** 204-206

LANGE, DOROTHEA (1895-1965), American photographer **9** 193-194

LANGLAND, WILLIAM (circa 1330-1400), English poet **9** 194-195

LANGLEY, SAMUEL PIERPONT (1834-1906), American scientist **9** 195-196

LANGMUIR, IRVING (1881-1957), American chemist **9** 196-197

LANGSTON, JOHN MERCER (1829-1897), American educator and diplomat **9** 197

LANGTON, STEPHEN (c. 1155-1228), English prelate and signer of the Magna Carta **21** 249-251

LANIER, JARON (born ca. 1961), American computer engineer **9** 198-199

LANIER, SIDNEY (1842-1881), American poet, critic, and musician **9** 199-200

LANSING, ROBERT (1864-1928), American lawyer and statesman **9** 200

LAO SHÊ (1899-1966), Chinese novelist **9** 200-201

LAO TZU (flourished 6th century B.C.), Chinese philosopher **9** 201-202

LAPLACE, MARQUIS DE (Pierre Simon; 1749-1827), French mathematician **9** 202-204

LARDNER, RINGGOLD WILMER (1885-1933), American author **9** 204-205

LARIONOV, MIKHAIL (1881-1964), Russian artist **9** 205-206

LARKIN, PHILIP (1922-1986), English poet **9** 206-207

LARKIN, THOMAS OLIVER (1802-1858), American merchant and diplomat **9** 208

LARSEN, NELLA (1893-1963), Harlem Renaissance writer **9** 209-210

LARSON, JONATHAN (1961-1996), American playwright, composer, and lyricist **18** 243-145

LAS CASAS, BARTOLOMÉ DE (1474-1566), Spanish Dominican missionary and historian **9** 211-212

LASCH, CHRISTOPHER (1932-1994), American historian and social critic **9** 212-214

LASHLEY, KARL SPENCER (1890-1958), American neuropsychologist **9** 214-215

LASKER, ALBERT (1880-1952), American advertising executive **21** 251-254

LASKER, EMANUEL (1868-1941), German chess grandmaster **20** 218-220

LASKI, HAROLD J. (1893-1950), English political scientist and Labour party leader **9** 215-216

LASKY, JESSE (1880-1958), American film producer **21** 254-256

LASSALLE, FERDINAND (1825-1864), German socialist leader **9** 216

LASSUS, ROLAND DE (1532-1594), Franco-Flemish composer **9** 216-218

LASSWELL, HAROLD DWIGHT (born 1902), American political scientist **9** 218-219

Last Year at Marienbad (film) Resnais, Alain **23** 333-335

LÁSZLÓ I, KING OF HUNGARY (ca. 1040-1095), king of Hungary and saint **9** 219-221

LATIMER, HUGH (circa 1492-1555), English Protestant bishop, reformer, and martyr **9** 221

LATIMER, LEWIS (1848-1928), American inventor and electrical engineer **19** 191-193

LATROBE, BENJAMIN HENRY (1764-1820), English-born American architect **9** 222-224

LAUD, WILLIAM (1573-1645), English archbishop of Canterbury **9** 224-225

LAUDER, ESTEE (née Josephine Esthe Menzer, born ca. 1908), founder of an international cosmetics empire **9** 225-226

LAUREL, SALVADOR H. (Doy; born 1928), member of the Philippine Congress and vice-president **9** 226-227

LAUREN, RALPH (Ralph Lipschitz; born 1939), American fashion designer **9** 228-229

LAURENCE, MARGARET (Jean Margaret Wemyss; 1926-1987), Canadian writer **9** 229-230

LAURENS, HENRI (1885-1954), French sculptor **9** 230-231

LAURENS, HENRY (1724-1792), American merchant and Revolutionary statesman **9** 232

LAURIER, SIR WILFRID (1841-1919), Canadian statesman, prime minister 1896-1911 **9** 232-234

LAURO, ACHILLE (1887-1984), Italian business and political leader **9** 234-235

LAUTARO (circa 1535-1557), Araucanian Indian chieftain in Chile **9** 235

LAVAL, FRANCOIS XAVIER DE (1623-1708), French bishop in Canada **9** 235-236

LAVAL, PIERRE (1883-1945), French politician, chief Vichy minister **9** 237-238

LAVALLEJA, JUAN ANTONIO (1778-1853), Uruguayan independence leader **9** 238-239

LAVIGERIE, CHARLES MARTEL ALLEMAND (1825-1892), French cardinal **9** 240

LAVISSE, ERNEST (1842-1922), French historian **9** 241

LAVOISIER, ANTOINE LAURENT (1743-1794), French chemist **9** 241-244

LAVOISIER, MARIE PAULZE (1758-1836), French chemist **22** 292-294

Law
commercial
Murray, William **23** 256-258
legal education
Langdell, Christopher Columbus **23** 204-206
legal reform
Romilly, Samuel **23** 348-351

LAW, JOHN (1671-1729), Scottish monetary theorist and banker **9** 244-245

LAW, WILLIAM (1686-1761), English devotional writer **9** 245-246

LAWRENCE, ABBOTT (1792-1855), American manufacturer and diplomat **9** 246

LAWRENCE, DAVID HERBERT (1885-1930), English novelist, poet, and essayist **9** 247-248

LAWRENCE, ERNEST ORLANDO (1901-1958), American physicist **9** 248-250

LAWRENCE, JACOB (born 1917), African American painter **9** 250-251

LAWRENCE, JAMES (1781-1813), American naval officer **9** 251-252

LAWRENCE, SIR THOMAS (1769-1830), English portrait painter **9** 252-253

LAWRENCE, THOMAS EDWARD (1888-1935), British soldier and author **9** 253-254

LAWSON, HENRY (1867-1922), Australian poet and short-story writer **9** 254-255

LAWSON, THOMAS WILLIAM (1857-1925), American entrepreneur and reformer **9** 255-256

Lawyers
see Jurists

LAYAMON (flourished circa 1200), English poet **9** 256-257

LAYE, CAMARA (1928-1980), Guinean novelist **9** 257-259

LAZARSFELD, PAUL F. (1901-1976), American sociologist **9** 259-260

LAZARUS, EMMA (1849-1887), American poet and playwright **9** 260-261

LE BON, GUSTAVE (1841-1931), French social scientist and philosopher **9** 268-269

LE BRUN, CHARLES (1619-1690), French painter, decorator, and draftsman **9** 269-270

LE CARRE, JOHN (born David Cornwell, 1931), British spy novelist **9** 270-271

LE CORBUSIER (Charles Édouard eanneret-Gris; 1887-1965), Swiss architect, city planner, and painter **9** 274-275
Maekawa, Kunio **23** 239-242

LE DUAN (1908-1986), North Vietnamese leader and later head of the government of all Vietnam **9** 278-280

LE FANU, JOSEPH SHERIDAN (1814-1873), Irish author **23** 206-208

LE GUIN, URSULA KROEBER (born 1929), American author **18** 249-251

LE JEUNE, CLAUDE (circa 1530-1600), Flemish composer **9** 314-315

LE NAIN BROTHERS, 17th-century French painters **9** 321-322

LE NÔTRE, ANDRÉ (or Le Nostre; 1613-1700), French landscape architect **9** 328-329

LE PEN, JEAN MARIE (born 1928), French political activist of the radical right **9** 348-350

LE PLAY, GUILLAUME FRÉDÉRIC (1806-1882), French sociologist and economist **9** 350-351

LE VAU, LOUIS (1612-1670), French architect **9** 360-361

LEA, HENRY CHARLES (1825-1909), American historian **9** 261-262

LEADBELLY (Huddie William Leadbetter; 1885-1949), African American folk singer **23** 208-211

League of Nations (1919-1946)
supporters (Europe)
Murray, Gilbert **23** 250-253

LEAKEY, LOUIS SEYMOUR BAZETT (1903-1972), British anthropologist **9** 262

LEAKEY, MARY DOUGLAS (1913-1996), English archaeologist **9** 263-264

LEAKEY, RICHARD ERSKINE FRERE (born 1944), Kenyan researcher in human prehistory and wildlife conservationist **9** 264-265

LEAR, EDWARD (1812-1888), English writer and artist **9** 265-266

LEAR, NORMAN (born 1922), American author and television director and producer **19** 193-195

LEARY, TIMOTHY (1920-1996), American psychologist, author, lecturer, and cult figure **9** 266-267

LEASE, MARY ELIZABETH CLYENS (1853-1933), American writer and politician **9** 268

LEAVITT, HENRIETTA SWAN (1868-1921), American astronomer **23** 211-213

LEBED, ALEXANDER IVANOVICH (1950-2002), Russian general and politician **18** 245-247

LEBLANC, NICOLAS (1742-1806), French industrial chemist **21** 256-258

LECKY, WILLIAM EDWARD HARTPOLE (1838-1903), Anglotrish historian and essayist **9** 271-272

LECLERC, JACQUES PHILIPPE (1902-1947), French general **9** 272-273

LECONTE DE LISLE, CHARLES MARIE RENÉ (1818-1894), French poet **9** 273-274

LECUONA, ERNESTO (Ernesto Sixto de la Asuncion Lecuona y Casado; 1896-1963), Cuban musician **23** 213-216

LED ZEPPELIN (1968-1980), British "Heavy Metal" band **23** 216-218

LEDERBERG, JOSHUA (born 1925), Nobel Prize winning geneticist **9** 275-277

LEDOUX, CLAUDE NICOLAS (1736-1806), French architect **9** 277-278

LEE, MOTHER ANN (1736-1784), religious and social reformer and founder of the Shakers **9** 289-290

LEE, ARTHUR (1740-1792), American statesman and diplomat **9** 288-289

LEE, BRUCE (1940-1973), Asian American actor and martial arts master **18** 247-249

LEE, CHARLES (1731-1782), American general **22** 294-297

LEE, HARPER (Nelle Harper Lee; born 1926), American author **20** 220-222

LEE, MING CHO (born 1930), American scene designer for theater and opera **9** 289-290

LEE, RICHARD HENRY (1732-1794), American patriot and statesman **9** 291-292

LEE, ROBERT EDWARD (1807-1870), American army officer and Confederate general in chief **9** 292-294

LEE, ROSE (Rose Hum; 1904-1964), American sociologist **21** 258-260

LEE, SPIKE (born Sheldon Jackson Lee; born 1957), African American actor, author, and filmmaker **9** 295-299

LEE, TSUNG-DAO (born 1926), Chinese-born American physicist **9** 299-300

LEE, YUAN TSEH (born 1936), Taiwanese American scientist and educator **23** 218-220

LEE HSIEN LOONG (born 1952), Singaporean soldier and deputy prime minister **9** 280-281

LEE KUAN YEW (born 1923), prime minister of Singapore (1959-1988) **9** 281-283

LEE TENG-HUI (born 1923), president of the Republic of China (1988-) **9** 283-285

LEEUWENHOEK, ANTON VAN (1632-1723), Dutch naturalist and microscopist **9** 300-301

LEFEBVRE, GEORGES (1874-1959), French historian **9** 301-302

Legal reform
see Law—legal reform

LÉGER, FERNAND (1881-1955), French painter **9** 302-303

LEGHARI, SARDAR FAROOQ AHMED KHAN (born 1940), president of the Islamic Republic of Pakistan **9** 303-305

LEGINSKA, ETHEL (Ethel Liggins; 1886-1970), English American musician **23** 220-222

LEGUÍA Y SALCEDO, AUGUSTO BERNARDINO (1863-1932), Peruvian president 1908-12 and 1919-30 **9** 305-306

LEHMAN, HERBERT HENRY (1878-1963), American banker and statesman **9** 306-307

LEHMBRUCK, WILHELM (1881-1919), German sculptor **9** 307

LEIBNIZ, GOTTFRIED WILHELM VON (1646-1716), German mathematician and philosopher **9** 307-310

LEIBOVITZ, ANNIE (born 1949), Ameircan photographer **9** 310-312

LEICESTER, EARL OF (Robert Dudley; 1532?-1588), English politician **9** 312-313

LEIGH, MIKE (born 1943), British director and screenwriter **23** 222-225

LEIGH, VIVIEN (Vivian Mary Hartley; 1913-1967), British actress **18** 251-253

LEISLER, JACOB (1640-1691), American colonial leader **9** 313-314

LEITZEL, LILLIAN (born Leopoldina Altitza Pelikan; 1892-1931), German aerialist **23** 225-227

Leland Stanford Junior University
see Stanford University

LELY, SIR PETER (1618-1680), German-born painter active in England **9** 315

LEMAÎTRE, ABBÈ GEORGES ÉDOUARD (1894-1966), Belgian astronomer **9** 315-316

LEMAY, CURTIS E. (1906-1990), United States combat leader (World War II) and Air Force chief of staff **9** 316-318

LEMBEDE, ANTON (1913-1947), leader of black resistance to white supremacy in South Africa **9** 318-319

LEMIEUX, MARIO (born 1965), Canadian hockey player and team owner **20** 222-224

LEMMON, JACK (John Uhler Lemmon; 1925-2001), American actor **22** 297-299

LEMNITZER, LYMAN LOUIS (Lem; 1899-1988), American soldier-statesman and strategist and NATO architect **9** 319-320

L'ENFANT, PIERRE CHARLES (1754-1825), French-born American architect **9** 322-323

L'ENGLE, MADELEINE (born 1918), American author **18** 253-255

LENGLEN, SUZANNE (1899-1938), French tennis player **19** 195-197

LENIN, VLADIMIR ILICH (1870-1924), Russian statesman **9** 323-326

LEO I (circa 400-461), saint and pope 440-461 **9** 329-330

LEO III (the Isaurian; circa 680-741), Byzantine emperor 717-741 **9** 330-332

LEO IX, SAINT (Bruno of Egisheim; 1002-1054), pope 1049-1054 **9** 332

LEO X (Giovanni de' Medici; 1475-1521), pope 1513-1521 **9** 332-334

LEO XIII (Vincenzo Gioacchino Pecci; 1810-1903), pope 1878-1903 **9** 334-336

Leon-Castilla (kingdom, Northern Spain) Urraca **23** 417-418

LEON, MOSES DE (circa 1250-1305), Jewish mystic **9** 336

LEONARD, DANIEL (1740-1829), American loyalist lawyer and essayist **9** 336-337

LEONARDO DA VINCI (1452-1519), Italian painter, sculptor, architect, and scientist **9** 337-340

LEONIDAS I (ca. 530 B.C. - 480 B.C.), Spartan king **9** 340-343

LÉONIN (Leoninus; flourished circa 1165-1185), French composer **9** 343-344

LEOPARDI, CONTE GIACOMO (1798-1837), Italian poet **9** 344-345

LEOPOLD I (1790-1865), king of Belgium 1831-1865 **9** 345-346

LEOPOLD II (1747-1792), Holy Roman emperor 1790-1792 **9** 346

LEOPOLD II (1835-1909), king of Belgium 1865-1909 **9** 346-347

LEOPOLD III (1901-1983), king of Belgium 1934-1951 **9** 347-348

LERDO DE TEJADA, MIGUEL (1812-1861), Mexican liberal politician **9** 351-352

LERMONTOV, MIKHAIL YURIEVICH (1814-1841), Russian poet and prose writer **9** 352-353

LERNER, ALAN JAY (1918-1986), American lyricist/librettist **20** 224-226

LESAGE, ALAIN RENÉ (1668-1747), French novelist and playwright **9** 353-354

LESCOT, PIERRE (1500/1515-1578), French architect **9** 354

LESSEPS, VICOMTE DE (Ferdinand Marie; 1805-1894), French diplomat **9** 354-355

LESSING, DORIS (Doris May Taylor; born 1919), South African expatriate writer **9** 355-357

LESSING, GOTTHOLD EPHRAIM (1729-1781), German philosopher, dramatist, and critic **9** 357-359

LETCHER, JOHN (1813-1884), American politician **9** 359-360

LEVANT, OSCAR (1906-1972), American composer and pianist **19** 197-199

LEVERRIER, URBAIN JEAN JOSEPH (1811-1877), French mathematical astronomer **9** 361-362

LÉVESQUE, RENÉ (1922-1987), premier of the province of Quebec, Canada (1976-1985) **9** 362-363

LEVI BEN GERSHON (1288-circa 1344); French Jewish scientist, philosopher, and theologian **9** 363-364

LEVI, CARLO (1902-1975), Italian writer and painter **9** 364

LEVI, PRIMO (1919-1987), Italian author and chemist **9** 365-366

LEVI-MONTALCINI, RITA (born 1909) Italian and American biologist who discovered the nerve growth factor **9** 366-368

LÉVI-STRAUSS, CLAUDE GUSTAVE (born 1908), French social anthropologist **9** 371-372

LEVINAS, EMMANUEL (1906-1995), Jewish philosopher **9** 368-369

LEVINE, JAMES (born 1943), American conductor and pianist **9** 369-371

LEVITT, WILLIAM (1907-1994), American real estate developer **19** 199-201

LEVY, BERNARD-HENRI (born 1948), French moralist and political philosopher **9** 372-373

LEVY, DAVID (born 1937), Israeli minister of foreign affairs and deputy prime minister **9** 373-374

LÉVY-BRUHL, LUCIEN (1857-1939), French philosopher and anthropologist **9** 374-375

LEWIN, KURT (1890-1947), German-American social psychologist **9** 375-376

LEWIS, ANDREW (circa 1720-1781), American general in the Revolution **9** 376-377

LEWIS, CARL (born Frederick Carlton Lewis; born 1961), African American track and field athlete **9** 377-380

LEWIS, CECIL DAY (1904-1972), British poet and essayist **9** 380

LEWIS, CLARENCE IRVING (1883-1964), American philosopher **9** 381

LEWIS, CLIVE STAPLES (C.S.; 1898-1963), British novelist and essayist **9** 381-382

LEWIS, ESSINGTON (1881-1961), Australian industrial leader **9** 382-384

LEWIS, GILBERT NEWTON (1875-1946), American physical chemist **9** 384-385

LEWIS, HARRY SINCLAIR (1885-1951), American novelist **9** 385-387

LEWIS, JOHN LLEWELLYN (1880-1969), American labor leader **9** 387-388

LEWIS, JOHN ROBERT (born 1940), United States civil rights activist and representative from Georgia **9** 388-390

LEWIS, MATTHEW GREGORY (1775-1818), English novelist and playwright **9** 390-391

LEWIS, MERIWETHER (1774-1809), American explorer and army officer **9** 391-392

LEWIS, OSCAR (1914-1970), American anthropologist **9** 392-393

LEWITT, SOL (born 1928), American Minimalist and Conceptualist artist **9** 393-395

LI HUNG-CHANG (1823-1901), Chinese soldier, statesman, and industrialist **9** 407-409

LI PENG (born 1928), premier of the People's Republic of China **9** 433-435

LI PO (701-762), Chinese poet **9** 437-439

LI SSU (280?-208 B.C.), Chinese statesman **9** 442-443

LI TA-CHAO (1889-1927), Chinese Communist revolutionist **9** 447

LI TZU-CH'ENG (circa 1606-1645), Chinese bandit and rebel leader **9** 452

LIANG CH'I-CH'AO (1873-1929), Chinese intellectual and political reformer **9** 395-396

LIANG WU-TI (464-549), Chinese emperor of Southern dynasties **9** 396-397

LIAQUAT ALI KHAN (1896-1951), Pakistani statesman **9** 397

LIBBY, WILLARD FRANK (1908-1980), American chemist **9** 397-398

LICHTENSTEIN, ROY (1923-1997), American painter, sculptor, and printmaker **9** 398-399

LIE, TRYGVE HALVDAN (1896-1968), Norwegian statesman and UN secretary general **9** 400-401

LIEBER, FRANCIS (circa 1798-1872), German American political scientist **9** 401-402

LIEBERMANN, MAX (1847-1935), German painter **9** 402-403

LIEBIG, BARON JUSTUS VON (1803-1873), German chemist **9** 403-404

LIGACHEV, YEGOR KUZ'MICH (born 1920), member of the Central Committee of the Communist Party of the Soviet Union (1966-1990) **9** 404-406

LIGETI, GYÖRGY (born 1923), Austrian composer **9** 406-407

LIGHTNER, CANDY (born 1946), American activist and founder of Mothers Against Drunk Driving **19** 201-203

LILBURNE, JOHN (1615-1657), English political activist and pamphleteer **9** 409-410

LILIENTHAL, DAVID ELI (1899-1981), American public administrator **9** 410-411

LILIENTHAL, OTTO (1848-1896), Prussian design engineer **21** 260-262

LILIUOKALANI, LYDIA KAMAKAEHA (1838-1917), queen of the Hawaiian Islands **9** 411-412

LIMBOURG BROTHERS (flourished circa 1399-1416), Netherlandish illuminators **9** 412-413

LIMÓN, JOSÉ ARCADIA (1908-1972), Mexican American dancer and choreographer **23** 227-229 Humphrey, Doris **23** 157-159

LIN, MAYA YING (born 1959), American architect **9** 413-415

LIN PIAO (1907-1971), Chinese Communist military and political leader **9** 429-430

LIN TSE-HSÜ (1785-1850), Chinese official **9** 431-432

LINCOLN, ABRAHAM (1809-1865), American statesman, president 1861-1865 **9** 415-418 in literature and biography Beveridge, Albert Jeremiah **23** 39-41

LINCOLN, BENJAMIN (1733-1810), American military officer **9** 418-419

LIND, JAKOV (Heinz "Henry" Landwirth; born 1927), Austrian autobiographer, short-story writer, novelist, and playwright **9** 419-420

LINDBERGH, ANNE MORROW (born 1906), American author and aviator **9** 420-421

LINDBERGH, CHARLES AUGUSTUS (1902-1974), American aviator **9** 421-423

LINDSAY, JOHN VLIET (born 1921), U.S. congressman (1959-1965) and mayor of New York (1966-1973) **9** 423-424

LINDSAY, VACHEL (1879-1931), American folk poet **9** 424-425

LINDSEY, BENJAMIN BARR (1869-1943), American jurist and reformer **9** 425-426

LINH, NGUYEN VAN (1915-1998), secretary-general of the Vietnamese Communist Party (1986-1991) **9** 426-427

LINNAEUS, CARL (Carl von Linné; 1707-1778), Swedish naturalist **9** 427-429

LINTON, RALPH (1893-1953), American anthropologist **9** 431

Lion of Lucerne (sculpture) Thorvaldsen, Bertel **23** 403-406

LIPCHITZ, JACQUES (1891-1973), Lithuanian-born American sculptor **9** 432-433

LIPPI, FRA FILIPPO (circa 1406-1469), Italian painter **9** 439

LIPPMANN, WALTER (1889-1974), American journalist **9** 439-440

LIPPOLD, RICHARD (1915-2002), American Constructivist sculptor **9** 440-442

LIST, GEORG FRIEDRICH (1789-1846), German economist **9** 443-444

LISTER, JOSEPH (1st Baron Lister of Lyme Regis; 1827-1912), English surgeon **9** 444-445

LISZT, FRANZ (1811-1886), Hungarian composer **9** 445-447

Literary criticism Brandes, Georg **23** 45-47

Literature for children England Nesbit, E(dith) **23** 263-265 United States Austin, Mary Hunter **23** 23-25 Rollins, Charlemae Hill **23** 346-348

LITTLE, ROYAL (born 1896), American textile tycoon **9** 449-451

Little Karoo, The (book) Smith, Pauline **23** 372-373

LITTLE RICHARD (Richard Penniman; born 1932), American rock 'n' roll musician **9** 447-449

LITTLE WOLF (1818?-1904), Cheyenne chief **18** 255-257

LITVINOV, MAXIM MAXIMOVICH (1876-1951), Soviet diplomat **9** 451-452

LIU HSIEH (circa 465-522), Chinese literary critic **9** 452-453

LIU PANG (Han Kao-tsu or Liu Chi; 256 B.C.-195 B.C.), Chinese emperor **9** 453

LIU SHAO-CH'I (born 1900), Chinese Communist party leader **9** 453-455

LIU TSUNG-YÜAN (773-819), Chinese poet and prose writer **9** 455-456

LIUZZO, VIOLA (1925-1965), American civil rights activist **19** 203-205

LIVERIGHT, HORACE B. (1886-1933), American publisher **23** 229-231

LIVERPOOL, 2ND EARL OF (Robert Barks Jenkinson; 1770-1828), English statesman, prime minister 1812-1827 **9** 456-457

LIVIA (ca. 58 B.C. - 29 A.D.), Roman empress, wife of Augustus **9** 457-460

LIVINGSTON, EDWARD (1764-1836), American jurist and statesman **9** 460-461

LIVINGSTON, ROBERT (1654-1728), American colonial politician **9** 461-462

LIVINGSTON, ROBERT R. (1746-1813), American jurist and diplomat **9** 462-463

LIVINGSTONE, DAVID (1813-1873), Scottish missionary and explorer in Africa **9** 463-465

LIVY (Titus Livius; circa 64 B.C.-circa 12 A.D.), Roman historian **9** 465-467

LLERAS CAMARGO, ALBERTO (1906-1990), Colombian statesman, twice president **9** 467

LLEWELYN AP GRUFFYDD (died 1282), Prince of Wales **9** 468

LLOYD, HENRY DEMAREST (1847-1903), American social reformer **9** 468-469

LLOYD GEORGE, DAVID, (1st Earl of Dwyfor; 1863-1945), English statesman, prime minister 1916-1922 **9** 469-471

LLOYD, HAROLD (1893-1971), American actor **20** 226-229

LLOYD-JONES, ESTHER MCDONALD (born 1901), school personnel specialist who focused on development of the whole person **9** 471-472

LOBACHEVSKII, NIKOLAI IVANOVICH (1792-1856), Russian mathematician **9** 472-474

LOBENGULA (died circa 1894), South African Ndebele king **9** 474-475

Local color (American literature) see Regionalism and local color

LOCHNER, STEPHAN (circa 1410-1451), German painter **9** 475

LOCKE, ALAIN (1886-1954), African American educator, editor, and author **9** 475-478

LOCKE, JOHN (1632-1704), English philosopher and political theorist **9** 478-480

LOCKWOOD, BELVA (1830-1917), American lawyer, suffragist, and reformer **19** 205-207

LODGE, DAVID (born 1935), English novelist **9** 480-482

LODGE, HENRY CABOT (1850-1924), American political leader **9** 482-483

LODGE, HENRY CABOT, JR. (1902-1985), American congressman, senator, ambassador, and presidential adviser **9** 483-485

LOEB, JACQUES (Isaak Loeb; 1859-1924), German-American biophysiologist **22** 299-301

LOESSER, FRANK (Francis Henry Loesser; 1910-1969), American lyricist **18** 257-259

LOEW, MARCUS (1870-1927), founder of a theater chain and Metro-Goldwyn-Mayer **9** 485-486

LOEWI, OTTO (1873-1961), German-American pharmacologist and physiologist **9** 486-487

LOFTING, HUGH (1886-1947), British author of children's books **19** 207-209

LOGAN, GEORGE (1753-1821), American politician and diplomat **23** 231-234

LOGAN, JAMES (1674-1751), American colonial statesman and jurist **9** 487-488

LOGAN, SIR WILLIAM EDMOND (1798-1875), Canadian geologist **9** 488-489

Logarithms (mathematics) Oughtred, William **23** 277-279

Logic (philosophy) antilogism Ladd-Franklin, Christine **23** 202-204

LOISY, ALFRED FIRMIN (1857-1940), French theologian and biblical historian **9** 489-490

Lola Montès (film) Ophüls, Max **23** 275-277

LOMBARD, PETER (circa 1095-1160), Italian bishop and theologian **9** 490-491

LOMBARDI, VINCE (1913-1970), American football coach **9** 491-492

LOMBARDO, GUY (Gaetano Alberto Lombardo; 1902-1977), Canadian band leader **23** 234-236

LOMBROSO, CESARE (1835-1909), Italian criminologist **9** 493

LOMONOSOV, MIKHAIL VASILEVICH (1711-1765), Russian chemist and physicist **9** 494

LONDON, JACK (1876-1916), American author **9** 494-495

LONG, CRAWFORD WILLIAMSON (1815-1878), American physician **9** 495-496

LONG, HUEY PIERCE (1893-1935), American politician **9** 496-497

LONG, IRENE D. (born 1951), African American aerospace medicine physician **9** 497-498

LONGFELLOW, HENRY WADSWORTH (1807-1882), American poet **9** 499-500

LONGINUS (flourished 1st or 3rd century), Latin author and rhetorician **9** 500-501

LONGSTREET, JAMES (1821-1904), American army officer **22** 301-305

LONGUS (flourished 3rd century), Greek author **20** 229-230

LONSDALE, KATHLEEN (born Kathleen Yardley; 1903-1971), Irish crystallographer **9** 501-502

LOOS, ADOLF (1870-1933), Viennese architect **9** 502-503

LOOS, ANITA (1893-1981), American actress and writer **21** 262-265

LOPE FÉLIX DE VEGA CARPIO (1562-1635), Spanish dramatist **9** 503-506

LÓPEZ, CARLOS ANTONIO (1792-1862), Paraguayan president-dictator 1844-1862 **9** 506-507

LÓPEZ, FRANCISCO SOLANO (1826-1870), Paraguayan president-dictator **9** 507-508

LÓPEZ, NARCISO (1798-1851), Venezuelan military leader **9** 508

LOPEZ ARELLANO, OSWALDO (born 1921), Honduran military officer and president **20** 230-231

LÓPEZ DE AYALA, PEDRO (1332-1407), Spanish statesman, historian, and poet **9** 508-509

LÓPEZ MATEOS, ADOLFO (1910-1970), president of Mexico (1958-1964) **9** 509-510

LÓPEZ PORTILLO, JOSÉ (born 1920), president of Mexico (1976-1982) **9** 510-511

LORCA, FEDERICO GARCÍA (1898-1936), Spanish poet and playwright **9** 511-513

LORDE, AUDRE (1934-1992), African American poet **9** 513-515

LOREN, SOPHIA (Sofia Villani Scicolene; born 1936), Italian actress and author **18** 259-261

LORENTZ, HENDRIK ANTOON (1853-1928), Dutch physicist **9** 515-516

LORENZ, KONRAD Z. (1903-1989), animal psychologist **9** 516-517

LORENZETTI, PIERRE AND AMBROGIO (flourished 14th century), Italian painters **9** 517-518

LOTI, PIERRE (1850-1923), French novelist **9** 519-520

LOTT, TRENT (Chester Trent Lott; born 1941), American congressman **18** 262-264

LOTTO, LORENZO (circa 1480-1556), Italian painter **9** 520-521

LOTZE, RUDOLF HERMANN (1817-1881), German idealist philosopher **9** 521-522

LOUIS I (778-840), Holy Roman emperor and king of France and Germany 814-840 **9** 522-523

LOUIS VI (1081-1137), king of France 1108-1137 **9** 523-524

LOUIS VII (circa 1120-1180), king of France 1137-1180 **9** 524-525

LOUIS IX (1214-1270), king of France 1226-1270 **9** 525-526

LOUIS XI (1423-1483), king of France 1461-1483 **9** 526-528

LOUIS XII (1462-1515), king of France 1498-1515 **9** 528-529

LOUIS XIII (1601-1643), king of France 1610-1643 **9** 529-531

LOUIS XIV (1638-1715), king of France 1643-1715 **9** 531-533

LOUIS XV (1710-1774), king of France 1715-1774 **9** 533-534

LOUIS XVI (1754-1793), king of France 1774-1792 **9** 534-535

LOUIS XVIII (1755-1824), king of France 1814-1824 **9** 535-536

LOUIS, JOE (Joe Louis Barrow; 1914-1981), American boxer **9** 537-538

LOUIS, MORRIS (Bernstein; 1912-1962), American painter **9** 538-539

LOUIS, PIERRE CHARLES ALEXANDRE (1787-1872), French physician **9** 540

LOUIS PHILIPPE (1773-1850), king of the French 1830-1848 **9** 536-537

LOVE, NAT (1854-1921), African American champion cowboy **10** 1-2

LOVE, SUSAN M. (born 1948), American surgeon and medical researcher **10** 2-3

LOVECRAFT, H. P. (1890-1937), American author **10** 3-6

LOVEJOY, ARTHUR ONCKEN (1873-1962), American philosopher **10** 6

LOVEJOY, ELIJAH PARISH (1802-1837), American newspaper editor and abolitionist **10** 6-7

LOVELACE, ADA BYRON (Countess of Lovelace, Augusta Ada King Byron; 1815-1852), English mathematician and author **18** 264-266

LOVELACE, RICHARD (circa 1618-circa 1657), English Cavalier poet **10** 7-8

LOVELL, SIR ALFRED CHARLES BERNARD (born 1913), English astronomer **10** 8-9

LOW, JULIETTE GORDON (born Juliette Magill Kinzie Gordon; 1860-1927), American reformer and founder of the Girl Scouts **10** 10-11

LOW, SETH (1850-1916), American politician and college president **10** 11-12

LOWELL, ABBOTT LAWRENCE (1856-1943), American educator and political scientist **10** 12-13

LOWELL, AMY (1874-1925), American poet, critic, and biographer **10** 13

LOWELL, FRANCIS CABOT (1775-1817), American merchant and manufacturer **10** 13-14

LOWELL, JAMES RUSSELL (1819-1891), American poet and diplomat **10** 14-15

LOWELL, JOSEPHINE SHAW (1843-1905), American social reformer and philanthropist **10** 15-16

LOWELL, ROBERT TRAIL SPENCE, JR. (1917-1977), American poet **10** 16-17

LOWIE, ROBERT HARRY (1883-1957), Austrian-born American anthropologist **10** 18

LOWRY, MALCOLM (1909-1957), English author **19** 209-211

LU CHI (261-303), Chinese poet and critic **10** 24

LU CHIU-YUAN (Lu Hsiang-shan; 1139-1193), Chinese philosopher **10** 24-25

LU HSÜN (pen name of Chou Shu-jen; 1881-1936), Chinese author and social critic **10** 35-37

LUBITSCH, ERNST (1892-1947), German-American film director **10** 18-19

LUCARIS, CYRIL (1572-1637), Greek Orthodox patriarch and theologian **10** 20

LUCAS, GEORGE (born 1944), American filmmaker **19** 211-213

LUCAS VAN LEYDEN (1494-1533), Dutch engraver and painter **10** 20-21

LUCE, CLARE BOOTHE (1903-1987), playwright and U.S. congresswoman **10** 21-23

LUCE, HENRY ROBINSON (1898-1967), American magazine editor and publisher **10** 23-24

LUCIAN (circa 120-circa 200), Greek satirist **10** 25-26

LUCIANO, LUCKY (Charles Luciano, Salvatore Lucania; 1897-1962), Italian American mobster **19** 214-215

LUCID, SHANNON (born 1943), American astronaut **19** 215-217

LUCRETIUS (Titus Lucretius Carus; circa 94-circa 55 B.C.), Latin poet and philosopher **10** 26-27

LUDENDORFF, ERICH FRIEDRICH WILHELM (1865-1937), German general **10** 27-28

LUDLUM, ROBERT (a.k.a. Jonathan Ryder and Michael Shepherd; born 1927), American suspense novelist **10** 28-29

LUDWIG, DANIEL KEITH (1897-1992), American shipping magnate **10** 29-31

LUDWIG, KARL FRIEDRICH WILHELM (1816-1895), German physiologist **10** 31

LUGARD, FREDERICK JOHN DEALTRY (1st Baron Lugard; 1858-1945), British soldier and colonial administrator in Africa **10** 31-32

LUHAN, MABEL DODGE (1879-1962), American writer, salon hostess, and patron of artists, writers, and political radicals **10** 32-34

LUHMANN, NIKLAS (born 1927), German sociologist who developed a general sociological systems theory **10** 34-35

LUKÁCS, GYORGY (1885-1971), Hungarian literary critic and philosopher **10** 37-38

LUKE, SAINT (flourished A.D. 50), Evangelist and biblical author **10** 38

LUKS, GEORGE BENJAMIN (1867-1933), American painter **10** 38-39

LULL, RAYMOND (1232/35-1316), Spanish theologian, poet, and missionary **10** 39-40

LULLY, JEAN BAPTISTE (1632-1687), Italian-born French composer **10** 40-41

LUMET, SIDNEY (born 1924), American filmmaker and television director **22** 305-307

LUMIÈRE BROTHERS (Auguste Marie Louis, 1862-1954, and Louis Jean, 1864-1948), French inventors **10** 41-43

LUMUMBA, PATRICE EMERY (1925-1961), Congolese statesman **10** 43-45

LUNDY, BENJAMIN (1789-1839), American journalist **10** 45-46

LUNS, JOSEPH (1911-2002), West European political leader **10** 46-47

LURIA, ISAAC BEN SOLOMON ASHKENAZI (1534-1572), Jewish mystic **10** 47-48

LUTHER, MARTIN (1483-1546), German religious reformer **10** 48-51

LUTHULI, ALBERT JOHN (1898-1967), South African statesman **10** 51-52

LUTOSLAWSKI, WITOLD (1913-1994), Polish composer **10** 52-53

LUTYENS, EDWIN LANDSEER (1869-1944), English architect **10** 54-55

LUXEMBURG, ROSA (1870-1919), Polish revolutionary **10** 55-56

LUZ, ARTURO ROGERIO (born 1926), Philippine painter and sculptor **10** 56-57

LUZHKOV, YURI MIKHAYLOVICH (born 1936), mayor of Moscow **18** 266-268

LUZZATO, MOSES HAYYIM (1707-1747), Jewish mystic and poet **10** 57-58

LUZZI, MONDINO DE' (circa 1265/70-1326), Italian anatomist **10** 58

LWOFF, ANDRÉ (1902-1994), French microbiologist and geneticist **10** 58-59

LY, ABDOULAYE (born 1919), Senegalese politician and historian **10** 60

LYAUTEY, LOUIS HUBERT GONZALVE (1854-1934), French marshal and colonial administrator **10** 60-61

LYDGATE, JOHN (circa 1370-1449/50), English poet **10** 61-62

LYELL, SIR CHARLES (1797-1875), Scottish geologist **10** 62-63

LYND, HELEN MERRELL (1896-1982), American sociologist and educator **10** 63-64

LYND, ROBERT STAUGHTON (1892-1970), American sociologist **10** 64-65

LYND, STAUGHTON (born 1929), historian and peace militant **10** 65-66

LYNDSAY, SIR DAVID (circa 1485-1555), Scottish poet and courtier **10** 66-67

LYON, MARY (1797-1849), American educator, religious leader, and women's rights advocate **10** 67-69

LYONS, JOSEPH ALOYSIUS (1879-1939), Australian statesman, prime minister 1932-39 **10** 69-70

LYSANDER (died 395 B.C.), Spartan military commander and statesman **10** 70

LYSENKO, TROFIM DENISOVICH (1898-1976), Soviet agronomist and geneticist **10** 71

M

MA, YO-YO (born 1955), American cellist **20** 232-234

MAATHAI, WANGARI MUTA (born 1940), Kenyan environmental activist **18** 269-271

MABILLON, JEAN (1632-1707), French monk and historian **10** 72

MABINI, APOLINARIO (1864-1903), Filipino political philosopher **10** 72-73

MABUCHI, KAMO (1697-1769), Japanese writer and scholar **10** 73-74

MACAPAGAL, DIOSDADO P. (born 1910), Filipino statesman **10** 74-76

MACARTHUR, DOUGLAS (1880-1964), American general **10** 76-78

MACARTHUR, JOHN (circa 1767-1834), Australian merchant, sheep breeder, and politician **10** 78

MACAULAY, HERBERT (1864-1945), Nigerian politician **10** 78-79

MACAULAY, THOMAS BABINGTON (1st Baron Macaulay of Rothley; 1800-1859), English essayist, historian, and politician **10** 79-80

MACBETH (died 1057), king of Scotland 1040-1057 **10** 81

MACBRIDE, SEAN (1904-1988), Irish statesman **19** 218-220

MacCREADY, PAUL (born 1925), American aeronautical engineer **20** 234-237

MACDONALD, DWIGHT (1906-1982), American editor, journalist, essayist, and critic **10** 81-83

MACDONALD, ELEANOR JOSEPHINE (born 1906), American epidemiologist **10** 83-84

MACDONALD, JAMES RAMSAY (1866-1937), British politician **10** 84-85

MACDONALD, SIR JOHN ALEXANDER (1815-1891), Canadian statesman **10** 85-87

MACDOWELL, EDWARD ALEXANDER (1861-1908), American pianist and composer **10** 87-88

MACEO, ANTONIO (1845-1896), Cuban general and patriot **10** 88-90

MACH, ERNST (1838-1916), Austrian physicist **10** 90-91

MACHADO DE ASSIS, JOAQUIM MARIA (1839-1908), Brazilian novelist **10** 91-92

MACHADO Y MORALES, GERARDO (1871-1939), Cuban general and president **10** 92-93

MACHAUT, GUILLAUME DE (circa 1300-1377), French composer and poet **10** 93-94

MACHEL, SAMORA MOISES (1933-1986), socialist revolutionary and first president of Mozambique **10** 94-96

MACHIAVELLI, NICCOLÒ (1469-1527), Italian author and statesman **10** 97-99

MacINTYRE, ALASDAIR CHALMERS (born 1929), Scottish-born philosopher and ethicist **10** 99-100

MACIVER, ROBERT MORRISON (1882-1970), Scottish-American sociologist, political philosopher, and educator **10** 100-101

MACK, CONNIE (Cornelius Alexander McGillicuddy; 1862-1956), American baseball player and manager **19** 220-222

MACKAY, JOHN WILLIAM (1831-1902), American miner and business leader **10** 101-102

MACKE, AUGUST (1887-1914), Expressionist painter **10** 102-103

MACKENZIE, SIR ALEXANDER (circa 1764-1820), Scottish explorer, fur trader, and businessman **10** 103-104

MACKENZIE, ALEXANDER (1822-1892), Scottish-born Canadian statesman, prime minister 1873-1878 **10** 104

MACKENZIE, WILLIAM LYON (1795-1861), Scottish-born Canadian journalist, politician, and rebel **10** 104-106

MACKERRAS, ALAN CHARLES (Sir Charles Mackerrras; born 1925), Australian conductor **23** 237-239

MACKILLOP, MARY (1842-1909), first Australian candidate for sainthood in the Roman Catholic Church and foundress of the Sisters of Saint Joseph of the Sacred Heart **10** 106-107

MACKINTOSH, CHARLES RENNIE (1868-1928), Scottish artist, architect, and interior/furniture/textile designer **10** 107-108

MACLEAN, GEORGE (1801-1847), Scottish soldier and agent of British expansion **10** 108-109

MACLEISH, ARCHIBALD (born 1892), American poet, playwright, and public official **10** 109-110

MACLENNAN, HUGH (1907-1990), Canadian novelist, essayist, and academic **10** 110-111

MACMILLAN, DONALD BAXTER (1874-1970), American explorer and scientist **10** 111-112

MACMILLAN, HAROLD (born 1894), British statesman **10** 112-113

MACNEICE, LOUIS (1907-1964), British poet **10** 113-114

MACON, NATHANIEL (1758-1837), American statesman **10** 114-115

MACQUARIE, LACHLAN (1762-1824), British officer, governor of New South Wales 1810-1822 **10** 115-116

MACQUARRIE, JOHN (born 1919), Anglican theologian **10** 116-117

MACY, ANNE SULLIVAN (Johanna "Annie" Sullivan; 1866-1936), American teacher **20** 237-239

MADERNO, CARLO (1556-1629), Italian architect **10** 117-118

MADERO, FRANCISCO INDALECIO (1873-1913), Mexican politician, president 1911-13 **10** 118-119

MADHVA (Vasudeva; Madhwa; Anande Tirtha; Purna Prajna; c.1199-c.1276), Indian theologian and philosopher **22** 308-309

MADISON, DOLLY (wife of James Madison, born Dorothea Payne; 1768-1849), American First Lady **10** 119-121

MADISON, JAMES (1751-1836), American statesman, president 1809-1817 **10** 121-123

MADONNA (Madonna Louise Veronica Ciccone, born 1958), American singer and actress **10** 123-125

MAEKAWA, KUNIO (1905-1986), Japanese architect **23** 239-242

MAETERLINCK, COUNT MAURICE (1863-1949), Belgian poet, dramatist, and essayist **10** 125-126

MAGELLAN, FERDINAND (1480-1521), Portuguese explorer **10** 126-127

MAGNASCO, ALESSANDRO (1667-1749), Italian painter **10** 127-128

MAGRITTE, RENÉ (1890-1967), Surrealist painter **10** 128-130

MAGSAYSAY, RAMON (1907-1957), Philippine statesman, president 1953-1957 **10** 130-131

MAHAL, HAZRAT (Iftikarun-nisa; 1820?-1879), Indian revolutionary **18** 271-273

MAHAN, ALFRED THAYER (1840-1914), American naval historian and strategist **10** 131-132

MAHARISHI MAHESH YOGI (born 1911?), Indian guru and founder of the Transcendental Meditation movement **10** 132-133

MAHATHIR MOHAMAD (born 1925), prime minister of Malaysia **10** 134-135

MAHDI, THE (Mohammed Ahmed; circa 1844-1885), Islamic reformer and Sudanese military leader **10** 137-138

MAHENDRA, KING (Bir Bikram Shah Dev; 1920-1972), ninth Shah dynasty ruler of Nepal (1955-1972) **10** 138-139

MAHERERO, SAMUEL (ca. 1854-1923), Supreme Chief of the Herero naion in southwest Africa **10** 139-142

MAHFUZ, NAJIB (born 1912), Egyptian novelist **10** 142-144

MAHLER, GUSTAV (1860-1911), Bohemian-born composer and conductor **10** 144-145

MAHMUD II (1785-1839), Ottoman sultan 1808-1839 **10** 145-147

MAHMUD OF GHAZNI (971-1030); Ghaznavid sultan in Afghanistan **10** 147

MAHONE, WILLIAM (1826-1895), American politician and Confederate general **10** 147-148

MAILER, NORMAN KINGSLEY (born 1923), American author, producer, and director **10** 148-150

MAILLOL, ARISTIDE (1861-1944), French sculptor **10** 150-151

MAIMONIDES (1135-1204), Jewish philosopher **10** 151-152

MAINE, SIR HENRY JAMES SUMNER (1822-1888), English legal historian and historical anthropologist **10** 152

MAISONEUVE, SIEUR DE (Paul de Chomedey; 1612-1676), French explorer and colonizer in Canada **10** 153

MAISTRE, JOSEPH DE (1753-1821), French political philosopher **10** 153-154

MAITLAND, FREDERIC WILLIAM (1850-1906), English historian, lawyer, and legal scholar **10** 154-155

MAJOR, JOHN (born 1943), British prime minister **10** 155-157

MAKARIOS III (Michael Christodoulou Mouskos; 1913-1977), archbishop and ethnarch of the Orthodox Church of Cyprus and first president of the Republic of Cyprus (1959-1977) **10** 157-158

MAKEBA, MIRIAM (Zensi Miriam Makeba; born 1932), South African singer and activist **22** 309-312

MAKEMIE, FRANCIS (1658-1708), Irish-born Presbyterian missionary **10** 158-159

MAKI, FUMIHIKO (born 1928), Japanese architect **10** 159-161

MAKIBI, KIBI-NO (693-775), Japanese courtier and statesman **10** 161

MÄKONNEN ENDALKAČÄW (1892-1963), Ethiopian writer and official **10** 161-162

Malagueña (song) Lecuona, Ernesto **23** 213-216

MALAMUD, BERNARD (1914-1986), American novelist and short-story writer **10** 162-163

MALAN, DANIEL FRANCOIS (1874-1959), South African pastor, journalist, and prime minister 1948-1954 **10** 163-164

MALCOLM III (died 1093), king of Scotland 1058-1093 **10** 164-165

MALCOLM X (1925-1965), African American civil rights leader **10** 165-166

MALEBRANCHE, NICOLAS (1638-1715), French philosopher and theologian **10** 166-167

MALENKOV, GEORGY MAKSIMILIANOVICH (1902-1988), head of the Soviet government and leader of its Communist Party (1953) **10** 168

MALEVICH, KASIMIR (1878-1935), Russian painter **10** 168-169

MALHERBE, FRANÇOIS DE (1555-1628), French poet **10** 169-170

MALINOWSKI, KASPAR BRONISLAW (1884-1942), Austrian-born British social anthropologist **10** 170-171

MALIPIERO, GIAN FRANCESCO (1882-1973), Italian composer **10** 171

MALKAM KHAN, MIRZA (1831-1908), Persian diplomat **10** 172

MALLARMÉ, STÉPHANE (1842-1898), French poet **10** 172-173

MALLE, LOUIS (1932-1995), French film director and producer **18** 273-275

MALLON, MARY (Typhoid Mary; 1869-1938), Irish woman who unwittingly infected many with typhoid fever **21** 266-268

MALLORY, GEORGE (1886-1924), English mountain climber **21** 268-271

MALONE, ANNIE TURNBO (Annie Minerva Turnbo Malone; 1869-1957), African American entrepreneur and philanthropist **23** 242-243

MALONE, DUMAS (1892-1986), American historian and editor **10** 174-175

MALORY, SIR THOMAS (flourished 15th century), English author **10** 175-176

MALPIGHI, MARCELLO (1628-1694), Italian anatomist **10** 176-178

MALRAUX, ANDRÉ (1901-1976), French novelist, essayist, and politician **10** 178-180

MALTHUS, THOMAS ROBERT (1766-1834), English economist **10** 180-181

MAMET, DAVID ALAN (born 1947), American author **10** 181-182

MAMUN, ABDALLAH AL- (786-833), Abbasid caliph **10** 183

Man Who Loved Children, The (book) Stead, Christina Ellen **23** 378-380

MANASSEH BEN ISRAEL (1604-1657), Dutch rabbi and theologian **10** 183-184

MANCINI, HENRY (Enrico Mancini; 1924-1994), American composer, pianist, and film music scorer **18** 275-276

MANCO CAPAC (circa 1500-1545), Inca emperor **10** 184-185

MANDELA, NELSON ROLIHLAHLA (born 1918), South African leader **10** 185-186

MANDELA, WINNIE (Nomzamo Winifred Madikizela; born 1936), South African anti-apartheid leader **10** 187-189

MANDELBROT, BENOIT B. (born 1924), Polish-born French-American mathematician who invented fractals **10** 189-191

MANDELSTAM, OSIP EMILYEVICH (1891-1938), Russian poet **10** 191

MANDEVILLE, BERNARD (circa 1670-1733), English satirist and moral philosopher **10** 192

MANDEVILLE, SIR JOHN (flourished 14th century), pen name of English author **10** 192-193

MANET, ÉDOUARD (1832-1883), French painter **10** 193-194

MANGAS COLORADAS (ca. 1790-1863), Apache military leader **10** 194-196

MANI (216-276/277), Persian prophet **10** 196-197

MANIN, DANIELE (1804-1857), Venetian patriot **10** 197-198

MANKILLER, WILMA (born 1945), Native American activist and Cherokee chief **10** 198-199

MANLEY, MICHAEL NORMAN (1924-1997), Jamaican prime minister (1972-1980) **10** 200-201

MANN, HEINRICH (1871-1950), German novelist, essayist, and social critic **10** 201-202

MANN, HORACE (1796-1859), American educational reformer and humanitarian **10** 202-204

MANN, THOMAS (1875-1955), German novelist and essayist **10** 204-207

MANNERHEIM, BARON CARL GUSTAV EMIL VON (1867-1951), Finnish military leader and statesman, president 1944-46 **10** 207-208

MANNHEIM, KARL (1893-1947), Hungarian-born sociologist and educator **10** 208-209

MANNING, HENRY EDWARD (1808-1892), English cardinal **10** 209-210

MANNIX, DANIEL (1864-1963), Irish-born Australian archbishop **10** 210

MANRIQUE, JORGE (1440?-1478), Spanish poet and soldier **10** 210-211

MANSART, FRANÇOIS (1598-1666), French architect **10** 211

MANSART, JULES HARDOUIN (1646-1708), French architect **10** 212

MANSFIELD, KATHERINE (born Kathleen Mansfield Beauchamp; 1888-1923), New Zealander short-story writer and poet **10** 213-214

MANSUR, ABU JAFAR IBN MUHAMMAD AL (712-775), Abbasid caliph **10** 214-215

MANTEGNA, ANDREA (circa 1430-1506), Italian painter and engraver **10** 215-216

MANTLE, MICKEY (1931-1995), American baseball player **10** 216-218

MANUEL I (1469-1521), king of Portugal 1495-1521 **10** 219-220

MANUEL I COMNENUS (circa 1123-1180), Byzantine emperor 1143-1180 **10** 218-219

MANUELITO (1818-1894), Navajo tribal leader **10** 220-222

Manufacturers
see Business and industrial leaders

MANZONI, ALESSANDRO (1785-1873), Italian novelist and playwright **10** 222-224

MANZÙ, GIACOMO (born 1908), Italian sculptor **10** 224-225

MAO ZEDONG (1893-1976), Chinese statesman **10** 225-227

MAPPLETHORPE, ROBERT (1946-1989), controversial American photographer **10** 227-228

MARADONA, DIEGO (born 1961), Argentine soccer player **20** 239-241

MARAGHI, AL-MUSTAFĀ (1881-1945), Egyptian jurist and educator **10** 228-229

MARAT, JEAN PAUL (1743-1793), French journalist and political leader **10** 230-231

MARBLE, ALICE (1913-1990), American tennis player **21** 271-273

MARC, FRANZ (1880-1916), German painter **10** 231

MARCEAU, MARCEL (born 1923), world's greatest practitioner of pantomine **10** 231-233

MARCEL, GABRIEL (1889-1973), French philosopher **10** 233-234

MARCHAND, JEAN-BAPTISTE (1863-1934), French explorer and soldier **10** 234-237

MARCIANO, ROCKY (1923-1969), American boxer **10** 237-238

MARCION (flourished mid-2nd century), Christian theologian **10** 238-239

MARCONI, GUGLIELMO (1874-1937), Italian inventor **10** 239-240

MARCOS, FERDINAND (1917-1989), president of the Republic of the Philippines (1965-1986) **10** 240-242

MARCOS, IMELDA ROMUALDEZ (born 1930), wife of Philippine President Ferdinand Marcos and governor of Metro Manila **10** 242-243

MARCOS DE NIZA, FRIAR (circa 1500-1558), Franciscan missionary in Spanish America **10** 240

MARCUS AURELIUS ANTONINUS (121-180), Roman emperor 161-180 **10** 243-245

MARCUS, STANLEY (1905-2002), American businessman **19** 222-224

MARCUSE, HERBERT (1898-1979), German-American philosopher **10** 245-247

MARCY, WILLIAM LEARNED (1786-1857), American statesman **10** 247-248

MARENZIO, LUCA (1553/54-1599), Italian composer **10** 248

MARGAI, SIR MILTON AUGUSTUS STRIERY (1895-1964), Sierra Leonean physician and statesman **10** 248-249

MARGARET OF ANJOU (1430-1482), queen consort of Henry VI of England **10** 249-250

MARGARET OF DENMARK (born Margaret Valdemarsdottir; 1353-1412), queen of Denmark **10** 250-252

MARGARET OF SCOTLAND, SAINT (1045-1093), wife of Malcolm III of Scotland **10** 252-253

MARGGRAF, ANDREAS (1709-1782), German chemist **21** 273-275

MARGULIS, LYNN (born 1938), American biologist **10** 253-254

MARIA THERESA (1717-1780), Holy Roman empress 1740-1780 **10** 256-258

MARIANA, JUAN DE (1536-1624), Spanish Jesuit historian **10** 254-255

MARIÁTEGUI, JOSÉ CARLOS (1895-1930), Peruvian writer **10** 255-256

MARIE ANTOINETTE (1755-1793), queen of France 1774-1793 **10** 258-259

MARIE DE FRANCE (flourished late 12th century), French poet **10** 259

MARIN, JOHN, III (1870-1953), American painter **10** 259-260

MARINI, MARINO (1901-1980), Italian sculptor **10** 260-262

MARION, FRANCIS (1732-1795), American Revolutionary War leader **10** 262-263

MARITAIN, JACQUES (1882-1973), French Catholic philosopher **10** 263

MARIUS GAIUS (circa 157-86 B.C.), Roman general and politician **10** 264-265

MARIVAUX, PIERRE CARLET DE CHAMBLAIN DE (1688-1763), French novelist and dramatist **10** 265-266

MARK, SAINT (flourished 1st century), Apostle of Jesus **10** 266-267

MARKHAM, BERYL (1902-1986), British aviator, author, and horse trainer **20** 241-243

MARKHAM, EDWIN (1852-1940), American poet **10** 267

MARKIEVICZ, CONSTANCE (1868-1927), Irish nationalist, labor activist, and feminist **10** 267-271

MARLBOROUGH, 1ST DUKE OF (John Churchill; 1650-1722), English general and statesman **10** 271-272

MARLOWE, CHRISTOPHER (1564-1593), English dramatist **10** 272-274

MÁRMOL, JOSÉ (1817-1871), Argentine writer and intellectual **10** 274

MARQUETTE, JACQUES (1637-1675), French Jesuit, missionary and explorer **10** 274-275

MARSALIS, WYNTON (born 1961), American trumpeter and bandleader **19** 224-226

MARSH, GEORGE PERKINS (1801-1882), American diplomat, philologist, and conservationist **21** 275-277

MARSH, NGAIO (Edith Ngaio Marsh; 1899-1982), New Zealander author and playwright **19** 226-228

MARSH, OTHNIEL CHARLES (1831-1899), American paleontologist **10** 275-276

MARSH, REGINALD (1898-1954), American painter and printmaker **10** 276-277

MARSHALL, ALFRED (1842-1924), English economist **10** 277-278

MARSHALL, GEORGE CATLETT (1880-1959), American soldier and statesman **10** 278-279

MARSHALL, JOHN (1755-1835), American jurist, chief justice of United States. Supreme Court 1801-1835 **10** 279-281
Beveridge, Albert Jeremiah **23** 39-41

MARSHALL, PAULE BURKE (born 1929), American author **10** 281-282

MARSHALL, THURGOOD (1908-1993), African American jurist **10** 282-284

MARSILIUS OF PADUA (1275/80-1342), Italian political philosopher **10** 284

MARTEL, CHARLES (circa 690-741), Frankish ruler **10** 285

MARTÍ, JOSÉ (1853-1895), Cuban revolutionary, poet, and journalist **10** 285-286

MARTIAL (Marcus Valerias Martialis; circa 38/41-circa 104), Roman epigrammatist **10** 286-287

MARTIN V (Oddone Colonna; 1368-1431), pope 1417-1431 **10** 287-288

MARTIN, AGNES (born 1912), American painter **10** 288-289

MARTIN, GREGORY (circa 1540-1582), British Bible translator and scholar **21** 277-279

MARTIN, LUTHER (1748-1826), American lawyer and Revolutionary patriot **10** 289-290

MARTIN, LYNN MORLEY (born 1939), Republican representative from Illinois and secretary of labor under George Bush **10** 290-292

MARTIN, MARY (1913-1990), popular stage actress, singer, and dancer and a television and film star **10** 292-293

MARTIN, WILLIAM MCCHESNEY, JR. (1906-1998), American business executive and federal government official **10** 293-295

MARTIN DU GARD, ROGER (1881-1958), French author **10** 295-296

MARTINEAU, HARRIET (1802-1876), English writer and philosopher **10** 296-297

MARTÍNEZ, MAXIMILIANO HERNÁNDEZ (1882-1966), president of El Salvador (1931-1944) **10** 297-298

MARTINEZ, VILMA SOCORRO (born 1943), Hispanic American attorney and activist **18** 276-279

MARTINI, SIMONE (flourished 1315-1344), Italian painter **10** 298-299

MARTINU, BOHUSLAV (1890-1959), Czech composer **10** 299-300

MARTY, MARTIN E. (born 1928), Lutheran pastor, historian of American religion, and commentator **10** 300-301

MARVELL, ANDREW (1621-1678), English poet and politician **10** 301-303

MARX, KARL (1818-1883), German political philosopher **10** 304-308

MARX BROTHERS, 20th-century American stage and film comedians **10** 303-304

MARY, QUEEN OF SCOTS (1542-1587), queen of France and Scotland **10** 308-309

MARY, SAINT (Blessed Virgin Mary; late 1st century B.C.-1st century A.D.), New Testament figure, mother of Jesus **10** 308-309

MARY I (1516-1558), queen of England 1553-1558 **10** 308-309

MARY II (1662-1694), queen of England, Scotland, and Ireland 1689-1694 **10** 309-310

MASACCIO (1401-1428), Italian painter **10** 312-313

MASARYK, JAN (1886-1948), Czech foreign minister **20** 243-246

MASARYK, TOMÁŠ GARRIGUE (1850-1937), Czech philosopher and statesman, president 1919-1935 **10** 314-315

MASINISSA, KING OF NUMIDIA (240 B.C. - 148 B.C.), prince of the Massylians who consolidated the Numidian tribes to form a North African kingdom **10** 315-317

MASIRE, QUETT KETUMILE (born 1925), a leader of the fight for independence and president of Botswana **10** 318-319

MASON, BRIDGET (Biddy Mason; 1818-1891), African American nurse, midwife, and entrepreneur **22** 312-314

MASON, GEORGE (1725-1792), American statesman **10** 319-320

MASON, JAMES MURRAY (1796-1871), American politician and Confederate diplomat **10** 320-321

MASON, LOWELL (1792-1872), American composer and music educator **10** 321-322

MASSASOIT (1580-1661), Native American tribal chief **10** 322-324

MASSEY, WILLIAM FERGUSON (1856-1925), New Zealand prime minister 1912-1925 **10** 324

MASSINGER, PHILIP (1583-1640), English playwright **10** 324-325

MASSYS, QUENTIN (1465/66-1530), Flemish painter **10** 325-326

MASTERS, EDGAR LEE (1869-1950), American author and lawyer **10** 326-327

MASTERS, WILLIAM HOWELL (born 1915), American psychologist and sex therapist **10** 327-328

MASUDI, ALI IBN AL- HUSAYN AL- (died 956), Arab historian **10** 328-329

MASUR, KURT (born 1927), German conductor and humanist **20** 246-248

MATA HARI (Margaretha Geertruida Zelle; 1876-1917), Dutch spy **21** 279-282

MATAMOROS, MARINO (1770-1814), Mexican priest and independence hero **10** 329-330

Mathematics
  Fermat's last theorem
    Wiles, Andrew J. **23** 442-444
  geometry
    Scott, Charlotte Angas **23** 364-367
    Theano **23** 399-401
  group theory
    Wilson, Kenneth Geddes **23** 446-448
  projective geometry
    Steiner, Jakob **23** 380-382
  symbols
    Oughtred, William **23** 277-279
  theory of games
    Bernoulli, Jakob **23** 37-39

MATHER, COTTON (1663-1728), American Puritan clergyman and historian **10** 330-332

MATHER, INCREASE (1639-1723), American Puritan clergymen, educator, and author **10** 332-333

MATHEWSON, CHRISTY (Christopher Mathewson; 1880-1925), American baseball player **21** 282-284

MATHIAS, BOB (Robert Bruce Mathias; born 1930), American track and field star **21** 284-286

MATHIEZ, ALBERT (1874-1932), French historian **10** 333-334

MATILDA OF TUSCANY (ca. 1046-1115), Italian countess **10** 334-336

MATISSE, HENRI (1869-1954), French painter and sculptor **10** 336-337

MATLIN, MARLEE (born 1965), American actress **19** 228-230

MATLOVICH, LEONARD (1943-1988), American gay rights activist **20** 248-250

MATSUNAGA, SPARK MASAYUKI (1916-1990), Asian American U.S. senator **18** 279-281

MATSUSHITA, KONOSUKE (1918-1989), Japanese inventor and businessman **19** 230-232

MATTEI, ENRICO (1906-1962), Italian entrepreneur **10** 337-339

MATTEOTTI, GIACOMO (1885-1924), Italian political leader **10** 339-340

MATTHAU, WALTER (Walter Matthow; Walter Matuschanskayasky; 1920-2000), American Actor **22** 314-316

MATTHEW, SAINT (flourished Ist century), Apostle and Evangelist **10** 340-341

MATTHEW PARIS (circa 1200-1259), English Benedictine chronicler **10** 341-342

MATTINGLY, GARRETT (1900-1962), American historian, professor, and author of novel-like histories **10** 342-344

MATZELIGER, JAN (1852-1889), American inventor and shoemaker **19** 232-234

MAUCHLY, JOHN (1907-1980), American computer entrepreneur **20** 250-252

MAUDSLAY, HENRY (1771-1831), British engineer and inventor **21** 286-288

MAUGHAM, WILLIAM SOMERSET (1874-1965), English author **10** 344-345

MAULBERTSCH, FRANZ ANTON (1724-1796), Austrian painter **10** 345

MAULDIN, BILL (1921-2003), cartoon biographer of the ordinary GI in World War II **10** 345-346

MAUPASSANT, HENRI RENÉ ALBERT GUY DE (1850-1893), French author **10** 347

MAURIAC, FRANÇOIS (1885-1970), French author **10** 347-348

MAURICE, JOHN FREDERICK DENISON (1805-1872), English theologian and Anglican clergyman **10** 349-350

MAURICE OF NASSAU, PRINCE OF ORANGE (1567-1625), Dutch general and statesman **10** 348-349

MAURRAS, CHARLES MARIE PHOTIUS (1868-1952), French political writer and reactionary **10** 350-351

MAURY, ANTONIA (1866-1952), American astronomer and conservationist **20** 252-254

MAURY, MATTHEW FONTAINE (1806-1873), American naval officer and oceanographer **10** 351-352

MAUSS, MARCEL (1872-1950), French sociologist and anthropologist **10** 352-353

MAWDUDI, ABU-I A'LA (1903-1979), Muslim writer and religious and political leader in the Indian sub-continent **10** 353-354

MAWSON, SIR DOUGLAS (1882-1958), Australian scientist and Antarctic explorer **10** 354-355

MAXIM, SIR HIRAM STEVENS (1840-1916), American-born British inventor **10** 355-356

MAXIMILIAN I (1459-1519), Holy Roman emperor 1493-1519 **10** 356-357

MAXIMILIAN II (1527-1576), Holy Roman emperor 1564-1576 **10** 357-358

MAXIMILIAN OF HAPSBURG (1832-1867), archduke of Austria and emperor of Mexico **10** 358-360

MAXWELL, IAN ROBERT (née Ludvik Hock; 1923-1991), British publishing magnate **10** 360-361

MAXWELL, JAMES CLERK (1831-1879), Scottish physicist **10** 361-364

MAYAKOVSKY, VLADIMIR VLADIMIROVICH (1893-1930), Russian poet **10** 364-365

MAYER, JEAN (born 1920), nutritionist, researcher, consultant to government and international organizations, and president of Tufts University **10** 365-366

MAYER, LOUIS BURT (Eliezer Mayer; 1885-1957), American motion picture producer **19** 234-235

MAYNARD, ROBERT CLYVE (1937-1993), African American journalist and publisher **10** 366-367

MAYO, WILLIAM J. (1861-1939) and CHARLES H. (1865-1939), American physicians **10** 367-369

MAYOR ZARAGOSA, FEDERICO (born 1934), Spanish biochemist who was director-general of UNESCO (United Nations Educational, Scientific, and Cultural Organization) **10** 369-371

MAYO-SMITH, RICHMOND (1854-1901), American statistician and sociologist **10** 371-372

MAYR, ERNST (born 1904), American evolutionary biologist **10** 372-374

MAYS, BENJAMIN E. (1894-1984), African American educator and civil rights activist **10** 374-376

MAYS, WILLIE (William Howard Mays, Jr.; born 1931), African American baseball player **10** 376-379

MAZARIN, JULES (1602-1661), French cardinal and statesman **10** 379-380

MAZEPA, IVAN STEPANOVICH (circa 1644-1709), Ukrainian Cossack leader **10** 381

MAZZINI, GIUSEPPE (1805-1872), Italian patriot **10** 381-383

M'BOW, AMADOU-MAHTAR (born 1921), director general of UNESCO (United Nations Educational, Scientific, and Cultural Organization) **10** 383-384

MBOYA, THOMAS JOSEPH (1930-1969), Kenyan political leader **10** 384-385

MCADOO, WILLIAM GIBBS (1863-1941), American statesman **10** 385-386

MCAULIFFE, ANTHONY (1898-1975), American army officer **19** 236-239

MCAULIFFE, CHRISTA (nee Sharon Christa Corrigan; 1948-1986), American teacher **20** 254-257

MCCANDLESS, BRUCE (born 1937), American astronaut **23** 243-246

MCCARTHY, EUGENE JOSEPH (born 1916), American statesman **10** 386-388

MCCARTHY, JOSEPH RAYMOND (1908-1957), American politician **10** 388-389

MCCARTHY, MARY T. (born 1912), American writer **10** 389-391

MCCAY, WINSOR (Zenas Winsor McKay; 1871?-1934), American cartoonist and animator **21** 288-291

MCCLELLAN, GEORGE BRINTON (1826-1885), American general **10** 391-392

MCCLELLAN, JOHN LITTLE (1896-1977), U.S. senator from Arkansas **10** 392-393

MCCLINTOCK, BARBARA (1902-1992), geneticist and winner of the Nobel Prize in physiology **10** 393-394

MCCLINTOCK, SIR FRANCIS LEOPOLD (1819-1907), British admiral and Arctic explorer **10** 394-395

MCCLOSKEY, JOHN (1810-1885), American cardinal **10** 395

MCCLUNG, NELLIE LETITIA (1873-1951), Canadian suffragist, social reformer, legislator, and author **10** 396-397

MCCLURE, SIR ROBERT (1807-1873), English explorer and navy officer **10** 398-399

MCCLURE, SAMUEL SIDNEY (1857-1949), American editor and publisher **10** 398-399

MCCORMACK, JOHN WILLIAM (1891-1980), U.S. congressman and Speaker of the House **10** 399-400

MCCORMICK, CYRUS HALL (1809-1884), American inventor, manufacturer, and philanthropist **10** 400-401

MCCORMICK, ROBERT RUTHERFORD (1880-1955), American publisher **10** 401-402

MCCOSH, JAMES (1811-1894), Scottish-American minister, philosopher, and college president **10** 402-403

MCCOY, ELIJAH (1843-1929), American engineer and inventor **19** 239-241

MCCOY, ISAAC (1784-1846), American Indian agent and missionary **10** 403

MCCOY, JOSEPH GEITING (1837-1915), American cattleman **10** 403-404

MCCULLERS, CARSON (Lula Carson Smith; 1917-1967), American novelist and playwright **18** 281-283

MCCULLOCH, HUGH (1808-1895), American banker and lawyer **10** 404-405

MCDANIEL, HATTIE (1898-1952), African American actress **10** 405-408

MCDUFFIE, GEORGE (1790-1851), American statesman **10** 408

MCENROE, JOHN PATRICK, JR. (born 1959), American tennis player **10** 408-411

MCGILL, RALPH EMERSON (1898-1969), American journalist **10** 411-412

MCGILLIVRAY, ALEXANDER (circa 1759-1793), American Creek Indian chief **10** 412

MCGOVERN, GEORGE STANLEY (born 1922), American statesman **10** 412-414

MCGUFFEY, WILLIAM HOLMES (1800-1873), American educator **10** 414-415

MCINTIRE, SAMUEL (1757-1811), American builder and furniture maker **10** 415

MCKAY, CLAUDE (1890-1948), African American poet and novelist **10** 416

MCKAY, DONALD (1810-1880), American ship builder **10** 416-417

MCKIM, CHARLES FOLLEN (1847-1909), American architect **10** 417-418

MCKINLEY, WILLIAM (1843-1901), American statesman, president 1897-1901 **10** 418-420

MCKISSICK, FLOYD B., (1922-1991), African American civil rights leader **10** 420-422

MCLEAN, JOHN (1785-1861), American jurist and politician **10** 422-423

MCLOUGHLIN, JOHN (1784-1857), Canadian pioneer and trader **10** 423-424

MCLUHAN, MARSHALL (Herbert Marshall McLuhan; 1911-1980), Canadian professor of literature and culture **10** 424-426

MCMASTER, JOHN BACH (1852-1932), American historian **10** 426-427

MCMILLAN, TERRY (born 1951), African American novelist and short story writer **10** 427-428

MCMURRAY, BETTE CLAIR (1924-1980), American inventor and businesswoman **10** 429

MCNAMARA, ROBERT S. (born 1916), U.S. secretary of defense and president of the World Bank **10** 429-431

MCNAUGHTON, ANDREW (1887-1966), Canadian soldier and diplomat **10** 431-432

MCNEALY, SCOTT (born 1954), American businessman **19** 241-243

MCNICKLE, D'ARCY (born William D'Arcy McNickle; 1904-1977), Native American author, historian, and activist **10** 433

MCPHERSON, AIMEE SEMPLE (1890-1944), American evangelist **10** 434

MCQUEEN, BUTTERFLY (born Thelma McQueen; 1911-1995), African American actress **10** 434-437

MEAD, GEORGE HERBERT (1863-1931), American philosopher and social psychologist **10** 437-438

MEAD, MARGARET (1901-1978), American anthropologist **10** 438-440

MEADE, GEORGE GORDON (1815-1872), American general **10** 440-441

MEANS, RUSSELL (born 1939), Native American activist **10** 441-444

MEANY, GEORGE (1894-1980), American labor leader **10** 444

MECIAR, VLADIMIR (born 1942), Slovak prime minister **18** 283-285

Medal of Honor
see Congressional Medal of Honor

MEDAWAR, PETER BRIAN (1915-1987), British zoologist **10** 444-445

MEDICI, CATHERINE DE' (1519-1589), Italian queen of France **10** 445-449

MEDICI, COSIMO DE' (1389-1464), Italian statesman and merchant prince **10** 449-450

MEDICI, LORENZO DE' (1449-1492), Italian statesman, ruler of Florence 1469-1492 **10** 450-451

Medicine
slow virus diseases
Prusiner, Stanley Ben **23** 320-323

MEDILL, JOSEPH (1823-1899), American abolitionist editor and publisher **10** 451-452

MEGAWATI SUKARNOPUTRI (born 1947), Indonesian prime minister **20** 257-259

MEHMED THE CONQUEROR (a.k.a. Mehmed II and Mehmed Celebi; ca. 1432-1481), Turkish sultan **10** 452-454

MEHTA, SIR PHEROZESHAH (1845-1915), Indian statesman **10** 455

MEHTA, ZUBIN (born 1936), India born American conductor **10** 455-456

MEIER, RICHARD (born 1934), New York architect **10** 456-458

MEIGGS, HENRY (1811-1877), American railroad builder **10** 458-459

MEIGHEN, ARTHUR (1874-1960), Canadian lawyer, prime minister 1920-21, 1926 **10** 459-460

MEINECKE, FRIEDRICH (1862-1954), German historian **10** 460-461

MEINESZ, FELIX ANDRIES VENING (1887-1966), Dutch geodesist and geophysicist **10** 461

MEINONG, ALEXIUS RITTER VON HANDSCHUCHSHEIM (1853-1920), Austrian philosopher **10** 461-462

MEIR, GOLDA (1898-1978), Israeli prime minister **10** 462-463

MEITNER, LISE (born Elise Meitner; 1878-1968), Austrian-born American nuclear physicist **10** 463-466

MELANCTHON, PHILIP (1497-1560), German theologian and humanist **10** 466-467

MELAND, BERNARD EUGENE (born 1899), American historian of liberal theology **10** 467-468

MELBOURNE, 2ND VISCOUNT (William Lamb; 1779-1848), English statesman, prime minister 1834 and 1835-1841 **10** 468-469

MELLON, ANDREW WILLIAM (1855-1937), American businessman **10** 469-470

MELLON, RICHARD KING (1899-1970), American business leader and philanthropist **20** 259-261

MELNIKOV, KONSTANTIN STEPANOVICH (1890-1974), Russian avant-grant architect **10** 470-471

MELVILLE, GEORGE WALLACE (1841-1912), American naval officer and explorer **10** 472

MELVILLE, HERMAN (1819-1891), American author **10** 472-476

MEMLING, HANS (circa 1440-1494), German-born painter active in Flanders **10** 476

MEMMINGER, CHRISTOPHER GUSTAVUS (1803-1888), American politician **10** 476-477

MENANDER (342-291 B.C.), Athenian comic playwright **10** 477-478

MENCHÚ, RIGOBERTA (born 1959), Guatemalan human rights activist who won the Nobel Peace Prize **10** 479-480

MENCIUS (circa 371-circa 289 B.C.), Chinese philosopher **10** 480-481

MENCKEN, HENRY LOUIS (1880-1956), American journalist, editor, critic, and philologist **10** 481-483

MENDAÑA DE NEYRA, ÁLVARO DE (1541-1595), Spanish explorer **10** 483

MENDEL, JOHANN GREGOR (1822-1884), Moravian natural scientist and Augustinian abbot **10** 483-486

MENDELEEV, DMITRII IVANOVICH (1834-1907), Russian chemist **10** 486-488

MENDELSOHN, ERICH (1887-1953), German architect **10** 488

MENDELSSOHN, MOSES (1729-1786), German Jewish philosopher **10** 488-489

MENDELSSOHN-BARTHOLDY, FELIX JAKOB LUDWIG (1809-1847), German composer **10** 489-491

MENDENHALL, DOROTHY REED (1874-1964), American physician **10** 491-492

MENDES, CHICO (Francisco Mendes; 1944-1988), Brazilian environmental activist **19** 243-245

MENDÈS FRANCE, PIERRE (1907-1982), French prime minister (1954-1955) and politician **10** 492-493

MENDES PINTO, FERNAO (1509-1583), Portugese adventurer **10** 493-494

MENDOZA, ANTONIO DE (1490-1552), Spanish viceroy in Mexico and Peru **10** 494-495

MENDOZA, DANIEL (1764-1836), English boxer **20** 261-263

MENELIK II (born Sahle Mariam; 1844-1913), Ethiopian emperor 1889-1913 **10** 495-497

MENEM, CARLOS SÁUL (born 1930), Peronist president of Argentina **10** 497-499

MENÉNDEZ DE AVILÉS, PEDRO (1519-1574), Spanish seaman and colonizer **10** 499-500

MENES (King of Egypt; ca. 3420 B.C. - 3345 B.C.), unifier of Egypt **10** 500-502

MENGELE, JOSEF (1911-1979), German physician and war criminal **10** 502-503

MENGISTU HAILE MARIAM (born 1937), head of state of Ethiopia **10** 503-505

MENGS, ANTON RAPHAEL (1728-1779), German painter **10** 505

MENKEN, ALAN (born 1949), American composer **20** 263-266

MENNO SIMONS (circa 1496-1561), Dutch reformer **10** 505-506

MENOCAL, MARIO GARCIA (1866-1941), Cuban statesman, president 1913-1921 **10** 506-507

MENON, VENGALIL KRISHNAN KRISHNA (born 1897), Indian statesman **10** 507-509

MENOTTI, GIAN CARLO (born 1911), Italian-born American composer **10** 509-510

MENUHIN, YEHUDI (1916-1999), American and British violinist and conductor **20** 266-268

MENZIES, SIR ROBERT GORDON (born 1894), Australian statesman **10** 510-511

MENZIES, WILLIAM CAMERON (1896-1957), American film director, producer, and set designer **21** 291-293

MERCATOR, GERHARDUS (1512-1594), Flemish cartographer **10** 511-512

MEREDITH, GEORGE (1828-1909), English novelist and poet **10** 512-513

MEREDITH, JAMES H. (born 1933), African American civil rights activist and politician **10** 514-515

MEREZHKOVSKY, DMITRY SERGEYEVICH (1865-1941), Russian writer and literary critic **10** 515-516

MERGENTHALER, OTTMAR (1854-1899), German-American inventor of the Linotype **10** 516-517

MERIAN, MARIA SIBYLLA (1647-1717), German artist and entomologist **20** 268-269

MERICI, ANGELA (St. Angela; 1474-1530), Italian nun and educator **21** 293-295

MÉRIMÉE, PROSPER (1803-1870), French author **10** 517

MERLEAU-PONTY, MAURICE (1908-1961), French philosopher **10** 518

MERMAN, ETHEL (Ethel Agnes Zimmermann; 1909-1984), American singer and actress **21** 295-297

MERRIAM, CHARLES EDWARD (1874-1953), American political scientist **10** 518-519

MERRILL, CHARLES E. (1885-1956), founder of the world's largest brokerage firm **10** 519-520

MERRILL, JAMES (1926-1995), American novelist, poet, and playwright **10** 521-522

MERTON, ROBERT K. (1910-2003), American sociologist and educator **10** 522-523

MERTON, THOMAS (1915-1968), Roman Catholic writer, social critic, and spiritual guide **10** 523-525

MERULO, CLAUDIO (1533-1604), Italian composer, organist, and teacher **10** 525-526

MESMER, FRANZ ANTON (1734-1815), German physician **10** 526-527

MESSALI HADJ (1898-1974), founder of the Algerian nationalist movement **10** 527-528

MESSIAEN, OLIVIER (1908-1992), French composer and teacher **10** 528-529

MESSNER, REINHOLD (born 1944), Austrian mountain climber and author **22** 316-318

METACOM (a.k.a. King Philip; 1640-1676), Wampanoag cheiftain **10** 529-531

METCALFE, CHARLES THEOPHILUS (1st Baron Metcalfe; 1785-1846), British colonial administrator **10** 531-532

METCHNIKOFF, ÉLIE (1845-1916), Russian physiologist and bacteriologist **10** 532-533

METHODIUS, SAINT (825-885), Greek missionary and bishop **4** 362-363

Metropolitan Opera Co. (New York City) Bori, Lucrezia **23** 44-45

METTERNICH, KLEMENS VON (1773-1859), Austrian politician and diplomat **10** 533-536

MEYERBEER, GIACOMO (1791-1864), German composer **10** 536-537

MEYERHOF, OTTO FRITZ (1884-1951), German biochemist **10** 537-539

MEYERHOLD, VSEVOLOD EMILIEVICH (1874-1942?), Russian director **10** 539

MFUME, KWEISI (born Frizzell Gray; born 1948), African American civil rights activist and congressman **10** 539-542

MI FEI (1051-1107), Chinese painter, calligrapher, and critic **11** 12-13

MICAH (flourished 8th century B.C.), prophet of ancient Israel **10** 542-543

MICHAEL VIII (Palaeologus; 1224/25-1282), Byzantine emperor 1259-1282 **11** 1-2

MICHELANGELO BUONARROTI (1475-1564), Italian sculptor, painter, and architect **11** 2-5

MICHELET, JULES (1798-1874), French historian **11** 5-6

MICHELOZZO (circa 1396-1472), Italian architect and sculptor **11** 6-7

MICHELSON, ALBERT ABRAHAM (1852-1931), American physicist **11** 7-8

MICHENER, JAMES (1907-1997), American author **19** 245-247

MIDDLETON, THOMAS (1580-1627), English playwright **11** 8-9

MIDGELY, MARY BURTON (born 1919), British philosopher who focused on the philosophy of human motivation and ethics **11** 9-10

MIES VAN DER ROHE, LUDWIG (1886-1969), German-born American architect **11** 10-12

MIKAN, GEORGE (born 1924), American basketball player **21** 297-299

MIKULSKI, BARBARA (born 1936), United States senator from Maryland **11** 13-15

MILÁN, LUIS (circa 1500-after 1561), Spanish composer **11** 15-16

MILES, NELSON APPLETON (1839-1925), American general **11** 16-17

MILHAUD, DARIUS (born 1892), French composer and teacher **11** 17-18

Military leaders, Albanian
Kastrioti-Skanderbeg, Gjergj **23** 187-189

Military leaders, Angolan
Nzinga, Anna **23** 270-271

Military leaders, Georgian
Tamara **23** 388-390

Military leaders, Indian (Asian)
Razia **23** 326-329

Military leaders, Swiss
Jomini, Antoine Henri **23** 177-179

Military strategy
treatises
Jomini, Antoine Henri **23** 177-179

MILIUKOV, PAVEL NIKOLAYEVICH (1859-1943), Russian historian and statesman **11** 18-19

MILK, HARVEY BERNARD (1930-1978), American politician and gay rights activist **11** 19-21

MILKEN, MICHAEL (born 1946), American businessman **19** 247-249

MILL, JAMES (1773-1836), Scottish philosopher and historian **11** 21

MILL, JOHN STUART (1806-1873), English philosopher and economist **11** 21-23

MILLAIS, SIR JOHN EVERETT (1829-1896), English painter **11** 23-24

MILLAY, EDNA ST. VINCENT (1892-1950), American lyric poet **11** 24-25

MILLER, ARTHUR (born 1915), American playwright, novelist, and film writer **11** 25-26

MILLER, GLENN (Alton Glenn Miller; 1904-1944), American musician **19** 250-251

MILLER, HENRY (born 1891), American author **11** 26-27

MILLER, JOAQUIN (1837-1913), American writer **11** 27-28

MILLER, PERRY (1905-1963), American historian **11** 28-29

MILLER, SAMUEL FREEMAN (1816-1890), American jurist **11** 29-30

MILLER, WILLIAM (1782-1849), American clergyman **11** 30-31

MILLET, JEAN FRANÇOIS (1814-1875), French painter **11** 31

MILLET, KATE (born 1934), American feminist author and sculptor **11** 31

MILLIKAN, ROBERT ANDREWS (1868-1953), American physicist **11** 33-35

MILLS, BILLY (Makata Taka Hela; born 1938), Native American runner and businessman **19** 251-253

MILLS, C. WRIGHT (1916-1962), American sociologist and political polemicist **11** 35-36

MILLS, ROBERT (1781-1855), American architect **11** 36-37

MILNE, ALAN ALEXANDER (A.A. Milne; 1882-1956), British author **19** 253-254

MILNE, DAVID BROWN (1882-1953), Canadian painter and etcher **11** 37-38

MILNER, ALFRED (1st Viscount Milner; 1854-1925), British statesman **11** 38-39

MILOSEVIC, SLOBODAN (born 1941), president of Serbia **11** 39-40

MILOSZ, CZESLAW (born 1911), Nobel Prize winning Polish author and poet **11** 40-42

MILTIADES (circa 549-488 B.C.), Athenian military strategist and statesman **11** 42-43

MILTON, JOHN (1608-1674), English poet and controversialist **11** 43-46

MIN (1851-1895), Korean queen **11** 46-47

MINDON MIN (ruled 1852-1878), Burmese king **11** 47

MINDSZENTY, CARDINAL JÓZSEF (1892-1975), Roman Catholic primate of Hungary **11** 47-49

Mining (metallurgy)
industry
Tyrrell, Joseph Burr **23** 410-412

MINK, PATSY TAKEMOTO (1927-2003), Asian American congresswoman **18** 287-289

MINTZ, BEATRICE (born 1921), American embryologist **11** 49-50

MINUIT, PETER (1580-1638), Dutch colonizer **11** 50

MIRABEAU, COMTE DE (Honoré Gabriel Victor de Riqueti; 1749-1791), French statesman and author **11** 51-52

MIRANDA, FRANCISCO DE (1750-1816), Latin American patriot **11** 52-53

MIRÓ, JOAN (1893-1983), Spanish painter **11** 53-54

MISHIMA, YUKIO (1925-1970), Japanese novelist and playwright **11** 54-55

MISTRAL, GABRIELA (1889-1957), Chilean poet and educator **11** 55-56

MITCHELL, BILLY (1879-1936), American military officer and aviator **20** 269-272

MITCHELL, EDGAR DEAN (born 1930), American astronaut **22** 318-320

MITCHELL, GEORGE JOHN (born 1933), Maine Democrat and majority leader in the United States Senate **11** 56-58

MITCHELL, JOHN (1870-1919), American labor leader **11** 58-59

MITCHELL, JONI (Roberta Joan Anderson; born 1943), Canadian American singer **23** 246-248

MITCHELL, MARGARET (Munnerlyn; 1900-1949), American author of Gone With the Wind **11** 59-60

MITCHELL, MARIA (1818-1889), American astronomer and educator **11** 61
Whitney, Mary Watson **23** 440-442

MITCHELL, WESLEY CLAIR (1874-1948), American economist **11** 61-62

MITRE, BARTOLOMÉ (1821-1906), Argentine historian and statesman, president 1862-1868 **11** 62-63

MITTERRAND, FRANÇOIS (born 1916), French politician and statesman and president (1981-1990) **11** 63-66

MIZOGUCHI, KENJI (1898-1956), Japanese film director **23** 248-250

MIZRAHI, ISAAC (born 1961), American designer **11** 66-67

MLADIC, RATKO (born 1943), Bosnian Serb military leader **11** 68-69

MOBUTU SESE SEKO (Joseph Désiré Mobuto; 1930-1997), Congolese president **11** 69-71

MODEL, LISETTE (nee Lisette Seyberg; 1906?-1983), American photographer and educator **19** 254-256

Modern dance
Limón, José Arcadia **23** 227-229
Tamiris, Helen **23** 390-392

Modern Library of the World's Greatest Books (publishing house)
Liveright, Horace B. **23** 229-231

MODERSOHN-BECKER, PAULA (1876-1907), German painter **11** 71-72

MODIGLIANI, AMEDEO (1884-1920), Italian painter and sculptor **11** 72-73

MOFFETT, WILLIAM ADGER (1869-1933), American naval officer **21** 299-301

MOFOLO, THOMAS (1876-1948), Lesothoan author **11** 74

MOGILA, PETER (1596/1597-1646), Russian Orthodox churchman and theologian **11** 74-75

Mogul empire
see India–1000-1600

MOHAMMAD REZA SHAH PAHLAVI (1919-1980), king of Iran **11** 75-76

MOHAMMED (circa 570-632), founder of Islam **11** 76-78

MOHAMMED V (Mohammed Ben Youssef; 1911-1961), king of Morocco **11** 79-81

MOHAMMED ALI (1769-1849), Ottoman pasha of Egypt 1805-1848 **11** 81-82

MOHOLY-NAGY, LÁSZLÓ (1895-1946), Hungarian painter and designer **11** 82-83

MOI, DANIEL ARAP (born Daniel Toroitich arap Moi; born 1924), president of Kenya **11** 83-86

Molecular biology
see Biology, molecular

MOLIÈRE (1622-1673), French dramatist **11** 86-88

MOLINARI, SUSAN K. (born 1958), American newscaster **18** 289-291

MOLINOS, MIGUEL DE (1628-1696), Spanish priest **11** 88-89

MOLOTOV, VYACHESLAV MIKHAILOVICH (1890-1986), Soviet statesman **11** 89-90

MOLTKE, COUNT HELMUTH KARL BERNARD VON (1800-1891), Prussian military leader **11** 90-91

MOLTMANN, JÖURGEN (born 1926), German Protestant theologian **11** 91-92

MOMADAY, N. SCOTT (born 1934), Native American author **11** 92-94

MOMMSEN, THEODOR (1817-1903), German historian and philologist **11** 94-95

MONAGHAN, TOM (Thomas Stephen Monaghan; born 1937), American businessman and philanthropist **19** 256-258

MONASH, JOHN (1865-1931), Australian soldier, engineer, and administrator **11** 95-96

MONCK, GEORGE (1st Duke of Albemarle; 1608-1670), English general and statesman **11** 96-97

MONDALE, WALTER F. (Fritz; born 1928), United States senator and vice president **11** 97-99

MONDAVI, ROBERT (born 1913), American winemaker **19** 258-260

MONDLANE, EDUARDO CHIVAMBO (1920-1969), Mozambican educator and nationalist **11** 100-101

MONDRIAN, PIET (1872-1944), Dutch painter **11** 101-102

MONET, CLAUDE (1840-1926), French painter **11** 102-104

MONGKUT (Rama IV; 1804-1868), king of Thailand 1851-1868 **11** 104

MONK, THELONIOUS (1917-1982), African American jazz musician **11** 104-108

MONMOUTH AND BUCCLEUGH, DUKE OF (James Scott; 1649-1685), English claimant to the throne **11** 108-109

MONNET, JEAN (1888-1979), French economist and diplomat **11** 109-110

MONOD, JACQUES (1910-1976), French biologist who discovered messenger RNA **11** 110-111

MONROE, JAMES (1758-1831), American diplomat and statesman, president 1817-1825 **11** 111-113

MONROE, MARILYN (Norma Jean Baker; 1926-1962), film actress **11** 113-114

MONTAGNIER, LUC (born 1932), French virologist **11** 114-116

MONTAGU, ASHLEY (Israel Ehrenberg; 1905-1999), British-born American anthroplogist and author **22** 320-322

MONTAGU, JOHN, FOURTH EARL OF SANDWICH (1718-1792), English politician and first lord of the admiralty **21** 301-303

MONTAGU, MARY WORTLEY (1689-1762), English poet **18** 291-293

MONTAIGNE, MICHEL EYQUEM DE (1533-1592), French essayist **11** 116-117

MONTALE, EUGENIO (1896-1981), Italian poet and critic **11** 117-118

MONTALEMBERT, COMTE DE (Charles Forbes; 1810-1870), French political writer **11** 118-119

MONTALVO, JUAN MARÍA (1832-1889), Ecuadorian writer **11** 119-120

MONTANA, JOE (born 1956), American football player **11** 120-121

MONTANUS (flourished 2nd century), Early Christian founder of schismatic sect **11** 122

MONTCALM DE SAINT-VÉRAN, MARQUIS DE (1712-1759), French general in Canada **11** 122-123

MONTEFIORE, MOSES (1784-1885), English Zionist and philanthropist **20** 272-274

MONTESQUIEU, BARON DE (Charles Louis de Secondat; 1689-1755), French man of letters **11** 123-125

MONTESSORI, MARIA (1870-1952), Italian educator and physician **11** 125-126

MONTEVERDI, CLAUDIO GIOVANNI ANTONIO (1567-1643), Italian composer **11** 126-128

MONTEZUMA I (Motecuhzoma I; Moctezuma I; 1397-1469), Aztec ruler **22** 322-324

MONTEZUMA II (1466?-1520), Aztec emperor 1502-1520 **11** 128-129

MONTEZUMA, CARLOS (born Wassaja; ca. 1865-1923), Native American physician and political leader **11** 129-132

MONTFORT, SIMON DE (6th Earl of Leicester; 1208-1265), English statesman and soldier **11** 132-133

MONTGOLFIER, JACQUES ÉTIENNE (1745-1799), French inventor and industrialist **11** 133-134

MONTGOLFIER, JOSEPH MICHEL (1740-1810), French inventor and industrialist **11** 133-134

MONTGOMERY, BERNARD LAW (1st Viscount Montgomery of Alamein; born 1887), English field marshal **11** 135-136

MONTGOMERY, LUCY MAUD (1874-1942), Canadian author **11** 136-138

MONTGOMERY, RICHARD (1736-1775), colonial American general **11** 138-139

Montreal Canadiens (hockey team) Roy, Patrick **23** 351-353

MONTREUIL, PIERRE DE (flourished circa 1231-1266/67), French architect **11** 139

MONTT TORRES, MANUEL (1809-1880), Chilean statesman, president 1851-1861 **11** 139-140

MOODIE, SUSANNA (1803-1885), Canadian poet, novelist, and essayist **11** 140-141

MOODY, DWIGHT L. (1837-1899), American evangelist **11** 141-142

MOON, SUN MYUNG (born 1920), founder of the Unification Church **11** 142-143

MOORE, CHARLES WILLARD (1925-1993), American architect and educator **11** 143-145

MOORE, CHARLOTTE E. (1898-1990), American astrophysicist **11** 145-146

MOORE, GEORGE EDWARD (1873-1958), English philosopher **11** 146

MOORE, HENRY (1898-1986), English sculptor **11** 146-148

MOORE, MARIANNE (1887-1972), American poet and translator **11** 148-149

MORALES, LUIS DE (circa 1519-1586), Spanish painter **11** 150

MORALES-BERMÚDEZ CERRUTI, FRANCISCO (born 1921), president of Peru (1975-1980) **11** 150-151

MORAN, THOMAS (1837-1926), American painter and graphic artist **11** 151-152

MORANDI, GIORGIO (1890-1964), Italian painter of still lifes **11** 152-153

MORAVIA, ALBERTO (1907-1990), Italian author **11** 153-155

MORAZÁN, JOSÉ FRANCISCO (1792-1842), Central American general and statesman **11** 155

MORE, SIR THOMAS (1478-1535), English humanist and statesman **11** 156-157

MOREAU, GUSTAVE (1826-1898), French artist and professor **22** 324-326

MORELOS, JOSÉ MARÍA (1765-1815), Mexican priest and revolutionary leader **11** 157-158

MORENO, MARIANO (1778-1811), Argentine revolutionary **20** 274-275

MORGAGNI, GIOVANNI BATTISTA (1682-1771), Italian anatomist **11** 158-159

MORGAN, CONWAY LLOYD (1852-1936), English psychologist **11** 159-160

MORGAN, DANIEL (circa 1735-1802), American soldier and tactician **11** 160-161

MORGAN, GARRETT A. (1877-1963), African American inventor and publisher **11** 161-162

MORGAN, JOHN (1735-1789), American physician **11** 162-163

MORGAN, JOHN PIERPONT (1837-1913), American banker **11** 163-165

MORGAN, JOHN PIERPONT, II (1867-1943), American banker **11** 165

MORGAN, JULIA (1872-1957), American architect **11** 165-166

MORGAN, JUNIUS SPENCER (1813-1890), American banker **11** 166-167

MORGAN, LEWIS HENRY (1818-1881), American anthropologist **11** 167-168

MORGAN, ROBIN (born 1941), feminist writer, editor, poet, and political activist **11** 168-170

MORGAN, THOMAS HUNT (1866-1945), American zoologist and geneticist **11** 170-171

MORGENTHAU, HANS J. (1904-1979), American political scientist **11** 171-172

MORGENTHAU, HENRY, JR. (1891-1967), American statesman **11** 172-173

MORIN, PAUL (1889-1963), French-Canadian poet **11** 174

MORÍNIGO, HIGINIO (1897-1985), Paraguayan statesman **11** 174-175

MORISON, SAMUEL ELIOT (1887-1976), American historian and biographer **11** 175-176

MORISOT, BERTHE (1841-1895), French painter **21** 303-305

MORITA, AKIO (born 1921), Japanese industrial leader **11** 176-178

MORLEY, JOHN (Viscount Morley of Blackburn; 1838-1923), English statesman and author **11** 178-179

MORLEY, THOMAS (circa 1557-1602/08), English composer and organist **11** 179-180

MORO, ALDO (1916-1978), leader of Italy's Christian Democratic Party **11** 180-181

MORRICE, JAMES WILSON (1865-1924), Canadian painter **11** 181-182

MORRILL, JUSTIN SMITH (1810-1898), American legislator **11** 182

MORRIS, GOUVERNEUR (1752-1816), American statesman and diplomat **11** 182-183

MORRIS, LEWIS (1671-1746), American colonial official **11** 183-184

MORRIS, MARK (born 1956), American choreographer **11** 184-185

MORRIS, ROBERT (1734-1806), American financer and statesman **11** 185-187

MORRIS, WILLIAM (1834-1896), English man of letters, artist, and politician **11** 187-188

MORRISON, JIM (James Douglas Morrison; 1943-1971), American singer and songwriter **18** 293-295

MORRISON, TONI (Chloe Anthony Wofford; born 1931), African American novelist **11** 188-190

MORROW, DWIGHT WHITNEY (1873-1931), American banker and diplomat **11** 190-191

MORSE, JEDIDIAH (1761-1826), American geographer and clergyman **11** 191-192

MORSE, SAMUEL FINLEY BREESE (1791-1872), American artist and inventor **11** 192-193

MORSE, WAYNE L. (1900-1974), United States senator from Oregon **11** 193-194

MORTIMER, JOHN CLIFFORD (born 1923), British author of novels, stories, and plays for radio, stage, television, and film **11** 194-195

MORTON, NELLE KATHERINE (1905-1987), activist for racial justice, teacher of Christian educators, and proponent of feminist theology **11** 195-197

MORTON, OLIVER HAZARD PERRY THROCK (1823-1877), American politician **11** 197-198

MORTON, WILLIAM THOMAS GREEN (1819-1868), American dentist **11** 198-199

MOSELY-BRAUN, CAROL (born 1947), African American Democratic senator from Illinois **11** 199-200

MOSES (circa 1392-circa 1272 B.C.), Hebrew prophet and lawgiver **11** 200-201

MOSES, EDWIN (born 1955), African American track and field star **20** 275-277

MOSES, GRANDMA (Anna Mary Robertson; 1860-1961), American painter **11** 201-202

MOSES, ROBERT (1888-1981), New York City's builder of public works **11** 202-203

MOSHWESHWE (Moshesh; circa 1787-1868), South African king **11** 203-205

MOSQUERA, TOMÁS CIPRIANO DE (1798-1878), Colombian statesman **11** 205-206

MOSSADEGH, MOHAMMAD (Musaddiq; 1882-1967), Iranian nationalist politician and prime minister (1951-1953) **11** 206-207

MÖSSBAUER, RUDOLF (born 1929), German physicist **11** 208-209

MOTHERWELL, ROBERT (1915-1991), American painter **11** 210-211

Motion pictures (Asia)
Kobayashi, Masaki **23** 199-201
Mizoguchi, Kenji **23** 248-250
Ozu, Yasujiro **23** 279-281

Motion pictures (Australia)
Campion, Jane **23** 58-60

Motion pictures (Europe)
Almodovar, Pedro **23** 6-9
Leigh, Mike **23** 222-225
Ophüls, Max **23** 275-277
Pabst, G. W. **23** 282-284
Polanski, Roman **23** 310-312
Resnais, Alain **23** 333-335
Tarkovsky, Andrei **23** 392-395
Vigo, Jean **23** 429-431

Motion pictures (Russia)
Tarkovsky, Andrei **23** 392-395

Motion pictures (United States)
directors
Brooks, Mel **23** 48-50
Polanski, Roman **23** 310-312

experimental
Nauman, Bruce **23** 259-261
musicals
Brooks, Mel **23** 48-50
"talkies" and after
Peterson, Oscar Emanuel **23** 304-306
theater chains
Redstone, Sumner Murray **23** 329-331

MOTLEY, CONSTANCE BAKER (born 1921), African American judge and attorney **18** 295-297

MOTLEY, JOHN LOTHROP (1814-1877), American historian and diplomat **11** 211-212

MOTLEY, Willard Francis (1909-1965), African American author **22** 326-328

MOTT, JOHN R. (1865-1955), American Protestant leader **11** 212

MOTT, LUCRETIA COFFIN (1793-1880), American feminist and abolitionist **11** 212-213

MOUNT, WILLIAM SIDNEY (1807-1868), American painter **11** 213-214

MOUNTBATTEN, LOUIS FRANCIS ALBERT VICTOR NICHOLAS (1900-1979), English Navy officer and viceroy of India **18** 297-299

MOYERS, BILLY DON ("Bill"; born 1934), television journalist, author, and press secretary to president Lyndon B. Johnson **11** 214-216

MOYNIHAN, DANIEL PATRICK ("Pat"; 1927-2003), United States senator from New York **11** 216-218

MOZART, WOLFGANG AMADEUS (1756-1791), Austrian composer **11** 218-221
interpretations
Uchida, Mitsuko **23** 413-415

MPHAHLELE, EZEKIEL (a.k.a. Bruno Eseki; born 1919), South African author and scholar **11** 221-223

MQHAYI, SAMUEL EDWARD KRUNE (1875-1945), South African novelist and poet **11** 223

MUAWIYA IBN ABU SUFYAN (died 680), Umayyad caliph **11** 223-224

MUBARAK, HOSNI (born 1928), president of Egypt **11** 225-226

MUELLER, OTTO (1874-1930), German expressionist painter **11** 226-227

MUGABE, ROBERT GABRIEL (born 1924), Zimbabwe's first elected black prime minister **11** 227-229

MUHAMMAD, ELIJAH (Poole; 1897-1975), leader of the Nation of Islam ("Black Muslims") **11** 230-231

MUHAMMAD BIN TUGHLUQ (ruled 1325-1351), Moslem sultan of Delhi **11** 229

MUHAMMAD TURE, ASKIA (circa 1443-1538), ruler of the West African Songhay empire **11** 231-232

MÜHLENBERG, HEINRICH MELCHIOR (1711-1787), German-born American Lutheran clergyman **11** 232-233

MUHLENBERG, WILLIAM AUGUSTUS (1796-1877); American Episcopalian clergyman **11** 233-234

MUIR, JOHN (1838-1914), American naturalist **11** 234

MUJIBUR RAHMAN, SHEIK (1920-1975), Bengal leader who helped found Bangladesh **11** 234-236

MUKERJI, DHAN GOPAL (1890-1936), Indian author and Hindu priest **22** 328-330

MULDOWNEY, SHIRLEY (born ca. 1940), American race car driver **11** 236-238

MULLER, HERMANN JOSEPH (1890-1967), American geneticist **11** 238-239

MÜLLER, JOHANNES PETER (1801-1858), German physiologist and anatomist **11** 239-240

MÜLLER, KARL ALEXANDER (born 1927), Swiss-born solid-state physicist **11** 240-241

MÜLLER, PAUL HERMANN (1899-1965), Swiss chemist **11** 241-242

MULRONEY, MARTIN BRIAN (born 1939), prime minister of Canada **11** 242-246

MUMFORD, LEWIS (1895-1990), American social philosopher and architectural critic **11** 246-247

MUNCH, EDVARD (1863-1944), Norwegian painter and graphic artist **11** 247-248

MUNDELEIN, GEORGE WILLIAM (1872-1939), American Roman Catholic cardinal **11** 248-249

MUÑOZ MARÍN, JOSÉ LUÍS ALBERTO (1898-1980), Puerto Rican political leader **11** 249-250

MUÑOZ RIVERA, LUÍS (1859-1916), Puerto Rican political leader **11** 250

MUNSEY, FRANK ANDREW (1854-1925), American publisher **11** 251

MÜNZER, THOMAS (1489?-1525), German Protestant reformer **11** 251-252

Murad II (1403?-1451), Ottoman sultan 1421-1451
Kastrioti-Skanderbeg, Gjergj **23** 187-189

MURASAKI SHIKIBU (circa 976-circa 1031), Japanese writer **11** 252-253

MURAT, JOACHIM (1767-1815), French marshal, king of Naples 1808-1815 **11** 253-254

MURATORI, LODOVICO ANTONIO (1672-1750), Italian historian and antiquary **11** 254-255

MURCHISON, SIR RODERICK IMPEY (1792-1871), British geologist **11** 255-256

MURDOCH, JEAN IRIS (1919-1999), British novelist **11** 256-257

MURDOCH, RUPERT (born 1931), Australian newspaper publisher **11** 257-258

MURILLO, BARTOLOMÉ ESTEBAN (1617-1682), Spanish painter **11** 258-259

MURNAU, F.W. (Friedrich Wilhelm Plumpe; 1888-1913), German film director **22** 330-332

MURPHY, AUDIE (1924-1971), American army officer and actor **18** 299-301

MURPHY, CHARLES FRANCIS (1858-1924), American politician **11** 259-260

MURPHY, FRANK (1890-1949), American jurist and diplomat **11** 260-261

MURRAY, GILBERT (George Gilbert Aime Murray; 1886-1957), English scholar **23** 250-253

MURRAY, JAMES (1721-1794), British general **11** 261-262

MURRAY, JOSEPH (born 1919), American physician **18** 301-303

MURRAY, LESLIE ALLAN (born 1938), Australian poet and literary critic **11** 262-263

MURRAY, PAULI (Anna Pauline Murray; 1910-1985), African American/Native American civil right activist and priest **23** 253-256

MURRAY, PHILIP (1886-1952), American labor leader **11** 264-265

MURRAY, WILLIAM (Lord Mansfield; 1705-1793), English judge **23** 256-258

MURROW, EDWARD ROSCOE (1908-1965), American radio and television news broadcaster **11** 265-266

MUSA MANSA (died 1337), king of the Mali empire in West Africa ca. 1312-1337 **11** 266

MUSGRAVE, THEA (born 1928), Scottish-born composer **11** 266-268

MUSHARRAF, PERVEZ (born 1943), Pakistani head of sate **22** 332-335

MUSIAL, STAN (Stanislaus Musial, Stanley Frank Musial; born 1920), American baseball **19** 260-262

Music
experimental forms
Badings, Henk **23** 26-28
recording of
Burlin, Natalie Curtis **23** 50-52

Musicals (United States)
choreographers
Tamiris, Helen **23** 390-392
directors
Brooks, Mel **23** 48-50

Musicians, American
composers (19th-20th century)
Beach, Amy **23** 30-32
composers (20th century)
Armstrong, Lillian Hardin **23** 15-17
Leginska, Ethel **23** 220-222
Rands, Bernard **23** 324-326
Williams, Mary Lou **23** 444-446
conductors
Leginska, Ethel **23** 220-222
Rands, Bernard **23** 324-326
country singers
Pride, Charley Frank **23** 317-319
folk singers
Leadbelly **23** 208-211
Mitchell, Joni **23** 246-248
guitarists
Leadbelly **23** 208-211
lyricists
Mitchell, Joni **23** 246-248
pianists
Armstrong, Lillian Hardin **23** 15-17
Beach, Amy **23** 30-32
Leginska, Ethel **23** 220-222
Williams, Mary Lou **23** 444-446
singers
Bailey, Mildred **23** 28-30

Musicians, Australian
Mackerras, Alan Charles **23** 237-239

Musicians, Canadian
Lombardo, Guy **23** 234-236
Mitchell, Joni **23** 246-248
Peterson, Oscar Emanuel **23** 304-306

Musicians, Chilean
Arrau, Claudio **23** 17-18

Musicians, Cuban
Lecuona, Ernesto **23** 213-216

Musicians, Danish
Nørgård, Per **23** 265-267

Musicians, English
composers (19th-20th century)
Leginska, Ethel **23** 220-222
conductors
Leginska, Ethel **23** 220-222

Heavy Metal
Led Zeppelin **23** 216-218
pianists
Leginska, Ethel **23** 220-222

Musicians, Estonian
Pärt, Arvo **23** 295-297

Musicians, Japanese
Uchida, Mitsuko **23** 413-415

Musicians, Spanish
Bori, Lucrezia **23** 44-45
Peña, Paco **23** 299-301

MUSIL, ROBERT EDLER VON (1880-1942), Austrian novelist, dramatist, and short story writer **11** 268-269

MUSKIE, EDMUND SIXTUS (1914-1996), United States senator and Democratic vice-presidential nominee **11** 269-271

MUSSET, LOUIS CHARLES ALFRED DE (1810-1857), French poet, dramatist, and fiction writer **11** 271-272

MUSSOLINI, BENITO (1883-1945), Italian Fascist dictator 1922-1943 **11** 272-274

MUSSORGSKY, MODEST PETROVICH (1839-1881), Russian composer **11** 274-276

MUSTE, ABRAHAM JOHANNES (1885-1967), American pacifist and labor leader **11** 276-277

MUTESA I (circa 1838-1884), African monarch of Buganda **11** 277

MUTESA II (1924-1969), Monarch of Buganda **11** 277-278

MUTIS, JOSÉ CELESTINO (1732-1808), Spanish-Colombian naturalist **11** 278-279

MUTSUHITO (a.k.a. Meiji; 1852-1912), Japanese emperor **11** 279-282

MUYBRIDGE, EADWEARD (1830-1904), English photographer **21** 305-308

MWANGA (circa 1866-1901), Monarch of Buganda **11** 282-283

MYDANS, CARL (born 1907), American photojournalist **11** 283-284

MYRDAL, KARL GUNNAR (1898-1987), Swedish economist and sociologist **11** 284

MYRON (flourished circa 470-450 B.C.), Greek sculptor **11** 285

MZILIKAZI (circa 1795-1868), South African warrior leader **11** 285-286

N

NAACP
see National Association for the Advancement of Colored People

NABOKOV, VLADIMIR (1899-1977), Russian-born American writer, critic, and lepidopterist **11** 287-288

NABUCO DE ARAUJO, JOAQUIM AURELIO (1849-1910), Brazilian abolitionist, statesman, and author **11** 288-289

NADELMAN, ELIE (1882-1946), Polish-American sculptor and graphic artist **11** 289-290

NADER, RALPH (born 1934), American lawyer and social crusader **11** 290-291

NADIR SHAH (born Nadir Kouli; 1685-1747), Emperor of Persia **20** 278-281

NAGEL, ERNEST (1901-1985), American philosopher of science **11** 291-292

NAGUMO, CHUICHI (1887-1944), Japanese admiral **19** 263-266

NAGURSKI, BRONKO (Bronislaw Nagurski; 1908-1990), Canadian football player **21** 309-311

NAGY, IMRE (1896-1958), prime minister of Hungary (1953-55, 1956) **11** 292-293

NAHMANIDES (1194-1270), Spanish Talmudist **11** 293-294

NAIDU, SAROJINI (1879-1949), Indian poet and nationalist **11** 294-295

NAIPAUL, V. S. (born 1932), Trinidadian author of English-language prose **11** 295-296

NAISMITH, JAMES (1861-1939), Canadian inventor of basketball **21** 311-313

NAJIBULLAH, MOHAMMAD (born 1947), Soviet-selected ruler of the Republic of Afghanistan **11** 296-298

NAKASONE, YASUHIRO (born 1918), prime minister of Japan (1982-1987) **11** 298-300

NAMATJIRA, ALBERT (1902-1959), Australian Aboriginal artist **11** 300-301

NAMIER, SIR LEWIS BERNSTEIN (1888-1960), English historian **11** 301-303

NANAK (1469-1538), Indian reformer, founder of Sikhism **11** 303

Naked (film)
Leigh, Mike **23** 222-225

NANSEN, FRIDTJOF (1861-1930), Norwegian polar explorer, scientist, and statesman **11** 304-305

NAOROJI, DADABHAI (1825-1917), Indian nationalist leader **11** 305

NAPIER, JOHN (1550-1617), Scottish mathematician **11** 306

NAPOLEON I (1769-1821), emperor of the French 1804-1815 **11** 306-310
military strategy
Jomini, Antoine Henri, Baron **23** 177-179

NAPOLEON III (Louis Napoleon; 1808-1873), emperor of the French 1852-1870 **11** 310-312

NARAYAN, JAYAPRAKASH (1902-1979), Indian nationalist and social reformer **11** 312-313

NARAYAN, R. K. (Narayanswami; born 1906), Indian author **11** 313-314

NARIÑO, ANTONIO (1765-1823), Colombian patriot **11** 314-315

NARVÁEZ, PÁNFILO DE (1478?-1528), Spanish soldier and explorer **11** 315

NASH, JOHN (1752-1835), English architect and town planner **11** 316

NASH, JOHN FORBES, JR. (born 1928), American mathematician **22** 336-338

NASH, OGDEN (Fredric Ogden Nash; 1902-1971), American poet **18** 304-306

NASMYTH, JAMES (1808-1890), Scottish engineer and inventor **11** 316-317

NASSER, GAMAL ABDEL (1918-1970), Egyptian statesman, president 1956-1970 **11** 317-318

NAST, CONDÉ (1873-1942), American publisher **19** 266-268

NAST, THOMAS (1840-1902), American caricaturist and painter **11** 318-319

NATHAN, GEORGE JEAN (1882-1958), American author, editor, and critic **11** 319-321

NATION, CARRY AMELIA MOORE (1846-1911), American temperance reformer **11** 321-322

National American Woman Suffrage Association (NAWSA)
Terrell, Mary Church **23** 397-399

National Association for the Advancement of Colored People (inc. 1910)
formation
Terrell, Mary Church **23** 397-399

National Association of Colored Women (United States)
Terrell, Mary Church **23** 397-399

National Organization for Women (United States, established 1966)
Murray, Pauli **23** 253-256

National Socialism
see Nazism

Native Americans
and the American Revolution
Ward, Nancy **23** 436-438
medicine
Sanapia **23** 358-360
society and culture
religion
Tekakwitha, Kateri **23** 395-397
tribal leaders
Ward, Nancy **23** 436-438

NATIVIDAD, IRENE (born 1948), Asian American activist and women's rights advocate **11** 322-324

NATSUME, SOSEKI (or Kinnosuke; 1867-1916), Japanese novelist and essayist **11** 324-325

Naturalism (art)
Asia
Okyo, Maruyama **23** 272-274
Europe
North, Marianne **23** 268-270

NAUMAN, BRUCE (born 1941), American artist **23** 259-261

NAVRATILOVA, MARTINA (born 1956), American tennis player **11** 325-327

NAYLOR, GLORIA (born 1950), African American novelist **11** 328-329

Nazi party
see Nazism

Nazism (National Socialism)
Films relating to
Pabst, G. W. **23** 282-284

NAZZAM, IBRAHIM IBN SAYYAR AL- (died circa 840), Moslem thinker and theologian **11** 329

N'DOUR, YOUSSOU (born 1959), Senegalese musician **22** 338-340

NE WIN (1911-2002), Burmese political leader **11** 364-365

NEAL, PATRICIA (Patsy Louise Neal; born 1926), American actress **19** 268-270

NEBUCHADNEZZAR (ruled 605-562 B.C.), king of Babylon **11** 330

NECKER, JACQUES (1732-1804), French financier and statesman **11** 330-331

NEEL, ALICE (Alice Hartley Neel; 1900-1984), American artist **23** 261-263

NEFERTITI (flourished first half 14th century B.C.), Egyptian queen **11** 331-332

Negro Spirituals (dances)
Tamiris, Helen **23** 390-392

NEHRU, JAWAHARLAL (1889-1964), Indian nationalist, prime minister 1947-1964 **11** 332-334

NEHRU, MOTILAL (1861-1931), Indian lawyer and statesman **11** 334-335

NEILL, ALEXANDER SUTHERLAND (1883-1973), Scottish psychologist **11** 335-336

NEILSON, JOHN SHAW (1872-1942), Australian author **22** 340-342

Nejd (Arabic Kingdom)
see Saudi Arabia

NELSON, HORATIO (Viscount Nelson; 1758-1805), English admiral **11** 336-338

NELSON, RICK (Eric Hillard Nelson; 1940-1985), American musician and actor **21** 314-316

NEMEROV, HOWARD (1920-1991), American author and third poet laureate of the United States **11** 338-340

Neoclassicism (art)
Denmark
Thorvaldsen, Bertel **23** 403-406

Neoimpressionism (art)
Signac, Paul **23** 369-372

NERI, ST. PHILIP (1515-1595), Italian reformer **11** 340

NERNST, WALTHER (born Hermann Walther Nernst; 1864-1941), German chemist and inventor **11** 340-342

NERO CLAUDIUS CAESAR (37-68), Roman emperor 54-68 **11** 342-344

NERUDA, PABLO (Neftalí Ricardo Reyes Basoalto; 1904-73), Chilean poet, Nobel prize winner 1971 **11** 344-345

NERVAL, GÉRARD DE (1808-1855), French poet **11** 345-346

NERVI, PIER LUIGI (1891-1979), Italian architect and engineer **11** 346-348

NESBIT, E(DITH) (Edith Nesbit Bland; Fabian Bland; 1885-1924), English author and activist **23** 263-265

NESSELRODE, COUNT KARL ROBERT (1780-1862), Russian diplomat **11** 348-349

NESTORIUS (died circa 453), Syrian patriarch of Constantinople and heresiarch **11** 349-350

NETANYAHU, BINYAMIN (born 1949), Israeli ambassador to the United Nations (1984-1988), head of the Likud Party, and prime minister **11** 350-351

NETO, ANTÓNIO AGOSTINHO (1922-1979), Angolan intellectual and nationalist and first president of the People's Republic of Angola **11** 351-352

NEUFELD, ELIZABETH F. (born 1928), American biochemist **11** 352-353

NEUMANN, BALTHASAR (1687-1753), German architect **11** 354-355

NEUTRA, RICHARD JOSEPH (1892-1970), Austrian-born American architect **11** 355-356

NEVELSON, LOUISE (1900-1988), American abstract sculptor **11** 356-357

NEVERS, ERNIE (Ernest Alonzo Nevers; 1903-1976), American athlete **20** 281-283

NEVIN, JOHN WILLIAMSON (1803-1886), American Protestant theologian **11** 357

NEVINS, ALLAN (1890-1971), American historian **11** 357-359

NEVSKY, ALEXANDER (ca. 1220-1262), Russian grand duke and prince **11** 359

New France
see Canada

NEWBERY, JOHN (1713-1767), English publisher **11** 360-361

NEWCOMB, SIMON (1835-1909), American astronomer **11** 361-362

NEWCOMEN, THOMAS (1663-1729), English inventor and engineer **11** 362

NEWHOUSE, SAMUEL IRVING (1895-1979), American media tycoon **11** 362-364

NEWMAN, BARNETT (1905-1970), American painter **11** 365

NEWMAN, JOHN HENRY (1801-1890), English cardinal and theologian **11** 365-367

NEWMAN, PAUL LEONARD (born 1925), American actor and humanitarian **18** 306-308

NEWTON, HUEY P. (born 1942), co-founder of the Black Panther Party **11** 367-369

NEWTON, SIR ISAAC (1642-1727), English scientist and mathematician **11** 369-372

NEXØ, MARTIN ANDERSON (1869-1954), Danish author **11** 372

NEY, MICHEL (1769-1815), French marshal **11** 372-373

NEYMAN, JERZY (1894-1981), American statistician **21** 316-318

NGALA, RONALD GIDEON (1923-1972), Kenyan politician **11** 373-374

NGATA, SIR APIRANA TURUPA (1874-1950), Maori leader, politician, and scholar **11** 374-375

NGOYI, LILLIAN (1911-1980), South African civil rights activist **20** 283-284

NGUGI WA THIONG'O (James Ngugi; born 1938), Kenyan writer **11** 375-376

NI TSAN (1301-1374), Chinese painter **11** 400

NICHIREN (1222-1282), Japanese Buddhist monk **11** 376-377

NICHOLAS I (1796-1855), czar of Russia 1825-1855 **11** 377-378

NICHOLAS II (1868-1918), czar of Russia 1894-1917 **11** 378-380

NICHOLAS OF ORESME (circa 1320-1382), French bishop, writer and translator **11** 380

NICHOLSON, BEN (1894-1982), English painter **11** 380-381

NICHOLSON, SIR FRANCIS (1655-1728), English colonial governor **11** 381-382

NICKLAUS, JACK (born 1940), American golfer **11** 382-383

Nicknames
alchemical artist
Polke, Sigmar **23** 312-315
Black Patti
Joyner, Matilda Sissieretta **23** 179-181
father of the English ghost story
Le Fanu, Joseph Sheridan **23** 206-208
father of modern day Pentecostalism
Parham, Charles Fox **23** 291-293
father of South African poetry
Pringle, Thomas **23** 319-320
first lady of jazz
Williams, Mary Lou **23** 444-446
Hurricane Camille
Paglia, Camille **23** 286-288
lily of the Mohawk
Tekakwitha, Kateri **23** 395-397
queen of the air
Leitzel, Lillian **23** 225-227

NICHOLAS, SAINT (Santa Claus; died 345), Lycian bishop **20** 284-285

NICHOLS, MIKE (Michael Igor Peschkowsky; born 1931), American film and theater director and producer **20** 285-288

NICOLSON, HAROLD GEORGE (1886-1968), British diplomat, historian, biographer, critic and journalist, and diarist **11** 383-384

NICOLSON, MARJORIE HOPE (1894-1981), American educator **11** 384-385

NIDETCH, JEAN (born 1927), founder of Weight Watchers **21** 318-320

NIEBUHR, BARTHOLD GEORG (1776-1831), German historian and statesman **11** 385-386

NIEBUHR, HELMUT RICHARD (1894-1962), American Protestant theologian **11** 386-387

NIEBUHR, REINHOLD (1892-1971), American Protestant theologian **11** 387-388

NIELSEN, CARL AUGUST (1865-1931), Danish composer **11** 388-389

NIEMEYER SOARES FILHO, OSCAR (born 1907), Brazilian architect **11** 389-390

NIETZSCHE, FRIEDRICH (1844-1900), German philosopher and poet **11** 390-392
associates
Brandes, Georg **23** 45-47

NIGHTINGALE, FLORENCE (1820-1910), English nurse **11** 392-393

NIJINSKY, VASLAV (1890-1950), Russian ballet dancer **11** 393-395

NIKON, NIKITA MINOV (1605-1681), patriarch of the Russian Orthodox Church 1652-1666 **11** 395

NIMITZ, CHESTER WILLIAM (1885-1966), American admiral **11** 395-396

NIN, ANAIS (1903-1977), American author **11** 397-398

NIN-CULMELL, JOAQUÍN MARÍA (born 1908), American composer, pianist, and conductor **11** 398

NIRENBERG, MARSHALL WARREN (born 1927), American biochemist **11** 399-400

NIWANO, NIKKYO (Shikazo Niwano; born 1906), Buddhist Japanese religious leader **11** 400-401

NIXON, RICHARD MILHOUS (1913-1994), president of the United States (1969-1974) **11** 401-404

NIZAMI, KHALIQ AHMAD (born 1925), Indian historian, religious scholar, and diplomat **11** 405

NKOMO, JOSHUA MQABUKO (1917-1999), leading African nationalist in former colony of Rhodesia and president of the Zimbabwe African People's Union **11** 405-407

NKOSI, LEWIS (born 1936), South African author and literary critic **11** 407-408

NKRUMAH, KWAME (Francis Nwa Nkrumah; 1909-1972), Ghanaian statesman, president 1960-1966 **11** 408-410

NOBEL, ALFRED BERNHARD (1833-1896), Swedish chemist **11** 410-411

Nobel Prize winners
chemistry
Altman, Sidney **23** 9-11
Lee, Yuan Tseh **23** 218-220
medicine and physiology
Prusiner, Stanley Ben **23** 320-323
physics
Leavitt, Henrietta Swan **23** 211-213
Penzias, Arno Allen **23** 301-304
Ting, Samuel Chao Chung **23** 406-408

NOBILE, UMBERTO (1885-1978), Italian explorer and airship designer **11** 411-412

NOBUNAGA, ODA (1534-1582), Japanese general and statesman **11** 413-414

NOETHER, EMMY (born Amalie Emmy Noether; 1882-1935), German American mathematician **11** 414-416

NOGUCHI, ISAMU (1904-1988), American sculptor and designer **11** 416-418

NOLAN, SIDNEY ROBERT (1917-1992), Australian expressionist painter **11** 418

NOLAND, KENNETH (born 1924), American color-field painter **11** 418-419

NOLDE, EMIL (1867-1956), German expressionist painter **11** 419-420

NONO, LUIGI (1924-1990), Italian composer **11** 420-421

NORDENSKJÖLD, BARON NILS ADOLF ERIK (1832-1901), Finnish-Swedish polar explorer and mineralogist **11** 421-422

NORDENSKOLD, NILS OTTO GUSTAF (1869-1928), Swedish polar explorer and geologist **11** 422-423

NORDSTROM, JOHN (Johan W. Nordstrom; 1871-1963), American shoe retailer **19** 270-272

NORFOLK, 3D DUKE OF (Thomas Howard; 1473-1554), English soldier and councilor **11** 423

NØRGÅRD, PER (born 1932), Danish composer **23** 265-267

NORIEGA, MANUEL A. (born 1934), strongman of Panama (1980s) forced out in 1989 by the United States **11** 423-425

NORMAN, JESSYE (born 1945), American singer **11** 425-427

NORRIS, BENJAMIN FRANKLIN, JR. (1870-1902), American novelist and critic **11** 427-428

NORRIS, GEORGE WILLIAM (1861-1944), American statesman **11** 428-429

NORTH, FREDERICK (2nd Earl of Guilford; 1732-1792), English statesman **11** 429-430

NORTH, MARIANNE (1830-1890), English naturalist and painter **23** 268-270

North Pole
see Arctic exploration

NORTHROP, JOHN HOWARD (1891-1987), American biological chemist **11** 430-431

NORTHUMBERLAND, DUKE OF (John Dudley; circa 1502-1553), English soldier and statesman **11** 431-432

Nostalghia (film)
Tarkovsky, Andrei Arsenyevich **23** 392-395

NOSTRADAMUS (born Michel de Notredame; 1503-1566), French physician, astrologist, and author **11** 432-434

NOVALIS (1772-1801), German poet and author **11** 435

NOVELLO, ANTONIA (Antonia Coello; born 1944), Puerto Rican American pediatrician **18** 308-310

NOYCE, ROBERT (1927-1990), American physicist and inventor **11** 436-437

NOYES, JOHN HUMPHREY (1811-1886), American founder of the Oneida Community **11** 437-438

NOZICK, ROBERT (1938-2002), American philosopher and polemical advocate of radical libertarianism **11** 438-439

NU, U (1907-1995), Burmese statesman **11** 439-441

Nuclear physics (science)
elementary particles
Ting, Samuel Chao Chung **23** 406-408
subatomic particles
Ting, Samuel Chao Chung **23** 406-408

NUJOMA, SHAFIIHUNA ("Sam"; born 1929), first president of independent Namibia **11** 441-443

NUNN, SAM (born 1938), United States senator from Georgia **11** 443-444

NUREDDIN (Malik al-Adil Nur-al-Din Mahmud; 1118-1174), sultan of Syria and Egypt **11** 444-445

NUREYEV, RUDOLPH (born 1938), Russian-born dancer and choreographer **11** 445-446

NURI AL-SA'ID (1888-1958), Iraqi army officer, statesman, and nationalist **11** 446-447

NURMI, PAAVO (1897-1973), Finnish runner **19** 272-274

NYE, GERALD (1892-1971), American senator **21** 320-323

NYERERE, JULIUS KAMBERAGE (born 1922), Tanzanian statesman **11** 447-449

NYGREN, ANDERS (1890-1978), Lutheran bishop of Lund and representative of the so-called Lundensian school of theology **11** 449-451

NZINGA, ANNA (Pande Dona Ana Souza; 1582-1663), queen of Angola **23** 270-271

NZINGA NKUWU (died 1506), king of Kongo **11** 451-452

O

OAKLEY, ANNIE (1860-1926), American markswoman and Wild West star **11** 453-454

OATES, JOYCE CAROL (born 1938), American author **11** 454-456

OATES, TITUS (1649-1705), English leader of the Popish Plot **11** 456

OBOTE, APOLO MILTON (born 1925), Ugandan politician **11** 457

OBRECHT, JACOB (1450-1505), Dutch composer **11** 457-458

OBREGÓN, ÀLVARO (1880-1928), Mexican revolutionary general and president **11** 458-459

O'BRIEN, WILLIS (1886-1962), American film special effects pioneer **21** 324-326

O'CASEY, SEAN (1880-1964), Irish dramatist **11** 459-460

OCHOA, ELLEN (born 1958), Hispanic American electrical engineer and astronaut **11** 460-461

OCHOA, SEVERO (1905-1993), Spanish biochemist **11** 461-464

OCHS, ADOLPH SIMON (1858-1935), American publisher and philanthropist **11** 464

OCKEGHEM, JOHANNES (circa 1425-1495), Netherlandish composer **11** 464-465

O'CONNELL, DANIEL (1775-1847), Irish statesman **11** 465-467

O'CONNOR, CARROLL (1924-2001), American actor **22** 343-345

O'CONNOR, JOHN JOSEPH (1920-2000), American Roman Catholic cardinal and archbishop **22** 345-347

O'CONNOR, (MARY) FLANNERY (1925-1964), American author of short stories and novels **11** 467-468

O'CONNOR, SANDRA DAY (born 1930), United States Supreme Court justice **11** 468-470

ODETS, CLIFFORD (1906-1963), American playwright and film director **11** 470-471

ODINGA, AJUMA JARAMOGI OGINGA (born 1912), Kenyan politician **11** 471-473

ODOACER (433-493), Germanic chieftain **11** 473

ODRIÁ AMORETTI, MANUEL APOLINARIO (1897-1974), Peruvian army officer, dictator-president, and politician **11** 473-474

ODUM, HOWARD WASHINGTON (1884-1954), American sociologist, educator, and academic administrator **11** 474-476

ODUMEGWU OJUKWU, CHUKWUEMEKA (born 1933), Nigerian army general and rebel **18** 311-313

OERSTED, HANS CHRISTIAN (1777-1851), Danish physicist **11** 476-478

OERTER, AL (Alfred Adolph Oerter Jr.; born 1936), American discus thrower **21** 326-328

OFFENBACH, JACQUES (1819-1880), German-French composer **11** 478-479

OGATA, SADAKO (born 1927), United Nations High Commissioner for Refugees **11** 479-480

OGBURN, WILLIAM FIELDING (1886-1959), American sociologist **11** 480

OGDEN, PETER SKENE (1794-1854), Canadian fur trader and explorer **11** 480-481

OGILVY, DAVID MACKENZIE (1911-1999), British-American advertising executive **11** 481-482

OGLETHORPE, JAMES EDWARD (1696-1785), English general and colonizer **11** 482-483

OGOT, GRACE EMILY AKINYI (born 1930), Kenyan author and politician **11** 483-484

O'HAIR, MADALYN MURRAY (born 1919), American atheist author and radio commentator **11** 484-485

O'HARA, JOHN (1905-1970), American novelist **11** 485

O'HIGGINS, BERNARDO (1778-1842), Chilean soldier and statesman **11** 486

OHM, GEORG SIMON (1789-1854), German physicist **11** 486-487

O'KEEFFE, GEORGIA (1887-1986), American painter **11** 487-489

OKUBO, TOSHIMICHI (1830-1878), Japanese statesman **11** 489-490

OKUMA, SHIGENOBU (1838-1922), Japanese statesman **11** 490

OKYO, MARUYAMA (1733-1795), Japanese artist **23** 272-274

OLAF I TRYGGVASON (968-1000), Viking warrior and king of Norway **11** 490-493

OLAF II (circa 990-1030), king of Norway **11** 493-494

OLBRICH, JOSEPH MARIA (1867-1908), Austrian Art Nouveau architect and a founder of the Vienna Secession **11** 494-495

Old Testament
see Bible

OLDENBARNEVELT, JOHAN VAN (1547-1619), Dutch statesman **11** 495-496

OLDENBURG, CLAES (born 1929), American artist **11** 496-498

OLDS, RANSOM ELI (1864-1950), American inventor and automobile manufacturer **18** 313-315

OLIPHANT, PATRICK BRUCE (born 1935), American newspaper editorial cartoonist **11** 498-500

OLIVER, JAMES (1823-1908), American inventor and manufacturer **11** 500-501

OLIVETTI, ADRIANO (1901-1960), Italian manufacturer of typewriters, calculators, and computers **11** 501-502

OLIVIER, LAURENCE (1907-1989), English actor and director **11** 502-503

OLLER, FRANCISCO MANUEL (1833-1917), Puerto Rican artist **23** 274-275

OLMSTED, FREDERICK LAW (1822-1903), American landscape architect **11** 503-504

OLNEY, RICHARD (1835-1917), American statesman **11** 504-505

OLSEN, TILLIE (nee Tillie Lerner; born 1913), American author **20** 289-291

OLSON, CHARLES (1910-1970), American poet **11** 505-506

Olympic Games
athletes
Albright, Tenley Emma **23** 3-6
Blair, Bonnie **23** 42-44
Button, Dick **23** 55-57
Kckkonen, Urho Kaleva **23** 189-191
Spitz, Mark **23** 376-378

OLYMPIO, SYLVANUS E. (1902-1963), first president of the Republic of Togo **11** 506-507

OMAR AL-MUKHTAR (circa 1860-1931), national hero of Libya and member of the Senusy **11** 507-508

OMAR IBN AL-KHATTAB (died 644); second caliph of the Moslems **11** 508-509

OMAR IBN SAID TAL, AL-HAJJ (circa 1797-1864), West African Moslem leader **11** 509-510

OMAR KHAYYAM (1048-circa 1132), Persian astronomer, mathematician, and poet **11** 510-511

ONASSIS, JACQUELINE LEE BOUVIER KENNEDY (1929-1994), American First Lady **11** 511-513

OÑATE, JUAN DE (circa 1549-circa 1624), Spanish explorer **11** 513-514

ONDAATJE, MICHAEL (Philip Michael Ondaatji; born 1943), Canadian author and poet **18** 315-317

O'NEILL, EUGENE (1888-1953), American dramatist **11** 514-516

O'NEILL, TERENCE MARNE (1914-1990), Northern Ireland prime minister **11** 516-517

O'NEILL, THOMAS P. ("Tip"; 1912-1994), American politician **11** 517-519

ONG TENG CHEONG (1936-2002), Singapore's fifth president **11** 519-520

ONSAGER, LARS (1903-1976), American chemist **11** 520-523

OORT, JAN HENDRIK (1900-1992), Dutch astronomer **11** 523-524

Opera (musical form)
American
Bori, Lucrezia **23** 44-45
Leginska, Ethel **23** 220-222
Australian
Mackerras, Alan Charles **23** 237-239
Danish
Nørgård, Per **23** 265-267
English
Mackerras, Alan Charles **23** 237-239

OPHÜLS, MAX (Max Oppenheimer; 1902-1957), German film director and screenwriter **23** 275-277

OPPENHEIM, MERET (1913-1985), Swiss Surrealist artist **11** 524-525

OPPENHEIMER, J. ROBERT (1904-1967), American physicist **11** 525-526

ORCAGNA (1308?-1368?), Italian painter, sculptor, and architect **11** 526-527

ORELLANA, FRANCISCO DE (circa 1511-1546), Spanish explorer **11** 527-528

ORIGEN (Origenes Adamantius; circa 185-circa 254), Early Christian theologian **11** 528-529

ORLANDO, VITTORIO EMMANUELE (1860-1952), Italian statesman **11** 529-530

ORLÉANS, CHARLES (1394-1465), French prince and poet **11** 530

ORLÉANS, PHILIPPE II (1674-1723), French statesman, regent 1715-23 **11** 530-531

OROZCO, JOSÉ CLEMENTE (1883-1949), Mexican painter **12** 1-2

ORR, BOBBY (Robert Gordon Orr; born 1948), Canadian hockey player **12** 2-4

ORR, JOHN BOYD (1st Baron Orr of Brechin; 1880-1971), Scottish nutritionist and UN official **12** 4-5

ORTEGA, DANIEL (born 1945), leader of the Sandinista National Liberation Front and president of Nicaragua **12** 5-7

ORTEGA Y GASSET, JOSÉ (1883-1955), Spanish philosopher and essayist **12** 7-8

ORTELIUS, ABRAHAM (Abraham, Ortels; 1527-1598), Flemish cartographer **12** 8-9

ORTIZ, SIMON J. (born 1941), Native American author and storyteller **12** 9-12

ORTON, JOHN KINGSLEY ("Joe;" 1933-1967), British playwright **12** 12-14

ORWELL, GEORGE (1903-1950), British novelist and essayist **12** 14-15

OSBORNE, JOHN (1929-1994), English playwright **12** 16-17

OSBORNE, THOMAS MOTT (1859-1926), American reformer **12** 17-18

OSCEOLA (circa 1800-1838), Seminole Indian war chief **12** 18

OSGOOD, HERBERT LEVI (1855-1918), American historian **12** 18-19

OSLER, SIR WILLIAM (1849-1919), Canadian physician **12** 19-20

OSMAN I (Othman; 1259-1326), Turkish warrior-leader who established the Ottoman state as an independent entity **12** 20-22

OSMEÑA, SERGIO (1878-1961), Philippine lawyer and statesman **12** 22-24

OSWALD, LEE HARVEY (1939-1963), presumed assassin of John F. Kennedy **21** 328-330

OTIS, ELISHA GRAVES (1811-1861), American manufacturer and inventor **12** 24

OTIS, HARRISON GRAY (1765-1848), American statesman **12** 25

OTIS, JAMES, JR. (1725-1783), American Revolutionary statesman **12** 25-27

OTTERBEIN, PHILIP WILLIAM (1726-1813), American clergyman **12** 27-28

OTTO I (912-973), Holy Roman emperor 936-973 **12** 28-29

OTTO III (980-1002), Holy Roman emperor 996-1002 and German king 983-1002 **12** 29-30

OTTO, LOUIS KARL RUDOLF (1869-1937), German interpreter of religion **12** 30-32

OTTO, NIKOLAUS AUGUST (1832-1891), German engineer and inventor **21** 331-333

OTTO OF FREISING (circa 1114-1158), German historiographer and philosopher of history **12** 30

OUD, JACOBUS JOHANNES PIETER (1890-1963), Dutch architect **12** 32

OUGHTRED, WILLIAM (1574-1660), English mathematician **23** 277-279

OUSMANE, SEMBENE (born 1923), Senegalese novelist and film maker **12** 32-33

OU-YANG HSIU (1007-1072), Chinese author and statesman **12** 33-34

OVID (Publius Ovidius Naso; 43 B.C.-circa. A.D. 18), Roman elegiac and epic poet **12** 34-36

OVINGTON, MARY WHITE (1865-1951), civil rights reformer and a founder of the National Association for the Advancement of Colored People **12** 36-37

OWEN, DAVID ANTHONY LLEWELLYN (born 1938), English peace envoy in former Yugoslavia for the European Community **12** 37-39

OWEN, SIR RICHARD (1804-1892), English zoologist **12** 39

OWEN, ROBERT (1771-1858), British socialist pioneer **12** 39-40

OWEN, ROBERT DALE (1801-1877), Scottish-born American legislator **12** 40-41

OWEN, RUTH BRYAN (1885-1954), American congresswoman, diplomat, and author **12** 41-43

OWEN, WILFRED (1893-1918), English poet **20** 291-293

OWENS, JESSE (1913-1980), African American track star **12** 43-44

OXENSTIERNA, COUNT AXEL GUSTAFSSON (1583-1654), Swedish statesman **12** 44-45

Oxford Committee for Famine Relief (Oxfam)
Murray, Gilbert **23** 250-253

OZ, AMOS (born 1939), Israeli author **12** 45-47

OZAL, TURGUT (born 1927), Turkish prime minister and president **12** 47-49

OZAWA, SEIJI (born 1935), Japanese musician and conductor **12** 49-51

OZU, YASUJIRO (1903-1963), Japanese film director **23** 279-281

P

PA CHIN (pen name of Li Fei-kan; born 1904), Chinese novelist **12** 53-54

PABST, G. W. (Georg Wilhelm Pabst; 1885-1967), Austrian film director **23** 282-284

PACHELBEL, JOHANN (1653-1706), German composer and organist **12** 52

PACHER, MICHAEL (circa 1435-98), Austro-German painter and wood carver **12** 53

PACINO, AL (Alfredo James Pacino; born 1940), American actor and film director **23** 284-286

PACKARD, DAVID (1912-1996), cofounder of Hewlett-Packard Company and deputy secretary of defense under President Nixon **12** 54-56

PADEREWSKI, IGNACE JAN (1860-1941), Polish pianist, composer, and statesman **12** 56-57

PADMORE, GEORGE (1902/03-1959), Trinidadian leftist political activist **12** 57-58

PÁEZ, JOSÉ ANTONIO (1790-1873), Venezuelan general and president 1831-46 **12** 58

PAGANINI, NICCOLO (1782-1840), Italian violinist and composer **12** 58-59

Page, Robert (born 1944), British guitarist
Led Zeppelin **23** 216-218

PAGE, THOMAS NELSON (1853-1922), American author and diplomat **12** 59-60

PAGE, WALTER HINES (1855-1918), American journalist and diplomat **12** 60-61

PAGELS, ELAINE HIESEY (born 1943), historian of religion **12** 61-62

PAGLIA, CAMILLE (born 1947), American author and social critic **23** 286-288

PAIGE, SATCHEL (Leroy Robert Paige; 1906-1982), African American baseball player **12** 62-65

PAINE, JOHN KNOWLES (1839-1905), American composer **12** 65

PAINE, THOMAS (1737-1809), English-born American journalist and Revolutionary propagandist **12** 66-67

PAISLEY, IAN K. (born 1926), political leader and minister of religion in Northern Ireland **12** 67-69

PALACKÝ, FRANTIŠEK (1798-1876), Czech historian and statesman **12** 69-70

PALAMAS, KOSTES (1859-1943), Greek poet **12** 70

PALESTRINA, GIOVANNI PIERLUIGI DA (circa 1525-94), Italian composer **12** 70-72

PALEY, GRACE (born, 1922), American author and activist **22** 348-350

PALEY, WILLIAM (1743-1805), English theologian and moral philosopher **12** 72

PALEY, WILLIAM S. (1901-1990), founder and chairman of the Columbia Broadcasting System **12** 72-75

PALLADIO, ANDREA (1508-1580), Italian architect **12** 75-77

PALMA, RICARDO (1833-1919), Peruvian poet, essayist, and short-story writer **12** 77

PALMER, ALEXANDER MITCHELL (1872-1936), American politician and jurist **12** 77-78

PALMER, ARNOLD DANIEL (born 1929), American golfer **12** 78-80

PALMER, NATHANIEL BROWN (1799-1877), American sea captain **12** 80-81

PALMER, PHOEBE WORRALL (1807-1847), American evangelist **23** 288-290

PALMERSTON, 3D VISCOUNT (Henry John Temple; 1784-1865), English prime minister 1855-65 **12** 81-83

PAN KU (32-92), Chinese historian and man of letters **12** 86-87

PANDIT, VIJAYA LAKSHMI (1900-1990), Indian diplomat and politician **12** 83-84

Pandora's Box (film)
Pabst, G. W. **23** 282-284

PANETTA, LEON E. (born 1938), Democratic congressman from California and chief of staff to President Clinton **12** 84-85

PANKHURST, CHRISTABEL HARRIETTE (1880-1948), English reformer and suffragette **22** 350-352

PANKHURST, EMMELINE (1858-1928), English reformer **12** 85-86

PANNENBERG, WOLFHART (born 1928), German Protestant theologian **12** 87-88

Papacy (Roman Catholic Church)
political powers
Paul V **23** 297-299

PAPANDREOU, ANDREAS (1919-1996), Greek scholar and statesman and prime minister **12** 88-91

PAPINEAU, LOUIS-JOSEPH (1786-1871), French-Canadian radical political leader **12** 91

PARACELSUS, PHILIPPUS AUREOLUS (1493-1541), Swiss physician and alchemist **12** 91-93

PARBO, ARVI (born 1926), Australian industrial giant **12** 93-94

PARÉ, AMBROISE (1510-1590), French military surgeon **12** 94-95

PARETO, VILFREDO (1848-1923), Italian sociologist, political theorist, and economist **12** 95-96

PARHAM, CHARLES FOX (1873-1929), American evangelist **23** 291-293

PARIZEAU, JACQUES (born 1930), Canadian politician and premier of Quebec **12** 96-99

PARK, CHUNG HEE (1917-1979), Korean soldier and statesman **12** 99-102

PARK, MAUD WOOD (1871-1955), suffragist and first president of the League of Women Voters **12** 102

PARK, ROBERT E. (1864-1944), American sociologist **12** 102-104

PARK, WILLIAM HALLOCK (1863-1939), American physician **12** 104-105

PARKER, CHARLES CHRISTOPHER, JR. (Charlie Parker; 1920-55), American jazz musician **12** 105-106

PARKER, DOROTHY ROTHSCHILD (1893-1967), American writer **12** 106

PARKER, ELY SAMUEL (Ha-sa-no-an-da; 1828-1895), Native American tribal leader **12** 106-108

PARKER, HORATIO WILLIAM (1863-1919), American composer **12** 109

PARKER, QUANAH (c. 1845-1911), Native American religious leader **12** 109-112

PARKER, THEODORE (1810-1860), American Unitarian clergyman **12** 112-113

PARKES, ALEXANDER (1813-1890), British metallurgist and inventor of plastic **21** 334-336

PARKES, SIR HENRY (1815-1896), Australian statesman **12** 113

PARKMAN, FRANCIS (1823-1893), American historian **12** 113-115

PARKS, GORDON (born 1912), American photographer, composer, and filmmaker **19** 275-277

PARKS, ROSA LEE MCCAULEY (born 1913), American civil rights leader **12** 115-116

PARMENIDES (flourished 475 B.C.), Greek philosopher **12** 116-117

PARMIGIANINO (1503-1540), Italian painter **12** 117

PARNELL, CHARLES STEWART (1846-1891), Irish nationalist leader **12** 117-119

Parochial schools (United States) *see* Education (United States)

PARRINGTON, VERNON LOUIS (1871-1929), American historian **12** 119-120

PARSONS, SIR CHARLES ALGERNON (1854-1931), British engineer **12** 120-121

PARSONS, FRANK (1854-1908), American educator and reformer **12** 121-122

PARSONS, LOUELLA (Louella Oetlinger; 1881-1972), American gossip columnist **21** 336-338

PARSONS, LUCY GONZÁLEZ (1853-1942), Mexican American activist and author **23** 293-295

PARSONS, TALCOTT (1902-1979), American sociologist **12** 122

PÄRT, ARVO (born 1935), Estonian musician **23** 295-297

PASCAL, BLAISE (1623-1662), French scientist and philosopher **12** 122-124

PASHA, ENVER (1881-1922), Turkish soldier and Young Turk leader **5** 290-291

PASHA, TEWFIK (1852-1892), khedive of Egypt 1879-92 **15** 157-158

PASTERNAK, BORIS LEONIDOVICH (1890-1960), Russian poet, novelist, and translator **12** 124-125

PASTEUR, LOUIS (1822-1895), French chemist and biologist **12** 125-127

PATCHEN, KENNETH (1911-1972), American experimental poet and novelist **12** 128-129

PATEL, VALLABHBHAI (1875-1950), Indian political leader **12** 129-130

PATER, WALTER HORATIO (1839-1894), English author **12** 130-131

PATERSON, ANDREW BARTON (1864-1941), Australian folk poet **12** 131-132

PATERSON, WILLIAM (1745-1806), American jurist **12** 132-133

PATIÑO, SIMÓN ITURRI (1862-1947), Bolivian industrialist and entrepreneur **12** 133-134

PATON, ALAN STEWART (1903-1988), South African writer and liberal leader **12** 134-135

PATRICK, JENNIE R. (born 1949), African American chemical engineer **12** 136-137

PATRICK, RUTH (born 1907), American limnologist **12** 137-138

PATRICK, SAINT (died circa 460), British missionary bishop to Ireland **12** 135-136

PATTEN, SIMON NELSON (1852-1922), American economist **12** 138-139

PATTERSON, FREDERICK DOUGLAS (1901-1988), African American educator **12** 139-140

PATTON, GEORGE SMITH, JR. (1885-1945), American Army officer **12** 140-141

PAUL I (1754-1801), Russian czar 1796-1801 **12** 143-144

PAUL III (Alessandro Farnese; 1468-1549), pope 1534-49 **12** 144-145

PAUL IV (Giampietro Carafa; 1476-1559), pope 1555-59 **12** 145-146

PAUL V (Camillo Borghese; 1550-1621), Italian pope **23** 297-299

PAUL VI (Giovanni Battista Montini; 1897-1978), pope **12** 146-148

PAUL, ALICE (1885-1977), American feminist and women's rights activist **19** 277-280

PAUL, SAINT (died 66/67), Christian theologian and Apostle **12** 141-143

PAULI, WOLFGANG ERNST (1900-1958), Austrian theoretical physicist **12** 149

PAULING, LINUS CARL (born 1901), American chemist **12** 150-152

PAVAROTTI, LUCIANO (born 1935), Italian tenor **12** 152-154

PAVESE, CESARE (1908-1950), Italian novelist, poet, and critic **12** 154-155

PAVLOV, IVAN PETROVICH (1849-1936), Russian physiologist **12** 155-157

PAVLOVA, ANNA (1881-1931), Russian ballet dancer **12** 157-159

PAYNE, JOHN HOWARD (1791-1852), American actor, playwright, and songwriter **12** 159

PAYNE-GAPOSCHKIN, CECILIA (1900-1979), American astronomer **12** 159-161

PAYTON, WALTER (1954-1999), American football player **20** 294-296

PAZ, OCTAVIO (1914-1998), Mexican diplomat, critic, editor, translator, poet, and essayist **12** 161-162

PAZ ESTENSSORO, VICTOR (1907-2001), Bolivian statesman and reformer **12** 163-164

PAZ ZAMORA, JAIME (born 1939), president of Bolivia (1989-) **12** 165-167

PÁZMÁNY, PÉTER (1570-1637), Hungarian archbishop **12** 164-165

PEABODY, ELIZABETH PALMER (1804-1894), American educator and author **12** 167-168

PEABODY, GEORGE (1795-1869), American merchant, financier, and philanthropist **12** 168

PEACOCK, THOMAS LOVE (1785-1866), English novelist and satirist **12** 169

PEALE, CHARLES WILLSON (1741-1827), American painter and scientist **12** 169-171

PEALE, NORMAN VINCENT (1898-1993), American religious leader who blended psychotherapy and religion **12** 171-172

PEALE, REMBRANDT (1778-1860), American painter **12** 172-173

PEARSE, PATRICK HENRY (1879-1916), Irish poet, educator, and revolutionary **12** 173-174

PEARSON, LESTER BOWLES (1897-1972), Canadian statesman and diplomat, prime minister **12** 174-175

PEARY, ROBERT EDWIN (1856-1920), American explorer **12** 175-176

PECHSTEIN, HERMANN MAX (1881-1955), German Expressionist painter and graphic artist **12** 176-177

PECK, ROBERT NEWTON (born 1928), American author of children's literature **12** 177-178

PECKINPAH, SAM (1925-1984), American film director **21** 338-340

PEDRARIAS (Pedro Arias de Ávila; circa 1440-1531), Spanish conqueror and colonial governor **12** 179

PEDRO I (1798-1834), emperor of Brazil and king of Portugal **12** 179-180

PEDRO II (1825-1891), emperor of Brazil 1831-89 **12** 180-181

PEEL, SIR ROBERT (1788-1850), English statesman, prime minister 1834-35 and 1841-46 **12** 181-183

PÉGUY, CHARLES PIERRE (1873-1914), French poet **12** 183-184

PEI, I. M. (Ieoh Ming Pei; born 1917), Chinese-American architect **12** 184-187

PEIRCE, BENJAMIN (1809-1880), American mathematician **21** 340-342

PEIRCE, CHARLES SANDERS (1839-1914), American scientist and philosopher **12** 187-188

PEIXOTO, FLORIANO (1839-1895), Brazilian marshal, president 1891-94 **12** 188-189

PELAGIUS (died circa 430), British theologian **12** 189-190

PELE (Edson Arantes Do Nascimento Pele; born 1940), Brazilian soccer player **12** 190-191

PELLI, CESAR (born 1926), Hispanic American architect and educator **12** 191-192

PELTIER, LEONARD (born 1944), Native American activist **12** 193-195

PEÑA, PACO (Francisco Peña Pérez; born 1942), Spanish guitarist and composer **23** 299-301

PENDERECKI, KRZYSZTOF (born 1933), Polish composer **12** 195-197

PENDLETON, EDMUND (1721-1803), American political leader **12** 197-198

PENDLETON, GEORGE HUNT (1825-1889), American politician **12** 198

PENFIELD, WILDER GRAVES (1891-1976), Canadian neurosurgeon **12** 198-200

PENN, WILLIAM (1644-1718), English Quaker, founder of Pennsylvania **12** 200-202

PENNEY, J. C. (James Cash Penney; 1875-1971), American chain store executive and philanthropist **12** 202-203

PENNINGTON, MARY ENGLE (1872-1952), American chemist **22** 352-355

Pennsylvania (state, United States) politics
Logan, George **23** 231-234

PENROSE, BOIES (1860-1921), American senator and political boss **12** 203-204

PENROSE, ROGER (born 1931), British mathematician and physicist **12** 204-205

PENSKE, ROGER (born 1937), American businessman and race car team owner **19** 280-282

Pentecostal sects (religion)
Parham, Charles Fox **23** 291-293

PENZIAS, ARNO ALLEN (born 1932), German American physicist **23** 301-304

PEP, WILLIE (William Guiglermo Papaleo; born 1922), American boxer **21** 342-344

PEPPER, CLAUDE DENSON (1900-1989), Florida attorney, state representative, U.S. senator, and U.S. representative **12** 205-206

PEPPERELL, SIR WILLIAM (1696-1759), American merchant and soldier **12** 206-207

PEPYS, SAMUEL (1633-1703), English diarist **12** 207-208

PERCY, WALKER (1916-1990), American author **19** 282-284

PEREGRINUS, PETRUS (flourished 1261-69), French scholastic and scientist **12** 208

PERELMAN, S. J. (Sidney Jerome Perelman; 1904-1979), American cartoonist, satirist, and parodist **12** 209-210

PERES, SHIMON (born 1923), head of the Israel Labour Party and Israeli prime minister (1984-1986) **12** 210-211

PERETZ, ISAAC LOEB (1851-1915), Jewish poet, novelist, and playwright **12** 212

PÉREZ, CARLOS ANDRÉS (born 1922), president of Venezuela (1989-1993) **12** 212-214

PÉREZ DE CUÉLLAR, JAVIER (born 1920), Peruvian foreign service officer

and secretary general of the United Nations (1982-) **12** 214-215

PÉREZ ESQUIVEL, ADOLFO (born 1931), Argentine artist and human rights activist **12** 215-217

PÉREZ JIMENEZ, MARCOS (1914-2001), Venezuelan dictator **12** 217-218

PERGOLESI, GIOVANNI BATTISTA (1710-1736), Italian composer **12** 218-219

PERICLES (circa 495-429 B.C.), Athenian statesman **12** 219-221

PERKINS, FRANCES (1882-1965), American statesman and social worker **12** 221-222

PERKINS, GEORGE WALBRIDGE (1862-1920), American businessman and banker **21** 344-347

PERKINS, WILLIAM MAXWELL EVARTS (1884-1947), American editor of fiction who discovered and developed brilliant authors **12** 222-223

PERLE, GEORGE (born 1915), American musician **12** 223-224

PERLMAN, ITZHAK (born 1945), American musician **18** 318-320

PERÓN, EVA (MARÍA) DUARTE DE (1919-1952), the second wife and political partner of President Juan Perón of Argentina **12** 225-226

PERÓN, ISABEL MARTINEZ DE (born 1931), first woman president of Argentina (1974-1976) **12** 226-228

PERÓN, JUAN DOMINGO (1895-1974), Argentine statesman, president 1946-55 **12** 228-230

PEROT, HENRY ROSS (born 1930), American businessman and activist **12** 230-231

PÉROTIN (Perotinus; flourished circa 1185-1205), French composer and musician **12** 231-232

PERRAULT, CLAUDE (1613-1688), French scientist and architect **12** 232-233

PERRET, AUGUSTE (1874-1954), French architect **12** 233

PERRIN, JEAN BAPTISTE (1870-1942), French physicist **12** 233-236

PERRY, HAROLD ROBERT (1916-1991), African American Roman Catholic bishop **12** 236-237

PERRY, MATTHEW CALBRAITH (1794-1858), American naval officer **12** 237-239

PERRY, OLIVER HAZARD (1785-1819), American naval officer **12** 239

PERRY, RALPH BARTON (1876-1957), American philosopher **12** 239-240

PERRY, WILLIAM JAMES (born 1927), President Clinton's secretary of defense (1994-) **12** 240-242

PERSE, SAINT-JOHN (Alexis Saint-Léger Léger; 1887-1975), French poet and diplomat **12** 242-243

PERSHING, JOHN JOSEPH (1860-1948), American general **12** 243-244

PERTH, 16TH EARL OF (James Eric Drummond; 1876-1951), English statesman **12** 244-245

PERUGINO (circa 1450-1523), Italian painter **12** 245-246

PERUTZ, MAX (1914-2002), English crystallographer and biochemist **12** 246-248

PESOTTA, ROSE (1896-1965), American union organizer **12** 248-249

PESTALOZZI, JOHANN HEINRICH (1746-1827), Swiss educator **12** 249-250

PÉTAIN, HENRI PHILIPPE (1856-1951), French general and statesman **12** 250-252

PETER I (Peter the Great; 1672-1725), czar of Russia 1682-1725 **12** 253-256

PETER I (1844-1921), king of Serbia 1903-18, and of the Serbs, Croats, and Slovenes 1918-21 **12** 256

PETER III (Pedro; circa 1239-85), king of Aragon 1276-85 **12** 256-257

PETER, SAINT (died circa 65), apostle and bishop of Rome **12** 252-253

PETERS, CARL (1856-1918), German explorer and colonizer **12** 257-258

PETERSON, EDITH R. (born Edith Elizabeth Runne; 1914-1992), American medical researcher **12** 258-259

PETERSON, OSCAR (born 1925), Canadian pianist **23** 304-306

PETO, JOHN FREDERICK (1854-1907), American painter **12** 259

PETÖFI, SÁNDOR (1823-1849), Hungarian poet and revolutionary leader **23** 306-308

PETRARCH (Francesco Petrarca; 1304-74), Italian poet **12** 259-261

PETRIE, SIR WILLIAM MATTHEW FLINDERS (1853-1942), English archeologist **12** 261-262

PETRONIUS ARBITER (died circa 66), Roman author **12** 262-263

PEVSNER, ANTOINE (1886-1962), Russian sculptor and painter **12** 263-264

PHAEDRUS (c. 15 BC-c. 50), Greek/Roman fabulists **20** 296-297

Pharmacology (science)
Plotkin, Mark J. **23** 308-310

PHIBUN SONGKHRAM, LUANG (1897-1964), Thai statesman, prime minister 1938-1944 and 1948-1957 **12** 264-265

PHIDIAS (flourished circa 475-425 B.C.), Greek sculptor **12** 265-267

Philanthropists, American
20th century
Malone, Annie Turnbo **23** 242-243

Philanthropists, Spanish
Bori, Lucrezia **23** 44-45

PHILIDOR, FRANÇOIS-ANDRÉ (François-André Danican-Philidor; 1726-1795), French composer and chess player **21** 347-349

PHILIP (died 1676), American Wampanoag Indian chief 1662-76 **12** 267-268

PHILIP II (382-336 B.C.), king of Macedon 359-336 **12** 269-271

PHILIP II (Philip Augustus; 1165-1223), king of France 1180-1223 **12** 268-269

PHILIP II (1527-1598), king of Spain 1556-1598 **12** 271-273

PHILIP III (1578-1621), king of Spain 1598-1621 **12** 273-274

PHILIP IV (the Fair; 1268-1314), king of France 1285-1314 **12** 274

PHILIP IV (1605-1665), king of Spain 1621-65 **12** 275

PHILIP V (1683-1746), king of Spain 1700-46 **12** 276-277

PHILIP VI (1293-1350), king of France 1328-50 **12** 277-278

PHILIP THE GOOD (1396-1467), duke of Burgundy 1419-67 **12** 278-279

PHILLIP, ARTHUR (1738-1814), English governor of New South Wales **12** 279-280

PHILLIPS, DAVID GRAHAM (1867-1911), American journalist and novelist **12** 280-281

PHILLIPS, WENDELL (1811-1884), American abolitionist and social reformer **12** 281-282

PHIPS, SIR WILLIAM (1650/51-95), American shipbuilder and colonial governor **12** 283

PHOTIUS (circa 820-891), Byzantine patriarch **12** 283-284

Photography
as art form
Richter, Gerhard **23** 338-340
Wall, Jeff **23** 434-436
of celebrities
Karsh, Yousuf **23** 184-187

PHYFE, DUNCAN (1768-1854), American cabinetmaker **12** 284-285

Physics (science)
electrodynamics
Wilson, Kenneth Geddes **23** 446-448

Physiology (science)
blood
Pool, Judith Graham **23** 315-316

PIAF, EDITH (Edith Giovanna Gassion; 1915-63), French music hall/cabaret singer **12** 285-287

PIAGET, JEAN (1896-1980), Swiss psychologist and educator **12** 287-288

Pianist, The (film)
Polanski, Roman **23** 310-312

PIANKHI (ruled circa 741-circa 712 B.C.), Nubian king **12** 288-289

Piano (musical instrument)
Armstrong, Lillian Hardin **23** 15-17
Arrau, Claudio **23** 17-18
Beach, Amy **23** 30-32
Lecuona, Ernesto **23** 213-216
Leginska, Ethel **23** 220-222
Pärt, Arvo **23** 295-297
Peterson, Oscar Emanuel **23** 304-306
Uchida, Mitsuko **23** 413-415
Williams, Mary Lou **23** 444-446

Piano, The (film)
Campion, Jane **23** 58-60

PIANO, RENZO (born 1937), Italian architect, lecturer, and designer **12** 289-291

PICABIA, FRANCIS (1879-1953), French artist, writer, and bon vivant **12** 291-292

PICASSO, PABLO (1881-1973), Spanish painter, sculptor, and graphic artist **12** 292-295

PICASSO, PALOMA (born 1949), Spanish fashion designer **12** 295-297

PICCARD, AUGUSTE (1884-1962), Swiss scientist **12** 297-298

PICCARD, JACQUES ERNEST JEAN (born 1922), Swiss explorer, scientist, oceanographer, and engineer **18** 320-322

PICKENS, THOMAS BOONE JR. (T. Boone Pickens; born 1928), American businessman **19** 284-286

PICKERING, EDWARD CHARLES (1846-1919), American astronomer **12** 298

PICKERING, TIMOTHY (1745-1829), American Revolutionary soldier and statesman **12** 298-299

PICKETT, BILL (1870-1932), American rodeo cowboy **19** 286-288

PICKFORD, MARY (Gladys Louise Smith; 1893-1979), Canadian-American actress, screenwriter, and film producer **19** 288-290

PICO DELLA MIRANDOLA, CONTE GIOVANNI (1463-1494), Italian philosopher and humanist **12** 299-300

PIERCE, FRANKLIN (1804-1869), American statesman, president 1853-57 **12** 300-301

PIERCE, JOHN ROBINSON (born 1910), American electronics engineer and author **21** 349-351

PIERO DELLA FRANCESCA (circa 1415/20-92), Italian painter **12** 301-302

PIGOU, ARTHUR CECIL (1877-1959), English economist **12** 302

PIKE, ZEBULON (1779-1813), American soldier and explorer **12** 302-304

PILLSBURY, CHARLES ALFRED (1842-1899), American businessman **12** 304

PILON, GERMAIN (circa 1535-90), French sculptor **12** 305

PILSUDSKI, JOSEPH (1867-1935), Polish general, president 1918-21 **12** 305-306

PINCHBACK, PINCKNEY BENTON STEWART (1837-1921), African American politician **12** 306-308

PINCHOT, GIFFORD (1865-1946), American conservationist and public official **12** 308-309

PINCKNEY, CHARLES (1757-1824), American politician and diplomat **12** 309-310

PINCKNEY, CHARLES COTESWORTH (1745-1825), American statesman **12** 310

PINCUS, GREGORY GOODWIN (1903-1967), American biologist **12** 310-312

PINDAR (552/518-438 B.C.), Greek lyric poet **12** 312-313

PINEL, PHILIPPE (1745-1826), French physician **12** 313-314

PINERO, ARTHUR WING (1855-1934), English playwright **18** 322-324

PINKERTON, ALLEN (1819-1884), American detective **12** 314-315

PINKHAM, LYDIA ESTES (1819-1883), American patent medicine manufacturer **21** 351-353

PINKNEY, WILLIAM (1764-1822), American attorney, diplomat, and statesman **22** 355-357

PINOCHET UGARTE, AUGUSTO (born 1915), Chilean military leader and dictator **12** 315-317

PINTER, HAROLD (born 1930), English playwright **12** 317-318

PINTO, ISAAC (1720-1791), Jewish merchant and scholar **12** 318

PINZÓN, MARTIN ALONSO (1440?-1493), Spanish navigator **22** 358-360

PINZÓN, VICENTE YÁÑEZ (1460?-1524?), Spanish navigator **22** 360-361

PIO, PADRE (Francesco Forgione; 1887-1968), Italian priest **20** 297-299

PIPPIN, HORACE (1888-1946), African American painter **12** 318-319

PIRANDELLO, LUIGI (1867-1936), Italian playwright novelist, and critic **12** 319-321

PIRANESI, GIOVANNI BATTISTA (1720-1778), Italian engraver and architect **12** 321-322

PIRENNE, JEAN HENRI (Jean Henri Otto Lucien Marie Pirenne; 1862-1935), Belgian historian **12** 322-323

PISANELLO (Antonio Pisano; before 1395-1455), Italian painter and medalist **12** 323-324

PISANO, GIOVANNI (circa 1250-1314/17), Italian sculptor **12** 324-325

PISANO, NICOLA (Nicola d'Apulia; circa 1220/25-1278/84), Italian sculptor **12** 325

PISSARO, CAMILLE (1830-1903), French painter **12** 326-327

PISTON, WALTER (born 1894), American composer **12** 327-328

PITT, WILLIAM, THE ELDER (1708-1778), English statesman **12** 328-329

PITT, WILLIAM, THE YOUNGER (1759-1806), English statesman **12** 329-331

PIUS II (Enea Silvio de'Piccolomini; 1405-64), pope 1458-64 **12** 331

PIUS IV (Giovanni Angelo de' Medici; 1499-1565), pope 1559-65 **12** 332

PIUS V (Antonio Ghislieri; 1504-72), pope 1566-72 **12** 332-333

PIUS VI (Gianangelo Braschi; 1717-99), pope 1775-99 **12** 333-334

PIUS VII (Luigi Barnabà Chiaramonti; 1740-1823), pope 1880-23 **12** 334-335

PIUS IX (Giovanni Maria Mastai-Ferretti; 1792-1878), pope 1846-78 **12** 335-336

PIUS X (Giuseppe Melchiorre Sarto; 1835-1914), pope 1903-14 **12** 336-337

PIUS XI (Ambrogio Damiano Achille Ratti; 1857-1939), pope 1922-39 **12** 337-339

PIUS XII (Eugenio Maria Giuseppe Pacelli; 1876-1958), pope 1939-58 **12** 339-340

PIZARRO, FRANCISCO (circa 1474-1541), Spanish conquistador in Peru **12** 340-341

PLAATJE, SOLOMON TSHEKISHO (1878-1932), South African writer **12** 341-342

PLANCK, MAX KARL ERNST LUDWIG (1858-1947), German physicist **12** 342-344

Plane geometry
see Geometry–plane

Plant, Robert (born 1948), British singer Led Zeppelin **23** 216-218

Plants, medicinal
Plotkin, Mark J. **23** 308-310

PLATH, SYLVIA (1932-1963), American poet and novelist **12** 344-345

PLATO (428-347 B.C.), Greek philosopher **12** 345-347

PLATT, THOMAS COLLIER (1833-1910), American politician **12** 347-348

PLAUTUS (circa 254-circa 184 B.C.), Roman writer **12** 348-350

PLAZA LASSO, GALO (1906-1987), Ecuadorian statesman **12** 350-351

PLEKHANOV, GEORGI VALENTINOVICH (1856-1918), Russian revolutionist and social philosopher **12** 351-352

PLENTY COUPS (c. 1848-1932), Native American tribal leader and Crow chief **12** 352-355

PLINY THE ELDER (23/24-79), Roman encyclopedist **12** 355-356

PLINY THE YOUNGER (circa 61-circa 113), Roman author and administrator **12** 356

PLISETSKAYA, MAYA MIKHAILOVNA (born 1925), Russian ballet dancer **12** 356-358

PLOTINUS (205-270), Greek philosopher, founder of Neoplatonism **12** 358-359

PLOTKIN, MARK (born 1955), American ethnobotanist and environmentalist **23** 308-310

PLUTARCH (circa 46-circa 120), Greek biographer **12** 359-360

PO CHÜ-I (772-846), Chinese poet **12** 362-363

POBEDONOSTSEV, KONSTANTIN PETROVICH (1827-1907), Russian statesman and jurist **12** 360-361

POCAHONTAS (circa 1595-1617), American Indian princess **12** 361-362

POE, EDGAR ALLAN (1809-1849), American writer **12** 363-365

POINCARÉ, JULES HENRI (1854-1912), French mathematician **12** 365-366

POINCARÉ, RAYMOND (1860-1934), French statesman **12** 366-368

POIRET, PAUL (1879-1944), French fashion designer **19** 291-293

POITIER, SIDNEY (born 1927), African American actor and director **12** 368-370

POL POT (1928-1998), Cambodian Communist and premier of Democratic Kampuchéa (1976-1979) **12** 382-384

POLANSKI, ROMAN (born 1933), Polish filmmaker and director **23** 310-312

POLANYI, JOHN CHARLES (born 1929), Canadian scientist and Nobel Prize winner **12** 370-372

POLANYI, KARL (1886-1964), Hungarian economic historian **12** 372

POLANYI, MICHAEL (1891-1976), Hungarian medical doctor, physical chemist, social thinker, and philosopher **12** 372-373

POLIZIANO, ANGELO (Politian; 1454-94), Italian poet **12** 373-374

POLK, JAMES KNOX (1795-1849), American statesman, president 1845-49 **12** 374-376

POLK, LEONIDAS LAFAYETTE (1837-1892), American agrarian crusader and editor **12** 376-377

POLKE, SIGMAR (born 1941), German painter **23** 312-315

POLLAIUOLO, ANTONIO (circa 1432-98), Italian painter, sculptor, goldsmith, and engraver **12** 377-378

POLLARD, ALBERT FREDERICK (1869-1948), English historian **12** 378

POLLOCK, JACKSON (1912-1956), American painter **12** 379-380

POLO, MARCO (circa 1254-circa 1324), Venetian traveler and writer **12** 380-382

POLYBIOS (circa 203-120 B.C.), Greek historian **12** 384-385

POLYKLEITOS (flourished circa 450-420 B.C.), Greek sculptor **12** 385-386

POMBAL, MARQUÊS DE (Sebastião José de Carvalho e Mello; 1699-1782), Portuguese statesman **12** 386-387

POMPEY (106-48 B.C.), Roman general and statesman **12** 387-389

POMPIDOU, GEORGES (1911-1974), second president of the French Fifth Republic (1969-1974) **12** 389-390

POMPONAZZI, PIETRO (1462-1525), Italian Aristotelian philosopher **12** 390-391

PONCE DE LEÓN, JUAN (1460?-1521), Spanish conqueror and explorer **12** 391-392

PONIATOWSKA, ELENA (born 1933), Mexican journalist, novelist, essayist, and short-story writer **12** 392-393

PONTIAC (circa 1720-69), Ottawa Indian chief **12** 393-394

PONTORMO (1494-1556), Italian painter **12** 394-395

POOL, JUDITH GRAHAM (1919-1975), American physiologist **23** 315-316

POPE, ALEXANDER (1688-1744), English poet and satirist **12** 395-397

POPE, JOHN RUSSELL (1874-1937), American architect in the classical tradition **12** 397-399

POPHAM, WILLIAM JAMES (born 1930), American educator active in educational test development **12** 399-401

POPOVA, LIUBOV SERGEEVNA (1889-1924), Russian and Soviet avant-garde artist **12** 401-402

POPPER, SIR KARL RAIMUND (1902-1994), Austrian philosopher **12** 402

PORSCHE, FERDINAND SR. (1875-1951), Austrian German automobile designer and engineer **19** 293-295

PORTA, GIACOMO DELLA (circa 1537-1602), Italian architect **12** 402-403

PORTA, GIAMBATTISTA DELLA (1535-1615), Italian scientist and dramatist **12** 403-404

PORTALES PLAZAZUELOS, DIEGO JOSÉ VÍCTOR (1793-1837), Chilean statesman **12** 404

PORTER, COLE ALBERT (1891-1964), American composer **12** 405-406

PORTER, EDWIN STRATTON (1870-1941), American filmmaker **20** 299-301

PORTER, KATHERINE ANNE (1890-1980), American writer **12** 406-407

PORTINARI, CÂNDIDO (1903-1962), Brazilian painter **12** 407-408

PORTOLÁ, GASPAR DE (circa 1723-1784), Spanish explorer and colonial governor **12** 408

Portrait Gallery of Canada (Toronto)
Karsh, Yousuf **23** 184-187

Portugal (Portuguese Republic; nation, Europe)
• EMPIRE and DECLINE
colonization (Africa)
Nzinga, Anna **23** 270-271

PORTZAMPARC, CHRISTIAN DE (born 1944), French architect **18** 324-326

POST, CHARLES WILLIAM (1854-1914), American pioneer in the manufacture and mass-marketing of breakfast cereals **12** 408-409

POST, EMILY PRICE (1873-1960), American authority on etiquette **12** 409-410

POTEMKIN, GRIGORI ALEKSANDROVICH (1739-1791), Russian administrator and field marshal **12** 411-412

POTTER, BEATRIX (Helen Beatrix Potter; 1866-1943), English author and illustrator **18** 326-328

POTTER, DAVID M. (1910-1971), American historian **12** 412

POTTER, DENNIS (1935-1994), British essayist, playwright, screenwriter, and novelist **12** 412-414

POULENC, FRANCIS (1899-1963), French composer **12** 414-415

POUND, EZRA LOOMIS (1885-1972), American poet, editor, and critic **12** 415-417

POUND, ROSCOE (1870-1964), American jurist and botanist **12** 417-418

POUSSIN, NICOLAS (1594-1665), French painter **12** 418-420

POWDERLY, TERENCE VINCENT (1849-1924), American labor leader **12** 420-421

POWELL, ADAM CLAYTON, JR. (1908-1972), African American political leader and Baptist minister **12** 421-422

POWELL, ANTHONY (1905-2000), English novelist **12** 422-423

POWELL, COLIN LUTHER (born 1937), African American chairman of the Joint Chiefs of Staff **12** 424-425

POWELL, JOHN WESLEY (1834-1902), American geologist, anthropologist, and explorer **12** 425-426

POWELL, LEWIS F., JR. (1907-1998), U.S. Supreme Court justice (1972-1987) **12** 426-428

POWERS, HIRAM (1805-1873), American sculptor **12** 428-429

POWHATAN (circa 1550-1618), Native American tribal chief **12** 429-430

PRADO UGARTECHE, MANUEL (1889-1967), Peruvian statesman **12** 430-431

PRAETORIUS, MICHAEL (circa 1571-1621), German composer and theorist **12** 431-432

PRAN, DITH (born 1942), Cambodian American journalist and activist **18** 328-331

PRANDTAUER, JAKOB (1660-1726), Austrian baroque architect **12** 432

PRASAD, RAJENDRA (1884-1963), Indian nationalist, first president of the Republic **12** 433

PRAXITELES (flourished circa 370-330 B.C.), Greek sculptor **12** 433-434

PREBISCH, RAÚL (1901-1986), Argentine economist active in the United Nations **12** 434-436

PREGL, FRITZ (1869-1930), Austrian physiologist and medical chemist **12** 436-437

PREM TINSULANONDA (born 1920), military leader and prime minister of Thailand (1979-1988) **12** 437

PREMADASA, RANASINGHE (born 1924), president of Sri Lanka (1988-) **12** 437-439

PREMCHAND (1880-1936), Indian novelist and short-story writer **12** 439

PREMINGER, OTTO (1895-1986), Austrian filmmaker and theater producer/director **18** 331-332

PRENDERGAST, MAURICE BRAZIL (1859-1924), American painter **12** 440

PRESCOTT, WILLIAM HICKLING (1796-1859), American historian **12** 440-441

PRESLEY, ELVIS ARON (1935-1977), American singer and actor **12** 441-442

PRESTES, LUIZ CARLOS (1898-1990), Brazilian revolutionary and Communist leader **12** 442-444

PRETORIUS, ANDRIES (1798-1853), South African politician and general **12** 444-445

PREVIN, ANDRE (Andreas Ludwig Priwin; born 1929), German American composer and conductor **18** 333-334

PRÉVOST, ABBÉ (1697-1763), French novelist, journalist, and cleric **12** 445-446

PRICE, LEONTYNE (Mary Leontyne Price; born 1927), American prima donna soprano **12** 446-447

PRICE, RICHARD (1723-1791), English Nonconformist minister and political philosopher **12** 447-448

PRICHARD, DIANA GARCÍA (born 1949), Hispanic American chemical physicist **12** 448-449

PRIDE, CHARLEY FRANK (born 1938), African American musician **23** 317-319

PRIDI PHANOMYONG (1901-1983), Thai political leader **12** 449

PRIEST, IVY MAUDE BAKER (1905-1975), treasurer of the United States (1953-1960) **12** 450-451

PRIESTLEY, J(OHN) B(OYNTON) (1894-1984), English author of novels, essays, plays, and screenplays **12** 451-452

PRIESTLEY, JOSEPH (1733-1804), English clergyman and chemist **12** 452-453

PRIMATICCIO, FRANCESCO (1504-1570), Italian painter, sculptor, and architect **12** 453-454

PRIMO DE RIVERA Y ORBANEJA, MIGUEL (1870-1930), Spanish general, dictator 1923-30 **12** 454-455

PRINCE, HAL (Harold Smith Prince; born 1928), American theatrical producer and director **19** 295-298

PRINCIP, GAVRILO (1894-1918), Serbian nationalist and assassin **21** 353-355

PRINGLE, THOMAS (1789-1834), Scottish author and abolitionist **23** 319-320

PRITCHETT, V(ICTOR) S(AWDON) (born 1900), English short story writer, novelist, literary critic, journalist, travel writer, biographer, and autobiographer **12** 455-457

Probability (mathematics) development of theory Bernoulli, Jakob **23** 37-39

PROCLUS DIADOCHUS (born 410), Byzantine philosopher **12** 457

PROCOPIUS OF CAESAREA (circa 500-circa 565), Byzantine historian **12** 457-458

PROCTER, WILLIAM COOPER (1862-1934), American businessman **19** 298-300

Progressive movement (U.S. politics) leaders Beveridge, Albert Jeremiah **23** 39-41

PROKOFIEV, SERGEI SERGEEVICH (1891-1953), Russian composer **12** 458-460

Prophets see Bible–Old Testament

PROSSER, GABRIEL (circa 1775-1800), Afro-American slave rebel **12** 460-461

PROTAGORAS (circa 484-circa 414 B.C.), Greek philosopher **12** 461

Protein (chemistry) Prusiner, Stanley Ben **23** 320-323

PROUDHON, PIERRE JOSEPH (1809-1864), French anarchist political philosopher and journalist **12** 461-463

PROULX, E. ANNIE (born 1935), American author **12** 463-465

PROUST, MARCEL (1871-1922), French novelist **12** 465-467

PROXMIRE, WILLIAM (born 1915), Democratic senator for Wisconsin **12** 467-468

PRUD'HON, PIERRE PAUL (1758-1823), French painter **12** 469

PRUSINER, STANLEY BEN (born 1942), American biomedical researcher **23** 320-323

PRYOR, RICHARD (born 1940), American entertainer **19** 300-302

PRZHEVALSKY, NIKOLAI MIKHAILOVICH (1839-1888), Russian general and traveler **12** 469-470

PTOLEMY I (367/366-283 B.C.), Macedonian general, king of Egypt 323-285 **12** 470-472

PTOLEMY II (308-246 B.C.), king of Egypt 285-246 **12** 472-473

PTOLEMY, CLAUDIUS (circa 100-circa 170), Greek astronomer and geographer **12** 473-474

Public school (United States) see Education (United States)

Publishers, American books and/or educational materials Liveright, Horace B. **23** 229-231

PUCCINI, GIACOMO (1858-1924), Italian composer **12** 474-476

Puerto Rico (United States commonwealth; island, Greater Antilles)
Rodríguez de Tío, Lola **23** 345-346

PUFENDORF, BARON SAMUEL VON (1632-1694), German jurist and historian **12** 477-478

PUGACHEV, EMELYAN IVANOVICH (1742-1775), Russian Cossack soldier **12** 478-479

PUGIN, AUGUSTUS WELBY NORTHMORE (1812-1852), English architect **12** 479-480

PULASKI, CASIMIR (1747/48-79), Polish patriot **12** 480-481

PULCI, LUIGI (1432-1484), Italian poet **12** 481

PULITZER, JOSEPH (1847-1911), American editor and publisher **12** 481-482

Pulitzer Prize winners
Beveridge, Albert Jeremiah **23** 39-41

PULLMAN, GEORGE MORTIMER (1831-1897), American industrial innovator **12** 482-483

PUPIN, MICHAEL IDVORSKY (1858-1935), Serbo-American physicist and inventor **12** 483-484

PURCELL, HENRY (1659-1695), English composer and organist **12** 484-485

PURVIS, ROBERT (1810-1898), African American abolitionist **12** 485-486

PURYEAR, MARTIN (born 1941), African American artist **12** 486-487

PUSEY, EDWARD BOUVERIE (1800-1882), English clergyman and scholar **12** 488-489

PUSHKIN, ALEKSANDR SERGEEVICH (1799-1837), Russian poet and prose writer **12** 489-491

PUTIN, VLADIMIR (born 1952), Russian president **21** 355-358

PUTNAM, ISRAEL (1718-1790), American Revolutionary War general **12** 491-492

PUVIS DE CHAVANNES, PIERRE (1824-1898), French painter **12** 492-493

PYLE, ERNIE (Earnest Taylor Pyle; 1900-1945), American war correspondent during World War II **12** 493-494

PYM, FRANCIS (Francis Leslie Pym; born 1922), British statesman **12** 494-495

PYM, JOHN (1584-1643), English statesman **12** 495-496

PYNCHON, THOMAS (Thomas Ruggles Pynchon, Jr.; born 1937), American writer **12** 496-498

PYTHAGORAS (circa 575-circa 495 B.C.), Greek philosopher, scientist, and religious teacher **12** 498-499
associates
Theano **23** 399-401

PYTHEAS (c. 380 B.C.-c. 300 B.C.), Greek explorer **12** 499-500

Q

QABOOS IBN SA'ID (born 1940), ruler of the Sultanate of Oman **12** 501-502

QIANLONG (Ch'ien-lung and Hung-li; 1711-1799), Chinese emperor **12** 502-505

QUANT, MARY (born 1934), British fashion designer and businesswoman **19** 303-305

Quantum theory (physics)
and chemical reactions
Fukui, Kenichi **23** 111-112
quantum electrodynamics
Wilson, Kenneth Geddes **23** 446-448

Quark (hypothetical particle)
Ting, Samuel Chao Chung **23** 406-408

QUASIMODO, SALVATORE (1901-1968), Italian poet, translator, and critic **12** 506

QUAY, MATTHEW STANLEY (1833-1904), American politician **12** 507

QUAYLE, J(AMES) DANFORTH (born 1947), vice president under George Bush **12** 507-509

QUERCIA, JACOPO DELLA (1374?-1438), Italian sculptor and architect **12** 509

QUÉTELET, LAMBERT ADOLPHE JACQUES (1796-1874), Belgian statistician and astronomer **12** 510-511

QUEVEDO Y VILLEGAS, FRANCISCO GÓMEZ DE (1580-1645), Spanish poet, satirist, and novelist **12** 511

QUEZON, MANUEL LUIS (1878-1944), Philippine statesman **12** 511-513

QUINE, WILLARD VAN ORMAN (born 1908), American philosopher **12** 514-515

QUINN, ANTHONY (Antonio Rudolph Oaxaca Quinn; born 1915), Hispanic American actor and artist **20** 302-304

QUINTILIAN (circa 35-circa 99), Roman rhetorician and literary critic **12** 518-519

QUIRINO, ELPIDIO (1890-1956), Philippine statesman **12** 519-520

QUIROGA, HORACIO (1878-1937), Uruguayan writer **12** 520-521

QUIROGA, JUAN FACUNDO (1788/1790-1835), Argentine caudillo **12** 521-522

QUISLING, VIDKIN (1887-1945), Norwegian traitor **20** 304-306

R

Rabbis
see Religious leaders, Jewish

RABEARIVELO, JEAN JOSEPH (1901-1937), Malagasy poet **12** 523-524

RABELAIS, FRANÇOIS (circa 1494-circa 1553), French humanist, doctor, and writer **12** 524-526

RABI, ISIDOR ISAAC (1898-1988), American physicist **12** 526-527

RABIN, YITZCHAK (1922-1995), Israeli statesman **12** 527-529

RACHMANINOV, SERGEI VASILIEVICH (1873-1943), Russian composer, pianist, and conductor **12** 531-532

RACINE, JEAN BAPTISTE (1639-1699), French dramatist **12** 532-535

RADCLIFFE-BROWN, A(LFRED) R(EGINALD) (1881-1955), English anthropologist **12** 535-536

RADEK, KARL BERNARDOVICH (1885-1939), Russian Communist leader **12** 536-537

RADHAKRISHNAN, SARVEPALLI (1888-1995), Indian philosopher and statesman **12** 537-538

Radiation
see Radioactivity

RADIN, PAUL (1883-1959), American anthropologist and ethnographer **12** 538-539

Radio (communications)
personalities
Lombardo, Guy **23** 234-236

Radioactivity (physics)
radioactive decay
Gleditsch, Ellen **23** 124-126

Radiochemistry (science)
Gleditsch, Ellen **23** 124-126

RADISSON, PIERRE-ESPRIT (circa 1636-1710), French explorer **12** 539-540

Radium (element–chemistry)
Gleditsch, Ellen **23** 124-126

RAFFLES, SIR THOMAS STAMFORD (1781-1826), English colonial administrator **13** 1-2

RAFINESQUE, CONSTANTINE SAMUEL (1783-1840), French naturalist **21** 359-361

RAFSANJANI, AKBAR HASHEMI (born 1934), president of Iran **13** 3-4

RAHNER, KARL (1904-1984), German Catholic theologian **13** 4-5

RAI, LALA LAJPAT (1865-1928), Indian nationalist leader **13** 5-6

Railway Children, The (book) Nesbit, E(dith) **23** 263-265

RAINEY, MA (Gertrude Pridgett; 1886-1939), American singer **19** 306-308

RAINIER III, PRINCE OF MONACO (born 1923), ruler of the principality of Monaco **18** 335-337

RAJAGOPALACHARI, CHAKRAVARTI (1879-1972), Indian nationalist leader **13** 6-7

RAJARAJA I (985-1014), Indian statesman **13** 7

RAJNEESH, BHAGWAN SHREE (Rahneesh Chandra Mohan; 1931-1990), Indian religious leader **13** 7-9

RALEIGH, SIR WALTER (or Ralegh; circa 1552-1618), English statesman, soldier, courtier, explorer, and poet **13** 9-11
Harriot, Thomas **23** 137-139

RAMA KHAMHAENG (circa 1239-circa 1299), king of Sukhothai in Thailand **13** 11

RAMAKRISHNA, SRI (1833-1886), Indian mystic, reformer, and saint **13** 11-13

RAMAN, SIR CHANDRASEKHAR VENKATA (1888-1970), Indian physicist **13** 13-14

RAMANUJA (Ramanujacarya; c. 1017-1137), Indian theologian and philosopher **21** 361-362

RAMANUJAN AIYANGAR, SRINIVASA (1887-1920), India mathematician **13** 14-15

RAMAPHOSA, MATEMELA CYRIL (born 1952), general secretary of the National Union of Mineworkers (NUM) in South Africa and secretary general of the African National Congress **13** 15-16

RAMAZZINI, BERNARDINO (1633-1714), Italian physician **21** 362-364

RAMEAU, JEAN PHILIPPE (1683-1764), French music theorist and composer **13** 17-18

RAMOS, FIDEL VALDEZ (born 1928), president of the Philippines (1992-) **13** 18-19

RAMPAL, JEAN-PIERRE LOUIS (1922-2000), French flutist **22** 362-364

RAMPHAL, SHRIDATH SURENDRANATH (born 1928), Guyanese barrister, politician, and international civil servant **13** 19-20

RAMSAY, DAVID (1749-1815), American historian **13** 21

RAMSAY, SIR WILLIAM (1852-1916), British chemist and educator **13** 21-22

RAMSES II (ruled 1304-1237 B.C.), pharaoh of Egypt **13** 22-23

RAMSEY, ARTHUR MICHAEL (1904-1988), archbishop of Canterbury and president of the World Council of Churches **13** 23-25

RAMSEY, FRANK PLUMPTON (1903-1930), English mathematician and philosopher **13** 25

RAMSEY, NORMAN FOSTER, JR. (born 1915), American physicist **13** 25-27

RAMUS, PETRUS (1515-1572), French humanist, logician and mathematician **13** 27-28

RAND, AYN (1905-1982), American author and philosoher **20** 307-309

RANDOLPH, A. PHILIP (1889-1979), African American labor and civil rights leader **13** 28-29

RANDOLPH, EDMUND (1753-1813), American statesman **13** 29-30

RANDOLPH, JOHN (1773-1833), American statesman **13** 30

RANDOLPH, PEYTON (1721-1775), American statesman **18** 337-339

RANDS, BERNARD (born 1934), American musician **23** 324-326

RANGEL, CHARLES B. (born 1930), Democratic U.S. representative from New York City **13** 31-32

RANJIT SINGH (1780-1839), ruler of the Punjab **13** 32-33

RANK, OTTO (1884-1939), Austrian psychotherapist **13** 33

RANKE, LEOPOLD VON (1795-1886), German historian **13** 33-35

RANKIN, JEANNETTE PICKERING (1880-1973), first woman elected to the U.S. Congress **13** 35-37

RANNARIDH, PRINCE NORODOM (born 1944), first prime minister of Cambodia **13** 37-39

RANSOM, JOHN CROWE (1888-1974), American poet and critic **13** 39-40

RAPHAEL (1483-1520), Italian painter and architect **13** 40-42

RAPP, GEORGE (1757-1847), German-American religious leader **13** 42-43

RASHI (1040-1105), French Jewish scholar and commentator **13** 43

RASMUSSEN, KNUD JOHAN VICTOR (1879-1933), Danish Arctic explorer and ethnologist **13** 44

RASPUTIN, GRIGORI EFIMOVICH (1872-1916), Russian monk **13** 44-45

RATANA, TAUPOTIKI WIREMU (1870-1939), spiritual and political leader of the New Zealand Maori people **13** 46

RATHBONE, ELEANOR (Eleanor Florence Rathbone; 1872-1946), British politician and social reformer **13** 47-48

RATHENAU, WALTHER (1867-1922), German industrialist and statesman **13** 48-49

RATTLE, SIMON DENIS (born 1955), conductor of England's City of Birmingham Symphony Orchestra **13** 49-50

RATZEL, FRIEDRICH (1844-1904), German geographer **13** 50-51

RAU, JOHANNES (born 1931), German Social Democrat politician **13** 51-52

RAUSCHENBERG, ROBERT (born 1925), American painter and printmaker **13** 52-53

RAUSCHENBUSCH, WALTER (1861-1918), American Baptist clergyman **13** 53-54

RAVEL, MAURICE JOSEPH (1875-1937), French composer **13** 54-55

RAWLS, JOHN (1921-2002), American political philosopher **13** 55-56

RAY, DIXY LEE (1914-1994), marine biologist and governor of Washington **13** 56-57

RAY, JOHN (1627-1705), English naturalist **13** 57-59

RAY, MAN (1890-1976), American painter, photographer, and object maker **13** 59-60

RAY, NICHOLAS (Raymond Nicholas Kienzle; 1911-1978), American film director **22** 364-366

RAY, SATYAJIT (1921-1992), Indian film director **13** 60-61

RAYBURN, SAMUEL TALIAFERRO (1882-1961), American statesman **13** 61-62

RAYLEIGH, 3D BARON (John William Strutt; 1842-1919), English physicist **13** 62

RAZI (Abu Bakr Muhammad ibn Zakariya al-Razi; circa 865-925), Persian physician **13** 63-64

RAZIA (Raziya; c. 1210-1240), sultana of Delhi **23** 326-329

READING, 1ST MARQUESS OF (Rufus Daniel Isaacs; 1860-1935), English lawyer and statesman **13** 64

REAGAN, RONALD W. (born 1911), governor of California (1967-1975) and U.S. president (1981-1989) **13** 65-68

REBER, GROTE (1911-2002), American radio astronomer **21** 364-366

Reconquista
see Spain–Islamic

RECORDE, ROBERT (1510-1558), English mathematician **13** 68-69

RECTO, CLARO M. (1890-1960), Philippine nationalist and statesman **13** 69-70

RED CLOUD (1822-1909), American Oglala Sioux Indian chief **13** 70-71

RED JACKET (Sagoyewatha; 1758-1830), Seneca tribal leader **13** 71-73

Red scare (U.S. history)
Robeson, Eslanda Goode **23** 340-342

REDFIELD, ROBERT (1897-1958), American anthropologist **13** 73-74

REDFORD, ROBERT (Charles Robert Redford, Jr.; born 1937), American actor, producer, and director **18** 339-342

REDGRAVE, VANESSA (born 1937), British actress and political activist **13** 74-75

REDON, ODILON (1840-1916), French painter and graphic artist **13** 75-76

REDSTONE, SUMNER MURRAY (born 1932), American businessman **23** 329-331

REED, ISHMAEL (Emmett Coleman; born 1938), African American author **23** 331-333

REED, JOHN SILAS (1887-1920), American revolutionist, poet, and journalist **13** 76-77

REED, THOMAS BRACKETT (1839-1902), American statesman and parliamentarian **13** 77

REED, WALTER (1851-1902), American military surgeon **13** 78

REES, LLOYD FREDERIC (1895-1988), Australian artist **13** 78-79

REEVE, CHRISTOPHER (born 1952), American actor and activist **18** 342-344

REEVE, TAPPING (1744-1823), American jurist **13** 79-80

Reform, social
see Social reform

Reformers, educational
see also Social scientists–educators
White, Ellen Gould **23** 438-440

Reformers, legal
see Jurists

Reformers, social
American (19th-20th century)
Walker, Mary Edwards **23** 432-434
Australian
Spence, Catherine Helen **23** 374-375

REGAN, DONALD (Donald Thomas Regan; born 1918), American secretary of the treasury and White House chief of staff under Reagan **13** 80-81

REGIOMONTANUS (1436-1476), German astronomer and mathematician **13** 81-82

Regionalism and local color (American literature)
West
Atherton, Gertrude **23** 21-23
Austin, Mary Hunter **23** 23-25

REHNQUIST, WILLIAM HUBBS (born 1924), U.S. Supreme Court chief justice **13** 82-84

REICH, STEVE (born 1936), American composer **13** 84-85

REICHSTEIN, TADEUS (1897-1996), Polish-Swiss chemist **13** 85-87

REID, THOMAS (1710-1796), Scottish philosopher, clergyman, and teacher **13** 87-88

REID, WILLIAM RONALD (Bill Reid; 1920-1998), Canadian artist **13** 88-89

Reign of Terror
see French Revolution–1792-95 (Reign of Terror)

REINHARDT, MAX (Max Goldman; 1873-1943), Austrian stage director **13** 89-90

Religious leaders, Catholic (since 1517)
nuns
Tekakwitha, Kateri **23** 395-397
popes
Benedict XIV **23** 32-35
Innocent IV **23** 165-167
Paul V **23** 297-299

Religious leaders, Christian (to 1517)
bishops
Clement I **23** 78-81
Fathers of the Church
Clement I **23** 78-81
martyrs
Clement I **23** 78-81
monks and abbots
David, Saint **23** 83-85
popes
Vigilius **23** 427-429

Religious leaders, Jewish
rabbis
Schindler, Alexander Moshe **23** 360-362

Religious leaders, Protestant
Adventists
White, Ellen Gould **23** 438-440
evangelists (Great Awakening)
Palmer, Phoebe Worrall **23** 288-290
Parham, Charles Fox **23** 291-293
Methodist ministers
Parham, Charles Fox **23** 291-293
Methodist missionaries
Palmer, Phoebe Worrall **23** 288-290
Seventh-Day Adventists
White, Ellen Gould **23** 438-440

REMARQUE, ERICH MARIA (Erich Paul Remark; 1898-1970), German novelist **13** 91

REMBRANDT HARMENSZ VAN RIJN (1606-1669), Dutch painter and etcher **13** 91-95

REMINGTON, FREDERIC (1861-1909), American painter, sculptor, and illustrator **18** 344-346 91-95

REMOND, CHARLES LENNOX (1810-1873), American black abolitionist **13** 95

RENAN, ERNEST (1823-1892), French author and philologist **13** 95-96

RENDELL, RUTH (Ruth Grasemann Rendell; born 1930), English writer of mysteries and suspense thrillers **13** 96-97

RENI, GUIDO (1575-1642), Italian painter **13** 97-98

RENNER, KARL (1870-1950), Austrian statesman, president 1945-50 **13** 98-99

RENO, JANET (born 1938), U.S. attorney general (1993-) **13** 99-101

RENOIR, JEAN (1894-1979), French-American film director, producer, and screenwriter **22** 366-369

RENOIR, PIERRE AUGUSTE (1841-1919), French impressionist painter **13** 101-102

RENWICK, JAMES (1818-1895), American architect **13** 102-103

Republican party (United States)
leaders
Ashcroft, John **23** 18-21

RESNAIS, ALAIN (born 1922), French filmmaker **23** 333-335

RESNIK, JUDITH ARLENE (Judy Resnik; 1949-1986), American astronaut **22** 369-371

RESPIGHI, OTTORINO (1879-1936), Italian composer **13** 103-104

RESTON, JAMES BARRETT ("Scotty"; born 1909), American journalist and political commentator **13** 104-105

RETIEF, PIETER (1780-1838), South African Boer leader **13** 105-106

REUCHLIN, JOHANN (1455-1522), German humanist and jurist **13** 106-107

REUTER, PAUL JULIUS VON (Isreal Beer Josaphat; 1816-1899), French journalist **21** 366-367

REUTHER, WALTER PHILIP (1907-1970), American labor leader **13** 107-108

REVEL, BERNARD (1885-1940), Talmudic scholar and educator **13** 108-109

REVELS, HIRAM RHOADES (1822-1901), African American clergyman, statesman, and educator **13** 109-110

REVERE, PAUL (1735-1818), American patriot, silversmith, and engraver **13** 110-111

REVILLAGIGEDO, CONDE DE (Juan Vicente Güemes Pacheco y Padilla; 1740-1799), Spanish colonial administrator, viceroy of New Spain **13** 111-112

Revolution of 1848 (Europe)
Hungary
Petöfi, Sándor **23** 306-308

REYES, ALFONSO (1889-1959), Mexican author and diplomat **13** 112-113

REYES, RAFAEL (1850-1920), Colombian military leader, president 1904-09 **13** 113

REYNOLDS, ALBERT (born 1932), prime minister of Ireland **13** 113-115

REYNOLDS, SIR JOSHUA (1723-1792), English portrait painter **13** 115-116

REYNOLDS, RICHARD JOSHUA JR. (R.J. Reynolds; 1906-1964), American businessman and philanthropist **19** 308-310

REZA SHAH PAHLAVI (Reza Khan; 1878-1944), Shah of Iran 1925-41 **13** 116-117

RHEE, SYNGMAN (1875-1965), Korean independence leader, South Korean president 1948-60 **13** 117-120

RHETT, ROBERT BARNWELL (1800-1876) American statesman **13** 120

RHODES, CECIL JOHN (1853-1902), English imperialist and financier **13** 120-122

RHODES, JAMES FORD (1848-1927), American historian **13** 122

RHYS, JEAN (Ella Gwendolen Rees Williams; 1890-1979), English author **19** 310-312

RIBERA, JUSEPE DE (1591-1652), Spanish painter **13** 122-123

RICARDO, DAVID (1772-1823), English economist **13** 123-124

RICCI, MATTEO (1552-1610), Italian Jesuit missionary **13** 124-125

RICE, ANNE (born 1941), American author **13** 125-126

RICE, CONDOLEEZZA (born 1954), African American national security advisor **23** 335-338

RICE, ELMER (1892-1967), American playwright and novelist **13** 126-127

RICE, JOSEPH MAYER (1857-1934), American education reformer **13** 127-128

RICH, ADRIENNE (born 1929), American poet **13** 128-130

RICHARD I (1157-1199), king of England 1189-99 **13** 130

RICHARD II (1367-1400), king of England 1377-99 **13** 130-131

RICHARD III (1452-1485), king of England 1483-85 **13** 132-133

RICHARD, MAURICE ("Rocket" Richard; born 1921), Canadian hockey player **19** 312-313

RICHARDS, ANN WILLIS (born 1933), Democratic governor of Texas **13** 133-134

RICHARDS, ELLEN H. (born Ellen Henrietta Swallow; 1842-1911), American chemist and educator **13** 134-136

RICHARDS, IVOR ARMSTRONG (1893-1979), English-born American semanticist and literary critic **13** 137

RICHARDS, THEODORE WILLIAM (1868-1928), American chemist **13** 137-138

RICHARDSON, HENRY HANDEL (pen name of Ethel Florence Lindesay Richardson; 1870-1946), expatriate Australian novelist **13** 139

RICHARDSON, HENRY HOBSON (1838-1886), American architect **13** 139-141

RICHARDSON, SAMUEL (1689-1761), English novelist **13** 141-142

RICHELIEU, ARMAND JEAN DU PLESSIS DE (1585-1642), French statesman and cardinal **13** 142-144

RICHET, CHARLES ROBERT (1850-1935), French physiologist **13** 144-145

RICHIER, GERMAINE (1904-1959), French sculptor **13** 145-146

RICHLER, MORDECAI (1931-2001), Canadian author **22** 371-373

RICHTER, CHARLES F. (1900-1985), American seismologist **13** 146-148

RICHTER, CONRAD MICHAEL (1890-1968), American novelist and short-story writer **13** 148-149

RICHTER, GERHARD (born 1932), German artist **23** 338-340

RICHTER, HANS (Johann Siegried Richter; 1888-1976), German-born film director **13** 149-150

RICHTER, JOHANN PAUL FRIEDRICH (1763-1825), German humorist and prose writer **13** 150-151

RICIMER, FLAVIUS (died 472), Germanic Roman political chief **13** 151-152

RICKENBACKER, EDWARD VERNON (1890-1973), World War I fighter pilot and airline president **13** 152-153

RICKEY, WESLEY BRANCH (1881-1965), innovative baseball executive **13** 153-155

RICKOVER, HYMAN GEORGE (1900-1986), U.S. Navy officer **13** 155-157

RICOEUR, PAUL (born 1913), French exponent of hermeneutical philosophy **13** 157-158

RIDE, SALLY (born 1951), American astronaut and physicist **13** 158-160

RIDGE, JOHN ROLLIN (Yellow Bird; 1827-1867), Native American author **22** 373-375

RIDGWAY, MATTHEW BUNKER (1895-1993), American general **13** 160-161

RIEFENSTAHL, LENI (born 1902), German film director **13** 161-163

RIEL, LOUIS (1844-1885), Canadian rebel **13** 163-164

RIEMANN, GEORG FRIEDRICH BERNARD (1826-1866), German mathematician **13** 164-165

RIEMENSCHNEIDER, TILMAN (1468-1531), German sculptor **13** 166

RIENZI, COLA DI (or Rienzo; 1313/14-1354), Italian patriot, tribune of Rome **13** 166-167

RIESMAN, DAVID (1909-2002), American sociologist, writer, and social critic **13** 167-168

RIETVELD, GERRIT THOMAS (1888-1964), Dutch architect and furniture designer **13** 169

RIIS, JACOB AUGUST (1849-1914), Danish-born American journalist and reformer **13** 169-170

RILEY, JAMES WHITCOMB (1849-1916), American poet **13** 170-171

RILKE, RAINER MARIA (1875-1926), German lyric poet **13** 171-172

RILLIEUX, NORBERT (1806-1894), American inventor **20** 309-311

RIMBAUD, (JEAN NICOLAS) ARTHUR (1854-1891), French poet **13** 172-174

RIMMER, WILLIAM (1816-1879), American sculptor, painter, and physician **13** 174

RIMSKY-KORSAKOV, NIKOLAI ANDREEVICH (1844-1908), Russian composer and conductor **13** 174-175

RINGGOLD, FAITH (Faith Jones; born 1930), African American painter, sculptress, and performer **13** 175-177

Ringling Bros. and Barnum and Bailey Circus
Leitzel, Lillian **23** 225-227

RIO BRANCO, BARÃO DO (José Maria da Silva Paranhos; 1845-1912), Brazilian political leader **13** 177

RIORDAN, RICHARD JOSEPH (born 1930), American politician; mayor of Los Angeles **13** 177-179

RIPKEN, CAL, JR. (Calvin Edwin Ripken, Jr.; born 1960), American baseball player **18** 346-349

RIPLEY, GEORGE (1802-1880), American Unitarian minister and journalist **13** 179-180

RITSCHL, ALBRECHT BENJAMIN (1822-1889), German theologian **13** 180

RITTENHOUSE, DAVID (1732-1796), American astronomer and instrument maker **13** 180-181

RITTER, KARL (1779-1859), German geographer **13** 181-182

RIVADAVIA, BERNARDINO (1780-1845), Argentine independence leader, president 1826-27 **13** 182-183

RIVAS, DUQUE DE (Angel de Saavedra; 1791-1865), Spanish poet, dramatist, and statesman **13** 398

RIVERA, DIEGO (1886-1957), Mexican painter **13** 183-184

RIVERA, FRUCTUOSO (circa 1788-1854), Uruguayan statesman **13** 184-185

RIVERA, JOSÉ EUSTACIO (1888-1928), Colombian novelist **13** 185-186

RIVERS, LARRY (Yitzroch Loiza Grossberg; 1923-2002), American artist **13** 186-187

RIVLIN, ALICE M. (born 1931), American economist and political advisor **18** 349-350

RIZAL, JOSÉ (1861-1896), Philippine national hero **13** 187-189

ROBARDS, JASON (Jason Nelson Robards, JR.; 1922-2000), American Actor **22** 375-378

ROBBE-GRILLET, ALAIN (born 1922), French novelist **13** 189-190

ROBBIA, LUCA DELLA (1400-1482), Italian sculptor **10** 19-20

ROBBINS, JEROME (Rabinowitz; 1918-1998), American director and choreographer **13** 190-192

ROBERT I (1274-1329), king of Scotland 1306-29 **13** 192-194

ROBERT II (1316-1390), king of Scotland 1371-90 **13** 194

ROBERT III (circa 1337-1406), king of Scotland 1390-1406 **13** 194-195

ROBERT, HENRY MARTYN (1837-1923), American engineer and parliamentarian **21** 367-370

ROBERT, SHAABAN (1909-1962), Tanzanian author who wrote in the Swahili language **14** 128-129

ROBERTS, FREDERICK SLEIGH (1st Earl Roberts of Kandhar, Pretoria, and Waterford; 1832-1914), British field marshal **13** 195-196

ROBERTSON, SIR DENNIS HOLME (1890-1963), English economist **13** 196

ROBERTSON, MARION G. (Pat Robertson; born 1930), television evangelist who founded the Christian Broadcasting Network and presidential candidate **13** 196-198

ROBERTSON, OSCAR (born 1938), African American basketball player **20** 311-313

ROBESON, ESLANDA GOODE (born Eslanda Cardozo Goode; 1896-1965), African American cultural anthropologist **23** 340-342

ROBESON, PAUL LEROY (1898-1976), American singer, actor, and political activist **13** 198-199
Robeson, Eslanda Goode **23** 340-342

ROBESPIERRE, MAXIMILIEN FRANÇOIS MARIE ISIDORE DE (1758-1794), French Revolutionary leader **13** 199-201

ROBINSON, EDDIE (born 1919), African American college football coach **18** 351-352

ROBINSON, EDWIN ARLINGTON (1869-1935), American poet and playwright **13** 201-202

ROBINSON, FRANK, JR. (born 1935), African American baseball player and manager **13** 202-203

ROBINSON, HARRIET HANSON (1825-1911), American author and suffragist **13** 203-207

ROBINSON, JACK ROOSEVELT (Jackie Robinson; 1919-72), African American baseball player; first African American player in the major leagues **13** 207-208

ROBINSON, JAMES HARVEY (1863-1936), American historian **13** 208

ROBINSON, JOAN VIOLET MAURICE (1903-1983), English economist **13** 209-210

ROBINSON, SIR JOHN BEVERLEY (1791-1863), Canadian political leader and jurist **13** 215-217

ROBINSON, JULIA (1919-1985), American mathematician **13** 210-211

ROBINSON, MARY BOURKE (born 1944), first woman president of Ireland **13** 211-213

ROBINSON, MAX (1939-1988), African American television news anchor **13** 213-215

ROBINSON, RANDALL (born 1941), American author and activist **23** 342-345

ROBINSON, SMOKEY (born 1940), African American performer and composer **13** 215-217

ROBINSON, SUGAR RAY (Walker Smith Jr.; 1921-1989), American boxer **19** 313-315

ROBINSON, THEODORE (1852-1896), American painter **13** 217

ROCA, JULIO ARGENTINO (1843-1914), Argentine general and president **13** 218

ROCARD, MICHEL (born 1930), French left-wing politician **13** 218-220

ROCHAMBEAU, COMTE DE (Jean Baptiste Donatien de Vimeur, 1725-1807), French general **13** 220-221

ROCHBERG, GEORGE (born 1918), American composer **13** 221-222

ROCHE, KEVIN (born 1922), Irish-American architect **13** 222-224

ROCK, ARTHUR (born 1926), American businessman **19** 316-317

ROCK, JOHN (1825-1866), American physician, lawyer, and abolitionist **21** 370-372

Rock and Roll Hall of Fame
Leadbelly **23** 208-211
Led Zeppelin **23** 216-218

ROCKEFELLER, DAVID (born 1915), chairman of the Chase Manhattan Bank **13** 224-225

ROCKEFELLER, JOHN D., JR. (1874-1960), American philanthropist and industrial relations expert **13** 225-226

ROCKEFELLER, JOHN DAVISON (1839-1937), American industrialist and philanthropist **13** 226-228

ROCKEFELLER, NELSON ALDRICH (1908-1979), four-term governor of New York and vice-president of the United States **13** 228-230

ROCKINGHAM, 2D MARQUESS OF (Charles Watson-Wentworth; 1730-82), English statesman **13** 230-231

ROCKNE, KNUTE (1888-1931), American football coach **13** 231

ROCKWELL, NORMAN PERCEVEL (1894-1978), American illustrator **13** 231-233

RODCHENKO, ALEXANDER MIKHAILOVICH (1891-1956), Russian abstract painter, sculptor, photographer, and industrial designer **13** 233-234

RODGERS, JIMMIE (James Charles Rodgers; 1897-1933), American musician **19** 317-319

RODGERS, RICHARD CHARLES (1902-1972), American composer **13** 234-236

RODIN, AUGUSTE (1840-1917), French sculptor **13** 236-238
influence of
Hoffman, Malvina Cornell **23** 148-150
students of
Fuller, Meta Warrick **23** 112-114

RODINO, PETER WALLACE, JR. (born 1909), Democratic U.S. representative from New Jersey **13** 238-239

RODNEY, GEORGE BRYDGES (1st Baron Rodney; 1718-92), British admiral **13** 239-240

RODÓ, JOSÉ ENRIQUE (1872-1917), Uraguayan essayist and literary critic **13** 240-241

RODRÍGUEZ DE TÍO, LOLA (1834-1924), Puerto Rican/Cuban poet and nationalist **23** 345-346

ROEBLING, JOHN AUGUSTUS (1806-1869), German-born American engineer **13** 241-242

ROEBLING, WASHINGTON AUGUSTUS (1837-1926), American engineer and manufacturer **13** 243

ROETHKE, THEODORE (1908-1963), American poet and teacher **13** 243-244

ROGER II (1095-1154), king of Sicily 1130-54 **13** 244-245

ROGERS, CARL RANSOM (1902-1987), American psychotherapist **13** 245-247

ROGERS, EDITH NOURSE (1881-1960), U.S. congresswoman from Massachusetts **13** 247-248

ROGERS, FRED ("Mr." Rogers; 1928-2003), American television host **18** 352-354

ROGERS, JOHN (1829-1904), American sculptor **13** 248

ROGERS, RICHARD (born 1933), British architect **13** 248-250

ROGERS, ROBERT (1731-1795), American frontiersman and army officer **13** 250-251

ROGERS, WILL (1879-1935), American actor, humorist, journalist, and performer **13** 251-252

ROH TAE WOO (born 1932), president of the Republic of Korea **13** 253-255

ROHDE, RUTH BRYAN OWEN (1885-1954), U.S. congresswoman **13** 252-253

ROJAS PINILLA, GUSTAVO (1900-1975), Colombian general and politician **13** 255-256

ROLAND, MADAME (Marie-Jeanne Phlipon; 1754-1793), French author and revolutionary **13** 256-259

ROLFE, JOHN (1585-1622), English colonist in Virginia **13** 259-260

ROLLAND, ROMAIN (1866-1944), French writer **13** 260

ROLLE OF HAMPOLE, RICHARD (circa 1290-1349), English prose and verse writer **13** 260-261

ROLLING STONES, THE (formed in 1963), rock and roll band **13** 261-264

ROLLINS, CHARLEMAE HILL (1897-1979), African American librarian and author **23** 346-348

ROLLO (Rolf; circa 860-circa 932), Viking adventurer **13** 264-265

RÖLVAAG, OLE EDVART (1876-1931), Norwegian-American writer **13** 265

Roman Catholic Church
Latin America
Benedict XIV **23** 32-35
monophysite dispute
Vigilius **23** 427-429
political role
Innocent IV **23** 165-167
Spain
Benedict XIV **23** 32-35

Roman Catholic Church (United States)
17th century
Tekakwitha, Kateri **23** 395-397

Romanian literature
Caragiale, Ion Luca **23** 62-64

ROMANOV, ANASTASIA NICHOLAIEVNA (1901-1918), Russian grand duchess **18** 354-357

ROMERO, ARCHBISHOP OSCAR (1917-1980), archbishop of San Salvador **13** 265-267

ROMERO BARCELÓ, CARLOS (born 1932), Puerto Rican political leader and governor **13** 267-268

ROMILLY, SAMUEL (1757-1818), English legal reformer **23** 348-351

ROMMEL, ERWIN (1891-1944), German field marshal **13** 268-269

ROMNEY, GEORGE (1734-1802), English painter **13** 269-270

ROMNEY, GEORGE (1907-1995), American businessman and politician **20** 313-316

RÓMULO, CARLOS P. (1899-1985), Filipino journalist and diplomat **13** 270-271

RONDON, CANDIDO MARIANO DA SILVA (1865-1958), Brazilian militarist **13** 271

RONSARD, PIERRE DE (1524-1585), French poet **13** 271-273

RÖNTGEN, WILHELM CONRAD (1845-1923), German physicist **13** 273-275

ROOSEVELT, ANNA ELEANOR (1884-1962), American lecturer and author, first lady 1933-45 **13** 275-277

ROOSEVELT, FRANKLIN DELANO (1882-1945), American statesman, president 1933-45 **13** 277-280

ROOSEVELT, THEODORE (1858-1919), American statesman, president 1901-09 **13** 280-283

ROOT, ELIHU (1845-1937), American statesman **13** 283-284

ROOT, JOHN WELLBORN (1850-1891), American architect **21** 372-374

ROREM, NED (born 1923), American composer of art songs **13** 284-286

RORSCHACH, HERMANN (1884-1922), Swiss psychiatrist **13** 286-288

RORTY, RICHARD (born 1931), American philosopher and man of letters **13** 288-289

ROSA, SALVATOR (1615-1673), Italian painter and poet **13** 289-290

ROSAS, JUAN MANUEL DE (1793-1877), Argentine dictator 1829-52 **13** 290-291

ROSE, PETE (Peter Edward Rose; born 1941), American baseball player **21** 374-376

ROSENBERG, JULIUS AND ETHEL (died 1953), Americans executed for atomic espionage **13** 291-293

ROSENWALD, JULIUS (1862-1932), American retailer and philanthropist **13** 293

ROSENZWEIG, FRANZ (1886-1929), Jewish philosopher and writer **13** 294

ROS-LEHTINEN, ILEANA (born 1952) Hispanic American U.S. congresswoman **13** 294-296

ROSMINI-SERBATI, ANTONIO (1797-1855), Italian philosopher and priest **13** 296-297

ROSS, BETSY (Elizabeth Griscom; 1752-1836), American upholsterer who made the first U.S. flag **13** 297-298

ROSS, DIANA (born 1944), African American singer **13** 298-300

ROSS, EDWARD ALSWORTH (1866-1951), American sociologist **13** 300

ROSS, HAROLD (Harold Wallace Ross; 1892-1951), founder and editor of the *New Yorker* magazine **13** 300-302

ROSS, SIR JAMES CLARK (1800-1862), English admiral and polar explorer **13** 302-303

ROSS, SIR JOHN (1777-1856), British explorer **22** 378-380

ROSS, JOHN (1790-1866), American Cherokee Indian chief **13** 303-304

ROSS, MARY G. (born 1908), Native American aerospace engineer **13** 304-305

ROSS, NELLIE TAYLOE (1876-1977), American politician **13** 305-306

ROSSELLINI, ROBERTO (1906-1977), Italian film director **20** 316-318

ROSSETTI, CHRISTINA GEORGINA (1830-1894), English poet **13** 307-308

ROSSETTI, DANTE GABRIEL (1828-1882), English painter and poet **13** 308-309

ROSSI, ALDO (born 1931), Italian architect **13** 309-310

ROSSI, LUIGI (circa 1598-1653), Italian composer **13** 310-311

ROSSINI, GIOACCHINO (1792-1868), Italian composer **13** 311-312

ROSSO, IL (Giovanni Battista di Jacopo; 1495-1540), Italian painter **13** 312-313

ROSSO, MEDARDO (1858-1928), Italian sculptor **13** 313-315

ROSTOVTZEFF, MICHAEL IVANOVICH (1870-1952), Russian-born American historian and classical scholar **13** 315

ROSTOW, WALT WHITMAN (1916-2003), American educator, economist, and government official **13** 315-317

ROSTROPOVICH, MSTISLAV LEOPOLDOVICH (Slava Rostropovich; born 1927), Russian cellist and conductor **13** 317-318

ROTH, PHILIP (born 1933), American author **13** 318-320

ROTHKO, MARK (1903-1970), American painter **13** 320-321

ROTHSCHILD, MAYER (1744-1812), German merchant banker **20** 318-320

ROTTMAYR, JOHANN MICHAEL (1654-1730), Austrian painter **13** 321

ROUAULT, GEORGES (1871-1958), French painter and graphic artist **13** 321-322

ROUS, FRANCIS PEYTON (1879-1970), American pathologist and virologist **13** 322-323

ROUSSEAU, HENRI (1844-1910), French painter **13** 323-324

ROUSSEAU, JEAN JACQUES (1712-1778), Swiss-born French philosopher and author **13** 324-328

ROUSSEAU, THÉODORE (1812-1867), French painter and draftsman **13** 328

ROUSSEL, ALBERT (1869-1937), French composer **13** 328-329

ROWAN, CARL T. (born 1925), American journalist, author, and ambassador **13** 329-330

ROWLAND, HENRY AUGUSTUS (1848-1901), American physicist **13** 330-331

ROXAS, MANUEL (1892-1948), Filipino statesman, president 1946-48 **13** 331-332

ROY, PATRICK (born 1965), Canadian hockey player **23** 351-353

ROY, RAM MOHUN (1772-1833), Bengali social and religious reformer **13** 18

Royal Botanical Gardens (Kew Gardens, London)
North, Marianne **23** 268-270

Royal Canadians (band)
Lombardo, Guy **23** 234-236

ROYBAL-ALLARD, LUCILLE (born 1941), Hispanic American U.S. congresswoman **13** 332-334

ROYCE, JOSIAH (1855-1916), American philosopher **13** 334-335

ROYDEN, AGNES MAUDE (1876-1956), British preacher, lecturer, and author **13** 335-337

ROYKO, MIKE (1932-1997), American columnist **13** 337-339

ROZELLE, PETE (Alvin Ray Rozelle; 1926-1996), American commissioner of the National Football League (NFL) **19** 319-322

RUBENS, PETER PAUL (1577-1640), Flemish painter and diplomat **13** 339-342

RUBENSTEIN, HELENA (1870-1965), Polish-born beauty expert and businesswoman **13** 342-343

RUBENSTEIN, RICHARD L. (born 1924), American Jewish theologian and writer **13** 343-344

RUBIN, JERRY (1938-1994), activist, writer, lecturer, and businessman **13** 344-346

RUBIN, VERA COOPER (born 1928), American Astronomer **22** 380-382

RUDKIN, MARGARET FOGARTY (1897-1976), founder and president of Pepperidge Farm Inc. **13** 346-347

RUDOLF I (Rudolf of Hapsburg; circa 1218-91), Holy Roman emperor-elect 1273-91 **13** 347-348

RUDOLPH, PAUL MARVIN (1918-1997), American architect **13** 348-350

RUDOLPH, WILMA (1940-1994), African American track and field athlete and coach **13** 350-352

RUEF, ABRAHAM (1864-1936), American political boss **13** 352-353

RUETHER, ROSEMARY RADFORD (born 1936), American church historian, theologian, writer, and teacher specializing in the area of women and religion **13** 353-354

RUFFIN, EDMUND (1794-1865), American agriculturist **13** 354-355

RUGG, HAROLD (1886-1960), American teacher, historian, and educational theorist **13** 355-357

RUISDAEL, JACOB VAN (1628/29-82), Dutch landscape painter **13** 357-358

RUÍZ, JOSÉ MARTÍNEZ (1873-1967), Spanish writer **13** 358

RUIZ, JUAN (1283?-1350?), Spanish poet **13** 358-359

RUIZ CORTINES, ADOLFO (1890-1973), president of Mexico (1952-1958) **13** 359-360

RUMFORD, COUNT (Benjamin Thompson; 1753-1814), American-born British physicist **13** 360-362

RUMI, JALAI ED-DIN (1207-1273), Persian poet and Sufi mystic **13** 362-363

RUMSFELD, DONALD HAROLD (born 1932), American statesman **23** 353-355

RUNDSTEDT, KARL RUDOLF GERD VON (1875-1953), German field marshal **13** 363-364

RURIK (died circa 873), Norman warrior **13** 364

RUSH, BENJAMIN (1745-1813), American physician **13** 364-365

RUSH, WILLIAM (1756-1833), American sculptor **13** 365-366

RUSHDIE, AHMED SALMAN (born 1947), Indian/British author **13** 366-368

RUSK, DAVID DEAN (1909-1994), American secretary of state (1961-1969) **13** 368-370

RUSKA, ERNST AUGUST FRIEDRICH (1906-1988), German engineer **13** 370-371

RUSKIN, JOHN (1819-1900), English critic and social theorist **13** 371-372

RUSSELL, BERTRAND ARTHUR WILLIAM (3rd Earl Russell; 1872-1970), British mathematician, philosopher, and social reformer **13** 373-374

RUSSELL, BILL (William Felton Russell; born 1934), African American basketball player and coach **20** 320-322

RUSSELL, CHARLES EDWARD (1860-1941), American journalist and reformer **13** 374-375

RUSSELL, CHARLES MARION (1864-1926), American painter **13** 375-376

RUSSELL, CHARLES TAZE (1852-1916), American religious leader **13** 376-377

RUSSELL, ELIZABETH SHULL (born 1913), American geneticist **13** 377-379

RUSSELL, JAMES EARL (1864-1945), educator and college dean who developed Teachers College **13** 379-380

RUSSELL, JOHN (1792-1878), English statesman, Prime minister 1846-52 **13** 380-381

Russian art
Kabakov, Ilya **23** 182-184

Russian Orthodox Church
Tamara **23** 388-390

RUSSWURM, JOHN BROWN (1799-1851), African American and Liberian journalist, educator, and governor **13** 381-382

RUSTIN, BAYARD (1910-1987), American social activist **13** 382-383

RUTAN, BURT (Elbert L. Rutan; born 1943), American aeronautical engineer **20** 322-325

RUTAN, DICK (Richard Glenn Rutan; born 1938), American aviator **20** 325-326

RUTH, GEORGE HERMAN, JR. (Babe Ruth; 1895-1948), American baseball player **13** 384

RUTHERFORD, ERNEST (1st Baron Rutherford of Nelson; 1871-1937), British physicist **13** 384-387

RUTLEDGE, JOHN (1739-1800), American jurist and statesman **13** 387-388

RUYSBROECK, JAN VAN (1293-1381), Flemish mystic **13** 388-389

RYAN, LYNN NOLAN (born 1947), American baseball player and author **13** 389-391

RYDER, ALBERT PINKHAM (1847-1917), American painter **13** 391-392

RYERSON, (ADOLPHUS) EGERTON (1803-1882), Canadian Methodist clergyman and educator **13** 392-393

RYLE, GILBERT (1900-1976), English philosopher **13** 393-394

S

SÁ, MEM DE (1504-1572), Portuguese jurist and governor general of Brazil **13** 395

SAADIA BEN JOSEPH AL-FAYUMI (882-942), Jewish scholar **13** 396

SAARINEN, EERO (1910-1961), Finnish-American architect and industrial designer **13** 396-398

SAARINEN, ELIEL (1873-1950), Finnish-American architect and industrial designer **13** 396-398

SABATIER, PAUL (1854-1941), French chemist **13** 398-399

SÁBATO, ERNESTO (born 1911), Argentine novelist and essayist **13** 399-400

SABBATAI ZEVI (1626-1676), Jewish mystic and pseudo-Messiah **13** 400-401

SABIN, ALBERT BRUCE (1906-1993), Polish-American physician and virologist who developed polio vaccine **13** 401-402

SABIN, FLORENCE RENA (1871-1953), American anatomist **13** 402-405

SACAJAWEA (c. 1784-c. 1812), Native American translator/interpreter, and guide **13** 405-408

SACCO, NICOLA (1891-1927) AND VANZETTI, BARTOLOMEO (1887-1927), Italian-born American anarchists **13** 408-410

SACHS, HANS (1494-1576), German poet **13** 410-411

SACHS, NELLY (1891-1970), German-born Jewish poet and playwright **13** 411-412

SADAT, ANWAR (1918-1981), Egyptian president **13** 412-414

SADAT, JIHAN (born 1933), Egyptian women's rights activist **13** 414-415

SADDAM HUSSEIN (born 1937), socialist president of the Iraqi Republic and strongman of the ruling Ba'th regime **13** 415-416

SADE, COMTE DE (Donatien Alphonse François, Marquis de Sade; 1740-1814), French writer **13** 416-418.

SA'DI (circa 1200-1291), Persian poet **13** 418-419

SADR, MUSA AL- (Imam Musa; 1928-?), Lebanese Shi'ite Moslem religious and political leader **13** 420-422

SAFIRE, WILLIAM (born 1929), American journalist **13** 422-424

SAGAN, CARL E. (born 1934), American astronomer and popularizer of science **13** 424-425

SAGER, RUTH (1918-1997), American biologist and geneticist **13** 425-426

SAICHO (767-822), Japanese Buddhist monk **13** 426-428

SAID, SEYYID (1790-1856), Omani sultan **13** 428-429

SAIGO, TAKAMORI (1827-1877), Japanese rebel and statesman **13** 429

ST. CLAIR, ARTHUR (1736-1818), Scottish-born American soldier and politician **13** 429-430

ST. DENIS, RUTH (1878?-1968), American dancer and choreographer **13** 430-431

ST. LAURENT, LOUIS STEPHEN (born 1882), Canadian statesman **13** 434

SAINTE-BEUVE, CHARLES AUGUSTIN (1804-1869), French literary critic **13** 438

SAINT-EXUPÉRY, ANTOINE DE (1900-1944), French novelist, essayist, and pilot **13** 431-432

SAINT-GAUDENS, AUGUSTUS (1848-1907), American sculptor **13** 432

SAINT-JUST, LOUIS ANTOINE LÉON DE (1767-1794), French radical political leader **13** 433

ST. LAURENT, YVES (born 1936), French fashion designer **20** 327-329

SAINT-PIERRE, ABBÉ DE (Charles Irénée Castel; 1658-1743), French political and economic theorist **13** 434-435

SAINT-SAËNS, CHARLES CAMILLE (1835-1921), French composer **13** 435-436

SAINT-SIMON, COMTE DE (Claude Henri de Rouvroy; 1760-1825), French social philosopher and reformer **13** 436-437

SAINT-SIMON, DUC DE (Louis de Rouvroy; 1675-1755), French writer **13** 436

SAIONJI, KIMMOCHI (1849-1940), Japanese elder statesman **13** 438-439

SAKHAROV, ANDREI (1921-1989), Russian theoretical physicist and "father of the Soviet atomic bomb" **13** 439-441

SALADIN (Salah-ad-Din Yusuf ibn Aiyub; 1138-93), Kurdish ruler of Egypt and Syria **13** 441-442

SALAZAR, ANTÓNIO DE OLIVEIRA (1889-1970), Portuguese statesman **13** 442-443

SALIH, ALI'ABDALLAH (born 1942), president of the Yemeni Arab Republic (North Yemen) and first president of the United Republic of Yemen **13** 443-445

SALINAS DE GORTARI, CARLOS (born 1948), president of Mexico (1988-) **13** 445-447

SALINGER, J. D. (born 1919), American author **13** 447-448

SALISBURY, HARRISON EVANS (born 1908), American journalist **13** 449-451

SALISBURY, 3D MARQUESS OF (Robert Arthur Talbot Gascoyne-Cecil; 1830-1903), English statesman and diplomat **13** 448-449

SALK, JONAS EDWARD (1914-1995), American physician, virologist, and immunologist **13** 451-452

SALLE, DAVID (born 1952), American artist **13** 452-453

SALLUST (Gaius Sallustius Crispus; 86-circa 35 B.C.), Roman statesman and historian **13** 454

SALOMON, CHARLOTTE (1917-1943), German artist **13** 454-455

SALOMON, HAYM (c. 1740-1785), American financier **20** 329-331

SALVEMINI, GAETANO (1873-1957), Italian historian **13** 455-456

SAMPSON, EDITH (nee Edith Spurlock; 1901-1979), African American social worker, judge, and promoter of the United States **23** 356-358

SAMUEL (circa 1056-1004 B.C.), Hebrew prophet, last judge of Israel **13** 457-458

SAMUELSON, PAUL ANTHONY (born 1915), American economist **13** 458-459

SAN MARTÍN, JOSÉ DE (1778-1850), Argentine soldier and statesman **13** 468-469

SANAPIA (Mary Poafpybitty; 1895-1979), Comanche medicine woman **23** 358-360

SANDAGE, ALLAN REX (born 1926), American astronomer **21**

SANCTORIUS (1561-1636), Italian physician and physiologist **13** 459

SAND, GEORGE (1804-1876), French novelist **13** 459-461

SANDBURG, CARL (1878-1967), American poet, anthologist, and biographer **13** 461-462

SANDERS, COLONEL (Harland David Sanders; 1890-1980), American businessman **19** 323-325

SANDINO, AUGUSTO C. (1894-1934), Nicaraguan guerrilla leader **13** 462-463

SANDYS, SIR EDWIN (1561-1629), English statesman and colonizer in America **13** 463-464

SANGALLO FAMILY (flourished late 15th-mid-16th century), Italian artists and architects **13** 464-466

SANGER, FREDERICK (born 1918), English biochemist **13** 466-467

SANGER, MARGARET HIGGINS (1884-1966), American leader of birth control movement **13** 467-468

SANMICHELI, MICHELE (circa 1484-1559), Italian architect and military engineer **13** 469-470

SANSOVINO, JACOPO (1486-1570), Italian sculptor and architect **13** 470-471

SANTA ANA, ANTONIO LÓPEZ DE (1794-1876), Mexican general and statesman, six times president **13** 471-472

SANTA CRUZ, ANDRÉS DE (1792-1865), Bolivian general and statesman, president 1829-39 **13** 472-473

SANTAMARIA, BARTHOLOMEW AUGUSTINE (born 1915), Australian Roman Catholic publicist and organizer **13** 473-474

SANTANA, PEDRO (1801-1864), Dominican military leader, three times president **13** 474-475

SANTANDER, FRANCISCO DE PAULA (1792-1840), Colombian general and statesman **13** 475

SANTAYANA, GEORGE (Jorge Agustin de Santayana; 1863-1952), Spanish-American philosopher **13** 475-477

SANTOS-DUMONT, ALBERTO (1873-1932), Brazilian inventor **13** 477-478

SAPIR, EDWARD (1884-1939), American anthropologist **13** 478-479

SAPPHO (circa 625-570 B.C.), Greek lyric poet **13** 479-480

SAPRU, SIR TEJ BAHADUR (1875-1949), Indian lawyer and statesman **13** 480-481

SARANDON, SUSAN (Susan Abigail Tomalin; born 1946), American actress and activist **18** 358-360

SARGENT, JOHN SINGER (1856-1925), American portrait painter **13** 481-482

SARGON II (ruled 722-705 B.C.), king of Assyria **13** 482

SARGON OF AGADE (circa 2340-2284 B.C.), first Semitic king of Mesopotamia **13** 483

SARIT THANARAT (1908-1963), Thai army officer, prime minister 1957-63 **13** 483-484

SARMIENTO, DOMINGO FAUSTINO (1811-1888), Argentine statesman, president 1868-74 **13** 484-485

SARNOFF, DAVID (1891-1971), American television and radio broadcasting executive **13** 485-486

SAROYAN, WILLIAM (1908-1981), American short-story writer, dramatist, and novelist **13** 486-487

SARPI, PAOLO (1552-1623), Italian prelate and statesman **13** 487-488

SARRAUTE, NATHALIE TCHERNIAK (1900-1999), French author of novels, essays, and plays **13** 488-490

SARTON, GEORGE (1884-1956), Belgian-born American historian of science **13** 490-491

SARTRE, JEAN PAUL (1905-1980), French philosopher and author **13** 491-492

SASSETTA (circa 1400-50), Italian painter **13** 492

SASSOON, SIEGFRIED (1886-1967), English poet **13** 492-493

SATANTA (White Bear; 1830-1878), Native American orator and leader of the Kiowa tribe **13** 493-494

Satellites, artificial see Space exploration

SATIE, ERIK (1866-1925), French composer **13** 494-495

SATO, EISAKU (1901-1975), Japanese statesman, prime minister 1964-72 **13** 495-496

Saudi Arabia, Kingdom of (nation, South Western Asia) Khalid bin Abdul Aziz Al-Saud **23** 194-196

SAUER, CARL ORTWIN (1889-1975), American geographer and anthropologist **13** 496-497

SAUGUET, HENRI (born 1901), French composer, writer, and thinker on art and music **13** 497-498

SAUL (circa 1020-1000 B.C.), first King of Israel **13** 498

SAUNDERS, SIR CHARLES EDWARD (1867-1937), Canadian cerealist **13** 498-499

SAVAGE, AUGUSTA CHRISTINE (born Augusta Christine Fells; 1892-1962), African American sculptor and teacher **13** 499-501

SAVAGE, MICHAEL JOSEPH (1872-1940), New Zealand labor leader, prime minister 1935-40 **13** 501-502

SAVIGNY, FRIEDRICH KARL VON (1779-1861), German jurist **13** 502-503

SAVIMBI, JONAS MALHEIROS (1934-2002), founder and leader of UNITA (National Union for the Total Independence of Angola) **13** 503-505

SAVONAROLA, GIROLAMO (1452-1498), Italian religious reformer and dictator of Florence **13** 505-506

SAW MAUNG (born 1928), leader of armed forces that took power in Burma (now Myanmar) in a 1988 military coup **13** 506-507

SAXE, COMTE DE (1696-1750), marshal of France **13** 507-508

SAY, JEAN BAPTISTE (1767-1832), French economist **13** 508-509

SAYERS, GALE (born 1943), American football player **21** 377-379

SAYRE, FRANCIS BOWES (1885-1972), American lawyer and administrator **13** 509

SAYYID QUTB (1906-1966), Egyptian writer, educator, and religious leader **13** 509-511

SCALFARO, OSCAR LUIGI (born 1918), Christian Democratic leader and president of the Italian Republic **13** 511-512

SCALIA, ANTONIN (born 1936), U.S. Supreme Court justice **13** 513-514

SCARGILL, ARTHUR (born 1938), president of the British National Union of Mineworkers **13** 514-515

SCARLATTI, DOMENICO (1685-1757), Italian harpsichordist and composer **13** 515-517

SCARLATTI, PIETRO ALESSANDRO GASPARE (1660-1725), Italian composer **13** 517-518

Scent of a Woman (film) Pacino, Al **23** 284-286

SCHACHT, HJALMAR HORACE GREELEY (1877-1970), German economist and banker **13** 518-519

SCHAFF, PHILIP (1819-1893), Swiss-born American religious scholar **13** 519-520

SCHAPIRO, MIRIAM (born 1923), Artist **13** 520-521

SCHARNHORST, GERHARD JOHANN DAVID VON (1755-1813), Prussian general **13** 521-522

SCHARPING, RUDOLF (born 1947), minister-president of Rhineland-Palatinate and chairman of the German Social Democratic Party **13** 522-524

SCHECHTER, SOLOMON (1849-1915), Romanian-American Jewish scholar and religious leader **13** 524

SCHEELE, KARL WILHELM (1742-1786), Swedish pharmacist and chemist **13** 525-526

SCHELLING, FRIEDRICH WILHELM JOSEPH VON (1775-1854), German philosopher **13** 526-527

SCHIELE, EGON (1890-1918), Austrian Expressionist painter and draftsman **14** 1-2

SCHIESS, BETTY BONE (born 1923), American Episcopalian priest **18** 360-362

SCHIFF, JACOB HENRY (1847-1920), German-American banker **14** 2-3

SCHILLEBEECKX, EDWARD (born 1914), Belgian Roman Catholic theologian **14** 3-4

SCHILLER, JOHANN CHRISTOPH FRIEDRICH VON (1759-1805), German dramatist, poet, and historian **14** 4-7

SCHINDLER, ALEXANDER MOSHE (1925-2000), American Jewish leader **23** 360-362

SCHINDLER, OSKAR (1908-1974), German businessman and humanitarian **18** 362-365

SCHINDLER, SOLOMON (1842-1915), German-American rabbi and social theorist **14** 7-8

SCHINKEL, KARL FRIEDRICH (1781-1841), German architect, painter and designer **14** 8

SCHLAFLY, PHYLLIS (born 1924), American political activist and author **14** 9-10

SCHLEGEL, FRIEDRICH VON (1772-1829), German critic and author **14** 10-11

SCHLEIERMACHER, FRIEDRICH ERNST DANIEL (1768-1834), German theologian and philosopher **14** 11-12

SCHLEMMER, OSKAR (1888-1943), German painter, sculptor, and stage designer **14** 12-13

SCHLESINGER, ARTHUR MEIER (1888-1965), American historian **14** 13

SCHLESINGER, ARTHUR MEIER, JR. (born 1917), American historian and Democratic party activist **14** 13-15

SCHLESINGER, JAMES RODNEY (born 1929), American government official **14** 15-16

SCHLICK, FRIEDRICH ALBERT MORITZ (1882-1936), German physicist and philosopher **14** 16-17

SCHLIEMANN, HEINRICH (1822-1890), German merchant and archeologist **14** 17-18

SCHLÜTER, ANDREAS (circa 1660-1714), German sculptor and architect **14** 18-19

SCHMIDT, HELMUT (born 1918), Social Democrat and chancellor of the Federal Republic of Germany (the former West Germany), 1974-82 **14** 19-21

SCHMITT, JACK (Harrison Hagan Schmitt; borm 1935), American astronaut and geologist **22** 385-386

SCHMOLLER, GUSTAV FRIEDRICH VON (1838-1917), German economist **14** 21

SCHNEERSON, MENACHEM MENDEL (The Rebbe; 1902-1994), Russian-American Hassidic Jewish leader **22** 386-388

SCHNEIDERMAN, ROSE (1882-1972), labor organizer and activist for the improvement of working conditions for women **14** 22-23

SCHNITZLER, ARTHUR (1862-1931), Austrian dramatist and novelist **14** 23-24

SCHOENBERG, ARNOLD (1874-1951), Austrian composer **14** 24-26

SCHOLEM, GERSHOM (1897-1982), Jewish scholar **14** 26

SCHONGAUER, MARTIN (circa 1435-91), German engraver and painter **14** 26-28

SCHÖNHUBER, FRANZ XAVER (born 1923), German right-wing political leader **14** 28-29

SCHOOLCRAFT, HENRY ROWE (1793-1864), American explorer and ethnologist **14** 29

SCHOPENHAUER, ARTHUR (1788-1860), German philosopher **14** 29-31

SCHOUTEN, WILLIAM CORNELIUS (circa 1580-1625), Dutch explorer and navigator **14** 31

SCHREINER, OLIVE (Olive Emilie Albertina Schreiner; Ralph Iron; 1855-1920), South African author **23** 362-364

SCHREMPP, JUERGEN (born 1944), German automobile industry executive **20** 331-332

SCHRODER, GERHARD (born 1944), German chancellor **19** 325-327

SCHRÖDINGER, ERWIN (1887-1961), Austrian physicist **14** 31-33

SCHROEDER, PATRICIA SCOTT (born 1940), first U.S. congresswoman from Colorado **14** 33-35

SCHUBERT, FRANZ PETER (1797-1828), Austrian composer **14** 35-37

SCHULLER, GUNTHER (born 1925), American musician **14** 37-38

SCHULZ, CHARLES M. (1922-2000), American cartoonist and creator of "Peanuts" **14** 38-39

SCHUMACHER, KURT (1895-1952), German socialist statesman **14** 40-41

SCHUMAN, ROBERT (1886-1963), French statesman **14** 41

SCHUMAN, WILLIAM HOWARD (1910-1992), American composer and educator **22** 388-391

SCHUMANN, ROBERT ALEXANDER (1810-1856), German composer and critic **14** 41-43

SCHUMPETER, JOSEPH ALOIS (1883-1950), Austrian economist **14** 43-44

SCHURZ, CARL (1829-1906), American soldier, statesman, and journalist **14** 44-45

SCHUSCHNIGG, KURT VON (1897-1977), Austrian statesman, chancellor of Austria 1934-38 **14** 45-46

SCHÜSSLER FIORENZA, ELIZABETH (born 1938), biblical scholar and theologian **14** 46-48

SCHÜTZ, HEINRICH (1585-1672), German composer **14** 48-49

SCHUYLER, PHILIP JOHN (1733-1804), American Revolutionary War general **14** 49-50

SCHWAB, CHARLES MICHAEL (1862-1939), American industrialist **14** 50-51

SCHWANN, THEODOR (1810-1882), German biologist **14** 51-52

SCHWARTZ, DELMORE (1913-1966), American poet **19** 327-329

SCHWARZKOPF, NORMAN (born 1934), American army general **14** 52-54

SCHWEITZER, ALBERT (1875-1965), Alsatian-German philosopher and medical missionary **14** 55-56

SCHWENCKFELD, KASPER VON (1489/90-1561), Silesian nobleman and theologian **14** 56-57

SCHWIMMER, ROSIKA (1877-1948), Hungarian women's rights activist **14** 57-60

SCHWITTERS, KURT (1887-1948), German painter, collagist, typographer, and poet and creator of MERZ-art **14** 60-61

Science
philosophy of
Cavendish, Margaret Lucas **23** 66-67

Scientists, American
astronomers
Leavitt, Henrietta Swan **23** 211-213
Penzias, Arno Allen **23** 301-304
Whitney, Mary Watson **23** 440-442
biochemists
Prusiner, Stanley Ben **23** 320-323
biomedical researchers
Prusiner, Stanley Ben **23** 320-323
botanists
Plotkin, Mark J. **23** 308-310
chemists (20th century)
Lee, Yuan Tseh **23** 218-220
inventors (20th century)
Lee, Yuan Tseh **23** 218-220
molecular biologists
Cech, Thomas Robert **23** 68-70
Gilbert, Walter **23** 122-124
Ho, David Da-I **23** 145-148
physicians (19th-20th century)
Walker, Mary Edwards **23** 432-434
physicians (20th century)
Sanapia **23** 358-360
physicists (20th century)
Penzias, Arno Allen **23** 301-304
Ting, Samuel Chao Chung **23** 406-408
Wilson, Kenneth Geddes **23** 446-448
physiologists
Pool, Judith Graham **23** 315-316
psychologists
Ladd-Franklin, Christine **23** 202-204
virologists
Ho, David Da-I **23** 145-148

Scientists, Canadian
Altman, Sidney **23** 9-11
Tyrrell, Joseph Burr **23** 410-412

Scientists, English
astronomers
Harriot, Thomas **23** 137-139
mathematicians
Harriot, Thomas **23** 137-139
Oughtred, William **23** 277-279
Scott, Charlotte Angas **23** 364-367
Wiles, Andrew J. **23** 442-444
naturalists
Cavendish, Margaret Lucas **23** 66-67
North, Marianne **23** 268-270
physicians and surgeons
Jex-Blake, Sophia **23** 168-170

Scientists, German
biochemists
Deisenhofer, Johann **23** 90-93
mathematicians
Fraenkel, Abraham Adolf **23** 109-111

Scientists, Greek
mathematicians
Theano **23** 399-401
physicians
Theano **23** 399-401

Scientists, Japanese
Fukui, Kenichi **23** 111-112

Scientists, Swiss
mathematicians
Bernoulli, Jakob **23** 37-39
Steiner, Jakob **23** 380-382

Scientists, Taiwanese
Lee, Yuan Tseh **23** 218-220

SCIPIO AFRICANUS MAJOR, PUBLIUS CORNELIUS (236-184/183 B.C.), Roman general **14** 61-62

SCIPIO AFRICANUS MINOR, PUBLIUS CORNELIUS AEMILIANUS (185/184-129 B.C.), Roman general **14** 62-63

SCORSESE, MARTIN (born 1942), American filmmaker and screenwriter **14** 63-65

SCOTT, CHARLOTTE ANGAS (1858-1931), English mathematician **23** 364-367

SCOTT, DRED (1795-1858), African American revolutionary **14** 65-66

SCOTT, FRANCIS REGINALD (1899-1985), Canadian poet, political activist, and constitutional theorist **14** 66-67

SCOTT, GEORGE CAMPBELL (1927-1999), American actor and director **22** 391-393

SCOTT, ROBERT FALCON (1868-1912), English naval officer and polar explorer **14** 67-68

SCOTT, THOMAS ALEXANDER (1823-1881), American railroad builder **21**

SCOTT, SIR WALTER (1771-1832), Scottish novelist and poet **14** 68-70

SCOTT, WINFIELD (1786-1866), American general **14** 70-71

SCRIABIN, ALEXANDER NIKOLAYEVICH (1871-1915), Russian composer and pianist **14** 71-72

SCRIPPS, EDWARD WYLLIS (1854-1926), American newspaper publisher **14** 72-73

Scripture studies
see Bible

SCULLIN, JAMES HENRY (1876-1953), Australian politician **14** 73

SEABORG, GLENN THEODORE (1912-1999), American chemist and chairman of the Atomic Energy Commission **14** 74-76

SEABURY, SAMUEL (1729-1796), American theologian **14** 76

SEALE, ROBERT GEORGE (Bobby; born 1936), militant activist and a founder of the Black Panther Party **14** 77-78

SEAMAN, ELIZABETH COCHRANE (1864-1922), American journalist and reformer **14** 78-80

SEATTLE (c. 1788-1866), Native American tribal chief **14** 80-81

Secrets and Lies (film)
Leigh, Mike **23** 222-225

SEDDON, RICHARD JOHN (1845-1906), New Zealand politician **14** 81-82

SEDGWICK, ADAM (1785-1873), English geologist **14** 82-83

SEEGER, PETE (born 1919), American folksinger and activist **14** 83-84

SEFERIS, GEORGE (Georgios Seferiadis; 1900-71), Greek poet and statesman **14** 84-85

SEGAL, GEORGE (born 1924), American sculptor **14** 85-87

SEGOVIA, ANDRÉS (1893-1987), Spanish guitarist **14** 87-88

Segregation (racial, United States)
see African American history (United States)

SEIBERT, FLORENCE B. (1897-1991), American biochemist **14** 89-90

SEJO (1417-1468), king of Korea 1453-68 **14** 90-91

SEJONG (1397-1450), king of Korea 1418-50 **14** 91-92

SELENA (Selena Quintanilla-Perez; 1971-1995), Hispanic-American singer **18** 365-367

SELEUCUS I (circa 358-281 B.C.), Macedonian general, king of Babylonia and Syria **14** 92-93

SELIGMAN, EDWIN ROBERT ANDERSON (1861-1939), American economist and editor **14** 93-94

SELIM I (circa 1470-1520), Ottoman sultan 1512-20 **14** 94-95

SELIM III (1761-1808), Ottoman sultan 1789-1807 **14** 95-96

SELKIRK, 5TH EARL OF (Thomas Douglas; 1771-1820), Scottish colonizer in Canada **14** 96

SELLARS, WILFRED (1912-1989), American philosopher **14** 96-98

SELLERS, PETER RICHARD HENRY (1925-1980), British comedy genius of theater, radio, television, and movies **14** 98-99

SELZNICK, DAVID OLIVER (1902-1965), American filmmaker **20** 333-335

SEMENOV, NIKOLAI NIKOLAEVICH (1896-1986), Russian physicist and physical chemist **14** 101

SEMMELWEIS, IGNAZ PHILIPP (1818-1865), Hungarian physician **14** 101-102

SEMMES, RAPHAEL (1809-1877), American Confederate naval officer **14** 102-103

SEN, RAM CAMUL (1783-1844), Bengali intellectual and entrepreneur **13** 16-17

SENDAK, MAURICE (born 1928), American author, artist, and illustrator **19** 329-331

SENECA THE YOUNGER, LUCIUS ANNAEUS (circa 4 B.C.-A.D. 65), Roman philosopher **14** 103-105

SENFL, LUDWIG (circa 1486-circa 1543), Swiss-born German composer **14** 105-106

SENGHOR, LÉOPOLD SÉDAR (born 1906), Senegalese poet, philosopher, and statesman **14** 106-107

SENNACHERIB (ruled 705-681 B.C.), king of Assyria **14** 108

SENNETT, MACK (1884-1960), American film producer and director **14** 108-109

SEQUOYAH (circa 1770-1843), American Cherokee Indian scholar **14** 110-111

SERRA, JUNIPERO (Miguel José Serra; 1713-84), Spanish Franciscan missionary, founder of California missions **14** 111-112

SERRANO ELÍAS, JORGE ANTONIO (born 1945), president of Guatemala (1991-1993) **14** 112-113

SERTÜRNER, FRIEDRICH (Friedrich Wilhelm Adam Ferdinand Sertürner; 1783-1841), Prussian pharmacist **21** 379-381

SERVAN-SCHREIBER, JEAN-JACQUES (born 1924), French journalist and writer on public affairs **14** 113-115

SERVETUS, MICHAEL (circa 1511-53), Spanish religious philosopher **14** 115-116

SESSHU, TOYA (1420-1506), Japanese painter and Zen priest **14** 116-117

SESSIONS, ROGER HUNTINGTON (1896-1985), American composer **14** 117-118

Set theory (mathematics)
Fraenkel, Abraham Adolf **23** 109-111

SETON, ELIZABETH ANN BAYLEY (1774-1821), American Catholic leader **14** 118-119

SETON, ERNEST THOMPSON (1860-1946), Canadian author and co-founder of the Boy Scouts of America **14** 119-120

SETTIGNANO, DESIDERIO DA (1428/31-1464), Italian sculptor **4** 509

SEURAT, GEORGES PIERRE (1859-1891), French painter **14** 120-122

SEVAREID, ERIC (Arnold Eric Sevareid 1912-1992), American broadcast journalist and author **22** 395-397

Seventh-Day Adventist Church
White, Ellen Gould **23** 438-440

SEVERINI, GINO (1883-1966), Italian painter **14** 122

SEVERUS, LUCIUS SEPTIMIUS (146-211), Roman emperor 193-211 **14** 109-110

SEVIER, JOHN (1745-1815), American frontiersman, soldier, and politician **14** 122-123

SEWALL, SAMUEL (1652-1730), American jurist and diarist **14** 123-124

SEWARD, WILLIAM HENRY (1801-1872), American statesman **14** 124-125

SEXTON, ANNE (Anne Gray Harvey; 1928-74), American ''confessional'' poet **14** 125-126

SEYMOUR, HORATIO (1810-1886), American politician **14** 126-127

SEYMOUR, JANE (1509-1537), third wife and queen consort of Henry VIII of England **18** 367-368

SFORZA, LODOVICO (1452-1508), duke of Milan **14** 127-128

SHABAKA (ruled circa 712-circa 696 B.C.), Nubian king, pharaoh of Egypt **14** 130

SHABAZZ, BETTY (1936-1997), African American educator, activist, and health administrator **14** 130-132

SHACKLETON, SIR ERNEST HENRY (1874-1922), British explorer **14** 132-133

SHAFFER, PETER LEVIN (born 1926), English/American playwright **14** 133-135

SHAFTESBURY, 1ST EARL OF (Anthony Ashley Cooper; 1621-83), English statesman **14** 135-136

SHAFTESBURY, 3D EARL OF (Anthony Ashley Cooper; 1671-1713), English moral philosopher **14** 136-137

SHAFTESBURY, 7TH EARL OF (Anthony Ashley Cooper; 1801-85), English social reformer **14** 137-138

SHAH JAHAN (1592-1666), Mogul emperor of India 1628-58 **14** 138-139

SHAHN, BEN (1898-1969), American painter, graphic artist, and photographer **14** 139-140

SHAHPUR II (310-379), king of Persia **14** 140-141

SHAKA (circa 1787-1828), African Zulu military monarch **14** 141-142

SHAKESPEARE, WILLIAM (1564-1616), English playwright, poet, and actor **14** 142-145

SHALIKASHVILI, JOHN MALCHASE DAVID (born 1936), chairman of the U.S. Joint Chiefs of Staff **14** 145-147

SHAMIR, YITZCHAK (Yizernitsky; born 1914), Israeli prime minister and leader of the Likud Party **14** 147-149

SHAMMAI (flourished 1st century B.C.), Jewish sage **14** 149

SHANG YANG (circa 390-338 B.C.), Chinese statesman and political philosopher **14** 149-150

SHANGE, NTOZAKE (Paulette Linda Williams; born 1948), African American author **23** 367-369

SHANKARA (Shankaracharya; circa 788-820), Indian philosopher and reformer **14** 150-151

SHANKAR, RAVI (Robindra Shankar; born 1920), Indian musician **22** 397-399

SHANKER, ALBERT (1928-1977), American education leader **14** 151-153

SHANNON, CLAUDE ELWOOD (born 1916), American mathematician **14** 153-154

SHAPEY, RALPH (1921-2002), American composer, conductor, and teacher **14** 154-155

SHAPLEY, HARLOW (1885-1972), American astronomer **14** 155-156

SHARIATI, ALI (1933-1977), ''Ideologue of the Iranian Revolution'' **14** 156-157

SHARIF, NAWAZ (Niam Nawaz Sharif; born 1949), Pakistani prime minister **19** 331-333

SHARON, ARIEL (Arik; born 1928), Israeli politician and defense minister **14** 157-159

SHARPTON, AL (born 1954), African American civil rights leader and minister **14** 159-162

SHAW, ANNA HOWARD (1847-1919), American suffragist leader, reformer, and women's rights activist **14** 162-163

SHAW, GEORGE BERNARD (1856-1950), British playwright, critic, and pamphleteer **14** 163-164

SHAW, LEMUEL (1781-1861), American jurist **14** 164-165

SHAW, MARY (born 1943), American computer science professor **14** 165-167

SHAW, RICHARD NORMAN (1831-1912), British architect **14** 167-168

SHAWN, WILLIAM (1907-1992), American editor **19** 333-335

SHAYS, DANIEL (circa 1747-1825), American Revolutionary War Captain **14** 168

SHCHARANSKY, ANATOLY BORISOVICH (born 1948), prominent figure of the Helsinki Watch Group **14** 168-170

SHEELER, CHARLES (1883-1965), American painter **14** 170-171

SHEEN, FULTON J. (1895-1979), American Roman Catholic bishop and television host **14** 171-172

SHELDON, CHARLES M. (1857-1946), American social reformer who also wrote *In His Steps* **14** 172-174

SHELLEY, MARY WOLLSTONECRAFT (1797-1851), English author **14** 174-176

SHELLEY, PERCY BYSSHE (1792-1822), English romantic poet **14** 176-178

SHEPARD, ALAN (1923-1998), American astronaut **14** 178-180

SHEPARD, SAM (Samuel Shepard Rogers VII; born 1943), American playwright, rock performer, and film actor **14** 180-181

SHERATON, THOMAS (1751-1806), English furniture designer **14** 181-182

SHERIDAN, PHILIP HENRY (1831-1888), American general **14** 182-183

SHERIDAN, RICHARD BRINSLEY (1751-1816), British playwright and orator **14** 183-184

SHERMAN, CINDY (Cynthia Morris Sherman; born 1954), American photographer **19** 335-337

SHERMAN, JOHN (1823-1900), American politician **14** 184-185

SHERMAN, ROGER (1721-1793), American patriot **14** 185-186

SHERMAN, WILLIAM TECUMSEH (1820-1891), American general **14** 186-187

SHERRINGTON, SIR CHARLES SCOTT (1857-1952), English physiologist **14** 187-189

SHERWOOD, ROBERT EMMET (1896-1955), American playwright **14** 189-190

SHESTOV, LEV (Lev Isaakovich Schwarzmann; 1866-1938), Russian Jewish thinker and literary critic **14** 190-191

SHEVARDNADZE, EDUARD AMVROSEVICH (born 1928), foreign minister of the U.S.S.R. (1985-1990) **14** 191-193

SHIH KO-FA (died 1644), Chinese scholar-soldier **14** 194-195

SHIH LE (274-333), Chinese emperor 330-333 **14** 195

SHIHAB, FU'AD (1903-1973), Father of the Lebanese Army and president of Lebanon (1958-1964) **14** 193-194

SHILS, EDWARD ALBERT (born 1911), American sociologist **14** 195-197

SHINRAN (1173-1262), Japanese Buddhist monk **14** 197

SHIPPEN, EDWARD (1728-1806), American jurist **14** 197-198

SHIRER, WILLIAM L. (born 1904), American journalist and historian who wrote on the history of Nazi Germany **14** 198-199

Shochiku Motion Picture Company Ozu, Yasujiro **23** 279-281

SHOCKLEY, WILLIAM (1910-1989), American physicist **14** 200-202

SHOEMAKER, GENE (Eugene Merle Shoemaker; 1928-1997), American geologist and planetary scientist **20** 335-338

SHOEMAKER, WILLIE (Billy Lee Shoemaker; born 1931), American jockey and horse trainer **21** 381-383

SHOLEM ALEICHEM (Sholem Rabinowitz; 1859-1916), Russian-born American author **14** 202-203

SHOLES, CHRISTOPHER LATHAM (1819-1890), American publisher, inventor, and social reformer **21** 383-385

SHOLOKHOV, MIKHAIL ALEKSANDROVICH (1905-1984), Russian novelist **14** 203-204

SHORT, WALTER (1880-1949), American army officer **19** 337-339

SHOSTAKOVICH, DMITRI DMITRIEVICH (1906-1975), Russian composer **14** 204-205

SHOTOKU TAISHI (573-621), Japanese regent, statesman, and scholar **14** 205-207

Show Boat (musical) Tamiris, Helen **23** 390-392

SHREVE, HENRY MILLER (1785-1851), American steamboat designer and builder **14** 207

SHRIVER, EUNICE KENNEDY (born 1921), American activist **19** 339-341

SHUBERT BROTHERS (1883-1963), theatrical managers **14** 207-209

SHULTZ, GEORGE PRATT (born 1920), labor and economics specialist, educator, businessman, and international negotiator **14** 209-211

SIBELIUS, JEAN JULIUS CHRISTIAN (1865-1957), Finnish composer **14** 211-212

SICKERT, WALTER RICHARD (1860-1942), English painter **14** 212-213

SICKLES, DANIEL EDGAR (1819-1914), American politician and diplomat **21** 385-388

SIDGWICK, HENRY (1838-1900), English philosopher and moralist **14** 213

SIDNEY, SIR PHILIP (1554-1586), English poet, courtier, diplomat, and soldier **14** 214-215

SIEBERT, MURIEL (born 1932), American businesswoman **18** 368-370

SIEGEL, BENJAMIN ("Bugsy"; 1906-1947), American gangster **14** 215-216

SIENKIEWICZ, HENRYK (1846-1916), Polish novelist and short-story writer **14** 216-217

SIERRA, JUSTO (1848-1912), Mexican educator, writer, and historian **14** 217

SIEYÈS, COMTE EMMANUEL JOSEPH (1748-1836), French statesman and political writer **14** 217-218

SIFTON, SIR CLIFFORD (1861-1929), politician who helped turn the Canadian West into a premier agricultural area **14** 219-220

SIGISMUND (1368-1437), Holy Roman emperor 1411-37, king of Bohemia 1420-37, and king of Hungary 1385-1437 **14** 220-221

SIGNAC, PAUL (1863-1935), French painter **23** 369-372

SIGNORELLI, LUCA (circa 1445/50-1523), Italian painter **14** 221-222

SIHANOUK, PRINCE NORODOM (born 1922), Cambodian nationalist and political leader **14** 222-223

SIKORSKY, IGOR (1889-1972), Russian-American aeronautical engineer, aircraft manufacturer, and inventor **14** 223-224

SIKORSKI, WLADYSLAW (1881-1943), Polish military leader and prime minister **20** 338-340

SILBER, JOHN (born 1926), American philosopher and educator **14** 224-226

SILES ZUAZO, HERNAN (1914-1996), Bolivian politician **18** 370-373

SILKO, LESLIE (Leslie Marmon Silko; born 1948), Native American author and poet **14** 226-227

SILKWOOD, KAREN (1946-1974), American antinuclear activist **14** 227-229

SILLIMAN, BENJAMIN (1779-1864), American chemist, naturalist, and editor **14** 229-230

SILLS, BEVERLY (Belle Miriam Silverman; born 1929), American child performer, coloratura soprano, and operatic superstar **14** 230-231

SILONE, IGNAZIO (1900-1978), Italian novelist and essayist **14** 231-232

SILVER, ABBA HILLEL (1893-1963), American rabbi and Zionist leader **14** 232-233

SILVERSTEIN, SHEL (1932-1999), American author and poet **19** 341-343

SIMENON, GEORGES (1903-1989), Belgian novelist **14** 233-234

SIMMEL, GEORG (1858-1918), German sociologist and philosopher **14** 234-235

SIMMS, WILLIAM GILMORE (1806-1870), American author **14** 235-236

SIMON, HERBERT ALEXANDER (born 1916), American Nobelist in economics **14** 236-237

SIMON, JULES FRANÇOIS (1814-1896), French philosopher, writer, and statesman **14** 237-238

SIMON, NEIL (Marvin Neil Simon; born 1927), American playwright **18** 373-374

SIMON, PAUL (born 1928), newspaper publisher, Illinois state legislator, lieutenant governor, and U.S. representative and senator **14** 238-239

SIMONOV, KONSTANTIN MIKHAILOVICH (1915-1979), Soviet poet and novelist **14** 239-240

SIMPSON, GEORGE GAYLORD (1902-1984), American paleontologist **14** 240-242

SIMPSON, LOUIS ASTON MARANTZ (born 1923), American poet, critic, and educator **14** 243-244

SIMPSON, WALLIS (Bessie Wallis Warfield Simpson, Duchess of Windsor; 1896-1986), American socialite and wife of Edward VIII, King of England **19** 343-345

SIMS, WILLIAM SOWDEN (1858-1936), American admiral **14** 244

SIN, JAIME L. (born 1928), Filipino cardinal of the Roman Catholic Church **14** 244-245

SINAN, KODJA MIMAR (1489-1578), Ottoman architect **14** 245-246

SINATRA, FRANCIS ALBERT (Frank Sinatra; 1915-1998), American singer **14** 246-248

SINCLAIR, UPTON BEALE, JR. (1878-1968), American novelist and political writer **14** 248-249

SINGER, ISAAC BASHEVIS (1904-1991), Polish-American author **14** 249-250

SINGER, ISAAC M. (1811-1875), American inventor of the sewing machine **14** 250

SINGER, MAXINE (born Maxine Frank, 1931), American biochemist and geneticist **14** 251-252

SINGER, PETER ALBERT DAVID (born 1946), Australian philosopher and author of Animal Liberation **14** 253-254

SINGH, VISHWANATH PRATAP (born 1931), prime minister of India (1989-1990) **14** 254-256

SIQUEIROS, DAVID ALFARO (1896-1974), Mexican mural painter **14** 256

SIRANI, ELISABETTA (1638-1665), Italian artist **22** 399-401

SIRICA, JOHN JOSEPH (1904-1992), U.S. district court judge who presided over the Watergate affair **14** 257-258

SISMONDI, JEAN CHARLES LÉONARD SIMONDE DE (1773-1842), Swiss-born historian and political economist **14** 258-259

SISULU, NONTSIKELELO ALBERTINA (1918-2003), leader of the anti-apartheid movement in South Africa **14** 259-261

SISULU, WALTER MAX ULYATE (born 1912), leader of the African National Congress (ANC) of South Africa **14** 261-262

SITHOLE, NDABANINGI (born 1920), African nationalist **14** 262-264

SITTING BULL (circa 1834-90), American Indian leader and medicine man **14** 264-265

SITWELL, DAME EDITH (1887-1964), English poet and critic **14** 265-266

ŚIVAJT (1627-1680), Indian warrior and leader of a Hindu nation **14** 266-267

SIXTUS V (Felice Perreti; 1520-90), pope 1585-90 **14** 267-268

SIZA, ALVARO (Alvaro Joaquim Melo Siza Vieria; born 1933), Portugese architect **18** 375-376

SKELTON, JOHN (circa 1460-1529), English poet and humanist **14** 268-269

SKINNER, BURRHUS FREDERIC (1904-1990), American experimental psychologist **14** 269-270

SKINNER, CORNELIA OTIS (1901-1979), American actress and author **19** 346-348

SLÁNSKÝ, RUDOLF SALZMANN (1901-1952), founding member of the Czechoslovak Communist Party and vice-premier of the former Czechoslovakia **14** 270-271

SLATER, SAMUEL (1768-1835), English-born American manufacturer **14** 272-273

SLIDELL, JOHN (1793-1871), American politician **14** 273

SLIM, WILLIAM JOSEPH (a.k.a. Anthony Mills; 1891-1970), English general and governor-general of Australia **18** 377-378

SLOAN, ALFRED PRITCHARD, JR. (1875-1966), American automobile executive **14** 274

SLOAN, JOHN (1871-1951), American painter **14** 274-275

SLUTER, CLAUS (circa 1350-1405/1406), Dutch-Burgundian sculptor **14** 275-276

SLYE, MAUD (1879-1954), American pathologist **14** 276-277

SMALL, ALBION WOODBURY (1854-1926), American sociologist and educator **14** 277

SMALLS, ROBERT (1839-1916), African American statesman **14** 277-278

SMEAL, ELEANOR (Eleanor Marie Cutri Smeal; born 1939), American women's rights activist and president of the National Organization for Women **14** 278-280

SMEATON, JOHN (1724-1792), English civil engineer **14** 280-281

SMETANA, BEDŘICH (1824-1884), Czech composer **14** 281-282

SMIBERT, JOHN (1688-1751), Scottish-born American painter **14** 282

SMITH, ADAM (1723-1790), Scottish economist and moral philosopher **14** 283-284

SMITH, ALFRED EMMANUEL (1873-1944), American politician **14** 284-285

SMITH, BESSIE (1894-1937), African American blues singer **14** 285-287

SMITH, DAVID (1906-1965), American sculptor **14** 287-288

SMITH, DEAN EDWARDS (born 1931), American college basketball coach **18** 378-380

SMITH, DONALD ALEXANDER (1st Baron Strathcona and Mount Royal; 1820-1914), Canadian politician and philanthropist **14** 288-289

SMITH, DORA VALENTINE (1893-1985), American educator **14** 289-290

SMITH, GERRIT (1797-1874), American philanthropist and reformer **14** 290-291

SMITH, IAN DOUGLAS (born 1919), African prime minister **14** 291-293

SMITH, JAMES MCCUNE (1813-1865), African American physician and author **14** 293-294

SMITH, JEDEDIAH S. (1799-1831), American trapper, fur trader, and explorer **14** 294-295

SMITH, JOHN (circa 1580-1631), English colonist in America **14** 295-297

SMITH, JOSEPH (1805-1844), American Mormon leader **14** 297-298

SMITH, LILLIAN EUGENIA (1897-1966), Southern writer and critic of white supremacy and segregation **14** 298-299

SMITH, MARGARET CHASE (1897-1995), first woman elected to both houses of Congress **14** 299-300

SMITH, PAULINE (Pauline Janet Urmson Smith; Janet Tamson; 1882-1959), South African author **23** 372-373

SMITH, WILLIAM (1727-1803), American educator and churchman **14** 301

SMITH, WILLIAM EUGENE (1918-1978), American photojournalist **19** 348-350

SMITHSON, ROBERT (1938-1973), American sculptor, essayist, and filmmaker **14** 301-303

SMOHALLA (1815-1895), Native American warrior, medicine man, and spiritual leader **14** 303-305

SMOLLETT, TOBIAS GEORGE (1721-1771), English novelist and satirist **14** 305-307

SMUIN, MICHAEL (born 1938), American dancer-choreographer-director **14** 307-309

SMUTS, JAN CHRISTIAN (1870-1950), South African soldier and statesman **14** 309-310

SNEAD, SAM (Samuel Jackson Snead; 1912-2002), American golfer **21** 388-390

SNOW, CHARLES PERCY (1905-1972), English novelist and physicist **14** 311-312

SNOW, EDGAR (1905-1972), American journalist and author **14** 312-313

SNOWE, OLYMPIA (born Olympia Jean Bouchles, 1947), U.S. congresswoman and senator **14** 313-314

SOANE, SIR JOHN (1753-1837), English architect **14** 314-315

SOARES, MÁRIO (Mário Alberto Nobre Lopes Soares; born 1924), first socialist president of Portugal **14** 315-316

SOBCHAK, ANATOLY ALEXANDROVICH (1937-2000), popular democratic leader of Russia elected mayor of St. Petersburg in 1990 **14** 317-318

SOBUKWE, ROBERT MANGALISO (1924-1978), South African politician **14** 318-319

Social reform
Australia
Spence, Catherine Helen **23** 374-375
Europe
Romilly, Samuel **23** 348-351
United States
Paglia, Camille **23** 286-288
Walker, Mary Edwards **23** 432-434

Social scientists, American
anthropologists (20th century)
Robeson, Eslanda Goode **23** 340-342
historians (20th century)
Beveridge, Albert Jeremiah **23** 39-41
librarians
Rollins, Charlemae Hill **23** 346-348

Social scientists, Taiwanese
Lee, Yuan Tseh **23** 218-220

SOCRATES (469-399 B.C.), Greek philosopher and logican **14** 320-321

SODDY, FREDERICK (1877-1956), English chemist **14** 321-323

SÖDERBLOM, NATHAN (Lars Jonathan Söderblom; 1866-1931), Swedish Lutheran archbishop **14** 323-324

SOELLE, DOROTHEE (1929-2003), German theologian, political activist, and feminist **14** 324-325

SOL CH'ONG (circa 680-750), Korean Confucian scholar **14** 325-326

Solaris (film)
Tarkovsky, Andrei Arsenyevich **23** 392-395

SOLÍS, JUAN DÍAZ DE (circa 1470-1516), Spanish explorer **14** 326

SOLOMON (ruled circa 965-circa 925 B.C.), king of the ancient Hebrews **14** 326-327

SOLON (active 594 B.C.), Greek statesman and poet **14** 327-328

SOLOVEITCHIK, JOSEPH BAER (1903-1993), Jewish theologian and philosopher **14** 328-329

SOLOVIEV, VLADIMIR SERGEEVICH (1853-1900), Russian philosopher and religious thinker **14** 329-330

SOLZHENITSYN, ALEXANDER ISAYEVICH (born 1918), Soviet novelist **14** 330-332

SOMBART, WERNER (1863-1941), German economic historian **14** 332-333

SOMERSET, DUKE OF (Edward Seymour; 1506-52), English statesman **14** 333-334

SOMERVILLE, EDITH ANNE ŒNONE (1858-1949), Irish author **14** 334-335

SOMERVILLE, MARY (1780-1872), Scottish mathematician, physicist, and geographer **20** 340-342

Somerville and Ross (pseudonym)
see Edith Anna Œnone Somerville

SOMOZA, ANASTASIO (1896-1956), Nicaraguan dictator and military leader **14** 335-336

SOMOZA DEBAYLE, ANASTASIO (1925-1980), president of Nicaragua (1967-1979) **14** 336-337

SONDHEIM, STEPHEN (born 1930), American composer and lyricist **14** 337-338

SONG SISTERS (Ailing Song, 1890-1973; Meiling Song, 1898-1919; and Qingling Song, 1890-1981) Chinese political and social activists **14** 338-341

SONJO (1552-1608), king of Korea 1567-1608 **14** 341-342

SONTAG, SUSAN (born 1933), American essayist **14** 342-343

Sophie's Choice (book, film)
Streep, Meryl Louise **23** 384-387

SOPHOCLES (496-406 B.C.), Greek playwright **14** 343-345

SOPWITH, THOMAS OCTAVE MURDOCH (1888-1989), British aviation industrialist and pioneer pilot **14** 345-346

SORDELLO (ca. 1180-ca. 1269), Italian poet and troubadour **20** 342-343

SOREL, ALBERT (1842-1906), French diplomatic historian **14** 346-347

SOREL, GEORGES (1847-1922), French philosopher **14** 347-348

SOROKIN, PITIRIM A. (1889-1968), Russian-American sociologist **14** 348-349

SOTATSU, TAWARAYA (circa 1570-circa 1643), Japanese painter **14** 349

SOUFFLOT, JACQUES GERMAIN (1713-1780), French architect **14** 349-350

SOULAGES, PIERRE (born 1919), French painter **14** 350-351

SOULÉ, PIERRE (1801-1870), American politician and diplomat **14** 351-352

SOUSA, HENRIQUE TEIXEIRA DE (born 1919), Cape Verdean novelist **14** 352-353

SOUSA, JOHN PHILIP (1854-1932), American bandmaster and composer **14** 353-354

SOUSA, MARTIM AFONSO DE (circa 1500-64), Portuguese colonizer and statesman **14** 354-355

SOUTER, DAVID H. (born 1939), U.S. Supreme Court justice **14** 355-356

South Africa, Republic of
• INDEPENDENCE
dissidents
Schreiner, Olive **23** 362-364

South African literature
Pringle, Thomas **23** 319-320
Schreiner, Olive **23** 362-364
Smith, Pauline **23** 372-373

SOUTHEY, ROBERT (1774-1843), English poet and author **18** 381-382

SOUTINE, CHAIM (1894-1943), Russian painter **14** 356-357

SOUVANNA PHOUMA (1901-1984), Laotian prince and premier **14** 357-358

SOWELL, THOMAS (born 1930), American economist and author **19** 350-352

SOYINKA, WOLE (Oluwole Akinwande Soyinka; born 1934), first African to win the Nobel Prize for Literature (1986) **14** 358-359

SPAAK, PAUL HENRI (1899-1972), Belgian statesman and diplomat **14** 359-360

SPAATZ, CARL (1891-1974), American army and air force officer **19** 352-355

Space exploration
manned flights
McCandless, Bruce, II **23** 243-246

Spain (Spanish State; nation, Europe)
• ISLAMIC (756-1492)
Castile and León
Urraca **23** 417-418

SPALLANZANI, LAZZARO (Abbé Spallanzani; 1729-99) Italian naturalist **14** 360-361

Spanish literature
modern
Almodovar, Pedro **23** 6-9

Spanish music
Cugat, Xavier **23** 81-82

SPARK, MURIEL SARAH (born 1918), British author **14** 361-362

SPARKS, JARED (1789-1866), American historian **14** 363

SPARTACUS (died 71 B.C.), Thracian galdiator **14** 363-364

SPAULDING, CHARLES CLINTON (1874-1952), African American business executive **14** 364-365

Speakers of the House
see Statesmen, American

SPEER, ALBERT (1905-1981), German architect and Nazi **19** 355-356

SPEKE, JOHN HANNING (1827-1864), English explorer **14** 366-367

SPELLMAN, CARDINAL FRANCIS JOSEPH (1889-1967), Roman Catholic archbishop **14** 367

SPEMANN, HANS (1869-1941), German experimental embryologist **14** 368-369

SPENCE, CATHERINE HELEN (1825-1910), Australian author and activist **23** 374-375

SPENCER, HERBERT (1820-1903), English philosopher **14** 369-370

SPENDER, STEPHEN HAROLD (born 1909), English poet and critic **14** 370-371

SPENER, PHILIPP JAKOB (1635-1705), German theologian **14** 372

SPENGLER, OSWALD (1880-1936), German philosopher **14** 372-373

SPENSER, EDMUND (circa 1552-99), English poet **14** 373-376

SPERANSKI, COUNT MIKHAIL MIKHAILOVICH (1772-1839), Russian statesman and reformer **14** 376-377

SPERRY, ELMER A. (1860-1930), American inventor **14** 377-379

SPIELBERG, STEVEN (born 1947), American filmmaker **14** 379-381

SPINOZA, BARUCH (Benedict Spinoza; 1632-77), Dutch philosopher **14** 381-383

SPITZ, MARK (born 1950), American swimmer **23** 376-378

SPOCK, BENJAMIN McLANE (1903-1998), American pediatrician and political activist and author of *Baby and Child Care* **14** 383-385

Sports
see Athletes, American

SPOTSWOOD, ALEXANDER (1676-1740), British general and colonial governor **14** 385

SPRAGUE, FRANK JULIAN (1857-1934), American electrical engineer and inventor **14** 385-386

SQUIBB, EDWARD ROBINSON (1819-1900), American physician and pharmacist **21** 390-392

SSU-MA CH'IEN (145-circa 90 B.C.), Chinese historian **14** 388-389

SSU-MA HSIANG-JU (circa 179-117 B.C.), Chinese poet **14** 389-390

SSU-MA KUANG (1019-1086), Chinese statesman **14** 390-391

STAËL, GERMAINE DE (1766-1817), French-Swiss novelist and woman of letters **14** 391-392

STAËL, NICOLAS DE (1914-1955), French painter **14** 392

STAHL, GEORG ERNST (1660-1734), German chemist and medical theorist **14** 392-393

Stairway to Heaven (song)
Led Zeppelin **23** 216-218

STALIN, JOSEPH (1879-1953), Soviet statesman **14** 393-396

STANDISH, MYLES (circa 1584-1656), English military adviser to the Pilgrims **14** 396-397

STANFORD, LELAND (1824-1893), American railroad builder and politician **14** 397-398

Stanford University (Palo Alto, California)
Rice, Condoleezza **23** 335-338

STANISLAVSKY, CONSTANTIN (1863-1938), Russian actor and director **14** 398-399

STANLEY, SIR HENRY MORTON (1841-1904), British explorer and journalist **14** 399-400

STANLEY, WENDELL MEREDITH (1904-1971), American virologist **14** 400-401

STANTON, EDWIN McMASTERS (1814-1869), American statesman **14** 401-402

STANTON, ELIZABETH CADY (1815-1902), American feminist and reformer **14** 402-403

STARHAWK (Miriam Simos; born 1951), theoretician and practitioner of feminist Wicca (witchcraft) in the United States **14** 403-404

STARLEY, JAMES (1831-1881), British inventor and businessman **21** 392-393

STARZL, THOMAS (born 1926), American surgeon **21** 393-395

State, U.S. Secretaries of
see Statesmen, American–Executive (secretaries of state)

Statesmen, American
• EXECUTIVE (CABINET)
attorneys general
Ashcroft, John **23** 18-21
national security advisors
Rice, Condoleezza **23** 335-338
secretaries of defense
Rumsfeld, Donald Harold **23** 353-355
• LEGISLATIVE
senators (19th century)
Logan, George **23** 231-234
senators (20th century)
Ashcroft, John **23** 18-21
Beveridge, Albert Jeremiah **23** 39-41
• STATE and LOCAL
state representatives
Logan, George **23** 231-234

Statesmen, Angolan
Nzinga, Anna **23** 270-271

Statesmen, Cherokee
Ward, Nancy **23** 436-438

Statesmen, Dutch
pensionaries
Cats, Jacob **23** 64-66

Statesmen, English
members of Parliament
Romilly, Samuel **23** 348-351

Statesmen, Georgian (Asia Minor)
Tamara **23** 388-390

Statesmen, Indian (Asian)
UN officials
Razia **23** 326-329

Statesmen, Israelite
see Bible–Old Testament; Jewish history

Statesmen, Saudi Arabian
Khalid Bin Abdul Aziz Al-Saud **23** 194-196

Statesmen, Spanish
queens
Urraca **23** 417-418

STEAD, CHRISTINA ELLEN (1902-1983), Australian author **23** 378-380

STEEL, DANIELLE (born 1947), American author and poet **14** 404-406

STEEL, DAVID MARTIN SCOTT (born 1938), Scottish member of Parliament and leader of the Liberal Party **14** 406-407

STEEL, DAWN (1946-1997), American movie producer and studio executive **18** 383-384

STEELE, SIR RICHARD (1672-1729), British essayist, dramatist, and politician **14** 407-409

STEFANSSON, VILHJALMUR (1879-1962), Canadian-American Arctic explorer and scientist **14** 409-410

STEFFENS, LINCOLN (1866-1936), American journalist **14** 410-411

STEGNER, WALLACE (1909-1993), American author **19** 356-358

STEICHEN, EDWARD (1879-1973), American photographer, painter, and museum curator **14** 411-412

STEIN, EDITH (1891-1942), German philosopher **14** 412-414

STEIN, GERTRUDE (1874-1946), American writer **14** 414-415

STEIN, BARON HEINRICH FRIEDRICH KARL VOM UND ZUM (1757-1831), Prussian statesman **14** 415-416

STEINBECK, JOHN ERNST (1902-1968), American author **14** 416-417

STEINEM, GLORIA (born 1934), American feminist and journalist **14** 418-419

STEINER, JAKOB (1796-1863), Swiss mathematician **23** 380-382

STEINITZ, WILHELM (1836-1900), Bohemian American chess player **20** 343-346

STEINMETZ, CHARLES PROTEUS (Karl August Rudolf Steinmetz; 1865-1923), German-born American mathematician and electrical engineer **14** 419-420

STELLA, FRANK (born 1936), American painter **14** 420-422

STELLA, JOSEPH (1877-1946), Italian-born American painter **14** 422

STENDHAL (Marie Henri Beyle; 1783-1842), French author **14** 422-425

STENGEL, CASEY (Charles Dillon Stengel; 1890-1975), American baseball player and manager **19** 361-363

STENO, NICOLAUS (Niels Stensen; 1638-86), Danish naturalist **14** 425-426

STEPHEN (1096?-1154), king of England 1135-54 **14** 426-427

STEPHEN I (c. 973-1038), king of Hungary **14** 427-428

STEPHEN, SIR LESLIE (1832-1904), English historian **14** 429

STEPHEN HARDING, ST. (died 1134), English abbot and monastic reformer **14** 428-429

STEPHENS, ALEXANDER HAMILTON (1812-1883), American statesman **14** 429-430

STEPHENS, HELEN (1918-1994), American athlete **19** 363-365

STEPHENS, JAMES (1882-1950), Irish novelist and poet **14** 430-431

STEPHENS, URIAH (1821-1882), American labor leader **14** 431-432

STEPHENSON, GEORGE (1781-1848), English railway engineer **14** 432-433

STEPHENSON, ROBERT (1803-1859), English railway engineer **14** 432-433

STEPINAC, ALOJZIJE (1898-1960), Croatian nationalist, Catholic, and anti-Communist **14** 433-435

STEPTOE, PATRICK (1913-1988), British physician **20** 346-348

STERN, ISAAC (born 1920), American violinist **19** 365-367

STERN, OTTO (1888-1969), German-born American physicist **14** 435

STERNE, LAURENCE (1713-1768), British novelist **14** 435-437

STETTINIUS, EDWARD R., JR. (1900-1949), American industrialist and statesman **14** 437-438

STEUBEN, BARON FREDERICK WILLIAM AUGUSTUS VON (1730-1794), German officer in the American Revolution **14** 438-439

STEVENS, GEORGE COOPER (1904-1975), American Film Director and Producer **22** 401-403

STEVENS, JOHN (1749-1838), American engineer and inventor **14** 439-440

STEVENS, JOHN PAUL (born 1920), U.S. Supreme Court justice **14** 440-441

STEVENS, NETTIE MARIA (1861-1912), American biologist and geneticist **14** 441-442

STEVENS, THADDEUS (1792-1868), American politician **14** 442-443

STEVENS, WALLACE (1879-1955), American poet **14** 443-445

STEVENSON, ADLAI EWING (1900-1965), American statesman and diplomat **14** 445-446

STEVENSON, ROBERT LOUIS (1850-1894), Scottish novelist, essayist and poet **14** 446-448

STEVIN, SIMON (Simon Stevinus; 1548-1620), Dutch mathematician **21** 395-398

STEWART, ALEXANDER TURNEY (1803-1876), American dry-goods merchant **14** 448-449

STEWART, DUGALD (1753-1828), Scottish philosopher **14** 449

STEWART, ELLEN (born 1920), African-American theater founder and director **20** 348-352

STEWART, JIMMY (James Maitland Stewart; 1908-1997), American actor **18** 385-386

STEWART, MARTHA (nee Martha Kostyra; born 1941), American author, entertainer, and businesswoman **19** 367-369

STEWART, POTTER (1915-1985), liberal U.S. Supreme Court justice **14** 449-451

STIEGEL, HENRY WILLIAM (1729-1785), German born American iron founder and glassmaker **14** 451

STIEGLITZ, ALFRED (1864-1946), American photographer, editor, and art gallery director **14** 451-452

STILICHO, FLAVIUS (died 408), Roman general **14** 452-453

STILL, CLYFFORD (1904-1980), American Abstract Expressionist artist **14** 453-454

STILL, WILLIAM (1821-1902), African American abolitionist, philanthropist, and businessman **14** 454-455

STILL, WILLIAM GRANT (born 1895), African American composer **14** 455-456

STILWELL, JOSEPH WARREN (1883-1946), American general **14** 456-457

STIMSON, HENRY LEWIS (1867-1950), American lawyer and statesman **14** 457-458

STIRLING, JAMES (1926-1992), British architect and city planner **14** 458-459

STIRNER, MAX (1806-1856), German philosopher **14** 459-460

STOCKHAUSEN, KARLHEINZ (born 1928), German composer **14** 460-461

STOCKTON, ROBERT FIELD (1795-1866), American naval officer and politician **14** 461-462

STODDARD, SOLOMON (1643-1728/29), American colonial Congregational clergyman **14** 462-463

STOKER, BRAM (Abraham Stoker; 1847-1912), Irish author **14** 463-464

STOKES, CARL B. (1927-1996), African American politician **14** 464-465

STOLYPIN, PIOTR ARKADEVICH (1862-1911), Russian statesman and reformer **14** 465-466

STONE, EDWARD DURRELL (1902-1978), American architect, educator, and designer **14** 466-468

STONE, HARLAN FISKE (1872-1946), American jurist; chief justice of U.S. Supreme Court 1914-46 **14** 468-470

STONE, I. F. (Isador Feinstein; 1907-1989), American journalist **14** 470-471

STONE, LUCY (1818-1893), American abolitionist and women's suffrage leader **14** 471-472

STONE, OLIVER (born 1946), American filmmaker **14** 472-475

STONE, ROBERT ANTHONY (born 1937), American novelist **14** 475-476

STOPES, MARIE (1880-1958), British scientist and birth control advocate **14** 476-478

STOPPARD, THOMAS (Thomas Straussler; born 1937), English playwright **14** 478-479

STORM, THEODOR (1817-1888), German poet and novelist **14** 479-480

STORY, JOSEPH (1779-1845), American jurist and statesman **14** 480-481

Story of an African Farm, The (book) Schreiner, Olive **23** 362-364

STOSS, VEIT (circa 1445-1533), German sculptor **14** 481-482

STOUFFER, SAMUEL A. (1900-1960), American sociologist and statistician **14** 482-483

STOUT, JUANITA KIDD (1919-1998), African American judge **23** 382-384

STOVALL, LUTHER McKINLEY (born 1937), American silkscreen artist **14** 483-484

STOWE, HARRIET ELIZABETH BEECHER (1811-1896), American writer **14** 484-485

STRABO (circa 64 B.C.-circa A.D. 23), Greek geographer and historian **14** 485-486

STRACHAN, JOHN (1778-1867), Canadian Anglican bishop **14** 486-487

STRACHEY, GILES LYTTON (1880-1932), English biographer and critic known for his satire of the Victorian era **14** 487-488

STRACHEY, JOHN (Evelyn John St. Loe Strachey; 1901-1963), British author and politician **20** 352-354

STRADIVARI, ANTONIO (circa 1644-1737), Italian violin maker **14** 488-490

STRAFFORD, 1ST EARL OF (Thomas Wentworth; 1593-1641), English statesman **14** 490-491

STRAND, MARK (born 1934), fourth Poet Laureate of the United States **14** 491-493

STRAND, PAUL (1890-1976), American photographer **19** 369-371

STRANG, RUTH MAY (1895-1971), American educator **14** 493-494

STRASBERG, LEE (Israel Strasberg; 1901-82), American acting instructor, director, and founding member of the Group Theatre **14** 494-495

STRAUS, ISIDOR (1845-1912), American merchant **14** 496

STRAUSS, DAVID FRIEDRICH (1808-1874), German historian and Protestant theologian **14** 496-497

STRAUSS, FRANZ JOSEF (1915-1988), West German politician **14** 497-498

STRAUSS, JOHANN, JR. (1825-1899), Austrian composer **14** 498-499

STRAUSS, LEO (1899-1973), German Jewish Socratic political philosopher **14** 499-500

STRAUSS, LEVI (Loeb Strauss; 1829-1902), American businessman **20** 354-356

STRAUSS, RICHARD (1864-1949), German composer and conductor **14** 500-501

STRAUSS, ROBERT SCHWARZ (born 1918), Democratic fundraiser and strategist **14** 501-502

STRAVINSKY, IGOR FEDOROVICH (1882-1971), Russian-born composer **14** 502-506

STRAWSON, SIR PETER FREDRICK (born 1919), English philosopher **14** 506-507

STREEP, MERYL LOUISE (born 1949), American actress **23** 384-387

STREETON, SIR ARTHUR ERNEST (1867-1943), Australian landscape painter **14** 507-508

STREISAND, BARBRA (Barbara Joan Streisand; born 1942), American entertainer **18** 386-388

STRESEMANN, GUSTAV (1878-1929), German statesman and diplomat **14** 508-509

STRINDBERG, AUGUST (1849-1912), Swedish author **14** 509-511

STROESSNER, ALFREDO (born 1912), Paraguayan statesman **14** 511-512

STRONG, JOSIAH (1847-1916), American clergyman and social activist **14** 512-513

STRUSS, KARL (1886-1981), American photographer and cinematographer **21** 398-399

STRUVE, FRIEDRICH GEORG WILHELM VON (1793-1864), German-born Russian astronomer and geodesist **14** 513

STUART, GILBERT (1755-1828), American painter **14** 513-515

STUART, JAMES EWELL BROWN (Jeb; 1833-64), Confederate cavalry officer **14** 515-516

STUDENT, KURT (1890-1978), German general **20** 356-358

STUDI, WES (born Wesley Studie; born circa 1944), Native American actor **15** 1-2

STURGES, PRESTON (Edmund Preston Biden; 1898-1959), American playwright, screenwriter, director, and businessman **19** 371-374

STURLUSON, SNORRI (1179-1241), Icelandic statesman and historian **14** 310-311

STURT, CHARLES (1795-1869), British officer, explorer, and colonial administrator **15** 2-3

STURTEVANT, A. H. (Alfred Henry Sturtevant; 1891-1970), American geneticist **15** 3-5

STUYVESANT, PETER (circa 1610-72), Dutch colonial administrator **15** 5-6

STYRON, WILLIAM (born 1925), American southern writer of novels and articles **15** 6-8

SUÁREZ, FRANCISCO (1548-1617), Spanish philosopher and theologian **15** 8

SUAZO CÓRDOVA, ROBERTO (born 1927), physician and president of Honduras (1982-1986) **15** 8-10

SUCKLING, SIR JOHN (1609-1642), English poet and playwright **15** 10-11

SUCRE, ANTONIO JOSÉ DE (1795-1830), Venezuelan general, Bolivian president 1826-28 **15** 11-12

SUDERMANN, HERMANN (1857-1928), German dramatist and novelist **15** 12-13

SUETONIUS TRANQUILLUS, GAIUS (circa 70-circa 135), Roman administrator and writer **15** 13

SUHARTO (born 1921), second president after Indonesia's independence **15** 14-15

SUI WEN-TI (541-604) Chinese emperor **15** 16-18

SUIKO (554-628), empress of Japan 593-628 **15** 15-16

SUKARNO (1901-1970), Indonesian statesman, president 1945-66 **15** 18-20

SULEIMAN I (the Magnificent; 1494-1566), Ottoman sultan 1520-66 **15** 20-21

SULLA, LUCIUS CORNELIUS I (138-78 B.C.), Roman general, dictator 82-79 B.C. **15** 21-22

SULLIVAN, SIR ARTHUR SEYMOUR (1842-1900), English composer **15** 23

SULLIVAN, ED (Edward Vincent Sullivan; 1902-1974), American television emcee, screenwriter, and author **19** 374-376

SULLIVAN, HARRY STACK (1892-1949), American psychiatrist **15** 23-24

SULLIVAN, JOHN LAWRENCE (1858-1918), American boxer **15** 24-25

SULLIVAN, LEON HOWARD (1922-2001), African American civil rights leader and minister **15** 25-27

SULLIVAN, LOUIS HENRI (1856-1924), American architect **15** 27-28

SULLY, THOMAS (1783-1872), English-born American painter **22** 403-404

SULZBERGER, ARTHUR OCHS (born 1926), publisher of the *New York Times* **15** 28-30

SULZBERGER, ARTHUR OCHS JR. (born 1951), American newspaper publisher **19** 376-378

SUMNER, CHARLES (1811-1874), American statesman **15** 30-31

SUMNER, WILLIAM GRAHAM (1840-1910), American sociologist and educator **15** 32

SUN YAT-SEN (1866-1925), Chinese statesman, leader of republican revolution **15** 35-39

SUNDAY, WILLIAM ASHLEY ("Billy"; 1862-1935), American evangelist **15** 32-33

SUNDIATA KEITA (circa 1210-circa 1260), founder of Mali empire in West Africa **15** 33-34

SU-SHIH (Su Tung-p'o; 1037-1101), Chinese author and artist **15** 39-40

SUTHERLAND, GRAHAM (1903-1980), English painter **15** 40-41

SUTHERLAND, JOAN (born 1926), Australian opera singer **22** 404-407

SUTTER, JOHN AUGUSTUS (1803-1880), German-born American adventurer and colonizer **15** 41-42

SUTTNER, BERTHA VON (born Countess Bertha Kinsky; 1843-1914), Austrian author and activist **15** 42-44

SUVOROV, ALEKSANDR VASILIEVICH (1730-1800), Russian general **15** 44-45

SUZMAN, HELEN (born 1917), member of the South African House of Assembly for the Progressive Party **15** 45-46

SUZUKI, DAISETZ TEITARO (1870-1966), Japanese translator, teacher, and interpreter of Zen Buddhist thought **15** 46-47

SVEVO, ITALO (pseudonym of Ettore Schmitz; 1861-1928), Italian novelist **15** 47-48

SWAMMERDAM, JAN (1637-1680), Dutch naturalist **15** 48-49

SWEDENBORG, EMANUEL (1688-1772), Swedish scientist, theologian, and mystic **15** 49-50

SWEELINCK, JAN PIETERSZOON (1562-1621), Dutch composer, organist, and teacher **15** 50-51

SWIFT, GUSTAVUS FRANKLIN (1839-1903), American businessman **22** 407-409

SWIFT, JONATHAN (1667-1745), English-Irish poet, political writer, and clergyman **15** 51-54

Swimming (sport) Spitz, Mark **23** 376-378

SWINBURNE, ALGERNON CHARLES (1837-1909), English poet, dramatist, and critic **15** 54-55

SWITZER, MARY E. (1900-1971), American champion of rehabilitation **15** 55-56

SWOPE, GERARD (1872-1957), president of General Electric **15** 56-58

SYDENHAM, BARON (Charles Edward Poulett Thomson; 1799-1841), English merchant and politician **15** 59-60

SYDENHAM, THOMAS (1624-1689), English physician **15** 59-60

SYED AHMED KHAN (1817-1898), Moslem religious leader, educationalist, and politician **15** 60

SYLVIS, WILLIAM (1828-1869), American labor leader **15** 60-61

Symphony (music) Denmark Nørgård, Per **23** 265-267

SYNGE, EDMUND JOHN MILLINGTON (1871-1909), Irish dramatist **15** 61-62

SZENT-GYÖRGYI, ALBERT VON (1893-1986), Hungarian-American biochemist **15** 62-64

SZILARD, LEO (1898-1964), Hungarian-born nuclear physicist **15** 64-66

SZOLD, HENRIETTA (1860-1945), American Jewish leader **15** 66-67

SZYMANOWSKI, KAROL (1882-1937), Polish composer **15** 67-68

T

TABARI, MUHAMMAD IBN JARIR AL- (839-923), Moslem historian and religious scholar **15** 69-70

TABOR, HORACE AUSTIN WARNER (1830-1899), American mining magnate and politician **15** 70

TACITUS (56/57-circa 125), Roman orator and historian **15** 70-72

TAEUBER-ARP, SOPHIE (1889-1943), Swiss-born painter, designer, and dancer **15** 73-74

TAEWON'GUN, HŬNGSON (1820-1898), Korean imperial regent **15** 74-75

TAFAWA BALEWA, SIR ABUBAKAR (1912-1966), Nigerian statesman, prime minister 1957-1966 **15** 75

TAFT, LORADO (1860-1936), American sculptor **15** 75-76

TAFT, ROBERT ALPHONSO (1889-1953), American senator **15** 76-78

TAFT, WILLIAM HOWARD (1857-1930), American statesman, president 1909-1913 **15** 78-81

TAGORE, RABINDRANATH (1861-1941), Bengali poet, philosopher, social reformer, and dramatist **12** 529-531

TAHARQA (reigned circa 688-circa 663 B.C.), Nubian pharaoh of Egypt **15** 81-82

TAINE, HIPPOLYTE ADOLPHE (1828-1893), French critic and historian **15** 82-83

T'AI-TSUNG, T'ANG (600-649), Chinese emperor **15** 83-84

TAKAHASHI, KOREKIYO (1854-1936), Japanese statesman **15** 84-85

TAL, JOSEF (Josef Gruenthal; born 1910), Israeli composer, pianist, and professor of music **15** 85-86

TALBERT, MARY MORRIS BURNETT (1866-1923), American educator, feminist, civil rights activist, and lecturer **15** 86-88

TALLCHIEF, MARIA (born 1925), Native American prima ballerina **15** 88-89

TALLEYRAND, CHARLES MAURICE DE (Duc de Tallyrand-Périgord; 1754-1838), French statesman **15** 89-90

TALLIS, THOMAS (circa 1505-85), English composer and organist **15** 91

TALON, JEAN (1626-1694), French intendant of New France **15** 91-92

TAMARA (Tamar; 1159-1212), Queen of Georgia (1184-1212) **23** 388-390

TAMBO, OLIVER REGINALD (1917-1993), serves as acting president of the African National Congress **15** 92-94

TAMERLANE (1336-1405), Turko-Mongol conqueror **15** 94-95

TAMIRIS, HELEN (Helen Becker; 1905-1966), American dancer and choreographer **23** 390-392

TAN, AMY (born 1952), American author **15** 95-96

TANAKA, KAKUEI (1918-1993), prime minister of Japan (1972-1974) **15** 96-98

TANEY, ROGER BROOKE (1777-1864), American political leader, chief justice of U.S. Supreme Court **15** 98-99

TANGE, KENZO (born 1913), Japanese architect and city planner **15** 99-101

TANGUY, YVES (1900-1955), French painter **15** 101

TANIZAKI, JUNICHIRO (1886-1965), Japanese novelist, essayist, and playwright **15** 101-102

TANNER, HENRY OSSAWA (1859-1937), African American painter **15** 102-103

T'AO CH'IEN (365-427), Chinese poet **15** 104-105

TAO-AN (312-385), Chinese Buddhist monk **15** 103-104

TAO-HSÜAN (596-667), Chinese Buddhist monk **15** 105

TAPPAN BROTHERS (19th century), American merchants and reformers **15** 105-106

TAQI KHAN AMIR-E KABIR, MIRZA (circa 1806-52), Iranian statesman **15** 106-107

TARBELL, IDA MINERVA (1857-1944), American journalist **15** 107-108

TARDE, JEAN GABRIEL (1843-1904), French philosopher and sociologist **15** 108-109

TARKINGTON, NEWTON BOOTH (1869-1946), American author **15** 109

TARKOVSKY, ANDREI ARSENYEVICH (1932-1986), Russian film director **23** 392-395

TARLETON, SIR BANASTRE (1754-1833), English soldier; fought in American Revolution **15** 110

TARSKI, ALFRED (1902-1983), Polish-American mathematician and logician **15** 110-111

TARTAGLIA, NICCOLO (1500-1557), Italian mathematician **15** 111-112

TARTINI, GIUSEPPE (1692-1770), Italian violinist, composer, and theorist **15** 112-113

TASMAN, ABEL JANSZOON (circa 1603-59), Dutch navigator **15** 113-114

TASSO, TORQUATO (1544-1595), Italian poet **15** 114-116

TATE, ALLEN (1899-1979), American poet, critic and editor **15** 116

TATLIN, VLADIMIR EVGRAFOVICH (1885-1953), Russian avant garde artist **15** 117-118

TATI, JACQUES (Jacques Tatischeff; 1908-1982), French actor and director **22** 410-412

TAUSSIG, HELEN BROOKE (1898-1986), American physician **15** 118-120

TAWNEY, RICHARD HENRY (1880-1962), British economic historian and social philosopher **15** 120-121

TAYLOR, BROOK (1685-1731), English mathematician **15** 121-122

TAYLOR, EDWARD (circa 1642-1729), American Puritan poet and minister **15** 122-123

TAYLOR, EDWARD PLUNKET (1901-1989), Canadian-born financier and thoroughbred horse breeder **15** 123-124

TAYLOR, ELIZABETH ROSEMUND (born 1932), American film actress **15** 124-125

TAYLOR, FREDERICK WINSLOW (1856-1915), American industrial manager and production engineer **21** 400-402

TAYLOR, JOHN (1753-1824), American politician and political theorist **15** 126

TAYLOR, MAXWELL (1901-1987), American soldier-statesman-scholar **15** 126-127

TAYLOR, SUSIE KING (1848-1912), African American nurse **15** 127-128

TAYLOR, ZACHARY (1784-1850), American statesman; president 1849-50 **15** 128-130

TCHAIKOVSKY, PETER ILYICH (1840-1893), Russian composer **15** 130-132

TCHEREPNIN, ALEXANDER (Nikolayevich; 1899-1977), Russian-French and later American composer **15** 132-133

TE KANAWA, KIRI (born 1944), lyric soprano from New Zealand **15** 136-137

TECUMSEH (circa 1768-1813), American Shawnee Indian tribal chief **15** 133

TEDDER, ARTHUR (1890-1967), British military leader **19** 379-381

TEGGART, FREDERICK J. (1870-1946), comparative historian, librarian, sociologist, and educator who initiated sociology at the University of California **15** 133-134

TEILHARD DE CHARDIN, MARIE JOSEPH PIERRE (1881-1955), French theologian and paleontologist **15** 134-136

TEKAKWITHA, KATERI (Catherine Tegakovita; 1656-1680), Native American nun **23** 395-397

TELEMANN, GEORG PHILIPP (1681-1767), German composer **15** 137-138

Telephone (communications) Vail, Theodore Newton **23** 419-421

TELESIO, BERNARDINO (1509-1588), Italian philosopher of nature **15** 138-139

Television (Great Britain)
screenwriters for
Leigh, Mike **23** 222-225

Television (United States)
cable TV
Redstone, Sumner Murray **23** 329-331
personalities
Burnett, Carol **23** 52-55
Button, Dick **23** 55-57
producers
Burnett, Carol **23** 52-55
scriptwriters for
Burnett, Carol **23** 52-55
sportscasters
Button, Dick **23** 55-57

TELLER, EDWARD (born 1908), Hungarian-American physicist **15** 139-141

TEMPLE, WILLIAM (1881-1944), ecumenicist and archbishop of Canterbury **15** 141-143

TENGKU, ABDUL RAHMAN ("the Tengku"; born 1903), first prime minister of the Federation of Malaya and later of Malaysia **15** 340-341

TENNENT, GILBERT (1703-1764), American Presbyterian clergyman and evangelist **15** 143-144

TENNYSON, ALFRED (1st Baron Tennyson; 1809-92), English poet **15** 144-146

TENSKWATAWA (Lalewithaka; 1775-1836), Shawnee religious leader **20** 359-362

TENZING NORGAY (born 1914), Nepalese mountain climber **20** 362-364

TER BORCH, GERARD (1617-1681), Dutch painter **15** 146

TERENCE (Publius Terentius After; 195-159 B.C.), Roman comic playwright **15** 146-148

TERESA (Mother Teresa; Agnes Gonxha Bojaxhiu; 1910-1997), Catholic nun and missionary; Noble Prize for Peace recipient **15** 148-151

TERESA OF AVILA (Teresa Sanchez de Cepeda y Ahumada; 1515-1582), Spanish nun **20** 364-366

TERESHKOVA, VALENTINA (born 1937), Russian cosmonaut **15** 151-152

TERKEL, LOUIS ("Studs"; born 1912), American radio personality and author **15** 152-153

TERMAN, LEWIS MADISON (1877-1956), American psychologist **15** 153-154

TERRA, GABRIEL (1873-1942), Uruguayan politician, president 1933-38 **15** 154-155

TERRELL, MARY CHURCH (Mary Eliza Church Terrell; 1863-1954), African American activist and feminist **23** 397-399

Terror, Reign of
see French Revolution—1792-95 (Reign of Terror)

TERTULLIAN (Quintus Septimius Florens Tertullianus; circa 160-circa 220), North African theologian and apologist **15** 155-156

TESLA, NIKOLA (1856-1943), Croatian-American inventor and electrical engineer **15** 156-157

TEWODROS II (1820-1868), emperor of Ethiopia **15** 158-159

THACKERAY, WILLIAM MAKEPEACE (1811-1863), British novelist **15** 159-161

THALBERG, IRVING (1899-1936), American filmmaker **20** 366-368

THALES (circa 624-circa 545 B.C.), Greek natural philosopher **15** 161

THANT, U (1909-1974), Burmese statesman and UN secretary general **15** 161-162

THARP, MARIE (born 1920), American geologist and oceanographic cartologist **15** 162-164

THARP, TWYLA (born 1941), American dancer and choreographer **15** 164-165

THATCHER, MARGARET HILDA (born 1925), prime minister of Great Britain (1979-1990) **15** 165-168

THAYER, ELI (1819-1899), American reformer, agitator, and promoter **15** 168

THAYER, SYLVANUS (1785-1872), American educator and engineer **15** 168-169

THEANO (born c. 546 BC), Greek mathematician and physician **23** 399-401

THEILER, MAX (1899-1972), American epidemiologist and microbiologist **15** 169-170

THEMISTOCLES (circa 528-462 B.C.), Athenian politician **15** 170-171

THEOCRITUS (circa 310-circa 245 B.C.), Greek poet **15** 171-172

THEODORIC THE GREAT (453/454-526), king of the Ostrogoths **15** 175-176

THEODOSIUS (circa 346-395), Roman emperor 379-395 **15** 176

THEORELL, AXEL HUGO THEODOR (born 1903), Swedish biochemist **15** 176-177

THERESA, SAINT (Theresa of Ávila; 1515-82), Spanish nun **15** 178-179

THEROUX, PAUL (born 1941), expatriate American writer of fiction and of chronicles of train travels **15** 179-180

THIBAUT IV (Thibaut I of Navarre; 1201-53), Count of Champagne and Brie **15** 180-181

THIERS, LOUIS ADOLPHE (1797-1877), French journalist, historian, and statesman **15** 181-182

THIEU, NGUYEN VAN (1923-2001), South Vietnamese president **15** 182-183

THOMAS, ALMA WOODSEY (1891-1978), African American artist **23** 401-403

THOMAS, CLARENCE (born 1948), U.S. Supreme Court justice **15** 186-188

THOMAS, DAVE (R. David Thomas; 1932-2002), American businessman **18** 389-397

THOMAS, DYLAN MARLAIS (1914-1953), British poet **15** 188-190

THOMAS, GEORGE HENRY (1816-1870), American general **15** 190-191

THOMAS, HELEN (born 1920), American journalist **19** 381-384

THOMAS, NORMAN MATTOON (1884-1968), American Socialist politician, author, and lecturer **15** 191-192

THOMAS, THEODORE (1835-1905), American orchestral conductor **15** 192-193

THOMAS, WILLIAM ISAAC (1863-1947), American sociologist and educator **15** 193

THOMAS AQUINAS, SAINT (circa 1224-74), Italian philosopher and theologian **15** 183-186

THOMASIUS (1655-1728), German philosopher and jurist **15** 193-194

THOMPSON, DALEY (Francis Ayodele Thompson; born 1958), English track and field athlete **20** 368-370

THOMPSON, DAVID (1770-1857), Canadian explorer, cartographer, and surveyor **15** 194-195

THOMPSON, DOROTHY (1894-1961), conservative American journalist **15** 195-196

THOMPSON, HUNTER STOCKTON (born 1939), American journalist **15** 196-198

THOMSON, SIR GEORGE PAGET (1892-1975), English atomic physicist **15** 198-199

THOMSON, JAMES (1700-1748), British poet **15** 199-200

THOMSON, SIR JOSEPH JOHN (1856-1940), English physicist **15** 200-201

THOMSON, KENNETH (born 1923), Canadian print and broadcast journalism magnate **15** 201-202

THOMSON, TOM (1877-1917), Canadian painter **15** 202

THOMSON, VIRGIL (1896-1989), American composer, critic, and conductor **15** 202-203

THOREAU, HENRY DAVID (1817-1862), American writer and transcendentalist **15** 203-205

THOREZ, MAURICE (1900-1964), headed the French Communist Party from 1930 to 1964 **15** 206-207

THORN, GASTON (born 1928), prime minister of Luxembourg **15** 207-208

THORNDIKE, EDWARD LEE (1874-1949), American psychologist and educator **15** 208-209

THORPE, JIM (James Francis Thorpe; 1888-1953), American track star and professional football and baseball player **15** 209-211

THORVALDSEN, BERTEL (Albert Bertel Thorvaldsen; 1770-1848), Danish sculptor **23** 403-406

THUCYDIDES (circa 460-circa 401 B.C.), Greek historian **15** 211-212

THUKU, HARRY (1895-1970), Kenyan politician **15** 212-213

THURBER, JAMES GROVE (1894-1961), American writer and artist **15** 213-214

THURMOND, JAMES STROM (born 1902), American lawyer and statesman **15** 214-215

THURSTONE, LOUIS LEON (1887-1955), American psychologist **15** 215-216

THUTMOSE III (1504-1450 B.C.), Egyptian king **15** 216-217

TIBERIUS JULIUS CAESAR AUGUSTUS (42 B.C. -A.D. 37), emperor of Rome 14-37 **15** 217-218

TIECK, LUDWIG (1773-1853), German author **15** 218-219

TIEPOLO, GIOVANNI BATTISTA (1696-1770), Italian painter **15** 219-220

TIFFANY, LOUIS COMFORT (1848-1933), American painter and designer **15** 220-221

TIGLATH-PILESER III (ruled 745-727 B.C.), king of Assyria **15** 221-222

TILDEN, BILL (William Tatem Tilden II; 1893-1953), American tennis player **20** 370-372

TILDEN, SAMUEL JONES (1814-1886), American politician **15** 222-223

TILLEY, SIR SAMUEL LEONARD (1818-1896), Canadian statesman **15** 223-224

TILLICH, PAUL JOHANNES (1886-1965), German-American Protestant theologian and philosopher **15** 224-225

TILLMAN, BENJAMIN RYAN (1847-1918), American statesman and demagogue **15** 225-226

TILLY, GRAF VON (Johann Tserclaes; 1559-1632), Flemish general **20** 372-374

TIMERMAN, JACOBO (1923-1999), Argentine journalist and human rights advocate **15** 226-228

TINBERGEN, JAN (1903-1994), Dutch economist **15** 228-229

TINBERGEN, NIKOLAAS (1907-1988), English ethologist and zoologist **15** 229-230

TING, SAMUEL CHAO CHUNG (born 1936), American nuclear physicist **23** 406-408

TINGUELY, JEAN (1925-1991), Swiss sculptor **15** 230-232

TINTORETTO (1518-1594), Italian painter **15** 232-234

TIPPETT, MICHAEL KEMP, SIR (1905-1998), English composer and conductor **15** 234-235

TIPPU TIP (Hamed bin Mohammed bin Juma bin Rajab el Murjebi; circa 1840-1905), Zanzibari trader **15** 235-236

TIPU SULTAN (1750-1799), Moslem ruler of Mysore **15** 236

TIRADENTES (José Joaquim da Silva Xavier; 1748-92), Brazilian national hero **15** 237

TIRPITZ, ALFRED VON (1849-1930), German admiral and politician **20** 374-376

TIRSO DE MOLINA (1584-1648), Spanish dramatist **15** 237-238

TISCH BROTHERS (1923-), real estate developers **15** 238-240

TISELIUS, ARNE WILHELM KAURIN (1902-1971), Swedish biochemist **15** 240-241

TITCHENER, EDWARD BRADFORD (1867-1927), English-American psychologist **15** 241-242

TITIAN (1488/90-1576), Italian painter **15** 242-244

TITO, MARSHAL (1892-1980), Yugoslav president **15** 244-246

TITULESCU, NICOLAE (1882-1941), Romanian statesman **15** 246-247

TITUS FLAVIUS VESPASIANUS (39-81), Roman general, emperor 79-81 **15** 247-248

TOBA SOJO (1053-1140), Japanese painter-priest **15** 248-249

TOBEY, MARK (1890-1976), American painter **15** 249-250

TOCQUEVILLE, ALEXIS CHARLES HENRI MAURICE CLÉREL DE (1805-1859), French statesman and historian **15** 250-251

TODD, ALEXANDER (1907-1997), English chemist **15** 251-253

TODD, MIKE (Avron Hirsch Goldenbogen; 1907-1958), American theater and film producer **21** 402-404

TODD, REGINALD STEPHEN GARFIELD (1908-2002), prime minister of Southern Rhodesia and supporter of Zimbabwean independence **18** 391-393

TOGLIATTI, PALMIRO (1893-1964), Italian statesman and a founder of the Italian Communist Party **15** 253-254

TOGO, HEIHACHIRO (1847-1934), Japanese admiral **20** 376-379

TOJO, HIDEKI (1884-1948), Japanese general, premier 1941-1944 **15** 254-256

TOKUGAWA IEYASU (1542-1616), founder of Tokugawa shogunate **8** 103-106

Tokyo Metropolitan Festival Hall (Japan) Maekawa, Kunio **23** 239-242

Tokyo Story (film) Ozu, Yasujiro **23** 279-281

TOLAND, GREGG (1904-1948), American cinematographer **21** 405-407

TOLAND, JOHN (1670-1722), British scholar **15** 256

TOLEDANO, VICENTE LOMBARDO (1894-1968), Mexican intellectual and politician **15** 256-257

TOLEDO, FRANCISCO DE (1515-1584), Spanish viceroy of Peru **15** 257-259

TOLKIEN, J. R. R. (1892-1973), English author **15** 259-261

TOLLER, ERNST (1893-1939), German playwright **15** 261

TOLMAN, EDWARD CHACE (1886-1959), American psychologist **15** 261-262

TOLSTOY, LEO (1828-1910), Russian novelist and moral philosopher **15** 262-265

TOMONAGA, SIN-ITIRO (1906-1979), Japanese physicist **15** 265-266

TÖNNIES, FERDINAND (1855-1936), German sociologist **15** 266-267

TOOMBS, ROBERT AUGUSTUS (1810-1885), American statesman **15** 267-268

TOOMER, JEAN (Nathan Eugene Pinchback Toomer; 1894-1967), American author **23** 408-410

TORQUEMADA, TOMAS DE (1420-1498), leader of the Spanish Inquisition **21** 407-409

TORRENCE, JACKIE (born 1944), American storyteller **19** 384-386

TORRICELLI, EVANGELISTA (1608-1647), Italian mathematician and physicist **15** 268-269

TORRIJOS, OMAR (1929-1981), Panamanian strongman **15** 269-270

TORSTENSSON, LENNART (1603-1651), Swedish military leader **20** 379-381

TOSCANINI, ARTURO (1867-1957), Italian conductor **15** 270-271

TOSOVSKY, JOSEF (born 1950), banker and prime minister of the Czech Republic **18** 393-395

TOULMIN, STEPHEN EDELSTON (born 1922), British-American ethical philosopher **15** 271-273

TOULOUSE-LAUTREC, HENRI DE (1864-1901), French painter **15** 273-274

TOURAINE, ALAIN (born 1925), French sociologist **15** 274-275

TOURÉ, SAMORY (1830-1900), Sudanese ruler and state builder **15** 275-277

TOURÉ, SÉKOU (1922-1984), African statesman, president of Guinea **15** 275-277

TOURGÉE, ALBION WINEGAR (1838-1905), American jurist and writer **15** 277-278

TOUSSAINT L'OUVERTURE, FRANÇOIS DOMINIQUE (1743-1803), Haitian military leader **15** 278-279

TOWER, JOAN (born 1938), American composer **15** 279-281

TOWNES, CHARLES HARD (born 1915), American physicist **15** 281-282

TOWNSEND, FRANCIS EVERITT (1867-1960), American physician **15** 282-283

TOYNBEE, ARNOLD JOSEPH (1889-1975), English historian and philosopher of history **15** 283-284

TOYODA, EIJI (born 1913), Japanese automobile manufacturing executive **15** 284-286

TOYOTOMI HIDEYOSHI (1536-1598), Japanese warrior commander **15** 286-289

TRACY, SPENCER BONAVENTURE (1900-1967), American film actor **15** 289-290

TRAILL, CATHARINE PARR (1802-1899), Canadian naturalist and author **15** 291

TRAJAN (Marcus Ulpius Trajanus; circa 53-117), Roman emperor 98-117 **15** 291-292

TransAfrica (lobbying group; U.S.) Robinson, Randall **23** 342-345

TRAVIS, WILLIAM BARRET (1809-1836), American cavalry commander **15** 292-293

TREITSCHKE, HEINRICH VON (1834-1896), German historian and publicist **15** 293-294

TREVELYAN, GEORGE MACAULAY (1876-1962), English historian **15** 294-295

TREVOR, WILLIAM (born 1928), British novelist, television dramatist, playwright, and short-story writer **15** 295-297

TRIMBLE, DAVID (William David Trimble; born 1944), Irish political leaders **19** 386-388

TRIPPE, JUAN TERRY (1899-1981), American overseas aviation industry pioneer **15** 297-298

TRIST, NICHOLAS PHILIP (1800-1874), American lawyer and diplomat **15** 298-299

TROELTSCH, ERNST (1865-1923), German theologian, historian, and sociologist **15** 299-300

TROGER, PAUL (1698-1762), Austrian painter **15** 300

TROLLOPE, ANTHONY (1815-1882), English novelist **15** 300-302

Tropical medicine Plotkin, Mark J. **23** 308-310

TROTSKY, LEON (1879-1940), Russian revolutionist **15** 302-305

TROTTER, MILDRED (1899-1991), American anatomist **15** 305-306

TROTTER, WILLIAM MONROE (1872-1934), African American newspaper editor and protest leader **15** 306-307

TRUDEAU, GARRETSON BEEKMAN ("Garry"; born 1948), comic-strip artist, playwright, and animator **15** 308-309

TRUDEAU, PIERRE ELLIOTT (born 1919), leader of the Liberal Party and Canada's prime minister (1968-1984) **15** 309-311

TRUFFAUT, FRANÇOIS (1932-1984), French film director and critic **15** 311-313

TRUJILLO MOLINA, RAFAEL LEONIDAS (1891-1961), dictator of the Dominican Republic **15** 313-314

TRUMAN, HARRY S. (1884-1972), American statesman, president 1945-53 **15** 314-316

TRUMBO, DALTON (James Dalton Trumbo; 1905-1976), American screenwriter **21** 409-411

TRUMBULL, JOHN (1756-1843), American painter **15** 316-317

TRUMBULL, LYMAN (1813-1896), American statesman **15** 317-318

TRUMP, DONALD JOHN (born 1946), American real estate developer **15** 318-319

TRUONG CHINH (1909-1988), Vietnamese Communist leader **15** 319-320

TRUTH, SOJOURNER (circa 1797-1883), African American freedom fighter and orator **15** 320-321

TRYON, WILLIAM (1729-1788), English colonial governor in America **15** 321

TS'AI YÜAN-P'EI (1867-1940), Chinese educator **15** 322

TS'AO TS'AO (155-220), Chinese general, statesman, and folk hero **15** 322-323

TSCHERNICHOWSKY, SAUL (1875-1943), Hebrew poet, translator, and physician **15** 323

TSENG KUO-FAN (1811-1872), Chinese statesman, general and scholar **15** 324-325

TSHOMBE, MOÏSE KAPENDA (1919-1969), Congolese political leader **15** 325-326

TSIOLKOVSKY, KONSTANTIN EDUARDOVICH (1857-1935), Russian scientist **15** 326-328 associates

TSO TSUNG-T'ANG (1812-1885), Chinese general and statesman **15** 328-329

TSOU YEN (flourished late 4th century B.C.), Chinese philosopher **15** 329-330

TU FU (712-770), Chinese poet **15** 335-336

TUBMAN, HARRIET ROSS (circa 1820-1913), African American Underground Railroad agent **15** 330-331

TUBMAN, WILLIAM VACANARAT SHADRACH (1895-1971), Liberian statesman, president 1943-71 **15** 331

TUCHMAN, BARBARA (born 1912), American Pulitzer Prize-winning historian and journalist **15** 331-332

TUCKER, C. DELORES (Cynthia DeLores Nottage; born 1927), African American civil rights activist **18** 395-397

TUCKER, GEORGE (1775-1861), American historian **15** 332-333

TUCKER, PRESTON (1903-1956), American businessman and automobile designer **18** 397-399

TUDJMAN, FRANJO (1922-1999), Croatian president **15** 333-335

TUGWELL, REXFORD GUY (1891-1979), American politician, educator, and public servant **15** 336-339

TULL, JETHRO (1674-1741), English agriculturist and inventor **21** 411-413

TUNG CH'I-CH'ANG (1555-1636), Chinese calligrapher, painter, and historian **15** 339-340

TÚPAC AMARU, JOSÉ GABRIEL (1742-1781), Peruvian revolutionist, last of the Incas **15** 341

TUPOLEV, ANDREI NIKOLAEVICH (1888-1972), Soviet aeronautical engineer and army officer **15** 341-342

TUPPER, SIR CHARLES (1821-1915),Canadian statesman, prime minister 1896 **15** 342-343

TURA, COSIMO (1430-1495), Italian painter **15** 343-344

TURABI, HASSAN ABDULLAH AL- (born 1932), major leader of the Sudan's Islamic fundamentalist movement **15** 344-345

TURENNE, VICOMTE DE (Henri de la Tour d'Auvergne; 1611-1675), French military commander **20** 381-383

TURGENEV, IVAN SERGEYEVICH (1818-1883), Russian novelist, dramatist, and short-story writer **15** 345-348

TURGOT, ANNE ROBERT JACQUES (Baron de l'Aulne; 1721-81), French economist **15** 348-349

TURING, ALAN MATHISON (1912-1954), British mathematician **15** 349-350

TURNER, FREDERICK JACKSON (1861-1932), American historian **15** 350-351

TURNER, HENRY MCNEAL (1834-1915), African American racial leader **15** 351-352

TURNER, JOSEPH MALLORD WILLIAM (1775-1851), English painter **15** 352-354

TURNER, LANA (Julia Jean Mildred Frances Turner; 1920-1995), American actress **19** 388-390

TURNER, NATHANIEL (1800-1831), African American slave leader **15** 354

TURNER, TED (Robert Edward Turner; born 1938), American television entrepreneur **15** 355-357

TURNER, TINA (Anna Mae Bullock; born 1939), African American singer, dancer, and actress **15** 357-359

TUTANKHAMEN (reigned 1361-1352 B.C.), twelfth king of the Eighteenth Egyptian Dynasty **15** 359-360

TUTU, ARCHBISHOP DESMOND (born 1931), South African Anglican archbishop and opponent of apartheid **15** 360-361

TUTUOLA, AMOS (born 1920), Nigerian writer **15** 361-362

TWACHTMAN, JOHN HENRY (1853-1902), American painter **15** 362-363

TWAIN, MARK (Samuel Langhorne Clemens; 1835-1910), American humorist and novelist **15** 363-366

TWEED, WILLIAM MARCY (1823-1878), American politician and leader of Tammany Hall **15** 366-367

TYLER, ANNE (born 1941), American author **15** 367-368

TYLER, JOHN (1790-1862), American statesman, president 1841-45 **15** 368-369

TYLER, MOSES COIT (1835-1900), American historian **15** 369-370

TYLER, RALPH W. (born 1902), American educator/scholar **15** 370-371

TYLER, ROYALL (1757-1826), American playwright, novelist, and jurist **15** 371-372

TYLOR, SIR EDWARD BURNETT (1832-1917), English anthropologist **15** 372-373

TYNDALE, WILLIAM (circa 1495-1536), English biblical scholar **15** 373-374

TYNDALL, JOHN (1820-1893), Irish physicist **15** 374

Typhoid Mary
see Mallon, Mary

TYRRELL, GEORGE (1861-1909), Irish-English Jesuit priest and theologian **15** 374-375

TYRRELL, JOSEPH BURR (J.B. Tyrrell; 1858-1957), Canadian geologist and explorer **23** 410-412

TZ'U-HSI (1835-1908), empress dowager of China 1860-1908 **15** 375-376

U

UBICO Y CASTAÑEDA, GENERAL JORGE (1878-1946), president of Guatemala (1931-1944) **15** 377-378

UCCELLO, PAOLO (1397-1475), Italian painter **15** 378-379

UCHIDA, MITSUKO (born 1948), Japanese pianist **23** 413-415

UEBERROTH, PETER VICTOR (born 1937), Former baseball commissioner **15** 379-381

UELSMANN, JERRY (born 1934), American photographer **20** 384-385

UHLENBECK, KAREN (born 1942), American mathematician **15** 381-382

ULANOVA, GALINA (1910-1998), Russian ballerina **15** 382-383

ULBRICHT, WALTER (1893-1973), East German political leader **15** 383-384

ULFILAS (circa 311-circa 382), Arian bishop of the Visigoths **15** 384

ULPIAN, DOMITIUS (died 228), Roman jurist **15** 385-386

UNAMUNO Y JUGO, MIGUEL DE (1864-1936), Spanish philosopher and writer **15** 386-387

UNÁNUE, JOSÉ HIPÓLITO (1755-1833), Peruvian intellectual, educator, and scientist **15** 387-388

UNDERHILL, JOHN (circa 1597-1672), American military leader and magistrate **15** 388

UNDSET, SIGRID (1882-1949), Norwegian novelist **15** 388-389

UNGARETTI, GIUSEPPE (1888-1970), Italian poet **15** 389-390

UNITAS, JOHNNY (John Constantine Unitas; 1933-2002), American football player **20** 385-387

United Kingdom
see Great Britain; Northern Ireland

United Nations
supporters
Murray, Gilbert **23** 250-253

U.S. House of Representatives
House Committee on Un-American
Activities (HUAC)
Robeson, Eslanda Goode **23**
340-342

UNSER, AL, SR. (born 1939), American
race car driver **23** 415-417

UPDIKE, JOHN (born 1932), American
author of poems, short stories, essays,
and novels **15** 390-392

UPJOHN, RICHARD (1802-1878),
English-born American architect **15**
392

URBAN II (Otto de Lagery; 1042-99),
pope 1088-99 **15** 393

URBAN VI (Bartolomeo Prignano; 1318-
89), pope 1378-89 **15** 394

URBAN, MATT (1919-1995), American
solider **19** 391-392

UREY, HAROLD CLAYTON (1893-1981),
American chemical physicist and
geochemist **15** 394-396

URQUIZA, JUSTO JOSÉ (1801-1870),
Argentine dictator, general, and
statesman **15** 396-397

URRACA (c. 1078-1126), Queen of
Leon-Castilla) **23** 417-418

UTAMARO, KITAGAWA (1753-1806),
Japanese printmaker **15** 397

UTHMAN DON FODIO (1755-1816),
Moslem teacher and theologian **15**
397-398

V

VADIM, ROGER (Roger Vadim
Plemiannikov; 1928-2000), Russian/
French filmaker and author **22**
413-415

VAIL, THEODORE NEWTON (1845-
1920), American businessman **23**
419-421

VAJPAYEE, ATAL BEHARI (born 1926),
prime minister of India **19** 393-395

VALDEZ, LUIS (born 1940), Hispanic
American playwright and filmmaker **15**
399-400

VALDIVIA, PEDRO DE (circa 1502-53),
Spanish conquistador and professional
soldier **15** 400-401

VALENS, RITCHIE (Richard Steven
Valenzuela; 1941-1959), Hispanic
American musician **22** 415-417

VALENTI, JACK JOSEPH (born 1921),
presidential adviser and czar of the
American film industry **15** 401-403

VALENTINO, RUDOLPH (Rodolfo
Alfonso Raffaelo Pierre Filibert de
Valentina d'Antonguolla Guglielmi;
1895-1926), Italian/American actor **20**
388-390

VALENZUELA, LUISA (born 1938),
Argentine author **23** 421-423

VALERA Y ALCALÁ GALIANO, JUAN
(1824-1905), Spanish novelist and
diplomat **15** 403

VALERIAN (Publius Licinius Valerianus;
circa 200-circa 260), Roman emperor
253-260 **15** 404-405

VALÉRY, PAUL AMBROISE (1871-1945),
French poet, philosopher, and critic **15**
405-406

VALLA, LORENZO (circa 1407-57),
Italian humanist **15** 406

VALLANDIGHAM, CLEMENT LAIRD
(1820-1871), American politician **15**
406-407

VALLE INCLÁN, RAMÓN MARIA DEL
(circa 1866-1936), Spanish novelist,
playwright, and poet **15** 407-408

VALLEJO, CÉSAR ABRAHAM (1892-
1938), Peruvian poet **15** 408-409

VAN BUREN, MARTIN (1782-1862),
American statesman, president 1837-
41 **15** 410-411

VAN DER GOES, HUGO (flourished
1467-82), Flemish painter **15** 416-417

VAN DIEMEN, ANTHONY MEUZA
(1593-1645), Dutch colonial official
and merchant **15** 420

VAN DOESBURG, THEO (1883-1931),
Dutch painter **15** 421

VAN DONGEN, KEES (Cornelis
Theodorus Marie Van Dongen; 1877-
1968), Fauvist painter, portraitist, and
socialite **15** 421-422

VAN DUYN, MONA (born 1921), first
woman to be appointed poet laureate
of the United States **15** 422-423

VAN DYCK, ANTHONY (1599-1641),
Flemish painter **15** 423-425

VAN EEKELEN, WILLEM FREDERIK (born
1931), Dutch secretary-general of the
Western European Union **15** 426-427

VAN GOGH, VINCENT (1853-1890),
Dutch painter **15** 427-429

**VAN HORNE, SIR WILLIAM
CORNELIUS** (1843-1915), American-
born Canadian railroad entrepreneur
15 429-430

VAN PEEBLES, MELVIN (Melvin Peebles;
born 1932), American film director
and producer, actor, author, and
musician **21** 414-416

VAN RENSSELAER, KILIAEN (circa 1580-
1643), Dutch merchant and colonial
official in America **15** 430-431

VAN VECHTEN, CARL (1880-1964),
American writer and photographer **18**
400-402

VANBRUGH, SIR JOHN (1664-1726),
English architect and dramatist **15**
409-410

VANCE, CYRUS R. (1917-2002),
American secretary of the army and
secretary of state **15** 411-413

VANCE, ZEBULON BAIRD (1830-1894),
American politician **15** 413-414

VANCOUVER, GEORGE (1758-1798),
English explorer and navigator **15**
414-415

VANDER ZEE, JAMES (1886-1983),
photographer of the people of Harlem
15 418-419

VANDERBILT, CORNELIUS (1794-1877),
American financier, steamship and
railroad builder **15** 415-416

VANDERBILT, GLORIA (born 1924),
American designer, artist, and author
19 395-397

VANDERLYN, JOHN (1775-1852),
American painter **15** 417

VANE, SIR HENRY (1613-1662), English
statesman **15** 425-426

VAN'T HOFF, JACOBUS HENDRICUS
(1852-1911), Dutch physical chemist
15 431-432

VARDHAMANA MAHAVIRA (circa 540-
470 B.C.), Indian ascetic philosopher
10 135-137

VARÈSE, EDGARD (1883-1965), French-
American composer **15** 432-433

VARGAS, GETULIO DORNELLES (1883-
1954), Brazilian political leader **15**
433-434

VARGAS LLOSA, MARIO (born 1936),
Peruvian novelist, critic, journalist,
screenwriter, and essayist **15** 434-436

VARMUS, HAROLD ELIOT (born 1939),
medical research expert and director of
the National Institutes of Health
(1993-) **15** 436-437

**VARNHAGEN, FRANCISCO ADOLFO
DE** (1816-1878), Brazilian historian **15**
437-438

VARRO, MARCUS TERENTIUS (116-27
B.C.), Roman scholar and writer **15**
438-439

VARTHEMA, LUDOVICO DI (circa 1470-circa 1517), Italian traveler and adventurer **15** 439-440

VASARELY, VICTOR (1908-1997), Hungarian-French artist **15** 440-442

VASARI, GIORGIO (1511-1570), Italian painter, architect, and author **15** 442-443

VASCONCELOS, JOSÉ (1882-1959), Mexican educator and author **15** 443-444

Vassar College (Poughkeepsie, New York State)
Whitney, Mary Watson **23** 440-442

VAUBAN, SEBASTIEN LE PRESTRE DE (1633-1707), French military engineer **18** 402-404

VAUDREUIL-CAVAGNAL, MARQUIS DE (Pierre Franşcois de Regaud; 1698-1778), Canadian-born governor of New France **15** 444

VAUGHAN, HENRY (1621/22-95), British poet **15** 444-445

VAUGHAN, SARAH LOIS (1924-1990), jazz singer **15** 445-446

VAUGHAN WILLIAMS, RALPH (1872-1958), English composer **15** 446-447

VAVILOV, NIKOLAI IVANOVICH (1887-1943), Russian botanist and geneticist **15** 447-448

VÁZQUEZ, HORACIO (1860-1936), president of the Dominican Republic 1903-04 and 1924-30 **15** 448-449

VÁZQUEZ ARCE Y CEBALLOS, GREGORIO (1638-1711), Colombian artist **23** 423-425

VEBLEN, THORSTEIN BUNDE (1857-1929), American political economist and sociologist **15** 449-450

VELASCO, JOSÉ MARÍA (1840-1912), Mexican painter **15** 450-451

VELASCO, LUIS DE (1511-1564), Spanish colonial administrator **15** 450-451

VELASCO ALVARADO, JUAN (1910-1977), Peruvian army officer who seized power in 1968 **15** 451-452

VELASCO IBARRA, JOSÉ MARÍA (1893-1979), Ecuadorian statesman, five time president **15** 452-454

VELÁZQUEZ, DIEGO RODRÍGUEZ DE SILVA Y (1599-1660), Spanish painter **15** 454-456

VELÁZQUEZ, NYDIA MARGARITA (born 1953), Hispanic American politician **15** 456-459

VELÁZQUEZ DE CUÉLLAR, DIEGO (circa 1465-1523), Spanish conqueror, founder of Cuba **15** 459

VELDE, HENRY VAN DE (1863-1957), Belgian painter, designer, and architect **15** 419-420

Venezia, Domenico di Bartolomeo da see Veneziano, Domenico

VENEZIANO, DOMENICO (Domenico di Bartolomeo da Venezia; 1410?-1461), Italian painter **15** 459-460

VENIZELOS, ELEUTHERIOS (1864-1936), Greek statesman **15** 460-461

VENTURI, ROBERT (born 1925), American architect **15** 461-463

VERA, YVONNE (born 1964), Zimbabwean author **23** 425-427

VERCINGETORIX (circa 75-circa 46 B.C.), Celtic chieftain and military leader **19** 397-399

VERDI, GIUSEPPE FORTUNINO FRANCESCO (1813-1901), Italian opera composer **15** 463-465

VERLAINE, PAUL MARIE (1844-1896), French poet **15** 465-466

VERMEER, JAN (1632-1675), Dutch painter **15** 466-467

VERNE, JULES (1828-1905), French novelist **15** 467-469

VERONESE, PAOLO (1528-1588), Italian painter **15** 469-470

VERRAZANO, GIOVANNI DA (circa 1485-circa 1528), Italian navigator and explorer **15** 470-471

VERROCCHIO, ANDREA DEL (1435-1488), Italian sculptor and painter **15** 471-472

VERSACE, GIANNI (1946-1997), Italian fashion designer **19** 399-401

VERWOERD, HENDRIK FRENSCH (1901-1966), South African statesman, prime minister 1958-66 **15** 472-473

VESALIUS, ANDREAS (1514-1564), Belgian anatomist **15** 473-475

VESEY, DENMARK (1767-1822), American slave leader **15** 475

VESPASIAN (9-79), Roman emperor 69-79 **15** 475-476

VESPUCCI, AMERIGO (1454-1512), Italian navigator **15** 476-478

Viacom (media corporation)
Redstone, Sumner Murray **23** 329-331

VIANNEY, ST. JEAN BAPTISTE (1786-1859), French priest **15** 478-479

VICENTE, GIL (circa 1465-circa 1536), Portuguese dramatist and poet **15** 479-480

VICO, GIAMBATTISTA (1668-1744), Italian philosopher and jurist **15** 480-481

VICTOR AMADEUS II (1666-1732), Duke of Savoy, king of Sicily, and king of Sardinia **15** 482-483

VICTOR EMMANUEL II (1820-1878), king of Sardinia 1849-61 and of Italy 1861-78 **15** 483-484

VICTOR EMMANUEL III (1869-1947), king of Italy 1900-46 **15** 484-485

VICTORIA (1819-1901), queen of Great Britain and Ireland 1837-1901 and empress of India 1876-1901 **15** 485-487

VICTORIA, TOMÁS LUIS DE (circa 1548-1611), Spanish composer **15** 487-488

VIDAL, EUGENE LUTHER GORE (born 1925), American author of novels, essays, plays, and short stories **15** 488-490

VIDAL DE LA BLACHE, PAUL (1845-1918), French geographer **15** 490

VIDELA, JORGE RAFAÉL (born 1925), military president of Argentina (1976-1981) who violated human rights **15** 490-492

VIEIRA, ANTÔNIO (1608-1697), Portuguese orator and Jesuit missionary **15** 492

VIGEE LEBRUN, ELISABETH (1755-1842), French painter **19** 402-403

VIGILIUS (died 555), pope (537-555) **23** 427-429

VIGNOLA, GIACOMO DA (1507-1573), Italian architect **15** 493-494

VIGNY, COMTE DE (Alfred Victor Vigny; 1797-1863), French poet **15** 494-495

VIGO, JEAN (Jean Bonaventure de Vigo; 1905-1934), French filmmaker **23** 429-431

VILLA, PANCHO (Francisco Villa; 1878-1923), Mexican revolutionary **15** 495-496

VILLA-LOBOS, HEITOR (1887-1959), Brazilian composer **15** 496-497

VILLANI, GIOVANNI (circa 1270-1348), Italian chronicler **15** 497-498

VILLARD, OSWALD GARRISON (1872-1949), American journalist **15** 498-499

VILLEHARDOUIN, GEFFROI DE (circa 1150-1213), French historian and soldier **15** 499

VILLEDA MORALES, RAMON (1909-1971), Honduran president, 1957-1963 **20** 390-392

VILLON, FRANÇOIS (1431-after 1463), French poet **15** 499-501

VINCENT, JOHN HEYL (1832-1920), American educator and religious leader **15** 502-503

VINCENT DE PAUL, ST. (1581-1660), French priest **15** 501-502

VINCENT OF BEAUVAIS (circa 1190-1264), French writer and theologian **21** 416-418

VINOGRADOFF, SIR PAUL GAVRILOVITCH (1854-1925), Russian educator and historian **15** 503

VINSON, FRED (Frederic Moore Vinson; 1890-1953), chief justice of the U.S. Supreme Court **15** 503-505

Violin (musical instrument)
Chung, Kyung Wha **23** 74-76
Cugat, Xavier **23** 81-82

VIOLLET-LE-DUC, EUGÈNE EMMANUEL (1814-1879), French architect and theorist **15** 505-506

VIRCHOW, RUDOLF LUDWIG CARL (1821-1902), German medical scientist, anthropologist, and politician **15** 506-507

VIRGIL (Publius Vergilius Maro; 70-19 B.C.), Roman poet **15** 507-510

Virus (medical)
Ho, David Da-I **23** 145-148

VISCONTI, GIAN GALEAZZO (Duke of Milan; 1351-1402), Italian despot **15** 510-511

VISSER 'T HOOFT, WILLEM ADOLF (1900-1985), Reformed churchman and ecumenist who was the first general secretary of the World Council of Churches **15** 511-512

VITORIA, FRANCISCO DE (circa 1483-1546), Spanish theologian and political theorist **16** 1-2

VITRY, PHILIPPE DE (1291-1360), French poet, composer, and churchman-statesman **16** 2

VITTORINI, ELIO (1908-1966), Italian novelist, editor, and journalist **16** 2-3

VIVALDI, ANTONIO (1678-1741), Italian violinist and composer **16** 3-4

VIVEKANANDA (1863-1902), Indian reformer, missionary, and spiritual leader **16** 4-5

VLADIMIR I (died 1015), grand prince of Kievan Russia 980-1015 **16** 5-6

VLAMINCK, MAURICE (1876-1958), French painter **16** 6

VOEGELIN, ERIC (1901-1985), German-Austrian political theorist **16** 6-8

VOGEL, HANS-JOCHEN (born 1926), West German political leader **16** 8-9

VOGEL, SIR JULIUS (1835-1899), New Zealand statesman, twice prime minister **16** 9-10

VOGELWEIDE, WALTHER VON DER (circa 1170-1229), German poet, composer, and singer **16** 10-11

VOLCKER, PAUL (born 1927), chairman of the U.S. Federal Reserve Board (1979-1987) **16** 11-12

VOLTA, ALESSANDRO (1745-1827), Italian physicist **16** 12-14

VOLTAIRE (1694-1778), French poet, dramatist, historian, and philosopher **16** 14-16

VON AUE, HARTMANN (Aue von Hartman; c.1160 - c.1250), German poet and troubadour **22** 417-419

VON BINGEN, HILDEGARD (Hildegard of Bingen; 1098-1179), German composer, scientist, and theologian **22** 240-242

VON BRAUN, WERNHER (1912-1977), German-born American space scientist **16** 17-18

VON FURSTENBERG, DIANE (Diane Simone Michelle Halfin; born 1946), American fashion designer and businesswoman **16** 20-21

VON HÜGEL, BARON FRIEDRICH (1852-1925), philosopher of Christianity **16** 21-22

VON LAUE, MAX (1879-1960), German physicist **16** 23-24

VON MEHREN, ROBERT BRANDT (born 1922), American lawyer who helped create the International Atomic Energy Agency **16** 24-25

VON MISES, LUDWIG (born 1881), Austrian economist and social philosopher **16** 25

VON NEUMANN, JOHN (1903-1957), Hungarian-born American mathematician **16** 27-28

VON PAPEN, FRANZ (1879-1969), conservative German politician who helped prepare the way for the Third Reich **16** 28-29

VON RAD, GERHARD (1901-1971), German theologian **16** 29-30

VON STROHEIM, ERICH (Erich Oswald Stroheim; 1885-1957), Austrian actor and director **21** 418-420

VONDEL, JOOST VAN DEN (1587-1679), Dutch poet and dramatist **16** 19-20

VONNEGUT, KURT, JR. (born 1922), American author **16** 25-27

VORSTER, BALTHAZAR JOHANNES (1915-1983), South African political leader **16** 30-32

VOS SAVANT, MARILYN (born 1946), American columnist and consultant **16** 32-33

VUILLARD, JEAN ÉDOUARD (1868-1940), French painter **16** 36

VYSHINSKY, ANDREI (1883-1954), state prosecutor in Stalin's purge trials and head of the U.S.S.R.'s foreign ministry (1949-1953) **16** 36-37

W

WAALS, JOHANNES DIDERIK VAN DER (1837-1923), Dutch physicist **15** 417-418

WADE, BENJAMIN FRANKLIN (1800-1878), American lawyer and politician **16** 38-39

WAGNER, HONUS (Johannes Peter Wagner; 1874-1955), American baseball player **20** 393-395

WAGNER, OTTO (1841-1918), Austrian architect and teacher **16** 39-40

WAGNER, RICHARD (1813-1883), German operatic composer **16** 40-43

WAGNER, ROBERT F. (1910-1991), New York City Tammany Hall mayor (1954-1965) **16** 44-45

WAGNER, ROBERT FERDINAND (1877-1953), American lawyer and legislator **16** 43

WAINWRIGHT, JONATHAN MAYHEW (1883-1953), American general **16** 45-46

WAITE, MORRISON REMICK (1816-1888), American jurist, chief justice of U.S. Supreme Court 1874-88 **16** 46

WAITE, TERRY (born 1939), official of the Church of England and hostage in Lebanon **16** 47-48

WAKEFIELD, EDWARD GIBBON (1796-1862), British colonial reformer and promoter **16** 48-49

WAKSMAN, SELMAN ABRAHAM (1888-1973), American microbiologist **16** 49-50

WALCOTT, DEREK ALTON (born 1930), West Indian poet and dramatist **16** 50-51

WALD, GEORGE (born 1906), American biochemist interested in vision **16** 51-53

WALD, LILLIAN (1867-1940), American social worker and reformer **16** 53-54

WALDEMAR IV (Wlademar Atterdag; 1320-1375), King of Denmark, 1340-1375 **20** 395-397

WALDHEIM, KURT (born 1918), Austrian statesman and president **16** 54-55

WALDO, PETER (flourished 1170-84), French religious leader **16** 55-56

WALDSEEMÜLLER, MARTIN (circa 1470-circa 1518), German geographer and cartographer **16** 56

Wales (political region, Great Britain) David, Saint **23** 83-85

WALESA, LECH (born 1943), Polish Solidarity leader and former president **16** 57-59

WALKER, ALICE MALSENIOR (born 1944), African American novelist, poet, and short story writer **16** 59-61

WALKER, MADAME C. J. (Sarah Breedlove; 1867-1919), African American entrepreneur **16** 61-62

WALKER, DAVID (1785-1830), African American pamphleteer and activist **16** 62-63

WALKER, JOSEPH REDDEFORD (1798-1876), American fur trader **16** 63-64

WALKER, LEROY TASHREAU (born 1918), U.S. sports official, university chancellor, educator, and track coach **16** 64-65

WALKER, MAGGIE LENA (1867-1934), American entrepreneur and civic leader **16** 65-66

WALKER, MARGARET (born 1915), American novelist, poet, scholar, and teacher **16** 67

WALKER, MARY EDWARDS (1832-1919), American physician and feminist **23** 432-434

WALKER, ROBERT JOHN (1801-1869), American politician **16** 67-68

WALKER, WILLIAM (1824-1860), American adventurer and filibuster **16** 68-69

WALL, JEFF (born 1946), Canadian photographer and artist **23** 434-436

WALLACE, ALFRED RUSSEL (1823-1913), English naturalist and traveler **16** 69-70

WALLACE, DeWITT (1889-1981), American publisher and founder of *Reader's Digest* **16** 70-71

WALLACE, GEORGE CORLEY (1919-1998), American political leader **16** 71-72

WALLACE, HENRY (1836-1916), American agricultural publicist and editor **16** 73

WALLACE, HENRY AGARD (1888-1965), American statesman, vice-president 1940-1944 **16** 73-74

WALLACE, LEWIS (1827-1905), American general and author **16** 74-75

WALLACE, SIR WILLIAM (circa 1270-1305), Scottish soldier **16** 75-76

WALLACE-JOHNSON, ISAAC THEOPHILUS AKUNNA (1895-1965), West African political leader and pan-Africanist **16** 76-77

WALLAS, GRAHAM (1858-1932), English sociologist and political scientist **16** 77-78

WALLENBERG, RAOUL (1912-?), Swedish diplomat **16** 78-80

WALLENSTEIN, ALBRECHT WENZEL EUSEBIUS VON (1583-1634), Bohemian soldier of fortune **16** 80-81

WALLER, THOMAS WRIGHT (Fats; 1904-43), American jazz singer, pianist, organist, bandleader, and composer **16** 81-82

WALPOLE, ROBERT (1st Earl of Oxford; 1676-1745), English statesman **16** 82-84

WALRAS, MARIE ESPRIT LÉON (1834-1910), French economist **16** 84-85

WALSH, STELLA (Stanislawa Walasiewiczowna; 1911-1980), Polish American athlete **19** 404-406

WALSH, THOMAS JAMES (1859-1933), American statesman **16** 85-86

WALTER, JOHANN (1496-1570), German composer **16** 86

WALTERS, BARBARA (born 1931), American network newscast anchor **16** 86-88

WALTON, ERNEST (1903-1995), Irish physicist **16** 88-90

WALTON, IZAAK (1593-1683), English writer and biographer **16** 90-91

WALTON, SAM MOORE (1918-1992), American businessman who co-founded Wal-Mart **16** 91-92

WALTON, SIR WILLIAM TURNER (1902-1983), English composer **16** 91-92

WANG, AN (1920-1990), Chinese-American inventor, electronics expert, and businessman **16** 93-95

WANG AN-SHIH (1021-1086), Chinese reformer, poet, and scholar **16** 95-97

WANG CHING-WEI (1883-1944), Chinese revolutionary leader **16** 98

WANG CH'UNG (27-circa 100), Chinese philosopher **16** 98-99

WANG FU-CHIH (1619-1692), Chinese philosopher **16** 99-101

WANG KON (877-943), Korean king **16** 101

WANG MANG (45 B.C.-A.D. 23), Chinese statesman, emperor 9-23 **16** 101-103

WANG MING (Chen Shaoyu; 1904-74), leader of the "Internationalist" group within the Chinese Communist Party **16** 103-104

WANG PI (226-249), Chinese philosopher **16** 104-105

WANG T'AO (1828-1897), Chinese reformer and scholar **16** 105-106

WANG WEI (699-759), Chinese poet and painter **16** 106-108

WANG YANG-MING (1472-1529), Chinese philosopher and government official **16** 108-109

WARBURG, OTTO (1883-1970), German biochemist **16** 109-111

WARBURG, PAUL MORITZ (1868-1932), German-American banker **16** 111-112

WARD, AARON MONTGOMERY (1843-1913), American merchant **16** 112

WARD, ARTEMUS (1834-1867), American journalist and humorist **16** 112-113

WARD, JAY (J Troplong Ward; 1920-1989), American television producer **21** 421-423

WARD, LESTER FRANK (1841-1913), American paleobotanist and sociologist **16** 113-114

WARD, NANCY (Tsituna-Gus-Ke; Nanye'hi; Ghihau; 1738-1822), Cherokee tribal leader **23** 436-438

WARHOL, ANDY (Andrew Warhola; ca. 1927-1987), American pop artist and film maker **16** 114-115

WARMERDAM, DUTCH (Cornelius Warmerdam; 1915-2001), American pole vaulter **21** 423-425

WARNER, JACK (Jacob Eichelbaum; 1892-1978), American film producer and studio executive **19** 406-408

WARNOCK, HELEN MARY WILSON (born 1924), British philosopher 16 115-117

WARREN, EARL (1891-1974), American jurist, chief justice of U.S. Supreme Court 1953-69 16 117-120

WARREN, MERCY OTIS (1728-1814), American writer 16 120-121

WARREN, ROBERT PENN (1905-1989), American man of letters 16 121-122

WARWICK AND SALISBURY, EARL OF (Richard Neville; 1428-71), English military and political leader 16 122-123

WASHAKIE (circa 1804-1900), Native American Shoshoni tribal leader 16 123-125

WASHINGTON, BOOKER TALIAFERRO (1856-1915), African American educator and racial leader 16 125-126

Washington, D.C. (federal city)
cultural programs
Thomas, Alma Woodsey 23 401-403
integration
Terrell, Mary Church 23 397-399

WASHINGTON, GEORGE (1732-1799), American Revolutionary commander in chief, president 1789-97 16 126-129

WASMOSY, JUAN CARLOS (born 1939), president of Paraguay (1993-) 16 129-130

WASSERMANN, JAKOB (1873-1934), German author 16 130-131

WATERHOUSE, BENJAMIN (1754-1846), American physician 16 131-132

WATERS, MAXINE (born 1938), African American congresswoman 16 132-134

WATERS, MUDDY (born McKinley Morganfield; 1915-1983), African American blues musician 16 134-136

WATSON, ELKANAH (1758-1842), American merchant and banker 16 136

WATSON, JAMES DEWEY (born 1928), American biologist 16 137-138

WATSON, JOHN BROADUS (1878-1958), American psychologist 16 138-139

WATSON, THOMAS EDWARD (1856-1922), American lawyer and politician 16 139

WATSON, THOMAS J. (1874-1956), American business executive 16 140

WATSON, THOMAS J. JR. (1914-1993), American businessman 19 408-410

WATSON-WATT, SIR ROBERT ALEXANDER (1892-1973), British scientific civil servant 16 140-141

WATT, JAMES (1736-1819), British instrument maker and engineer 16 141-143

WATTEAU, ANTOINE (1684-1721), French painter 16 143-144

WATTLETON, FAYE (Alyce Faye Wattleton, born 1943), African American women's rights activist 18 405-407

WATTS, ALAN WILSON (1915-1973), naturalized American author and lecturer 16 144-145

WATTS, J.C. (Julius Caesar Watts, Jr.; born 1957), African American politician 18 407-409

WAUGH, EVELYN ARTHUR ST. JOHN (1903-1966), English author 16 145-147

WAUNEKA, ANNIE DODGE (1910-1997), Navajo nation leader and Native American activist 18 409-410

WAVELL, ARCHIBALD PERCIVAL (1st Earl Wavell; 1883-1950), English general, statesman, and writer 16 147-148

WAYLAND, FRANCIS (1796-1865), American educator and clergyman 16 148-149

WAYNE, ANTHONY (1745-1796), American soldier 16 149-150

WAYNE, JOHN (Marion Mitchell Morrison; 1907-79), American actor 16 150-151

WEAVER, JAMES BAIRD (1833-1912), American political leader 16 151-152

WEAVER, PAT (Sylvester Laflin Weaver, Jr.; 1908-2002), American television executive 19 410-413

WEAVER, ROBERT C. (1907-1997), first African American U.S. cabinet officer 16 152-153

WEBB, BEATRICE POTTER (1858-1943), English social reformer 16 153-154

WEBB, SIDNEY JAMES (Baron Passfield; 1859-1947), English social reformer, historian, and statesman 16 154-155

WEBBER, ANDREW LLOYD (born 1948), British composer 16 155-156

WEBER, CARL MARIA FRIEDRICH ERNST VON (1786-1826), German composer and conductor 16 156-157

WEBER, MAX (1864-1920), German social scientist 16 157-160

WEBER, MAX (1881-1961), American painter 16 160

WEBERN, ANTON (1883-1945), Austrian composer 16 160-162

WEBSTER, DANIEL (1782-1852), American lawyer, orator, and statesman 16 162-164

WEBSTER, JOHN (circa 1580-circa 1634), English dramatist 16 164

WEBSTER, NOAH (1758-1843), American lexicographer 16 164-166

WEDEKIND, FRANK (Benjamin Franklin Wedekind; 1864-1918), German dramatist, cosmopolite, and libertarian 16 166-167

WEDGWOOD, CICELY VERONICA (1910-1997), British writer and historian 16 167-168

WEDGWOOD, JOSIAH (1730-1795), English potter 16 168-169

WEED, THURLOW (1797-1882), American politician 16 169-170

WEEMS, MASON LOCKE (1759-1825), American Episcopal minister and popular writer 16 170

WEGENER, ALFRED LOTHAR (1880-1930), German meteorologist, Arctic explorer, and geophysicist 16 170-171

WEI HSIAO-WEN-TI (467-499), Chinese emperor 8 5

WEI JINGSHENG (born 1950), Chinese human rights activist 18 410-412

WEI YÜAN (1794-1856), Chinese historian and geographer 16 180-181

WEIDENREICH, FRANZ (1873-1948), German anatomist and physical anthropologist 16 171-172

WEIL, SIMONE (1909-1943), French thinker, political activist, and religious mystic 16 172-174

WEILL, KURT (1900-1950), German-American composer 16 174-175

WEINBERG, STEVEN (born 1933), Nobel Prize-winning physicist 16 175-177

WEINBERGER, CASPER WILLARD (born 1917), U.S. public official under three presidents 16 177-178

WEISMANN, AUGUST FREIDRICH LEOPOLD (1834-1914), German biologist 16 178-180

WEISSMULLER, JOHNNY (Peter John Weissmuller; 1904-1984), American swimmer and actor 21 425-427

WEIZMAN, EZER (born 1924), Israeli air force commander and president of Israel (1993-) 16 181-182

WEIZMANN, CHAIM (1874-1952), Israeli statesman, president 1949-52 **16** 183-184

WELCH, JACK (John Francis Welch, Jr.; born 1935), American businessman **19** 413-415

WELCH, ROBERT (1899-1985), founder of the John Birch Society **16** 184-185

WELCH, WILLIAM HENRY (1850-1934), American pathologist, bacteriologist, and medical educator **16** 185-186

WELD, THEODORE DWIGHT (1803-1895), American reformer, preacher, and editor **16** 186

WELDON, FAY BIRKINSHAW (born 1931 or 1933), British novelist, dramatist, essayist, and feminist **16** 186-188

WELENSKY, SIR ROY (1907-1991), Rhodesian statesman **16** 188

WELK, LAWRENCE (1903-1992), American bandleader and television host **22** 420-422

WELLES, GIDEON (1802-1878), American statesman **16** 188-190

WELLES, ORSON (1915-1985), Broadway and Hollywood actor, radio actor, and film director **16** 190-191

WELLES, SUMNER (1892-1961), American diplomat **16** 191-192

WELLESLEY, RICHARD COLLEY (1st Marquess Wellesley; 1760-1842), British colonial administrator **16** 192-193

WELLHAUSEN, JULIUS (1844-1918), German historian **20** 397-400

WELLS, HERBERT GEORGE (1866-1946), English author **16** 195-196

WELLS, HORACE (1815-1848), American dentist **16** 196

WELLS, MARY GEORGENE BERG (born 1928), American businesswoman **16** 197-198

WELLS-BARNETT, IDA B. (1862-1931), American journalist and activist **16** 198-199

WELTY, EUDORA (born 1909), American author and essayist **16** 199-201

WEN T'IEN-HSIANG (1236-1283), Chinese statesman **16** 203

WENCESLAS (Vaclav; 903?-935?), Czech feudal lord **20** 400-402

WENCESLAUS (Wenceslaus IV of Bohemia; 1361-1419), Holy Roman emperor 1376-1400, and king of Bohemia 1378-1419 **16** 201-202

WEN-HSIANG (1818-1876), Manchu official and statesman **16** 202-203

WENTWORTH, WILLIAM CHARLES (1790-1872), Australian statesman, writer, and explorer **16** 203-204

WERFEL, FRANZ (1890-1945), Austrian poet, novelist, and playwright **16** 204-205

WERNER, ABRAHAM GOTTLOB (1749-1817), German naturalist **16** 205-207

WERNER, HELMUT (born 1936), German business executive **19** 415-417

WERTHEIMER, MAX (1880-1943), German psychologist **16** 207-208

WESLEY, CHARLES (1707-1788), English hymn writer and preacher **16** 208-209

WESLEY, JOHN (1703-1791), English evangelical clergyman, preacher, and writer **16** 209-210

WEST, BENJAMIN (1738-1820), English American painter **16** 210-212

WEST, CORNEL (born 1953), American philosopher **16** 212-213

WEST, JERRY (born 1938), American basketball player and coach **21** 428-430

WEST, MAE (Mary Jane West; 1893-1980), American actress **19** 417-419

WEST, NATHANAEL (1903-1940), American novelist **16** 213-214

Western Health Reform Institute
White, Ellen Gould **23** 438-440

WESTHEIMER, RUTH KAROLA (a.k.a. "Dr. Ruth;" born 1928), German American psychologist, author, and media personality **16** 214-215

WESTINGHOUSE, GEORGE (1846-1914), American inventor and manufacturer **16** 215

WESTMORELAND, WILLIAM CHILDS (born 1914), commander of all American forces in the Vietnam War (1964-1968) and chief of staff of the U.S. Army **16** 216-217

WESTON, EDWARD (1886-1958), American photographer **19** 419-421

WESTWOOD, VIVIENNE (born 1941), British designer **16** 217-218

WEXLER, NANCY (born 1945), American psychologist **16** 218-219

WEYDEN, ROGIER VAN DER (1399-1464), Flemish painter **16** 219-221

WHARTON, EDITH (1861-1937), American author **16** 221

WHEATLEY, PHILLIS (circa 1753-84), African American poet **16** 221-222

WHEELOCK, ELEAZAR (1711-1779), American clergyman and educator **16** 222-223

WHEELWRIGHT, WILLIAM (1798-1873), American entrepreneur **16** 223-224

WHIPPLE, GEORGE HOYT (1878-1976), American pathologist **16** 224-225

WHISTLER, JAMES ABBOTT MCNEILL (1834-1903), American painter, etcher, and lithographer **16** 225-226

WHITE, ANDREW DICKSON (1832-1918), American educator and diplomat **16** 226-227

WHITE, BYRON R. (1917-2002), deputy U.S. attorney general and associate justice of the U.S. Supreme Court **16** 227-228

WHITE, E. B. (Elwyn Brooks White; 1899-1985), American essayist and author of children's books **16** 228-230

WHITE, ELLEN GOULD (Ellen Gould Harmon White; 1827-1915), American religious leader and reformer **23** 438-440

WHITE, KEVIN H. (born 1929), mayor of Boston (1967-1983) **16** 231-232

WHITE, LESLIE A. (1900-1975), American anthropologist **16** 232-233

WHITE, PATRICK VICTOR MARTINDALE (1912-1990), Australian novelist and playwright **16** 233-235

WHITE, RYAN (1971-1990), American AIDS activist **19** 421-423

WHITE, STANFORD (1853-1906), American architect **16** 235-236

WHITE, T. H. (1915-1986), American journalist **16** 236-237

WHITE, WALTER FRANCIS (1893-1955), general secretary of the National Association for the Advancement of Colored People **16** 238-239

WHITE, WILLIAM ALANSON (1870-1937), American psychiatrist **16** 239-240

WHITE, WILLIAM ALLEN (1868-1944), American journalist **16** 240-241

WHITEFIELD, GEORGE (1714-1770), English evangelist **16** 241-242

WHITEHEAD, ALFRED NORTH (1861-1947), English-American mathematician and philosopher **16** 242-244

WHITLAM, EDWARD GOUGH (Gof; born 1916), prime minister of Australia (1972-1975) **16** 244-245

WHITMAN, CHRISTINE TODD (born c. 1947), American politician **16** 245-248

WHITMAN, MARCUS (1802-1847), American physician, missionary, and pioneer **16** 248-249

WHITMAN, WALT (1819-1892), American poet **16** 249-251

WHITMIRE, KATHRYN JEAN NIEDERHOFER (born 1946), first female mayor of Houston, Texas (1982-1992) **16** 252-253

WHITNEY, ELI (1765-1825), American inventor and manufacturer **16** 253-254

WHITNEY, JOSIAH DWIGHT (1819-1896), American chemist and geologist **16** 254-255

WHITNEY, MARY WATSON (1847-1921), American astronomer **23** 440-442

WHITTAKER, CHARLES EVANS (1901-1973), U.S. Supreme Court justice **16** 255-256

WHITTIER, JOHN GREENLEAF (1807-1892), American poet **16** 256-257

WHITTLE, SIR FRANK (1907-1996), English Air Force officer and engineer **16** 257-258

WIDNALL, SHEILA E. (born 1938), American aeronautical engineer **16** 258-259

WIELAND, CHRISTOPH MARTIN (1733-1813), German poet and author **16** 260-261

WIEMAN, HENRY NELSON (1884-1975), American philosopher and theologian **16** 261-262

WIENER, NORBERT (1894-1964), American mathematician **16** 262-263

WIESEL, ELIE (born 1928), writer, orator, teacher, and chairman of the United States Holocaust Memorial Council **16** 263-264

WIESENTHAL, SIMON (born 1908), Ukrainian Jew who tracked down Nazi war criminals **16** 264-266

WIGGLESWORTH, MICHAEL (1631-1705), American Puritan poet and minister **16** 266-267

WIGMAN, MARY (Marie Wiegmann; 1886-1973), German dancer, choreographer, and teacher **16** 267-268

WIGNER, EUGENE PAUL (1902-1995), Hungarian-born American physicist **16** 268-269

WILBERFORCE, WILLIAM (1759-1833), English statesman and humanitarian **16** 269-270

WILBUR, RICHARD PURDY (born 1921), translator and poet laureate of the United States (1987-1988) **16** 271-272

WILDE, OSCAR FINGALL O'FLAHERTIE WILLS (1854-1900), British author **16** 272-273

WILDER, AMOS NIVEN (1895-1993), American New Testament scholar, poet, minister, and literary critic **16** 273-274

WILDER, BILLY (Samuel Wilder; 1906-2002), American film director, screenwriter, and producer **21** 430-432

WILDER, LAURA INGALLS (1867-1957), American author and pioneer **18** 413-414

WILDER, LAWRENCE DOUGLAS (born 1931), first African American elected governor in the United States **16** 274-276

WILDER, THORNTON NIVEN (1897-1975), American novelist and playwright **16** 276-277

WILES, ANDREW J. (born 1953), English mathematician **23** 442-444

WILEY, HARVEY WASHINGTON (1844-1930), American chemist **16** 277-278

WILHELMINA (1880-1962), queen of the Netherlands 1890-1948 **16** 278-279

WILKES, CHARLES (1798-1877), American naval officer **16** 279-280

WILKES, JOHN (1727-1797), English politician **16** 280-281

WILKINS, SIR GEORGE HUBERT (1888-1958), Australian explorer, scientist, and adventurer **16** 281-282

WILKINS, MAURICE HUGH FREDERICK (born 1916), English biophysicist **18** 415-416

WILKINS, ROY (1901-1981), African American civil rights leader **16** 282-283

WILKINSON, ELLEN (1891-1947), British Labour politician and crusader for the unemployed **16** 283-284

WILKINSON, JAMES (1757-1825), American army general and frontier adventurer **16** 284-286

WILL, GEORGE FREDERICK (born 1941), syndicated columnist and television commentator **16** 286-287

WILLAERT, ADRIAN (circa 1480-1562), Franco-Flemish composer active in Italy **16** 287-288

WILLARD, EMMA HART (1787-1870), American educator and author **16** 288-289

WILLARD, FRANCES ELIZABETH CAROLINE (1839-1898), American temperance and women's suffrage leader **16** 289-290

WILLIAM I (the Conqueror; 1027/28-1087), king of England 1066-1087 **16** 290-291

WILLIAM I (1772-1843), king of the Netherlands 1815-40 **16** 291-292

WILLIAM I (1797-1888), emperor of Germany 1871-88 and king of Prussia 1861-88 **16** 292-293

WILLIAM II (William Rufus; circa 1058-1100), king of England 1087-1100 **16** 293-294

WILLIAM II (1859-1941), emperor of Germany and king of Prussia 1888-1918 **16** 294-295

WILLIAM III (1650-1702), king of England, Scotland, and Ireland 1689-1702 **16** 295-296

WILLIAM IV (1765-1837), king of Great Britain and Ireland 1830-37 **16** 296-297

WILLIAM OF MALMESBURY (circa 1090-circa 1142), English historian **16** 297-298

WILLIAM OF OCKHAM (circa 1284-1347), English philosopher and theologian **16** 298-299

WILLIAM OF SENS (Guillaume de Sens; died 1180), French architect **21** 432-434

WILLIAM OF TYRE (circa 1130-84/85), French archbishop, chancellor of the Latin Kingdom of Jerusalem **16** 299-300

WILLIAM THE SILENT (1533-1584), prince of Orange and stadholder of the Netherlands **16** 300-302

WILLIAMS, DANIEL HALE (1856-1931), African American surgical pioneer **16** 302-303

WILLIAMS, EDWARD BENNETT (1920-1988), American lawyer and sports club owner **22** 422-424

WILLIAMS, HANK (Hiram King Williams; 1923-1953), American singer and songwriter **20** 402-404

WILLIAMS, HENRY SYLVESTER (1869-1911), Trinidadian lawyer and pan-African leader **16** 303-304

WILLIAMS, JOE (Joseph Goreed; 1918-1999), American singer **20** 404-407

WILLIAMS, MARY LOU (Mary Lou Burley; Mary Elfrieda Scruggs; Mary Elfreda Winn; 1910-1981), African American musician **23** 444-446

WILLIAMS, ROGER (circa 1603-83), Puritan clergyman in colonial America **16** 304-305

WILLIAMS, SHIRLEY VIVIEN TERESA BRITTAIN (born 1930), British politician **16** 305-306

WILLIAMS, TED (Theodore Samuel Williams; 1918-2002), American baseball player **19** 423-426

WILLIAMS, TENNESSEE (Thomas Lanier Williams; born 1914), American dramatist and fiction writer **16** 306-308

WILLIAMS, WILLIAM CARLOS (1883-1963), American poet and pediatrician **16** 308-309

WILLS, HELEN (1905-1998), American tennis player **19** 426-428

WILLYS, JOHN (1873-1935), American businessman **20** 407-409

WILMOT, DAVID (1814-1868), American politician **16** 312-313

WILMUT, IAN (born 1944), British embryologist **20** 409-411

WILSON, ALEXANDER (1766-1813), Scottish-American ornithologist and poet **16** 313-314

WILSON, AUGUST (Frederick August Kittell; born 1945), African American playwright **16** 314-316

WILSON, CHARLES ERWIN (1890-1961), engineer, businessman, and secretary of defense **16** 316-317

WILSON, CHARLES THOMSON REES (1869-1959), Scottish physicist **16** 317-318

WILSON, EDMUND (1895-1972), American critic **16** 318-319

WILSON, EDWARD OSBORNE (born 1929), American biologist **16** 319-320

WILSON, HARRIET E. (circa 1827-circa 1863), African American author **16** 320-322

WILSON, HENRY (1812-1875), American politician **16** 322-323

WILSON, JAMES (1742-1798), American statesman **16** 323-324

WILSON, JAMES HAROLD (born 1916), English statesman, prime minister 1964-70 **16** 324-325

WILSON, JOSEPH CHAMBERLAIN (1909-1971), American businessman **16** 325-326

WILSON, KENNETH GEDDES (born 1936), American scientist **23** 446-448

WILSON, PETE (born 1933), American politician **16** 326-329

WILSON, RICHARD (1713/14-82), British painter **16** 329-330

WILSON, THOMAS WOODROW (1856-1924), American statesman, president 1913-21 **16** 330-332

WINCKELMANN, JOHANN JOACHIM (1717-1768), German archeologist **16** 332-333

Windsor, Duchess of
see Simpson, Wallis

WINFREY, OPRAH GAIL (born 1954), America's first lady of talk shows **16** 333-336

WINNEMUCCA, SARAH (a.k.a. Thocmetony; circa 1844-1891), Native American rights activist **16** 336-338

WINSLOW, EDWARD (1595-1655), Pilgrim leader in colonial America **16** 338-339

WINTHROP, JOHN (1588-1649), American colonial politician and historian **16** 339-341

WINTHROP, JOHN (1606-1676), American colonial statesman and scientist **16** 341

WINTHROP, JOHN (1714-1779), American educator and scientist **16** 341-342

WIRTH, LOUIS (1897-1952), American sociologist and activist **21** 434-436

WISE, ISAAC MAYER (1819-1900), American Jewish religious leader **16** 342-343

WISE, JOHN (1652-1725), American Congregational minister **16** 343-344

WISE, STEPHEN SAMUEL (1874-1949), American Jewish religious leader **16** 344-345

WISEMAN, FREDERICK (born 1930), American documentary filmmaker **16** 345-346

WITHERSPOON, JOHN (1723-1794), Scottish-born American Presbyterian divine and educator **16** 346-348

WITT, JOHAN DE (1625-1672), Dutch statesman **16** 348-349

WITTE, COUNT SERGEI YULYEVICH (1849-1915), Russian statesman **16** 349-350

WITTGENSTEIN, LUDWIG (1889-1951), Austrian philosopher **16** 350-351

WITZ, KONRAD (circa 1410-46), German painter **16** 351-352

Wobblies
see Industrial Workers of the World

WO-JEN (1804-1871), Chinese official **16** 352

WOLF, FRIEDRICH AUGUST (1759-1824), German classical scholar and philologist **16** 352-353

WOLFE, JAMES (1727-1759), English general **16** 354-355

WOLFE, THOMAS CLAYTON (1900-1938), American novelist **16** 355-356

WOLFE, THOMAS KENNERLY, JR. ("Tom"; born 1931), American journalist and novelist **16** 356-357

WOLFF, BARON CHRISTIAN VON (1679-1754), German philosopher **16** 358

WOLFF, HUGH (born 1953), American conductor **16** 358-360

WOLFRAM VON ESCHENBACH (circa 1170-circa 1230), German writer **16** 360-361

WOLFSON, HARRY AUSTRYN (1887-1974), American scholar and educator **16** 361-362

WOLPE, STEFAN (1902-1972), German-born composer **16** 362-364

WOLSELEY, GARNET (1833-1913), Irish army officer **20** 411-413

WOLSEY, THOMAS (circa 1475-1530), English statesman and cardinal **16** 364-366

Women athletes
Albright, Tenley Emma **23** 3-6

Women judges
Stout, Juanita Kidd **23** 382-384

Women on the Verge of a Nervous Breakdown (film)
Almodovar, Pedro **23** 6-9

Women politicians
Indian (Asian)
Razia **23** 326-329

Women scientists
astronomers
Leavitt, Henrietta Swan **23** 211-213
chemists
Gleditsch, Ellen **23** 124-126
mathematicians
Theano **23** 399-401
physiologists
Pool, Judith Graham **23** 315-316
psychologists
Ladd-Franklin, Christine **23** 202-204

Women's rights
dress reform movement
Walker, Mary Edwards **23** 432-434
equal education opportunity
Jex-Blake, Sophia **23** 168-170
political activists
de Gouges, Marie Olympe **23** 85-88
Height, Dorothy Irene **23** 139-141
Murray, Pauli **23** 253-256

Women's suffrage (Australia)
Spence, Catherine Helen **23** 374-375

Women's suffrage (United States)
leaders
Terrell, Mary Church **23** 397-399

WONDER, STEVIE (Stevland Judkins Morris; born 1950), American singer, songwriter, and musician **19** 428-430

WONG, ANNA MAY (born Wong Liu Tsong; 1905-1961), Asian American actress **16** 366-367

WOOD, FERNANDO (1812-1881), American politician **16** 367-368

WOOD, GRANT (1891-1942), American painter **16** 368-369

WOOD, LEONARD (1860-1927), American Army officer and colonial administrator **16** 369-370

WOOD, ROBERT ELKINGTON (1879-1969), American Army officer and business executive **16** 370-371

WOODHULL, VICTORIA C. (1838-1927), American women's rights activist **16** 371-372

WOODRUFF, ROBERT W. (1889-1985), American businessman and philanthropist **16** 372-374

WOODS, ROBERT ARCHEY (1865-1925), American social worker **16** 374

WOODS, TIGER (born 1975), African American/Asian American golfer **18** 416-418

WOODSON, CARTER GODWIN (1875-1950), African American historian **16** 374-376

WOODSWORTH, JAMES SHAVER (1874-1942), Canadian humanitarian, reformer, and political leader **16** 376

WOODWARD, COMER VANN (born 1908), American historian **16** 378-379

WOODWARD, ELLEN S. (1887-1971), director of work relief programs for women during the New Deal **16** 379-381

WOODWARD AND BERNSTEIN, investigative reporting team of Woodward, Robert Upshur (born 1943), and Bernstein, Carl (born 1944) **16** 376-378

WOOLF, VIRGINIA STEPHEN (1882-1941), English novelist, critic, and essayist **16** 381-382

WOOLMAN, JOHN (1720-1772), American Quaker merchant and minister **16** 382-383

WOOLWORTH, FRANK WINFIELD (1852-1919), American merchant **16** 383-384

WOOTTON, BARBARA ADAM (1897-1988), British social scientist and member of Parliament **16** 384-385

WORDSWORTH, WILLIAM (1770-1850), English poet **16** 385-388

WORK, MONROE (1866-1945), American sociologist and publisher **16** 388-389

Workingmen's party (U.S. politics)
Parsons, Lucy González **23** 293-295

WORNER, MANFRED (born 1934), West German statesman **16** 389-390

WORTH, CHARLES FREDERICK (1825-1895), English-born French fashion designer **21** 436-438

WOVOKA (a.k.a Jack Wilson; circa 1856-1932), Native American religious leader and mystic **16** 390-393

WOZNIAK, STEVE (Stephen Gary Wozniak; born 1950), American inventor and computer designer **19** 430-432

WREN, SIR CHRISTOPHER (1632-1723), English architect **16** 393-394

WRIGHT, CARROLL DAVIDSON (1840-1909), American statistician and social economist **16** 396

WRIGHT, ELIZUR (1804-1885), American reformer **16** 396-397

WRIGHT, FRANCES (1795-1852), Scottish-American socialist, feminist, and reformer **16** 397-398

WRIGHT, FRANK LLOYD (1869-1959), American architect **16** 398-401

WRIGHT, RICHARD (1908-1960), African American author **16** 401-402

WRIGHT, WILBUR (1867-1919) AND ORVILLE (1871-1948), American aviation pioneers **16** 394-396

WRIGLEY, WILLIAM, JR. (1861-1932), American businessman and baseball team owner **20** 413-415

WU CHAO (Wu Hou/Wu Tse T'ien; 625-705), Empress of China, 690-705 **20** 415-417

WU CHIEN-SHIUNG (1912-1997), American physicist **19** 432-434

WU P'EI-FU (1874-1939), Chinese warlord **16** 404-405

WU TAO-TZU (circa 689-after 758), Chinese painter **16** 405-406

WU TSE-T'IEN (623-705), empress of China **16** 408

WU WANG (died circa 1116 B.C.), first ruler of the Chou dynasty of China 1122-1116 B.C. **16** 408-409

WUNDT, WILHELM MAX (1832-1920), German psychologist and philosopher **16** 402-403

WUORINEN, CHARLES (born 1938), American composer, conductor, and pianist **16** 404

WU-TI (a.k.a. Han Wuti; 156 B.C.-circa 87 B.C.), Chinese emperor **16** 406-408

WYANT, ALEXANDER HELWIG (1836-1892), American painter **16** 409-410

WYATT, SIR THOMAS (1503-1542), English poet and diplomat **16** 410-411

WYCHERLEY, WILLIAM (circa 1640-1716), English dramatist **16** 411-412

WYCLIF, JOHN (1330/32-84), English theologian and reformer **16** 412-413

WYETH, ANDREW NEWELL (born 1917), American painter **16** 413-415

WYLER, WILLIAM (1902-1981), American film director **22** 424-426

WYNN, EARLY (Gus Wynn; 1920-1999), American baseball player **20** 417-419

WYTHE, GEORGE (1726-1806), American jurist **16** 415

X

XENAKIS, IANNIS (born 1922), Greek-French composer and architect **16** 416-418

XENOPHON (circa 430-circa 355 B.C.), Greek historian, essayist, and military expert **16** 418-420

XERXES (ruled 486-465 B.C.), king of Persia **16** 420

XIANG JINGYU (born Xiang Qunxian; 1895-1928), Chinese feminist **16** 421-422

XU GUANGQI (a.k.a. Kuang-ch'i Hsü; 1562-1633), Chinese politician **16** 422-425

Y

YAKUB AL-MANSUR, ABU YUSUF (reigned 1184-99), Almohad caliph in Spain **16** 426

YALOW, ROSALYN S. (Sussman; born 1921), American physicist who developed radioimmunoassay **16** 427-428

YAMAGATA, ARITOMO (1838-1922), Japanese general **16** 428-429

YAMAMOTO, ISOROKU (born Takano Isoroku; 1884-1943), Japanese admiral **16** 429-433

YAMANI, AHMED ZAKI (born 1930), Saudi Arabian lawyer and minister of petroleum and mineral resources (1962-1986) **16** 433-435

YAMASHITA, TOMOYUKI (1885-1946), Japanese general **16** 435-436

YANCEY, WILLIAM LOWNDES (1814-1863), American politician **16** 436-437

YANG, CHEN NING (born 1922), Chinese-born American physicist **16** 437-438

YARD, MARY ALEXANDER ("Molly"; born 1912), American feminist, political organizer, and social activist **16** 438-439

YASUI, MINORU (1917-1987), Asian American attorney **16** 440-444

YEAGER, CHUCK (born 1923), American pilot **16** 444-445

YEAGER, JEANA (born 1952), American pilot **23** 449-451

YEATS, WILLIAM BUTLER (1865-1939), Irish poet and dramatist **16** 445-447

YEH-LÜ CH'U-TS'AI (1189-1243), Mongol administrator **16** 447-449

YEKUNO AMLAK (ruled circa 1268-1283), Ethiopian king **16** 449

YELTSIN, BORIS NIKOLAEVICH (born 1931), president of the Russian Republic (1990-) **16** 449-452

YEN FU (1853-1921), Chinese translator and scholar **16** 452

YEN HSI-SHAN (1883-1960), Chinese warlord **16** 452-453

YEN LI-PEN (died 673), Chinese painter **16** 453-454

YERKES, ROBERT MEARNS (1876-1956), American psychologist **16** 454-455

YEVTUSHENKO, YEVGENY ALEXANDROVICH (born 1933), Soviet poet **16** 455-456

YI HWANG (1501-1570), Korean philosopher, poet, scholar, and educator **16** 457

YI SNG-GYE (1335-1408), Korean military leader, founder of the Yi dynasty **16** 458-459

YI SUNSIN (1545-1598), Korean military strategist and naval hero **16** 459-461

YO FEI (Yo P'eng-chü; 1103-41), Chinese general **16** 462

YOGANANDA (Mukunda Lal Ghose; 1893-1952), Indian yogi **16** 462-463

YÔNGJO (1694-1776), king of Korea 1724-76 **16** 461-462

YORITOMO, MINAMOTO (1147-1199), Japanese warrior chieftain **16** 463-464

YOSHIDA, SHIGERU (1878-1967), Japanese diplomat and prime minister **16** 464-465

YOSHIMUNE, TOKUGAWA (1684-1751), Japanese shogun **16** 465-466

YOULOU, FULBERT (1917-1972), Congolese president **16** 466-467

YOUNG, ANDREW JACKSON JR. (born 1932), African American preacher, civil rights activist, and politician **16** 467-469

YOUNG, BRIGHAM (1801-1877), American Mormon leader and colonizer **16** 469-470

YOUNG, COLEMAN ALEXANDER (1918-1997), first African American mayor of Detroit **16** 470-471

YOUNG, LESTER WILLIS ("Prez";1909-59), American jazz musician **16** 471-473

YOUNG, LORETTA (Gretchen Michaela Young; 1913-2000), American Actress **22** 427-430

YOUNG, OWEN D. (1874-1962), American industrialist and monetary authority **16** 473-474

YOUNG, STARK (1881-1963), drama critic, editor, translator, painter, playwright, and novelist **16** 474-475

YOUNG, THOMAS (1773-1829), English physicist **16** 475-476

YOUNG, WHITNEY MOORE, JR. (1921-1971), African American civil rights leader and social work administrator **16** 476-477

Young Women's Christian Association (YWCA)
Height, Dorothy Irene **23** 139-141

YOUNGHUSBAND, SIR FRANCIS EDWARD (1863-1942), English soldier and explorer **16** 477

YOURCENAR, MARGUERITE (Marguerite Antoinette Ghislaine; 1903-87), French novelist, poet, essayist, dramatist, world traveller, and translator **16** 477-479

YÜAN, MA (flourished circa 1190-circa 1229), Chinese painter **10** 379

YÜAN MEI (1716-1798), Chinese author **16** 479-480

YÜAN SHIH-K'AI (1859-1916), Chinese military leader **16** 480-481

YUKAWA, HIDEKI (1907-1981), Japanese physicist **16** 481-482

YUN SONDO (1587-1671), Korean sijo poet **16** 483

YUNG-LO (1360-1424), Chinese emperor **16** 482-483

YWCA
see Young Women's Christian Association

YZERMAN, STEVE (born 1965), Canadian hockey player **23** 451-453

Z

ZADKINE, OSSIP JOSELYN (1890-1967), Russian sculptor **16** 484

ZAGHLUL PASHA, SAAD (1859-1927), Egyptian political leader **16** 485-486

ZAH, PETERSON (born 1937), Native American leader and activist **16** 486-487

ZAHARIAS, MILDRED DIDRIKSON ("Babe"; 1913-56), Olympic athlete and golfer **16** 487-488

ZAHIR SHAH, MUHAMMAD (born 1914); Afghani King **22** 431-433

ZANGWILL, ISRAEL (1864-1926), Jewish author and philosopher **16** 488-489

ZANUCK, DARRYL F. (1902-1979), American film producer and executive **19** 435-437

ZAPATA, EMILIANO (circa 1879-1919), Mexican agrarian leader and guerrilla fighter **16** 489-490

ZARLINO, GIOSEFFO (1517-1590), Italian music theorist and composer **16** 490-491

ZATOPEK, EMIL (born 1922), Czechoslovakian runner **20** 420-422

ZAYID BIN SULTAN AL-NAHYAN (born 1923), president of the United Arab Emirates (1971-) **16** 491-492

ZEAMI, KANZE (1364-1444), Japanese actor, playwright, and critic **16** 492-493

ZEDILLO PONCE DE LEON, ERNESTO (born 1951), president of Mexico **16** 493-495

ZEFFIRELLI, FRANCO (born 1923), Italian stage, opera, and film director, set designer, and politician **18** 419-421

ZELAYA, JOSÉ SANTOS (1853-1919), Nicaraguan statesman, three-time president **16** 495-496

ZEMURRAY, SAMUEL (1877-1961), Russian-born U.S. fruit importer **16** 496-497

ZENGER, JOHN PETER (1697-1746), American printer **16** 497-498

ZENO OF CITIUM (335-263 B.C.), Greek philosopher **16** 499-500

ZENO OF ELEA (born circa 490 B.C.), Greek philosopher and logician **16** 500

ZENOBIA (died 273), queen of Palmyra **16** 500-503

Zero for Conduct (film) Vigo, Jean **23** 429-431

ZETKIN, CLARA (1857-1933), German political activist **16** 504-505

ZHAO KUANG-YIN (a.k.a. Song Tai Zu or Sung T'ai Tsu; 927-976), Chinese emperor **16** 505-508

ZHAO ZIYANG (Zhao Xiusheng; born 1919), Chinese statesman **16** 508-509

ZHIRINOVSKY, VLADIMIR VOLFOVICH (born 1946), Russian politician **16** 509-510

ZHIVKOV, TODOR (1911-1998), leader of the Bulgarian Communist Party and head of the Bulgarian government (1962-) **16** 510-512

ZHUKOV, GEORGI KONSTANTINOVICH (1896-1974), Russian general **16** 512-513

ZIA, HELEN (born 1952), Asian American activist and journalist **18** 421-423

ZIA UL-HAQ, MOHAMMAD (1924-1988), president of Pakistan (1978-1988) **16** 513-515

ZIAUR RAHMAN (1936-1981), Bangladesh president (1975-1981) **16** 515-516

ZIEGFELD, FLORENZ (1869-1932), American musical producer **16** 516-517

Zimbabwean literature Vera, Yvonne **23** 425-427

ZIMMERMANN, BERND ALOIS (1918-1970), German composer **16** 517-518

ZIMMERMANN BROTHERS, German artists **16** 518

ZINDEL, PAUL (1936-2003), American children's author and playwright **18** 423-425

ZINE EL ABIDINE BEN ALI (born 1936), president of Tunisia **16** 518-520

ZINN, HOWARD (born 1922), American political scientist and historian **16** 520-521

ZINOVIEV, GRIGORI EVSEEVICH (1883-1936), Soviet politician **16** 521-522

ZINZENDORF, COUNT NIKOLAUS LUDWIG VON (1700-1760), German-born Moravian clergyman **16** 522-523

ZNANIECKI, FLORIAN (1882-1958), Polish-American sociologist and educator **16** 523-524

ZOË (circa 978-1050), Byzantine empress 1028-34 **16** 524-525

ZOG I (Ahmed Bey Zog; 1895–1961), Albanian king **16** 525-526

ZOLA, ÉMILE (1840-1902), French novelist **16** 526-528

ZORACH, WILLIAM (1887-1966), American sculptor and painter **16** 528

ZOROASTER (flourished 1st millennium B.C.), prophet and founder of Iranian national religion **16** 528-530

ZORRILLA DE SAN MARTIN, JUAN (1855-1931), Uruguayan poet and newspaperman **16** 530-531

ZOSER (flourished circa 2686 B.C.), Egyptian king **16** 531

ZUKERMAN, PINCHAS (born 1948), Israeli musician **22** 433-435

ZUKOR, ADOLPH (1873-1976), American film producer and executive **19** 437-439

ZUMÁRRAGA, JUAN DE (circa 1468-1548), Spanish churchman, first archbishop of Mexico **16** 531-532

ZUMWALT, ELMO RUSSELL, JR. ("Bud"; 1920-2000), commander of U.S. naval forces in Vietnam **16** 532-534

ZUNZ, LEOPOLD (1794-1886), German-born Jewish scholar **16** 534

ZURBARÁN, FRANCISCO DE (1598-1644), Spanish painter **16** 534-535

ZWILICH, ELLEN TAAFFE (born 1939), American composer **16** 536-537

ZWINGLI, HULDREICH (1484-1531), Swiss Protestant reformer **16** 537-538

ZWORYKIN, VLADIMIR KOSMA (1889-1982), Russian-American physicist and radio engineer **16** 539-540